An Introduction to

LITERATURE

~~In Praise of your Poise~~ The Silken Tent

She is as ~~on the lawn~~ in a field a silken ~~tent~~
At midday when a ~~sunny~~ summer breeze
Has dried the dew and all its ~~ropes~~ relent,
So that in guys it gently sways at ease,

And its supporting central cedar pole,
That is its ~~summit~~ pinnacle to ~~pointing~~ heavenward
And signifies the sureness of the soul,
Seems to owe ~~nothing~~ naught to any single cord,

But strictly held by none, is loosely bound
By countless silken ties of love and ~~thought~~
To every thing on ~~earth~~ the compass round,
And only by one's going slightly taut
In the capriciousness of ~~of~~ summer air,
Is of the slightest bondage made aware.

An Introduction to

LITERATURE

Tenth Edition

Fiction / Poetry / Drama

Edited by

Sylvan Barnet
Tufts University

Morton Berman
Boston University

William Burto
University of Lowell

HarperCollins*CollegePublishers*

Acquisitions Editor: Lisa Moore
Developmental Editor: Judith Leet
Project Coordination, Text and Cover Design: PC&F, Inc.
Cover Illustration: Emmi Whitehorse (Navajo)
  Mt. Taylor Early Morning, 1987, oil and chalk on paper, 37¾" x 50".
  Courtesy LewAllen Gallery, Santa Fe, NM
Photo Researchers: Kelly Mountain/Judy Ladendorf
Production/Manufacturing: Michael Weinstein/Paula Keller
Compositor: PC&F, Inc.
Printer and Binder: R.R. Donnelley & Sons Company
Cover Printer: The Lehigh Press, Inc.

For permission to use copyrighted material, grateful
acknowledgment is made to the copyright holders on pp.
887–893, which are hereby made part of this copyright page.

AN INTRODUCTION TO LITERATURE: FICTION,
POETRY, DRAMA, Tenth Edition

Library of Congress Cataloging-in-Publication Data

An Introduction to literature : fiction, poetry, drama / edited by
  Sylvan Barnet, Morton Berman, William Burto. — 10th ed.
      p.   cm.
    Includes index.
    ISBN 0-673-52183-4 (student edition) ISBN 0-673-52184-2 (teacher edition)
    1. Literature—Collections. I. Barnet, Sylvan. II. Berman,
  Morton. III. Burto, William.
  PN6014.I57   1992   92-1499
  808—dc20   CIP

92 93 94 95 9 8 7 6 5 4 3 2 1

Contents

🖎   Selection followed by Topics for Discussion and Writing.

────────────

✍   Selection followed by Topics for Discussion and Writing.

9 *Observations on the Novel* 404

─────────────────────

✍ Selection followed by Topics for Discussion and Writing.

✍   Selection followed by Topics for Discussion and Writing.

───────────────

✍   Selection followed by Topics for Discussion and Writing.

✍ Selection followed by Topics for Discussion and Writing.

✍   Selection followed by Topics for Discussion and Writing.

PART THREE

Drama

──────────

✍   Selection followed by Topics for Discussion and Writing.

APPENDIX

A *Writing Essays about Literature*   1236

✍   Selection followed by Topics for Discussion and Writing.

APPENDIX

B   *Remarks about Manuscript Form*   1277

Preface

In producing the tenth edition of AN INTRODUCTION TO LITERA-
TURE, we have kept in mind Dr. Johnson's maxim: "Books that you
may . . . hold readily in your hand are the most useful after all." Aware
that many instructors and students have found bulky textbooks an obstacle to the enjoyment of literature (and burdensome to carry to class), the
editors and publisher have made every effort to introduce students to the
pleasures of reading—emotional and intellectual pleasures—by maintaining this book's convenient size and manageable length.

About half of the selections in this edition are works that for many
decades—in some cases even for centuries—have given readers great pleasure. Writers such as Shakespeare, Walt Whitman, Emily Dickinson, and
Kate Chopin have stood the test of time, including the test of today's
students and teachers in introductory courses. The other half is contemporary material, some of it by writers who established their reputations
a couple of decades ago (for instance, John Updike and Alice Walker), but
much of it by writers who are still young (for instance, Amy Tan and Sandra
Cisneros). We have tried to read widely in today's writing, and we think
we have found some new voices with stories, poems, and plays that are
exceptionally strong—pieces worth the time of busy students and busy
instructors.

Our editorial material introduces students to the elements of literature and assists them to read actively. To this end, we include several extended interpretations (some by students) in the introductory chapters on
responding to literature; and we provide questions on about half of the
selections and brief chapters on getting ideas for writing. We also include
material on manuscript form. For the most part, however, we try to keep
ourselves in the background. We know, as teachers, that the proper place
for extended discussion of stories, poems, and plays is not the textbook
but the classroom.

In providing some apparatus, but not too much, we have kept in
mind Robert Frost's remark: "You don't chew a poem—macerate a
poem—for an evening's pleasure, for a Roman holiday. You touch it. You
are aware that a good deal of it is missed."

WHAT'S NEW IN THIS EDITION?

This book is both old and new. It retains material (literature and apparatus) that instructors have indicated has worked well in class, but it includes

many new selections as well as new apparatus. Fifteen of the stories (out of 40), 37 poems (out of 170), and 7 plays (out of 12) are new to this edition. Some familiar authors are now represented by relatively unfamiliar works (Chekhov by "Enemies," Maupassant by "Mademoiselle," Chopin by "Ripe Figs" and "The Storm" as well as by the familiar "Story of an Hour"), and many talented new writers are included (for instance, Judith Ortiz Cofer, Carolyn Forché, Rita Dove, Li-Young Lee, David Mura, Tim O'Brien, and Maria Viramontes). While choosing the material, whether classic or contemporary, we have kept in mind the advice a tightrope walker gave to a student who was trying to learn her art: "Whenever you feel yourself falling toward one side, lean toward the other."

The first chapter, "Reading and Responding to Literature," is almost entirely new. It begins by juxtaposing a canonical work, Frost's "Immigrants," with a relatively unknown work by a contemporary writer, "Immigrants" by Pat Mora. Further, two new chapters introduce students to the active reading of fiction and poetry—by means of annotating, free writing, and journal entries. For fiction, the work we use is Hemingway's unjustly neglected "Cat in the Rain"; for poetry, Langston Hughes's "Harlem."

We now also present some authors in greater depth than before. In the fiction section, Flannery O'Connor is represented by three stories and also by a selection from her comments about literature. The poetry section includes many poems by Emily Dickinson and Robert Frost, along with some of their letters and observations on literature.

In the drama section, Sophocles is represented by two tragedies, Shakespeare by a comedy and a tragedy; Ibsen, Tennessee Williams, Arthur Miller, Joyce Carol Oates, Luis Valdez, and August Wilson are all represented not only by plays but also by their comments on the plays. Works by Susan Glaspell and Wendy Wasserstein (a one-act comedy) are also reprinted in the drama section.

USING THE BOOK

Probably most instructors first teach fiction, then poetry, and then drama—the order followed here. But the three sections can be taught in any sequence because each is relatively independent. For example, symbolism is discussed in each of the three sections, and although the three discussions have a cumulative effect, any of the three can be used first. This flexibility runs throughout the book; one can teach everything straight through, or skip one's way through a section, or bring in (whenever one wishes) the anthologized stories, poems, and plays that conclude the sections. Perhaps the only chapter that ought to be taught at a specific time, or not taught at all, is Chapter 1, "Reading and Responding to Literature." Or perhaps one might assign it late in the term, after the students have read a fair amount of literature, and then invite them to evaluate the chapter.

Assuming that instructors teach fiction before poetry and drama, we suggest that they assign Chapter 1, then Chapter 2 ("A First Approach to Fiction: Responding in Writing"), then some stories, and, before the first writing assignment, Chapter 6 ("In Brief: Getting Ideas for Writing about Fiction") and the Appendixes A and B ("Writing Essays about Literature" and "Remarks about Manuscript Form").

ACKNOWLEDGMENTS

Finally, after this elaborate explanation of what has been done, we wish to thank the people who helped us do it. For the preparation of the tenth edition, we own a special debt to Judith Leet and Lisa Moore, of Harper-Collins, to Virginia Creeden for permissions assistance, and to the following instructors: Ken Anderson, Floyd College; Alfred Arteaga, University of California, Berkeley; Rance Baker, San Antonio College; Lois Birky, Illinois Central College; Carol Boyd, Black Hawk College; Lois Bragg, Gallaudet University; Robert Coltrane, Lock Haven University; Charles Darling, Greater Hartford Community College; Richard Dietrich, University of South Florida; Gail Duffy, Dean Junior College; Marilyn Edelstein, Santa Clara University; Toni Empringham, El Camino College; Craig Etchison, Glenville State College; Robert Farrell, Housatonic Community College; Elaine Fitzpatrick, Massasoit College; Donna Galati, University of South Dakota; Marvin P. Garrett, University of Cincinnati; Francis B. Hanify, Luzerne County Community College; Blair Hemstock, Keyano College (Canada); Paula Hester, Indian Hills Community College; Edwina Jordan, Illinois Central College; Kate Kiefer, Colorado State University; Sandra Lakey, Pennsylvania College of Technology; Cecilia G. Martyn, Montclair State College; Paul McVeigh, Northern Virginia Community College; William S. Nicholson, Eastern Shore Community College; Stephen O'Neill, Bucks County Community College; Betty Jo Hicks Peters, Morehead State University; Frank Perkins, Quincy College; Barbara Pokdowka, Commonwealth College; Patricia R. Rochester, University of Southwestern Louisiana; Betty Rhodes, Faulkner State College; Martha Saunders, West Georgia College; Allison Shumsky, Northwestern Michigan College; Isabel B. Stanley, East Tennessee State University; LaVonne Swanson, National College; Beverly Taylor, University of North Carolina, Chapel Hill; Merle Thompson, North Virginia Community College; Cyrilla Vessey, North Virginia Community College; Mildred White, Oholone College; Margaret Whitt, University of Denver; Betty J. Williams, East Tennessee State University; Donald R. Williams, North Shore Community College; Donnie Yeilding, Central Texas College.

Our thanks also to the many users of the earlier editions who gave us advice on how and where to make improvements: Linda Bamber, David

Cavitch, Robert Cyr, Arthur Friedman, Nancy Grayson, Martha Hicks-Courant, Billie Ingram, Martha Lappen, Judy Maas, Deirdre McDonald, Patricia Meier, Ronald E. Pepin, William Roberts, Clair Seng-Niemoeller, Virginia Shine, and Charles L. Walker.

We are especially grateful for the comments and suggestions offered by the following scholars: Priscilla B. Bellair, Carroll Britch, Don Brunn, Malcolm B. Clark, Terence A. Dalrymple, Franz Douskey, Gerald Duchovnay, Peter Dumanis, Estelle Easterly, Adam Fischer, Martha Flint, Robert H. Fossum, Gerald Hasham, Richard Henze, Catharine M. Hoff, Grace S. Kehrer, Nancy E. Kensicki, Linda Kraus, Juanita Laing, Vincent J. Liesenfeld, Martha McGowan, John H. Meagher III, Stuart Millner, Edward Anthony Nagel, Peter L. Neff, Robert F. Panara, Ronald E. Pepin, Jane Pierce, Robert M. Post, Kris Rapp, Mark Reynolds, John Richardson, Donald H. Sanborn, Marlene Sebeck, Frank E. Sexton, Peggy Skaggs, David Stuehler, James E. Tamer, Carol Teaff, C. Uejio, Hugh Whitmeyer, Manfred Wolf, Joseph Zaitchik.

Finally, we are also grateful for valuable suggestions made by Charles Christensen, Joan Feinberg, X. J. Kennedy, Carolyn Potts, Marcia Stubbs, Helen Vendler, and Ann Chalmers Watts.

Sylvan Barnet
Morton Berman
William Burto

Publisher's Note:
An Introduction to Literature, Tenth Edition, is accompanied by an extensive multimedia teaching resource package. Professors Barnet, Berman, and Burto have prepared an instructors' manual, *Teaching An Introduction to Literature,* with suggestions for teaching every selection in the book.

In addition, HarperCollins has provided an exclusive set of videotapes designed specifically to accompany this book: "Writers on Writers" (produced by the BBC, WGBH, and HarperCollins). "Writers on Writers" comprises two complementary videos, a dramatization of Chekhov's "Enemies" (the story is included in *An Introduction to Literature*) and a companion video tape in which Jamaica Kincaid—who wrote the screen play for the dramatization of "Enemies," and who is also represented in this book—discusses Chekhov's story and also her own work.

Numerous videotapes and audiotapes of other literary works are also available to enhance the student's experience of literature. To receive more information, and to request a copy of *Teaching An Introduction to Literature,* contact your HarperCollins representative, or write to

Humanities Marketing Manager
HarperCollins College Publishers
10 East 53rd Street
New York, New York 10022

1

Reading and Responding to Literature

WHAT IS LITERATURE?

Large books have been written on this subject, and large books will continue to be written on it. But we can offer a few brief generalizations that may be useful.

First, the word "literature" can be used to refer to anything written. The Department of Agriculture will, upon request, send an applicant "literature on canning tomatoes." People who ask for such material expect it to be clear and informative, but they do not expect it to be interesting in itself. They do not read it for the experience of reading it; they read it only if they are thinking about canning tomatoes.

There is, however, a sort of literature that people *do* read without expecting a practical payoff. They read the sort of writing that is in *An Introduction to Literature* because they expect it to hold their interest and to provide pleasure. They may vaguely feel that it will be good for them, but they don't read it *because* it will be good for them, any more than they dance because dancing provides healthful exercise. Dancing may indeed be healthful, but that's not why people dance. They dance because dancing affords a special kind of pleasure. For similar reasons people watch athletic contests and go to concerts or to the theater. We participate in activities such as these not because we expect some sort of later reward but because we know that the experience of participating is in itself rewarding. Perhaps the best explanation is that the experiences are absorbing — which is to say that they take us out of ourselves for a while — and that (especially in the case of concerts, dance performances, and athletic contests) they allow us to appreciate excellence, to admire achievement. Most of us can swim or toss a ball and maybe even hit a ball, but when we go to a swimming meet or to a ball game we see a level of performance that evokes our admiration.

Looking at an Example:
Robert Frost's ''Immigrants''

Let's begin, then, by thinking of literature as (to quote Robert Frost) "a performance in words." And let's begin with a very short poem by Frost (1874–1963), probably America's best-known poet. Frost wrote these lines for a pageant at Plymouth, Massachusetts, celebrating the three-hundredth anniversary of the arrival of the Mayflower from England.

Immigrants

No ship of all that under sail or steam
Have gathered people to us more and more
But Pilgrim-manned the Mayflower in a dream
Has been her anxious convoy in to shore.

[1920]

To find this poem—this performance in words—of any interest, a reader probably has to know that the Mayflower brought the Pilgrims to America. Second, a reader has to grasp a slightly unfamiliar construction: "No ship . . . but . . . has . . . ," which means, in effect, "every ship has." (Compare: "No human being but is born of woman," which means "Every human being is born of woman.")

If, then, we *paraphrase* the poem—translate it into other words in the same language—we get something roughly along these lines:

> Every ship of all the ships (whether sailing vessels or steamships)
> that have collected people in increasing numbers and brought them
> to this country has had the Mayflower, with its Pilgrims, as its
> eager (or worried?) escort to the coast.

We have tried to make this paraphrase as accurate and as concise as possible, but for reasons that we'll explain in a moment, we have omitted giving an equivalent for Frost's "in a dream." Why, one might ask, is our paraphrase so much less interesting than the original?

Performance   First, the poem is metrical. With only a few exceptions, every second syllable is accented more than the preceding syllable. Take the first line. Although "No" probably receives at least as much stress as the word that follows it, "ship," in the rest of the line the pattern is clear;

No shíp of all that únder sáil or steám

(Of course not all of the stresses are equally heavy. When you read the line aloud you will probably put less emphasis on the first syllable of "under," for instance, than you put on "sail" or "steam.")

The language, then, is highly patterned, and you doubtless have ex-perienced the force of patterned language—of rhythmic thought—whether from other poems or songs ("We shall overcome, / We shall overcome") or football chants ("Block that kick! Block that kick!"). Take a moment to reread the first line, without heavily emphasizing the stressed syllables but with some awareness of them. (Don't read the line mechanically; read it for sense, not for fixed pattern—but you'll *feel* a pattern.)

No ship of all that under sail or steam . . .

Further, repetition is not limited to the pattern of stresses in the lines. We get the same number of syllables (ten) in each line. (There may be a few variations. For instance, in the third line if we pronounce "Mayflower" with three syllables, the line has eleven syllables. Probably we should pronounce it with two syllables: "Mayflow'r," maybe something like "Mayflar.") And of course we also get repetitions of sounds at the ends of the lines: "steam" rhymes with "dream," and "more" with "shore."

Probably, too, the repetition of *s* in "*s*ail or *s*team" catches the ear. The two words are somewhat alike in that they are both monosyllables, they both begin with the same sound, and they both evoke images of ships. Compare "sail or steam" with "sail or gas" or "sail or engine" and you will probably agree that the original is more pleasing and more interesting.

One can see what Frost meant when he said that a poem is a per-formance in words: four lines, each with the same basic pattern of stresses, each ending with a word that rhymes, and all this in a single grammatical sentence. The thing looks easy enough, but we know that it took great skill to make the words behave properly, that is, to get the right words in the right order. Frost went into the lions' cage, did his act, and came out unharmed.

Significance　　We've been talking about Frost's skill in handling words, but we haven't said anything (except in our clumsy paraphrase) about *what* Frost is saying in "Immigrants." One of the things that literature does is to make us see—hear, feel, love—what the author thinks is a valuable part of the experience of living. A thousand years ago a Japanese writer, Lady Murasaki, made this point when she had one of the characters in her book talk about what motivates an author:

> Again and again something in one's own life or in that around one will seem so important that one cannot bear to let it pass into oblivion. There must never come a time, the writer feels, when people do not know about this.

We can probably agree with Lady Murasaki that writers of litera-ture try to get at something important in their experiences, emotions, or visions, and try to make the reader feel the importance. And so writers show us what it is like (for instance) to be in love (plenty of room for comedy as well as tragedy here), or what forgiveness is like, or what is at the heart of immigration to America.

We can't be certain about what Frost really thought of the Pilgrims and of the Mayflower, but we do have the poem, and that's what we are concerned with. It celebrates the anniversary, of course, but it also celebrates at least two other things: the continuing arrival of new immigrants and the close connection between the early and the later immigrants.

Persons whose ancestors came over on the Mayflower have a reputation for being rather sniffy about later arrivals, but Frost reminds his Yankee audience that their ancestors, the Mayflower passengers, were themselves immigrants. However greatly the histories and the experiences of the early immigrants differed from those of later immigrants, the experience of emigration and the hopes for a better life link the Mayflower passengers with more recent arrivals.

The poem says, if our paraphrase is roughly accurate, that the Mayflower and its passengers accompany all later immigrants. Now, what does this mean? Literally, of course, it is nonsense. The Mayflower and its passengers disappeared centuries ago.

TOPICS FOR DISCUSSION AND WRITING

1. In our paraphrase, in an effort to avoid complexities, we did not give any equivalent for "in a dream." The time has now come to face this puzzle in line 3: "But Pilgrim-manned the Mayflower in a dream." Some readers take Frost to be saying that the long-deceased passengers of the Mayflower still dream of others following them. Other readers, however, interpret the line as saying that later immigrants dream of the Mayflower. Now, this paraphrase, even if accurate, makes an assertion that is not strictly true, since many later immigrants probably had never even heard of the Mayflower. But in a larger sense the statement is true. The later immigrants—with the terrible exception of involuntary immigrants who were brought here in chains—dreamed of a better life, just as the Mayflower passengers did. Some hoped for religious freedom, some hoped to escape political oppression or starvation, but again, all were seeking a better life.

2. In our paraphrase we mentioned that "anxious" might be paraphrased either as "eager" or as "worried." (Contrast, for instance, "She was anxious to serve the community" and "She was anxious about the exam.") Is Frost's "anxious convoy" *eagerly* accompanying the ships with immigrants, or is it *nervously* accompanying them, perhaps worried that these new arrivals may not be the right sort of people, or worried that the new arrivals may not be able to get on in the new

country? Or does the word "anxious," which seems to modify "convoy" (here, the Mayflower), really refer to the new immigrants, who are worried that they may not succeed? Or perhaps they are worried that America may not in fact correspond to their hopes.

Read the poem aloud two or three times, and then think about which of these meanings—or some other meanings that you come up with—you find most rewarding. You might consider, too, whether more than one meaning can be present. Frost himself in a letter wrote that he liked to puzzle his readers a bit—to baffle them and yet (or thereby) propel them forward:

> My poems—I should suppose everybody's poems—are all set to trip the reader head foremost into the boundless. Ever since infancy I have had the habit of leaving my blocks carts chairs and such like ordinaries where people would be pretty sure to fall forward over them in the dark. Forward, you understand, *and* in the dark.

What we have been saying is this: a reader of a work of literature finds meanings in the work, but also (even when the meaning is uncertain) takes delight in the details, takes delight in the way that the work has been constructed, takes delight in (again) the performance. When we have got at what we think may be the "meaning" of a work, we do not value or hold on to the meaning only and turn away from the work itself; rather, we value even more the craftsmanship that the work displays. And we come to see that the meaning is inseparable from all of the details that go to make up the work.

3. "Pilgrim-manned" may disturb some readers. Conscious of sexist language, today we try to avoid saying things like "This shows the greatness of man" or "Man is a rational animal" when we are speaking not about males but about all people. If Frost's "Pilgrim-manned" strikes you as slighting women, bear in mind the fact that most if not all of the physical handling of the ship was indeed done by males. Moreover, remember that Frost wrote the poem some three-quarters of a century ago, when such language was not questioned. The expression may remain offensive, but the offense is not so much Frost's as the age's.

4. We have already mentioned that Frost's poem cannot possibly be thought to describe involuntary immigrants. Is this a weakness in the poem? If so, how serious a weakness? All readers will come up with their own answers.

5. Frost's poem celebrates immigration and does not consider its effect on the Native American population. The poem does not, so to speak, tell the whole truth; but no statement, however long, could tell the "whole truth" about such a complex topic. Even if the poem doesn't give us the whole truth, perhaps we get enough if the poem reminds us of *a* truth.

Looking at a Second Example: Pat Mora's "Immigrants"

Pat Mora, after graduating from Texas Western College, earned a master's degree at the University of Texas at El Paso. She is best known for her poems, but she has also published essays on Chicano culture.

Immigrants

wrap their babies in the American flag,
feed them mashed hot dogs and apple pie,
name them Bill and Daisy,
buy them blonde dolls that blink blue
eyes or a football and tiny cleats
before the baby can even walk,
speak to them in thick English,
    hallo, babee, hallo.
whisper in Spanish or Polish
when the babies sleep, whisper
in a dark parent bed, that dark
parent fear, "Will they like
our boy, our girl, our fine american
boy, our fine american girl?"

[1986]

Pat Mora's experience—that of a Mexican-American woman in the United States—obviously must be very different from that of Frost, an Anglo-Saxon male and almost the official poet of the country. Further, Mora is writing in our own time, not three-quarters of a century ago. A reader expects, and finds, a very different sort of poem. We won't discuss this poem at length, but we will say that in our view she too gets at something important. Among the many things in this verbal performance that give us pleasure are these:

1. the wit of making the title part of the first sentence. A reader expects the title to be relevant to the poem but does not expect it to be grammatically the first word of the poem. We like the fresh way in which the title is used.
2. We also like the aptness with which Mora has caught the immigrants' eager yet worried attempt to make their children "100% American."
3. We like the mimicry of the immigrants talking to their children: "hallo, babee, hallo." Of course if this mimicry came from an outsider it would be condescending and offensive, but since it is written by someone known for her concern with Mexican-American culture, it probably is not offensive. It is almost affectionate.

TOPICS FOR DISCUSSION AND WRITING

1. The last comment may be right, so far as it goes, but isn't it too simple? Reread the poem — preferably aloud — and then try to decide exactly what Mora's attitude is toward the immigrants. Do you think that she fully approves of their hopes? On what do you base your answer?

2. What does it mean to say that someone — a politician, for instance — "wraps himself in the American flag"? What does Mora mean when she says that immigrants "wrap their babies in the American flag"? How would you paraphrase the line?

3. After reading the poem aloud two or three times, what elements of "verbal performance" — we might say of skillful play — do you notice? Mora does not use rhyme, but she does engage in some verbal play. What examples can you point to?

4. What is your own attitude toward the efforts of some immigrants to assimilate themselves to an Anglo-American model? How does your attitude affect your reading of the poem?

THINKING ABOUT A STORY: THE PARABLE OF THE PRODIGAL SON

Good prose narratives, too, like good poems, are carefully constructed. Let's look at a story, one told by Jesus, and reported in the fifteenth chapter of the Gospel according to St. Luke. Jesus here tells a **parable,** a short story from which a lesson is to be drawn. Luke reports that just before Jesus told the story, the Pharisees and scribes — persons whom the Gospels depict as opposed to Jesus because he sometimes found their traditions and teachings inadequate — complained that Jesus was a man of loose morals, one who "receives sinners and eats with them." According to Luke, Jesus responded thus:

And he said, "A certain man had two sons: and the younger of them said to his father, 'Father, give me the portion of goods that falleth to me.' And he divided unto them his living. And not many days after, the younger son gathered all together, and took his journey into a far country, and there wasted his substance with riotous living.

And when he had spent all, there arose a mighty famine in that land, and he began to be in want. And he went and joined himself to a citizen of that country, and he sent him into his fields to feed swine. And he would fain have filled his belly with the husks that the swine did eat: and no man gave unto him.

And when he came to himself he said, 'How many hired servants of my father's have bread enough and to spare, and I perish with hunger? I will arise and go to my father, and will say unto him, "Father, I have sinned against heaven, and before thee. And am no more worthy to be called thy son: make me as one of thy hired servants."'

And he arose, and came to his father. But when he was yet a great way off, his father saw him, and had compassion, and ran, and fell on his neck, and kissed him. And the son said unto him, 'Father, I have sinned against heaven, and in thy sight, and am no more worthy to be called thy son.' But the father said to his servants, 'Bring forth the best robe, and put it on him, and put a ring on his hand, and shoes on his feet. And bring hither the fatted calf and kill it, and let us eat, and be merry. For this my son was dead, and is alive again; he was lost, and is found.' And they began to be merry.

Now his elder son was in the field, and as he came and drew nigh to the house, he heard music and dancing. And he called one of the servants, and asked what these things meant. And he said unto him, 'Thy brother is come, and thy father hath killed the fatted calf, because he hath received him safe and sound.' And he was angry, and would not go in: therefore came his father out, and entreated him. And he answering said to his father, 'Lo, these many years do I serve thee, neither transgressed I at any time thy commandment, and yet thou never gavest me a kid, that I might make merry with my friends: but as soon as this thy son was come, which hath devoured thy living with harlots, thou has killed for him the fatted calf.' And he said unto him, 'Son, thou art ever with me, and all that I have is thine. It was meet that we should make merry, and be glad: for this thy brother was dead, and is alive again: and was lost, and is found.'"

Now, to begin with a small point, it is not likely that any but strictly observant Jews, or perhaps Moslems (who, like these Jews, do not eat pork), can feel the disgust that Jesus' audience must have felt at the thought that the son was reduced to feeding swine and that he even envied the food that swine ate. Further, some of us may be vegetarians; if so, we are not at all delighted at the thought that the father kills the fatted calf (probably the wretched beast has been force-fed) in order to celebrate the son's return.

And, of course, some of us do not believe in God, and hence are not prepared to take the story, as many people take it, as a story whose message is that we, like God (the father in this parable is usually taken to stand for God), ought to rejoice in the restoration of the sinner. Probably, then, for all sorts of obvious reasons none of us can put ourselves back into the first century A.D. and hear the story exactly as Jesus' hearers heard it.

Still, most of us can probably agree on what we take to be the gist of the story, and, second, we can enjoy the skillful way in which it is told.

This skill will become apparent, however, only after several sympathetic readings. What are some examples of superb storytelling here, and what can a reader gain from a sympathetic, thoughtful reading? We can begin by noting a few points:

1. Although the story is customarily called "The Parable of the Prodigal Son" or "The Parable of the Lost Son," it tells of two sons, not of one. When we reread the story, we increasingly see that these brothers are compared and contrasted: the prodigal leaves his father's house for a different way of life—he thus seems lost to the father—but then he repents and returns to the father, whereas the older son, who physically remains with the father, is spiritually remote from the father, or is lost in a different way. By virtue of his self-centeredness the older son is remote from the father in feeling or spirit.

2. Again, reading and rereading reveal small but telling details. For instance, when the prodigal plans to return home, he thinks of what he will say to his father. He has come to his senses and repudiated his folly, but he still does not understand his father, for we will see in a moment that the prodigal has no need of this speech. Jesus tells us that as soon as the father saw the prodigal returning, he "had compassion, and ran, and fell on his neck, and kissed him." And (another very human touch) the prodigal—although already forgiven—nevertheless cannot refrain from uttering his heartfelt but, under the circumstances, unnecessary speech of repentance.

3. The elder son, learning that the merrymaking is for the returning prodigal, "was angry, and would not go in." This character is sketched only briefly, but a reader immediately recognizes the type: self-centered, unforgiving, and petulant. The older son does not realize it, but he is as distant from his father as the younger son had been. What is the father's response to this son, who is so different from the forgiving father?

> Therefore came his father out, and entreated him.

The father goes out to the dutiful son, just as he had gone out to the prodigal son. (What the father *does* is as important as what he *says*.) Notice, too, speaking of sons, that the older son, talking to his father, somewhat distances himself from his brother, disdainfully referring to the prodigal as "this thy son." And what is the father's response? To the elder son's "this thy son," the father replies, "this thy brother."

No matter how closely we look, however, we will not be able to find certain pieces of information; certain **blanks** or **gaps** will remain. For instance, we are not given information about the relationship of the brothers before the story begins. Nor are we told if the older son learns a lesson, and repents of his nasty behavior. We can offer guesses based on our understanding of others and based on our own nature, but the story is not explicit about these matters, and other readers may offer different guesses. We may even, perhaps, deny that the stay-at-home's behavior *is* nasty, and we may say that the father was sentimental and foolish to forgive the prodigal so easily.

There may also be **indeterminacies** in a story, passages that remain unclear even to careful readers of the story. Thus, the father says to the older son, "All that I have is thine," but is this true? After all, he has just killed the fatted calf, and has never offered even "a kid" (young goat) to the older son. And—a very large issue—readers may even question the historical accuracy of the picture of the Pharisees and scribes, for sources other than the Gospels depict them more sympathetically.

Such thoughts may come to mind, because, again, we inevitably bring ourselves to all that we experience (and reading is an experience). It may turn out that, finally, we will (so to speak) go against the story and give it a **counter-reading,** a reading that challenges or replaces the more obvious meaning we might at first give it. Just as a reader of Frost's "Immigrants" might argue that it gives a white New Englander's view of immigration and overlooks the disastrous effects of colonization on Native Americans and on black slaves, so a reader may feel that the Parable of the Prodigal Son obscures another story and that the son should show his repentence in more than words. Or a reader may interpret the story from a psychoanalytic perspective as a story of sibling rivalry. We may come to feel that this whole story of a father and his two sons is an example of the sort of male-dominated or patriarchal thinking that (one might argue) gives little or no value to women; these sons seem to have no mother, and the only women mentioned are harlots.

Thoughtful, plausible responses of this sort, based on a close reading, can be valuable, and it is useful to set them forth in writing so that we share them with our colleagues. If, however, we let the work of literature merely trigger our stock responses rather than try to let it induce new, deeper responses, we may be the losers. We may, to put it bluntly, simply retain our prejudices and miss the experience of encountering something more important, more substantial.

TOPIC FOR DISCUSSION AND WRITING

This story is traditionally called the Parable of the Prodigal Son. Can a case be made for the view that it ought to be called the Parable of the Prodigal Father? Forget, if you can, the traditional title, and ask yourself if the story tells of a father who is prodigal with his property and who at the end is prodigal with his love. Explain why you accept or reject this interpretation.

STORIES TRUE AND FALSE

The word "story" comes from "history"; the stories that historians, biographers, and journalists narrate are supposed to be true accounts of what happened. The stories of novelists and short-story writers, however, are admittedly untrue; they are "fiction," things made up, imagined, manufactured. As readers, we come to a supposedly true story with expectations different from those we bring to fiction.

Consider the difference between reading a narrative in a newspaper and one in a book of short stories. If, while reading a newspaper, we come across a story of, say, a subway accident, we assume that the account is true, and we read it for the information about a relatively unusual event. Anyone hurt? What sort of people? In our neighborhood? Whose fault? When we read a book of fiction, however, we do not expect to encounter literal truths; we read novels and short stories not for facts but for pleasure and for some insight or for a sense of what an aspect of life means to the writer. Consider the following short story by Grace Paley.

Grace Paley

Born in 1922 in New York City, Grace Paley attended Hunter College and New York University, but left without a degree. (She now teaches at Sarah Lawrence College.) While raising two children she wrote poetry and then, in the 1950s, turned to writing fiction.

Paley's chief subject is the life of little people struggling in the Big City. Of life she has said, "How daily life is lived is a mystery to me. You write about what's mysterious to you. What is it like? Why do people do this?" Of the short story she has said, "It can be just telling a little tale, or writing a complicated philosophical story. It can be a song, almost."

Samuel

Some boys are very tough. They're afraid of nothing. They are the ones who climb a wall and take a bow at the top. Not only are they brave on the roof, but they make a lot of noise in the darkest part of the cellar where even the super hates to go. They also jiggle and hop on the platform between the locked doors of the subway cars.

Four boys are jiggling on the swaying platform. Their names are Alfred, Calvin, Samuel, and Tom. The men and the women in the cars on either side watch them. They don't like them to jiggle or jump but don't want to interfere. Of course some of the men in the cars were once brave boys like these. One of them had ridden the tail of a speeding truck from New York to Rockaway Beach without getting off, without his sore fingers losing hold. Nothing happened to him then or later. He had made a compact with other boys who preferred to watch: Starting at Eighth Avenue and Fifteenth Street, he would get to some specified place, maybe Twenty-third and the river, by hopping the tops of the moving trucks. This was hard to do when one truck turned a corner in the wrong direction and the nearest truck was a couple of feet too high. He made three or four starts before succeeding. He had gotten his idea from a film at school called *The Romance of Logging.* He had finished high school, married a good friend, was in a responsible job and going to night school.

These two men and others looked at the four boys jumping and jiggling on the platform and thought, It must be fun to ride that way, especially now the weather is nice and we're out of the tunnel and way high over the Bronx. Then they thought, These kids do seem to be acting sort of stupid. They *are* little. Then they thought of some of the brave things they had done when they were boys and jiggling didn't seem so risky.

The ladies in the car became very angry when they looked at the four boys. Most of them brought their brows together and hoped the boys could see their extreme disapproval. One of the ladies wanted to get up and say, Be careful you dumb kids, get off that platform or I'll call a cop. But three of the boys were Negroes and the fourth was something else she couldn't tell for sure. She was afraid they'd be fresh and laugh at her and embarrass her. She wasn't afraid they'd hit her, but she was afraid of embarrassment. Another lady thought, Their mothers never know where they are. It wasn't true in this particular case. Their mothers all knew that they had gone to see the missile exhibit on Fourteenth Street.

Out on the platform, whenever the train accelerated, the boys would raise their hands and point them up to the sky to act like rockets going off, then they rat-tat-tatted the shatterproof glass pane like machine guns, although no machine guns had been exhibited.

For some reason known only to the motorman, the train began a sudden slowdown. The lady who was afraid of embarrassment saw the boys jerk forward and backward and grab the swinging guard chains. She had her own boy at home. She stood up with determination and went to the door. She slid it open and said, "You boys will be hurt. You'll be killed. I'm going to call the conductor if you don't just go into the next car and sit down and be quiet."

Two of the boys said, "Yes'm," and acted as though they were about to go. Two of them blinked their eyes a couple of times and pressed their lips together. The train resumed its speed. The door slid shut, parting the lady and the boys. She leaned against the side door because she had to get off at the next stop.

The boys opened their eyes wide at each other and laughed. The lady blushed. The boys looked at her and laughed harder. They began to pound each other's back. Samuel laughed the hardest and pounded Alfred's back until Alfred coughed and the tears came. Alfred held tight to the chain hook. Samuel pounded him even harder when he saw the tears. He said, "Why you bawling? You a baby, huh?" and laughed. One of the men whose boyhood had been more watchful than brave became angry. He stood up straight and looked at the boys for a couple of seconds. Then he walked in a citizenly way to the end of the car, where he pulled the emergency cord. Almost at once, with a terrible hiss, the pressure of air abandoned the brakes and the wheels were caught and held.

People standing in the most secure places fell forward, then backward. Samuel had let go of his hold on the chain so he could pound Tom as well as Alfred. All the passengers in the cars whipped back and forth, but he pitched only forward and fell head first to be crushed and killed between the cars.

The train had stopped hard, halfway into the station, and the conductor called at once for the trainmen who knew about this kind of death and how to take the body from the wheels and brakes. There was silence except for passengers from other cars who asked, What happened! What happened! The ladies waited around wondering if he might be an only child. The men recalled other afternoons with very bad endings. The little boys stayed close to each other, leaning and touching shoulders and arms and legs.

When the policeman knocked at the door and told her about it, Samuel's mother began to scream. She screamed all day and moaned all night, though the doctors tried to quiet her with pills.

Oh, oh, she hopelessly cried. She did not know how she could ever find another boy like that one. However, she was a young woman and she became pregnant. Then for a few months she was hopeful. The child born to her was a boy. They brought him to be seen and nursed. She smiled. But immediately she saw that this baby wasn't Samuel. She and her husband together have had other children, but never again will a boy exactly like Samuel be known.

[1968]

You might think about the ways in which "Samuel" differs from a newspaper story of an accident in a subway. (You might even want to write a newspaper version of the happening.) In some ways, of course, Paley's story faintly resembles an account that might appear in a newspaper. Journalists are taught to give information about Who, What, When, Where, and Why, and Paley does provide this. Thus, the *characters* (Samuel and others) are the journalist's Who; the *plot* (the boys were jiggling on the platform, and when a man pulled the emergency cord one of them was killed) is the What; the *setting* (the subway, presumably in modern times) is the When and the Where; the *motivation* (the irritation of the man who pulls the emergency cord) is the Why.

Ask yourself questions about each of these elements, and think about how they work in Paley's story. You might also think about responses to the following questions. Your responses will teach you a good deal about what literature is and about some of the ways in which it works.

TOPICS FOR DISCUSSION AND WRITING

1. Paley wrote the story, but an unspecified person *tells* it. Describe the voice of this narrator in the first paragraph. Is the voice neutral and objective, or do you hear some sort of attitude, a point of view? If you do hear an attitude, what words or phrases in the story indicate it?
2. What do you know about the setting of "Samuel"? What can you infer about the neighborhood?
3. In the fourth paragraph we are told that "three of the boys were Negroes and the fourth was something else." Is race important in this story? Is Samuel "Negro" or "something else"? Does it matter?
4. Exactly *why* did a man walk "in a citizenly way to the end of the car, where he pulled the emergency cord"? Do you think the author blames him? What evidence can you offer to support your view? Do *you* blame him? Or do you blame the boys? Or anyone? Explain.
5. The story is called "Samuel," and it is, surely, about him. But what happens after Samuel dies? (You might want to list the events.) What else is the story about? (You might want to comment on why you believe the items in your list are important.)
6. Can you generalize about what the men think of the jigglers and about what the women think? Is Paley saying something about the sexes? About the attitudes of onlookers in a big city?

WHAT'S PAST IS PROLOGUE

The two poems and two stories that you have just read cannot, of course, stand for all works of literature. For one thing, although Mora's "Immigrants" and the two prose fictions include some dialogue, none of these works is in dramatic form, designed for presentation on a stage. Still, these four examples, as well as works of literature that you are already familiar with, will provide something of a background against which you can read the other works in this book. For instance, if you read a story that, like the Parable of the Prodigal Son, seems strongly to imply a moral, think about how the moral is controlled by what the characters *do* as well as by what they *say,* and how one character is defined by being set against another. If you read a poem that, like Mora's "Immigrants," seems to play one tone of voice against another (for instance, the voice of the speaker of the poem against a voice quoted within the poem), think about how the voices relate to each other and how they perhaps harmonize to create a complex vision.

In short, a work of literature is not a nut to be cracked open so that a kernel of meaning can be extracted and devoured, and the rest thrown away; the whole — a performance in words — is something to be experienced and enjoyed.

FICTION

2

A First Approach to Fiction: Responding in Writing

The next four chapters will look at specific elements, one by one, in fiction—plot, symbolism, and so on—but first let's read a brief story by Ernest Hemingway and then talk about it (and see how one student talked about it) with little or no technical language.

Ernest Hemingway

Ernest Hemingway (1899–1961) was born in Oak Park, Illinois. After graduating from high school in 1917 he worked on the Kansas City Star, *but left to serve as a volunteer ambulance driver in Italy, where he was wounded in action. He returned home, married, and then served as European correspondent for the Toronto* Star, *but he soon gave up journalism for fiction. In 1922 he settled in Paris, where he moved in a circle of American expatriates that included Ezra Pound, Gertrude Stein, and F. Scott Fitzgerald. It was in Paris that he wrote stories and novels about what Gertrude Stein called a "lost generation" of rootless Americans in Europe. (For Hemingway's reminiscences of the Paris years, see his posthumously published* A Moveable Feast.) *He served as a journalist during the Spanish Civil War and during the Second World War, but he was also something of a private soldier.*

After the Second World War his reputation sank, though he was still active as a writer (for instance, he wrote The Old Man and the Sea *in 1952). In 1954 Hemingway was awarded the Nobel Prize in Literature, but in 1961, depressed by a sense of failing power, he took his own life.*

Cat in the Rain

There were only two Americans stopping at the hotel. They did not know any of the people they passed on the stairs on their way to and from their room. Their room was on the second floor facing the sea. It also faced the public garden and the war monument. There were big palms and green benches in the public garden. In the good weather there was always an artist with his easel. Artists liked the way the palms grew and the bright colors of the hotels facing the gardens and the sea. Italians came from a long way off to look up at the war monument. It was made of bronze and glistened in the rain. It was raining. The rain dripped from the palm trees. Water stood in pools on the gravel paths. The sea broke in a long line in the rain and slipped back down the beach to come up and break again in a long line in the rain. The motor cars were gone from the square by the war monument. Across the square in the doorway of the café a waiter stood looking out at the empty square.

The American wife stood at the window looking out. Outside right under their window a cat was crouched under one of the dripping green tables. The cat was trying to make herself so compact that she would not be dripped on.

"I'm going down and get that kitty," the American wife said.

"I'll do it," her husband offered from the bed.

"No, I'll get it. The poor kitty out trying to keep dry under a table."

The husband went on reading, lying propped up with the two pillows at the foot of the bed.

"Don't get wet," he said.

The wife went downstairs and the hotel owner stood up and bowed to her as she passed the office. His desk was at the far end of the office. He was an old man and very tall.

"Il piove,"[1] the wife said. She liked the hotel-keeper.

"Si, si, Signora, brutto tempo. It is very bad weather."

He stood behind his desk in the far end of the dim room. The wife liked him. She liked the deadly serious way he received any complaints. She liked his dignity. She like the way he wanted to serve her. She liked the way he felt about being a hotel-keeper. She liked his old, heavy face and big hands.

Liking him she opened the door and looked out. It was raining harder. A man in a rubber cape was crossing the empty square to the café. The cat would be around to the right. Perhaps she could go along under the eaves. As she stood in the doorway an umbrella opened behind her. It was the maid who looked after their room.

"You must not get wet," she smiled, speaking Italian. Of course, the hotel-keeper had sent her.

---

[1] **Il piove**   It's raining (Italian)

With the maid holding the umbrella over her, she walked along the gravel path until she was under their window. The table was there, washed bright green in the rain, but the cat was gone. She was suddenly disappointed. The maid looked up at her.

"Ha perduto qualque cosa, Signora?"[2]

"There was a cat," said the American girl.

"A cat?"

"Si, il gatto."

"A cat?" the maid laughed. "A cat in the rain?"

"Yes," she said, "under the table." Then, "Oh, I wanted it so much. I wanted a kitty."

When she talked English the maid's face tightened.

"Come, Signora," she said. "We must get back inside. You will be wet."

"I suppose so," said the American girl.

They went back along the gravel path and passed in the door. The maid stayed outside to close the umbrella. As the American girl passed the office, the padrone bowed from his desk. Something felt very small and tight inside the girl. The padrone made her feel very small and at the same time really important. She had a momentary feeling of being of supreme importance. She went on up the stairs. She opened the door of the room. George was on the bed, reading.

"Did you get the cat?" he asked, putting the book down.

"It was gone."

"Wonder where it went to," he said, resting his eyes from reading.

She sat down on the bed.

"I wanted it so much," she said. "I don't know why I wanted it so much. I wanted that poor kitty. It isn't any fun to be a poor kitty out in the rain."

George was reading again.

She went over and sat in front of the mirror of the dressing table looking at herself with the hand glass. She studied her profile, first one side and then the other. Then she studied the back of her head and her neck.

"Don't you think it would be a good idea if I let my hair grow out?" she asked, looking at her profile again.

George looked up and saw the back of her neck, clipped close like a boy's.

"I like it the way it is."

"I get so tired of it," she said. "I get so tired of looking like a boy."

George shifted his position in the bed. He hadn't looked away from her since she started to speak.

"You look pretty darn nice," he said.

---

[2]**Ha . . . Signora**   Have you lost something, Madam?

She laid the mirror down on the dresser and went over to the window and looked out. It was getting dark.

"I want to pull my hair back tight and smooth and make a big knot at the back that I can feel," she said. "I want to have a kitty to sit on my lap and purr when I stroke her."

"Yeah?" George said from the bed.

"And I want to eat at a table with my own silver and I want candles. And I want it to be spring and I want to brush my hair out in front of a mirror and I want a kitty and I want some new clothes."

"Oh, shut up and get something to read," George said. He was reading again.

His wife was looking out of the window. It was quite dark now and still raining in the palm trees.

"Anyway, I want a cat," she said, "I want a cat. I want a cat now. If I can't have long hair or any fun, I can have a cat."

George was not listening. He was reading his book. His wife looked out of the window where the light had come on in the square.

Someone knocked at the door.

"Avanti,"[3] George said. He looked up from his book.

In the doorway stood the maid. She held a big tortoise-shell cat pressed tight against her and swung down against her body.

"Excuse me," she said, "the padrone asked me to bring this for the Signora."

[1925]

RESPONSES: ANNOTATIONS AND JOURNAL ENTRIES

When you read a story—or, perhaps more accurately, when you reread a story before discussing it or writing about it—you'll find it helpful to jot an occasional note (for instance, a brief response or a question) in the margins and to underline or highlight passages that strike you as especially interesting. Here is part of the story, with a student's annotations.

> The cat was trying to make herself so compact that she would not be dripped on.
>
> "I'm going down and get that kitty," the American wife said.
>
> "I'll do it," her husband offered from the bed.   *He doesn't make a move*
>
> "No, I'll get it. The poor kitty out trying to keep dry under a table."

[3] **Avanti**   Come in (Italian)

still doesn't move!

The husband <u>went on reading,</u> lying propped up with the two pillows at the foot of the bed.

"<u>Don't get wet,</u>" he said.

← is he making a joke? or maybe he just isn't even thinking about what he is saying?

The wife went downstairs and the <u>hotel owner</u> stood up and bowed to her as she passed the office.

contrast with the husband

His desk was at the far end of the office. He was an old man and very tall.

"Il piove," the wife said. She liked the hotel-keeper.

"Si, si, Signora, brutto tempo. It is very bad weather."

He stood behind his desk in the far end of the dim room. <u>The wife liked him.</u> She liked the deadly serious way he received any complaints. <u>She liked his</u> dignity. She liked the way he wanted to serve her. She liked the way he felt about being a hotel-keeper. She liked his old, heavy face and big hands.

She respects him and she is pleased by the attention he shows

to emphasize the bad weather??

Liking him she opened the door and looked out. It was raining harder. <u>A man in a rubber cape</u> was crossing the <u>empty square</u> to the café. The cat would be around to the right.

Of course *everything* in a story presumably is important, but having read the story once, probably something has especially interested (or puzzled) you, for instance the relationship between two people, or the way the end of the story is connected to the beginning. On rereading, then, pen in hand, you'll find yourself noticing things that you missed or didn't find especially significant on your first reading. Now that you know the end of the story, you will read the beginning in a different way.

And of course if your instructor asks you to think about certain questions, you'll keep these in mind while you reread, and you will find ideas coming to you. For instance, in "Cat in the Rain" suppose you are asked (or you ask yourself) if the story might just as well be about a dog in the rain. Would anything be lost?

Here are a few questions that you can ask of almost any story. After scanning the questions, you probably will want to reread the story, pen in hand, and then jot down your responses on a sheet of paper. As you write, doubtless you will go back and reread the story or at least parts of it.

1. What happens? In two or three sentences—say 25–50 words—summarize the gist of what happens in the story.
2. What sorts of people are the chief characters? In "Cat in the Rain" the chief characters are George, George's wife, and the innkeeper (the

padrone). Jot down the traits that each seems to possess, and next
to each trait briefly give some supporting evidence.

3. What especially pleased or displeased you in the story? Devote at
least a sentence or two to the end of the story. Do you find the end
satisfying? Why or why not?

4. Have you any thoughts about the title? If so, what are they? If the
story did not have a title, what would you call it?

After you have made your own jottings, compare them with these
responses by a student. Obviously no two readers will respond in exactly
the same way, but all readers can examine their responses and try to account for them, at least in part. If your responses are substantially different, how do you account for the differences?

```
1.  A summary. A young wife, stopping with her
    husband at an Italian hotel, from her room sees
    a cat in the rain. She goes to get it, but it is
    gone, and so she returns empty-handed. A moment
    later the maid knocks at the door, holding a
    tortoise-shell cat.
2.  The characters: The woman.
    kind-hearted (pities cat in rain)
    appreciates innkeeper's courtesy ("liked
         the way he wanted to serve her") and
         admires him ("She liked his dignity")
    unhappy (wants a cat, wants to change her hair,
         wants to eat at a table with her own silver)
    The husband, George.
    not willing to put himself out (says he'll go to
         garden to get cat but doesn't move)
    doesn't seem very interested in wife (hardly
         talks to her--he's reading; tells her to
         "shut up")
    but he does say he finds her attractive ("You
         look pretty darn nice")
    The innkeeper.
    serious, dignified ("She liked the deadly serious
         way he received any complaints. She liked
         his dignity")
    courteous, helpful (sends maid with umbrella; at
         end sends maid with cat)
3.  Dislikes and likes. "Dislikes" is too strong,
    but I was disappointed that more didn't happen
    at the end. What is the husband's reaction to
    the cat? Or his final reaction to his wife? I
```

mean, what did he think about his wife when the
maid brings the cat? And, for that matter, what
is the wife's reaction? Is she satisfied? Or
does she realize that the cat can't really make
her happy? Now for the likes. (1) I guess I did
like the way it turned out; it's sort of a happy
ending, I think, since she wants the cat and
gets it. (2) I also especially like the innkeeper. Maybe I like him partly because the wife
likes him, and if she likes him he must be nice.
And he is nice--very helpful. And I also like
the the way Hemingway shows the husband. I don't
mean that I like the man himself, but I like the
way Hemingway shows he is such a bastard--not
getting off the bed to get the cat, telling his
wife to shut up and read.

Another thing about him is that the one
time he says something nice about her, it's
about her hair, and she isn't keen on the way
her hair is. She says it makes her look "like a
boy," and she is "tired" of looking like a boy.
There's something wrong with this marriage.
George hardly pays attention to his wife, but he
wants her to look like a boy. Maybe the idea is
that this macho guy wants to keep her looking
like an inferior (immature) version of himself.
Anyway, he certainly doesn't seem interested in
letting her fulfill herself as a woman.

I think my feelings add up to this: I like
the way Hemingway shows us the relation between
the husband and wife (even though the relation
is pretty bad), and I like the innkeeper. In a
way, even if the relation with the couple ends
unhappily, the story has a sort of happy ending,
so far as it goes, since the innkeeper does what
he can to please his guest: he sends the maid,
with the cat. There's really nothing more that
he can do.

More about the ending. The more I think about
it, the more I feel that the ending is as happy
as it can be. George is awful. When his wife
says "I want a cat and I want a cat now," Hemingway tells us "George was not listening." And
then, a moment later, almost like a good fairy
the maid appears and grants the wife's wish.

4. The title. I don't suppose that I would have
   called it "Cat in the Rain," but I don't know
   what I would have called it. Maybe "An American
   Couple in Italy." Or maybe "The Innkeeper." I
   really do think that the innkeeper is very important, even though he only has a few lines.
   He's very impressive--not only to the girl, but
   to me (and maybe to all readers), since at the
   end of the story we see how careful the innkeeper is.

   But the more I think about Hemingway's
   title, the more I think that maybe it also
   refers to the girl. Like the "poor kitty" in the
   rain, the wife is in a pretty bad situation. "It
   isn't any fun to be a poor kitty out in the
   rain." Of course the woman is indoors, but her
   husband generates lots of unpleasant weather.
   She may as well be out in the rain. She says "I
   want to have a kitty to sit on my lap and purr
   when I stroke it." This shows that she wants to
   be affectionate and that she also wants to have
   someone respond to her affection. She is like a
   cat in the rain.

   Oh, I just noticed that the wife at first
   calls the cat "her" rather than "it." ("The cat
   was trying to make herself compact. . . .")
   Later she says "it," but at first she thinks of
   the cat as female--because (I think) she identifies with the cat.

The responses of this student probably include statements that you want
to take issue with. Or perhaps you feel that the student did not even mention some things that you think are important. You may want to jot down
some notes and raise some questions in class.

TOPICS FOR DISCUSSION AND WRITING

1. Can we be certain that the cat at the end of the story is the cat that
   the woman saw in the rain? (When we first hear about the cat in the
   rain we are not told anything about its color, and at the end of the
   story we are not told that the tortoise-shell cat is wet.) Does
   it matter if there are two cats?
2. One student argued that the cat represents the child that the girl wants
   to have. Do you think there is something to this idea? How might
   you support or refute it?

3. Consider the following passage:

> As the American girl passed the office, the padrone bowed from his desk. Something felt very small and tight inside the girl. The padrone made her feel very small and at the same time really important. She had a momentary feeling of being of supreme importance.

Do you think there is anything sexual here? And if so, that the passage tells us something about her relations with her husband? Support your view.

4. What do you suppose Hemingway's attitude was toward each of the three chief characters? How might you support your hunch?

5. Hemingway wrote the story in Italy, when his wife Hadley was pregnant. In a letter to F. Scott Fitzgerald he said,

> Cat in the Rain wasn't about Hadley. . . . When I wrote that we were at Rapallo but Hadley was 4 months pregnant with Bumby. The Inn Keeper was the one at Cortina D'Ampezzo. . . . Hadley never made a speech in her life about wanting a baby because she had been told various things by her doctor and I'd—no use going into all that. (*Letters,* p. 180)

According to some biographers, the story shows that Hemingway knew his marriage was going on the rocks (Hemingway and Hadley divorced). Does knowing that Hemingway's marriage turned out unhappily help you to understand the story? Does it make the story more interesting? And do you think that the story tells a biographer something about Hemingway's life?

And here is one more question:

6. It is sometimes said that a good short story does two things at once: It provides a believable picture of the surface of life, and it also illuminates some moral or psychological complexity that we feel is part of the essence of human life. This dual claim may not be true, but for the moment accept it. Do you think that Hemingway's story fulfills either or both of these specifications? Support your view.

Later chapters will offer some technical vocabulary and will examine specific elements of fiction, but familiarity with technical vocabulary will not in itself assure that you will understand and enjoy fiction. There is no substitute for reading carefully, thinking about your responses, and (pen in hand) rereading the text, looking for evidence that accounts for your responses or that will lead you to different and perhaps richer responses. The essays that you will submit to your instructor are, finally, rooted in the annotations that you make in your text and the notes in which you record and explore your responses.

3
Stories and Meanings

People tell stories for many reasons, including the sheer egotistical delight of talking, but probably most of the best storytelling proceeds from one of two more commendable desires: a desire to entertain or a desire to instruct. Among the most famous of the stories designed to instruct are the parables that Jesus told, for instance, The Parable of the Prodigal Son, which we discussed in the previous chapter. (*Parable* comes from the Greek word meaning "to throw beside," that is, "to compare." We are to compare these little stories with our own behavior.) We can say that the parable is told for the sake of the point; we also can say that it is told for our sake, because we are implicitly invited to see ourselves in the story, and to live our lives in accordance with it. This simple but powerful story, with its memorable characters—though nameless and briefly sketched—makes us feel the point in our hearts.

Even older than Jesus' parables are the fables attributed to Aesop, some of which go back to the seventh century before Jesus. These stories also teach lessons by telling brief incidents from which homely morals may easily be drawn, even though the stories are utterly fanciful. Among famous examples are the stories of the hare and the tortoise, the boy who cried "Wolf," the ant and the grasshopper, and a good many others that stick in the mind because of the sharply contrasted characters in sharply imagined situations. The fables just mentioned take only four or five sentences apiece, but, brief as they are, Aesop told some briefer ones. Here is the briefest of all:

> A vixen sneered at a lioness because she never bore more than
> one cub. "Only one," the lioness replied, "but a lion."

Just that: a situation with a conflict (the mere confrontation of a fox and a lion brings together the ignoble and the noble) and a resolution (*something* must come out of such a confrontation). There is no setting (we are not told that "one day in June a vixen, walking down a road, met a lioness"), but none is needed here. What there is—however briefly set forth—is characterization. The fox's baseness is effectively communicated through the verb "sneered" and through her taunt, and the lioness's nobility is even more effectively communicated through the brevity and decisiveness of her reply. This reply at first seems to agree with the fox ("Only one") and then, after a suspenseful delay provided by the words "the lioness replied," the reply is tersely and powerfully completed ("but a lion"), placing the matter firmly in a new light. Granted that the story is not much of a story, still, it is finely told, and more potent—more memorable, more lively, we might even say more real, despite its talking animals—than the mere moral. "Small-minded people confuse quantity with quality."

Here is a much later short tale, from nineteenth-century Japan. It is said to be literally true, but whether it really occurred or not is scarcely of any importance. It is the story, not the history, that counts.

> Two monks, Tanzan and Ekido, were once traveling together down a muddy road. A heavy rain was still falling.
>
> Coming around a bend, they met a lovely girl in a silk kimono and sash, unable to cross the intersection.
>
> "Come on, girl," said Tanzan at once. Lifting her in his arms, he carried her over the mud.
>
> Ekido did not speak again until that night when they reached a lodging temple. Then he no longer could restrain himself. "We monks don't go near females," he told Tanzan, "especially not young and lovely ones. It is dangerous. Why did you do that?"
>
> "I left the girl there," said Tanzan. "Are you still carrying her?"

A superb story. The opening paragraph, though simple and matter-of-fact, holds our attention: we sense that something interesting is going to happen during this journey along a muddy road on a rainy day. Perhaps we even sense, somehow, by virtue of the references to the mud and the rain, that the journey itself rather than the travelers' destination will be the heart of the story: getting there will be more than half the fun. And then, after the introduction of the two **characters** and the **setting,** we quickly get the **complication,** the encounter with the girl. Still there is apparently no **conflict,** though in "Ekido did not speak again until that night" we sense an unspoken conflict, an action (or, in this case, an inaction) that must be explained, an imbalance that must be righted before we are finished. At last Ekido, no longer able to contain his thoughts, lets his indignation burst out: "We monks don't go near females . . ., especially not young and lovely ones. It is dangerous. Why did you do that?" His statement and his question reveal not only his moral principles, but also his insecurity and the anger that grows from it. And now, when the conflict is out in the open, comes the brief reply that reveals Tanzan's very

different character as clearly as the outburst revealed Ekido's. This reply —
though we could not have predicted it — strikes us as exactly right, bringing the story to a perfect end, i.e., to a point (like the ends of Jesus' parable
and Aesop's fable) at which there is no more to be said. It provides the
dénouement (literally, "unknotting"), or resolution.

Let's look now at another short piece, though this one is somewhat
longer than the stories we have just read, and it is less concerned than
they are with teaching a lesson.

Anton Chekhov

*Anton Chekhov (1860–1904) was born in Russia, the son of a shop-
keeper. While a medical student at Moscow University, Chekhov
wrote stories, sketches, and reviews to help support his family and
to finance his education. In 1884 he received his medical degree,
began to practice medicine, published his first book of stories, and
suffered the first of a series of hemorrhages from tuberculosis. In
his remaining twenty years, in addition to writing several hundred
stories, he wrote plays, half a dozen of which have established themselves as classics. He died from tuberculosis at the age of forty-four.*

Misery

Translated by Constance Garnett

"*To Whom Shall I Tell My Grief?*"

The twilight of evening. Big flakes of wet snow are whirling lazily about
the street lamps, which have just been lighted, and lying in a thin soft
layer on roofs, horses' backs, shoulders, caps. Iona Potapov, the sledge-
driver, is all white like a ghost. He sits on the box without stirring, bent
as double as the living body can be bent. If a regular snowdrift fell on
him it seems as though even then he would not think it necessary to shake
it off. . . . His little mare is white and motionless too. Her stillness, the
angularity of her lines, and the stick-like straightness of her legs make her
look like a halfpenny gingerbread horse. She is probably lost in thought.
Anyone who has been torn away from the plough, from the familiar gray
landscapes, and cast into this slough, full of monstrous lights, of unceas-
ing uproar and hurrying people, is bound to think.

It is a long time since Iona and his nag have budged. They came
out of the yard before dinner-time and not a single fare yet. But now the

shades of evening are falling on the town. The pale light of the street lamps changes to a vivid color, and the bustle of the street grows noisier.

"Sledge to Vyborgskaya!" Iona hears. "Sledge!"

Iona starts, and through his snow-plastered eyelashes sees an officer in a military overcoat with a hood over his head.

"To Vyborgskaya," repeats the officer. "Are you asleep? To Vyborgskaya!"

In token of assent Iona gives a tug at the reins which sends cakes of snow flying from the horse's back and shoulders. The officer gets into the sledge. The sledge-driver clicks to the horse, cranes his neck like a swan, rises in his seat, and more from habit than necessity brandishes his whip. The mare cranes her neck, too, crooks her stick-like legs, and hesitatingly sets off. . . .

"Where are you shoving, you devil?" Iona immediately hears shouts from the dark mass shifting to and fro before him. "Where the devil are you going? Keep to the r–right!"

"You don't know how to drive! Keep to the right," says the officer angrily.

A coachman driving a carriage swears at him; a pedestrian crossing the road and brushing the horse's nose with his shoulder looks at him angrily and shakes the snow off his sleeve. Iona fidgets on the box as though he were sitting on thorns, jerks his elbows, and turns his eyes about like one possessed, as though he did not know where he was or why he was there.

"What rascals they all are!" says the officer jocosely. "They are simply doing their best to run up against you or fall under the horse's feet. They must be doing it on purpose."

Iona looks at his fare and moves his lips. . . . Apparently he means to say something, but nothing comes out but a sniff.

"What?" inquires the officer.

Iona gives a wry smile, and straining his throat, brings out huskily: "My son . . ., er . . . my son died this week, sir."

"H'm! What did he die of?"

Iona turns his whole body round to his fare, and says:

"Who can tell! It must have been from fever. . . . He lay three days in the hospital and then he died. . . . God's will."

"Turn round, you devil!" comes out of the darkness. "Have you gone cracked, you old dog? Look where you are going!"

"Drive on! drive on! . . . " says the officer. "We shan't get there till tomorrow going on like this. Hurry up!"

The sledge-driver cranes his neck again, rises in his seat, and with heavy grace swings his whip. Several times he looks round at the officer, but the latter keeps his eyes shut and is apparently disinclined to listen. Putting his fare down at Vyborgskaya, Iona stops by a restaurant, and again sits huddled up on the box. . . . Again the wet snow paints him and his horse white. One hour passes, and then another. . . .

Three young men, two tall and thin, one short and hunchbacked, come up, railing at each other and loudly stamping on the pavement with their galoshes.

"Cabby, to the Police Bridge!" the hunchback cries in a cracked voice. "The three of us, . . . twenty kopecks!"

Iona tugs at the reins and clicks to his horse. Twenty kopecks is not a fair price, but he has no thoughts for that. Whether it is a rouble or whether it is five kopecks does not matter to him now so long as he has a fare. . . . The three young men, shoving each other and using bad language, go up to the sledge, and all three try to sit down at once. The question remains to be settled: Which are to sit down and which one is to stand? After a long altercation, ill-temper, and abuse, they come to the conclusion that the hunchback must stand because he is the shortest.

"Well, drive on," says the hunchback in his cracked voice, settling himself and breathing down Iona's neck. "Cut along! What a cap you've got, my friend! You wouldn't find a worse one in all Petersburg. . . ."

"He-he! . . . he-he! . . ." laughs Iona. "It's nothing to boast of!"

"Well, then, nothing to boast of, drive on! Are you going to drive like this all the way? Eh? Shall I give you one in the neck?"

"My head aches," says one of the tall ones. "At the Dukmasovs' yesterday Vaska and I drank four bottles of brandy between us."

"I can't make out why you talk such stuff," says the other tall one angrily. "You lie like a brute."

"Strike me dead, it's the truth! . . ."

"It's about as true as that a louse coughs."

"He-he!" grins Iona. "Me-er-ry gentlemen!"

"Tfoo! the devil take you!" cries the hunchback indignantly. "Will you get on, you old plague, or won't you? Is that the way to drive? Give her one with the whip. Hang it all, give it her well."

Iona feels behind his back the jolting person and quivering voice of the hunchback. He hears abuse addressed to him, he sees people, and the feeling of loneliness begins little by little to be less heavy on his heart. The hunchback swears at him, till he chokes over some elaborately whimsical string of epithets and is overpowered by his cough. His tall companions begin talking of a certain Nadyezhda Petrovna. Iona looks round at them. Waiting till there is a brief pause, he looks round once more and says:

"This week . . . er . . . my . . . er . . . son died!"

"We shall all die, . . ." says the hunchback with a sigh, wiping his lips after coughing. "Come, drive on! drive on! My friends, I simply cannot stand crawling like this! When will he get us there?"

"Well, you give him a little encouragement . . . one in the neck!"

"Do you hear, you old plague? I'll make you smart. If one stands on ceremony with fellows like you one may as well walk. Do you hear, you old dragon? Or don't you care a hang what we say?"

And Iona hears rather than feels a slap on the back of his neck.

"He-he! . . ." he laughs. "Merry gentlemen . . . God give you health!"

"Cabman, are you married?" asks one of the tall ones.

"I? He-he! Me-er-ry gentlemen. The only wife for me now is the damp earth. . . . He-ho-ho! . . . The grave that is! . . . Here my son's dead and I am alive. . . . It's a strange thing, death has come in at the wrong door. . . . Instead of coming for me it went for my son. . . ."

And Iona turns round to tell them how his son died, but at that point the hunchback gives a faint sigh and announces that, thank God! they have arrived at last. After taking his twenty kopecks, Iona gazes for a long while after the revelers, who disappear into a dark entry. Again he is alone and again there is silence for him. . . . The misery which has been for a brief space eased comes back again and tears his heart more cruelly than ever. With a look of anxiety and suffering Iona's eyes stray restlessly among the crowds moving to an fro on both sides of the street: can he not find among those thousands someone who will listen to him? But the crowds flit by heedless of him and his misery. . . . His misery is immense, beyond all bounds. If Iona's heart were to burst and his misery to flow out, it would flood the whole world, it seems, but yet it is not seen. It has found a hiding-place in such an insignificant shell that one would not have found it with a candle by daylight. . . .

Iona sees a house-porter with a parcel and makes up his mind to address him.

"What time will it be, friend?" he asks.

"Going on for ten. . . . Why have you stopped here? Drive on!"

Iona drives a few paces away, bends himself double, and gives himself up to his misery. He feels it is no good to appeal to people. But before five minutes have passed he draws himself up, shakes his head as though he feels a sharp pain, and tugs at the reins. . . . He can bear it no longer.

"Back to the yard!" he thinks. "To the yard!"

And his little mare, as though she knew his thoughts, falls to trotting. An hour and a half later Iona is sitting by a big dirty stove. On the stove, on the floor, and on the benches are people snoring. The air is full of smells and stuffiness. Iona looks at the sleeping figures, scratches himself, and regrets that he has come home so early. . . .

"I have not earned enough to pay for the oats, even," he thinks. "That's why I am so miserable. A man who knows how to do his work, . . . who has had enough to eat, and whose horse has had enough to eat, is always at ease. . . ."

In one of the corners a young cabman gets up, clears his throat sleepily, and makes for the waterbucket.

"Want a drink?" Iona asks him.

"Seems so."

"May it do you good. . . . But my son is dead, mate. . . . Do you hear? This week in the hospital. . . . It's queer business. . . ."

Iona looks to see the effect produced by his words, but he sees nothing. The young man has covered his head over and is already asleep. The old man sighs and scratches himself. . . . Just as the young man had been thirsty for water, he thirsts for speech. His son will soon have been dead a week, and he has not really talked to anybody yet. . . . He wants to talk of it properly, with deliberation. . . . He wants to tell how his son was taken ill, how he suffered, what he said before he died, how he died. . . . He wants to describe the funeral, and how he went to the hospital to get his son's clothes. He still has his daughter Anisya in the country. . . . And he wants to talk about her too. . . . Yes, he has plenty to talk about now. His listener ought to sigh and exclaim and lament. . . . It would be even better to talk to women. Though they are silly creatures, they blubber at the first word.

"Let's go out and have a look at the mare," Iona thinks. "There is always time for sleep. . . . You'll have sleep enough, no fear. . . ."

He puts on his coat and goes into the stables where his mare is standing. He thinks about oats, about hay, about the weather. . . . He cannot think about his son when he is alone. . . . To talk about him with someone is possible, but to think of him and picture him is insufferable anguish. . . .

"Are you munching?" Iona asks his mare, seeing her shining eyes. "There, munch away, munch away. . . . Since we have not earned enough for oats, we will eat hay. . . . Yes, . . . I have grown too old to drive. . . . My son ought to be driving, not I. . . . He was a real coachman. . . . He ought to have lived. . . ."

Iona is silent for a while, and then he goes on:

"That's how it is, old girl. . . . Kuzma Ionitch is gone. . . . He said good-by to me. . . . He went and died for no reason. . . . Now, suppose you had a little colt, and you were own mother to that little colt. . . . And all at once that same little colt went and died. . . . You'd be sorry, wouldn't you? . . ."

The little mare munches, listens, and breathes on her master's hands. Iona is carried away and tells her all about it.

[1886]

Let's look at Chekhov's "Misery" as a piece of craftsmanship. The happenings (here, a cabman seeks to tell his grief to several people, but is rebuffed and finally tells it to his horse) are the **plot;** the participants (cabman, officer, drunks, etc.) are the **characters;** the locale, time, and social circumstances (a snowy city in Russia, in the late nineteenth century) are the **setting;** and (though, as we will urge later, this word should be used with special caution) the meaning or point is the **theme.**

The traditional plot has this structure:

1. **Exposition** (setting forth of the initial situation)
2. **Conflict** (a complication that moves to a climax)
3. **Dénouement** (the outcome of the conflict; the resolution)

Chekhov's first paragraph, devoted to **exposition,** begins by introducing a situation that seems to be static: it briefly describes a motionless cabdriver, who "is all white like a ghost," and the cabdriver's mare, whose immobility and angularity "make her look like a halfpenny gingerbread horse." A reader probably anticipates that something will intrude into this apparently static situation; some sort of conflict will be established, and then in all probability will be (in one way or another) resolved. In fact, the inertia described at the very beginning is disturbed even before the paragraph ends, when Chekhov rather surprisingly takes us into the mind not of the cabdriver but of the horse, telling us that if we were in such a situation as the horse finds itself, we "too would find it difficult not to think."

By the middle of the first paragraph, we have been given a brief but entirely adequate view of the **setting:** a Russian city in the days of horse-drawn sleighs, that is, in Chekhov's lifetime. Strictly speaking, of course, the paragraph does not specify Russia or the period, but the author is a Russian writing in the late nineteenth century, the character has a Russian name, and there is lots of snow so one concludes that the story is set in Russia. (A reader somewhat familiar with Chekhov does not even have to read the first paragraph of this story to know the setting, since all of Chekhov's work is set in the Russia of his day.)

One might almost say that by the end of the first paragraph we have met all the chief **characters**—though, of course, we can't know this until we finish the story. In later paragraphs we will meet additional figures, but the chief characters—the characters whose fates we are concerned with, one might say—are simply the cabdriver and the horse. It's odd, of course, to call the horse a character, but, as we noticed, even in the first paragraph Chekhov takes us into the mind of the horse. Notice, too, how Chekhov establishes connections between the man and the horse; for instance, when the first fare gets into the sleigh, the driver "cranes his neck" and then "the mare cranes her neck, too." By the end of the story, the horse seems almost a part of Iona. Perhaps the horse will be the best possible listener, since perhaps grief of Iona's sort can be told only to the self.

Before talking further about the characters, we should point out that the word "character" has two chief meanings:

1. a figure in a literary work (thus Iona is a character, the officer who hires the cab is another character, and the drunks are additional characters).

2. personality, as when we say that Iona's character is described only briefly, or that Hamlet's character is complex, or that So-and-So's character is unpleasant.

Usually the context makes clear the sense in which the word is used, but in your own writing, make sure that there is no confusion.

It is sometimes said that figures in literature are either **flat characters** (one-dimensional figures, figures with simple personalities) or **round characters** (complex figures). The usual implication is that good writers give us round characters, believeable figures who are more than cardboard cutouts holding up signs saying "jealous lover," "cruel landlord," "kind mother," and so forth. But a short story scarecely has space to show the complexity or roundness of several characters, and in fact, many good stories do not give even their central characters much complexity. In "Misery," for instance, Iona is shown chiefly as a grieving father aching to speak of the death of his son. We don't know what sort of food he likes, whether he ever gets drunk, what he thinks of the Czar, or whether he belongs to the church. But it is hard to imagine that knowing any of these things would be relevant and would increase our interest in him. Similarly, the other characters in the story are drawn with a few simple lines. The officer who first hires the cab is arrogant ("Sledge to Vyborgskaya! . . . Are you asleep? To Vyborgskaya!"), and though he at first makes a little joke that leads Iona to think the officer will listen to his story, the officer quickly changes the subject. We know of him only that he wants to get to Vyborg. The three noisy drunks whom Iona next picks up can probably be fairly characterized as just that—three noisy drunks. Again, we can hardly imagine that the story would be better if we knew much more about these drunks.

On the other hand, Iona is not quite so flat as we have perhaps implied. A careful reader notices, for instance, that Iona reveals other things about himself in addition to his need to express his grief. For instance, he treats his horse as kindly as possible. When the officer gets into the cab, Iona "more from habit than necessity brandishes his whip"—but he gets the horse moving by making a clicking sound, and he actually whips the horse only when the officer tells him to hurry. Later the hunchback will say of the mare, "Give her one with the whip. Hang it all, give it her well," but we feel that Iona uses his horse as gently as is possible.

It should be noted, however, that the drunks, though they are not much more than drunks, are not less than drunks either. They are quarrelsome and they even display touches of cruelty, but we cannot call them villains. In some degree, the fact that they are drunk excuses their "bad language," their "ill-tempers," and even their displays of cruelty. If these characters are fairly flat, they nevertheless are thoroughly believable, and we know as much about them as we need to know for the purposes of the story. Furthermore, the characters in a story help to characterize other characters, by their resemblances or their differences. How Iona might behave if he were an officer, or if he were drunk, we do not know, but he is in some degree contrasted with the other characters and thus gains some complexity, to the extent that we can at least say that he is *not* drunk, arrogant, or quarrelsome.

We need hardly ask if there is **motivation** (compelling grounds, external and also within one's personality) for Iona's final action. He has tried to express his grief to the officer, and then to the drunks. Next, his eyes search the crowds to "find someone who will listen to him." After speaking to the house-porter, Iona sees, Chekhov tells us, that "it is no good to appeal to people." When we read this line, we probably do not think, or at least do not think consciously, that he will turn from people to the mare, but when at the end of the story he does turn to the mare, the action seems entirely natural, inevitable.

In some stories, of course, we are chiefly interested in plot (the arrangement of happenings or doings), in others we are chiefly interested in character (the personalities of the doers), but on the whole the two are so intertwined that interest in one involves interest in the other. Happenings occur (people cross paths), and personalities respond, engendering further happenings. As Henry James rhetorically asked, "What is character but the determination of incident? What is incident but the illustration of character?" Commonly, as a good story proceeds and we become increasingly familiar with the characters, we get intimations of what they may do in the future. We may not know precisely how they will act, but we have a fairly good idea, and when in fact we see their subsequent actions, we usually recognize the appropriateness. Sometimes there are hints of what is to come, and because of this **foreshadowing,** we are not shocked by what happens later, but rather we experience suspense as we wait for the expected to come about. Coleridge had Shakespeare's use of foreshadowing in mind when he praised him for giving us not surprise, but expectation — the active reader participates in the work by reading it responsively — and then the fulfillment of expectation. E. M. Forster, in *Aspects of the Novel,* has a shrewd comment on the importance of both fulfilling expectation and offering a slight surprise: "Shock, followed by the feeling, 'Oh, that's all right,' is a sign that all is well with plot: characters, to be real, ought to run smoothly, but a plot ought to cause surprise."

Finally, a few words about **theme.** Usually we feel that a story is about something, it has a point — a theme. (What happens is the plot; what the happenings add up to is the theme.) But a word of caution is needed here. What is the theme of "Misery"? One student formulated the theme thus:

Human beings must utter their grief, even if only to an animal.

Another student formulated it thus:

Human beings are indifferent to the sufferings of others.

Still another student offered this:

> Deep suffering is incommunicable, but the sufferer must try to find an outlet.

And, of course, many other formulations are possible. Probably there is no "right" statement of the theme of "Misery" or of any other good story: a story is not simply an illustration of an abstract statement of theme. A story has a complex variety of details that modify any summary statement we may offer when we try to say what it is about. And what lives in our memory is not an abstract statement—certainly not a thesis, i.e., a proposition offered and argued, such as "We should pay attention to the suffering of others." What lives is an image that by every word in the story has convinced us that it is a representation, if not of "reality," of at least an aspect of reality.

Still, the writer is guided by a theme in the choice of details; of many possible details, Chekhov decided to present only a few. The musical sense of the word "theme" can help us to understand what a theme in literature is: "a melody constituting the basis of variation, development, or the like." The variations and the development cannot be random, but must have a basis. (We have already suggested that the episodes in "Misery"—the movement from the officer to the drunks and then to the house-porter and the other cabman—are not random, but somehow seem exactly "right," just as the remarks about the man and the horse both stretching their necks seem "right.") What is it, Robert Frost asks, that prevents the writer from jumping "from one chance suggestion to another in all directions as of a hot afternoon in the life of a grasshopper?" Frost's answer: "Theme alone can steady us down."

We can, then, talk about the theme—again, what the story adds up to—as long as we do not think a statement of the theme is equivalent to or is a substitute for the whole story. As Flannery O'Connor said, "Some people have the notion that you can read the story and then climb out of it into the meaning, but for the fiction writer himself the whole story is the meaning." A theme, she said, is not like a string tying a sack of chicken feed, to be pulled out so that the feed can be got at. "A story is a way to say something that can't be said any other way." That "something"—which can't be said in any other way—is the theme. (On theme, see also page 100.)

TOPICS FOR DISCUSSION AND WRITING

1. What do you like or not like about Chekhov's story? Why?
2. Try to examine in detail your response to the ending. Do you think the ending is, in a way, a happy ending? Would you prefer a different ending? For instance, should the story end when the young cabman falls asleep? Or when Iona sets out for the stable? Or can you imagine a better ending? If so, what?

KATE CHOPIN: THREE STORIES

Kate Chopin

Kate Chopin (1851–1904)—the name is pronounced in the French way, somewhat like "show pan"—was born in St. Louis, with the name Katherine O'Flaherty. Her father was an immigrant from Ireland, and her mother was descended from an old Creole family. (In the United States, a Creole is a person descended from the original French settlers in Louisiana or the original Spanish settlers in the Gulf States.) At the age of nineteen she married Oscar Chopin, a cotton broker in New Orleans. They had six children, and though Kate Chopin had contemplated a literary career, she did not turn seriously to writing until after her husband's death in 1883. Most of her fiction concerns the lives of the descendants of the French who had settled in Louisiana.

Ripe Figs

Maman-Nainaine said that when the figs were ripe Babette might go to visit her cousins down on the Bayou-Lafourche where the sugar cane grows. Not that the ripening of figs had the least thing to do with it, but that is the way Maman-Nainaine was.

It seemed to Babette a very long time to wait; for the leaves upon the trees were tender yet, and the figs were like little hard, green marbles.

But warm rains came along and plenty of strong sunshine, and though Maman-Nainaine was as patient as the statue of la Madone, and Babette as restless as a humming-bird, the first thing they both knew it was hot summer-time. Every day Babette danced out to where the fig-trees were in a long line against the fence. She walked slowly beneath them, carefully peering between the gnarled, spreading branches. But each time she came disconsolate away again. What she saw there finally was something that made her sing and dance the whole long day.

When Maman-Nainaine sat down in her stately way to breakfast, the following morning, her muslin cap standing like an aureole about her white, placid face, Babette approached. She bore a dainty porcelain platter, which she set down before her godmother. It contained a dozen purple figs, fringed around with their rich, green leaves.

"Ah," said Maman-Nainaine arching her eyebrows, "how early the figs have ripened this year!"

"Oh," said Babette. "I think they have ripened very late."

"Babette," continued Maman-Nainaine, as she peeled the very plum-pest figs with her pointed silver fruit-knife, "you will carry my love to them all down on Bayou-Lafourche. And tell your Tante[1] Frosine I shall look for her at Toussaint—when the chrysanthemums are in bloom."

[1893]

TOPICS FOR DISCUSSION AND WRITING

1. Compare and constrast Maman-Nainaine and Babette.
2. Two questions here: What, if anything, "happens" in "Ripe Figs"? And what, in your opinion, is the story about?
3. What, if anything, would be lost if the last line were omitted? (If you can think of a better final line, write it, and explain why your version is preferable.)

The Story of an Hour

Knowing that Mrs. Mallard was afflicted with a heart trouble, great care was taken to break to her as gently as possible the news of her husband's death.

It was her sister Josephine who told her, in broken sentences, veiled hints that revealed in half concealing. Her husband's friend Richards was there, too, near her. It was he who had been in the newspaper office when intelligence of the railroad disaster was received, with Brently Mallard's name leading the list of "killed." He had only taken the time to assure himself of its truth by a second telegram, and had hastened to forestall any less careful, less tender friend in bearing the sad message.

She did not hear the story as many women have heard the same, with a paralyzed inability to accept its significance. She wept at once, with sudden, wild abandonment, in her sister's arms. When the storm of grief had spent itself she went away to her room alone. She would have no one follow her.

There stood, facing the open window, a comfortable, roomy arm-chair. Into this she sank, pressed down by a physical exhaustion that haunted her body and seemed to reach into her soul.

She could see in the open square before her house the tops of trees that were all aquiver with the new spring life. The delicious breath of rain was in the air. In the street below a peddler was crying his wares. The notes of a distant song which some one was singing reached her faintly, and countless sparrows were twittering in the eaves.

[1]**Tante**   aunt (French)

There were patches of blue sky showing here and there through the clouds that had met and piled above the other in the west facing her window.

She sat with her head thrown back upon the cushion of the chair quite motionless, except when a sob came up into her throat and shook her, as a child who has cried itself to sleep continues to sob in its dreams.

She was young, with a fair, calm face, whose lines bespoke repression and even a certain strength. But now there was a dull stare in her eyes, whose gaze was fixed away off yonder on one of those patches of blue sky. It was not a glance of reflection, but rather indicated a suspension of intelligent thought.

There was something coming to her and she was waiting for it, fearfully. What was it? She did not know; it was too subtle and elusive to name. But she felt it, creeping out of the sky, reaching toward her through the sounds, the scents, the color that filled the air.

Now her bosom rose and fell tumultuously. She was beginning to recognize this thing that was approaching to possess her, and she was striving to beat it back with her will—as powerless as her two white slender hands would have been.

When she abandoned herself a little whispered word escaped her slightly parted lips. She said it over and over under her breath: "Free, free, free!" The vacant stare and the look of terror that had followed it went from her eyes. They stayed keen and bright. Her pulses beat fast, and the coursing blood warmed and relaxed every inch of her body.

She did not stop to ask if it were not a monstrous joy that held her. A clear and exalted perception enabled her to dismiss the suggestion as trivial.

She knew that she would weep again when she saw the kind, tender hands folded in death; the face that had never looked save with love upon her, fixed and gray and dead. But she saw beyond that bitter moment a long procession of years to come that would belong to her absolutely. And she opened and spread her arms out to them in welcome.

There would be no one to live for her during those coming years; she would live for herself. There would be no powerful will bending her in that blind persistence with which men and women believe they have a right to impose a private will upon a fellow creature. A kind intention or a cruel intention made the act seem no less a crime as she looked upon it in that brief moment of illumination.

And yet she had loved him—sometimes. Often she had not. What did it matter! What could love, the unsolved mystery, count for in face of this possession of self-assertion which she suddenly recognized as the strongest impulse of her being.

"Free! Body and soul free!" she kept whispering.

Josephine was kneeling before the closed door with her lips to the keyhole, imploring for admission. "Louise, open the door! I beg; open the door—you will make yourself ill. What are you doing, Louise? For heaven's sake open the door."

"Go away. I am not making myself ill." No; she was drinking in a very elixir of life through that open window.

Her fancy was running riot along those days ahead of her. Spring days, and summer days, and all sorts of days that would be her own. She breathed a quick prayer that life might be long. It was only yesterday she had thought with a shudder that life might be long.

She arose at length and opened the door to her sister's importunities. There was a feverish triumph in her eyes, and she carried herself unwittingly like a goddess of Victory. She clasped her sister's waist, and together they descended the stairs. Richards stood waiting for them at the bottom.

Some one was opening the front door with a latchkey. It was Brently Mallard who entered, a little travel-stained, composedly carrying his grip-sack and umbrella. He had been far from the scene of accident, and did not even know there had been one. He stood amazed at Josephine's piercing cry; at Richards' quick motion to screen him from the view of his wife.

But Richards was too late.

When the doctors came they said she had died of heart disease—of joy that kills.

[1894]

TOPICS FOR DISCUSSION AND WRITING

1. Is Mrs. Mallard's grief sincere?
2. In the first half of the story, how does Chopin help to prepare for Mrs. Mallard's words, "Free, free, free"?
3. How accurate is the doctors' final diagnosis?

The Storm

I

The leaves were so still that even Bibi thought it was going to rain. Bobinôt, who was accustomed to converse on terms of perfect equality with his little son, called the child's attention to certain sombre clouds that were rolling with sinister intention from the west, accompanied by a sullen, threatening roar. They were at Friedheimer's store and decided to remain there till the storm had passed. They sat within the door on two empty kegs. Bibi was four years old and looked very wise.

"Mama'll be 'fraid, yes," he suggested with blinking eyes.

"She'll shut the house. Maybe she got Sylvie helpin' her this evenin'," Bobinôt responded reassuringly.

"No; she ent got Sylvie. Sylvie was helpin' her yistiday," piped Bibi.

Bobinôt arose and going across to the counter purchased a can of shrimps, of which Calixta was very fond. Then he returned to his perch on the keg and sat stolidly holding the can of shrimps while the storm burst. It shook the wooden store and seemed to be ripping great furrows in the distant field. Bibi laid his little hand on his father's knee and was not afraid.

II

Calixta, at home, felt no uneasiness for their safety. She sat at a side window sewing furiously on a sewing machine. She was greatly occupied and did not notice the approaching storm. But she felt very warm and often stopped to mop her face on which the perspiration gathered in beads. She unfastened her white sacque at the throat. It began to grow dark, and suddenly realizing the situation she got up hurriedly and went about closing windows and doors.

Out on the small front gallery she had hung Bobinôt's Sunday clothes to air and she hastened out to gather them before the rain fell. As she stepped outside, Alcée Laballière rode in at the gate. She had not seen him very often since her marriage, and never alone. She stood there with Bobinôt's coat in her hands, and the big rain drops began to fall. Alcée rode his horse under the shelter of a side projection where the chickens had huddled and there were plows and a harrow piled up in the corner.

"May I come and wait on your gallery till the storm is over, Calixta?" he asked.

"Come 'long in, M'sieur Alcée."

His voice and her own startled her as if from a trance, and she seized Bobinôt's vest. Alcée, mounting to the porch, grabbed the trousers and snatched Bibi's braided jacket that was about to be carried away by a sudden gust of wind. He expressed an intention to remain outside, but it was soon apparent that he might as well have been out in the open: the water beat in upon the boards in driving sheets, and he went inside, closing the door after him. It was even necessary to put something beneath the door to keep the water out.

"My! what a rain! It's good two years sence it rain' like that," exclaimed Calixta as she rolled up a piece of bagging and Alcée helped her to thrust it beneath the crack.

She was a little fuller of figure than five years before when she married; but she had lost nothing of her vivacity. Her blue eyes still retained their melting quality; and her yellow hair, dishevelled by the wind and rain, kinked more stubbornly than ever about her ears and temples.

The rain beat upon the low, shingled roof with a force and clatter that threatened to break an entrance and deluge them there. They were in the dining room—the sitting room—the general utility room. Adjoining was her bed room, with Bibi's couch along side her own. The door stood open, and the room with its white, monumental bed, its closed shutters, looked dim and mysterious.

Alcée flung himself into a rocker and Calixta nervously began to gather up from the floor the lengths of a cotton sheet which she had been sewing.

"If this keeps up, *Dieu sait*[1] if the levees goin' to stan' it!" she exclaimed.

"What have you got to do with the levees?"

"I got enough to do! An' there's Bobinôt with Bibi out in that storm—if he only didn' left Friedheimer's!"

"Let us hope, Calixta, that Bobinôt's got sense enough to come in out of a cyclone."

She went and stood at the window with a greatly disturbed look on her face. She wiped the frame that was clouded with moisture. It was stiflingly hot. Alcée got up and joined her at the window, looking over her shoulder. The rain was coming down in sheets obscuring the view of far-off cabins and enveloping the distant wood in a gray mist. The playing of the lightning was incessant. A bolt struck a tall chinaberry tree at the edge of the field. It filled all visible space with a blinding glare and the crash seemed to invade the very boards they stood upon.

Calixta put her hands to her eyes, and with a cry, staggered backward. Alcée's arm encircled her, and for an instant he drew her close and spasmodically to him.

"*Bonte!*"[2] she cried, releasing herself from his encircling arm and retreating from the window, "the house'll go next! If I only knew w'ere Bibi was!" She would not compose herself; she would not be seated. Alcée clasped her shoulders and looked into her face. The contact of her warm, palpitating body when he had unthinkingly drawn her into his arms, had aroused all the old-time infatuation and desire for her flesh.

"Calixta," he said, "don't be frightened. Nothing can happen. The house is too low to be struck, with so many tall trees standing about. There! aren't you going to be quiet? say, aren't you?" He pushed her hair back from her face that was warm and steaming. Her lips were as red and moist as pomegranate seed. Her white neck and a glimpse of her full, firm bosom disturbed him powerfully. As she glanced up at him the fear in her liquid blue eyes had given place to a drowsy gleam that unconsciously betrayed

---

[1] *Dieu sait* God only knows
[2] *Bonte!* Heavens!

a sensuous desire. He looked down into her eyes and there was nothing for him to do but to gather her lips in a kiss. It reminded him of Assumption.[3]

"Do you remember—in Assumption, Calixta?" he asked in a low voice broken by passion. Oh! she remembered; for in Assumption he had kissed her and kissed and kissed her; until his senses would well nigh fail, and to save her he would resort to a desperate flight. If she was not an immaculate dove in those days, she was still inviolate; a passionate creature whose very defenselessness had made her defense, against which his honor forbade him to prevail. Now—well, now—her lips seemed in a manner free to be tasted, as well as her round, white throat and her whiter breasts.

They did not heed the crashing torrents, and the roar of the elements made her laugh as she lay in his arms. She was a revelation in that dim, mysterious chamber; as white as the couch she lay upon. Her firm, elastic flesh that was knowing for the first time its birthright, was like a creamy lily that the sun invites to contribute its breath and perfume to the undying life of the world.

The generous abundance of her passion, without guile or trickery, was like a white flame which penetrated and found response in depths of his own sensuous nature that had never yet been reached.

When he touched her breasts they gave themselves up in quivering ecstasy, inviting his lips. Her mouth was a fountain of delight. And when he possessed her, they seemed to swoon together at the very borderland of life's mystery.

He stayed cushioned upon her, breathless, dazed, enervated, with his heart beating like a hammer upon her. With one hand she clasped his head, her lips lightly touching his forehead. The other hand stroked with a soothing rhythm his muscular shoulders.

The growl of the thunder was distant and passing away. The rain beat softly upon the shingles, inviting them to drowsiness and sleep. But they dared not yield.

The rain was over; and the sun was turning the glistening green world into a palace of gems. Calixta, on the gallery, watched Alcée ride away. He turned and smiled at her with a beaming face; and she lifted her pretty chin in the air and laughed aloud.

III

Bobinôt and Bibi, trudging home, stopped without at the cistern to make themselves presentable.

"My! Bibi, w'at will yo' mama say! You ought to be ashame'. You oughtn' put on those good pants. Look at 'em! An' that mud on yo' collar! How you got that mud on yo' collar, Bibi? I never saw such a boy!"

---

[3]**Assumption** a church feast on 15 August celebrating Mary's bodily ascent to heaven

Bibi was the picture of pathetic resignation. Bobinôt was the embodiment of serious solicitude as he strove to remove from his own person and his son's the signs of their tramp over heavy roads and through wet fields. He scraped the mud off Bibi's bare legs and feet with a stick and carefully removed all traces from his heavy brogans. Then, prepared for the worst—the meeting with an over-scrupulous housewife, they entered cautiously at the back door.

Calixta was preparing supper. She had set the table and was dripping coffee at the hearth. She sprang up as they came in.

"Oh, Bobinôt! You back! My! but I was uneasy. W'ere you been during the rain? An' Bibi? he ain't wet? he ain't hurt?" She had clasped Bibi and was kissing him effusively. Bobinôt's explanations and apologies which he had been composing all along the way, died on his lips as Calixta felt him to see if he were dry, and seemed to express nothing but satisfaction at their safe return.

"I brought you some shrimps, Calixta," offered Bobinôt, hauling the can from his ample side pocket and laying it on the table.

"Shrimps! Oh, Bobinôt! you too good fo' anything!" and she gave him a smacking kiss on the cheek that resounded. *"J'vous reponds,*[4] we'll have a feas' to night! umph-umph!"

Bobinôt and Bibi began to relax and enjoy themselves, and when the three seated themselves at table they laughed much and so loud that anyone might have heard them as far away as Laballière's.

IV

Alcée Laballière wrote to his wife, Clarisse, that night. It was a loving letter, full of tender solicitude. He told her not to hurry back, but if she and the babies liked it at Biloxi, to stay a month longer. He was getting on nicely; and though he missed them, he was willing to bear the separation a while longer—realizing that their health and pleasure were the first things to be considered.

V

As for Clarisse, she was charmed upon receiving her husband's letter. She and the babies were doing well. The society was agreeable; many of her old friends and acquaintances were at the bay. And the first free breath since her marriage seemed to restore the pleasant liberty of her maiden days. Devoted as she was to her husband, their intimate conjugal life was something which she was more than willing to forego for a while.

So the storm passed and everyone was happy.

[1898]

---

[4]*J'vous reponds*   Take my word; let me tell you

TOPICS FOR DISCUSSION AND WRITING

1. How would you characterize Calixta?
2. In Part III do you think Calixta is insincere in her expressions of solicitude for Bobinôt? Why, or why not?
3. Do you take Part IV to imply that Alcée and Calixta will continue their affair for another month? Support your answer.
4. Why does Chopin bother, in Part V, to tell us about Clarisse? And exactly what do you make of the last line of the story?
5. Do you think it is fair to say that the story is cynical? Explain.

4
Narrative Point of View

Every story is told by someone. Mark Twain wrote *The Adventures of Huckleberry Finn,* but he does not tell the story; Huck tells the story, and he begins thus:

> You don't know about me without you have read a book by the name of *The Adventures of Tom Sawyer,* but that ain't no matter. That book was made by Mr. Mark Twain, and he told the truth, mainly. There was things which he stretched, but mainly he told the truth.

Similarly, Edgar Allan Poe wrote "The Cask of Amontillado," but the story is told by a man whose name, we learn later, is Montresor. Here is the opening:

> The thousand injuries of Fortunato I had borne as I best could, but when he ventured upon insult, I vowed revenge.

Each of these passages gives a reader a very strong sense of the narrator, that is, of the invented person who tells the story, and it turns out that the works are chiefly about the speakers. Compare those opening passages, however, with two others, which sound far more objective. The first comes from Chekhov's "Misery" (page 30):

> The twilight of evening. Big flakes of wet snow are whirling lazily about the street lamps, which have just been lighted, and lying in a thin soft layer on roofs, horses' backs, shoulders, caps. Iona Potapov, the sledge-driver, is all white like a ghost. He sits on the box without stirring, bent as double as the living body can be bent.

And another example, this one from Hawthorne's "Young Goodman Brown" (page 74):

> Young Goodman Brown came forth at sunset into the street at Salem village; but put his head back, after crossing the threshold, to exchange a parting kiss with his young wife. And Faith, as the wife was aptly named, thrust her own pretty head into the street, letting the wind play with the pink ribbons of her cap while she called to Goodman Brown.

In each of these two passages, a reader is scarcely aware of the personality of the narrator; our interest is almost entirely in the scene that each speaker reveals, not in the speaker's response to the scene.

The narrators of *Huckleberry Finn* and of "The Cask of Amontillado" immediately impress us with their distinctive personalities. We realize that whatever happenings they report will be colored by the special ways in which such personalities see things. But what can we say about the narrators of "Misery" and of "Young Goodman Brown"? A reader is scarcely aware of them, at least in comparison with Huck and Montresor. We look, so to speak, not *at* these narrators, but at others (the cabman and Goodman Brown and Faith).

Of course, it is true that as we read "Misery" and "Young Goodman Brown" we are looking through the eyes of the narrators, but these narrators seem (unlike Huck and Montresor) to have 20/20 vision. This is not to say, however, that these apparently colorless narrators really are colorless or invisible. For instance, the narrator of "Misery" seems, at least if we judge from the opening sentences, to want to evoke an atmosphere. He describes the setting in some detail, whereas the narrator of "Young Goodman Brown" seems chiefly concerned with reporting the actions of people whom he sees. Moreover, if we listen carefully to Hawthorne's narrator, perhaps we can say that when he mentions that Faith was "aptly" named, he makes a judgment. Still, it is clear that the narrative voices we hear in "Misery" and "Young Goodman Brown" are at least relatively impartial and relatively inconspicuous; when we hear them, we feel, for the most part, that they are chiefly talking about something objective, about something "out there." These narrative voices will produce stories very different from the narrative voices used by Twain and Poe. The voice that the writer chooses, then, will in large measure shape the story; different voices, different stories.

The narrative point of view of *Huckleberry Finn* and of "The Cask of Amontillado (and of any other story in which a character in the story tells the story) is a **participant** (or **first-person**) point of view. The point of view of "Young Goodman Brown" (and of any other story in which a nearly invisible outsider tells the story) is a **nonparticipant** (or **third-person**) point of view.

PARTICIPANT (OR FIRST-PERSON) POINTS OF VIEW

In John Updike's "A & P" on page 54, the narrator is, like Mark Twain's Huck and Poe's Montresor, a major character. Updike has invented an adolescent boy who undergoes certain experiences and who comes to certain perceptions. Since the story is narrated by one of its characters, we can say that the author uses a first-person (or participant) point of view.

It happens that in Updike's "A & P" the narrator is the central character, the character whose actions — whose life, we might say — most interests the reader. But sometimes a first-person narrator tells a story that focuses on another character; the narrator still says "I" (thus the point of view is first person), but the reader feels that the story is not chiefly about this "I" but is about some other figure. For instance, the narrator may be a witness to a story about Jones, and our interest is chiefly in what happens to Jones, though we get the story of Jones filtered through, say, the eyes of Jones's friend, or brother, or cat.

When any of us tells a story (for instance, why we quit a job), our hearers may do well to take what we say with a grain of salt. After all, we are giving *our* side, our version of what happened. And so it is with first-person narrators of fiction. They may be reliable, in which case the reader can pretty much accept what they say, or they may be **unreliable narrators,** perhaps because they have an ax to grind, perhaps because they are not perceptive enough to grasp the full implications of what they report, or perhaps because they are mentally impaired, even insane. Poe's Montresor, in "The Cask of Amontillado," is so obsessed that we cannot be certain that Fortunato really did inflict a "thousand injuries" on him.

One special kind of unreliable first-person narrator (whether major or minor) is the **innocent eye:** the narrator is naive (usually a child, or a not-too-bright adult), telling what he or she sees and feels; the contrast between what the narrator perceives and what the reader understands produces an ironic effect. Such a story, in which the reader understands more than the teller himself does, is Ring Lardner's "Haircut," a story told by a garrulous barber who does not perceive that the "accident" he is describing is in fact a murder.

NONPARTICIPANT (OR THIRD-PERSON) POINTS OF VIEW

In a nonparticipant (third-person) point of view, the teller of the tale is not a character in the tale. The narrator has receded from the story. If the point of view is **omniscient,** the narrator relates what he or she wishes about the thoughts as well as the deeds of the characters. The omniscient teller can at any time enter the mind of any or all of the characters; whereas the first-person narrator can only say, "I was angry," or "Jones seemed angry to me," the omniscient narrator can say, "Jones was inwardly angry but gave no sign; Smith continued chatting, but he sensed Jones's anger."

Furthermore, a distinction can be made between **neutral omniscience** (the narrator recounts deeds and thoughts, but does not judge) and **editorial omniscience** (the narrator not only recounts, but also judges). The narrator in Hawthorne's "Young Goodman Brown" knows what goes on in the mind of Brown, and he comments approvingly or disapprovingly: "With this excellent resolve for the future, Goodman Brown felt himself justified in making more haste on his present evil purpose."

Because a short story can scarcely hope to develop effectively a picture of several minds, an author may prefer to limit his or her omniscience to the minds of only a few of the characters, or even to that of one of the characters; that is, the author may use **selective omniscience** as the point of view. Selective omniscience provides a focus, especially if it is limited to a single character. When thus limited, the author hovers over the shoulder of one character, seeing him or her from outside and from inside and seeing other characters only from the outside and from the impact they make on the mind of this selected receptor. In "Young Goodman Brown" the reader sees things mostly as they make their impact on the protagonist's mind.

> He could have well-nigh sworn that the shape of his own dead father beckoned him to advance, looking downward from a smoke wreath, while a woman, with dim features of despair, threw out her hand to warn him back. Was it his mother? But he had no power to retreat one step, nor to resist, even in thought, when the minister and good old Deacon Gookin seized his arms and led him to the blazing rock.

When selective omniscience attempts to record mental activity ranging from consciousness to the unconscious, from clear perceptions to confused longings, it is sometimes labeled the **stream-of-consciousness** point of view. The following example is from Katherine Anne Porter's "The Jilting of Granny Weatherall" (page 233):

> Her eyelids wavered and let in streamers of blue-gray light like tissue paper over her eyes. She must get up and pull the shades down or she'd never sleep. She was in bed again and the shades were not down. How could that happen? Better turn over, hide from the light, sleeping in the light gave you nightmares. "Mother, how do you feel now?" and a stinging wetness on her forehead. But I don't like having my face washed in cold water!

In an effort to reproduce the unending activity of the mind, some authors who use the stream-of-consciousness point of view dispense with conventional word order, punctuation, and logical transitions. The last forty-six pages in James Joyce's *Ulysses* are an unpunctuated flow of one character's thoughts.

Finally, sometimes a third-person narrator does not enter even a single mind, but records only what crosses a dispassionate eye and ear. Such a point of view is **objective** (sometimes called **the camera** or **fly-on-the-wall**). The absence of editorializing and of dissection of the mind often produces the effect of a play; we see and hear the characters in action. Much of Hemingway's "Cat in the Rain" (page 20) is objective, consisting of bits of dialogue that make the story look like a play:

> "I'm going down and get the kitty," the American wife said.
> "I'll do it," her husband offered from the bed.
> "No, I'll get it. The poor kitty out trying to keep dry under a table."
> The husband went on reading, lying propped up with the two pillows at the foot of the bed.
> "Don't get wet," he said.

The absence of comment on the happenings forces readers to make their own evaluations of the happenings. For instance, in the passage just quoted, when Hemingway writes "'Don't get wet,' he said," readers probably are forced to think (and to sense that Hemingway is guiding them to think) that the husband is outrageously indifferent to his wife. After all, how can she go out into the rain and not get wet? A writer can use an objective point of view, then, and still control the feelings of the reader.

THE POINT OF A POINT OF VIEW

Generalizations about the effect of a point of view are risky, but two have already been made: that the innocent eye can achieve an ironic effect otherwise unattainable, and that an objective point of view (because we hear dialogue but get little or no comment about it) is dramatic. Three other generalizations are often made: (1) that a first-person point of view lends a sense of immediacy or reality, (2) that an omniscient point of view suggests human littleness, and (3) that the point of view must be consistent.

To take the first of these: it is true that when Poe begins a story "The thousand injuries of Fortunato I had borne as I best could, but when he ventured upon insult, I vowed revenge," we feel that the author has gripped us by the lapels; but, on the other hand, we know that we are only reading a piece of fiction, and we do not really believe in the existence of the "I" or of Fortunato; and furthermore, when we pick up a story that begins with *any* point of view, we agree (by picking up the book) to pretend to believe the fictions we are being told. That is, all fiction—whether in the first person or not—is known to be literally false but is read with the pretense that it is true (probably because we hope to get some sort of insight, or truth). The writer must hold our attention, and make us feel that the fiction is meaningful, but the use of the first-person pronoun does not of itself confer reality.

The second generalization, that an omniscient point of view can make puppets of its characters, is equally misleading; this point of view also can reveal in them a depth and complexity quite foreign to the idea of human littleness.

The third generalization, that the narrator's point of view must be consistent lest the illusion of reality be shattered, has been much preached by the followers of Henry James. But E. M. Forster has suggested, in *Aspects of the Novel,* that what is important is not consistency but "the power of the writer to bounce the reader into accepting what he says." Forster notes that in *Bleak House* Dickens uses in Chapter I an omniscient point of view, in Chapter II a selective omniscient point of view, and in Chapter III a first-person point of view. "Logically," Forster says, "*Bleak House* is all to pieces, but Dickens bounces us, so that we do not mind the shiftings of the viewpoint."

Perhaps the only sound generalizations possible are these:

1. Because point of view is one of the things that gives form to a story, a good author chooses the point (or points) of view that he or she feels best for the particular story.
2. The use of any other point or points of view would turn the story into a different story.

John Updike

John Updike (b. 1932) grew up in Shillington, Pennsylvania, where his father was a teacher and his mother a writer. After receiving a B.A. degree in 1954 from Harvard, where he edited the Harvard Lampoon *(for which he both wrote and drew), he studied drawing at Oxford for a year, but an offer from* The New Yorker *brought him back to the United States. He was hired as a reporter for the magazine but soon began contributing poetry, essays, and fiction. In 1957 he left* The New Yorker *in order to write independently fulltime, though his stories and book reviews appear fairly regularly in it.*

*In 1959 Updike published his first book of stories (*The Same Door*) and also his first novel (*The Poorhouse Fair*); the next year*

he published Rabbit, Run, *an enormously successful novel whose pro-
tagonist, "Rabbit" Angstrom, has reappeared in three later novels,*
Rabbit Redux *(1971),* Rabbit Is Rich *(1981), and* Rabbit at Rest *(1990).
The first and the last Rabbit books each won a Pulitzer Prize.*

A & P

In walks these three girls in nothing but bathing suits. I'm in the
third checkout slot, with my back to the door, so I don't see them until
they're over by the bread. The one that caught my eye first was the one
in the plaid green two-piece. She was a chunky kid, with a good tan and
a sweet broad soft-looking can with those two crescents of white just under
it, where the sun never seems to hit, at the top of the backs of her legs.
I stood there with my hand on a box of HiHo crackers trying to remember if I rang it up or not. I ring it up again and the customer starts giving
me hell. She's one of these cash-register-watchers, a witch about fifty with
rouge on her cheekbones and no eyebrows, and I know it made her day
to trip me up. She'd been watching cash registers for fifty years and probably never seen a mistake before.

By the time I got her feathers smoothed and her goodies into a
bag—she gives me a little snort in passing, if she'd been born at the right
time they would have burned her over in Salem—by the time I get her
on her way the girls had circled around the bread and were coming back,
without a pushcart, back my way along the counters, in the aisle between
the checkouts and the Special bins. They didn't even have shoes on. There
was this chunky one, with the two-piece—it was bright green and the
seams on the bra were still sharp and her belly was still pretty pale so
I guessed she just got it (the suit)—there was this one, with one of those
chubby berry-faces, the lips all bunched together under her nose, this one,
and a tall one, with black hair that hadn't quite frizzed right, and one of
these sunburns right across under the eyes, and a chin that was too long—
you know, the kind of girl other girls think is very "striking" and "attractive" but never quite makes it, as they very well know, which is why they
like her so much—and then the third one, that wasn't quite so tall. She
was the queen. She kind of led them, the other two peeking around and
making their shoulders round. She didn't look around, not this queen, she
just walked straight on slowly, on these long white prima-donna legs. She
came down a little hard on her heels, as if she didn't walk in her bare feet
that much, putting down her heels and then letting the weight move along
to her toes as if she was testing the floor with every step, putting a little
deliberate extra action into it. You never know for sure how girls' minds
work (do they really think it's a mind in there or just a little buzz like
a bee in a glass jar?) but you got the idea she had talked the other two

into coming in here with her, and now she was showing them how to do it, walk slow and hold yourself straight.

She had on a kind of dirty pink — beige maybe, I don't know — bathing suit with a little nubble all over it and, what got me, the straps were down. They were off her shoulders looped loose around the cool tops of her arms, and I guess as a result the suit had slipped on her, so all around the top of the cloth there was this shining rim. If it hadn't been there you wouldn't have known there could have been anything whiter than those shoulders. With the straps pushed off, there was nothing between the top of the suit and the top of her head except just *her,* this clean bare plane of the top of her chest down from the shoulder bones like a dented sheet of metal tilted in the light. I mean, it was more than pretty.

She had sort of oaky hair that the sun and salt had bleached, done up in a bun that was unravelling, and a kind of prim face. Walking into the A & P with your straps down, I suppose it's the only kind of face you *can* have. She held her head so high her neck, coming up out of those white shoulders, looked kind of stretched, but I didn't mind. The longer her neck was, the more of her there was.

She must have felt in the corner of her eye me and over my shoulder Stokesie in the second slot watching, but she didn't tip. Not this queen. She kept her eyes moving across the racks, and stopped, and turned so slow it made my stomach rub the inside of my apron, and buzzed to the other two, who kind of huddled against her for relief, and then they all three of them went up the cat and dog food-breakfast cereal-macaroni-rice-raisins-seasonings-spreads-spaghetti-soft drinks-crackers-and-cookies aisle. From the third slot I look straight up this aisle to the meat counter, and I watched them all the way. The fat one with the tan sort of fumbled with the cookies, but on second thought she put the package back. The sheep pushing their carts down the aisle — the girls were walking against the usual traffic (not that we have one-way signs or anything) — were pretty hilarious. You could see them, when Queenie's white shoulders dawned on them, kind of jerk, or hop, or hiccup, but their eyes snapped back to their own baskets and on they pushed. I bet you could set off dynamite in the A & P and the people would by and large keep reaching and checking oatmeal off their lists and muttering "Let me see, there was a third thing, began with A, asparagus, no, ah, yes, applesauce!" or whatever it is they do mutter. But there was no doubt, this jiggled them. A few house slaves in pin curlers even look around after pushing their carts past to make sure what they had seen was correct.

You know, it's one thing to have a girl in a bathing suit down on the beach, where what with the glare nobody can look at each other much anyway, and another thing in the cool of the A & P, under the fluorescent lights, against all those stacked packages, with her feet paddling along naked over our checker-board green-and-cream rubber-tile floor.

"Oh, Daddy," Stokesie said beside me. "I feel so faint."

"Darling," I said. "Hold me tight." Stokesie's married, with two babies chalked up on his fuselage already, but as far as I can tell that's the only difference. He's twenty-two, and I was nineteen this April.

"Is it done?" he asks, the responsible married man finding his voice. I forgot to say he thinks he's going to be a manager some sunny day, maybe in 1990 when it's called the Great Alexandrov and Petrooshki Tea Company or something.

What he meant was, our town is five miles from a beach, with a big summer colony out on the Point, but we're right in the middle of town, and the women generally put on a shirt or shorts or something before they get out of the car into the street. And anyway these are usually women with six children and varicose veins mapping their legs and nobody, including them, could care less. As I say, we're right in the middle of town, and if you stand at our front doors you can see two banks and the Congregational church and the newspaper store and three real estate offices and about twenty-seven old freeloaders tearing up Central Street because the sewer broke again. It's not as if we're on the Cape; we're north of Boston and there's people in this town haven't seen the ocean for twenty years.

The girls had reached the meat counter and were asking McMahon something. He pointed, they pointed, and they shuffled out of sight behind a pyramid of Diet Delight peaches. All that was left for us to see was old McMahon patting his mouth and looking after them sizing up their joints. Poor kids, I began to feel sorry for them, they couldn't help it.

Now here comes the sad part of the story, at least my family says it's sad, but I don't think it's so sad myself. The store's pretty empty, it being Thursday afternoon, so there was nothing much to do except lean on the register and wait for the girls to show up again. The whole store was like a pinball machine and I didn't know which tunnel they'd come out of. After a while they come around out of the far aisle, around the light bulbs, records at discount of the Caribbean Six or Tony Martin Sings or some such gunk you wonder they waste the wax on, sixpacks of candy bars, and plastic toys done up in cellophane that fall apart when a kid looks at them anyway. Around they come, Queenie still leading the way, and holding a little gray jar in her hand. Slots Three through Seven are unmanned and I could see her wondering between Stokes and me, but Stokesie with his usual luck draws an old party in baggy gray pants who stumbles up with four giant cans of pineapple juice (what do these bums *do* with all that pineapple juice? I've often asked myself) so the girls come to me. Queenie puts down the jar and I take it into my fingers icy cold. Kingfish Fancy Herring Snacks in Pure Sour Cream: 49¢. Now her hands are empty, not a ring or a bracelet, bare as God made them, and I wonder where the money's coming from. Still with the prim look she lifts a folded dollar bill out of the hollow at the center of her nubbled pink top. The jar went heavy in my hand. Really, I thought that was so cute.

Then everybody's luck begins to run out. Lengel comes in from haggling with a truck full of cabbages on the lot and is about to scuttle into the door marked MANAGER behind which he hides all day when the girls touch his eye. Lengel's pretty dreary, teaches Sunday school and the rest, but he doesn't miss that much. He comes over and says, "Girls, this isn't the beach."

Queenie blushes, though maybe it's just a brush of sunburn I was noticing for the first time, now that she was so close. "My mother asked me to pick up a jar of herring snacks." Her voice kind of startled me, the way voices do when you see the people first, coming out so flat and dumb yet kind of tony, too, the way it ticked over "pick up" and "snacks." All of a sudden I slid right down her voice into her living room. Her father and the other men were standing around in ice-cream coats and bow ties and the women were in sandals picking up herring snacks on toothpicks off a big glass plate and they were all holding drinks the color of water with olives and sprigs of mint in them. When my parents have somebody over they get lemonade and if it's a real racy affair Schlitz in tall glasses with "They'll Do It Every Time" cartoons stencilled on.

"That's all right," Lengel said. "But this isn't the beach." His repeating this struck me as funny, as if it had just occurred to him, and he had been thinking all these years the A & P was a great big dune and he was the head lifeguard. He didn't like my smiling — as I say he doesn't miss much — but he concentrates on giving the girls that sad Sunday-school-superintendent stare.

Queenie's blush is no sunburn now, and the plump one in plaid, that I liked better from the back — a really sweet can — pipes up, "We weren't doing any shopping. We just came in for the one thing."

"That makes no difference," Lengel tells her, and I could see from the way his eyes went that he hadn't noticed she was wearing a two-piece before. "We want you decently dressed when you come in here."

"We *are* decent," Queenie says suddenly, her lower lip pushing, getting sore now that she remembers her place, a place from which the crowd that runs the A & P must look pretty crummy. Fancy Herring Snacks flashed in her very blue eyes.

"Girls, I don't want to argue with you. After this come in here with your shoulders covered. It's our policy." He turns his back. That's policy for you. Policy is what the kingpins want. What the others want is juvenile delinquency.

All this while, the customers had been showing up with their carts but, you know, sheep, seeing a scene, they had all bunched up on Stokesie, who shook open a paper bag as gently as peeling a peach, not wanting to miss a word. I could feel in the silence everybody getting nervous, most of all Lengel, who asks me, "Sammy, have you rung up this purchase?"

I thought and said "No" but it wasn't about that I was thinking. I go through the punches, 4, 9, GROC, TOT — it's more complicated than you think and after you do it often enough, it begins to make a little song, that you hear words to, in my case "Hello *(bing)* there, you *(gung)* hap-py *pee*pul *(splat)*!"—the *splat* being the drawer flying out. I uncrease the bill, tenderly as you may imagine, it just having come from between the two smoothest scoops of vanilla I had ever known were there, and pass a half and a penny into her narrow pink palm and nestle the herrings in a bag and twist its neck and hand it over, all the time thinking.

The girls, and who'd blame them, are in a hurry to get out, so I say "I quit" to Lengel quick enough for them to hear, hoping they'll stop and watch me, their unsuspected hero. They keep right on going, into the electric eye; the door flies open and they flicker across the lot to their car, Queenie and Plaid and Big Tall Goony-Goony (not that as raw material she was so bad), leaving me with Lengel and a kink in his eyebrow.

"Did you say something, Sammy?"

"I said I quit."

"I thought you did."

"You didn't have to embarrass them."

"It was they who were embarrassing us."

I started to say something that came out "Fiddle-de-doo." It's a saying of my grandmother's, and I know she would have been pleased.

"I don't think you know what you're saying," Lengel said.

"I know you don't," I said. "But I do." I pull the bow at the back of my apron and start shrugging it off my shoulders. A couple customers that had been heading for my slot begin to knock against each other, like scared pigs in a chute.

Lengel sighs and begins to look very patient and old and gray. He's been a friend of my parents for years. "Sammy, you don't want to do this to your Mom and Dad," he tells me. It's true, I don't. But it seems to me that once you begin a gesture it's fatal not to go through with it. I fold the apron, "Sammy" stitched in red on the pocket, and put it on the counter, and drop the bow tie on top of it. The bow tie is theirs, if you've ever wondered. "You'll feel this for the rest of your life," Lengel says, and I know that's true, too, but remembering how he made that pretty girl blush makes me so scrunchy inside I punch the No Sale tab and the machine whirs "pee-pul" and the drawer splats out. One advantage to this scene taking place in summer, I can follow this up with a clean exit, there's no fumbling around getting your coat and galoshes, I just saunter into the electric eye in my white shirt that my mother ironed the night before, and the door heaves itself open, and outside the sunshine is skating around on the asphalt.

I look around for my girls, but they're gone, of course. There wasn't anybody but some young married screaming with her children about some candy they didn't get by the door of a powder-blue Falcon station wagon. Looking back in the big windows, over the bags of peat moss and aluminum lawn furniture stacked on the pavement, I could see Lengel in my place in the slot, checking the sheep through. His face was dark gray and his back stiff, as if he'd just had an injection of iron, and my stomach kind of fell as I felt how hard the world was going to be to me hereafter.

[1962]

TOPICS FOR DISCUSSION AND WRITING

1. What is Sammy's image of himself? What is your image of Sammy?
2. What is Sammy's social background? (Point to some passages in which Sammy's language provides clues.)
3. In your opinion, why does Sammy defy Lengel? As a matter of principle? To impress the girls? Both, or neither? Or what?
4. Write a paragraph from Lengel's point of view, describing some part of the episode.

Here is a second story by Updike, written from a different point of view.

The Rumor

Frank and Sharon Whittier had come from the Cincinnati area and, with an inheritance of hers and a sum borrowed from his father, had opened a small art gallery on the fourth floor of a narrow building on West Fifty-seventh Street. They had known each other as children; their families had been in the same country-club set. They had married in 1971, when Frank was freshly graduated from Oberlin and Vietnam-vulnerable and Sharon was only nineteen, a sophomore at Antioch majoring in dance. By the time, six years later, they arrived in New York, they had two small children; the birth of a third led them to give up their apartment and the city struggle and move to a house in Hastings, a low stucco house with a wide-eaved Wright-style roof and a view, through massive beeches at the bottom of the yard, of the leaden, ongliding Hudson. They were happy, surely. They had dry midwestern taste, and by sticking to representational painters and abstract sculptors they managed to survive the uglier Eighties styles — faux graffiti, neo-German expressionism, cathode-ray prole play, ecological-protest trash art — and bring their quiet, chaste string of fourth-floor rooms into the calm lagoon of Nineties eclectic revivalism and subdued recession chic. They prospered; their youngest child turned twelve, their oldest was filling out college applications.

When Sharon first heard the rumor that Frank had left her for a young homosexual with whom he was having an affair, she had to laugh, for, far from having left her, there he was, right in the lamplit study with her, ripping pages out of *ARTnews*.

"I don't think so, Avis," she said to the graphic artist on the other end of the line. "He's right here with me. Would you like to say hello?" The easy refutation was made additionally sweet by the fact that, some years before, there had been a brief (Sharon thought) romantic flare-up between her husband and this caller, an overanimated redhead with protuberant cheeks and chin. Avis was a second-wave appropriationist who made color Xeroxes of masterpieces out of art books and then signed them in an ink mixed of her own blood and urine. How could she, who had actually slept with Frank, be imagining this grotesque thing?

The voice on the phone gushed as if relieved and pleased. "I know, it's wildly absurd, but I heard it from two sources, with absolutely solemn assurance."

"Who were these sources?"

"I'm not sure they'd like you to know. But it was Ed Jaffrey and then that boy who's been living with Walton Forney, what does he call himself, one of those single names like Madonna—Jojo!"

"Well, then," Sharon began.

"But I've heard it from still others," Avis insisted. "All over town— it's in the air. Couldn't you and Frank *do* something about it, if it's not true?"

"'If,'" Sharon protested, and her thrust of impatience carried, when she put down the receiver, into her conversation with Frank. "Avis says you're supposed to have run off with your homosexual lover."

"I don't have a homosexual lover," Frank said, too calmly, ripping an auction ad out of the magazine.

"She says all New York says you do."

"Well, what are you going to believe, all New York or your own experience? Here I sit, faithful to a fault, straight as a die, whatever that means. We made love just two nights ago."

It seemed possibly revealing to her that he so distinctly remembered, as if heterosexual performance were a duty he checked off. He was—had always been, for over twenty years—a slim blond man several inches under six feet tall, with a narrow head he liked to keep trim, even during those years when long hair was in fashion, milky-blue eyes set at a slight tilt, such as you see on certain taut Slavic or Norwegian faces, and a small, precise mouth he kept pursed over teeth a shade too prominent and yellow. He was reluctant to smile, as if giving something away, and was vain of his flat belly and lithe collegiate condition. He weighed himself every morning on the bathroom scale, and if he weighed a pound more than yesterday, he skipped lunch. In this, and in his general attention to his own person, he was as quietly fanatic as—it for the first time occured to her—a woman.

"You know I've never liked the queer side of this business," he went on. "I've just gotten used to it. I don't even think anymore, who's gay and who isn't."

"Avis was *ju*bilant," Sharon said. "How could she think it?"

It took him a moment to focus on the question and realize that his answer was important to her. He became nettled. "Ask *her* how," he said. "Our brief and regrettable relationship, if that's what interests you, seemed satisfactory to me at least. What troubles and amazes me, if I may say so, is how *you* can be taking this ridiculous rumor so seriously."

"I'm *not*, Frank," she insisted, then backtracked. "But why would such a rumor come out of thin air? Doesn't there have to be *something*? Since we moved up here, we're not together so much, naturally, some days when I can't come into town you're gone sixteen hours. . . ."

"But *Shar*on," he said, like a teacher restoring discipline, removing his reading glasses from his almond-shaped eyes, with their stubby fair lashes. "Don't you *know* me? Ever since after that dance when you were sixteen, that time by the lake? . . ."

She didn't want to reminisce. Their early sex had been difficult for her; she had submitted to his advances out of a larger, more social, rather idealistic attraction. She knew that together they would have the strength to get out of Cincinnati and, singly or married to others, they would stay. "Well," she said, enjoying this sensation, despite the chill the rumor had awakened in her, of descending to a deeper level of intimacy than usual, "how well do you know even your own spouse? People are fooled all the time. Peggy Jacobson, for instance, when Henry ran off with that physical therapist, couldn't believe, even when the evidence was right there in front of her—"

"I'm *deeply* insulted," Frank interrupted, his mouth tense in that way he had when making a joke but not wanting to show his teeth. "My masculinity is insulted." But he couldn't deny himself a downward glance into his magazine; his tidy white hand jerked, as if wanting to tear out yet another item that might be useful to their business. Intimacy had always made him nervous. She kept at it, rather hopelessly. "Avis said two separate people had solemnly assured her."

"Who, exactly?"

When she told him, he said, exactly as she had done, "Well, then." He added, "You know how gays are. Malicious. Mischievous. They have all that time and money on their hands."

"You sound jealous." Something about the way he was arguing with her strengthened Sharon's suspicion that, outageous as the rumor was— indeed, *because* it was outrageous—it was true.

In the days that followed, now that she was alert to the rumor's vaporous presence, she imagined it everywhere—on the poised young faces of their staff, in the delicate negotiatory accents of their artists' agents, in the heartier tones of their repeat customers, even in the gruff, self-occupied ramblings of the artists themselves. People seemed startled when she and Frank entered a room together: The desk receptionist and the security guard in their gallery halted their daily morning banter, and the waiters in their pet restaurant, over on Fifty-ninth, appeared especially effusive and attentive. Handshakes lasted a second too long, women embraced her with an extra squeeze, she felt herself ensnared in a soft net of unspoken pity.

Frank sensed her discomfort and took a certain malicious pleasure in it, enacting all the while his perfect innocence. He composed himself to appear, from her angle, aloof above the rumor. Dealing professionally in so much absurdity—the art world's frantic attention-getting, studied grotesqueries—he merely intensified the fastidious dryness that had sustained their gallery through wave after wave of changing fashion, and that had, like a rocket's heat-resistant skin, insulated their launch, their escape from the comfortable riverine smugness of this metropolis of dreadful freedom. The rumor amused him, and it amused him, too, to notice how she helplessly watched to see if in the metropolitan throngs his eyes now followed young men as once they had noticed and followed young women. She observed his gestures—always a bit excessively graceful and precise—distrustfully, and listened for the buttery, reedy tone of voice that might signal an invisible sex change.

That even in some small fraction of her she was willing to believe the rumor justified a certain maliciousness on his part. He couldn't help teasing her—glancing over at her, say, when an especially magnetic young waiter served them, or at home, in their bedroom, pushing more brusquely than was his style at her increasing sexual unwillingness. More than once, at last away from the countless knowing eyes of their New York milieu, in the privacy of their Hastings upstairs, beneath the wide midwestern eaves, she burst into tears and struck out at him, his infuriating, impervious apparent blamelessness. He was like one of those photo-realist nudes, merciless in every detail and yet subtly, defiantly not there, not human. "You're distant," she accused him. "You've always been."

"I don't mean to be. You didn't used to mind my manner. You thought it was quietly masterful."

"I was a teenage girl. I deferred to you."

"It worked out," he pointed out, lifting his hands in an effete, disclaiming way from his sides, to take in their room, their expensive house, their joint career. "What is it that bothers you, Sharon? The idea of losing me? Or the insult to your female pride? The people who started this ridiculous rumor don't even *see* women. Women to them are just background noise."

"It's *not* ridiculous—if it were, why does it keep on and on, even though we're seen together all the time?"

For, ostensibly to quiet her and to quench the rumor, he had all but ceased to go to the city alone, and took her with him even though it meant some neglect of the house and their sons.

Frank asked, "Who *says* it keeps on all the time? I've *never* heard it, never once, except from you. Who's mentioned it lately?"

"Nobody."

"Well, then." He smiled, his lips not quite parting on his curved teeth, tawny like a beaver's.

"You bastard!" Sharon burst out. "You have some stinking little secret!"

"I don't," he serenely half-lied.

The rumor had no factual basis. But was there, Frank asked himself, some truth to it after all? Not circumstantial truth, but some higher, inner truth? As a young man, slight of build, with artistic interests, had he not been fearful of being mistaken for a homosexual? Had he not responded to homosexual overtures as they arose, in bars and locker rooms, with a disproportionate terror and repugnance? Had not his early marriage, and then, ten years later, his flurry of adulterous womanizing, been an escape of sorts, into safe, socially approved terrain? When he fantasized, or saw a pornographic movie, was not the male organ the hero of the occasion for him, at the center of every scene? Were not those slavish, lapping starlets his robotlike delegates, with glazed eyes and undisturbed coiffures venturing where he did not dare? Did he not, perhaps, envy women their privilege of worshiping the phallus? But, Frank asked himself, in fairness, arguing both sides of the case, can homosexual strands be entirely disentangled from heterosexual in that pink muck of carnal excitement, of dream made flesh, of return to the presexual womb?

More broadly, had he not felt more comfortable with his father than with his mother? Was not this in itself a sinister reversal of the usual biology? His father had been a genteel Fourth Street lawyer, of no particular effectuality save that most of his clients were from the same social class, with the same accents and comfortably narrowed aspirations, here on this plateau by the swelling Ohio. Darker and taller than Frank, with the same long teeth and primly set mouth, his father had had the lawyer's gift of silence, of judicious withholding, and in his son's scattered memories of times together—a trip downtown on the trolley to buy Frank his first suit, each summer's one or two excursions to see the Reds play at old Crosley Field—the man said little. This prim reserve, letting so much go unstated and unacknowledged, was a relief after the daily shower of words and affection and advice Frank received from his mother. As an adult he was attracted, he had noticed, to stoical men, taller than he and nursing an unexpressed sadness; his favorite college roommate had been of this saturnine type, and his pet tennis partner in Hastings, and artists he especially favored and encouraged—dour, weathered landscapists and virtually illiterate sculptors, welded solid into their crafts and stubborn obsessions. With these men he became a catering, wifely, subtly agitated presence that Sharon would scarcely recognize.

Frank's mother, once a fluffy belle from Louisville, had been gaudy, strident, sardonic, volatile, needy, demanding, loving; from her he had inherited his "artistic" side, as well as his pretty blondness, but he was not especially grateful. Less—as was proposed by a famous formula he didn't know as a boy—would have been more. His mother had given him an impression of women as complex, brightly-colored traps, attractive but treacherous, their petals apt to harden in an instant into knives. A certain wistful pallor, indeed, a limp helplessness, had drawn him to Sharon and, after the initial dazzlement of the Avises of the world faded and fizzled, always drew him back. Other women asked more than he could provide; he was aware of other, bigger, warmer men they had had. But with Sharon he had been a rescuing knight, slaying the dragon of the winding Ohio. Yet what more devastatingly, and less forgivably, confirmed the rumor's essential truth than her willingness, she who knew him best and owed him most, to entertain it? Her instinct had been to believe Avis even though, far from run off, he was sitting there right in front of her eyes.

He was unreal to her, he could not help but conclude: all those years of uxorious cohabitation, those nights of lovemaking and days of homemaking ungratefully absorbed and now suddenly dismissed because of an apparition, a shadow of gossip. On the other hand, now that the rumor existed, Frank had become more real in the eyes of José, the younger, daintier of the two security guards, whose daily greetings had edged beyond the perfunctory; a certain mischievous dance in the boy's sable eyes animated their employer-employee courtesies. And Jennifer, too, the severely beautiful receptionist, with her rather Sixties-reminiscent bangs and shawls and serapes, now treated him more relaxedly, even offhandedly, as if he had somehow dropped out of her calculations. She assumed with him a comradely slanginess—"The boss was in earlier but she went out to exchange something at Bergdorf's"—as if both he and she were in roughly parallel ironic bondage to "the boss." Frank's heart felt a reflex loyalty to Sharon, a single sharp beat, but then he too relaxed, as if his phantom male lover and the weightless, scandal-veiled life that lived with him in some glowing apartment had bestowed at last what the city had withheld from the overworked, child-burdened married couple who had arrived fourteen years ago—a halo of glamour, of debonair uncaring.

In Hastings, when he and his wife attended a suburban party, the effect was less flattering. The other couples, he imagined, were slightly unsettled by the Whittiers' stubbornly appearing together and became disjointed in their presence, the men drifting off in distaste, the women turning supernormal and laying up a chinkless wall of conversation about children's college applications, local zoning, and Wall Street layoffs. The women, it seemed to Frank, edged, with an instinctive animal movement, a few inches closer to Sharon and touched her with a deft, protective flicking on the shoulder or forearm, to express solidarity and sympathy.

Wes Robertson, Frank's favorite tennis partner, came over to him and grunted, "How's it going?"

"*Fine,*" Frank said, staring up at Wes with what he hoped weren't unduly starry eyes. Wes, who had recently turned fifty, had an old motorcycle-accident scar on one side of his chin, a small pale rose of discoloration that seemed to concentrate the man's self-careless manliness. Frank gave him more of an answer than he might have wanted: "In the art game we're feeling the slowdown like everybody else, but the Japanese are keeping the roof from caving in. The trouble with the Japanese, though, is, from the standpoint of a marginal gallery like ours, they aren't adventurous—they want blue chips, they want guaranteed value, they can't grasp that in art, value has to be subjective to an extent. Look at their own stuff—it's all standardized. Who the hell can tell a Hiroshige from a Hokusai?[1] When you think about it, their whole society, their whole success, really, is based on everybody being alike, everybody agreeing. The notion of art as a struggle, a gamble, as the dynamic embodiment of an existential problem, they just don't get it." He was talking too much, he knew, but he couldn't help it; Wes's scowling presence, his melancholy scarred face, and his stringy alcoholic body, which nevertheless could still whip a backhand right across the forecourt, perversely excited Frank, made him want to flirt.

Wes grimaced and contemplated Frank glumly. "Be around for a game Sunday?" Meaning, had he really run off?

"Of course. Why wouldn't I be?" This was teasing the issue, and Frank tried to sober up, to rein in. He felt a flush on his face and a stammer coming on. He asked, "The usual time? Ten forty-five, more or less?"

Wes nodded. "Sure."

Frank chattered on: "Let's try to get court 5 this time. Those brats having their lessons on court 2 drove me crazy last time. We spent all our time retrieving their damn balls. And listening to their moronic chatter."

Wes didn't grant this attempt at evocation of past liaisons even a word, just continued his melancholy, stoical nodding. This was one of the things, it occurred to Frank, that he liked about men: their relational minimalism, their gender-based realization that the cupboard of life, emotionally speaking, was pretty near bare. There wasn't that tireless, irksome, bright-eyed *hope* women kept fluttering at you.

Once, years ago, on a stag golfing trip to Bermuda, he and Wes had shared a room with two single beds, and Wes had fallen asleep within a minute and started snoring, keeping Frank awake for much of the night.

[1]**Hiroshige . . . Hokusai** Ando Hiroshige (1797–1858) and Katsushika Hokusai (1760–1849) are chiefly known as designers of landscape prints.

Contemplating the unconscious male body on its moonlit bed, Frank had been struck by the tragic dignity of this supine form, like a stone knight eroding on a tomb — the snoring profile in motionless gray silhouette, the massive, sacred warrior weight helpless as Wes's breathing struggled from phase to phase of the sleep cycle, from deep to REM to a near-wakefulness that brought a few merciful minutes of silence. The next morning, Wes said Frank should have reached over and poked him in the side; that's what his wife did. But he wasn't his wife, Frank thought, though in the course of that night's ordeal, he had felt his heart make many curious motions, among them the heaving, all-but-impossible effort women's hearts make in overcoming men's heavy grayness and achieving — a rainbow born of drizzle — love.

At the opening of Ned Forschheimer's show — Forschheimer, a shy, rude, stubborn, and now elderly painter of tea-colored, wintry Connecticut landscapes, was one of Frank's pets, unfashionable yet sneakily salable — none other than Walton Forney came up to Frank, his round face lit by white wine and odd, unquenchable self-delight, and said, "Say, Frank, old boy. Methinks I owe you an apology. It was Charlie Whit*field,* who used to run that framing shop down on Eighth Street, who left his wife suddenly, with some little Guatemalan boy he was putting through CCNY on the side. They took off for Mexico and left the missus sitting with the shop mortgaged up to its attic and about a hundred prints of wild ducks left unframed. The thing that must have confused me, Charlie came from Ohio, too — Columbus or Cleveland, one of those. It was — what do they call it — a Freudian slip, an understandable confusion. Avis Wasserman told me Sharon wasn't all that thrilled to get the word a while ago, and you must have wondered yourself what the hell was up."

"We ignored it," Frank said, in a voice firmer and less catering than his usual one. "We rose above it." Walton was a number of inches shorter than Frank, with yet a bigger head; his gleaming, thin-skinned face, bearing smooth jowls that had climbed into his sideburns, was shadowed blue here and there, like the moon. His bruised and powdered look somehow went with his small, spaced teeth and the horizontal red tracks his glasses had left in the fat in front of his ears.

The man gazed at Frank with a gleaming, sagging lower lip, his nearsighted little eyes trying to assess the damage, the depth of the grudge. "Well, mea culpa, mea culpa, I guess, though I *didn't* tell Jojo and that *poisonous* Ed Jaffrey to go blabbing it all over town."

"Well, thanks for telling me, Wally, I guess." Depending on which man he was standing with, Frank felt large and straight and sonorous or, as with Wes, gracile and flighty. Sharon, scenting blood amid the vacuous burble of the party, pushed herself through the crowd and joined the two men. To deny Walton the pleasure, Frank quickly told her, "Wally just

confessed to me he started the rumor because Charlie Whitfield downtown, who did run off with somebody, came from Ohio, too. Toledo, as
I remember."

"Oh, that rumor," Sharon said, blinking once, as if her party mas-
cara were sticking. "I'd forgotten it. Who could believe it, of Frank?"

"Everybody, evidently," Frank said. It was possible, given the strange,
willful ways of women, that she had forgotten it, even while Frank had
been brooding over its possible justice. If the rumor were truly dispersed—
and Walton would undoubtedly tell the story of his Freudian slip around
town as a self-promoting joke on himself—Frank would feel diminished.
He would lose that small sadistic power to make her watch him watching
waiters in restaurants, and to bring her into town as his chaperon. He would
feel emasculated if she no longer thought he had a secret. Yet that night,
at the party, Walton Forney's Jojo had come up to him. He had seemed,
despite an earring the size of a faucet washer and a stripe of bleach in the
center of his hair, unexpectedly intelligent and low-key, offering, not in
so many words, a kind of apology, and praising the tea-colored landscapes
being offered for sale. "I've been thinking, in my own work, of going,
you know, more traditional. You get this feeling of, like, a dead end with
abstraction." The boy had a bony, rueful face, with a silvery line of a scar
under one eye, and seemed uncertain in manner, hesitantly murmurous,
as if at a point in life where he needed direction. The fat fool Forney could
certainly not provide that, and it pleased Frank to imagine that Jojo was
beginning to realize it.

The car as he and Sharon drove home together along the Hudson
felt close; the heater fan blew oppressively, parchingly. "*You* were willing
to believe it at first," he reminded her.

"Well, Avis seemed so definite. But you convinced me."

"How?"

She placed her hand high on his thigh and dug her fingers in, annoyingly, infuriatingly. "You know," she said, in a lower register, meant
to be sexy, but almost inaudible with the noise of the heater fan.

"That could be mere performance," he warned her. "Women are
fooled that way all the time."

"Who says?"

"Everybody. Books. Proust.[2] People aren't that simple."

"They're simple enough," Sharon said, in a neutral, defensive tone,
removing her presumptuous hand.

"If you say so," he said, somewhat stoically, his mind drifting. That
silvery line of a scar under Jojo's left eye . . . lean long muscles snugly

wrapped in white skin . . . lofts . . . Hellenic fellowship,[3] exercise machines
. . . direct negotiations, a simple transaction among equals. The rumor
might be dead in the world, but in him it had come alive.

[1990]

TOPICS FOR DISCUSSION AND WRITING

1. What point of view is used in the first paragraph of the story?
2. Consider the following line from the story:

   "I don't have a homosexual lover," Frank said, too calmly, ripping an auction ad out of the catalog.

   What is the point of view?
3. How would you characterize the point of view in the following passage, from near the end of the story?

   She placed her hand high on his thigh and dug her fingers in,
   annoyingly, infuriatingly. "You know," she said in a lower register,
   meant to be sexy, but almost inaudible with the noise of the heater
   fan.

4. Suppose the story had been told entirely from Sharon's point of view.
   What might have been gained? What might have been lost?
5. In an essay on fiction, Updike wrote:

   I want stories to startle and engage me within the first few sentences, and in their middle to widen or deepen or sharpen my
   knowledge of human activity, and to end by giving me a sensation of completed statement.

   Is this what you want from stories? If not, in what ways do your
   desires differ from Updike's? A second question: Do you think "The
   Rumor" meets Updike's criteria? Explain.

[3]**Hellenic fellowship**   Greek friendship, with the implication of erotic love between a mature
man and a youth

5
Allegory and Symbolism

In Chapter 3 we looked at some fables, short fictions that were evidently meant to teach us: the characters clearly stood for principles of behavior, and the fictions as a whole evidently taught lessons. If you think of a fable such as The Ant and the Grasshopper (the ant wisely collects food during the summer in order to provide for the winter, whereas the grasshopper sings all summer and goes hungry in the winter), you can easily see that the characters may stand for something other than themselves. The ant, let's say, is the careful, foresighted person, and the grasshopper is the person who lives for the moment. Similarly, in the fable of the tortoise and the hare, the tortoise represents the person who is slow but steady, the rabbit the person who is talented but overly confident and, in the end, foolish.

A story in which each character is understood to have an equivalent is an **allegory.** Further, in an allegory, not only characters but also things (roads, forests, houses) have fairly clear equivalents. Thus, in John Bunyan's *The Pilgrim's Progress,* we meet characters with names such as Christian, Mr. Worldly Wiseman, and the Giant Despair; and we also encounter places such as Vanity Fair, City of Destruction, and, finally (Christian's goal), the Celestial City. Bunyan tells us of a man named Christian, who, on the road to the Celestial City, comes to a place called Vanity Fair and encounters, among others, Giant Despair, Mr. Worldly Wiseman, and Faithful. What all of these are equivalent to is clear from their names. It is also clear that Christian's journey stands for the trials of the soul in this world. There is, so to speak, a one-to-one relationship: A = , B = , and so on. If, for example, we are asked what the road represents in *The Pilgrim's Progress,* we can confidently say that it stands for the journey of life. Thus, *The Pilgrim's Progress* tells two stories, the surface story of a man making a trip, during which he meets various figures and visits various places, and a second story, understood through the first, of the trials that afflict the soul during its quest for salvation.

Modern short stories rarely have the allegory's clear system of equivalents, but we may nevertheless feel that at least certain characters and certain things in the story stand for more than themselves, or hint at larger meanings. We feel, that is, that they are **symbolic.** But here we must be careful. How does one know that this or that figure or place is symbolic? In Hemingway's "Cat in the Rain" (page 20), is the cat symbolic? Is the inn keeper? Is the rain? Reasonable people may differ in their answers. Again, in Chopin's "The Story of an Hour" (page 40) is the railroad accident a symbol? Is Josephine a symbol? Is the season (springtime) a symbol? And again, reasonable people may differ in their responses.

Let's assume for the moment, however, that if writers use symbols, they want readers to perceive—at least faintly—that certain characters or places or seasons or happenings have rich implications, stand for something more than what they are on the surface. How do writers help us to perceive these things? By emphasizing them—for instance, by describing them at some length, or by introducing them at times when they might not seem strictly necessary, or by calling attention to them repeatedly.

Consider, for example, Chopin's treatment of the season in which "The Story of an Hour" takes place. The story has to take place at *some* time, but Chopin does not simply say, "On a spring day," or an autumn day, or whatever, and let things go at that. Rather, she tells us about the sky, the trees, the rain, the twittering sparrows—and all of this in an extremely short story where we might think there is no time for talk about the setting. After all, none of this material is strictly necessary to a story about a woman who has heard that her husband was killed in an accident, who grieves, then recovers, and then dies when he suddenly reappears.

Why, then, does Chopin give such emphasis to the season? Because, we think, she is using the season symbolically. In this story, the spring is not just a bit of detail added for realism. It is rich with suggestions of renewal, of the new life that Louise achieves for a moment. But here, a caution. We think that the spring in this story is symbolic, but this is not to say that whenever spring appears in a story, it always stands for renewal, any more than whenever winter appears it always symbolizes death. Nor does it mean that since spring recurs, Louise will be reborn. In short, in *this* story Chopin uses the season to convey certain specific implications.

Is the railroad accident also a symbol? Our answer is no—though we don't expect all readers to agree with us. We think that the railroad accident in "The Story of an Hour" is just a railroad accident. It's our sense that Chopin is *not* using this event to say something about (for instance) modern travel, or about industrialism. The steam-propelled railroad train could of course be used, symbolically, to say something about industrialism displacing an agrarian economy, but does Chopin give her train any such suggestion? We don't think so. Had she wished to do so, we think, she would probably have talked about the enormous power of the train, the shriek of its whistle, the smoke pouring out of the smokestack, the intense fire burning in the engine, its indifference as it charged through the countryside, and so forth. Had she done so, the story would be a different story. Or she might have made the train a symbol of fate overriding human desires, but, again in our opinion, Chopin does not endow her train with such suggestions. She gives virtually no emphasis to the train, and so we believe it has virtually no significance for the reader.

What of Chopin's "Ripe Figs" (page 39)? Maman-Nainaine tells Babette that when the figs are ripe Babette can visit her cousins. Of course Maman may merely be setting an arbitrary date, but as we read the story we probably feel—because of the emphasis on the *ripening* of the figs, which occurs in the spring or early summer—that the ripening of the figs in some way suggests the maturing of Babette. If we do get such ideas, we will in effect be saying that the story is not simply an anecdote about an old woman whose behavior is odd. True, the narrator of the story, after telling us of Maman-Nainaine's promise, adds, "Not that the ripening of figs had the least thing to do with it, but that is the way Maman-Nainaine was." That is, the narrator sees nothing special—merely Maman-Nainaine's eccentricity—in the connection between the ripening of the figs and Babette's visit to her cousins. Readers, however, may see more than the narrator sees or says. They may see in Babette a young girl maturing; they may see in Maman-Nainaine an older woman who, almost collaborating with nature, helps Babette to mature.

And here, of course, as we talk about symbolism we are getting into the theme of the story. An apparently inconsequential and even puzzling action, such as is set forth in "Ripe Figs," may cast a long shadow. As Robert Frost once said,

> There is no story written that has any value at all, however straightforward it looks and free from doubleness, double entendre, that you'd value at all if it didn't have intimations of something more than itself.

The stranger, the more mysterious the story, of course, the more likely we are to suspect some sort of significance, but even realistic stories such as Chopin's "The Storm" and "The Story of an Hour" may be rich in suggestions. This is not to say, however, that the suggestions (rather than the details of the surface) are what count. A reader does not discard the richly detailed, highly specific narrative (Mrs. Mallard learned that her husband was dead and reacted in such-and-such a way) in favor of some supposedly universal message or theme that it implies. We do not throw away the specific narrative—the memorable characters, for example, or the interesting thing that happens in the story—and move on to some "higher truth." Robert Frost went on to say, "The anecdote, the parable, the surface meaning has got to be good and got to be sufficient in itself."

Between these two extremes—on the one hand, writing that is almost all a richly detailed surface and, on the other hand, writing that has a surface so thin that we are immediately taken up with the implications or meanings—are stories in which we strongly feel both the surface happenings and their implications. In *Place in Fiction,* Eudora Welty uses an image of a china lamp to explain literature that presents an interesting surface texture filled with rich significance. When unlit, the lamp showed London; when lit, it showed the Great Fire of London. Like a painted porcelain lamp that, when illuminated, reveals an inner picture shining through the outer, the physical details in a work are illuminated from within by the author's imaginative vision. The outer painting (the literal details) presents "a continuous, shapely, pleasing, and finished surface to the eye," but this surface is not the whole. Welty happens to be talking about the novel, but her words apply equally to the short story:

> The lamp alight is the combination of internal and external, glow-
> ing at the imagination as one; and so is the good novel. . . . The
> good novel should be steadily alight, revealing.

Details that glow, that are themselves and are also something more than themselves, are symbols. Of course readers may disagree about whether in any particular story something is or is not symbolic—let's say the figs and chrysanthemums in Chopin's "Ripe Figs," or the season in "The Story of an Hour." And certainly an ingenious reader may over-complicate or overemphasize the symbolism of a work or may distort it by omitting some of the details and by unduly focusing on others. In many works the details glow, but the glow is so gentle and subtle that even to talk about the details is to overstate them and to understate other equally important aspects of the work.

Yet if it is false to overstate the significance of a detail, it is also false to understate a significant detail. For example, the let's-have-no-nonsense literal reader who holds that "the figure of a man" whom Brown meets in the forest in Hawthorne's "Young Goodman Brown" is simply a man— rather than the Devil—impoverishes the story by neglecting the rich implications just as much as the symbol-hunter impoverishes "The Story of an Hour" by losing sight of Mrs. Mallard in an interpretation of the story as a symbolic comment on industrialism. To take only a single piece of evidence: the man whom Brown encounters holds a staff, "which bore the likeness of a great black snake, so curiously wrought that it might almost be seen to twist and wriggle itself like a living serpent." If we are familiar with the story of Adam and Eve, in which Satan took the form of a serpent, it is hard not to think that Hawthorne is here implying that Brown's new acquaintance is Satan. And, to speak more broadly, as one reads the story one can hardly not set up opposing meanings (or at least suggestions) for the village (from which Brown sets out) and the forest (into which he enters). The village is associated with daylight, faith, and goodness; the forest with darkness, loss of faith, and evil. This is not to say that the story sets up neat categories. If you read the story, you will find that Hawthorne is careful to be ambiguous. Even in the passage quoted, about the serpent-staff, you'll notice that he does not say it twisted and wriggled, but that it "might almost be seen to twist and wriggle."

A NOTE ON SETTING

The **setting** of a story—not only the physical locale but also the time of day or year or century—may or may not be symbolic. Sometimes the setting is lightly sketched, presented only because the story has to take place somewhere and at some time. Often, however, the setting is more important, giving us the feel of the people who move through it. But if scenery is drawn in detail, yet adds up to nothing, we share the impatience Robert Louis Stevenson expressed in a letter: "'Roland approached the house; it had green doors and window blinds; and there was a scraper on the upper step.' To hell with Roland and the scraper."

Yes, of course, but if the green doors and the scraper were to tell us something about the tenant, they could be important. For instance, in Eudora Welty's "Livvie" (included in this chapter), we learn that in front of old Solomon's house there is "a clean dirt yard with every vestige of grass patiently uprooted." Now, such a yard *must* tell us something about the man who lives on the property. You'll notice, too, if you read Welty's story, that the property-owner Solomon is contrasted with a man named Cash, who is explicitly said to be a field hand. In the context of the story, the house and yard "say" one thing, and the fields and field hands "say" another. In short, the characters are related to their surroundings. As the novelist Elizabeth Bowen has said, "Nothing can happen nowhere. The locale of the happening always colors the happening, and often, to a degree, shapes it." And as Henry James neatly said, in fiction "landscape is character." But don't believe it simply because Bowen and James say it. Read the stories, and test the view for yourself.

Nathaniel Hawthorne

Nathaniel Hawthorne (1804–64) was born in Salem, Massachusetts, the son of a sea captain and a descendant of a judge who had persecuted Quakers and of another judge who had served at the Salem witch trials. After graduating from Bowdoin College in Maine, he returned to Salem, Massachusetts, in order to write in relative seclusion. In 1835 he published "Young Goodman Brown" in a magazine.

In his stories and novels Hawthorne keeps returning to the Puritan past, studying guilt, sin, and isolation.

Young Goodman Brown

Young Goodman[1] Brown came forth, at sunset, into the street at Salem village; but put his head back, after crossing the threshold, to exchange a parting kiss with his young wife. And Faith, as the wife was aptly named, thrust her pretty head into the street, letting the wind play with the pink ribbons of her cap while she called to Goodman Brown.

"Dearest heart," whispered she, softly and rather sadly, when her lips were close to his ear, "prithee put off your journey until sunrise and sleep in your own bed to-night. A lone woman is troubled with such dreams and such thoughts that she's afeared of herself sometimes. Pray tarry with me this night, dear husband, of all nights in the year."

"My love and my Faith," replied young Goodman Brown, "of all nights in the year, this one night must I tarry away from thee. My journey, as thou callest it, forth and back again, must needs be done 'twixt now and sunrise. What, my sweet, pretty wife, dost thou doubt me already, and we but three months married?"

"Then God bless you!" said Faith, with the pink ribbons; "and may you find all well when you come back."

"Amen!" cried Goodman Brown. "Say thy prayers, dear Faith, and go to bed at dusk, and no harm will come to thee."

So they parted; and the young man pursued his way until, being about to turn the corner by the meeting-house, he looked back and saw the head of Faith still peeping after him with a melancholy air, in spite of her pink ribbons.

"Poor little Faith!" thought he, for his heart smote him. "What a wretch am I to leave her on such an errand! She talks of dreams, too. Methought as she spoke there was trouble in her face, as if a dream had warned her what work is to be done to-night. But no, no; 'twould kill her to think it. Well, she's a blessed angel on earth; and after this one night, I'll cling to her skirts and follow her to heaven."

With this excellent resolve for the future, Goodman Brown felt himself justified in making more haste on his present evil purpose. He had taken a dreary road, darkened by all the gloomiest trees of the forest, which barely stood aside to let the narrow path creep through, and closed immediately behind. It was all as lonely as could be; and there is this peculiarity in such a solitude, that the traveller knows not who may be

---

[1]**Goodman**   polite term of address for a man of humble standing

concealed by the innumerable trunks and the thick boughs overhead; so that with lonely footsteps he may yet be passing through an unseen multitude.

"There may be a devilish Indian behind every tree," said Goodman Brown, to himself and he glanced fearfully behind him as he added, "What if the devil himself should be at my very elbow!"

His head being turned back, he passed a crook of the road, and, looking forward again, beheld the figure of a man, in grave and decent attire, seated at the foot of an old tree. He arose at Goodman Brown's approach and walked onward side by side with him.

"You are late, Goodman Brown," said he. "The clock of the Old South was striking as I came through Boston, and that is full fifteen minutes agone."

"Faith kept me back a while," replied the young man, with a tremor in his voice, caused by the sudden appearance of his companion, though not wholly unexpected.

It was now deep dusk in the forest, and deepest in that part of it where these two were journeying. As nearly as could be discerned, the second traveller was about fifty years old, apparently in the same rank of life as Goodman Brown, and bearing a considerable resemblance to him, though perhaps more in expression than features. Still they might have been taken for father and son. And yet, though the elder person was as simply clad as the younger, and as simple in manner too, he had an indescribable air of one who knew the world, and who would not have felt abashed at the governor's dinner table, or in King William's court, were it possible that his affairs should call him thither. But the only thing about him that could be fixed upon as remarkable was his staff, which bore the likeness of a great black snake, so curiously wrought that it might almost be seen to twist and wriggle itself like a living serpent. This, of course, must have been an ocular deception, assisted by the uncertain light.

"Come, Goodman Brown," cried his fellow-traveller, "this is a dull pace for the beginning of a journey. Take my staff, if you are so soon weary."

"Friend," said the other, exchanging his slow pace for a full stop, "having kept covenant by meeting thee here, it is my purpose now to return whence I came. I have scruples touching the matter thou wot'st[2] of."

"Sayest thou so?" replied he of the serpent, smiling apart. "Let us walk on, nevertheless, reasoning as we go; and if I convince thee not thou shalt turn back. We are but a little way in the forest yet."

"Too far! too far!" exclaimed the goodman, unconsciously resuming his walk. "My father never went into the woods on such an errand, nor his father before him. We have been a race of honest men and good

[2]**wot'st**   knowest

Christians since the days of the martyrs; and shall I be the first of the name of Brown that ever took this path and kept—"

"Such company, thou wouldst say," observed the elder person, interpreting his pause. "Well said, Goodman Brown! I have been as well acquainted with your family as with ever a one among the Puritans; and that's no trifle to say. I helped your grandfather, the constable, when he lashed the Quaker woman so smartly through the streets of Salem; and it was I that brought your father a pitch-pine knot, kindled at my own hearth, to set fire to an Indian village, in King Philip's war.[3] They were my good friends, both; and many a pleasant walk have we had along this path, and returned merrily after midnight. I would fain be friends with you for their sake."

"If it be as thou sayest," replied Goodman Brown, "I marvel they never spoke of these matters, or, verily, I marvel not, seeing that the least rumor of the sort would have driven them from New England. We are a people of prayer, and good works to boot, and abide no such wickedness."

"Wickedness or not," said the traveller with the twisted staff, "I have a very general acquaintance here in New England. The deacons of many a church have drunk the communion wine with me; the selectmen of divers towns make me their chairman; and a majority of the Great and General Court are firm supporters of my interest. The governor and I, too—But these are state secrets."

"Can this be so!" cried Goodman Brown, with a stare of amazement at his undisturbed companion. "Howbeit, I have nothing to do with the governor and council; they have their own ways, and are no rule for a simple husbandman[4] like me. But, were I to go on with thee, how should I meet the eye of that good old man, our minister, at Salem village? Oh, his voice would make me tremble both Sabbath day and lecture day!"

Thus far the elder traveller had listened with due gravity; but now burst into a fit of irrepressible mirth, shaking himself so violently that his snake-life staff actually seemed to wriggle in sympathy.

"Ha! ha! ha!" shouted he again and again; then composing himself, "Well, go on, Goodman Brown, go on; but, prithee, don't kill me with laughing."

"Well, then, to end the matter at once," said Goodman Brown, considerably nettled, "there is my wife, Faith. It would break her dear little heart; and I'd rather break my own."

"Nay, if that be the case," answered the other, "e'en go thy ways, Goodman Brown. I would not for twenty old women like the one hobbling before us that Faith should come to any harm."

---

[3] **King Philip's war**   war waged by the Colonists (1675–76) against the Wampanoag Indian leader Metacom, known as "King Philip"
[4] **husbandman**   farmer, or, more generally, any man of humble standing

As he spoke he pointed his staff at a female figure on the path, in whom Goodman Brown recognized a very pious and exemplary dame, who had taught him his catechism in youth, and was still his moral and spiritual adviser, jointly with the minister and Deacon Gookin.

"A marvel, truly, that Goody[5] Cloyse should be so far in the wilderness at night fall," said he. "But with your leave, friend, I shall take a cut through the woods until we have left this Christian woman behind. Being a stranger to you, she might ask whom I was consorting with and whither I was going."

"Be it so," said his fellow-traveller. "Betake you the woods, and let me keep the path."

Accordingly the young man turned aside, but took care to watch his companion, who advanced softly along the road until he had come within a staff's length of the old dame. She, meanwhile, was making the best of her way, with singular speed for so aged a woman, and mumbling some indistinct words—a prayer, doubtless—as she went. The traveller put forth his staff and touched her withered neck with what seemed the serpent's tail.

"The devil!" screamed the pious old lady.

"Then Goody Cloyse knows her old friend?" observed the traveller, confronting her and leaning on his writhing stick.

"Ah, forsooth, and is it your worship indeed?" cried the good dame. "Yea, truly is it, and in the very image of my old gossip, Goodman Brown, the grandfather of the silly fellow that now is. But—would your worship believe it?—my broomstick hath strangely disappeared, stolen, as I suspect, by that unhanged witch, Goody Cory, and that, too, when I was all anointed with the juice of smallage and cinquefoil and wolf's bane—"

"Mingled with fine wheat and the fat of a new-born babe," said the shape of old Goodman Brown.

"Ah, your worship knows the recipe," cried the old lady, cackling aloud. "So, as I was saying, being all ready for the meeting, and no horse to ride on, I made up my mind to foot it; for they tell me there is a nice young man to be taken into communion to-night. But now your good worship will lend me your arm, and we shall be there in a twinkling."

"That can hardly be," answered her friend. "I may not spare you my arm, Goody Cloyse; but here is my staff, if you will."

So saying, he threw it down at her feet, where, perhaps, it assumed life, being one of the rods which its owner had formerly lent to the Egyptian magi. Of this fact, however, Goodman Brown could not take cognizance. He had cast up his eyes in astonishment, and, looking down again, beheld neither Goody Cloyse nor the serpentine staff but his fellow-traveller alone, who waited for him as calmly as if nothing had happened.

---

[5] **Goody**   contraction of Goodwife, a polite term of address for a married woman of humble standing

"That old woman taught me my catechism," said the young man; and there was a world of meaning in this simple comment.

They continued to walk onward, while the elder traveller exhorted his companion to make good speed and persevere in the path, discoursing so aptly that his arguments seemed rather to spring up in the bosom of his auditor than to be suggested by himself. As they went, he plucked a branch of maple to serve for a walking-stick, and began to strip it of the twigs and little boughs, which were wet with evening dew. The moment his fingers touched them they became strangely withered and dried up as with a week's sunshine. Thus the pair proceeded, at a good free pace, until suddenly, in a gloomy hollow of the road, Goodman Brown sat himself down on the stump of a tree and refused to go any farther.

"Friend," said he, stubbornly, "my mind is made up. Not another step will I budge on this errand. What if a wretched old woman do choose to go to the devil when I thought she was going to heaven: is that any reason why I should quit my dear Faith and go after her?"

"You will think better of this by and by," said his acquaintance, composedly. "Sit here and rest yourself a while; and when you feel like moving again, there is my staff to help you along."

Without more words, he threw his companion the maple stick, and was as speedily out of sight as if he had vanished into the deepening gloom. The young man sat a few moments by the roadside, applauding himself greatly, and thinking with how clear a conscience he should meet the minister in his morning walk, nor shrink from the eye of good old Deacon Gookin. And what calm sleep would be his that very night, which was to have been spent so wickedly, but so purely and sweetly now, in the arms of Faith! Amidst these pleasant and praiseworthy meditations, Goodman Brown heard the tramp of horses along the road, and deemed it advisable to conceal himself within the verge of the forest, conscious of the guilty purpose that had brought him thither, though now so happily turned from it.

On came the hoof-tramps and the voices of the riders, two grave old voices, conversing soberly as they drew near. These mingled sounds appeared to pass along the road, within a few yards of the young man's hiding-place; but, owing doubtless to the depth of the gloom at that particular spot, neither the travellers nor their steeds were visible. Though their figures brushed the small boughs by the wayside, it could not be seen that they intercepted, even for a moment, the faint gleam from the strip of bright sky athwart which they must have passed. Goodman Brown alternately crouched and stood on tiptoe, pulling aside the branches and thrusting forth his head as far as he durst without discerning so much as a shadow. It vexed him the more, because he could have sworn, were such a thing possible, that he recognized the voices of the minister and Deacon Gookin, jogging along quietly, as they were wont to do, when bound to some ordination or ecclesiastical council. While yet within hearing, one of the riders stopped to pluck a switch.

"Of the two, reverend sir," said the voice like the deacon's, "I had rather miss an ordination dinner than to-night's meeting. They tell me that some of our community are to be here from Falmouth and beyond, and others from Connecticut and Rhode Island, besides several of the Indian powwows, who, after their fashion, know almost as much deviltry as the best of us. Moreover, there is a goodly young woman to be taken into communion."

"Mighty well, Deacon Gookin!" replied the solemn old tones of the minister. "Spur up, or we shall be late. Nothing can be done, you know, until I get on the ground."

The hoofs clattered again; and the voices, talking so strangely in the empty air, passed on through the forest, where no church had ever been gathered or solitary Christian prayed. Whither, then, could these holy men be journeying so deep into the heathen wilderness? Young Goodman Brown caught hold of a tree for support, being ready to sink down on the ground, faint and overburdened with the heavy sickness of his heart. He looked up to the sky, doubting whether there really was a heaven above him. Yet, there was the blue arch, and the stars brightening in it.

"With heaven above, and Faith below, I will yet stand firm against the devil!" cried Goodman Brown.

While he still gazed upward into the deep arch of the firmament and had lifted his hands to pray, a cloud, though no wind was stirring, hurried across the zenith and hid the brightening stars. The blue sky was still visible, except directly overhead, where this black mass of cloud was sweeping swiftly northward. Aloft in the air, as if from the depths of the cloud, came a confused and doubtful sound of voices. Once the listener fancied that he could distinguish the accents of towns-people of his own, men and women, both pious and ungodly, many of whom he had met at the communion table, and had seen others rioting at the tavern. The next moment, so indistinct were the sounds, he doubted whether he had heard aught but the murmur of the old forest, whispering without a wind. Then came a stronger swell of those familiar tones, heard daily in the sunshine at Salem village, but never until now from a cloud of night. There was one voice, of a young woman, uttering lamentations, yet with an uncertain sorrow, and entreating for some favor, which, perhaps, it would grieve her to obtain; and all the unseen multitude, both saints and sinners, seemed to encourage her onward.

"Faith!" shouted Goodman Brown, in a voice of agony and desperation; and the echoes of the forest mocked him, crying, "Faith! Faith!" as if bewildered wretches were seeking her all through the wilderness.

The cry of grief, rage, and terror was yet piercing the night, when the unhappy husband held his breath for a response. There was a scream, drowned immediately in a louder murmur of voices, fading into far-off laughter, as the dark cloud swept away, leaving the clear and silent sky above Goodman Brown. But something fluttered lightly down through the air and caught on the branch of a tree. The young man seized it, and beheld a pink ribbon.

"My Faith is gone!" cried he, after one stupefied moment. "There is no good on earth; and sin is but a name. Come, devil; for to thee is this world given."

And, maddened with despair, so that he laughed loud and long, did Goodman Brown grasp his staff and set forth again, at such a rate that he seemed to fly along the forest path, rather than to walk or run. The road grew wilder and drearier and more faintly traced, and vanished at length, leaving him in the heart of the dark wilderness, still rushing onward with the instinct that guides mortal man to evil. The whole forest was peopled with frightful sounds—the creaking of the trees, the howling of wild beasts, and the yell of Indians; while sometimes the wind tolled like a distant church bell, and sometimes gave a broad roar around the traveller, as if all Nature were laughing him to scorn. But he was himself the chief horror of the scene, and shrank not from its other horrors.

"Ha! ha! ha!" roared Goodman Brown when the wind laughed at him. "Let us hear which will laugh loudest! Think not to frighten me with your deviltry! Come witch, come wizard, come Indian powwow, come devil himself, and here comes Goodman Brown. You may as well fear him as he fear you!"

In truth, all through the haunted forest there could be nothing more frightful than the figure of Goodman Brown. On he flew among the black pines, brandishing his staff with frenzied gestures, now giving vent to an inspiration of horrid blasphemy, and now shouting forth such laughter as set all the echoes of the forest laughing like demons around him. The fiend in his own shape is less hideous than when he rages in the breast of man. Thus sped the demoniac on his course, until, quivering among the trees, he saw a red light before him, as when the felled trunks and branches of a clearing have been set on fire, and throw up their lurid blaze against the sky, at the hour of midnight. He paused, in a lull of the tempest that had driven him onward, and heard the swell of what seemed a hymn, rolling solemnly from a distance with the weight of many voices. He knew the tune; it was a familiar one in the choir of the village meeting-house. The verse died heavily away, and was lengthened by a chorus, not of human voices, but of all the sounds of the benighted wilderness pealing in awful harmony together. Goodman Brown cried out; and his cry was lost to his own ear by its unison with the cry of the desert.

In the interval of silence he stole forward until the light glared full upon his eyes. At one extremity of an open space, hemmed in by the dark wall of the forest, arose a rock, bearing some rude, natural resemblance either to an altar or a pulpit, and surrounded by four blazing pines, their tops aflame, their stems untouched, like candles at an evening meeting.

The mass of foliage that had overgrown the summit of the rock was all on fire, blazing high into the night and fitfully illuminating the whole field. Each pendent twig and leafy festoon was in a blaze. As the red light arose and fell, a numerous congregation alternately shone forth, then disappeared in shadow, and again grew, as it were, out of the darkness, peopling the heart of the solitary woods at once.

"A grave and dark-clad company," quoth Goodman Brown.

In truth, they were such. Among them, quivering to-and-fro between gloom and splendor, appeared faces that would be seen next day at the council board of the province, and others which, Sabbath after Sabbath, looked devoutly heavenward, and benignantly over the crowded pews, from the holiest pulpits in the land. Some affirm that the lady of the governor was there. At least there were high dames well known to her, and wives of honored husbands, and widows, a great multitude, and ancient maidens, all of excellent repute, and fair young girls, who trembled lest their mothers should espy them. Either the sudden gleams of light flashing over the obscure field bedazzled Goodman Brown, or he recognized a score of the church-members of Salem village famous for their especial sanctity. Good old Deacon Gookin had arrived, and waited at the skirts of that venerable saint, his revered pastor. But, irreverently consorting with these grave, reputable, and pious people, these elders of the church, these chaste dames and dewy virgins, there were men of dissolute lives and women of spotted fame, wretches given over to all mean and filthy vice, and suspected even of horrid crimes. It was strange to see, that the good shrank not from the wicked, nor were the sinners abashed by the saints. Scattered also among their pale-faced enemies were the Indian priests, or powwows, who had often scared their native forest with more hideous incantations than any known to English witchcraft.

"But, where is Faith?" thought Goodman Brown; and, as hope came into his heart, he trembled.

Another verse of the hymn arose, a slow and mournful strain, such as the pious love, but joined to words which expressed all that our nature can conceive of sin, and darkly hinted at far more. Unfathomable to mere mortals is the lore of fiends. Verse after verse was sung; and still the chorus of the desert swelled between, like the deepest tone of a mighty organ; and with the final peal of that dreadful anthem there came a sound, as if the roaring wind, the rushing streams, the howling beasts, and every other voice of the unconcerted wilderness were mingling and according with the voice of guilty man in homage to the prince of all. The four blazing pines threw up a loftier flame, and obscurely discovered shapes and visages of horror on the smoke wreaths above the impious assembly. At the same moment the fire on the rock shot redly forth and formed a glowing arch above its base, where now appeared a figure. With reverence be it spoken, the figure bore no slight similitude, both in garb and manner, to some grave divine of the New England churches.

"Bring forth the converts!" cried a voice that echoed through the field and rolled into the forest.

At the word, Goodman Brown stepped forth from the shadow of the trees and approached the congregation, with whom he felt a loathful brotherhood by the sympathy of all that was wicked in his heart. He could have well nigh sworn that the shape of his own dead father beckoned him to advance, looking downward from a smoke wreath, while a woman, with dim features of despair, threw out her hand to warn him back. Was it his mother? But he had no power to retreat one step, nor to resist, even in thought, when the minister and good old Deacon Gookin seized his arms and led him to the blazing rock. Thither came also the slender form of a veiled female, led between Goody Cloyse, that pious teacher of the catechism, and Martha Carrier, who had received the devil's promise to be queen of hell. A rampant hag was she. And there stood the proselytes beneath the canopy of fire.

"Welcome, my children," said the dark figure, "to the communion of your race. Ye have found thus young your nature and your destiny. My children, look behind you!"

They turned; and flashing forth, as it were, in a sheet of flame, the fiend worshippers were seen; the smile of welcome gleamed darkly on every visage.

"There," resumed the sable form, "are all whom ye have reverenced from youth. Ye deemed them holier than yourselves, and shrank from your own sin, contrasting it with their lives of righteousness and prayerful aspirations heavenward. Yet here are they all in my worshipping assembly. This night it shall be granted you to know their secret deeds: how hoary-bearded elders of the church have whispered wanton words to the young maids of their households; how many a woman, eager for widow's weeds, has given her husband a drink at bedtime, and let him sleep his last sleep in her bosom; how beardless youths have made haste to inherit their fathers' wealth; and how fair damsels—blush not, sweet ones—have dug little graves in the garden, and bidden me, the sole guest, to an infant's funeral. By the sympathy of your human hearts for sin ye shall scent out all the places—whether in church, bed-chamber, street, field, or forest—where crime has been committed, and shall exult to behold the whole earth one stain of guilt, one mighty blood spot. Far more than this. It shall be yours to penetrate, in every bosom, the deep mystery of sin, the fountain of all wicked arts, and which inexhaustibly supplies more evil impulses than human power—than my power at its utmost—can make manifest in deeds. And now, my children, look upon each other."

They did so; and, by the blaze of the hell-kindled torches, the wretched man beheld his Faith, and the wife her husband, trembling before that unhallowed altar.

"Lo, there ye stand, my children," said the figure, in a deep and solemn tone, almost sad with its despairing awfulness, as if his once angelic nature could yet mourn for our miserable race. "Depending upon one another's hearts, ye had still hoped that virtue were not all a dream. Now are ye undeceived. Evil is the nature of mankind. Evil must be your only happiness. Welcome, again, my children, to the communion of your race."

"Welcome," repeated the fiend worshippers, in one cry of despair and triumph.

And there they stood, the only pair, as it seemed, who were yet hesitating on the verge of wickedness in this dark world. A basin was hollowed, naturally, in the rock. Did it contain water, reddened by the lurid light? or was it blood? or, perchance, a liquid flame? Herein did the shape of evil dip his hand and prepare to lay the mark of baptism upon their foreheads, that they might be partakers of the mystery of sin, more conscious of the secret guilt of others, both in deed and thought, than they could now be of their own. The husband cast one look at his pale wife, and Faith at him. What polluted wretches would the next glance show them to each other, shuddering alike at what they disclosed and what they saw!

"Faith! Faith!" cried the husband, "look up to heaven, and resist the wicked one."

Whether Faith obeyed he knew not. Hardly had he spoken when he found himself amid calm night and solitude, listening to a roar of the wind which died heavily away through the forest. He staggered against the rock, and felt it chill and damp; while a hanging twig, that had been all on fire, besprinkled his cheek with the coldest dew.

The next morning young Goodman Brown came slowly into the street of Salem village, staring around him like a bewildered man. The good old minister was taking a walk along the graveyard to get an appetite for breakfast and meditate his sermon, and bestowed a blessing, as he passed, on Goodman Brown. He shrank from the venerable saint as if to avoid an anathema. Old Deacon Gookin was at domestic worship, and the holy words of his prayer were heard through the open window. "What God doth the wizard pray to?" quoth Goodman Brown. Goody Cloyse, that excellent old Christian, stood in the early sunshine at her own lattice, catechizing a little girl who had brought her a pint of morning's milk. Goodman Brown snatched away the child as from the grasp of the fiend himself. Turning the corner by the meeting-house, he spied the head of Faith, with the pink ribbons, gazing anxiously forth, and bursting into such joy at sight of him that she skipped along the street and almost kissed her husband before the whole village. But Goodman Brown looked sternly and sadly into her face, and passed on without a greeting.

Had Goodman Brown fallen asleep in the forest and only dreamed a wild dream of a witch-meeting?

Be it so, if you will; but, alas! it was a dream of evil omen for young Goodman Brown. A stern, a sad, a darkly meditative, a distrustful, if not a desperate man did he become from the night of that fearful dream. On the Sabbath day, when the congregation were singing a holy psalm, he could not listen because an anthem of sin rushed loudly upon his ear and drowned all the blessed strain. When the minister spoke from the pulpit with power and fervid eloquence, and, with his hand on the open Bible, of the sacred truths of our religion, and of saint-like lives and triumphant deaths, and of future bliss or misery unutterable, then did Goodman Brown turn pale, dreading lest the roof should thunder down upon the gray blasphemer and his hearers. Often, awakening suddenly at midnight, he shrank from the bosom of Faith; and at morning or eventide, when the family knelt down at prayer, he scowled and muttered to himself, and gazed sternly at his wife, and turned away. And when he had lived long, and was borne to his grave a hoary corpse, followed by Faith, an aged woman, and children and grandchildren, a goodly procession, besides neighbors, not a few, they carved no hopeful verse upon his tombstone, for his dying hour was gloom.

[1835]

TOPICS FOR DISCUSSION AND WRITING

1. Do you take Faith to stand only for religious faith, or can she here also stand for one's faith in one's fellow human beings? Explain.
2. Hawthorne describes the second traveler as "about fifty years old, apparently in the same rank as Goodman Brown, and bearing a considerable resemblance to him." Further, "they might have been taken for father and son." What do you think Hawthorne is getting at here?
3. In the forest Brown sees (or thinks he sees) Goody Cloyse, the minister, Deacon Gookin, and others. Does he in fact meet them, or does he dream of them? Or does he encounter "figures" and "forms" (rather than real people) whom the devil conjures up in order to deceive Brown?
4. Evaluate the view that when Brown enters the dark forest he is really entering his own evil mind.

Eudora Welty

Eudora Welty (b. 1909) was born in Jackson, Mississippi. Although she earned a bachelor's degree at the University of Wisconsin and spent a year studying advertising in New York City at the Columbia University Graduate School of Business, she has lived almost all of her life in Jackson.

In the preface to her Collected Stories *she says,*

I have been told, both in approval and in accusation, that I seem to love all my characters. What I do in writing of any character is to try to enter into the mind, heart and skin of a human being who is not myself. Whether this happens to be a man or a woman, old or young, with skin black or white, the primary challenge lies in making the jump itself. It is the act of a writer's imagination that I set most high.

In addition to writing stories and novels, Welty has written a book about fiction, The Eye of the Story *(1977), and a memoir,* One Writer's Beginnings *(1984).*

Livvie

Solomon carried Livvie twenty-one miles away from her home when he married her. He carried her away up on the Old Natchez Trace into the deep country to live in his house. She was sixteen — an only girl, then. Once people said he thought nobody would ever come along there. He told her himself that it had been a long time, and a day she did not know about, since that road was a traveled road with *people* coming and going. He was good to her, but he kept her in the house. She had not thought that she could not get back. Where she came from, people said an old man did not want anybody in the world to ever find his wife, for fear they would steal her back from him. Solomon asked her before he took her, "Would she be happy?" — very dignified, for he was a colored man that owned his land and had it written down in the courthouse; and she said, "Yes, sir," since he was an old man and she was young and just listened and answered. He asked her, if she was choosing winter, would she pine for spring, and she said, "No indeed." Whatever she said, always, was because he was an old man . . . while nine years went by. All the time, he got old, and he got so old he gave out. At least he slept the whole day in bed, and she was young still.

It was a nice house, inside and outside both. In the first place, it had three rooms. The front room was papered in holly paper, with green palmettos from the swamp spaced at careful intervals over the walls. There was fresh newspaper cut with fancy borders on the mantleshelf, on which were propped photographs of old or very young men printed in faint yellow — Solomon's people. Solomon had a houseful of furniture. There was a double settee, a tall scrolled rocker and an organ in the front room, all around a three-legged table with a pink marble top, on which was set a lamp with three gold feet, beside a jelly glass with pretty hen feathers in it. Behind the front room, the other room had the bright iron bed with the polished knobs like a throne, in which Solomon slept all day. There

were snow-white curtains of wiry lace at the window, and a lace bed-
spread belonged on the bed. But what old Solomon slept sound under
was a big feather-stitched piece-quilt in the pattern "Trip Around the
World," which had twenty-one different colors, four hundred and forty
pieces, and a thousand yards of thread, and that was what Solomon's
mother made in her life and old age. There was a table holding the Bible,
and a trunk with a key. On the wall were two calendars, and a diploma
from somewhere in Solomon's family, and under that Livvie's one possession was nailed, a picture of the little white baby of the family she
worked for, back in Natchez before she was married. Going through that
room and on to the kitchen, there was a big wood stove and a big round
table always with a wet top and with the knives and forks in one jelly
glass and the spoons in another, and a cut-glass vinegar bottle between,
and going out from those, many shallow dishes of pickled peaches, fig
preserves, watermelon pickles and blackberry jam always sitting there. The
churn sat in the sun, the doors of the safe were always both shut, and
there were four baited mouse-traps in the kitchen, one in every corner.

The outside of Solomon's house looked nice. It was not painted, but
across the porch was an even balance. On each side there was one easy
chair with high springs, looking out, and a fern basket hanging over it
from the ceiling, and a dishpan of zinnia seedlings growing at its foot on
the floor. By the door was a plow-wheel, just a pretty iron circle, nailed
up on one wall and a square mirror on the other, a turquoise-blue comb
stuck up in the frame, with the wash stand beneath it. On the door was
a wooden knob with a pearl in the end, and Solomon's black hat hung
on that, if he was in the house.

Out front was a clean dirt yard with every vestige of grass patiently
uprooted and the ground scarred in deep whorls from the strike of Livvie's broom. Rose bushes with tiny blood-red roses blooming every month
grew in threes on either side of the steps. On one side was a peach tree,
on the other a pomegranate. Then coming around up the path from the
deep cut of the Natchez Trace below was a line of bare crape-myrtle trees
with every branch of them ending in a colored bottle, green or blue. There
was no word that fell from Solomon's lips to say what they were for, but
Livvie knew that there could be a spell put in trees, and she was familiar
from the time she was born with the way bottle trees kept evil spirits from
coming into the house—by luring them inside the colored bottles, where
they cannot get out again. Solomon had made the bottle trees with his
own hands over the nine years, in labor amounting to about a tree a year,
and without a sign that he had any uneasiness in his heart, for he took
as much pride in his precautions against spirits coming in the house as
he took in the house, and sometimes in the sun the bottle trees looked
prettier than the house did.

It was a nice house. It was in a place where the days would go by
and surprise anyone that they were over. The lamplight and the firelight

would shine out the door after dark, over the still and breathing country, lighting the roses and the bottle trees, and all was quiet there.

But there was nobody, nobody at all, not even a white person. And if there had been anybody, Solomon would not have let Livvie look at them, just as he would not let her look at a field hand, or a field hand look at her. There was no house near, except for the cabins of the tenants that were forbidden to her, and there was no house as far as she had been, stealing away down the still, deep Trace. She felt as if she waded a river when she went, for the dead leaves on the ground reached as high as her knees, and when she was all scratched and bleeding she said it was not like a road that went anywhere. One day, climbing up the high bank, she had found a graveyard without a church; with ribbon-grass growing about the foot of an angel (she had climbed up because she thought she saw angel wings), and in the sun, trees shining like burning flames through the great caterpillar nets which enclosed them. Scarey thistles stood looking like the prophets in the Bible in Solomon's house. Indian paint brushes grew over her head, and the mourning dove made the only sound in the world. Oh for a stirring of the leaves, and a breaking of the nets! But not by a ghost, prayed Livvie, jumping down the bank. After Solomon took to his bed, she never went out, except one more time.

Livvie knew she made a nice girl to wait on anybody. She fixed things to eat on a tray like a surprise. She could keep from singing when she ironed, and to sit by a bed and fan away the flies, she could be so still she could not hear herself breathe. She could clean up the house and never drop a thing, and wash the dishes without a sound, and she would step outside to churn, for churning sounded too sad to her, like sobbing, and if it made her home-sick and not Solomon, she did not think of that.

But Solomon scarcely opened his eyes to see her, and scarcely tasted his food. He was not sick or paralyzed or in any pain that he mentioned, but he was surely wearing out in the body, and no matter what nice hot thing Livvie would bring him to taste, he would only look at it now, as if he was past seeing how he could add anything more to himself. Before she could beg him, he would go fast asleep. She could not surprise him any more, if he would not taste, and she was afraid that he was never in the world going to taste another thing she brought him—and so how could he last?

But one morning it was breakfast time and she cooked his eggs and grits, carried them in on a tray, and called his name. He was sound asleep. He lay in a dignified way with his watch beside him, on his back in the middle of the bed. One hand drew the quilt up high, though it was the first day of spring. Through the white lace curtains a little puffy wind was blowing as if it came from round cheeks. All night the frogs had sung out in the swamp, like a commotion in the room, and he had not stirred, though she lay wide awake and saying, "Shh, frogs!" for fear he would mind them.

He looked as if he would like to sleep a little longer, and so she put back the tray and waited a little. When she tiptoed and stayed so quiet, she surrounded herself with a little reverie, and sometimes it seemed to her when she was so stealthy that the quiet she kept was for a sleeping baby, and that she had a baby and was its mother. When she stood at Solomon's bed and looked down at him, she would be thinking, "He sleeps so well," and she would hate to wake him up. And in some other way, too, she was afraid to wake him up because even in his sleep he seemed to be such a strict man.

Of course, nailed to the wall over the bed—only she would forget who it was—there was a picture of him when he was young. Then he had a fan of hair over his forehead like a king's crown. Now his hair lay down on his head, the spring had gone out of it. Solomon had a lightish face, with eyebrows scattered but rugged, the way privet grows, strong eyes, with second sight, a strict mouth, and a little gold smile. This was the way he looked in his clothes, but in bed in the daytime he looked like a different and smaller man, even when he was wide awake, and holding the Bible. He looked like somebody kin to himself. And then sometimes when he lay in sleep and she stood fanning the flies away, and the light came in, his face was like new, so smooth and clear that it was like a glass of jelly held to the window, and she could almost look through his forehead and see what he thought.

She fanned him and at length he opened his eyes and spoke her name, but he would not taste the nice eggs she had kept warm under a pan.

Back in the kitchen she ate heartily, his breakfast and hers, and looked out the open door at what went on. The whole day, and the whole night before, she had felt the stir of spring close to her. It was as present in the house as a young man would be. The moon was in the last quarter and outside they were turning the sod and planting peas and beans. Up and down the red fields, over which smoke from the brush-burning hung showing like a little skirt of sky, a white horse and a white mule pulled the plow. At intervals hoarse shouts came through the air and roused her as if she dozed neglectfully in the shade, and they were telling her, "Jump up!" She could see how over each ribbon of field were moving men and girls, on foot and mounted on mules, with hats set on their heads and bright with tall hoes and forks as if they carried streamers on them and were going to some place on a journey—and how as if at a signal now and then they would all start at once shouting, hollering, cajoling, calling and answering back, running, being leaped on and breaking away, flinging to earth with a shout and lying motionless in the trance of twelve o'clock. The old women came out of the cabins and brought them food they had ready for them, and then all worked together, spread evenly out. The little children came too, like a bouncing stream overflowing the fields, and set upon the men, the women, the dogs, the rushing birds, and the wave-like rows of earth, their little voices almost too high to be heard. In the middle distance like some white-and-gold towers were the haystacks, with black cows coming around to eat their edges. High above everything, the wheel of fields, house, and cabins, and the deep road surrounding like a moat to keep them in, was the turning sky, blue with long, far-flung white mare's tail clouds, serene and still as high flames. And sound asleep while all this went around him that was his, Solomon was like a little still spot in the middle.

Even in the house the earth was sweet to breathe. Solomon had never let Livvie go any farther than the chicken house and the well. But what if she would walk now into the heart of the fields and take a hoe and work until she fell stretched out and drenched with her efforts, like other girls, and laid her cheek against the laid-open earth, and shamed the old man with her humbleness and delight? To shame him! A cruel wish would come in uninvited and so fast while she looked out the back door. She washed the dishes and scrubbed the table. She could hear the cries of the little lambs. Her mother, that she had not seen since her wedding day, had said one time, "I rather a man be anything, than a woman be mean."

So all morning she kept tasting the chicken broth on the stove, and when it was right she poured off a nice cupful. She carried it in to Solomon, and there he lay having a dream. Now what did he dream about? For she saw him sigh gently as if not to disturb some whole thing he held round in his mind, like a fresh egg. So even an old man dreamed about something pretty. Did he dream of her, while his eyes were shut and sunken, and his small hand with the wedding ring curled close in sleep around the quilt? He might be dreaming of what time it was, for even through his sleep he kept track of it like a clock, and knew how much of it went by, and waked up knowing where the hands were even before he consulted the silver watch that he never let go. He would sleep with the watch in his palm, and even holding it to his cheek like a child that loves a plaything. Or he might dream of journeys and travels on a steamboat to Natchez. Yet she thought he dreamed of her; but even while she scrutinized him, the rods of the foot of the bed seemed to rise up like a rail fence between them, and she could see that people never could be sure of anything as long as one of them was asleep and the other awake. To look at him dreaming of her when he might be going to die frightened her a little, as if he might carry her with him that way, and she wanted to run out of the room. She took hold of the bed and held on, and Solomon opened his eyes and called her name, but he did not want anything. He would not taste the good broth.

Just a little after that, as she was taking up the ashes in the front room for the last time in the year, she heard a sound. It was somebody coming. She pulled the curtains together and looked through the slit.

Coming up the path under the bottle trees was a white lady. At first she looked young, but then she looked old. Marvelous to see, a little car stood steaming like a kettle out in the field-track—it had come without a road.

Livvie stood listening to the long, repeated knockings at the door, and after a while she opened it just a little. The lady came in through the crack, though she was more than middle-sized and wore a big hat.

"My name is Miss Baby Marie," she said.

Livvie gazed respectfully at the lady and at the little suitcase she was holding close to her by the handle until the proper moment. The lady's eyes were running over the room, from palmetto to palmetto, but she was saying, "I live at home . . . out from Natchez . . . and get out and show these pretty cosmetic things to the white people and the colored people both . . . all around . . . years and years. . . . Both shades of powder and rouge. . . . It's the kind of work a girl can do and not go clear 'way from home. . . . " And the harder she looked, the more she talked. Suddenly she turned up her nose and said, "It's not Christian or sanitary to put feathers in a vase," and then she took a gold key out of the front of her dress and began unlocking the locks on her suitcase. Her face drew the light, the way it was covered with intense white and red, with a little patty-cake of white between the wrinkles by her upper lip. Little red tassels of hair bobbed under the rusty wires of her picture-hat, as with an air of triumph and secrecy she now drew open her little suitcase and brought out bottle after bottle and jar after jar, which she put down on the table, the mantelpiece, the settee, and the organ.

"Did you ever see so many cosmetics in your life?" cried Miss Baby Marie.

"No'm," Livvie tried to say, but the cat had her tongue.

"Have you ever applied cosmetics?" asked Miss Baby Marie next.

"No'm," Livvie tried to say.

"Then look!" she said, and pulling out the last thing of all, "Try this!" she said. And in her hand was unclenched a golden lipstick which popped open like magic. A fragrance came out of it like incense, and Livvie cried out suddenly, "Chinaberry flowers!"

Her hand took the lipstick, and in an instant she was carried away in the air through the spring, and looking down with a half-drowsy smile from a purple cloud she saw from above a chinaberry tree, dark and smooth and neatly leaved, neat as a guinea hen in the dooryard, and there was her home that she had left. On one side of the tree was her mama holding up her heavy apron, and she could see it was loaded with ripe figs, and on the other side was her papa holding a fish-pole over the pond, and she could see it transparently, the little clear fishes swimming up to the brim.

"Oh, no, not chinaberry flowers—secret ingredients," said Miss Baby Marie, "My cosmetics have secret ingredients—not chinaberry flowers."

"It's purple," Livvie breathed, and Miss Baby Marie said, "Use it freely. Rub it on."

Livvie tiptoed out to the wash stand on the front porch and before the mirror put the paint on her mouth. In the wavery surface her face danced before her like a flame. Miss Baby Marie followed her out, took a look at what she had done, and said, "That's it."

Livvie tried to say "Thank you" without moving her parted lips where the paint lay so new.

By now Miss Baby Marie stood behind Livvie and looked in the mirror over her shoulder, twisting up the tassels of her hair. "The lipstick I can let you have for only two dollars," she said, close to her neck.

"Lady, but I don't have no money, never did have," said Livvie.

"Oh, but you don't pay the first time. I make another trip, that's the way I do. I come back again—later."

"Oh," said Livvie, pretending she understood everything so as to please the lady.

"But if you don't take it now, this may be the last time I'll call at your house," said Miss Baby Marie sharply. "It's far away from anywhere, I'll tell you that. You don't live close to anywhere."

"Yes'm. My husband, he keep the *money*," said Livvie, trembling. "He is strict as he can be. He don't know *you* walk in here—Miss Baby Marie!"

"Where is he?"

"Right now, he in yonder sound asleep, an old man. I wouldn't ever ask him for anything."

Miss Baby Marie took back the lipstick and packed it up. She gathered up the jars for both black and white and got them all inside the suitcase, with the same little fuss of triumph with which she had brought them out. She started away.

"Goodbye," she said, making herself look grand from the back, but at the last minute she turned around in the door. Her old hat wobbled as she whispered, "Let me see your husband."

Livvie obediently went on tiptoe and opened the door to the other room. Miss Baby Marie came behind her and rose on her toes and looked in.

"My, what a little tiny old, old man!" she whispered, clasping her hands and shaking her head over them. "What a beautiful quilt! What a tiny old, old man!"

"He can sleep like that all day," whispered Livvie proudly.

They looked at him awhile so fast asleep, and then all at once they looked at each other. Somehow that was as if they had a secret, for he had never stirred. Livvie then politely, but all at once, closed the door.

"Well! I'd certainly like to leave you with a lipstick!" said Miss Baby Marie vivaciously. She smiled in the door.

"Lady, but I told you I don't have no money, and never did have."

"And never will?" In the air and all around, like a bright halo around the white lady's nodding head, it was a true spring day.

"Would you take eggs, lady?" asked Livvie softly.

"No, I have plenty of eggs—plenty," said Miss Baby Marie.

"I still don't have no money," said Livvie, and Miss Baby Marie took her suitcase and went on somewhere else.

Livvie stood watching her go, and all the time she felt her heart beating in her left side. She touched the place with her hand. It seemed as if her heart beat and her whole face flamed from the pulsing color of her lips. She went to sit by Solomon and when he opened his eyes he could not see a change in her. "He's fixin' to die," she said inside. That was the secret. That was when she went out of the house for a little breath of air.

She went down the path and down the Natchez Trace a way, and she did not know how far she had gone, but it was not far, when she saw a sight. It was a man, looking like a vision—she standing on one side of the Old Natchez Trace and he standing on the other.

As soon as this man caught sight of her, he began to look himself over. Starting at the bottom with his pointed shoes, he began to look up, lifting his peg-top pants the higher to see fully his bright socks. His coat long and wide and leaf-green he opened like doors to see his high-up tawny pants and his pants he smoothed downward from the points of his collar, and he wore a luminous baby-pink satin shirt. At the end, he reached gently above his wide platter-shaped round hat, the color of a plum, and one finger touched at the feather, emerald green, blowing in the spring winds.

No matter how she looked, she could never look so fine as he did, and she was not sorry for that, she was pleased.

He took three jumps, one down and two up, and was by her side.

"My name is Cash," he said.

He had a guinea pig in his pocket. They began to walk along. She stared on and on at him, as if he were doing some daring spectacular thing, instead of just walking beside her. It was not simply the city way he was dressed that made her look at him and see hope in its insolence looking back. It was not only the way he moved along kicking the flowers as if he could break through everything in the way and destroy anything in the world, that made her eyes grow bright. It might be, if he had not appeared the way he did appear that day she would never have looked so closely at him, but the time people come makes a difference.

They walked through the still leaves of the Natchez Trace, the light and the shade falling through trees about them, the white irises shining like candles on the banks and the new ferns shining like green stars up in the oak branches. They came out at Solomon's house, bottle trees and all. Livvie stopped and hung her head.

Cash began whistling a little tune. She did not know what it was, but she had heard it before from a distance, and she had a revelation. Cash was a field hand. He was a transformed field hand. Cash belonged to Solomon. But he had stepped out of his overalls into this. There in front of Solomon's house he laughed. He had a round head, a round face, all of him was young, and he flung his head up, rolled it against the mare's-tail sky in his round hat, and he could laugh just to see Solomon's house sitting there. Livvie looked at it, and there was Solomon's black hat hanging on the peg on the front door, the blackest thing in the world.

"I been to Natchez," Cash said, wagging his head around the sky. "*I* taken a trip, *I* ready for Easter!"

How was it possible to look so fine before the harvest? Cash must have stolen the money, stolen it from Solomon. He stood in the path and lifted his spread hand high and brought it down again and again in his laughter. He kicked up his heels. A little chill went through her. It was as if Cash was bringing that strong hand down to beat a drum or to rain blows upon a man, such an abandon and menace were in his laugh. Frowning, she went closer to him and his swinging arm drew her in at once and the fright was crushed from her body, as a little match-flame might be smothered out by what it lighted. She gathered the folds of his coat behind him and fastened her red lips to his mouth, and she was dazzled by herself then, the way he had been dazzled with himself to begin with.

In that instant she felt something that could not be told—that Solomon's death was at hand, that he was the same to her as if he were dead now. She cried out, and uttering little cries turned and ran for the house.

At once Cash was coming, following after, he was running behind her. He came close, and half-way up the path he laughed and passed her. He even picked up a stone and sailed it into the bottle trees. She put her hands over her head, and sounds clattered through the bottle trees like cries of outrage. Cash stamped and plunged zigzag up the front steps and in at the door.

When she got there, he had stuck his hands in his pockets and was turning slowly about in the front room. The little guinea pig peeped out. Around Cash, the pinned-up palmettos looked as if a lazy green monkey had walked up and down and around the walls leaving green prints of his hands and feet.

She got through the room and his hands were still in his pockets, and she fell upon the closed door to the other room and pushed it open. She ran to Solomon's bed, calling "Solomon! Solomon!" The little shape of the old man never moved at all, wrapped under the quilt as if it were winter still.

"Solomon!" She pulled the quilt away, but there was another one under that, and she fell on her knees beside him. He made no sound except a sigh, and then she could hear in the silence the light springy steps of Cash walking and walking in the front room, and the ticking of Solomon's silver watch, which came from the bed. Old Solomon was far away in his sleep, his face looked small, relentless, and devout, as if he were walking somewhere where she could imagine the snow falling.

Then there was a noise like a hoof pawing the floor, and the door gave a creak, and Cash appeared beside her. When she looked up, Cash's face was so black it was bright, and so bright and bare of pity that it looked sweet to her. She stood up and held up her head. Cash was so powerful that his presence gave her strength even when she did not need any.

Under their eyes Solomon slept. People's faces tell of things and places not known to the one who looks at them while they sleep, and while Solomon slept under the eyes of Livvie and Cash his face told them like a mythical story that all his life he had built, little scrap by little scrap, respect. A beetle could not have been more laborious or more ingenious in the task of its destiny. When Solomon was young, as he was in his picture overhead, it was the infinite thing with him, and he could see no end to the respect he would contrive and keep in a house. He had built a lonely house, the way he would make a cage, but it grew to be the same with him as a great monumental pyramid and sometimes in his absorption of getting it erected he was like the builder-slaves of Egypt who forgot or never knew the origin and meaning of the thing to which they gave all their strength of their bodies and used up all their days. Livvie and Cash could see that as a man might rest from a life-labor he lay in his bed, and they could hear how, wrapped in his quilt, he sighed to himself comfortably in sleep, while in his dreams he might have been an ant, a beetle, a bird, an Egyptian, assembling and carrying on his back and building with his hands, or he might have been an old man of India or a swaddled baby, about to smile and brush all away.

Then without warning old Solomon's eyes flew wide open under the hedgelike brows. He was wide awake.

And instantly Cash raised his quick arm. A radiant sweat stood on his temples. But he did not bring his arm down—it stayed in the air, as if something might have taken hold.

It was not Livvie—she did not move. As if something said "Wait," she stood waiting. Even while her eyes burned under motionless lids, her lips parted in a stiff grimace, and with her arms stiff at her sides she stood above the prone old man and the panting young one, erect and apart.

Movement when it came came in Solomon's face. It was an old and strict face, a frail face, but behind it, like a covered light, came an animation that could play hide and seek, that would dart and escape, had always escaped. The mystery flickered in him, and invited from his eyes. It was that very mystery that Cash with his quick arm would have to strike, and that Livvie could not weep for. But Cash only stood holding his arm in the air, when the gentlest flick of his great strength, almost a puff of his breath, would have been enough, if he had known how to give it, to send the old man over the obstruction that kept him away from death.

If it could not be that the tiny illumination in the fragile and ancient face caused a crisis, a mystery in the room that would not permit a blow to fall, at least it was certain that Cash, throbbing in his Easter clothes, felt a pang of shame that the vigor of a man would come to such an end that he could not be struck without warning. He took down his hand and stepped back behind Livvie, like a round-eyed schoolboy on whose unsuspecting head the dunce cap has been set.

"Young ones can't wait," said Solomon.

Livvie shuddered violently, and then in a gush of tears she stooped for a glass of water and handed it to him, but he did not see her.

"So here come the young man Livvie wait for. Was no prevention. No prevention. Now I lay eyes on young man and it come to be somebody I know all the time, and been knowing since he were born in a cotton patch, and watched grow up year to year, Cash McCord, growed to size, growed up to come in my house in the end—ragged and barefoot."

Solomon gave a cough of distaste. Then he shut his eyes vigorously, and his lips began to move like a chanter's.

"When Livvie married, her husband were already somebody. He had paid great cost for his land. He spread sycamore leaves over the ground from wagon to door, day he brought her home, so her foot would not have to touch ground. He carried her through his door. Then he growed old and could not lift her, and she were still young."

Livvie's sobs followed his words like a soft melody repeating each thing as he stated it. His lips moved for a little without sound, or she cried too fervently, and unheard he might have been telling his whole life, and then he said, "God forgive Solomon for sins great and small. God forgive Solomon for carrying away too young girl for wife and keeping her away from her people and from all the young people would clamor for her back."

Then he lifted up his right hand toward Livvie where she stood by the bed and offered her his silver watch. He dangled it before her eyes, and she hushed crying; her tears stopped. For a moment the watch could be heard ticking as it always did, precisely in his proud hand. She lifted it away. Then he took hold of the quilt; then he was dead.

Livvie left Solomon dead and went out of the room. Stealthily, nearly without noise, Cash went beside her. He was like a shadow, but his shiny shoes moved over the floor in spangles, and the green downy feather shone like a light in his hat. As they reached the front room, he seized her deftly as a long black cat and dragged her hanging by the waist round and round him, while he turned in a circle, his face bent down to hers. The first moment, she kept one arm and its hand stiff and still, the one that held Solomon's watch. Then the fingers softly let go, all of her was limp, and the watch fell somewhere on the floor. It ticked away in the still room, and all at once there began outside the full song of a bird.

They moved around and around the room and into the brightness of the open door, then he stopped and shook her once. She rested in silence in his trembling arms, unprotesting as a bird on a nest. Outside the redbirds were flying and criss-crossing, the sun was in all the bottles

on the prisoned trees, and the young peach was shining in the middle of
them with the bursting light of spring.

[1943]

TOPICS FOR DISCUSSION AND WRITING

1. Of another of her stories, Eudora Welty wrote:

    > Above all I had no wish to sound mystical, but did expect to sound
    > mysterious now and then, if I could: this was a circumstantial
    > realistic story in which the reality *was* mystery.

    "Livvie," too, can be described as a "realistic story in which the real-
    ity *was* mystery." Which details do you find that make the story both
    "realistic" and mysterious? Why does the story take place shortly be-
    fore Easter? Why are Cash's clothes "luminous" and green and brown?
    What do you make out of the fact that Cash is described as "look-
    ing like a vision" (page 92)?
2. To a large extent the story is one of contrast, both explicit and im-
    plicit. What are some of the contrasting elements? In your opinion,
    how do they reflect or illuminate the story's theme? Compare and
    contrast the four characters. Are any of their names significant? How?
3. Do you think Livvie feels confined? Do you feel that Livvie is con-
    fined? Explain.
4. Though there is a basic conflict between young Livvie and old Solo-
    mon, how does Welty avoid a simple "good-bad" dichotomy?
5. What do you make out of the appearance of Miss Baby Marie? Do
    you think she is introduced merely for comic relief?
6. What do you make out of the bottle trees and Solomon's watch?

6

In Brief: Getting Ideas for Writing about Fiction

Here are some questions that may help to stimulate ideas about stories. Not every question is, of course, relevant to every story, but if after reading a story and thinking about it, you then run your eye over these pages, you will probably find some questions that will help you to think further about the story—in short, that will help you to get ideas.

It's best to do your thinking with a pen or pencil in hand. If some of the following questions seem to you to be especially relevant to the story you will be writing about, jot down—freely, without worrying about spelling—your initial responses, interrupting your writing only to glance again at the story when you feel the need to check the evidence.

PLOT

1. Does the plot grow out of the characters, or does it depend on chance or coincidence? Did something at first strike you as irrelevant that later you perceived as relevant? Do some parts continue to strike you as irrelevant?
2. Does surprise play an important role, or does foreshadowing? If surprise is very important, can the story be read a second time with any interest? If so, what gives it this further interest?
3. What conflicts does the story include? Conflicts of one character against another? Of one character against the setting, or against society? Conflicts within a single character?
4. Are certain episodes narrated out of chronological order? If so, were you puzzled? Annoyed? On reflection, does the arrangement of episodes seem effective? Why or why not? Are certain situations repeated? If so, what do you make out of the repetitions?

CHARACTER

1. Which character chiefly engages your interest? Why?
2. What purposes do minor characters serve? Do you find some who by their similarities and differences help to define each other or help to define the major character? How else is a particular character defined — by his or her words, actions (including thoughts and emotions), dress, setting, narrative point of view? Do certain characters act differently in the same, or in a similar, situation?
3. How does the author reveal character? By explicit authorial (editorial) comment, for instance, or, on the other hand, by revelation through dialogue? Through depicted action? Through the actions of other characters? How are the author's methods expecially suited to the whole of the story?
4. Is the behavior plausible — that is, are the characters well motivated?
5. If a character changes, why and how does he or she change? (You may want to jot down each event that influences a change.) Or did you change your attitude toward a character not because the character changes but because you came to know the character better?
6. Are the characters round or flat? Are they complex, or, on the other hand, highly typical (for instance, one-dimensional representatives of a social class or age)? Are you chiefly interested in a character's psychology, or does the character strike you as standing for something, such as honesty or the arrogance of power?
7. How has the author caused you to sympathize with certain characters? How does your response — your sympathy or lack of sympathy — contribute to your judgment of the conflict?

POINT OF VIEW

1. Who tells the story? How much does the narrator know? Does the narrator strike you as reliable? What effect is gained by using this narrator?
2. How does the point of view help shape the theme? After all, the basic story of "Little Red Riding Hood" — what happens — remains unchanged whether told from the wolf's point of view or the girl's, but (to simplify grossly) if we hear the story from the wolf's point of view, we may feel that the story is about terrifying yet pathetic compulsive behavior; if from the girl's point of view, about terrified innocence and male violence.
3. Does the narrator's language help you to construct a picture of the narrator's character, class, attitude, strengths, and limitations? (Jot

down some evidence, such as colloquial or—on the other hand—formal expressions, ironic comments, figures of speech.) How far can you trust the narrator? Why?

SETTING

1. Do you have a strong sense of the time and place? Is the story very much about, say, New England Puritanism, or race relations in the South in the late nineteenth century, or midwestern urban versus small-town life? If time and place are important, how and at what points in the story has the author conveyed this sense? If you do not strongly feel the setting, do you think the author should have made it more evident?

2. What is the relation of the setting to the plot and the characters? (For instance, do houses or rooms or their furnishings say something about their residents?) Would anything be lost if the descriptions of the setting were deleted from the story or the setting were changed?

SYMBOLISM

1. Do certain characters seem to you to stand for something in addition to themselves? Does the setting—whether a house, a farm, a landscape, a town, a period—have an extra dimension?)

2. If you do believe that the story has symbolic elements, do you think they are adequately integrated within the story, or do they strike you as being too obviously stuck in?

STYLE

(Style may be defined as *how* the writer says what he or she says. It is the writer's manner of expression. The writer's choice of words, of sentence structure, and of sentence length are all aspects of style. Example: "Shut the door," and "Would you mind closing the door, please," differ substantially in style. Another example: Lincoln begins the Gettysburg Address by speaking of "Four score and seven years ago," i.e., by using language that has a Biblical overtone. If he had said "Eighty-seven years ago," his style would have been different.)

1. How would you characterize the style? Simple? Understated? Figurative? Or what, and why?
2. How has the point of view shaped or determined the style?
3. Do you think that the style is consistent? If it isn't—for instance, if there are shifts from simple sentences to highly complex ones— what do you make of the shifts?

THEME

1. Is the title informative? What does it mean or suggest? Did the meaning seem to change after you read the story? Does the title help you to formulate a theme? If you had written the story, what title would you use?
2. Do certain passages—dialogue or description—seem to you to point especially toward the theme? Do you find certain repetitions of words or pairs of incidents highly suggestive and helpful in directing your thoughts toward stating a theme? Flannery O'Connor, in *Mystery and Manners,* says, "In good fiction, certain of the details will tend to accumulate meaning from the action of the story itself, and when that happens, they become symbolic in the way they work." Does this story work that way?
3. Is the meaning of the story embodied in the whole story, or does it seem stuck in, for example in certain passages of editorializing?
4. Suppose someone asked you to state the point—the theme—of the story. Could you? And if you could, would you say that the theme of a particular story reinforces values you hold, or does it to some degree challenge them? (It is sometimes said that the best writers are subversive, forcing readers to see something that they do not want to see.)

7

A Fiction Writer in Depth: Flannery O'Connor

We read stories by authors we are unfamiliar with, just as we try new foods or play new games or listen to the music of new groups, because we want to extend our experience. But we also sometimes stay with the familiar, for pretty much the same reason, oddly. We want, so to speak, to taste more fully, to experience not something utterly unfamiliar but a variation on a favorite theme. Having read, say, one story by Poe or by Alice Walker, we want to read another, and another, because we like the sort of thing that this author does, and we find that with each succeeding story we get deeper into an interesting mind talking about experiences that interest us.

This chapter includes three stories by Flannery O'Connor, along with some of her comments on her own work. You'll find, we think, that each of O'Connor's stories takes on a richer significance when thought of together with the others and with her comments.

Flannery O'Connor: Three Stories and Observations on Literature

Flannery O'Connor (1925–64)—her first name was Mary but she did not use it—was born in Savannah, Georgia, but spent most of her life in Milledgeville, Georgia, where her family moved when she was twelve. She was educated in parochial schools and at the local college and then went to the School for Writers at the University of Iowa where she earned an M.F.A. in 1946. For a few months she lived at a writers' colony in Saratoga Springs, New York, and then for a few weeks she lived in New York City, but most of her life was spent back in Milledgeville, where she tended her peacocks and wrote

2

~~Of course she~~ *the grandmother* was the first one ready to load up the next morning at six
o'clock. She had Baby Brother's bucking bronco ~~that~~ and ~~hxxxxxxxx~~ what she
called her "g*et*" and Pitty Sing, the cat, ~~all three~~ packed in the car before
Boatwrite had a chance to ~~get anything xxxxxxx~~ ~~come out of the door with the~~ *get the*
rest of the luggage out of the ha~~ll~~. They got off at seven-thirty, Boatwrite
and ~~Emby~~ the children's mother in the front and Granny, John Wesley, Baby Brother,
Little Sister Mary Ann, Pitty Sing, and the bucking bronco in the back.

"Why the hell did you bring that goddam rocking horse?" Boatwrite asked
because as soon as ~~the car began to move,~~ *they were out of the city + on the smooth highway* Baby Brother began to squall to get
on the bucking bronco. "He can't get on that thing in this car and that's final,"
his father who was a stern man said.

"Can we open the lunch now?" Little Sister ~~Maxxxxx~~ asked. "It'll shut
Baby Brother up. Mamma, can we open up the lunch?"

"No," their grandmother said. *It's only eight-thirty*

Their mother was ~~xxxxx~~ reading SCREEN MOTHERS AND THEIR CHILDREN. "Yeah,
sure," she said without looking up. She was all dressed up today. She had on
a purple silk dress and a hat and ~~xxxxxxxxxx~~ a choker of pink beads and a new
pocket book, and high heel *her red* pumps.

"Let's go through Georgia quick so we won't have to look at it much," John
Wesley said. ~~"I seen enough of it already."~~

"You should see Tennessee," his grandmother said. "Now there is a *beautiful* state."

"Like hell," John Wesley said. "That's just a hillbilly dumping ground."

"Ha*w*," his mother said, and nudged Boatwrite. "Didjer hear that?" ~~She was~~
from Arkansas.
They ate their lunch and got along fine ~~after that~~ for a while until Pitty
Sing who had been asleep jumped into the front of the car and caused Boatwrite
to swerve to the right into a ditch. Pitty Sing was a large grey-striped cat
with a yellow hind leg and a ~~x large~~ *big* soiled white face. Granny thought that she
was the only person in the world that he really loved but he had never ~~really~~ *the truth was*
looked ~~xxxxxxxxxxxxx~~ *much* farther than her middle and he didn't even
like other cats. He jumped snarling into the front seat and Boatwrite's shoulders

Manuscript page from Flannery O'Connor's "A Good Man Is Hard to Find."

stories, novels, essays (posthumously published as Mystery and Manners *[1970]), and letters (posthumously published under the title of* The Habit of Being *[1979]).*

In 1951, when she was twenty-five, Flannery O'Connor discovered that she was a victim of lupus erythematosus, an incurable degenerative blood disease that had crippled and then killed her father ten years before. She died at the age of thirty-nine. O'Connor faced her illness with stoic courage, Christian fortitude—and tough humor. Here is a glimpse, from one of her letters, of how she dealt with those who pitied her:

> An old lady got on the elevator behind me and as soon as I turned around she fixed me with a moist gleaming eye and said in a loud voice, "Bless you, darling!" I felt exactly like the Misfit [in "A Good Man Is Hard To Find"] and I gave her a weakly lethal look, whereupon greatly encouraged she grabbed my arm and whispered (very loud) in my ear, "Remember what they said to John at the gate, darling!" It was not my floor but I got off and I suppose the old lady was astounded at how quick I could get away on crutches. I have a one-legged friend and I asked her what they said to John at the gate. She said she reckoned they said, "The lame shall enter first." This may be because the lame will be able to knock everybody else aside with their crutches.

A devout Catholic, O'Connor forthrightly summarized the relation between her belief and her writing:

> I see from the standpoint of Christian orthodoxy. This means that for me the meaning of life is centered in our Redemption by Christ and what I see in the world I see in its relation to that.

A Good Man Is Hard to Find

The grandmother didn't want to go to Florida. She wanted to visit some of her connections in east Tennessee and she was seizing at every chance to change Bailey's mind. Bailey was the son she lived with, her only boy. He was sitting on the edge of his chair at the table, bent over the orange sports section of the *Journal.* "Now look here, Bailey," she said, "see here, read this," and she stood with one hand on her thin hip and the other rattling the newspaper at his bald head. "Here this fellow that calls himself The Misfit is aloose from the Federal Pen and headed toward Florida and you read here what it says he did to these people. Just you read it. I wouldn't take my children in any direction with a criminal like that aloose in it. I couldn't answer to my conscience if I did."

Bailey didn't look up from his reading so she wheeled around then and faced the children's mother, a young woman in slacks, whose face was as broad and innocent as a cabbage and was tied round with a green head-kerchief that had two points on the top like rabbit's ears. She was sitting on the sofa, feeding the baby his apricots out of a jar. "The children have been to Florida before," the old lady said. "You all ought to take them somewhere else for a change so they would see different parts of the world and be broad. They never have been to east Tennessee."

The children's mother didn't seem to hear her but the eight-year-old boy, John Wesley, a stocky child with glasses, said, "If you don't want to go to Florida, why dontcha stay at home?" He and the little girl, June Star, were reading the funny papers on the floor.

"She wouldn't stay at home to be queen for a day," June Star said without raising her yellow head.

"Yes and what would you do if this fellow, The Misfit, caught you?" the grandmother said.

"I'd smack his face," John Wesley said.

"She wouldn't stay at home for a million bucks," June Star said. "Afraid she'd miss something. She has to go everywhere we go."

"All right, Miss," the grandmother said. "Just remember that the next time you want me to curl your hair."

June Star said her hair was naturally curly.

The next morning the grandmother was the first one in the car, ready to go. She had her big black valise that looked like the head of a hippopotamus in one corner, and underneath it she was hiding a basket with Pitty Sing, the cat, in it. She didn't intend for the cat to be left alone in the house for three days because he would miss her too much and she was afraid he might brush against one of the gas burners and accidentally asphyxiate himself. Her son, Bailey, didn't like to arrive at a motel with a cat.

She sat in the middle of the back seat with John Wesley and June Star on either side of her. Bailey and the children's mother and the baby sat in front and they left Atlanta at eight forty-five with the mileage on the car at 55890. The grandmother wrote this down because she thought it would be interesting to say how many miles they had been when they got back. It took them twenty minutes to reach the outskirts of the city.

The old lady settled herself comfortably, removing her white cotton gloves and putting them up with her purse on the shelf in front of the back window. The children's mother still had on slacks and still had her hair tied up in a green kerchief, but the grandmother had on a navy blue straw sailor hat with a bunch of white violets on the brim and a navy blue dress with a small white dot in the print. Her collars and cuffs were white organdy trimmed with lace and at her neckline she had pinned a purple spray of cloth violets containing a sachet. In case of an accident, anyone seeing her dead on the highway would know at once that she was a lady.

She said she thought it was going to be a good day for driving, neither too hot nor too cold, and she cautioned Bailey that the speed limit was fifty-five miles an hour and that the patrolmen hid themselves behind billboards and small clumps of trees and sped out after you before you had a chance to slow down. She pointed out interesting details of the scenery: Stone Mountain; the blue granite that in some places came up to both sides of the highway; the brilliant red clay banks slightly streaked with purple; and the various crops that made rows of green lace-work on the ground. The trees were full of silver-white sunlight and the meanest of them sparkled. The children were reading comic magazines and their mother had gone back to sleep.

"Let's go through Georgia fast so we won't have to look at it much," John Wesley said.

"If I were a little boy," said the grandmother, "I wouldn't talk about my native state that way. Tennessee has the mountains and Georgia has the hills."

"Tennessee is just a hillbilly dumping ground," John Wesley said, "and Georgia is a lousy state too."

"You said it," June Star said.

"In my time," said the grandmother, folding her thin veined fingers, "children were more respectful of their native states and their parents and everything else. People did right then. Oh look at the cute little pickaninny!" she said and pointed to a Negro child standing in the door of a shack. "Wouldn't that make a picture, now?" she asked and they all turned and looked at the little Negro out of the back window. He waved.

"He didn't have any britches on," June Star said.

"He probably didn't have any," the grandmother explained. "Little niggers in the country don't have things like we do. If I could paint, I'd paint that picture," she said.

The children exchanged comic books.

The grandmother offered to hold the baby and the children's mother passed him over the front seat to her. She set him on her knee and bounced him and told him about the things they were passing. She rolled her eyes and screwed up her mouth and stuck her leathery thin face into his smooth bland one. Occasionally he gave her a faraway smile. They passed a large cotton field with five or six graves fenced in the middle of it, like a small island. "Look at the graveyard!" the grandmother said, pointing it out. "That was the old family burying ground. That belonged to the plantation."

"Where's the plantation?" John Wesley asked.

"Gone With the Wind," said the grandmother. "Ha. Ha."

When the children finished all the comic books they had brought, they opened the lunch and ate it. The grandmother ate a peanut butter sandwich and an olive and would not let the children throw the box and the paper napkins out the window. When there was nothing else to do they played a game by choosing a cloud and making the other two guess what shape it suggested. John Wesley took one the shape of a cow and June Star guessed a cow and John Wesley said, no, an automobile, and June Star said he didn't play fair, and they began to slap each other over the grandmother.

The grandmother said she would tell them a story if they would keep quiet. When she told a story, she rolled her eyes and waved her head and was very dramatic. She said once when she was a maiden lady she had been courted by a Mr. Edgar Atkins Teagarden from Jasper, Georgia. She said he was a very good-looking man and a gentleman and that he brought her a watermelon every Saturday afternoon with his initials cut in it, E. A. T. Well, one Saturday, she said, Mr. Teagarden brought the watermelon and there was nobody at home and he left it on the front porch and returned in his buggy to Jasper, but she never got the water-melon, she said, because a nigger boy ate it when he saw the initials, E. A. T.! This story tickled John Wesley's funny bone and he giggled and giggled but June Star didn't think it was any good. She said she wouldn't marry a man that just brought her a watermelon on Saturday. The grand-mother said she would have done well to marry Mr. Teagarden because he was a gentleman and had bought Coca-Cola stock when it first came out and that he had died only a few years ago, a very wealthy man.

They stopped at The Tower for barbecued sandwiches. The Tower was a part stucco and part wood filling station and dance hall set in a clear-ing outside of Timothy. A fat man named Red Sammy Butts ran it and there were signs stuck here and there on the building and for miles up and down the highway saying, TRY RED SAMMY'S FAMOUS BARBECUE. NONE LIKE FAMOUS RED SAMMY'S! RED SAM! THE FAT BOY WITH THE HAPPY LAUGH. A VETERAN! RED SAMMY'S YOUR MAN!

Red Sammy was lying on the bare ground outside The Tower with his head under a truck while a gray monkey about a foot high, chained to a small chinaberry tree, chattered nearby. The monkey sprang back into the tree and got on the highest limb as soon as he saw the children jump out of the car and run toward him.

Inside, The Tower was a long dark room with a counter at one end and tables at the other and dancing space in the middle. They all sat down at a broad table next to the nickelodeon and Red Sam's wife, a tall burnt-brown woman with hair and eyes lighter than her skin, came and took their order. The children's mother put a dime in the machine and played "The Tennessee Waltz," and the grandmother said that tune always made her want to dance. She asked Bailey if he would like to dance but he only glared at her. He didn't have a naturally sunny disposition like she did and trips made him nervous. The grandmother's brown eyes were very bright. She swayed her head from side to side and pretended she was danc-ing in her chair. June Star said play something she could tap to so the children's mother put in another dime and played a fast number and June Star stepped out onto the dance floor and did her tap routine.

"Ain't she cute?" Red Sam's wife said, leaning over the counter. "Would you like to come be my little girl?"

"No I certainly wouldn't," June Star said. "I wouldn't live in a broken-down place like this for a million bucks!" and she ran back to the table.

"Ain't she cute?" the woman repeated, stretching her mouth politely.

"Aren't you ashamed?" hissed the grandmother.

Red Sam came in and told his wife to quit lounging on the counter and hurry with these people's order. His khaki trousers reached just to his hip bones and his stomach hung over them like a sack of meal swaying under his shirt. He came over and sat down at a table nearby and let out a combination sigh and yodel. "You can't win," he said. "You can't win," and he wiped his sweating red face off with a gray handkerchief. "These days you don't know who to trust," he said. "Ain't that the truth?"

"People are certainly not nice like they used to be," said the grandmother.

"Two fellers come in here last week," Red Sammy said, "driving a Chrysler. It was a old beat-up car but it was a good one and these boys looked all right to me. Said they worked at the mill and you know I let them fellers charge the gas they bought? Now why did I do that?"

"Because you're a good man!" the grandmother said at once.

"Yes'm, I suppose so," Red Sam said as if he were struck with this answer.

His wife brought the orders, carrying the five plates all at once without a tray, two in each hand and one balanced on her arm. "It isn't a soul in this green world of God's that you can trust," she said. "And I don't count nobody out of that, not nobody," she repeated, looking at Red Sammy.

"Did you read about that criminal, The Misfit, that's escaped?" asked the grandmother.

"I wouldn't be a bit surprised if he didn't attack this place right here," said the woman. "If he hears about it being here, I wouldn't be none surprised to see him. If he hears it's two cent in the cash register, I wouldn't be a tall surprised if he . . ."

"That'll do," Red Sam said. "Go bring these people their Co'Colas," and the woman went off to get the rest of the order.

"A good man is hard to find," Red Sammy said. "Everything is getting terrible. I remember the day you could go off and leave your screen door unlatched. Not no more."

He and the grandmother discussed better times. The old lady said that in her opinion Europe was entirely to blame for the way things were now. She said the way Europe acted you would think we were made of money and Red Sam said it was no use talking about it, she was exactly right. The children ran outside into the white sunlight and looked at the monkey in the lacy chinaberry tree. He was busy catching fleas on himself and biting each one carefully between his teeth as if it were a delicacy.

They drove off again into the hot afternoon. The grandmother took cat naps and woke up every five minutes with her own snoring. Outside of Toombsboro she woke up and recalled an old plantation that she had visited in this neighborhood once when she was a young lady. She said the house had six white columns across the front and that there was an avenue of oaks leading up to it and two little wooden trellis arbors on either side in front where you sat down with your suitor after a stroll in the garden. She recalled exactly which road to turn off to get to it. She knew that Bailey would not be willing to lose any time looking at an old house, but the more she talked about it, the more she wanted to see it once again and find out if the little twin arbors were still standing. "There was a secret panel in this house," she said craftily, not telling the truth but wishing that she were, "and the story went that all the family silver was hidden in it when Sherman came through but it was never found . . ."

"Hey!" John Wesley said. "Let's go see it! We'll find it! We'll poke all the woodwork and find it! Who lives there? Where do you turn off at? Hey, Pop, can't we turn off there?"

"We never have seen a house with a secret panel!" June Star shrieked. "Let's go to the house with the secret panel! Hey Pop, can't we go see the house with the secret panel!"

"It's not far from here, I know," the grandmother said. "It wouldn't take over twenty minutes."

Bailey was looking straight ahead. His jaw was as rigid as a horseshoe. "No," he said.

The children began to yell and scream that they wanted to see the house with the secret panel. John Wesley kicked the back of the front seat and June Star hung over her mother's shoulder and whined desperately into her ear that they never had any fun even on their vacation, that they could never do what THEY wanted to do. The baby began to scream and John Wesley kicked the back of the seat so hard that his father could feel the blows in his kidney.

"All right!" he shouted and drew the car to a stop at the side of the road. "Will you all shut up? Will you all just shut up for one second? If you don't shut up, we won't go anywhere."

"It would be very educational for them," the grandmother murmured.

"All right," Bailey said, "but get this: this is the only time we're going to stop for anything like this. This is the one and only time."

"The dirt road that you have to turn down is about a mile back," the grandmother directed. "I marked it when we passed."

"A dirt road," Bailey groaned.

After they had turned around and were headed toward the dirt road, the grandmother recalled other points about the house, the beautiful glass over the front doorway and the candle-lamp in the hall. John Wesley said that the secret panel was probably in the fireplace.

"You can't go inside this house," Bailey said. "You don't know who lives there."

"While you all talk to the people in front, I'll run around behind and get in a window," John Wesley suggested.

"We'll all stay in the car," his mother said.

They turned onto the dirt road and the car raced roughly along in a swirl of pink dust. The grandmother recalled the times when there were no paved roads and thirty miles was a day's journey. The dirt road was hilly and there were sudden washes in it and sharp curves on dangerous embankments. All at once they would be on a hill, looking down over the blue tops of trees for miles around, then the next minute, they would be in a red depression with the dust-coated trees looking down on them.

"This place had better turn up in a minute," Bailey said, "or I'm going to turn around."

The road looked as if no one had traveled on it in months.

"It's not much farther," the grandmother said and just as she said it, a horrible thought came to her. The thought was so embarrassing that she turned red in the face and her eyes dilated and her feet jumped up, upsetting her valise in the corner. The instant the valise moved, the newspaper top she had over the basket under it rose with a snarl and Pitty Sing, the cat, sprang onto Bailey's shoulder.

The children were thrown to the floor and their mother, clutching the baby, was thrown out the door onto the ground, the old lady was thrown into the front seat. The car turned over once and landed right-sideup in a gulch on the side of the road. Bailey remained in the driver's seat with the cat—gray-striped with a broad white face and an orange nose—clinging to his neck like a caterpillar.

As soon as the children saw they could move their arms and legs, they scrambled out of the car, shouting, "We've had an ACCIDENT!" The grandmother was curled up under the dashboard, hoping she was injured so that Bailey's wrath would not come down on her all at once. The horrible thought she had had before the accident was that the house she had remembered so vividly was not in Georgia but in Tennessee.

Bailey removed the cat from his neck with both hands and flung it out the window against the side of a pine tree. Then he got out of the car and started looking for the children's mother. She was sitting against the side of the red gutted ditch, holding the screaming baby, but she only had a cut down her face and a broken shoulder. "We've had an ACCIDENT!" the children screamed in a frenzy of delight.

"But nobody's killed," June Star said with disappointment as the grandmother limped out of the car, her hat still pinned to her head but the broken front brim standing up at a jaunty angle and the violet spray hanging off the side. They all sat down in the ditch, except the children, to recover from the shock. They were all shaking.

"Maybe a car will come along," said the children's mother hoarsely.

"I believe I have injured an organ," said the grandmother, pressing her side, but no one answered her. Bailey's teeth were clattering. He had on a yellow sport shirt with bright blue parrots designed in it and his face was as yellow as the shirt. The grandmother decided that she would not mention that the house was in Tennessee.

The road was about ten feet above and they could see only the tops of the trees on the other side of it. Behind the ditch they were sitting in there were more woods, tall and dark and deep. In a few minutes they saw a car some distance away on top of a hill, coming slowly as if the occupants were watching them. The grandmother stood up and waved both her arms dramatically to attract their attention. The car continued to come on slowly, disappeared around a bend and appeared again, moving even slower, on top of the hill they had gone over. It was a big black battered hearse-like automobile. There were three men in it.

It came to a stop just over them and for some minutes, the driver looked down with a steady expressionless gaze to where they were sitting, and didn't speak. Then he turned his head and muttered something to the other two and they got out. One was a fat boy in black trousers and a red sweat shirt with a silver stallion embossed on the front of it. He moved around on the right side of them and stood staring, his mouth partly open in a kind of loose grin. The other had on khaki pants and a blue striped coat and a gray hat pulled down very low, hiding most of his face. He came around slowly on the left side. Neither spoke.

The driver got out of the car and stood by the side of it, looking down at them. He was an older man than the other two. His hair was just beginning to gray and he wore silver-rimmed spectacles that gave him a scholarly look. He had a long creased face and didn't have on any shirt or undershirt. He had on blue jeans that were too tight for him and was holding a black hat and a gun. The two boys also had guns.

"We've had an ACCIDENT!" the children screamed.

The grandmother had the peculiar feeling that the bespectacled man was some one she knew. His face was as familiar to her as if she had known him all her life but she could not recall who he was. He moved away from the car and began to come down the embankment, placing his feet carefully so that he wouldn't slip. He had on tan and white shoes and no socks, and his ankles were red and thin. "Good afternoon," he said. "I see you all had you a little spill."

"We turned over twice!" said the grandmother.

"Oncet," he corrected. "We seen it happen. Try their car and see will it run, Hiram," he said quietly to the boy with the gray hat.

"What you got that gun for?" John Wesley asked. "Whatcha gonna do with that gun?"

"Lady," the man said to the children's mother, "would you mind calling them children to sit down by you? Children make me nervous. I want all you all to sit down right together there where you're at."

"What are you telling us what to do for?" June Star asked.

Behind them the line of woods gaped like a dark open mouth. "Come here," said their mother.

"Look here now," Bailey began suddenly, "we're in a predicament! We're in . . ."

The grandmother shrieked. She scrambled to her feet and stood staring. "You're The Misfit!" she said. "I recognized you at once!"

"Yes'm," the man said, smiling slightly as if he were pleased in spite of himself to be known, "but it would have been better for all of you, lady, if you hadn't of recognized me."

Bailey turned his head sharply and said something to his mother that shocked even the children. The old lady began to cry and The Misfit reddened.

"Lady," he said, "don't you get upset. Sometimes a man says things he don't mean. I don't reckon he meant to talk to you thataway."

"You wouldn't shoot a lady, would you?" the grandmother said and removed a clean handkerchief from her cuff and began to slap at her eyes with it.

The Misfit pointed the toe of his shoe into the ground and made a little hole and then covered it up again. "I would hate to have to," he said.

"Listen," the grandmother almost screamed, "I know you're a good man. You don't look a bit like you have common blood. I know you must come from nice people!"

"Yes ma'm," he said, "finest people in the world." When he smiled he showed a row of strong white teeth. "God never made a finer woman than my mother and my daddy's heart was pure gold," he said. The boy with the red sweat shirt had come around behind them and was standing with his gun at his hip. The Misfit squatted down on the ground. "Watch them children, Bobby Lee," he said. "You know they make me nervous." He looked at the six of them huddled together in front of him and he seemed to be embarrassed as if he couldn't think of anything to say. "Ain't a cloud in the sky," he remarked, looking up at it. "Don't see no sun but don't see no cloud neither."

"Yes, it's a beautiful day," said the grandmother. "Listen," she said, "you shouldn't call yourself The Misfit because I know you're a good man at heart. I can just look at you and tell."

"Hush!" Bailey yelled. "Hush! Everybody shut up and let me handle this!" He was squatting in the position of a runner about to sprint forward but he didn't move.

"I pre-chate that, lady," The Misfit said and drew a little circle in the ground with the butt of his gun.

"It'll take a half a hour to fix this here car," Hiram called, looking over the raised hood of it.

"Well, first you and Bobby Lee get him and that little boy to step over yonder with you," The Misfit said, pointing to Bailey and John Wesley.

"The boys want to ask you something," he said to Bailey. "Would you mind stepping back in them woods there with them?"

"Listen," Bailey began, "we're in a terrible predicament. Nobody realizes what this is," and his voice cracked. His eyes were as blue and intense as the parrots in his shirt and he remained perfectly still.

The grandmother reached up to adjust her hat brim as if she were going to the woods with him but it came off in her hand. She stood staring at it and after a second she let it fall on the ground. Hiram pulled Bailey up by the arm as if he were assisting an old man. John Wesley caught hold of his father's hand and Bobby Lee followed. They went off toward the woods and just as they reached the dark edge, Bailey turned and supporting himself against a gray naked pine trunk, he shouted, "I'll be back in a minute, Mamma, wait on me!"

"Come back this instant!" his mother shrilled but they all disappeared into the woods.

"Bailey Boy!" the grandmother called in a tragic voice but she found she was looking at The Misfit squatting on the ground in front of her. "I just know you're a good man," she said desperately. "You're not a bit common!"

"Nome, I ain't a good man," The Misfit said after a second as if he had considered her statement carefully, "but I ain't the worst in the world neither. My daddy said I was a different breed of dog from my brothers and sisters. 'You know,' Daddy said, 'it's some that can live their whole life out without asking about it and it's others has to know why it is, and this boy is one of the latters. He's going to be into everything!'" He put on his black hat and looked up suddenly and then away deep into the woods as if he were embarrassed again. "I'm sorry I don't have on a shirt before you ladies," he said, hunching his shoulders slightly. "We buried our clothes that we had on when we escaped and we're just making do until we can get better. We borrowed these from some folks we met," he explained.

"That's perfectly all right," the grandmother said. "Maybe Bailey has an extra shirt in his suitcase."

"I'll look and see terrectly," The Misfit said.

"Where are they taking him?" the children's mother screamed.

"Daddy was a card himself," The Misfit said. "You couldn't put anything over on him. He never got in trouble with the Authorities though. Just had the knack of handling them."

"You could be honest too if you'd only try," said the grandmother. "Think how wonderful it would be to settle down and live a comfortable life and not have to think about somebody chasing you all the time."

The Misfit kept scratching in the ground with the butt of his gun as if he were thinking about it. "Yes'm, somebody is always after you," he murmured.

The grandmother noticed how thin his shoulder blades were just behind his hat because she was standing up looking down on him. "Do you ever pray?" she asked.

He shook his head. All she saw was the black hat wiggle between shoulder blades. "Nome," he said.

There was a pistol shot from the woods, followed closely by another. Then silence. The old lady's head jerked around. She could hear the wind move through the tree tops like a long satisfied insuck of breath. "Bailey Boy!" she called.

"I was a gospel singer for a while," The Misfit said. "I been most everything. Been in the arm service, both land and sea, at home and abroad, been twict married, been an undertaker, been with the railroads, plowed Mother Earth, been in a tornado, seen a man burnt alive oncet," and he looked up at the children's mother and the little girl who were sitting close together, their faces white and their eyes glassy; "I even seen a woman flogged," he said.

"Pray, pray," the grandmother began, "pray, pray. . . ."

"I never was a bad boy that I remember of," The Misfit said in an almost dreamy voice, "but somewheres along the line I done something wrong and got sent to the penitentiary. I was buried alive," and he looked up and held her attention to him by a steady stare.

"That's when you should have started to pray," she said. "What did you do to get sent up to the penitentiary that first time?"

"Turn to the right, it was a wall," The Misfit said, looking up again at the cloudless sky. "Turn to the left, it was a wall. Look up it was a ceiling, look down it was a floor. I forget what I done, lady. I set there and set there, trying to remember what it was I done and I ain't recalled it to this day. Oncet in a while, I would think it was coming to me, but it never come."

"Maybe they put you in by mistake," the old lady said vaguely.

"Nome," he said. "It wasn't no mistake. They had the papers on me."

"You must have stolen something," she said.

The Misfit sneered slightly. "Nobody had nothing I wanted," he said. "It was a head–doctor at the penitentiary said what I had done was kill my daddy but I know that for a lie. My daddy died in nineteen ought nineteen of the epidemic flu and I never had a thing to do with it. He was buried in the Mount Hopewell Baptist churchyard and you can go there and see for yourself."

"If you would pray," the old lady said, "Jesus would help you."

"That's right," The Misfit said.

"Well then, why don't you pray?" she asked trembling with delight suddenly.

"I don't want no hep," he said. "I'm doing all right by myself."

Bobby Lee and Hiram came ambling back from the woods. Bobby Lee was dragging a yellow shirt with bright blue parrots in it.

"Throw me that shirt, Bobby Lee," The Misfit said. The shirt came flying at him and landed on his shoulder and he put it on. The grandmother couldn't name what the shirt reminded her of. "No, lady," The Misfit said while he was buttoning it up, "I found out the crime don't matter. You can do one thing or you can do another, kill a man or take a tire off his car, because sooner or later you're going to forget what it was you done and just be punished for it."

The children's mother had begun to make heaving noises as if she couldn't get her breath. "Lady," he asked, "would you and that little girl like to step off yonder with Bobby Lee and Hiram and join your husband?"

"Yes, thank you," the mother said faintly. Her left arm dangled helplessly and she was holding the baby, who had gone to sleep, in the other. "Hep that lady up, Hiram," The Misfit said as she struggled to climb out of the ditch, "and Bobby Lee, you hold onto that little girl's hand."

"I don't want to hold hands with him," June Star said. "He reminds me of a pig."

The fat boy blushed and laughed and caught her by the arm and pulled her off into the woods after Hiram and her mother.

Alone with The Misfit, the grandmother found that she had lost her voice. There was not a cloud in the sky nor any sun. There was nothing around her but woods. She wanted to tell him that he must pray. She opened and closed her mouth several times before anything came out. Finally she found herself saying, "Jesus, Jesus," meaning, Jesus will help you, but the way she was saying it, it sounded as if she might be cursing.

"Yes'm," The Misfit said as if he agreed. "Jesus thown everything off balance. It was the same case with Him as with me except He hadn't committed any crime and they could prove I had committed one because they had the papers on me. Of course," he said, "they never shown me my papers. That's why I sign myself now. I said long ago, you get you a signature and sign everything you do and keep a copy of it. Then you'll know what you done and you can hold up the crime to the punishment and see do they match and in the end you'll have something to prove you ain't been treated right. I call myself The Misfit," he said, "because I can't make what all I done wrong fit what all I gone through in punishment."

There was a piercing scream from the woods, followed closely by a pistol report. "Does it seem right to you, lady, that one is punished a heap and another ain't punished at all?"

"Jesus!" the old lady cried. "You've got good blood! I know you wouldn't shoot a lady! I know you come from nice people! Pray! Jesus, you ought not to shoot a lady. I'll give you all the money I've got!"

"Lady," The Misfit said, looking beyond her far into the woods, "there never was a body that give the undertaker a tip."

There were two more pistol reports and the grandmother raised her head like a parched old turkey hen crying for water and called, "Bailey Boy, Bailey Boy!" as if her heart would break.

"Jesus was the only One that ever raised the dead," The Misfit continued, "and He shouldn't have done it. He thown everything off balance. If He did what He said, then it's nothing for you to do but thow away everything and follow Him, and if He didn't, then it's nothing for you to do but enjoy the few minutes you got left the best way you can—by killing somebody or burning down his house or doing some other meanness to him. No pleasure but meanness," he said and his voice had become almost a snarl.

"Maybe He didn't raise the dead," the old lady mumbled, not knowing what she was saying and feeling so dizzy that she sank down in the ditch with her legs twisted under her.

"I wasn't there so I can't say He didn't," The Misfit said. "I wisht I had of been there," he said, hitting the ground with his fist. "It ain't right I wasn't there because if I had of been there I would of known. Listen lady," he said in a high voice, "if I had of been there I would of known and I wouldn't be like I am now." His voice seemed about to crack and the grandmother's head cleared for an instant. She saw the man's face twisted close to her own as if he were going to cry and she murmured, "Why you're one of my babies. You're one of my own children!" She reached out and touched him on the shoulder. The Misfit sprang back as if a snake had bitten him and shot her three times through the chest. Then he put his gun down on the ground and took off his glasses and began to clean them.

Hiram and Bobby Lee returned from the woods and stood over the ditch, looking down at the grandmother who half sat and half lay in a puddle of blood with her legs crossed under her like a child's and her face smiling up at the cloudless sky.

Without his glasses, The Misfit's eyes were red-rimmed and pale and defenseless-looking. "Take her off and thow her where you thown the others," he said, picking up the cat that was rubbing itself against his leg.

"She was a talker, wasn't she?" Bobby Lee said, sliding down the ditch with a yodel.

"She would of been a good woman," The Misfit said, "if it had been somebody there to shoot her every minute of her life."

"Some fun!" Bobby Lee said.

"Shut up, Bobby Lee," The Misfit said. "It's no real pleasure in life."

[1953]

Revelation

The doctor's waiting room, which was very small, was almost full when the Turpins entered and Mrs. Turpin, who was very large, made it look even smaller by her presence. She stood looming at the head of the magazine table set in the center of it, a living demonstration that the room was inadequate and ridiculous. Her little bright black eyes took in all the patients as she sized up the seating situation. There was one vacant chair and a place on a sofa occupied by a blond child in a dirty blue romper who should have been told to move over and make room for the lady. He was five or six, but Mrs. Turpin saw at once that no one was going to tell him to move over. He was slumped down in the seat, his arms idle at his sides and his eyes idle in his head; his nose ran unchecked.

Mrs. Turpin put a firm hand on Claud's shoulder and said in a voice that included anyone who wanted to listen, "Claud, you sit in that chair there," and gave him a push down into the vacant one. Claud was florid and bald and sturdy, somewhat shorter than Mrs. Turpin, but he sat down as if he were accustomed to doing what she told him to.

Mrs. Turpin remained standing. The only man in the room besides Claud was a lean stringy old fellow with a rusty hand spread out on each knee, whose eyes were closed as if he were asleep or dead or pretending to be so as not to get up and offer her his seat. Her gaze settled agreeably on a well-dressed grey-haired lady whose eyes met hers and whose expression said: If that child belonged to me, he would have some manners and move over—there's plenty of room there for you and him too.

Claud looked up with a sigh and made as if to rise.

"Sit down," Mrs. Turpin said. "You know you're not supposed to stand on that leg. He has an ulcer on his leg," she explained.

Claud lifted his foot onto the magazine table and rolled his trouser leg up to reveal a purple swelling on a plump marble-white calf.

"My!" the pleasant lady said. "How did you do that?"

"A cow kicked him," Mrs. Turpin said.

"Goodness!" said the lady.

Claud rolled his trouser leg down.

"Maybe the little boy would move over," the lady suggested, but the child did not stir.

"Somebody will be leaving in a minute," Mrs. Turpin said. She could not understand why a doctor—with as much money as they made charging five dollars a day to just stick their head in the hospital door and look at you—couldn't afford a decent-sized waiting room. This one was hardly bigger than a garage. The table was cluttered with limp-looking magazines and at one end of it there was a big green glass ash tray full of cigaret butts and cotton wads with little blood spots on them. If she had had anything to do with the running of the place, that would have been emptied every so often. There were no chairs against the wall at the head of the room. It had a rectangular-shaped panel in it that permitted a view of the office where the nurse came and went and the secretary listened to the radio. A plastic fern in a gold pot sat in the opening and trailed its fronds down almost to the floor. The radio was softly playing gospel music.

Just then the inner door opened and a nurse with the highest stack of yellow hair Mrs. Turpin had ever seen put her face in the crack and called for the next patient. The woman sitting beside Claud grasped the two arms of her chair and hoisted herself up; she pulled her dress free from her legs and lumbered through the door where the nurse had disappeared.

Mrs. Turpin eased into the vacant chair, which held her tight as a corset. "I wish I could reduce," she said, and rolled her eyes and gave a comic sigh.

"Oh, *you* aren't fat," the stylish lady said.

"Ooooo I am too," Mrs. Turpin said. "Claud he eats all he wants to and never weighs over one hundred and seventy-five pounds, but me I just look at something good to eat and I gain some weight," and her stomach and shoulders shook with laughter. "You can eat all you want to, can't you, Claud?" she asked, turning to him.

Claud only grinned.

"Well, as long as you have such a good disposition," the stylish lady said, "I don't think it makes a bit of difference what size you are. You just can't beat a good disposition."

Next to her was a fat girl of eighteen or nineteen, scowling into a thick blue book which Mrs. Turpin saw was entitled *Human Development.* The girl raised her head and directed her scowl at Mrs. Turpin as if she did not like her looks. She appeared annoyed that anyone should speak while she tried to read. The poor girl's face was blue with acne and Mrs. Turpin thought how pitiful it was to have a face like that at that age. She gave the girl a friendly smile but the girl only scowled the harder. Mrs. Turpin herself was fat but she had always had good skin, and, though she was forty-seven years old, there was not a wrinkle in her face except around her eyes from laughing too much.

Next to the ugly girl was the child, still in exactly the same position, and next to him was a thin leathery old woman in a cotton print dress. She and Claud had three sacks of chicken feed in their pump house that was in the same print. She had seen from the first that the child belonged with the old woman. She could tell by the way they sat — kind of vacant and white-trashy, as if they would sit there until Doomsday if nobody called and told them to get up. And at right angles but next to the well-dressed pleasant lady was a lank-faced woman who was certainly the child's mother. She had on a yellow sweat shirt and wine-colored slacks, both gritty-looking, and the rims of her lips were stained with snuff. Her dirty yellow hair was tied behind with a little piece of red paper ribbon. Worse than niggers any day, Mrs. Turpin thought.

The gospel hymn playing was, "When I looked up and He looked down," and Mrs. Turpin, who knew it, supplied the last line mentally, "And wona these days I know I'll we-eara crown."

Without appearing to, Mrs. Turpin always noticed people's feet. The well-dressed lady had on red and grey suede shoes to match her dress.

Mrs. Turpin had on her good black patent leather pumps. The ugly girl had on Girl Scout shoes and heavy socks. The old woman had on tennis shoes and the white-trashy mother had on what appeared to be bedroom slippers, black straw with gold braid threaded through them—exactly what you would have expected her to have on.

Sometimes at night when she couldn't go to sleep, Mrs. Turpin would occupy herself with the question of who she would have chosen to be if she couldn't have been herself. If Jesus had said to her before he made her, "There's only two places available for you. You can either be a nigger or white-trash," what would she have said? "Please, Jesus, please," she would have said, "just let me wait until there's another place available," and he would have said, "No, you have to go right now and I have only those two places so make up your mind." She would have wiggled and squirmed and begged and pleaded but it would have been no use and finally she would have said, "All right, make me a nigger then—but that don't mean a trashy one." And he would have made her a neat clean respectable Negro-woman, herself but black.

Next to the child's mother was a red-headed youngish woman, reading one of the magazines and working a piece of chewing gum, hell for leather, as Claud would say. Mrs. Turpin could not see the woman's feet. She was not white-trash, just common. Sometimes Mrs. Turpin occupied herself at night naming the classes of people. On the bottom of the heap were most colored people, not the kind she would have been if she had been one, but most of them; then next to them—not above, just away from—were the white-trash; then above them were the homeowners, and above them the home-and-land owners, to which she and Claud belonged. Above she and Claud were people with a lot of money and much bigger houses and much more land. But here the complexity of it would begin to bear in on her, for some of the people with a lot of money were common and ought to be below she and Claud and some of the people who had good blood had lost their money and had to rent and then there were colored people who owned their homes and land as well. There was a colored dentist in town who had two red Lincolns and a swimming pool and a farm with registered white-face cattle on it. Usually by the time she had fallen asleep all the classes of people were moiling and roiling around in her head, and she would dream they were all crammed in together in a box car, being ridden off to be put in a gas oven.

"That's a beautiful clock," she said and nodded to her right. It was a big wall clock, the face encased in a brass sunburst.

"Yes, it's very pretty," the stylish lady said agreeably. "And right on the dot too," she added, glancing at her watch.

The ugly girl beside her cast an eye upward at the clock, smirked, then looked directly at Mrs. Turpin and smirked again. Then she returned her eyes to her book. She was obviously the lady's daughter because, although they didn't look anything alike as to disposition, they both had

the same shape of face and the same blue eyes. On the lady they sparkled
pleasantly but in the girl's seared face they appeared alternately to smolder
and to blaze.

What if Jesus had said, "All right, you can be white-trash or a nigger
or ugly"!

Mrs. Turpin felt an awful pity for the girl, though she thought it
was one thing to be ugly and another to act ugly.

The woman with the snuff-stained lips turned around in her chair
and looked up at the clock. Then she turned back and appeared to look
a little to the side of Mrs. Turpin. There was a cast in one of her eyes.
"You want to know wher you can get one of themther clocks?" she asked
in a loud voice.

"No, I already have a nice clock," Mrs. Turpin said. Once somebody like her got a leg in the conversation, she would be all over it.

"You can get you one with green stamps," the woman said. "That's
most likely wher he got hisn. Save you up enough, you can get you most
anythang. I got me some joo'ry."

Ought to have got you a wash rag and some soap, Mrs. Turpin
thought.

"I get contour sheets with mine," the pleasant lady said.

The daughter slammed her book shut. She looked straight in front
of her, directly through Mrs. Turpin and on through the yellow curtain
and the plate glass window which made the wall behind her. The girl's
eyes seemed lit all of a sudden with a peculiar light, an unnatural light
like night road signs give. Mrs. Turpin turned her head to see if there was
anything going on outside that she should see, but she could not see anything. Figures passing cast only a pale shadow through the curtain. There
was no reason the girl should single her out for her ugly looks.

"Miss Finley," the nurse said, cracking the door. The gum chewing
woman got up and passed in front of her and Claud and went into the
office. She had on red high-heeled shoes.

Directly across the table, the ugly girl's eyes were fixed on Mrs. Turpin
as if she had some very special reason for disliking her.

"This is wonderful weather, isn't it?" the girl's mother said.

"It's good weather for cotton if you can get the niggers to pick it,"
Mrs. Turpin said, "but niggers don't want to pick cotton any more. You
can't get the white folks to pick it and now you can't get the niggers—
because they got to be right up there with the white folks."

"They gonna *try* anyways," the white-trash woman said, leaning
forward.

"Do you have one of those cotton-picking machines?" the pleasant
lady asked.

"No," Mrs. Turpin said, "they leave half the cotton in the field. We
don't have much cotton anyway. If you want to make it farming now,
you have to have a little of everything. We got a couple of acres of cotton

and a few hogs and chickens and just enough white-face that Claud can look after them himself."

"One thang I don't want," the white-trash woman said, wiping her mouth with the back of her hand. "Hogs. Nasty stinking things, a-gruntin and a-rootin all over the place."

Mrs. Turpin gave her the merest edge of her attention. "Our hogs are not dirty and they don't stink," she said. "They're cleaner than some children I've seen. Their feet never touch the ground. We have a pig-parlor—that's where you raise them on concrete," she explained to the pleasant lady, "and Claud scoots them down with the hose every afternoon and washes off the floor." Cleaner by far than that child right there, she thought. Poor nasty little thing. He had not moved except to put the thumb of his dirty hand into his mouth.

The woman turned her face away from Mrs. Turpin. "I know I wouldn't scoot down no hog with no hose," she said to the wall.

You wouldn't have no hog to scoot down, Mrs. Turpin said to herself.

"A-gruntin and a-rootin and a-groanin," the woman muttered.

"We got a little of everything," Mrs. Turpin said to the pleasant lady. "It's no use in having more than you can handle yourself with help like it is. We found enough niggers to pick our cotton this year but Claud he has to go after them and take them home again in the evening. They can't walk that half a mile. No they can't. I tell you," she said and laughed merrily, "I sure am tired of buttering up niggers, but you got to love em if you want em to work for you. When they come in the morning, I run out and I say, 'Hi yawl this morning?' and when Claud drives them off to the field I just wave to beat the band and they just wave back." And she waved her hand rapidly to illustrate.

"Like you read out of the same book," the lady said, showing she understood perfectly.

"Child, yes," Mrs. Turpin said. "And when they come in from the field, I run out with a bucket of icewater. That's the way it's going to be from now on," she said. "You may as well face it."

"One thang I know," the white-trash woman said. "Two thangs I ain't going to do: love no niggers or scoot down no hog with no hose." And she let out a bark of contempt.

The look that Mrs. Turpin and the pleasant lady exchanged indicated they both understood that you had to *have* certain things before you could *know* certain things. But every time Mrs. Turpin exchanged a look with the lady, she was aware that the ugly girl's peculiar eyes were still on her, and she had trouble bringing her attention back to the conversation.

"When you got something," she said, "you got to look after it." And when you ain't got a thing but breath and britches, she added to herself, you can afford to come to town every morning and just sit on the Court House coping and spit.

A grotesque revolving shadow passed across the curtain behind her and was thrown palely on the opposite wall. Then a bicycle clattered down against the outside of the building. The door opened and a colored boy glided in with a tray from the drug store. It had two large red and white paper cups on it with tops on them. He was a tall, very black boy in discolored white pants and a green nylon shirt. He was chewing gum slowly, as if to music. He set the tray down in the office opening next to the fern and stuck his head through to look for the secretary. She was not in there. He rested his arms on the ledge and waited, his narrow bottom stuck out, swaying slowly to the left and right. He raised a hand over his head and scratched the base of his skull.

"You see that button there, boy?" Mrs. Turpin said. "You can punch that and she'll come. She's probably in the back somewhere."

"Is that right?" the boy said agreeably, as if he had never seen the button before. He leaned to the right and put his finger on it. "She sometime out," he said and twisted around to face his audience, his elbows behind him on the counter. The nurse appeared and he twisted back again. She handed him a dollar and he rooted in his pocket and made the change and counted it out to her. She gave him fifteen cents for a tip and he went out with the empty tray. The heavy door swung to slowly and closed at length with the sound of suction. For a moment no one spoke.

"They ought to send all them niggers back to Africa," the white-trash woman said. "That's wher they come from in the first place."

"Oh, I couldn't do without my good colored friends," the pleasant lady said.

"There's a heap of things worse than a nigger," Mrs. Turpin agreed. "It's all kinds of them just like it's all kinds of us."

"Yes, and it takes all kinds to make the world go round," the lady said in her musical voice.

As she said it, the raw-complexioned girl snapped her teeth together. Her lower lip turned downwards and inside out, revealing the pale pink inside of her mouth. After a second it rolled back up. It was the ugliest face Mrs. Turpin had ever seen anyone make and for a moment she was certain that the girl had made it at her. She was looking at her as if she had known and disliked her all her life—all of Mrs. Turpin's life, it seemed too, not just all the girl's life. Why, girl, I don't even know you, Mrs. Turpin said silently.

She forced her attention back to the discussion. "It wouldn't be practical to send them back to Africa," she said. "They wouldn't want to go. They got it too good here."

"Wouldn't be what they wanted—if I had anythang to do with it," the woman said.

"It wouldn't be a way in the world you could get all the niggers back over there," Mrs. Turpin said. "They'd be hiding out and lying down and turning sick on you and wailing and hollering and raring and pitch-ing. It wouldn't be a way in the world to get them over there."

"They got over here," the trashy woman said. "Get back like they got over."

"It wasn't so many of them then," Mrs. Turpin explained.

The woman looked at Mrs. Turpin as if here was an idiot indeed but Mrs. Turpin was not bothered by the look, considering where it came from.

"Nooo," she said, "they're going to stay here where they can go to New York and marry white folks and improve their color. That's what they all want to do, every one of them, improve their color."

"You know what comes of that, don't you?" Claud asked.

"No, Claud, what?" Mrs. Turpin said.

Claud's eyes twinkled. "White-faced niggers," he said with never a smile.

Everybody in the office laughed except the white-trash and the ugly girl. The girl gripped the book in her lap with white fingers. The trashy woman looked around her from face to face as if she thought they were all idiots. The old woman in the feed sack dress continued to gaze expres-sionless across the floor at the high-top shoes of the man opposite her, the one who had been pretending to be asleep when the Turpins came in. He was laughing heartily, his hands still spread out on his knees. The child had fallen to the side and was lying now almost face down in the old woman's lap.

While they recovered from their laughter, the nasal chorus on the radio kept the room from silence.

> You go to blank blank
> And I'll go to mine
> But we'll all blank along
> To-geth-ther,
> And all along the blank
> We'll hep each other out
> Smile-ling in any kind of
> Weath-ther!

Mrs. Turpin didn't catch every word but she caught enough to agree with the spirit of the song and it turned her thoughts sober. To help any-body out that needed it was her philosophy of life. She never spared her-self when she found somebody in need, whether they were white or black, trash or decent. And of all she had to be thankful for, she was most thankful that this was so. If Jesus had said, "You can be high society and have all the money you want and be thin and svelte-like, but you can't be a good woman with it," she would have had to say, "Well don't make me that then. Make me a good woman and it don't matter what else, how fat or how ugly or how poor!" Her heart rose. He had not made her a nigger or white-trash or ugly! He had made her herself and given her a little of everything. Jesus, thank you! she said. Thank you thank you thank you! Whenever she counted her blessings she felt as buoyant as if she weighed one hundred and twenty-five pounds instead of one hundred and eighty.

"What's wrong with your little boy?" the pleasant lady asked the white-trashy woman.

"He has a ulcer," the woman said proudly. "He ain't give me a minute's peace since he was born. Him and her are just alike," she said, nodding at the old woman, who was running her leathery fingers through the child's pale hair. "Look like I can't get nothing down them two but Co'Cola and candy."

That's all you try to get down em, Mrs. Turpin said to herself. Too lazy to light the fire. There was nothing you could tell her about people like them that she didn't know already. And it was not just that they didn't have anything. Because if you gave them everything, in two weeks it would all be broken or filthy or they would have chopped it up for lightwood. She knew all this from her own experience. Help them you must, but help them you couldn't.

All at once the ugly girl turned her lips inside out again. Her eyes were fixed like two drills on Mrs. Turpin. This time there was no mistaking that there was something urgent behind them.

Girl, Mrs. Turpin exclaimed silently, I haven't done a thing to you! The girl might be confusing her with somebody else. There was no need to sit by and let herself be intimidated. "You must be in college," she said boldly, looking directly at the girl. "I see you reading a book there."

The girl continued to stare and pointedly did not answer.

Her mother blushed at this rudeness. "The lady asked you a question, Mary Grace," she said under her breath.

"I have ears," Mary Grace said.

The poor mother blushed again. "Mary Grace goes to Wellesley College," she explained. She twisted one of the buttons on her dress. "In Massachusetts," she added with a grimace. "And in the summer she just keeps right on studying. Just reads all the time, a real book worm. She's done real well at Wellesley; she's taking English and Math and History and Psychology and Social Studies," she rattled on, "and I think it's too much. I think she ought to get out and have fun."

The girl looked as if she would like to hurl them all through the plate glass window.

"Way up north," Mrs. Turpin murmured and thought, well, it hasn't done much for her manners.

"I'd almost rather to have him sick," the white-trash woman said, wrenching the attention back to herself. "He's so mean when he ain't. Look like some children just take natural to meanness. It's some gets bad when they get sick but he was the opposite. Took sick and turned good. He don't give me no trouble now. It's me waitin to see the doctor," she said.

If I was going to send anybody back to Africa, Mrs. Turpin thought, it would be your kind, woman. "Yes, indeed," she said aloud, but looking up at the ceiling, "it's a heap of things worse than a nigger." And dirtier than a hog, she added to herself.

"I think people with bad dispositions are more to be pitied than anyone on earth," the pleasant lady said in a voice that was decidedly thin.

"I thank the Lord he has blessed me with a good one," Mrs. Turpin said. "The day has never dawned that I couldn't find something to laugh at."

"Not since she married me anyways," Claud said with a comical straight face.

Everybody laughed except the girl and the white-trash.

Mrs. Turpin's stomach shook. "He's such a caution," she said, "that I can't help but laugh at him."

The girl made a loud ugly noise through her teeth.

Her mother's mouth grew thin and tight. "I think the worst thing in the world," she said, "is an ungrateful person. To have everything and not appreciate it. I know a girl," she said, "who has parents who would give her anything, a little brother who loves her dearly, who is getting a good education, who wears the best clothes, but who can never say a kind word to anyone, who never smiles, who just criticizes and complains all day long."

"Is she too old to paddle?" Claud asked.

The girl's face was almost purple.

"Yes," the lady said, "I'm afraid there's nothing to do but leave her to her folly. Some day she'll wake up and it'll be too late."

"It never hurt anyone to smile," Mrs. Turpin said. "It just makes you feel better all over."

"Of course," the lady said sadly, "but there are just some people you can't tell anything to. They can't take criticism."

"If it's one thing I am," Mrs. Turpin said with feeling, "it's grateful. When I think who all I could have been besides myself and what all I got, a little of everything, and a good disposition besides, I just feel like shouting, 'Thank you, Jesus, for making everything the way it is!' It could have been different!" For one thing, somebody else could have got Claud. At the thought of this, she was flooded with gratitude and a terrible pang of joy ran through her. "Oh thank you, Jesus, Jesus, thank you!" she cried aloud.

The book struck her directly over her left eye. It struck almost at the same instant that she realized the girl was about to hurl it. Before she could utter a sound, the raw face came crashing across the table toward her, howling. The girl's fingers sank like clamps into the soft flesh of her neck. She heard the mother cry out and Claud shout, "Whoa!" There was an instant when she was certain that she was about to be in an earthquake.

All at once her vision narrowed and she saw everything as if it were happening in a small room far away, or as if she were looking at it through the wrong end of a telescope. Claud's face crumpled and fell out of sight.

The nurse ran in, then out, then in again. Then the gangling figure of the doctor rushed out of the inner door. Magazines flew this way and that as the table turned over. The girl fell with a thud and Mrs. Turpin's vision suddenly reversed itself and she saw everything large instead of small. The eyes of the white-trashy woman were staring hugely at the floor. There the girl, held down on one side by the nurse and on the other by her mother, was wrenching and turning in their grasp. The doctor was kneeling astride her, trying to hold her arm down. He managed after a second to sink a long needle into it.

Mrs. Turpin felt entirely hollow except for her heart which swung from side to side as if it were agitated in a great empty drum of flesh.

"Somebody that's not busy call for the ambulance," the doctor said in the off-hand voice young doctors adopt for terrible occasions.

Mrs. Turpin could not have moved a finger. The old man who had been sitting next to her skipped nimbly into the office and made the call, for the secretary still seemed to be gone.

"Claud!" Mrs. Turpin called.

He was not in his chair. She knew she must jump up and find him but she felt like some one trying to catch a train in a dream, when everything moves in slow motion and the faster you try to run the slower you go.

"Here I am," a suffocated voice, very unlike Claud's, said.

He was doubled up in the corner on the floor, pale as paper, holding his leg. She wanted to get up and go to him but she could not move. Instead, her gaze was drawn slowly downward to the churning face on the floor, which she could see over the doctor's shoulder.

The girl's eyes stopped rolling and focused on her. They seemed a much lighter blue than before, as if a door that had been tightly closed behind them was now open to admit light and air.

Mrs. Turpin's head cleared and her power of motion returned. She leaned forward until she was looking directly into the fierce brilliant eyes. There was no doubt in her mind that the girl did know her, knew her in some intense and personal way, beyond time and place and condition. "What you got to say to me?" she asked hoarsely and held her breath, waiting, as for a revelation.

The girl raised her head. Her gaze locked with Mrs. Turpin's. "Go back to hell where you came from, you old wart hog," she whispered. Her voice was low but clear. Her eyes burned for a moment as if she saw with pleasure that her message had struck its target.

Mrs. Turpin sank back in her chair.

After a moment the girl's eyes closed and she turned her head wearily to the side.

The doctor rose and handed the nurse the empty syringe. He leaned over and put both hands for a moment on the mother's shoulders, which were shaking. She was sitting on the floor, her lips pressed together, holding Mary Grace's hand in her lap. The girl's fingers were gripped like a baby's around her thumb. "Go on to the hospital," he said. "I'll call and make the arrangements."

"Now let's see that neck," he said in a jovial voice to Mrs. Turpin. He began to inspect her neck with his first two fingers. Two little moon-shaped lines like pink fish bones were indented over her windpipe. There was the beginning of an angry red swelling above her eye. His fingers passed over this also.

"Lea' me be," she said thickly and shook him off. "See about Claud. She kicked him."

"I'll see about him in a minute," he said and felt her pulse. He was a thin gray-haired man, given to pleasantries. "Go home and have yourself a vacation the rest of the day," he said and patted her on the shoulder.

Quit your pattin me, Mrs. Turpin growled to herself.

"And put an ice pack over that eye," he said. Then he went and squatted down beside Claud and looked at his leg. After a moment he pulled him up and Claud limped after him into the office.

Until the ambulance came, the only sounds in the room were the tremulous moans of the girl's mother, who continued to sit on the floor. The white-trash woman did not take her eyes off the girl. Mrs. Turpin looked straight ahead at nothing. Presently the ambulance drew up, a long dark shadow, behind the curtain. The attendants came in and set the stretcher down beside the girl and lifted her expertly onto it and carried her out. The nurse helped the mother gather up her things. The shadow of the ambulance moved silently away and the nurse came back in the office.

"That ther girl is going to be a lunatic, ain't she?" the white-trash woman asked the nurse, but the nurse kept on to the back and never answered her.

"Yes, she's going to be a lunatic," the white-trash woman said to the rest of them.

"Po' critter," the old woman murmured. The child's face was still in her lap. His eyes looked idly out over her knees. He had not moved during the disturbance except to draw one leg up under him.

"I thank Gawd," the white-trash woman said fervently, "I ain't a lunatic."

Claud came limping out and the Turpins went home.

As their pick-up truck turned into their own dirt road and made the crest of the hill, Mrs. Turpin gripped the window ledge and looked out suspiciously. The land sloped gracefully down through a field dotted with lavender weeds and at the start of the rise their small yellow frame house, with its little flower beds spread out around it like a fancy apron, sat primly in its accustomed place between two giant hickory trees. She would not have been startled to see a burnt wound between two blackened chimneys.

Neither of them felt like eating so they put on their house clothes and lowered the shade in the bedroom and lay down, Claud with his leg on a pillow and herself with a damp washcloth over her eye. The instant she was flat on her back, the image of a razor-backed hog with warts on its face and horns coming out behind its ears snorted into her head. She moaned, a low quiet moan.

"I am not," she said tearfully, "a wart hog. From hell." But the denial had no force. The girl's eyes and her words, even the tone of her voice, low but clear, directed only to her, brooked no repudiation. She had been singled out for the message, though there was trash in the room to whom it might justly have been applied. The full force of this fact struck her only now. There was a woman there who was neglecting her own child but she had been overlooked. The message had been given to Ruby Turpin, a respectable, hard-working, church-going woman. The tears dried. Her eyes began to burn instead with wrath.

She rose on her elbow and the washcloth fell into her hand. Claud was lying on his back, snoring. She wanted to tell him what the girl had said. At the same time she did not wish to put the image of herself as a wart hog from hell into his mind.

"Hey, Claud," she muttered and pushed his shoulder.

Claud opened one pale baby blue eye.

She looked into it warily. He did not think about anything. He just went his way.

"Wha, whasit?" he said and closed the eye again.

"Nothing," she said. "Does your leg pain you?"

"Hurts like hell," Claud said.

"It'll quit terreckly," she said and lay back down. In a moment Claud was snoring again. For the rest of the afternoon they lay there. Claud slept. She scowled at the ceiling. Occasionally she raised her fist and made a small stabbing motion over her chest as if she was defending her innocence to invisible guests who were like the comforters of Job, reasonable-seeming but wrong.

About five-thirty Claud stirred. "Got to go after those niggers," he sighed, not moving.

She was looking straight up as if there were unintelligible handwriting on the ceiling. The protuberance over her eye had turned a greenish-blue. "Listen here," she said.

"What?"

"Kiss me."

Claud leaned over and kissed her loudly on the mouth. He pinched her side and their hands interlocked. Her expression of ferocious concentration did not change. Claud got up, groaning and growling, and limped off. She continued to study the ceiling.

She did not get up until she heard the pick-up truck coming back with the Negroes. Then she rose and thrust her feet in her brown ox-fords, which she did not bother to lace, and stumped out onto the back porch and got her red plastic bucket. She emptied a tray of ice cubes into it and filled it half full of water and went out into the back yard. Every afternoon after Claud brought the hands in, one of the boys helped him put out hay and the rest waited in the back of the truck until he was ready to take them home. The truck was parked in the shade under one of the hickory trees.

"Hi yawl this evening?" Mrs. Turpin asked grimly, appearing with the bucket and the dipper. There were three women and a boy in the truck.

"Us doin nicely," the oldest woman said. "Hi you doin?" and her gaze stuck immediately on the dark lump on Mrs. Turpin's forehead. "You done fell down, ain't you?" she asked in a solicitous voice. The old woman was dark and almost toothless. She had on an old felt hat of Claud's set back on her head. The other two women were younger and lighter and they both had new bright green sun hats. One of them had hers on her head; the other had taken hers off and the boy was grinning beneath it.

Mrs. Turpin set the bucket down on the floor of the truck. "Yawl hep yourselves," she said. She looked around to make sure Claud had gone. "No. I didn't fall down," she said, folding her arms. "It was something worse than that."

"Ain't nothing bad happen to you!" the old woman said. She said it as if they all knew Mrs. Turpin was protected in some special way by Divine Providence. "You just had you a little fall."

"We were in town at the doctor's office for where the cow kicked Mr. Turpin," Mrs. Turpin said in a flat tone that indicated they could leave off their foolishness. "And there was this girl there. A big fat girl with her face all broke out. I could look at that girl and tell she was peculiar but I couldn't tell how. And me and her mama were just talking and going along and all of a sudden WHAM! She throws this big book she was reading at me and . . ."

"Naw!" the old woman cried out.

"And then she jumps over the table and commences to choke me."

"Naw!" they all exclaimed, "naw!"

"Hi come she do that?" the old woman asked. "What ail her?"

Mrs. Turpin only glared in front of her.

"Somethin ail her," the old woman said.

"They carried her off in an ambulance," Mrs. Turpin continued, "but before she went she was rolling on the floor and they were trying to hold her down to give her a shot and she said something to me." She paused. "You know what she said to me?"

"What she say?" they asked.

"She said," Mrs. Turpin began, and stopped, her face very dark and heavy. The sun was getting whiter and whiter, blanching the sky overhead so that the leaves of the hickory tree were black in the face of it. She could not bring forth the words. "Something real ugly," she muttered.

"She sho shouldn't said nothin ugly to you," the old woman said. "You so sweet. You the sweetest lady I know."

"She pretty too," the one with the hat on said.

"And stout," the other one said. "I never knowed no sweeter white lady."

"That's the truth befo' Jesus," the old woman said. "Amen! You des as sweet and pretty as you can be."

Mrs. Turpin knew just exactly how much Negro flattery was worth and it added to her rage. "She said," she began again and finished this time with a fierce rush of breath, "that I was an old wart hog from hell."

There was an astounded silence.

"Where she at?" the youngest woman cried in a piercing voice. "Lemme see her. I'll kill her!"

"I'll kill her with you!" the other one cried.

"She b'long in the sylum," the old woman said emphatically. "You the sweetest white lady I know."

"She pretty too," the other two said. "Stout as she can be and sweet. Jesus satisfied with her!"

"Deed he is," the old woman declared.

Idiots! Mrs. Turpin growled to herself. You could never say anything intelligent to a nigger. You could talk at them but not with them. "Yawl ain't drunk your water," she said shortly. "Leave the bucket in the truck when you're finished with it. I got more to do than just stand around and pass the time of day," and she moved off and into the house.

She stood for a moment in the middle of the kitchen. The dark protuberance over her eye looked like a miniature tornado cloud which might any moment sweep across the horizon of her brow. Her lower lip protruded dangerously. She squared her massive shoulders. Then she marched into the front of the house and out the side door and started down the road to the pig parlor. She had the look of a woman going single-handed, weaponless, into battle.

The sun was a deep yellow now like a harvest moon and was riding westward very fast over the far tree line as if it meant to reach the hogs before she did. The road was rutted and she kicked several good-sized stones out of her path as she strode along. The pig parlor was on a little knoll at the end of a lane that ran off from the side of the barn. It was a square of concrete as large as a small room, with a board fence about four feet high around it. The concrete floor sloped slightly so that the hog wash could drain off into a trench where it was carried to the field for fertilizer. Claud was standing on the outside, on the edge of the concrete, hanging onto the top board, hosing down the floor inside. The hose was connected to the faucet of a water trough nearby.

Mrs. Turpin climbed up beside him and glowered down at the hogs inside. There were seven long-snouted bristly shoats in it—tan with liver-colored spots—and an old sow a few weeks off from farrowing. She was lying on her side grunting. The shoats were running about shaking themselves like idiot children, their little slit pig eyes searching the floor for anything left. She had read that pigs were the most intelligent animal. She doubted it. They were supposed to be smarter than dogs. There had even been a pig astronaut. He had performed his assignment perfectly but died of a heart attack afterwards because they left him in his electric suit, sitting upright throughout his examination when naturally a hog should be on all fours.

A-gruntin and a-rootin and a-groanin.

"Gimme that hose," she said, yanking it away from Claud. "Go on and carry them niggers home and then get off that leg."

"You look like you might have swallowed a mad dog," Claud observed, but he got down and limped off. He paid no attention to her humors.

Until he was out of earshot, Mrs. Turpin stood on the side of the pen, holding the hose and pointing the stream of water at the hind quarter of any shoat that looked as if it might try to lie down. When he had had time to get over the hill, she turned her head slightly and her wrathful eyes scanned the path. He was nowhere in sight. She turned back again and seemed to gather herself up. Her shoulders rose and she drew in her breath.

"What do you send me a message like that for?" she said in a low fierce voice, barely above a whisper but with the force of a shout in its concentrated fury. "How am I a hog and me both? How am I saved and from hell too?" Her free fist was knotted and with the other she gripped the hose, blindly pointing the stream of water in and out of the eye of the old sow whose outraged squeal she did not hear.

The pig parlor commanded a view of the back pasture where their twenty beef cows were gathered around the hay-bales Claud and the boy had put out. The freshly cut pasture sloped down to the highway. Across it was their cotton field and beyond that a dark green dusty wood which they owned as well. The sun was behind the wood, very red, looking over the paling of trees like a farmer inspecting his own hogs.

"Why me?" she rumbled. "It's no trash around here, black or white, that I haven't given to. And break my back to the bone every day working. And do for the church."

She appeared to be the right size woman to command the arena before her. "How am I a hog?" she demanded. "Exactly how am I like them?" and she jabbed the stream of water at the shoats. "There was plenty of trash there. It didn't have to be me."

"If you like trash better, go get yourself some trash then," she railed. "You could have made me trash. Or a nigger. If trash is what you wanted why didn't you make me trash?" She shook her fist with the hose in it and a watery snake appeared momentarily in the air. "I could quit working and take it easy and be filthy," she growled. "Lounge about the sidewalks all day drinking root beer. Dip snuff and spit in every puddle and have it all over my face. I could be nasty."

"Or you could have made me a nigger. It's too late for me to be a nigger," she said with deep sarcasm, "but I could act like one. Lay down in the middle of the road and stop traffic. Roll on the ground."

In the deepening light everything was taking on a mysterious hue. The pasture was growing a peculiar glassy green and the streak of highway had turned lavender. She braced herself for a final assault and this time her voice rolled out over the pasture. "Go on," she yelled, "call me a hog! Call me a hog again. From hell. Call me a wart hog from hell. Put that bottom rail on top. There'll still be a top and bottom!"

A garbled echo returned to her.

A final surge of fury shook her and she roared, "Who do you think you are?"

The color of everything, field and crimson sky, burned for a moment with a transparent intensity. The question carried over the pasture and across the highway and the cotton field and returned to her clearly like an answer from beyond the wood.

She opened her mouth but no sound came out of it.

A tiny truck, Claud's, appeared on the highway, heading rapidly out of sight. Its gears scraped thinly. It looked like a child's toy. At any moment a bigger truck might smash into it and scatter Claud's and the niggers' brains all over the road.

Mrs. Turpin stood there, her gaze fixed on the highway, all her muscles rigid, until in five or six minutes the truck reappeared, returning. She waited until it had had time to turn into their own road. Then like a monumental statue coming to life, she bent her head slowly and gazed, as if through the very heart of the mystery, down into the pig parlor at the hogs. They had settled all in one corner around the old sow who was grunting softly. A red glow suffused them. They appeared to pant with a secret life.

Until the sun slipped finally behind the tree line, Mrs. Turpin remained there with her gaze bent to them as if she were absorbing some abysmal life-giving knowledge. At last she lifted her head. There was only a purple streak in the sky, cutting through a field of crimson and leading, like an extension of the highway, into the descending dusk. She raised her hands from the side of the pen in a gesture hieratic and profound. A visionary light settled in her eyes. She saw the streak as a vast swinging bridge extending upward from the earth through a field of living fire. Upon it a vast horde of souls were rumbling toward heaven. There were whole companies of white-trash, clean for the first time in their lives, and bands of black niggers in white robes, and battalions of freaks and lunatics shouting and clapping and leaping like frogs. And bringing up the end of the procession was a tribe of people whom she recognized at once as those who, like herself and Claud, had always had a little of everything and the God-given wit to use it right. She leaned forward to observe them closer. They were marching behind the others with great dignity, accountable

as they had always been for good order and common sense and respectable behavior. They alone were on key. Yet she could see by their shocked
and altered faces that even their virtues were being burned away. She lowered her hands and gripped the rail of the hog pen, her eyes small but
fixed unblinkingly on what lay ahead. In a moment the vision faded but
she remained where she was, immobile.

At length she got down and turned off the faucet and made her slow
way on the darkening path to the house. In the woods around her the
invisible cricket choruses had struck up, but what she heard were the voices
of the souls climbing upward into the starry field and shouting hallelujah.

[1964]

Parker's Back

Parker's wife was sitting on the front porch floor, snapping beans. Parker
was sitting on the step, some distance away, watching her sullenly. She
was plain, plain. The skin on her face was thin and drawn as tight as the
skin on an onion and her eyes were grey and sharp like the points of two
icepicks. Parker understood why he had married her—he couldn't have
got her any other way—but he couldn't understand why he stayed with
her now. She was pregnant and pregnant women were not his favorite
kind. Nevertheless, he stayed as if she had him conjured. He was puzzled
and ashamed of himself.

The house they rented sat alone save for a single tall pecan tree on a
high embankment overlooking a highway. At intervals a car would shoot
past below and his wife's eyes would swerve suspiciously after the sound
of it and then come back to rest on the newspaper full of beans in her
lap. One of the things she did not approve of was automobiles. In addition
to her other bad qualities, she was forever sniffing up sin. She did not smoke
or dip,[1] drink whiskey, use bad language or paint her face, and God knew
some paint would have improved it, Parker thought. Her being against
color, it was the more remarkable she had married him. Sometimes he
supposed that she had married him because she meant to save him. At
other times he had a suspicion that she actually liked everything she said
she didn't. He could account for her one way or another; it was himself
he could not understand.

She turned her head in his direction and said, "It's no reason you
can't work for a man. It don't have to be a woman."

"Aw shut your mouth for a change," Parker muttered.

If he had been certain she was jealous of the woman he worked for
he would have been pleased but more likely she was concerned with the

---

[1] **dip**   use snuff

sin that would result if he and the woman took a liking to each other. He had told her that the woman was a hefty young blonde; in fact she was nearly seventy years old and too dried up to have an interest in any-thing except getting as much work out of him as she could. Not that an old woman didn't sometimes get an interest in a young man, particularly if he was as attractive as Parker felt he was, but this old woman looked at him the way she looked at her old tractor—as if he had to put up with it because it was all she had. The tractor had broken down the second day Parker was on it and she had set him at once to cutting bushes, saying out of the side of her mouth to the nigger, "Everything he touches, he breaks." She also asked him to wear his shirt when he worked; Parker had removed it even though the day was not sultry; he put it back on reluctantly.

This ugly woman Parker married was his first wife. He had had other women but he had planned never to get himself tied up legally. He had first seen her one morning when his truck broke down on the highway. He had managed to pull it off the road into a neatly swept yard on which sat a peeling two-room house. He got out and opened the hood of the truck and began to study the motor. Parker had an extra sense that told him when there was a woman nearby watching him. After he had leaned over the motor a few minutes, his neck began to prickle. He cast his eye over the empty yard and porch of the house. A woman he could not see was either nearby beyond a clump of honeysuckle or in the house, watch-ing him out the window.

Suddenly Parker began to jump up and down and fling his hand about as if he had mashed it in the machinery. He doubled over and held his hand close to his chest. "God dammit!" he hollered, "Jesus Christ in hell! Jesus God Almighty damm! God dammit to hell!" he went on, flinging out the same few oaths over and over as loud as he could.

Without warning a terrible bristly claw slammed the side of his face and he fell backwards on the hood of the truck. "You don't talk no filth here!" a voice close to him shrilled.

Parker's vision was so blurred that for an instant he thought he had been attacked by some creature from above, a giant hawk-eyed angel wield-ing a hoary weapon. As his sight cleared, he saw before him a tall raw-boned girl with a broom.

"I hurt my hand," he said. "I HURT my hand." He was so incensed that he forgot that he hadn't hurt his hand. "My hand may be broke," he growled although his voice was still unsteady.

"Lemme see it," the girl demanded.

Parker stuck out his hand and she came closer and looked at it. There was no mark on the palm and she took the hand and turned it over. Her own hand was dry and hot and rough and Parker felt himself jolted back to life by her touch. He looked more closely at her. I don't want nothing to do with this one, he thought.

The girl's sharp eyes peered at the back of the stubby reddish hand she held. There emblazoned in red and blue was a tattooed eagle perched on a cannon. Parker's sleeve was rolled to the elbow. Above the eagle a serpent was coiled about a shield and in the spaces between the eagle and the serpent there were hearts, some with arrows through them. Above the serpent there was a spread hand of cards. Every space on the skin of Parker's arm, from wrist to elbow, was covered in some loud design. The girl gazed at this with an almost stupefied smile of shock, as if she had accidentally grasped a poisonous snake; she dropped the hand.

"I got most of my other ones in foreign parts," Parker said. "These here I mostly got in the United States. I got my first one when I was only fifteen year old."

"Don't tell me," the girl said, "I don't like it. I ain't got any use for it."

"You ought to see the ones you can't see," Parker said and winked.

Two cirlces of red appeared like apples on the girl's cheeks and softened her appearance. Parker was intrigued. He did not for a minute think that she didn't like the tattoos. He had never yet met a woman who was not attracted to them.

Parker was fourteen when he saw a man in a fair, tattooed from head to foot. Except for his loins which were girded with a panther hide, the man's skin was patterned by what seemed from Parker's distance—he was near the back of the tent, standing on a bench—a single intricate design of brilliant color. The man, who was small and sturdy, moved about on the platform, flexing his muscles so that the arabesque of men and beasts and flowers on his skin appeared to have a subtle motion of its own. Parker was filled with emotion, lifted up as some people are when the flag passes. He was a boy whose mouth habitually hung open. He was heavy and earnest, as ordinary as a loaf of bread. When the show was over, he had remained standing on the bench, staring where the tattooed man had been, until the tent was almost empty.

Parker had never before felt the least motion of wonder in himself. Until he saw the man at the fair, it did not enter his head that there was anything out of the ordinary about the fact that he existed. Even then it did not enter his head, but a peculiar unease settled in him. It was as if a blind boy had been turned so gently in a different direction that he did not know his destintion had been changed.

He had his first tattoo some time after—the eagle perched on the cannon. It was done by a local artist. It hurt very little, just enough to make it appear to Parker to be worth doing. This was peculiar too for before he had thought that only what did not hurt was worth doing. The next year he quit school because he was sixteen and could. He went to the trade school for a while, then he quit the trade school and worked for six months in a garage. The only reason he worked at all was to pay for more tattoos. His mother worked in a laundry and could support him, but she would not pay for any tattoo except her name on a heart, which he had put on, grumbling. However, her name was Betty Jean and nobody had to know it was his mother. He found out that the tattoos were attractive to the kind of girls he liked but who had never liked him before. He began to drink beer and get in fights. His mother wept over what was becoming of him. One night she dragged him off to a revival with her, not telling him where they were going. When he saw the big lighted church, he jerked out of her grasp and ran. The next day he lied about his age and joined the navy.

Parker was large for the tight sailor's pants but the silly white cap, sitting low on his forehead, made his face by contrast look thoughtful and almost intense. After a month or two in the navy, his mouth ceased to hang open. His features hardened into the features of a man. He stayed in the navy five years and seemed a natural part of the grey mechanical ship, except for his eyes, which were the same pale slate-color as the ocean and reflected the immense spaces around him as if they were a microcosm of the mysterious sea. In port Parker wandered about comparing the run-down places he was in to Birmingham, Alabama. Everywhere he went he picked up more tattoos.

He had stopped having lifeless ones like anchors and crossed rifles. He had a tiger and a panther on each shoulder, a cobra coiled about a torch on his chest, hawks on his thighs, Elizabeth II and Philip over where his stomach and liver were respectively. He did not care much what the subject was so long as it was colorful; on his abdomen he had a few obscenities but only because that seemed the proper place for them. Parker would be satisfied with each tattoo about a month, then something about it that had attracted him would wear off. Whenever a decent-sized mirror was available, he would get in front of it and study his overall look. The effect was not of one intricate arabesque of colors but of something haphazard and botched. A huge dissatisfaction would come over him and he would go off and find another tattooist and have another space filled up. The front of Parker was almost completely covered but there were no tattoos on his back. He had no desire for one anywhere he could not readily see it himself. As the space on the front of him for tattoos decreased, his dissatisfaction grew and became general.

After one of his furloughs, he didn't go back to the navy but remained away without official leave, drunk, in a rooming house in a city he did not know. His dissatisfaction, from being chronic and latent, had suddenly become acute and raged in him. It was as if the panther and the lion and the serpents and the eagles and the hawks had penetrated his skin and lived inside him in a raging warfare. The navy caught up with him, put him in the brig for nine months and then gave him a dishonorable discharge.

After that Parker decided that country air was the only kind fit to breathe. He rented the shack on the embankment and bought the old truck and took various jobs which he kept as long as it suited him. At the time he met his future wife, he was buying apples by the bushel and selling them for the same price by the pound to isolated homesteaders on back country roads.

"All that there," the woman said, pointing to his arm, "is no better than what a fool Indian would do. It's a heap of vanity." She seemed to have found the word she wanted. "Vanity of vanities,"[2] she said.

Well what the hell do I care what she thinks of it? Parker asked himself, but he was plainly bewildered. "I reckon you like one of these better than another anyway," he said, dallying until he thought of something that would impress her. He thrust the arm back at her. "Which you like best?"

"None of them," she said, "but the chicken is not as bad as the rest."

"What chicken?" Parker almost yelled.

She pointed to the eagle.

"That's an eagle," Parker said. "What fool would waste their time having a chicken put on themself?"

"What fool would have any of it?" the girl said and turned away. She went slowly back to the house and left him there to get going. Parker remained for almost five minutes, looking agape at the dark door she had entered.

The next day he returned with a bushel of apples. He was not one to be outdone by anything that looked like her. He liked women with meat on them, so you didn't feel their muscles, much less their bones. When he arrived, she was sitting on the top step and the yard was full of children, all as thin and poor as herself; Parker remembered it was Saturday. He hated to be making up to a woman when there were children around, but it was fortunate he had brought the bushel of apples off the truck. As the children approached him to see what he carried, he gave each child an apple and told it to get lost; in that way he cleared out the whole crowd.

The girl did nothing to acknowledge his presence. He might have been a stray pig or goat that had wandered into the yard and she too tired to take up the broom and send it off. He set the bushel of apples down next to her on the step. He sat down on a lower step.

"Hep yourself," he said, nodding at the basket; then he lapsed into silence.

She took an apple quickly as if the basket might disappear if she didn't make haste. Hungry people made Parker nervous. He had always had plenty to eat himself. He grew very uncomfortable. He reasoned he had nothing to say so why should he say it? He could not think now why he had come or why he didn't go before he wasted another bushel of apples on the crowd of children. He supposed they were her brothers and sisters.

She chewed the apple slowly but with a kind of relish of concentration, bent slightly but looking out ahead. The view from the porch

---

[2] **Vanity of Vanities**   a quotation from Ecclesiastes 1:2

stretched off across a long incline studded with iron weed and across the highway to a vast vista of hills and one small mountain. Long views depressed Parker. You look out into space like that and you begin to feel as if someone were after you, the navy or the government or religion.

"Who them children belong to, you?" he said at length.

"I ain't married yet," she said. "They belong to momma." She said as if it were only a matter of time before she would be married.

Who in God's name would marry her? Parker thought.

A large barefooted woman with a wide gap-toothed face appeared in the door behind Parker. She had apparently been there for several minutes.

"Good evening," Parker said.

The woman crossed the porch and picked up what was left of the bushel of apples. "We thank you," she said and returned with it into the house.

"That your old woman?" Parker muttered.

The girl nodded. Parker knew a lot of sharp things he could have said like "You got my sympathy," but he was gloomily silent. He just sat there, looking at the view. He thought he must be coming down with something.

"If I pick up some peaches tomorrow I'll bring you some," he said.

"I'll be much obliged to you," the girl said.

Parker had no intention of taking any basket of peaches back there but the next day he found himself doing it. He and the girl had almost nothing to say to each other. One thing he did say was, "I ain't got any tattoo on my back."

"What you got on it?" the girl said.

"My shirt," Parker said. "Haw."

"Haw, haw," the girl said politely.

Parker thought he was losing his mind. He could not believe for a minute that he was attracted to a woman like this. She showed not the least interest in anything but what he brought until he appeared the third time with two cantaloups. "What's you name?" she asked.

"O. E. Parker," he said.

"What does the O.E. stand for?"

"You can jut call me O.E.," Parker said. "Or Parker. Don't nobody call me by my name."

"What's it stand for?" she persisted.

"Never mind," Parker said. "What's yours?"

"I'll tell you when you tell me what them letters are the short of," she said. There was just a hint of flirtatiousness in her tone and it went rapidly to Parker's head. He had never revealed the name to any man or woman, only to the files of the navy and the government, and it was on his baptismal record which he got at the age of a month; his mother was a Methodist. When the name leaked out of the navy files, Parker narrowly missed killing the man who used it.

"You'll go blab it around," he said.

"I'll swear I'll never tell nobody," she said. "On God's holy word I swear it."

Parker sat for a few minutes in silence. Then he reached for the girl's neck, drew her ear close to his mouth and revealed the name in a low voice.

"Obadiah," she whispered. Her face slowly brightened as if the name came as a sign to her. "Obadiah," she said.

The name still stank in Parker's estimation.

"Obadiah Elihue,"[3] she said in a reverent voice.

"If you call me that aloud. I'll bust your head open," Parker said. "What's yours?"

"Sarah Ruth Cates," she said.

"Glad to meet you, Sarah Ruth," Parker said.

Sarah Ruth's father was a Straight Gospel preacher but he was away, spreading it in Florida. Her mother did not seem to mind his attention to the girl so long as he brought a basket of something with him when he came. As for Sarah Ruth herself, it was plain to Parker after he had visited three times that she was crazy about him. She liked him even though she insisted that pictures on the skin were vanity of vanities and even after hearing him curse, and even after she had asked him if he was saved and he had replied that he didn't see it was anything in particular to save him from. After that, inspired, Parker had said, "I'd be saved enough if you was to kiss me."

She scowled. "That ain't being saved," she said.

Not long after that she agreed to take a ride in his truck. Parker parked it on a deserted road and suggested to her that they lie down together in the back of it.

"Not until after we're married," she said—just like that.

"Oh that ain't necessary," Parker said and as he reached for her, she thrust him away with such force that the door of the truck came off and he found himself flat on his back on the ground. He made up his mind then and there to have nothing further to do with her.

They were married in the County Ordinary's office because Sarah Ruth thought churches were idolatrous. Parker had no opinion about that one way or the other. The Ordinary's office was lined with cardboard file boxes and record books with dusty yellow slips of paper hanging on out of them. The Ordinary was an old woman with red hair who had held office for forty years and looked as dusty as her books. She married them from behind the iron-grill of a stand-up desk and when she finished, she

---

[3]**Obadiah Elihue**   both names occur in the Hebrew Bible. Obadiah ("worshipper," or "servant of Yahweh") is used of at least eleven different people, including a prophet. Elihue, a young man who claims divine inspiration but who chiefly repeats what others have said, appears in Job 32–37.

said with a flourish, "Three dollars and fifty cents and till death do you part!" and yanked some forms out of a machine.

Marriage did not change Sarah Ruth a jot and it made Parker gloomier than ever. Every morning he decided he had had enough and would not return that night; every night he returned. Whenever Parker couldn't stand the way he felt, he would have another tattoo, but the only surface left on him now was his back. To see a tattoo on his own back he would have to get two mirrors and stand between them in just the correct position and this seemed to Parker a good way to make an idiot of himself. Sarah Ruth who, if she had had better sense, could have enjoyed a tattoo on his back, would not even look at the ones he had elsewhere. When he attempted to point out especial details of them, she would shut her eyes tight and turn her back as well. Except in total darkness, she preferred Parker dressed and with his sleeves rolled down.

"At the judgement seat of God, Jesus is going to say to you, 'What you been doing all your life besides have pictures drawn all over you?'" she said.

"You don't fool me none." Parker said, "you're just afraid that hefty girl I work for'll like me so much she'll say, 'Come on, Mr. Parker, let's you and me . . .'"

"You're tempting sin," she said, "and at the judgement seat of God you'll have to answer for that too. You ought to go back to selling the fruits of the earth."

Parker did nothing much when he was at home but listen to what the judgement seat of God would be like for him if he didn't change his ways. When he could, he broke in with tales of the hefty girl he worked for. "'Mr. Parker,'" he said she said, "'I hired you for your brains.'" (She had added, "So why don't you use them?")

"And you should have seen her face the first time she saw me without my shirt," he said. "'Mr. Parker,' she said, 'you're a walking panner-rammer!'" This had, in fact, been her remark but it had been delivered out of one side of her mouth.

Dissatisfaction began to grow so great in Parker that there was no containing it outside of a tattoo. It had to be his back. There was no help for it. A dim half-formed inspiration began to work in his mind. He visualized having a tattoo put there that Sarah Ruth would not be able to resist—a religious subject. He thought of an open book with HOLY BIBLE tattooed under it and an actual verse printed on the page. This seemed just the thing for a while; then he began to hear her say, "Ain't I already got a real Bible? what you think I want to read the same verse over and over for when I can read it all?" He needed something better even than the Bible! He thought about it so much that he began to lose sleep. He was already losing flesh—Sarah Ruth just threw food in the pot and let it boil. Not knowing for certain why he continued to stay with a woman who was both ugly and pregnant and no cook made him generally nervous and irritable, and he developed a little tic in the side of his face.

Once or twice he found himself turning around abruptly as if someone were trailing him. He had had a granddaddy who had ended in the state mental hospital, although not until he was seventy-five, but as urgent as it might be for him to get a tattoo, it was just as urgent that he get exactly the right one to bring Sarah Ruth to heel. As he continued to worry over it, his eyes took on a hollow preoccupied expression. The old woman he worked for told him that if he couldn't keep his mind on what he was doing, she knew where she could find a fourteen-year-old colored boy who could. Parker was too preoccupied to be offended. At any time previous, he would have left her then and there, saying drily, "Well, you go ahead on and get him then."

Two or three mornings later he was baling hay with the old woman's sorry baler and her broken down tractor in a large field, cleared save for one enormous old tree standing in the middle of it. The old woman was the kind who would not cut down a large old tree because it was a large old tree. She had pointed it out to Parker as if he didn't have eyes and told him to be careful not to hit it as the machine picked up hay near it. Parker began at the outside of the field and made circles inward toward it. He had to get off the tractor every now and then and untangle the baling cord or kick a rock out of the way. The old woman had told him to carry the rocks to the edge of the field, which he did when she was there watching. When he thought he could make it, he ran over them. As he circled the field his mind was on a suitable design for his back. The sun, the size of a golf ball, began to switch regularly from in front to behind him, but he appeared to see it both places as if he had eyes in the back of his head. All at once he saw the tree reaching out to grasp him. A ferocious thud propelled him into the air, and he heard himself yelling in an unbelievably loud voice, "GOD ABOVE!"

He landed on his back while the tractor crashed upside-down into the tree and burst into flame. The first thing Parker saw were his shoes, quickly being eaten by the fire; one was caught under the tractor, the other was some distance away, burning by itself. He was not in them. He could feel the hot breath of the burning tree on his face. He scrambled backwards, still sitting, his eyes cavernous, and if he had known how to cross himself he would have done it.

His truck was on a dirt road at the edge of the field. He moved toward it, still sitting, still backwards, but faster and faster; halfway to it he got up and began a kind of forward-bent run from which he collapsed on his knees twice. His legs felt like two old rusted rain gutters. He reached the truck finally and took off in it, zigzagging up the road. He drove past his house on the embankment and straight for the city, fifty miles distant.

Parker did not allow himself to think on the way to the city. He only knew that there had been a great change in his life, a leap forward into a worse unknown, and that there was nothing he could do about it. It was for all intents accomplished.

The artist had two large cluttered rooms over a chiropodist's office on a back street. Parker, still barefooted, burst silently in on him at a little after three in the afternoon. The artist, who was about Parker's own age — twenty-eight — but thin and bald, was behind a small drawing table, tracing a design in green ink. He looked up with an annoyed glance and did not seem to recognize Parker in the hollow-eyed creature before him.

"Let me see the book you got with all the pictures of God in it," Parker said breathlessly. "The religious one."

The artist continued to look at him with his intellectual, superior stare. "I don't put tattoos on drunks," he said.

"You know me!" Parker cried indignantly. "I'm O. E. Parker! You done work for me before and I always paid!"

The artist looked at him another moment as if he were not altogether sure. "You've fallen off some," he said. "You must have been in jail."

"Married," Parker said.

"Oh," said the artist. With the aid of mirrors the artist had tattooed on the top of his head a miniature owl, perfect in every detail. It was about the size of a half-dollar and served him as a show piece. There were cheaper artists in town but Parker had never wanted anything but the best. The artist went over to a cabinet at the back of the room and began to look over some art books. "Who are you interested in?" he said, "saints, angels, Christs or what?"

"God," Parker said.

"Father, Son or Spirit?"

"Just God," Parker said impatiently. "Christ. I don't care. Just so it's God."

The artist returned with a book. He moved some papers off another table and put the book down on it and told Parker to sit down and see what he liked. "The up-t-date ones are in the back," he said.

Parker sat down with the book and wet his thumb. He began to go through it, beginning at the back where the up-to-date pictures were. Some of them he recognized — The Good Shepherd, Forbid Them Not, The Smiling Jesus, Jesus the Physician's Friend, but he kept turning rapidly backwards and the pictures became less and less reassuring. One showed a gaunt green dead face streaked with blood. One was yellow with sagging purple eyes. Parker's heart began to beat faster and faster until it appeared to be roaring inside him like a great generator. He flipped the pages quickly, feeling that when he reached the one ordained, a sign would come. He continued to flip through until he had almost reached the front of the book. On one of the pages a pair of eyes glanced at him swiftly. Parker sped on, then stopped. His heart too appeared to cut off; there was absolute silence. It said as plainly as if silence were a language itself, GO BACK.

Parker returned to the picture—the haloed head of a flat stern Byzantine Christ[4] with all-demanding eyes. He sat there trembling; his heart began slowly to beat again as if it were being brought to life by a subtle power.

"You found what you want?" the artist asked.

Parker's throat was too dry to speak. He got up and thrust the book at the artist, opened at the picture.

"That'll cost you plenty," the artist said. "You don't want all those little blocks though, just the outline and some better features."

"Just like it is," Parker said, "just like it is or nothing."

"It's your funeral," the artist said, "but I don't do that kind of work for nothing."

"How much?" Parker asked.

"It'll take maybe two days work."

"How much?" Parker said.

"On time or cash?" the artist asked. Parker's other jobs had been on time, but he had paid.

"Ten down and ten for every day it takes," the artist said.

Parker drew ten dollar bills out of his wallet; he had three left in.

"You come back in the morning," the artist said, putting the money in his own pocket. "First I'll have to trace that out of the book."

"No no!" Parker said. "Trace it now or gimme my money back," and his eyes blared as if he were ready for a fight.

The artist agreed. Any one stupid enough to want a Christ on his back, he reasoned, would be just as likely as not to change his mind the next minute, but once the work was begun he could hardly do so.

While he worked on the tracing, he told Parker to go wash his back at the sink with the special soap he used there. Parker did it and returned to pace back and forth across the room, nervously flexing his shoulders. He wanted to go look at the picture again but at the same time he did not want to. The artist got up finally and had Parker lie down on the table. He swabbed his back with ethyl chloride and then began to outline the head on it with his iodine pencil. Another hour passed before he took up his electric instrument. Parker felt no particular pain. In Japan he had had a tattoo of the Buddha done on his upper arm with ivory needles; in Burma, a little brown root of a man had made a peacock on each of his knees using thin pointed sticks, two feet long; amateurs had worked on him with pins and soot. Parker was usually so relaxed and easy under the hand of the artist that he often went to sleep, but this time he remained awake, every muscle taut.

[4]**Byzantine Christ**   in Byzantine art (fifth to thirteenth century) the usual image of Christ is not the incarnate Messiah (the humble and humane teacher) but the all-powerful ruler enthroned in heaven. The most famous of such images, in San Vitale, Ravenna, is a sixth-century mosaic, hence the reference a little later in the story to "all those little blocks," i.e. inlaid bits of colored stone or tile set in mortar to form a picture.

At midnight the artist said he was ready to quit. He propped one mirror, four feet square, on a table by the wall and took a smaller mirror off the lavatory wall and put it in Parker's hands. Parker stood with his back to the one on the table and moved the other until he saw a flashing burst of color reflected from his back. It was almost completely covered with little red and blue and ivory and saffron squares; from them he made out the lineaments of the face—a mouth, the beginning of heavy brows, a straight nose, but the face was empty; the eyes had not yet been put in. The impression for the moment was almost as if the artist had tricked him and done the Physician's Friend.

"It don't have eyes," Parker cried out.

"That'll come," the artist said, "in due time. We have another day to go on it yet."

Parker spent the night on a cot at the Haven of Light Christian Mission. He found these the best places to stay in the city because they were free and included a meal of sorts. He got the last available cot and because he was still barefooted, he accepted a pair of second-hand shoes which, in his confusion, he put on to go to bed; he was still shocked from all that had happened to him. All night he lay awake in the long dormitory of cots with lumpy figures on them. The only light was from a phosphorescent cross glowing at the end of the room. The tree reached out to grasp him again, then burst into flame; the shoe burned quietly by itself; the eyes in the book said to him distinctly GO BACK and at the same time did not utter a sound. He wished that he were not in this city, not in this Haven of Light Mission, not in a bed by himself. He longed miserably for Sarah Ruth. Her sharp tongue and icepick eyes were the only comfort he could bring to mind. He decided he was losing it. Her eyes appeared soft and dilatory compared with the eyes in the book, for even though he could not summon up the exact look of those eyes, he could still feel their penetration. He felt as though, under their gaze, he was as transparent as the wing of a fly.

The tattooist had told him not to come until ten in the morning, but when he arrived at that hour, Parker was sitting in the dark hallway on the floor, waiting for him. He had decided upon getting up that, once the tattoo was on him, he would not look at it, that all his sensations of the day and night before were those of a crazy man and that he would return to doing things according to his own sound judgement.

The artist began where he left off. "One thing I want to know," he said presently as he worked over Parker's back, "why do you want this on you? Have you gone and got religion? Are you saved?" he asked in a mocking voice.

Parker's throat felt salty and dry. "Naw," he said, "I ain't go not use for none of that. A man can't save his self from whatever it is he don't deserve none of my sympathy." These words seemed to leave his mouth like wraiths and to evaporate at once as if he had never uttered them.

"Then why . . ."

"I married this woman that's saved," Parker said. "I never should have done it. I ought to leave her. She's done gone and got pregnant."

"That's too bad," the artist said. "Then it's her making you have this tattoo."

"Naw," Parker said, "she don't know nothing about it. It's a surprise for her."

"You think she'll like it an lay off you a while?"

"She can't hep herself," Parker said. "She can't say she don't like the looks of God." He decided he had told the artist enough of his business. Artists were all right in their place but he didn't like them poking their noses into the affairs of regular people. "I didn't get no sleep last night," he said. "I think I'll get some now."

That closed the mouth of the artist but it did not bring him any sleep. He lay there, imagining how Sarah Ruth would be struck speechless by the face on his back and every now and then this would be interrupted by a vision of the tree of fire and his empty shoe burning beneath it.

The artist worked steadily until nearly four o'clock, not stopping to have lunch, hardly pausing with the electric instrument except to wipe the dripping dye off Parker's back as he went along. Finally he finished. "You can get up and look at it now," he said.

Parker sat up but he remained on the edge of the table.

The artist was pleased with his work and wanted Parker to look at it at once. Instead Parker continued to sit on the edge of the table, bent forward slightly but with a vacant look. "What ails you?" the artist said. "Go look at it."

"Ain't nothing ail me," Parker said in a sudden belligerent voice. "That tattoo ain't going nowhere. It'll be there when I get there." He reached for his shirt and began gingerly to put it on.

The artist took him roughly by the arm and propelled him between the two mirrors. "Now *look*," he said, angry at having his work ignored.

Parker looked, turned white and moved away. The eyes in the reflected face continued to look at him—still, straight, all-demanding, enclosed in silence.

"It was your idea, remember," the artist said. "I would have advised something else."

Parker said nothing. He put on his shirt and went out the door while the artist shouted, "I'll expect all of my money!"

Parker headed toward a package shop on the corner. He bought a pint of whiskey and took it into a nearby alley and drank it all in five minutes. Then he moved on to a pool hall nearby which he frequented when he came to the city. It was a well-lighted barn-like place with a bar up one side and gambling machines on the other and pool tables in the back. As soon as Parker entered, a large man in a red and black checkered

shirt hailed him by slapping him on the back and yelling, "Yeyyyyyy bo!
O. E. Parker!"

"Parker was not yet ready to be struck on the back. "Lay off," he
said, "I got a fresh tattoo there."

"What you got this time?" the man asked and then yelled to a few
at the machines. "O.E.'s got him another tattoo."

"Nothing special this time," Parker said and slunk over to a machine
that was not being used.

"Come on," the big man said, "let's have a look at O.E.'s tattoo,"
and while Parker squirmed at their hands, they pulled up his shrt. Parker
felt all the hands drop away instantly and his shirt fell again like a veil
over the face. There was a silence in the pool room which seemed to Parker
to grow from the cirle around him until it extended to the foundations
under the building and upward through the beams in the roof.

Finally some one said, "Christ!" Then they all broke into noise at
once. Parker turned around, an uncertain grin on his face.

"Leave it to O.E.!" the man in the checkered shirt said. "That boy's
a real card!"

"Maybe he's gone and got religion," some one yelled.

"Not on your life," Parker said.

"O.E.'s got religion and is witnessing for Jesus, ain't you, O.E.?" a
little man with a piece of cigar in his mouth said wryly. "An original way
to do it if I ever saw one."

"Leave it to Parker to think of a new one!" the fat man said.

"Yyeeeeeeyyyyyyy bo!" someone yelled and they all began to whistle
and curse in compliment until Parker said, "Aaa shut up."

"What'd you do it for?" somebody asked.

"For laughs," Parker said. "What's it to you?"

"Why ain't you laughing then?" somebody yelled. Parker lunged into
the midst of them and like a whirlwind on a summer's day there began
a fight that raged and overturned tables and swinging fists until two of
them grabbed him and ran to the door with him and threw him out. Then
a calm descended on the pool hall as nerve shattering as if the long barn-
like room were the ship from which Jonah had been cast into the sea.

Parker sat for a long time on the ground in the alley behind the pool
hall, examining his soul. He saw it as a spider web of facts and lies that
was not at all important to him but which appeared to be necessary in
spite of his opinion. The eyes that were now forever on his back were
eyes to be obeyed. He was as certain of it as he had ever been of anything.
Throughout his life, grumbling and sometimes cursing, often afraid, once
in rapture, Parker had obeyed whatever instinct of this kind had come to
him—in rapture when his spirit had lifted at the sight of the tattooed man
at the fair, afraid when he had joined the navy, grumbling when he had
married Sarah Ruth.

The thought of her brought him slowly to his feet. She would know what he had to do. She would clear up the rest of it, and she would at least be pleased. It seemed to him that, all along, that was what he wanted, to please her. His truck was still parked in front of the building where the artist had his place, but it was not far away. He got in it and drove out of the city and into the country night. His head was almost clear of liquor and he observed that his dissatisfaction was gone, but he felt not quite like himself. It was as if he were himself but a stranger to himself, driving into a new country though everything he saw was familiar to him, even at night.

He arrived finally at the house on the embankment, pulled the truck under the pecan tree and got out. He made as much noise as possible to assert that he was still in charge here, that his leaving her for a night without word meant nothing except it was the way he did things. He slammed the car door, stamped up the two steps and across the porch and rattled the door knob. It did not respond to his touch. "Sarah Ruth!" he yelled, "let me in."

There was no lock on the door and she had evidently placed the back of a chair against the knob. He began to beat on the door and rattle the knob at the same time.

He heard the bed springs creak and bent down and put his head to the keyhole, but it was stopped up with paper. "Let me in!" he hollered, bamming on the door again. "What you got me locked out for?"

A sharp voice close to the door said, "Who's there?"

"Me," Parker said, "O.E."

He waited a moment.

"Me," he said impatiently, "O.E."

Still no sound from inside.

He tried once more. "O.E.," he said, bamming the door two or three more times. "O. E. Parker. You know me."

There was a silence. Then the voice said slowly, "I don't know no O.E."

"Quit fooling," Parker pleaded. "You ain't got any business doing me this way. It's me, old O.E., I'm back. You ain't afraid of me."

"Who's there?" the same unfeeling voice said.

Parker turned his head as if he expected someone behind him to give him the answer. The sky had lightened slightly and there were two or three streaks of yellow floating above the horizon. Then as he stood there, a tree of light burst over the skyline.

Parker fell back against the door as if he had been pinned there by a lance.

"Who's there?" the voice from inside said and there was a quality about it now that seemed final. The knob rattled and the voice said peremptorily, "Who's there, I ast you?"

Parker bent down and put his mouth near the stuffed keyhold. "Obadiah," he whispered and all at once he felt the light pouring through him, turning his spider web soul into a perfect arabesque of colors, a garden of trees and birds and beasts.

"Obadiah Elihue!" he whispered.

The door opened and he stumbled in. Sarah Ruth loomed there, hands on her hips. She began at once, "That was no hefty blonde woman you was working for and you'll have to pay her every penny on her tractor you busted up. She don't keep insurance on it. She came here and her and me had a long talk and I . . ."

Trembling, Parker set about lighting the kerosene lamp.

"What's the matter with you, wasting that kerosene this near daylight?" she demanded. "I ain't got to look at you."

A yellow glow enveloped them. Parker put the match down and began to unbutton his shirt.

"And you ain't going to have none of me this near morning," she said.

"Shut your mouth," he said quietly. "Look at this and then I don't want to hear no more out of you." He removed the shirt and turned his back to her.

"Another picture," Sarah Ruth growled. "I might have known you was off after putting some more trash on yourself."

Parker's knees went hollow under him. He wheeled around and cried, "Look at it! Don't just say that! *Look* at it!"

"I done looked," she said.

"Don't you know who it is?" he cried in anguish.

"No, who is it?" Sarah Ruth said. "It ain't anybody I know."

"It's him," Parker said.

"Him who?"

"God!" Parker cried.

"God? God don't look like that!"

"What do you know how he looks?" Parker moaned. "You ain't seen him."

"He don't *look*," Sarah Ruth said. "He's a spirit. No man shall see his face."

"Aw listen," Parker groaned, "this is just a picture of him."

"Idolatry!" Sarah Ruth screamed. "Idolatry! Enflaming yourself with idols under every green tree! I can put up with lies and vanity but I don't want no idolator in this house!" and she grabbed up the broom and began to thrash him across the shoulders with it.

Parker was too stunned to resist. He sat there and let her beat him until she had nearly knocked him senseless and large welts had formed on the face of the tattooed Christ. Then he staggered up and made for the door.

She stamped the broom two or three times on the floor and went to the window and shook it out to get the taint of him off it. Still gripping

it, she looked toward the pecan tree and her eyes hardened still more. There
he was—who called himself Obadiah Elihue—leaning against the tree, crying like a baby.

[1964]

On Fiction: Remarks from Essays and Letters

from "The Fiction Writer and His Country"

In the greatest fiction, the writer's moral sense coincides with his dramatic
sense, and I see no way for it to do this unless his moral judgment is part
of the very act of seeing, and he is free to use it. I have heard it said
that belief in Christian dogma is a hindrance to the writer, but I myself
have found nothing further from the truth. Actually, it frees the story-
teller to observe. It is not a set of rules which fixes what he sees in the
world. If affects his writing primarily by guaranteeing his respect for
mystery.

When I look at stories I have written I find that they are, for the
most part, about people who are poor, who are afflicted in both mind
and body, who have little—or at best a distorted—sense of spiritual purpose,
and whose actions do not apparently give the reader a great assurance of
the joy of life.
Yet how is this? For I am no disbeliever in spiritual purpose and no
vague believer. I see from the standpoint of Christian orthodoxy. This
means that for me the meaning of life is centered in our Redemption by
Christ and what I see in the world I see in its relation to that.

The novelist with Christian concerns will find in modern life distortions which are repugnant to him, and his problem will be to make
these appear as distortions to an audience which is used to seeing them
as natural; and he may well be forced to take ever more violent means
to get his vision across to this hostile audience. When you can assume
that your audience holds the same beliefs you do, you can relax a little
and use more normal means of talking to it; when you have to assume
that it does not, then you have to make your vision apparent by shock—
to the hard of hearing you shout, and for the almost-blind you draw large
and startling figures.

from "Some Aspects of The Grotesque in Southern Fiction"

If the writer believes that our life is and will remain essentially mysterious, if he looks upon us as beings existing in a created order to whose laws we freely respond, then what he sees on the surface will be of interest to him only as he can go through it into an experience of mystery itself. His kind of fiction will always be pushing its own limits outward toward the limits of mystery, because for this kind of writer, the meaning of a story does not begin except at a depth where adequate motivation and adequate psychology and the various determinations have been exhausted. Such a writer will be interested in what we don't understand rather than in what we do. He will be interested in possibility rather than in probability. He will be interested in characters who are forced out to meet evil and grace and who act on a trust beyond themselves—whether they know very clearly what is is they act upon or not. To the modern mind, this kind of character, and his creator, are typical Don Quixotes, tilting at what is not there.

from "The Nature and Aim of Fiction"

The novel works by a slower accumulation of detail than the short story does. The short story requires more drastic procedures than the novel because more has to be accomplished in less space. The details have to carry more immediate weight. In good fiction, certain of the details will tend to accumulate meaning from the story itself, and when his happens, they become symbolic in their action.

Now the word *symbol* scares a good many people off, just as the word *art* does. They seem to feel that a symbol is some mysterious thing put in arbitrarily by the writer to frighten the common reader—sort of a literary Masonic grip that is only for the initiated. They seem to think that it is a way of saying something that you aren't actually saying, and so if they can be got to read a reputedly symbolic work at all, they approach it as if it were a problem in algebra. Find *x*. And when they do find or think they find this abstraction, *x*, then they go off with an elaborate sense of satisfaction and the notion that they have "understood" the story. Many students confuse the *process* of understanding a thing with understanding it.

I think that for the fiction writer himself, symbols are something he uses simply as a matter of course. You might say that these are details that, while having their essential place in the literal level of the story, operate in depth as well as on the surface, increasing the story in every direction.

People have a habit of saying, "What is the theme of your story?" and they expect you to give them a statement: "The theme of my story

is the economic pressure of the machine on the middle class" — or some
such absurdity. And when they've got a statement like that, they go off
happy and feel it is no longer necessary to read the story.

Some people have the notion that you read the story and then climb
out of it into the meaning, but for the fiction writer himself the whole
story is the meaning, because it is an experience, not an abstraction.

from "Writing Short Stories"

Being short does not mean being slight. A short story should be long
in depth and should give us an experience of meaning.

Meaning is what keeps the short story from being short. I prefer
to talk about the meaning in a story rather than the theme of a story. People talk about the theme of a story as if the theme were like the string
that a sack of chicken feed is tied with. They think that if you can pick
out the theme, the way you pick the right thread in the chicken-feed sack,
you can rip the story open and feed the chickens. But this is not the way
meaning works in fiction.

When you can state the theme of a story, when you can separate
it from the story itself, then you can be sure the story is not a very good
one. The meaning of a story has to be embodied in it, has to be made
concrete in it. A story is a way to say something that can't be said any
other way, and it takes every word in the story to say what the meaning
is. You tell a story because a statement would be inadequate. When anybody
asks what a story is about, the only proper thing is to tell him to read
the story. The meaning of fiction is not abstract meaning but experienced
meaning, and the purpose of making statements about the meaning of a
story is only to help you to experience that meaning more fully.

"A Reasonable Use of the Unreasonable"

Last fall I received a letter from a student who said she would be "gra-
ciously appreciative" if I would tell her "just what enlightenment" I expected
her to get from each of my stories. I suspect she had a paper to write.
I wrote her back to forget about the enlightenment and just try to enjoy
them. I knew that was the most unsatisfactory answer I could have given
because, of course, she didn't want to enjoy them, she just wanted to figure
them out.

In most English classes the short story has become a kind of literary
specimen to be dissected. Every time a story of mine appears in a Fresh-
man anthology, I have a vision of it, with its little organs laid open, like
a frog in a bottle.

I realize that a certain amount of this what-is-the-significance has to go on, but I think something has gone wrong in the process when, for so many students, the story becomes simply a problem to be solved, something which you evaporate to get Instant Enlightenment.

A story really isn't any good unless it successfully resists paraphrase, unless it hangs on and expands in the mind. Properly, you analyze to enjoy, but it's equally true that to analyze with any discrimination, you have to have enjoyed already, and I think that the best reason to hear a story read is that it should stimulate that primary enjoyment.

I don't have any pretensions to being an Aeschylus or Sophocles and providing you in this story with a cathartic experience out of your mythic background, though this story I'm going to read certainly calls up a good deal of the South's mythic background, and it should elicit from you a degree of pity and terror, even though its way of being serious is a comic one. I do think, though, that like the Greeks you should know what is going to happen in this story so that any element of suspense in it will be transferred from its surface to its interior.

I would be most happy if you have already read it, happier still if you knew it well, but since experience has taught me to keep my expectations along these lines modest, I'll tell you that this is the story of a family of six which, on its way driving to Florida, gets wiped out by an escaped convict who calls himself the Misfit. The family is made up of the Grandmother and her son, Bailey, and his children, John Wesley and June Star and the baby, and there is also the cat and the children's mother. The cat is named Pitty Sing, and the Grandmother is taking him with them, hidden in a basket.

Now I think it behooves me to try to establish with you the basis on which reason operates in this story. Much of my fiction takes its character from a reasonable use of the unreasonable, though the reasonableness of my use of it may not always be apparent. The assumptions that underlie this use of it, however, are those of the central Christian mysteries. These are assumptions to which a large part of the modern audience takes exception. About this I can only say that there are perhaps other ways than my own in which this story could be read, but none other by which it could have been written. Belief, in my own case anyway, is the engine that makes perception operate.

The heroine of this story, the Grandmother, is in the most significant position life offers the Christian. She is facing death. And to all appearances she, like the rest of us, is not too well prepared for it. She would like to see the event postponed. Indefinitely.

I've talked to a number of teachers who use this story in class and who tell their students that the Grandmother is evil, that in fact, she's a witch, even down to the cat. One of these teachers told me that his students, and particularly his Southern students, resisted this interpretation with a certain bemused vigor, and he didn't understand why. I had to tell him that they resisted it because they all had grandmothers or great-aunts just like her at home, and they knew, from personal experience, that the old lady lacked comprehension, but that she had a good heart. The Southerner is usually tolerant of those weaknesses that proceed from innocence, and he knows that a taste for self-preservation can be readily combined with the missionary spirit.

This same teacher was telling his students that morally the Misfit was several cuts above the Grandmother. He had a really sentimental attachment to the Misfit. But then a prophet gone wrong is almost always more interesting than your grandmother, and you have to let people take their pleasures where they find them.

It is true that the old lady is a hypocritical old soul; her wits are no match for the Misfit's, nor is her capacity for grace equal to his; yet I think the unprejudiced reader will feel that the Grandmother has a special kind of triumph in this story which instinctively we do not allow to someone altogether bad.

I often ask myself what makes a story work, and what makes it hold up as a story, and I have decided that it is probably some action, some gesture of a character that is unlike any other in the story, one which indicates where the real heart of the story lies. This would have to be an action or a gesture which was both totally right and totally unexpected; it would have to be one that was both in character and beyond character; it would have to suggest both the world and eternity. The action or gesture I'm talking about would have to be on the anagogical level, that is, the level which has to do with the Divine life and our participation in it. It would be a gesture that transcended any neat allegory that might have been intended or any pat moral categories a reader could make. It would be a gesture which somehow made contact with mystery.

There is a point in this story where such a gesture occurs. The Grandmother is at last alone, facing the Misfit. Her head clears for an instant and she realizes, even in her limited way, that she is responsible for the man before her and joined to him by ties of kinship which have their roots deep in the mystery she has been merely prattling about so far. And at this point, she does the right thing, she makes the right gesture.

I find that students are often puzzled by what she says and does here, but I think myself that if I took out this gesture and what she says with it, I would have no story. What was left would not be worth your attention. Our age not only does not have a very sharp eye for the almost imperceptible intrusions of grace, it no longer has much feeling for the nature of the violences which precede and follow them. The devil's greatest wile, Baudelaire has said, is to convince us that he does not exist.

I suppose the reasons for the use of so much violence in modern fiction will differ with each writer who uses it, but in my own stories I have found that violence is strangely capable of returning my characters to reality and preparing them to accept their moment of grace. Their heads are so hard that almost nothing else will do the work. This idea, that reality is something to which we must be returned at considerable cost, is one which is seldom understood by the casual reader, but it is one which is implicit in the Christian view of the world.

I don't want to equate the Misfit with the devil. I prefer to think that, however unlikely this may seem, the old lady's gesture, like the mustard-seed, will grow to be a great crow-filled tree in the Misfit's heart, and will be enough of a pain to him there to turn him into the prophet he was meant to become. But that's another story.

This story has been called grotesque, but I prefer to call it literal. A good story is literal in the same sense that a child's drawing is literal. When a child draws, he doesn't intend to distort but to set down exactly what he sees, and as his gaze is direct, he sees the lines that create motion. Now the lines of motion that interest the writer are usually invisible. They are lines of spiritual motion. And in this story you should be on the lookout for such things as the action of grace in the Grandmother's soul, and not for the dead bodies.

We hear many complaints about the prevalance of violence in modern fiction, and it is always assumed that this violence is a bad thing and meant to be an end in itself. With the serious writer, violence is never an end in itself. It is the extreme situation that best reveals what we are essentially, and I believe these are times when writers are more interested in what we are essentially than in the tenor of our daily lives. Violence is a force which can be used for good or evil, and among other things taken by it is the kingdom of heaven. But regardless of what can be taken by it, the man in the violent situation reveals those qualities least dispensable in his personality, those qualities which are all he will have to take into eternity with him; and since the characters in this story are all on the verge of eternity, it is appropriate to think of what they take with them. In any case, I hope that if you consider these points in connection with the story, you will come to see it as something more than an account of a family murdered on the way to Florida.

[1957]

On Interpreting "A Good Man Is Hard to Find"

A professor of English had sent Flannery the following letter: "I am writing as spokesman for three members of our department and some ninety university students in three classes who for a week now have been discussing you story 'A Good Man Is Hard to Find.' We have debated at length several possible interpretations, none of which fully satisfies us. In general we believe that the appearance of the Misfit is not 'real' in the same sense that the incidents of the first half of the story are real. Bailey, we believe, imagines the appearance of the Misfit, whose activities have been called to his attention on the night before the trip and again during the stopover at the roadside restaurant. Bailey, we further believe, identifies himself with the Misfit and so plays two roles in the imaginary last half of the story. But we cannot, after great effort, determine the point at which reality fades into illusion or reverie. Does the accident literally occur, or is it a part of Bailey's dream? Please believe me when I say we are not seeking an easy way out of our difficulty. We admire your story and have examined it with great care, but we are convinced that we are missing something important which you intended for us to grasp. We will all be very grateful if you comment on the interpretation which I have outlined above and if you will give us further comments about your intention in writing 'A Good Man is Hard to Find.'"

She replied:

To a Professor of English

28 March 61

The interpretation of your ninety students and three teachers is fantastic and about as far from my intentions as it could get to be. If it were a legitimate interpretation, the story would be little more than a trick and its interest would be simply for abnormal psychology. I am not interested in abnormal psychology.

There is a change of tension from the first part of the story to the second where the Misfit enters, but this is no lessening of reality. This story is, of course, not meant to be realistic in the sense that it portrays the everyday doings of people in Georgia. It is stylized and its conventions are comic even though its meaning is serious.

Bailey's only importance is as the Grandmother's boy and the driver of the car. It is the Grandmother who first recognizes the Misfit and who is most concerned with him throughout. The story is a duel of sorts between the Grandmother and her superficial beliefs and the Misfit's more profoundly felt involvement with Christ's action which set the world off balance for him.

The meaning of a story should go on expanding for the reader the more he thinks about it, but meaning cannot be captured in an interpretation. If teachers are in the habit of approaching a story as if it were a research problem for which any answer is believable so long as it is not obvious, then I think students will never learn to enjoy fiction. Too much interpretation is certainly worse than too little and where feeling for a story is absent, theory will not supply it.

My tone is not meant to be obnoxious. I am in a state of shock.

8
A Collection of Short Fiction

The stories of Cain and Abel, Ruth, Samson, and Joseph in the Hebrew Bible and the parables of Jesus in the New Testament are sufficient evidence that brief narratives existed in ancient times. The short tales in Boccaccio's *Decameron* and Chaucer's *Canterbury Tales* (the latter an amazing variety of narrative poems ranging from bawdy stories to legends of saints) are medieval examples of the ancient form. But, speaking generally, short narratives before the nineteenth century were either didactic pieces, with the narrative existing for the sake of a moral point, or they were "curious and striking" tales (to use Somerset Maugham's words for his favorite kind of story) recounted in order to entertain.

The contemporary short story is rather different from both of these genres, which can be called the parable and the anecdote. Like the parable, the contemporary short story has a point, a meaning; but unlike the parable, it has a richness of surface as well as depth, so that it is interesting whether or not the reader goes on to ponder "the meaning." Like the ancecdote, the short story relates a happening, but whereas the happening in the anecdote is curious and is the center of interest, the happening in the contemporary story often is less interesting in itself than as a manifestation of a character's state of mind. A good short story usually has a psychological interest that an anecdote lacks.

The anecdotal story is what "story" means for most readers. It is an interesting happening or series of happenings, usually with a somewhat surprising ending. The anecdotal story, however, is quite different from most of the contemporary short stories in this book. The anecdote is good entertainment, and good entertainment should not be lightly dismissed. But it has two elements within it that prevent it (unless it is something in addition to an anecdote) from taking a high place among the world's literature. First, it cannot be reread with increasing or even continued pleasure. Even when it is well told, once we know the happening we may lose patience with the telling. Second, effective anecdotes are often highly implausible. Now, implausible anecdotes alleged to be true have a special impact by virtue of their alleged truth: they make us say to ourselves, "Truth is stranger than fiction." But the invented anecdote lacks this power; its unlikely coincidence, its unconvincing ironic situation, its surprise ending, are both untrue and unbelievable. It is entertaining but it is usually not especially meaningful.

The short story of the last hundred and fifty years is not an anecdote and is not an abbreviated novel. If it were the latter, *Reader's Digest* condensation of novels would be short stories. But they aren't; they are only eviscerated novels. Novelists usually cover a long period of time, presenting not only a few individuals but also something of a society. They often tell of the development of several many-sided figures. In contrast, short-story writers, having only a few pages, usually focus on a single figure episode, revealing a character rather than recording its developement.

Whereas the novel is narrative, the contemporary short story often seems less narrative than lyric or dramatic: in the short story we have a sense of a present mood or personality revealed, rather than the sense of a history reported. The revelation in a story is presented through incidents, of course, but the interest commonly resides in the character revealed through the incidents, rather than in the incidents themselves. Little "happens," in the sense that there is little rushing from place to place. What does "happen" is usually a mental reaction to an experience, and the mental reaction, rather than the external experience, is the heart of the story. In older narratives the plot usually involves a conflict that is resolved, bringing about a change in the protagonist's condition; in contemporary stories the plot usually is designed to reveal a protagonist's state of mind. This de-emphasis of overt actions results in an affinity with the lyric and the drama.

One way of looking at the matter is to distinguish between literature of *resolution* and literature of *revelation,* that is, between (1) literature that resolves a plot (literature that stimulates us to ask, "And what happened next?" and that finally leaves us with a settled state of affairs) and (2) literature that reveals a condition (literature that causes us to say, "Ah, now I understand how these people feel"). Two great writers of the later nineteenth century can be taken as representatives of the two kinds: Guy de Maupassant (1850–93) usually puts the emphasis on resolution, Anton Chekhov (1860–1904) usually on revelation. Maupassant's tightly plotted stories move to a decisive end, ordinarily marked by a great change in fortune (usually to the characters' disadvantage). Chekhov's stories, on the other hand, seem loosely plotted and may end with the characters pretty much in the condition they were in at the start, but *we* see them more clearly, even if *they* have not achieved any self-knowledge.

A slightly different way of putting the matter is this: much of the best short fiction from Chekhov onward is less concerned with *what happens* than it is with how a character (often the narrator) *feels* about the happenings. Thus the emphasis is not on external action but on inner action, feeling. Perhaps one can say that the reader is left with a mood rather than with an awareness of a decisive happening.

The distinction between a story of resolution and a story of revelation will probably be clear enough if you are familiar with stories by Maupassant and Chekhov, but of course the distinction should not be overemphasized. These are poles; most stories exist somewhere in between, closer to one pole or the other, but not utterly apart from the more remote pole. Consider again The Parable of the Prodigal Son, in Chapter 1. Insofar as the story stimulates responses such as "The son left, *and then what happened? Did he prosper?"*, it is a story of resolution. Insofar as it makes increasingly evident the unchanging love of the father, it is a story of revelation.

The de-emphasis on narrative in the contemporary short story is not an invention of the twentieth-century mind. It goes back at least to three important American writers of the early nineteenth century—Washington Irving, Nathaniel Hawthorne, and Edgar Allan Poe. In 1824 Irving wrote:

> I fancy much of what I value myself upon in writing, escapes the observation of the great mass of my readers: who are intent more upon the story than the way in which it is told. For my part I consider a story merely as a frame on which to stretch my materials. It is the play of thought, and sentiments and language; the weaving in of characters, lightly yet expressively delineated; the familiar and faithful exhibition of scenes in common life; and the half-concealed vein of humor that is often playing through the whole—these are among what I aim at, and upon which I felicitate myself in proportion as I think I succeed.

Hawthorne and Poe may seem stranger than Irving as forebears of the contemporary short story: both are known for their fantastic narratives (and, in addition, Poe is known as the inventor of the detective story, a genre in which there is strong interest in curious happenings). But because Hawthorne's fantastic narratives are, as he said, highly allegorical, the reader's interest is pushed beyond the narrative to the moral significance. Poe's "arabesques," as he called his fanciful tales (in distinction from his detective tales of "ratiocination"), are aimed at revealing and arousing unusual mental states. The weird happenings and personages are symbolic representations of the mind or soul. In "The Cask of Amontillado," for instance, perhaps the chief interest is not in what happens but rather in the representation of an almost universal fear of being buried alive. But, it must be noted, in both Hawthorne and Poe we usually get what is commonly called the tale rather than the short story: we get short prose fiction dealing with the strange rather than the usual. (The distinction between the wondrous and the ordinary is discussed at some length in Chapter 9, "Observations on the Novel," page 404.)

A paragraph from Poe's review (1842) of Hawthorne's *Twice Told Tales*, though more useful in revealing Poe's theory of fiction than Hawthorne's, illuminates something of the kinship between the contemporary short story and the best short fictions of the earlier nineteenth century. In the review Poe has been explaining that because "unity of effect or impression" is essential, a tale (Poe doubtless uses "tale" to mean short fiction in general, rather than the special type just discussed) that can be read at a single sitting has an advantage over the novel.

> A skillful artist has contructed a tale. He has not fashioned his thoughts to accommodate his incidents, but having deliberately conceived a certain single effect to be wrought, he then invents such incidents, he then combines such events, and discusses them in such tone as may best serve him in establishing this preconceived effect. If his very first sentence tends not to the outbringing of this effect, then in his very first step has he committed a blunder. In the whole composition there should be no word written of which the tendency, direct or indirect, is not to the one pre-established design. And by such means, with such care and skill a picture is at length painted which leaves in the mind of him who contemplates it with a kindred art, a sense of the fullest satisfaction. The idea of the tale, its thesis, has been presented unblemished, because undisturbed—an end absolutely demanded, yet, in the novel, altogether unattainable.

Nothing that has been said here should be construed as suggesting that short fiction from the mid-nineteenth century to the present is necessarily better than older short narratives.

The object of these comments has been less to evaluate than to call attention to the characteristics dominating short fiction of the last century and a half. It should not be thought, of course, that all of this fiction is of a piece; the stories in this book demonstrate something of its variety. Readers who do not like one need not despair; they need only (in the words of an early writer of great short fiction) "turne over the leef and chese another tale."

Edgar Allan Poe (American; 1809–49)

The Cask of Amontillado

The thousand injuries of Fortunato I had borne as I best could, but when he ventured upon insult, I vowed revenge. You, who so well know the nature of my soul, will not suppose, however, that I gave utterance to a threat. At *length* I would be avenged; this was a point definitely settled—

but the very definitiveness with which it was resolved precluded the idea of risk. I must not only punish, but punish with impunity. A wrong is unredressed when retribution overtakes its redresser. It is equally unredressed when the avenger fails to make himself felt as such to him who has done the wrong.

It must be understood that neither by word nor deed had I given Fortunato cause to doubt my good will. I continued, as was my wont, to smile in his face, and he did not perceive that my smile *now* was at the thought of his immolation.

He had a weak point—this Fortunato—although in other regards he was a man to be respected and even feared. He prided himself on his connoisseurship in wine. Few Italians have the true virtuoso spirit. For the most part their enthusiasm is adopted to suit the time and opportunity to practice imposture upon the British and Austrian *millionaires.* In painting and gemmary Fortunato, like his countrymen, was a quack, but in the matter of old wines he was sincere. In this respect I did not differ from him materially;—I was skillful in the Italian vintages myself, and bought largely whenever I could.

It was about dusk, one evening during the supreme madness of the carnival season, that I encountered my friend. He accosted me with excessive warmth, for he had been drinking much. The man wore motley. He had on a tight-fitting parti-striped dress, and his head was surmounted by the conical cap and bells. I was so pleased to see him, that I thought I should never have done wringing his hand.

I said to him—"My dear Fortunato, you are luckily met. How remarkably well you are looking to-day! But I have received a pipe[1] of what passes for Amontillado, and I have my doubts."

"How?" said he, "Amontillado? A pipe? Impossible! And in the middle of the carnival?"

"I have my doubts," I replied; "and I was silly enough to pay the full Amontillado price without consulting you in the matter. You were not to be found, and I was fearful of losing a bargain."

"Amontillado!"

"I have my doubts."

"Amontillado!"

"And I must satisfy them."

"Amontillado!"

"As you are engaged, I am on my way to Luchesi. If any one has a critical turn, it is he. He will tell me—"

"Luchesi cannot tell Amontillado from Sherry."

"And yet some fools will have it that his taste is a match for your own."

"Come, let us go."

[1]**pipe** wine cask

"Whither?"

"To your vaults."

"My friend, no; I will not impose upon your good nature. I perceive you have an engagement. Luchesi—"

"I have no engagement; come."

"My friend, no. It is not the engagement, but the severe cold with which I perceive you are afflicted. The vaults are insufferably damp. They are encrusted with nitre."

"Let us go, nevertheless. The cold is merely nothing. Amontillado! You have been imposed upon; and as for Luchesi, he cannot distinguish Sherry from Amontillado."

Thus speaking, Fortunato possessed himself of my arm. Putting on a mask of black silk, and drawing a *roquelaure*[2] closely about my person, I suffered him to hurry me to my palazzo.

There were no attendants at home; they had absconded to make merry in honor of the time. I had told them that I should not return until the morning, and had given them explicit orders not to stir from the house. These orders were sufficient, I well knew, to insure their immediate disappearance, one and all, as soon as my back was turned.

I took from their sconces two flambeaux, and giving one to Fortunato, bowed him through several suites of rooms to the archway that led into the vaults. I passed down a long and winding staircase, requesting him to be cautious as he followed. We came at length to the foot of the descent, and stood together on the damp ground of the catacombs of the Montresors.

The gait of my friend was unsteady, and the bells upon his cap jingled as he strode.

"The pipe," said he.

"It is farther on," said I; "but observe the white web-work which gleams from these cavern walls."

He turned towards me, and looked into my eyes with two filmy orbs that distilled the rheum of intoxication.

"Nitre?" he asked, at length.

"Nitre," I replied. "How long have you had that cough?"

"Ugh! ugh! ugh!—ugh! ugh! ugh!—ugh! ugh! ugh!—ugh! ugh! ugh!—ugh! ugh! ugh!"

My poor friend found it impossible to reply for many minutes.

"It is nothing," he said, at last.

"Come," I said, with decision, "we will go back; your health is precious. You are rich, respected, admired, beloved; you are happy, as once I was. You are a man to be missed. For me it is no matter. We will go back; you will be ill, and I cannot be responsible. Besides, there is Luchesi—"

[2]**roquelaure**   short cloak

"Enough," he said; "the cough is a mere nothing: it will not kill me. I shall not die of a cough."

"True—true," I replied; "and, indeed, I had no intention of alarming you unnecessarily—but you should use all proper caution. A draught of this Medoc will defend us from the damps."

Here I knocked off the neck of a bottle which I drew from a long row of its fellows that lay upon the mould.

"Drink," I said, presenting him the wine.

He raised it to his lips with a leer. He paused and nodded to me familiarly, while his bells jingled.

"I drink," he said, "to the buried that repose around us."

"And I to your long life."

He again took my arm, and we proceeded.

"These vaults," he said, "are extensive."

"The Montresors," I replied, "were a great and numerous family."

"I forget your arms."

"A huge human foot d'or, in a field azure; the foot crushes a serpent rampant whose fangs are imbedded in the heel."

"And the motto?"

"Nemo me impune lacessit."[3]

"Good!" he said.

The wine sparkled in his eyes and the bells jingled. My own fancy grew warm with the Medoc. We had passed through walls of piled bones, with casks and puncheons intermingling, into the inmost recesses of the catacombs. I paused again, and this time I made bold to seize Fortunato by an arm above the elbow.

"The nitre!" I said; "see, it increases. It hangs like moss upon the vaults. We are below the river's bed. The drops of moisture trickle among the bones. Come, we will go back ere it is too late. Your cough—"

"It is nothing," he said; "let us go on. But first, another draught of the Medoc."

I broke and reached him a flagon of De Grâve. He emptied it at a breath. His eyes flashed with a fierce light. He laughed and threw the bottle upwards with a gesticulation I did not understand.

I looked at him in surprise. He repeated the movement—a grotesque one.

"You do not comprehend?" he said.

"Not I," I replied.

"Then you are not of the brotherhood."

"How?"

"You are not of the masons."

"Yes, yes," I said, "yes, yes."

"You? Impossible! A mason?"

[3] **Nemo me impune lacessit**   No one dare attack me with impunity (the motto of Scotland)

"A mason," I replied.

"A sign," he said.

"It is this," I answered, producing a trowel from beneath the folds of my *roquelaure.*

"You jest," he exclaimed, recoiling a few paces. "But let us proceed to the Amontillado."

"Be it so," I said, replacing the tool beneath the cloak, and again offering him my arm. He leaned upon it heavily. We continued our route in search of the Amontillado. We passed through a range of low arches, descended, passed on, and descending again, arrived at a deep crypt, in which the foulness of the air caused our flambeaux rather to glow than flame.

At the most remote end of the crypt there appeared another less spacious. Its walls had been lined with human remains piled to the vault overhead, in the fashion of the great catacombs of Paris. Three sides of this interior crypt were still ornamented in this manner. From the fourth the bones had been thrown down, and lay promiscuously upon the earth, forming at one point a mound of some size. Within the wall thus exposed by the displacing of the bones, we perceived a still interior recess, in depth about four feet, in width three, in height six or seven. It seemed to have been constructed for no especial use within itself, but formed merely the interval between two of the colossal supports of the roof of the catacombs, and was backed by one of their circumscribing walls of solid granite.

It was in vain that Fortunato, uplifting his dull torch, endeavored to pry into the depths of the recess. Its termination the feeble light did not enable us to see.

"Proceed," I said; "herein is the Amontillado. As for Luchesi— "

"He is an ignoramus," interrupted my friend, as he stepped unsteadily forward, while I followed immediately at his heels. In an instant he had reached the extremity of the niche, and finding his progress arrested by the rock, stood stupidly bewildered. A moment more and I had fettered him to the granite. In its surface were two iron staples, distant from each other about two feet, horizontally. From one of these depended a short chain, from the other a padlock. Throwing the links about his waist, it was but the work of a few seconds to secure it. He was too much astounded to resist. Withdrawing the key I stepped back from the recess.

"Pass your hand," I said, "over the wall; you cannot help feeling the nitre. Indeed it is *very* damp. Once more let me *implore* you to return. No? Then I must positively leave you. But I must first render you all the little attentions in my power."

"The Amontillado!" ejaculated my friend, not yet recovered from his astonishment.

"True," I replied; "the Amontillado."

As I said these words I busied myself among the pile of bones of which I have before spoken. Throwing them aside, I soon uncovered a quantity of building-stone and mortar. With these materials and with the aid of my trowel, I began vigorously to wall up the entrance of the niche.

I had scarcely laid the first tier of masonry when I discovered that the intoxication of Fortunato had in a great measure worn off. The earliest indication I had of this was a low moaning cry from the depth of the recess. It was *not* the cry of a drunken man. There was then a long and obstinate silence. I laid the second tier, and the third, and the fourth; and then I heard the furious vibrations of the chain. The noise lasted for several minutes, during which, that I might hearken to it with the more satisfaction, I ceased my labors and sat down upon the bones. When at last the clanking subsided, I resumed the trowel, and finished without interruption the fifth, the sixth, and the seventh tier. The wall was now nearly upon a level with my breast. I again paused, and holding the flambeaux over the masonwork, threw a few feeble rays upon the figure within.

A succession of loud and shrill screams, bursting suddenly from the throat of the chained form, seemed to thrust me violently back. For a brief moment I hesitated—I trembled. Unsheathing my rapier, I began to grope with it about the recess; but the thought of an instant reassured me. I placed my hand upon the solid fabric of the catacombs, and felt satisfied. I reapproached the wall. I replied to the yells of him who clamored. I re-echoed—I aided—I surpassed them in volume and in strength. I did this, and the clamorer grew still.

It was now midnight, and my task was drawing to a close. I had completed the eighth, the ninth, and the tenth tier. I had finished a portion of the last and the eleventh; there remained but a single stone to be fitted and plastered in. I struggled with its weight; I placed it partially in its destined position. But now there came from out the niche a low laugh that erected the hairs upon my head. It was succeeded by a sad voice, which I had difficulty in recognizing as that of the noble Fortunato. The voice said—

"Ha! ha! ha!—he! he! he!—a very good joke indeed—an excellent jest. We will have many a rich laugh about it at the palazzo—he! he! he!—over our wine—he! he! he!"

"The Amontillado!" I said.

"He! he! he!—he! he! he!—yes, the Amontillado. But is it not getting late? Will not they be awaiting us at the palazzo, the Lady Fortunato and the rest? Let us be gone."

"Yes," I said, "let us be gone."

"For the love of God, Montresor!"

"Yes," I said, "for the love of God!"

But to these words I hearkened in vain for a reply. I grew impatient. I called aloud;

"Fortunato!"

No answer. I called again;

"Fortunato!"

No answer still, I thrust a torch through the remaining aperture and let it fall within. There came forth in return only a jingling of the bells. My heart grew sick—on account of the dampness of the catacombs. I hastened to make an end of my labor. I forced the last stone into its position; I plastered it up. Against the new masonry I reerected the old rampart of bones. For the half of a century no mortal has disturbed them. *In pace requiescat!*[4]

[1846]

Guy de Maupassant (French; 1850–93)

Mademoiselle

English version by Jane Saretta

He had been registered under the names of Jean Marie[1] Mathieu Valot, but he was never called anything but "Mademoiselle." He was the village simpleton, but not one of those wretched, ragged simpletons who live on public charity. He lived comfortably on a small income which his mother had left him, and which his guardian paid him regularly, and so he was rather envied than pitied. And then, he was not one of those idiots with wild looks and the manners of an animal, for he was by no means unattractive, with his half-open lips and smiling eyes, and especially in his constant make-up in female dress. For he dressed like a girl, and thus showed how little he objected to being called Mademoiselle.

And why should he not like the nickname which his mother had given him affectionately, when he was a mere child, so delicate and weak, and with a fair complexion—poor little diminutive lad not as tall as many girls of the same age? It was in pure love that, in his earlier years, his mother whispered that tender Mademoiselle to him, while his old grandmother used to say jokingly:

"The fact is, as for his male equipment, it's really not worth mentioning—no offense to God in saying so." And his grandfather, who was equally fond of a joke, used to add: "I only hope it won't disappear as he grows up."

And they treated him as if he had really been a girl and coddled him, the more so as they were very prosperous and did not have to worry about making ends meet.

---

[4] *In pace requiescat!* May he rest in peace!
[1] **Jean Marie** Although this name may strike American readers as a female name, in French it is unambiguously a male name.

When his mother and grandparents were dead, Mademoiselle was almost as happy with his paternal uncle, an unmarried man, who had carefully attended the simpleton and who had grown more and more attached to him by dint of looking after him; and the worthy man continued to call Jean Marie Mathieu Valot, Mademoiselle.

He was called so in all the country round as well, not with the slightest intention of hurting his feelings, but, on the contrary, because all thought they would please the poor gentle creature who harmed nobody by his behavior.

The very street boys meant no harm by it, accustomed as they were to call the tall idiot in a frock and cap by the nickname; but it would have struck them as very extraordinary, and would have led them to crude jokes, if they had seen him dressed like a boy.

Mademoiselle, however, took care of that, for his dress was as dear to him as his nickname. He delighted in wearing it, and, in fact, cared for nothing else, and what gave it a particular zest was that he knew that he was not a girl, and that he was living in disguise. And this was evident by the exaggerated feminine bearing and walk he put on; as if to show that it was not natural to him. His enormous, carefully arranged cap was adorned with large variegated ribbons. His petticoat, with numerous flounces, was distended behind by many hoops. He walked with short steps, and with exaggerated swaying of the hips, while his folded arms and crossed hands were distorted into pretensions of comical coquetry.

On such occasions, if anybody wished to make friends with him, it was necessary to say:

"Ah! Mademoiselle, what a nice girl you make."

That put him into a good humor, and he used to reply, much pleased:

"Don't I? But people can see I only do it for a joke."

But, nevertheless, when they were dancing at village festivals in the neighborhood, he would always be invited to dance as Mademoiselle, and would never ask any of the girls to dance with him; and one evening when somebody asked him the reason for this, he opened his eyes wide, laughed as if the man had said something stupid, and replied:

"I cannot ask the girls, because I am not dressed like a boy. Just look at my dress, you fool!"

As his interrogator was a judicious man, he said to him:

"Then dress like one, Mademoiselle."

He thought for a moment, and then said with a cunning look:

"But if I dress like a boy, I won't be a girl anymore; and then I am a girl," and he shrugged his shoulders as he said it.

But the remark seemed to make him think.

For some time afterward, when he met the same person, he would ask him abruptly:

"If I dress like a boy, will you still call me Mademoiselle?"

"Of course, I will," the other replied. "You will always be called so."

The simpleton appeared delighted, for there was no doubt that he thought more of his nickname than he did of his dress, and the next day he made his appearance in the village square, without his petticoats and dressed as a man. He had taken a pair of trousers, a coat, and a hat from his guardian's closet. This created quite a disturbance in the neighborhood, for the people who had been in the habit of smiling at him kindly when he was dressed as a woman, looked at him in astonishment and almost in fear, while the indulgent could not help laughing, and visibly making fun of him.

The involuntary hostility of some, and the too evident ridicule of others, the disagreeable surprise of all, were too palpable for him not to see it, and to be hurt by it, and it was still worse when a street urchin said to him in a jeering voice, as he danced round him:

"Oh! oh! Mademoiselle, you wear trousers! Oh! oh! Mademoiselle!"

And it grew worse and worse, when a whole band of these vagabonds were on his heels, hooting and yelling after him, as if he had been somebody in a masquerading dress during the Carnival.

It was quite certain that the unfortunate creature looked more in disguise now than he had formerly. By dint of living like a girl, and by even exaggerating the feminine walk and manners, he had totally lost all masculine looks and ways. His smooth face, his long flax-like hair, required a cap with ribbons, and became a caricature under the high stove-pipe hat of the old doctor, his grandfather.

Mademoiselle's shoulders, and especially her swelling stern, danced about wildly in this old-fashioned coat and wide trousers. And nothing was as funny as the contrast between his odd dress and delicate walk, the winning way he used his head, and the elegant movements of his hands, with which he fanned himself like a girl.

Soon the older lads and girls, the old women, men of ripe age and even the Judicial Councilor, joined the little brats, and hooted Mademoiselle, while the astonished fellow ran away, and rushed into the house with terror. There he put both hands to his poor head, and tried to comprehend the matter. Why were they angry with him? For it was quite evident that they were angry with him. What wrong had he done, and whom had he injured, by dressing as a boy? Was he not a boy, after all? For the first time in his life, he felt a horror for his nickname, for had he not been insulted through it? But immediately he was seized with a horrible doubt.

"Suppose that, after all, I am a girl?"

He wanted to ask his guardian about it but he was reluctant to do so, for he somehow felt, although only obscurely, that he, worthy man, might not tell him the truth, out of kindness. And, besides, he preferred to find out for himself, without asking anyone.

All his idiot's cunning, which had been lying latent up till then, because he never had any occasion to make use of it, now came out and urged him to a solitary and dark action.

The next day he dressed himself as a girl again, and made his appearance as if he had perfectly forgotton his escapade of the day before, but the people, especially the street boys, had not forgotten it. They looked at him sideways, and, even the best of them, could not help smiling, while the little blackguards ran after him and said:

"Oh! oh! Mademoiselle, you were wearing pants!"

But he pretended not to hear, or even to guess what they were alluding to. He seemed as happy and glad to look about him as he usually did, with half-open lips and smiling eyes. As usual, he wore an enormous cap with vareigated ribbons, and the same large petticoats; he walked with short, mincing steps, swaying and wriggling his hips and gesticulating like a coquette, and licked his lips when they called him Mademoiselle, while really he would have liked to have jumped at the throats of those who called him so.

Days and months passed, and by degrees people forgot all about his strange escapade. But he had never left off thinking about it, or trying to find out—for which he was always on the alert—how he could ascertain his qualities as a boy, and how to assert them victoriously. Really innocent, he had reached the age of twenty without knowing anything or without ever having any natural impulse, but being tenacious of purpose, curious and dissembling, he asked no questions, but observed all that was said and done.

Often at their village dances, he had heard young fellows boasting about girls whom they had seduced, and girls praising such and such a young fellow, and, often, also, after a dance, he saw the couples go away together, with their arms round each other's waists. They paid no attention to him, and he listened and watched, until, at last, he discovered what was going on.

And then, one night, when dancing was over, and the couples were going away with their arms round each other's waists, a terrible screaming was heard at the corner of the woods through which those going to the next village had to pass. It was Josephine, pretty Josephine, and when her screams were heard, they ran to her assistance, and arrived only just in time to rescue her, half strangled, from Mademoiselle's clutches.

The idiot had watched her and had thrown himself upon her in order to treat her as the other young fellows did the girls, but she resisted him so stoutly that he took her by the throat and squeezed it with all his might until she could not breathe, and was nearly dead.

In rescuing Josephine from him, they had thrown him on the ground, but he jumped up again immediately, foaming at the mouth and slobbering, and exclaimed:

"I am not a girl any longer, I am a young man, I am a young man, I tell you."

Anton Chekhov (Russian; 1860–1904)

Enemies

Between nine and ten on a dark September evening the only son of the district doctor, Kirilov, a child of six, called Andrey, died of diphtheria. Just as the doctor's wife sank on her knees by the dead child's bedside and was overwhelmed by the first rush of despair there came a sharp ring at the bell in the entry.

All the servants had been sent out of the house that morning on account of the diphtheria. Kirilov went to open the door just as he was, without his coat on, with his waistcoat unbuttoned, without wiping his wet face or his hands which were scalded with carbolic. It was dark in the entry and nothing could be distinguished in the man who came in but medium height, a white scarf, and a large, extremely pale face, so pale as its entrance seemed the make the passage lighter.

"Is the doctor at home?" the newcomer asked quickly.

"I am at home," answered Kirilov. "What do you want?"

"Oh, it's you? I am very glad," said the stranger in a tone of relief, and he began feeling in the dark for the doctor's hand, found it and squeezed it tightly in his own. "I am very . . . very glad! We are acquainted. My name is Abogin, and I had the honour of meeting you in the summer at Gnutchev's. I am very glad I have found you at home. . . . For God's sake don't refuse to come back with me at once. . . . My wife has been taken dangerously ill. . . . And the carriage is waiting. . . ."

From the voice and gestures of the speaker it could be seen that he was in a state of great excitement. Like a man terrified by a house on fire or a mad dog, he could hardly restrain his rapid breathing and spoke quickly in a shaking voice, and there was a note of sincerity and childish alarm in his voice. As people always do who are frightened and overwhelmed, he spoke in brief, jerky sentences and uttered a great many unnecessary, irrelevant words.

"I was afraid I might not find you in," he went on. "I was in a perfect agony as I drove here. Put on your things and let us go, for God's sake . . . . This is how it happened. Alexandr Semyonovitch Paptchinsky, whom you know, came to see me. . . . We talked a little then we sat down to tea; suddenly my wife cried out, clutched at her heart, and fell back on her chair. We carried her to bed and . . . and I rubbed her forehead with ammonia and sprinkled her with water . . . she lay as though she were dead . . . I am afraid it is aneurism. . . . Come along . . . her father died of aneurism."

Kirilov listened and said nothing, as though he did not understand Russian.

When Abogin mentioned again Paptchinsky and his wife's father and once more began feeling in the dark for his hand the doctor shook his head and said apathetically, dragging out each word:

"Excuse me, I cannot come . . . my son died . . . five minutes ago!"

"Is it possible!" whispered Abogin, stepping back a pace. "My God, at what an unlucky moment I have come! A wonderfully unhappy day . . . wonderfully. What a coincidence. . . . It's as though it was on purpose!"

Abogin took hold of the door-handle and bowed his head. He was evidently hesitating and did not know what to do—whether to go away or to continue entreating the doctor.

"Listen," he said fervently, catching hold of Kirilov's sleeve. "I well understand your position! God is my witness that I am ashamed of attempting at such a moment to intrude on your attention, but what am I to do? Only think, to whom can I go? There is no other doctor here, you know. For God's sake come! I am not asking you for myself. . . . I am not the patient!"

A silence followed. Kirilov turned his back on Abogin, stood still a moment, and slowly walked into the drawing-room. Judging from his unsteady, mechanical step, from the attention with which he set straight the fluffy shade on the unlighted lamp in the drawing-room and glanced into a thick book lying on the table, at that instant he had no intention, no desire, was thinking of nothing and most likely did not remember that there was a stranger in the entry. The twilight and stillness of the drawing-room seemed to increase his numbness. Going out of the drawing-room into his study he raised his right foot higher than was necessary, and felt for the doorposts with his hands, and as he did so there was an air of perplexity about his whole figure as though he were in somebody else's house, or were drunk for the first time in this life and were now abandoning himself with surprise to the new sensation. A broad streak of light stretched across the bookcase on one wall of the study; this light came together with the close, heavy smell of carbolic and ether from the door into the bedroom, which stood a little way open. . . . The doctor sank into a low chair in front of the table; for a minute he stared drowsily at his books, which lay with the light on them, then got up and went into the bedroom.

Here in the bedroom reigned a dead silence. Everything to the smallest detail was eloquent of the storm that had been passed through, of exhaustion, and everything was at rest. A candle standing among a crowd of bottles, boxes, and pots on a stool and a big lamp on the chest of drawers threw a brilliant light over all the room. On the bed under the window lay a boy with open eyes and a look of wonder on his face. He did not move, but his open eyes seemed every moment growing darker and sinking further into his head. The mother was kneeling by the bed with her arms on his body and her head hidden in the bedclothes. Like the child, she did not stir; but what throbbing life was suggested in the curves of her body and in her arms! She leaned against the bed with all her being, pressing against it greedily with all her might, as though she were afraid of disturbing the peaceful and comfortable attitude she had found at last for her exhausted body. The bedclothes, the rags and bowls, the splashes of water on the floor, the little paint-brushes and spoons thrown down here and there, the white bottle of lime water, the very air, heavy and stifling—were all hushed and seemed plunged in repose.

The doctor stopped close to his wife, thrust his hands in his trouser pockets, and slanting his head on one side fixed his eyes on his son. His face bore an expression of indifference, and only from the drops that glittered on his beard it could be seen that he had just been crying.

That repellent horror which is thought of when we speak of death was absent from the room. In the numbness of everything, in the mother's attitude, in the indifference on the doctor's face there was something that attracted and touched the heart, that subtle, almost elusive beauty of human sorrow which men will not for a long time learn to understand and describe, and which it seems only music can convey. There was a feeling of beauty, too, in the austere stillness. Kirilov and his wife were silent and not weeping, as though besides the bitterness of their loss they were conscious, too, of all the tragedy of their position; just as once their youth had passed away, so now together with this boy their right to have children had gone for ever to all eternity! The doctor was forty-four, his hair was grey and he looked like an old man; his faded and invalid wife was thirty-five. Andrey was not merely the only child, but the last child.

In contrast to his wife the doctor belonged to the class of people who at times of spiritual suffering feel a craving for movement. After standing for five minutes by his wife, he walked, raising his right foot high, from the bedroom into the little room which was half filled up by a big sofa; from there he went into the kitchen. After wandering by the stove and the cook's bed he bent down and went by a little door into the passage.

There he saw again the white scarf and the white face.

"At last," sighed Abogin, reaching towards the door-handle. "Let us go, please."

The doctor started, glanced at him, and remembered. . . .

"Why, I have told you already that I can't go!" he said, growing more animated. "How strange!"

"Doctor, I am not a stone, I fully understand your position . . . I feel for you," Abogin said in an imploring voice, laying his hand on his scarf. "But I am not asking you for myself. My wife is dying. If you had heard that cry, if you had seen her face, you would understand my pertinacity. My God, I thought you had gone to get ready! Doctor, time is precious. Let us go, I entreat you."

"I cannot go," said Kirilov emphatically, and he took a step into the drawing-room.

Abogin followed him and caught hold of his sleeve.

"You are in sorrow, I understand. But I'm not asking you to a case of toothache, or to a consultation, but to save a human life!" he went on entreating like a beggar. "Life comes before any personal sorrow! Come, I ask for courage, for heroism! For the love of humanity!"

"Humanity—that cuts both ways," Kirilov said irritably. "In the name of humanity I beg you not to take me. And how queer it is, really! I can hardly stand and you talk to me about humanity! I am fit for nothing just now. . . . Nothing will induce me to go, and I can't leave my wife alone. No, no. . . ."

Kirilov waved his hands and staggered back.

"And . . . and don't ask me," he went on in a tone of alarm. "Excuse me. By No. XIII of the regulations I am obliged to go and you have the right to drag me by my collar . . . drag me if you like, but . . . I am not fit . . . I can't even speak . . . excuse me."

"There is no need to take that tone to me, doctor!" said Abogin, again taking the doctor by his sleeve. "What do I care about No. XIII! To force you against your will I have no right whatever. If you will, come; if you will not—God forgive you; but I am not appealing to your will, but to your feelings. A young woman is dying. You were just speaking of the death of your son. Who should understand my horror if not you?"

Abogin's voice quivered with emotion; that quiver and his tone were far more persuasive than his words. Abogin was sincere, but it was remarkable that whatever he said his words sounded stilted, soulless, and inappropriately flowery, and even seeemed an outrage on the atmosphere of the doctor's home and on the woman who was somewhere dying. He felt this himself, and so, afraid of not being understood, did his utmost to put softness and tenderness into his voice so that the sincerity of his tone might prevail if his words did not. As a rule, however fine and deep a phrase may be, it only affects the indifferent, and cannot fully satisfy those who are happy or unhappy; that is why dumbness is most often the highest expression of happiness or unhappiness; lovers understand each other better when they are silent, and a fervent, passionate speech delivered by the grave only touches outsiders, while to the widow and children of the dead man it seems cold and trivial.

Kirilov stood in silence. When Abogin uttered a few more phrases concerning the noble calling of a doctor, self-sacrifice, and so on, the doctor asked sullenly: "Is it far?"

"Something like eight or nine miles. I have capital horses, doctor! I give you my word of honour that I will get you there and back in an hour. Only one hour."

These words had more effect on Kirilov than the appeals to humanity or the noble calling of the doctor. He thought a moment and said with a sigh: "Very well, let us go!"

He went rapidly with a more certain step to his study, and afterwards came back in a long frock-coat. Abogin, greatly relieved, fidgeted round him and scraped with his feet as he helped him on with his overcoat, and went out of the house with him.

It was dark out of doors, though lighter than in the entry. The tall, stooping figure of the doctor, with his long, narrow beard and aquiline nose, stood out distinctly in the darkness. Abogin's big head and the little student's cap that barely covered it could be seen now as well as his pale face. The scarf showed white only in front, behind it was hidden by his long hair.

"Believe me, I know how to appreciate your generosity," Abogin muttered as he helped the doctor into the carriage. "We shall get there quickly. Drive as fast as you can, Luka, there's a good fellow! Please!"

The coachman drove rapidly. At first there was a row of indistinct buildings that stretched alongside the hospital yard; it was dark everywhere except for a bright light from a window that gleamed through the fence into the furthest part of the yard while three windows of the upper storey of the hospital looked paler than the surrounding air. Then the carriage drove into dense shadow; here there was the smell of dampness and mushrooms, and the sound of rustling trees; the crows, awakened by the noise of the wheels, stirred among the foliage and uttered prolonged plaintive cries as though they knew the doctor's son was dead and that Abogin's wife was ill. Then came glimpses of separate trees, of bushes; a pond, on which great black shadows were slumbering, gleamed with a sullen light—and the carriage rolled over a smooth level ground. The clamour of the crows sounded dimly far away and soon ceased altogether.

Kirilov and Abogin were silent almost all the way. Only once Abogin heaved a deep sigh and muttered:

"It's an agonizing state! One never loves those who are near one so much as when one is in danger of losing them."

And when the carriage slowly drove over the river, Kirilov started all at once as though the splash of the water had frightened him, and made a movement.

"Listen—let me go," he said miserably. "I'll come to you later. I must just send my assistant to my wife. She is alone, you know!"

Abogin did not speak. The carriage swaying from side to side and crunching over the stones drove up the sandy bank and rolled on its way. Kirilov moved restlessly and looked about him in misery. Behind them in the dim light of the stars the road could be seen and the riverside willows vanishing into the darkness. On the right lay a plain as uniform and as boundless as the sky; here and there in the distance, probably on the peat marshes, dim lights were glimmering. On the left, parallel with the

road, ran a hill tufted with small bushes, and above the hill stood motionless a big, red half-moon, slightly veiled with mist and encircled by tiny
clouds, which seemed to be looking round at it from all sides and watching that it did not go away.

In all nature there seemed to be a feeling of hopelessness and pain.
The earth, like a ruined woman sitting alone in the dark room and trying
not to think of the past, was brooding over memories of spring and summer and apathetically waiting for the inevitable winter. Wherever one
looked, on all sides, nature seemed like a dark, infinitely deep, cold pit
from which neither Kirilov nor Abogin nor the red half-moon could
escape. . . .

The nearer the carriage got to its goal the more impatient Abogin
became. He kept moving, leaping up, looking over the coachman's shoulder.
And when at last the carriage stopped before the entrance, which was elegantly curtained with stiped linen, and when he looked at the lighted windows of the second storey there was an audible catch in his breath.

"If anything happens . . . I shall not survive it," he said, going into
the hall with the doctor, and rubbing his hands in agitation. "But there
is no commotion, so everything must be going well, so far," he added,
listening in the stillness.

There was no sound in the hall of steps or voices and all the house
seemed asleep in spite of the lighted windows. Now the doctor and Abogin, who till then had been in darkness, could see each other clearly. The
doctor was tall and stooped, was untidily dressed and not good-looking.
There was an unpleasantly harsh, morose, and unfriendly look about his
lips, thick as a negro's, his aquiline nose, and listless, apathetic eyes. His
unkempt head and sunken temples, the premature greyness of his long,
narrow beard through which his chin was visible, the pale grey hue of
his skin and his careless, uncouth manners — the harshness of all this was
suggestive of years of poverty, of ill fortune, of weariness with life and
with men. Looking at his frigid figure one could hardly believe that this
man had a wife, that he was capable of weeping over his child. Abogin
presented a very different appearance. He was a thick-set, sturdy-looking,
fair man with a big head and large, soft features; he was elegantly dressed
in the very latest fashion. In his carriage, his closely buttoned coat, his
long hair, and his face there was a suggestion of something generous, leo-
nine; he walked with his head erect and his chest squared, he spoke in
an agreeable baritone, and there was a shade of refined almost feminine
elegance in the manner in which he took off his scarf and smoothed his
hair. Even his paleness and the childlike terror with which he looked up
at the stairs as he took off his coat did not detract from his dignity nor
diminish the air of sleekness, health, and aplomb which characterized his
whole figure.

"There is nobody and no sound," he said going up the stairs. "There
is no commotion. God grant all is well."

He led the doctor through the hall into a big drawing-room where there was a black piano and a chandelier in a white cover; from there they both went into a very snug, pretty little drawing-room full of agreeable, rosy twilight.

"Well, sit down here, doctor, and I . . . will be back directly. I will go and have a look and prepare them."

Kirilov was left alone. The luxury of the drawing-room, the agreeably subdued light and his own presence in the stanger's unfamiliar house, which had something of the character of an adventure, did not apparently affect him. He sat in a low chair and scrutinized his hands, which were burnt with carbolic. He only caught a passing glimpse of the bright red lamp-shade and the violoncello case, and glancing in the direction where the clock was ticking he noticed a stuffed wolf as substantial and sleek-looking as Abogin himself.

It was quiet. . . . Somewhere far away in the adjoining rooms someone uttered a loud exclamation:

"Ah!" There was a clang of a glass door, probably of a cupboard, and again all was still. After waiting five minutes Kirilov left off scrutinizing his hands and raised his eyes to the door by which Abogin had vanished.

In the doorway stood Abogin, but he was not the same as when he had gone out. The look of sleekness and refined elegance had disappeared—his face, his hands, his attitude were contorted by a revolting expression of something between horror and agonizing physical pain. His nose, his lips, his moustache, all his features were moving and seemed trying to tear themselves from his face, his eyes looked as though they were laughing with agony. . . .

Abogin took a heavy stride into the drawing-room, bent forward, moaned, and shook his fists.

"She has deceived me," he cried, with a strong emphasis on the second syllable of the verb. "Deceived me, gone away. She fell ill and sent me for the doctor only to run away with that clown Paptchinsky! My God!"

Abogin took a heavy step towards the doctor, held out his soft white fists in his face, and shaking them went on yelling:

"Gone away! Deceived me! But why this deception? My God! My God! What need of this dirty, scoundrelly trick, this diabolical, snakish farce? What have I done to her? Gone away!"

Tears gushed from his eyes. He turned on one foot and began pacing up and down the drawing-room. Now in his short coat, his fashionable narrow trousers which made his legs look disproportionately slim, with his big head and long mane he was extremely like a lion. A gleam of curiosity came into the apathetic face of the doctor. He got up and looked at Abogin.

"Excuse me, where is the patient?" he said.

"The patient! The patient!" cried Abogin, laughing, crying, and still brandishing his fists. "She is not ill, but accursed! The baseness! The vileness!

The devil himself could not have imagined anything more loathsome! She sent me off that she might run away with a buffoon, a dull-witted clown, an Alphonse! Oh God, better she had died! I cannot bear it! I cannot bear it!"

The doctor drew himself up. His eyes blinked and filled with tears, his narrow beard began moving to right and to left together with his jaw.

"Allow me to ask what's the meaning of this?" he asked, looking round him with curiosity. "My child is dead, my wife is in grief alone in the whole house. . . . I myself can scarcely stand up, I have not slept for three nights. . . . And here I am forced to play a part in some vulgar farce, to play the part of a stage property! I don't . . . don't understand it."

Abogin unclenched one fist, flung a crumpled note on the floor, and stamped on it as though it were an insect he wanted to crush.

"And I didn't see, didn't understand," he said through clenched teeth, brandishing one fist before his face with an expression as though some one had trodden on his corns. "I did not notice that he came every day! I did not notice that he came today in a closed carriage! What did he come in a closed carriage for? And I did not see it! Noodle!"

I don't understand . . ." muttered the doctor. "Why, what's the meaning of it? Why, it's an outrage on personal dignity, a mockery of human suffering! It's incredible. . . . It's the first time in my life I have had such an experience!"

With the dull surprise of a man who has only just realized that he has been bitterly insulted the doctor shrugged his shoulders, flung wide his arms, and not knowing what to do or to say sank helplessly into a chair.

"If you have ceased to love me and love another — so be it; but why this deceit, why this vulgar, treacherous trick?" Abogin said in a tearful voice. "What is the object of it? And what is there to justify it? And what have I done to you? Listen, doctor," he said hotly, going up to Kirilov. "You have been the involuntary witness of my misfortune and I am not going to conceal the truth from you. I swear that I loved the woman, loved her devotedly, like a slave! I have sacrificed everything for her; I have quarrelled with my own people, I have given up the service and music, I have forgiven her what I could not have forgiven my own mother or sister. . . . I have never looked askance at her. . . . I have never gainsaid her in anything. Why this deception? I do not demand love, but why this loathsome duplicity? If she did not love me, why did she not say so openly, honestly, especially as she knows my views on the subject? . . ."

With tears in his eyes, trembling all over, Abogin opened his heart to the doctor with perfect sincerity. He spoke warmly, pressing both hands on his heart, exposing the secrets of his private life without the faintest hesitation, and even seemed to be glad that at last these secrets were no longer pent up in his breast. If he had talked in this way for an hour or two, and opened his heart, he would undoubtedly have felt better. Who knows, if the doctor had listened to him and had sympathized with him like a friend, he might perhaps, as often happens, have reconciled himself to his trouble without protest, without doing anything needless and absurd. . . . But what happened was quite different. While Abogin was speaking the outraged doctor perceptibly changed. The indifference and wonder on his face gradually gave way to an expression of bitter resentment, indignation, and anger. The features of his face became even harsher, coarser, and more unpleasant. When Abogin held out before his eyes the photograph of a young woman with a handsome face as cold and expressionless as a nun's and asked him whether, looking at that face, one could conceive that it was capable of duplicity, the doctor suddenly flew out, and with flashing eyes said, rudely rapping out each word:

"What are you telling me all this for? I have no desire to hear it! I have no desire to!" he shouted and brought his fist down on the table. "I don't want your vulgar secrets! Damnation take them! Don't dare to tell me of such vulgar doings! Do you consider that I have not been insulted enough already? That I am a flunkey whom you can insult without restraint? Is that it?"

Abogin staggered back from Kirilov and stared at him in amazement.

"Why did you bring me here?" the doctor went on, his beard quivering. "If you are so puffed up with good living that you go and get married and then act a farce like this, how do I come in? What have I to do with your love affairs? Leave me in peace! Go on squeezing money out of the poor in your gentlemanly way. Make a display of humane ideas, play (the doctor looked sideways at the violoncello case) play the bassoon and the trombone, grow as fat as capons, but don't dare to insult personal dignity! If you cannot respect it, you might at least spare it your attention!"

"Excuse me, what does all this mean?" Abogin asked, flushing red.

"It means that it's base and low to play with people like this! I am a doctor; you look upon doctors and people generally who work and don't stink of perfume and prostitution as your menials and *mauvais ton*[1]; well, you may look upon them so, but no one has given you the right to treat a man who is suffering as a stage property!"

"How dare you say that to me!" Abogin said quietly, and his face began working again, and this time unmistakably from anger.

"No, how dared you, knowing of my sorrow, bring me here to listen to these vulgarities!" shouted the doctor, and he again banged on the table with his fist. "Who has given you the right to make a mockery of another man's sorrow?"

"You have taken leave of your senses," shouted Abogin. "It is ungenerous. I am intensely unhappy myself and . . . and . . ."

---

[1] *mauvais ton*   a crude lot

"Unhappy!" said the doctor, with a smile of contempt. "Don't utter that word, it does not concern you. The spendthrift who cannot raise a loan calls himself unhappy, too. The capon, sluggish from over-feeding, is unhappy, too. Worthless people!"

"Sir, you forget yourself," shrieked Abogin. "For saying things like that . . . people are thrashed! Do you understand?"

Abogin hurriedly felt in his side pocket, pulled out a pocket-book, and extracting two notes flung them on the table.

"Here is the fee for your visit," he said, his nostrils dilating. "You are paid."

"How dare you offer me money?" shouted the doctor and he brushed the notes off the table onto the floor. "An insult cannot be paid for in money!"

Abogin and the doctor stood face to face, and in their wrath continued flinging undeserved insults at each other. I believe that never in their lives, even in delirium, had they uttered so much that was unjust, cruel, and absurd. The egoism of the unhappy was conspicuous in both. The unhappy are egoistic, spiteful, unjust, cruel, and less capable of understanding each other than fools. Unhappiness does not bring people together but draws them apart, and even where one would fancy people should be united by the similarity of their sorrow, far more injustice and cruelty is generated than in comparatively placid surroundings.

"Kindly let me go home!" shouted the doctor, breathing hard.

Abogin rang the bell sharply. When no one came to answer the bell he rang again and angrily flung the bell on the floor; it fell on the carpet with a muffled sound, and uttered a plaintive note as though at the point of death. A footman came in.

"Where have you been hiding yourself, the devil take you?" His master flew at him, clenching his fists. "Where were you just now? Go and tell them to bring the victoria round for this gentleman, and order the closed carriage to be got ready for me. Stay," he cried as the footman turned to go out. "I won't have a single traitor in the house by to-morrow! Away with you all! I will engage fresh servants! Reptiles!"

Abogin and the doctor remained in silence waiting for the carriage. The first regained his expression of sleekness and his refined elegance. He paced up and down the room, tossed his head elegantly, and was evidently meditating on something. His anger had not cooled, but he tried to appear not to notice his enemy . . . .The doctor stood, leaning with one hand on the edge of the table, and looked at Abogin with that profound and somewhat cynical, ugly contempt only to be found in the eyes of sorrow and indigence when they are confronted with well-nourished comfort and elegance.

When a little later the doctor got into the victoria and drove off there was still a look of contempt in his eyes. It was dark, much darker than it had been an hour before. The red half-moon had sunk behind the hill and the clouds that had been guarding it lay in dark patches near the stars. The carriage with red lamps rattled along the road and soon overtook the doctor. It was Abogin driving off to protest, to do absurd things. . . .

All the way home the doctor thought not of his wife, nor of his Andrey, but of Abogin and the people in the house he had just left. His thoughts were unjust and inhumanly cruel. He condemned Abogin and his wife and Paptchinsky and all who lived in rosy, subdued light among sweet perfumes, and all the way home he hated and despised them till his head ached. And a firm conviction concerning those people took shape in his mind.

Time will pass and Kirilov's sorrow will pass, but that conviction, unjust and unworthy of the human heart, will not pass, but will remain in the doctor's mind to the grave.

[1887]

Charlotte Perkins Gilman (American; 1860–1935)

The Yellow Wallpaper

It is very seldom that mere ordinary people like John and myself secure ancestral halls for the summer.

A colonial mansion, a hereditary estate, I would say a haunted house, and reach the height of romantic felicity—but that would be asking too much of fate!

Still I will proudly declare that there is something queer about it.

Else, why should it be let so cheaply? And why have stood so long untenanted?

John laughs at me, of course, but one expects that in marriage.

John is practical in the extreme. He has no patience with faith, an intense horror of superstition, and he scoffs openly at any talk of things not to be felt and seen and put down in figures.

John is a physician, and *perhaps*—(I would not say it to a living soul, of course, but this is dead paper and a great relief to my mind)—*perhaps* that is one reason I do not get well faster.

You see he does not believe I am sick!

And what can one do?

If a physician of high standing, and one's own husband, assures friends and relatives that there is really nothing the matter with one but temporary nervous depression—a slight hysterical tendency—what is one to do?

My brother is also a physician, and also of high standing, and he says the same thing.

So I take phosphates or phosphites—whichever it is, and tonics, and journeys, and air, and exercise, and am absolutely forbidden to "work" until I am well again.

Personally, I disagree with their ideas.

Personally, I believe that congenial work, with excitement and change, would do me good.

But what is one to do?

I did write for a while in spite of them; but it *does* exhaust me a good deal—having to be so sly about it, or else meet with heavy opposition.

I sometimes fancy that in my condition if I had less opposition and more society and stimulus—but John says the very worst thing I can do is to think about my condition, and I confess it always makes me feel bad.

So I will let it alone and talk about the house.

The most beautiful place! It is quite alone, standing well back from the road, quite three miles from the village. It makes me think of English places that you read about, for there are hedges and walls and gates that lock, and lots of separate little houses for the gardeners and people.

There is a *delicious* garden! I never saw such a garden—large and shady, full of box-bordered paths, and lined with long grapecovered arbors with seats under them.

There were greenhouses, too, but they are all broken now. There was some legal trouble, I believe, something about the heirs and coheirs; anyhow, the place has been empty for years.

That spoils my ghostliness, I am afraid, but I don't care—there is something strange about the house—I can feel it.

I even said so to John one moonlight evening, but he said what I felt was a *draught,* and shut the window.

I get unreasonably angry with John sometimes. I'm sure I never used to be so sensitive. I think it is due to this nervous condition.

But John says if I feel so, I shall neglect proper self-control; so I take pains to control myself—before him, at least, and that makes me very tired.

I don't like our room a bit. I wanted one downstairs that opened on the piazza and had roses all over the window, and such pretty old-fashioned chintz hangings! but John would not hear of it.

He said there was only one window and not room for two beds, and no near room for him if he took another.

He is very careful and loving, and hardly lets me stir without special direction.

I have a schedule prescription for each hour in the day; he takes all care from me, and so I feel basely ungrateful not to value it more.

He said we came here solely on my account, that I was to have perfect rest and all the air I could get. "Your exercise depends on your strength, my dear," said he, "and your food somewhat on your appetite; but air you can absorb all the time." So we took the nursery at the top of the house.

It is a big, airy room, the whole floor nearly, with windows that look all ways, and air and sunshine galore. It was nursery first and then playroom and gymnasium, I should judge; for the windows are barred for little children, and there are rings and things in the walls.

The paint and paper look as if a boys' school had used it. It is stripped off—the paper—in great patches all around the head of my bed, about as far as I can reach, and in a great place on the other side of the room low down. I never saw a worse paper in my life.

One of those sprawling flamboyant patterns committing every artistic sin.

It is dull enough to confuse the eye in following, pronounced enough to constantly irritate and provoke study, and when you follow the lame uncertain curves for a little distance they suddenly commit suicide—plunge off at outrageous angles, destroy themselves in unheard of contradictions.

The color is repellent, almost revolting; a smouldering unclean yellow, strangely faded by the slow-turning sunlight.

It is a dull yet lurid orange in some places, a sickly sulphur tint in others.

No wonder the children hated it! I should hate it myself if I had to live in this room long.

There comes John, and I must put this away,—he hates to have me write a word.

We have been here two weeks, and I haven't felt like writing before, since that first day.

I am sitting by the window now, up in this atrocious nursery, and there is nothing to hinder my writing as much as I please, save lack of strength.

John is away all day, and even some nights when his cases are serious.

I am glad my case is not serious!

But these nervous troubles are dreadfully depressing.

John does not know how much I really suffer. He knows there is no *reason* to suffer, and that satisfies him.

Of course it is only nervousness. It does weigh on me so not to do my duty in any way!

I meant to be such a help to John, such a real rest and comfort, and here I am a comparative burden already!

Nobody would believe what an effort it is to do what little I am able,—to dress and entertain, and order things.

It is fortunate Mary is so good with the baby. Such a dear baby!

And yet I *cannot* be with him, it makes me so nervous.

I suppose John never was nervous in his life. He laughs at me so about this wallpaper!

At first he meant to repaper the room, but afterwards he said that I was letting it get the better of me, and that nothing was worse for a nervous patient than to give way to such fancies.

He said that after the wallpaper was changed it would be the heavy bedstead, and then the barred windows, and then that gate at the head of the stairs, and so on.

"You know the place is doing you good," he said, "and really, dear, I don't care to renovate the house just for a three months' rental."

"Then do let us go downstairs," I said, "there are such pretty rooms there."

Then he took me in his arms and called me a blessed little goose, and said he would go down to the cellar, if I wished, and have it whitewashed into the bargain.

But he is right enough about the beds and windows and things.

It is an airy and comfortable room as any one need wish, and, of course, I would not be so silly as to make him uncomfortable just for a whim.

I'm really getting quite fond of the big room, all but that horrid paper.

Out of one window I can see the garden, those mysterious deep-shaded arbors, the riotous old-fashioned flowers, and bushes and gnarly trees.

Out of another I get a lovely view of the bay and a little private wharf belonging to the estate. There is a beautiful shaded lane that runs down there from the house. I always fancy I see people walking in these numerous paths and arbors, but John has cautioned me not to give way to fancy in the least. He says that with my imaginative power and habit of story-making, a nervous weakness like mine is sure to lead to all manner of excited fancies, and that I ought to use my will and good sense to check the tendency. So I try.

I think sometimes that if I were only well enough to write a little it would relieve the press of ideas and rest me.

But I find I get pretty tired when I try.

It is so discouraging not have any advice and companionship about my work. When I get really well, John says we will ask Cousin Henry and Julia down for a long visit; but he says he would as soon put fireworks in my pillow-case as to let me have those stimulating people about now.

I wish I could get well faster.

But I must not think about that. This paper looks to me as if it *knew* what a vicious influence it had!

There is a recurrent spot where the pattern lolls like a broken neck and two bulbous eyes stare at you upside down.

I get positively angry with the impertinence of it and the everlastingness. Up and down and sideways they crawl, and those absurd, unblinking eyes are everywhere. There is one place where two breadths didn't match, and the eyes go all up and down the line, one a little higher than the other.

I never saw so much expression in an inanimate thing before, and we all know how much expression they have! I used to lie awake as a child and get more entertainment and terror out of blank walls and plain furniture than most children could find in a toystore.

I remember what a kindly wink the knobs of our big, old bureau used to have, and there was one chair that always seemed like a strong friend.

I used to feel that if any of the other things looked too fierce I could always hop into that chair and be safe.

The furniture in this room is no worse than inharmonious, however, for we had to bring it all from downstairs. I suppose when this was used as a playroom they had to take the nursery things out, and no wonder! I never saw such ravages as the children have made here.

The wallpaper, as I said before, is torn off in spots, and it sticketh closer than a brother—they must have had perseverance as well as hatred.

Then the floor is scratched and gouged and splintered, the plaster itself is dug out here and there, and this great heavy bed which is all we found in the room, looks as if it had been through the wars.

But I don't mind it a bit—only the paper.

There comes John's sister. Such a dear girl as she is, and so careful of me! I must not let her find me writing.

She is a perfect and enthusiastic housekeeper, and hopes for no better profession. I verily believe she thinks it is the writing which made me sick!

But I can write when she is out, and see her a long way off from these windows.

There is one that commands the road, a lovely shaded winding road, and one that just looks off over the country. A lovely country, too, full of great elms and velvet meadows.

This wallpaper has a kind of sub-pattern in a different shade, a particularly irritating one, for you can only see it in certain lights, and not clearly then.

But in the places where it isn't faded and where the sun is just so—I can see a strange, provoking, formless sort of figure, that seems to skulk about behind that silly and conspicuous front design.

There's sister on the stairs!

Well, the Fourth of July is over! The people are all gone and I am tired out. John thought it might do me good to see a little company, so we just had mother and Nellie and the children down for a week.

Of course I didn't do a thing. Jennie sees to everything now. But it tired me all the same.

John says if I don't pick up faster he shall send me to Weir Mitchell in the fall.

But I don't want to go there at all. I had a friend who was in his hands once, and she says he is just like John and my brother, only more so!

Besides, it is such an undertaking to go so far.

I don't feel as if it was worth while to turn my hand over for anything, and I'm getting dreadfully fretful and querulous.

I cry at nothing, and cry most of the time.

Of course I don't when John is here, or anybody else, but when I am alone.

And I am alone a good deal just now. John is kept in town very often by serious cases, and Jennie is good and lets me alone when I want her to.

So I walk a little in the garden or down that lovely lane, sit on the porch under the roses, and lie down up here a good deal.

I'm getting really fond of the room in spite of the wallpaper. Perhaps *because* of the wallpaper.

It dwells in my mind so!

I lie here on this great immovable bed—it is nailed down, I believe—and follow that pattern about by the hour. It is as good as gymnastics, I assure you. I start, we'll say, at the bottom, down in the corner over there where it has not been touched, and I determine for the thousandth time that I *will* follow that pointless pattern to some sort of a conclusion.

I know a little of the principle of design, and I know this thing was not arranged on any laws of radiation, or alternation, or repetition, or symmetry, or anything else that I ever heard of.

It is repeated, of course, by the breadths, but not otherwise.

Looked at in one way each breadth stands alone, the bloated curves and flourishes—a kind of "debased Romanesque" with *delirium tremens*—go waddling up and down in isolated columns of fatuity.

But, on the other hand, they connect diagonally, and the sprawling outlines run off in great slanting waves of optic horror, like a lot of wallowing seaweeds in full chase.

The whole thing goes horizontally, too, at least it seems so, and I exhaust myself in trying to distinguish the order of its going in that direction.

They have used a horizontal breadth for a frieze, and that adds wonderfully to the confusion.

There is one end of the room where it is almost intact, and there, when the crosslights fade and the low sun shines directly upon it, I can almost fancy radiation after all,—the interminable grotesques seem to form around a common center and rush off in headlong plunges of equal distraction.

It makes me tired to follow it. I will take a nap I guess.

I don't know why I should write this.

I don't want to.

I don't feel able.

And I know John would think it absurd. But I *must* say what I feel and think in some way—it is such a relief.

But the effort is getting to be greater than the relief!

Half the time now I am awfully lazy, and lie down ever so much.

John says I mustn't lose my strength, and has me take cod liver oil and lots of tonics and things, to say nothing of ale and wine and rare meat.

Dear John! He loves me very dearly, and hates to have me sick. I tried to have a real earnest reasonable talk with him the other day, and tell him how I wish he would let me go and make a visit to Cousin Henry and Julia.

But he said I wasn't able to go, nor able to stand it after I got there; and I did not make out a very good case for myself, for I was crying before I had finished.

It is getting to be a great effort for me to think straight. Just this nervous weakness I suppose.

And dear John gathered me up in his arms, and just carried me upstairs and laid me on the bed, and sat by me and read to me till it tired my head.

He said I was his darling and his comfort and all he had, and that I must take care of myself for his sake, and keep well.

He says no one but myself can help me out of it, that I must use my will and self-control and not let any silly fancies run away with me.

There's one comfort, the baby is well and happy, and does not have to occupy this nursery with the horrid wallpaper.

If we had not used it, that blessed child would have! What a fortunate escape! Why, I wouldn't have a child of mine, an impressionable little thing, live in such a room for worlds.

I never thought of it before, but it is lucky that John kept me here after all, I can stand it so much easier than a baby, you see.

Of course I never mention it to them any more—I am too wise,—but I keep watch of it all the same.

There are things in that paper that nobody knows but me, or ever will.

Behind that outside pattern the dim shapes get clearer every day.

It is always the same shape, only very numerous.

And it is like a woman stooping down and creeping about behind that pattern. I don't like it a bit. I wonder—I begin to think—I wish John would take me away from here!

It is so hard to talk with John about my case, because he is so wise, and because he loves me so.

But I tried last night.

It was moonlight. The moon shines in all around just as the sun does.

I hate to see it sometimes, it creeps so slowly, and always comes in by one window or another.

John was asleep and I hated to waken him, so I kept still and watched the moonlight on that undulating wallpaper till I felt creepy.

The faint figure behind seemed to shake the pattern, just as if she wanted to get out.

I got up softly and went to feel and see if the paper *did* move, and when I came back John was awake.

"What is it, little girl?" he said. "Don't go walking about like that—you'll get cold."

I thought it was a good time to talk, so I told him that I really was not gaining here, and that I wished he would take me away.

"Why darling!" said he, "our lease will be up in three weeks, and I can't see how to leave before.

"The repairs are not done at home, and I cannot possibly leave town just now. Of course if you were in any danger, I could and would, but you really are better, dear, whether you can see it or not. I am a doctor, dear, and I know. You are gaining flesh and color, your appetite is better, I feel really much easier about you."

"I don't weigh a bit more," said I, "nor as much; and my appetite may be better in the evening when you are here, but it is worse in the morning when you are away!"

"Bless her little heart!" said he with a big hug, "she shall be as sick as she pleases! But now let's improve the shining hours by going to sleep, and talk about it in the morning!"

"And you won't go away?" I asked gloomily.

"Why, how can I, dear? It is only three weeks more and then we will take a nice little trip of a few days while Jennie is getting the house ready. Really dear you are better!"

"Better in body perhaps—" I began, and stopped short, for he sat up straight and looked at me with such a stern, reproachful look that I could not say another word.

"My darling," said he, "I beg of you, for my sake and for our child's sake, as well as for your own, that you will never for one instant let that idea enter your mind! There is nothing so dangerous, so fascinating, to a temperament like yours. It is a false and foolish fancy. Can you not trust me as a physician when I tell you so?"

So of course I said no more on that score, and we went to sleep before long. He thought I was asleep first, but I wasn't, and lay there for hours trying to decide whether that front pattern and the back pattern really did move together or separately.

On a pattern like this, by daylight, there is a lack of sequence, a defiance of law, that is a constant irritant to a normal mind.

The color is hideous enough, and unreliable enough, and infuriating enough, but the pattern is torturing.

You think you have mastered it, but just as you get well under-way in following, it turns a back-somersault and there you are. It slaps you in the face, knocks you down, and tramples upon you. It is like a bad dream.

The outside pattern is a florid arabesque, reminding one of a fungus. If you can imagine a toadstool in joints, an interminable string of toadstools, budding and sprouting in endless convolutions—why, that is something like it.

That is, sometimes!

There is one marked peculiarity about this paper, a thing nobody seems to notice but myself, and that is that it changes as the light changes.

When the sun shoots in through the east window—I always watch for that first long, straight ray—it changes so quickly that I never can quite believe it.

That is why I watch it always.

By moonlight—the moon shines in all night when there is a moon—I wouldn't know it was the same paper.

At night in any kind of light, in twilight, candle light, lamplight, and worst of all by moonlight, it becomes bars! The outside pattern I mean, and the woman behind it is as plain as can be.

I didn't realize for a long time what the thing was that showed behind, that dim sub-pattern, but now I am quite sure it is a woman.

By daylight she is subdued, quiet. I fancy it is the pattern that keeps her so still. It is so puzzling. It keeps me quiet by the hour.

I lie down ever so much now. John says it is good for me, and to sleep all I can.

Indeed he started the habit by making me lie down for an hour after each meal.

It is a very bad habit I am convinced, for you see I don't sleep.

And that cultivates deceit, for I don't tell them I'm awake—O no!

The fact is I am getting a little afraid of John.

He seems very queer sometimes, and even Jennie has an inexplicable look.

It strikes me occasionally, just as a scientific hypothesis,—that perhaps it is the paper!

I have watched John when he did not know I was looking, and come into the room suddenly on the most innocent excuses, and I've caught him several times *looking at the paper!* And Jennie too. I caught Jennie with her hand on it once.

She didn't know I was in the room, and when I asked her in a quiet, a very quiet voice, with the most restrained manner possible, what she was doing with the paper—she turned around as if she had been caught stealing, and looked quite angry—asked me why I should frighten her so!

Then she said that the paper stained everything it touched, that she had found yellow smooches on all my clothes and John's, and she wished we would be more careful!

Did not that sound innocent? But I know she was studying that pattern, and I am determined that nobody shall find it out but myself!

Life is very much more exciting now than it used to be. You see I have something more to expect, to look forward to, to watch. I really do eat better, and am more quiet than I was.

John is so pleased to see me improve! He laughed a little the other day, and said I seemed to be flourishing in spite of my wallpaper.

I turned it off with a laugh. I had no intention of telling him it was *because* of the wallpaper—he would make fun of me. He might even want to take me away.

I don't want to leave now until I have found it out. There is a week more, and I think that will be enough.

I'm feeling ever so much better! I don't sleep much at night, for it is so interesting to watch developments; but I sleep a good deal in the daytime.

In the daytime it is tiresome and perplexing.

There are always new shoots on the fungus, and new shades of yellow all over it. I cannot keep count of them, though I have tried conscientiously.

It is the strangest yellow, that wallpaper! It makes me think of all the yellow things I ever saw—not beautiful ones like buttercups, but old foul, bad yellow things.

But there is something else about that paper—the smell! I noticed it the moment we came into the room, but with so much air and sun it was not bad. Now we have had a week of fog and rain, and whether the windows are open or not, the smell is here.

It creeps all over the house.

I find it hovering in the dining-room, skulking in the parlor, hiding in the hall, lying in wait for me on the stairs.

It gets into my hair.

Even when I go to ride, if I turn my head suddenly and surprise it—there is that smell!

Such a peculiar odor, too! I have spent hours in trying to analyze it, to find what it smelled like.

It is not bad—at first, and very gentle, but quite the subtlest, most enduring odor I ever met.

In this damp weather it is awful, I wake up in the night and find it hanging over me.

It used to disturb me at first. I thought seriously of burning the house—to reach the smell.

But now I am used to it. The only thing I can think of that it is like the *color* of the paper! A yellow smell.

There is a very funny mark on this wall, low down, near the mopboard. A streak that runs round the room. It goes behind every piece of furniture, except the bed, a long, straight, even *smooch,* as if it had been rubbed over and over.

I wonder how it was done and who did it, and what they did it for. Round and round and round—round and round and round—it makes me dizzy!

I really have discovered something at last.

Through watching so much at night, when it changes so, I have finally found out.

The front pattern *does* move—and no wonder! The woman behind shakes it!

Sometimes I think there are a great many women behind, and sometimes only one, and she crawls around fast, and her crawling shakes it all over.

Then in the very bright spots she keeps still, and in the very shady spots she just takes hold of the bars and shakes them hard.

And she is all the time trying to climb through. But nobody could climb through that pattern—it strangles so; I think that is why it has so many heads.

They get through, and then the pattern strangles them off and turns them upside down, and makes their eyes white!

If those heads were covered or taken off it would not be half so bad.

I think that woman gets out in the daytime!

And I'll you tell why—privately—I've seen her!

I can see her out of every one of my windows!

It is the same woman, I know, for she is always creeping, and most women do not creep by daylight.

I see her on that long road under the trees, creeping along, and when a carriage comes she hides under the blackberry vines.

I don't blame her a bit. It must be very humiliating to be caught creeping by daylight!

I always lock the door when I creep by daylight. I can't do it at night, for I know John would suspect something at once.

And John is so queer now, that I don't want to irritate him. I wish he would take another room! Besides, I don't want anybody to get that woman out at night but myself.

I often wonder if I could see her out of all the windows at once.

But, turn as fast as I can, I can only see out of one at one time. And though I always see her, she *may* be able to creep faster than I can turn!

I have watched her sometimes away off in the open country, creeping as fast as a cloud shadow in a high wind.

If only that top pattern could be gotten off from the under one! I mean to try it, little by little.

I have found out another funny thing, but I shan't tell at this time! It does not do to trust people too much.

There are only two more days to get this paper off, and I believe John is beginning to notice. I don't like the look in his eyes.

And I heard him ask Jennie a lot of professional questions about me. She had a very good report to give.

She said I slept a good deal in the daytime.

John knows I don't sleep very well at night, for all I'm so quiet!

He asked me all sorts of questions, too, and pretended to be very loving and kind.

As if I couldn't see through him!

Still, I don't wonder he acts so, sleeping under this paper for three months.

It only interests me, but I feel sure John and Jennie are secretly affected by it.

Hurrah! This is the last day, but it is enough. John to stay in town over night, and won't be out until this evening.

Jennie wanted to sleep with me—the sly thing! But I told her I should undoubtedly rest better for a night all alone.

That was clever, for really I wasn't alone a bit! As soon as it was moonlight and that poor thing began to crawl and shake the pattern, I got up and ran to help her.

I pulled and she shook, I shook and she pulled, and before morning we had peeled off yards of that paper.

A strip about as high as my head and half round the room. And then when the sun came and that awful pattern began to laugh at me, I declared I would finish it to-day!

We go away to-morrow, and they are moving all the furniture down again to leave things as they were before.

Jennie looked at the wall in amazement, but I told her merrily that I did it out of pure spite at the vicious thing.

She laughed and said she wouldn't mind doing it herself, but I must not get tired.

How she betrayed herself that time!

But I am here, and no person touches this paper but me—not *alive!*

She tried to get me out of the room—it was too patent! But I said it was so quiet and empty and clean now that I believed I would lie down again and sleep all I could; and not to wake me even for dinner—I would call when I woke.

So now she is gone, and the servants are gone, and the things are gone, and there is nothing left but that great bedstead nailed down, with the canvas mattress we found on it.

We shall sleep downstairs to-night, and take the boat home to-morrow.

I quite enjoy the room, now it is bare again.

How those children did tear about here!

This bedstead is fairly gnawed!

But I must get to work.

I have locked the door and thrown the key down into the front path.

I don't want to go out, and I don't want to have anybody come in, till John comes.

I want to astonish him.

I've got a rope up here that even Jennie did not find. If that woman does get out, and tries to get away, I can tie her!

But I forgot I could not reach far without anything to stand on! This bed will *not* move!

I tried to lift and push it until I was lame, and then I got so angry I bit off a little piece at one corner—but it hurt my teeth.

Then I peeled off all the paper I could reach standing on the floor. It sticks horribly and the pattern just enjoys it! All those strangled heads and bulbous eyes and waddling fungus growths just shriek with derision!

I am getting angry enough to do something desperate. To jump out of the window would be admirable exercise, but the bars are too strong even to try.

Besides I wouldn't do it. Of course not. I know well enough that a step like that is improper and might be misconstrued.

I don't like to *look* out of the windows even—there are so many of those creeping women, and they creep so fast.

I wonder if they all come out of that wallpaper as I did?

But I am securely fastened now by my well-hidden rope—you don't get *me* out in the road there!

I suppose I shall have to get back behind the pattern when it comes night, and that is hard!

It is so pleasant to be out in this great room and creep around as I please!

I don't want to go outside. I won't, even if Jennie asks me to.

For outside you have to creep on the ground, and everything is green instead of yellow.

But here I can creep smoothly on the floor, and my shoulder just fits in that long smooch around the wall, so I cannot lose my way.

Why there's John at the door!

It is no use, young man, you can't open it!

How he does call and pound!

Now he's crying for an axe.

It would be a shame to break down that beautiful door!

"John dear!" said I in the gentlest voice, "the key is down by the front steps, under a plantain leaf!"

That silenced him for a few moments.

Then he said—very quietly indeed, "Open the door, my darling!"

"I can't," said I. "The key is down by the front door under a plantain leaf!"

And then I said it again, several times, very gently and slowly, and said it so often that he had to go and see, and he got it of course, and came in. He stopped short by the door.

"What is the matter?" he cried. "For God's sake, what are you doing!"

I kept on creeping just the same, but I looked at him over my shoulder.

"I've got out at last," said I, "in spite of you and Jane. And I've pulled off most of the paper, so you can't put me back!"

Now why should that man have fainted? But he did, and right across my path by the wall, so that I had to creep over him every time!

[1892]

James Joyce *(Irish; 1882–1941)*

Araby

North Richmond Street, being blind,[1] was a quiet street except at the hour when the Christian Brothers' School set the boys free. An uninhabited house of two stories stood at the blind end, detached from its neighbors in a square ground. The other houses of the street, conscious of decent lives within them, gazed at one another with brown imperturbable faces.

The former tenant of our house, a priest, had died in the back drawing-room. Air, musty from having long been enclosed, hung in all the rooms, and the waste room behind the kitchen was littered with old useless papers. Among these I found a few papercovered books, the pages of which were curled and damp: *The Abbot,* by Walter Scott, *The Devout Communicant* and *The Memoirs of Vidocq*[2]. I liked the last best because its leaves were yellow. The wild garden behind the house contained a central apple-tree and a few straggling bushes under one of which I found the

[1]**blind** a dead-end street
[2]*The Abbot* was one of Scott's popular historical romances. *The Devout Communicant* was a Catholic religious manual; *The Memoirs of Vidocq* were the memoirs of the chief of the French detective force.

late tenant's rusty bicycle-pump. He had been a very charitable priest; in his will he had left all his money to institutions and the furniture of his house to his sister.

When the short days of winter came dusk fell before we had well eaten our dinners. When we met in the street the houses had grown sombre. The space of sky above us was the colour of everchanging violet and towards it the lamps of the street lifted their feeble lanterns. The cold air stung us and we played till our bodies glowed. Our shouts echoed in the silent street. The career of our play brought us through the dark muddy lanes behind the houses where we ran the gauntlet of the rough tribes from the cottages, to the back doors of the dark dripping gardens where odours arose from the ashpits, to the dark odorous stables where a coach-man smoothed and combed the horse or shook music from the buckled harness. When we returned to the street light from the kitchen windows had filled the areas. If my uncle was seen turning the corner we hid in the shadow until we had seen him safely housed. Or if Mangan's sister came out on the doorstep to call her brother in to his tea we watched her from our shadow peer up and down the street. We waited to see whether she would remain or go in and, if she remained, we left our shadow and walked up to Mangan's steps resignedly. She was waiting for us, her figure defined by the light from the half-opened door. Her brother always teased her before he obeyed and I stood by the railings looking at her. Her dress swung as she moved her body and the soft rope of her hair tossed from side to side.

Every morning I lay on the floor in the front parlour watching her door. The blind was pulled down to within an inch of the sash so that I could not be seen. When she came out on the doorstep my heart leaped. I ran to the hall, seized my books and followed her. I kept her brown figure always in my eye and, when we came near the point at which our ways diverged, I quickened my pace and passed her. This happened morning after morning. I had never spoken to her, except for a few casual words, and yet her name was like a summons to all my foolish blood.

Her image accompanied me even in places the most hostile to romance. On Saturday evenings when my aunt went marketing I had to go to carry some of the parcels. We walked through the flaring streets, jostled by drunken men and bargaining women, amid the curses of labourers, the shrill litanies of shop-boys who stood on guard by the bar-rels of pigs' cheeks, the nasal chanting of street-singers, who sang a *come-all-you* about O'Donovan Rossa,[3] or a ballad about the troubles in our na-tive land. These noises converged in a single sensation of life for me: I imagined that I bore my chalice safely through a throng of foes. Her name

---

[3]Jeremiah O'Donovan (1831–1915), a popular Irish leader who was jailed by the British for advocating violent rebellion. A "come-all-you" was a topical song that began "Come all you gallant Irishmen."

sprang to my lips at moments in strange prayers and praises which I myself did not understand. My eyes were often full of tears (I could not tell
why) and at times a flood from my heart seemed to pour itself out into
my bosom. I thought little of the future. I did not know whether I would
ever speak to her or not or, if I spoke to her, how I could tell her of my
confused adoration. But my body was like a harp and her words and
gestures were like fingers running upon the wires.

One evening I went into the back drawing-room in which the priest
had died. It was a dark rainy evening and there was no sound in the house.
Through one of the broken panes I heard the rain impinge upon the earth,
the fine incessant needles of water playing in the sodden beds. Some
distant lamp or lighted window gleamed below me. I was thankful that
I could see so little. All my senses seemed to desire to veil themselves
and, feeling that I was about to slip from them, I pressed the palms of
my hands together until they trembled, murmuring: *O love! O love!* many
times.

At last she spoke to me. When she addressed the first words to me
I was so confused that I did not know what to answer. She asked me was
I going to Araby.

I forget whether I answered yes or no. It would be a splendid bazaar,
she said; she would love to go.

—And why can't you? I asked.

While she spoke she turned a silver bracelet round and round her
wrist. She could not go, she said, because there would be a retreat that
week in her convent. Her brother and two other boys were fighting for
their caps and I was alone at the railings. She held one of the spikes, bowing her head towards me. The light from the lamp opposite our door caught
the white curve of her neck, lit up her hair that rested there and, falling,
lit up the hand upon the railing. It fell over one side of her dress and caught
the white border of a petticoat, just visible as she stood at ease.

—It's well for you, she said.

—If I go, I said, I will bring you something.

What innumerable follies laid waste my waking and sleeping thoughts
after that evening! I wished to annihilate the tedious intervening days. I
chafed against the work of school. At night in my bedroom and by day
in the classroom her image came between me and the page I strove to
read. The syllables of the word *Araby* were called to me through the silence in which my soul luxuriated and cast an Eastern enchantment over
me. I asked for leave to go to the bazaar on Saturday night. My aunt was
surprised and hoped it was not some Freemason[4] affair. I answered few
questions in class, I watched my master's face pass from amiability to sternness; he hoped I was not beginning to idle. I could not call my wandering

---

[4]Irish Catholics viewed the Masons as their Protestant enemies.

thoughts together. I had hardly any patience with the serious work of life which, now that it stood between me and my desire, seemed to me child's play, ugly monotonous child's play.

On Saturday morning I reminded my uncle that I wished to go to the bazaar in the evening. He was fussing at the hallstand, looking for the hat-brush, and answered me curtly:

—Yes, boy, I know.

As he was in the hall I could not go into the front parlour and lie at the window. I left the house in bad humour and walked slowly towards the school. The air was pitilessly raw and already my heart misgave me.

When I came home to dinner my uncle had not yet been home. Still it was early. I sat staring at the clock for some time and, when its ticking began to irritate me, I left the room. I mounted the staircase and gained the upper part of the house. The high cold empty gloomy rooms liberated me and I went from room to room singing. From the front window I saw my companions playing below in the street. Their cries reached me weakened and indistinct and, leaning my forehead against the cool glass, I looked over at the dark house where she lived. I may have stood there for an hour, seeing nothing but the brown-clad figure cast by my imagination, touched discreetly by the lamplight at the curved neck, at the hand upon the railings and at the border below the dress.

When I came downstairs again I found Mrs Mercer sitting at the fire. She was an old garrulous woman, a pawnbroker's widow, who collected used stamps for some pious purpose. I had to endure the gossip of the tea-table. The meal was prolonged beyond an hour and still my uncle did not come. Mrs Mercer stood up to go: she was sorry she couldn't wait any longer, but it was after eight o'clock and she did not like to be out late, as the night air was bad for her. When she had gone I began to walk up and down the room, clenching my fists. My aunt said:

—I'm afraid you may put off your bazaar for this night of Our Lord.

At nine o'clock I heard my uncle's latchkey in the halldoor. I heard him talking to himself and heard the hallstand rocking when it had received the weight of his overcoat. I could interpret these signs. When he was midway through his dinner I asked him to give me the money to go to the bazaar. He had forgotten.

—The people are in bed and after their first sleep now, he said.

I did not smile. My aunt said to him energetically:

—Can't you give him the money and let him go? You've kept him late enough as it is.

My uncle said he was very sorry he had forgotten. He said he believed in the old saying: *All work and no play makes Jack a dull boy.* He asked me where I was going and, when I had told him a second time he asked me did I know *The Arab's Farewell to His Steed*[5]. When I left the kitchen he was about to recite the opening lines of the piece to my aunt.

I held a florin tightly in my hand as I strode down Buckingham Street towards the station. The sight of the streets thronged with buyers and glaring with gas recalled to me the purpose of my journey. I took my seat in a third-class carriage of a deserted train. After an intolerable delay the train moved out of the station slowly. It crept onward among ruinous houses and over the twinkling river. At Westland Row Station a crowd of people pressed to the carriage doors; but the porters moved them back, saying that it was a special train for the bazaar. I remained alone in the bare carriage. In a few minutes the train drew up beside an improvised wooden platform. I passed out on to the road and saw by the lighted dial of a clock that it was ten minutes to ten. In front of me was a large building which displayed the magical name.

I could not find any sixpenny entrance and, fearing that the bazaar would be closed, I passed in quickly through a turnstile, handing a shilling to a weary-looking man. I found myself in a big hall girdled at half its height by a gallery. Nearly all the stalls were closed and the greater part of the hall was in darkness. I recognised a silence like that which pervades a church after a service. I walked into the center of the bazaar timidly. A few people were gathered about the stalls which were still open. Before a curtain, over which the words *Café Chantant* were written in coloured lamps, two men were counting money on a salver. I listened to the fall of the coins.

Remembering with difficulty why I had come I went over to one of the stalls and examined porcelain vases and flowered teasets. At the door of the stall a young lady was talking and laughing with two young gentlemen. I remarked their English accents and listened vaguely to their conversation.

—O, I never said such a thing!

—O, but you did!

—O, but I didn't!

—Didn't she say that?

—Yes! I heard her.

—O, there's a . . . fib!

Observing me the young lady came over and asked me did I wish to buy anything. The tone of her voice was not encouraging; she seemed to have spoken to me out of a sense of duty. I looked humbly at the great jars that stood like eastern guards at either side of the dark entrance to the stall and murmured:

—No, thank you.

[5]"The Arab to His Favorite Steed" was a popular sentimental poem by Caroline Norton (1808–77).

The young lady changed the position of one of the vases and went back to the two young men. They began to talk of the same subject. Once or twice the young lady glanced at me over her shoulder.

I lingered before her stall, though I knew my stay was useless, to make my interest in her wares seem the more real. Then I turned away slowly and walked down the middle of the bazaar. I allowed the two pennies to fall against the sixpence in my pocket. I heard a voice call from one end of the gallery that the light was out. The upper part of the hall was now completely dark.

Gazing up into the darkness I saw myself as a creature driven and derided by vanity; and my eyes burned with anguish and anger.

[1905]

Franz Kafka *(Czechoslovakian; 1883–1924)*

The Metamorphosis

Translated by Willa and Edwin Muir

I

As Gregor Samsa awoke one morning from uneasy dreams he found himself transformed in his bed into a gigantic insect. He was lying on his hard, as it were armor-plated, back and when he lifted his head a little he could see his dome-like brown belly divided into stiff arched segments on top of which the bed quilt could hardly keep in position and was about to slide off completely. His numerous legs, which were pitifully thin compared to the rest of his bulk, waved helplessly before his eyes.

What has happened to me? he thought. It was no dream. His room, a regular human bedroom, only rather too small, lay quiet between the four familiar walls. Above the table on which a collection of cloth samples was unpacked and spread out—Samsa was a commercial traveler— hung the picture which he had recently cut out of an illustrated magazine and put into a pretty gilt frame. It showed a lady, with a fur cap on and a fur stole, sitting upright and holding out to the spectator a huge fur muff into which the whole of her forearm had vanished!

Gregor's eyes turned next to the window, and the overcast sky— one could hear rain drops beating on the window gutter—made him quite melancholy. What about sleeping a little longer and forgetting all this nonsense, he thought, but it could not be done, for he was accustomed to sleep on his right side and in his present condition he could not turn himself over. However violently he forced himself towards his right side he always rolled on to his back again. He tried it at least a hundred times, shutting his eyes to keep from seeing his struggling legs, and only desisted when he began to feel in his side a faint dull ache he had never experienced before.

Oh God, he thought, what an exhausting job I've picked on! Traveling about day in, day out. It's much more irritating work than doing the actual business in the office, and on top of that there's the trouble of constant traveling, of worrying about train connections, the bed and irregular meals, casual acquaintances that are always new and never become intimate friends. The devil take it all! He felt a slight itching up on his belly; slowly pushed himself on his back nearer to the top of the bed so that he could lift his head more easily; identified the itching place which was surrounded by many small white spots the nature of which he could not understand and made to touch it with a leg, but drew the leg back immediately, for the contact made a cold shiver run through him.

He slid down again into his former position. This getting up early, he thought, makes one quite stupid. A man needs his sleep. Other commercials live like harem women. For instance, when I come back to the hotel of a morning to write up the orders I've got, these others are only sitting down to breakfast. Let me just try that with my chief; I'd be sacked on the spot. Anyhow, that might be quite a good thing for me, who can tell? If I didn't have to hold my hand because of my parents I'd have given notice long ago, I'd have gone to the chief and told him exactly what I think of him. That would knock him endways from his desk! It's a queer way of doing, too, this sitting on high at a desk and talking down to employees, especially when they have to come quite near because the chief is hard of hearing. Well, there's still hope; once I've saved enough money to pay back my parents' debts to him—that should take another five or six years—I'll do it without fail. I'll cut myself completely loose then. For the moment, though, I'd better get up, since my train goes at five.

He looked at the alarm clock ticking on the chest. Heavenly Father! he thought. It was half-past six o'clock and the hands were quietly moving on, it was even past the half-hour, it was getting on toward a quarter to seven. Had the alarm clock not gone off? From the bed one could see that it had been properly set for four o'clock; of course it must have gone off. Yes, but was it possible to sleep quietly through that ear-splitting noise? Well, he had not slept quietly, yet apparently all the more soundly for that. But what was he to do now? The next train went at seven o'clock; to catch that he would need to hurry like mad and his samples weren't even packed up, and he himself wasn't feeling particularly fresh and active. And even if he did catch the train he wouldn't avoid a row with the chief, since the firm's porter would have been waiting for the five o'clock train and would have long since reported his failure to turn up. The porter was a creature of the chief's, spineless and stupid. Well, supposing he were to say he was sick? But that would be most unpleasant and would look suspicious, since during his five years' employment he had not been ill once. The chief himself would be sure to come with the sick-insurance doctor, would reproach his parents with their son's laziness and would cut all excuses short by referring to the insurance doctor, who of course regarded all mankind as perfectly healthy malingerers. And would he be so far wrong on this occasion? Gregor really felt quite well, apart from a drowsiness that was utterly superfluous after such a long sleep, and he was even unusually hungry.

As all this was running through his mind at top speed without his being able to decide to leave his bed—the alarm clock had just struck a quarter to seven—there came a cautious tap at the door behind the head of his bed. "Gregor," said a voice—it was his mother's—"it's a quarter to seven. Hadn't you a train to catch?" That gentle voice! Gregor had a shock as he heard his own voice answering hers, unmistakably his own voice, it was true, but with a persistent horrible twittering squeak behind it like an undertone, that left the words in their clear shape only for the first moment and then rose up reverberating round them to destroy their sense, so that one could not be sure one had heard them rightly. Gregor wanted to answer at length and explain everything, but in the circumstances he confined himself to saying: "Yes, yes, thank you, Mother, I'm getting up now." The wooden door between them must have kept the change in his voice from being noticeable outside, for his mother contented herself with this statement and shuffled away. Yet this brief exchange of words had made the other members of the family aware that Gregor was still in the house, as they had not expected, and at one of the side doors his father was already knocking, gently, yet with his fist. "Gregor, Gregor," he called, "what's the matter with you?" And after a little while he called again in a deeper voice: "Gregor! Gregor!" At the other side door his sister was saying in a low, plaintive tone: "Gregor? Aren't you well? Are you needing anything?" He answered them both at once: "I'm just ready," and did his best to make his voice sound as normal as possible by enunciating the words very clearly and leaving long pauses between them. So his father went back to his breakfast, but his sister whispered: "Gregor, open the door, do." However, he was not thinking of opening the door, and felt thankful for the prudent habit he had acquired in traveling of locking all doors during the night, even at home.

His immediate intention was to get up quietly without being disturbed, to put on his clothes and above all eat his breakfast, and only then to consider what else was to be done, since in bed, he was well aware, his meditations would come to no sensible conclusion. He remembered that often enough in bed he had felt small aches and pains, probably caused by awkward postures, which had proved purely imaginary once he got up, and he looked forward eagerly to seeing this morning's delusions gradually fall away. That the change in his voice was nothing but the precursor of a severe chill, a standing ailment of commercial travelers, he had not the least possible doubt.

To get rid of the quilt was quite easy; he had only to inflate himself a little and it fell off by itself. But the next move was difficult, especially because he was so uncommonly broad. He would have needed arms and hands to hoist himself up; instead he had only the numerous little legs which never stopped waving in all directions and which he could not control in the least. When he tried to bend one of them it was the first to stretch itself straight; and did he succeed at last in making it do what he wanted, all the other legs meanwhile waved the more wildly in a high degree of unpleasant agitation. "But what's the use of lying idle in bed," said Gregor to himself.

He thought that he might get out of bed with the lower part of his body first, but this lower part, which he had not yet seen and of which he could form no clear conception, proved too difficult to move; it shifted so slowly; and when finally, almost wild with annoyance, he gathered his forces together and thrust out recklessly, he had miscalculated the direction and bumped heavily against the lower end of the bed, and the stinging pain he felt informed him that precisely this lower part of his body was at the moment probably the most sensitive.

So he tried to get the top part of himself out first, and cautiously moved his head towards the edge of the bed. That proved easy enough, and despite its breadth and mass the bulk of his body at last slowly followed the movement of his head. Still, when he finally got his head free over the edge of the bed he felt too scared to go on advancing, for after all if he let himself fall in this way it would take a miracle to keep his head from being injured. And at all costs he must not lose consciousness now, precisely now; he would rather stay in bed.

But when after a repetition of the same efforts he lay in his former position again, sighing, and watched his little legs struggling against each other more wildly than ever, if that were possible, and saw no way of bringing any order into this arbitrary confusion, he told himself again that it was impossible to stay in bed and that the most sensible course was to risk everything for the smallest hope of getting away from it. At the same time he did not forget meanwhile to remind himself that cool reflection, the coolest possible, was much better than desperate resolves. In such moments he focused his eyes as sharply as possible on the window, but, unfortunately, the prospect of the morning fog, which muffled even the other side of the narrow street, brought him little encouragement and comfort. "Seven o'clock already," he said to himself when the alarm clock chimed again, "seven o'clock already and still such a thick fog." And for a little while he lay quiet, breathing lightly, as if perhaps expecting such complete repose to restore all things to their real and normal condition.

But then he said to himself: "Before it strikes a quarter past seven I must be quite out of this bed, without fail. Anyhow, by that time someone will have come from the office to ask for me, since it opens before seven." And he set himself to rocking his whole body at once in a regular rhythm, with the idea of swinging it out of the bed. If he tipped himself out in that way he could keep his head from injury by lifting it at an acute angle when he fell. His back seemed to be hard and was not likely to suffer from a fall on the carpet. His biggest worry was the loud crash he would not be able to help making, which would probably cause anxiety, if not terror, behind all the doors. Still, he must take the risk.

When he was already half out of the bed—the new method was more a game than an effort, for he needed only to hitch himself across by rocking to and fro—it struck him how simple it would be if he could get help. Two strong people—he thought of his father and the servant girl—would be amply sufficient; they would only have to thrust their arms under his convex back, lever him out of the bed, bend down with their burden and then be patient enough to let him turn himself right over on to the floor, where it was to be hoped his legs would then find their proper function. Well, ignoring the fact that the doors were all locked, ought he really to call for help? In spite of his misery he could not suppress a smile at the very idea of it.

He had got so far that he could barely keep his equilibrium when he rocked himself strongly, and he would have to nerve himself very soon for the final decision since in five minutes' time it would be a quarter past seven—when the front doorbell rang. "That's someone from the office," he said to himself, and grew almost rigid, while his little legs only jigged about all the faster. For a moment everything stayed quiet. "They're not going to open the door," said Gregor to himself, catching at some kind of irrational hope. But then of course the servant girl went as usual to the door with her heavy tread and opened it. Gregor needed only to hear the first good morning of the visitor to know immediately who it was—the chief clerk himself. What a fate, to be condemned to work for a firm where the smallest omission at once gave rise to the gravest suspicion! Were all employees in a body nothing but scoundrels, was there not among them one single loyal devoted man who, had he wasted only an hour or so of the firm's time in a morning, was so tormented by conscience as to be driven out of his mind and actually incapable of leaving his bed? Wouldn't it really have been sufficient to send an apprentice to inquire—if any inquiry were necessary at all—did the chief clerk himself have to come and thus indicate to the entire family, an innocent family, that this suspicious circumstance could be investigated by no one less versed in affairs than himself? And more through the agitation caused by these reflections than through any act of will Gregor swung himself out of bed with all his strength. There was a loud thump, but it was not really a crash. His fall was broken to some extent by the carpet, his back, too, was less stiff than he thought, and so there was merely a dull thud, not so very startling.

Only he had not lifted his head carefully enough and had hit it; he turned it and rubbed it on the carpet in pain and irritation.

"That was something falling down in there," said the chief clerk in the next room to the left. Gregor tried to suppose to himself that something like what had happened to him today might some day happen to the chief clerk; one really could not deny that it was possible. But as if in brusque reply to this supposition the chief clerk took a couple of firm steps in the next-door room and his patent leather boots creaked. From the right-hand room his sister was whispering to inform him of the situation: "Gregor, the chief clerk's here." "I know," muttered Gregor to himself; but he didn't dare to make his voice loud enough for his sister to hear it.

"Gregor," said his father now from the left-hand room, "the chief clerk has come and wants to know why you didn't catch the early train. We don't know what to say to him. Besides, he wants to talk to you in person. So open the door, please. He will be good enough to excuse the untidiness of your room." "Good morning, Mr. Samsa," the chief clerk was calling amiably meanwhile. "He's not well," said his mother to the visitor, while his father was still speaking through the door, "he's not well, sir, believe me. What else would make him miss a train! The boy thinks about nothing but his work. It makes me almost cross the way he never goes out in the evenings; he's been here the last eight days and has stayed at home every single evening. He just sits there quietly at the table reading a newspaper or looking through railway timetables. The only amusement he gets is doing fretwork. For instance, he spent two or three evenings cutting out a little picture frame; you would be surprised to see how pretty it is; it's hanging in his room; you'll see it in a minute when Gregor opens the door. I must say I'm glad you've come, sir; we should never have got him to unlock the door by ourselves; he's so obstinate; and I'm sure he's unwell, though he wouldn't have it to be so this morning." "I'm just coming," said Gregor slowly and carefully, not moving an inch for fear of losing one word of the conversation. "I can't think of any other explanation, madam," said the chief clerk, "I hope it's nothing serious. Although on the other hand I must say that we men of business—fortunately or unfortunately—very often simply have to ignore any slight indisposition, since business must be attended to." "Well, can the chief clerk come in now?" asked Gregor's father impatiently, again knocking on the door. "No," said Gregor. In the left-hand room a painful silence followed this refusal, in the right-hand room his sister began to sob.

Why didn't his sister join the others? She was probably newly out of bed and hadn't even begun to put on her clothes yet. Well, why was she crying? Because he wouldn't get up and let the chief clerk in, because he was in danger of losing his job, and because the chief would begin dunning his parents again for the old debts? Surely these were things one didn't need to worry about for the present. Gregor was still at home and not in the least thinking of deserting the family. At the moment, true, he was lying on the carpet and no one who knew the condition he was in could seriously expect him to admit the chief clerk. But for such a small discourtesy, which could plausibly be explained away somehow later on, Gregor could hardly be dismissed on the spot. And it seemed to Gregor that it would be much more sensible to leave him in peace for the present than to trouble him with tears and entreaties. Still, of course, their uncertainty bewildered them all and excused their behavior.

"Mr. Samsa," the chief clerk called now in a louder voice, "what's the matter with you? Here you are, barricading yourself in your room, giving only 'yes' and 'no' for answers, causing your parents a lot of unnecessary trouble and neglecting—I mention this only in passing—neglecting your business duties in an incredible fashion. I am speaking here in the name of your parents and of your chief, and I beg you quite seriously to give me an immediate and precise explanation. You amaze me, you amaze me. I thought you were a quiet, dependable person, and now all at once you seem bent on making a disgraceful exhibition of yourself. The chief did hint to me early this morning a possible explanation for your disappearance—with reference to the cash payments that were entrusted to you recently—but I almost pledged my solemn word of honor that this could not be so. But now that I see how incredibly obstinate you are, I no longer have the slightest desire to take your part at all. And your position in the firm is not so unassailable. I came with the intention of telling you all this in private, but since you are wasting my time so needlessly I don't see why your parents shouldn't hear it too. For some time past your work has been most unsatisfactory; this is not the season of the year for a business boom, of course, we admit that, but a season of the year for doing no business at all, that does not exist, Mr. Samsa, must not exist."

"But, sir," cried Gregor, beside himself and in his agitation forgetting everything else. "I'm just going to open the door this very minute. A slight illness, an attack of giddiness, has kept me from getting up. I'm still lying in bed. But I feel all right again. I'm getting out of bed now. Just give me a moment or two longer! I'm not quite so well as I thought. But I'm all right, really. How a thing like that can suddenly strike one down! Only last night I was quite well, my parents can tell you, or rather I did have a slight presentiment. I must have showed some sign of it. Why didn't I report it at the office! But one always thinks that an indisposition can be got over without staying in the house. Oh sir, do spare my parents! All that you're reproaching me with now has no foundation; no one has ever said a word to me about it. Perhaps you haven't looked at the last orders I sent in. Anyhow, I can still catch the eight o'clock train, I'm much the better for my few hours' rest. Don't let me detain you here, sir; I'll be attending to business very soon, and do be good enough to tell the chief so and to make my excuses to him!"

And while all this was tumbling out pell-mell and Gregor hardly knew what he was saying, he had reached the chest quite easily, perhaps because of the practice he had had in bed, and was now trying to lever himself upright by means of it. He meant actually to open the door, actually to show himself and speak to the chief clerk; he was eager to find out what the others, after all their insistence, would say at the sight of him. If they were horrified then the responsibility was no longer his and he could stay quiet. But if they took it calmly, then he had no reason either to be upset, and could really get to the station for the eight o'clock train if he hurried. At first he slipped down a few times from the polished surface of the chest, but at length with a last heave he stood upright; he paid no more attention to the pains in the lower part of his body, however they smarted. Then he let himself fall against the back of a nearby chair, and clung with his little legs to the edges of it. That brought him into control of himself again and he stopped speaking, for now he could listen to what the chief clerk was saying.

"Did you understand a word of it?" the chief clerk was asking; "surely he can't be trying to make fools of us?" "Oh dear," cried his mother, in tears, "perhaps he's terribly ill and we're tormenting him. Grete! Grete!" she called out then. "Yes Mother?" called his sister from the other side. They were calling to each other across Gregor's room. "You must go this minute for the doctor. Gregor is ill. Go for the doctor, quick. Did you hear how he was speaking?" "That was no human voice," said the chief clerk in a voice noticeably low beside the shrillness of the mother's. "Anna! Anna!" his father was calling through the hall to the kitchen, clapping his hands, "get a locksmith at once!" And the two girls were already running through the hall with a swish of skirts—how could his sister have got dressed so quickly?—and were tearing the front door open. There was no sound of its closing again; they had evidently left it open as one does in houses where some great misfortune has happened.

But Gregor was now much calmer. The words he uttered were no longer understandable, apparently, although they seemed clear enough to him, even clearer than before, perhaps because his ear had grown accustomed to the sound of them. Yet at any rate people now believed that something was wrong with him, and were ready to help him. The positive certainty with which these first measures had been taken comforted him. He felt himself drawn once more into the human circle and hoped for great and remarkable results from both the doctor and the locksmith, without really distinguishing precisely between them. To make his voice as clear as possible for the decisive conversation that was now imminent he coughed a little, as quietly as he could, of course, since this noise too might not sound like a human cough for all he was able to judge. In the next room meanwhile there was complete silence. Perhaps his parents were sitting at the table with the chief clerk, whispering, perhaps they were all leaning against the door and listening.

Slowly Gregor pushed the chair towards the door, then let go of it, caught hold of the door for support—the soles at the end of his little legs were somewhat sticky—and rested against it for a moment after his efforts. Then he set himself to turning the key in the lock with his mouth. It seemed, unhappily, that he hadn't really any teeth—what could he grip the key with?—but on the other hand his jaws were certainly very strong; with their help he did manage to set the key in motion, heedless of the fact that he was undoubtedly damaging them somewhere, since a brown fluid issued from his mouth, flowed over the key and dripped on the floor. "Just listen to that," said the chief clerk next door; "he's turning the key." That was a great encouragement to Gregor; but they should all have shouted encouragement to him, his father and mother too: "Go on, Gregor," they should have called out, "keep going, hold on to that key!" And in the belief that they were all following his efforts intently, he clenched his jaws recklessly on the key with all the force at his command. As the turning of the key progressed he circled round the lock, holding on now only with his mouth, pushing on the key, as required, or pulling it down again with all the weight of his body. The louder click of the finally yielding lock literally quickened Gregor. With a deep breath of relief he said to himself. "So I didn't need the locksmith," and laid his head on the handle to open the door wide.

Since he had to pull the door towards him, he was still invisible when it was really wide open. He had to edge himself very slowly round the near half of the double door, and to do it very carefully if he was not to fall plump upon his back just on the threshold. He was still carrying out this difficult manoeuvre, with no time to observe anything else, when he heard the chief clerk utter a loud "Oh!"—it sounded like a gust of wind—and now he could see the man, standing as he was nearest to the door, clapping one hand before his open mouth and slowly backing away as if driven by some invisible steady pressure. His mother—in spite of the chief clerk's being there her hair was still undone and sticking up in all directions—first clasped her hands and looked at his father, then took two steps towards Gregor and fell on the floor among her outspread skirts, her face quite hidden on her breast. His father knotted his fist with a fierce expression on his face as if he meant to knock Gregor back into his room, then looked uncertainly round the living room, covered his eyes with his hands and wept till his great chest heaved.

Gregor did not go now into the living room, but leaned against the inside of the firmly shut wing of the door, so that only half his body was visible and his head above it bending sideways to look at the others. The light had meanwhile strengthened; on the other side of the street one could see clearly a section of the endlessly long, dark gray building opposite—it was a hospital—abruptly punctuated by its row of regular windows; the rain was still falling, but only in large singly discernible and literally singly splashing drops. The breakfast dishes were set out on the table lavishly, for breakfast was the most important meal of the day to Gregor's father, who lingered it out for hours over various newspapers. Right opposite Gregor on the wall hung a photograph of himself on military service, as a lieutenant, hand on sword, a carefree smile on his face, inviting one to respect his uniform and military bearing. The door leading to the hall was open, and one could see that the front door stood open too, showing the landing beyond and the beginning of the stairs going down.

"Well," said Gregor, knowing perfectly that he was the only one who had retained any composure, "I'll put my clothes on at once, pack up my samples and start off. Will you only let me go? You see, sir, I'm not obstinate, and I'm willing to work; traveling is a hard life, but I couldn't live without it. Where are you going, sir? To the office? Yes? Will you give a true account of all this? One can be temporarily incapacitated, but that's just the moment for remembering former services and bearing in mind that later on, when the incapacity has been got over, one will certainly work with all the more industry and concentration. I'm loyally bound to serve the chief, you know that very well. Besides, I have to provide for my parents and my sister. I'm in great difficulties, but I'll get out of them again. Don't make things any worse for me than they are. Stand up for me in the firm. Travelers are not popular there, I know. People think they earn sacks of money and just have a good time. A prejudice there's no particular reason for revising. But you, sir, have a more comprehensive view of affairs than the rest of the staff, yes, let me tell you in confidence, a more comprehensive view than the chief himself, who, being the owner, lets his judgment easily be swayed against one of his employees. And you know very well that the traveler, who is never seen in the office almost the whole year round, can so easily fall a victim to gossip and ill luck and unfounded complaints, which he mostly knows nothing about, except when he comes back exhausted from his rounds, and only then suffers in person from their evil consequences, which he can no longer trace back to the original causes. Sir, sir, don't go away without a word to me to show that you think me in the right at least to some extent!"

But at Gregor's very first words the chief clerk had already backed away and only stared at him with parted lips over one twitching shoulder. And while Gregor was speaking he did not stand still one moment but stole away towards the door, without taking his eyes off Gregor, yet only an inch at a time, as if obeying some secret injunction to leave the room. He was already at the hall, and the suddenness with which he took his last step out of the living room would have made one believe he had burned the sole of his foot. Once in the hall he stretched his right arm before him towards the staircase, as if some supernatural power were waiting there to deliver him.

Gregor perceived that the chief clerk must on no account be allowed to go away in this frame of mind if his position in the firm were not to be endangered to the utmost. His parents did not understand this so well;

they had convinced themselves in the course of years that Gregor was settled for life in this firm, and besides they were so occupied with their immediate troubles that all foresight had forsaken them. Yet Gregor had this
foresight. The chief clerk must be detained, soothed, persuaded and finally won over; the whole future of Gregor and his family depended on
it! If only his sister had been there! She was intelligent; she had begun
to cry while Gregor was still lying quietly on his back. And no doubt
the chief clerk, so partial to ladies, would have been guided by her; she
would have shut the door of the flat and in the hall talked him out of
his horror. But she was not there, and Gregor would have to handle the
situation himself. And without remembering that he was still unaware what
powers of movement he possessed, without even remembering that his
words in all possibility, indeed in all likelihood, would again be unintelligible, he let go the wing of the door, pushed himself through the opening, started to walk towards the chief clerk, who was already ridiculously
clinging with both hands to the railing on the landing; but immediately,
as he was feeling for a support, he fell down with a little cry upon all
his numerous legs. Hardly was he down when he experienced for the first
time this morning a sense of physical comfort; his legs had firm ground
under them; they were completely obedient, as he noted with joy; they
even strove to carry him forward in whatever direction he chose; and he
was inclined to believe that a final relief from all his sufferings was at hand.
But in the same moment as he found himself on the floor, rocking with
suppressed eagerness to move, not far from his mother, indeed just in front
of her, she, who had seemed so completely crushed, sprang all at once
to her feet, her arms and fingers outspread, cried: "Help, for God's sake,
help!" bent her head down as if to see Gregor better, yet on the contrary
kept backing senselessly away; had quite forgotten that the laden table stood
behind her; sat upon it hastily, as if in absence of mind, when she bumped
into it; and seemed altogether unaware that the big coffee pot beside her
was upset and pouring coffee in a flood over the carpet.

    "Mother, Mother," said Gregor in a low voice, and looked up at her.
The chief clerk, for the moment, had quite slipped from his mind; instead
he could not resist snapping his jaws together at the sight of the streaming coffee. That made his mother scream again, she fled from the table
and fell into the arms of his father, who hastened to catch her. But Gregor
had now no time to spare for his parents; the chief clerk was already on
the stairs; with his chin on the banisters he was taking one last backward
look. Gregor made a spring, to be as sure as possible of overtaking him;
the chief clerk must have divined his intention, for he leaped down several
steps and vanished; he was still yelling "Ugh!" and it echoed through the
whole staircase.

    Unfortunately, the flight of the chief clerk seemed completely to upset
Gregor's father, who had remained relatively calm until now, for instead
of running after the man himself, or at least not hindering Gregor in his

pursuit, he seized in his right hand the walking stick which the chief clerk had left behind on a chair, together with a hat and greatcoat, snatched in his left hand a large newspaper from the table and began stamping his feet and flourishing the stick and the newspaper to drive Gregor back into his room. No entreaty of Gregor's availed, indeed no entreaty was even understood; however humbly he bent his head his father only stamped on the floor the more loudly. Behind his father his mother had torn open a window, despite the cold weather, and was leaning far out of it with her face in her hands. A strong draught set in from the street to the staircase, the window curtain blew in, the newspapers on the table fluttered, stray pages whisked over the floor. Pitilessly Gregor's father drove him back, hissing and crying "Shoo!" like a savage. But Gregor was quite unpracticed in walking backwards, it really was a slow business. If he only had a chance to turn round he could get back to his room at once, but he was afraid of exasperating his father by the slowness of such a rotation and at any moment the stick in his father's hand might hit him a fatal blow on the back or on the head. In the end, however, nothing else was left for him to do since to his horror he observed that in moving backwards he could not even control the direction he took; and so, keeping an anxious eye on his father all the time over his shoulder, he began to turn round as quickly as he could, which was in reality very slowly. Perhaps his father noted his good intentions, for he did not interfere except every now and then to help in the manoeuvre from a distance with the point of the stick. If only he would have stopped making that unbearable hissing noise! It made Gregor quite lose his head. He had turned almost completely round when the hissing noise so distracted him that he even turned a little the wrong way again. But when at last his head was fortunately right in front of the doorway, it appeared that his body was too broad simply to get through the opening. His father, of course, in his present mood was far from thinking of such a thing as opening the other half of the door, to let Gregor have enough space. He had merely the fixed idea of driving Gregor back into his room as quickly as possible. He would have never suffered Gregor to make the circumstantial preparations for standing up on end and perhaps slipping his way through the door. Maybe he was now making more noise than ever to urge Gregor forward as if no obstacle impeded him; to Gregor, anyhow, the noise in his rear sounded no longer like the voice of one single father; this was really no joke, and Gregor thrust himself—come what might—into the doorway. One side of his body rose up, he was tilted at an angle in the doorway, his flank was quite bruised, horrid blotches stained the white door, soon he was stuck fast and, left to himself, could not have moved at all, his legs on one side fluttered trembling in the air, those on the other were crushed painfully to the floor—when from behind his father gave him a strong push which was literally a deliverance and he flew far into the room, bleeding freely. The door was slammed behind him with the stick, and then at last there was silence.

II

Not until it was twilight did Gregor awake out of a deep sleep, more like a swoon than a sleep. He would certainly have waked up of his own accord not much later, for he felt himself sufficiently rested and well-slept, but it seemed to him as if a fleeting step and a cautious shutting of the door leading into the hall had aroused him. The electric lights in the street cast a pale sheen here and there on the ceiling and the upper surfaces of the furniture, but down below, where he lay, it was dark. Slowly, awkwardly trying out his feelers, which he now first learned to appreciate, he pushed his way to the door to see what had been happening there. His left side felt like one single long, unpleasantly tense scar, and he had actually to limp on his two rows of legs. One little leg, moreover, had been severely damaged in the course of that morning's events—it was almost a miracle that only one had been damaged—and trailed uselessly behind him.

He had reached the door before he discovered what had really drawn him to it: the smell of food. For there stood a basin filled with fresh milk in which floated little sops of white bread. He could almost have laughed with joy, since he was now still hungrier than in the morning, and dipped his head almost over the eyes straight into the milk. But soon in disappointment he withdrew it again; not only did he find it difficult to feed because of his tender left side—and he could only feed with the palpitating collaboration of his whole body—he did not like the milk either, although milk had been his favorite drink and that was certainly why his sister had set it there for him, indeed it was almost with repulsion that he turned away from the basin and crawled back to the middle of the room.

He could see through the crack of the door that the gas was turned on in the living room, but while usually at this time his father made a habit of reading the afternoon newspaper in a loud voice to his mother and occasionally to his sister as well, not a sound was now to be heard. Well, perhaps his father had recently given up this habit of reading aloud, which his sister had mentioned so often in conversation and in her letters. But there was the same silence all around, although the flat was certainly not empty of occupants. "What a quiet life our family has been leading," said Gregor to himself, and as he sat there motionless staring into the darkness he felt great pride in the fact that he had been able to provide such a life for his parents and sister in such a fine flat. But what if all the quiet, the comfort, the contentment were now to end in horror? To keep himself from being lost in such thoughts Gregor took refuge in movement and crawled up and down the room.

Once during the long evening one of the side doors was opened a little and quickly shut again, later the other side door too; someone had apparently wanted to come in and then thought better of it. Gregor now stationed himself immediately before the living room door, determined to persuade any hesitating visitor to come in or at least to discover who it might be; but the door was not opened again and he waited in vain. In the early morning, when the doors were locked, they had all wanted to come in, now that he had opened one door and the other had apparently been opened during the day, no one came in and even the keys were on the other side of the doors.

It was late at night before the gas went out in the living room, and Gregor could easily tell that his parents and his sister had all stayed awake until then, for he could clearly hear the three of them stealing away on tiptoe. No one was likely to visit him, not until the morning, that was certain; so he had plenty of time to meditate at his leisure on how he was to arrange his life afresh. But the lofty, empty room in which he had to lie flat on the floor filled him with an apprehension he could not account for, since it had been his very own room for the past five years—and with a half-unconscious action, not without a slight feeling of shame, he scuttled under the sofa, where he felt comfortable at once, although his back was a little cramped and he could not lift his head up, and his only regret was that his body was too broad to get the whole of it under the sofa.

He stayed there all night, spending the time partly in a light slumber, from which his hunger kept waking him up with a start, and partly in worrying and sketching vague hopes, which all led to the same conclusion, that he must lie low for the present and, by exercising patience and the utmost consideration, help the family to bear the inconvenience he was bound to cause them in his present condition.

Very early in the morning, it was still almost night, Gregor had the chance to test the strength of his new resolutions, for his sister, nearly fully dressed, opened the door from the hall and peered in. She did not see him at once, yet when she caught sight of him under the sofa—well, he had to be somewhere, he couldn't have flown away, could he?—she was so startled that without being able to help it she slammed the door shut again. But as if regretting her behavior she opened the door again immediately and came in on tiptoe, as if she were visiting an invalid or even a stranger. Gregor had pushed his head forward to the very edge of the sofa and watched her. Would she notice that he had left the milk standing, and not for lack of hunger, and would she bring in some other kind of food more to his taste? If she did not do it of her own accord, he would rather starve than draw her attention to the fact, although he felt a wild impulse to dart out from under the sofa, throw himself at her feet and beg her for something to eat. But his sister at once noticed, with surprise, that the basin was still full, except for a little milk that had been spilt all around it, she lifted it immediately, not with her bare hands, true, but with a cloth and carried it away. Gregor was wildly curious to know what she would bring instead, and made various speculations about it. Yet what she actually did next, in the goodness of her heart, he could never have guessed at. To find out what he liked she brought him a whole selection of food, all set out on an old newspaper. There were old, half-decayed vegetables, bones from last night's supper covered with a white sauce that had thickened; some raisins and almonds; a piece of cheese that Gregor would have called un-eatable two days ago; a dry roll of bread, a buttered roll, and a roll both buttered and salted. Besides all that, she set down again the same basin, into which she had poured some water, and which was apparently to be reserved for his exclusive use. And with fine tact, knowing that Gregor would not eat in her presence, she withdrew quickly and even turned the key, to let him understand that he could take his ease as much as he liked. Gregor's legs all whizzed towards the food. His wounds must have healed completely, moreover, for he felt no disability, which amazed him and made him reflect how more than a month ago he had cut one finger a little with a knife and had still suffered pain from the wound only the day before yesterday. Am I less sensitive now? he thought, and sucked greedily at the cheese, which above all the other edibles attracted him at once and strongly. One after another and with tears of satisfaction in his eyes he quickly devoured the cheese, the vegetables and the sauce; the fresh food, on the other hand, had no charms for him, he could not even stand the smell of it and actually dragged away to some little distance the things he could eat. He had long finished his meal and was only lying lazily on the same spot when his sister turned the key slowly as a sign for him to retreat. That roused him at once, although he was nearly asleep, and he hurried under the sofa again. But it took considerable self-control for him to stay under the sofa, even for the short time his sister was in the room, since the large meal had swollen his body somewhat and he was so cramped he could hardly breathe. Slight attacks of breathlessness afflicted him and his eyes were starting a little out of his head as he watched his unsuspect-ing sister sweeping together with a broom not only the remains of what he had eaten but even the things he had not touched, as if these were now of no use to anyone, and hastily shoveling it all into a bucket, which she covered with a wooden lid and carried away. Hardly had she turned her back when Gregor came from under the sofa and stretched and puffed himself out.

In this manner Gregor was fed, once in the early morning while his parents and the servant girl were still asleep, and a second time after they had all had their midday dinner, for then his parents took a short nap and the servant girl could be sent out on some errand or other by his sister. Not that they would have wanted him to starve, of course, but perhaps they could not have borne to know more about his feeding than from hearsay, perhaps too his sister wanted to spare them such little anxi-eties wherever possible, since they had quite enough to bear as it was.

Under what pretext the doctor and the locksmith had been got rid of on that first morning Gregor could not discover, for since what he said was not understood by the others it never struck any of them, not even his sister, that he could understand what they said, and so whenever his sister came into his room he had to content himself with hearing her utter only a sigh now and then and an occasional appeal to the saints. Later on, when she had got a little used to the situation—of course she could never get completely used to it—she sometimes threw out a remark which was kindly meant or could be so interpreted. "Well, he liked his dinner today," she would say when Gregor had made a good clearance of his food; and when he had not eaten, which gradually happened more and more often, she would say almost sadly: "Everything's been left standing again."

But although Gregor could get no news directly, he overheard a lot from the neighboring rooms, and as soon as voices were audible, he would run to the door of the room concerned and press his whole body against it. In the first few days especially there was no conversation that did not refer to him somehow, even if only indirectly. For two whole days there were family consultations at every mealtime about what should be done; but also between meals the same subject was discussed, for there were always at least two members of the family at home, since no one wanted to be alone in the flat and to leave it quite empty was unthinkable. And on the very first of these days the household cook—it was not quite clear what and how much she knew of the situation—went down on her knees to his mother and begged leave to go, and when she departed, a quarter of an hour later, gave thanks for her dismissal with tears in her eyes as if for the greatest benefit that could have been conferred on her, and without any prompting swore a solemn oath that she would never say a single word to anyone about what had happened.

Now Gregor's sister had to cook too, helping her mother; true, the cooking did not amount to much, for they ate scarcely anything. Gregor was always hearing one of the family vainly urging another to eat and getting no answer but: "Thanks, I've had all I want," or something similar. Perhaps they drank nothing either. Time and again his sister kept asking if he wouldn't like some beer and offered kindly to go and fetch it herself, and when he made no answer suggested that she could ask the concierge to fetch it, so that he need feel no sense of obligation, but then a round "No" came from his father and no more was said about it.

In the course of that very first day Gregor's father explained the family's financial position and prospects to both his mother and his sister. Now and then he rose from the table to get some voucher or memorandum out of the small safe he had rescued from the collapse of his business five years earlier. One could hear him opening the complicated lock and rustling papers out and shutting it again. This statement made by his father was the first cheerful information Gregor had heard since his imprisonment. He had been of the opinion that nothing at all was left over from his father's business, at least his father had never said anything to the contrary, and of course he had not asked him directly. At that time Gregor's sole desire was to do his utmost to help the family to forget as soon as possible the catastrophe which had overwhelmed the business and thrown them all into a state of complete despair. And so he had set to work with unusual ardor and almost overnight had become a commercial traveler instead of a little clerk, with of course much greater chances of earning money, and his success was immediately translated into good round coin which he could lay on the table for his amazed and happy family. These had been fine times, and they had never recurred, at least not with the same sense of glory, although later on Gregor had earned so much money that he was able to meet the expenses of the whole household and did so. They had simply got used to it, both the family and Gregor; the money was gratefully accepted and gladly given, but there was no special uprush of warm feeling. With his sister alone had he remained intimate, and it was a secret plan of his that she, who loved music, unlike himself, and could play movingly on the violin, should be sent next year to study at the Conservatorium, despite the great expense that would entail, which must be made up in some other way. During his brief visits home the Conservatorium was often mentioned in the talks he had with his sister, but always merely as a beautiful dream which could never come true, and his parents discouraged even these innocent references to it; yet Gregor had made up his mind firmly about it and meant to announce the fact with due solemnity on Christmas Day.

Such were the thoughts, completely futile in his present condition, that went through his head as he stood clinging upright to the door and listening. Sometimes out of sheer weariness he had to give up listening and let his head fall negligently against the door, but he always had to pull himself together again at once, for even the slight sound his head made was audible next door and brought all conversation to a stop. "What can he be doing now?" his father would say after a while, obviously turning towards the door, and only then would the interrupted conversation gradually be set going again.

Gregor was now informed as amply as he could wish—for his father tended to repeat himself in his explanations, partly because it was a long time since he had handled such matters and partly because his mother could not always grasp things at once—that a certain amount of investments, a very small amount it was true, had survived the wreck of their fortunes and had even increased a little because the dividends had not been touched meanwhile. And besides that, the money Gregor brought home every month—he had kept only a few dollars for himself—had never been quite used up and now amounted to a small capital sum. Behind the door Gregor nodded his head eagerly, rejoiced at this evidence of unexpected thrift and foresight. True, he could really have paid off some more of his father's debts to the chief with this extra money, and so brought much nearer the day on which he could quit his job, but doubtless it was better the way his father had arranged it.

Yet this capital was by no means sufficient to let the family live on the interest of it; for one year, perhaps, or at the most two, they could live on the principal, that was all. It was simply a sum that ought not to be touched and should be kept for a rainy day; money for living expenses would have to be earned. Now his father was still hale enough but an old man, and he had done no work for the past five years and could not be expected to do much; during these five years, the first years of leisure in his laborious though unsuccessful life, he had grown rather fat and become sluggish. And Gregor's old mother, how was she to earn a living with her asthma, which troubled her even when she walked through the flat and kept her lying on a sofa every other day panting for breath beside an open window? And was his sister to earn her bread, she who was still a child of seventeen and whose life hitherto had been so pleasant, consisting as it did in dressing herself nicely, sleeping long, helping in the housekeeping, going out to a few modest entertainments and above all playing the violin? At first whenever the need for earning money was mentioned Gregor let go his hold on the door and threw himself down on the cool leather sofa beside it, he felt so hot with shame and grief.

Often he just lay there the long nights through without sleeping at all, scrabbling for hours on the leather. Or he nerved himself to the great effort of pushing an armchair to the window, then crawled up over the window sill and, braced against the chair, leaned against the window panes, obviously in some recollection of the sense of freedom that looking out of a window always used to give him. For in reality day by day things that were even a little way off were growing dimmer to his sight; the hospital across the street, which he used to execrate for being all too often before his eyes, was not quite beyond his range of vision, and if he had not known that he lived in Charlotte Street, a quiet street but still a city street, he might have believed that his window gave on a desert waste where gray sky and gray land blended indistinguishably into each other. His quick-witted sister only needed to observe twice that the armchair stood by the window; after that whenever she had tidied the room she always pushed the chair back to the same place at the window and even left the inner casements open.

If he could have spoken to her and thanked her for all she had to do for him, he could have borne her ministrations better; as it was, they oppressed him. She certainly tried to make as light as possible of whatever was disagreeable in her task, and as time went on she succeeded, of course, more and more, but time brought more enlightenment to Gregor too. The very way she came in distressed him. Hardly was she in the room when she rushed to the window, without even taking time to shut the door, careful as she was usually to shield the sight of Gregor's room from the others, and as if she were almost suffocating tore the casements open with hasty fingers, standing them in the open draught for a while even in the bitterest cold and drawing deep breaths. This noisy scurry of hers upset Gregor twice a day; he would crouch trembling under the sofa all the time, knowing quite well that she would certainly have spared him such a disturbance had she found it at all possible to stay in his presence without opening the window.

On one occasion, about a month after Gregor's metamorphosis, when there was surely no reason for her to be still startled at his appearance, she came a little earlier than usual and found him gazing out of the window, quite motionless, and thus well placed to look like a bogey. Gregor would not have been surprised had she not come in at all, for she could not immediately open the window while he was there, but not only did she retreat, she jumped back as if in alarm and banged the door shut; a stranger might well have thought that he had been lying in wait for her there meaning to bite her. Of course he hid himself under the sofa at once, but he had to wait until midday before she came again, and she seemed more ill at ease than usual. This made him realize how repulsive the sight of him still was to her, and that it was bound to go on being repulsive, and what an effort it must cost her not to run away even from the sight of the small portion of his body that stuck out from under the sofa. In order to spare her that, therefore, one day he carried a sheet on his back to the sofa—it cost him four hours' labor—and arranged it there in such a way as to hide him completely, so that even if she were to bend down she could not see him. Had she considered the sheet unnecessary, she would certainly have stripped it off the sofa again, for it was clear enough that this curtaining and confining of himself was not likely to conduce Gregor's comfort, but she left it where it was, and Gregor even fancied that he caught a thankful glance from her eye when he lifted the sheet carefully a very little with his head to see how she was taking the new arrangement.

For the first fortnight his parents could not bring themselves to the point of entering his room, and he often heard them expressing their appreciation of his sister's activities, whereas formerly they had frequently scolded her for being as they thought a somewhat useless daughter. But now, both of them often waited outside the door, his father and his mother, while his sister tidied his room, and as soon as she came out she had to tell them exactly how things were in the room, what Gregor had eaten, how he had conducted himself this time and whether there was not perhaps some slight improvement in his condition. His mother, moreover, began relatively soon to want to visit him, but his father and sister dissuaded her at first with arguments which Gregor listened to very attentively and altogether approved. Later, however, she had to be held back by main force, and when she cried out: "Do let me in to Gregor, he is my unfortunate son! Can't you understand that I must go to him?" Gregor thought that it might be well to have her come in, not every day, of course, but perhaps once a week; she understood things, after all, much better than his sister, who was only a child despite the efforts she was making and had perhaps taken on so difficult a task merely out of childish thoughtlessness.

Gregor's desire to see his mother was soon fulfilled. During the day-time he did not want to show himself at the window, out of consideration for his parents, but he could not crawl very far around the few square yards of floor space he had, nor could he bear lying quietly at rest all during the night, while he was fast losing any interest he had ever taken in food, so that for mere recreation he had formed the habit of crawling crisscross over the walls and ceiling. He especially enjoyed hanging suspended from the ceiling; it was much better than lying on the floor. One could breathe more freely; one's body swung and rocked lightly; and in the almost blissful absorption induced by this suspension it could happen to his own surprise that he let go and fell plump on the floor. Yet he now had his body much better under control than formerly, and even such a big fall did him no harm. His sister at once remarked the new distraction Gregor had found for himself—he left traces behind him of the sticky stuff on his soles wherever he crawled—and she got the idea in her head of giving him as wide a field as possible to crawl in and of removing the pieces of furniture that hindered him, above all the chest of drawers and the writing desk. But that was more than she could manage all by herself, she did not dare ask her father to help her; and as for the servant girl, a young creature of sixteen who had had the courage to stay on after the cook's departure, she could not be asked to help, for she had begged as an especial favor that she might keep the kitchen door locked and open it only on a definite summons; so there was nothing left but to apply to her mother at an hour when her father was out. And the old lady did come, with exclamations of joyful eagerness, which, however, died away at the door of Gregor's room. Gregor's sister, of course, went in first, to see that everything was in order before letting his mother enter. In great haste Gregor pulled the sheet lower and tucked it more in folds so that it really looked as if it had been thrown accidentally over the sofa. And this time he did not peer out from under it; he renounced the pleasure of seeing his mother on this occasion and was only glad that she had come at all. "Come in, he's out of sight," said his sister, obviously leading her mother by the hand. Gregor could now hear the two women struggling to shift the heavy old chest from its place, and his sister claiming the greater part of the labor for herself, without listening to the admonitions of her mother who feared she might overstrain herself. It took a long time. After at least a quarter of an hour's tugging his mother objected that the chest had better be left where it was, for in the first place it was too heavy and could never be got out before his father came home, and standing in the middle of the room like that it would only hamper Gregor's movements, while in the second place it was not at all certain that removing the furniture would be doing a service to Gregor. She was inclined to think to the contrary; the sight of the naked walls made her own heart heavy, and why shouldn't Gregor have the same feeling, considering that he had been used to his furniture for so long and might feel forlorn without it. "And doesn't it look," she concluded in a low voice—in fact she had been almost whispering all the time as if to avoid letting Gregor, whose exact whereabouts she did not know, hear even the tones of her voice, for she was convinced that he could not understand her words—"doesn't it look as if we were showing him, by taking away his furniture, that we have given up hope of his ever getting better and are just leaving him coldly to himself? I think it would be best to keep his room exactly as it has always been, so that when he comes back to us he will find everything unchanged and be able all the more easily to forget what has happened in between."

On hearing these words from his mother Gregor realized that the lack of all direct human speech for the past two months together with the monotony of family life must have confused his mind, otherwise he could not account for the fact that he had quite earnestly looked forward to having his room emptied of furnishing. Did he really want his warm room, so comfortably fitted with old family furniture, to be turned into a naked den in which he would certainly be able to crawl unhampered in all directions but at the price of shedding simultaneously all recollection of his human background? He had indeed been so near the brink of forgetfulness that only the voice of his mother, which he had not heard for so long, had drawn him back from it. Nothing should be taken out of his room; everything must stay as it was; he could not dispense with the good influence of the furniture on his state of mind; and even if the furniture did hamper him in his senseless crawling round and round, that was no drawback but a great advantage.

Unfortunately his sister was of the contrary opinion; she had grown accustomed, and not without reason, to consider herself an expert in Gregor's affairs as against her parents, and so her mother's advice was now enough to make her determined on the removal not only of the chest and the writing desk, which had been her first intention, but of all the furniture except the indispensable sofa. This determination was not, of course, merely the outcome of childish recalcitrance and of the self-confidence she had recently developed so unexpectedly and at such cost; she had in fact perceived that Gregor needed a lot of space to crawl about in, while on the other hand he never used the furniture at all, so far as could be seen. Another factor might have been also the enthusiastic temperament of an adolescent girl, which seeks to indulge itself on every opportunity and which now tempted Grete to exaggerate the horror of her brother's circumstances in order that she might do all the more for him. In a room where Gregor lorded it all alone over empty walls no one save herself was likely ever to set foot.

And so she was not to be moved from her resolve by her mother who seemed moreover to be ill at ease in Gregor's room and therefore unsure of herself, was soon reduced to silence and helped her daughter as best she could to push the chest outside. Now, Gregor could do without the chest, if need be, but the writing desk he must retain. As soon as the two women had got the chest out of his room, groaning as they pushed it, Gregor stuck his head out from under the sofa to see how he might intervene as kindly and cautiously as possible. But as bad luck would have it, his mother was the first to return, leaving Grete clasping the chest in the room next door where she was trying to shift it all by herself, without of course moving it from the spot. His mother however was not accustomed to the sight of him, it might sicken her and so in alarm Gregor backed quickly to the other end of the sofa, yet could not prevent the sheet from swaying a little in front. That was enough to put her on the alert. She paused, stood still for a moment and then went back to Grete.

Although Gregor kept reassuring himself that nothing out of the way was happening, but only a few bits of furniture were being changed round, he soon had to admit that all this trotting to and fro of the two women, their little ejaculations and the scraping of furniture along the floor affected him like a vast disturbance coming from all sides at once, and however much he tucked in his head and legs and cowered to the very floor he was bound to confess that he would not be able to stand it for long. They were clearing his room out; taking away everything he loved; the chest in which he kept his fret saw and other tools was already dragged off, they were now loosening the writing desk which had almost sunk into the floor, the desk at which he had done all his homework when he was at the commercial academy, at the grammar school before that, and, yes, even at the primary school—he had no more time to waste in weighing the good intentions of the two women, whose existence he had by now almost forgotten, for they were so exhausted that they were laboring in silence and nothing could be heard but the heavy scuffling of their feet.

And so he rushed out—the women were just leaning against the writing desk in the next room to give themselves a breather—and four times changed his direction, since he really did not know what to rescue first, then on the wall opposite, which was already otherwise cleared, he was struck by the picture of the lady muffled in so much fur and quickly crawled up to it and pressed himself to the glass, which was a good surface to hold on to and comforted his hot belly. This picture at least, which was entirely hidden beneath him, was going to be removed by nobody. He turned his head towards the door of the living room so as to observe the women when they came back.

They had not allowed themselves much of a rest and were already coming; Grete had twined her arm round her mother and was almost supporting her. "Well, what shall we take now?" said Grete, looking round. Her eyes met Gregor's from the wall. She kept her composure, presumably because of her mother, bent her head down to her mother, to keep her from looking up, and said, although in a fluttering, unpremeditated voice: "Come, hadn't we better go back to the living room for a moment?" Her intentions were clear enough to Gregor, she wanted to bestow her mother in safety and then chase him down from the wall. Well, just let her try it! He clung to his picture and would not give it up. He would rather fly in Grete's face.

But Grete's words had succeeded in disquieting her mother, who took a step to one side, caught sight of the huge brown mass on the flowered wallpaper, and before she was really conscious that what she saw was Gregor screamed in a loud, hoarse voice: "Oh God, oh God!" fell with outspread arms over the sofa as if giving up and did not move. "Gregor!" cried his sister, shaking her fist and glaring at him. This was the first time she had directly addressed him since his metamorphosis. She ran into the next room for some aromatic essence with which to rouse her mother from her fainting fit. Gregor wanted to help too—there was still time to rescue the picture—but he was stuck fast to the glass and had to tear himself loose; he then ran after his sister into the next room as if he could advise her, as he used to do; but then had to stand helplessly behind her; she meanwhile searched among various small bottles and when she turned round started in alarm at the sight of him; one bottle fell on the floor and broke; a splinter of glass cut Gregor's face and some kind of corrosive medicine splashed him; without pausing a moment longer Grete gathered up all the bottles she could carry and ran to her mother with them; she banged the door shut with her foot. Gregor was now cut off from his mother, who was perhaps nearly dying because of him; he dared not open the door for fear of frightening away his sister, who had to stay with her mother; there was nothing he could do but wait; and harassed by self-reproach and worry he began now to crawl to and fro, over everything, walls, furniture and ceiling, and finally in his despair, when the whole room seemed to be reeling round him, fell down on to the middle of the big table.

A little while elapsed, Gregor was still lying there feebly and all around was quiet, perhaps that was a good omen. Then the doorbell rang. The servant girl was of course locked in her kitchen, and Grete would have to open the door. It was his father. "What's been happening?" were his first words; Grete's face must have told him everything. Grete answered in a muffled voice, apparently hiding her head on his breast: "Mother has been fainting, but she's better now. Gregor's broken loose." "Just what I expected," said his father, "just what I've been telling you, but you women would never listen." It was clear to Gregor that his father had taken the worst interpretation of Grete's all too brief statement and was assuming that Gregor had been guilty of some violent act. Therefore Gregor must now try to propitiate his father, since he had neither time nor means for an explanation. And so he fled to the door of his own room and crouched against it, to let his father see as soon as he came in from the hall that his son had the good intention of getting back into his room immediately and that it was not necessary to drive him there, but that if only the door were opened he would disappear at once.

Yet his father was not in the mood to perceive such fine distinctions. "Ah!" he cried as soon as he appeared, in a tone which sounded at once angry and exultant. Gregor drew his head back from the door and lifted it to look at his father. Truly, this was not the father he had imagined to himself, admittedly he had been too absorbed of late in his new recreation of crawling over the ceiling to take the same interest as before in what was happening elsewhere in the flat, and he ought really to be prepared for some changes. And yet, and yet, could that be his father? The man who used to lie wearily sunk in bed whenever Gregor set out on a business journey; who welcomed him back of an evening lying in a long chair in a dressing gown; who could not really rise to his feet but only lifted his arms in greeting, and on the rare occasions when he did go out with his family, on one or two Sundays a year and on high holidays, walked between Gregor and his mother, who were slow walkers anyhow, even more slowly than they did, muffled in his old greatcoat, shuffling laboriously forward with the help of his crook-handled stick which he set down most cautiously at every step and, whenever he wanted to say anything, nearly always came to a full stop and gathered his escort around him? Now he was standing there in fine shape; dressed in a smart blue uniform with gold buttons, such as bank messengers wear; his strong double chin bulged over the stiff high collar of his jacket; from under his bushy eyebrows his black eyes darted fresh and penetrating glances; his one-time tangled white hair had been combed flat on either side of a shining and carefully exact parting. He pitched his cap, which bore a gold monogram, probably the badge of some bank, in a wide sweep across the whole room on to a sofa and with the tail-ends of his jacket thrown back, his hands in his trouser pockets, advanced with a grim visage towards Gregor. Likely enough he did not himself know what he meant to do; at any rate he lifted his feet uncommonly high, and Gregor was dumbfounded at the enormous size of his shoe soles. But Gregor could not risk standing up to him, aware as he had been from the very first day of his new life that his father believed only the severest measures suitable for dealing with him. And so he ran before his father, stopping when he stopped and scuttling forward again when his father made any kind of move. In this way they circled the room several times without anything decisive happening, indeed the whole operation did not even look like a pursuit because it was carried out so slowly. And so Gregor did not leave the floor, for he feared that his father might take as a piece of peculiar wickedness any excursion of his over the walls or the ceiling. All the same, he could not stay this course much longer, for while his father took one step he had to carry out a whole series of movements. He was already beginning to feel breathless, just as in his former life his lungs had not been very dependable. As he was staggering along, trying to concentrate his energy on running, hardly keeping his eyes open; in his dazed state never even thinking of any other escape than simply going forward; and having almost forgotten that the walls were free to him, which in his room were well provided with finely carved pieces of furniture full of knobs and crevices—suddenly something lightly flung landed close behind him and rolled before him. It was an apple; a second apple followed immediately; Gregor came to

a stop in alarm; there was no point in running on, for his father was determined to bombard him. He had filled his pockets with fruit from the
dish on the sideboard and was now shying apple after apple, without taking particularly good aim for the moment. The small red apples rolled
about the floor as if magnetized and cannoned into each other. An apple
thrown without much force grazed Gregor's back and glanced off harmlessly. But another following immediately landed right on his back and
sank in; Gregor wanted to drag himself forward, as if this startling, incredible pain could be left behind him; but he felt as if nailed to the spot
and flattened himself out in a complete derangement of all his senses. With
his last conscious look he saw the door of his room being torn open and
his mother rushing out ahead of his screaming sister, in her underbodice,
for her daughter had loosened her clothing to let her breathe more freely
and recover from her swoon, he saw his mother rushing towards his father,
leaving one after another behind her on the floor her loosened petticoats,
stumbling over her petticoats straight to his father and embracing him,
in complete union with him—but here Gregor's sight began to fail—with
her hands clasped round his father's neck as she begged for her son's life.

III

The serious injury done to Gregor, which disabled him for more
than a month—the apple went on sticking in his body as a visible reminder,
since no one ventured to remove it—seemed to have made even his father
recollect that Gregor was a member of the family, despite his present unfortunate and repulsive shape, and ought not to be treated as an enemy,
that, on the contrary, family duty required the suppression of disgust and
the exercise of patience, nothing but patience.

And although his injury had impaired, probably for ever, his power
of movement, and for the time being it took him long, long minutes to
creep across his room like an old invalid—there was no question now of
crawling up the wall—yet in his own opinion he was sufficiently com-
pensated for this worsening of his condition by the fact that towards evening
the living-room door, which he used to watch intently for an hour or
two beforehand, was always thrown open, so that lying in the darkness
of his room, invisible to the family, he could see them all at the lamplit
table and listen to their talk, by general consent as it were, very different
from his earlier eavesdropping.

True, their intercourse lacked the lively character of former times,
which he had always called to mind with a certain wistfulness in the small
hotel bedrooms where he had been wont to throw himself down, tired
out, on damp bedding. They were now mostly very silent. Soon after supper his father would fall asleep in his armchair; his mother and sister would
admonish each other to be silent; his mother, bending low over the lamp,
stitched at fine sewing for an underwear firm; his sister, who had taken
a job as a salesgirl, was learning shorthand and French in the evenings

on the chance of bettering herself. Sometimes his father woke up, and as if quite unaware that he had been sleeping said to his mother: "What a lot of sewing you're doing today!" and at once fell asleep again, while the two women exchanged a tired smile.

With a kind of mulishness his father persisted in keeping his uniform on even in the house; his dressing gown hung uselessly on its peg and he slept fully dressed where he sat, as if he were ready for service at any moment and even here only at the beck and call of his superior. As a result, his uniform, which was not brand-new to start with, began to look dirty, despite all the loving care of the mother and sister to keep it clean, and Gregor often spent whole evenings gazing at the many greasy spots on the garment, gleaming with gold buttons always in a high state of polish, in which the old man sat sleeping in extreme discomfort and yet quite peacefully.

As soon as the clock struck ten his mother tried to rouse his father with gentle words and to persuade him after that to get into bed, for sitting there he could not have a proper sleep and that was what he needed most, since he had to go to duty at six. But with the mulishness that had obsessed him since he became a bank messenger he always insisted on staying longer at the table, although he regularly fell asleep again and in the end only with the greatest trouble could be got out of his armchair and into his bed. However insistently Gregor's mother and sister kept urging him with gentle reminders, he would go on slowly shaking his head for a quarter of an hour, keeping his eyes shut, and refuse to get to his feet. The mother plucked at his sleeve, whispering endearments in his ear, the sister left her lessons to come to her mother's help, but Gregor's father was not to be caught. He would only sink down deeper in his chair. Not until the two women hoisted him up by the armpits did he open his eyes and look at them both, one after the other, usually with the remark: "This is a life. This is the peace and quiet of my old age." And leaning on the two of them he would heave himself up, with difficulty, as if he were a great burden to himself, suffer them to lead him as far as the door and then wave them off and go on alone, while the mother abandoned her needlework and the sister her pen in order to run after him and help him farther.

Who could find time, in this overworked and tired-out family, to bother about Gregor more than was absolutely needful? The household was reduced more and more; the servant girl was turned off; a gigantic bony charwoman with white hair flying round her head came in morning and evening to do the rough work; everything else was done by Gregor's mother, as well as great piles of sewing. Even various family ornaments, which his mother and sister used to wear with pride at parties and celebrations, had to be sold, as Gregor discovered of an evening from hearing them all discuss the prices obtained. But what they lamented most was the fact that they could not leave the flat which was too big for their present circumstances, because they could not think of any way to shift Gregor. Yet Gregor saw well enough that consideration for him was not the main difficulty preventing the removal, for they could have easily shifted him in some suitable box with a few air holes in it; what really kept them from moving into another flat was rather their own complete hopelessness and the belief that they had been singled out for a misfortune such as had never happened to any of their relations or acquaintances. They fulfilled to the uttermost all that the world demands of poor people, the father fetched breakfast for the small clerks in the bank, the mother devoted her energy to making underwear for strangers, the sister trotted to and fro behind the counter at the behest of customers, but more than this they had not the strength to do. And the wound in Gregor's back began to nag at him afresh when his mother and sister, after getting his father into bed, came back again, left their work lying, drew close to each other and sat cheek by cheek; when his mother, pointing towards his room, said: "Shut that door now, Grete," and he was left again in darkness, while next door the women mingled their tears or perhaps sat dry-eyed staring at the table.

Gregor hardly slept at all by night or by day. He was often haunted by the idea that next time the door opened he would take the family's affairs in hand again just as he used to do; once more, after this long interval, there appeared in his thoughts the figures of the chief and the chief clerk, the commercial travelers and the apprentices, the porter who was so dull-witted, two or three friends in other firms, a chambermaid in one of the rural hotels, a sweet and fleeting memory, a cashier in a milliner's shop, whom he had wooed earnestly but too slowly—they all appeared, together with strangers or people he had quite forgotten, but instead of helping him and his family they were one and all unapproachable and he was glad when they vanished. At other times he would not be in the mood to bother about his family, he was only filled with rage at the way they were neglecting him, and although he had no clear idea of what he might care to eat he would make plans for getting into the larder to take the food that was after all his due, even if he were not hungry. His sister no longer took thought to bring him what might especially please him, but in the morning and at noon before she went to business hurriedly pushed into his room with her foot any food that was available, and in the evening cleared it out again with one sweep of the broom, heedless of whether it had been merely tasted, or—as most frequently happened—left untouched. The cleaning of his room, which she now did always in the evenings, could not have been more hastily done. Streaks of dirt stretched along the walls, here and there lay balls of dust and filth. At first Gregor used to station himself in some particularly filthy corner when his sister arrived, in order to reproach her with it, so to speak. But he could have sat there for weeks without getting her to make any improvements; she could see the dirt as well as he did, but she had simply made up her mind to leave it alone. And yet, with a touchiness that was new to her, which seemed anyhow to have infected the whole family, she jealously guarded her claim to be the sole caretaker of Gregor's room. His mother once subjected his room to a thorough cleaning, which was achieved only by means of several buckets of water—all this dampness of course upset Gregor too and he lay widespread, sulky and motionless on the sofa—but she was well punished for it. Hardly had his sister noticed the changed aspect of his room that evening than she rushed in high dudgeon into the living room and, despite the imploringly raised hands of her mother, burst into a storm of weeping, while her parents—her father had of course been startled out of his chair—looked on at first in helpless amazement; then they too began to go into action; the father reproached the mother on his right for not having left the cleaning of Gregor's room to his sister; shrieked at the sister on his left that never again was she to be allowed to clean Gregor's room; while the mother tried to pull the father into his bedroom, since he was beyond himself with agitation; the sister, shaken with sobs, then beat upon the table with her small fists; and Gregor hissed loudly with rage because not one of them thought of shutting the door to spare him such a spectacle and so much noise.

Still, even if the sister, exhausted by her daily work, had grown tired of looking after Gregor as she did formerly, there was no need for his mother's intervention or for Gregor's being neglected at all. The charwoman was there. This old widow, whose strong bony frame had enabled her to survive the worst a long life could offer, by no means recoiled from Gregor. Without being in the least curious she had once by chance opened the door of his room and at the sight of Gregor, who, taken by surprise, began to rush to and fro although no one was chasing him, merely stood there with her arms folded. From that time she never failed to open his door a little for a moment, morning and evening, to have a look at him. At first she even used to call him to her, with words which apparently she took to be friendly; such as: "Come along, then, you old dung beetle!" or "Look at the old dung beetle, then!" To such allocutions Gregor made no answer, but stayed motionless where he was, as if the door had never been opened. Instead of being allowed to disturb him so senselessly whenever the whim took her, she should rather have been ordered to clean out his room daily, that charwoman! Once, early in the morning—heavy rain was lashing on the windowpanes, perhaps a sign that spring was on the way—Gregor was so exasperated when she began addressing him again that he ran for her, as if to attack her, although slowly and feebly enough. But the charwoman instead of showing fright merely lifted high a chair that happened to be beside the door, and as she stood there with her mouth wide open it was clear that she meant to shut it only when she brought the chair down on Gregor's back. "So you're not coming any nearer?" she asked, as Gregor turned away again, and quietly put the chair back into the corner.

Gregor was now eating hardly anything. Only when he happened to pass the food laid out for him did he take a bit of something in his mouth as a pastime, kept it there for an hour at a time and usually spat it out again. At first he thought it was chagrin over the state of his room that prevented him from eating, yet he soon got used to the various changes in his room. It had become a habit in the family to push into his room things there was no room for elsewhere, and there were plenty of these now, since one of the rooms had been let to three lodgers. These serious gentlemen—all three of them with full beards, as Gregor once observed through a crack in the door—had a passion for order, not only in their own room but, since they were now members of the household, in all its arrangements, especially in the kitchen. Superfluous, not to say dirty, objects they could not bear. Besides, they had brought with them most of the furnishings they needed. For this reason many things could be dispensed with that it was no use trying to sell but that should not be thrown away either. All of them found their way into Gregor's room. The ash can likewise and the kitchen garbage can. Anything that was not needed for the moment was simply flung into Gregor's room by the charwoman, who did everything in a hurry; fortunately Gregor usually saw only the object, whatever it was, and the hand that held it. Perhaps she intended to take the things away again as time and opportunity offered, or to collect them until she could throw them all out in a heap, but in fact they just lay wherever she happened to throw them, except when Gregor pushed his way through the junk heap and shifted it somewhat, at first out of necessity, because he had not room enough to crawl, but later with increasing enjoyment, although after such excursions, being sad and weary to death, he would lie motionless for hours. And since the lodgers often ate their supper at home in the common living room, the living-room door stayed shut many an evening, yet Gregor reconciled himself quite easily to the shutting of the door, for often enough on evenings when it was opened he had disregarded it entirely and lain in the darkest corner of his room, quite unnoticed by the family. But on one occasion the charwoman left the door open a little and it stayed ajar even when the lodgers came in for supper and the lamp was lit. They set themselves at the top end of the table where formerly Gregor and his father and mother had eaten their meals, unfolded their napkins and took knife and fork in hand. At once his mother appeared in the doorway with a dish of meat and close behind her his sister with a dish of potatoes piled high. The food steamed with a thick vapor. The lodgers bent over the food set before them as if to scrutinize it before eating, in fact the man in the middle, who seemed to pass for an authority with the other two, cut a piece of meat as it lay on the dish, obviously to discover if it were tender or should be sent back to the kitchen. He showed satisfaction, and Gregor's mother and sister, who had been watching anxiously, breathed freely and began to smile.

The family itself took its meals in the kitchen. None the less, Gregor's father came into the living room before going into the kitchen and with one prolonged bow, cap in hand, made a round of the table. The lodgers all stood up and murmured something in their beards. When they were alone again they ate their food in almost complete silence. It seemed remarkable to Gregor that among the various noises coming from the table he could always distinguish the sound of their masticating teeth, as if this were a sign to Gregor that one needed teeth in order to eat, and that with toothless jaws even of the finest make one could do nothing. "I'm hungry enough," said Gregor sadly to himself, "but not for that kind of food. How these lodgers are stuffing themselves, and here am I dying of starvation!"

On that very evening—during the whole of his time there Gregor could not remember ever having heard the violin—the sound of violin-playing came from the kitchen. The lodgers had already finished their supper, the one in the middle had brought out a newspaper and given the other two a page apiece, and now they were leaning back at ease reading and smoking. When the violin began to play they pricked up their ears, got to their feet, and went on tiptoe to the hall door where they stood huddled together. Their movements must have been heard in the kitchen, for Gregor's father called out: "Is the violin-playing disturbing you gentlemen? It can be stopped at once." "On the contrary," said the middle lodger, "could not Fräulein Samsa come and play in this room, beside us, where it is much more convenient and comfortable?" "Oh certainly," cried Gregor's father, as if he were the violin player. The lodgers came back into the living room and waited. Presently Gregor's father arrived with the music stand, his mother carrying the music and his sister with the violin. His sister quietly made everything ready to start playing; his parents, who had never let rooms before and so had an exaggerated idea of the courtesy due to lodgers, did not venture to sit down on their own chairs; his father leaned against the door, the right hand thrust between two buttons of his livery coat, which was formally buttoned up; but his mother was offered a chair by one of the lodgers and, since she left the chair just where he had happened to put it, sat down in a corner to one side.

Gregor's sister began to play; the father and mother, from either side, intently watched the movements of her hands. Gregor, attracted by the playing, ventured to move forward a little until his head was actually inside the living room. He felt hardly any surprise at his growing lack of consideration for the others; there had been a time when he prided himself on being considerate. And yet just on this occasion he had more reason than ever to hide himself, since owing to the amount of dust which lay thick in his room and rose into the air at the slightest movement, he too was covered with dust; fluff and hair and remnants of food trailed with him, caught on his back and along his sides; his indifference to everything was much too great for him to turn on his back and scrape himself clean on the carpet, as once he had done several times a day. And in spite of his condition, no shame deterred him from advancing a little over the spotless floor of the living room.

To be sure, no one was aware of him. The family was entirely absorbed in the violin-playing; the lodgers, however, who first of all had stationed themselves, hands in pockets, much too close behind the music stand so that they could all have read the music, which must have bothered his sister, had soon retreated to the window, half-whispering with downbent heads, and stayed there while his father turned an anxious eye on them. Indeed, they were making it more than obvious that they had been disappointed in their expectation of hearing good or enjoyable violin-playing, that they had had more than enough of the performance and only out of courtesy suffered a continued disturbance of their peace. From the way they all kept blowing the smoke of their cigars high in the air through nose and mouth one could divine their irritation. And yet Gregor's sister was playing so beautifully. Her face leaned sideways, intently and sadly her eyes followed the notes of music. Gregor crawled a little farther forward and lowered his head to the ground so that it might be possible for his eyes to meet hers. Was he an animal, that music had such an effect upon him? He felt as if the way were opening before him to the unknown nourishment he craved. He was determined to push forward till he reached his sister, to pull at her skirt and so let her know that she was to come into his room with her violin, for no one here appreciated her playing as he would appreciate it. He would never let her out of his room, at least, not so long as he lived; his frightful appearance would become, for the first time, useful to him; he would watch all the doors of his room at once and spit at intruders; but his sister should need no constraint, she should stay with him of her own free will; she should sit beside him on the sofa, bend down her ear to him and hear him confide that he had had the firm intention of sending her to the Conservatorium, and that, but for his mishap, last Christmas—surely Christmas was long past?—he would have announced it to everybody without allowing a single objection. After this confession his sister would be so touched that she would burst into tears, and Gregor would then raise himself to her shoulder and kiss her on the neck, which, now that she went to business, she kept free of any ribbon or collar.

"Mr. Samsa!" cried the middle lodger, to Gregor's father, and pointed, without wasting any more words, at Gregor, now working himself slowly forwards. The violin fell silent, the middle lodger first smiled to his friends with a shake of the head and then looked at Gregor again. Instead of driving Gregor out, his father seemed to think it more needful to begin by soothing down the lodgers, although they were not at all agitated and apparently found Gregor more entertaining than the violin-playing. He hurried towards them and, spreading out his arms, tried to urge them back into their own room and at the same time to block their view of Gregor.

They now began to be really a little angry, one could not tell whether because of the old man's behavior or because it just dawned on them that all unwittingly they had such a neighbor as Gregor next door. They demanded explanations of his father, they waved their arms like him, tugged uneasily at their beards, and only with reluctance backed towards their room. Meanwhile Gregor's sister, who stood there as if lost when her playing was so abruptly broken off, came to life again, pulled herself together all at once after standing for a while holding violin and bow in nervelessly hanging hands and staring at her music, pushed her violin into the lap of her mother, who was still sitting in her chair fighting asthmatically for breath, and ran into the lodgers' room to which they were now being shepherded by her father rather more quickly than before. One could see the pillows and blankets on the beds flying under her accustomed fingers and being laid in order. Before the lodgers had actually reached their room she had finished making the beds and slipped out.

The old man seemed once more to be so possessed by his mulish self-assertiveness that he was forgetting all the respect he should show to his lodgers. He kept driving them on and driving them on until in the very door of the bedroom the middle lodger stamped his foot loudly on the floor and so brought him to a halt. "I beg to announce," said the lodger, lifting one hand and looking also at Gregor's mother and sister, "that because of the disgusting conditions prevailing in this household and family"—here he spat on the floor with emphatic brevity—"I give you notice on the spot. Naturally I won't pay you a penny for the days I have lived here, on the contrary I shall consider bringing an action for damages against you, based on claims—believe me—that will be easily susceptible of proof." He ceased and stared straight in front of him, as if he expected something. In fact his two friends at once rushed into the breach with these words: "And we too give notice on the spot." On that he seized the door-handle and shut the door with a slam.

Gregor's father, groping with his hands, staggered forward and fell into his chair; it looked as if he were stretching himself there for his ordinary evening nap, but the marked jerkings of his head, which was as if uncontrollable, showed that he was far from asleep. Gregor had simply stayed quietly all the time on the spot where the lodgers had espied him. Disappointment at the failure of his plan, perhaps also the weakness arising from extreme hunger, made it impossible for him to move. He feared, with a fair degree of certainty, that at any moment the general tension would discharge itself in a combined attack upon him, and he lay waiting. He did not react even to the noise made by the violin as it fell off his mother's lap from under her trembling fingers and gave out a resonant note.

"My dear parents," said his sister, slapping her hand on the table by way of introduction, "things can't go on like this. Perhaps you don't realize that, but I do. I won't utter my brother's name in the presence of this creature, and so all I say is: we must try to get rid of it. We've tried to look after it and to put up with it as far as is humanly possible, and I don't think anyone could reproach us in the slightest."

"She is more than right," said Gregor's father to himself. His mother, who was still choking for lack of breath, began to cough hollowly into her hand with a wild look in her eyes.

His sister rushed over to her and held her forehead. His father's thoughts seemed to have lost their vagueness at Grete's words, he sat more upright, fingering his service cap that lay among the plates still lying on the table from the lodgers' supper, and from time to time looked at the still form of Gregor.

"We must try to get rid of it," his sister now said explicitly to her father, since her mother was coughing too much to hear a word, "it will be the death of both of you. I can see that coming. When one has to work as hard as we do, all of us, one can't stand this continual torment at home on top of it. At least I can't stand it any longer." And she burst into such a passion of sobbing that her tears dropped on her mother's face, where she wiped them off mechanically.

"My dear," said the old man sympathetically, and with evident understanding, "but what can we do?"

Gregor's sister merely shrugged her shoulders to indicate the feeling of helplessness that had now overmastered her during her weeping fit, in contrast to her former confidence.

"If he could understand us," said her father, half questioningly; Grete, still sobbing, vehemently waved a hand to show how unthinkable that was.

"If he could understand us," repeated the old man, shutting his eyes to consider his daughter's conviction that understanding was impossible, "then perhaps we might come to some agreement with him. But as it is—"

"He must go," cried Gregor's sister, "that's the only solution, Father. You must just try to get rid of the idea that this is Gregor. The fact that we've believed it for so long is the root of all our trouble. But how can it be Gregor? If this were Gregor, he would have realized long ago that human beings can't live with such a creature, and he'd have gone away on his own accord. Then we wouldn't have any brother, but we'd be able to go on living and keep his memory in honor. As it is, this creature persecutes us, drives away our lodgers, obviously wants the whole apartment to himself and would have us all sleep in the gutter. Just look, Father," she shrieked all at once, "he's at it again!" And in an access of panic that was quite incomprehensible to Gregor she even quitted her mother, literally thrusting the chair from her as if she would rather sacrifice her mother than stay so near to Gregor, and rushed behind her father, who also rose up, being simply upset by her agitation, and half-spread his arms out as if to protect her.

Yet Gregor had not the slightest intention of frightening anyone, far less his sister. He had only begun to turn round in order to crawl back to his room, but it was certainly a startling operation to watch, since because of his disabled condition he could not execute the difficult turning movements except by lifting his head and then bracing it against the floor over and over again. He paused and looked around. His good intentions seemed to have been recognized; the alarm had only been momentary. Now they were all watching him in melancholy silence. His mother lay in her chair, her legs stiffly outstretched and pressed together, her eyes almost closing for sheer weariness; his father and his sister were sitting beside each other, his sister's arm around the old man's neck.

Perhaps I can go on turning round now, thought Gregor, and began his labors again. He could not stop himself from panting with the effort, and had to pause now and then to take breath. Nor did anyone harass him, he was left entirely to himself. When he had completed the turn-round he began at once to crawl straight back. He was amazed at the distance separating him from his room and could not understand how in his weak state he had managed to accomplish the same journey so recently, almost without remarking it. Intent on crawling as fast as possible, he barely noticed that not a single word, not an ejaculation from his family, interfered with his progress. Only when he was already in the doorway did he turn his head round, not completely, for his neck muscles were getting stiff, but enough to see that nothing had changed behind him except that his sister had risen to her feet. His last glance fell on his mother, who was not quite overcome by sleep.

Hardly was he well inside his room when the door was hastily pushed shut, bolted and locked. The sudden noise in his rear startled him so much that his little legs gave beneath him. It was his sister who had shown such haste. She had been standing ready waiting and had made a light spring forward. Gregor had not even heard her coming, and she cried "At last!" to her parents as she turned the key in the lock.

"And what now?" said Gregor to himself, looking round in the darkness. Soon he made the discovery that he was now unable to stir a limb. This did not surprise him, rather it seemed unnatural that he should ever actually have been able to move on these feeble little legs. Otherwise he felt relatively comfortable. True, his whole body was aching, but it seemed that the pain was gradually growing less and would finally pass away. The rotting apple in his back and the inflamed area around it, all covered with soft dust, already hardly troubled him. He thought of his family with tenderness and love. The decision that he must disappear was one that he held to even more strongly than his sister, if that were possible. In this state of vacant and peaceful meditation he remained until the tower clock struck three in the morning. The first broadening of light in the world outside the window entered his consciousness once more. Then his head sank to the floor of its own accord and from his nostrils came the last faint flicker of his breath.

When the charwoman arrived early in the morning—what between her strength and her impatience she slammed all the doors so loudly, never mind how often she had been begged not to do so, that no one in the whole apartment could enjoy any quiet sleep after her arrival—she noticed nothing unusual as she took her customary peep into Gregor's room. She thought he was lying motionless on purpose, pretending to be in the sulks; she credited him with every kind of intelligence. Since she happened to have the longhandled broom in her hand she tried to tickle him up with it from the doorway. When that too produced no reaction she felt provoked and poked at him a little harder, and only when she had pushed him along the floor without meeting any resistance was her attention aroused. It did not take her long to establish the truth of the matter, and her eyes widened, she let out a whistle, yet did not waste much time over it but tore open the door of the Samsas' bedroom and yelled into the darkness at the top of her voice: "Just look at this, it's dead; it's lying here dead and done for!"

Mr. and Mrs. Samsa started up in their double bed and before they realized the nature of the charwoman's announcement had some difficulty in overcoming the shock of it. But then they got out of bed quickly, one on either side, Mr. Samsa throwing a blanket over his shoulders, Mrs. Samsa in nothing but her nightgown; in this array they entered Gregor's room. Meanwhile the door of the living room opened, too, where Grete had been sleeping since the advent of the lodgers; she was completely dressed as if she had not been to bed, which seemed to be confirmed also by the paleness of her face. "Dead?" said Mrs. Samsa, looking questioningly at the charwoman, although she could have investigated for herself, and the fact was obvious enough without investigation. "I should say so," said the charwoman, proving her words by pushing Gregor's corpse a long way to one side with her broomstick. Mrs. Samsa made a movement as if to stop her, but checked it. "Well," said Mr. Samsa, "now thanks be to God." He crossed himself, and the three women followed his example. Grete, whose eyes never left the corpse, said: "Just see how thin he was. It's such a long time since he's eaten anything. The food came out again just as it went in." Indeed, Gregor's body was completely flat and dry, as could only now be seen when it was no longer supported by the legs and nothing prevented one from looking closely at it.

"Come in beside us, Grete, for a little while," said Mrs. Samsa with a tremulous smile, and Grete, not without looking back at the corpse, followed her parents into their bedroom. The charwoman shut the door and opened the window wide. Although it was so early in the morning a certain softness was perceptible in the fresh air. After all, it was already the end of March.

The three lodgers emerged from their room and were surprised to see no breakfast; they had been forgotten. "Where's our breakfast?" said the middle lodger peevishly to the charwoman. But she put her finger to her lips and hastily, without a word, indicated by gestures that they should go into Gregor's room. They did so and stood, their hands in the pockets of their somewhat shabby coats, around Gregor's corpse in the room where it was now fully light.

At that the door of the Samsas' bedroom opened and Mr. Samsa appeared in his uniform, his wife on one arm, his daughter on the other. They all looked a little as if they had been crying; from time to time Grete hid her face on her father's arm.

"Leave my house at once!" said Mr. Samsa, and pointed to the door without disengaging himself from the women. "What do you mean by that?" said the middle lodger, taken somewhat aback, with a feeble smile. The two others put their hands behind them and kept rubbing them together, as if in gleeful expectation of a fine set-to in which they were bound to come off the winners. "I mean just what I say," answered Mr. Samsa, and advanced in a straight line with his two companions towards the lodger. He stood his ground at first quietly, looking at the floor as if his thoughts were taking a new pattern in his head. "Then let us go, by all means," he said and looked up at Mr. Samsa as if in a sudden access of humility he were expecting some renewed sanction for this decision. Mr. Samsa merely nodded briefly once or twice with meaning eyes. Upon that the lodger really did go with long strides into the hall, his two friends had been listening and had quite stopped rubbing their hands for some moments and now went scuttling after him as if afraid that Mr. Samsa might get into the hall before them and cut them off from their leader. In the hall they all three took their hats from the rack, their sticks from the umbrella stand, bowed in silence and quitted the apartment. With a suspiciousness which proved quite unfounded Mr. Samsa and the two women followed them out to the landing; leaning over the banister they watched the three figures slowly but surely going down the long stairs, vanishing from sight at a certain turn of the staircase on every floor and coming into view again after a moment or so; the more they dwindled, the more the Samsa family's interest in them dwindled, and when a butcher's boy met them and passed them on the stairs coming up proudly with a tray on his head, Mr. Samsa and the two women soon left the landing and as if a burden had been lifted from them went back into their apartment.

They decided to spend this day in resting and going for a stroll; they had not only deserved such a respite from work, but absolutely needed it. And so they sat down at the table and wrote three notes of excuse, Mr. Samsa to his board of management, Mrs. Samsa to her employer and Grete to the head of her firm. While they were writing, the charwoman came in to say that she was going now, since her morning's work was finished. At first they only nodded without looking up, but as she kept hovering there they eyed her irritably. "Well?" said Mr. Samsa. The charwoman stood grinning in the doorway as if she had good news to impart to the family but meant not to say a word unless properly questioned. The small ostrich feather standing upright on her hat, which had annoyed Mr. Samsa ever since she was engaged, was waving gaily in all directions. "Well, what is it then?" asked Mrs. Samsa, who obtained more respect from the charwoman than the others. "Oh," said the charwoman, giggling so amiably that she could not at once continue, "just this, you don't need to bother about how to get rid of the thing next door. It's been seen to already." Mrs. Samsa and Grete bent over their letters again, as if preoccupied; Mr. Samsa, who perceived that she was eager to begin describing it all in detail, stopped her with a decisive hand. But since she was not allowed to tell her story, she remembered the great hurry she was in, being obviously deeply huffed: "Bye, everybody," she said, whirling off violently, and departed with a frightful slamming of doors.

"She'll be given notice tonight," said Mr. Samsa, but neither from his wife nor his daughter did he get any answer, for the charwoman seemed to have shattered again the composure they had barely achieved. They rose, went to the window and stayed there, clasping each other tight. Mr. Samsa turned in his chair to look at them and quietly observed them for a little. Then he called out: "Come along, now, do. Let bygones be bygones. And you might have some consideration for me." The two of them complied at once, hastened to him, caressed him and quickly finished their letters.

Then they all three left the apartment together, which was more than they had done for months, and went by tram into the open country outside the town. The tram, in which they were the only passengers, was filled with warm sunshine. Leaning comfortably back in their seats they canvassed their prospects for the future, and it appeared on closer inspection that these were not at all bad, for the jobs they had got, which so far they had never really discussed with each other, were all three admirable and likely to lead to better things later on. The greatest immediate improvement in their condition would of course arise from moving to another house; they wanted to take a smaller and cheaper but also better situated and more easily run apartment than the one they had, which Gregor had selected. While they were thus conversing, it struck both Mr. and Mrs. Samsa, almost at the same moment, as they became aware of their daughter's increasing vivacity, that in spite of all the sorrow of recent times, which had made her cheeks pale, she had bloomed into a pretty girl with a good figure. They grew quieter and half unconsciously exchanged glances of complete agreement, having come to the conclusion that it would soon be time to find a good husband for her. And it was like a confirmation of their new dreams and excellent intentions that at the end of their journey their daughter sprang to her feet first and stretched her young body.

[1915]

Katherine Anne Porter (American; 1890–1980)

The Jilting of Granny Weatherall

She flicked her wrist neatly out of Doctor Harry's pudgy careful fingers and pulled the sheet up to her chin. The brat ought to be in knee breeches. Doctoring around the country with spectacles on his nose! "Get along now, take your schoolbooks and go. There's nothing wrong with me."

Doctor Harry spread a warm paw like a cushion on her forehead where the forked green vein danced and made her eyelids twitch. "Now, now, be a good girl, and we'll have you up in no time."

"That's no way to speak to a woman nearly eighty years old just because she's down. I'd have you respect your elders, young man."

"Well, Missy, excuse me." Doctor Harry patted her cheek. "But I've got to warn you, haven't I? You're a marvel, but you must be careful or you're going to be good and sorry."

"Don't tell me what I'm going to be. I'm on my feet now, morally speaking. It's Cornelia. I had to go to bed to get rid of her."

Her bones felt loose, and floated around in her skin, and Doctor Harry floated like a balloon around the foot of the bed. He floated and pulled down his waistcoat and swung his glasses on a cord. "Well, stay where you are, it certainly can't hurt you."

"Get along and doctor your sick," said Granny Weatherall. "Leave a well woman alone. I'll call for you when I want you. . . . Where were you forty years ago when I pulled through milk-leg and double pneumonia? You weren't even born. Don't let Cornelia lead you on," she shouted, because Doctor Harry appeared to float up to the ceiling and out. "I pay my own bills, and I don't throw my money away on nonsense!"

She meant to wave good-bye, but it was too much trouble. Her eyes closed of themselves, it was like a dark curtain drawn around the bed. The pillow rose and floated under her, pleasant as a hammock in a light wind. She listened to the leaves rustling outside the window. No, somebody was swishing newspapers: no, Cornelia and Doctor Harry were whispering together. She leaped broad awake, thinking they whispered in her ear.

"She was never like this, *never* like this!" "Well, what can we expect?" "Yes, eighty years old. . . ."

Well, and what if she was? She still had ears. It was like Cornelia to whisper around doors. She always kept things secret in such a public way. She was always being tactful and kind. Cornelia was dutiful; that was the trouble with her. Dutiful and good: "So good and dutiful," said Granny, "and I'd like to spank her." She saw herself spanking Cornelia and making a fine job of it.

"What'd you say, Mother?"

Granny felt her face tying up in hard knots.

"Can't a body think, I'd like to know?"

"I thought you might want something."

"I do. I want a lot of things. First off, go away and don't whisper."

She lay and drowsed, hoping in her sleep that the children would keep out and let her rest a minute. It had been a long day. Not that she was tired. It was always pleasant to snatch a minute now and then. There was always so much to be done, let me see: tomorrow.

Tomorrow was far away and there was nothing to trouble about. Things were finished somehow when the time came; thank God there was always a little margin over for peace; then a person could spread out the plan of life and tuck in the edges orderly. It was good to have everything clean and folded away, with the hair brushes and tonic bottles sitting straight on the white embroidered linen: the day started without fuss and the pantry shelves laid out with rows of jelly glasses and brown jugs and white stone-china jars and blue whirligigs and words painted on them: coffee, tea, sugar, ginger, cinnamon, allspice: and the bronze clock with the lion on top nicely dusted off. The dust that lion could collect in twenty-four hours! The box in the attic with all those letters tied up, she'd have to go through that tomorrow. All those letters — George's letters and John's letters and her letters to them both — lying around for the children to find afterwards made her uneasy. Yes, that would be tomorrow's business. No use to let them know how silly she had been once.

While she was rummaging around she found death in her mind and it felt clammy and unfamiliar. She had spent so much time preparing for death there was no need for bringing it up again. Let it take care of itself now. When she was sixty she had felt very old, finished, and went around making farewell trips to see her children and grandchildren, with a secret in her mind: This is the very last of your mother, children! Then she made her will and came down with a long fever. That was all just a notion like a lot of other things, but it was lucky too, for she had once for all got over the idea of dying for a long time. Now she couldn't be worried. She hoped she had better sense now. Her father had lived to be one hundred and two years old and had drunk a noggin of strong hot toddy at his last birthday. He told the reporters it was his daily habit, and he owed his long life to that. He had made quite a scandal and was very pleased about it. She believed she'd just plague Cornelia a little.

"Cornelia! Cornelia!" No footsteps, but a sudden hand on her cheek. "Bless you, where have you been?"

"Here, Mother."

"Well, Cornelia, I want a noggin of hot toddy."

"Are you cold, darling?"

"I'm chilly, Cornelia. Lying in bed stops the circulation. I must have told you that a thousand times."

Well, she could just hear Cornelia telling her husband that Mother was getting a little childish and they'd have to humor her. The thing that most annoyed her was that Cornelia thought she was deaf, dumb, and blind. Little hasty glances and tiny gestures tossed around her and over her head saying, "Don't cross her, let her have her way, she's eighty years old," and she sitting there as if she lived in a thin glass cage. Sometimes Granny almost made up her mind to pack up and move back to her own house where nobody could remind her every minute that she was old. Wait, wait, Cornelia, till your own children whisper behind your back!

In her day she had kept a better house and had got more work done. She wasn't too old yet for Lydia to be driving eighty miles for advice when one of the children jumped the track, and Jimmy still dropped in and talked things over: "Now, Mammy, you've a good business head, I want to know what you think of this? . . ." Old. Cornelia couldn't change the furniture around without asking. Little things, little things! They had been so sweet when they were little. Granny wished the old days were back again with the children young and everything to be done over. It had been a hard pull, but not too much for her. When she thought of all the food she had cooked, and all the clothes she had cut and sewed, and all the gardens she had made—well, the children showed it. There they were, made out of her, and they couldn't get away from that. Sometimes she wanted to see John again and point to them and say, Well, I didn't do so badly, did I? But that would have to wait. That was for tomorrow. She used to think of him as a man, but now all the children were older than their father, and he would be a child beside her if she saw him now. It seemed strange and there was something wrong in the idea. Why, he couldn't possibly recognize her. She had fenced in a hundred acres once, digging the post holes herself and clamping the wires with just a negro boy to help. That changed a woman. John would be looking for a young woman with the peaked Spanish comb in her hair and the painted fan. Digging post holes changed a woman. Riding country roads in the winter when women had their babies was another thing: sitting up nights with sick horses and sick negroes and sick children and hardly ever losing one. John, I hardly ever lost one of them! John would see that in a minute, that would be something he could understand, she wouldn't have to explain anything!

It made her feel like rolling up her sleeves and putting the whole place to rights again. No matter if Cornelia was determined to be everywhere at once, there were a great many things left undone on this place. She would start tomorrow and do them. It was good to be strong enough for everything, even if all you made melted and changed and slipped under your hands, so that by the time you finished you almost forgot what you were working for. What was it I set out to do? she asked herself intently, but she could not remember. A fog rose over the valley, she saw it marching across the creek swallowing the trees and moving up the hill like an army of ghosts. Soon it would be at the near edge of the orchard, and then it was time to go in and light the lamps. Come in, children, don't stay out in the night air.

Lighting the lamps had been beautiful. The children huddled up to her and breathed like little calves waiting at the bars in the twilight. Their eyes followed the match and watched the flame rise and settle in a blue curve, then they moved away from her. The lamp was lit, they didn't have to be scared and hang on to mother any more. Never, never, never more. God, for all my life I thank Thee. Without Thee, my God, I could never have done it. Hail, Mary, full of grace.

I want you to pick all the fruit this year and see that nothing is wasted. There's always someone who can use it. Don't let good things rot for want of using. You waste life when you waste good food. Don't let things get lost. It's bitter to lose things. Now, don't let me get to thinking, not when I am tired and taking a little nap before supper. . . .

The pillow rose about her shoulders and pressed against her heart and the memory was being squeezed out of it: oh, push down that pillow, somebody: it would smother her if she tried to hold it. Such a fresh breeze blowing and such a green day with no threats in it. But he had not come, just the same. What does a woman do when she has put on the white veil and set out the white cake for a man and he doesn't come? She tried to remember. No, I swear he never harmed me but in that. He never harmed me but in that . . . and what if he did? There was the day, the day, but a whirl of dark smoke rose and covered it, crept up and over into the bright field where everything was planted so carefully in orderly rows. That was hell, she knew hell when she saw it. For sixty years she had prayed against remembering him and against losing her soul in the deep pit of hell, and now the two things were mingled in one and the thought of him was a smoky cloud from hell that moved and crept in her head when she had just got rid of Doctor Harry and was trying to rest a minute. Wounded vanity, Ellen, said a sharp voice in the top of her mind. Don't let your wounded vanity get the upper hand of you. Plenty of girls get jilted. You were jilted, weren't you? Then stand up to it. Her eyelids wavered and let in streamers of blue-gray light like tissue paper over her eyes. She must get up and pull the shades down or she'd never sleep. She was in bed again and the shades were not down. How could that happen? Better turn over, hide from the light, sleeping in the light gave you nightmares. "Mother, how do you feel now?" and a stinging wetness on her forehead. But I don't like having my face washed in cold water!

Hapsy? George? Lydia? Jimmy? No, Cornelia, and her features were swollen and full of little puddles. "They're coming, darling, they'll all be here soon." Go wash your face, child, you look funny.

Instead of obeying, Cornelia knelt down and put her head on the pillow. She seemed to be talking but there was no sound. "Well, are you tongue-tied? Whose birthday is it? Are you going to give a party?"

Cornelia's mouth moved urgently in strange shapes. "Don't do that, you bother me, daughter."

"Oh, no, Mother. Oh, no. . . ."

Nonsense. It was strange about children. They disputed your every word. "No what, Cornelia?"

"Here's Doctor Harry."

"I won't see that boy again. He just left five minutes ago."

"That was this morning, Mother. It's night now. Here's the nurse."

"This is Doctor Harry, Mrs. Weatherall. I never saw you look so young and happy!"

"Ah, I'll never be young again—but I'd be happy if they'd let me lie in peace and get rested."

She thought she spoke up loudly, but no one answered. A warm weight on her forehead, a warm bracelet on her wrist, and a breeze went on whispering, trying to tell her something. A shuffle of leaves in the ever-lasting hand of God. He blew on them and they danced and rattled. "Mother, don't mind, we're going to give you a little hypodermic." "Look here, daughter, how do ants get in this bed? I saw sugar ants yesterday." Did you send for Hapsy too?

It was Hapsy she really wanted. She had to go a long way back through a great many rooms to find Hapsy standing with a baby on her arm. She seemed to herself to be Hapsy also, and the baby on Hapsy's arm was Hapsy and himself and herself, all at once, and there was no surprise in the meeting. Then Hapsy melted from within and turned flimsy as gray gauze and the baby was a gauzy shadow, and Hapsy came up close and said, "I thought you'd never come," and looked at her very searchingly and said, "You haven't changed a bit!" They leaned forward to kiss, when Cornelia began whispering from a long way off, "Oh, is there anything you want to tell me? Is there anything I can do for you?"

Yes, she had changed her mind after sixty years and she would like to see George. I want you to find George. Find him and be sure to tell him I forgot him. I want him to know I had my husband just the same and my children and my house like any other woman. A good house too and a good husband that I loved and fine children out of him. Better than I hoped for even. Tell him I was given back everything he took away and more. Oh, no, oh, God, no, there was something else besides the house and the man and the children. Oh, surely they were not all? What was it? Something not given back. . . . Her breath crowded down under her ribs and grew into a monstrous frightening shape with cutting edges; it bored up into her head, and the agony was unbelievable: Yes, John, get the doctor now, no more talk, my time has come.

When this one was born it should be the last. The last. It should have been born first, for it was the one she had truly wanted. Everything came in good time. Nothing left out, left over. She was strong, in three days she would be as well as ever. Better. A woman needed milk in her to have her full health.

"Mother, do you hear me?"

"I've been telling you—"

"Mother, Father Connolly's here."

"I went to Holy Communion only last week. Tell him I'm not so sinful as all that."

"Father just wants to speak to you."

He could speak as much as he pleased. It was like him to drop in and inquire about her soul as if it were a teething baby, and then stay on for a cup of tea and a round of cards and gossip. He always had a funny story of some sort, usually about an Irishman who made his little mistakes and confessed them, and the point lay in some absurd thing he would blurt out in the confessional showing his struggles between native piety and original sin. Granny felt easy about her soul. Cornelia, where are your manners? Give Father Connolly a chair. She had her secret comfortable understanding with a few favorite saints who cleared a straight road to God for her. All as surely signed and sealed as the papers for the new Forty Acres. Forever . . . heirs and assigns forever. Since the day the wedding cake was not cut, but thrown out and wasted. The whole bottom dropped out of the world, and there she was blind and sweating and nothing under her feet and the walls falling away.

His hand had caught her under the breast, she had not fallen, there was the freshly polished floor with the green rug on it, just as before. He had cursed like a sailor's parrot and said, "I'll kill him for you." Don't lay a hand on him, for my sake leave something to God. "Now, Ellen, you must believe what I tell you. . . ."

So there was nothing, nothing to worry about any more, except sometimes in the night one of the children screamed in a nightmare, and they both hustled out shaking and hunting for the matches and calling, "There, wait a minute, here we are!" John, get the doctor now, Hapsy's time has come. But there was Hapsy standing by the bed in a white cap. "Cornelia, tell Hapsy to take off her cap. I can't see her plain."

Her eyes opened very wide and the room stood out like a picture she had seen somewhere. Dark colors with the shadows rising toward the ceiling in long angles. The tall black dresser gleamed with nothing on it but John's picture, enlarged from a little one, with John's eyes very black when they should have been blue. You never saw him, so how do you know how he looked? But the man insisted the copy was perfect, it was very rich and handsome. For a picture, yes, but it's not my husband. The table by the bed had a linen cover and a candle and a crucifix. The light was blue from Cornelia's silk lampshades. No sort of light at all, just frippery. You had to live forty years with kerosene lamps to appreciate honest electricity. She felt very strong and she saw Doctor Harry with a rosy nimbus around him.

"You look like a saint, Doctor Harry, and I vow that's as near as you'll ever come to it."

"She's saying something."

"I heard you, Cornelia. What's all this carrying on?"

"Father Connolly's saying—"

Cornelia's voice staggered and bumped like a cart in a bad road. It rounded corners and turned back again and arrived nowhere. Granny stepped up in the cart very lightly and reached for the reins, but a man sat beside her and she knew him by his hands, driving the cart. She did not look in his face, for she knew without seeing, but looked instead down the road where the trees leaned over and bowed to each other and a thousand birds were singing a Mass. She felt like singing too, but she put her hand in the bosom of her dress and pulled out a rosary, and Father Connolly murmured Latin in a very solemn voice and tickled her feet. My God, will you stop that nonsense? I'm a married woman. What if he did run away and leave me to face the priest by myself? I found another a whole world better. I wouldn't have exchanged my husband for anybody except St. Michael himself, and you may tell him that for me with a thank you in the bargain.

Light flashed on her closed eyelids, and a deep roaring shook her. Cornelia, is that lightning? I hear thunder. There's going to be a storm. Close all the windows. Call the children in. . . . "Mother, here we are, all of us." "Is that you, Hapsy?" "Oh, no, I'm Lydia. We drove as fast as we could." Their faces drifted above her, drifted away. The rosary fell out of her hands and Lydia put it back. Jimmy tried to help, their hands fumbled together, and Granny closed two fingers around Jimmy's thumb. Beads wouldn't do, it must be something alive. She was so amazed her thoughts ran round and round. So, my dear Lord, this is my death and I wasn't even thinking about it. My children have come to see me die. But I can't, it's not time. Oh, I always hated surprises. I wanted to give Cornelia the amethyst set—Cornelia, you're to have the amethyst set, but Hapsy's to wear it when she wants, and, Doctor Harry, do shut up. Nobody sent for you. Oh, my dear Lord, do wait a minute. I meant to do something about the Forty Acres, Jimmy doesn't need it and Lydia will later on, with that worthless husband of hers. I meant to finish the altar cloth and send six bottles of wine to Sister Borgia for her dyspepsia. I want to send six bottles of wine to Sister Borgia, Father Connolly, now don't let me forget.

Cornelia's voice made short turns and tilted over and crashed. "Oh, Mother, oh, Mother, oh, Mother. . . ."

"I'm not going, Cornelia. I'm taken by surprise. I can't go."

You'll see Hapsy again. What about her? "I thought you'd never come." Granny made a long journey outward, looking for Hapsy. What if I don't find her? What then? Her heart sank down and down, there was no bottom to death, she couldn't come to the end of it. The blue light from Cornelia's lampshade drew into a tiny point in the center of her brain, it flickered and winked like an eye, quietly it fluttered and dwindled. Granny lay curled down within herself, amazed and watchful, starting at the point of light that was herself; her body was now only a deeper mass of shadow in an endless darkness and this darkness would curl around the light and swallow it up. God, give a sign!

For the second time there was no sign. Again no bridegroom and the priest in the house. She could not remember any other sorrow because this grief wiped them all away. Oh, no, there's nothing more cruel than this — I'll never forgive it. She stretched herself with a deep breath and blew out the light.

[1929]

William Faulkner (*American; 1897–1962*)

A Rose for Emily

I

When Miss Emily Grierson died, our whole town went to her funeral: the men through a sort of respectful affection for a fallen monument, the women mostly out of curiosity to see the inside of her house, which no one save an old manservant — a combined gardener and cook — had seen in at least ten years.

It was a big, squarish frame house that had once been white, decorated with cupolas and spires and scrolled balconies in the heavily lightsome style of the seventies, set on what had once been our most select street. But garages and cotton gins had encroached and obliterated even the august names of that neighborhood; only Miss Emily's house was left, lifting its stubborn and coquettish decay above the cotton wagons and the gasoline pumps — an eyesore among eyesores. And now Miss Emily had gone to join the representatives of those august names where they lay in the cedar-bemused cemetery among the ranked and anonymous graves of Union and Confederate soldiers who fell at the battle of Jefferson.

Alive, Miss Emily had been a tradition, a duty, and a care; a sort of hereditary obligation upon the town, dating from that day in 1894 when Colonel Sartoris, the mayor — he who fathered the edict that no Negro woman should appear on the streets without an apron — remitted her taxes, the dispensation dating from the death of her father on into perpetuity. Not that Miss Emily would have accepted charity. Colonel Sartoris invented an involved tale to the effect that Miss Emily's father had loaned money to the town, which the town, as a matter of business, preferred this way of repaying. Only a man of Colonel Sartoris' generation and thought could have invented it, and only a woman could have believed it.

When the next generation, with its more modern ideas, became mayors and aldermen, this arrangement created some little dissatisfaction. On the first of the year they mailed her a tax notice. February came, and there was no reply. They wrote her a formal letter, asking her to call at the sheriff's office at her convenience. A week later the mayor wrote her himself, offering to call or to send his car for her, and received in reply a note on paper of an archaic shape, in a thin, flowing calligraphy in faded ink, to the effect that she no longer went out at all. The tax notice was also enclosed, without comment.

They called a special meeting of the Board of Aldermen. A deputation waited upon her, knocked at the door through which no visitor had passed since she ceased giving china-painting lessons eight or ten years earlier. They were admitted by the old Negro into a dim hall from which a staircase mounted into still more shadow. It smelled of dust and disuse—a close, dank smell. The Negro led them into the parlor. It was furnished in heavy, leather-covered furniture. When the Negro opened the blinds of one window, they could see that the leather was cracked; and when they sat down, a faint dust rose sluggishly about their thighs, spinning with slow motes in the single sunray. On a tarnished gilt easel before the fireplace stood a crayon portrait of Miss Emily's father.

They rose when she entered—a small, fat woman in black, with a thin gold chain descending to her waist and vanishing into her belt, leaning on an ebony cane with a tarnished gold head. Her skeleton was small and spare; perhaps that was why what would have been merely plumpness in another was obesity in her. She looked bloated, like a body long submerged in motionless water, and of that pallid hue. Her eyes, lost in the fatty ridges of her face, looked like two small pieces of coal pressed into a lump of dough as they moved from one face to another while the visitors stated their errand.

She did not ask them to sit. She just stood in the door and listened quietly until the spokesman came to a stumbling halt. Then they could hear the invisible watch ticking at the end of the gold chain.

Her voice was dry and cold. "I have no taxes in Jefferson. Colonel Sartoris explained it to me. Perhaps one of you can gain access to the city records and satisfy yourselves."

"But we have. We are the city authorities, Miss Emily. Didn't you get a notice from the sheriff, signed by him?"

"I received a paper, yes," Miss Emily said. "Perhaps he considers himself the sheriff. . . . I have no taxes in Jefferson."

"But there is nothing on the books to show that, you see. We must go by the—"

"See Colonel Sartoris. I have no taxes in Jefferson."

"But, Miss Emily—"

"See Colonel Sartoris." (Colonel Sartoris had been dead almost ten years.) "I have no taxes in Jefferson. Tobe!" The Negro appeared. "Show these gentlemen out."

II

So she vanquished them, horse and foot, just as she had vanquished their fathers thirty years before about the smell. That was two years after her father's death and a short time after her sweetheart—the one we believed would marry her—had deserted her. After her father's death she went out very little; after her sweetheart went away, people hardly saw her at all. A few of the ladies had the temerity to call, but were not received, and the only sign of life about the place was the Negro man—a young man then—going in and out with a market basket.

"Just as if a man—any man—could keep a kitchen properly," the ladies said; so they were not surprised when the smell developed. It was another link between the gross, teeming world and the high and mighty Griersons.

A neighbor, a woman, complained to the mayor, Judge Stevens, eighty years old.

"But what will you have me do about it, madam?" he said.

"Why, send her word to stop it," the woman said. "Isn't there a law?"

"I'm sure that won't be necessary," Judge Stevens said. "It's probably just a snake or a rat that nigger of hers killed in the yard. I'll speak to him about it."

The next day he received two more complaints, one from a man who came in diffident deprecation. "We really must do something about it, Judge. I'd be the last one in the world to bother Miss Emily, but we've got to do something." That night the Board of Aldermen met—three gray-beards and one younger man, a member of the rising generation.

"It's simple enough," he said. "Send her word to have her place cleaned up. Give her a certain time to do it in, and if she don't . . . "

"Dammit, sir," Judge Stevens said, "will you accuse a lady to her face of smelling bad?"

So the next night, after midnight, four men crossed Miss Emily's lawn and slunk about the house like burglars, sniffing along the base of the brickwork and at the cellar openings while one of them performed a regular sowing motion with his hand out of a sack slung from his shoulder. They broke open the cellar door and sprinkled lime there, and in all the outbuildings. As they recrossed the lawn, a window that had been dark was lighted and Miss Emily sat in it, the light behind her, and her upright torso motionless as that of an idol. They crept quietly across the lawn and into the shadow of the locusts that lined the street. After a week or two the smell went away.

That was when people had begun to feel really sorry for her. People in our town, remembering how old lady Wyatt, her great-aunt, had gone completely crazy at last, believed that the Griersons held themselves a little too high for what they really were. None of the young men were quite good enough for Miss Emily and such. We had long thought of them as a tableau; Miss Emily a slender figure in white in the background, her father a spraddled silhouette in the foreground, his back to her and clutching a horsewhip, the two of them framed by the back-flung front door. So when she got to be thirty and was still single, we were not pleased exactly, but vindicated; even with insanity in the family she wouldn't have turned down all of her chances if they had really materialized.

When her father died, it got about that the house was all that was left to her; and in a way, people were glad. At last they could pity Miss Emily. Being left alone, and a pauper, she had become humanized. Now she too would know the old thrill and the old despair of a penny more or less.

The day after his death all the ladies prepared to call at the house and offer condolence and aid, as is our custom. Miss Emily met them at the door, dressed as usual and with no trace of grief on her face. She told them that her father was not dead. She did that for three days, with the ministers calling on her, and the doctors, trying to persuade her to let them dispose of the body. Just as they were about to resort to law and force, she broke down, and they buried her father quickly.

We did not say she was crazy then. We believed she had to do that. We remembered all the young men her father had driven away, and we knew that with nothing left, she would have to cling to that which had robbed her, as people will.

III

She was sick for a long time. When we saw her again, her hair was cut short, making her look like a girl, with a vague resemblance to those angels in colored church windows—sort of tragic and serene.

The town had just let the contracts for paving the sidewalks, and in the summer after her father's death they began the work. The construction company came with niggers and mules and machinery, and a foreman named Homer Barron, a Yankee—a big, dark, ready man, with a big voice and eyes lighter than his face. The little boys would follow in groups to hear him cuss the niggers, and the niggers singing in time to the rise and fall of picks. Pretty soon he knew everybody in town. Whenever you heard a lot of laughing anywhere about the square, Homer Barron would be in the center of the group. Presently we began to see him and Miss Emily on Sunday afternoons driving in the yellow-wheeled buggy and the matched team of bays from the livery stable.

At first we were glad that Miss Emily would have an interest, because the ladies all said, "Of course a Grierson would not think seriously of a Northerner, a day laborer." But there were still others, older people, who said that even grief could not cause a real lady to forget *noblesse oblige*—without calling it *noblesse oblige.* They just said, "Poor Emily. Her kinsfolk should come to her." She had some kin in Alabama; but years ago her father had fallen out with them over the estate of old lady Wyatt, the crazy woman, and there was no communication between the two families. They had not even been represented at the funeral.

And as soon as the old people said, "Poor Emily," the whispering began. "Do you suppose it's really so?" they said to one another. "Of course it is. What else could . . . " This behind their hands; rustling of craned silk and satin behind jalousies closed upon the sun of Sunday afternoon as the thin, swift clop-clop-clop of the matched team passed: "Poor Emily."

She carried her head high enough—even when we believed that she was fallen. It was as if she demanded more than ever the recognition of her dignity as the last Grierson; as if it had wanted that touch of earthiness to reaffirm her imperviousness. Like when she bought the rat poison, the arsenic. That was over a year after they had begun to say "Poor Emily," and while the two female cousins were visiting her.

"I want some poison," she said to the druggist. She was over thirty then, still a slight woman, though thinner than usual, with cold, haughty black eyes in a face the flesh of which was strained across the temples and about the eyesockets as you imagine a lighthousekeeper's face ought to look. "I want some poison," she said.

"Yes, Miss Emily. What kind? For rats and such? I'd recom—"

"I want the best you have. I don't care what kind."

The druggist named several. "They'll kill anything up to an elephant. But what you want is—"

"Arsenic," Miss Emily said. "Is that a good one?"

"Is . . . arsenic? Yes, ma'am. But what you want—"

"I want arsenic."

The druggist looked down at her. She looked back at him, erect, her face like a strained flag. "Why, of course," the druggist said. "If that's what you want. But the law requires you to tell what you are going to use it for."

Miss Emily just stared at him, her head tilted back in order to look him eye for eye, until he looked away and went and got the arsenic and wrapped it up. The Negro delivery boy brought her the package; the druggist didn't come back. When she opened the package at home there was written on the box, under the skull and bones: "For rats."

IV

So the next day we all said, "She will kill herself"; and we said it would be the best thing. When she had first begun to be seen with Homer Barron, we had said, "She will marry him." Then we said, "She will persuade him yet," because Homer himself had remarked—he liked men, and it was known that he drank with the younger men in the Elks' Club— that he was not a marrying man. Later we said, "Poor Emily" behind the jalousies as they passed on Sunday afternoon in the glittering buggy, Miss Emily with her head high and Homer Barron with his hat cocked and a cigar in his teeth, reins and whip in a yellow glove.

Then some of the ladies began to say that it was a disgrace to the town and a bad example to the young people. The men did not want to interfere, but at last the ladies forced the Baptist minister—Miss Emily's people were Episcopal—to call upon her. He would never divulge what happened during that interview, but he refused to go back again. The next Sunday they again drove about the streets, and the following day the minister's wife wrote to Miss Emily's relations in Alabama.

So she had blood-kin under her roof again and we sat back to watch developments. At first nothing happened. Then we were sure that they were to be married. We learned that Miss Emily had been to the jeweler's and ordered a man's toilet set in silver, with the letters H. B. on each piece. Two days later we learned that she had bought a complete outfit of men's clothing, including a nightshirt, and we said, "They are married." We were really glad. We were glad because the two female cousins were even more Grierson than Miss Emily had ever been.

So we were surprised when Homer Barron—the streets had been finished some time since—was gone. We were a little disappointed that there was not a public blowing-off, but we believed that he had gone on to prepare for Miss Emily's coming, or to give her a chance to get rid of the cousins. (By that time it was a cabal, and we were all Miss Emily's allies to help circumvent the cousins.) Sure enough, after another week they departed. And, as we had expected all along, within three days Homer Barron was back in town. A neighbor saw the Negro man admit him at the kitchen door at dusk one evening.

And that was the last we saw of Homer Barron. And of Miss Emily for some time. The Negro man went in and out with the market basket, but the front door remained closed. Now and then we would see her at a window for a moment, as the men did that night when they sprinkled the lime, but for almost six months she did not appear on the streets. Then we knew that this was to be expected too; as if that quality of her father which had thwarted her woman's life so many times had been too virulent and too furious to die.

When we next saw Miss Emily, she had grown fat and her hair was turning gray. During the next few years it grew grayer and grayer until it attained an even pepper-and-salt iron-gray, when it ceased turning. Up to the day of her death at seventy-four it was still that vigorous iron-gray, like the hair of an active man.

From that time on her front door remained closed, save for a period of six or seven years, when she was about forty, during which she gave lessons in china-painting. She fitted up a studio in one of the downstairs rooms, where the daughters and grand-daughters of Colonel Sartoris' contemporaries were sent to her with the same regularity and in the same spirit that they were sent to church on Sundays with a twenty-five-cent piece for the collection plate. Meanwhile her taxes had been remitted.

Then the newer generation became the backbone and the spirit of the town, and the painting pupils grew up and fell away and did not send their children to her with boxes of color and tedious brushes and pictures cut from the ladies' magazines. The front door closed upon the last one and remained closed for good. When the town got free postal delivery, Miss Emily alone refused to let them fasten the metal numbers above her door and attach a mailbox to it. She would not listen to them.

Daily, monthly, yearly we watched the Negro grow grayer and more stooped, going in and out with the market basket. Each December we sent her a tax notice, which would be returned by the post office a week later, unclaimed. Now and then we would see her in one of the downstairs windows—she had evidently shut up the top floor of the house—like the carven torso of an idol in a niche, looking or not looking at us, we could never tell which. Thus she passed from generation to generation—dear, inescapable, impervious, tranquil, and perverse.

And so she died. Fell ill in the house filled with dust and shadows, with only a doddering Negro man to wait on her. We did not even know she was sick; we had long since given up trying to get any information from the Negro. He talked to no one, probably not even to her, for his voice had grown harsh and rusty, as if from disuse.

She died in one of the downstairs rooms, in a heavy walnut bed with a curtain, her gray head propped on a pillow yellow and moldy with age and lack of sunlight.

V

The Negro met the first of the ladies at the front door and let them in, with their hushed, sibilant voices and their quick, curious glances, and then he disappeared. He walked right through the house and out the back and was not seen again.

The two female cousins came at once. They held the funeral on the second day, with the town coming to look at Miss Emily beneath a mass of bought flowers, with the crayon face of her father musing profoundly above the bier and the ladies sibilant and macabre; and the very old men—some in their brushed Confederate uniforms—on the porch and the lawn, talking of Miss Emily as if she had been a contemporary of theirs, believing that they had danced with her and courted her perhaps, confusing time with its mathematical progression, as the old do, to whom all the past is not a diminishing road but, instead, a huge meadow which no winter ever quite touches, divided from them now by the narrow bottleneck of the most recent decade of years.

Already we knew that there was one room in that region above stairs which no one had seen in forty years, and which would have to be forced. They waited until Miss Emily was decently in the ground before they opened it.

The violence of breaking down the door seemed to fill this room with pervading dust. A thin, acrid pall as of the tomb seemed to lie every-where upon this room decked and furnished as for a bridal: upon the valance curtains of faded rose color, upon the rose-shaded lights, upon the dressing table, upon the delicate array of crystal and the man's toilet things backed with tarnished silver, silver so tarnished that the monogram was obscured. Among them lay collar and tie, as if they had just been re-moved, which, lifted, left upon the surface a pale crescent in the dust. Upon a chair hung the suit, carefully folded; beneath it the two mute shoes and the discarded socks.

The man himself lay in the bed.

For a long while we just stood there, looking down at the profound and fleshless grin. The body had apparently once lain in the attitude of an embrace, but now the long sleep that outlasts love, that conquers even the grimace of love, had cuckolded him. What was left of him, rotted beneath what was left of the nightshirt, had become inextricable from the bed in which he lay; and upon him and upon the pillow beside him lay that even coating of the patient and biding dust.

Then we noticed that in the second pillow was the indentation of a head. One of us lifted something from it, and leaning forward, that faint and invisible dust dry and acrid in the nostrils, we saw a long strand of iron-gray hair.

[1930]

Zora Neale Hurston (American; 1901–60)

Sweat

It was eleven o'clock of a Spring night in Florida. It was Sunday. Any other night, Delia Jones would have been in bed for two hours by this time. But she was a washwoman, and Monday morning meant a great deal to her. So she collected the soiled clothes on Saturday when she returned the clean things. Sunday night after church, she sorted them and put the white things to soak. It saved her almost a half day's start. A great hamper in the bedroom held the clothes that she brought home. It was so much neater than a number of bundles lying around.

She squatted in the kitchen floor beside the great pile of clothes, sort-ing them into small heaps according to color, and humming a song in a mournful key, but wondering through it all where Sykes, her husband, had gone with her horse and buckboard.[1]

[1]**buckboard** an open wagon

Just then something long, round, limp and black fell upon her shoulders and slithered to the floor beside her. A great terror took hold of her. It softened her knees and dried her mouth so that it was a full minute before she could cry out or move. Then she saw that it was the big bull whip her husband liked to carry when he drove.

She lifted her eyes to the door and saw him standing there bent over with laughter at her fright. She screamed at him.

"Sykes, what you throw dat whip on me like dat? You know it would skeer me—looks just like a snake, an' you knows how skeered Ah is of snakes."

"Course Ah knowed it! That's how come Ah done it." He slapped his leg with his hand and almost rolled on the ground in his mirth. "If you such a big fool dat you got to have a fit over a earth worm or a string, Ah don't keer how bad Ah skeer you."

"You aint got no business doing it. Gawd knows it's a sin. Some day Ah'm gointuh drop dead from some of yo' foolishness. 'Nother thing, where you been wid mah rig? Ah feeds dat pony. He aint fuh you to be drivin' wid no bull whip."

"Yo sho is one aggravatin' nigger woman!" he declared and stepped into the room. She resumed her work and did not answer him at once. "Ah done tole you time and again to keep them white folks' clothes outa dis house."

He picked up the whip and glared down at her. Delia went on with her work. She went out into the yard and returned with a galvanized tub and set it on the washbench. She saw that Sykes had kicked all of the clothes together again, and now stood in her way truculently, his whole manner hoping, *praying,* for an argument. But she walked calmly around him and commenced to re-sort the things.

"Next time, Ah'm gointer to kick 'em outdoors," he threatened as he struck a match along the leg of his corduroy breeches.

Delia never looked up from her work, and her thin, stooped shoulders sagged further.

"Ah aint for no fuss t'night Sykes. Ah just come from taking sacrament at the church house."

He snorted scornfully. "Yeah, you just come from de church house on a Sunday night, but heah you is gone to work on them clothes. You ain't nothing but a hypocrite. One of them amen-corner Christians— sing, whoop, shout, then come home and wash white folks clothes on the Sabbath."

He stepped roughly upon the whitest pile of things, kicking them helter-skelter as he crossed the room. His wife gave a little scream of dismay, and quickly gathered them together again.

"Sykes, you quit grindin' dirt into these clothes! How can Ah git through by Sat'day if Ah don't start on Sunday?"

"Ah don't keer if you never git through. Anyhow, Ah done promised Gawd and a couple of other men, Ah aint gointer have it in mah house. Don't gimme no lip neither, else Ah'll throw 'em out and put mah fist up side yo' head to boot."

Delia's habitual meekness seemed to slip from her shoulders like a blown scarf. She was on her feet; her poor little body, her bare knuckly hands bravely defying the strapping hulk before her.

"Looka heah, Sykes, you done gone too fur. Ah been married to you fur fifteen years, and Ah been takin' in washin' for fifteen years. Sweat, sweat, sweat! Work and sweat, cry and sweat, pray and sweat!"

"What's that got to do with me?" he asked brutally.

"What's it to got to do with you, Sykes? Mah tub of suds is filled yo' belly with vittles more times than yo' hands is filled it. Mah sweat is done paid for this house and Ah reckon Ah kin keep on sweatin' in it."

She seized the iron skillet from the stove and struck a defensive pose, which act surprised him greatly, coming from her. It cowed him and he did not strike her as he usually did.

"Naw you won't," she panted, "that ole snaggle-toothed black woman you runnin' with aint comin' heah to pile up on *mah* sweat and blood. You aint paid for nothin' on this place, and Ah'm gointer stay right heah till Ah'm toted out foot foremost."

"Well, you better quit gittin' me riled up, else they'll be totin' you out sooner than you expect. Ah'm so tired of you Ah don't know whut to do. Gawd! how Ah hates skinny wimmen!"

A little awed by this new Delia, he sidled out of the door and slammed the back gate after him. He did not say where he had gone, but she knew too well. She knew very well that he would not return until nearly daybreak also. Her work over, she went on to bed but not to sleep at once. Things had come to a pretty pass!

She lay awake, gazing upon the debris that cluttered their matrimonial trail. Not an image left standing along the way. Anything like flowers had long ago been drowned in the salty stream that had been pressed from her heart. Her tears, her sweat, her blood. She had brought love to the union and he had brought a longing for the flesh. Two months after the wedding, he had given her the first brutal beating. She had the memory of numerous trips to Orlando with all of his wages when he had returned to her penniless, even before the first year had passed. She was young and soft then, but now she thought of her knotty, muscled limbs, her harsh knuckly hands, and drew herself up into an unhappy little ball in the middle of the big feather bed. Too late now to hope for love, even if it were not Bertha it would be someone else. This case differed from the others only in that she was bolder than the others. Too late for everything except her little home. She had built it for her old days, and planted one by one the trees and flowers there. It was lovely to her, lovely.

Somehow before sleep came, she found herself saying aloud: "Oh well, whatever goes over the Devil's back, is got to come under his belly. Sometime or ruther, Sykes, like everybody else, is gointer reap his sowing." After that she was able to build a spiritual earthworks against her husband. His shells could no longer reach her. *Amen.* She went to sleep and slept until he announced his presence in bed by kicking her feet and rudely snatching the cover away.

"Gimme some kivah heah, an' git yo' damn foots over on yo' own side! Ah oughter mash you in yo' mouf fuh drawing dat skillet on me."

Delia went clear to the rail without answering him. A triumphant indifference to all that he was or did.

The week was as full of work for Delia as all other weeks, and Saturday found her behind her little pony, collecting and delivering clothes.

It was a hot, hot day near the end of July. The village men on Joe Clarke's porch even chewed cane listlessly. They did not hurl the caneknots as usual. They let them dribble over the edge of the porch. Even conversation had collapsed under the heat.

"Heah comes Delia Jones," Jim Merchant said, as the shaggy pony came 'round the bend of the road towards them. The rusty buckboard was heaped with baskets of crisp, clean laundry.

"Yep," Joe Lindsay agreed. "Hot or col', rain or shine, jes ez reg'lar ez de weeks roll roun' Delia carries 'em an' fetches 'em on Sat'day."

"She better if she wanter eat," said Moss. "Syke Jones aint wuth de shot an' powder hit would tek tuh kill 'em. Not to *bub* he aint."

"He sho' aint," Walter Thomas chimed in. "It's too bad, too, cause she wuz a right pritty lil trick when he got huh. Ah'd uh mah'ied huh mahseff if he hadnter beat me to it."

Delia nodded briefly at the men as she drove past.

"Too much knockin' will ruin *any* 'oman. He done beat huh 'nough tuh kill three women, let 'lone change they looks," said Elijah Mosely. "How Syke kin stommuck dat big black greasy Mogul[2] he's layin' roun' wid, gits me. Ah swear dat eight-rock couldn't kiss a sardine can Ah done thowed out de back do' 'way las' yeah."

"Aw, she's fat, thass how come. He's allus been crazy 'bout fat women," put in Merchant. "He'd a' been tied up wid one long time ago if he could a' found one tuh have him. Did Ah tell yuh 'bout him come sidlin' roun' *mah* wife—bringin' her a basket uh pee-cans outa his yard fuh a present? Yes-sir, mah wife! She tol' him tuh take 'em right straight back home, cause Delia works so hard ovah dat washtub she reckon everything en de place taste lak sweat an' soapsuds. Ah jus' wisht Ah'd a' caught 'im 'roun' dere! Ah'd a' made his hips ketch on fiah down dat shell road."

[2]**Mongul** big person

"Ah know he done it, too. Ah sees 'im grinnin' at every 'oman dat passes," Walter Thomas said. "But even so, he useter eat some mighty big hunks uh humble pie tuh git dat lil' 'oman he got. She wuz ez pritty ez a speckled pup! Dat wuz fifteen yeahs ago. He useter be so skeered uh losin' huh, she could make him do some parts of a husband's duty. Dey never wuz de same in de mind."

"There oughter be a law about him," said Lindsay. "He aint fit tuh carry guts tuh a bear."

Clarke spoke for the first time. "Taint no law on earth dat kin make a man be decent if it aint in 'im. There's plenty men dat takes a wife lak dey do a joint uh sugar-cane. It's round, juicy an' sweet when dey gits it. But dey squeeze an' grind, squeeze an' grind an' wring tell dey wring every drop uh pleasure dat's in 'em out. When dey's satisfied dat dey is wrung dry, dey treats 'em jes lak dey do a cane-chew. Dey thows 'em away. Dey knows whut dey is doin' while dey is at it, an' hates theirselves fuh it but they keeps on hangin' after huh tell she's empty. Den dey hates huh fuh bein' a cane-chew an' in de way."

"We oughter take Syke an' dat stray 'oman uh his'n down in Lake Howell swamp an' lay on de rawhide till they cain't say 'Lawd a' mussy.' He allus wuz uh ovahbearin' niggah, but since dat white 'oman from up north done teached 'im how to run a automobile, he done got too biggety to live—an' we oughter kill 'im," Old Man Anderson advised.

A grunt of approval went around the porch. But the heat was melting their civic virtue and Elijah Moseley began to bait Joe Clarke.

"Come on, Joe, git a melon outa dere an' slice it up for yo' customers. We'se all sufferin' wid de heat. De bear's done got *me!*"

"Thass right, Joe, a watermelon is jes' whut Ah needs tuh cure de eppizudicks,"[3] Walter Thomas joined forces with Moseley. "Come on dere, Joe. We all is steady customers an' you aint set us up in a long time. Ah chooses dat long, bowlegged Floridy favorite."

"A god, an' be dough. You all gimme twenty cents and slice away," Clarke retorted. "Ah needs a col' slice m'self. Heah, everybody chip in. Ah'll lend y'll mah meat knife."

The money was quickly subscribed and the huge melon brought forth. At that moment, Sykes and Bertha arrived. A determined silence fell on the porch and the melon was put away again.

Merchant snapped down the blade of his jackknife and moved toward the store door.

"Come on in, Joe, an' gimme a slab uh sow belly an' uh pound uh coffee—almost fuhgot 'twas Sat'day. Got to git on home." Most of the men left also.

Just then Delia drove past on her way home, as Sykes was ordering magnificently for Bertha. It pleased him for Delia to see.

[3]**eppizudicks** i.e., epizootic, an epidemic among animals

"Git whutsover yo' heart desires, Honey. Wait a minute, Joe. Give huh two botles uh strawberry soda-water, uh quart uh parched ground-peas, an' a block uh chewin' gum."

With all this they left the store, with Sykes reminding Bertha that this was his town and she could have it if she wanted it.

The men returned soon after they left, and held their watermelon feast. "Where did Syke Jones git dat 'oman from nohow?" Lindsay asked.

"Ovah Apopka. Guess dey musta been cleanin' out de town when she lef'. She don't look lak a thing but a hunk uh liver wid hair on it."

"Well, she sho' kin squall," Dave Carter contributed. "When she gits ready tuh laff, she jes' opens huh mouf an' latches it back tuh de las' notch. No ole grandpa alligator down in Lake Bell ain't got nothin' on huh."

Bertha had been in town three months now. Sykes was still paying her room rent in Della Lewis'—the only house in town that would have taken her in. Sykes took her frequently to Winter Park to "stomps."[4] He still assured her that he was the swellest man in the state.

"Sho' you kin have dat lil' ole house soon's Ah kin git dat 'oman outa dere. Everything b'longs tuh me an' you sho' kin have it. Ah sho' 'bominates uh skinny 'oman. Lawdy, you sho' is got one portly shape on you! You kit git *anything* you wants. Dis is *mah* town an' you sho' kin have it."

Delia's work-worn knees crawled over the earth in Gethsemane and on the rocks of Calvary[5] many, many times during these months. She avoided the villagers and meeting places in her efforts to be blind and deaf. But Bertha nullified this to a degree, by coming to Delia's house to call Sykes out to her at the gate.

Delia and Sykes fought all the time now with no peaceful interludes. They slept and ate in silence. Two or three times Delia had attempted a timid friendliness, but she was repulsed each time. It was plain that the breaches must remain agape.

The sun had burned July to August. The heat streamed down like a million hot arrows, smiting all things living upon the earth. Grass withered, leaves browned, snakes went blind in shedding and men and dogs went mad. Dog days!

Delia came home one day and found Sykes there before her. She wondered, but started to go on into the house without speaking, even though he was standing in the kitchen door and she must either stoop under his arm or ask him to move. He made no room for her. She noticed a soap box beside the steps, but paid no particular attention to it, knowing that he must have brought it there. As she was stooping to pass under his outstretched arm, he suddenly pushed her backward, laughingly.

"Look in de box dere Delia, Ah done brung yuh somethin'!"

She nearly fell upon the box in her stumbling, and when she saw what it held, she all but fainted outright.

"Syke! Syke, mah Gawd! You take dat rattlesnake 'way from heah! You *gottuh*. Oh, Jesus, have mussy!"

"Ah aint gut tuh do nuthin' uh de kin'—fact is Ah aint got tuh do nothin' but die. Taint no use uh you puttin' on airs makin' out lak you skeered uh dat snake—he's gointer stay right heah tell he die. He wouldn't bite me cause Ah knows how tuh handle 'im. Nohow he wouldn't risk breakin' out his fangs 'gin yo' skinny laigs."

"Naw, now Syke, don't keep dat thing 'roun' heah tuh skeer me tuh death. You knows Ah'm even feared uh earth worms. Thass de biggest snake Ah evah did see. Kill 'im Syke, please."

"Doan ast me tuh do nothin' fuh yuh. Goin' 'roun' tryin' to be so dam asterperious. Naw, Ah aint' gonna kill it. Ah think uh damn sight mo' uh him dan you! Dat's a nice snake an' anybody doan lak 'im kin jes' hit de grit."

The village soon heard that Sykes had the snake, and came to see and ask questions.

"How de hen-fire did you ketch dat six-foot rattler, Syke?" Thomas asked.

"He's full uh frogs so he caint hardly move, thass how Ah eased up on'm. But Ah'm a snake charmer an' knows how tuh handle 'em. Shux, dat aint nothin'. Ah could ketch one eve'y day if Ah so wanted tuh."

"Whut he needs is a heavy hick'ry club leaned real heavy on his head. Dat's de bes 'way tuh charm a rattlesnake."

"Naw, Walt, y'll jes' don't understand dese diamon' backs lak Ah do," said Sykes in a superior tone of voice.

The village agreed with Walter, but the snake stayed on. His box remained by the kitchen door with its screen wire covering. Two or three days later it had digested its meal of frogs and literally came to life. It rattled at every movement in the kitchen or the yard. One day as Delia came down the kitchen steps she saw his chalky-white fangs curved like scimitars hung in the wire meshes. This time she did not run away with averted eyes as usual. She stood for a long time in the doorway in a red fury that grew bloodier for every second that she regarded the creature that was her torment.

That night she broached the subject as soon as Sykes sat down to the table.

"Syke, Ah wants you tuh take dat snake 'way fum heah. You done starved me an' Ah put up widcher, you done beat me an Ah took dat, but you done kilt all mah insides bringin' dat varmint heah."

Sykes poured out a saucer full of coffee and drank it deliberately before he answered her.

"A whole lot Ah keer 'bout how you feels inside uh out. Dat snake aint goin' no damn wheah till Ah gits ready fuh 'im tuh go. So fur as beatin' is concerned, yuh aint took near all dat you gointer take ef yuh stay 'roun' *me.*"

Delia pushed back her plate and got up from the table. "Ah hates you, Sykes," she said calmly. "Ah hates you tuh de same degree dat Ah useter love yuh. Ah done took an' took till mah belly is full up tuh mah neck. Dat's de reason Ah got mah letter fum de church an' moved mah membership tuh Woodbridge—so Ah don't haftuh take no sacrament wid yuh. Ah don't wantuh see yuh 'round me atall. Lay 'roun' wid dat 'oman all yuh wants tuh, but gwan 'way fum me an' mah house. Ah hates yuh lak uh suck-egg dog."

Syles almost let the huge wad of corn bread and collard greens he was chewing fall out of his mouth in amazement. He had a hard time whipping himself to the proper fury to try to answer Delia.

"Well, Ah'm glad you does hate me. Ah'm sho' tiahed uh you hangin' ontuh me. Ah don't want yuh. Look at yuh stringey ole neck! Yo' raw-bony laigs an' arms is enough tuh cut uh man tuh death. You looks jes' lak de devvul's doll-baby tuh *me.* You cain't hate me no worse dan Ah hates you. Ah been hatin' *you* fuh years."

"Yo' ole black hide don't look lak nothin' tuh me, but uh passle uh wrinkled up rubber, wid yo' big ole yeahs flappin' on each side lak uh paih uh buzzard wings. Don't think Ah'm gointuh be run 'way fum mah house neither. Ah'm goin' tuh de white folks about *you,* mah young man, de very nex' time you lay yo' han's on me. Mah cup is done run ovah." Delia said this with no signs of fear and Sykes departed from the house, threatening her, but made not the slightest move to carry out any of them.

That night he did not return at all, and the next day being Sunday, Delia was glad that she did not have to quarrel before she hitched up her pony and drove the four miles to Woodbridge.

She stayed to the night service—"love feast"—which was very warm and full of spirit. In the emotional winds her domestic trials were borne far and wide so that she sang as she drove homeward.

> "Jurden water,[6] black an' col'
> Chills de body, not de soul
> An' Ah wantah cross Jurden in uh calm time."

She came from the barn to the kitchen door and stopped.

"Whut's de mattah, ol' satan, you aint kickin' up yo' racket?" She addressed the snake's box. Complete silence. She went on into the house

---

[6]**Jurden water**   the River Jordan, which the Jews had to cross in order to reach the promised land

with a new hope in its birth struggles. Perhaps her threat to go to the white folks had frightened Sykes! Perhaps he was sorry! Fifteen years of misery and suppression had brought Delia to the place where she would hope *anything* that looked towards a way over or through her wall of inhibitions.

She felt in the match safe behind the stove at once for a match. There was only one there.

"Dat niggah wouldn't fetch nothin' heah tuh save his rotten neck, but he kin run thew whut Ah brings quick enough. Now he done toted off nigh on tuh haff uh box uh matches. He done had dat 'oman heah in mah house, too."

Nobody but a woman could tell how she knew this even before she struck the match. But she did and it put her into a new fury.

Presently she brought in the tubs to put the white things to soak. This time she decided she need not bring the hamper out of the bedroom; she would go in there and do the sorting. She picked up the pot-bellied lamp and went in. The room was small and the hamper stood hard by the foot of the white iron bed. She could sit and reach through the bedposts—resting as she worked.

"Ah wantah cross Jurden in uh calm time." She was singing again. The mood of the "love feast" had returned. She threw back the lid of the basket almost gaily. Then, moved by both horror and terror, she sprang back toward the door. *There lay the snake in the basket!* He moved sluggishly at first, but even as she turned round and round, jumped up and down in an insanity of fear, he began to stir vigorously. She saw him pouring his awful beauty from the basket upon the bed, then she seized the lamp and ran as fast as she could to the kitchen. The wind from the open door blew out the light and the darkness added to her terror. She sped to the darkness of the yard, slamming the door after her before she thought to set down the lamp. She did not feel safe even on the ground, so she climbed up in the hay barn.

There for an hour or more she lay sprawled upon the hay a gibbering wreck.

Finally she grew quiet, and after that, coherent thought. With this, stalked through her a cold, bloody rage. Hours of this. A period of introspection, a space of retrospection, then a mixture of both. Out of this an awful calm.

"Well, Ah done de bes' Ah could. If things aint right, Gawd knows taint mah fault."

She went to sleep—a twitchy sleep—and woke up to a faint gray sky. There was a loud hollow sound below. She peered out. Sykes was at the wood-pile, demolishing a wire-covered box.

He hurried to the kitchen door, but hung outside there some minutes before he entered, and stood some minutes more inside before he closed it after him.

The gray in the sky was spreading. Delia descended without fear now, and crouched beneath the low bedroom window. The drawn shade shut out the dawn, shut in the night. But the thin walls held back no sound.

"Dat ol' scratch is woke up now!" She mused at the tremendous whirr inside, which every woodsman knows, is one of the sound illusions. The rattler is a ventriloquist. His whirr sounds to the right, to the left, straight ahead, behind, close under foot—everywhere but where it is. Woe to him who guesses wrong unless he is prepared to hold up his end of the argument! Sometimes he strikes without rattling at all.

Inside, Sykes heard nothing until he knocked a pot lid off the stove while trying to reach the match safe in the dark. He had emptied his pockets at Bertha's.

The snake seemed to wake up under the stove and Sykes made a quick leap into the bedroom. In spite of the gin he had had, his head was clearing now.

"Mah Gawd!" he chattered, "ef Ah could on'y strack uh light!"

The rattling ceased for a moment as he stood paralyzed. He waited. It seemed that the snake waited also.

"Oh, fuh de light! Ah thought he'd be too sick"—Sykes was muttering to himself when the whirr began again, closer, right underfoot this time. Long before this, Sykes' ability to think had been flattened down to primitive instinct and he leaped—onto the bed.

Outside Delia heard a cry that might have come from a maddened chimpanzee, a stricken gorilla. All the terror, all the horror, all the rage that man possibly could express, without a recognizable human sound.

A tremendous stir inside there, another series of animal screams, the intermittent whirr of the reptile. The shade torn violently down from the window, letting in the red dawn, a huge brown hand seizing the window stick, great dull blows upon the wooden floor punctuating the gibberish of sound long after the rattle of the snake had abruptly subsided. All this Delia could see and hear from her place beneath the window, and it made her ill. She crept over to the four-o'clocks[7] and stretched herself on the cool earth to recover.

She lay there. "Delia, Delia!" She could hear Sykes calling in a most despairing tone as one who expected no answer. The sun crept on up, and he called. Delia could not move—her legs were gone flabby. She never moved, he called, and the sun kept rising.

"Mah Gawd!" She heard him moan, "Mah Gawd fum Heben!" She heard him stumbling about and got up from her flower-bed. The sun was growing warm. As she approached the door she heard him call out hopefully, "Delia, is dat you Ah heah?"

[7] **four-o'clock** tropical American plants, especially *Mirabilis japala,* a garden plant whose yellow, red, or white flowers open in the late afternoon

She saw him on his hands and knees as soon as she reached the door. He crept an inch or two toward her—all that he was able, and she saw his horribly swollen neck and his one open eye shining with hope. A surge of pity too strong to support bore her away from that eye that must, could not, fail to see the tubs. He would see the lamp. Orlando with its doctors was too far. She could scarcely reach the Chinaberry tree, where she waited in the growing heat while inside she knew the cold river was creeping up and up to extinguish that eye which must know by now that she knew.

[1926]

Frank O'Connor (Irish; 1903–66)

Guests of the Nation

I

At dusk the big Englishman, Belcher, would shift his long legs out of the ashes and say, "Well, chums, what about it?" and Noble or me would say "All right, chum" (for we had picked up some of their curious expressions), and the little Englishman, Hawkins, would light the lamp and bring out the cards. Sometimes Jeremiah Donovan would come up and supervise the game and get excited over Hawkins's cards, which he always played badly, and shout at him as if he was one of our own "Ah, you divil, you, why didn't you play the tray?"

But ordinarily Jeremiah was a sober and contented poor devil like the big Englishman, Belcher, and was looked up to only because he was a fair hand at documents, though he was slow enough even with them. He wore a small cloth hat and big gaiters over his long pants, and you seldom saw him with his hands out of his pockets. He reddened when you talked to him, tilting from toe to heel and back, and looking down all the time at his big farmer's feet. Noble and me used to make fun of his broad accent, because we were from the town.

I couldn't at the time see the point of me and Noble guarding Belcher and Hawkins at all, for it was my belief that you could have planted that pair down anywhere from this to Claregalway and they'd have taken root there like a native weed. I never in my short experience seen two men to take to the country as they did.

They were handed on to us by the Second Battalion when the search for them became too hot, and Noble and myself, being young, took over with a natural feeling of responsibility, but Hawkins made us look like fools when he showed that he knew the country better than we did.

"You're the bloke they calls Bonaparte," he says to me. "Mary Brigid O'Connell told me to ask you what you done with the pair of her brother's socks you borrowed."

For it seemed, as they explained it, that the Second used to have little evenings, and some of the girls of the neighborhood turned in, and, seeing they were such decent chaps, our fellows couldn't leave the two Englishmen out of them. Hawkins learned to dance "The Walls of Limerick," "The Siege of Ennis," and "The Waves of Tory" as well as any of them, though, naturally, we couldn't return the compliment, because our lads at that time did not dance foreign dances on principle.

So whatever privileges Belcher and Hawkins had with the Second they just naturally took with us, and after the first day or two we gave up all pretense of keeping a close eye on them. Not that they could have got far, for they had accents you could cut with a knife and wore khaki tunics and overcoats with civilian pants and boots. But it's my belief that they never had any idea of escaping and were quite content to be where they were.

It was a treat to see how Belcher got off with the old woman of the house where we were staying. She was a great warrant to scold, and cranky even with us, but before ever she had a chance of giving our guests, as I may call them, a lick of her tongue, Belcher had made her his friend for life. She was breaking sticks, and Belcher, who hadn't been more than ten minutes in the house, jumped up from his seat and went over to her.

"Allow me, madam," he says, smiling his queer little smile, "please allow me"; and he takes the bloody hatchet. She was struck too paralytic to speak, and after that, Belcher would be at her heels, carrying a bucket, a basket, or a load of turf, as the case might be. As Noble said, he got into looking before she leapt, and hot water, or any little thing she wanted, Belcher would have it ready for her. For such a huge man (and though I am five foot ten myself I had to look up at him) he had an uncommon shortness—or should I say lack?—of speech. It took us some time to get used to him, walking in and out, like a ghost, without a word. Especially because Hawkins talked enough for a platoon, it was strange to hear big Belcher with his toes in the ashes come out with a solitary "Excuse me, chum," or "That's right, chum." His one and only passion was cards, and I will say for him that he was a good cardplayer. He could have fleeced myself and Noble, but whatever we lost to him Hawkins lost to us, and Hawkins played with the money Belcher gave him.

Hawkins lost to us because he had too much old gab, and we probably lost to Belcher for the same reason. Hawkins and Noble would spit at one another about religion into the early hours of the morning, and Hawkins worried the soul out of Noble, whose brother was a priest, with a string of questions that would puzzle a cardinal. To make it worse, even in treating of holy subjects. Hawkins had a deplorable tongue. I never in all my career met a man who could mix such a variety of cursing and bad language into an argument. He was a terrible man, and a fright to argue. He never did a stroke of work, and when he had no one else to talk to, he got stuck in the old woman.

He met his match in her, for one day when he tried to get her to complain profanely of the drought, she gave him a great comedown by blaming it entirely on Jupiter Pluvius (a deity neither Hawkins nor I had ever heard of, though Noble said that among the pagans it was believed that he had something to do with the rain). Another day he was swearing at the capitalists for starting the German war when the old lady laid down her iron, puckered up her little crab's mouth, and said: "Mr. Hawkins, you can say what you like about the war, and think you'll deceive me because I'm only a simple poor countrywoman, but I know what started the war. It was the Italian Count that stole the heathen divinity out of the temple in Japan. Believe me, Mr. Hawkins, nothing but sorrow and want can follow the people that disturb the hidden powers."

A queer old girl, all right.

II

We had our tea one evening, and Hawkins lit the lamp and we all sat into cards. Jeremiah Donovan came in too, and sat down and watched us for a while, and it suddenly struck me that he had no great love for the two Englishmen. It came as a great surprise to me, because I hadn't noticed anything about him before.

Late in the evening a really terrible argument blew up between Hawkins and Noble, about capitalists and priests and love of your country.

"The capitalists," says Hawkins with an angry gulp, "pays the priests to tell you about the next world so as you won't notice what the bastards are up to in this."

"Nonsense, man!" says Noble, losing his temper. "Before ever a capitalist was thought of, people believed in the next world."

Hawkins stood up as though he was preaching a sermon.

"Oh, they did, did they?" he says with a sneer. "They believed all the things you believe, isn't that what you mean? And you believe that God created Adam, and Adam created Shem, and Shem created Jehoshaphat. You believe all that silly old fairytale about Eve and Eden and the apple. Well, listen to me, chum. If you're entitled to hold a silly belief like that, I'm entitled to hold my silly belief—which is that the first thing your God created was a bleeding capitalist, with morality and Rolls-Royce complete. Am I right, chum?" he says to Belcher.

"You're right, chum," says Belcher with his amused smile, and got up from the table to stretch his long legs into the fire and stroke his moustache. So, seeing that Jeremiah Donovan was going, and that there was no knowing when the argument about religion would be over, I went out with him. We strolled down to the village together, and then he stopped and started blushing and mumbling and saying I ought to be behind, keeping guard on the prisoners. I didn't like the tone he took with me, and anyway I was bored with life in the cottage, so I replied by asking him what the hell we wanted guarding them at all for. I told him I'd talked it over with Noble, and that we'd both rather be out with a fighting column.

"What use are those fellows to us?" says I.

He looked at me in surprise and said: "I thought you knew we were keeping them as hostages."

"Hostages?" I said.

"The enemy have prisoners belonging to us," he says, "and now they're talking of shooting them. If they shoot our prisoners, we'll shoot theirs."

"Shoot them?" I said.

"What else did you think we were keeping them for?" he says.

"Wasn't it very unforeseen of you not to warn Noble and myself of that in the beginning?" I said.

"How was it?" says he. "You might have known it."

"We couldn't know it, Jeremiah Donovan," says I. "How could we when they were on our hands so long?"

"The enemy have our prisoners as long and longer," says he.

"That's not the same thing at all," says I.

"What difference is there?" says he.

I couldn't tell him, because I knew he wouldn't understand. If it was only an old dog that was going to the vet's, you'd try and not get too fond of him, but Jeremiah Donovan wasn't a man that would ever be in danger of that.

"And when is this thing going to be decided?" says I.

"We might hear tonight," he says. "Or tomorrow or the next day at latest. So if it's only hanging round here that's a trouble to you, you'll be free soon enough."

It wasn't the hanging round that was a trouble to me at all by this time. I had worse things to worry about. When I got back to the cottage the argument was still on. Hawkins was holding forth in his best style, maintaining that there was no next world, and Noble was maintaining that there was; but I could see that Hawkins had had the best of it.

"Do you know what, chum?" he was saying with a saucy smile. "I think you're just as big a bleeding unbeliever as I am. You say you believe in the next world, and you know just as much about the next world as I do, which is sweet damn-all. What's heaven? You don't know. Where's heaven? You don't know. You know sweet damn-all! I ask you again, do they wear wings?"

"Very well, then," says Noble, "they do. Is that enough for you? They do wear wings."

"Where do they get them, then? Who makes them? Have they a factory for wings? Have they a sort of store where you hands in your chit and takes your bleeding wings?"

"You're an impossible man to argue with," says Noble. "Now, listen to me—" And they were off again.

It was long after midnight when we locked up and went to bed. As I blew out the candle I told Noble what Jeremiah Donovan was after telling me. Noble took it very quietly. When we'd been in bed about an hour he asked me did I think we ought to tell the Englishmen. I didn't think we should, because it was more than likely that the English wouldn't shoot our men, and even if they did, the brigade officers, who were always up and down with the Second Battalion and knew the Englishmen well, wouldn't be likely to want them plugged. "I think so too," says Noble. "It would be great cruelty to put the wind up them now."

"It was very unforeseen of Jeremiah Donovan anyhow," says I.

It was next morning that we found it so hard to face Belcher and Hawkins. We went about the house all day scarcely saying a word. Belcher didn't seem to notice; he was stretched into the ashes as usual, with his usual look of waiting in quietness for something unforeseen to happen, but Hawkins noticed and put it down to Noble's being beaten in the argument of the night before.

"Why can't you take a discussion in the proper spirit?" he says severely. "You and your Adam and Eve! I'm a Communist, that's what I am. Communist or anarchist, it all comes to much the same thing." And for hours he went round the house, muttering when the fit took him. "Adam and Eve! Adam and Eve! Nothing better to do with their time than picking bleeding apples!"

III

I don't know how we got through that day, but I was very glad when it was over, the tea things were cleared away, and Belcher said in his peaceable way: "Well, chums, what about it?" We sat round the table and Hawkins took out the cards, and just then I heard Jeremiah Donovan's footsteps on the path and a dark presentiment crossed my mind. I rose from the table and caught him before he reached the door.

"What do you want?" I asked.

"I want those two soldier friends of yours," he says, getting red.

"Is that the way, Jeremiah Donovan?" I asked.

"That's the way. There were four of our lads shot this morning, one of them a boy of sixteen."

"That's bad," I said.

At that moment Noble followed me out, and the three of us walked down the path together, talking in whispers. Feeney, the local intelligence officer, was standing by the gate.

"What are you going to do about it?" I asked Jeremiah Donovan.

"I want you and Noble to get them out; tell them they're being shifted again; that'll be the quietest way."

"Leave me out of that," says Noble under his breath.

Jeremiah Donovan looks at him hard.

"All right," he says. "You and Feeney get a few tools from the shed and dig a hole by the far end of the bog. Bonaparte and myself will be after you. Don't let anyone see you with the tools. I wouldn't like it to go beyond ourselves."

We saw Feeney and Noble go round to the shed and went in ourselves. I left Jeremiah Donovan to do the explanations. He told them that he had orders to send them back to the Second Battalion. Hawkins let out a mouthful of curses, and you could see that though Belcher didn't say anything, he was a bit upset too. The old woman was for having them stay in spite of us, and she didn't stop advising them until Jeremiah Donovan lost his temper and turned on her. He had a nasty temper, I noticed. It was pitch-dark in the cottage by this time, but no one thought of lighting the lamp, and in the darkness the two Englishmen fetched their topcoats and said good-bye to the old woman.

"Just as a man makes a home of a bleeding place, some bastard at headquarters thinks you're too cushy and shunts you off," says Hawkins, shaking her hand.

"A thousand thanks, madam," says Belcher. "A thousand thanks for everything"—as though he'd made it up.

We went round to the back of the house and down towards the bog, it was only then that Jeremiah Donovan told them. He was shaking with excitement.

"There were four of our fellows shot in Cork this morning and now you're to be shot as a reprisal."

"What are you talking about?" snaps Hawkins. "It's bad enough being mucked about as we are without having to put up with your funny jokes."

"It isn't a joke," says Donovan. "I'm sorry, Hawkins, but it's true," and begins on the usual rigmarole about duty and how unpleasant it is.

I never noticed that people who talk a lot about duty find it much of a trouble to them.

"Oh, cut it out!" says Hawkins.

"Ask Bonaparte," says Donovan, seeing that Hawkins isn't taking him seriously. "Isn't it true, Bonaparte?"

"It is," I say, and Hawkins stops.

"Ah, for Christ's sake, chum."

"I mean it, chum," I say.

"You don't sound as if you meant it."

"If he doesn't mean it, I do," says Donovan, working himself up.

"What have you against me, Jeremiah Donovan?"

"I never said I had anything against you. But why did your people take out four of our prisoners and shoot them in cold blood?"

He took Hawkins by the arm and dragged him on, but it was impossible to make him understand that we were in earnest. I had the Smith and Wesson in my pocket and I kept fingering it and wondering what

I'd do if they put up a fight for it or ran, and wishing to God they'd do one or the other. I knew if they did run for it, that I'd never fire on them. Hawkins wanted to know was Noble in it, and when we said yes, he asked us why Noble wanted to plug him. Why did any of us want to plug him? What had he done to us? Weren't we all chums? Didn't we understand him and didn't he understand us? Did we imagine for an instant that he'd shoot us for all the so-and-so officers in the so-and-so British Army?

By this time we'd reached the bog, and I was so sick I couldn't even answer him. We walked along the edge of it in the darkness, and every now and then Hawkins would call a halt and begin all over again, as if he was wound up, about our being chums, and I knew that nothing but the sight of the grave would convince him that we had to do it. And all the time I was hoping that something would happen; that they'd run for it or that Noble would take over the responsibility from me. I had the feeling that it was worse on Noble than on me.

IV

At last we saw the lantern in the distance and made towards it. Noble was carrying it, and Feeney was standing somewhere in the darkness behind him, and the picture of them so still and silent in the bogland brought it home to me that we were in earnest, and banished the last bit of hope I had.

Belcher, on recognizing Noble, said: "Hallo, chum," in his quiet way, but Hawkins flew at him at once, and the argument began all over again, only this time Noble had nothing to say for himself and stood with his head down, holding the lantern between his legs.

It was Jeremiah Donovan who did the answering. For the twentieth time, as though it was haunting his mind, Hawkins asked if anybody thought he'd shoot Noble.

"Yes, you would," says Jeremiah Donovan.

"No, I wouldn't, damn you!"

"You would, because you'd know you'd be shot for not doing it."

"I wouldn't, not if I was to be shot twenty times over. I wouldn't shoot a pal. And Belcher wouldn't—isn't that right, Belcher?"

"That's right, chum," Belcher said, but more by way of answering the question than of joining in the argument. Belcher sounded as though whatever unforeseen thing he'd always been waiting for had come at last.

"Anyway, who says Noble would be shot if I wasn't? What do you think I'd do if I was in his place, out in the middle of a blasted bog?"

"What would you do?" asks Donovan.

"I'd go with him wherever he was going, of course. Share my last bob with him and stick by him through thick and thin. No one can ever say of me that I let down a pal."

"We had enough of this," says Jeremiah Donovan, cocking his revolver. "Is there any message you want to send?"

"No, there isn't."

"Do you want to say your prayers?"

Hawkins came out with a cold-blooded remark that even shocked me and turned on Noble again.

"Listen to me, Noble," he says. "You and me are chums. You can't come over to my side, so I'll come over to your side. That show you I mean what I say? Give me a rifle and I'll go along with you and the other lads."

Nobody answered him. We knew that was no way out.

"Hear what I'm saying?" he says. "I'm through with it. I'm a deserter or anything else you like. I don't believe in your stuff, but it's no worse than mine. That satisfy you?"

Noble raised his head, but Donovan began to speak and he lowered it again without replying.

"For the last time, have you any messages to send?" says Donovan in a cold, excited sort of voice.

"Shut up, Donovan! You don't understand me, but these lads do. They're not the sort to make a pal and kill a pal. They're not the tools of any capitalist."

I alone of the crowd saw Donovan raise his Webley to the back of Hawkins's neck, and as he did so I shut my eyes and tried to pray. Hawkins had begun to say something else when Donovan fired, and as I opened my eyes at the bang, I saw Hawkins stagger at the knees and lie out flat at Noble's feet, slowly and as quiet as a kid falling asleep, with the lantern-light on his lean legs and bright farmer's boots. We all stood very still, watching him settle out in the last agony.

Then Belcher took out a handkerchief and began to tie it about his own eyes (in our excitement we'd forgotten to do the same for Hawkins), and, seeing it wasn't big enough, turned and asked for the loan of mine. I gave it to him and he knotted the two together and pointed with his foot at Hawkins.

"He's not quite dead," he says. "Better give him another." Sure enough, Hawkins's left knee is beginning to rise. I bend down and put my gun to his head; then, recollecting myself, I get up again. Belcher understands what's in my mind.

"Give him his first," he says. "I don't mind. Poor bastard, we don't know what's happening to him now."

I knelt and fired. By this time I didn't seem to know what I was doing. Belcher, who was fumbling a bit awkwardly with the handkerchiefs, came out with a laugh as he heard the shot. It was the first time I heard him laugh and it sent a shudder down my back; it sounded so unnatural.

"Poor bugger!" he said quietly. "And last night he was so curious about it all. It's very queer, chums, I always think. Now he knows as much about it as they'll ever let him know, and last night he was all in the dark."

Donovan helped him to tie the handkerchiefs about his eyes. "Thanks, chum," he said. Donovan asked if there were any messages he wanted sent.

"No, chum," he says. "Not for me. If any of you would like to write to Hawkins's mother, you'll find a letter from her in his pocket. He and his mother were great chums. But my missus left me eight years ago. Went away with another fellow and took the kid with her. I like the feeling of a home, as you may have noticed, but I couldn't start again after that."

It was an extraordinary thing, but in those few minutes Belcher said more than in all the weeks before. It was just as if the sound of the shot had started a flood of talk in him and he could go on the whole night like that, quite happily, talking about himself. We stood round like fools now that he couldn't see us any longer. Donovan looked at Noble, and Noble shook his head. Then Donovan raised his Webley, and at that moment Belcher gives his queer laugh again. He may have thought we were talking about him, or perhaps he noticed the same thing I'd noticed and couldn't understand it.

"Excuse me, chums," he says. "I feel I'm talking the hell of a lot, and so silly, about my being so handy about a house and things like that. But this thing came on me suddenly. You'll forgive me, I'm sure."

"You don't want to say a prayer?" asked Donovan.

"No, chum," he says. "I don't think it would help. I'm ready, and you boys want to get it over."

"You understand that we're only doing our duty?" says Donovan.

Belcher's head was raised like a blind man's, so that you could only see his chin and the tip of his nose in the lantern-light.

"I never could make out what duty was myself," he said. "I think you're all good lads, if that's what you mean. I'm not complaining."

Noble, just as if he couldn't bear any more of it, raised his fist at Donovan, and in a flash Donovan raised his gun and fired. The big man went over like a sack of meal, and this time there was no need of a second shot.

I don't remember much about the burying, but that it was worse than all the rest because we had to carry them to the grave. It was all mad lonely with nothing but a patch of lantern-light between ourselves and the dark, and birds hooting and screeching all round, disturbed by the guns. Noble went through Hawkins's belongings to find the letter from his mother, and then joined his hands together. He did the same with Belcher. Then, when we'd filled in the grave, we separated from Jeremiah Donovan and Feeney and took our tools back to the shed. All the way we didn't speak a word. The kitchen was dark and cold as we'd left it, and the old woman was sitting over the hearth, saying her beads. We walked past her into the room, and Noble struck a match to light the lamp. She rose quietly and came to the doorway with all her cantankerousness gone.

"What did ye do with them?" she asked in a whisper, and Noble started so that the match went out in his hand.

"What's that?" he asked without turning round.

"I heard ye," she said.

"What did you hear?" asked Noble.

"I heard ye. Do ye think I didn't hear ye, putting the spade back in the houseen?"

Noble struck another match and this time the lamp lit for him.

"Was that what ye did to them?" she asked.

Then, by God, in the very doorway, she fell on her knees and began praying, and after looking at her for a minute or two Noble did the same by the fireplace. I pushed my way out past her and left them at it. I stood at the door, watching the stars and listening to the shrieking of the birds dying out over the bogs. It is so strange what you feel at times like that you can't describe it. Noble says he saw everything ten times the size, as though there were nothing in the whole world but that little patch of bog with the two Englishmen stiffening into it, but with me it was as if the patch of bog where the Englishmen were was a million miles away, and even Noble and the old woman, mumbling behind me, and the birds and the bloody stars were all far away, and I was somehow very small and very lost and lonely like a child astray in the snow. And anything that happened to me afterwards, I never felt the same about again.

[1931]

Shirley Jackson (American; 1919–65)

The Lottery

The morning of June 27th was clear and sunny, with the fresh warmth of a full-summer day; the flowers were blossoming profusely and the grass was richly green. The people of the village began to gather in the square, between the post office and the bank, around ten o'clock; in some towns there were so many people that the lottery took two days and had to be started on June 26th, but in this village, where there were only about three hundred people, the whole lottery took less than two hours, so it could begin at ten o'clock in the morning and still be through in time to allow the villagers to get home for noon dinner.

The children assembled first, of course. School was recently over for the summer, and the feeling of liberty sat uneasily on most of them; they tended to gather together quietly for a while before they broke into boisterous play, and their talk was still of the classroom and the teacher, of books and reprimands. Bobby Martin had already stuffed his pockets full of stones, and the other boys soon followed his example, selecting the smoothest and roundest stones; Bobby and Harry Jones and Dickie Delacroix—the villagers pronounced this name "Dellacroy"—eventually made a great pile of stones in one corner of the square and guarded it against the raids of the other boys. The girls stood aside, talking among themselves, looking over their shoulders at the boys, and the very small children rolled in the dust or clung to the hands of their older brothers or sisters.

Soon the men began to gather, surveying their own children, speaking of planting and rain, tractors and taxes. They stood together, away from the pile of stones in the corner, and their jokes were quiet and they smiled rather than laughed. The women, wearing faded house dresses and sweaters, came shortly after their menfolk. They greeted one another and exchanged bits of gossip as they went to join their husbands. Soon the women, standing by their husbands, began to call to their children, and the children came reluctantly, having to be called four or five times. Bobby Martin ducked under his mother's grasping hand and ran, laughing, back to the pile of stones. His father spoke up sharply, and Bobby came quickly and took his place between his father and his oldest brother.

The lottery was conducted—as were the square dances, the teenage club, the Halloween program—by Mr. Summers, who had time and energy to devote to civic activities. He was a round-faced, jovial man and he ran the coal business, and people were sorry for him, because he had no children and his wife was a scold. When he arrived in the square, carrying the black wooden box, there was a murmur of conversation among the villagers and he waved and called, "Little late today, folks." The postmaster, Mr. Graves, followed him, carrying a three-legged stool, and the stool was put in the center of the square and Mr. Summers set the black box down on it. The villagers kept their distance, leaving a space between themselves and the stool, and when Mr. Summers said, "Some of you fellows want to give me a hand?" there was a hesitation before two men, Mr. Martin and his oldest son, Baxter, came forward to hold the box steady on the stool while Mr. Summers stirred up the papers inside it.

The original paraphernalia for the lottery had been lost long ago, and the black box now resting on the stool had been put into use even before Old Man Warner, the oldest man in town, was born. Mr. Summers spoke frequently to the villagers about making a new box, but no one liked to upset even as much tradition as was represented by the black box. There was a story that the present box had been made with some pieces of the box that had preceded it, the one that had been constructed when the first people settled down to make a village here. Every year, after the lottery, Mr. Summers began talking again about a new box, but every year the subject was allowed to fade off without anything's being done. The black box grew shabbier each year; by now it was no longer completely black but splintered badly along one side to show the original wood color, and in some places faded or stained.

Mr. Martin and his oldest son, Baxter, held the black box securely on the stool until Mr. Summers had stirred the papers thoroughly with his hand. Because so much of the ritual had been forgotten or discarded, Mr. Summers had been successful in having slips of paper substituted for the chips of wood that had been used for generations. Chips of wood, Mr. Summers had argued, had been all very well when the village was tiny, but now that the population was more than three hundred and likely to keep on growing, it was necessary to use something that would fit more easily into the black box. The night before the lottery, Mr. Summers and Mr. Graves made up the slips of paper and put them in the box, and it was then taken to the safe of Mr. Summers's coal company and locked up until Mr. Summers was ready to take it to the square next morning. The rest of the year, the box was put away, sometimes one place, sometimes another; it had spent one year in Mr. Graves's barn and another year underfoot in the post office, and sometimes it was set on a shelf in the Martin grocery and left there.

There was a great deal of fussing to be done before Mr. Summers declared the lottery open. There were lists to make up—of heads of families, heads of households in each family, members of each household in each family. There was the proper swearing-in of Mr. Summers by the postmaster, as the official of the lottery; at one time, some people remembered, there had been a recital of some sort, performed by the official of the lottery, a perfunctory, tuneless chant that had been rattled off duly each year; some people believed that the official of the lottery used to stand just so when he said or sang it, others believed that he was supposed to walk among the people, but years and years ago this part of the ritual had been allowed to lapse. There had been, also, a ritual salute, which the official of the lottery had had to use in addressing each person who came up to draw from the box, but this also had changed with time, until now it was felt necessary only for the official to speak to each person approaching. Mr. Summers was very good at all this; in his clean white shirt and blue jeans, with one hand resting carelessly on the black box, he seemed very proper and important as he talked interminably to Mr. Graves and the Martins.

Just as Mr. Summers finally left off talking and turned to the assembled villagers, Mrs. Hutchinson came hurriedly along the path to the square, her sweater thrown over her shoulders, and slid into place in the back of the crowd. "Clean forgot what day it was," she said to Mrs. Delacroix, who stood next to her, and they both laughed softly. "Thought my old man was out back stacking wood," Mrs. Hutchinson went on, "and then I looked out the window and the kids were gone, and then I remembered it was the twenty-seventh and came a-running." She dried her hands on her apron, and Mrs. Delacroix said, "You're in time, though. They're still talking away up there."

Mrs. Hutchinson craned her neck to see through the crowd and found her husband and children standing near the front. She tapped Mrs. Delacroix on the arm as a farewell and began to make her way through the crowd. The people separated good humoredly to let her through; two or three people said, in voices just loud enough to be heard across the crowd, "Here comes your Missus, Hutchinson," and "Bill, she made it after all." Mrs. Hutchinson reached her husband, and Mr. Summers, who had been waiting, said cheerfully, "Thought we were going to have to get on without you, Tessie." Mrs. Hutchinson said, grinning, "Wouldn't have me leave m'dishes in the sink, now would you, Joe?," and soft laughter ran through the crowd as the people stirred back into position after Mrs. Hutchinson's arrival.

"Well, now," Mr. Summers said soberly, "guess we better get started, get this over with, so's we can go back to work. Anybody ain't here?"

"Dunbar," several people said. "Dunbar, Dunbar."

Mr. Summers consulted his list. "Clyde Dunbar," he said. "That's right. He's broke his leg, hasn't he? Who's drawing for him?"

"Me, I guess," a woman said, and Mr. Summers turned to look at her. "Wife draws for her husband," Mr. Summers said. "Don't you have a grown boy to do it for you, Janey?" Although Mr. Summers and everyone else in the village knew the answer perfectly well, it was the business of the official of the lottery to ask such questions formally. Mr. Summers waited with an expression of polite interest while Mrs. Dunbar answered.

"Horace's not but sixteen yet," Mrs. Dunbar said regretfully. "Guess I gotta fill in for the old man this year."

"Right," Mr. Summers said. He made a note on the list he was holding. Then he asked, "Watson boy drawing this year?"

A tall boy in the crowd raised his hand. "Here," he said. "I'm drawing for m'mother and me." He blinked his eyes nervously and ducked his head as several voices in the crowd said things like "Good fellow, Jack," and "Glad to see your mother's got a man to do it."

"Well," Mr. Summers said, "guess that's everyone. Old Man Warner make it?"

"Here," a voice said, and Mr. Summers nodded.

A sudden hush fell on the crowd as Mr. Summers cleared his throat and looked at the list. "All ready?" he called. "Now, I'll read the names — heads of families first — and the men come up and take a paper out of the box. Keep the paper folded in your hand without looking at it until everyone has had a turn. Everything clear?"

The people had done it so many times that they only half listened to the directions; most of them were quiet, wetting their lips, not looking around. Then Mr. Summers raised one hand high and said, "Adams." A man disengaged himself from the crowd and came forward. "Hi, Steve," Mr. Summers said, and Mr. Adams said, "Hi, Joe." They grinned at one another humorlessly and nervously. Then Mr. Adams reached into the black box and took out a folded paper. He held it firmly by one corner as he turned and went hastily back to his place in the crowd, where he stood a little apart from his family, not looking down at his hand.

"Allen," Mr. Summers said. "Anderson. . . . Bentham."

"Seems like there's no time at all between lotteries any more," Mrs. Delacroix said to Mrs. Graves in the back row. "Seems like we got through with the last one only last week."

"Time sure goes fast," Mrs. Graves said.

"Clark. . . . Delacroix."

"There goes my old man," Mrs. Delacroix said. She held her breath while her husband went forward.

"Dunbar," Mr. Summers said, and Mrs. Dunbar went steadily to the box while one of the women said, "Go on, Janey," and another said, "There she goes."

"We're next," Mrs. Graves said. She watched while Mr. Graves came around from the side of the box, greeted Mr. Summers gravely, and selected a slip of paper from the box. By now, all through the crowd there were men holding the small folded papers in their large hands, turning them over and over nervously. Mrs. Dunbar and her two sons stood together, Mrs. Dunbar holding the slip of paper.

"Harburt. . . . Hutchinson."

"Get up there, Bill," Mrs. Hutchinson said, and the people near her laughed.

"Jones."

"They do say," Mr. Adams said to Old Man Warner, who stood next to him, "that over in the north village they're talking of giving up the lottery."

Old Man Warner snorted. "Pack of crazy fools," he said. "Listening to the young folks, nothing's good enough for *them*. Next thing you know, they'll be wanting to go back to living in caves, nobody work any more, live *that* way for a while. Used to be a saying about 'Lottery in June, corn be heavy soon.' First thing you know, we'd all be eating stewed chickweed and acorns. There's *always* been a lottery," he added petulantly. "Bad enough to see young Joe Summers up there joking with everybody."

"Some places have already quit lotteries," Mrs. Adams said.

"Nothing but trouble in *that,*" Old Man Warner said stoutly. "Pack of young fools."

"Martin." And Bobby Martin watched his father go forward. "Overdyke. . . . Percy."

"I wish they'd hurry," Mrs. Dunbar said to her older son. "I wish they'd hurry."

"They're almost through," her son said.

"You get ready to run tell Dad," Mrs. Dunbar said.

Mr. Summers called his own name and then stepped forward precisely and selected a slip from the box. Then he called, "Warner."

"Seventy-seventh year I been in the lottery," Old Man Warner said as he went through the crowd. "Seventy-seventh time."

"Watson." The tall boy came awkwardly through the crowd. Someone said, "Don't be nervous, Jack," and Mr. Summers said, "Take your time, son."

"Zanini."

After that, there was a long pause, a breathless pause, until Mr. Summers, holding his slip of paper in the air, said, "All right, fellows." For a minute, no one moved, and then all the slips of paper were opened. Suddenly, all women began to speak at once, saying, "Who is it?" "Who's got it?" "Is it the Dunbars?" "Is it the Watsons?" Then the voices began to say, "It's Hutchinson. It's Bill." "Bill Hutchinson's got it."

"Go tell your father," Mrs. Dunbar said to her older son.

People began to look around to see the Hutchinsons. Bill Hutchinson was standing quiet, staring down at the paper in his hand. Suddenly, Tessie Hutchinson shouted to Mr. Summers, "You didn't give him time enough to take any paper he wanted. I saw you. It wasn't fair!"

"Be a good sport, Tessie," Mrs. Delacroix called, and Mrs. Graves said, "All of us took the same chance."

"Shut up, Tessie," Bill Hutchinson said.

"Well, everyone," Mr. Summers said, "that was done pretty fast, and now we've got to be hurrying a little more to get done in time." He consulted his next list. "Bill," he said, "you draw for the Hutchinson family. You got any other households in the Hutchinsons?"

"There's Don and Eva," Mrs. Hutchinson yelled. "Make *them* take their chance!"

"Daughters draw with their husbands' families, Tessie," Mr. Summers said gently. "You know that as well as anyone else."

"It wasn't fair," Tessie said.

"I guess not, Joe," Bill Hutchinson said regretfully. "My daughter draws with her husband's family, that's only fair. And I've got no other family except the kids."

"Then, as far as drawing for families is concerned, it's you," Mr. Summers said in explanation, "and as far as drawing for households is concerned, that's you, too. Right?"

"Right," Bill Hutchinson said.

"How many kids, Bill?" Mr. Summers asked formally.

"Three," Bill Hutchinson said. "There's Bill, Jr., and Nancy, and little Dave. And Tessie and me."

"All right, then," Mr. Summers said. "Harry, you got their tickets back?"

Mr. Graves nodded and held up the slips of paper. "Put them in the box, then," Mr. Summers directed. "Take Bill's and put it in."

"I think we ought to start over," Mrs. Hutchinson said, as quietly as she could. "I tell you it wasn't *fair*. You didn't give him time enough to choose. *Every*body saw that."

Mr. Graves had selected the five slips and put them in the box, and he dropped all the papers but those onto the ground, where the breeze caught them and lifted them off.

"Listen, everybody," Mrs. Hutchinson was saying to the people around her.

"Ready, Bill?" Mr. Summers asked, and Bill Hutchinson, with one quick glance around at his wife and children, nodded.

"Remember," Mr. Summers said, "take the slips and keep them folded until each person has taken one. Harry, you help little Dave." Mr. Graves took the hand of the little boy, who came willingly with him up to the box. "Take a paper out of the box, Davy," Mr. Summers said. Davy put his hand into the box and laughed. "Take just *one* paper," Mr. Summers said. "Harry, you hold it for him." Mr. Graves took the child's hand and removed the folded paper from the tight fist and held it while little Dave stood next to him and looked up at him wonderingly.

"Nancy next," Mr. Summers said. Nancy was twelve, and her school friends breathed heavily as she went forward, switching her skirt, and took a slip daintily from the box. "Bill, Jr.," Mr. Summers said, and Billy, his face red and his feet over-large, nearly knocked the box over as he got a paper out. "Tessie," Mr. Summers said. She hesitated for a minute, looking around defiantly, and then set her lips and went up to the box. She snatched a paper out and held it behind her.

"Bill," Mr. Summers said, and Bill Hutchinson reached into the box and felt around, bringing his hand out at last with the slip of paper in it.

The crowd was quiet. A girl whispered, "I hope it's not Nancy," and the sound of the whisper reached the edges of the crowd.

"It's not the way it used to be," Old Man Warner said clearly. "People ain't the way they used to be."

"All right," Mr. Summers said. "Open the papers. Harry, you open little Dave's."

Mr. Graves opened the slip of paper and there was a general sigh through the crowd as he held it up and everyone could see that it was blank. Nancy and Bill, Jr., opened theirs at the same time, and both beamed and laughed, turning around to the crowd and holding their slips of paper above their heads.

"Tessie," Mr. Summers said. There was a pause, and then Mr. Summers looked at Bill Hutchinson, and Bill unfolded his paper and showed it. It was blank.

"It's Tessie," Mr. Summers said, and his voice was hushed. "Show us her paper, Bill."

Bill Hutchinson went over to his wife and forced the slip of paper out of her hand. It had a black spot on it, the black spot Mr. Summers had made the night before with the heavy pencil in the coal-company office. Bill Hutchinson held it up, and there was a stir in the crowd.

"All right, folks," Mr. Summers said, "let's finish quickly."

Although the villagers had forgotten the ritual and lost the original black box, they still remembered to use stones. The pile of stones the boys had made earlier was ready; there were stones on the ground with the blowing scraps of paper that had come out of the box. Mrs. Delacroix selected a stone so large she had to pick it up with both hands and turned to Mrs. Dunbar. "Come on," she said. "Hurry up."

Mrs. Dunbar had small stones in both hands, and she said, gasping for breath, "I can't run at all. You'll have to go ahead and I'll catch up with you."

The children had stones already, and someone gave little Davy Hutchinson a few pebbles.

Tessie Hutchinson was in the center of a cleared space by now, and she held her hands out desperately as the villagers moved in on her. "It isn't fair," she said. A stone hit her on the side of the head.

Old Man Warner was saying, "Come on, come on, everyone." Steve Adams was in the front of the crowd of villagers, with Mrs. Graves beside him.

"It isn't fair, it isn't right," Mrs. Hutchinson screamed, and then they were upon her.

[1948]

Hisaye Yamamoto (American; b. 1921)

Yoneko's Earthquake

Yoneko Hosoume became a free-thinker on the night of March 10, 1933, only a few months after her first actual recognition of God. Ten years old at the time, of course she had heard rumors about God all along, long before Marpo came. Her cousins who lived in the city were all Christians, living as they did right next door to a Baptist church exclusively for Japanese people. These city cousins, of whom there were several, had been baptized en masse, and were very proud of their condition. Yoneko was impressed when she heard of this and thereafter was given to referring to them as "my cousins, the Christians." She, too, yearned at times after Christianity, but she realized the absurdity of her whim, seeing that there was no Baptist church for Japanese in the rural community she lived in. Such a church would have been impractical, moreover, since Yoneko, her father, her mother, and her little brother Seigo, were the only Japanese thereabouts. They were the only ones, too, whose agriculture was so diverse as to include blackberries, cabbages, rhubarb, potatoes, cucumbers, onions, and cantaloupes. The rest of the countryside there was like one vast orange grove.

Yoneko had entered her cousins' church once, but she could not recall the sacred occasion without mortification. It had been one day when the cousins had taken her and Seigo along with them to Sunday school. The church was a narrow, wooden building mysterious-looking because of its unusual bluish-gray paint and its steeple, but the basement schoolroom inside had been disappointingly ordinary, with desks, a blackboard, and erasers. They had all sung "Let Us Gather at the River" in Japanese. This goes:

> *Mamonaku kanata no*
> *Nagare no soba de*
> *Tanoshiku ai-masho*
> *Mata tomodachi to*
>
> *Mamonaku ai-masho*
> *Kirei-na, kirei-na kawa de*
> *Tanoshiku ai-masho*
> *Mata tomodachi to.*

Yoneko had not known the words at all, but always clever in such situations, she had opened her mouth and grimaced nonchalantly to the rhythm. What with everyone else singing at the top of his lungs, no one had noticed that she was not making a peep. Then everyone had sat down again and the man had suggested, "Let us pray." Her cousins and the rest had promptly curled their arms on the desks to make nests for their heads, and Yoneko had done the same. But not Seigo. Because when the room had become so still that one was aware of the breathing, the creaking, and the chittering in the trees outside, Seigo, sitting with her, had suddenly flung his arm around her neck and said with concern, "Sis, what are you crying for? Don't cry." Even the man had laughed and Yoneko had been terribly ashamed that Seigo should thus disclose them to be interlopers. She had pinched him fiercely and he had begun to cry, so she had had to drag him outside, which was a fortunate move, because he had immediately wet his pants. But he had been only three then, so it was not very fair to expect dignity of him.

So it remained for Marpo to bring the word of God to Yoneko, Marpo with the face like brown leather, the thin mustache like Edmund Lowe's,[1] and the rare, breathtaking smile like white gold. Marpo, who was twenty-seven years old, was a Filipino and his last name was lovely,

---

[1]**Edmund Lowe**   a movie actor popular in the 1930s

something like Humming Wing, but no one ever ascertained the spelling of it. He ate principally rice, just as though he were Japanese, but he never sat down to the Hosoume table, because he lived in the bunkhouse out by the barn and cooked on his own kerosene stove. Once Yoneko read somewhere that Filipinos trapped wild dogs, starved them for a time, then, feeding them mountains of rice, killed them at the peak of their bloatedness, thus insuring themselves meat ready to roast, stuffing and all, without further ado. This, the book said, was considered a delicacy. Unable to hide her disgust and her fascination, Yoneko went straightway to Marpo and asked, "Marpo, is it true that you eat dogs?" and he, flashing that smile, answered "Don't be funny, honey!" This caused her no end of amusement, because it was a poem, and she completely forgot about the wild dogs.

Well, there seemed to be nothing Marpo could not do. Mr. Hosoume said Marpo was the best hired man he had ever had, and he said this often, because it was an irrefutable fact among Japanese in general that Filipinos in general were an indolent lot. Mr. Hosoume ascribed Marpo's industry to his having grown up in Hawaii, where there is known to be considerable Japanese influence. Marpo had gone to a missionary school there and he owned a Bible given him by one of his teachers. This had black leather covers that gave as easily as cloth, golden edges, and a slim purple ribbon for a marker. He always kept it on the little table by his bunk, which was not a bed with springs but a low, three-plank shelf with a mattress only. On the first page of the book, which was stiff and black, his teacher had written in large swirls of white ink, "As we draw near to God, He will draw near to us."

What, for instance, could Marpo do? Why, it would take an entire, leisurely evening to go into his accomplishments adequately, because there was not only Marpo the Christian and Marpo the best hired man, but Marpo the athlete, Marpo the musician (both instrumental and vocal), Marpo the artist, and Marpo the radio technician:

(1) As an athlete, Marpo owned a special pair of black shoes, equipped with sharp nails on the soles, which he kept in shape with the regular application of neatsfoot oil. Putting these on, he would dash down the dirt road to the highway, a distance of perhaps half a mile, and back again. When he first came to work for the Hosoumes, he undertook this sprint every evening before he went to get his supper but, as time went on, he referred to these shoes less and less and, in the end, when he left, he had not touched them for months. He also owned a muscle-builder sent him by Charles Atlas which, despite his unassuming size, he could stretch the length of his outspread arms; his teeth gritted then and his whole body became temporarily victim to a jerky vibration. (2) As an artist, Marpo painted larger-than-life water colors of his favorite movie stars, all of whom were women and all of whom were blonde, like Ann Harding and Jean Harlow, and tacked them up on his walls. He also made for Yoneko a

folding contraption of wood holding two pencils, one with lead and one without, with which she, too, could obtain double-sized likenesses of any picture she wished. It was a fragile instrument, however, and Seigo splintered it to pieces one day when Yoneko was away at school. He claimed he was only trying to copy Boob McNutt from the funny paper when it failed. (3) As a musician, Marpo owned a violin for which he had paid over one hundred dollars. He kept this in a case whose lining was red velvet, first wrapping it gently in a brilliant red silk scarf. This scarf, which weighed nothing, he tucked under his chin when he played, gathering it up delicately by the center and flicking it once to unfurl it—a gesture Yoneko prized. In addition to this, Marpo was a singer, with a soft tenor which came out in professional quavers and rolled r's when he applied a slight pressure to his Adam's apple with thumb and forefinger. His violin and vocal repertoire consisted of the same numbers, mostly hymns and Irish folk airs. He was especially addicted to "The Rose of Tralee" and the "Londonderry Air." (4) Finally, as a radio technician who had spent two previous winters at a specialists' school in the city, Marpo had put together a bulky table-size radio which brought in equal proportions of static and entertainment. He never got around to building a cabinet to house it and its innards of metal and glass remained public throughout its lifetime. This was just as well, for not a week passed without Marpo's deciding to solder one bit or another. Yoneko and Seigo became a part of the great listening audience with such fidelity that Mr. Hosoume began remarking the fact that they dwelt more with Marpo than with their own parents. He eventually took a serious view of the matter and bought the naked radio from Marpo, who thereupon put away his radio manuals and his soldering iron in the bottom of his steamer trunk and divided more time among his other interests.

However, Marpo's versatility was not revealed, as it is here, in a lump. Yoneko uncovered it fragment by fragment every day, by dint of unabashed questions, explorations among his possessions, and even silent observation, although this last was rare. In fact, she and Seigo visited with Marpo at least once a day and both of them regularly came away amazed with their findings. The most surprising thing was that Marpo was, after all this, a rather shy young man meek to the point of speechlessness in the presence of Mr. and Mrs. Hosoume. With Yoneko and Seigo, he was somewhat more self-confident and at ease.

It is not remembered now just how Yoneko and Marpo came to open their protracted discussion on religion. It is sufficient here to note that Yoneko was an ideal apostle, adoring Jesus, desiring Heaven, and fearing Hell. Once Marpo had enlightened her on these basics, Yoneko never questioned their truth. The questions she put up to him, therefore, sought neither proof of her exegeses nor balm for her doubts, but simply additional color to round out her mental images. For example, who did Marpo suppose was God's favorite movie star? Or, what sound did Jesus' laughter have (it must be like music, she added, nodding sagely, answering herself to her own satisfaction), and did Marpo suppose that God's sense of humor would have appreciated the delicious chant she had learned from friends at school today:

> There ain't no bugs on us,
> There ain't no bugs on us,
> There may be bugs on the rest of you mugs,
> But there ain't no bugs on us!

Or, did Marpo believe Jesus to have been exempt from stinging eyes when he shampooed that long, naturally wavy hair of his?

To shake such faith, there would have been required a most monstrous upheaval of some sort, and it might be said that this is just what happened. For early on the evening of March 10, 1933, a little after five o'clock this was, as Mrs. Hosoume was getting supper, as Marpo was finishing up in the fields alone because Mr. Hosoume had gone to order some chicken fertilizer, and as Yoneko and Seigo were listening to Skippy, a tremendous roar came out of nowhere and the Hosoume house began shuddering violently as though some giant had seized it in his two hands and was giving it a good shaking. Mrs. Hosoume, who remembered similar, although milder experiences, from her childhood in Japan, screamed, *"Jishin, jishin!"*[2] before she ran and grabbed Yoneko and Seigo each by a hand and dragged them outside with her. She took them as far as the middle of the rhubarb patch near the house, and there they all crouched, pressed together, watching the world about them rock and sway. In a few minutes, Marpo, stumbling in from the fields, joined them, saying, "Earthquake, earthquake!" and he gathered them all in his arms, as much to protect them as to support himself.

Mr. Hosoume came home later that evening in a stranger's car, with another stranger driving the family Reo. Pallid, trembling, his eyes wildly staring, he could have been mistaken for a drunkard, except that he was famous as a teetotaler. It seemed that he had been on the way home when the first jolt came, that the old green Reo had been kissed by a broken live wire dangling from a suddenly leaning pole. Mr. Hosoume, knowing that the end had come by electrocution, had begun to writhe and kick and this had been his salvation. His hands had flown from the wheel, the car had swerved into a ditch, freeing itself from the sputtering wire. Later, it was found that he was left permanently inhibited about driving automobiles and permanently incapable of considering electricity with calmness.

[2]*jishin*   earthquake (Japanese)

He spent the larger part of his later life weakly, wandering about the house or fields and lying down frequently to rest because of splitting headaches and sudden dizzy spells.

So it was Marpo who went back into the house as Yoneko screamed, "No, Marpo, no!" and brought out the Hosoumes' kerosene stove, the food, the blankets, while Mr. Hosoume huddled on the ground near his family.

The earth trembled for days afterwards. The Hosoumes and Marpo Humming Wing lived during that time on a natural patch of Bermuda grass between the house and the rhubarb patch remembering to take three meals a day and retire at night. Marpo ventured inside the house many times despite Yoneko's protests and reported the damage slight: a few dishes had been broken; a gallon jug of mayonnaise had fallen from the top pantry shelf and spattered the kitchen floor with yellow blobs and pieces of glass.

Yoneko was in constant terror during this experience. Immediately on learning what all the commotion was about, she began praying to God to end this violence. She entreated God, flattered Him, wheedled Him, commanded Him, but He did not listen to her at all—inexorably, the earth went on rumbling. After three solid hours of silent, desperate prayer, without any results whatsoever, Yoneko began to suspect that God was either powerless, callous, downright cruel, or nonexistent. In the murky night, under a strange moon wearing a pale ring of light, she decided upon the last as the most plausible theory. "Ha," was one of the things she said tremulously to Marpo, when she was not begging him to stay out of the house, "you and your God!"

The others soon oriented themselves to the catastrophe with philosophy, saying how fortunate they were to live in the country where the peril was less than in the city and going so far as to regard the period as a sort of vacation from work, with their enforced alfresco existence a sort of camping trip. They tried to bring Yoneko to partake of this pleasant outlook, but she, shivering with each new quiver, looked on them as dreamers who refused to see things as they really were. Indeed, Yoneko's reaction was so notable that the Hosoume household thereafter spoke of the event as "Yoneko's earthquake."

After the earth subsided and the mayonnaise was mopped off the kitchen floor, life returned to normal, except that Mr. Hosoume stayed at home most of the time. Sometimes, if he had a relatively painless day, he would have supper on the stove when Mrs. Hosoume came in from the fields. Mrs. Hosoume and Marpo did all the field labor now, except on certain overwhelming days when several Mexicans were hired to assist them. Marpo did most of the driving, too, and it was now he and Mrs. Hosoume who went into town on the weekly trip for groceries. In fact, Marpo became indispensable and both Mr. and Mrs. Hosoume often told each other how grateful they were for Marpo.

When summer vacation began and Yoneko stayed at home, too, she found the new arrangement rather inconvenient. Her father's presence cramped her style: for instance, once when her friends came over and it was decided to make fudge, he would not permit them, saying fudge used too much sugar and that sugar was not a plaything; once when they were playing paper dolls, he came along and stuck his finger up his nose and pretended he was going to rub some snot off onto the dolls. Things like that. So, on some days, she was very much annoyed with her father.

Therefore when her mother came home breathless from the fields one day and pushed a ring at her, a gold-colored ring with a tiny glasslike stone in it, saying, "Look, Yoneko, I'm going to give you this ring. If your father asks where you got it, say you found it on the street." Yoneko was perplexed but delighted both by the unexpected gift and the chance to have some secret revenge on her father, and she said, certainly, she was willing to comply with her mother's request. Her mother went back to the fields then and Yoneko put the pretty ring on her middle finger, taking up the loose space with a bit of newspaper. It was similar to the rings found occasionally in boxes of Crackerjack, except that it appeared a bit more substantial.

Mr. Hosoume never asked about the ring; in fact, he never noticed she was wearing one. Yoneko thought he was about to, once, but he only reproved her for the flamingo nail polish she was wearing, which she had applied from a vial brought over by Yvonne Fournier, the French girl two orange groves away. "You look like a Filipino," Mr. Hosoume said sternly, for it was another irrefutable fact among Japanese in general that Filipinos in general were a gaudy lot. Mrs. Hosoume immediately came to her defense, saying that in Japan, if she remembered correctly, young girls did the same thing. In fact, she remembered having gone to elaborate lengths to tint her fingernails: she used to gather, she said, the petals of the red *tsubobana* or the purple *kogane* (which grows on the underside of stones), grind them well, mix them with some alum powder, then cook the mixture and leave it to stand overnight in an envelope of either persimmon or sugar potato leaves (both very strong leaves). The second night, just before going to bed, she used to obtain threads by ripping a palm leaf (because real thread was dear) and tightly bind the paste to her fingernails under shields of persimmon or sugar potato leaves. She would be helpless for the night, the fingertips bound so well that they were alternately numb or aching, but she would grit her teeth and tell herself that the discomfort indicated the success of the operation. In the morning, finally releasing her fingers, she would find the nails shining with a translucent red-orange color.

Yoneko was fascinated, because she usually thought of her parents as having been adults all their lives. She thought that her mother must have been a beautiful child, with or without bright fingernails, because, though surely past thirty, she was even yet a beautiful person. When she herself was younger, she remembered, she had at times been so struck with her mother's appearance that she had dropped to her knees and mutely clasped her mother's legs in her arms. She had left off this habit as she learned to control her emotions, because at such times her mother had usually walked away, saying, "My, what a clinging child you are. You've got to learn to be a little more independent." She also remembered she had once heard someone comparing her mother to "a dewy, half-opened rosebud."

Mr. Hosoume, however, was irritated. "That's no excuse for Yoneko to begin using paint on her fingernails," he said. "She's only ten."

"Her Japanese age is eleven,[3] and we weren't much older," Mrs. Hosoume said.

"Look," Mr. Hosoume said, "if you're going to contradict every piece of advice I give the children, they'll end up disobeying us both and doing what they very well please. Just because I'm ill just now is no reason for them to start being disrespectful."

"When have I ever contradicted you before?" Mrs. Hosoume said.

"Countless times," Mr. Hosoume said.

"Name one instance," Mrs. Hosoume said.

Certainly there had been times, but Mr. Hosoume could not happen to mention the one requested instance on the spot and he became quite angry. "That's quite enough of your insolence," he said. Since he was speaking in Japanese, his exact accusation was that she was *nama-iki,* which is a shade more revolting than being merely insolent.

"Nama-iki, nama-iki?" said Mrs. Hosoume. "How dare you? I'll not have anyone calling me *nama-iki!"*

At that, Mr. Hosoume went up to where his wife was ironing and slapped her smartly on the face. It was the first time he had ever laid hands on her. Mrs. Hosoume was immobile for an instant, but she resumed her ironing as though nothing had happened, although she glanced over at Marpo, who happened to be in the room reading a newspaper. Yoneko and Seigo forgot they were listening to the radio and stared at their parents, thunderstruck.

"Hit me again," said Mrs. Hosoume quietly, as she ironed. "Hit me all you wish."

Mr. Hosoume was apparently about to, but Marpo stepped up and put his hand on Mr. Hosoume's shoulder. "The children are here," said Marpo, "the children."

"Mind your own business," said Mr. Hosoume in broken English. "Get out of here!"

---

[3] **Her Japanese age is eleven** By Japanese reckoning a child becomes one year old on the first New Year's Day following his or her birth.

Marpo left, and that was about all. Mrs. Hosoume went on ironing, Yoneko and Seigo turned back to the radio, and Mr. Hosoume muttered that Marpo was beginning to forget his place. Now that he thought of it, he said, Marpo had been increasingly impudent towards him since his illness. He said just because he was temporarily an invalid was no reason for Marpo to start being disrespectful. He added that Marpo had better watch his step or that he might find himself jobless one of these fine days.

And something of the sort must have happened. Marpo was here one day and gone the next, without even saying good-bye to Yoneko and Seigo. That was also the day the Hosoume family went to the city on a weekday afternoon, which was most unusual. Mr. Hosoume, who now avoided driving as much as possible, handled the cumbersome Reo as though it were a nervous stallion, sitting on the edge of the seat and hugging the steering wheel. He drove very fast and about halfway to the city struck a beautiful collie which had dashed out barking from someone's yard. The car jerked with the impact, but Mr. Hosoume drove right on and Yoneko, wanting suddenly to vomit, looked back and saw the collie lying very still at the side of the road.

When they arrived at the Japanese hospital, which was their destination, Mr. Hosoume cautioned Yoneko and Seigo to be exemplary children and wait patiently in the car. It seemed hours before he and Mrs. Hosoume returned, she walking with very small, slow steps and he assisting her. When Mrs. Hosoume got in the car, she leaned back and closed her eyes. Yoneko inquired as to the source of her distress, for she was obviously in pain, but she only answered that she was feeling a little under the weather and that the doctor had administered some necessarily astringent treatment. At that, Mr. Hosoume turned around and advised Yoneko and Seigo that they must tell no one of coming to the city on a weekday afternoon, absolutely no one, and Yoneko and Seigo readily assented. On the way home, they passed the place of the encounter with the collie, and Yoneko looked up and down the stretch of road but the dog was nowhere to be seen.

Not long after that, the Hosoumes got a new hired hand, an old Japanese man who wore his gray hair in a military cut and who, unlike Marpo, had no particular interests outside working, eating, sleeping, and playing an occasional game of *goh*[4] with Mr. Hosoume. Before he came Yoneko and Seigo played sometimes in the empty bunkhouse and recalled Marpo's various charms together. Privately, Yoneko was wounded more than she would admit even to herself that Marpo should have subjected her to such an abrupt desertion. Whenever her indignation became too great to endure gracefully, she would console herself by telling Seigo that, after all, Marpo was a mere Filipino, an eater of wild dogs.

[4]***goh*** a Japanese game for two, played with pebblelike counters on a board

Seigo never knew about the disappointing new hired man, because he suddenly died in the night. He and Yoneko had spent the hot morning in the nearest orange grove, she driving him to distraction by repeating certain words he could not bear to hear: she had called him Serge, a name she had read somewhere, instead of Seigo; and she had chanted off the name of the tires they were rolling around like hoops as Goodrich Silver-TO-town, Goodrich Silver-TO-town, instead of Goodrich Silvertown. This had enraged him, and he had chased her around the trees most of the morning. Finally she had taunted him from several trees away by singing "You're a Yellow-streaked Coward," which was one of several small songs she had composed. Seigo had suddenly grinned and shouted, "Sure!" and walked off, leaving her, as he intended, with a sense of emptiness. In the afternoon, they had perspired and followed the potato-digging machine and the Mexican workers, both hired for the day, around the field, delighting in unearthing marble-sized, smooth-skinned potatoes that both the machine and the men had missed. Then, in the middle of the night, Seigo began crying, complaining of a stomach ache. Mrs. Hosoume felt his head and sent her husband for the doctor, who smiled and said Seigo would be fine in the morning. He said it was doubtless the combination of green oranges, raw potatoes, and the July heat. But as soon as the doctor left, Seigo fell into a coma and a drop of red blood stood out on his underlip, where he had evidently bit it. Mr. Hosoume again fetched the doctor, who was this time very grave and wagged his head, saying several times, "It looks very bad." So Seigo died at the age of five.

Mrs. Hosoume was inconsolable and had swollen eyes in the morning for weeks afterwards. She now insisted on visiting the city relatives each Sunday, so that she could attend church services with them. One Sunday, she stood up and accepted Christ. It was through accompanying her mother to many of these services that Yoneko finally learned the Japanese words to "Let Us Gather at the River." Mrs. Hosoume also did not seem interested in discussing anything but God and Seigo. She was especially fond of reminding visitors how adorable Seigo had been as an infant, how she had been unable to refrain from dressing him as a little girl and fixing his hair in bangs until he was two. Mr. Hosoume was very gentle with her and when Yoneko accidently caused her to giggle once, he nodded and said, "Yes, that's right, Yoneko, we must make your mother laugh and forget about Seigo." Yoneko herself did not think about Seigo at all. Whenever the thought of Seigo crossed her mind, she instantly began composing a new song, and this worked very well.

One evening, when the new hired man had been with them a while, Yoneko was helping her mother with the dishes when she found herself being examined with such peculiarly intent eyes that, with a start of guilt, she began searching in her mind for a possible crime she had lately committed. But Mrs. Hosoume only said, "Never kill a person, Yoneko, because if you do, God will take from you someone you love."

"Oh, that," said Yoneko quickly, "I don't believe in that, I don't believe in God." And her words tumbling pell-mell over one another, she
went on eagerly to explain a few of her reasons why. If she neglected to
mention the test she had given God during the earthquake, it was probably because she was a little upset. She had believed for a moment that
her mother was going to ask about the ring (which, alas, she had lost already, somewhere in the flumes⁵ along the cantaloupe patch).

[1951]

Gabriel García Márquez (*Colombian; b. 1928*)

A Very Old Man With Enormous Wings: A Tale for Children

Translated by Gregory Rabassa

On the third day of rain they had killed so many crabs inside the house
that Pelayo had to cross his drenched courtyard and throw them into the
sea, because the newborn child had a temperature all night and they thought
it was due to the stench. The world had been sad since Tuesday. Sea and
sky were a single ash-gray thing and the sands of the beach, which on
March nights glimmered like powdered light, had become a stew of mud
and rotten shellfish. The light was so weak at noon that when Pelayo was
coming back to the house after throwing away the crabs, it was hard for
him to see what it was that was moving and groaning in the rear of the
courtyard. He had to go very close to see that it was an old man, a very
old man, lying face down in the mud, who, in spite of his tremendous
efforts, couldn't get up, impeded by his enormous wings.

Frightened by that nightmare, Pelayo ran to get Elisenda, his wife,
who was putting compresses on the sick child, and he took her to the
rear of the courtyard. They both looked at the fallen body with mute stupor.
He was dressed like a ragpicker. There were only a few faded hairs left
on his bald skull and very few teeth in his mouth, and his pitiful condition of a drenched great-grandfather had taken away any sense of grandeur he might have had. His huge buzzard wings, dirty and half-plucked,
were forever entangled in the mud. They looked at him so long and so
closely that Pelayo and Elisenda very soon overcame their surprise and
in the end found him familiar. Then they dared speak to him, and he
answered in an incomprehensible dialect with a strong sailor's voice. That
was how they skipped over the inconvenience of the wings and quite intelligently concluded that he was a lonely castaway from some foreign ship

wrecked by the storm. And yet, they called in a neighbor woman who knew everything about life and death to see him, and all she needed was one look to show them their mistake.

"He's an angel," she told them. "He must have been coming for the child, but the poor fellow is so old that the rain knocked him down."

On the following day everyone knew that a flesh-and-blood angel was held captive in Pelayo's house. Against the judgment of the wise neighbor woman, for whom angels in those times were the fugitive survivors of a celestial conspiracy, they did not have the heart to club him to death. Pelayo watched over him all afternoon from the kitchen, armed with his bailiff's club, and before going to bed he dragged him out of the mud and locked him up with the hens in the wire chicken coop. In the middle of the night, when the rain stopped, Pelayo and Elisenda were still killing crabs. A short time afterward the child woke up without a fever and with a desire to eat. Then they felt magnanimous and decided to put the angel on a raft with fresh water and provisions for three days and leave him to his fate on the high seas. But when they went out into the courtyard with the first light of dawn, they found the whole neighborhood in front of the chicken coop having fun with the angel, without the slightest reverence, tossing him things to eat through the openings in the wire as if he weren't a supernatural creature but a circus animal.

Father Gonzaga arrived before seven o'clock, alarmed at the strange news. By that time onlookers less frivolous than those at dawn had already arrived and they were making all kinds of conjectures concerning the captive's future. The simplest among them thought that he should be named mayor of the world. Others of sterner mind felt that he should be promoted to the rank of five-star general in order to win all wars. Some visionaries hoped that he could be put to stud in order to implant on earth a race of winged wise men who could take charge of the universe. But Father Gonzaga, before becoming a priest, had been a robust woodcutter. Standing by the wire, he reviewed his catechism in an instant and asked them to open the door so that he could take a close look at that pitiful man who looked more like a huge decrepit hen among the fascinated chickens. He was lying in a corner drying his open wings in the sunlight among the fruit peels and breakfast leftovers that the early risers had thrown him. Alien to the impertinences of the world, he only lifted his antiquarian eyes and murmured something in his dialect when Father Gonzaga went into the chicken coop and said good morning to him in Latin. The parish priest had his first suspicion of an imposter when he saw that he did not understand the language of God or know how to greet His ministers. Then he noticed that seen close up he was much too human: he had an unbearable smell of the outdoors, the back side of his wings was strewn with parasites and his main feathers had been mistreated by terrestrial winds, and nothing about him measured up to the proud dignity of angels. Then he came out of the chicken coop and in a brief sermon warned the curious against the risks of being ingenuous. He reminded them that the devil had the bad habit of making use of carnival tricks in order to confuse the unwary. He argued that if wings were not the essential element in determining the difference between a hawk and an airplane, they were even less so in the recognition of angels. Nevertheless, he promised to write a letter to his bishop so that the latter would write to his primate so that the latter would write to the Supreme Pontiff in order to get the final verdict from the highest courts.

His prudence fell on sterile hearts. The news of the captive angel spread with such rapidity that after a few hours the courtyard had the bustle of a marketplace and they had to call in troops with fixed bayonets to disperse the mob that was about to knock the house down. Elisenda, her spine all twisted from sweeping up so much marketplace trash, then got the idea of fencing in the yard and charging five cents admission to see the angel.

The curious came from far away. A traveling carnival arrived with a flying acrobat who buzzed over the crowd several times, but no one paid any attention to him because his wings were not those of an angel but, rather, those of a sidereal bat. The most unfortunate invalids on earth came in search of health: a poor woman who since childhood had been counting her heartbeats and had run out of numbers; a Portuguese man who couldn't sleep because the noise of the stars disturbed him; a sleepwalker who got up at night to undo the things he had done while awake; and many others with less serious ailments. In the midst of that shipwreck disorder that made the earth tremble, Pelayo and Elisenda were happy with fatigue, for in less than a week they had crammed their rooms with money and the line of pilgrims waiting their turn to enter still reached beyond the horizon.

The angel was the only one who took no part in his own act. He spent his time trying to get comfortable in his borrowed nest, befuddled by the hellish heat of the oil lamps and sacramental candles that had been placed along the wire. At first they tried to make him eat some mothballs, which, according to the wisdom of the wise neighbor woman, were the food prescribed for angels. But he turned them down, just as he turned down the papal lunches that the penitents brought him, and they never found out whether it was because he was an angel or because he was an old man that in the end he ate nothing but eggplant mush. His only supernatural virtue seemed to be patience. Especially during the first days, when the hens pecked at him, searching for the stellar parasites that proliferated in his wings, and the cripples pulled out feathers to touch their defective parts with, and even the most merciful threw stones at him, trying to get him to rise so they could see him standing. The only time they succeeded in arousing him was when they burned his side with an iron for branding steers, for he had been motionless for so many hours that they thought he was dead. He awoke with a start, ranting in his hermetic language and with tears in his eyes, and he flapped his wings a couple of times, which brought on a whirlwind of chicken dung and lunar dust and a gale of panic that did not seem to be of this world. Although many thought that his reaction had been one not of rage but of pain, from then on they were careful not to annoy him, because the majority understood that his passivity was not that of a hero taking his ease but that of a cataclysm in repose.

Father Gonzaga held back the crowd's frivolity with formulas of maidservant inspiration while awaiting the arrival of a final judgment on the nature of the captive. But the mail from Rome showed no sense of urgency. They spent their time finding out if the prisoner had a navel, if his dialect had any connection with Aramaic, how many times he could fit on the head of a pin, or whether he wasn't just a Norwegian with wings. Those meager letters might have come and gone until the end of time if a providential event had not put an end to the priest's tribulations.

It so happened that during those days, among so many other carnival attractions, there arrived in town the traveling show of the woman who had been changed into a spider for having disobeyed her parents. The admission to see her was not only less than the admission to see the angel, but people were permitted to ask her all manner of questions about her absurd state and to examine her up and down so that no one would ever doubt the truth of her horror. She was a frightful tarantula the size of a ram and with the head of a sad maiden. What was most heart-rending, however, was not her outlandish shape but the sincere affliction with which she recounted the details of her misfortune. While still practically a child she had sneaked out of her parents' house to go to a dance, and while she was coming back through the woods after having danced all night without permission, a fearful thunderclap rent the sky in two and through the crack came the lightning bolt of brimstone that changed her into a spider. Her only nourishment came from the meatballs that charitable souls chose to toss into her mouth. A spectacle like that, full of so much human truth and with such a fearful lesson, was bound to defeat without even trying that of a haughty angel who scarcely deigned to look at mortals. Besides, the few miracles attributed to the angel showed a certain mental disorder, like the blind man who didn't recover his sight but grew three new teeth, or the paralytic who didn't get to walk but almost won the lottery, and the leper whose sores sprouted sunflowers. Those consolation miracles, which were more like mocking fun, had already ruined the angel's reputation when the woman who had been changed into a spider finally crushed him completely. That was how Father Gonzaga was cured forever of his insomnia and Pelayo's courtyard went back to being as empty as during the time it had rained for three days and crabs walked through the bedrooms.

The owners of the house had no reason to lament. With the money they saved they built a two-story mansion with balconies and gardens and high netting so that crabs wouldn't get in during the winter, and with iron bars on the windows so that angels couldn't get in. Pelayo also set up a rabbit warren close to town and gave up his job as bailiff for good, and Elisenda bought some satin pumps with high heels and many dresses of iridescent silk, the kind worn on Sunday by the most desirable women in those times. The chicken coop was the only thing that didn't receive any attention. If they washed it down with creolin and burned tears of myrrh inside it every so often, it was not in homage to the angel but to drive away the dungheap stench that still hung everywhere like a ghost and was turning the new house into an old one. At first, when the child learned to walk, they were careful that he not get too close to the chicken coop. But then they began to lose their fears and got used to the smell, and before the child got his second teeth he'd gone inside the chicken coop to play, where the wires were falling apart. The angel was no less standoffish with him than with other mortals, but he tolerated the most ingenious infamies with the patience of a dog who had no illusions. They both came down with chicken pox at the same time. The doctor who took care of the child couldn't resist the temptation to listen to the angel's heart, and he found so much whistling in the heart and so many sounds in his kidneys that it seemed impossible for him to be alive. What surprised him most, however, was the logic of his wings. They seemed so natural on that completely human organism that he couldn't understand why other men didn't have them too.

When the child began school it had been some time since the sun and rain had caused the collapse of the chicken coop. The angel went dragging himself about here and there like a stray dying man. They would drive him out of the bedroom with a broom and a moment later find him in the kitchen. He seemed to be in so many places at the same time that they grew to think that he'd been duplicated, that he was reproducing himself all through the house, and the exasperated and unhinged Elisenda shouted that it was awful living in that hell full of angels. He could scarcely eat and his antiquarian eyes had also become so foggy that he went about bumping into posts. All he had left were the bare cannulae of his last feathers. Pelayo threw a blanket over him and extended him the charity of letting him sleep in the shed, and only then did they notice that he had a temperature at night, and was delirious with the tongue twisters of an old Norwegian. That was one of the few times they became alarmed, for they thought he was going to die and not even the wise neighbor woman had been able to tell them what to do with dead angels.

And yet he not only survived his worst winter, but seemed improved with the first sunny days. He remained motionless for several days in the farthest corner of the courtyard, where no one would see him, and at the beginning of December some large, stiff feathers began to grow on his wings, the feathers of a scarecrow, which looked more like another misfortune of decrepitude. But he must have known the reason for those changes, for he was quite careful that no one should notice them, that no one should hear the sea chanteys that he sometimes sang under the stars.

One morning Elisenda was cutting some bunches of onions for lunch when a wind that seemed to come from the high seas blew into the kitchen. Then she went to the window and caught the angel in his first attempts at flight. They were so clumsy that his fingernails opened a furrow in the vegetable patch and he was on the point of knocking the shed down with the ungainly flapping that slipped on the light and couldn't get a grip on the air. But he did manage to gain altitude. Elisenda let out a sigh of relief, for herself and for him, when she saw him pass over the last houses, holding himself up in some way with the risky flapping of a senile vulture. She kept watching him even when she was through cutting the onions and she kept on watching until it was no longer possible for her to see him, because then he was no longer an annoyance in her life but an imaginary dot on the horizon of the sea.

[1968]

Alice Munro *(Canadian; b. 1931)*

How I Met My Husband

We heard the plane come over at noon, roaring through the radio news, and we were sure it was going to hit the house, so we all ran out into the yard. We saw it come in over the treetops, all red and silver, the first close-up plane I ever saw. Mrs. Peebles screamed.

"Crash landing," their little boy said. Joey was his name.

"It's okay," said Dr. Peebles. "He knows what he's doing." Dr. Peebles was only an animal doctor, but had a calming way of talking, like any doctor.

This was my first job—working for Dr. and Mrs. Peebles, who had bought an old house out on the Fifth Line, about five miles out of town. It was just when the trend was starting of town people buying up old farms, not to work them but to live on them.

We watched the plane land across the road, where the fairgrounds used to be. It did make a good landing field, nice and level for the old race track, and the barns and display sheds torn down now for scrap lumber so there was nothing in the way. Even the old grandstand bays had burned.

"All right," said Mrs. Peebles, snappy as she always was when she got over her nerves. "Let's go back in the house. Let's not stand here gawking like a set of farmers."

She didn't say that to hurt my feelings. It never occurred to her.

I was just setting the dessert down when Loretta Bird arrived, out of breath, at the screen door.

"I thought it was going to crash into the house and kill youse all!"

She lived on the next place and the Peebleses thought she was a countrywoman, they didn't know the difference. She and her husband didn't farm, he worked on the roads and had a bad name for drinking. They had seven children and couldn't get credit at the HiWay Grocery. The Peebleses made her welcome, not knowing any better, as I say, and offered her dessert.

Dessert was never anything to write home about, at their place. A dish of Jell-O or sliced bananas or fruit out of a tin. "Have a house without a pie, be ashamed until you die," my mother used to say, but Mrs. Peebles operated differently.

Loretta Bird saw me getting the can of peaches.

"Oh, never mind," she said. "I haven't got the right kind of a stomach to trust what comes out of those tins, I can only eat home canning."

I could have slapped her. I bet she never put down fruit in her life.

"I know what he's landed here for," she said. "He's got permission to use the fairgrounds and take people up for rides. It costs a dollar. It's the same fellow who was over at Palmerston last week and was up the lakeshore before that. I wouldn't go up, if you paid me."

"I'd jump at the chance," Dr. Peebles said. "I'd like to see this neighborhood from the air."

Mrs. Peebles said she would just as soon see it from the ground. Joey said he wanted to go and Heather did, too. Joey was nine and Heather was seven.

"Would you, Edie?" Heather said.

I said I didn't know. I was scared, but I never admitted that, especially in front of children I was taking care of.

"People are going to be coming out here in their cars raising dust and trampling your property, if I was you I would complain." Loretta said. She hooked her legs around the chair rung and I knew we were in for a lengthy visit. After Dr. Peebles went back to his office or out on his next call and Mrs. Peebles went for her nap, she would hang around me while I was trying to do the dishes. She would pass remarks about the Peebleses in their own house.

"She wouldn't find time to lay down in the middle of the day, if she had seven kids like I got."

She asked me did they fight and did they keep things in the dresser drawer not to have babies with. She said it was a sin if they did. I pretended I didn't know what she was talking about.

I was fifteen and away from home for the first time. My parents had made the effort and sent me to high school for a year, but I didn't like it. I was shy of strangers and the work was hard, they didn't make it nice for you or explain the way they do now. At the end of the year the averages were published in the paper, and mine came out at the very bottom, 37 percent. My father said that's enough and I didn't blame him. The last thing I wanted, anyway, was to go on and end up teaching school. It happened the very day the paper came out with my disgrace in it, Dr. Peebles was staying at our place for dinner, having just helped one of the cows have twins, and he said I looked smart to him and his wife was looking for a girl to help. He said she felt tied down, with the two children, out in the country. I guess she would, my mother said, being polite, though I could tell from her face she was wondering what on earth it would be like to have only two children and no barn work, and then to be complaining.

When I went home I would describe to them the work I had to do, and it made everybody laugh. Mrs. Peebles had an automatic washer and dryer, the first I ever saw. I have had those in my own home for such a long time now it's hard to remember how much of a miracle it was to me, not having to struggle with the wringer and hang up and haul down. Let alone not having to heat water. Then there was practically no baking. Mrs. Peebles said she couldn't make pie crust, the most amazing thing I ever heard a woman admit. I could, of course, and I could make light biscuits and a white cake and dark cake, but they didn't want it, she said they watched their figures. The only thing I didn't like about working there, in fact, was feeling half hungry a lot of the time. I used to bring back a box of doughnuts made out at home, and hide them under my bed. The children found out, and I didn't mind sharing, but I thought I better bind them to secrecy.

The day after the plane landed Mrs. Peebles put both children in the car and drove over to Chesley, to get their hair cut. There was a good woman then at Chesley for doing hair. She got hers done at the same place, Mrs. Peebles did, and that meant they would be gone a good while. She had to pick a day Dr. Peebles wasn't going out into the country, she didn't have her own car. Cars were still in short supply then, after the war.

I loved being left in the house alone, to do my work at leisure. The kitchen was all white and bright yellow, with fluorescent lights. That was before they ever thought of making the appliances all different colors and doing the cupboards like dark old wood and hiding the lighting. I loved light. I loved the double sink. So would anybody new-come from washing dishes in a dishpan with a rag-plugged hole on an oilcloth-covered table by light of a coal-oil lamp. I kept everything shining.

The bathroom too. I had a bath in there once a week. They wouldn't have minded if I took one oftener, but to me it seemed like asking too much, or maybe risking making it less wonderful. The basin and the tub and the toilet were all pink, and there were glass doors with flamingoes painted on them, to shut off the tub. The light had a rosy cast and the mat sank under your feet like snow, except that it was warm. The mirror was three-way. With the mirror all steamed up and the air like a perfume cloud, from things I was allowed to use, I stood up on the side of the tub and admired myself naked, from three directions. Sometimes I thought about the way we lived out at home and the way we lived here and how one way was so hard to imagine when you were living the other way. But I thought it was still a lot easier, living the way we lived at home, to picture something like this, the painted flamingoes and the warmth and the soft mat, than it was anybody knowing only things like this to picture how it was the other way. And why was that?

I was through my jobs in no time, and had the vegetables peeled for supper and sitting in cold water besides. Then I went into Mrs. Peebles' bedroom. I had been in there plenty of times, cleaning, and I always took a good look in her closet, at the clothes she had hanging there. I wouldn't have looked in her drawers, but a closet is open to anybody. That's a lie. I would have looked in drawers, but I would have felt worse doing it and been more scared she could tell.

Some clothes in her closet she wore all the time, I was quite familiar with them. Others she never put on, they were pushed to the back. I was disappointed to see no wedding dress. But there was one long dress I could just see the skirt of, and I was hungering to see the rest. Now I took note of where it hung and lifted it out. It was satin, a lovely weight on my arm, light bluish-green in color, almost silvery. It had a fitted, pointed waist and a full skirt and an off-the-shoulder fold hiding the little sleeves.

Next thing was easy. I got out of my own things and slipped it on. I was slimmer at fifteen than anybody would believe who knows me now and the fit was beautiful. I didn't, of course, have a strapless bra on, which was what it needed, I just had to slide my straps down my arms under the material. Then I tried pinning up my hair, to get the effect. One thing led to another. I put on rouge and lipstick and eyebrow pencil from her dresser. The heat of the day and the weight of the satin and all the excitement made me thirsty, and I went out to the kitchen, got-up as I was, to get a glass of ginger ale with ice cubes from the refrigerator. The Peebleses drank ginger ale, or fruit drinks, all day, like water, and I was getting so I did too. Also there was no limit on ice cubes, which I was so fond of I would even put them in a glass of milk.

I turned from putting the ice tray back and saw a man watching me through the screen. It was the luckiest thing in the world I didn't spill the ginger ale down the front of me then and there.

"I never meant to scare you. I knocked but you were getting the ice out, you didn't hear me."

I couldn't see what he looked like, he was dark the way somebody is pressed up against a screen door with the bright daylight behind them. I only knew he wasn't from around here.

"I'm from the plane over there. My name is Chris Watters and what I was wondering was if I could use that pump."

There was a pump in the yard. That was the way the people used to get their water. Now I noticed he was carrying a pail.

"You're welcome," I said. "I can get it from the tap and save you pumping." I guess I wanted him to know we had piped water, didn't pump ourselves.

"I don't mind the exercise." He didn't move, though, and finally he said, "Were you going to a dance?"

Seeing a stranger there had made me entirely forgot how I was dressed.

"Or is that the way ladies around here generally get dressed up in the afternoon?"

I didn't know how to joke back then. I was too embarrassed.

"You live here? Are you the lady of the house?"

"I'm the hired girl."

Some people change when they find that out, their whole way of looking at you and speaking to you changes, but his didn't.

"Well, I just wanted to tell you you look very nice. I was so surprised when I looked in the door and saw you. Just because you looked so nice and beautiful."

I wasn't even old enough then to realize how out of the common it is, for a man to say something like that to a woman, or somebody he is treating like a woman. For a man to say a word like *beautiful.* I wasn't old enough to realize or to say anything back, or in fact to do anything but wish he would go away. Not that I didn't like him, but just that it upset me so, having him look at me, and me trying to think of something to say.

He must have understood. He said good-bye, and thanked me, and went and started filling his pail from the pump. I stood behind the Venetian blinds in the dining room, watching him. When he had gone, I went into the bedroom and took the dress off and put it back in the same place. I dressed in my own clothes and took my hair down and washed my face, wiping it on Kleenex, which I threw in the wastebasket.

The Peebleses asked me what kind of man he was. Young, middle-aged, short, tall? I couldn't say.

"Good-looking?" Dr. Peebles teased me.

I couldn't think a thing but that he would be coming to get his water again, he would be talking to Dr. or Mrs. Peebles, making friends with them, and he would mention seeing me that first afternoon, dressed up. Why not mention it? He would think it was funny. And no idea of the trouble it would get me into.

After supper the Peebleses drove into town to go to a movie. She wanted to go somewhere with her hair fresh done. I sat in my bright kitchen wondering what to do, knowing I would never sleep. Mrs. Peebles might not fire me, when she found out, but it would give her a different feeling about me altogether. This was the first place I ever worked but I already had picked up things about the way people feel when you are working for them. They like to think you aren't curious. Not just that you aren't dishonest, that isn't enough. They like to feel you don't notice things, that you don't think or wonder about anything but what they liked to eat and how they liked things ironed, and so on. I don't mean they weren't kind to me, because they were. They had me eat my meals with them (to tell the truth I expected to, I didn't know there were families who don't) and sometimes they took me along in the car. But all the same.

I went up and checked on the children being asleep and then I went out. I had to do it. I crossed the road and went in the old fairgrounds gate. The plane looked unnatural sitting there, and shining with the moon. Off at the far side of the fairgrounds where the bush was taking over, I saw his tent.

He was sitting outside it smoking a cigarette. He saw me coming.

"Hello, were you looking for a plane ride? I don't start taking people up till tomorrow." Then he looked again and said, "Oh, it's you. I didn't know you without your long dress on."

My heart was knocking away, my tongue was dried up. I had to say something. But I couldn't. My throat was closed and I was like a deaf-and-dumb.

"Did you want a ride? Sit down. Have a cigarette."

I couldn't even shake my head to say no, so he gave me one.

"Put it in your mouth or I can't light it. It's a good thing I'm used to shy ladies."

I did. It wasn't the first time I had smoked a cigarette, actually. My girlfriend out home, Muriel Lowe, used to steal them from her brother.

"Look at your hand shaking. Did you just want to have a chat, or what?"

In one burst I said, "I wisht you wouldn't say anything about that dress."

"What dress? Oh, the long dress."

"It's Mrs. Peebles'."

"Whose? Oh, the lady you work for? She wasn't home so you got dressed up in her dress, eh? You got dressed up and played queen. I don't blame you. You're not smoking the cigarette right. Don't just puff. Draw it in. Did anybody ever show you how to inhale? Are you scared I'll tell on you? Is that it?"

I was so ashamed at having to ask him to connive this way I couldn't nod. I just looked at him and he saw *yes*.

"Well I won't. I won't in the slightest way mention it or embarrass you. I give you my word of honor."

Then he changed the subject, to help me out, seeing I couldn't even thank him.

"What do you think of this sign?"

It was board sign lying practically at my feet.

SEE THE WORLD FROM THE SKY. ADULTS $1.00, CHILDREN 50¢. QUALI-FIED PILOT.

"My old sign was getting pretty beat up, I thought I'd make a new one. That's what I've been doing with my time today."

The lettering wasn't all that handsome, I thought. I could have done a better one in half an hour.

"I'm not an expert at sign making."

"It's very good," I said.

"I don't need it for publicity, word of mouth is usually enough. I turned away two carloads tonight. I felt like taking it easy. I didn't tell them ladies were dropping in to visit me."

Now I remembered the children and I was scared again, in case one of them had waked up and called me and I wasn't there.

"Do you have to go so soon?"

I remembered some manners. "Thank you for the cigarette."

"Don't forget. You have my word of honor."

I tore off across the fairgrounds, scared I'd see the car heading home from town. My sense of time was mixed up, I didn't know how long I'd been out of the house. But it was all right, it wasn't late, the children were asleep. I got in my bed myself and lay thinking what a lucky end to the day, after all, and among things to be grateful for I could be grateful Loretta Bird hadn't been the one who caught me.

The yard and borders didn't get trampled, it wasn't as bad as that. All the same it seemed very public, around the house. The sign was on the fairgrounds gate. People came mostly after supper but a good many in the afternoon, too. The Bird children all came without fifty cents between them and hung on the gate. We got used to the excitement of the plane coming in and taking off, it wasn't excitement anymore. I never went over, after that one time, but would see him when he came to get his water. I would be out on the steps doing sitting-down work, like preparing vegetables, if I could.

"Why don't you come over? I'll take you up in my plane."

"I'm saving my money," I said, because I couldn't think of anything else.

"For what? For getting married?"

I shook my head.

"I'll take you up for free if you come sometime when it's slack. I thought you would come, and have another cigarette."

I made a face to hush him, because you never could tell when the children would be sneaking around the porch, or Mrs. Peebles herself listening in the house. Sometimes she came out and had a conversation with him. He told her things he hadn't bothered to tell me. But then I hadn't thought to ask. He told her he had been in the war, that was where he learned to fly a plane, and how he couldn't settle down to ordinary life, this was what he liked. She said she couldn't imagine anybody liking such a thing. Though sometimes, she said, she was almost bored enough to try anything herself, she wasn't brought up to living in the country. It's all my husband's idea, she said. This was news to me.

"Maybe you ought to give flying lessons," she said.

"Would you take them?"

She just laughed.

Sunday was a busy flying day in spite of it being preached against from two pulpits. We were all sitting out watching. Joey and Heather were over on the fence with the Bird kids. Their father had said they could go, after their mother saying all week they couldn't.

A car came down the road past the parked cars and pulled up right in the drive. It was Loretta Bird who got out, all importance, and on the driver's side another woman got out, more sedately. She was wearing sunglasses.

"This is a lady looking for the man that flies the plane," Loretta Bird said. "I heard her inquire in the hotel coffee shop where I was having a Coke and I brought her out."

"I'm sorry to bother you," the lady said. "I'm Alice Kelling, Mr. Watters' fiancée."

This Alice Kelling had on a pair of brown and white checked slacks and a yellow top. Her bust looked to me rather low and bumpy. She had a worried face. Her hair had had a permanent, but had grown out, and she wore a yellow band to keep it off her face. Nothing in the least pretty or even young-looking about her. But you could tell from how she talked she was from the city, or educated, or both.

Dr. Peebles stood up and introduced himself and his wife and me and asked her to be seated.

"He's up in the air right now, but you're welcome to sit and wait. He gets his water here and he hasn't been yet. He'll probably take his break about five."

"That is him, then?" said Alice Kelling, wrinkling and straining at the sky.

"He's not in the habit of running out on you, taking a different name?" Dr. Peebles laughed. He was the one, not his wife, to offer iced tea. Then she sent me into the kitchen to fix it. She smiled. She was wearing sunglasses too.

"He never mentioned his fiancée," she said.

I loved fixing iced tea with lots of ice and slices of lemon in tall glasses. I ought to have mentioned before, Dr. Peebles was an abstainer, at least around the house, or I wouldn't have been allowed to take the place. I had to fix a glass for Loretta Bird too, though it galled me, and when I went out she had settled in my lawn chair, leaving me the steps.

"I knew you was a nurse when I first heard you in that coffee shop."

"How would you know a thing like that?"

"I get my hunches about people. Was that how you met him, nursing?"

"Chris? Well yes. Yes, it was."

"Oh, were you overseas?" said Mrs. Peebles.

"No, it was before he went overseas. I nursed him when he was stationed at Centralia and had a ruptured appendix. We got engaged and then he went overseas. My, this is refreshing, after a long drive."

"He'll be glad to see you," Dr. Peebles said. "It's a rackety kind of life, isn't it, not staying one place long enough to really make friends."

"Youse've had a long engagement," Loretta Bird said.

Alice Kelling passed that over. "I was going to get a room at the hotel, but when I was offered directions I came on out. Do you think I could phone them?"

"No need," Dr. Peebles said. "You're five miles away from him if you stay at the hotel. Here, you're right across the road. Stay with us. We've got rooms on rooms, look at this big house."

Asking people to stay, just like that, is certainly a country thing, and maybe seemed natural to him now, but not to Mrs. Peebles, from the way she said, oh yes, we have plenty of room. Or to Alice Kelling, who kept protesting, but let herself be worn down. I got the feeling it was a temptation to her, to be that close. I was trying for a look at her ring. Her nails were painted red, her fingers were freckled and wrinkled. It was a tiny stone. Muriel Lowe's cousin had one twice as big.

Chris came to get his water, late in the afternoon just as Dr. Peebles had predicted. He must have recognized the car from a way off. He came smiling.

"Here I am chasing after you to see what you're up to," called Alice Kelling. She got up and went to meet him and they kissed, just touched, in front of us.

"You're going to spend a lot on gas that way," Chris said.

Dr. Peebles invited Chris to stay for supper, since he had already put up the sign that said: NO MORE RIDES TILL 7 P.M. Mrs. Peebles wanted it served in the yard, in spite of the bugs. One thing strange to anybody from the country is this eating outside. I had made a potato salad earlier and she had made a jellied salad, that was one thing she could do, so it was just a matter of getting those out, and some sliced meat and cucumbers and fresh leaf lettuce. Loretta Bird hung around for some time saying, "Oh, well, I guess I better get home to those yappers," and, "It's so nice just sitting here, I sure hate to get up," but nobody invited her, I was relieved to see, and finally she had to go.

That night after rides were finished Alice Kelling and Chris went off somewhere in her car. I lay awake till they got back. When I saw the car lights sweep my ceiling I got up to look down on them through the slats of my blind. I don't know what I thought I was going to see. Muriel Lowe and I used to sleep on her front veranda and watch her sister and her sister's boy friend saying good night. Afterward we couldn't get to sleep, for longing for somebody to kiss us and rub against us and we would talk about suppose you were out in a boat with a boy and he wouldn't bring you in to shore unless you did it, or what if somebody got you trapped in a barn, you would have to, wouldn't you, it wouldn't be your fault. Muriel said her two girl cousins used to try with a toilet paper roll that one of them was a boy. We wouldn't do anything like that; just lay and wondered.

All that happened was that Chris got out of the car on one side and she got out on the other and they walked off separately—him toward the fairgrounds and her toward the house. I got back in bed and imagined about me coming home with him, not like that.

Next morning Alice Kelling got up late and I fixed a grapefruit for her the way I had learned and Mrs. Peebles sat down with her to visit and have another cup of coffee. Mrs. Peebles seemed pleased enough now, having company. Alice Kelling said she guessed she better get used to putting in a day just watching Chris take off and come down, and Mrs. Peebles said she didn't know if she should suggest it because Alice Kelling was the one with the car, but the lake was only twenty-five miles away and what a good day for a picnic.

Alice Kelling took her up on the idea and by eleven o'clock they were in the car, with Joey and Heather and a sandwich lunch I had made. The only thing was that Chris hadn't come down, and she wanted to tell him where they were going.

"Edie'll go over and tell him," Mrs. Peebles said. "There's no problem."

Alice Kelling wrinkled her face and agreed.

"Be sure and tell him we'll be back by five!"

I didn't see that he would be concerned about knowing this right away, and I thought of him eating whatever he ate over there, alone, cooking on his camp stove, so I got to work and mixed up a crumb cake and baked it, in between the other work I had to do; then, when it was a bit cooled, wrapped it in a tea towel. I didn't do anything to myself but take off my apron and comb my hair. I would like to have put some makeup on, but I was too afraid it would remind him of the way he first saw me, and that would humiliate me all over again.

He had come and put another sign on the gate: NO RIDES THIS P.M. APOLOGIES. I worried that he wasn't feeling well. No sign of him outside and the tent flap was down. I knocked on the pole.

"Come in," he said, in a voice that would just as soon have said *Stay out.*

I lifted the flap.

"Oh, it's you. I'm sorry. I didn't know it was you."

He had been just sitting on the side of the bed, smoking. Why not at least sit and smoke in the fresh air?

"I brought a cake and hope you're not sick," I said.

"Why would I be sick? Oh—that sign. That's all right. I'm just tired of talking to people. I don't mean you. Have a seat." He pinned back the tent flap. "Get some fresh air in here."

I sat on the edge of the bed, there was no place else. It was one of those fold-up cots, really; I remembered and gave him his fiancée's message.

He ate some of the cake. "Good."

"Put the rest away for when you're hungry later."

"I'll tell you a secret. I won't be around here much longer."

"Are you getting married?"

"Ha ha. What time did you say they'd be back?"

"Five o'clock."

"Well, by that time this place will have seen the last of me. A plane can get further than a car." He unwrapped the cake and ate another piece of it, absent-mindedly.

"Now you'll be thirsty."

"There's some water in the pail."

"It won't be very cold. I could bring some fresh. I could bring some ice from the refrigerator."

"No," he said. "I don't want you to go. I want a nice long time of saying good-bye to you."

He put the cake away carefully and sat beside me and started those little kisses, so soft, I can't ever let myself think about them, such kindness in his face and lovely kisses, all over my eyelids and neck and ears, all over, then me kissing back as well as I could (I had only kissed a boy on a dare before, and kissed my own arms for practice) and we lay back on the cot and pressed together, just gently, and he did some other things, not bad things or not in a bad way. It was lovely in the tent, that smell of grass and hot tent cloth with the sun beating down on it, and he said, "I wouldn't do you any harm for the world." Once, when he had rolled on top of me and we were sort of rocking together on the cot, he said softly, "Oh, no," and freed himself and jumped up and got the water pail. He splashed some of it on his neck and face, and the little bit left, on me lying there.

"That's to cool us off, miss."

When we said good-bye I wasn't at all sad, because he held my face and said "I'm going to write you a letter. I'll tell you where I am and maybe you can come and see me. Would you like that? Okay then. You wait." I was really glad I think to get away from him, it was like he was piling presents on me I couldn't get the pleasure of till I considered them alone.

No consternation at first about the plane being gone. They thought he had taken somebody up, and I didn't enlighten them. Dr. Peebles had phoned he had to go to the country, so there was just us having supper, and then Loretta Bird thrusting her head in the door and saying, "I see he's took off."

"What?" said Alice Kelling, and pushed back her chair.

"The kids come and told me this afternoon he was taking down his tent. Did he think he'd run through all the business there was around here? He didn't take off without letting you know, did he?"

"He'll send me word," Alice Kelling said. "He'll probably phone tonight. He's terribly restless, since the war."

"Edie, he didn't mention to you, did he?" Mrs. Peebles said. "When you took over the message?"

"Yes," I said. So far so true.

"Well why didn't you say?" All of them were looking at me. "Did he say where he was going?"

"He said he might try Bayfield," I said. What made me tell such a lie? I didn't intend it.

"Bayfield, how far is that?" said Alice Kelling.

Mrs. Peebles said, "Thirty, thirty-five miles."

"That's not far. Oh, well, that's really not far at all. It's on the lake, isn't it?"

You'd think I'd be ashamed of myself, setting her on the wrong track. I did it to give him more time, whatever time he needed. I lied for him, and also, I have to admit, for me. Women should stick together and not do things like that. I see that now, but didn't then. I never thought of myself as being in any way like her, or coming to the same troubles, ever.

She hadn't taken her eyes off me. I thought she suspected my lie.

"When did he mention this to you?"

"Earlier."

"When you were over at the plane?"

"Yes."

"You must've stayed and had a chat." She smiled at me, not a nice smile. "You must've stayed and had a little visit with him."

"I took a cake," I said, thinking that telling some truth would spare me telling the rest.

"We didn't have a cake," said Mrs. Peebles rather sharply.

"I baked one."

Alice Kelling said, "That was very friendly of you."

"Did you get permission," said Loretta Bird. "You never know what these girls'll do next," she said. "It's not they mean harm so much, as they're ignorant."

"The cake is neither here nor there," Mrs. Peebles broke in. "Edie, I wasn't aware you knew Chris that well."

I didn't know what to say.

"I'm not surprised," Alice Kelling said in a high voice. "I knew by the look of her as soon as I saw her. We get them at the hospital all the

time." She looked hard at me with her stretched smile. "Having their babies. We have to put them in a special ward because of their diseases. Little
country tramps. Fourteen and fifteen years old. You should see the babies
they have, too."

"There was a bad woman here in town had a baby that pus was
running out of its eyes," Loretta Bird put in.

"Wait a minute," said Mrs. Peebles. "What is this talk? Edie. What
about you and Mr. Watters? Were you intimate with him?"

"Yes," I said. I was thinking of us lying on the cot and kissing, wasn't
that intimate? And I would never deny it.

They were all one minute quiet, even Loretta Bird.

"Well," said Mrs. Peebles. "I am surprised. I think I need a cigarette.
This is the first of any such tendencies I've seen in her," she said, speaking
to Alice Kelling, but Alice Kelling was looking at me.

"Loose little bitch." Tears ran down her face. "Loose little bitch, aren't
you? I knew as soon as I saw you. Men despise girls like you. He just
made use of you and went off, you know that, don't you? Girls like you
are just nothing, they're just public conveniences, just filthy little rags!"

"Oh, now," said Mrs. Peebles.

"Filthy," Alice Kelling sobbed. "Filthy little rags!"

"Don't get yourself upset," Loretta Bird said. She was swollen up
with pleasure at being in on this scene. "Men are all the same."

"Edie, I'm very surprised," Mrs. Pebbles said. "I thought your parents were so strict. You don't want to have a baby, do you?"

I'm still ashamed of what happened next. I lost control, just like a
six-year-old, I started howling. "You don't get a baby from just doing that!"

"You see. Some of them are that ignorant," Loretta Bird said.

But Mrs. Peebles jumped up and caught my arms and shook me.
"Calm down. Don't get hysterical. Calm down. Stop crying. Listen
to me. Listen I'm wondering, if you know what being intimate means.
Now tell me. What did you think it meant?"

"Kissing," I howled.

She let go. "Oh, Edie. Stop it. Don't be silly. It's all right. It's all
a misunderstanding. Being intimate means a lot more than that. Oh, I
wondered."

"She's trying to cover up, now," said Alice Kelling. "Yes. She's not
so stupid. She sees she got herself in trouble."

"I believe her," Mrs. Peebles said. "This is an awful scene."

"Well there is one way to find out," said Alice Kelling, getting up.
"After all, I am a nurse."

Mrs. Peebles drew a breath and said, "No. No. Go to your room,
Edie. And stop that noise. This is too disgusting."

I heard the car start in a little while. I tried to stop crying, pulling
back each wave as it started over me. Finally I succeeded, and lay heaving
on the bed.

Mrs. Peebles came and stood in the doorway.

"She's gone," she said. "That Bird woman too. Of course, you know you should never have gone near that man and that is the cause of all this trouble. I have a headache. As soon as you can, go and wash your face in cold water and get at the dishes and we will not say any more about this."

Nor we didn't. I didn't figure out till years later the extent of what I had been saved from. Mrs. Peebles was not very friendly to me afterward, but she was fair. Not very friendly is the wrong of describing what she was. She had never been very friendly. It was just that now she had to see me all the time and it got on her nerves, a little.

As for me, I put it all out of my mind like a bad dream and concentrated on waiting for my letter. The mail came every day except Sunday, between one-thirty and two in the afternoon, a good time for me because Mrs. Peebles was always having her nap. I would get the kitchen all cleaned and then go up to the mailbox and sit in the grass, waiting. I was perfectly happy, waiting. I forgot all about Alice Kelling and her misery and awful talk and Mrs. Peebles and her chilliness and the embarrassment of whether she told Dr. Peebles and the face of Loretta Bird, getting her fill of other people's troubles. I was always smiling when the mailman got there, and continued smiling even after he gave me the mail and I saw today wasn't the day. The mailman was a Carmichael. I knew by his face because there are a lot of Carmichaels living out by us and so many of them have a sort of sticking-out top lip. So I asked his name (he was a young man, shy, but good-humored, anybody could ask him anything) and then I said, "I knew by your face!" He was pleased by that and always glad to see me and got a little less shy. "You've got the smile I've been waiting for all day!" he used to holler out the car window.

It never crossed my mind for a long time a letter might not come. I believed in it coming just like I believed the sun would rise in the morning. I just put off my hope from day to day, and there was the goldenrod out around the mailbox and the children gone back to school, and the leaves turning, and I was wearing a sweater when I went to wait. One day walking back with the hydro bill stuck in my hand, that was all, looking across at the fairgrounds with the full-blown milkweed and dark teasels, so much like fall, it just struck me: *No letter was ever going to come.* It was an impossible idea to get used to. No, not impossible. If I thought about Chris's face when he said he was going to write me, it was impossible, but if I forgot that and thought about the actual tin mailbox, empty, it was plain and true. I kept on going to meet the mail, but my heart was heavy now like a lump of lead. I only smiled because I thought of the mailman counting on it, and he didn't have an easy life, with the winter driving ahead.

Till it came to me one day there were women doing this with their lives, all over. There were women just waiting and waiting by mailboxes for one letter or another. I imagined me making this journey day after day and year after year, and my hair starting to get gray, and I thought, I was never made to go on like that. So I stopped meeting the mail. If there were women all through life waiting, and women busy and not waiting, I knew which I had to be. Even though there might be things the second kind of women have to pass up and never know about, it still is better. I was surprised when the mailman phoned the Peebleses' place in the evening and asked for me. He said he missed me. He asked if I would like to go to Goderich, where some well-known movie was on, I forget now what. So I said yes, and I went out with him for two years and he asked me to marry him, and we were engaged a year more while I got my things together, and then we did marry. He always tells the children the story of how I went after him by sitting by the mailbox every day, and naturally I laugh and let him, because I like for people to think what pleases them and makes them happy.

[1974]

Joyce Carol Oates (American; b. 1938)

Where Are You Going, Where Have You Been?

To Bob Dylan

Her name was Connie. She was fifteen and she had a quick nervous giggling habit of craning her neck to glance into mirrors or checking other people's faces to make sure her own was all right. Her mother, who noticed everything and knew everything and who hadn't much reason any longer to look at her own face, always scolded Connie about it. "Stop gawking at yourself, who are you? You think you're so pretty?" she would say. Connie would raise her eyebrows at these familiar complaints and look right through her mother, into a shadowy vision of herself as she was right at that moment: she knew she was pretty and that was everything. Her mother had been pretty once too, if you could believe those old snapshots in the album, but now her looks were gone and that was why she was always after Connie.

"Why don't you keep your room clean like your sister? How've you got your hair fixed—what the hell stinks? Hair spray? You don't see your sister using that junk."

Her sister June was twenty-four and still lived at home. She was a secretary in the high school Connie attended, and if that wasn't bad enough—with her in the same building—she was so plain and chunky and steady that Connie had to hear her praised all the time by her mother and her mother's sisters. June did this, June did that, she saved money and helped clean the house and cooked and Connie couldn't do a thing, her mind was all filled with trashy daydreams. Their father was away at work most of the time and when he came home he wanted supper and he read the newspaper at supper and after supper he went to bed. He didn't bother talking much to them, but around his bent head Connie's mother kept picking at her until Connie wished her mother was dead and she herself was dead and it was all over. "She makes me want to throw up sometimes," she complained to her friends. She had a high, breathless, amused voice which made everything she said sound a little forced, whether it was sincere or not.

There was one good thing: June went places with girlfriends of hers, girls who were just as plain and steady as she, and so when Connie wanted to do that her mother had no objections. The father of Connie's best girlfriend drove the girls the three miles to town and left them off at a shopping plaza, so that they could walk through the stores or go to a movie, and when he came to pick them up again at eleven he never bothered to ask what they had done.

They must have been familiar sights, walking around that shopping plaza in their shorts and flat ballerina slippers that always scuffed the sidewalk, with charm bracelets jingling on their thin wrists; they would lean together to whisper and laugh secretly if someone passed by who amused or interested them. Connie had long dark blond hair that drew anyone's eye to it, and she wore part of it pulled up on her head and puffed out and the rest of it she let fall down her back. She wore a pull-over jersey blouse that looked one way when she was at home and another way when she was away from home. Everything about her had two sides to it, one for home and one for anywhere that was not home: her walk that could be childlike and bobbing, or languid enough to make anyone think she was hearing music in her head, her mouth which was pale and smirking most of the time, but bright and pink on these evenings out, her laugh which was cynical and drawling at home—"Ha, ha, very funny"—but high-pitched and nervous anywhere else, like the jingling of the charms on her bracelet.

Sometimes they did go shopping or to a movie, but sometimes they went across the highway, ducking fast across the busy road, to a drive-in restaurant where older kids hung out. The restaurant was shaped like a big bottle, though squatter than a real bottle, and on its cap was a revolving figure of a grinning boy who held a hamburger aloft. One night in midsummer they ran across, breathless with daring, and right away someone leaned out a car window and invited them over, but it was just a boy from high school they didn't like. It made them feel good to be able to ignore him. They went up through the maze of parked and cruising cars to the bright-lit, fly-infested restaurant, their faces pleased and expectant as if they were entering a sacred building that loomed out of the night to give them what haven and what blessing they yearned for. They sat at the counter and crossed their legs at the ankles, their thin shoulders rigid with excitement, and listened to the music that made everything so good: the music was always in the background like music at a church service, it was something to depend upon.

A boy named Eddie came in to talk with them. He sat backward on his stool, turning himself jerkily around in semicircles and then stopping and turning again, and after a while he asked Connie if she would like something to eat. She said she did and so she tapped her friend's arm on her way out—her friend pulled her face up into a brave droll look— and Connie said she would meet her at eleven, across the way. "I just hate to leave her like that," Connie said earnestly, but the boy said that she wouldn't be alone for long. So they went out to his car and on the way Connie couldn't help but let her eyes wander over the windshields and faces all around her, her face gleaming with a joy that had nothing to do with Eddie or even this place; it might have been the music. She drew her shoulders up and sucked in her breath with the pure pleasure of being alive, and just at that moment she happened to glance at a face just a few feet from hers. It was a boy with shaggy black hair, in a convertible jalopy painted gold. He stared at her and then his lips widened into a grin. Connie slit her eyes at him and turned away, but she couldn't help glancing back and there he was still watching her. He wagged a finger and laughed and said, "Gonna get you, baby," and Connie turned away again without Eddie noticing anything.

She spent three hours with him, at the restaurant where they ate hamburgers and drank Cokes in wax cups that were always sweating, and then down an alley a mile or so away, and when he left her off at five to eleven only the movie house was still open at the plaza. Her girlfriend was there, talking with a boy. When Connie came up the two girls smiled at each other and Connie said, "How was the movie?" and the girl said, "*You* should know." They rode off with the girl's father, sleepy and pleased, and Connie couldn't help but look at the darkened shopping plaza with its big empty parking lot and its signs that were faded and ghostly now, and over at the drive-in restaurant where cars were still circling tirelessly. She couldn't hear the music at this distance.

Next morning June asked her how the movie was and Connie said, "So-so."

She and that girl and occasionally another girl went out several times a week that way, and the rest of the time Connie spent around the house—it was summer vacation—getting in her mother's way and thinking, dreaming, about the boys she met. But all the boys fell back and dissolved into a single face that was not even a face, but an idea, a feeling, mixed up with the urgent insistent pounding of the music and the humid night air of July. Connie's mother kept dragging her back to the daylight by finding things for her to do or saying, suddenly, "What's this about the Pettinger girl?"

And Connie would say nervously, "Oh, her. That dope." She always drew thick clear lines between herself and such girls, and her mother was simple and kindly enough to believe her. Her mother was so simple, Connie thought, that it was maybe cruel to fool her so much. Her mother went scuffling around the house in old bedroom slippers and complained over the telephone to one sister about the other, then the other called up and the two of them complained about the third one. If June's name was mentioned her mother's tone was approving, and if Connie's name was mentioned it was disapproving. This did not really mean she disliked Connie and actually Connie thought that her mother preferred her to June because she was prettier, but the two of them kept up a pretense of exasperation, a sense that they were tugging and struggling over something of little value to either of them. Sometimes, over coffee, they were almost friends, but something would come up—some vexation that was like a fly buzzing suddenly around their heads—and their faces went hard with contempt.

One Sunday Connie got up at eleven—none of them bothered with church—and washed her hair so that it could dry all day long, in the sun. Her parents and sister were going to a barbecue at an aunt's house and Connie said no, she wasn't interested, rolling her eyes to let her mother know just what she thought of it. "Stay home alone then," her mother said sharply. Connie sat out back in a lawn chair and watched them drive away, her father quiet and bald, hunched around so that he could back the car out, her mother with a look that was still angry and not at all softened through the windshield, and in the back seat poor old June all dressed up as if she didn't know what a barbecue was, with all the running yelling kids and the flies. Connie sat with her eyes closed in the sun, dreaming and dazed with the warmth about her as if this were a kind of love, the caresses of love, and her mind slipped over onto thoughts of the boy she had been with the night before and how nice he had been, how sweet it always was, not the way someone like June would suppose but sweet, gentle, the way it was in movies and promised in songs; and when she opened her eyes she hardly knew where she was, the back yard ran off into weeds and a fence line of trees and behind it the sky was perfectly blue and still. The asbestos "ranch house" that was now three years old startled her—it looked small. She shook her head as if to get awake.

It was too hot. She went inside the house and turned on the radio to drown out the quiet. She sat on the edge of her bed, barefoot, and listened for an hour and a half to a program called XYZ Sunday Jamboree, record after record of hard, fast, shrieking songs she sang along with, interspersed by exclamations from "Bobby King": "An' look here you girls at Napoleon's—Son and Charley want you to pay real close attention to this song coming up!"

And Connie paid close attention herself, bathed in a glow of slow-pulsed joy that seemed to rise mysteriously out of the music itself and lay languidly about the airless little room, breathed in and breathed out with each gentle rise and fall of her chest.

After a while she heard a car coming up the drive. She sat up at once, startled, because it couldn't be her father so soon. The gravel kept crunching all the way in from the road—the driveway was long—and Connie ran to the window. It was a car she didn't know. It was an open jalopy, painted a bright gold that caught the sunlight opaquely. Her heart began to pound and her fingers snatched at her hair, checking it, and she whispered "Christ, Christ," wondering how bad she looked. The car came to a stop at the side door and the horn sounded four short taps as if this were a signal Connie knew.

She went into the kitchen and approached the door slowly, then hung out the screen door, her bare toes curling down off the step. There were two boys in the car and now she recognized the driver: he had shaggy, shabby black hair that looked crazy as a wig and he was grinning at her.

"I ain't late, am I?" he said.

"Who the hell do you think you are?" Connie said.

"Toldja I'd be out, didn't I?"

"I don't even know who you are."

She spoke sullenly, careful to show no interest or pleasure, and he spoke in a fast bright monotone. Connie looked past him to the other boy, taking her time. He had fair brown hair, with a lock that fell onto his forehead. His sideburns gave him a fierce, embarrassed look, but so far he hadn't even bothered to glance at her. Both boys wore sunglasses. The driver's glasses were metallic and mirrored everything in miniature.

"You wanta come for a ride?" he said.

Connie smirked and let her hair fall loose over one shoulder.

"Don'tcha like my car? New paint job," he said. "Hey."

"What?"

"You're cute."

She pretended to fidget, chasing flies away from the door.

"Don'tcha believe me, or what?" he said.

"Look, I don't even know who you are," Connie said in disgust.

"Hey, Ellie's got a radio, see. Mine's broke down." He lifted his friend's arm and showed her the little transistor the boy was holding, and now Connie began to hear the music. It was the same program that was playing inside the house.

"Bobby King?" she said.

"I listen to him all the time. I think he's great."

"He's kind of great," Connie said reluctantly.

"Listen, that guy's *great*. He knows where the action is."

Connie blushed a little, because the glasses made it impossible for her to see just what this boy was looking at. She couldn't decide if she liked him or if he was just a jerk, and so she dawdled in the doorway and wouldn't come down or go back inside. She said, "What's all that stuff painted on your car?"

"Can'tcha read it?" He opened the door very carefully, as if he was afraid it might fall off. He slid out just as carefully, planting his feet firmly on the ground, the tiny metallic world in his glasses slowing down like gelatine hardening and in the midst of it Connie's bright green blouse. "This here is my name, to begin with," he said. ARNOLD FRIEND was written in tarlike black letters on the side, with a drawing of a round grinning face that reminded Connie of a pumpkin, except it wore sunglasses. "I wanta introduce myself, I'm Arnold Friend and that's my real name and I'm gonna be your friend, honey, and inside the car's Ellie Oscar, he's kinda shy." Ellie brought his transistor radio up to his shoulder and balanced it there. "Now these numbers are a secret code, honey," Arnold Friend explained. He read off the numbers 33, 19, 17 and raised his eyebrows at her to see what she thought of that, but she didn't think much of it. The left rear fender had been smashed and around it was written, on the gleaming gold background: DONE BY CRAZY WOMAN DRIVER. Connie had to laugh at that. Arnold Friend was pleased at her laughter and looked up at her. "Around the other side's a lot more—you wanta come and see them?"

"No."

"Why not?"

"Why should I?"

"Don'tcha wanta see what's on the car? Don'tcha wanta go for a ride?"

"I don't know."

"Why not?"

"I got things to do."

"Like what?"

"Things."

He laughed as if she had said something funny. He slapped his thighs. He was standing in a strange way, leaning back against the car as if he were balancing himself. He wasn't tall, only an inch or so taller than she would be if she came down to him. Connie liked the way he was dressed, which was the way all of them dressed: tight faded jeans stuffed into black, scuffed boots, a belt that pulled his waist in and showed how lean he was, and a white pullover shirt that was a little soiled and showed the hard small muscles of his arms and shoulders. He looked as if he probably did hard work, lifting and carrying things. Even his neck looked muscular. And his face was a familiar face, somehow: the jaw and chin and cheeks slightly darkened, because he hadn't shaved for a day or two, and the nose long and hawklike, sniffing as if she were a treat he was going to gobble up and it was all a joke.

"Connie, you ain't telling the truth. This is your day set aside for a ride with me and you know it," he said, still laughing. The way he straightened and recovered from his fit of laughing showed that it had been all fake.

"How do you know what my name is?" she said suspiciously.

"It's Connie."

"Maybe and maybe not."

"I know my Connie," he said, wagging his finger. Now she remembered him even better, back at the restaurant, and her cheeks warmed at the thought of how she sucked in her breath just at the moment she passed him—how she must have looked to him. And he had remembered her. "Ellie and I come out here especially for you," he said. "Ellie can sit in back. How about it?"

"Where?"

"Where what?"

"Where're we going?"

He looked at her. He took off the sunglasses and she saw how pale the skin around his eyes was, like holes that were not in shadow but instead in light. His eyes were like chips of broken glass that catch the light in an amiable way. He smiled. It was as if the idea of going for a ride somewhere, to some place, was a new idea to him.

"Just for a ride, Connie sweetheart."

"I never said my name was Connie," she said.

"But I know what it is. I know your name and all about you, lots of things," Arnold Friend said. He had not moved yet but stood still leaning back against the side of his jalopy. "I took a special interest in you, such a pretty girl, and found out all about you like I know your parents and sister are gone somewheres and I know where and how long they're going to be gone, and I know who you were with last night, and your best girlfriend's name is Betty. Right?"

He spoke in a simple lilting voice, exactly as if he were reciting the words to a song. His smile assured her that everything was fine. In the car Ellie turned up the volume on his radio and did not bother to look around at them.

"Ellie can sit in the back seat," Arnold Friend said. He indicated his friend with a casual jerk of his chin, as if Ellie did not count and she should not bother with him.

"How'd you find out all that stuff?" Connie said.

"Listen: Betty Schultz and Tony Fitch and Jimmy Pettinger and Nancy Pettinger," he said, in a chant. "Raymond Stanley and Bob Hutter—"

"Do you know all those kids?"

"I know everybody."

"Look, you're kidding. You're not from around here."

"Sure."

"But—how come we never saw you before?"

"Sure you saw me before," he said. He looked down at his boots, as if he were a little offended. "You just don't remember."

"I guess I'd remember you," Connie said.

"Yeah?" He looked up at this, beaming. He was pleased. He began to mark time with the music from Ellie's radio, tapping his fists lightly together. Connie looked away from his smile to the car, which was painted so bright it almost hurt her eyes to look at it. She looked at that name, ARNOLD FRIEND. And up at the front fender was an expression that was familiar — MAN THE FLYING SAUCERS. It was an expression kids had used the year before, but didn't use this year. She looked at it for a while as if the words meant something to her that she did not yet know.

"What're you thinking about? Huh?" Arnold Friend demanded. "Not worried about your hair blowing around in the car, are you?"

"No."

"Think I maybe can't drive good?"

"How do I know?"

"You're a hard girl to handle. How come?" he said. "Don't you know I'm your friend? Didn't you see me put my sign in the air when you walked by?"

"What sign?"

"My sign." And he drew an X in the air, leaning out toward her. They were maybe ten feet apart. After his hand fell back to his side the X was still in the air, almost visible. Connie let the screen door close and stood perfectly still inside it, listening to the music from her radio and the boy's blend together. She stared at Arnold Friend. He stood there so stiffly relaxed, pretending to be relaxed, with one hand idly on the door handle as if he were keeping himself up that way and had no intention of ever moving again. She recognized most things about him, the tight jeans that showed his thighs and buttocks and the greasy leather boots and the tight shirt, and even that slippery friendly smile of his, that sleepy dreamy smile that all the boys used to get across ideas they didn't want to put into words. She recognized all this and also the singsong way he talked, slightly mocking, kidding, but serious and a little melancholy, and she recognized the way he tapped one fist against the other in homage to the perpetual music behind him. But all these things did not come together.

She said suddenly, "Hey, how old are you?"

His smile faded. She could see then that he wasn't a kid, he was much older — thirty, maybe more. At this knowledge her heart began to pound faster.

"That's a crazy thing to ask. Can'tcha see I'm your own age?"

"Like hell you are."

"Or maybe a coupla years older, I'm eighteen."

"Eighteen?" she said doubtfully.

He grinned to reassure her and lines appeared at the corners of his mouth. His teeth were big and white. He grinned so broadly his eyes became slits and she saw how thick the lashes were, thick and black as if painted with a black tarlike material. Then he seemed to become embarrassed, abruptly, and looked over his shoulder at Ellie. "*Him,* he's crazy," he said. "Ain't he a riot, he's a nut, a real character." Ellie was still listening to the music. His sunglasses told nothing about what he was thinking. He wore a bright orange shirt unbuttoned halfway to show his chest, which was a pale, bluish chest and not muscular like Arnold Friend's. His shirt collar was turned up all around and the very tips of the collar pointed out past his chin as if they were protecting him. He was pressing the transistor radio up against his ear and sat there in a kind of daze, right in the sun.

"He's kinda strange," Connie said.

"Hey, she says you're kinda strange! Kinda strange!" Arnold Friend cried. He pounded on the car to get Ellie's attention. Ellie turned for the first time and Connie saw with shock that he wasn't a kid either—he had a fair, hairless face, cheeks reddened slightly as if the veins grew too close to the surface of his skin, the face of a forty-year-old baby. Connie felt a wave of dizziness rise in her at this sight and she stared at him as if waiting for something to change the shock of the moment, make it all right again. Ellie's lips kept shaping words, mumbling along, with the words blasting in his ear.

"Maybe you two better go away," Connie said faintly.

"What? How come?" Arnold Friend cried. "We come out here to take you for a ride. It's Sunday." He had the voice of the man on the radio now. It was the same voice, Connie thought. "Don'tcha know it's Sunday all day and honey, no matter who you were with last night today you're with Arnold Friend and don't you forget it!—Maybe you better step out here," he said, and this last was in a different voice. It was a little flatter, as if the heat was finally getting to him.

"No. I got things to do."

"Hey."

"You two better leave."

"We ain't leaving until you come with us."

"Like hell I am—"

"Connie, don't fool around with me. I mean, I mean, don't fool *around,*" he said, shaking his head. He laughed incredulously. He placed his sunglasses on top of his head, carefully, as if he were indeed wearing a wig, and brought the stems down behind his ears. Connie stared at him, another wave of dizziness and fear rising in her so that for a moment he wasn't even in focus but was just a blur, standing there against his gold car, and she had the idea that he had driven up the driveway all right but had come from nowhere before that and belonged nowhere and that everything about him and even about the music that was so familiar to her was only half real.

"If my father comes and sees you—"

"He ain't coming. He's at a barbecue."

"How do you know that?"

"Aunt Tillie's. Right now they're—uh—they're drinking. Sitting around," he said vaguely, squinting as if he were staring all the way to town and over to Aunt Tillie's back yard. Then the vision seemed to get clear and he nodded energetically. "Yeah. Sitting around. There's your sister in a blue dress, huh? And high heels, the poor sad bitch—nothing like you, sweetheart! And your mother's helping some fat woman with the corn, they're cleaning the corn—husking the corn—"

"What fat woman?" Connie cried.

"How do I know what fat woman. I don't know every goddam fat woman in the world!" Arnold Friend laughed.

"Oh, that's Mrs. Hornby . . . . Who invited her?" Connie said. She felt a little light-headed. Her breath was coming quickly.

"She's too fat. I don't like them fat. I like them the way you are, honey," he said, smiling sleepily at her. They stared at each other for a while, through the screen door. He said softly, "Now what you're going to do is this: you're going to come out that door. You're going to sit up front with me and Ellie's going to sit in the back, the hell with Ellie, right? This isn't Ellie's date. You're my date. I'm your lover, honey."

"What? You're crazy—"

"Yes, I'm your lover. You don't know what that is but you will," he said. "I know that too. I know all about you. But look: it's real nice and you couldn't ask for nobody better than me, or more polite. I always keep my word. I'll tell you how it is, I'm always nice at first, the first time. I'll hold you so tight you won't think you have to try to get away or pretend anything because you'll know you can't. And I'll come inside you where it's all secret and you'll give in to me and you'll love me—"

"Shut up! You're crazy!" Connie said. She backed away from the door. She put her hands against her ears as if she'd heard something terrible, something not meant for her. "People don't talk like that, you're crazy," she muttered. Her heart was almost too big now for her chest and its pumping made sweat break out all over her. She looked out to see Arnold Friend pause and then take a step toward the porch lurching. He almost fell. But, like a clever drunken man, he managed to catch his balance. He wobbled in his high boots and grabbed hold of one of the porch posts.

"Honey?" he said. "You still listening?"

"Get the hell out of here!"

"Be nice, honey. Listen."

"I'm going to call the police—"

He wobbled again and out of the side of his mouth came a fast spat curse, an aside not meant for her to hear. But even this "Christ!" sounded forced. Then he began to smile again. She watched this smile come, awkward as if he were smiling from inside a mask. His whole face was a mask, she thought wildly, tanned down onto his throat but then running out as if he had plastered makeup on his face but had forgotten about his throat.

"Honey—? Listen, here's how it is. I always tell the truth and I promise you this: I ain't coming in that house after you."

"You better not! I'm going to call the police if you—if you don't—"

"Honey," he said, talking right through her voice, "honey, I'm not coming in there but you are coming out here. You know why?"

She was panting. The kitchen looked like a place she had never seen before, some room she had run inside but which wasn't good enough, wasn't going to help her. The kitchen window had never had a curtain, after three years, and there were dishes in the sink for her to do—probably—and if you ran your hand across the table you'd probably feel something sticky there.

"You listening, honey? Hey?"

"—going to call the police—"

"Soon as you touch the phone I don't need to keep my promise and can come inside. You won't want that."

She rushed forward and tried to lock the door. Her fingers were shaking. "But why lock it," Arnold Friend said gently, talking right into her face. "It's just a screen door. It's just nothing." One of his boots was at a strange angle, as if his foot wasn't in it. It pointed out to the left, bent at the ankle. "I mean, anybody can break through a screen door and glass and wood and iron or anything else if he needs to, anybody at all and specially Arnold Friend. If the place got lit up with a fire honey you'd come runnin' out into my arms, right into my arms an' safe at home—like you knew I was your lover and'd stopped fooling around. I don't mind a nice shy girl but I don't like no fooling around." Part of those words were spoken with a slight rhythmic lilt, and Connie somehow recognized them—the echo of a song from last year, about a girl rushing into her boyfriend's arms and coming home again—

Connie stood barefoot on the linoleum floor, staring at him. "What do you want?" she whispered.

"I want you," he said.

"What?"

"Seen you that night and thought, that's the one, yes sir. I never needed to look any more."

"But my father's coming back. He's coming to get me. I had to wash my hair first—" She spoke in a dry, rapid voice, hardly raising it for him to hear.

"No, your Daddy is not coming and yes, you had to wash your hair and you washed it for me. It's nice and shining and all for me, I thank you, sweetheart," he said, with a mock bow, but again he almost lost his balance. He had to bend and adjust his boots. Evidently his feet did not go all the way down; the boots must have been stuffed with something so that he would seem taller. Connie stared out at him and behind him Ellie in the car, who seemed to be looking off toward Connie's right into nothing. This Ellie said, pulling the words out of the air one after another as if he were just discovering them, "You want me to pull out the phone?"

"Shut your mouth and keep it shut," Arnold Friend said, his face red from bending over or maybe from embarrassment because Connie had seen his boots. "This ain't none of your business."

"What—what are you doing? What do you want?" Connie said. "If I call the police they'll get you, they'll arrest you—"

"Promise was not to come in unless you touch that phone, and I'll keep that promise," he said. He resumed his erect position and tried to force his shoulders back. He sounded like a hero in a movie, declaring something important. He spoke too loudly and it was as if he were speaking to someone behind Connie. "I ain't made plans for coming in that house where I don't belong but just for you to come out to me, the way you should. Don't you know who I am?"

"You're crazy," she whispered. She backed away from the door but did not want to go into another part of the house, as if this would give him permission to come through the door. "What do you . . . You're crazy, you . . ."

"Huh? What're you saying, honey?"

Her eyes darted everywhere in the kitchen. She could not remember what it was, this room.

"This is how it is, honey: you come out and we'll drive away, have a nice ride. But if you don't come out we're gonna wait till your people come home and then they're all going to get it."

"You want that telephone pulled out?" Ellie said. He held the radio away from his ear and grimaced, as if without the radio the air was too much for him.

"I toldja shut up, Ellie," Arnold Friend said, "you're deaf, get a hearing aid, right? Fix yourself up. This little girl's no trouble and's gonna be nice to me, so Ellie keep to yourself, this ain't your date—right? Don't hem in on me. Don't hog. Don't crush. Don't bird dog. Don't trail me," he said in a rapid meaningless voice, as if he were running through all the expressions he'd learned but was no longer sure which one of them was in style, then rushing on to new ones, making them up with his eyes closed, "Don't crawl under my fence, don't squeeze in my chipmunk hole, don't sniff my glue, suck my popsicle, keep your own greasy fingers on yourself!" He shaded his eyes and peered in at Connie, who was backed against the kitchen table. "Don't mind him honey he's just a creep. He's a dope. Right? I'm the boy for you and like I said you come out here nice like a lady and give me your hand, and nobody else gets hurt, I mean, your nice old bald-headed daddy and your mummy and your sister in her high heels. Because listen: why bring them in this?"

"Leave me alone," Connie whispered.

"Hey, you know that old woman down the road, the one with the chickens and stuff—you know her?"

"She's dead!"

"Dead? What? You know her?" Arnold Friend said.

"She's dead—"

"Don't you like her?"

"She's dead—she's—she isn't here any more—"

"But don't you like her, I mean, you got something against her? Some grudge or something?" Then his voice dipped as if he were conscious of a rudeness. He touched the sunglasses perched on top of his head as if to make sure they were still there. "Now you be a good girl."

"What are you going to do?"

"Just two things, or maybe three," Arnold Friend said. "But I promise it won't last long and you'll like me the way you get to like people you're close to. You will. It's all over for you here, so come on out. You don't want your people in any trouble, do you?"

She turned and bumped against a chair or something, hurting her leg, but she ran into the back room and picked up the telephone. Something roared in her ear, a tiny roaring, and she was so sick with fear that she could do nothing but listen to it—the telephone was clammy and very heavy and her fingers groped down to the dial but were too weak to touch it. She began to scream into the phone, into the roaring. She cried out, she cried for her mother, she felt her breath start jerking back and forth in her lungs as if it were something Arnold Friend were stabbing her with again and again with no tenderness. A noisy sorrowful wailing rose all about her and she was locked inside it the way she was locked inside the house.

After a while she could hear again. She was sitting on the floor with her wet back against the wall.

Arnold Friend was saying from the door, "That's a good girl. Put the phone back."

She kicked the phone away from her.

"No, honey. Pick it up. Put it back right."

She picked it up and put it back. The dial tone stopped.

"That's a good girl. Now come outside."

She was hollow with what had been fear, but what was now just an emptiness. All that screaming had blasted it out of her. She sat, one leg cramped under her, and deep inside her brain was something like a pinpoint of light that kept going and would not let her relax. She thought, I'm not going to see my mother again. She thought, I'm not going to sleep in my bed again. Her bright green blouse was all wet.

Arnold Friend said, in a gentle-loud voice that was like a stage voice, "The place where you came from ain't there any more, and where you had in mind to go is canceled out. This place you are now—inside your daddy's house—is nothing but a cardboard box I can knock down any time. You know that and always did know it. You hear me?"

She thought, I have got to think. I have to know what to do.

"We'll go out to a nice field, out in the country here where it smells so nice and it's sunny," Arnold Friend said. "I'll have my arms tight around you so you won't need to try to get away and I'll show you what love is like, what it does. The hell with this house! It looks solid all right," he said. He ran a fingernail down the screen and the noise did not make Connie shiver, as it would have the day before. "Now put your hand on your heart, honey. Feel that? That feels solid too but we know better, be nice to me, be sweet like you can because what else is there for a girl like you but to be sweet and pretty and give in?—and get away before her people come back?"

She felt her pounding heart. Her hand seemed to enclose it. She thought for the first time in her life that it was nothing that was hers, that belonged to her, but just a pounding, living thing inside this body that wasn't really hers either.

"You don't want them to get hurt," Arnold Friend went on. "Now get up, honey. Get up all by yourself."

She stood up.

"Now turn this way. That's right. Come over here to me—Ellie, put that away, didn't I tell you? You dope. You miserable creepy dope," Arnold Friend said. His words were not angry but only part of an incantation. The incantation was kindly. "Now come out through the kitchen to me honey, and let's see a smile, try it, you're a brave sweet little girl and now they're eating corn and hot dogs cooked to bursting over an outdoor fire, and they don't know one thing about you and never did and honey you're better than them because not a one of them would have done this for you."

Connie felt the linoleum under her feet; it was cool. She brushed her hair back out of her eyes. Arnold Friend let go of the post tentatively and opened his arms for her, his elbows pointing in toward each other and his wrists limp, to show that this was an embarrassed embrace and a little mocking, he didn't want to make her self-conscious.

She put out her hand against the screen. She watched herself push the door slowly open as if she were safe back somewhere in the other doorway, watching this body and this head of long hair moving out into the sunlight where Arnold Friend waited.

"My sweet little blue-eyed girl," he said, in a half-sung sigh that had nothing to do with her brown eyes but was taken up just the same by the vast sunlit reaches of the land behind him and on all sides of him, so much land that Connie had never seen before and did not recognize except to know that she was going to it.

[1966]

Raymond Carver (American; 1938–88)

Cathedral

This blind man, an old friend of my wife's, he was on his way to spend the night. His wife had died. So he was visiting the dead wife's relatives in Connecticut. He called my wife from his in-laws'. Arrangements were made. He would come by train, a five-hour trip, and my wife would meet him at the station. She hadn't seen him since she worked for him one summer in Seattle ten years ago. But she and the blind man had kept in touch. They made tapes and mailed them back and forth. I wasn't enthusiastic about his visit. He was no one I knew. And his being blind bothered me. My idea of blindness came from the movies. In the movies, the blind moved slowly and never laughed. Sometimes they were led by seeing-eye dogs. A blind man in my house was not something I looked forward to.

That summer in Seattle she had needed a job. She didn't have any money. The man she was going to marry at the end of the summer was in officers' training school. He didn't have any money, either. But she was in love with the guy, and he was in love with her, etc. She'd seen something in the paper: HELP WANTED—*Reading to Blind Man,* and a telephone number. She phoned and went over, was hired on the spot. She'd worked with this blind man all summer. She read stuff to him, case studies, reports, that sort of thing. She helped him organize his little office in the county social-service department. They'd become good friends, my wife and the blind man. How do I know these things? She told me. And she told me something else. On her last day in the office, the blind man asked if he could touch her face. She agreed to this. She told me he touched his fingers to every part of her face, her nose—even her neck! She never forgot it. She even tried to write a poem about it. She was always trying to write a poem. She wrote a poem or two every year, usually after something really important had happened to her.

When we first started going out together, she showed me the poem. In the poem, she recalled his fingers and the way they had moved around over her face. In the poem, she talked about what she had felt at the time, about what went through her mind when the blind man touched her nose and lips. I can remember I didn't think much of the poem. Of course, I didn't tell her that. Maybe I just don't understand poetry. I admit it's not the first thing I reach for when I pick up something to read.

Anyway, this man who'd first enjoyed her favors, the officer-to-be, he'd been her childhood sweetheart. So okay. I'm saying that at the end of the summer she let the blind man run his hands over her face, said good-bye to him, married her childhood etc., who was now a commissioned officer, and she moved away from Seattle. But they'd kept in touch, she and the blind man. She made the first contact after a year or so. She called him up one night from an Air Force base in Alabama. She wanted to talk. They talked. He asked her to send a tape and tell him about her life. She did this. She sent the tape. On the tape, she told the blind man about her husband and about their life together in the military. She told the blind man she loved her husband but she didn't like it where they lived and she didn't like it that he was part of the military-industrial thing. She told the blind man she'd written a poem and he was in it. She told him that she was writing a poem about what it was like to be an Air Force officer's wife. The poem wasn't finished yet. She was still writing it. The blind man made a tape. He sent her the tape. She made a tape. This went on for years. My wife's officer was posted to one base and then another. She sent tapes from Moody AFB, McGuire, McConnell, and finally Travis, near Sacramento, where one night she got to feeling lonely and cut off from people she kept losing in that moving-around life. She got to feeling she couldn't go it another step. She went in and swallowed all the pills and capsules in the medicine chest and washed them down with a bottle of gin. Then she got into a hot bath and passed out.

But instead of dying, she got sick. She threw up. Her officer—why should he have a name? he was the childhood sweetheart, and what more does he want?—came home from somewhere, found her, and called the ambulance. In time, she put it all on a tape and sent the tape to the blind man. Over the years, she put all kinds of stuff on tapes and sent the tapes off lickety-split. Next to writing a poem every year, I think it was her chief means of recreation. On one tape, she told the blind man she'd decided to live away from her officer for a time. On another tape, she told him about her divorce. She and I began going out, and of course she told her blind man about it. She told him everything, or so it seemed to me. Once she asked me if I'd like to hear the latest tape from the blind man. This was a year ago. I was on the tape, she said. So I said okay, I'd listen to it. I got us drinks and we settled down in the living room. We made ready to listen. First she inserted the tape into the player and adjusted a couple of dials. Then she pushed a lever. The tape squeaked and someone began to talk in this loud voice. She lowered the volume. After a few minutes of harmless chitchat, I heard my own name in the mouth of this stranger, this blind man I didn't even know! And then this: "From all you've said about him, I can only conclude—" But we were interrupted, a knock at the door, something, and we didn't ever get back to the tape. Maybe it was just as well. I'd heard all I wanted to.

Now this same blind man was coming to sleep in my house.

"Maybe I could take him bowling," I said to my wife. She was at the draining board doing scalloped potatoes. She put down the knife she was using and turned around.

"If you love me," she said, "you can do this for me. If you don't love me, okay. But if you had a friend, any friend, and the friend came to visit, I'd make him feel comfortable." She wiped her hands with the dish towel.

"I don't have any blind friends," I said.

"You don't have *any* friends," she said. "Period. Besides," she said, "goddamn it, his wife's just died! Don't you understand that? The man's lost his wife!"

I didn't answer. She'd told me a little about the blind man's wife. Her name was Beulah. Beulah! That's a name for a colored woman.

"Was his wife a Negro?" I asked.

"Are you crazy?" my wife said. "Have you just flipped or something?" She picked up a potato. I saw it hit the floor, then roll under the stove. "What's wrong with you?" she said. "Are you drunk?"

"I'm just asking," I said.

Right then my wife filled me in with more detail than I cared to know. I made a drink and sat at the kitchen table to listen. Pieces of the story began to fall into place.

Beulah had gone to work for the blind man the summer after my wife had stopped working for him. Pretty soon Beulah and the blind man had themselves a church wedding. It was a little wedding—who'd want to go to such a wedding in the first place?—just the two of them, plus the minister and the minister's wife. But it was a church wedding just the same. It was what Beulah had wanted, he'd said. But even then Beulah must have been carrying the cancer in her glands. After they had been inseparable for eight years—my wife's word, *inseparable*—Beulah's health went into a rapid decline. She died in a Seattle hospital room, the blind man sitting beside the bed and holding on to her hand. They'd married, lived and worked together, slept together—had sex, sure—and then the blind man had to bury her. All this without his having ever seen what the goddamned woman looked like. It was beyond my understanding. Hearing this, I felt sorry for the blind man for a little bit. And then I found myself thinking what a pitiful life this woman must have led. Imagine a woman who could never see herself as she was seen in the eyes of her loved one. A woman who could go on day after day and never receive the smallest compliment from her beloved. A woman whose husband could never read the expression on her face, be it misery or something better. Someone who could wear makeup or not—what difference to him? She could, if she wanted, wear green eye-shadow around one eye, a straight pin in her nostril, yellow slacks, and purple shoes, no matter. And then to slip off into death, the blind man's hand on her hand, his blind eyes streaming tears—I'm imagining now—her last thought maybe this: that he never even knew what she looked like, and she on an express to the grave. Robert was left with a small insurance policy and a half of a twenty-peso Mexican coin. The other half of the coin went into the box with her. Pathetic.

So when the time rolled around, my wife went to the depot to pick him up. With nothing to do but wait—sure, I blamed him for that—I was having a drink and watching the TV when I heard the car pull into the drive. I got up from the sofa with my drink and went to the window to have a look.

I saw my wife laughing as she parked the car. I saw her get out of the car and shut the door. She was still wearing a smile. Just amazing. She went around to the other side of the car to where the blind man was already starting to get out. This blind man, feature this, he was wearing a full beard! A beard on a blind man! Too much, I say. The blind man reached into the back seat and dragged out a suitcase. My wife took his arm, shut the car door, and, talking all the way, moved him down the drive and then up the steps to the front porch. I turned off the TV. I finished my drink, rinsed the glass, dried my hands. Then I went to the door.

My wife said, "I want you to meet Robert. Robert, this is my husband. I've told you all about him." She was beaming. She had this blind man by his coat sleeve.

The blind man let go of his suitcase and up came his hand. I took it. He squeezed hard, held my hand, and then he let it go.

"I feel like we've already met," he boomed.

"Likewise," I said. I didn't know what else to say. Then I said, "Welcome. I've heard a lot about you." We began to move then, a little group, from the porch into the living room, my wife guiding him by the arm. The blind man was carrying his suitcase in his other hand. My wife said things like, "To your left here, Robert. That's right. Now watch it, there's a chair. That's it. Sit down right here. This is the sofa. We just bought this sofa two weeks ago."

I started to say something about the old sofa. I'd liked that old sofa. But I didn't say anything. Then I wanted to say something else, small-talk, about the scenic ride along the Hudson. How going *to* New York, you should sit on the right-hand side of the train, and coming *from* New York, the left-hand side.

"Did you have a good train ride?" I said. "Which side of the train did you sit on, by the way?"

"What a question, which side!" my wife said. "What's it matter which side?" she said.

"I just asked," I said.

"Right side," the blind man said. "I hadn't been on a train in nearly forty years. Not since I was a kid. With my folks. That's been a long time. I'd nearly forgotten the sensation. I have winter in my beard now," he said. "So I've been told, anyway. Do I look distinguished, my dear?" the blind man said to my wife.

"You look distinguished, Robert," she said. "Robert," she said. "Robert, it's just so good to see you."

My wife finally took her eyes off the blind man and looked at me. I had the feeling she didn't like what she saw. I shrugged.

I've never met, or personally known, anyone who was blind. This blind man was late forties, a heavy-set, balding man with stooped shoulders, as if he carried a great weight there. He wore brown slacks, brown shoes, a light-brown shirt, a tie, a sports coat. Spiffy. He also had this full beard. But he didn't use a cane and he didn't wear dark glasses. I'd always thought dark glasses were a must for the blind. Fact was, I wished he had a pair. At first glance, his eyes looked like anyone else's eyes. But if you looked close, there was something different about them. Too much white in the iris, for one thing, and the pupils seemed to move around in the sockets without his knowing it or being able to stop it. Creepy. As I stared at his face, I saw the left pupil turn in toward his nose while the other made an effort to keep in one place. But it was only an effort, for that eye was on the roam without his knowing it or wanting it to be.

I said, "Let me get you a drink. What's your pleasure? We have a little of everything. It's one of our pastimes."

"Bub, I'm a Scotch man myself," he said fast enough in this big voice.

"Right," I said. Bub! "Sure you are. I knew it."

He let his fingers touch his suitcase, which was sitting alongside the sofa. He was taking his bearings. I didn't blame him for that.

"I'll move that up to your room," my wife said.

"No, that's fine," the blind man said loudly. "It can go up when I go up."

"A little water with the Scotch?" I said.

"Very little," he said.

"I knew it," I said.

He said, "Just a tad. The Irish actor, Barry Fitzgerald? I'm like that fellow. When I drink water, Fitzgerald said, I drink water. When I drink whiskey, I drink whiskey." My wife laughed. The blind man brought his hand up under his beard. He lifted his beard slowly and let it drop.

I did the drinks, three big glasses of Scotch with a splash of water in each. Then we made ourselves comfortable and talked about Robert's travels. First the long flight from the West Coast to Connecticut, we covered that. Then from Connecticut up here by train. We had another drink concerning that leg of the trip.

I remembered having read somewhere that the blind didn't smoke because, as speculation had it, they couldn't see the smoke they exhaled. I thought I knew that much and that much only about blind people. But this blind man smoked his cigarette down to the nubbin and then lit another one. This blind man filled his ashtray and my wife emptied it.

When we sat down at the table for dinner, we had another drink. My wife heaped Robert's plate with cube steak, scalloped potatoes, green beans. I buttered him up two slices of bread. I said, "Here's bread and butter for you." I swallowed some of my drink. "Now let us pray," I said, and the blind man lowered his head. My wife looked at me, her mouth agape. "Pray the phone won't ring and the food doesn't get cold," I said.

We dug in. We ate everything there was to eat on the table. We ate like there was no tomorrow. We didn't talk. We ate. We scarfed. We grazed that table. We were into serious eating. The blind man had right away located his foods, he knew just where everything was on his plate. I watched with admiration as he used his knife and fork on the meat. He'd cut two pieces of meat, fork the meat into his mouth, and then go all out for the scalloped potatoes, the beans next, and then he'd tear off a hunk of buttered bread and eat that. He'd follow this up with a big drink of milk. It didn't seem to bother him to use his fingers once in a while, either.

We finished everything, including half a strawberry pie. For a few moments, we sat as if stunned. Sweat beaded on our faces. Finally, we got up from the table and left the dirty plates. We didn't look back. We took ourselves into the living room and sank into our places again. Robert and my wife sat on the sofa. I took the big chair. We had us two or three more drinks while they talked about the major things that had come to pass for them in the past ten years. For the most part, I just listened. Now and then I joined in. I didn't want him to think I'd left the room, and I didn't want her to think I was feeling left out. They talked of things that had happened to them—to them!—these past ten years. I waited in vain to hear my name on my wife's sweet lips: "And then my dear husband came into my life"—something like that. But I heard nothing of the sort. More talk of Robert. Robert had done a little of everything, it seemed, a regular blind jack-of-all-trades. But most recently he and his wife had had an Amway distributorship, from which, I gathered, they'd earned their living, such as it was. The blind man was also a ham radio operator. He talked in his loud voice about conversations he'd had with fellow operators in Guam, in the Philippines, in Alaska, and even in Tahiti. He said he'd have a lot of friends there if he ever wanted to go visit those places. From time to time, he'd turn his blind face toward me, put his hand under his beard, ask me something. How long had I been in my present position? (Three years.) Did I like my work? (I didn't.) Was I going to stay with it? (What were the options?) Finally, when I thought he was beginning to run down, I got up and turned on the TV.

My wife looked at me with irritation. She was heading toward a boil. Then she looked at the blind man and said, "Robert, do you have a TV?"

The blind man said, "My dear, I have two TVs. I have a color set and a black-and-white thing, an old relic. It's funny, but if I turn the TV on, and I'm always turning it on, I turn on the color set. It's funny, don't you think?"

I didn't know what to say to that. I had absolutely nothing to say to that. No opinion. So I watched the news program and tried to listen to what the announcer was saying.

"This is a color TV," the blind man said. "Don't ask me how, but I can tell."

"We traded up a while ago," I said.

The blind man had another taste of his drink. He lifted his beard, sniffed it, and let it fall. He leaned forward on the sofa. He positioned his ashtray on the coffee table, then put the lighter to his cigarette. He leaned back on the sofa and crossed his legs at the ankles.

My wife covered her mouth, and then she yawned. She stretched. She said, "I think I'll go upstairs and put on my robe. I think I'll change into something else. Robert, you make yourself comfortable," she said.

"I'm comfortable," the blind man said.

"I want you to feel comfortable in this house," she said.

"I am comfortable," the blind man said.

After she'd left the room, he and I listened to the weather report and then to the sports roundup. By that time, she'd been gone so long I didn't know if she was going to come back. I thought she might have gone to bed. I wished she'd come back downstairs. I didn't want to be left alone with a blind man. I asked him if he wanted another drink, and he said sure. Then I asked if he wanted to smoke some dope with me. I said I'd just rolled a number. I hadn't, but I planned to do so in about two shakes.

"I'll try some with you," he said.

"Damn right," I said. "That's the stuff."

I got our drinks and sat down on the sofa with him. Then I rolled us two fat numbers. I lit one and passed it. I brought it to his fingers. He took it and inhaled.

"Hold it as long as you can," I said. I could tell he didn't know the first thing.

My wife came back downstairs wearing her pink robe and her pink slippers.

"What do I smell?" she said.

"We thought we'd have us some cannabis," I said.

My wife gave me a savage look. Then she looked at the blind man and said, "Robert, I didn't know you smoked."

He said, "I do now, my dear. There's a first time for everything. But I don't feel anything yet."

"This stuff is pretty mellow," I said. "This stuff is mild. It's dope you can reason with," I said. "It doesn't mess you up."

"Not much it doesn't, bub," he said, and laughed.

My wife sat on the sofa between the blind man and me. I passed her the number. She took it and toked and then passed it back to me. "Which way is this going?" she said. Then she said, "I shouldn't be smoking this. I can hardly keep my eyes open as it is. That dinner did me in. I shouldn't have eaten so much."

"It was the strawberry pie," the blind man said. "That's what did it," he said, and he laughed his big laugh. Then he shook his head.

"There's more strawberry pie," I said.

"Do you want some more, Robert?" my wife said.

"Maybe in a little while," he said.

We gave our attention to the TV. My wife yawned again. She said, "Your bed is made up when you feel like going to bed, Robert. I know you must have had a long day. When you're ready to go to bed, say so." She pulled his arm. "Robert?"

He came to and said, "I've had a real nice time. This beats tapes, doesn't it?"

I said, "Coming at you," and I put the number between his fingers. He inhaled, held the smoke, and then let it go. It was like he'd been doing it since he was nine years old.

"Thanks, bub," he said. "But I think this is all for me. I think I'm beginning to feel it," he said. He held the burning roach out for my wife.

"Same here," she said. "Ditto. Me, too." She took the roach and passed it to me. "I may just sit here for a while between you two guys with my eyes closed. But don't let me bother you, okay? Either one of you. If it bothers you, say so. Otherwise, I may just sit here with my eyes closed until you're ready to go to bed," she said. "Your bed's made up, Robert, when you're ready. It's right next to our room at the top of the stairs. We'll show you up when you're ready. You wake me up now, you guys, if I fall asleep." She said that and then she closed her eyes and went to sleep.

The news program ended. I got up and changed the channel. I sat back down on the sofa. I wished my wife hadn't pooped out. Her head lay across the back of the sofa, her mouth open. She'd turned so that her robe slipped away from her legs, exposing a juicy thigh. I reached to draw her robe back over her, and it was then that I glanced at the blind man. What the hell! I flipped the robe open again.

"You say when you want some strawberry pie," I said.

"I will," he said.

I said, "Are you tired? Do you want me to take you up to your bed? Are you ready to hit the hay?"

"Not yet," he said. "No, I'll stay up with you, bub. If that's all right. I'll stay up until you're ready to turn in. We haven't had a chance to talk. Know what I mean? I feel like me and her monopolized the evening." He lifted his beard and he let it fall. He picked up his cigarettes and his lighter.

"That's all right," I said. Then I said, "I'm glad for the company."

And I guess I was. Every night I smoked dope and stayed up as long as I could before I fell asleep. My wife and I hardly ever went to bed at the same time. When I did go to sleep, I had these dreams. Sometimes I'd wake up from one of them, my heart going crazy.

Something about the church and the Middle Ages was on the TV. Not your run-of-the-mill TV fare. I wanted to watch something else. I turned to the other channels. But there was nothing on them, either. So I turned back to the first channel and apologized.

"Bub, it's all right," the blind man said. "It's fine with me. Whatever you want to watch is okay. I'm always learning something. Learning never ends. It won't hurt me to learn something tonight. I got ears," he said.

We didn't say anything for a time. He was leaning forward with his head turned at me, his right ear aimed in the direction of the set. Very disconcerting. Now and then his eyelids drooped and then they snapped open again. Now and then he put his fingers into his beard and tugged, like he was thinking about something he was hearing on the television.

On the screen, a group of men wearing cowls was being set upon and tormented by men dressed in skeleton costumes and men dressed as devils. The men dressed as devils wore devil masks, horns, and long tails. This pageant was part of a procession. The Englishman who was narrating the thing said it took place in Spain once a year. I tried to explain to the blind man what was happening.

"Skeletons," he said. "I know about skeletons," he said, and he nodded.

The TV showed this one cathedral. Then there was a long, slow look at another one. Finally, the picture switched to the famous one in Paris, with its flying buttresses and its spires reaching up to the clouds. The camera pulled away to show the whole of the cathedral rising above the skyline.

There were times when the Englishman who was telling the thing would shut up, would simply let the camera move around the cathedrals. Or else the camera would tour the countryside, men in fields walking behind oxen. I waited as long as I could. Then I felt I had to say something. I said, "They're showing the outside of this cathedral now. Gargoyles. Little statues carved to look like monsters. Now I guess they're in Italy. Yeah, they're in Italy. There's paintings on the walls of this one church."

"Are those fresco paintings, bub?" he asked, and he sipped from his drink.

I reached for my glass. But it was empty. I tried to remember what I could remember. "You're asking me are those frescoes?" I said. "That's a good question. I don't know."

The camera moved to a cathedral outside Lisbon. The differences in the Portuguese cathedral compared with the French and Italian were not that great. But they were there. Mostly the interior stuff. Then something occurred to me, and I said, "Something has occurred to me. Do you have any idea what a cathedral is? What they look like, that is? Do you follow me? If somebody says cathedral to you, do you have any notion what they're talking about? Do you know the difference between that and a Baptist church, say?"

He let the smoke dribble from his mouth. "I know they took hundreds of workers fifty or a hundred years to build," he said. "I just heard the man say that, of course. I know generations of the same families worked on a cathedral. I heard him say that, too. The men who began their life's work on them, they never lived to see the completion of their work. In that wise, bub, they're no different from the rest of us, right?" He laughed. Then his eyelids drooped again. His head nodded. He seemed to be snoozing. Maybe he was imagining himself in Portugal. The TV was showing another cathedral now. This one was in Germany. The Englishman's voice droned on. "Cathedrals," the blind man said. He sat up and rolled his head back and forth. "If you want the truth, bub, that's about all I know. What I just said. What I heard him say. But maybe you could describe one to me? I wish you'd do it. I'd like that. If you want to know, I really don't have a good idea."

I stared hard at the shot of the cathedral on the TV. How could I even begin to describe it? But say my life depended on it. Say my life was being threatened by an insane guy who said I had to do it or else.

I stared some more at the cathedral before the picture flipped off into the countryside. There was no use. I turned to the blind man and said, "To begin with, they're very tall." I was looking around the room for clues. "They reach way up. Up and up. Toward the sky. They're so big, some of them, they have to have these supports. To help hold them up, so to speak. These supports are called buttresses. They remind me of viaducts, for some reason. But maybe you don't know viaducts, either? Sometimes the cathedrals have devils and such carved into the front. Sometimes lords and ladies. Don't ask me why this is," I said.

He was nodding. The whole upper part of his body seemed to be moving back and forth.

"I'm not doing so good, am I?" I said.

He stopped nodding and leaned forward on the edge of the sofa. As he listened to me, he was running his fingers through his beard. I wasn't getting through to him, I could see that. But he waited for me to go on just the same. He nodded, like he was trying to encourage me. I tried to think what else to say. "They're really big," I said. "They're massive. They're built of stone. Marble, too, sometimes. In those olden days, when they built cathedrals, men wanted to be close to God. In those olden days, God was an important part of everyone's life. You could tell this from their cathedral-building. I'm sorry," I said, "but it looks like that's the best I can do for you. I'm just no good at it."

"That's all right, bub," the blind man said. "Hey, listen. I hope you don't mind my asking you. Can I ask you something? Let me ask you a simple question, yes or no. I'm just curious and there's no offense. You're my host. But let me ask if you are in any way religious? You don't mind my asking?"

I shook my head. He couldn't see that, though. A wink is the same as a nod to a blind man. "I guess I don't believe in it. In anything. Sometimes it's hard. You know what I'm saying?"

"Sure, I do," he said.

"Right," I said.

The Englishman was still holding forth. My wife sighed in her sleep. She drew a long breath and went on with her sleeping.

"You'll have to forgive me," I said. "But I can't tell you what a cathedral looks like. It just isn't in me to do it. I can't do any more than I've done."

The blind man sat very still, his head down, as he listened to me.

I said, "The truth is, cathedrals don't mean anything special to me. Nothing. Cathedrals. They're something to look at on late-night TV. That's all they are."

It was then that the blind man cleared his throat. He brought something up. He took a handkerchief from his back pocket. Then he said, "I get it, bub. It's okay. It happens. Don't worry about it," he said. "Hey, listen to me. Will you do me a favor? I got an idea. Why don't you find us some heavy paper? And a pen. We'll do something. We'll draw one together. Get us a pen and some heavy paper. Go on, bub, get the stuff," he said.

So I went upstairs. My legs felt like they didn't have any strength in them. They felt like they did after I'd done some running. In my wife's room, I looked around. I found some ballpoints in a little basket on her table. And then I tried to think where to look for the kind of paper he was talking about.

Downstairs, in the kitchen, I found a shopping bag with onion skins in the bottom of the bag. I emptied the bag and shook it. I brought it into the living room and sat down with it near his legs. I moved some things, smoothed the wrinkles from the bag, spread it out on the coffee table.

The blind man got down from the sofa and sat next to me on the carpet.

He ran his fingers over the paper. He went up and down the sides of the paper. The edges, even the edges. He fingered the corners.

"All right," he said. "All right, let's do her."

He found my hand, the hand with the pen. He closed his hand over my hand. "Go ahead, bub, draw," he said. "Draw. You'll see. I'll follow along with you. It'll be okay. Just begin now like I'm telling you. You'll see. Draw," the blind man said.

So I began. First I drew a box that looked like a house. It could have been the house I lived in. Then I put a roof on it. At either end of the roof, I drew spires. Crazy.

"Swell," he said. "Terrific. You're doing fine," he said. "Never thought anything like this could happen in your lifetime, did you, bub? Well, it's a strange life, we all know that. Go on now. Keep it up."

I put in windows with arches. I drew flying buttresses. I hung great doors. I couldn't stop. The TV station went off the air. I put down the pen and closed and opened my fingers. The blind man felt around over the paper. He moved the tips of his fingers over the paper, all over what I had drawn, and he nodded.

"Doing fine," the blind man said.

I took up the pen again, and he found my hand. I kept at it. I'm no artist. But I kept drawing just the same.

My wife opened up her eyes and gazed as us. She sat up on the sofa, her robe hanging open. She said, "What are you doing? Tell me, I want to know."

I didn't answer her.

The blind man said, "We're drawing a cathedral. Me and him are working on it. Press hard," he said to me. "That's right. That's good," he said. "Sure. You got it, bub, I can tell. You didn't think you could. But you can, can't you? You're cooking with gas now. You know what I'm saying? We're going to really have us something here in a minute. How's the old arm?" he said. "Put some people in there now. What's a cathedral without people?"

My wife said, "What's going on? Robert, what are you doing? What's going on?"

"It's all right," he said to her. "Close your eyes now," the blind man said to me.

I did it. I closed them just like he said.

"Are they closed?" he said. "Don't fudge."

"They're closed," I said.

"Keep them that way," he said. He said, "Don't stop now. Draw."

So we kept on with it. His fingers rode my fingers as my hand went over the paper. It was like nothing else in my life up to now.

Then he said, "I think that's it. I think you got it," he said. "Take a look. What do you think?"

But I had my eyes closed. I thought I'd keep them that way for a little longer. I thought it was something I ought to do.

"Well?" he said. "Are you looking?"

My eyes were still closed. I was in my house. I knew that. But I didn't feel like I was inside anything.

"It's really something," I said.

[1981]

Toni Cade Bambara *(American; b. 1939)*

The Lesson

Back in the days when everyone was old and stupid or young and foolish and me and Sugar were the only ones just right, this lady moved on our block with nappy hair and proper speech and no makeup. And quite natur- ally we laughed at her, laughed the way we did at the junk man who went about his business like he was some big-time president and his sorry-ass horse his secretary. And we kinda hated her too, hated the way we did the winos who cluttered up our parks and pissed on our handball walls and stank up our hallways and stairs so you couldn't halfway play hide- and-seek without a goddamn gas mask. Miss Moore was her name. The only woman on the block with no first name. And she was black as hell, cept for her feet, which were fish-white and spooky. And she was always planning these boring-ass things for us to do, us being my cousin, mostly, who lived on the block cause we all moved North the same time and to the same apartment then spread out gradual to breathe. And our parents would yank our heads into some kinda shape and crisp up our clothes so we'd be presentable for travel with Miss Moore, who always looked like she was going to church, though she never did. Which is just one of the things the grownups talked about when they talked behind her back like a dog. But when she came calling with some sachet she'd sewed up or some gingerbread she'd made or some book, why then they'd all be too embarrassed to turn her down and we'd get handed over all spruced up. She'd been to college and said it was only right that she should take responsibility for the young ones' education, and she not even related by marriage or blood. So they'd go for it. Specially Aunt Gretchen. She was the main gofer in the family. You got some old dumb shit foolishness you want somebody to go for, you send for Aunt Gretchen. She been screwed into the go-along for so long, it's a blood-deep natural thing with her. Which is how she got saddled with me and Sugar and Junior in the first place while our mothers were in a la-de-da apartment up the block hav- ing a good ole time.

So this one day Miss Moore rounds us all up at the mailbox and it's puredee hot and she's knockin herself out about arithmetic. And school suppose to let up in summer I heard, but she don't never let up. And the starch in my pinafore scratching the shit outta me and I'm really hating this nappy-head bitch and her goddamn college degree. I'd much rather go to the pool or to the show where it's cool. So me and Sugar leaning on the mailbox being surly, which is a Miss Moore word. And Flyboy checking out what everybody brought for lunch. And Fat Butt already wasting his peanut-butter-and-jelly sandwich like the pig he is. And June- bug punchin on Q.T.'s arm for potato chips. And Rosie Giraffe shifting from one hip to the other waiting for somebody to step on her foot or ask her if she from Georgia so she can kick ass, preferably Mercedes'. And Miss Moore asking us do we know what money is, like we a bunch of retards. I mean real money, she say, like it's only poker chips or monopoly papers we lay on the grocer. So right away I'm tired of this and say so. And would much rather snatch Sugar and go to the Sunset and terrorize the West Indian kids and take their hair ribbons and their money too. And Miss Moore files that remark away for next week's lesson on brotherhood, I can tell. And finally I say we oughta get to the subway cause it's cooler and besides we might meet some cute boys. Sugar done swiped her mama's lipstick, so we ready.

So we heading down the street and she's boring us silly about what things cost and what our parents make and how much goes for rent and how money ain't divided up right in this country. And then she gets to the part about we all poor and live in the slums, which I don't feature. And I'm ready to speak on that, but she steps out in the street and hails two cabs just like that. Then she hustles half the crew in with her and hands me a five-dollar bill and tells me to calculate 10 percent tip for the driver. And we're off. Me and Sugar and Junebug and Flyboy hangin out the window and hollering to everybody, putting lipstick on each other cause Flyboy a faggot anyway, and making farts with our sweaty armpits. But I'm mostly trying to figure how to spend this money. But they all fascinated with the meter ticking and Junebug starts laying bets as to how much it'll read when Flyboy can't hold his breath no more. Then Sugar lays bets as to how much it'll be when we get there. So I'm stuck. Don't nobody want to go for my plan, which is to jump out at the next light and run off to the first bar-b-que we can find. Then the driver tells us to get the hell out cause we there already. And the meter reads eighty-five cents. And I'm stalling to figure out the tip and Sugar say give him a dime. And I decide he don't need it bad as I do, so later for him. But then he tries to take off with Junebug foot still in the door so we talk about his mama something ferocious. Then we check out that we on Fifth Avenue and everybody dressed up in stockings. One lady in a fur coat, hot as it is. White folks crazy.

"This is the place," Miss Moore say, presenting it to us in the voice she uses at the museum. "Let's look in the windows before we go in."

"Can we steal?" Sugar asks very serious like she's getting the ground rules squared away before she plays. "I beg your pardon," say Miss Moore, and we fall out. So she leads us around the windows of the toy store and me and Sugar screamin, "This is mine, that's mine. I gotta have that, that was made for me. I was born for that," till Big Butt drowns us out.

"Hey, I'm goin to buy that there."

"That there? You don't even know what it is, stupid."

"I do so," he say punchin on Rosie Giraffe. "It's a microscope."

"Whatcha gonna do with a microscope, fool?"

"Look at things."

"Like what, Ronald?" ask Miss Moore. And Big Butt ain't got the first notion. So here go Miss Moore gabbing about the thousands of bacteria in a drop of water and the somethinorother in a speck of blood and the million and one living things in the air around us is invisible to the naked eye. And what she say that for? Junebug go to town on that "naked" and we rolling. Then Miss Moore ask what it cost. So we all jam into the window smudgin it up and the price tag say $300. So then she ask how long'd take for Big Butt and Junebug to save up their allowances. "Too long," I say. "Yeh," adds Sugar, "outgrown it by that time." And Miss Moore say no, you never outgrow learning instruments. "Why, even medical students and interns and," blah, blah, blah. And we ready to choke Big Butt for bringing it up in the first damn place.

"This here costs four hundred eighty dollars," say Rosie Giraffe. So we pile up all over her to see what she pointin out. My eyes tell me it's a chunk of glass cracked with something heavy, and different-color inks dripped into the splits, then the whole thing put into a oven or something. But for $480 it don't make sense.

"That's a paperweight made of semi-precious stones fused together under tremendous pressure," she explains slowly, with her hands doing the mining and all the factory work.

"So what's a paperweight?" asks Rosie Giraffe.

"To weigh paper with, dumbbell," say Flyboy, the wise man from the East.

"Not exactly," say Miss Moore, which is what she say when you warm or way off too. "It's to weigh paper down so it won't scatter and make your desk untidy." So right away me and Sugar curtsy to each other and then to Mercedes who is more the tidy type.

"We don't keep paper on top of the desk in my class," say Junebug, figuring Miss Moore crazy or lyin one.

"At home, then," she say. "Don't you have a calendar and a pencil case and a blotter and a letter-opener on your desk at home where you do your homework?" And she know damn well what our homes look like cause she nosys around in them every chance she gets.

"I don't even have a desk," say Junebug. "Do we?"

"No. And I don't get no homework neither," says Big Butt.

"And I don't even have a home," say Flyboy like he do at school to keep the white folks off his back and sorry for him. Send this poor kid to camp posters, is his specialty.

"I do," says Mercedes. "I have a box of stationery on my desk and a picture of my cat. My godmother bought the stationery and the desk. There's a big rose on each sheet and the envelopes smell like roses."

"Who wants to know about your smelly-ass stationery," say Rosie Giraffe fore I can get my two cents in.

"It's important to have a work area all your own so that . . . "

"Will you look at this sailboat, please," say Flyboy, cuttin her off and pointin to the thing like it was his. So once again we tumble all over each other to gaze at this magnificent thing in the toy store which is just big enough to maybe sail two kittens across the pond if you strap them to the posts tight. We all start reciting the price tag like we in assembly. "Hand-crafted sailboat of fiberglass at one thousand one hundred ninety-five dollars."

"Unbelievable," I hear myself say and am really stunned. I read it again for myself just in case the group recitation put me in a trance. Same thing. For some reason this pisses me off. We look at Miss Moore and she lookin at us, waiting for I dunno what.

"Who'd pay all that when you can buy a sailboat set for a quarter at Pop's, a tube of glue for a dime, and a ball of string for eight cents? It must have a motor and a whole lot else besides," I say. "My sailboat cost me about fifty cents."

"But will it take water?" say Mercedes with her smart ass.

"Took mine to Alley Pond Park once," say Flyboy. "String broke. Lost it. Pity."

"Sailed mine in Central Park and it keeled over and sank. Had to ask my father for another dollar."

"And you got the strap," laugh Big Butt. "The jerk didn't even have a string on it. My old man wailed on his behind."

Little Q.T. was staring hard at the sailboat and you could see he wanted it bad. But he too little and somebody'd just take it from him. So what the hell. "This boat for kids, Miss Moore?"

"Parents silly to buy something like that just to get all broke up," say Rosie Giraffe.

"That much money it should last forever," I figure.

"My father'd buy it for me if I wanted it."

"Your father, my ass," say Rosie Giraffe getting a chance to finally push Mercedes.

"Must be rich people shop here," say Q.T.

"You are a very bright boy," say Flyboy. "What was your first clue?" And he rap him on the head with the back of his knuckles, since Q.T. the only one he could get away with. Though Q.T. liable to come up behind you years later and get his licks in when you half expect it.

"What I want to know is," I says to Miss Moore though I never talk to her, I wouldn't give the bitch that satisfaction, "is how much a real boat costs? I figure a thousand'd get you a yacht any day."

"Why don't you check that out," she says, "and report back to the group?" Which really pains my ass. If you gonna mess up a perfectly good swim day least you could do is have some answers. "Let's go in," she say like she got something up her sleeve. Only she don't lead the way. So me and Sugar turn the corner to where the entrance is, but when we get there

I kinda hang back. Not that I'm scared, what's there to be afraid of, just a toy store. But I feel funny, shame. But what I got to be shamed about? Got as much right to go in as anybody. But somehow I can't seem to get hold of the door, so I step away for Sugar to lead. But she hangs back too. And I look at her and she looks at me and this is ridiculous. I mean, damn, I have never ever been shy about doing nothing or going nowhere. But then Mercedes steps up and then Rosie Giraffe and Big Butt crowd in behind and shove, and next thing we all stuffed into the doorway with only Mercedes squeezing past us, smoothing out her jumper and walking right down the aisle. Then the rest of us tumble in like a glued-together jigsaw done all wrong. And people lookin at us. And it's like the time me and Sugar crashed into the Catholic church on a dare. But once we got in there and everything so hushed and holy and the candles and the bowin and the handkerchiefs on all the drooping heads, I just couldn't go through with the plan. Which was for me to run up to the altar and do a tap dance while Sugar played the nose flute and messed around in the holy water. And Sugar kept givin me the elbow. Then later teased me so bad I tied her up in the shower and turned it on and locked her in. And she'd be there till this day if Aunt Gretchen hadn't finally figured I was lying about the boarder takin a shower.

Same thing in the store. We all walkin on tiptoe and hardly touchin the games and puzzles and things. And I watched Miss Moore who is steady watchin us like she waiting for a sign. Like Mama Drewery watches the sky and sniffs the air and takes note of just how much slant is in the bird formation. Then me and Sugar bump smack into each other, so busy gazing at the toys, 'specially the sailboat. But we don't laugh and go into our fat-lady bump-stomach routine. We just stare at that price tag. Then Sugar run a finger over the whole boat. And I'm jealous and want to hit her. Maybe not her, but I sure want to punch somebody in the mouth.

"Watcha bring us here for, Miss Moore?"

"You sound angry, Sylvia. Are you mad about something?" Givin me one of them grins like she tellin a grown-up joke that never turns out to be funny. And she's looking very closely at me like maybe she plannin to do my portrait from memory. I'm mad, but I won't give her that satisfaction. So I slouch around the store bein very bored and say, "Let's go."

Me and Sugar at the back of the train watchin the tracks whizzin by large then small then gettin gobbled up in the dark. I'm thinkin about this tricky toy I saw in the store. A clown that somersaults on a bar then does chin-ups just cause you yank lightly at his leg. Cost $35. I could see me askin my mother for a $35 birthday clown. "You wanna who that costs what?" she'd say, cocking her head to the side to get a better view of the hole in my head. Thirty-five dollars could buy new bunk beds for Junior and Gretchen's boy. Thirty-five dollars and the whole household could go visit Granddaddy Nelson in the country. Thirty-five dollars would pay for the rent and the piano bill too. Who are these people that spend that much for performing clowns and $1000 for toy sailboats? What kinda work they do and how they live and how come we ain't in on it? Where we are is who we are, Miss Moore always pointin out. But it don't necessarily have to be that way, she always adds then waits for somebody to say that poor people have to wake up and demand their share of the pie and don't none of us know what kind of pie she talkin about in the first damn place. But she ain't so smart cause I still got her four dollars from the taxi and she sure ain't gettin it. Messin up my day with this shit. Sugar nudges me in my pocket and winks.

Miss Moore lines us up in front of the mailbox where we started from, seem like years ago, and I got a headache for thinkin so hard. And we lean all over each other so we can hold up under the draggy-ass lecture she always finishes off with at the end before we thank her for borin us to tears. But she just looks at us like she readin tea leaves. Finally she say, "Well, what did you think of F. A. O. Schwarz?"

Rosie Giraffe mumbles, "White folks crazy."

"I'd like to go there again when I get my birthday money," says Mercedes, and we shove her out the pack so she has to lean on the mailbox by herself.

"I'd like a shower. Tiring day," say Flyboy.

Then Sugar surprises me by sayin, "You know, Miss Moore, I don't think all of us here put together eat in a year what that sailboat costs." And Miss Moore lights up like somebody goosed her. "And?" she say, urging Sugar on. Only I'm standin on her foot so she don't continue.

"Imagine for a minute what kind of society it is in which some people can spend on a toy what it would cost to feed a family of six or seven. What do you think?"

"I think," say Sugar pushing me off her feet like she never done before, cause I whip her ass in a minute, "that this is not much of a democracy if you ask me. Equal chance to pursue happiness means an equal crack at the dough, don't it?" Miss Moore is beside herself and I am disgusted with Sugar's treachery. So I stand on her foot one more time to see if she'll shove me. She shuts up, and Miss Moore looks at me, sorrowfully I'm thinkin. And somethin weird is goin on, I can feel it in my chest.

"Anybody else learn anything today?" lookin dead at me. I walk away and Sugar has to run to catch up and don't even seem to notice when I shrug her arm off my shoulder.

"Well, we got four dollars anyway," she says.

"Uh hunh."

"We could go to Hascombs and get half a chocolate layer and then go to the Sunset and still have plenty money for potato chips and ice cream sodas."

"Uh hunh."

"Race you to Hascombs," she say.

We start down the block and she gets ahead which is O.K. by me cause I'm going to the West End and then over to the Drive to think this day through. She can run if she want to and even run faster. But ain't nobody gonna beat me at nuthin.

[1972]

Margaret Atwood *(Canadian; b. 1939)*

Rape Fantasies

The way they're going on about it in the magazines you'd think it was just invented, and not only that but it's something terrific, like a vaccine for cancer. They put it in capital letters on the front cover, and inside they have these questionnaires like the ones they used to have about whether you were a good enough wife or an endomorph or an ectomorph,[1] remember that? with the scoring upside down on page 73, and then these numbered do-it-yourself dealies, you know? RAPE, TEN THINGS TO DO ABOUT IT, like it was ten new hairdos or something. I mean, what's so new about it?

So at work they all have to talk about it because no matter what magazine you open, there it is, staring you right between the eyes, and they're beginning to have it on the television, too. Personally I'd prefer a June Allyson[2] movie anytime but they don't make them anymore and they don't even have them that much on the Late Show. For instance, day before yesterday, that would be Wednesday, thank god it's Friday as they say, we were sitting around in the women's lunch room—the *lunch* room, I mean you'd think you could get some peace and quiet in there—and Chrissy closes up the magazine she's been reading and says, "How about it, girls, do you have rape fantasies?"

The four of us were having our game of bridge the way we always do, and I had a bare twelve points counting the singleton with not that much of a bid in anything. So I said one club, hoping Sondra would remember about the one club convention, because the time before when I used that she thought I really meant clubs and she bid us up to three, and all I had was four little ones with nothing higher than a six, and we went down two and on top of that we were vulnerable. She is not the world's best bridge player. I mean, neither am I but there's a limit.

---

[1] **endomorph, ectomorph**   body-types. An endomorph possesses a short, wide body; an ectomorph, a tall, narrow body.
[2] **June Allyson**   actress who portrayed the friendly, healthy girl in musical-comedy films of the 1940s and 50s

Darlene passed but the damage was done, Sondra's head went round like it was on ball bearings and she said, "*What* fantasies?"

"Rape fantasies," Chrissy said. She's a receptionist and she looks like one; she's pretty but cool as a cucumber, like she's been painted all over with nail polish, if you know what I mean. Varnished. "It says here all women have rape fantasies."

"For Chrissake, I'm eating an egg sandwich," I said, "and I bid one club and Darlene passed."

"You mean, like some guy jumping you in an alley or something," Sondra said. She was eating her lunch, we all eat our lunches during the game, and she bit into a piece of that celery she always brings and started to chew away on it with this thoughtful expression in her eyes and I knew we might as well pack it in as far as the game was concerned.

"Yeah, sort of like that," Chrissy said. She was blushing a little, you could see it even under her makeup.

"I don't think you should go out alone at night," Darlene said, "you put yourself in a position," and I may have been mistaken but she was looking at me. She's the oldest, she's forty-one though you wouldn't know it and neither does she, but I looked it up in the employees' file. I like to guess a person's age and then look it up to see if I'm right. I let myself have an extra pack of cigarettes if I am, though I'm trying to cut down. I figure it's harmless as long as you don't tell. I mean, not everyone has access to that file, it's more or less confidential. But it's all right if I tell you, I don't expect you'll ever meet her, though you never know, it's a small world. Anyway.

"For *heaven's* sake, it's only *Toronto*," Greta said. She worked in Detroit for three years and she never lets you forget it, it's like she thinks she's a war hero or something, we should all admire her just for the fact that she's still walking this earth, though she was really living in Windsor the whole time, she just worked in Detroit. Which for me doesn't really count. It's where you sleep, right?

"Well, do you?" Chrissy said. She was obviously trying to tell us about hers but she wasn't about to go first, she's cautious, that one.

"I certainly don't," Darlene said, and she wrinkled up her nose, like this, and I had to laugh. "I think it's disgusting." She's divorced, I read that in the file too, she never talks about it. It must've been years ago anyway. She got up and went over to the coffee machine and turned her back on us as though she wasn't going to have anything more to do with it.

"Well," Greta said. I could see it was going to be between her and Chrissy. They're both blondes, I don't mean that in a bitchy way but they do try to outdress each other. Greta would like to get out of Filing, she'd like to be a receptionist too so she could meet more people. You don't meet much of anyone in Filing except other people in Filing. Me, I don't mind it so much, I have outside interests.

"Well," Greta said, "I sometimes think about, you know my apartment? It's got this little balcony, I like to sit out there in the summer and I have a few plants out there. I never bother that much about locking the door to the balcony, it's one of those sliding glass ones, I'm on the eighteenth floor for heaven's sake, I've got a good view of the lake and the CN Tower and all. But I'm sitting around one night in my housecoat, watching TV with my shoes off, you know how you do, and I see this guy's feet, coming down past the window, and the next thing you know he's standing on the balcony, he's let himself down by a rope with a hook on the end of it from the floor above, that's the nineteenth, and before I can even get up off the chesterfield he's inside the apartment. He's all dressed in black with black gloves on"—I knew right away what show she got the black gloves off because I saw the same one—"and then he, well, you know."

"You know what?" Chrissy said, but Greta said, "And afterwards he tells me that he goes all over the outside of the apartment building like that, from one floor to another, with his rope and his hook . . . and then he goes out to the balcony and tosses his rope, and he climbs up it and disappears."

"Just like Tarzan," I said, but nobody laughed.

"Is that all?" Chrissy said. "Don't you ever think about, well, I think about being in the bathtub, with no clothes on . . . "

"So who takes a bath in their clothes?" I said, you have to admit it's stupid when you come to think of it, but she just went on, " . . . with lots of bubbles, what I use is Vitabath, it's more expensive but it's so relaxing, and my hair pinned up, and the door opens and this fellow's standing there . . . "

"How'd he get in?" Greta said.

"Oh, I don't know, through a window or something. Well, I can't very well get out of the bathtub, the bathroom's too small and besides he's blocking the doorway, so I just lie there, and he starts to very slowly take his own clothes off, and then he gets into the bathtub with me."

"Don't you scream or anything?" said Darlene. She'd come back with her cup of coffee, she was getting really interested. "I'd scream like bloody murder."

"Who'd hear me?" Chrissy said. "Besides, all the articles say it's better not to resist, that way you don't get hurt."

"Anyway you might get bubbles up your nose," I said, "from the deep breathing," and I swear all four of them looked at me like I was in bad taste, like I'd insulted the Virgin Mary or something. I mean, I don't see what's wrong with a little joke now and then. Life's too short, right?

"Listen," I said, "those aren't *rape* fantasies. I mean, you aren't getting *raped,* it's just some guy you haven't met formally who happens to be more attractive than Derek Cummins"—he's the Assistant Manager, he wears elevator shoes or at any rate they have these thick soles and he has this funny way of talking, we call him Derek Duck—"and you have a good time. Rape is when they've got a knife or something and you don't want to."

"So what about you, Estelle," Chrissy said, she was miffed because I laughed at her fantasy, she thought I was putting her down. Sondra was miffed too, by this time she'd finished her celery and she wanted to tell about hers, but she hadn't got in fast enough.

"All right, let me tell you one," I said. "I'm walking down this dark street at night and this fellow comes up and grabs my arm. Now it so happens that I have a plastic lemon in my purse, you know how it always says you should carry a plastic lemon in your purse? I don't really do it, I tried it once but the darn thing leaked all over my checkbook, but in this fantasy I have one, and I say to him, 'You're intending to rape me, right?' and he nods, so I open my purse to get the plastic lemon, and I can't find it! My purse is full of all this junk, Kleenex and cigarettes and my change purse and my lipstick and my driver's license, you know the kind of stuff; so I ask him to hold out his hands, like this, and I pile all this junk into them and down at the bottom there's the plastic lemon, and I can't get the top off. So I hand it to him and he's very obliging, he twists the top off and hands it back to me, and I squirt him in the eye."

I hope you don't think that's too vicious. Come to think of it, it is a bit mean, especially when he was so polite and all.

"*That's* your rape fantasy?" Chrissy says. "I don't believe it."

"She's a card," Darlene says, she and I are the ones that've been here the longest and she never will forget the time I got drunk at the office party and insisted I was going to dance under the table instead of on top of it, I did a sort of Cossack number but then I hit my head on the bottom of the table—actually it was a desk—when I went to get up, and I knocked myself out cold. She's decided that's the mark of an original mind and she tells everyone new about it and I'm not sure that's fair. Though I did do it.

"I'm being totally honest," I say. I always am and they know it. There's no point in being anything else, is the way I look at it, and sooner or later the truth will come out so you might as well not waste the time, right? "You should hear the one about the Easy-Off Oven Cleaner."

But that was the end of the lunch hour, with one bridge game shot to hell, and the next day we spent most of the time arguing over whether to start a new game or play out the hands we had left over from the day before, so Sondra never did get a chance to tell about her rape fantasy.

It started me thinking though, about my own rape fantasies. Maybe I'm abnormal or something, I mean I have fantasies about handsome strangers coming in through the window too, like Mr. Clean, I wish one would, please god somebody without flat feet and big sweat marks on his shirt, and over five feet five, believe me being tall is a handicap though it's getting better, tall guys are starting to like someone whose nose reaches higher than their belly button. But if you're being totally honest you can't count those as rape fantasies. In a real rape fantasy, what you should feel is this anxiety, like when you think about your apartment building catching on fire and whether you should use the elevator or the stairs or maybe just stick your head under a wet towel, and you try to remember everything you've read about what to do but you can't decide.

For instance, I'm walking along this dark street at night and this short, ugly fellow comes up and grabs my arm, and not only is he ugly, you know, with a sort of puffy nothing face, like those fellows you have to talk to in the bank when your account's overdrawn—of course I don't mean they're all like that—but he's absolutely covered in pimples. So he gets me pinned against the wall, he's short but he's heavy, and he starts to undo himself and the zipper gets stuck. I mean, one of the most significant moments in a girl's life, it's almost like getting married or having a baby or something, and he sticks the zipper.

So I say, kind of disgusted, "Oh for Chrissake," and he starts to cry. He tells me he's never been able to get anything right in his entire life, and this is the last straw, he's going to jump off a bridge.

"Look," I say, I feel so sorry for him, in my rape fantasies I always end up feeling sorry for the guy, I mean there has to be something *wrong* with them, if it was Clint Eastwood it'd be different but worse luck it never is. I was the kind of little girl who buried dead robins, know what I mean? It used to drive my mother nuts, she didn't like me touching them, because of the germs I guess. So I say, "Listen, I know how you feel. You really should do something about those pimples, if you got rid of them you'd be quite good looking, honest; then you wouldn't have to go around doing stuff like this. I had them myself once," I say, to comfort him, but in fact I did, and it ends up I give him the name of my old dermatologist, the one I had in high school, that was back in Leamington, except I used to go to St. Catharine's for the dermatologist. I'm telling you, I was really lonely when I first came here; I thought it was going to be such a big adventure and all, but it's a lot harder to meet people in a city. But I guess it's different for a guy.

Or I'm lying in bed with this terrible cold, my face is all swollen up, my eyes are red and my nose is dripping like a leaky tap, and this fellow comes in through the window and *he* has a terrible cold too, it's a new kind of flu that's been going around. So he says, "I'b goig do rabe you"—I hope you don't mind me holding my nose like this but that's the way I imagine it—and he lets out this terrific sneeze, which slows him down a bit, also I'm no object of beauty myself, you'd have to be some kind of pervert to want to rape someone with a cold like mine, it'd be like raping a bottle of LePage's mucilage the way my nose is running. He's looking wildly around the room, and I realize it's because he doesn't have a piece of Kleenex! "Id's ride here," I say, and I pass him the Kleenex, god knows why he even bothered to get out of bed, you'd think if you were going to go around climbing in windows you'd wait till you were healthier, right? I mean, that takes a certain amount of energy. So I ask him why doesn't he let me fix him a Neo-Citran and scotch, that's what I always take, you still have the cold but you don't feel it, so I do and we end up watching the Late Show together. I mean, they aren't all sex maniacs, the rest of the time they must lead a normal life. I figure they enjoy watching the Late Show just like anybody else.

I do have a scarier one though . . . where the fellow says he's hearing angel voices that're telling him he's got to kill me, you know, you read about things like that all the time in the papers. In this one I'm not in the apartment where I live now, I'm back in my mother's house in Leamington and the fellow's been hiding in the cellar, he grabs my arm when I go downstairs to get a jar of jam and he's got hold of the axe too, out of the garage, that one is really scary. I mean, what do you say to a nut like that?

So I start to shake but after a minute I get control of myself and I say, is he sure the angel voices have got the right person, because I hear the same angel voices and they've been telling me for some time that I'm going to give birth to the reincarnation of St. Anne who in turn has the Virgin Mary and right after that comes Jesus Christ and the end of the world, and he wouldn't want to interfere with that, would he? So he gets confused and listens some more, and then he asks for a sign and I show him my vaccination mark, you can see it's sort of an odd-shaped one, it got infected because I scratched the top off and that does it, he apologizes and climbs out the coal chute again, which is how he got in in the first place, and I say to myself there's some advantage in having been brought up a Catholic even though I haven't been to church since they changed the service into English, it just isn't the same, you might as well be a Protestant. I must write to Mother and tell her to nail up that coal chute, it always has bothered me. Funny, I couldn't tell you at all what this man looks like but I know exactly what kind of shoes he's wearing, because that's the last I see of him, his shoes going up the coal chute, and they're the old-fashioned kind that lace up the ankles, even though he's a young fellow. That's strange, isn't it?

Let me tell you though I really sweat until I see him safely out of there and I go upstairs right away and make myself a cup of tea. I don't think about that one much. My mother always said you shouldn't dwell on unpleasant things and I generally agree with that, I mean, dwelling on them doesn't make them go away. Though not dwelling on them doesn't make them go away either, when you come to think of it.

Sometimes I have these short ones where the fellow grabs my arm but I'm really a Kung-Fu expert, can you believe it, in real life I'm sure it would just be a conk on the head and that's that, like getting your tonsils out, you'd wake up and it would be all over except for the sore places, and you'd be lucky if your neck wasn't broken or something, I could never even hit the volleyball in gym and a volleyball is fairly large, you know?—and I just go *zap* with my fingers into his eyes and that's it, he falls over, or I flip him against a wall or something. But I could never really stick my fingers in anyone's eyes, could you? It would feel like hot jello and I don't even like cold jello, just thinking about it gives me the creeps. I feel a bit guilty about that one, I mean how would you like walking around knowing someone's been blinded for life because of you?

But maybe it's different for a guy.

The most touching one I have is when the fellow grabs my arm and I say, sad and kind of dignified, "You'd be raping a corpse." That pulls him up short and I explain that I've just found out I have leukemia and the doctors have only given me a few months to live. That's why I'm out pacing the streets alone at night, I need to think, you know, come to terms with myself. I don't really have leukemia but in the fantasy I do, I guess I chose that particular disease because a girl in my grade four class died of it, the whole class sent her flowers when she was in the hospital. I didn't understand then that she was going to die and I wanted to have leukemia too so I could get flowers. Kids are funny, aren't they? Well, it turns out that he has leukemia himself, and *he* only has a few months to live, that's why he's going around raping people, he's very bitter because he's so young and his life is being taken from him before he's really lived it. So we walk along gently under the street lights, it's spring and sort of misty, and we end up going for coffee, we're happy we've found the only other person in the world who can understand what we're going through, it's almost like fate, and after a while we just sort of look at each other and our hands touch, and he comes back with me and moves into my apartment and we spend our last months together before we die, we just sort of don't wake up in the morning, though I've never decided which one of us gets to die first. If it's him I have to go on and fantasize about the funeral, if it's me I don't have to worry about that, so it just about depends on how tired I am at the time. You may not believe this but sometimes I even start crying. I cry at the ends of movies, even the ones that aren't all that sad, so I guess it's the same thing. My mother's like that too.

The funny thing about these fantasies is that the man is always someone I don't know, and the statistics in the magazines, well, most of them anyway, they say it's often someone you do know, at least a little bit, like your boss or something—I mean, it wouldn't be *my* boss, he's over sixty and I'm sure he couldn't rape his way out of a paper bag, poor old thing, but it might be someone like Derek Duck, in his elevator shoes, perish the thought—or someone you just met, who invites you up for a drink, it's getting so you can hardly be sociable anymore, and how are you supposed to meet people if you can't trust them even that basic amount? You can't spend your whole life in the Filing Department or cooped up in your own apartment with all the doors and windows locked and the shades down. I'm not what you would call a drinker but I like to go out now and then for a drink or two in a nice place, even if I am by my-self, I'm with Women's Lib on that even though I can't agree with a lot of other things they say. Like here for instance, the waiters all know me and if anyone, you know, bothers me. . . . I don't know why I'm telling you all this, except I think it helps you get to know a person, especially at first, hearing some of the things they think about. At work they call me the office worry wart, but it isn't so much like worrying, it's more like figuring out what you should do in an emergency, like I said before.

Anyway, another thing about it is that there's a lot of conversation, in fact I spend most of my time, in the fantasy that is, wondering what I'm going to say and what he's going to say, I think it would be better if you could get a conversation going. Like, how could a fellow do that to a person he's just had a long conversation with, once you let them know you're human, you have a life too, I don't see how they could go ahead with it, right? I mean, I know it happens but I just don't understand it, that's the part I really don't understand.

[1975]

Garrison Keillor (American; b. 1942)

The Tip-Top Club

The idea of pouring warm soapy water into overshoes and wearing them around the house to give yourself a relaxing footbath while you work is one that all fans of WLT's "The Tip-Top Club" seem to have remembered over the years, along with the idea that if you're depressed you should sit down and write a letter to yourself praising all of your good qualities, and the idea of puffing cigarette smoke at violets to prevent aphids.

Every evening, Sunday through Thursday, at 10:00 P.M. ("and now . . . direct from the Tip-Top studio in downtown Minneapolis . . ."), WLT played the Tip-Top theme song—

Whenever you feel blue, think of something nice to do;
That's the motto of the Tip-Top crew.

Don't let it get you down, wear a smile and not a frown,
And you'll be feeling Tip-top too.

— and Bud Swenson came on the air with his friendly greeting: "Good evening, Tip-Toppers, and welcome to *your* show. This is your faithful recording secretary, chief cook and bottle-washer, Bud Swenson, calling the Club to order and waiting to hear from you." And of the hundreds of calls that came in on the Tip-Top line (847-8677, or T-I-P-T-O-P-S), and of the fifty or sixty that actually got on the air, many were from listeners who simply wanted Bud to know they were doing fine, feeling good, and enjoying the show. "And—oh, yes," they might add, "we got our boots on," referring to overshoes.

Every night, Bud got at least one request for a copy of the poem a woman had written about writing a letter to yourself. It was called "Dear Me," it was a hundred and eight lines long, WLT mailed out 18,000 copies of it in the six months after it was written (May 18, 1956), and it began:

> When I look around these days
> And hear blame instead of praise
> (For to bless is so much harder than to damn),
> It makes me feel much better
> To write myself a letter
> And tell myself how good I really am.
>
> Dear Me, Sorry it's been
> So long since I took pen
> In hand and scribbled off a word or two.
> I'm busy with my work and such,
> But I need to keep in touch
> Cause the very closest friend I have is you.
>
> Through times of strife and toil,
> You've always remained loyal
> And stuck with me when other friends were far,
> And because we are so close,
> I think of you the most
> And of just how near and dear to me you are.

As for puffing smoke at violets, it touched off a debate that lasted for years. For months after it was suggested by an elderly woman, Bud got call after call from listeners who said that smoke-puffing would *not* discourage aphids; that even if it would, there are *better* ways to discourage aphids; and, worse, that it might encourage young people to take up smoking.

The pro-puffers replied hotly that: (1) you don't have to *inhale* in order to *puff* on a plant; (2) the treatment should be given only once a week or so; and (3) anyone who wants to smoke probably will go ahead and do it *anyway,* violets or *no* violets.

As time passed, the issue became confused in the minds of some Tip-Toppers, who came to think that Bud himself was a smoker (he was not). To the very end (November 26, 1969), he got calls from listeners wanting to know if he didn't agree with them that smoking is a filthy habit. (He did.)

At Bud's retirement party, Roy Elmore, Jr., president of WLT, presented him with twenty-five potted violet plants, one for each year of service.

Controversy was the very thing that distinguished "The Tip-Top Club." It had none. Edgar Elmore, the founder of WLT, abhorred controversy, and the terms of his will bound his heir, Roy Jr., to abhor it also. Though Edgar never heard Bud's show, having died in 1940, eleven years before the Club was formed, he certainly would have enjoyed it very much, as Roy Jr. told Bud frequently. No conversation about religion or politics was permitted, nor were callers allowed to be pessimistic or moody on the air. If a person started in to be moody, he or she was told firmly and politely to hang up and *listen* to the show and it would cheer him or her up. Few had to be told.

Vacations and pets were favorite Tip-Top topics, along with household hints, children, gardening, memories of long ago, favorite foods, great persons, good health and how to keep it, and of course the weather. Even when the weather was bad, even in times of national crisis, the Tip-Toppers always came up with cheerful things to talk about.

One reason for the show's cheery quality and the almost complete absence of crank calls was Bud's phone policy. After the first year he never divulged the Tip-Top phone number over the air (nor, for that matter, over the phone). In fact, it was an unlisted number, and one could obtain it only from another Tip-Topper. This tended to limit participation to those who understood the rules and accepted them.

The main reason for the show's cheery quality was Bud himself and his radio personality. His voice wasn't deep but his style of speaking was warm and reassuring, and he always tried to look on the bright side, even as host of "The Ten o'Clock News" (starting July 1, 1944). On the newscast, Bud played up features and human-interest stories and he skimmed over what he called "the grim stuff." He might devote fifteen seconds to a major earthquake and three minutes to a story about a chimpanzee whose finger paintings had been exhibited at a New York gallery and fooled all the critics. His approach offended a few listeners ("the *New York Times* crowd," he called them), but most people liked it. Bud pulled in fifty or sixty fan letters a week, more than all other WLT newscasters combined.

After reading a few headlines, he'd say, "Oh, here's something you might be interested in," and he'd tell about a dog that had actually learned to sing and sing on key, or read a story about the world's largest known tomato, or about a three-year-old kid who was a whiz at chess; and then he'd talk about a dog that *he* knew, or a kid *he* knew, or a tomato *he* had seen, and then he'd say, "Well, I don't know. Let me know what *you* think."

At first, some letters said, "What happened to the news?" but they quickly dwindled. ("Anger doesn't last," Roy Jr. said. "Only love is lasting. Angry people spout off once and then get over it. The people who

love you are loyal to the end.") Most of the letters were about a story Bud
had read: the letter writer described a similar experience that *he* had had,
or quoted a poem or a saying that the story had reminded *her* of—and
Bud made sure to read every one of those letters on the air. One day in
the winter of 1950, Roy Jr. said, "It's time to close down the News. You
need a new shingle."

According to Bud, the Tip-Top Club was the idea of a woman in
St. Paul. "We love your show," she wrote in January 1951, "and feel that
truly it is our show too. When I listen, as I do every night, I feel as if
I am among friends and we are all members of a club that gathers around
our radios. We share ideas and experiences, we inspire each other with
beautiful thoughts, and I only wish I could meet personally every one of
the wonderful people who also write to you, for when they write to you,
they are truly writing to me also."

Bud read her letter on the air, and listeners responded favorably to
the idea of a club. (Since he had often referred to his stories as "News-
Toppers," Bud suggested the name Tip-Top Club and it stuck.)

Nobody at WLT quite remembers who came up with the phone idea.
WLT had been doing remote broadcasts over telephone lines for years, starting with the "WLT Barn Dance and Bean Feed" in 1938; all that needed
to be done to put a telephone signal on the air was wrap the bare end
of one wire around the bare end of another. One night, Bud's engineer,
Harlan, did just that, and a woman's voice came on describing dark thun-
derstorm clouds moving east toward Minneapolis.

"Is it raining there yet?" asked Bud.

"No," she said, "but it will be, any minute now. But I've got my
boots on!"

Roy Jr. was leery of the phone idea from the start. "Every foul-mouth
in town will be slobbering into his telephone for the chance to get on
the air," he told Bud. "Every creep who writes on toilet walls, every dummy,
every drunken son-of-a-bitch from hell to breakfast. We'll be running a
nuthouse. We'll lose our license in a week."

Then Harlan came forward with his tape loop. Harlan was one who
seldom cracked a smile, but when WLT bought its first tape recorders,
two big Ampexes, in 1949, he was like a boy with a new toy. He recorded
everything on tape, and he played around with it, and his favorite game
was to play around with Bud's voice. At first, he got a kick out of playing
Bud's voice at a faster speed so he sounded like a hysterical woman; then
backward, which sounded like Russian; then slower, so Bud sounded drunk;
and then Harlan became fascinated with editing Bud. With a razor blade
in hand, Harlan went through thousands of feet of Bud tape, finding a
word here and a word there, and a vowel sound here and a consonant
there, making new words, and snipping and splicing hundreds of little bits
of tape to form a few sentences spoken in Bud's own voice, in which Bud

spoke, in his own warm and reassuring tones, about having carnal relations with dogs, cats, tomatoes, small boys, chimpanzees, overshoes, fruit jars, lawn mowers. It was disgusting, and also an amazing feat of patience. In two years, Harlan assembled just three minutes of Bud.

Harlan solved the problem of loonies by the simple trick of threading a continuous loop of tape through two machines sitting side by side. Bud and his telephone caller could be recorded on the first machine, which fed the tape into the second machine, which played it back on the air three seconds later. If the caller said anything not befitting the show, Harlan, listening to the first machine, would have three seconds in which to turn off the second. "Can't beat it," said Harlan. "I hit the button and they die like rats."

Nevertheless, Roy Jr. was on hand for the first taped show and supervised the Stop button personally. "I trust you," he told Harlan, "but the way you talk, you might not notice profanity until it is too late." Bud explained the tape loop on the air and invited calls as Roy Jr. hunched over the machine, his finger in position, like a ship's gunner waiting for incoming aircraft. The first caller was a man who wanted to know more about the loop and if it might have useful applications in the home. He got flustered in mid-call and stopped. On his radio at home, he heard his own voice, delayed by tape, saying what he had said three seconds before. "Please turn your radio down," Bud said. It was a line that he was to repeat thousands of times in the next eighteen years.

"This has been an historic event," Roy Jr. said proudly when the show was over. He had cut off just two calls, the first one after the words "What in hell—" and the second at the mention of the Pope ("Probably nothing, but I wasn't about to take chances," he explained to Harlan).

Most of the calls were about the tape loop, with all callers favoring its use, howbeit with some trepidation that a mechanical failure or employee carelessness might lead to tragedy. Several were worried that certain persons might try to fool Bud, opening their calls with a few innocuous remarks and then slipping in a fast one. ("Thanks for the tip," said Bud. "I'm confident we can handle them.")

Communists, people agreed, might be particularly adept at subverting the tape loop. Communists, one man reported, learned these techniques at special schools, including how to insinuate their beliefs into a conversation without anyone being the wiser. ("Appreciate your concern, sir, and, believe me, we'll be on guard.")

It was three weeks before Roy Jr. turned over the guard duty to Harlan and Alice the switchboard girl. Alice was to screen all callers: no kids, no foreign accents, and nobody who seemed unusually intense or determined to get on the air. Harlan was the second line of defense. Roy Jr. instructed him to listen carefully to each call and try to anticipate what the caller was driving at; and if the conversation should drift toward deep waters—hit the button. No politics. No religion except for general belief in the Almighty, thankfulness for His gifts, wonder at His creation, etc. No criticism of others, not even the caller's kith and kin. Roy Jr. didn't want them to get dragged into family squabbles and maybe have to give equal time to a miffed husband or mother-in-law giving *their* side of it. No promotion of products, services, clubs, fund drives, or events.

"What's left to talk about?" Harlan wondered. "Not a goddamn helluva lot."

And, at first, the Tip-Toppers seemed unsure of what to talk about too. "Just thought I'd call and say hi," one would say. "Great. What are you doing tonight?" Bud would ask. "Oh, not much," the caller would reply. "Just sitting here listening to the show."

Gradually, though, they loosened up, and when Bud said to a caller, "Tell me about yourself," the caller generally did. Most Tip-Toppers seemed to be older persons leading quiet lives and keeping busy with hobbies and children and grandchildren, and, judging from the interest in household hints, their homes were neat as a pin and in good repair. They were unfailingly courteous ("The distinguished gentleman who spoke earlier on cats was very well-informed on most points, but I feel he may have overlooked the fact that cats will not shed if brushed regularly"), and soon Harlan was taking his finger off the button and relaxing in the control room and even leaving for a smoke now and then. The few nuts who called in Alice soon recognized by voice—she enjoyed talking with them, and after a few conversations they always asked for her and not for Bud. They sent her gifts, usually pamphlets or books but occasionally a box of cookies or a cake, which, on Harlan's advice, she did not eat. Three months went by, and not a single nut got past the loop; Roy Jr. raised Bud's salary and even gave him a contract—six months with an option of renewing for three more.

"It is so pleasant in this day and age when we are subjected to so much dissension and mud-slinging to take a rest and listen to a show that follows the old adage 'If you can't say something nice, don't say anything at all,'" a woman wrote to Bud. "I am a faithful listener-in and now have a telephone in my bedroom so that I can participate after turning in. I go to sleep listening to the show, and I believe I sleep better knowing it is there."

Sleep was a major item on the Tip-Top agenda: how much is needed? how to get it? what position is best? Many scorned the eight-hour quota as wasteful and self-indulgent and said four or five is enough for any adult. "The secret of longevity is to stay out of bed," said one oldster.

Most members disagreed; they felt they needed more sleep, and one call asking for a cure for insomnia would set off an avalanche of sleep tips—warm milk, a hot bath, a brisk walk, a brief prayer, a mild barbiturate—each of which had gotten the caller through some difficult nights. A doctor (he called in often, usually to settle somebody's hash on the value of vitamins, chiropractic medicine, and vegetarian diets) offered the opinion that worry causes 95 percent of all sleeplessness. He suggested that Tip-Toppers who go to bed with restless thoughts should fill their minds instead with pleasant memories and plans for vacations.

As for vacations, there were strong voices in the Club who argued that a Minnesotan's vacation money should be kept at home, not spent abroad. The rest of the world, it was said, could be seen perfectly well in the pages of the *National Geographic.* There was general agreement, however, that the purpose of a vacation is to rest and enjoy yourself and not necessarily to visit family members or to catch up on work around the house.

Housework was important, though, a sure antidote for grief and worry and feeling sorry for yourself. To scrub a floor or paint a wall or make a pie was better than going to a psychiatrist. At the same time, there was no use taking more time than necessary to get the job done, and every job had its shortcuts. "What's a quick way to get bubble gum out of hair?" a woman would ask, and minutes later, a legion of women who had faced that very problem would rally to her side. Give the Club a problem, and in short order the Club solved it, whether it be a wobbly table, a grape-juice stain, or a treacherous stair tread, and then it suggested two or three things you could do in the time you had saved, such as making lovely and useful gifts from egg cartons, Popsicle sticks, and bottle caps.

And then there were hobbies. Bud often asked callers, particularly the shyer ones, to talk about their hobbies. He *never* asked about their occupations, not after the first few times: the answers were always apologetic-sounding—"Oh, I'm just a truck driver," or "Oh, I just work for the Post Office." But ask someone what he did in his spare time and the answer might be good for five or ten minutes.

Club members tended to be collectors. It seemed as if every object of which there was more than one sort, type, shape, brand, color, or configuration was the object of some collector's affection. "I have match-book covers from more than thirty-five countries." "Some of my fruit jars have been appraised at ten dollars and more." "I hope someday to open a license-plate museum." "I plan to donate my nails to the historical society."

Bird-watching, a sort of collecting, was also popular, and Bud had to put a damper on the bird people, they were so fanatical. One might call in and say, "I wonder if anyone out there can help me identify a bird I heard this morning. Its call sounded something like this—" and then whistle, *"twee-twee, twee-twee,"* and suddenly Alice was swamped with calls, some identifying the bird, some saying they had heard it too and didn't know what it was either, and others wondering if the bird's call perhaps wasn't more of a *"twee-it, twee-it."*

Five nights a week, from 10:00 P.M. to sign-off, Bud sat in Studio B behind a table, the earphones clamped on, and scribbled notes on a pad as one Tip-Topper after another poured it out. After the first few months of the tape loop, he quit reading news stories, and after the Club had hit full stride, telephonically speaking, he himself said very little, aside from an occasional question. He became a listener. For eighteen years, from 1951 to 1969, he sat in the same chair, in the same position (slightly hunched, head down and supported with one hand, the other hand writing, feet on the floor), and heard the same stuff, until he seemed to lose whatever personality he had in the beginning. He became neutral. "A goddamn ghost," Harlan said. "When he comes in, I don't even see him anymore. He don't really exist, except on the air."

At the age of sixty-five, he quietly retired. He didn't mention his retirement on "The Tip-Top Club." Tip-Toppers didn't know he was gone until they tuned in one night and heart Wayne Bargy. Wayne was the only WLT announcer willing to take the show. Others had subbed for Bud before when he took vacations and they noted a certain snideness, a meanness, among the Tip-Toppers, who implied in their conversations that the new man, while adequate, was certainly no Bud. "Bud would *know* that," a caller might say. "Bud wouldn't have said that." "Maybe I'll talk to Bud about it. When is Bud coming back?"

So one night out of the clear blue it was "The Tip-Top Club with Wayne Bargy," and one can only imagine the shock that Bud's fans felt to hear a new theme song (Simon and Garfunkel's "Sounds of Silence") instead of the old Tip-Top song, and then Wayne Bargy delivering a tribute to Bud as if Bud were dead. He called him "an innovator" and "a genius" and "a man who was totally concerned about others." "I loved him," said Wayne. "He was a totally understanding, giving type of man. He was someone I could always talk to about my problems."

"Friends, I know you're as disappointed as I am that Bud won't be here with us anymore, and let me tell you, I'd give anything if he were, and I want to be honest with you and admit that I've never done this type of show before and I don't know how good I am at talking with people, and maybe some of you will even wonder what I'm doing in the radio business and I have to admit that you may have a point there, but I would rather be honest about this than sit here and pretend that I'm somebody that I'm not, because I think that honesty has a place in radio, I don't think a radio personality has to be some sort of star or an idol or anything, I think he can be a real person, and even if I should fail and would quit this show tomorrow, I'd still be satisfied knowing I had done it my way and not tried to be like somebody else."

The Tip-Toppers heard him out; there was a minute or so of lull at the switchboard (perhaps they were too dazed to dial, or else they were composing carefully what they would say); and then the first wave struck. Even Harlan was surprised by the abuse Wayne got.

First call: "Why wait until tomorrow? Why not quit tonight?" (Wayne: "Thanks for calling.") A man said: "Oh, don't worry that we'll consider you a star, Wayne. Don't worry about that for one minute!" (Wayne: "Okay, I won't.") A woman said it was the worst night of her life. (Wayne: "It's hard for all of us.") "You make me absolutely sick. You're the biggest mistake they've made down there!" ("I appreciate your honesty, sir. I don't necessarily agree with that statement, but I think it's important that you feel you can be honest with me.")

By midnight, Wayne had logged almost a hundred calls, most of them quite brief and most cut off by Harlan. The longest exchange was with a woman who wanted to know where Bud was. Wayne said that Bud had retired.

> SHE: Then I'd like his number.
> HE: I'm sorry?
> SHE: I want Bud's phone number.
> HE: I—ma'am, I wish I could give you that but I can't, it's against company policy. We don't give out announcers' home numbers to the general public.
> SHE: Well, *I'm* not the general public. I'm Grace Ritter and he knows me even if you don't.
> HE: I'm sorry, but—
> SHE: And this is his show, and I think he has a right to know what you're doing to it! (CLICK)

During the midnight newscast, Roy Jr. called and told Wayne he was doing great. "I knew it'd be tough sledding the first night," he said, "but you stick in there. They're sore about Bud, but in three weeks they'll get tired and give up and all you'll get is flowers."

It didn't work that way. For one thing, Wayne had little interest in the old Tip-Top topics. He was divorced and lived in an efficiency apartment (no lawn to keep up, no maintenance responsibilities) and had no pets or children. His major interest was psychology. "People fascinate me," he said. ("You don't fascinate *me*," someone said.) He read psychology books and talked about them on the air. He said that he was undergoing therapy, and it had helped him to understand himself better. ("What's to understand?")

His other interests were eating out in foreign restaurants, attending films, and planning a trip to the Far East. ("How about leaving tomorrow?") Occasionally, he got a friendly caller who also liked Szechuan cuisine or Carl Rogers or Woody Allen movies, and he reached out and hung onto that call for dear life. Those calls would last for fifteen, twenty minutes, as if the caller were an old college chum he hadn't heard from in ages, but when he hung up, the Tip-Toppers were waiting, more determined than ever.

> THEM: This show is so boring. You talk about stuff that nobody but you is interested in.

HIM: I really think you're mistaken about that, at least I hope you are, but more importantly, I think that I would have no business being here if I *didn't* talk about things that interest me, because, when all is said and done, I do have to be myself.

THEM: That's the problem, Wayne. Yourself. You're dull.

HIM: Well, I grant you I'm not slick or polished, and I'm not a comedian, but that's not my job. Basically, I'm a communicator, and whatever my faults or failures in relating to people, I do try to be positive.

THEM: You're positively boring.

HIM: Well, let's talk about that. Define your terms. What do you mean by "boring"?

What they meant was Wayne Bargy. For all he said about keeping an open mind ("You got a hole in your head, Wayne!") and not condemning others but trying to understand people who may be different from ourselves ("You're different from everybody, Wayne! You're a different species!"), the Club kept a united front against him.

One night, Wayne casually mentioned that it was his first anniversary hosting the show. The switchboard sizzled. One man said it was time for Club members to take action, and before Harlan could cut him off he announced a time and place for the meeting.

Word came back that the Tip-Toppers had elected officers and were putting together a mailing list for a monthly newsletter. It was said the Club was assigning members to "listening squads" with each squad assigned two hours of "Wayne duty" a week. The squad members were responsible for listening to the show and calling in frequently. The newsletter printed a list of things to say.

It was harder on Harlan than on Wayne. Harlan had started to assemble a special Wayne Bargy tape, but he had no time to work on it. What with Wayne giving out the phone number every fifteen minutes, the show was attracting oddballs, in addition to the legions of Tip-Toppers, and Harlan was cutting calls off the air by the dozens. One night, after Wayne had talked about his divorce (he said that he and his wife didn't "relate to each other sexually"), there passed a long half hour during which no call was fit to broadcast. "I was slapping them down like barnyard flies. We were up to our ears in crazies," said Harlan. "Finally, my fingers got sore, and Alice pulled the plug on the switchboard and her and me sat down and had a cup of coffee and left that poor dumb SOB sit and die by himself."

Wayne talked a long time that night. He said he'd had a typical middle-class upbringing until he went to college, which opened his mind up to new possibilities. He said he had gone into radio because it had tremendous possibilities for creative communication. This show was a tremendous opportunity to get people to open up their minds. He viewed himself as an educator of sorts.

"I'll be honest," he said. "The past year has been rough. There's a lot of anger and violence out there—and I don't say people shouldn't feel that way, but I do feel people should be willing to change. Life is change. We all change. I've changed. Frankly, when I started doing this show, I didn't come off very well. I didn't communicate well. I had a hard time relating to working-class people. I think I've improved. I'm learning. I've put my feelings on the line, and I've benefited from it. I'm going to keep on trying."

He did keep on trying, and the Tip-Toppers kept calling—"We won't go away, Wayne!" they said, and he said, "I don't want you to go away. I want you to stay and let's get to know each other." That summer WLT did a survey that showed that most of the Tip-Top Club audience was over forty (72 percent), the least desirable age group to advertisers, and in July the station switched the Tip-Top slot to what it called "a modified middle-of-the-road pop-rock format" with a disc jockey who never talked except to give time, temperature, and commercials. His name was Michael Keske, but he never said it on the air.

[1981]

José Armas (American; b. 1944)

El Tonto del Barrio[1]

Romero Estrado was called "El Cotoro"[2] because he was always whistling and singing. He made nice music even though his songs were spontaneous compositions made up of words with sounds that he liked but which seldom made any sense. But that didn't seem to bother either Romero or anyone else in the Golden Heights Centro where he lived. Not even the kids made fun of him. It just was not permitted.

Romero had a ritual that he followed almost every day. After breakfast he would get his broom and go up and down the main street of the Golden Heights Centro whistling and singing and sweeping the sidewalks for all the businesses. He would sweep in front of the Tortillería America,[3] the XXX Liquor Store, the Tres Milpas[4] Bar run by Tino Gabaldon, Barelas' Barber Shop, the used furniture store owned by Goldstein, El Centro Market of the Avila family, the Model Cities Office, and Lourdes Printing Store.

---

[1] **El Tonto del Barrio**   the barrio dummy (in the United States, a barrio is a Spanish-speaking community)
[2] **El Cotoro**   The Parrot
[3] **Tortillería America**   America Tortilla Factory
[4] **Tres Milpas**   Three Cornfields

Then, in the afternoons, he would come back and sit in Barelas' Barber Shop and spend the day looking at magazines and watching and waving to the passing people as he sang and composed his songs without a care in the world.

When business was slow, Barelas would let him sit in the barber's chair. Romero loved it. It was a routine that Romero kept every day except Sundays and Mondays when Barelas' Barber Shop was closed. After a period of years, people in the barrio got used to seeing Romero do his little task of sweeping the sidewalks and sitting in Barelas' Barber Shop. If he didn't show up one day someone assumed the responsibility to go to his house to see if he was ill. People would stop to say hello to Romero on the street and although he never initiated a conversation while he was sober, he always smiled and responded cheerfully to everyone. People passing the barber shop in the afternoons made it a point to wave even though they couldn't see him; they knew he was in there and was expecting some salutation.

When he was feeling real good, Romero would sweep in front of the houses on both sides of the block also. He took his job seriously and took great care to sweep cleanly, between the cracks and even between the sides of buildings. The dirt and small scraps went into the gutter. The bottles and bigger pieces of litter were put carefully in cardboard boxes, ready for the garbage man.

If he did it the way he wanted, the work took him the whole morning. And always cheerful—always with some song.

Only once did someone call attention to his work. Frank Avila told him in jest that Romero had forgotten to pick up an empty bottle of wine from his door. Romero was so offended and made such a commotion that it got around very quickly that no one should criticize his work. There was, in fact, no reason to.

Although it had been long acknowledged that Romero was a little "touched," he fit very well into the community. He was a respected citizen.

He could be found at the Tres Milpas Bar drinking his occasional beer in the evenings. Romero had a rivalry going with the Ranchera songs on the jukebox. He would try to outsing the songs using the same melody but inserting his own selection of random words. Sometimes, like all people, he would "bust out" and get drunk.

One could always tell when Romero was getting drunk because he would begin telling everyone that he loved them.

"I looov youuu," he would sing to someone and offer to compose them a song.

"Ta bueno, Romero. Ta bueno, ya bete,"[5] they would tell him.

Sometimes when he got too drunk he would crap in his pants and then Tino would make him go home.

[5]**Ta bueno, ya bete**   OK, now go away

Romero received some money from Social Security but it wasn't much. None of the merchants gave him any credit because he would always forget to pay his bills. He didn't do it on purpose, he just forgot and spent his money on something else. So instead, the businessmen preferred to do little things for him occasionally. Barelas would trim his hair when things were slow. The Tortillería America would give him menudo[6] and fresh-made tortillas at noon when he was finished with his sweeping. El Centro Market would give him the overripe fruit and broken boxes of food that no one else would buy. Although it was unspoken and unwritten, there was an agreement that existed between Romero and the Golden Heights Centro. Romero kept the sidewalks clean and the barrio looked after him. It was a contract that worked well for a long time.

Then, when Seferino, Barelas' oldest son, graduated from high school he went to work in the barber shop for the summer. Seferino was a conscientious and sensitive young man and it wasn't long before he took notice of Romero and came to feel sorry for him.

One day when Romero was in the shop Seferino decided to act.

"Mira, Romero. Yo te doy 50 centavos por cada dia que me barres la banqueta. Fifty cents for every day you sweep the sidewalk for us. Qué te parece?"[7]

Romero thought about it carefully.

"Hecho! Done!" he exclaimed. He started for home right away to get his broom.

"Why did you do that for, m'ijo?"[8] asked Barelas.

"It don't seem right, Dad. The man works and no one pays him for his work. Everyone should get paid for what they do."

"He don't need no pay. Romero has everything he needs."

"It's not the same, Dad. How would you like to do what he does and be treated the same way? It's degrading the way he has to go around getting scraps and handouts."

"I'm not Romero. Besides you don't know about these things, m'ijo. Romero would be unhappy if his schedule was upset. Right now everyone likes him and takes care of him. He sweeps the sidewalks because he wants something to do, not because he wants money."

"I'll pay him out of my money, don't worry about it then."

"The money is not the point. The point is that money will not help Romero. Don't you understand that?"

"Look, Dad. Just put yourself in his place. Would you do it? Would you cut hair for nothing?"

Barelas just knew his son was putting something over on him but he didn't know how to answer. It seemed to make sense the way Seferino

[6]**menudo**   tripe soup
[7]**Qué te parece?**   How does that strike you?
[8]**m'ijo** (mi hijo), my son

explained it. But it still went against his "instinct." On the other hand, Seferino had gone and finished high school. He must know something. There were few kids who had finished high school in the barrio, and fewer who had gone to college. Barelas knew them all. He noted (with some pride) that Seferino was going to be enrolled at Harvard University this year. That must count for something, he thought. Barelas himself had never gone to school. So maybe his son had something there. On the other hand . . . it upset Barelas that he wasn't able to get Seferino to see the issue. How can we be so far apart on something so simple, he thought. But he decided not to say anything else about it.

Romero came back right away and swept the front of Barelas' shop again and put what little dirt he found into the curb. He swept up the gutter, put the trash in a shoe box and threw it in a garbage can.

Seferino watched with pride as Romero went about his job and when he was finished he went outside and shook Romero's hand. Seferino told him he had done a good job. Romero beamed.

Manolo was coming into the shop to get his hair cut as Seferino was giving Romero his wages. He noticed Romero with his broom.

"What's going on?" He asked. Barelas shrugged his shoulders. "Qué tiene Romero?[9] Is he sick or something?"

"No, he's not sick," explained Seferino, who had now come inside. He told Manolo the story.

"We're going to make Romero a businessman" said Seferino. "Do you realize how much money Romero would make if everyone paid him just fifty cents a day? Like my dad says, 'Everyone should be able to keep his dignity, no matter how poor.' And he does a job, you know."

"Well, it makes sense," said Manolo.

"Hey. Maybe I'll ask people to do that," said Seferino. "That way the poor old man could make a decent wage. Do you want to help, Manolo? You can go with me to ask people to pay him."

"Well," said Manolo as he glanced at Barelas, "I'm not too good at asking people for money."

This did not discourage Seferino. He went out and contacted all the businesses on his own, but no one else wanted to contribute. This didn't discourage Seferino either. He went on giving Romero fifty cents a day.

After a while, Seferino heard that Romero had asked for credit at the grocery store. "See, Dad. What did I tell you? Things are getting better for him already. He's becoming his own man. And look. It's only been a couple of weeks." Barelas did not reply.

But then the next week Romero did not show up to sweep any sidewalks. He was around but he didn't do any work for anybody the entire week. He walked around Golden Heights Centro in his best gray work

---

[9]**Qué tiene Romero?**   What's with Romero?

pants and his slouch hat, looking important and making it a point to walk right past the barber shop every little while.

Of course, the people in the Golden Heights Centro noticed the change immediately, and since they saw Romero in the street, they knew he wasn't ill. But the change was clearly disturbing the community. They discussed him in the Tortillería America where people got together for coffee, and at the Tres Milpas Bar. Everywhere the topic of conversation was the great change that had come over Romero. Only Barelas did not talk about it.

The following week Romero came into the barber shop and asked to talk with Seferino in private. Barelas knew immediately something was wrong. Romero never initiated a conversation unless he was drunk.

They went into the back room where Barelas could not hear and then Romero informed Seferino, "I want a raise."

"What? What do you mean, a raise? You haven't been around for a week. You only worked a few weeks and now you want a raise?" Seferino was clearly angry but Romero was calm and insistent.

Romero correctly pointed out that he had been sweeping the side-walks for a long time. Even before Seferino finished high school.

"I deserve a raise," he repeated after an eloquent presentation.

Seferino looked coldly at Romero. It was clearly a stand-off.

Then Seferino said, "Look, maybe we should forget the whole thing. I was just trying to help you out and look at what you do."

Romero held his ground. "I helped you out too. No one told me to do it and I did it anyway. I helped you many years."

"Well, let's forget about the whole thing then," said Seferino.

"I quit then," said Romero.

"Quit?" exclaimed Seferino as he laughed at Romero.

"Quit! I quit!" said Romero as he walked out the front of the shop past Barelas who was cutting a customer's hair.

Seferino came out shaking his head and laughing.

"Can you imagine that old guy?"

Barelas did not seem too amused. He felt he could have predicted that something bad like this would happen.

Romero began sweeping the sidewalks again the next day with the exception that when he came to the barber shop he would go around it and continue sweeping the rest of the sidewalks. He did this for the rest of the week. And the following Tuesday he began sweeping the sidewalk all the way up to the shop and then pushing the trash to the sidewalk in front of the barber shop. Romero then stopped coming to the barber shop in the afternoon.

The barrio buzzed with fact and rumor about Romero. Tino commented that Romero was not singing anymore. Even if someone offered to buy him a beer he wouldn't sing. Frank Avila said the neighbors were complaining because he was leaving his TV on loud the whole day and night. He still greeted people but seldom smiled. He had run up a big bill at the liquor store and when the manager stopped his credit, he caught Romero stealing bottles of whiskey. He was also getting careless about his dress. He didn't shave and clean like he used to. Women complained that he walked around in soiled pants, that he smelled bad. Even one of the little kids complained that Romero had kicked his puppy, but that seemed hard to believe.

Barelas felt terrible. He felt responsible. But he couldn't convince Seferino that what he had done was wrong. Barelas himself stopped going to the Tres Milpas Bar after work to avoid hearing about Romero. Once he came across Romero on the street and Barelas said hello but with a sense of guilt. Romero responded, avoiding Barelas' eyes and moving past him awkwardly and quickly. Romero's behavior continued to get erratic and some people started talking about having Romero committed.

"You can't do that," said Barelas when he was presented with a petition.

"He's flipped," said Tino, who made up part of the delegation circulating the petition. "No one likes Romero more than I do, you know that Barelas."

"But he's really crazy," said Frank Avila.

"He was crazy before. No one noticed," pleaded Barelas.

"But it was a crazy we could depend on. Now he just wants to sit on the curb and pull up the women's skirts. It's terrible. The women are going crazy. He's also running into the street stopping the traffic. You see how he is. What choice do we have?"

"It's for his own good," put in one of the workers from the Model Cities Office. Barelas dismissed them as outsiders. Seferino was there and wanted to say something but a look from Barelas stopped him.

"We just can't do that," insisted Barelas. "Let's wait. Maybe he's just going through a cycle. Look. We've had a full moon recently, qué no?[10] That must be it. You know how the moon affects people in his condition."

"I don't know," said Tino. "What if he hurts. . . ."

"He's not going to hurt anyone," cut in Barelas.

"No, Barelas. I was going to say, what if he hurts himself. He has no one at home. I'd say, let him come home with me for a while but you know how stubborn he is. You can't even talk to him any more."

"He gives everyone the finger when they try to pull him out of the traffic," said Frank Avila. "The cops have missed him, but it won't be long before they see him doing some of his antics and arrest him. Then what? Then the poor guy is in real trouble."

"Well, look," said Barelas. "How many names you got on the list?"

Tino responded slowly, "Well, we sort of wanted you to start off the list."

[10]**qué no?**   right?

"Let's wait a while longer," said Barelas. "I just know that Romero will come around. Let's wait just a while, okay?"

No one had the heart to fight the issue and so they postponed the petition.

There was no dramatic change in Romero even though the full moon had completed its cycle. Still, no one initiated the petition again and then in the middle of August Seferino left for Cambridge to look for housing and to register early for school. Suddenly everything began to change again. One day Romero began sweeping the entire sidewalk again. His spirits began to pick up and his strange antics began to disappear.

At the Tortillería America the original committee met for coffee and the talk turned to Romero.

"He's going to be all right now," said a jubilant Barelas. "I guarantee it."

"Well, don't hold your breath yet," said Tino. "The full moon is coming up again."

"Yeah," said Frank Avila dejectedly.

When the next full moon was in force the group was together again drinking coffee and Tino asked, "Well, how's Romero doing?"

Barelas smiled and said, "Well. Singing songs like crazy."

[1982]

Alice Walker (American; b. 1944)

Everyday Use

For your grandmama

I will wait for her in the yard that Maggie and I made so clean and wavy yesterday afternoon. A yard like this is more comfortable than most people know. It is not just a yard. It is like an extended living room. When the hard clay is swept clean as a floor and the fine sand around the edges lined with tiny, irregular grooves anyone can come and sit and look up into the elm tree and wait for the breezes that never come inside the house.

Maggie will be nervous until after her sister goes: she will stand hopelessly in corners homely and ashamed of the burn scars down her arms and legs, eyeing her sister with a mixture of envy and awe. She thinks her sister has held life always in the palm of one hand, that "no" is a word the world never learned to say to her.

You've no doubt seen those TV shows where the child who has "made it" is confronted, as a surprise, by her own mother and father, tottering in weakly from backstage. (A pleasant surprise, of course: What would they do if parent and child came on the show only to curse out and insult each other?) On TV mother and child embrace and smile into each other's faces. Sometimes the mother and father weep, the child wraps them in her arms and leans across the table to tell how she would not have made it without their help. I have seen these programs.

Sometimes I dream a dream in which Dee and I are suddenly brought together on a TV program of this sort. Out of a dark and soft-seated limousine I am ushered into a bright room filled with many people. There I meet a smiling, gray, sporty man like Johnny Carson who shakes my hand and tells me what a fine girl I have. Then we are on the stage and Dee is embracing me with tears in her eyes. She pins on my dress a large orchid, even though she has told me once that she thinks orchids are tacky flowers.

In real life I am large, big-boned woman with rough, man-working hands. In the winter I wear flannel nightgowns to bed and overalls during the day. I can kill and clean a hog as mercilessly as a man. My fat keeps me hot in zero weather. I can work outside all day, breaking ice to get water for washing. I can eat pork liver cooked over the open fire minutes after it comes steaming from the hog. One winter I knocked a bull calf straight in the brain between the eyes with a sledge hammer and had the meat hung up to chill before nightfall. But of course all this does not show on television. I am the way my daughter would want me to be: a hundred pounds lighter, my skin like an uncooked barley pancake. My hair glistens in the hot bright lights. Johnny Carson has much to do to keep up with my quick and witty tongue.

But that is a mistake. I know even before I wake up. Who ever knew a Johnson with a quick tongue? Who can even imagine me looking a strange white man in the eye? It seems to me I have talked to them always with one foot raised in flight, with my head turned in whichever way is farthest from them. Dee, though. She would always look anyone in the eye. Hesitation was no part of her nature.

"How do I look, Mama?" Maggie says, showing just enough of her thin body enveloped in pink skirt and red blouse for me to know she's there, almost hidden by the door.

"Come out into the yard," I say.

Have you ever seen a lame animal, perhaps a dog run over by some careless person rich enough to own a car, sidle up to someone who is ignorant enough to be kind to him? That is the way my Maggie walks. She has been like this, chin on chest, eyes on ground, feet in shuffle, ever since the fire that burned the other house to the ground.

Dee is lighter than Maggie, with nicer hair and a fuller figure. She's a woman now, though sometimes I forget. How long ago was it that the other house burned? Ten, twelve years? Sometimes I can still hear the flames and feel Maggie's arms sticking to me, her hair smoking and her dress falling off her in little black papery flakes. Her eyes seemed stretched open, blazed open by the flames reflected in them. And Dee. I see her standing off under the sweet gum tree she used to dig gum out of; a look of concentration on her face as she watched the last dingy gray board of the house fall in toward the red-hot brick chimney. Why don't you do a dance around the ashes? I'd wanted to ask her. She had hated the house that much.

I used to think she hated Maggie, too. But that was before we raised the money, the church and me, to send her to Augusta to school. She used to read to us without pity; forcing words, lies, other folks' habits, whole lives upon us two, sitting trapped and ignorant underneath her voice. She washed us in a river of make-believe, burned us with a lot of knowledge we didn't necessarily need to know. Pressed us to her with the serious way she read, to shove us away at just the moment, like dimwits, we seemed about to understand.

Dee wanted nice things. A yellow organdy dress to wear to her graduation from high school; black pumps to match a green suit she'd made from an old suit somebody gave me. She was determined to stare down any disaster in her efforts. Her eyelids would not flicker for minutes at a time. Often I fought off the temptation to shake her. At sixteen she had a style of her own: and knew what style was.

I never had an education myself. After second grade the school was closed down. Don't ask me why: in 1927 colored asked fewer questions than they do now. Sometimes Maggie reads to me. She stumbles along good-naturedly but can't see well. She knows she is not bright. Like good looks and money, quickness passed her by. She will marry John Thomas (who has mossy teeth in an earnest face) and then I'll be free to sit here and I guess just sing church songs to myself. Although I never was a good singer. Never could carry a tune. I was always better at a man's job. I used to love to milk till I was hoofed in the side in '49. Cows are soothing and slow and don't bother you, unless you try to milk them the wrong way.

I have deliberately turned my back on the house. It is three rooms, just like the one that burned, except the roof is tin; they don't make shingle roofs any more. There are no real windows, just some holes cut in the sides, like the portholes in a ship, but not round and not square, with rawhide holding the shutters up on the outside. This house is in a pasture, too, like the other one. No doubt when Dee sees it she will want to tear it down. She wrote me once that no matter where we "choose" to live, she will manage to come see us. But she will never bring her friends. Maggie and I thought about this and Maggie asked me, "Mama, when did Dee ever *have* any friends?"

She had a few. Furtive boys in pink shirts hanging about on washday after school. Nervous girls who never laughed. Impressed with her they worshiped the well-turned phrase, the cute shape, the scalding humor that erupted like bubbles in lye. She read to them.

When she was courting Jimmy T she didn't have much time to pay to us, but turned all her faultfinding power on him. He *flew* to marry a cheap gal from a family of ignorant flashy people. She hardly had time to recompose herself.

When she comes I will meet—but there they are!

Maggie attempts to make a dash for the house, in her shuffling way, but I stay her with my hand. "Come back here," I say. And she stops and tries to dig a well in the sand with her toe.

It is hard to see them clearly through the strong sun. But even the first glimpse of leg out of the car tells me it is Dee. Her feet were always neat-looking, as if God himself had shaped them with a certain style. From the other side of the car comes a short, stocky man. Hair is all over his head a foot long and hanging from his chin like a kinky mule tail. I hear Maggie suck in her breath. "Uhnnnh," is what it sounds like. Like when you see the wriggling end of a snake just in front of your foot on the road. "Uhnnnh."

Dee next. A dress down to the ground, in this hot weather. A dress so loud it hurts my eyes. There are yellows and oranges enough to throw back the light of the sun. I feel my whole face warming from the heat waves it throws out. Earrings, too, gold and hanging down to her shoulders. Bracelets dangling and making noises when she moves her arm up to shake the folds of the dress out of her armpits. The dress is loose and flows, and as she walks closer, I like it. I hear Maggie go "Uhnnnh" again. It is her sister's hair. It stands straight up like the wool on a sheep. It is black as night and around the edges are two long pigtails that rope about like small lizards disappearing behind her ears.

"Wa-su-zo-Tean-o!" she says, coming on in that gliding way the dress makes her move. The short stocky fellow with the hair to his navel is all grinning and he follows up with "Asalamalakim, my mother and sister!" He moves to hug Maggie but she falls back, right up against the back of my chair. I feel her trembling there and when I look up I see the perspiration falling off her chin.

"Don't get up," says Dee. Since I am stout it takes something of a push. You can see me trying to move a second or two before I make it. She turns, showing white heels through her sandals, and goes back to the car. Out she peeks next with a Polaroid. She stoops down quickly and lines up picture after picture of me sitting there in front of the house with Maggie cowering behind me. She never takes a shot without making sure the house is included. When a cow comes nibbling around the edge of the yard she snaps it and me and Maggie *and* the house. Then she puts the Polaroid in the back seat of the car, and comes up and kisses me on the forehead.

Meanwhile Asalamalakim is going through the motions with Maggie's hand. Maggie's hand is as limp as a fish, and probably as cold, despite the sweat, and she keeps trying to pull it back. It looks like Asalamalakim wants to shake hands but wants to do it fancy. Or maybe he don't know how people shake hands. Anyhow, he soon gives up on Maggie.

"Well," I say. "Dee."

"No, Mama," she says. "Not 'Dee,' Wangero Leewanika Kemanjo!"

"What happened to 'Dee'?" I wanted to know.

"She's dead," Wangero said. "I couldn't bear it any longer being named after the people who oppress me."

"You know as well as me you was named after your aunt Dicie," I said. Dicie is my sister. She named Dee. We called her "Big Dee" after Dee was born.

"But who was *she* named after?" asked Wangero.

"I guess after Grandma Dee," I said.

"And who was she named after?" asked Wangero.

"Her mother," I said, and saw Wangero was getting tired. "That's about as far back as I can trace it," I said. Though, in fact, I probably could have carried it back beyond the Civil War through the branches.

"Well," said Asalamalakim, "there you are."

"Uhnnnh," I heard Maggie say.

"There I was not," I said, "before 'Dicie' cropped up in our family, so why should I try to trace it that far back?"

He just stood there grinning, looking down on me like somebody inspecting a Model A car. Every once in a while he and Wangero sent eye signals over my head.

"How do you pronounce this name?" I asked.

"You don't have to call me by it if you don't want to," said Wangero.

"Why shouldn't I?" I asked. "If that's what you want us to call you, we'll call you."

"I know it might sound awkward at first," said Wangero.

"I'll get used to it," I said. "Ream it out again."

Well, soon we got the name out of the way. Asalamalakim had a name twice as long and three times as hard. After I tripped over it two or three times he told me to just to call him Hakim-a-barber. I wanted to ask him was he a barber, but I didn't really think he was, so I didn't ask.

"You must belong to those beef-cattle peoples down the road," I said. They said "Asalamalakim" when they met you, too, but they didn't shake hands. Always too busy: feeding the cattle, fixing the fences, putting up salt-lick shelters, throwing down hay. When the white folks poisoned some of the herd the men stayed up all night with rifles in their hands. I walked a mile and a half just to see the sight.

Hakim-a-barber said, "I accept some of their doctrines, but farming and raising cattle is not my style." (They didn't tell me, and I didn't ask, whether Wangero [Dee] had really gone and married him.)

We sat down to eat and right away he said he didn't eat collards and pork was unclean. Wangero, though, went on through the chitlins and corn bread, the greens and everything else. She talked a blue streak over the sweet potatoes. Everything delighted her. Even the fact that we still used the benches her daddy made for the table when we couldn't afford to buy chairs.

"Oh, Mama!" she cried. Then turned to Hakim-a-barber. "I never knew how lovely these benches are. You can feel the rump prints," she said, running her hands underneath her and along the bench. Then she gave a sigh and her hand closed over Grandma Dee's butter dish. "That's it!" she said. "I knew there was something I wanted to ask you if I could have." She jumped up from the table and went over in the corner where the churn stood, the milk in it clabber by now. She looked at the churn and looked at it.

"This churn top is what I need," she said. "Didn't Uncle Buddy whittle it out of a tree you all used to have?"

"Yes," I said.

"Uh huh," she said happily. "And I want the dasher, too."

"Uncle Buddy whittle that, too?" asked the barber.

Dee (Wangero) looked up at me.

"Aunt Dee's first husband whittled the dash," said Maggie so low you almost couldn't hear her. "His name was Henry, but they called him Stash."

"Maggie's brain is like an elephant's," Wangero said, laughing. "I can use the churn top as a centerpiece for the alcove table," she said, sliding a plate over the churn, "and I'll think of something artistic to do with the dasher."

When she finished wrapping the dasher the handle stuck out. I took it for a moment in my hands. You didn't even have to look close to see where hands pushing the dasher up and down to make butter had left a kind of sink in the wood. In fact, there were a lot of small sinks; you could see where thumbs and fingers had sunk into the wood. It was beautiful light yellow wood, from a tree that grew in the yard where Big Dee and Stash had lived.

After dinner Dee (Wangero) went to the trunk at the foot of my bed and started rifling through it. Maggie hung back in the kitchen over the dishpan. Out came Wangero with two quilts. They had been pieced by Grandma Dee and then Big Dee and me had hung them on the quilt frames on the front porch and quilted them. One was in the Lone Star pattern. The other was Walk Around the Mountain. In both of them were scraps of dresses Grandma Dee had worn fifty and more years ago. Bits and pieces of Grandpa Jarrell's paisley shirts. And one teeny faded blue piece, about the piece of a penny matchbox, that was from Great Grandpa Ezra's uniform that he wore in the Civil War.

"Mama," Wangero said sweet as a bird. "Can I have these old quilts?"

I heard something fall in the kitchen, and a minute later the kitchen door slammed.

"Why don't you take one or two of the others?" I asked. "These old things was just done by me and Big Dee from some tops your grandma pieced before she died."

"No," said Wangero. "I don't want those. They are stitched around the borders by machine."

"That's make them last better," I said.

"That's not the point," said Wangero. "These are all pieces of dresses Grandma used to wear. She did all this stitching by hand. Imagine!" She held the quilts securely in her arms, stroking them.

"Some of the pieces, like those lavender ones, come from old clothes her mother handed down to her," I said, moving up to touch the quilts. Dee (Wangero) moved back just enough so that I couldn't reach the quilts. They already belonged to her.

"Imagine!" she breathed again, clutching them closely to her bosom.

"The truth is," I said, "I promised to give them quilts to Maggie, for when she marries John Thomas."

She gasped like a bee had stung her.

"Maggie can't appreciate these quilts!" she said. "She'd probably be backward enough to put them to everyday use."

"I reckon she would," I said. "God knows I been saving 'em for long enough with nobody using 'em. I hope she will!" I didn't want to bring up how I had offered Dee (Wangero) a quilt when she went away to college. Then she had told me they were old-fashioned, out of style.

"But they're *priceless!*" she was saying now, furiously; for she has a temper. "Maggie would put them on the bed and in five years they'd be in rags. Less than that!"

"She can always make some more," I said. "Maggie knows how to quilt."

Dee (Wangero) looked at me with hatred. "You just will not understand. The point is these quilts, *these* quilts!"

"Well," I said, stumped. "What would *you* do with them?"

"Hang them," she said. As if that was the only thing you *could* do with quilts.

Maggie by now was standing in the door. I could almost hear the sound her feet made as they scraped over each other.

"She can have them, Mama," she said, like somebody used to never winning anything, or having anything reserved for her. "I can 'member Grandma Dee without the quilts."

I looked at her hard. She had filled her bottom lip with checkerberry snuff and it gave her face a kind of dopey, hangdog look. It was Grandma Dee and Big Dee who taught her how to quilt herself. She stood there with her scarred hands hidden in the folds of her skirt. She looked at her sister with something like fear but she wasn't mad at her. This was Maggie's portion. This was the way she knew God to work.

When I looked at her like that something hit me in the top of my head and ran down to the soles of my feet. Just like when I'm in church and the spirit of God touches me and I get happy and shout. I did something I never had done before: hugged Maggie to me, then dragged her on into the room, snatched the quilts out of Miss Wangero's hands and dumped them into Maggie's lap. Maggie just sat there on my bed with her mouth open.

"Take one or two of the others," I said to Dee.

But she turned without a word and went out to Hakim-a-barber.

"You just don't understand," she said, as Maggie and I came out to the car.

"What don't I understand?" I wanted to know.

"Your heritage," she said. And then she turned to Maggie, kissed her, and said, "You ought to try to make something of yourself, too, Maggie. It's really a new day for us. But from the way you and Mama still live you'd never know it."

She put on some sunglasses that hid everything above the tip of her nose and her chin.

Maggie smiled; maybe at the sunglasses. But a real smile, not scared. After we watched the car dust settle I asked Maggie to bring me a dip of snuff. And then the two of us sat there just enjoying, until it was time to go in the house and go to bed.

[1973]

Tim O'Brien (American; b. 1947)

The Things They Carried

First Lieutenant Jimmy Cross carried letters from a girl named Martha, a junior at Mount Sebastian College in New Jersey. They were not love letters, but Lieutenant Cross was hoping, so he kept them folded in plastic at the bottom of his rucksack. In the late afternoon, after a day's march, he would dig his foxhole, wash his hands under a canteen, unwrap the letters, hold them with the tips of his fingers, and spend the last hour of light pretending. He would imagine romantic camping trips into the White Mountains in New Hampshire. He would sometimes taste the envelope flaps, knowing her tongue had been there. More than anything, he wanted

Martha to love him as he loved her, but the letters were mostly chatty, elusive on the matter of love. She was a virgin, he was almost sure. She was an English major at Mount Sebastian, and she wrote beautifully about her professors and roommates and midterm exams, about her respect for Chaucer and her great affection for Virginia Woolf. She often quoted lines of poetry; she never mentioned the war, except to say, Jimmy, take care of yourself. The letters weighed ten ounces. They were signed "Love, Martha," but Lieutenant Cross understood that Love was only a way of signing and did not mean what he sometimes pretended it meant. At dusk, he would carefully return the letters to his rucksack. Slowly, a bit distracted, he would get up and move among his men, checking the perimeter, then at full dark he would return to his hole and watch the night and wonder if Martha was a virgin.

The things they carried were largely determined by necessity. Among the necessities or near-necessities were P-38 can openers, pocket knives, heat tabs, wrist watches, dog tags, mosquito repellent, chewing gum, candy, cigarettes, salt tablets, packets of Kool-Aid, lighters, matches, sewing kits, Military Payment Certificates, C rations, and two or three canteens of water. Together, these items weighed between fifteen and twenty pounds, depending upon a man's habits or rate of metabolism. Henry Dobbins, who was a big man, carried extra rations; he was especially fond of canned peaches in heavy syrup over pound cake. Dave Jensen, who practiced field hygiene, carried a toothbrush, dental floss, and several hotel-size bars of soap he'd stolen on R&R[1] in Sydney, Australia. Ted Lavender, who was scared, carried tranquilizers until he was shot in the head outside the village of Than Khe in mid-April. By necessity, and because it was SOP,[2] they all carried steel helmets that weighed five pounds including the liner and camouflage cover. They carried the standard fatigue jackets and trousers. Very few carried underwear. On their feet they carried jungle boots — 2.1 pounds — and Dave Jensen carried three pairs of socks and a can of Dr. Scholl's foot powder as a precaution against trench foot. Until he was shot, Ted Lavender carried six or seven ounces of premium dope, which for him was a necessity. Mitchell Sanders, the RTO,[3] carried condoms. Norman Bowker carried a diary. Rat Kiley carried comic books. Kiowa, a devout Baptist, carried an illustrated New Testament that had been presented to him by his father, who taught Sunday school in Oklahoma City, Oklahoma. As a hedge against bad times, however, Kiowa also carried his grandmother's distrust of the white man, his grandfather's old hunting hatchet. Necessity dictated. Because the land was mined and booby-trapped, it was SOP for each man to carry a steel-centered, nylon-covered flak jacket,

[1]**R&R**   rest and rehabilitation leave
[2]**SOP**   standard operating procedure
[3]**RTO**   radio and telphone operator

which weighed 6.7 pounds, but which on hot days seemed much heavier. Because you could die so quickly, each man carried at least one large compress bandage, usually in the helmet band for easy access. Because the nights were cold, and because the monsoons were wet, each carried a green plastic poncho that could be used as a raincoat or groundsheet or makeshift tent. With its quilted liner, the poncho weighed almost two pounds, but it was worth every ounce. In April, for instance, when Ted Lavender was shot, they used his poncho to wrap him up, then to carry him across the paddy, then to lift him into the chopper that took him away.

They were called legs or grunts.

To carry something was to "hump" it, as when Lieutenant Jimmy Cross humped his love for Martha up the hills and through the swamps. In its intransitive form, "to hump" meant "to walk," or "to march," but it implied burdens far beyond the intransitive.

Almost everyone humped photographs. In his wallet, Lieutenant Cross carried two photographs of Martha. The first was a Kodachrome snapshot signed "Love," though he knew better. She stood against a brick wall. Her eyes were gray and neutral, her lips slightly open as she stared straight-on at the camera. At night, sometimes, Lieutenant Cross wondered who had taken the picture, because he knew she had boyfriends, because he loved her so much, and because he could see the shadow of the picture taker spreading out against the brick wall. The second photograph had been clipped from the 1968 Mount Sebastian yearbook. It was an action shot—women's volleyball—and Martha was bent horizontal to the floor, reaching, the palms of her hands in sharp focus, the tongue taut, the expression frank and competitive. There was no visible sweat. She wore white gym shorts. Her legs, he thought, were almost certainly the legs of a virgin, dry and without hair, the left knee cocked and carrying her entire weight, which was just over one hundred pounds. Lieutenant Cross remembered touching that left knee. A dark theater, he remembered, and the movie was *Bonnie and Clyde,* and Martha wore a tweed skirt, and during the final scene, when he touched her knee, she turned and looked at him in a sad, sober way that made him pull his hand back, but he would always remember the feel of the tweed skirt and the knee beneath it and the sound of the gunfire that killed Bonnie and Clyde, how embarrassing it was, how slow and oppressive. He remembered kissing her goodnight at the dorm door. Right then, he thought, he should've done something brave. He should've carried her up the stairs to her room and tied her to the bed and touched that left knee all night long. He should've risked it. Whenever he looked at the photographs, he thought of new things he should've done.

What they carried was partly a function of rank, partly of field specialty.

As a first lieutenant and platoon leader, Jimmy Cross carried a compass, maps, code books, binoculars, and a .45-caliber pistol that weighed 2.9 pounds fully loaded. He carried a strobe light and the responsibility for the lives of his men.

As an RTO, Mitchell Sanders carried the PRC-25 radio, a killer, twenty-six pounds with its battery.

As a medic, Rat Kiley carried a canvas satchel filled with morphine and plasma and malaria tablets and surgical tape and comic books and all the things a medic must carry, including M&M's[4] for especially bad wounds, for a total weight of nearly twenty pounds.

As a big man, therefore a machine gunner, Henry Dobbins carried the M-60, which weighed twenty-three pounds unloaded, but which was almost always loaded. In addition, Dobbins carried between ten and fifteen pounds of ammunition draped in belts across his chest and shoulders.

As PFCs or Spec 4s, most of them were common grunts and carried the standard M-16 gas-operated assault rifle. The weapon weighed 7.5 pounds unloaded, 8.2 pounds with its full twenty-round magazine. Depending on numerous factors, such as topography and psychology, the riflemen carried anywhere from twelve to twenty magazines, usually in cloth bandoliers, adding on another 8.4 pounds at minimum, fourteen pounds at maximum. When it was available, they also carried M-16 maintenance gear — rods and steel brushes and swabs and tubes of LSA oil — all of which weighed about a pound. Among the grunts, some carried the M-79 grenade launcher, 5.9 pounds unloaded, a reasonably light weapon except for the ammunition, which was heavy. A single round weighed ten ounces. The typical load was twenty-five rounds. But Ted Lavender, who was scared, carried thirty-four rounds when he was shot and killed outside Than Khe, and he went down under an exceptional burden, more than twenty pounds of ammunition, plus the flak jacket and helmet and rations and water and toilet paper and tranquilizers and all the rest, plus the unweighed fear. He was dead weight. There was no twitching or flopping. Kiowa, who saw it happen, said it was like watching a rock fall, or a big sandbag or something — just boom, then down — not like the movies where the dead guy rolls around and does fancy spins and goes ass over teakettle — not like that, Kiowa said, the poor bastard just flat-fuck fell. Boom. Down. Nothing else. It was a bright morning in mid-April. Lieutenant Cross felt the pain. He blamed himself. They stripped off Lavender's canteens and ammo, all the heavy things, and Rat Kiley said the obvious, the guy's dead, and Mitchell Sanders used his radio to report one U.S. KIA[5] and to request a chopper. Then they wrapped Lavender

---

[4]**M&M** joking term for medical supplies
[5]**KIA** killed in action

in his poncho. They carried him out to a dry paddy, established security, and sat smoking the dead man's dope until the chopper came. Lieutenant Cross kept to himself. He pictured Martha's smooth young face, thinking he loved her more than anything, more than his men, and now Ted Lavender was dead because he loved her so much and could not stop thinking about her. When the dust-off arrived, they carried Lavender aboard. Afterward they burned Than Khe. They marched until dusk, then dug their holes, and that night Kiowa kept explaining how you had to be there, how fast it was, how the poor guy just dropped like so much concrete. Boom-down, he said. Like cement.

In addition to the three standard weapons—the M-60, M-16, and M-79—they carried whatever presented itself, or whatever seemed appropriate as a means of killing or staying alive. They carried catch-as-catch-can. At various times, in various situations, they carried M-14s and CAR-15s and Swedish Ks and grease guns and captured AK-47s and Chi-Coms and RPGs and Simonov carbines and black-market Uzis and .38-caliber Smith & Wesson handguns and 66 mm LAWs and shotguns and silencers and blackjacks and bayonets and C-4 plastic explosives. Lee Strunk carried a slingshot; a weapon of last resort, he called it. Mitchell Sanders carried brass knuckles. Kiowa carried his grandfather's feathered hatchet. Every third or fourth man carried a Claymore antipersonnel mine—3.5 pounds with its firing device. They all carried fragmentation grenades—fourteen ounces each. They all carried at least one M-18 colored smoke grenade—twenty-four ounces. Some carried CS or tear-gas grenades. Some carried white-phosphorus grenades. They carried all they could bear, and then some, including a silent awe for the terrible power of the things they carried.

In the first week of April, before Lavender died, Lieutenant Jimmy Cross received a good-luck charm from Martha. It was a simple pebble, an ounce at most. Smooth to the touch, it was a milky-white color with flecks of orange and violet, oval-shaped, like a miniature egg. In the accompanying letter, Martha wrote that she had found the pebble on the Jersey shoreline, precisely where the land touched water at high tide, where things came together but also separated. It was this separate-but-together quality, she wrote, that had inspired her to pick up the pebble and to carry it in her breast pocket for several days, where it seemed weightless, and then to send it through the mail, by air, as a token of her truest feelings for him. Lieutenant Cross found this romantic. But he wondered what her truest feelings were, exactly, and what she meant by separate-but-together. He wondered how the tides and waves had come into play on that afternoon along the Jersey shoreline when Martha saw the pebble and bent down to rescue it from geology. He imagined bare feet. Martha was a poet, with the poet's sensibilities, and her feet would be brown and bare, the toenails unpainted, the eyes chilly and somber like the ocean in March, and though it was painful, he wondered who had been with her that afternoon. He imagined a pair of shadows moving along the strip of sand where things came together but also separated. It was phantom jealousy, he knew, but he couldn't help himself. He loved her so much. On the march, through the hot days of early April, he carried the pebble in his mouth, turning it with his tongue, tasting sea salts and moisture. His mind wandered. He had difficulty keeping his attention on the war. On occasion he would yell at his men to spread out the column, to keep their eyes open, but then he would slip away into daydreams, just pretending, walking barefoot along the Jersey shore, with Martha, carrying nothing. He would feel himself rising. Sun and waves and gentle winds, all love and lightness.

What they carried varied by mission.

When a mission took them to the mountains, they carried mosquito netting, machetes, canvas tarps, and extra bugjuice.

If a mission seemed especially hazardous, or if it involved a place they knew to be bad, they carried everything they could. In certain heavily mined AOs,[6] where the land was dense with Toe Poppers and Bouncing Betties, they took turns humping a twenty-eight-pound mine detector. With its headphones and big sensing plate, the equipment was a stress on the lower back and shoulders, awkward to handle, often useless because of the shrapnel in the earth, but they carried it anyway, partly for safety, partly for the illusion of safety.

On ambush, or other night missions, they carried peculiar little odds and ends. Kiowa always took along his New Testament and a pair of moccasins for silence. Dave Jensen carried night-sight vitamins high in carotin. Lee Strunk carried his slingshot; ammo, he claimed, would never be a problem. Rat Kiley carried brandy and M&M's. Until he was shot, Ted Lavender carried the starlight scope, which weighed 6.3 pounds with its aluminum carrying case. Henry Dobbins carried his girlfriend's panty hose wrapped around his neck as a comforter. They all carried ghosts. When dark came, they would move out single file across the meadows and paddies to their ambush coordinates, where they would quietly set up the Claymores and lie down and spend the night waiting.

Other missions were more complicated and required special equipment. In mid-April, it was their mission to search out and destroy the elaborate tunnel complexes in the Than Khe area south of Chu Lai. To blow the tunnels, they carried one-pound blocks of pentrite high explosives, four blocks to a man, sixty-eight pounds in all. They carried wiring, detonators, and battery-powered clackers. Dave Jensen carried earplugs. Most often, before blowing the tunnels, they were ordered by higher command to search them, which was considered bad news, but by and

[6]**AOs**   areas of operation

large they just shrugged and carried out orders. Because he was a big man, Henry Dobbins was excused from tunnel duty. The others would draw numbers. Before Lavender died there were seventeen men in the platoon, and whoever drew the number seventeen would strip off his gear and crawl in headfirst with a flashlight and Lieutenant Cross's .45-caliber pistol. The rest of them would fan out as security. They would sit down or kneel, not facing the hole, listening to the ground beneath them, imagining cobwebs and ghosts, whatever was down there—the tunnel walls squeezing in—how the flashlight seemed impossibly heavy in the hand and how it was tunnel vision in the very strictest sense, compression in all ways, even time, and how you had to wiggle in—ass and elbows—a swallowed-up feeling—and how you found yourself worrying about odd things—will your flashlight go dead? Do rats carry rabies? If you screamed, how far would the sound carry? Would your buddies hear it? Would they have the courage to drag you out? In some respects, though not many, the waiting was worse than the tunnel itself. Imagination was a killer.

On April 16, when Lee Strunk drew the number seventeen, he laughed and muttered something and went down quickly. The morning was hot and very still. Not good, Kiowa said. He looked at the tunnel opening, then out across a dry paddy toward the village of Than Khe. Nothing moved. No clouds or birds or people. As they waited, the men smoked and drank Kool-Aid, not talking much, feeling sympathy for Lee Strunk but also feeling the luck of the draw. You win some, you lose some, said Mitchell Sanders, and sometimes you settle for a rain check. It was a tired line and no one laughed.

Henry Dobbins ate a tropical chocolate bar. Ted Lavender popped a tranquilizer and went off to pee.

After five minutes, Lieutenant Jimmy Cross moved to the tunnel, leaned down, and examined the darkness. Trouble, he thought—a cave-in maybe. And then suddenly, without willing it, he was thinking about Martha. The stresses and fractures, the quick collapse, the two of them buried alive under all that weight. Dense, crushing love. Kneeling, watching the hole, he tried to concentrate on Lee Strunk and the war, all the dangers, but his love was too much for him, he felt paralyzed, he wanted to sleep inside her lungs and breathe her blood and be smothered. He wanted her to be a virgin and not a virgin, all at once. He wanted to know her. Intimate secrets—why poetry? Why so sad? Why that grayness in her eyes? Why so alone? Not lonely, just alone—riding her bike across campus or sitting off by herself in the cafeteria. Even dancing, she danced alone—and it was the aloneness that filled him with love. He remembered telling her that one evening. How she nodded and looked away. And how, later, when he kissed her, she received the kiss without returning it, her eyes wide open, not afraid, not a virgin's eyes, just flat and uninvolved.

Lieutenant Cross gazed at the tunnel. But he was not there. He was buried with Martha under the white sand at the Jersey shore. They were pressed together, and the pebble in his mouth was her tongue. He was smiling. Vaguely, he was aware of how quiet the day was, the sullen paddies, yet he could not bring himself to worry about matters of security. He was beyond that. He was just a kid at war, in love. He was twenty-two years old. He couldn't help it.

A few moments later Lee Strunk crawled out of the tunnel. He came up grinning, filthy but alive. Lieutenant Cross nodded and closed his eyes while the others clapped Strunk on the back and made jokes about rising from the dead.

Worms, Rat Kiley said. Right out of the grave. Fuckin' zombie.

The men laughed. They all felt great relief.

Spook City, said Mitchell Sanders.

Lee Strunk made a funny ghost sound, a kind of moaning, yet very happy, and right then, when Strunk made that high happy moaning sound, when he went *Ahhooooo,* right then Ted Lavender was shot in the head on his way back from peeing. He lay with his mouth open. The teeth were broken. There was a swollen black bruise under his left eye. The cheekbone was gone. Oh shit, Rat Kiley said, the guy's dead. The guy's dead, he kept saying, which seemed profound—the guy's dead. I mean really.

The things they carried were determined to some extent by superstition. Lieutenant Cross carried his good-luck pebble. Dave Jensen carried a rabbit's foot. Norman Bowker, otherwise a very gentle person, carried a thumb that had been presented to him as a gift by Mitchell Sanders. The thumb was dark brown, rubbery to the touch, and weighed four ounces at most. It had been cut from a VC corpse, a boy of fifteen or sixteen. They'd found him at the bottom of an irrigation ditch, badly burned, flies in his mouth and eyes. The boy wore black shorts and sandals. At the time of his death he had been carrying a pouch of rice, a rifle, and three magazines of ammunition.

You want my opinion, Mitchell Sanders said, there's a definite moral here.

He put his hand on the dead boy's wrist. He was quiet for a time, as if counting a pulse, then he patted the stomach, almost affectionately, and used Kiowa's hunting hatchet to remove the thumb.

Henry Dobbins asked what the moral was.

Moral?

You know. *Moral.*

Sanders wrapped the thumb in toilet paper and handed it across to Norman Bowker. There was no blood. Smiling, he kicked the boy's head, watched the flies scatter, and said, It's like with that old TV show—Paladin. Have gun, will travel.

Henry Dobbins thought about it.
Yeah, well, he finally said. I don't see no moral.
There it *is,* man.
Fuck off.

They carried USO stationery and pencils and pens. They carried
Sterno, safety pins, trip flares, signal flares, spools of wire, razor blades,
chewing tobacco, liberated joss sticks and statuettes of the smiling Buddha,
candles, grease pencils, *The Stars and Stripes,* fingernail clippers, Psy Ops
leaflets, bush hats, bolos, and much more. Twice a week, when the resupply choppers came in, they carried hot chow in green Mermite cans and
large canvas bags filled with iced beer and soda pop. They carried plastic
water containers, each with a two gallon capacity. Mitchell Sanders carried a set of starched tiger fatigues for special occasions. Henry Dobbins
carried Black Flag insecticide. Dave Jensen carried empty sandbags that
could be filled at night for added protection. Lee Strunk carried tanning
lotion. Some things they carried in common. Taking turns, they carried
the big PRC-77 scrambler radio, which weighed thirty pounds with its
battery. They shared the weight of memory. They took up what others
could no longer bear. Often, they carried each other, the wounded or weak.
They carried infections. They carried chess sets, basketballs, Vietnamese-
English dictionaries, insignia of rank, Bronze Stars and Purple Hearts, plastic
cards imprinted with the Code of Conduct. They carried diseases, among
them malaria and dysentery. They carried lice and ringworm and leeches
and paddy algae and various rots and molds. They carried the land itself—
Vietnam, the place, the soil—a powdery orange-red dust that covered their
boots and fatigues and faces. They carried the sky. The whole atmosphere,
they carried it, the humidity, the monsoons, the stink of fungus and decay,
all of it, they carried gravity. They moved like mules. By daylight they
took sniper fire, at night they were mortared, but it was not battle, it was
just the endless march, village to village, without purpose, nothing won
or lost. They marched for the sake of the march. They plodded along
slowly, dumbly, leaning forward against the heat, unthinking, all blood
and bone, simple grunts, soldiering with their legs, toiling up the hills and
down into the paddies and across the rivers and up again and down, just
humping, one step and then the next and then another, but no volition,
no will, because it was automatic, it was anatomy, and the war was entirely a matter of posture and carriage, the hump was everything, a kind
of inertia, a kind of emptiness, a dullness of desire and intellect and conscience and hope and human sensibility. Their principles were in their feet.
Their calculations were biological. They had no sense of strategy or mission. They searched the villages without knowing what to look for, nor
caring, kicking over jars of rice, frisking children and old men, blowing
tunnels, sometimes setting fires and sometimes not, then forming up and
moving on to the next village, then other villages, where it would always

be the same. They carried their own lives. The pressures were enormous. In the heat of early afternoon, they would remove their helmets and flak jackets, walking bare, which was dangerous but which helped ease the strain. They would often discard things along the route of march. Purely for comfort, they would throw away rations, blow their Claymores and grenades, no matter, because by nightfall the resupply choppers would arrive with more of the same, then a day or two later still more, fresh watermelons and crates of ammunition and sunglasses and woolen sweaters — the resources were stunning — sparklers for the Fourth of July, colored eggs for Easter. It was the great American war chest — the fruits of sciences, the smokestacks, the canneries, the arsenals at Hartford, the Minnesota forests, the machine shops, the vast fields of corn and wheat — they carried like freight trains; they carried it on their backs and shoulders — and for all the ambiguities of Vietnam, all the mysteries and unknowns, there was at least the single abiding certainty that they would never be at a loss for things to carry.

After the chopper took Lavender away, Lieutenant Jimmy Cross led his men into the village of Than Khe. They burned everything. They shot chickens and dogs, they trashed the village well, they called in artillery and watched the wreckage, then they marched for several hours through the hot afternoon, and then at dusk, while Kiowa explained how Lavender died, Lieutenant Cross found himself trembling.

He tried not to cry. With his entrenching tool, which weighed five pounds, he began digging a hole in the earth.

He felt shame. He hated himself. He had loved Martha more than his men, and as a consequence Lavender was now dead, and this was something he would have to carry like a stone in his stomach for the rest of the war.

All he could do was dig. He used his entrenching tool like an ax, slashing, feeling both love and hate, and then later, when it was full dark, he sat at the bottom of his foxhole and wept. It went on for a long while. In part, he was grieving for Ted Lavender, but mostly it was for Martha, and for himself, because she belonged to another world, which was not quite real, and because she was a junior at Mount Sebastian College in New Jersey, a poet and a virgin and uninvolved, and because he realized she did not love him and never would.

Like cement, Kiowa whispered in the dark. I swear to God — boom-down. Not a word.

I've heard this, said Norman Bowker.

A pisser, you know? Still zipping himself up. Zapped while zipping.

All right, fine. That's enough.

Yeah, but you had to see it, the guy just—

I *heard,* man. Cement. So why not shut the fuck *up?*

Kiowa shook his head sadly and glanced over at the hole where Lieutenant Jimmy Cross sat watching the night. The air was thick and wet. A warm, dense fog had settled over the paddies and there was the stillness that precedes rain.

After a time Kiowa sighed.

One thing for sure, he said. The lieutenant's in some deep hurt. I mean that crying jag—the way he was carrying on—it wasn't fake or anything, it was real heavy-duty hurt. The man cares.

Sure, Norman Bowker said.

Say what you want, the man does care.

We all got problems.

Not Lavender.

No, I guess not, Bowker said. Do me a favor, though.

Shut up?

That's a smart Indian. Shut up.

Shrugging, Kiowa pulled off his boots. He wanted to say more, just to lighten up his sleep, but instead he opened his New Testament and arranged it beneath his head as a pillow. The fog made things seem hollow and unattached. He tried not to think about Ted Lavender, but then he was thinking how fast it was, no drama, down and dead, and how it was hard to feel anything except surprise. It seemed unchristian. He wished he could find some great sadness, or even anger, but the emotion wasn't there and he couldn't make it happen. Mostly he felt pleased to be alive. He liked the smell of the New Testament under his cheek, the leather and ink and paper and glue, whatever the chemicals were. He liked hearing the sounds of night. Even his fatigue, it felt fine, the stiff muscles and the prickly awareness of his own body, a floating feeling. He enjoyed not being dead. Lying there, Kiowa admired Lieutenant Jimmy Cross's capacity for grief. He wanted to share the man's pain, he wanted to care as Jimmy Cross cared. And yet when he closed his eyes, all he could think was Boom-down, and all he could feel was the pleasure of having his boots off and the fog curling in around him and the damp soil and the Bible smells and the plush comfort of night.

After a moment Norman Bowker sat up in the dark.

What the hell, he said. You want to talk, *talk*. Tell it to me.

Forget it.

No, man, go on. One thing I hate, it's a silent Indian.

For the most part they carried themselves with poise, a kind of dignity. Now and then, however, there were times of panic, when they squealed or wanted to squeal but couldn't, when they twitched and made moaning sounds and covered their heads and said Dear Jesus and flopped around on the earth and fired their weapons blindly and cringed and sobbed and begged for the noise to stop and went wild and made stupid promises to themselves and to God and to their mothers and fathers, hoping not to die. In different ways, it happened to all of them. Afterward, when the firing ended, they would blink and peek up. They would touch their bodies, feeling shame, then quickly hiding it. They would force themselves to stand. As if in slow motion, frame by frame, the world would take on the old logic — absolute silence, then the wind, then sunlight, then voices. It was the burden of being alive. Awkwardly, the men would reassemble themselves, first in private, then in groups, becoming soldiers again. They would repair the leaks in their eyes. They would check for casualties, call in dust-offs, light cigarettes, try to smile, clear their throats and spit and begin cleaning their weapons. After a time someone would shake his head and say, No lie, I almost shit my pants, and someone else would laugh, which meant it was bad, yes, but the guy had obviously not shit his pants, it wasn't that bad, and in any case nobody would ever do such a thing and then go ahead and talk about it. They would squint into the dense, oppressive sunlight. For a few moments, perhaps, they would fall silent, lighting a joint and tracking its passage from man to man, inhaling, holding in the humiliation. Scary stuff, one of them might say. But then someone else would grin or flick his eyebrows and say, Roger-dodger, almost cut me a new asshole, *almost.*

There were numerous such poses. Some carried themselves with a sort of wistful resignation, others with pride or stiff soldierly discipline or good humor or macho zeal. They were afraid of dying but they were even more afraid to show it.

They found jokes to tell.

They used a hard vocabulary to contain the terrible softness. *Greased,* they'd say. *Offed, lit up, zapped while zipping.* It wasn't cruelty, just stage presence. They were actors and the war came at them in 3-D. When someone died, it wasn't quite dying, because in a curious way it seemed scripted, and because they had their lines mostly memorized, irony mixed with tragedy, and because they called it by other names, as if to encyst and destroy the reality of death itself. They kicked corpses. They cut off thumbs. They talked grunt lingo. They told stories about Ted Lavender's supply of tranquilizers, how the poor guy didn't feel a thing, how incredibly tranquil he was.

There's a moral here, said Mitchell Sanders.

They were waiting for Lavender's chopper, smoking the dead man's dope.

The moral's pretty obvious, Sanders said, and winked. Stay away from drugs. No joke, they'll ruin your day every time.

Cute, said Henry Dobbins.

Mind-blower, get it? Talk about wiggy — nothing left, just blood and brains.

They made themselves laugh.

There it is, they'd say, over and over, as if the repetition itself were an act of poise, a balance between crazy and almost crazy, knowing without going. There it is, which meant be cool, let it ride, because oh yeah, man, you can't change what can't be changed, there it is, there it absolutely and positively and fucking well *is.*

They were tough.

They carried all the emotional baggage of men who might die. Grief, terror, love, longing—these were intangibles, but the intangibles had their own mass and specific gravity, they had tangible weight. They carried shameful memories. They carried the common secret of cowardice barely restrained, the instinct to run or freeze or hide, and in many respects this was the heaviest burden of all, for it could never be put down, it required perfect balance and perfect posture. They carried their reputations. They carried the soldier's greatest fear, which was the fear of blushing. Men killed, and died, because they were embarrassed not to. It was what had brought them to the war in the first place, nothing positive, no dreams of glory or honor, just to avoid the blush of dishonor. They died so as not to die of embarrassment. They crawled into tunnels and walked point and advanced under fire. Each morning, despite the unknowns, they made their legs move. They endured. They kept humping. They did not submit to the obvious alternative, which was simply to close the eyes and fall. So easy, really. Go limp and tumble to the ground and let the muscles unwind and not speak and not budge until your buddies picked you up and lifted you into the chopper that would roar and dip its nose and carry you off to the world. A mere matter of falling, yet no one ever fell. It was not courage, exactly; the object was not valor. Rather, they were too frightened to be cowards.

By and large they carried these things inside, maintaining the masks of composure. They sneered at sick call. They spoke bitterly about guys who had found release by shooting off their own toes or fingers. Pussies, they'd say. Candyasses. It was fierce, mocking talk, with only a trace of envy or awe, but even so, the image played itself out behind their eyes.

They imagined the muzzle against flesh. They imagined the quick, sweet pain, then the evacuation to Japan, then a hospital with warm beds and cute geisha nurses.

They dreamed of freedom birds.

At night, on guard, staring into the dark, they were carried away by jumbo jets. They felt the rush of takeoff. *Gone!* they yelled. And then velocity, wings and engines, a smiling stewardess—but it was more than a plane, it was a real bird, a big sleek silver bird with feathers and talons and high screeching. They were flying. The weights fell off, there was nothing to bear. They laughed and held on tight, feeling the cold slap of wind and altitude, soaring, thinking *It's over, I'm gone!*—they were naked, they were light and free—it was all lightness, bright and fast and buoyant, light as light, a helium buzz in the brain, a giddy bubbling in the lungs as they were taken up over the clouds and the war, beyond duty, beyond gravity and mortification and global entanglements—*Sin loi!*[7] they yelled, *I'm sorry, motherfuckers, but I'm out of it, I'm goofed, I'm on a space cruise, I'm gone!*— and it was a restful, disencumbered sensation, just riding the light waves, sailing that big silver freedom bird over the mountains and oceans, over America, over the farms and great sleeping cities and cemeteries and highways and the Golden Arches of McDonald's. It was flight, a kind of fleeing, a kind of falling, falling higher and higher, spinning off the edge of the earth and beyond the sun and through the vast, silent vacuum where there were no burdens and where everything weighed exactly nothing. *Gone!* they screamed, *I'm sorry but I'm gone!* And so at night, not quite dreaming, they gave themselves over to lightness, they were carried, they were purely borne.

On the morning after Ted Lavender died, First Lieutenant Jimmy Cross crouched at the bottom of his foxhole and burned Martha's letters. Then he burned the two photographs. There was a steady rain falling, which made it difficult, but he used heat tabs and Sterno to build a small fire, screening it with his body, holding the photographs over the tight blue flame with the tips of his fingers.

He realized it was only a gesture. Stupid, he thought. Sentimental, too, but mostly just stupid.

Lavender was dead. You couldn't burn the blame.

Besides, the letters were in his head. And even now, without photographs, Lieutenant Cross could see Martha playing volleyball in her white gym shorts and yellow T-shirt. He could see her moving in the rain.

When the fire died out, Lieutenant Cross pulled his poncho over his shoulders and ate breakfast from a can.

There was no great mystery, he decided.

In those burned letters Martha had never mentioned the war, except to say, Jimmy, take care of yourself. She wasn't involved. She signed the letters "Love," but it wasn't love, and all the fine lines and technicalities did not matter.

The morning came up wet and blurry. Everything seemed part of everything else, the fog and Martha and the deepening rain.

It was a war, after all.

Half smiling, Lieutenant Jimmy Cross took out his maps. He shook his head hard, as if to clear it, then bent forward and began planning the day's march. In ten minutes, or maybe twenty, he would rouse the men and they would pack up and head west, where the maps showed the country to be green and inviting. They would do what they had always done. The rain might add some weight, but otherwise it would be one more day layered upon all the other days.

[7] *Sin loi* Sorry

He was realistic about it. There was that new hardness in his stomach. No more fantasies, he told himself.

Henceforth, when he thought about Martha, it would be only to think that she belonged elsewhere. He would shut down the daydreams. This was not Mount Sebastian, it was another world, where there were no pretty poems or midterm exams, a place where men died because of carelessness and gross stupidity. Kiowa was right. Boom-down, and you were dead, never partly dead.

Briefly, in the rain, Lieutenant Cross saw Martha's gray eyes gazing back at him.

He understood.

It was very sad, he thought. The things men carried inside. The things men did or felt they had to do.

He almost nodded at her, but didn't.

Instead he went back to his maps. He was now determined to perform his duties firmly and without negligence. It wouldn't help Lavender, he knew that, but from this point on he would comport himself as a soldier. He would dispose of his good-luck pebble. Swallow it, maybe, or use Lee Strunk's slingshot, or just drop it along the trail. On the march he would impose strict field discipline. He would be careful to send out flank security, to prevent straggling or bunching up, to keep his troops moving at the proper pace and at the proper interval. He would insist on clean weapons. He would confiscate the remainder of Lavender's dope. Later in the day, perhaps, he would call the men together and speak to them plainly. He would accept the blame for what had happened to Ted Lavender. He would be a man about it. He would look them in the eyes, keeping his chin level, and he would issue the new SOPs in a calm, impersonal tone of voice, an officer's voice, leaving no room for argument or discussion. Commencing immediately, he'd tell them, they would no longer abandon equipment along the route of march. They would police up their acts. They would get their shit together, and keep it together, and maintain it neatly and in good working order.

He would not tolerate laxity. He would show strength, distancing himself.

Among the men there would be grumbling, of course, and maybe worse, because their days would seem longer and their loads heavier, but Lieutenant Cross reminded himself that his obligation was not to be loved but to lead. He would dispense with love; it was not now a factor. And if anyone quarreled or complained, he would simply tighten his lips and arrange his shoulders in the correct command posture. He might give a curt little nod. Or he might not. He might just shrug and say Carry on, then they would saddle up and form into a column and move out toward the villages west of Than Khe.

[1986]

Leslie Marmon Silko (American; b. 1948)

The Man to Send Rain Clouds

One

They found him under a big cottonwood tree. His Levi jacket and pants were faded light-blue so that he had been easy to find. The big cottonwood tree stood apart from a small grove of winterbare cottonwoods which grew in the wide, sandy arroyo. He had been dead for a day or more, and the sheep had wandered and scattered up and down the arroyo. Leon and his brother-in-law, Ken, gathered the sheep and left them in the pen at the sheep camp before they returned to the cottonwood tree. Leon waited under the tree while Ken drove the truck through the deep sand to the edge of the arroyo. He squinted up at the sun and unzipped his jacket—it sure was hot for this time of year. But high and northwest the blue mountains were still deep in snow. Ken came sliding down the low, crumbling bank about fifty yards down, and he was bringing the red blanket.

Before they wrapped the old man, Leon took a piece of string out of his pocket and tied a small gray feather in the old man's long white hair. Ken gave him the paint. Across the brown wrinkled forehead he drew a streak of white and along the high cheekbones he drew a strip of blue paint. He paused and watched Ken throw pinches of corn meal and pollen into the wind that fluttered the small gray feather. Then Leon painted with yellow under the old man's broad nose, and finally, when he had painted green across the chin, he smiled.

"Send us rain clouds, Grandfather." They laid the bundle in the back of the pickup and covered it with a heavy tarp before they started back to the pueblo.

They turned off the highway onto the sandy pueblo road. Not long after they passed the store and post office they saw Father Paul's car coming toward them. When he recognized their faces he slowed his car and waved for them to stop. The young priest rolled down the car window.

"Did you find old Teofilo?" he asked loudly.

Leon stopped the truck. "Good morning, Father. We were just out to the sheep camp. Everything is O.K. now."

"Thank God for that. Teofilo is a very old man. You really shouldn't allow him to stay at the sheep camp alone."

"No, he won't do that any more now."

"Well, I'm glad you understand. I hope I'll be seeing you at Mass this week—we missed you last Sunday. See if you can get old Teofilo to come with you." The priest smiled and waved at them as they drove away.

Two

Louise and Teresa were waiting. The table was set for lunch, and the coffee was boiling on the black iron stove. Leon looked at Louise and then at Teresa.

"We found him under a cottonwood tree in the big arroyo near sheep camp. I guess he sat down to rest in the shade and never got up again." Leon walked toward the old man's bed. The red plaid shawl had been shaken and spread carefully over the bed, and a new brown flannel shirt and pair of stiff new Levis were arranged neatly beside the pillow. Louise held the screen door open while Leon and Ken carried in the red blanket. He looked small and shriveled, and after they dressed him in the new shirt and pants he seemed more shrunken.

It was noontime now because the church bells rang the Angelus.[1] They ate the beans with hot bread, and nobody said anything until after Teresa poured the coffee.

Ken stood up and put on his jacket. "I'll see about the gravediggers. Only the top layer of soil is frozen. I think it can be ready before dark."

Leon nodded his head and finished his coffee. After Ken had been gone for a while, the neighbors and clanspeople came quietly to embrace Teofilo's family and to leave food on the table because the grave-diggers would come to eat when they were finished.

Three

The sky in the west was full of pale-yellow light. Louise stood outside with her hands in the pockets of Leon's green army jacket that was too big for her. The funeral was over, and the old men had taken their candles and medicine bags and were gone. She waited until the body was laid into the pickup before she said anything to Leon. She touched his arm, and he noticed that her hands were still dusty from the corn meal that she had sprinkled around the old man. When she spoke, Leon could not hear her.

"What did you say? I didn't hear you."

"I said that I had been thinking about something."

"About what?"

"About the priest sprinkling holy water for Grandpa. So he won't be thirsty."

Leon stared at the new moccasins that Teofilo had made for the ceremonial dances in the summer. They were nearly hidden by the red blanket. It was getting colder, and the wind pushed gray dust down the narrow pueblo road. The sun was approaching the long mesa where it

---

[1]**Angelus**   a devotional prayer commemorating the Annunciation (the angel Gabriel's announcement of the Incarnation of God in the human form of Jesus)

disappeared during the winter. Louise stood there shivering and watching his face. Then he zipped up his jacket and opened the truck door. "I'll see if he's there."

Four

Ken stopped the pickup at the church, and Leon got out; and then Ken drove down the hill to the graveyard where people were waiting. Leon knocked at the old carved door with its symbols of the Lamb. While he waited he looked up at the twin bells from the king of Spain with the last sunlight pouring around them in their tower.

The priest opened the door and smiled when he saw who it was. "Come in! What brings you here this evening?"

The priest walked toward the kitchen, and Leon stood with his cap in his hand, playing with the earflaps and examining the living room—the brown sofa, the green armchair, and the brass lamp that hung down from the ceiling by links of chain. The priest dragged a chair out of the kitchen and offered it to Leon.

"No thank you, Father. I only came to ask you if you would bring your holy water to the graveyard."

The priest turned away from Leon and looked out the window at the patio full of shadows and the dining-room windows of the nuns' cloister across the patio. The curtains were heavy, and the light from within faintly penetrated; it was impossible to see the nuns inside eating supper. "Why didn't you tell me he was dead? I could have brought the Last Rites anyway."

Leon smiled. "It wasn't necessary, Father."

The priest stared down at his scuffed brown loafers and the worn hem of his cassock. "For a Christian burial it was necessary."

His voice was distant, and Leon thought that his blue eyes looked tired. "It's O.K., Father, we just want him to have plenty of water."

The priest sank down in the green chair and picked up a glossy missionary magazine. He turned the colored pages full of lepers and pagans without looking at them.

"You know I can't do that, Leon. There should have been the Last Rites and a funeral Mass at the very least."

Leon put on his green cap and pulled the flaps down over his ears. "It's getting late, Father. I've got to go."

When Leon opened the door Father Paul stood up and said, "Wait." He left the room and came back wearing a long brown overcoat. He followed Leon out the door and across the dim churchyard to the adobe steps in front of the church. They both stooped to fit through the low adobe entrance. And when they started down the hill to the graveyard only half of the sun was visible above the mesa.

The priest approached the grave slowly, wondering how they had managed to dig into the frozen ground; and then he remembered that this was New Mexico, and saw the pile of cold loose sand beside the hole. The people stood close to each other with little clouds of steam puffing from their faces. The priest looked at them and saw a pile of jackets, gloves, and scarves in the yellow, dry tumbleweeds that grew in the graveyard. He looked at the red blanket, not sure that Teofilo was so small, wondering if it wasn't some perverse Indian trick—something they did in March to ensure a good harvest—wondering if maybe old Teofilo was actually at sheep camp corraling the sheep for the night. But there he was, facing into a cold dry wind and squinting at the last sunlight, ready to bury a red wool blanket while the faces of the parishioners were in shadow with the last warmth of the sun on their backs.

His fingers were stiff, and it took them a long time to twist the lid off the holy water. Drops of water fell on the red blanket and soaked into dark icy spots. He sprinkled the grave and the water disappeared almost before it touched the dim, cold sand; it reminded him of something—he tried to remember what it was, because he thought if he could remember he might understand this. He sprinkled more water; he shook the container until it was empty, and the water fell through the light from sundown like August rain that fell while the sun was still shining, almost evaporating before it touched the wilted squash flowers.

The wind pulled at the priest's brown Franciscan robe and swirled away the corn meal and pollen that had been sprinkled on the blanket. They lowered the bundle into the ground, and they didn't bother to untie the stiff pieces of new rope that were tied around the ends of the blanket. The sun was gone, and over on the highway the eastbound lane was full of headlights. The priest walked away slowly. Leon watched him climb the hill, and when he had disappeared within the tall, thick walls, Leon turned to look up at the high blue mountains in the deep snow that reflected a faint red light from the west. He felt good because it was finished, and he was happy about the sprinkling of the holy water; now the old man could send them big thunderclouds for sure.

[1969]

Jamaica Kincaid (Antiguan: b. 1949)

Girl

Wash the white clothes on Monday and put them on the stone heap; wash the color clothes on Tuesday and put them on the clothesline to dry; don't walk barehead in the hot sun; cook pumpkin fritters in very hot sweet oil; soak your little clothes right after you take them off; when buying cotton to make yourself a nice blouse, be sure that it doesn't have gum on it, because that way it won't hold up well after a wash; soak salt fish overnight before you cook it; is it true that you sing benna[1] in Sunday School?; always eat your food in such a way that it won't turn someone else's stomach; on Sundays try to walk like a lady and not like the slut you are so bent on becoming; don't sing benna in Sunday School; you mustn't speak to wharf-rat boys, not even to give directions; don't eat fruits on the street—flies will follow you; *but I don't sing benna on Sundays at all and never in Sunday school;* this is how to sew on a button; this is how to make a buttonhole for the button you have just sewed on; this is how to hem a dress when you see the hem coming down and so to prevent yourself from looking like the slut I know you are so bent on becoming; this is how you iron your father's khaki shirt so that it doesn't have a crease; this is how you iron your father's khaki pants so that they don't have a crease; this is how you grow okra—far from the house, because okra tree harbors red ants; when you are growing dasheen, make sure it gets plenty of water or else it makes your throat itch when you are eating it; this is how you sweep a corner; this is how you sweep a whole house; this is how you sweep a yard; this is how you smile to someone you don't like too much; this is how you set a table for dinner with an important guest; this is how you smile to someone you don't like at all; this is how you smile to someone you like completely; this is how you set a table for tea; this is how you set a table for dinner; this is how you set a table for lunch; this is how you set a table for breakfast; this is how to behave in the presence of men who don't know you very well, and this way they won't recognize immediately the slut I have warned you against becoming; be sure to wash every day, even if it is with your own spit; don't squat down to play marbles—you are not a boy, you know; don't pick people's flowers—you might catch something; don't throw stones at blackbirds, because it might not be a blackbird at all; this is how to make a bread pudding; this is how to make doukona[2]; this is how to make pepper pot; this is how to make a good medicine for a cold; this is how to make a good medicine to throw away a child before it even becomes a child; this is how to catch a fish; this is how to throw back a fish you don't like, and that way something bad won't fall on you; this is how to bully a man; this is how a man bullies you; this is how to love a man, and if this doesn't work there are other ways, and if they don't work don't feel too bad about giving up; this is how to spit up in the air if you feel like it, and this is how to move quick so that it doesn't fall on you; this is how to make ends

---

[1]**benna** Calypso music
[2]**doukona** spicy pudding made of plantains

meet; always squeeze bread to make sure it's fresh; *but what if the baker won't let me feel the bread?*; you mean to say that after all you are really going to be the kind of woman who the baker won't let near the bread?

[1978]

Amy Tan (American; b. 1952)

Two Kinds

My mother believed you could be anything you wanted to be in America. You could open a restaurant. You could work for the government and get good retirement. You could buy a house with almost no money down. You could become rich. You could become instantly famous.

"Of course, you can be prodigy, too," my mother told me when I was nine. "You can be best anything. What does Auntie Lindo know? Her daughter, she is only best tricky."

America was where all my mother's hopes lay. She had come to San Francisco in 1949 after losing everything in China: her mother and father, her family home, her first husband, and two daughters, twin baby girls. But she never looked back with regret. Things could get better in so many ways.

We didn't immediately pick the right kind of prodigy. At first my mother thought I could be a Chinese Shirley Temple. We'd watch Shirley's old movies on TV as though they were training films. My mother would poke my arm and say, "*Ni kan.* You watch." And I would see Shirley tapping her feet, or singing a sailor song, or pursing her lips into a very round O while saying "Oh, my goodness."

"*Ni kan,*" my mother said, as Shirley's eyes flooded with tears. "You already know how. Don't need talent for crying!"

Soon after my mother got this idea about Shirley Temple, she took me to the beauty training school in the Mission District and put me in the hands of a student who could barely hold the scissors without shaking. Instead of getting big fat curls, I emerged with an uneven mass of crinkly black fuzz. My mother dragged me off to the bathroom and tried to wet down my hair.

"You look like Negro Chinese," she lamented, as if I had done this on purpose.

The instructor of the beauty training school had to lop off these soggy clumps to make my hair even again. "Peter Pan is very popular these days," the instructor assured my mother. I now had hair the length of a boy's, with curly bangs that hung at a slant two inches above my eyebrows. I liked the haircut, and it made me actually look forward to my future fame.

In fact, in the beginning I was just as excited as my mother, maybe even more so. I pictured this prodigy part of me as many different images, and I tried each one on for size. I was a dainty ballerina girl standing by the curtain, waiting to hear the music that would send me floating on my tiptoes. I was like the Christ child lifted out of the straw manger, crying with holy indignity. I was Cinderella stepping from her pumpkin carriage with sparkly cartoon music filling the air.

In all of my imaginings I was filled with a sense that I would soon become perfect. My mother and father would adore me. I would be beyond reproach. I would never feel the need to sulk, or to clamor for anything.

But sometimes the prodigy in me became impatient. "If you don't hurry up and get me out of here, I'm disappearing for good," it warned. "And then you'll always be nothing."

Every night after dinner my mother and I would sit at the Formica-topped kitchen table. She would present new tests, taking her examples from stories of amazing children that she read in *Ripley's Believe It or Not* or *Good Housekeeping, Reader's Digest,* or any of a dozen other magazines she kept in a pile in our bathroom. My mother got these magazines from people whose houses she cleaned. And since she cleaned many houses each week, we had a great assortment. She would look through them all, searching for stories about remarkable children.

The first night she brought out a story about a three-year-old boy who knew the capitals of all the states and even of most of the European countries. A teacher was quoted as saying that the little boy could also pronounce the names of the foreign cities correctly. "What's the capital of Finland?" my mother asked me, looking at the story.

All I knew was the capital of California, because Sacramento was the name of the street we lived on in Chinatown. "Nairobi!" I guessed, saying the most foreign word I could think of. She checked to see if that might be one way to pronounce *Helsinki* before showing me the answer.

The tests got harder—multiplying numbers in my head, finding the queen of hearts in a deck of cards, trying to stand on my head without using my hands, predicting the daily temperatures in Los Angeles, New York, and London. One night I had to look at a page from the Bible for three minutes and then report everything I could remember. "Now Jehoshaphat had riches and honor in abundance and . . . that's all I remember, Ma," I said.

And after seeing, once again, my mother's disappointed face, something inside me began to die. I hated the tests, the raised hopes and failed expectations. Before going to bed that night I looked in the mirror above the bathroom sink, and when I saw only my face staring back—and understood that it would always be this ordinary face—I began to cry. Such a sad, ugly girl! I made high-pitched noises like a crazed animal, trying to scratch out the face in the mirror.

And then I saw what seemed to be the prodigy side of me—a face I had never seen before. I looked at my reflection, blinking so that I could see more clearly. The girl staring back at me was angry, powerful. She and I were the same. I had new thoughts, willful thoughts—or, rather, thoughts filled with lots of won'ts. I won't let her change me, I promised myself. I won't be what I'm not.

So now when my mother presented her tests, I performed listlessly, my head propped on one arm. I pretended to be bored. And I was. I got so bored that I started counting the bellows of the foghorns out on the bay while my mother drilled me in other areas. The sound was comforting and reminded me of the cow jumping over the moon. And the next day I played a game with myself, seeing if my mother would give up on me before eight bellows. After a while I usually counted only one bellow, maybe two at most. At last she was beginning to give up hope.

Two or three months went by without any mention of my being a prodigy. And then one day my mother was watching the *Ed Sullivan Show* on TV. The TV was old and the sound kept shorting out. Every time my mother got halfway up from the sofa to adjust the set, the sound would come back on and Sullivan would be talking. As soon as she sat down, Sullivan would go silent again. She got up—the TV broke into loud piano music. She sat down—silence. Up and down, back and forth, quiet and loud. It was like a stiff, embraceless dance between her and the TV set. Finally, she stood by the set with her hand on the sound dial.

She seemed entranced by the music, a frenzied little piano piece with a mesmerizing quality, which alternated between quick, playful passages and teasing, lilting ones.

"*Ni kan,*" my mother said, calling me over with hurried hand gestures. "Look here."

I could see why my mother was fascinated by the music. It was being pounded out by a little Chinese girl, about nine years old, with a Peter Pan haircut. The girl had the sauciness of a Shirley Temple. She was proudly modest, like a proper Chinese child. And she also did a fancy sweep of a curtsy, so that the fluffy skirt of her white dress cascaded to the floor like the petals of a large carnation.

In spite of these warning signs, I wasn't worried. Our family had no piano and we couldn't afford to buy one, let alone reams of sheet music and piano lessons. So I could be generous in my comments when my mother badmouthed the little girl on TV.

"Play note right, but doesn't sound good!" my mother complained. "No singing sound."

"What are you picking on her for?" I said carelessly. "She's pretty good. Maybe she's not the best, but she's trying hard." I knew almost immediately that I would be sorry I had said that.

"Just like you," she said. "Not the best. Because you not trying." She gave a little huff as she let go of the sound dial and sat down on the sofa.

The little Chinese girl sat down also, to play an encore of "Anitra's Tanz," by Grieg.[1] I remember the song, because later on I had to learn how to play it.

Three days after watching the *Ed Sullivan Show* my mother told me what my schedule would be for piano lessons and piano practice. She had talked to Mr. Chong, who lived on the first floor of our apartment building. Mr. Chong was a retired piano teacher, and my mother had traded housecleaning services for weekly lessons and a piano for me to practice on every day, two hours a day, from four until six.

When my mother told me this, I felt as though I had been sent to hell. I whined, and then kicked my foot a little when I couldn't stand it anymore.

"Why don't you like me the way I am?" I cried. "I'm *not* a genius! I can't play the piano. And even if I could, I wouldn't go on TV if you paid me a million dollars!"

My mother slapped me. "Who ask you to be genius?" she shouted. "Only ask you be your best. For you sake. You think I want you to be genius? Hnnh! What for! Who ask you!"

"So ungrateful," I heard her mutter in Chinese. "If she had as much talent as she has temper, she'd be famous now."

Mr. Chong, whom I secretly nicknamed Old Chong, was very strange, always tapping his fingers to the silent music of an invisible orchestra. He looked ancient in my eyes. He had lost most of the hair on the top of his head, and he wore thick glasses and had eyes that always looked tired. But he must have been younger than I thought, since he lived with his mother and was not yet married.

I met Old Lady Chong once, and that was enough. She had a peculiar smell, like a baby that had done something in its pants, and her fingers felt like a dead person's, like an old peach I once found in the back of the refrigerator; its skin just slid off the flesh when I picked it up.

I soon found out why Old Chong had retired from teaching piano. He was deaf. "Like Beethoven!" he shouted to me. "We're both listening only in our head!" And he would start to conduct his frantic silent sonatas.

Our lessons went like this. He would open the book and point to different things, explaining their purpose: "Key! Treble! Bass! No sharps or flats! So this is C major! Listen now and play after me!"

---

[1] **"Anitra's Tanz," by Grieg**   a section from the incidental music that Edvard Grieg (1843–1907) wrote for *Peer Gynt,* a play by Henrik Ibsen

And then he would play the C scale a few times, a simple cord, and then, as if inspired by an old unreachable itch, he would gradually add more notes and running trills and a pounding bass until the music was really something quite grand.

I would play after him, the simple scale, the simple chord, and then just play some nonsense that sounded like a cat running up and down on top of garbage cans. Old Chong would smile and applaud and say, "Very good! But now you must learn to keep time!"

So that's how I discovered that Old Chong's eyes were too slow to keep up with the wrong notes I was playing. He went through the motions in half time. To help me keep rhythm, he stood behind me and pushed down on my right shoulder for every beat. He balanced pennies on top of my wrists so that I would keep them still as I slowly played scales and arpeggios. He had me curve my hand around an apple and keep that shape when playing chords. He marched stiffly to show me how to make each finger dance up and down, staccato, like an obedient little soldier.

He taught me all these things, and that was how I also learned I could be lazy and get away with mistakes, lots of mistakes. If I hit the wrong notes because I hadn't practiced enough, I never corrected myself. I just kept playing in rhythm. And Old Chong kept conducting his own private reverie.

So maybe I never really gave myself a fair chance. I did pick up the basics pretty quickly, and I might have become a good pianist at that young age. But I was so determined not to try, not to be anybody different, and I learned to play only the most ear-splitting preludes, the most discordant hymns.

Over the next year I practiced like this, dutifully in my own way. And then one day I heard my mother and her friend Lindo Jong both talking in a loud, bragging tone of voice so that others could hear. It was after church, and I was leaning against a brick wall, wearing a dress with stiff white petticoats. Auntie Lindo's daughter, Waverly, who was my age, was standing farther down the wall, about five feet away. We had grown up together and shared all the closeness of two sisters, squabbling over crayons and dolls. In other words, for the most part, we hated each other. I thought she was snotty. Waverly Jong had gained a certain amount of fame as "Chinatown's Littlest Chinese Chess Champion."

"She bring home too many trophy," Auntie Lindo lamented that Sunday. "All day she play chess. All day I have no time do nothing but dust off her winnings." She threw a scolding look at Waverly, who pretended not to see her.

"You lucky you don't have this problem," Auntie Lindo said with a sigh to my mother.

And my mother squared her shoulders and bragged: "Our problem worser than yours. If we ask Jing-mei wash dish, she hear nothing but music. It's like you can't stop this natural talent."

And right then I was determined to put a stop to her foolish pride.

A few weeks later Old Chong and my mother conspired to have me play in a talent show that was to be held in the church hall. But then my parents had saved up enough to buy me a secondhand piano, a black Wurlitzer spinet with a scarred bench. It was the showpiece of our living room.

For the talent show I was to play a piece called "Pleading Child," from Schumann's *Scenes From Childhood*.[2] It was a simple, moody piece that sounded more difficult than it was. I was supposed to memorize the whole thing. But I dawdled over it, playing a few bars and then cheating, looking up to see what notes followed. I never really listened to what I was playing. I daydreamed about being somewhere else, about being someone else.

The part I liked to practice best was the fancy curtsy: right foot out, touch the rose on the carpet with a pointed foot, sweep to the side, bend left leg, look up, and smile.

My parents invited all the couples from their social club to witness my debut. Auntie Lindo and Uncle Tin were there. Waverly and her two older brothers had also come. The first two rows were filled with children either younger or older than I was. The littlest ones got to go first. They recited simple nursery rhymes, squawked out tunes on miniature violins, and twirled hula hoops in pink ballet tutus, and when they bowed or curtsied, the audience would sigh in unison, "*Awww*," and then clap enthusiastically.

When my turn came, I was very confident. I remember my childish excitement. It was as if I knew, without a doubt, that the prodigy side of me really did exist. I had no fear whatsoever, no nervousness. I remember thinking, This is it! This is it! I looked out over the audience, at my mother's blank face, my father's yawn, Auntie Lindo's stiff-lipped smile, Waverly's sulky expression. I had on a white dress, layered with sheets of lace, and a pink bow in my Peter Pan haircut. As I sat down, I envisioned people jumping to their feet and Ed Sullivan rushing up to introduce me to everyone on TV.

And I started to play. Everything was so beautiful. I was so caught up in how lovely I looked that I wasn't worried about how I would sound. So I was surprised when I hit the first wrong note. And then I hit another, and another. A chill started at the top of my head and began to trickle down. Yet I couldn't stop playing, as though my hands were bewitched. I kept thinking my fingers would adjust themselves back, like a train switching to the right track. I played this strange jumble through to the end, the sour notes staying with me all the way.

[2] **Scenes from Childhood** piano work by Robert Schumann (1810–56) with twelve titled sections and an epilogue

When I stood up, I discovered my legs were shaking. Maybe I had just been nervous, and the audience, like Old Chong, had seen me go through the right motions and had not heard anything wrong at all. I swept my right foot out, went down on my knee, looked up, and smiled. The room was quiet, except for Old Chong, who was beaming and shouting, "Bravo! Bravo! Well done!" But then I saw my mother's face, her stricken face. The audience clapped weakly, and as I walked back to my chair, with my whole face quivering as I tried not to cry, I heard a little boy whisper loudly to his mother, "That was awful," and the mother whispered, "Well, she certainly tried."

And now I realized how many people were in the audience — the whole world, it seemed. I was aware of eyes burning into my back. I felt the shame of my mother and father as they sat stiffly through the rest of the show.

We could have escaped during intermission. Pride and some strange sense of honor must have anchored my parents to their chairs. And so we watched it all: The eighteen-year-old boy with a fake moustache who did a magic show and juggled flaming hoops while riding a unicycle. The breasted girl with white makeup who sang an aria from *Madame Butterfly* and got an honorable mention. And the eleven-year-old boy who won first prize playing a tricky violin song that sounded like a busy bee.

After the show the Hsus, the Jongs, and the St. Clairs, from the Joy Luck Club, came up to my mother and father.

"Lots of talented kids," Auntie Lindo said vaguely, smiling broadly.

"That was somethin' else," my father said, and I wondered if he was referring to me in a humorous way, or whether he even remembered what I had done.

Waverly looked at me and shrugged her shoulders. "You aren't a genius like me," she said matter-of-factly. And if I hadn't felt so bad, I would have pulled her braids and punched her stomach.

But my mother's expression was what devastated me: a quiet, blank look that said she had lost everything. I felt the same way, and everybody seemed now to be coming up, like gawkers at the scene of an accident, to see what parts were actually missing.

When we got on the bus to go home, my father was humming the busy-bee tune and my mother was silent. I kept thinking she wanted to wait until we got home before shouting at me. But when my father unlocked the door to our apartment, my mother walked in and went straight to the back, into the bedroom. No accusations. No blame. And in a way, I felt disappointed. I had been waiting for her to start shouting, so that I could shout back and cry and blame her for all my misery.

I had assumed that my talent-show fiasco meant that I would never have to play the piano again. But two days later, after school, my mother came out of the kitchen and saw me watching TV.

"Four clock," she reminded me, as if it were any other day. I was stunned, as though she were asking me to go through the talent-show torture again. I planted myself more squarely in front of the TV.

"Turn off TV," she called from the kitchen five minutes later.

I didn't budge. And then I decided. I didn't have to do what my mother said anymore. I wasn't her slave. This wasn't China. I had listened to her before, and look what happened. She was the stupid one.

She came out of the kitchen and stood in the arched entryway of the living room. "Four clock," she said once again, louder.

"I'm not going to play anymore," I said nonchalantly. "Why should I? I'm not a genius."

She stood in front of the TV. I saw that her chest was heaving up and down in an angry way.

"No!" I said, and I now felt stronger, as if my true self had finally emerged. So this was what had been inside me all along.

"No! I won't!" I screamed.

She snapped off the TV, yanked me by the arm and pulled me off the floor. She was frighteningly strong, half pulling, half carrying me toward the piano as I kicked the throw rugs under my feet. She lifted me up and onto the hard bench. I was sobbing by now, looking at her bitterly. Her chest was heaving even more and her mouth was open, smiling crazily as if she were pleased that I was crying.

"You want me to be someone that I'm not!" I sobbed. "I'll never be the kind of daughter you want me to be!"

"Only two kinds of daughters," she shouted in Chinese. "Those who are obedient and those who follow their own mind! Only one kind of daughter can live in this house. Obedient daughter!"

"Then I wish I weren't your daughter. I wish you weren't my mother," I shouted. As I said these things I got scared. It felt like worms and toads and slimy things crawling out of my chest, but it also felt good, that this awful side of me had surfaced, at last.

"Too late change this," my mother said shrilly.

And I could sense her anger rising to its breaking point. I wanted to see it spill over. And that's when I remembered the babies she had lost in China, the ones we never talked about. "Then I wish I'd never been born!" I shouted. "I wish I were dead! Like them."

It was as if I had said magic words. Alakazam! — her face went blank, her mouth closed, her arms went slack, and she backed out of the room, stunned, as if she were blowing away like a small brown leaf, thin, brittle, lifeless.

It was not the only disappointment my mother felt in me. In the years that followed, I failed her many times, each time asserting my will, my right to fall short of expectations. I didn't get straight *A*s. I didn't become class president. I didn't get into Stanford. I dropped out of college.

Unlike my mother, I did not believe I could be anything I wanted to be. I could only be me.

And for all those years we never talked about the disaster at the recital or my terrible declarations afterward at the piano bench. Neither of us talked about it again, as if it were a betrayal that was now unspeakable. So I never found a way to ask her why she had hoped for something so large that failure was inevitable.

And even worse, I never asked her about what frightened me the most: Why had she given up hope? For after our struggle at the piano, she never mentioned my playing again. The lessons stopped. The lid to the piano was closed, shutting out the dust, my misery, and her dreams.

So she surprised me. A few years ago she offered to give me the piano, for my thirtieth birthday. I had not played in all those years. I saw the offer as a sign of forgiveness, a tremendous burden removed.

"Are you sure?" I asked shyly. "I mean, won't you and Dad miss it?"

"No, this your piano," she said firmly. "Always your piano. You only one can play."

"Well, I probably can't play anymore," I said. "It's been years."

"You pick up fast," my mother said, as if she knew this was certain. "You have natural talent. You could be genius if you want to."

"No, I couldn't."

"You just not trying," my mother said. And she was neither angry nor sad. She said it as if announcing a fact that could never be disproved. "Take it," she said.

But I didn't at first. It was enough that she had offered it to me. And after that, every time I saw it in my parents' living room, standing in front of the bay window, it made me feel proud, as if it were a shiny trophy that I had won back.

Last week I sent a tuner over to my parents' apartment and had the piano reconditioned, for purely sentimental reasons. My mother had died a few months before, and I had been getting things in order for my father, a little bit at a time. I put the jewelry in special silk pouches. The sweaters she had knitted in yellow, pink, bright orange—all the colors I hated— I put in mothproof boxes. I found some old Chinese silk dresses, the kind with little slits up the sides. I rubbed the old silk against my skin, and then wrapped them in tissue and decided to take them home with me.

After I had the piano tuned, I opened the lid and touched the keys. It sounded even richer than I remembered. Really, it was a very good piano. Inside the bench were the same exercise notes with handwritten scales, the same secondhand music books with their covers held together with yellow tape.

I opened up the Schumann book to the dark little piece I had played at the recital. It was on the left-hand page, "Pleading Child." It looked more difficult than I remembered. I played a few bars, surprised at how easily the notes came back to me.

And for the first time, or so it seemed, I noticed the piece on the right-hand side. It was called "Perfectly Contented." I tried to play this one as well. It had a lighter melody but with the same flowing rhythm and turned out to be quite easy. "Pleading Child" was shorter but slower; "Perfectly Contented" was longer but faster. And after I had played them both a few times, I realized they were two halves of the same song.

[1989]

Sandra Cisneros (American; b. 1954)

One Holy Night

About the truth, if you give it to a person, then he has power over you. And if someone gives it to you, then they have made themselves your slave. It is a strong magic. You can never take it back.

Chaq Uxmal Paloquín

He said his name was Chaq. Chaq Uxmal Paloquín. That's what he told me. He was of an ancient line of Mayan kings. Here, he said, making a map with the heel of his boot, this is where I come from, the Yucatán, the ancient cities. This is what Boy Baby said.

It's been eighteen weeks since Abuelita[1] chased him away with the broom, and what I'm telling you I never told nobody, except Rachel and Lourdes, who know everything. He said he would love me like a revolution, like a religion. Abuelita burned the pushcart and sent me here, miles from home, in this town of dust, with one wrinkled witch woman who rubs my belly with jade, and sixteen nosy cousins.

I don't know how many girls have gone bad from selling cucumbers. I know I'm not the first. My mother took the crooked walk too, I'm told, and I'm sure my Abuelita has her own story, but it's not my place to ask.

---

[1]**Abuelita**   Grandma

Abuelita says it's Uncle Lalo's fault because he's the man of the family and if he had come home on time like he was supposed to and worked the pushcart on the days he was told to and watched over his goddaughter, who is too foolish to look after herself, nothing would've happened, and I wouldn't have to be sent to Mexico. But Uncle Lalo says if they had never left Mexico in the first place, shame enough would have kept a girl from doing devil things.

I'm not saying I'm not bad. I'm not saying I'm special. But I'm not like the Allport Street girls, who stand in doorways and go with men into alleys.

All I know is I didn't want it like that. Not against the bricks or hunkering in somebody's car. I wanted it come undone like gold thread, like a tent full of birds. The way it's supposed to be, the way I knew it would be when I met Boy Baby.

But you must know, I was no girl back then. And Boy Baby was no boy. Chaq Uxmal Paloquín. Boy Baby was a man. When I asked him how old he was he said he didn't know. The past and the future are the same thing. So he seemed boy and baby and man all at once, and the way he looked at me, how do I explain?

I'd park the pushcart in front of the Jewel food store Saturdays. He bought a mango on a stick the first time. Paid for it with a new twenty. Next Saturday he was back. Two mangoes, lime juice, and chili powder, keep the change. The third Saturday he asked for a cucumber spear and ate it slow. I didn't see him after that till the day he brought me Kool-Aid in a· plastic cup. Then I knew what I felt for him.

Maybe you wouldn't like him. To you he might be a bum. Maybe he looked it. Maybe. He had broken thumbs and burnt fingers. He had thick greasy fingernails he never cut and dusty hair. And all his bones were strong ones like a man's. I waited every Saturday in my same blue dress. I sold all the mango and cucumber, and then Boy Baby would come finally.

What I knew of Chaq was only what he told me, because nobody seemed to know where he came from. Only that he could speak a strange language that no one could understand, said his name translated into boy, or boy-child, and so it was the street people nicknamed him Boy Baby.

I never asked about his past. He said it was all the same and didn't matter, past and the future all the same to his people. But the truth has a strange way of following you, of coming up to you and making you listen to what it has to say.

Night time. Boy Baby brushes my hair and talks to me in his strange language because I like to hear it. What I like to hear him tell is how he is Chaq, Chaq of the people of the sun, Chaq of the temples, and what he says sounds sometimes like broken clay, and at other times like hollow sticks, or like the swish of old feathers crumbling into dust.

He lived behind Esparza & Sons Auto Repair in a little room that used to be a closet—pink plastic curtains on a narrow window, a dirty cot covered with newspapers, and a cardboard box filled with socks and rusty tools. It was there, under one bald bulb, in the back room of the Esparza garage, in the single room with pink curtains, that he showed me the guns—twenty-four in all. Rifles and pistols, one rusty musket, a machine gun, and several tiny weapons with mother-of-pearl handles that looked like toys. So you'll see who I am, he said, laying them all out on the bed of newspapers. So you'll understand. But I didn't want to know.

The stars foretell everything, he said. My birth. My son's. The boy-child who will bring back the grandeur of my people from those who have broken the arrows, from those who have pushed the ancient stones off their pedestals.

Then he told how he had prayed in the Temple of the Magician years ago as a child when his father had made him promise to bring back the ancient ways. Boy Baby had cried in the temple dark that only the bats made holy. Boy Baby who was man and child among the great and dusty guns lay down on the newspaper bed and wept for a thousand years. When I touched him, he looked at me with the sadness of stone.

You must not tell anyone what I am going to do, he said. And what I remember next is how the moon, the pale moon with its one yellow eye, the moon of Tikal, and Tulum, and Chichén, stared through the pink plastic curtains. Then something inside bit me, and I gave out a cry as if the other, the one I wouldn't be anymore, leapt out.

So I was initiated beneath an ancient sky by a great and mighty heir—Chaq Uxmal Paloquín. I, Ixchel, his queen.

The truth is, it wasn't a big deal. It wasn't any deal at all. I put my bloody panties inside my T-shirt and ran home hugging myself. I thought about a lot of things on the way home. I thought about all the world and how suddenly I became a part of history and wondered if everyone on the street, the sewing machine lady and the *panadería*[2] saleswomen and the woman with two kids sitting on the bus bench didn't all know. *Did I look any different? Could they tell?* We were all the same somehow, laughing behind our hands, waiting the way all women wait, and when we find out, we wonder why the world and a million years made such a big deal over nothing.

I know I was supposed to feel ashamed, but I wasn't ashamed. I wanted to stand on top of the highest building, the top-top floor, and yell, *I know.*

Then I understood why Abuelita didn't let me sleep over at Lourdes's house full of too many brothers, and why the Roman girl in the movies always runs away from the soldier, and what happens when the scenes in love stories begin to fade, and why brides blush, and how it is that sex isn't simply a box you check *M* or *F* on in the test we get at school.

[2]*panadería*   bakery

I was wise. The corner girls were still jumping into their stupid little hopscotch squares. I laughed inside and climbed the wooden stairs two by two to the second floor rear where me and Abuelita and Uncle Lalo live. I was still laughing when I opened the door and Abuelita asked, "Where's the pushcart?"

And then I didn't know what to do.

It's a good thing we live in a bad neighborhood. There are always plenty of bums to blame for your sins. If it didn't happen the way I told it, it really could've. We looked and looked all over for the kids who stole my pushcart. The story wasn't the best, but since I had to make it up right then and there with Abuelita staring a hole through my heart, it wasn't too bad.

For two weeks I had to stay home. Abuelita was afraid the street kids who had stolen the cart would be after me again. Then I thought I might go over to the Esparza garage and take the pushcart out and leave it in some alley for the police to find, but I was never allowed to leave the house alone. Bit by bit the truth started to seep out like a dangerous gasoline.

First the nosy woman who lives upstairs from the laundromat told my Abuelita she thought something was fishy, the pushcart wheeled into Esparza & Sons every Saturday after dark, how a man, the same dark Indian one, the one who never talks to anybody, walked with me when the sun went down and pushed the cart into the garage, that one there, and yes we went inside, there where the fat lady named Concha, whose hair is dyed a hard black, pointed a fat finger.

I prayed that we would not meet Boy Baby, and since the gods listen and are mostly good, Esparza said yes, a man like that had lived there but was gone, had packed a few things and left the pushcart in a corner to pay for his last week's rent.

We had to pay $20 before he would give us our pushcart back. Then Abuelita made me tell the real story of how the cart had disappeared, all of which I told this time, except for that one night, which I would have to tell anyway, weeks later, when I prayed for the moon of my cycle to come back, but it would not.

When Abuelita found out I was going to *dar a luz*,[3] she cried until her eyes were little, and blamed Uncle Lalo, and Uncle Lalo blamed this country, and Abuelita blamed the infamy of men. That is when she burned the cucumber pushcart and called me a *sinvergüenza* because I *am* without shame.

---

[3]***dar a luz***   have a baby

Then I cried too—Boy Baby was lost from me—until my head was hot with headaches and I fell asleep. When I woke up, the cucumber pushcart was dust and Abuelita was sprinkling holy water on my head.

Abuelita woke up early every day and went to the Esparza garage to see if news about that *demonio* had been found, had Chaq Uxmal Paloquín sent any letters, any, and when the other mechanics heard that name they laughed, and asked if we had made it up, that we could have some letters that had come for Boy Baby, no forwarding address, since he had gone in such a hurry.

There were three. The first, addressed "Occupant," demanded immediate payment for a four-month-old electric bill. The second was one I recognized right away—a brown envelope fat with cake-mix coupons and fabric-softener samples—because we'd gotten one just like it. The third was addressed in a spidery Spanish to a Señor C. Cruz, on paper so thin you could read it unopened by the light of the sky. The return address a convent in Tampico.

This was to whom my Abuelita wrote in hopes of finding the man who could correct my ruined life, to ask if the good nuns might know the whereabouts of a certain Boy Baby—and if they were hiding him it would be of no use because God's eyes see through all souls.

We heard nothing for a long time. Abuelita took me out of school when my uniform got tight around the belly and said it was a shame I wouldn't be able to graduate with the other eighth graders.

Except for Lourdes and Rachel, my grandma and Uncle Lalo, nobody knew about my past. I would sleep in the big bed I share with Abuelita same as always. I could hear Abuelita and Uncle Lalo talking in low voices in the kitchen as if they were praying the rosary, how they were going to send me to Mexico, to San Dionisio de Tlaltepango, where I have cousins and where I was conceived and would've been born had my grandma not thought it wise to send my mother here to the United States so that neighbors in San Dionisio de Tlaltepango wouldn't ask why her belly was suddenly big.

I was happy. I liked staying home. Abuelita was teaching me to crochet the way she had learned in Mexico. And just when I had mastered the tricky rosette stitch, the letter came from the convent which gave the truth about Boy Baby—however much we didn't want to hear.

He was born on a street with no name in a town called Miseria. His father, Eusebio, is a knife sharpener. His mother, Refugia, stacks apricots into pyramids and sells them on a cloth in the market. There are brothers. Sisters too of which I know little. The youngest, a Carmelite, writes me all this and prays for my soul, which is why I know it's all true.

Boy Baby is thirty-seven years old. His name is Chato which means
fat-face. There is no Mayan blood.

I don't think they understand how it is to be a girl. I don't think
they know how it is to have to wait your whole life. I count the
months for the baby to be born, and it's like a ring of water inside
me reaching out and out until one day it will tear from me with its own
teeth.

Already I can feel the animal inside me stirring in his own uneven
sleep. The witch woman says it's the dreams of weasels that make my child
sleep the way he sleeps. She makes me eat white bread blessed by the priest,
but I know it's the ghost of him inside me that circles and circles, and
will not let me rest.

Abuelita said they sent me here just in time, because a little later Boy
Baby came back to our house looking for me, and she had to chase him
away with the broom. The next thing we hear, he's in the newspaper clip-
pings his sister sends. A picture of him looking very much like stone, police
hooked on either arm . . . *on the road to* Las Grutas de Xtacumbilxuna, *the
Caves of the Hidden Girl . . . eleven female bodies . . . the last seven years . . .*

Then I couldn't read but only stare at the little black-and-white dots
that make up the face I am in love with.

All my girl cousins here either don't talk to me, or those who do,
ask questions they're too young to know *not* to ask. What they want to
know really is how it is to have a man, because they're too ashamed to
ask their married sisters.

They don't know what it is to lay so still until his sleep breathing
is heavy, for the eyes in the dim dark to look and look without worry
at the man-bones and the neck, the man-wrist and man-jaw thick and
strong, all the salty dips and hollows, the stiff hair of the brow and sour
swirl of sideburns, to lick the fat earlobes that taste of smoke, and stare
at how perfect is a man.

I tell them, "It's a bad joke. When you find out you'll be sorry."

I'm going to have five children. Five. Two girls. Two boys. And one
baby.

The girls will be called Lisette and Maritza. The boys I'll name Pablo
and Sandro.

And my baby. My baby will be named Alegre, because life will always be hard.

Rachel says that love is like a big black piano being pushed off the
top of a three-story building and you're waiting on the bottom to catch

it. But Lourdes says it's not that way at all. It's like a top, like all the colors in the world are spinning so fast they're not colors anymore and all that's left is a white hum.

There was a man, a crazy who lived upstairs from us when we lived on South Loomis. He couldn't talk, just walked around all day with this harmonica in his mouth. Didn't play it. Just sort of breathed through it, all day long, wheezing, in and out, in and out.

This is how it is with me. Love I mean.

[1988]

Helena Maria Viramontes (American; b. 1954)

The Moths

I was fourteen years old when Abuelita[1] requested my help. And it seemed only fair. Abuelita had pulled me through the rages of scarlet fever by placing, removing and replacing potato slices on the temples of my forehead; she had seen me through several whippings, an arm broken by a dare jump off Tío Enrique's toolshed, puberty, and my first lie. Really, I told Amá, it was only fair.

Not that I was her favorite granddaughter or anything special. I wasn't even pretty or nice like my older sisters and I just couldn't do the girl things they could do. My hands were too big to handle the fineries of crocheting or embroidery and I always pricked my fingers or knotted my colored threads time and time again while my sisters laughed and called me bull hands with their cute waterlike voices. So I began keeping a piece of jagged brick in my sock to bash my sisters or anyone who called me bull hands. Once, while we all sat in the bedroom, I hit Teresa on the forehead, right above her eyebrow and she ran to Amá with her mouth open, her hand over her eye while blood seeped between her fingers. I was used to the whippings by then.

I wasn't respectful either. I even went so far as to doubt the power of Abuelita's slices, the slices she said absorbed my fever. "You're still alive, aren't you?" Abuelita snapped back, her pasty gray eye beaming at me and burning holes in my suspicions. Regretful that I had let secret questions drop out of my mouth, I couldn't look into her eyes. My hands began to fan out, grow like a liar's nose until they hung by my side like low weights. Abuelita made a balm out of dried moth wings and Vicks and rubbed

[1]**Abuelita**   Grandma (Spanish); other Spanish words for relatives mentioned in the story are *Tío,* Uncle, *Amá,* Mother, and *Apá,* Dad.

my hands, shaped them back to size and it was the strangest feeling. Like bones melting. Like sun shining through the darkness of your eyelids. I didn't mind helping Abuelita after that, so Amá would always send me over to her.

In the early afternoon Amá would push her hair back, hand me my sweater and shoes, and tell me to go to Mama Luna's. This was to avoid another fight and another whipping, I knew. I would deliver one last direct shot on Marisela's arm and jump out of our house, the slam of the screen door burying her cries of anger, and I'd gladly go help Abuelita plant her wild lilies or jasmine or heliotrope or cilantro or hierbabuena in red Hills Brothers coffee cans. Abuelita would wait for me at the top step of her porch holding a hammer and nail and empty coffee cans. And although we hardly spoke, hardly looked at each other as we worked over root transplants, I always felt her gray eye on me. It made me feel, in a strange sort of way, safe and guarded and not alone. Like God was supposed to make you feel.

On Abuelita's porch, I would puncture holes in the bottom of the coffee cans with a nail and a precise hit of a hammer. This completed, my job was to fill them with red clay mud from beneath her rose bushes, packing it softly, then making a perfect hole, four fingers round, to nest a sprouting avocado pit, or the spidery sweet potatoes that Abuelita rooted in mayonnaise jars with toothpicks and daily water, or prickly chayotes[2] that produced vines that twisted and wound all over her porch pillars, crawling to the roof, up and over the roof, and down the other side, making her small brick house look like it was cradled within the vines that grew pear-shaped squashes ready for the pick, ready to be steamed with onions and cheese and butter. The roots would burst out of the rusted coffee cans and search for a place to connect. I would then feed the seedlings with water.

But this was a different kind of help, Amá said, because Abuelita was dying. Looking into her gray eye, then into her brown one, the doctor said it was just a matter of days. And so it seemed only fair that these hands she had melted and formed found use in rubbing her caving body with alcohol and marihuana, rubbing her arms and legs, turning her face to the window so that she could watch the Bird of Paradise blooming or smell the scent of clove in the air. I toweled her face frequently and held her hand for hours. Her gray wiry hair hung over the mattress. Since I could remember, she'd kept her long hair in braids. Her mouth was vacant and when she slept, her eyelids never closed all the way. Up close, you could see her gray eye beaming out the window, staring hard as if to remember everything. I never kissed her. I left the window open when I went to the market.

Across the street from Jay's Market there was a chapel. I never knew its denomination, but I went in just the same to search for candles. I sat

[2]**chayotes**   squash-like fruit

down on one of the pews because there were none. After I cleaned my fingernails, I looked up at the high ceiling. I had forgotten the vastness of these places, the coolness of the marble pillars and the frozen statues with blank eyes. I was alone. I knew why I had never returned.

That was one of Apá's biggest complaints. He would pound his hands on the table, rocking the sugar dish or spilling a cup of coffee and scream that if I didn't go to mass every Sunday to save my goddamn sinning soul, then I had no reason to go out of the house, period. Punto final.[3] He would grab my arm and dig his nails into me to make sure I understood the importance of catechism. Did he make himself clear? Then he strategically directed his anger at Amá for her lousy ways of bringing up daughters, being disrespectful and unbelieving, and my older sisters would pull me aside and tell me if I didn't get to mass right this minute, they were all going to kick the holy shit out of me. Why am I so selfish? Can't you see what it's doing to Amá, you idiot? So I would wash my feet and stuff them in my black Easter shoes that shone with Vaseline, grab a missal and veil, and wave good-bye to Amá.

I would walk slowly down Lorena to First to Evergreen, counting the cracks on the cement. On Evergreen I would turn left and walk to Abuelita's. I liked her porch because it was shielded by the vines of the chayotes and I could get a good look at the people and car traffic on Evergreen without them knowing. I would jump up the porch steps, knock on the screen door as I wiped my feet and call Abuelita? mi Abuelita? As I opened the door and stuck my head in, I would catch the gagging scent of toasting chile on the placa.[4] When I entered the sala,[5] she would greet me from the kitchen, wringing her hands in her apron. I'd sit at the corner of the table to keep from being in her way. The chiles made my eyes water. Am I crying? No, Mama Luna, I'm sure not crying. I don't like going to mass, but my eyes watered anyway, the tears dropping on the tablecloth like candle wax. Abuelita lifted the burnt chiles from the fire and sprinkled water on them until the skins began to separate. Placing them in front of me, she turned to check the menudo.[6] I peeled the skins off and put the flimsy, limp looking green and yellow chiles in the molcajete[7] and began to crush and crush and twist and crush the heart out of the tomato, the clove of garlic, the stupid chiles that made me cry, crushed them until they turned into liquid under my bull hand. With a wooden spoon, I scraped hard to destroy the guilt, and my tears were gone. I put the bowl of chile next to a vase filled with freshly cut roses. Abuelita touched my

---

[3]**Punto final**   period
[4]**placa**   round cast-iron griddle
[5]**sala**   living room
[6]**menudo**   tripe soup
[7]**molcajeta**   mixing vessel, mortar

hand and pointed to the bowl of menudo that steamed in front of me. I spooned some chile into the menudo and rolled a corn tortilla thin with the palms of my hands. As I ate, a fine Sunday breeze entered the kitchen and a rose petal calmly feathered down to the table.

I left the chapel without blessing myself and walked to Jay's. Most of the time Jay didn't have much of anything. The tomatoes were always soft and the cans of Campbell soups had rusted spots on them. There was dust on the tops of cereal boxes. I picked up what I needed: rubbing alcohol, five cans of chicken broth, a big bottle of Pine Sol. At first Jay got mad because I thought I had forgotten the money. But it was there all the time, in my back pocket.

When I returned from the market, I heard Amá crying in Abuelita's kitchen. She looked up at me with puffy eyes. I placed the bags of groceries on the table and began putting the cans of soup away. Amá sobbed quietly. I never kissed her. After a while, I patted her on the back for comfort. Finally: "¿Y mi Amá?"[8] she asked in a whisper, then choked again and cried into her apron.

Abuelita fell off the bed twice yesterday, I said, knowing that I shouldn't have said it and wondering why I wanted to say it because it only made Amá cry harder. I guess I became angry and just so tired of the quarrels and beatings and unanswered prayers and my hands just there hanging helplessly by my side. Amá looked at me again, confused, angry, and her eyes were filled with sorrow. I went outside and sat on the porch swing and watched the people pass. I sat there until she left. I dozed off repeating the words to myself like rosary prayers: when do you stop giving when do you start giving when do you . . . and when my hands fell from my lap, I awoke to catch them. The sun was setting, an orange glow, and I knew Abuelita was hungry.

There comes a time when the sun is defiant. Just about the time when moods change, inevitable seasons of a day, transitions from one color to another, that hour or minute or second when the sun is finally defeated, finally sinks into the realization that it cannot with all its power to heal or burn, exist forever, there comes an illumination where the sun and earth meet, a final burst of burning red orange fury reminding us that although endings are inevitable, they are necessary for rebirths, and when that time came, just when I switched on the light in the kitchen to open Abuelita's can of soup, it was probably then that she died.

The room smelled of Pine Sol and vomit and Abuelita had defecated the remains of her cancerous stomach. She had turned to the window and tried to speak, but her mouth remained open and speechless. I heard you, Abuelita, I said, stroking her cheek, I heard you. I opened the windows of the house and let the soup simmer and overboil on the stove. I turned the stove off and poured the soup down the sink. From the cabinet I got

[8]**¿Y mi Amá?**   And my Mother?

a tin basin, filled it with lukewarm water and carried it carefully to the room. I went to the linen closet and took out some modest bleached white towels. With the sacredness of a priest preparing his vestments, I unfolded the towels one by one on my shoulders. I removed the sheets and blankets from her bed and peeled off her thick flannel nightgown. I toweled her puzzled face, stretching out the wrinkles, removing the coils of her neck, toweled her shoulders and breasts. Then I changed the water. I returned to towel the creases of her stretch-marked stomach, her sporadic vaginal hairs, and her sagging thighs. I removed the lint from between her toes and noticed a mapped birthmark on the fold of her buttock. The scars on her back which were as thin as the life lines on the palms of her hands made me realize how little I really knew of Abuelita. I covered her with a thin blanket and went into the bathroom. I washed my hands, and turned on the tub faucets and watched the water pour into the tub with vitality and steam. When it was full, I turned off the water and undressed. Then, I went to get Abuelita.

She was not as heavy as I thought and when I carried her in my arms, her body fell into a V, and yet my legs were tired, shaky, and I felt as if the distance between the bedroom and bathroom was miles and years away. Amá, where are you?

I stepped into the bathtub one leg first, then the other. I bent my knees slowly to descend into the water slowly so I wouldn't scald her skin. There, there, Abuelita, I said, cradling her, smoothing her as we descended, I heard you. Her hair fell back and spread across the water like eagle's wings. The water in the tub overflowed and poured onto the tile of the floor. Then the moths came. Small, gray ones that came from her soul and out through her mouth fluttering to light, circling the single dull light bulb of the bathroom. Dying is lonely and I wanted to go to where the moths were, stay with her and plant chayotes whose vines would crawl up her fingers and into the clouds; I wanted to rest my head on her chest with her stroking my hair, telling me about the moths that lay within the soul and slowly eat the spirit up; I wanted to return to the waters of the womb with her so that we would never be alone again. I wanted. I wanted my Amá. I removed a few strands of hair from Abuelita's face and held her small light head within the hollow of my neck. The bathroom was filled with moths, and for the first time in a long time I cried, rocking us, crying for her, for me, for Amá, the sobs emerging from the depths of anguish, the misery of feeling half born, sobbing until finally the sobs rippled into circles and circles of sadness and relief. There, there, I said to Abuelita, rocking us gently, there, there.

[1982]

9
Observations on the Novel

Most of what has been said about short stories (on probability, narrative point of view, style) is relevant to the novel. And just as the short story of the last hundred years or so is rather different from earlier short fiction (see page 155), the novel—though here we must say of the last few hundred years—is different from earlier long fiction.

The ancient epic is at best a distant cousin to the novel, for though a narrative, the epic is in verse, and deals with god-like men and even with gods themselves. One has only to think of the *Odyssey* or the *Iliad,* or the *Aeneid* or *Beowulf* or *Paradise Lost* to recall that the epic does not deal with the sort of people one meets in *Tom Jones, David Copperfield, Crime and Punishment, The Return of the Native, The Portrait of a Lady, The Sun Also Rises, The Catcher in the Rye,* or *The Color Purple.*

The romance is perhaps a closer relative to the novel. Ancient romances were even in prose. But the hallmark of the romance, whether the romance is by a Greek sophist (Longus's *Daphnis and Chloe*) or by a medieval English poet (Chaucer's "The Knight's Tale") or by an American (Hawthorne's *The House of the Seven Gables*), is a presentation of the remote or the marvelous, rather than the local and the ordinary. The distinction is the same as that between the tale and the short story. "Tale" has the suggestion of a yarn, of unreality or of wondrous reality. (A case can be made for excluding Hawthorne's "Young Goodman Brown" from a collection of short stories on the ground that its remoteness and its allegorical implications mark it as a tale rather than a short story. This is not to say that it is inferior to a story, but only different.) In his preface to *The House of the Seven Gables* Hawthorne himself distinguishes between the romance and the novel:

> The latter form of composition is presumed to aim at a very minute
> fidelity, not merely to the possible, but to the probable and ordi-
> nary course of man's experience. The former—while, as a work

of art, it must rigidly subject itself to laws, and while it sins un-
pardonably so far as it may swerve aside from the truth of the
human heart—has fairly a right to present that truth under circumstances, to a great extent, of the writer's own choosing or
creation.

In his preface to *The Marble Faun* Hawthorne explains that he chose "Italy
as the site of his Romance" because it afforded him "a sort of poetic or
fairy precinct, where actualities would not be so terribly insisted upon as
the are . . . in America."

"Actualities . . . insisted upon." That, in addition to prose and length,
is the hallmark of the novel. The novel is a sort of long newspaper story;
the very word "novel" comes from an Italian word meaning a little new
thing, and is related to the French word that gives us "news." (It is notewor-
thy that the French cognate of Hawthorne's "actualities," *actualités,* means
"news" or "current events.") It is no accident that many novelists have been
newspapermen: Defoe, Dickens, Crane, Dreiser, Joyce, Hemingway, Camus.
And this connection with reportage perhaps helps to account for the relatively low esteem in which the novel is occasionally held: to some college
students, a course in the novel does not seem quite up to a course in poetry,
and people who read novels but not poetry are not likely to claim an interest in "literature."

Though Defoe's *Robinson Crusoe* is set in a far-off place, and thus
might easily have been a romance, in Defoe's day it was close to current
events, for it is a fictionalized version of events that had recently made
news—Alexander Selkirk's life on the island of Juan Fernandez. And the
story is not about marvelous happenings, but about a man's struggle for
survival in dismal surroundings. Crusoe is not armed with a magic sword,
nor does he struggle with monsters; he has a carpenter's chest of tools
and he struggles against commonplace nature. This chest was "much more
valuable than a shiploading of gold would have been at that time." The
world of romance contains splendid castles and enchanted forests, but Crusoe's world contains not much more than a plot of ground, some animals
and vegetables, and Friday. "I fancied I could make all but the wheel [of
a wheelbarrow Crusoe needed], but that I had no notion of, neither did
I know how to go about it; besides, I had no possible way to make the
iron gudgeons for the spindle or axis of the wheel to run in, so I gave
it over." The book, in short, emphasizes not the strange, but (given the
initial situation) the usual, the commonsensical, the probable. The world
of *Robinson Crusoe* is hardly different from the world we meet in the beginning of almost any novel:

> My father's family name being Pirrip, and my Christian name
> Philip, my infant tongue could make of both names nothing longer
> or more explicit than Pip. So I called myself Pip, and came to be
> called Pip.

> I give Pirrip as my father's family name, on the authority of his tombstone and my sister — Mrs. Joe Gargery, who married the blacksmith.

> Charles Dickens, *Great Expectations*

> If you really want to hear about it, the first thing you'll probably want to know is where I was born, and what my lousy childhood was like, and how my parents were occupied and all before they had me, and all that David Copperfield kind of crap, but I don't feel like going into it, if you want to know the truth.

> J. D. Salinger, *The Catcher in the Rye*

> It was June, 1933, one week after Commencement, when Kay Leiland Strong, Vassar '33, the first of her class to run around the table at the Class Day dinner, was married to Harald Petersen, Reed '27, in the chapel of St. George's Church, P.E., Karl F. Reiland, Rector. Outside, on Stuyvesant Square, the trees were in full leaf, and the wedding guests arriving by twos and threes in taxis heard the voices of children playing round the statue of Peter Stuyvesant in the park.

> Mary McCarthy, *The Group*

A boy who in boy's language seems reluctant to talk of his "lousy childhood"; a young woman who ran around the table at the Class Day dinner. In all these passages, and in the openings of most other novels, we are confronted with current biography. In contrast to these beginnings, look at the beginning of one of Chaucer's great romances:

> Whilom,° as olde stories tellen us,   *once*
> There was a duc that highte° Theseus;   *was named*
> Of Atthenes he was lord and governour,
> And in his tyme swich° a conquerour,   *such*
> That gretter was ther noon under the sonne.

"Whilom." "Olde stories." "Gretter was ther noon under the sonne." We are in a timeless past, in which unusual people dwell. But the novel is almost always set in the present or very recent past, and it deals with ordinary people. It so often deals with ordinary people, and presents them, apparently, in so ordinary a fashion that we sometimes wonder what is the point of it. Although the romance is often "escape" literature, it usually is didactic, holding up to us images of noble and ignoble behavior, revealing the rewards of courage and the power of love. In the preface to *The Marble Faun,* for instance, Hawthorne says he "proposed to himself to merely write a fanciful story, evolving a thoughtful moral, and did not propose attempting a portraiture of Italian manners and character." But portraiture is what the novelist gives us. Intent on revealing the world of real men and women going about their daily work and play, he does not simplify his characters into representatives of vices and virtues as does the romancer who wishes to evolve a thoughtful moral, but gives abundant detail— some of it apparently irrelevant. The innumerable details add up to a long book, although there need not be many physical happenings. The novel tells a story, of course, but the story is not only about what people overtly do but also about what they think (i.e., their mental doings) and about the society in which they are immersed and by which they are in part shaped. In the much-quoted preface to *Pierre and Jean,* Maupassant says:

> The skill of the novelist's plan will not reside in emotional effects, in attractive writing, in a striking beginning or a moving dénouement, but in the artful building up of solid details from which the essential meaning of the work will emerge.

As we read a novel we feel we are seeing not the "higher reality" or the "inner reality" so often mentioned by students of the arts, but the real reality.

The short story, too, is detailed, but commonly it reveals only a single character at a moment of crisis, whereas the novel commonly traces the development of an individual, a group of people, a world. The novelist, of course, has an attitude toward his world; he is not compiling an almanac but telling an invented story, making a work of art, offering not merely a representation of reality but a response to it, and he therefore selects and shapes his material. One way of selecting and shaping the material is through the chosen point of view: we do not get everything in nineteenth-century England, but only everything that Pip remembers or chooses to set down about his experiences, and what he sets down is colored by his personality. "I remember Mr. Hubble as a tough high-shouldered stooping old man, of a saw-dusty fragrance, with his legs extraordinarily wide apart: so that in my short days I always saw some miles of open country between them when I met him coming up the lane." In any case, the coherence in a novel seems inclusive rather than exclusive. The novelist usually conveys the sense that he, as distinct from his characters, is—in the words of Christopher Isherwood's *The Berlin Stories*—"a camera with its shutter open, quite passive, recording not thinking. Recording the man shaving at the windows opposite and the woman in the kimono washing her hair. Some day, all of this will have to be developed, carefully fixed, printed."

It is not merely that the novel gives us details. *Gulliver's Travels* has plenty of details about people six inches tall and people sixty feet tall, and about a flying island and rational horses. But these things are recognized as fanciful inventions, though they do turn our mind toward the real world. *Gulliver* is a satire that holds up to us a picuture of a fantastic world by which, paradoxically, we come to see the real world a little more clearly. The diminutive stature of the Lilliputians is an amusing and potent metaphor for the littleness of man, the flying island for abstract thinkers who have lost touch with reality, and so on. But the novelist who wants to show us the littleness of man invents not Lilliputians but a world of normal-sized people who do little things and have little thoughts.

Having spent so much time saying that the novel is not the epic or romance or fable, we must mention that a work may hover on the borderlines of these forms. Insofar as *Moby Dick* narrates with abundant realistic detail the experiences of a whaler ("This book," Dorothy Parker has said, "taught me more about whales than I ever wanted to know"), it is a novel; but in its evocation of mystery—Queequeg, the prophecies, Ishmael's miraculous rescue from the sea filled with sharks who "glided by as if with padlocks on their mouths"—it is a romance with strong symbolic implications.

The point is that although a reader of a long piece of prose fiction can complain that he did not get what he paid for, he should find out what he did get, rather than damn it for not being what it isn't. Bishop Butler's famous remark is relevant to literary criticism: "Everything is what it is and not another thing."

POETRY

10

A First Approach to Poetry

The title of this chapter is a bit misleading, since we have already spent a few pages discussing two poems in Chapter 1, "Reading and Responding to Literature." But here we will begin again, taking a different approach.

First, some brief advice.

1. Read the poem aloud, or, if you can't bring yourself to read aloud, at least sound the poem in your mind's ear. Try to catch the speaker's tone of voice.
2. Pay attention not only to the black marks on the white paper but also to the white spaces between groups of lines. If a space follows some lines, pause at least briefly, and take the preceding lines as a unit of thought.
3. Read the poem a second and a third time. Now that you know how it ends, you'll be able to see the connections between the beginning and what follows.

The following short poem is by Langston Hughes (1902–67), an African-American writer, born in Joplin, Mississippi, who lived part of his youth in Mexico, spent a year at Columbia Univeristy, served as a merchant seaman, and worked in a Paris nightclub, where he showed some of his poems to Dr. Alain Locke, a strong advocate of African-American literature. Encouraged by Locke, when Hughes returned to the United States he continued to write, publishing fiction, plays, essays, and biographies; he also founded theaters, gave public readings, and was, in short, a highly visible presence. The poem that we reprint, "Harlem" (1951), provided Lorraine Hansberry with the title of her well-known play, *A Raisin in the Sun* (1958).

Langston Hughes

Harlem

What happens to a dream deferred?

    Does it dry up
    like a raisin in the sun?
    Or fester like a sore—
    And then run?   5
    Does it stink like rotten meat?
    Or crust and sugar over—
    like a syrupy sweet?

    Maybe it just sags
    like a heavy load.   10

    Or does it explode?

[1951]

Read the poem at least twice, and then think about its effect on you.

Do you find the poem interesting? Why or why not?
Do some things in it interest you more than others? If so, why?
Does anything in it puzzle you? If so, what?

Before reading any further, you might jot down your responses to some of these questions. And, whatever your responses, how can you account for them?

Of course different readers will respond at least somewhat differently to any work. On the other hand, since writers want to communicate, they try to control their readers' responses, and they count on their readers to understand the meanings of words as they understand them. Thus, Hughes assumed that his readers knew that Harlem was the site of a large African-American community in New York City. A reader who confuses the title of the poem with Haarlem in the Netherlands will wonder what this poem is saying about the tulip-growing center in northern Holland.

Let's assume that the reader understands Hughes is talking about Harlem, New York, and, further, that the reader understands the "dream deferred" to refer to the unfulfilled hopes of African-Americans who live in a dominant white society. But Hughes does not say "hopes," he says "dream," and he does not say "unfulfilled," he says "deferred." You might ask yourself exactly what differences there are between these words. Next, when you have read the poem several times, you might think about which expression is better in the context, "Unfulfilled Hopes" or "Dream Deferred," and why?

Thinking about ''Harlem''

Let's turn to an analysis of the poem, an examination of how the parts fit. As you look at the poem, think about the parts, and jot down whatever notes come to mind. After you have written your own notes, consider the annotations of one student:

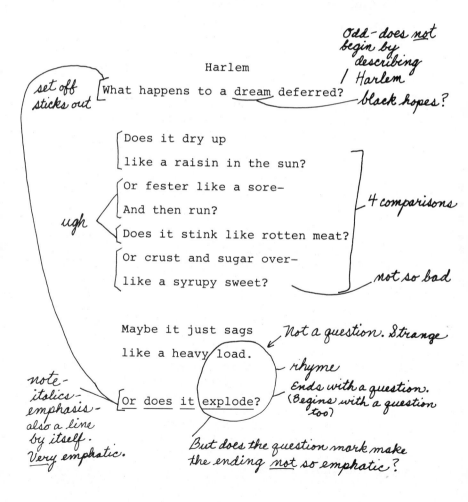

Harlem

Odd - does not begin by describing / Harlem black hopes?

set off / sticks out
What happens to a dream deferred?

Does it dry up
like a raisin in the sun?
Or fester like a sore—
And then run?
Does it stink like rotten meat?
Or crust and sugar over—
like a syrupy sweet?

ugh

4 comparisons

not so bad

Maybe it just sags
like a heavy load.

Not a question. Strange

rhyme

Or does it explode?

Ends with a question. (Begins with a question too)

note - italics - emphasis - also a line by itself. Very emphatic.

But does the question mark make the ending not so emphatic?

These annotations chiefly get at the structure of the poem, the relationship of the parts. The student notices that the poem begins with a line set off by itself and ends with a line set off by itself, and he also notices that each of these lines is a question. Further, he indicates that each of these two lines is emphasized in other ways: The first begins further to the left than any of the other lines—as though the other lines are subheadings or are in some way subordinate—and the last is italicized. In short, he comments on the *structure* of the poem.

Some Journal Entries

The student who made these annotations later wrote an entry in his journal:

Feb. 18. Since the title is "Harlem," it's obvious that the "dream" is by African-American people. Also, obvious that Hughes thinks that if the "dream" doesn't become real there may be riots ("explode"). I like "raisin in the sun" (maybe because I like the play), and I like the business about "a syrupy sweet"--much more pleasant than the festering sore and the rotten meat. But if the dream becomes "sweet," what's wrong with that? Why should something "sweet" explode?

Feb. 21. Prof. McCabe said to think of structure or form of a poem as a sort of architecture, a building with a foundation, floors, etc. topped by a roof-- but since we read a poem from top to bottom, it's like a building upside down. Title or first line is foundation (even though it's at top); last line is roof, capping the whole. As you read, you add layers. Foundation of "Harlem" is a question (first line). Then, set back a bit from foundation, or built on it by white space, a tall room (7 lines high, with 4 questions); then, on top of this room, another room (two lines, one statement, not a question). Funny; I thought that in poems all stanzas are the same number of lines. Then--more white space, so another unit--the roof. Man, this roof is going to fall in--"explode." Not just the roof, maybe the whole house.

Feb. 21, pm. I get it; one line at start, one line at end; both are questions, but the last sort of says (because it is in italics) that it is the most likely answer to the question of the first line. The last line is also a question, but it's still an answer. The big stanza (7 lines) has 4 questions: 2 lines, 2 lines, 1 line, 2 lines. Maybe the switch to 1 line is to give some variety, so as not to be dull? It's exactly in the middle of the poem. I get the progress from raisin in the sun (dried, but not so terrible), to festering sore and to stinking meat, but I still don't see what's so bad about "a syrupy sweet." Is Hughes saying that after things are very bad they will get better? But why, then, the explosion at the end?

Feb. 23. "Heavy load" and "sags" in next-to-last stanza seems to me to suggest slaves with bales of cotton, or maybe poor cotton pickers dragging big sacks of cotton. Or maybe people doing heavy labor in Harlem. Anyway, very tired. Different from running sore and stinking meat earlier; not disgusting, but pressing down, deadening. Maybe worse than a sore or rotten meat--a hard, hopeless life. And then the last line. Just one line, no fancy (and disgusting) simile. Boom! Not just pressed down and tired, like maybe some racist whites think (hope?) blacks will be? Bang! Will there be survivors?

Drawing chiefly on these notes, the student jotted down some key ideas to guide him through a draft of an analysis of the poem. (The organization of the draft posed no problem; the student simply followed the organization of the poem.)

On the following page, we give the notes.

11 lines; short, but powerful; explosive
Question (first line)
Answers (set off by space, & also indented)
"raisin in the sun": shrinking ⎫
"sore"   ⎬ *disgusting*
"rotten meat"   ⎭
"syrupy sweet": relief from disgusting comparisons
Final question (last line): explosion?
    explosive (powerful) because:
      short, condensed, packed
      in italics
      stands by self — like first line
      no fancy comparison; very direct

Final Draft

Here is the final analysis:

Langston Hughes's "Harlem"

"Harlem" is a poem that is only eleven lines long, but it is charged with power. It explodes. Hughes sets the stage, so to speak, by telling us in the title that he is talking about Harlem, and then he begins by asking "What happens to a dream deferred?" The rest of the poem is set off by being indented, as though it is the answer to his question. This answer is in three parts (three stanzas, of different lengths).

In a way, it's wrong to speak of the answer, since the rest of the poem consists of questions, but I think Hughes means that each question (for instance, does a "deferred" hope "dry up / like a raisin in the sun?") really is an answer, something that really has happened and that will happen again. The first question, "Does it dry up / like a raisin in the sun?" is a famous line. To compare hope to a raisin dried in the sun is to suggest a terrible shrinking. The next two comparisons are to a "sore" and to "rotten meat." These comparisons are less clever, but they are very effective because they are disgusting. Then, maybe because of the disgusting comparisons, he gives a comparison that is not at all disgusting. In this comparison he says that maybe the "dream deferred" will "crust over-- / like a syrupy sweet."

The seven lines with four comparisons are followed by a stanza of two lines with just one comparison:

Maybe it just sags

like a heavy load.

So if we thought that this postponed dream might finally turn into something "sweet," we were kidding ourselves. Hughes comes down to earth, in a short stanza, with an image of a heavy load, which probably also calls to mind images of people bent under heavy loads, maybe of cotton, or maybe just any sort of heavy load carried by African-Americans in Harlem and elsewhere.

The opening question ("What happens to a dream deferred?") was followed by four questions in seven lines, but now, with "Maybe it just sags / like a heavy load" we get a statement, as though the poet at last has found an answer. But at the end we get one more question, set off by itself and in italics: "Or does it explode?" This line itself is explosive for three reasons: it is short, it is italicized, and it is a stanza in itself. It's also interesting that this line, unlike the earlier lines, does not

```
use a simile. It's almost as though Hughes is say-
ing, "O.K., we've had enough fancy ways of talking
about this terrible situation; here it is, straight."
```

TOPICS FOR DISCUSSION AND WRITING

1. The student's analysis suggests that the comparison with "a syrupy sweet" is a deliberately misleading happy ending that serves to make the real ending even more powerful. In class another student suggested that Hughes may be referring to African-Americans who play the Uncle Tom, people who adopt a smiling manner in order to cope with an oppressive society. Which explanation do you prefer, and why? What do you think of combining the two? Or can you offer a different explanation?

2. Do you suppose that virtually all African-Americans respond to this poem in a way that is substantially different from the way virtually all Caucasians respond? Explain your position.

11
Lyric Poetry

For the ancient Greeks, a **lyric** was a song accompanied by a lyre. It was short, and it usually expressed a single emotion, such as joy or sorrow. The word is now used more broadly, referring to a poem that, neither narrative (telling a story) nor strictly dramatic (performed by actors), is an emotional or reflective soliloquy. Still, it is rarely very far from a singing voice. James Joyce saw the lyric as the "verbal vesture of an instant of emotion, a rhythmical cry such as ages ago cheered on the man who pulled at the oar." Such lyrics, too, were sung more recently than "ages ago." Here is a song that American slaves sang when rowing heavy loads.

Anonymous

Michael Row the Boat Ashore

Michael row the boat ashore, Hallelujah!
Michael's boat's a freedom boat, Hallelujah!
Sister, help to trim the sail, Hallelujah!
Jordan stream is wide and deep, Hallelujah!
Freedom stands on the other side, Hallelujah!

We might pause for a moment to comment on why people sing at work. There are at least three reasons: (1) work done rhythmically goes more efficiently; (2) the songs relieve the boredom of the work; and (3) the songs—whether narrative or lyrical—provide something of an outlet for the workers' frustrations.

Speaking roughly, we can say that whereas a narrative (whether in prose or poetry) is set in the past, telling what happened, a lyric is set in the present, catching a speaker in a moment of expression. But a lyric can, of course, glance backward or forward, as in this folk song, usually called "Careless Love."

Anonymous

Careless Love

Love, O love, O careless love,
You see what careless love can do.
When I wore my apron low,
Couldn't keep you from my do,°   *door*
    Fare you well, fare you well.
Now I wear my apron high,
Scarce see you passin' by,
    Fare you well, fare you well.

Notice, too, that a lyric, like a narrative, can have a sort of plot: "Michael" moves toward the idea of freedom, and "Careless Love" implies a story of desertion, but again, the emphasis is on a present state of mind.

Lyrics are sometimes differentiated among themselves. For example, if a lyric is melancholy or mournfully contemplative, especially if it laments a death, it may be called an **elegy.** If a lyric is rather long, elaborate, and on a lofty theme such as immortality or a hero's victory, it may be called an **ode** or a **hymn.** Distinctions among lyrics are often vague, and one person's ode may be another's elegy. Still, when writers use one of these words in their titles, they are inviting the reader to recall the tradition in which they are working. Of the poet's link to tradition T. S. Eliot said:

> No poet, no artist of any art, has his complete meaning alone.
> His significance, his appreciation is the appreciation of his relation to the dead poets and artists. You cannot value him alone; you must set him, for contrast and comparison, among the dead.

Although the lyric is often ostensibly addressed to someone (the "you" in "Careless Love"), the reader usually feels that the speaker is really talking to himself or herself. In "Careless Love," the speaker need not be in the presence of her man; rather, her heart is overflowing (the reader senses) and she pretends to address him.

A comment by John Stuart Mill on poetry is especially true of the lyric:

> Eloquence is *heard,* poetry is *over*heard. Eloquence supposes an audience; the peculiarity of poetry appears to us to lie in the poet's utter unconsciousness of a listener. Poetry is feeling confessing itself to itself, in moments of solitude.

This is particularly true, of course, in work-songs such as "Michael Row the Boat Ashore," where there is no audience: the singers sing for themselves, participating rather than performing. As one prisoner in Texas said: "They really be singing about the way they feel inside. Since they can't say it to nobody, they sing a song about it." The sense of "feeling confessing itself to itself, in moments of solitude" or of "singing about the way they feel inside" is strong and clear in this short cowboy song.

Anonymous

The Colorado Trail

Eyes like the morning star,
Cheeks like a rose,
Laura was a pretty girl
God Almighty knows.

Weep all ye little rains,
Wail winds wail,
All along, along, along
The Colorado trail.

Here is another anonymous poem, this one probably written in England in the early sixteenth century.

Anonymous

Western Wind

Westron wind, when will thou blow?
The small rain down can rain.
Christ, that my love were in my arms,
And I in my bed again.

TOPICS FOR DISCUSSION AND WRITING

1. In "Western Wind," what do you think is the tone of the speaker's voice in the first two lines? Angry? Impatient? Supplicating? Be as precise as possible. What is the tone in the next two lines?
2. In England, the west wind, warmed by the Gulf Stream, rises in the spring. What associations link the wind and rain of lines 1 and 2 with lines 3 and 4?
3. Ought we to have been told why the lovers are separated? Explain.

Li-Young Lee (American; b. 1957)

I Ask My Mother to Sing

She begins, and my grandmother joins her.
Mother and daughter sing like young girls.
If my father were alive, he would play
his accordian and sway like a boat.

I've never been in Peking, or the Summer Palace,
nor stood on the great Stone Boat to watch
the rain begin on Kuen Ming Lake, the picknickers
running away in the grass.

But I love to hear it sung;

how the waterlilies fill with rain until
they overturn, spilling water into water,
then rock back, and fill with more.

Both women have begun to cry.
But neither stops her song.

[1986]

TOPICS FOR DISCUSSION AND WRITING

1. Why might the speaker ask the women to sing?
2. Why do the women cry? Why do they continue to sing?

Langston Hughes *(American; 1902–67)*

Evenin' Air Blues

Folks, I come up North
Cause they told me de North was fine.
I come up North
Cause they told me de North was fine.
Been up here six months— *5*
I'm about to lose my mind.

This mornin' for breakfast
I chawed de mornin' air.
This mornin' for breakfast
Chawed de mornin' air. *10*
But this evenin' for supper,
I got evenin' air to spare.

Believe I'll do a little dancin'
Just to drive my blues away—
A little dancin' *15*
To drive my blues away,
Cause when I'm dancin'
De blues forgets to stay.

But if you was to ask me
How de blues they come to be, *20*
Says if you was to ask me
How de blues they come to be—
You wouldn't need to ask me:
Just look at me and see!

[1942]

TOPIC FOR DISCUSSION AND WRITING

In what ways (subject, language) does this poem resemble blues you
may have heard? Does it differ in any ways? If so, how?

Negro

I am a Negro:
   Black as the night is black,
   Black like the depths of my Africa.

I've been a slave:
   Caesar told me to keep his door-step clean.   *5*
   I brushed the boots of Washington.

I've been a worker:
   Under my hand the pyramids rose.
   I made mortar for the Woolworth Building.

I've been a singer: *10*
   All the way from Africa to Georgia
   I carried my sorrow songs.
   I made ragtime.

I've been a victim:
   The Belgians cut off my hands in the Congo.   *15*
   They lynch me still in Mississippi.

I am a Negro:
   Black as the night is black,
   Black like the depths of my Africa.

[1926]

The speaker of a lyric can usually be identified to some degree. The speaker of "Careless Love" (p. 420) is a woman—we know this because she says, "When I wore my apron low"—and the speaker of "The Colorado Trail" (p. 421) is presumably a man who loved a woman named Laura. Moreover, the speaker of a lyric usually expresses an emotion linked to a particular circumstance, for instance the death of Laura.

TOPICS FOR DISCUSSION AND WRITING

1. In what ways is the speaker of "Negro" different from the usual speaker of lyric?
2. Aside from the reference to "a slave" in line 4, the poem's strongest note of social protest is concentrated in the next-to-last stanza. Why do you suppose the poet went on to add another stanza—actually a repetition of the first stanza?

John Lennon (English; 1940–80)
Paul McCartney (English; b. 1942)

Eleanor Rigby

Ah, look at all the lonely people!
Ah, look at all the lonely people!

Eleanor Rigby
Picks up the rice in the church where a wedding has been,
Lives in a dream.   5
Waits at the window
Wearing the face that she keeps in a jar by the door.
Who is it for?

All the lonely people,
Where do they all come from?   10
All the lonely people,
Where do they all belong?

Father McKenzie,
Writing the words of a sermon that no one will hear,
No one comes near.   15

Look at him working,
Darning his socks in the night when there's nobody there.
What does he care?

All the lonely people,
Where do they all come from?   20
All the lonely people,
Where do they all belong?

Ah, look at all the lonely people!
Ah, look at all the lonely people!

Eleanor Rigby   25
Died in the church and was buried along with her name,
Nobody came.
Father McKenzie,
Wiping the dirt from his hands as he walks from the grave,
No one was saved.   30

All the lonely people,
Where do they all come from?
All the lonely people,
Where do they all belong?

Ah, look at all the lonely people!   *35*
Ah, look at all the lonely people!

[1966]

TOPICS FOR DISCUSSION AND WRITING

1. Is the poem chiefly about Eleanor Rigby?
2. What is Father McKenzie doing in the poem?

Edna St. Vincent Millay (American; 1892–1950)

The Spring and the Fall

In the spring of the year, in the spring of the year,
I walked the road beside my dear.
The trees were black where the bark was wet.
I see them yet, in the spring of the year.
He broke me a bough of the blossoming peach   *5*
That was out of the way and hard to reach.

In the fall of the year, in the fall of the year,
I walked the road beside my dear.
The rooks went up with a raucous trill.
I hear them still, in the fall of the year.   *10*
He laughed at all I dared to praise,
And broke my heart, in little ways.

Year be springing or year be falling,
The bark will drip and the birds be calling.
There's much that's fine to see and hear   *15*
In the spring of a year, in the fall of a year.
'Tis not love's going hurts my days,
But that it went in little ways.

[1923]

TOPICS FOR DISCUSSION AND WRITING

1. The first stanza describes the generally happy beginning of a love story. Where do you find the first hint of an unhappy ending?
2. Describe the rhyme scheme of the first stanza, including rhymes within lines. Do the second and third stanzas repeat the pattern, or are there some variations? What repetition of sounds other than rhyme do you note?
3. Put into your own words the last two lines. How do you react to the lines; that is, do you find the conclusion surprising, satisfying (or unsatisfying), recognizable from your own experience, anticlimactic, or what?
4. In two or three paragraphs explain how the imagery of the poem contributes to its meaning.

Wilfred Owen (English; 1893–1918)

Anthem for Doomed Youth

What passing-bells for these who die as cattle?
Only the monstrous anger of the guns.
Only the stuttering rifles' rapid rattle
Can patter out their hasty orisons.
No mockeries for them from prayers or bells,   *5*
Nor any voice of mourning save the choirs—
The shrill, demented choirs of wailing shells;
And bugles calling for them from sad shires.

What candles may be held to speed° them all?   *aid*
Not in the hands of boys, but in their eyes   *10*
Shall shine the holy glimmers of good-byes.
The pallor of girls' brows shall be their pall;
Their flowers the tenderness of patient minds,
And each slow dusk a drawing-down of blinds.

[1920]

TOPICS FOR DISCUSSION AND WRITING

1. Exactly what is an anthem? What are some of the words or phrases in this poem that might be found in a traditional anthem? What are some of the words or phrases that you would not expect in an anthem?
2. How would you characterize the speaker's state of mind? (Your response probably will require more than one word.)

Walt Whitman (*American; 1819–92*)

A Noiseless Patient Spider

A noiseless patient spider,
I mark'd where on a little promontory it stood isolated,
Mark'd how to explore the vacant vast surrounding,
It launch'd forth filament, filament, filament, out of itself,
Ever unreeling them, ever tirelessly speeding them.   *5*

And you O my soul where you stand,
Surrounded, detached, in measureless oceans of space,
Ceaselessly musing, venturing, throwing, seeking the spheres to
    connect them,
Till the bridge you will need be form'd, till the ductile anchor
    hold,
Till the gossamer thread you fling catch somewhere,
    O my soul.   *10*

[1862–63]

TOPICS FOR DISCUSSION AND WRITING

1. How are the suggestions in "launch'd" (line 4) and "unreeling" (line 5) continued in the second stanza?
2. How are the varying lengths of lines 1, 4, and 8 relevant to their ideas?
3. The second stanza is not a complete sentence. Why? The poem is unrhymed. What effect does the near-rhyme (hold: soul) in the last two lines have on you?

John Keats (*English; 1795–1821*)

Ode on a Grecian Urn

I

Thou still unravished bride of quietness,
    Thou foster-child of silence and slow time,
Sylvan historian, who canst thus express
    A flowery tale more sweetly than our rhyme:
What leaf-fringed legend haunts about thy shape   *5*

Of deities or mortals, or of both,
    In Tempe or the dales of Arcady?
What men or gods are these? What maidens loth?
What mad pursuit? What struggle to escape?
    What pipes and timbrels? What wild ecstasy?   *10*

II

Heard melodies are sweet, but those unheard
    Are sweeter; therefore, ye soft pipes, play on;
Not to the sensual° ear, but, more endeared,   *sensuous*
    Pipe to the spirit ditties of no tone:
Fair youth, beneath the trees, thou canst not leave   *15*
    Thy song, nor ever can those trees be bare;
        Bold Lover, never, never canst thou kiss,
Though winning near the goal—yet, do not grieve;
        She cannot fade, though thou hast not thy bliss,
    For ever wilt thou love, and she be fair!   *20*

III

Ah, happy, happy boughs! that cannot shed
    Your leaves, nor ever bid the Spring adieu;
And, happy melodist, unwearied,
    For ever piping songs for ever new;
More happy love! more happy, happy love!   *25*
    For ever warm and still to be enjoyed,
        For ever panting, and for ever young;
All breathing human passion far above,
    That leaves a heart high-sorrowful and cloyed,
        A burning forehead, and a parching tongue.   *30*

IV

Who are these coming to the sacrifice?
    To what green altar, O mysterious priest,
Lead'st thou that heifer lowing at the skies,
    And all her silken flanks with garlands drest?
What little town by river or sea shore,   *35*
    Or mountain-built with peaceful citadel,
        Is emptied of this folk, this pious morn?
And, little town, thy streets for evermore
    Will silent be; and not a soul to tell
        Why thou art desolate can e'er return.   *40*

V

O Attic shape! Fair attitude! with brede°   *design*
    Of marble men and maidens overwrought,
With forest branches and the trodden weed;
    Thou, silent form, dost tease us out of thought
As doth eternity: Cold Pastoral!   45
When old age shall this generation waste,
        Thou shalt remain, in midst of other woe
    Than ours, a friend to man, to whom thou say'st,
"Beauty is truth, truth beauty,"—that is all
    Ye know on earth, and all ye need to know.   50

[1820]

TOPICS FOR DISCUSSION AND WRITING

1. If you do not know the meaning of "sylvan," check a dictionary.
    Why does Keats call the urn a "sylvan" historian (line 3)? As the poem
    continues, what evidence is there that the urn cannot "express" (line
    3) a tale so sweetly as the speaker said?
2. What do you make of lines 11–14?
3. What do you think the urn may stand for in the first three stanzas?
    In the third stanza is the speaker caught up in the urn's world or
    is he sharply aware of his own?
4. Do you take "tease us out of thought" (line 44) to mean "draw us
    into a realm of imaginative experience superior to that of reason"
    or to mean "draw us into futile and frustrating questions"? Or both?
    Or neither? What suggestions do you find in "Cold Pastoral" (line
    45)?
5. Do lines 49–50 perhaps mean that imagination, stimulated by the
    urn, achieves a realm richer than the daily world? Or perhaps that
    art, the highest earthly wisdom, suggests there is a realm wherein
    earthly troubles are resolved? Support your response.

E. E. Cummings (American; 1894–1962)

anyone lived in a pretty how town

anyone lived in a pretty how town
(with up so floating many bells down)
spring summer autumn winter
he sang his didn't he danced his did.   4

Women and men(both little and small)
cared for anyone not at all
they sowed their isn't they reaped their same
sun moon stars rain   *8*

children guessed(but only a few
and down they forgot as up they grew
autumn winter spring summer)
that noone loved him more by more   *12*

when by now and tree by leaf
she laughed his joy she cried his grief
bird by snow and stir by still
anyone's any was all to her   *16*

someones married their everyones
laughed their cryings and did their dance
(sleep wake hope and then)they
said their nevers they slept their dream   *20*

stars rain sun moon
(and only the snow can begin to explain
how children are apt to forget to remember
with up so floating many bells down)   *24*

one day anyone died i guess
(and noone stooped to kiss his face)
busy folk buried them side by side
little by little and was by was   *28*

all by all and deep by deep
and more by more they dream their sleep
noone and anyone earth by april
wish by spirit and if by yes.   *32*

Women and men(both dong and ding)
summer autumn winter spring
reaped their sowing and went their came
sun moon stars rain   *36*

                                    [1940]

TOPICS FOR DISCUSSION AND WRITING

1. Put into normal order (as far as possible) the words of the first two stanzas and then compare your version with Cummings's. What does Cummings gain—or lose?

2. Characterize the "anyone" who "sang his didn't" and "danced his did." In your opinion, how does he differ from the people who "sowed their isn't they reaped the same"?

3. Some readers interpret "anyone died" (line 25) to mean that the child matured and became as dead as the other adults. How might you support or refute this interpretation?

12
The Speaking Tone of Voice

Everything written is as good as it is dramatic. . . . [A poem is] heard as sung or spoken by a person in a scene—in character, in a setting. By whom, where and when is the question. By the dreamer of a better world out in a storm in Autumn; by a lover under a window at night.

—Robert Frost, Preface, *A Way Out*

If we fall into the habit of saying "Whitman says, 'A noiseless patient spider, / I mark'd'" or "Sylvia Plath says, 'You do not,'" we neglect the important truth in Frost's comment: a poem is written by an author, but it is spoken by an invented speaker. The author counterfeits the speech of a person in a particular situation. The anonymous author of "Western Wind" (page 421) invents the speech of an unhappy lover who longs for the spring; John Keats, in "Ode on a Grecian Urn" (page 428), invents the speech of someone contemplating an ancient vase.

The speaker's voice, of course, often has the ring of the author's own voice, and to make a distinction between speaker and author may at times seem perverse. Robert Burns, for example, sometimes lets us know that the poem is spoken by "Rob"; he may address his wife by name; beneath the title "To a Mouse" he writes, "On Turning Up Her Nest with the Plow, November, 1785," and beneath the title "To a Mountain Daisy" he writes, "On Turning One Down with the Plow in April, 1786." Still, even in these allegedly autobiographical poems, it may be convenient to distinguish between author and speaker; the speaker is Burns the lover, or Burns the meditative man, or Burns the compassionate man, not simply Robert Burns the poet. Here are two poems by Burns; in the first the lover speaks, in the second we hear a different speaker. (If you read the poems aloud, the meanings of many of the Scots words will become clear. Thus, in line 5, "wad" is "would." And if you read the poems aloud, you will get a strong sense of the speakers.)

Robert Burns *(Scottish; 1759–96)*

Mary Morison

O Mary, at thy window be,
   It is the wished, the trysted hour!
Those smiles and glances let me see,
   That make the miser's treasure poor: *4*
How blithely wad I bide the stour,°   *endure the struggle*
   A weary slave frae sun to sun,
Could I the rich reward secure,
   The lovely Mary Morison.   *8*

Yestreen when to the trembling string
   The dance gaed° through the lighted ha'   *went*
To thee my fancy took its wing,
   I sat, but neither heard nor saw: *12*
Though this was fair, and that was braw,°   *handsome*
   And yon the toast of a' the town,
I sighed, and said amang them a',
   "Ye are na Mary Morison."   *16*

O Mary, canst thou wreck his peace,
   Wha for thy sake wad gladly die?
Or canst thou break that heart of his,
   Whase only faut° is loving thee?   *fault* *20*
If love for love thou wilt na gie,°   *give*
   At least be pity to me shown!
A thought ungentle canna be
   The thought o' Mary Morison.   *24*

[1788]

John Anderson My Jo

John Anderson my jo,° John,   *sweetheart*
   When we were first acquent,
Your locks were like the raven,
   Your bonnie brow was brent,°   *smooth* *4*
But now your brow is beld, John,
   Your locks are like the snaw,
But blessings on your frosty pow,°
   John Anderson my jo!   *8*

John Anderson my jo, John,
  We clamb the hill thegither,
And monie a cantie° day, John   *happy*
  We've had wi' ane anither: **12**
Now we maun° totter down, John,   *must*
  And hand in hand we'll go,
And sleep thegither at the foot,
  John Anderson my jo!   **16**

                    [1788]

TOPICS FOR DISCUSSION AND WRITING

1. In the first poem, do you think that the speaker is really addressing
   Mary Morison?
2. In "Mary Morison," how convincing are the assertions of the first
   stanza (that her smiles and glances are more valuable than great
   wealth; that he would willingly be a "weary slave" if only he could
   win her)? Does the third stanza somehow sound truer, more convincing? If so, why? The poem is excellent throughout, but many
   readers find the second stanza the best of the three. Do you?
3. In "John Anderson My Jo," the speaker cannot be identified with
   Burns, but do we feel that there is in the poem anything of the particular accent of an old lady? Why?

Although all poems are "dramatic" in Frost's sense of being uttered by
a speaker in a situation, and although most short poems are monologues,
the term **dramatic monologue** is reserved for those poems in which a
single character—not the poet—is speaking at a critical moment to a person or persons whose presence we strongly feel. The most famous example is Robert Browning's "My Last Duchess."

Robert Browning (English; 1812–89)

My Last Duchess

Ferrara°   *town in Italy*

That's my last Duchess painted on the wall,
Looking as if she were alive. I call

That piece a wonder, now; Frà Pandolf's° hands   *a fictitious painter*
Worked busily a day, and there she stands.
Will't please you sit and look at her? I said   *5*
"Frà Pandolf" by design, for never read
Strangers like you that pictured countenance,
The depth and passion of its earnest glance,
But to myself they turned (since none puts by
The curtain I have drawn for you, but I)   *10*
And seemed as they would ask me, if they durst,
How such a glance came there; so, not the first
Are you to turn and ask thus. Sir, 'twas not
Her husband's presence only, called that spot
Of joy into the Duchess' cheek; perhaps   *15*
Frà Pandolf chanced to say "Her mantle laps
Over my lady's wrist too much," or, "Paint
Must never hope to reproduce the faint
Half-flush that dies along her throat." Such stuff
Was courtesy, she thought, and cause enough   *20*
For calling up that spot of joy. She had
A heart—how shall I say?—too soon made glad,
Too easily impressed; she liked whate'er
She looked on, and her looks went everywhere.
Sir, 'twas all one! My favor at her breast,   *25*
The dropping of the daylight in the west,
The bough of cherries some officious fool
Broke in the orchard for her, the white mule
She rode with round the terrace—all and each
Would draw from her alike the approving speech,   *30*
Or blush, at least. She thanked men—good! but thanked
Somehow—I know not how—as if she ranked
My gift of a nine-hundred-years-old name
With anybody's gift. Who'd stoop to blame
This sort of trifling? Even had you skill   *35*
In speech—(which I have not)—to make your will
Quite clear to such an one, and say, "Just this
Or that in you disgusts me; here you miss,
Or there exceed the mark"—and if she let
Herself be lessoned so, nor plainly set   *40*
Her wits to yours, forsooth, and made excuse,
—E'en then would be some stooping; and I choose
Never to stoop. Oh, Sir, she smiled, no doubt,
Whene'er I passed her; but who passed without
Much the same smile? This grew; I gave commands;   *45*
Then all smiles stopped together. There she stands

As if alive. Will't please you rise? We'll meet
The company below, then. I repeat,
The Count your master's known munificence
Is ample warrant that no just pretense   *50*
Of mine for dowry will be disallowed;
Though his fair daughter's self, as I avowed
At starting, is my object. Nay, we'll go
Together down, Sir. Notice Neptune, though,
Taming a sea-horse, thought a rarity,   *55*
    Which Claus of Innsbruck° cast in bronze for me!   *a fictitious sculptor*

[1844]

TOPICS FOR DISCUSSION AND WRITING

1. Who is speaking to whom? On what occasion?
2. What words or lines do you think expecially convey the speaker's arrogance? What is your attitude toward the speaker? Loathing? Fascination? Respect? Explain.
3. The time and place are Renaissance Italy; how do they affect your attitude toward the duke? What would be the effect if the poem were set in the twentieth century?
4. Why does this poem sound more like talk and less like song than Burns's "John Anderson"?
5. Years after writing this poem, Browning explained that the duke's "commands" (line 45) were "that she should be put to death, or he might have had her shut up in a convent." Do you think the poem should have been more explicit? Does Browning's later uncertainty indicate that the poem is badly thought out? Suppose we did not have Browning's comment on line 45; could the line then could mean only that he commanded her to stop smiling and that she obeyed? Explain.

DICTION

From the whole of language, one consciously or unconsciously selects certain words and grammatical constructions; this selection constitutes one's **diction.** It is partly by the diction that we come to know the speaker of a poem. "Amang" and "frae sun to sun" tell us that that the speaker of "Mary Morison" is a Scot. In "My Last Duchess" such words as "countenance," "munificence," and "disallowed"—none of which is conceivable in Burns's poem—help us form our impression of the duke. Of course, some words are used in both poems: "I said," "and," "smile[s]," "glance[s]," etc. The fact remains, however, that although a large part of language is shared by all speakers, certain parts of language are used only by certain speakers.

Like some words, some grammatical constructions are used only by certain kinds of speakers. Consider these two passages:

> In Adam's fall
> We sinned all.
>
> —Anonymous, *The New England Primer*

> Of Man's first disobedience, and the fruit
> Of that forbidden tree whose mortal taste
> Brought death into the World, and all our woe.
> With loss of Eden, till one greater Man
> Restore us, and regain the blissful seat,
> Sing, Heavenly Muse, that, on the secret top
> Of Oreb, or of Sinai, didst inspire
> That shepherd who first taught the chosen seed
> In the beginning how the heaven and earth
> Rose out of Chaos. . . .
>
> —John Milton, *Paradise Lost*

There is an enormous difference in the diction of these two passages. Milton, speaking as an inspired poet, appropriately uses words and grammatical constructions somewhat removed from common life. Hence, while the anonymous author of the primer speaks directly of "Adam's fall," Milton speaks allusively of the fall, calling it "Man's first disobedience." Milton's sentence is nothing that any Englishman ever said in conversation; its genitive beginning ("Of". . .), its length (the sentence continues for six lines beyond the quoted passage), and its postponement of the main verb ("Sing") until the sixth line mark it as the utterance of a poet working in the tradition of Latin poetry. The primer's statement, by its choice of words as well as by its brevity, suggests a far less sophisticated speaker.

TONE

Speakers have attitudes toward themselves, their subjects, and their audiences, and (consciously or unconsciously) they choose their words, pitch, and modulation accordingly; all these add up to the **tone.** In written literature, tone must be detected without the aid of the ear; the reader must understand by the selection and sequence of words the way in which they are meant to be heard (that is, playfully, angrily, confidentially, sarcastically, etc.). The reader must catch what Frost calls "the speaking tone of voice somehow entangled in the words and fastened to the page of the ear of the imagination."*

Robert Herrick (*English; 1591–1674*)

To the Virgins, to Make Much of Time

Gather ye rosebuds while ye may,
    Old Time is still a-flying;
And this same flower that smiles today,
    Tomorrow will be dying. *4*

The glorious lamp of heaven, the sun,
    The higher he's a-getting,
The sooner will his race be run,
    And nearer he's to setting. *8*

That age is best which is the first,
    When youth and blood are warmer;
But being spent, the worse, and worst
    Times still succeed the former. *12*

Then be not coy, but use your time;
    And while ye may, go marry:
For having lost but once your prime,
    You may for ever tarry. *16*

[1648]

Carpe diem (Latin: "seize the day") is the theme. But if we want to get the full force of the poem, we must understand who is talking to whom. Look, for example, at "Old Time" in line 2. Time is "old," of course, in the sense of having been around a long while, but doesn't "old" in this context suggest also that the speaker regards Time with easy familiarity, almost affection? We visit the old school, and our friend is old George. Time is destructive, yes, and the speaker urges the young maidens to make the

---

*This discussion concentrates on the speaker's tone. But one can also talk of the author's tone, that is of the author's attitude toward the invented speaker. The speaker's tone might, for example, be angry, but the author's tone (as detected by the reader) might be humorous.

most of their spring, but the speaker is neither bitter nor importunate; rather, he seems to be the wise old man, the counselor, the man who has made his peace with Time and is giving advice to the young. Time moves rapidly in the poem (the rosebud of line 1 is already a flower in line 3), but the speaker is unhurried; in line 5 he has leisure to explain that the glorious lamp of heaven is the sun.

In "To the Virgins," the pauses, indicated by punctuation at the ends of the lines (except in line 11, where we tumble without stopping from "worst" to "Times"), slow the reader down. But even if there is no punctuation at the end of a line of poetry, the reader probably pauses slightly or gives the final word an additional bit of emphasis. Similarly, the space between stanzas slows a reader down, increasing the emphasis on the last word of one stanza and the first word of the next.

Thomas Hardy *(English; 1840–1928)*

The Man He Killed

"Had he and I but met
By some old ancient inn,
We should have sat us down to wet
Right many a nipperkin°!   *cup*

"But ranged as infantry,   *5*
And staring face to face,
I shot at him as he at me,
And killed him in his place.

"I shot him dead because—
Because he was my foe,   *10*
Just so: my foe of course he was;
That's clear enough; although

"He thought he'd 'list, perhaps,
Off-hand like—just as I—
Was out of work—had sold his traps°—   *personal belongings* *15*
No other reason why.

"Yes; quaint and curious war is!
You shoot a fellow down
You'd treat if met where any bar is,
Or help to half-a-crown."   *20*

[1902]

TOPICS FOR DISCUSSION AND WRITING

1. What do we learn about the speaker's life before he enlisted in the infantry? How does his diction characterize him?
2. What is the effect of the series of monosyllables in lines 7 and 8?
3. Consider the punctuation of the third and fourth stanzas. Why are the heavy, frequent pauses appropriate? Wht question is the speaker trying to answer?
4. In the last stanza what attitudes toward war does the speaker express? What, from the evidence of this poem, would you infer Hardy's attitude toward war to be?

Michael Drayton (*English; 1563–1631*)

Since There's No Help

Since there's no help, come let us kiss and part;
Nay, I have done, you get no more of me,
And I am glad, yea glad with all my heart
That thus so cleanly I myself can free;
Shake hands for ever, cancel all our vows,   5
And when we meet at any time again,
Be it not seen in either of our brows
That we one jot of former love retain.
Now at the last gasp of Love's latest breath,
When, his pulse failing, Passion speechless lies,   10
When Faith is kneeling by his bed of death,
And Innocence is closing up his eyes,
   Now if thou wouldst, when all have given him over,
   From death to life thou mightst him yet recover.

[1619]

TOPICS FOR DISCUSSION AND WRITING

1. What do you think is the tone of lines 1–8? What words especially establish this tone? What do you think is the tone of lines 9–14?
2. What is the significance of the shift from "you" (line 2) to "thou" (line 13)?

Elizabeth Bishop (American; 1911–79)

Filling Station

Oh, but it is dirty!
—this little filling station,
oil-soaked, oil-permeated
to a disturbing, over-all
black translucency.   5
Be careful with that match!

Father wears a dirty,
oil-soaked monkey suit
that cuts him under the arms,
and several quick and saucy   10
and greasy sons assist him
(it's a family filling station),
all quite thoroughly dirty.

Do they live in the station?
It has a cement porch   15
behind the pumps, and on it
a set of crushed and grease-
impregnated wickerwork;
on the wicker sofa
a dirty dog, quite comfy.   20

Some comic books provide
the only note of color—
of certain color. They lie
upon a big dim doily
draping a taboret°   *a low stool* 25
(part of the set), beside
a big hirsute begonia.

Why the extraneous plant?
Why the taboret?
Why, oh why, the doily?   30
(Embroidered in daisy stitch
with marguerites,° I think,   *daisies*
and heavy with gray crochet.)

Somebody embroidered the doily.
Somebody waters the plant,   35

or oils it, maybe. Somebody
arranges the rows of cans

so that they softly say:
ESSO°—so—so—so   *a brand of gasoline, now Exxon*
to high-strung automobiles.   40
Somebody loves us all.

[1965]

TOPICS FOR DISCUSSION AND WRITING

1. Elizabeth Bishop, though a woman, might have chosen to invent
   a male speaker. But she didn't. What words or phrases in "Filling
   Station" convince you that the speaker is a woman?
2. Taking into account only the first 14 lines, how would you characterize the speaker?
3. Would you agree that in the third stanza a reader begins to feel more
   sympathetic toward the speaker? Why? Because the speaker seems
   to be somewhat more sympathetic toward the family and the gas
   station? What do you make of "comfy" in line 20? Is it the speaker's
   word? Or is the speaker using a word that might be used by the
   owners of the gas station?
4. In lines 21–30, what evidence suggests that the speaker feels that
   her taste is superior to the taste of the family? Do you think that
   she changes her tone later? A little, a lot, or not at all?

Gerard Manley Hopkins (English; 1844–89)

Spring and Fall: To A Young Child

Márgarét are you gríeving
Over Goldengrove unleaving?
Léaves, líke the things of man, you
With your fresh thoughts care for, can you?
Áh! ás the heart grows older   5
It will come to such sights colder
By and by, nor spare a sigh
Though worlds of wanwood leafmeal lie;
And yet you will weep and know why.
Now no matter, child, the name: 10
Sórrow's spríngs áre the same.

Nor mouth had, no nor mind, expressed
What heart heard of, ghost° guessed: *spirit*
It ís the blight man was born for,
It ís Margaret you mourn for.   15

[1880]

TOPICS FOR DISCUSSION AND WRITING

1. About how old do you think the speaker is? What is his tone? What connection can you make between the title and the speaker and Margaret? What meanings do you think may be in "Fall"?
2. What is meant by Margaret's "fresh thoughts" (line 4)? Paraphrase lines 3–4 and lines 12–13.
3. "Wanwood" and "leafmeal" are words coined by Hopkins. What do they suggest to you?
4. How can you explain the apparent contradiction that Margaret weeps for herself (line 15) after the speaker has said that she weeps for "Goldengrove unleaving" (line 2)?

Ted Hughes (English; b. 1930)

Hawk Roosting

I sit in the top of the wood, my eyes closed.
Inaction, no falsifying dream
Between my hooked head and hooked feet:
Or in sleep rehearse perfect kills and eat.   *4*

The convenience of the high trees!
The air's buoyancy and the sun's ray
Are of advantage to me;
And the earth's face upward for my inspection.   *8*

My feet are locked upon the rough bark.
It took the whole of Creation
To produce my foot, my each feather:
Now I hold Creation in my foot   *12*

Or fly up, and revolve it all slowly—
I kill where I please because it is all mine.

There is no sophistry in my body:
My manners are tearing off heads —   *16*

The allotment of death.
For the one path of my flight is direct
Through the bones of the living.
No arguments assert my right: *20*

The sun is behind me.
Nothing has changed since I began.
My eye has permitted no change.
I am going to keep things like this.   *24*

[1959]

TOPICS FOR DISCUSSION AND WRITING

1. Many of the sentences are short — only one line long. What is the effect of these short sentences, expecially in the last stanza, where each of the four lines is a separate sentence?
2. Hawks cannot speak. Do you think this poem therefore is nonsense?

William Blake (*English; 1757–1827*)

The Clod and the Pebble

"Love seeketh not Itself to please,
Nor for itself hath any care;
But for another gives its ease,
And builds a Heaven in Hell's despair."   *4*

So sang a little Clod of Clay,
Trodden with the cattle's feet;
But a Pebble of the brook,
Warbled out these meters meet: *8*

"Love seeketh only Self to please,
To bind another to its delight;
Joys in another's loss of ease,
And builds a Hell in Heaven's despite."   *12*

[1794]

TOPICS FOR DISCUSSION AND WRITING

1. Can one reasonably say that the clod is feminine, the pebble masculine? Can one reasonably say that the clod needs the pebble, and the pebble needs the clod? Explain.
2. The clod and the pebble each express an uncompromising view. Does Blake express a preference for one or for the other? Or does he imply that both points of view have merit? Explain.

Countee Cullen (American; 1903–46)

For a Lady I Know

She even thinks that up in heaven
    Her class lies late and snores,
While poor black cherubs rise at seven
    To do celestial chores.

[1925]

TOPICS FOR DISCUSSION AND WRITING

1. What is the gist of what Cullen is saying?
2. How would you characterize the tone? Furious? Indifferent? Or what?

THE VOICE OF THE SATIRIST

E. E. Cummings (American; 1894–1962)

next to of course god america i

"next to of course god america i
love you land of the pilgrims' and so forth oh
say can you see by the dawn's early my
country 'tis of centuries come and go   *4*
and are no more what of it we should worry
in every language even deafanddumb
thy sons acclaim your glorious name by gorry
by jingo by gee by gosh by gum   *8*

why talk of beauty what could be more beautiful than these heroic happy dead
who rushed like lions to the roaring slaughter
they did not stop to think they died instead
then shall the voice of liberty be mute?"

He spoke. And drank rapidly a glass of water

[1926]

12

Cummings might have written, in the voice of a solid citizen or a good
poet, a direct attack on chauvinistic windbags; instead, he chose to invent
a windbag whose rhetoric punctures itself. Yet the last line tells that we
are really hearing someone who is recounting what the windbag said; that
is, the speaker of all the lines but the last is a sort of combination of the
chauvinist *and* the satiric observer of the chauvinist. (When Cummings
himself recited these lines there was mockery in his voice.)

Only in the final line of the poem does the author seem to speak
entirely on his own, and even here he adopts a matter-of-fact pose that
is far more potent than **invective** (direct abuse) would be. Yet the last line
is not totally free of explicit hostility. It might, for example, have run, "He
spoke. And poured slowly a glass of water." Why does this version lack
the punch of Cummings's? And what do you think is implied by the absence of a final period in line 14?

John Updike (American; b. 1932)

Youth's Progress

> *Dick Schneider of Wisconsin . . . was elected "Greek God"*
> *for an interfraternity ball.* —*Life*

When I was born, my mother taped my ears
So they lay flat. When I had aged ten years,
My teeth were firmly braced and much improved.
Two years went by; my tonsils were removed.

4

At fourteen, I began to comb my hair
A fancy way. Though nothing much was there,
I shaved my upper lip—next year, my chin.
At seventeen, the freckles left my skin.

8

Just turned nineteen, a nicely molded lad,
I said goodbye to Sis and Mother; Dad
Drove me to Wisconsin and set me loose.
At twenty-one, I was elected Zeus.   12

[1955]

TOPICS FOR DISCUSSION AND WRITING

1. Suppose the first two lines ran thus:

    > To keep them flat, my mother taped my ears;
    > And then, at last, when I had aged ten years. . . .

    How does this revision destroy the special tone of voice in the original
    two lines? (Notice that in the revision there is a heavy pause at the
    end of the first line.) Why, in the second line of the revision, is "at
    last" false to the "tone" or "voice" in the rest of the poem?
2. What do you think is the speaker's attitude toward himself? What
    is the author's attitude toward the speaker?

Marge Piercy (American; b. 1936)

Barbie Doll

This girlchild was born as usual
and presented dolls that did pee-pee
and miniature GE stoves and irons
and wee lipsticks the color of cherry candy.
Then in the magic of puberty, a classmate said: 5
You have a great big nose and fat legs.

She was healthy, tested intelligent,
possessed strong arms and back,
abundant sexual drive and manual dexterity.
She went to and fro apologizing.   10
Everyone saw a fat nose on thick legs.

She was advised to play coy,
exhorted to come on hearty,
exercise, diet, smile and wheedle.
Her good nature wore out   15
like a fan belt.

So she cut off her nose and her legs
and offered them up.

In the casket displayed on satin she lay
with the undertaker's cosmetics painted on,   *20*
a turned-up putty nose,
dressed in a pink and white nightie.
Doesn't she look pretty? everyone said.
Consummation at last.
To every woman a happy ending.   *25*

[1969]

TOPICS FOR DISCUSSION AND WRITING

1. Why is the poem called "Barbie Doll"?
2. What voice do you hear in lines 1–4? Line 6 is, we are told, the voice
   of "a classmate." How do these voices differ? What voice do you
   hear in the first three lines of the second stanza?
3. Explain in your own words what Piercy is saying about women in
   this poem. Does her view seem to you fair, slightly exaggerated, or
   greatly exaggerated?

Marge Piercy

What's That Smell in the Kitchen?

All over America women are burning dinners.
It's lambchops in Peoria; it's haddock
in Providence; it's steak in Chicago;
tofu delight in Big Sur; red
rice and beans in Dallas.   *5*
All over America women are burning
food they're supposed to bring with calico
smile on platters glittering like wax.
Anger sputters in her brainpan, confined
but spewing out missiles of hot fat.   *10*
Carbonized despair presses like a clinker
from a barbecue against the back of her eyes.
If she wants to grill anything, it's
her husband spitted over a slow fire.
If she wants to serve him anything   *15*

it's a dead rat with a bomb in its belly
ticking like the heart of an insomniac.
Her life is cooked and digested,
nothing but leftovers in Tupperware.
Look, she says, once I was roast duck   20
on your platter with parsley but now I am Spam.
Burning dinner is not incompetence but war.

[1982]

TOPICS FOR DISCUSSION AND WRITING

1. Suppose a friend told you that she didn't understand lines 20–21.
   How would you paraphrase the lines?
2. Who speaks the title?
3. If a poem begins, "All over America women are . . . ," what words
   might a reader reasonably expect next?
4. Do you take the poem to be chiefly comic? Superficially comic but
   essentially a work with a serious purpose? Or what?

Mitsuye Yamada (American; b. 1923)

To the Lady

The one in San Francisco who asked:
Why did the Japanese Americans let
the government put them in
those camps without protest?

Come to think of it I   5
        should've run off to Canada
        should've hijacked a plane to Algeria
        should've pulled myself up from my
        bra straps
        and kicked'm in the groin   10
        should've bombed a bank
        should've tried self-immolation

should've holed myself up in a
woodframe house
and let you watch me   *15*
burn up on the six o'clock news
should've run howling down the street
naked and assaulted you at breakfast
by AP wirephoto
should've screamed bloody murder   *20*
like Kitty Genovese[1]

Then
YOU would've
    come to my aid in shining armor
    laid yourself across the railroad track   *25*
    marched on Washington
    tatooed a Star of David on your arm
    written six million enraged
    letters to Congress

But we didn't draw the line   *30*
anywhere
law and order Executive Order 9066[2]
social order moral order internal order

YOU let'm
I let'm   *35*
All are punished.

[1976]

TOPICS FOR DISCUSSION AND WRITING

1. Has the lady's question (lines 2–4) ever crossed your mind? If so,
   what answers did you think of?
2. What, in effect, is the speaker really saying in lines 5–21? And in
   lines 24–29?
3. Explain the last line.

---

[1]**Kitty Genovese**   In 1964 Kitty Genovese of Kew Gardens, New York, was stabbed to
death when she left her car and walked toward her home. Thirty-eight persons heard her
screams, but no one came to her assistance.
[2]**Executive Order 9066**   an authorization, signed in 1941 by President Franklin D. Roosevelt, allowing military authorities to relocate Japanese and Japanese-Americans who resided
on the Pacific Coast of the United States

Louise Erdrich (American; b. 1954)

Dear John Wayne

August and the drive-in picture is packed.
We lounge on the hood of the Pontiac
surrounded by the slow-burning spirals they sell
at the window, to vanquish the hordes of mosquitoes.
Nothing works. They break through the smoke screen for blood.   5

Always the lookout spots the Indians first,
spread north to south, barring progress.
The Sioux or some other Plains bunch
in spectacular columns, ICBM missiles,
feathers bristling in the meaningful sunset.   10

The drum breaks. There will be no parlance.
Only the arrows whining, a death-cloud of nerves
swarming down on the settlers
who die beautifully, tumbling like dust weeds
into the history that brought us all here   15
together: this wide screen beneath the sign of the bear.

The sky fills, acres of blue squint and eye
that the crowd cheers. His face moves over us,
a thick cloud of vengeance, pitted
like the land that was once flesh. Each rut,   20
each scar makes a promise: *It is*
not over, this fight, not as long as you resist.

Everything we see belongs to us.

A few laughing Indians fall over the hood
slipping in the hot spilled butter.   25
The eye sees a lot, John, but the heart is so blind.
Death makes us owners of nothing.
He smiles, a horizon of teeth
the credits reel over, and then the white fields
again blowing in the true-to-life dark.   30
The dark films over everything.
We get into the car
scratching our mosquito bites, speechless and small
as people are when the movie is done.
We are back in our skins.   35

How can we help but keep hearing his voice,
the flip side of the sound track, still playing:
Come on, boys, we got them
where we want them, drunk, running.
They'll give us what we want, what we need.   40
Even his disease was the idea of taking everything.
Those cells, burning, doubling, splitting out of their skins.

[1984]

TOPICS FOR DISCUSSION AND WRITING

1. Who is the speaker of most of the poem? Who speaks the italicized lines?
2. There are curious shifts in the diction, for instance from "some other Plains bunch" (line 8) to "parlance" (line 11). Whose voice do we hear in "some . . . bunch"? Consider, too, the diction in "to vanquish the hordes of mosquitoes (line 4)." If you were talking about mosquitoes, you probably would not use the word "vanquish." What do you think Erdrich is up to?
3. What do you make of lines 24–25, talking of Indians "slipping in the hot spilled butter"? What connection do these lines have with what presumably is going on in the film?

13

Figurative Language: Simile, Metaphor, Personification, Apostrophe

HIPPOLYTA. 'Tis strange, my Theseus, that these lovers speak of.
THESEUS. More strange than true. I never may believe
These antique fables, nor these fairy toys.
Lovers and madmen have such seething brains,
Such shaping fantasies, that apprehend
More than cool reason ever comprehends.
The lunatic, the lover, and the poet,
Are of imagination all compact.
One sees more devils than vast hell can hold,
That is the madman. The lover, all as frantic,
Sees Helen's beauty in a brow of Egypt.
The poet's eye, in a fine frenzy rolling,
Doth glance from heaven to earth, from earth to heaven;
And as imagination bodies forth
The forms of things unknown, the poet's pen
Turns them to shapes, and gives to airy nothing
A local habitation and a name.
                    Shakespeare, *A Midsummer Night's Dream,* V.i.1–17

Theseus was neither the first nor the last to suggest that poets, like lunatics and lovers, freely employ their imagination. Terms such as "poetic license" and "poetic justice" imply that poets are free to depict a never-never land. One has only to leaf through any anthology of poetry to encounter numerous statements that are, from a logical point of view, lunacies. Here are a few:

> Look like th' innocent flower,
> But be the serpent under 't.
>
> —Shakespeare

Each outcry from the hunted hare
A fiber from the brain does tear.

—William Blake

The first of these is spoken by Lady Macbeth, when she urges her husband to murder King Duncan. How can a human being "Look like th' innocent flower," and how can a human being "be the serpent"? But Macbeth knows, and we know exactly what she means. We see and we feel her point, in a way that we would not if she had said, "Put on an innocent-looking face, but in fact kill the king."

And in the quotation from Blake, when we read that the hunted hare's plaintive cry serves to "tear" a "fiber" from our brain, we almost wince, even though we know that the statement is literally untrue.

On a literal level, then, such assertions are nonsense (so, too, is Theseus's notion that reason is cool). But of course they are not to be taken literally; rather, they employ **figures of speech** — departures from logical usage that are aimed at gaining special effects. Consider the lunacies that Robert Burns heaps up here.

Robert Burns (Scottish; 1759-96)

A Red, Red Rose

O, my luve is like a red, red rose,
    That's newly sprung in June.
O, my luve is like the melodie,
    That's sweetly played in tune.   *4*

As fair art thou, my bonnie lass,
    So deep in luve am I,
And I will luve thee still, my dear,
    Till a'° the seas gang° dry.   *all; go* *8*

Till a' the seas gang dry, my dear,
    And the rocks melt wi' the sun!
And I will luve thee still, my dear,
    While the sands o' life shall run.   *12*

And fare thee weel, my only luve,
    And fare thee weel awhile!
And I will come again, my luve,
    Though it were ten thousand mile!   *16*

[1796]

To the charge that these lines are lunacies or untruths, at least two replies can be made. First, it might be said that the speaker is not really making assertions about a woman; he is saying he feels a certain way. His words, it can be argued, are not assertions about external reality but expressions of his state of mind, just as a tune one whistles asserts nothing about external reality but expresses the whistler's state of mind. In this view, the nonlogical language of poetry (like a groan of pain or an exclamation of joy) is an expression of emotion; its further aim, if it has one, is to induce in the hearer an emotion.

Second, and more to the point here, it can be said that nonlogical language does indeed make assertions about external reality, and even gives the reader an insight into this reality that logical language cannot. The opening comparison in Burns's poem ("my luve is like a red, red rose") brings before our eyes the lady's beauty in a way that the reasonable assertion "She is beautiful" does not. By comparing the woman to a rose, the poet invites us to see the woman through a special sort of lens: she is fragrant; her lips (and perhaps her cheeks) are like a rose in texture and color; she will not keep her beauty long. Also, "my love is like a red, red rose" says something different from "like a red, red beet," or "a red, red cabbage."

The poet, then, has not only communicated a state of mind but also has discovered, through the lens of imagination, some things (both in the beloved and in the lover's own feelings) that interest us. The discovery is not world-shaking; it is less important than the discovery of America or the discovery that the meek are blessed, but it *is* a discovery and it leaves the reader with the feeling, "Yes, that's right. I hadn't quite thought of it that way, but that's right."

A poem, Robert Frost said, "assumes direction with the first line laid down, . . . runs a course of lucky events, and ends in a clarification of life — not necessarily a great clarification, such as sects and cults are founded on, but in a momentary stay against confusion." What is clarified? In another paragraph Frost gives an answer: "For me the initial delight is in the surprise of remembering something I didn't know I knew." John Keats made a similar statement: "Poetry . . . should strike the Reader as a wording of his own highest thoughts, and appear almost a Remembrance."

Some figures of speech are, in effect, riddling ways of speech. To call fishermen "farmers of the sea" — a metaphor — is to give a sort of veiled description of fishermen, bringing out, when the term is properly understood, certain aspects of a fisherman's activities. And a riddle, after all, is a veiled description — though intentionally obscure or deceptive — calling attention to characteristics, especially similarities, not usually noticed. ("Riddle," like "read," is from Old English *redan,* "to guess," "to interpret," and thus its solution provides knowledge.) "Two sisters upstairs, often looking but never seeing each other" is (after the riddle is explained) a way of calling attention to the curious fact that the eye, the instrument of vision, never sees its mate.

In the next poem the connection between riddles and metaphors is easily seen.

Sylvia Plath *(American; 1932-63)*

Metaphors

I'm a riddle in nine syllables,
An elephant, a ponderous house,
A melon strolling on two tendrils.
O red fruit, ivory, fine timbers!
This loaf's big with its yeasty rising.
Money's new-minted in this fat purse.
I'm a means, a stage, a cow in calf.
I've eaten a bag of green apples,
Boarded the train there's no getting off.

[1960]

The riddling speaker says that she is, among other things, "a ponderous house": and "a cow in calf." What is she?

SIMILE

In a **simile,** items from different classes are explicitly compared by a connective such as "like," "as," or "than" or by a verb such as "appears" or "seems." (If the objects compared are from the same class, e.g., "New York is like Chicago," no simile is present.)

Sometimes I feel like a motherless child.

—Anonymous

It is a beauteous evening, calm and free.
The holy time is quiet as a Nun,
Breathless with adoration.

—Wordsworth

How sharper than a serpent's tooth it is
To have a thankless child.

—Shakespeare

Seems he a dove? His feathers are but borrowed.

—Shakespeare

The following two lines constitute an entire poem.

Robert Herrick (*English; 1591–1674*)

Her Legs

Fain would I kiss my Julia's dainty leg,
Which is as white and hairless as an egg.

Richard Wilbur (*American; b. 1921*)

A Simile for Her Smile

Your smiling, or the hope, the thought of it,
Makes in my mind such pause and abrupt ease
As when the highway bridgegates fall,
Balking the hasty traffic, which must sit
On each side massed and staring, while   5
Deliberately the drawbridge starts to rise:

Then horns are hushed, the oilsmoke rarifies,
Above the idling motors one can tell
The packet's smooth approach, the slip,
Slip of the silken river past the sides,   10
The ringing of clear bells, the dip
And slow cascading of the paddle wheel.

[1950]

TOPIC FOR DISCUSSION AND WRITING

The title may lead you to think that the poet will compare the
woman's smile to something. But, in fact, the comparison is not between her smile and the passing scene. What *is* being compared to
the traffic?

METAPHOR

A **metaphor** asserts the identity, without a connective such as "like" or
a verb such as "appears," of terms that are literally incompatible.

She is the rose, the glory of the day.

—Spenser

O western orb sailing the heaven.

—Whitman

Notice how in the second example only one of the terms ("orb") is stated; the other ("ship") is implied in "sailing."

John Keats (English; 1795–1821)

On First Looking into Chapman's Homer*

Much have I traveled in the realms of gold,
And many goodly states and kingdoms seen;
Round many western islands have I been
Which bards in fealty to Apollo hold.   *4*
Oft of one wide expanse have I been told
That deep-browed Homer ruled as his demesne;
Yet did I never breathe its pure serene
Till I heard Chapman speak out loud and bold: *8*
Then felt I like some watcher of the skies
When a new planet swims into his ken;
Or like stout Cortez when with eagle eyes
He stared at the Pacific—and all his men   *12*
Looked at each other with a wild surmise—
Silent, upon a peak in Darien.

[1816]

TOPICS FOR DISCUSSION AND WRITING

1. In line 1, what do you think "realms of gold" stands for? Chapman was an Elizabethan; how does this fact add relevance to the metaphor in the first line?
2. Does line 9 introduce a totally new idea, or can you somehow connect it to the opening metaphor?

---

*George Chapman (1559–1634?), Shakespeare's contemporary, is chiefly known for his translations (from the Greek) of Homer's *Odyssey* and *Iliad*.

Marge Piercy (American; b. 1936)

A Work of Artifice

The bonsai tree
in the attractive pot
could have grown eighty feet tall
on the side of a mountain
till split by lightning.   5
But a gardener
carefully pruned it.
It is nine inches high.
Every day as he
whittles back the branches   10
the gardener croons,
It is your nature
to be small and cozy,
domestic and weak;
how lucky, little tree,   15
to have a pot to grow in.
With living creatures
one must begin very early
to dwarf their growth:
the bound feet,   20
the crippled brain,
the hair in curlers,
the hands you
love to touch.

[1973]

TOPICS FOR DISCUSSION AND WRITING

1. Piercy uses a bonsai tree as a metaphor—but a metaphor for what?
   (If you have never seen a bonsai tree, try to visit a florist or a nursery to take a close look at one. You can find a picture of a bonsai
   in *The American Heritage Dictionary.*)
2. The gardener "croons" (line 11) a song to the bonsai tree. If the tree
   could respond, what might it say?
3. Explain lines 17–24 to someone who doesn't get the point. In your
   response, explain how these lines are connected with "hair in curlers."

Explain, too, what "the hands you / love to touch" has to do with
the rest of the poem. What tone of voice do you hear in "the hands
you / love to touch"?

4. How does the form of the poem suggest its subject?

Two types of metaphor deserve special mention. In **metonymy,** something is named that replaces something closely related to it; "City Hall,"
for example, sometimes is used to stand for municipal authority. In the
following passage James Shirley names certain objects ("Scepter and crown,"
"scythe and spade"), using them to replace social classes (powerful people
and poor people) to which they are related:

Scepter and crown must tumble down
And in the dust be equal made
With the poor crooked scythe and spade.

In **synecdoche,** the whole is replaced by the part, or the part by
the whole. For example, "bread" in "Give us this day our daily bread"
replaces the whole class of edibles. Similarly, an automobile can be
"wheels," and workers are "hands." Robert Frost was fond of calling
himself "a Synecdochist" because he believed that it is the nature of poetry
to "have intimations of something more than itself. It almost always comes
under the head of synecdoche, a part, a hem of the garment for the whole
garment."

PERSONIFICATION

The attribution of human feelings or characteristics to abstractions or to
inanimate objects is called **personification.**

But Time did beckon to the flowers, and they
By noon most cunningly did steal away.

—Herbert

Herbert attributes a human gesture to Time and shrewdness to flowers.
Of all figures, personification most surely gives to airy nothings a local
habitation and a name:

There's Wrath who has learnt every trick of guerrilla warfare,
The shamming dead, the night-raid, the feinted retreat.

—Auden

Hope, thou bold taster of delight.

—Crashaw

APOSTROPHE

Crashaw's personification, "Hope, thou bold taster of delight," is also an example of the figure called **apostrophe,** an address to a person or thing not literally listening. Wordsworth begins a sonnet by apostrophizing John Milton:

> Milton, thou shouldst be living at this hour,

And Shelley begins an ode by apostrophizing a skylark:

> Hail to thee, blithe Spirit!

The following poem is largely built on apostrophe.

Edmund Waller (*English; 1606–87*)

Song

> Go, lovely rose,
> Tell her that wastes her time and me,
>   That now she knows,
> When I resemble her to thee,
>   How sweet and fair she seems to be.   5
>
>   Tell her that's young,
> And shuns to have her graces spied,
>   That hadst thou sprung
> In deserts where no men abide,
>   Thou must have uncommended died.   10
>
> Small is the worth
> Of beauty from the light retired:
>   Bid her come forth,
> Suffer her self to be desired,
>   And not blush so to be admired.   15
>
>   Then die, that she
> The common fate of all things rare
>   May read in thee,
>
> How small a part of time they share,
>   That are so wondrous sweet and fair.   20

[1645]

What conclusions, then, can we draw about **figurative language?** First, figurative language, with its literally incompatible terms, forces the reader to attend to the **connotations** (suggestions, associations) rather than to the **denotations** (dictionary definitions) of one of the terms.

Second, although figurative language is said to differ from ordinary discourse, it is found in ordinary discourse as well as in literature. "It rained cats and dogs," "War is hell," "Don't be a pig," and other tired figures are part of our daily utterances. But through repeated use, these (and most of the figures we use) have lost whatever impact they once had and are only a shade removed from expressions which, though once figurative, have become literal: the *eye* of a needle, a *branch* office, the *face* of a clock.

Third, good figurative language is usually (a) concrete, (b) condensed, and (c) interesting. The concreteness lends precision and vividness; when Keats writes that he felt "like some watcher of the skies / When a new planet swims into his ken," he more sharply characterizes his feelings than if he had said, "I felt exicited." His simile isolates for us a precise kind of excitement, and the metaphoric "swims" vividly brings up the oceanic aspect of the sky. The second of these three qualities, condensation, can be seen by attempting to paraphrase some of the figures. A paraphrase or rewording will commonly use more words than the original and will have less impact—as the gradual coming of night usually has less impact on us than a sudden darkening of the sky or as a prolonged push has less impact than a sudden blow. The third quality, interest, largely depends on the previous two: the successful figure often makes us open our eyes wider and take notice. Keats's "deep-browed Homer" arouses our interest in Homer as "thoughtful Homer" or "meditative Homer" does not. Similarly, when W. B. Yeats says (page 585):

> An aged man is but a paltry thing,
> A tattered coat upon a stick, unless
> Soul clap its hands and sing, and louder sing
> For every tatter in its mortal dress.

the metaphoric identification of an old man with a scarecrow jolts us out of all our usual unthinking attitudes about old men as kind, happy folk content to have passed from youth to senior citizenship.

Finally, the point must be made that although figurative language is one of the poet's chief tools, a poem does not have to contain figures. The anonymous ballad "Edward" (page 560) contains no figures, yet surely it is a poem and no one would say that the addition of figures would make it a better poem.

Here is another short poem. Does it contain any figures of speech?

William Carlos Williams (American; 1883–1963)

The Red Wheelbarrow

so much depends
upon

a red wheel
barrow

glazed with rain
water

beside the white
chickens.

[1923]

The following poems rely heavily on figures of speech.

Alfred, Lord Tennyson (English; 1809–92)

The Eagle

A Fragment

He clasps the crag with crooked hands;
Close to the sun in lonely lands,
Ringed with the azure world, he stands.
The wrinkled sea beneath him crawls:
He watches from his mountain walls,
And like a thunderbolt he falls.

[1851]

TOPICS FOR DISCUSSION AND WRITING

1. What figure is used in line 1? In line 4? In line 6? Can it be argued that the figures give us a sense of the eagle that is not to be found in a literal description?

2. In line 2 we get overstatement, or hyperbole, for the eagle is not really close to the sun. Suppose instead of "Close to the sun" Tennyson had written "Waiting on high"? Do you think the poem would be improved or worsened?

Christina Rossetti (English; 1830–94)

Uphill

Does the road wind uphill all the way?
    Yes, to the very end.
Will the day's journey take the whole long day?
    From morn to night, my friend.   *4*

But is there for the night a resting-place?
    A roof for when the slow dark hours begin.
May not the darkness hide it from my face?
    You cannot miss that inn.   *8*

Shall I meet other wayfarers at night?
    Those who have gone before.
Then must I knock, or call when just in sight?
    They will not keep you standing at that door.   *12*

Shall I find comfort, travel-sore and weak?
    Of labor you shall find the sum.
Will there be beds for me and all who seek?
    Yea, beds for all who come.   *16*

[1858]

TOPICS FOR DISCUSSION AND WRITING

1. Suppose that someone told you this poem is about a person preparing to go on a hike. The person is supposedly making inquiries about the road and the possible hotel arrangements. What would you reply?
2. Who is the questioner? A woman? A man? All human beings collectively? Can one say that in "Uphill" the questioner and the answerer are the same person?

3. Are the answers unambiguously comforting? Or can it, for instance, be argued that the "roof" is (perhaps among other things) the lid of a coffin—hence the questioner will certainly not be kept "standing at that door"? If the poem can be read along these lines, is it chilling rather than comforting?

Randall Jarrell (American; 1914–65)

The Death of the Ball Turret Gunner

From my mother's sleep I fell into the State,
And I hunched in its belly till my wet fur froze.
Six miles from earth, loosed from its dream of life,
I woke to black flak and the nightmare fighters.
When I died they washed me out of the turret with a hose.

[1955]

Jarrell has furnished an explanatory note: "A ball turret was a plexiglass sphere set into the belly of a B-17 or B-24, and inhabited by two .50 caliber machine-guns and one man, a short small man. When this gunner tracked with his machine-guns a fighter attacking his bomber from below, he revolved with the turret; hunched upside-down in his little sphere, he looked like a fetus in the womb. The fighters which attacked him were armed with cannon firing explosive shells. The hose was a steam hose."

TOPICS FOR DISCUSSION AND WRITING

1. What is implied in the first line? In "I woke to . . . nightmare"? Taking account of the title, do you think "wet fur" is literal or metaphoric or both? Do you find the simplicity of the last line anti-climactic? How does it continue the metaphor of birth?
2. Why do you think Jarrell ended each line with punctuation?

Seamus Heaney (Irish; b. 1939)

Digging

Between my finger and my thumb
The squat pen rests; snug as a gun.

Under my window, a clean rasping sound
When the spade sinks into gravelly ground:
My father, digging. I look down   5

Till his straining rump among the flowerbeds
Bends low, comes up twenty years away
Stooping in rhythm through potato drills
Where he was digging.

The coarse boot nestled on the lug, the shaft   10
Against the inside knee was levered firmly.
He rooted out tall tops, buried the bright edge deep
To scatter new potatoes that we picked
Loving their cool hardness in our hands.
By God, the old man could handle a spade.   15
Just like his old man.

My grandfather cut more turf in a day
Than any other man on Toner's bog.
Once I carried him milk in a bottle
Corked sloppily with paper. He straightened up   20
To drink it, then fell to right away

Nicking and slicing neatly, heaving sods
Over his shoulder, going down and down
For the good turf. Digging.

The cold smell of potato mould, the squelch and slap   25
Of soggy peat, the curt cuts of an edge
Through living roots awaken in my head.
But I've no spade to follow men like them.

Between my finger and my thumb
The squat pen rests.   30
I'll dig with it.

[1966]

TOPICS FOR DISCUSSION AND WRITING

1. The poem ends with the speaker saying that he will "dig" with his
   pen. Given all the preceding lines, what will he dig?
2. The first lines compare the pen with a gun. What implications are
   suggested by this comparison?

Louise Erdrich (American; b. 1954)

Indian Boarding School: The Runaways

Home's the place we head for in our sleep.
Boxcars stumbling north in dreams
don't wait for us. We catch them on the run.
The rails, old lacerations that we love,
shoot parallel across the face and break   5
just under Turtle Mountains.* Riding scars
you can't get lost. Home is the place they cross.

The lame guard strikes a match and makes the dark
less tolerant. We watch through cracks in boards
as the land starts rolling, rolling till it hurts   10
to be here, cold in regulation clothes.
We know the sheriff's waiting at midrun
to take us back. His car is dumb and warm.
The highway doesn't rock, it only hums
like a wing of long insults. The worn-down welts   15
of ancient punishment lead back and forth.

All runaways wear dresses, long green ones,
the color you would think shame was. We scrub
the sidewalks down because it's shameful work.
Our brushes cut the stone in watered arcs   20
and in the soak frail outlines shiver clear
a moment, things us kids pressed on the dark
face before it hardened, pale, remembering
delicate old injuries, the spines of names and leaves.

                                                        [1984]

TOPICS FOR DISCUSSION AND WRITING

1. In line 4 the railroad tracks are called "old lacerations." What is the connection between the two?
2. What other imagery of injury do you find in the poem? In lines 20–24, what—literally—is "the dark / face" that "hardened, pale"?

*__Turtle Mountains__   a mountain range in North Dakota and Manitoba

14

Figurative Language: Imagery and Symbolism

When we read the word "rose"—or, for that matter, "finger" or "thumb"—we may more or less call to mind a picture, an image. The term **imagery** is used to refer to whatever in a poem appeals to any of our sensations, including sensations of pressure and heat as well as of sight, smell, taste, touch, and sound.

Consider the opening lines of Seamus Heaney's "Digging" (page 466):

Between my finger and my thumb
The squat pen rests; snug as a gun.

We may, at least to some small degree, in our mind's eye see a finger, thumb, and pen; and perhaps, stimulated by "squat," we may almost feel the pen. Notice, too, that in Heaney's line the pen is compared to a gun, so there is yet another image in the line. In short, images are the sensory content of the work, whether literal (the finger, thumb, and pen) or figurative (the gun, to which the pen is compared). Edmund Waller's rose, in "Go, Lovely Rose" (page 462) is an image that happens to be compared in the first stanza to a woman ("I resemble her to thee"); later in the poem this image comes to stand for "all things rare." Yet we never forget that the rose is a rose, and that the poem is chiefly a revelation of the poet's attitude toward his beloved.

If a poet says "My rose" and is speaking about a rose, we have an image, even though we do not have a figure of speech. If a poet says "My rose" and, we gather, is speaking not really or chiefly about a rose but about something else—let's say the transience of beauty—we can say that the poet is using the rose as a symbol.

Some symbols are **natural symbols,** recognized as standing for something in particular even by people from different cultures. Rain, for instance, usually stands for fertility or the renewal of life. A forest often stands for some sort of mental darkness or chaos, a mountain for stability, a valley for a place of security, and so on. There are of course many exceptions, but by and large these meanings prevail.

Other symbols, however, are **conventional symbols,** which people have agreed to accept as standing for something other than themselves: a poem about the cross would probably be about Christianity. Similarly, the rose has long been a symbol for love. In Virginia Woolf's novel *Mrs. Dalloway,* the husband communicates his love by proffering this conventional symbol: "He was holding out flowers—roses, red and white roses. (But he could not bring himself to say he loved her; not in so many words.)" Objects that are not conventional symbols, however, also may give rise to rich, multiple, indefinable associations. The following poem uses the symbol of the rose but uses it in a nontraditional way.

William Blake *(English; 1757–1827)*

The Sick Rose

O rose, thou art sick!
The invisible worm
That flies in the night
In the howling storm

Has found out thy bed
Of crimson joy,
And his dark secret love
Does thy life destroy.

           [1794]

One might perhaps argue that the worm is "invisible" (line 2) merely because it is hidden within the rose, but an "invisible worm / That flies in the night" is more than a long, slender, soft-bodied creeping animal; and a rose that has, or is, a "bed / Of crimson joy" is more than a gardener's rose.

Blake's worm and rose suggest things beyond themselves—a stranger, more vibrant world than the world we are usually aware of. Many readers find themselves half-thinking, for example, that the worm is male, the rose female, and that the poem is about the violation of virginity. Or that the poem is about the destruction of beauty: woman's beauty, rooted in joy, is destroyed by a power that feeds on her. But these interpretations are not fully satisfying: the poem presents a worm and a rose, and yet it is not merely about a worm and a rose. These objects resonate, stimulating our thoughts toward something else, but the something else is elusive, whereas it is not elusive in Burns's "A Red, Red Rose" or in Waller's "Go, lovely rose."

A **symbol,** then, is an image so loaded with significance that it is not simply literal, and it does not simply stand for something else; it is both itself *and* something else that it richly suggests, a kind of manifestation of something too complex or too elusive to be otherwise revealed. Blake's poem is about a blighted rose and at the same time about much more. In a symbol, as Thomas Carlyle wrote, "the Infinite is made to blend with the Finite, to stand visible, and as it were, attainable there." Probably it is not fanciful to say that the American slaves who sang "Joshua fought the battle of Jericho, / And the walls came tumbling down" were singing both about an ancient occurrence *and* about a new embodiment of the ancient, the imminent collapse of slavery in the nineteenth century. Not one or the other, but both: the present partook of the past, and the past partook of the present.

Thomas Hardy (*English; 1840–1928*)

Neutral Tones

We stood by a pond that winter day,
And the sun was white, as though chidden of God,
And a few leaves lay on the starving sod;
— They had fallen from an ash, and were gray.   *4*

Your eyes on me were as eyes that rove
Over tedious riddles of years ago;
And some words played between us to and fro
    On which lost the more by our love.   *8*

The smile on your mouth was the deadest thing
Alive enough to have strength to die;
And a grin of bitterness swept thereby
    Like an ominous bird a-wing. . . .   *12*

Since then, keen lessons that love deceives,
And wrings with wrong, have shaped to me
Your face, and the God-cursed sun, and a tree,
    And a pond edged with grayish leaves.   *16*

[1898]

TOPICS FOR DISCUSSION AND WRITING

1. In a sentence or two, summarize the story implicit in the poem. What has happened between the time of the episode narrated and the time of this utterance?
2. Do you think that the speaker is actually addressing the woman, or is he recollecting her and addressing her image? Or does it matter?
3. Why do you think that "keen lessons that love deceives" always remind the speaker of this scene?
4. Characterize, in a sentence or two, the speaker's state of mind in the first stanza. Is he composed, or agitated? Bitter, or meditative? Or what? Next, characterize his mind as it seems to be revealed in the final stanza.

Edgar Allan Poe *(American; 1809–49)*

To Helen*

Helen, thy beauty is to me
    Like those Nicean° barks of yore,
That gently, o'er a perfumed sea,
    The weary, way-worn wanderer bore
    To his own native shore.   5

On desperate seas long wont to roam,
    Thy hyacinth hair,° thy classic face,
Thy Naiad° airs have brought me home
    To the glory that was Greece
And the grandeur that was Rome.   10

Lo! in yon brilliant window-niche
    How statue-like I see thee stand!
    The agate lamp within they hand

*Helen   Helen of Troy, considered the most beautiful woman of ancient times.
2 Nicean   perhaps referring to Nicea, an ancient city associated with the god Dionysus, or perhaps meaning "victorious," from Nike, Greek goddess of Victory   **7 hyacinth hair**   naturally curling hair, like that of Hyacinthus, beautiful Greek youth beloved by Apollo   **8 Naiad**   a nymph associated with lakes and streams

Ah! Psyche,° from the regions which
   Are Holy Land!°   *15*

[1831–43]

TOPICS FOR DISCUSSION AND WRITING

1. In the first stanza, to what is Helen's beauty compared? To whom does the speaker apparently compare himself? What does "way-worn" in line 4 suggest to you? To what in the speaker's experience might the "native shore" in line 5 correspond?
2. What do you take "desperate seas" to mean in line 6, and who has been traveling them? To what are they contrasted in line 8? How does "home" seem to be defined in this stanza (stanza 2)?
3. What further light is shed on the speaker's home or destination in stanza 3?
4. Do you think that "To Helen" can be a love poem and also a poem about spiritual beauty or about the love of art? Explain.

D. H. Lawrence (English; 1885–1930)

Snake

A snake came to my water-trough
On a hot, hot day, and I in pajamas for the heat,
To drink there.

In the deep, strange-scented shade of the great dark carob-tree
I came down the steps with my pitcher   *5*
And must wait, must stand and wait, for there he was at the
    trough before me.

He reached down from a fissure in the earth-wall in the gloom
And trailed his yellow-brown slackness soft-bellied down, over
    the edge of the stone trough
And rested his throat upon the stone bottom,
And where the water had dripped from the tap,
    in a small clearness,   *10*

14 Psyche Greek for "soul"   **15 Holy Land** ancient Rome or Athens, i.e., a sacred realm of art

He sipped with his straight mouth,
Softly drank through his straight gums, into his slack long body,
Silently.

Someone was before me at my water-trough,
And I, like a second comer, waiting.   15

He lifted his head from his drinking, as cattle do,
And looked at me vaguely, as drinking cattle do,
And flickered his two-forked tongue from his lips,
    and mused a moment,
And stooped and drank a little more,
Being earth-brown, earth-golden from the
    burning bowels of the earth   20
On the day of Sicilian July, with Etna smoking.

The voice of my education said to me
He must be killed,
For in Sicily the black, black snakes are innocent,
    the gold are venomous.

And voices in me said, If you were a man   25
You would take a stick and break him now, and finish him off.

But must I confess how I liked him,
How glad I was he had come like a guest in quiet,
    to drink at my water-trough
And depart peaceful, pacified, and thankless,
Into the burning bowels of this earth?   30

Was it cowardice, that I dared not kill him?
Was it perversity, that I longed to talk to him?
Was it humility, to feel so honored?
I felt so honored.

And yet those voices: 35
If you were not afraid, you would kill him!

And truly I was afraid, I was most afraid,
But even so, honored still more
That he should seek my hospitality
From out the dark door of the secret earth.   40

He drank enough
And lifted his head, dreamily, as one who has drunken,

And flickered his tongue like a forked night on the air, so black,
Seeming to lick his lips,
And looked around like a god, unseeing, into the air,   *45*
And slowly turned his head,
And slowly, very slowly, as if thrice adream,
Proceeded to draw his slow length curving round
And climb again the broken bank of my wall-face.

And as he put his head into that dreadful hole,   *50*
And as he slowly drew up, snake-easing his shoulders,
    and entered farther,
A sort of horror, a sort of protest against his withdrawing
    into that horrid black hole,
Deliberately going into the blackness, and slowly
    drawing himself after,
Overcame me now his back was turned.

I looked round, I put down my pitcher,   *55*
I picked up a clumsy log
And threw it at the water-trough with a clatter.

I think it did not hit him,
But suddenly that part of him that was left behind
    convulsed in undignified haste,
Writhed like lightning, and was gone   *526*
Into the black hole, the earth-lipped fissure in the wall-front,
At which, in the intense still noon, I started with fascination.

And immediately I regretted it.
I thought how paltry, how vulgar, what a mean act!
I despised myself and the voices of my accursed
    human education.   *65*
And I thought of the albatross,
And I wished he would come back, my snake.

For he seemed to me again like a king,
Like a king in exile, uncrowned in the underworld,
Now due to be crowned again.   *70*

And so, I missed my chance with one of the lords
Of life.
And I have something to expiate:
A pettiness.

[1923]

TOPICS FOR DISCUSSION AND WRITING

1. In line 6 and later Lawrence calls the snake "he"; in line 14, "some-one," thus elevating the snake. What other figures are used to give the snake dignity? How does Lawrence diminish himself?
2. What do you think Lawrence means by "The voice of my educa-tion" (line 22)? It explicitly speaks in lines 23–26. Where else in the poem do you hear this voice? What might you call the opposing voice?

Samuel Taylor Coleridge *(English; 1772–1834)*

Kubla Khan

Or, A Vision in a Dream. A Fragment.

In Xanadu did Kubla Khan
A stately pleasure-dome decree:
Where Alph, the sacred river, ran
Through caverns measureless to man
   Down to a sunless sea.   5
So twice five miles of fertile ground
With walls and towers were girdled round:
And here were gardens bright with sinuous rills,
Where blossomed many an incense-bearing tree;
And here were forests ancient as the hills,   10
Enfolding sunny spots of greenery.

But oh! that deep romantic chasm which slanted
Down the green hill athwart a cedarn cover!
A savage place! as holy and enchanted
As e'er beneath a waning moon was haunted   15
By woman wailing for her demon-lover!
And from this chasm, with ceaseless turmoil seething.
As if this earth in fast thick pants were breathing
A mighty fountain momently was forced;
Amid whose swift half-intermitted burst   20
Huge fragments vaulted like rebounding hail,
Or chaffy grain beneath the thresher's flail:
And 'mid these dancing rocks at once and ever
It flung up momently the sacred river.
Five miles meandering with a mazy motion   25

Through wood and dale the sacred river ran,
Then reached the caverns measureless to man,
And sank in tumult to a lifeless ocean:
And 'mid this tumult Kubla heard from far
Ancestral voices prophesying war!   *30*
    The shadow of the dome of pleasure
    Floated midway on the waves;
    Where was heard the mingled measure
    From the fountain and the caves.
It was a miracle of rare device,   *35*
A sunny pleasure-dome with caves of ice!

    A damsel with a dulcimer
    In a vision once I saw:
    It was an Abyssinian maid,
    And on her dulcimer she played,   *40*
    Singing of Mount Abora.
    Could I revive within me
    Her symphony and song,
    To such a deep delight 'twould win me,
That with music loud and long,   *45*
I would build that dome in air,
That sunny dome! those caves of ice!
And all who heard should see them there,
And all should cry, Beware! Beware!
His flashing eyes, his floating hair!   *50*
Weave a circle round him thrice,
And close your eyes with holy dread,
For he on honey-dew hath fed,
And drunk the milk of Paradise.

[1798]

When Coleridge published "Kubla Khan" in 1816, he prefaced it with this
explanatory note:

> The following fragment is here published at the request of a poet
> of great and deserved celebrity, and, as far as the author's own
> opinions are concerned, rather as a psychological curiosity, than
> on the ground of any supposed *poetic* merits.
>   In the summer of the year 1797, the author, then in ill health,
> had retired to a lonely farmhouse between Porlock and Linton,
> on the Exmoor confines of Somerset and Devonshire. In conse-
> quence of a slight indisposition, an anodyne had been prescribed,
> from the effects of which he fell asleep in his chair at the moment
> that he was reading the following sentence, or words of the same

substance, in *Purchas's Pilgrimage:* "Here the Khan Kubla commanded a palace to be built, and a stately garden thereunto. And thus ten miles of fertile ground were inclosed with a wall." The author continued for about three hours in a profound sleep, at least of the external senses, during which time he has the most vivid confidence that he could not have composed less than from two to three hundred lines; if that indeed can be called composition in which all the images rose up before him as *things,* with a parallel production of the correspondent expressions, without any sensation or consciousness of effort. On awaking he appeared to himself to have a distinct recollection of the whole, and taking his pen, ink, and paper, instantly and eagerly wrote down the lines that are here preserved. At this moment he was unfortunately called out by a person on business from Porlock, and detained by him above an hour, and on his return to his room, found, to his no small surprise and mortification, that though he still retained some vague and dim recollection of the general purport of the vision, yet, with the exception of some eight or ten scattered lines and images, all the rest had passed away like the images on the surface of a stream into which a stone has been cast, but, alas! without the after restoration of the latter!

> Then all the charm
> Is broken—all that phantom world so fair
> Vanishes, and a thousand circlets spread,
> And each misshape[s] the other. Stay awhile,
> Poor youth! who scarely dar'st lift up thine eyes—
> The stream will soon renew its smoothness, soon
> The visions will return! And lo, he stays,
> And soon the fragments dim of lovely forms
> Come trembling back, unite, and now once more
> The pool becomes a mirror.
>
> —Coleridge, *The Picture: or, the Lover's Resolution,*
> lines 91–100

Yet from the still surviving recollections in his mind, the author has frequently purposed to finish for himself what had been originally, as it were, given to him. Σαμεϱον αδιον ασω [today I shall sing more sweetly]: But the tomorrow is yet to come.

TOPICS FOR DISCUSSION AND WRITING

1. Coleridge changed the "palace" of his source into a "dome" (line 2). What do you think are the relevant associations of "dome"?
2. What pairs of contrasts (e.g., underground river, fountain) do you find? What do you think they contribute to the poem?

3. If Coleridge had not said that the poem is a fragment, might you take it as a complete poem, the first thirty-six lines describing the creative imagination, and the remainder lamenting the loss of poetic power?

Adrienne Rich (*American; b. 1929*)

Diving into the Wreck

First having read the book of myths,
and loaded the camera,
and checked the edge of the knife-blade,
I put on
the body-armor of black rubber   *5*
the absurd flippers
the grave and awkward mask.
I am having to do this
not like Cousteau* with his
assiduous team   *10*
aboard the sun-flooded schooner
but here alone.

There is a ladder.
The ladder is always there
hanging innocently   *15*
close to the side of the schooner.
We know what it is for,
we who have used it.
Otherwise
it's a piece of maritime floss   *20*
some sundry equipment.

I go down.
Rung after rung and still
the oxygen immerses me
the blue light   *25*
the clear atoms
of our human air.
I go down.

*Jacques Cousteau (b. 1910)   French underwater explorer

My flippers cripple me,
I crawl like an insect down the ladder   30
and there is no one
to tell me when the ocean
will begin.

First the air is blue and then
it is bluer and then green and then   35
black I am blacking out and yet
my mask is powerful
it pumps my blood with power
the sea is another story
the sea is not a question of power   40
I have to learn alone
to turn my body without force
in the deep element.

And now: it is easy to forget
what I came for   45
among so many who have always
lived here
swaying their crenellated fans
between the reefs
and besides   50
you breathe differently down here.

I came to explore the wreck.
The words are purposes.
The words are maps.
I came to see the damage that was done   55
and the treasures that prevail.
I stroke the beam of my lamp
slowly along the flank
of something more permanent
than fish or weed   60

the thing I came for:
the wreck and not the story of the wreck
the thing itself and not the myth
the drowned face always staring
toward the sun   65
the evidence of damage
worn by salt and sway into this threadbare beauty
the ribs of the disaster

curving their assertion
among the tentative haunters.   70

This is the place.
And I am here, the mermaid whose dark hair
streams black, the merman in his armored body
We circle silently
about the wreck   75
we dive into the hold.
I am she: I am he

whose drowned face sleeps with open eyes
whose breasts still bear the stress
whose silver, copper, vermeil cargo lies   80
obscurely inside barrels
half-wedged and left to rot
we are the half-destroyed instruments
that once held to a course
the water-eaten log   85
the fouled compass

We are, I am, you are
by cowardice or courage
the one who find our way
back to this scene   90
carrying a knife, a camera
a book of myths
in which
our names do not appear.

[1973]

TOPICS FOR DISCUSSION AND WRITING

1. Do you think the "wreck" can be defined fairly precisely? In any
   case, what do you think the wreck is?
2. In lines 62–63 the speaker says that she came to explore "the wreck
   and not the story of the wreck / the thing itself and not the myth."
   Lines 1 and 92 speak of a "book of myths." What sort of "myths"
   do you think the poet is talking about?
3. In line 72 the speaker is a mermaid; in line 73, a merman; in lines
   74 and 76, "we"; and in line 77, "I am she: I am he." What do you
   make of this?

Wallace Stevens (American; 1879–1955)

Anecdote of the Jar

I placed a jar in Tennessee,
And round it was, upon a hill.
It made the slovenly wilderness
Surround that hill.   4

The wilderness rose up to it,
And sprawled around, no longer wild.
The jar was round upon the ground
And tall and of a port in air.   8

It took dominion everywhere.
The jar was gray and bare.
It did not give of bird or bush,
Like nothing else in Tennessee.   12

[1923]

Stevens, asked for an interpretation of another poem, said (in *The Explicator,* November 1948): "Things that have their origin in the imagination or in the emotions (poems) . . . very often take on a form that is ambiguous or uncertain. It is not possible to attach a single, rational meaning to such things without destroying the imaginative or emotional ambiguity or uncertainty that is inherent in them and that is why poets do not like to explain. That the meanings given by others are sometimes meanings not intended by the poet or that were never present in his mind does not impair them as meanings."

TOPICS FOR DISCUSSION AND WRITING

1. What is the meaning of line 8? Check "port" in a dictionary.
2. Do you think the poem suggests that the jar organizes slovenly nature, or that the jar impoverishes abundant nature? Or both, or neither? What do you think of the view that the jar is a symbol of the imagination, or of the arts, or of material progress?

The Emperor of Ice-Cream

Call the roller of big cigars,
The muscular one, and bid him whip

In kitchen cups concupiscent curds.
Let the wenches dawdle in such dress
As they are used to wear, and let the boys   5
Bring flowers in last month's newspapers.
Let be be finale of seem.
The only emperor is the emperor of ice-cream.

Take from the dresser of deal,°   *fir or pine wood*
Lacking the three glass knobs, that sheet   10
On which she embroidered fantails once
And spread it so as to cover her face.
If her horny feet protrude, they come
To show how cold she is, and dumb.
Let the lamp affix its beam.   15
The only emperor is the emperor of ice-cream.

[1923]

TOPICS FOR DISCUSSION AND WRITING

What associations does the word "emperor" have for you? The word "ice-cream"? What, then, do you make of "the emperor of ice-cream"? The poem describes the preparations for a wake, and in line 15 ("Let the lamp affix its beam") it insists on facing the reality of death. In this context, then, what do you make of the last line of each stanza?

15
Irony and Paradox

There is a kind of discourse which, though nonliteral, need not use similes, metaphors, apostrophes, personification, or symbols. Without using these figures, speakers may say things that are not to be taken literally. They may, in short, employ **irony.**

In Greek comedy, the *eiron* was the sly underdog who, by dissembling inferiority, outwitted his opponent. As Aristotle puts it, irony (employed by the *eiron*) is a "pretense tending toward the underside" of truth. Later, Cicero somewhat altered the meaning of the word: he defined it as saying one thing and meaning another, and he held that Socrates, who feigned ignorance and let his opponents entrap themselves in their own arguments, was the perfect example of an ironist.

In **verbal irony,** as the term is now used, what is *stated* is in some degree negated by what is *suggested.* A classic example is Lady Macbeth's order to get ready for King Duncan's visit: "He that's coming / Must be provided for." The words seem to say that she and Macbeth must busy themselves with household preparations so that the king may be received in appropriate style, but this suggestion of hospitality is undercut by an opposite meaning: preparations must be made for the murder of the king. Two other examples of verbal irony are Melville's comment,

> What like a bullet can undeceive!

and the lover's assertion (in Marvell's "To His Coy Mistress") that

> The grave's a fine and private place,
> But none, I think, do there embrace.

Under Marvell's cautious words ("I think") we detect a wryness; the **understatement** masks yet reveals a deep-felt awareness of mortality and the barrenness of the grave. The self-mockery in this understatement proclaims modesty, but suggests assurance. The speaker here, like most ironists is both playful and serious at once. Irony packs a great deal into a few words.* What we call irony here, it should be mentioned, is often called **sarcasm,** but a distinction can be made: sarcasm is notably contemptuous and crude or heavyhanded ("You're a great guy, a real friend," said to a friend who won't lend you ten dollars). Sarcasm is only one kind of irony, and a kind almost never found in literature.

Overstatement (hyperbole), like understatement, is ironic when it contains a contradictory suggestion:

> For Brutus is an honorable man;
> So are they all, all honorable men.

The sense of contradiction that is inherent in verbal irony is also inherent in a paradox. **Paradox** has several meanings for philosophers, but we need only be concerned with its meaning of an apparent contradiction. In Gerard Manley Hopkins's "Spring and Fall" (page 443), there is an apparent contradiction in the assertions that Margaret is weeping for the woods (line 2) and for herself (line 15), but the contradiction is not real: both the woods and Margaret are parts of the nature blighted by Adam's sin. Other paradoxes are

> The child is father of the man;
>
> —Wordsworth

and (on the soldiers who died to preserve the British Empire)

> The saviors come not home tonight;
> Themselves they could not save;
>
> —Housman

and

> One short sleep past, we wake eternally,
> And Death shall be no more; Death, thou shalt die.
>
> —Donne

Donne's lines are a reminder that paradox is not only an instrument of the poet. Christianity embodies several paradoxes: God became a human being; through the death on the cross, human beings can obtain eternal life; human beings do not live fully until they die.

Some critics have put a high premium on ironic and paradoxical poetry. Briefly, the argument runs that great poetry recognizes the complexity of experience, and that irony and paradox are ways of doing justice to this complexity. I. A. Richards uses "irony" to denote "The bringing

---

*A word of caution: We have been talking about verbal irony, not **irony of situation.** Like ironic words, ironic situations have in them an element of contrast. A clown whose heart is breaking must make his audience laugh; an author's worst book is her only financial success; a fool solves a problem that vexes the wise.

in of the opposite, the complementary impulses," and suggests (in *The Principles of Literary Criticism*) that irony in this sense is a characteristic of poetry of "the highest order." It is dubious that all poets must always bring in the opposite, but it is certain that much poetry is ironic and paradoxical.

John Hall Wheelock *(American; 1908–78)*
Earth

"A planet doesn't explode of itself," said drily
The Martian astronomer, gazing off into the air—
"That they were able to do it is proof that highly
Intelligent beings must have been living there."

[1961]

TOPICS FOR DISCUSSION AND WRITING

1. What is the "it" (line 3) that has been done?
2. How do you think the Martian astronomer would characterize himself or herself? How do you think the author would characterize the astronomer?

Percy Bysshe Shelley *(English; 1792–1822)*
Ozymandias

I met a traveler from an antique land
Who said: Two vast and trunkless legs of stone
Stand in the desert . . . Near them, on the sand,
Half sunk, a shattered visage lies, whose frown,   4
And wrinkled lip, and sneer of cold command,
Tell that its sculptor well those passions read
Which yet survive, stamped on these lifeless things,
The hand that mocked them, and the heart that fed: 8
And on the pedestal these words appear:
"My name is Ozymandias, king of kings:
Look on my works, ye Mighty, and despair!"

Nothing beside remains. Round the decay   *12*
Of that colossal wreck, boundless and bare
The lone and level sands stretch far away.

[1817]

Lines 4–8 are somewhat obscure, but the gist is that the passions — still evident in the "shattered visage" — survive the sculptor's hand that "mocked" — that is, (1) copied, (2) derided — them, and the passions also survive the king's heart that had nourished them.

TOPIC FOR DISCUSSION AND WRITING

There is, of course, a sort of irony of plot here: Ozymandias believed that he created enduring works, but his intentions came to nothing. However, another sort of irony is also present: How are his words, in a way he did not intend, true?

Linda Pastan (American; b. 1932)

Ethics

In ethics class so many years ago
our teacher asked this question every fall:
if there were a fire in a museum
which would you save, a Rembrandt painting
or an old woman who hadn't many   *5*
years left anyhow? Restless on hard chairs
caring little for pictures or old age
we'd opt one year for life, the next for art
and always half-heartedly. Sometimes
the woman borrowed my grandmother's face   *10*
leaving her usual kitchen to wander
some drafty, half-imagined museum.
One year, feeling clever, I replied
why not let the woman decide herself?
Linda, the teacher would report, eschews   *15*
the burdens or responsibility.
This fall in a real museum I stand
before a real Rembrandt, old woman,
or nearly so, myself. The colors

within this frame are darker than autumn,   20
darker even than winter—the browns of earth,
though earth's most radiant elements burn
through the canvas. I know now that woman
and painting and season are almost one
and all beyond saving by children.   25

[1980]

TOPICS FOR DISCUSSION AND WRITING

1. What, if anything, do we know about the teacher in the poem? Do you imagine that you would like to take a course with this teacher? Why?
2. Lines 3–6 report a question that a teacher asked. Does the rest of the poem answer the question? If so, what is the answer? If not, what does the rest of the poem do?
3. Do you assume that, for this poem, the responses of younger readers (say 17–22) as a group would differ from those of older readers? If so, why?

Stevie Smith (English; 1902–71)

Not Waving but Drowning

Nobody heard him, the dead man,
But still he lay moaning:
I was much further out than you thought
And not waving but drowning.   4

Poor chap, he always loved larking
And now he's dead
It must have been too cold for him his heart gave way,
They said.   8

Oh, no no no, it was too cold always
(Still the dead one lay moaning)
I was much too far out all my life
And not waving but drowning.   12

[1957]

TOPICS FOR DISCUSSION AND WRITING

1. What sort of man did the friends of the dead man think he was? What sort of man do you think he was?
2. The first line, "Nobody heard him, the dead man," is of course literally true. Dead men do not speak. In what other ways is it true?

John Crowe Ransom *(American; 1888–1974)*

Bells for John Whiteside's Daughter

There was such speed in her little body,
And such lightness in her footfall,
It is no wonder her brown study
Astonishes us all.   *4*

Her wars were bruited in our high window.
We looked among orchard trees and beyond
Where she took arms against her shadow,
Or harried unto the pond   *8*

The lazy geese, like a snow cloud
Dripping their snow on the green grass,
Tricking and stopping, sleepy and proud,
Who cried in goose, Alas,   *12*

For the tireless heart within the little
Lady with rod that made them rise
From their noon apple-dreams and scuttle
Goose-fashion under the skies!   *16*

But now go the bells, and we are ready,
In one house we are sternly stopped
To say we are vexed at her brown study,
Lying so primly propped.   *20*

[1924]

TOPICS FOR DISCUSSION AND WRITING

1. What is the usual meaning of "a brown study" in line 3? For what is it an understatement here? What do you think the poet is referring

to when he speaks of "her wars" (line 5)? What are the literal and
figurative suggestions of "took arms against her shadow" in
line 7?
2. Why is "tireless heart" (line 13) ironic?
3. In line 17 the speaker says "we are ready." Ready for what? Do you
think he is ready?

Andrew Marvell (*English; 1621–78*)

To His Coy Mistress

Had we but world enough, and time,
This coyness, lady, were no crime.
We would sit down, and think which way
To walk, and pass our long love's day.
Thou by the Indian Ganges' side   5
Should'st rubies find: I by the tide
Of Humber would complain.° I would   *write love poems*
Love you ten years before the Flood,
And you should, if you please, refuse
Till the conversion of the Jews.   10
My vegetable° love should grow   *i.e., unconsciously growing*
Vaster than empires, and more slow.
An hundred years should go to praise
Thine eyes, and on thy forehead gaze:
Two hundred to adore each breast: 15
But thirty thousand to the rest.
An age at least to every part,
And the last age should show your heart.
For, lady, you deserve this state,
Nor would I love at lower rate.   20
    But at my back I always hear
Time's winged chariot hurrying near;
And yonder all before us lie
Deserts of vast eternity.
Thy beauty shall no more be found,   25
Nor in thy marble vault shall sound
My echoing song; then worms shall try
That long preserved virginity,
And your quaint honor turn to dust,
And into ashes all my lust.   30

The grave's a fine and private place,
But none, I think, do there embrace.
    Now therefore, while the youthful hue
Sits on thy skin like morning dew,
And while thy willing soul transpires   *35*
At every pore with instant fires,
Now let us sport us while we may;
And now, like am'rous birds of prey,
Rather at once our time devour,
Than languish in his slow-chapt° power,   *slowly devouring* **40**
Let us roll all our strength, and all
Our sweetness, up into one ball;
And tear our pleasures with rough strife
Thorough° the iron gates of life.   *through*
Thus, though we cannot make our sun   **45**
Stand still, yet we will make him run.

[1681]

TOPICS FOR DISCUSSION AND WRITING

1. Do you find the assertions in lines 1–20 so inflated that you detect behind them a plafully ironic tone? Explain. Why does the speaker say, in line 8, that he would love "ten years before the Flood," rather than merely "since the Flood"?

2. Explain lines 21–4. Why is time behind the speaker, and eternity in front of him? Is this "eternity" the same as the period discussed in lines 1–20? What do you make of the change in the speaker's tone after line 20.

3. Do you agree with the comment on pages 484–85 about the understatement in lines 31–2? What more can you say about these lines, in context?

4. Why "am'rous birds of prey" (line 38) rather than the conventional doves? Is the idea of preying continued in the poem?

5. Try to explain the last two lines, and characterize the speaker's tone. Do you find these lines anticlimactic?

6. The poem is organized in the form of an argument. Trace the steps.

John Donne (English; 1572–1631)

The Flea

Mark but this flea, and mark in this
How little that which thou deny'st me is;
It sucked me first, and now sucks thee,
And in this flea our two bloods mingled be;
Thou know'st that this cannot be said   5
A sin, nor shame, nor loss of maidenhead;
    Yet this enjoys before it woo,
      And pampered swells with one blood made of two,
      And this, alas, is more than we would do.

Oh stay, three lives in one flea spare,   10
Where we almost, yea, more than married are.
This flea is you and I, and this
Our marriage bed and marriage temple is;
Though parents grudge, and you, we are met
And cloistered in these living walls of jet.   15
    Though use° make you apt to kill me,   *custom*
    Let not to that, self-murder added be,
    And sacrilege, three sins in killing three.

Cruel and sudden, hast thou since
Purpled they nail in blood of innocence?   20
Wherein could this flea guilty be,
Except in that drop which it sucked from thee?
Yet thou triumph'st and say'st that thou
Find'st not thyself, nor me the weaker now.
    'Tis true. Then learn how false fears be: 25
    Just so much honor, when thou yield'st to me,
    Will waste, as this flea's death took life from thee.

[1633]

TOPICS FOR DISCUSSION AND WRITING

1. What is hyperbolic about line 10? Why does the speaker overstate
   the matter in the second stanza? How does the overstatement serve
   to diminish the subject?

2. What has the lady done between the second and third stanzas? In line 25 the speaker says that the lady's view is "true." Has he changed his mind during the course of the poem, or has he been leading up to this point?

Holy Sonnet XIV

Batter my heart, three-personed God; for you
As yet but knock, breathe, shine, and seek to mend;
That I may rise and stand, o'erthrow me, and bend
Your force, to break, blow, burn, and make me new.   *4*
I, like an usurped town, to another due,
Labor to admit you, but oh, to no end,
Reason, your viceroy in me, me should defend,
But is captived, and proves weak or untrue.   *8*
Yet dearly I love you, and would be loved fain,
But am betrothed unto your enemy:
Divorce me, untie, or break that knot again,
Take me to you, imprison me, for I   *12*
Except you enthrall me, never shall be free,
Nor ever chaste, except you ravish me.

[1633]

TOPICS FOR DISCUSSION AND WRITING

1. Explain the paradoxes in lines 1, 3, 13, and 14. Explain the double meanings of "enthrall" (line 13) and "ravish" (line 14).
2. In lines 1–4, what is God implicitly compared to (considering especially lines 2 and 4)? How does this comparison lead into the comparison that dominates lines 5–8? What words in lines 9–12 are especially related to the earlier lines?
3. What do you think is gained by piling up verbs in lines 2–4?
4. Do you find sexual references irreverent in a religious poem? Donne, incidentally, was an Anglican priest.

THREE POEMS BY LANGSTON HUGHES

Langston Hughes (American; 1902–67)

Dream Boogie

Good morning, daddy!
Ain't you heard
The boogie-woogie rumble
Of a dream deferred?
Listen closely: 5
You'll hear their feet
Beating out and beating out a—

    You think
    It's a happy beat?

Listen to it closely: 10
Ain't you heard
something underneath
like a—

    What did I say?

Sure,   15
I'm happy!
Take it away!

    Hey, pop!
    Re-bop!
    Mop!   20

    Y-e-a-h!

    What don't bug
    them white kids
    sure bugs me:
    We knows everybody   25
    ain't free!

Some of these young ones is cert'ly bad—
One batted a hard ball right through my window
and my gold fish et the glass.

> *What's written down*   30
> *for white folks*
> *ain't for us a-tall:*
> *"Liberty And Justice —*
> *Huh — For All."*

> *Oop-pop-a-da!*   35
> *Skee! Daddle-de-do!*
> *Be-bop!*

Salt'peanuts!

> *De-dop!*

          [1951]

TOPICS FOR DISCUSSION AND WRITING

1. What is boogie, or boogie-woogie?
2. Why did many whites assume that boogie was "a happy beat" (line 9)? In fact, what was boogie chiefly an expression of?
3. Why does Hughes in lines 32-4 quote part of the Pledge of Allegiance?

Theme for English B

The instructor said,

> *Go home and write*
> *a page tonight.*
> *And let that page come out of you —*
> *Then, it will be true.*

I wonder if it's that simple?   5
I am twenty-two, colored, born in Winston-Salem.*
I went to school there, then Durham, then here
to this college on the hill above Harlem.
I am the only colored student in my class.   10
The steps from the hill lead down into Harlem,
through a park, then I cross St. Nicholas,
Eighth Avenue, Seventh, and I come to the Y,

---

*Winston-Salem and Durham (line 8) are in North Carolina; the places later named are in New York; in line 24, Bessie Smith (1898?–1937) was an African-American singer of blues.

the Harlem Branch Y, where I take the elevator
up to my room, sit down, and write this page: *15*

It's not easy to know what is true for you or me
at twenty-two, my age. But I guess I'm what
I feel and see and hear, Harlem, I hear you:
hear you, hear me—we two—you, me, talk on this page.
(I hear New York, too.) Me—who?   *20*

Well, I like to eat, sleep, drink, and be in love.
I like to work, read, learn and understand life.
I like a pipe for a Christmas present,
or records—Bessie, bop, or Bach.
I guess being colored doesn't make me *not* like   *25*
the same things other folks like who are other races.
So will my page be colored that I write?

Being me, it will not be white.
But it will be
a part of you, instructor.   *30*
You are white—
yet a part of me, as I am a part of you.
That's American.
Sometimes perhaps you don't want to be a part of me.
Nor do I often want to be a part of you.   *35*
But we are, that's true!
As I learn from you,
I guess you learn from me—
although you're older—and white—
and somewhat more free.   *40*

This is my page for English B.

[1951]

TOPICS FOR DISCUSSION AND WRITING

1. On your first reading of the poem did the instructor's lines (2–5)
   sound sensible and convincing to you? On a second reading, how
   do they sound?
2. How much sense does it make for the speaker to say that his essay
   will be "a part of you, instructor," and "You are white— / yet a part
   of me, as I am a part of you" (lines 30–2)?
3. Do you think lines 37–40 are meant to be spoken with conscious
   verbal irony?

4. There are two voices, or speakers, in the poem—the instructor and the student. Which of the two strikes you as the more thoughtful?

Passing

On sunny summer Sunday afternoons in Harlem
when the air is one interminable ball game
and grandma cannot get her gospel hymns
from the Saints of God in Christ
on account of the Dodgers on the radio,   5
on sunny Sunday afternoons
when the kids look all new
and far too clean to stay that way,
and Harlem has its
washed-and-ironed-and-cleaned-best out,   10
the ones who've crossed the line
to live downtown
miss you,
Harlem of the bitter dream,
since their dream has   15
come true.

[1951]

TOPICS FOR DISCUSSION AND WRITING

1. What does the title mean? Given the title, what meanings do you find in "crosses the line" (line 11)?
2. What is ironic or paradoxical about the poem?

Martín Espada (American; b. 1957)

Tony Went to the Bodega* but He Didn't Buy Anything

para Angel Guadalupe

Tony's father left the family
and the Long Island city projects,

Bodega grocery and liquor store; in the dedication, after the title, *para* means "for."

leaving a mongrel-skinny puertorriqueño boy
nine years old
who had to find work.   5

Makengo the Cuban
let him work at the bodega.
In grocery aisles
he learned the steps of the dry-mop mambo,
banging the cash register   10
like piano percussion
in the spotlight of Machito's orchestra,
polite with the abuelas° who bought on credit,   *grandmothers*
practicing the grin on customers
he'd seen Makengo grin   15
with his bad yellow teeth.

Tony left the projects too,
with a scholarship for law school.
But he cursed the cold primavera°   *spring season*
in Boston;   20
the cooking of his neighbors
left no smell in the hallway,
and no one spoke Spanish
(not even the radio).

So Tony walked without a map   25
through the city,
a landscape of hostile condominiums
and the darkness of white faces,
sidewalk-searcher lost
till he discovered the projects.   30

Tony went to the bodega
but he didn't buy anything:
he sat by the doorway satisfied
to watch la gente° (people   *the people*
island-brown as him)   35
crowd in and out,
hablando español,°   *speaking Spanish*
thought: this is beautiful,
and grinned
his bodega grin.   40

This is a rice and beans
success story:

today Tony lives on Tremont Street,
above the bodega.

[1987]

TOPICS FOR DISCUSSION AND WRITING

1. Why do you suppose Espada included the information about Tony's father? The information about young Tony "practicing" a grin?
2. Why does Tony leave?
3. How would you characterize Tony?

Edna St. Vincent Millay *(American; 1892–1950)*

Love Is Not All: It Is Not Meat nor Drink

Love is not all: it is not meat nor drink
Nor slumber nor a roof against the rain;
Nor yet a floating spar to men that sink
And rise and sink and rise and sink again;   4
Love can not fill the thickened lung with breath,
Nor clean the blood, nor set the fractured bone;
Yet many a man is making friends with death
Even as I speak, for lack of love alone.   8
It well may be that in a difficult hour,
Pinned down by pain and moaning for release,
Or nagged by want past resolution's power,
I might be driven to sell your love for peace,   12
Or trade the memory of this night for food.
It well may be. I do not think I would.

[1931]

TOPICS FOR DISCUSSION AND WRITING

1. "Love Is Not All" is a sonnet. Using your own words, briefly summarize the argument of the octet (the first 8 lines). Next, paraphrase the sestet (the six lines from line 9 through line 14), line by line. On the whole, does the sestet repeat the idea of the octet, or does it add a new idea? Whom did you imagine to be speaking the octet? What does the sestet add to your knowledge of the speaker and the occasion? (And how did you paraphrase line 11?)

2. The first and last lines of the poem consist of words of one syllable, and both lines have a distinct pause in the middle. Do you imagine the lines to be spoken in the same tone of voice? If not, can you describe the difference and account for it?

3. Lines 7 and 8 appear to mean that the absence of love can be a cause of death. To what degree do you believe that to be true?

4. Would you call "Love Is Not All" a love poem? Why or why not? Describe the kind of person who might include the poem in a love letter or valentine, or who would be happy to receive it. (One of our friends recited it at her wedding. What do you think of that idea?)

16

Rhythm and Versification

Ezra Pound (*American; 1885–1972*)

An Immorality

Sing we for love and idleness,
Naught else is worth the having.

Though I have been in many a land,
There is naught else in living.

And I would rather have my sweet,
Though rose-leaves die of grieving,

Than do high deeds in Hungary
To pass all men's believing.

[1919]

A good poem. To begin with, it sings; as Pound said, "Poetry withers and dries out when it leaves music, or at least imagined music, too far behind it. Poets who are not interested in music are, or become, bad poets." Hymns and ballads, it must be remembered, are songs, and other poetry, too, is sung, especially by children. Children reciting a counting-out rhyme, or singing on their way home from school, are enjoying poetry:

> Pease-porridge hot,
>   Pease-porridge cold,
> Pease-porridge in the pot
>   Nine days old.

Nothing very important is being said, but for generations children have enjoyed the music of these lines, and adults, too, have recalled them with pleasure—though few people know what pease-porridge is.

The "music"—the catchiness of certain sounds—should not be underestimated. Here are lines chanted by the witches in *Macbeth:*

> Double, double, toil and trouble;
> Fire burn and cauldron bubble.

This is rather far from words that mean approximately the same thing: "Twice, twice, work and care; / Fire ignite, and pot boil." The difference is more in the sounds than in the instructions. What is lost in the paraphrase is the magic, the incantation, which resides in elaborate repetitions of sounds and stresses.

Rhythm (most simply, in English poetry, stresses at regular intervals) has a power of its own. A good march, said John Philip Sousa (the composer of "Stars and Stripes Forever") should make even someone with a wooden leg "step out." A highly pronounced rhythm is common in such forms of poetry as charms, college yells, and lullabies; all of them (like the witches' speech) are aimed at inducing a special effect magically. It is not surprising that *carmen,* the Latin word for poem or song, is also the Latin word for charm, and the word from which "charm" is derived.

> Rain, rain, go away;
> Come again another day.

> Block that kick! Block that kick! Block that kick!

> Rock-a-bye baby, on the tree top,
> When the wind blows, the cradle will rock.

In much poetry rhythm is only half-heard, but its omnipresence is suggested by the fact that when poetry is printed it is customary to begin each line with a capital letter. Prose (from Latin *prorsus,* "forward," "straight on") keeps running across the paper until the righthand margin is reached, and then, merely because the paper has given out, the writer or printer starts again at the left, with a small letter. But verse (Latin *versus,* "a turning") often ends well short of the righthand margin, and the next line begins at the left—usually with a capital—not because paper has run out but because the rhythmic pattern begins again. Lines of poetry are continually reminding us that they have a pattern.

Before turning to some other highly rhythmic pieces, a word of caution: a mechanical, unvarying rhythm may be good to put the baby to sleep, but it can be deadly to readers who wish to keep awake. Poets vary their rhythm according to their purpose; a poet ought not to be so regular that he or she is (in W. H. Auden's words) an "accentual pest." In competent hands, rhythm contributes to meaning; it says something. The rhythm in the lines from *Macbeth,* for example, helps suggest the strong binding power of magic. Again Ezra Pound has a relevant comment: "Rhythm *must* have meaning. It can't be merely a careless dash off, with no grip and no real hold to the words and sense, a tumty tum tumty tum tum ta." Some examples will be useful.

Consider this description of Hell from John Milton's *Paradise Lost* (the heavier stresses are marked by ´):

Rócks, cáves, lákes, féns, bógs, déns, aňd shádes ǒf déath.

Such a succession of stresses is highly unusual. Elsewhere in the poem Milton chiefly uses iambic feet—alternating unstressed and stressed syllables—but here he immediately follows one heavy stress with another, thereby helping to communicate the "meaning"—the impressive monotony of Hell. As a second example, consider the function of the rhythm in two lines by Alexander Pope:

Whěn Ájax strivěs sǒme róck's vást wěight tǒ thrów,

Thě líne tǒo lábǒrs, aňd thě wórds móve slów.

The heavier stresses (again, marked by ´) do not merely alternate with the lighter ones (marked ˇ); rather, the great weight of the rock is suggested by three consecutive stressed words, "rock's vast weight," and the great effort involved in moving it is suggested by another three consecutive stresses, "line too labors," and by yet another three, "words move slow." Note, also, the abundant pauses within the lines. In the first line, unless one's speech is slovenly, one must pause at least slightly after "Ajax," "strives," "rock's," "vast," "weight," and "throw." The grating sounds in "Ajax" and "rocks" do their work, too, and so do the explosive *t*'s. When Pope wishes to suggest lightness, he reverses his procedure and he groups unstressed syllables:

Not so, when swift Camilla scours the plain,

Fliés o'ěr th'unběndǐng córn, aňd skíms alǒng thě máin.

This last line has twelve syllables and is thus longer than the line about Ajax, but the addition of "along" helps to communicate lightness and swiftness because in this line (it can be argued) neither syllable of "along" is strongly stressed. If "along" is omitted, the line still makes grammatical sense and becomes more "regular," but it also becomes less imitative of lightness.

The very regularity of a line may be meaningful too. Shakespeare begins a sonnet thus:

Whěn Í dǒ cóunt thě clóck thǎt télls thě tíme.

This line about a mechanism runs with appropriate regularity. (It is worth noting, too, that "*c*ount the *c*lock" and "*t*ells the *t*ime" emphasize the regularity by the repetition of sounds and syntax.) But notice what Shakespeare does in the middle of the next line:

> And see the brave day sunk in hideous night.

What has he done? And what is the effect?

Here is another poem that refers to a clock. In England, until capital punishment was abolished, executions regularly took place at 8:00 A.M.

A. E. Housman (English; 1859–1936)

Eight O'Clock

He stood, and heard the steeple
  Sprinkle the quarters on the morning town.
One, two, three, four, to market-place and people
  It tossed them down.

Strapped, noosed, nighing his hour,
  He stood and counted them and cursed his luck;
And then the clock collected in the tower
  Its strength, and struck.

[1922]

The chief (but not unvarying) pattern is iambic, that is, the odd syllables are less emphatic than the even ones, as in

> He stood, and heard the steeple

Try to mark the syllables, stressed and unstressed, in the rest of the poem. Be guided by your ear, not by a mechanical principle, and don't worry too much about difficult or uncertain parts; different readers may reasonably come up with different results.

TOPICS FOR DISCUSSION AND WRITING

1. Where do you find two or more consecutive stresses? What explanations (related to meaning) can be offered?
2. What do you think is the effect of the short line at the end of each stanza? And what significance can you attach to the fact that these lines (unlike the first and third lines in each stanza) end with a stress?

Following are some poems in which the strongly felt pulsations are highly important.

William Carlos Williams *(American; 1883–1963)*

The Dance

In Breughel's great picture, The Kermess,°   *Carnival*
the dancers go round, they go round and
around, the squeal and the blare and the
tweedle of bagpipes, a bugle and fiddles
tipping their bellies (round as the thick-   *5*
sided glasses whose wash they impound)
their hips and their bellies off balance
to turn them. Kicking and rolling about
the Fair Grounds, swinging their butts, those
shanks must be sound to bear up under such   *10*
rollicking measures, prance as they dance
in Breughel's great picture, The Kermess.

[1944]

"The Carnival" by Pieter Breughel (1520?–1569). Kunsthistorisches Museum, Vienna.

TOPICS FOR DISCUSSION AND WRITING

1. Read the poem aloud several times, and decide where the heavy stresses fall. Mark the heavily stressed syllables (′), the lightly stressed ones (^), and the unstressed ones (˘). Are all the lines identical? What effect is thus gained, especially when read aloud? What does the parenthetical statement (lines 5–6) do to the rhythm? Does a final syllable often receive a heavy stress here? Are there noticeable pauses at the ends of the lines? What is the consequence? Are the dancers waltzing?

2. What syllables rhyme or are repeated (e.g., "round" in lines 2 and 5, and "–pound" in line 6; "–ing" in lines 5, 8, 9, and 11)? What effect do they have?

3. What do you think the absence at the beginning of each line of the customary capital contributes to the meaning? Why is the last line the same as the first?

Theodore Roethke (American; 1908–63)

My Papa's Waltz

The whiskey on your breath
Could make a small boy dizzy;
but I hung on like death:
Such waltzing was not easy.   4

We romped until the pans
Slid from the kitchen shelf;
My mother's countenance
Could not unfrown itself.   8

The hand that held my wrist
Was battered on one knuckle;
At every step you missed
My right ear scraped a buckle.   12

You beat time on my head
With a palm caked hard by dirt,
Then waltzed me off to bed
Still clinging to your shirt.   16

[1948]

TOPICS FOR DISCUSSION AND WRITING

1. Is the rhythm more regular than in Williams' "The Dance"? Do the syntactical pauses vary much from stanza to stanza? Be specific. Would you say that the rhythm suggests lightness? Why?
2. Does the rhythm parallel or ironically contrast with the episode described? Was the dance a graceful waltz? Explain.
3. What would you say is the function of the stresses in lines 13–4?

Gwendolyn Brooks *(American; b. 1917)*

We Real Cool

The Pool Players.

Seven at the Golden Shovel.

We real cool. We
Left school. We

Lurk late. We
Strike straight. We   *4*

Sing sin. We
Thin gin. We

Jazz June. We
Die soon.   *8*

      [1960]

TOPIC FOR DISCUSSION OR WRITING

The stanzas could, of course, have been written thus:

    We real cool.
    We left school.

    We lurk late.
    We strike straight.

And so forth. Why do you think Brooks wrote them, or printed them, the way she did?

Dylan Thomas (Welsh; 1914–53)

Do not go gentle into that good night

Do not go gentle into that good night,
Old age should burn and rave at close of day;
Rage, rage against the dying of the light.

Though wise men at their end know dark is right,
Because their words had forked no lightning they   5
Do not go gentle into that good night.

Good men, the last wave by, crying how bright
Their frail deeds might have danced in a green bay,
Rage, rage against the dying of the light.

Wild men who caught and sang the sun in flight,   10
And learn, too late, they grieved it on its way,
Do not go gentle into that good night.

Grave men, near death, who see with blinding sight
Blind eyes could blaze like meteors and be gay,
Rage, rage against the dying of the light.   15

And you, my father, there on the sad height,
Curse, bless, me now with your fierce tears, I pray.
Do not go gentle into that good night.
Rage, rage against the dying of the light.

[1952]

This poem is written in an elaborate French form, the **villanelle,** that is,
five tercets (stanzas of three lines each, the first and the third lines rhyming)
and a final quatrain (stanza of four lines, the first, third, and fourth lines
all rhyming with the first and third lines of the tercets, and the second
line rhyming with the middle lines of the tercets). Moreover, the first line
of the poem is the last line of the second and fourth tercets; the third line
of the poem is the last line of the third and fifth tercets, and these two
lines reappear yet again as a pair of rhyming lines at the end of the poem.

TOPIC FOR DISCUSSION OR WRITING

The intricate form of the villanelle might seem too fussy for a serious poem about dying. Do you find it too fussy? Or does the form here somehow succeed?

Robert Francis *(American; 1901–87)*

The Pitcher

His art is eccentricity, his aim
How not to hit the mark he seems to aim at,

His passion how to avoid the obvious,
His technique how to vary the avoidance. *4*

The others throw to be comprehended. He
Throws to be a moment misunderstood.

Yet not too much. Not errant, arrant, wild,
But every seeming aberration willed. *8*

Not to, yet still, still to communicate
Making the batter understand too late.

[1960]

If you read this poem aloud, pausing appropriately where the punctuation tells you to, you will hear the poet trying to represent something of the pitcher's "eccentricity." ("Eccentric," by the way, literally means "off center.") A pitcher tries to deceive a batter, perhaps by throwing a ball that will unexpectedly curve over the plate; the poet playfully deceives the reader, for instance, with unexpected pauses. In line 5, for example, he puts a heavy pause (indicated by a period) not at the end of the line, but just before the end.

TOPICS FOR DISCUSSION AND WRITING

1. Notice that some lines contain no pauses, but the next-to-last line contains two within it (indicated by commas) and no pause at the end of it. What do you suppose Francis is getting at?

2. What significance can be attached to the fact that only the last two lines really rhyme (communicate / late) whereas other lines do not quite rhyme?

VERSIFICATION: A GLOSSARY FOR REFERENCE

The technical vocabulary of **prosody** (the study of the principles of verse structure, including meter, rhyme and other sound effects, and stanzaic patterns) is large. An understanding of these terms will not turn anyone into a poet, but it will enable one to discuss some aspects of poetry more efficiently. A knowledge of them, like a knowledge of most other technical terms (e.g., "misplaced modifier," "woofer," "automatic transmission"), allows for quick and accurate communication. The following are the chief terms of prosody.

Meter

Most English poetry has a pattern of **stressed (accented)** sounds, and this pattern is the **meter** (from the Greek word for "measure"). Although in Old English poetry (poetry written in England before the Norman-French Conquest in 1066) a line may have any number of unstressed syllables in addition to four stressed syllables, most poetry written in England since the Conquest not only has a fixed number of stresses in a line, but also has a fixed number of unstressed syllables before of after each stressed one. (One really ought not to talk of "unstressed" or "unaccented" syllables, since to utter a syllable—however lightly—is to give it some stress. It is really a matter of *relative* stress, but the fact is that "unstressed"or "unaccented" are parts of the established terminology of versification.)

In a line of poetry, the **foot** is the basic unit of measurement. On rare occasions it is a single stressed syllable, but generally a foot consists of two or three syllables, one of which is stressed. (Stress is indicated by ´; lack of stress by ˘.) The repetition of feet, then, produces a pattern of stresses throughout the poem.

Two cautions:

1. A poem will seldom contain only one kind of foot throughout; significant variations usually occur, but one kind of foot is dominant.
2. In reading a poem one pays attention to the sense as well as to the metrical pattern. By paying attention to the sense, one often finds that the stress falls on a word that according to the metrical pattern would be unstressed. Or a word that according to the pattern would

be stressed may be seen to be unstressed. Furthermore, by reading for sense, one finds that not all stresses are equally heavy; some are almost as light as unstressed syllables, and sometimes there is a **hovering stress;** that is, the stress is equally distributed over two adjacent syllables. To repeat: one reads for sense, allowing the syntax to help indicate the stresses.

Metrical Feet.   The most common feet in English poetry are the six listed below.

Iamb (adjective: **iambic**): one unstressed syllable followed by one stressed syllable. The iamb, said to be the most common pattern in English speech, is surely the most common in English poetry. The following example has four iambic feet:

> My heart is like a sing-ing bird.
> > —Christina Rossetti

Trochee (trochaic): one stressed syllable followed by one unstressed.

> We were very tired, we were very merry
> > —Edna St. Vincent Millay

Anapest (anapestic): two unstressed syllables followed by one stressed.

> There are man-y who say that a dog has his day.
> > —Dylan Thomas

Dactyl (dactylic): one stressed syllable followed by two unstressed. This trisyllabic foot, like the anapest, is common in light verse or verse suggesting joy, but its use in not limited to such material, as Longfellow's *Evangeline* shows. Thomas Hood's sentimental "The Bridge of Sighs" begins:

> Take her up tenderly.

Spondee (spondaic): two stressed syllables; most often used as a sustitute for an iamb or trochee.

> Smart lad, to slip betimes away.
> > —A. E. Housman

Pyrrhic: two unstressed syllables; it is often not considered a legitimate foot in English.

Metrical Lines.   A metrical line consists of one or more feet and is named for the number of feet in it. The following names are used:

monometer: one foot   **pentameter:** five feet
dimeter: two feet   **hexameter:** six feet
trimeter: three feet   **heptameter:** seven feet
tetrameter: four feet   **octameter:** eight feet

A line is scanned for the kind and number of feet in it, and the **scansion** tells you if it is, say, anapestic trimeter (three anapests):

> Ăs Ĭ cáme tŏ thĕ édge ŏf thĕ wóods.
>
>   —Robert Frost

Or, in another example, iambic pentameter:

> Thĕ súm-mĕr thún-dĕr, lĭke ă wóod-ĕn béll
>
>   —Louise Bogan

A line ending with a stress has a **masculine ending;** a line ending with an extra unstressed syllable has a **feminine ending.** The **caesura** (usually indicated by the symbol / /) is a slight pause within the line. It need not be indicated by punctuation (notice the fourth and fifth lines in the following quotation), and it does not affect the metrical count:

> Awake, my St. John! / / leave all meaner things
> To low ambition, / / and the pride of kings.
> Let us / / (since life can little more supply
> Than just to look about us / / and to die)
> Expatiate free / / o'er all this scene of Man;
> A mighty maze! / / but not without a plan;
> A wild, / / where weeds and flowers promiscuous shoot;
> Or garden, / / tempting with forbidden fruit.
>
>   —Alexander Pope

The varying position of the caesura helps to give Pope's lines an informality that plays against the formality of the pairs of rhyming lines.

    An **end-stopped line** concludes with a distinct syntactical pause, but a **run-on line** has its sense carried over into the next line without syntactical pause. (The running-on of a line is called **enjambment.**) In the following passage, only the first is a run-on line:

> Yet if we look more closely we shall find
> Most have the seeds of judgment in their mind:
> Nature affords at least a glimmering light;
> The lines, though touched but faintly, are drawn right.
>
>   —Alexander Pope

    Meter produces **rhythm,** recurrences at equal intervals, but rhythm (from a Greek word meaning "flow") is usually applied to larger units than feet. Often it depends most obviously on pauses. Thus, a poem with run-on lines will have a different rhythm from a poem with end-stopped lines, even though both are in the same meter. And prose, though it is unmetrical, can have rhythm, too.

In addition to being affected by syntactical pause, rhythm is affected by pauses attributable to consonant clusters and to the length of words. Words of several syllables establish a different rhythm from words of one syllable, even in metrically identical lines. One can say, then, that rhythm is altered by shifts in meter, syntax, and the length and ease of pronunciation. But even with no such shift, even if a line is repeated word for word, a reader may sense a change in rhythm. The rhythm of the final line of a poem, for example, may well differ from that of the line before, even though in all other respects the lines are identical, as in Frost's "Stopping by Woods on a Snowy Evening" (page 541) which concludes by repeating "And miles to go before I sleep." One may simply sense that this final line ought to be spoken, say, more slowly and with more stress on "miles."

Patterns of Sound

Though rhythm is basic to poetry, **rhyme** — the repetition of the identical or similar stressed sound or sounds — is not. Rhyme is, presumably, pleasant in itself; it suggests order; and it may also be related to meaning, for it brings two words sharply together, often implying a relationship, as in the now trite *dove* and *love,* or in the more imaginative *throne* and *alone.*

Perfect, or **exact, rhyme:** Differing consonant sounds are followed by identical stressed vowel sounds, and the following sounds, if any, are identical *(foe — toe; meet — fleet; buffer — rougher).* Notice that perfect rhyme involves identity of sound, not of spelling. *Fix* and *sticks,* like *buffer* and *rougher,* are perfect rhymes.

Half-rhyme (or **off-rhyme**): Only the final consonant sounds of the words are identical; the stressed vowel sounds as well as the initial consonant sounds, if any, differ *(soul — oil; mirth — forth; trolley — bully).*

Eye-rhyme: The sounds do not in fact rhyme, but the words look as though they would rhyme *(cough — bough).*

Masculine rhyme: The final syllables are stressed and, after their differing initial consonant sounds, are identical in sound *(stark — mark; support — retort).*

Feminine rhyme (or **double rhyme**): Stressed rhyming syllables are followed by identical unstressed syllables *(revival — arrival; flatter — batter).* **Triple rhyme** is a kind of feminine rhyme in which identical stressed vowel sounds are followed by two identical unstressed syllables *(machinery — scenery; tenderly — slenderly).*

End rhyme (or **terminal rhyme**): The rhyming words occur at the ends of the lines.

Internal rhyme: At least one of the rhyming words occurs within the line (Oscar Wilde's "Each narrow *cell* in which we *dwell*").

Alliteration: sometimes defined as the repetition of initial sounds ("*A*ll the *a*wful *a*uguries," or "*B*ring me my *b*ow of *b*urning gold"), and sometimes as the prominent repetition of a consonant ("a*ft*er li*f*e's *f*it*f*ul *f*ever").

Assonance: the repetition, in words of proximity, of identical vowel sounds preceded and followed by differing consonant sounds. Whereas *tide* and *hide* are rhymes, *tide* and *mine* are assonantal.

Consonance: the repetition of identical consonant sounds and differing vowel sounds in words in proximity (*fail—feel; rough—roof; pitter—patter*). Sometimes consonance is more loosely defined merely as the repetition of a consonant (*fail—peel*). The following poem makes witty use of consonance and assonance.

George Starbuck (American; b. 1931)

Fable for Blackboard

Here is the grackle, people.
Here is the fox, folks.
The grackle sits in the bracken. The fox hopes.

Here are the fronds, friends,
that cover the fox.
The fronds get in a frenzy. The grackle looks.

Here are the ticks, tykes,
that live in the leaves, loves.
The fox is confounded,
and God is above.

[1960]

Onomatopoeia: the use of words that imitate sounds, such as *hiss* and *buzz*. There is a mistaken tendency to see onomatopoeia everywhere—for example, in *thunder* and *horror*. Many words sometimes thought to be onomatopoeic are not clearly imitative of the thing they refer to; they merely contain some sounds that, when we know what the word means, seem to have some resemblance to the thing they denote. Tennyson's lines from "Come down, O maid" are usually cited as an example of onomatopoeia:

The moan of doves in immemorial elms
And murmuring of innumerable bees.

Stanzaic Patterns

Lines of poetry are commonly arranged in a rhythmical unit called a stanza (from an Italian word meaning "room" or "stopping-place"). Usually all the stanzas in a poem have the same rhyme pattern. A stanza is sometimes called a **verse,** though **verse** may also mean a single line of poetry. (In discussing stanzas, rhymes are indicated by identical letters. Thus, *abab* indicates that the first and third lines rhyme with each other, while the second and fourth lines are linked by a different rhyme. An unrhymed line is denoted by *x.*) Common stanzaic forms in English poetry are the following:

Couplet: a stanza of two lines, usually, but not necessarily, with end-rhymes. *Couplet* is also used for a pair of rhyming lines. The **octosyllabic couplet** is iambic or trochaic tetrameter:

> Had we but world enough and time.
> This coyness, lady, were no crime.
>
> —Andrew Marvel

Heroic couplet: a rhyming couplet of iambic pentameter, often "closed," that is, containing a complete thought, with a fairly heavy pause at the end of the first line and a still heavier one at the end of the second. Commonly, there is a parallel or an *antithesis* (contrast) within a line or between the two lines. It is called heroic because in England, especially in the eighteenth century, it was much used for heroic (epic) poems.

> Some foreign writers, some our own despise;
> The ancients only, or the moderns, prize.
>
> —Alexander Pope

Triplet (or **tercet**): a three-line stanza, usually with one rhyme.

> Whenas in silks my Julia goes
> Then, then (methinks) how sweetly flows
> That liquefaction of her clothes.
>
> —Robert Herrick

Quatrain: a four-line stanza, rhymed or unrhymed. The **heroic** (or **elegiac**) **quatrain** is iambic pentameter, rhyming *abab.* That is, the first and third lines rhyme (so they are designated *a*), and the second and fourth lines rhyme (so they are designated *b*).

Sonnet: a fourteen-line poem, predominantly in iambic pentameter. The rhyme is usually according to one of two schemes. The **Italian** or **Petrarchan sonnet,** named for the Italian poet Francesco Petrarch (1304–74), has two divisions: The first eight lines (rhyming *abba abba*) are the octave, the last six (rhyming *cd cd cd,* or a variant) are the sestet. Gerard Manley Hopkins's "God's Grandeur" (page 582) is an Italian sonnet. The second kind of sonnet, the **English** (or **Shakespearean**) **sonnet,** is usually arranged into three quatrains and a couplet, rhyming *abab cdcd efef gg.* (For examples see pages 564–66.) In many sonnets there is a marked correspondence between the rhyme scheme and the development of the thought. Thus an Italian sonnet may state a generalization in the octave and a specific example in the sestet. Or an English sonnet may give three examples— one in each quatrain—and draw a conclusion in the couplet.

Why poets choose to imprison themselves in fourteen tightly rhymed lines is something of a mystery. Tradition has a great deal to do with it: the form, having been handled successfully by major poets, stands as a challenge. In writing a sonnet a poet gains a little of the authority of Petrarch, Shakespeare, Milton, Wordsworth, and other masters who showed that the sonnet is not merely a trick. A second reason perhaps resides in the very tightness of the rhymes, which can help as well as hinder. Many poets have felt, along with Richard Wilbur (in *Mid-Century American Poets,* ed. John Ciardi), that the need for a rhyme has suggested

> . . . arbitrary connections of which the mind may take advantage if it likes. For example, if one has to rhyme with *tide,* a great number of rhyme-words at once come to mind (ride, bide, shied, confide, Akenside, etc.). Most of these, in combination with *tide,* will probably suggest nothing apropos, but one of them may reveal precisely what one wanted to say. If none of them does, *tide* must be dispensed with. Rhyme, austerely used, may be a stimulus to discovery and a stretcher of the attention.

Here is a sonnet by X. J. Kennedy, written in the Petrarchan form. Kennedy alludes (line 4) to Milton's *Paradise Lost,* VII, 205–07: "Heaven opened wide / Her ever-during gates, harmonious sound / On golden hinges moving. . . ." For an account of the slaughter of the innocents, see Matthew 2:16. The Venerable Bede (673–735) in line 6, was an English theologian and historian.

X. J. Kennedy (American; b. 1929)

Nothing in Heaven Functions as it Ought

Nothing in Heaven functions as it ought:
Peter's bifocals, blindly sat on, crack;
His gates lurch wide with the cackle of a cock,
Not turn with a hush of gold as Milton had thought;
Gangs of the slaughtered innocents keep huffing
The nimbus off the Venerable Bede

Like that of an old dandelion gone to seed;
And the beatific choir keep breaking up, coughing.   *8*

But Hell, sleek Hell hath no freewheeling part:
None takes his own sweet time, none quickens pace.
Ask anyone, How come you here, poor heart?—
And he will slot a quarter through his face,   *12*
You'll hear an instant click, a tear will start
Imprinted with an abstract of his case.

[1965]

TOPIC FOR DISCUSSION AND WRITING

In the octave Kennedy uses off-rhymes (*crack, cock; huffing, coughing*)
but in the sestet all the rhymes are exact. How do the rhymes help
to convey the meaning? (Notice, too, that lines 3, 4, 5, 7, and 8 all
have more than the usual 10 syllables. Again, why?)

Blank Verse and Free Verse

A good deal of English poetry is unrhymed, much of it in **blank verse,**
that is, unrhymed iambic pentameter. Introduced into English poetry by
Henry Howard, the Earl of Surrey in the middle of the sixteenth century,
late in the century it became the standard medium (especially in the hands
of Marlowe and Shakespeare) of English drama. In the seventeenth century, Milton used it for *Paradise Lost,* and it has continued to be used in
both dramatic and nondramatic literature. For an example see the first one
hundred lines of *Othello* (pages 659–62). A passage of blank verse that has
a rhetorical unity is sometimes called a **verse paragraph.**

The second kind of unrhymed poetry fairly common in English, especially in the twentieth century, is **free verse** (or **vers libre**): rhythmical
lines varying in length, adhering to no fixed metrical pattern and usually
unrhymed. Such poetry may seem formless; Robert Frost, who strongly
preferred rhyme, said that he would not consider writing free verse any
more than he would consider playing tennis without a net. But free verse
does have a form or pattern, often largely based on repetition and parallel
grammatical structure. Whitman's "A Noiseless Patient Spider" (page 428)
is an example; Arnold's "Dover Beach" (page 578) is another example,
though less typical because it uses rhyme. Thoroughly typical is Whitman's "When I Heard the Learn'd Astronomer."

Walt Whitman (American; 1819–92)

When I Heard the Learn'd Astronomer

When I heard the learn'd astronomer,
When the proofs, the figures, were ranged in columns before me,
When I was shown the charts and diagrams, to add, divide, and
    measure them,
When I sitting heard the astronomer where he lectured with much
    applause in the lecture-room,
How soon unaccountable I became tired and sick,
Till rising and gliding out I wander'd off by myself,
In the mystical moist night-air, and from time to time,
Look'd up in perfect silence at the stars.

[1865]

What can be said about the rhythmic structure of this poem? Rhymes are
absent, and the lines vary greatly in the number of syllables, ranging from
nine (the first line) to twenty-three (the fourth line), but when we read
the poem we sense a rhythmic structure. The first four lines obviously
hang together, each beginning with "When"; indeed, three of these four
lines begin "When I." We may notice, too, that each of these four lines
has more syllables than its predecessor (the numbers are nine, fourteen,
eighteen, and twenty-three); this increase in length, like the initial repetition, is a kind of pattern. But then, with the fifth line, which speaks of
fatigue and surfeit, there is a shrinkage to fourteen syllables, offering an
enormous relief from the previous swollen line with its twenty-three syllables. The second half of the poem—the pattern established by "When"
in the first four lines is dropped, and in effect we get a new stanza, also
of four lines—does not relentlessly diminish the number of syllables in
each succeeding line, but it *almost* does so: fourteen, fourteen, thirteen, ten.

   The second half of the poem thus has a pattern too, and this pattern
is more or less the reverse of the first half of the poem. We may notice
too that the last line (in which the poet, now released from the oppressive
lecture hall, is in communion with nature) is very close to an iambic pentameter line; that is, the poem concludes with a metrical form said to be
the most natural in English. The effect of naturalness or ease in this final
line, moreover, is increased by the absence of repetitions (e.g., not only
of "When I," but even of such syntactic repetitions as "charts and diagrams,"
"tired and sick," "rising and gliding") that characterize most of the previous lines. But of course this final effect of naturalness is part of a carefully constructed pattern in which rhythmic structure is part of meaning.
Though at first glance free verse may appear unrestrained, as T. S. Eliot

(a practitioner) said, "No *vers* is *libre* for the man who wants to do a good job" — or for the woman who wants to do a good job.

The Prose Poem

The term prose poem is sometimes applied to a short work that looks like prose but that is highly rhythmical or rich in images, or both. Here is a modern example.

Carolyn Forché (American; b. 1950)

The Colonel

What you have heard is true. I was in his house. His wife carried a tray of coffee and sugar. His daughter filed her nails, his son went out for the night. There were daily papers, pet dogs, a pistol on the cushion beside him. The moon swung bare on its black cord over the house. On the television was a cop show. It was in English. Broken bottles were embedded in the walls around the house to scoop the kneecaps from a man's legs or cut his hands to lace. On the windows there were gratings like those in liquor stores. We had dinner, rack of lamb, good wine, a gold bell was on the table for calling the maid. The maid brought green mangoes, salt, a type of bread. I was asked how I enjoyed the country. There was a brief commercial in Spanish. His wife took everything away. There was some talk then of how difficult it had become to govern. The parrot said hello on the terrace. The colonel told it to shutup, and pushed himself from the table. My friend said to me with his eyes: say nothing. The colonel returned with a sack used to bring groceries home. He spilled many human ears on the table. They were like dried peach halves. There is no other way to say this. He took one of them in his hands, shook it in our faces, dropped it into a water glass. It came alive there. I am tired of fooling around he said. As for the rights of anyone, tell your people they can go fuck themselves. He swept the ears to the floor with his arm and held the last of his wine in the air. Something for your poetry, no? he said. Some of the ears on the floor caught this scrap of his voice. Some of the ears on the floor were pressed to the ground.

May 1978

[1982]

TOPICS FOR DISCUSSION AND WRITING

1. How would you characterize the colonel in a few sentences?
2. We are told that the colonel spoke of "how difficult it had become to govern." What do you suppose the colonel assumes is the purpose of government? What do *you* assume its purpose is?
3. How much do we know about the narrator? Can we guess the narrator's purpose in visiting the colonel? How would you characterize the narrator's tone? Do you believe the narrator?
4. What do you make of the last two lines?

17

In Brief: Getting Ideas for Writing about Poetry

If you are going to write about a fairly short poem (say, under thirty lines), it's not a bad idea to copy out the poem, writing or typing it double-spaced. By writing it out you will be forced to notice details, down to the punctuation. After you have copied the poem, proofread it carefully against the original. Catching an error—even the addition or omission of a comma—may help you to notice a detail in the original that you might otherwise have overlooked. And of course, now that you have the poem with ample space between the lines, you have a worksheet with room for jottings.

A good essay is based on a genuine response to a poem; a response may be stimulated in part by first reading the poem aloud and then considering the following questions.

FIRST RESPONSE

1. What was your response to the poem on first reading? Did some parts especially please or displease you, or puzzle you? After some study—perhaps checking the meanings of some of the words in a dictionary and reading the poem several times—did you modify your initial response to the parts and to the whole?

SPEAKER AND TONE

1. Who is the speaker? (Consider age, sex, personality, frame of mind, and tone of voice.) Is the speaker defined fairly precisely (for instance,

an older woman speaking to a child), or is the speaker simply a voice meditating? (Jot down your first impressions, then reread the poem and make further jottings, if necessary.)

2. Do you think the speaker is fully aware of what he or she is saying, or does the speaker unconsciously reveal his or her personality and values? What is your attitude toward this speaker?

3. Is the speaker narrating or reflecting on an earlier experience or attitude? If so, does he or she convey a sense of new awareness, such as of regret for innocence lost?

AUDIENCE

1. To whom is the speaker speaking? What is the situation (including time and place)? (In some poems, a listener is strongly implied, but in others, especially those in which the speaker is meditating, there may be no audience other than the reader, who "overhears" the speaker.)

STRUCTURE AND FORM

1. Does the poem proceed in a straightforward way, or at some point or points does the speaker reverse course, altering his or her tone or perception? If there is a shift, what do you make of it?

2. Is the poem organized into sections? If so, what are these sections—stanzas, for instance—and how does each section (characterized, perhaps, by a certain tone of voice, or a group of rhymes) grow out of what precedes it?

3. What is the effect on you of the form—say, quatrains (stanzas of four lines) or blank verse (unrhymed lines of ten syllables)? If the sense overflows the form, running without pause from (for example) one quatrain into the next, what effect is created?

CENTER OF INTEREST AND THEME

1. What is the poem about? Is the interest chiefly in a distinctive character, or in meditation? That is, is the poem chiefly psychological or chiefly philosophical?

2. Is the theme stated explicitly (directly) or implicitly? How might you state the theme in a sentence? What is lost by reducing the poem to a statement of a theme?

DICTION

1. How would you characterize the language? Colloquial, or elevated, or what?
2. Do certain words have rich and relevant associations that relate to other words and help to define the speaker or the theme or both?
3. What is the role of figurative language, if any? Does it help to define the speaker or the theme?
4. What do you think is to be taken figuratively or symbolically, and what literally?

SOUND EFFECTS

1. What is the role of sound effects, including repetitions of sound (for instance, alliteration) and of entire words, and shifts in versification?
2. If there are off-rhymes (for instance "dizzy" and "easy," or "home" and "come"), what effect do they have on you? Do they, for instance, add a note of tentativeness or uncertainty?
3. If there are unexpected stresses or pauses, what do they communicate about the speaker's experience? How do they affect you?

18
Two Poets in Depth: Emily Dickinson and Robert Frost

If you have read more than one work by an author, whether plays by Shakespeare or stories about Sherlock Holmes, you know that authors may return to certain themes, and that each treatment is different. *Hamlet, Macbeth,* and *Romeo and Juliet* are all tragedies, but each is highly distinctive.

When we read several works by an author, we may enjoy each one in itself, but we may also enjoy thinking about resemblances and differences. We enjoy seeing the author return to some theme (perhaps God or nature or love) or to some literary form (perhaps the sonnet, or perhaps stanzas of four lines each); and we may find, to our delight, that the author has done things differently and that we are getting a sense of the writer's variety and perhaps even of the the writer's development.

In this chapter we give fourteen poems and three letters by Emily Dickinson, and fifteen poems and three prose statements by Robert Frost. These numbers are hardly large—each author wrote hundreds of poems— but the works given here may help give you some sense of the pleasures of dipping into a body of work.

TWO POETS: EMILY DICKINSON AND ROBERT FROST

Emily Dickinson

Emily Dickinson (1830–86) was born into a proper New England family in Amherst, Massachusetts. Although she spent her seventeenth year a few miles away, at Mount Holyoke Seminary (now

Mount Holyoke College), in the next twenty years she left Amherst only five or six times, and in her last twenty years she may never have left her house. Her brother was probably right when he said that having seen something of the rest of the world—she had visited Washington with her father, when he was a member of Congress—"she could not resist the feeling that it was painfully hollow. It was to her so thin and unsatisfying in the face of the Great Realities of Life." Dickinson lived with her parents (a somewhat reclusive mother and an austere, remote father) and a younger sister; a married brother lived in the house next door. She did, however, form some passionate attachments, to women as well as men, but there is no evidence that they found physical expression.

By the age of twelve Dickinson was writing witty letters, but she apparently did not write more than an occasional poem before her late twenties. At her death—she died in the house where she was born—she left 1,775 poems, only seven of which had been published (anonymously) during her lifetime.

These Are the Days When Birds Come Back

These are the days when Birds come back—
A very few—a Bird or two—
To take a backward look.   *3*

These are days when skies resume
The old—old sophistries° of June—   *deceptively subtle arguments*
A blue and gold mistake.

O fraud that cannot cheat the Bee—
Almost thy plausibility
Induces my belief.   *9*

Till ranks of seeds their witness bear—
And softly thro' the altered air
Hurries a timid leaf.   *12*

Oh Sacrament of summer days,
Oh Last Communion in the Haze—
Permit a child to join.   *15*

Thy sacred emblems to partake—
Thy consecrated bread to take
And thine immortal wine!   *18*

[1859]

Wild Nights—Wild Nights!

Wild Nights—Wild Nights!
Were I with thee
Wild Nights should be
Our luxury!   *4*

Futile—the Winds—
To a Heart in port—
Done with the Compass—
Done with the Chart!   *8*

Rowing in Eden—
Ah, the Sea!
Might I but moor—Tonight—
In Thee!   *12*

[1861]

There's a certain Slant of light

There's a certain Slant of light,
Winter Afternoons—
That oppresses, like the Heft°   *weight*
Of Cathedral Tunes—   *4*

Heavenly Hurt, it gives us—
We can find no scar,
But internal difference,
Where the Meanings, are—   *8*

None may teach it—Any—
'Tis the Seal Despair—
An imperial affliction
Sent us of the Air—   *12*

When it comes, the Landscape listens—
Shadows—hold their breath—
When it goes, 'tis like the Distance
On the look of Death—   *16*

[c. 1861]

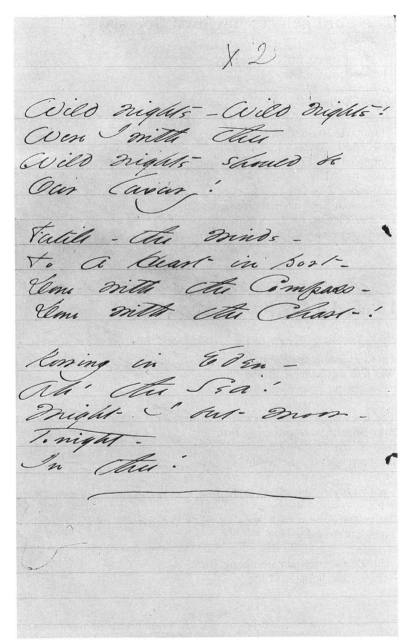

Page from Dickinson's notebooks, showing "Wild Nights."

The Soul selects her own Society

The Soul selects her own Society—
Then—shuts the Door—
To her divine Majority—
Present no more—   *4*

Unmoved—she notes the Chariots—pausing—
At her low Gate—
Unmoved—an Emperor be kneeling
Upon her Mat—   *8*

I've known her—from an ample nation—
Choose One—
Then—close the Valves* of her attention—
Like Stone—   *12*

[1862]

I heard a Fly buzz—when I died

I heard a Fly buzz—when I died—
The Stillness in the Room
Was like the Stillness in the Air—
Between the Heaves of Storm—   *4*

The Eyes around—had wrung them dry—
And Breaths were gathering firm
For the last Onset—when the King
Be witnessed—in the Room—   *8*

I willed my Keepsakes—Signed away
What portion of me be
Assignable—and then it was
There interposed a Fly—   *12*

With Blue—uncertain stumbling Buzz—
Between the light—and me—

---

*The two halves of a hinged door, such as is now found on telephone booths. Possibly also an allusion to a bivalve, such as an oyster or a clam, having a shell consisting of two hinged parts

And then the Windows failed—and then
I could not see to see—   *16*

[1862]

This World is not Conclusion

This World is not Conclusion.
A Species stands beyond—
Invisible, as Music—
But positive, as Sound—   *4*
It beckons, and it baffles—
Philosophy—dont know—
And through a Riddle, at the last—
Sagacity, must go—   *8*
To guess it, puzzles scholars—
To gain it, Men have borne
Contempt of Generations
And Crucifixion, shown—   *12*
Faith slips—and laughs, and rallies—
Blushes, if any see—
Plucks at a twig of Evidence—
And asks a Vane, the way—   *16*
Much Gesture, from the Pulpit—
Strong Hallelujahs roll—
Narcotics cannot still the Tooth
That nibbles at the soul—   *20*

[c. 1862]

I like to see it lap the Miles

I like to see it lap the Miles—
And lick the Valleys up—
And stop to feed itself at Tanks—
And then—prodigious step   *4*

Around a Pile of Mountains—
And supercilious peer
In Shanties—by the sides of Roads—
And then a Quarry pare   *8*

To fit its Ribs
And crawl between
Complaining all the while
In horrid—hooting stanza—   *12*
Then chase itself down Hill—

And neigh like Boanerges[1]—
Then—punctual as a Star
Stop—docile and omnipotent   *16*
At its own stable door—

[1862]

Because I could not stop for Death

Because I could not stop for Death—
He kindly stopped for me—
The Carriage held but just Ourselves—
And Immortality.   *4*

We slowly drove—He knew no haste
And I had put away
My labor and my leisure too,
For His Civility—   *8*

We passed the School, where Children strove
At Recess—in the Ring—
We passed the Fields of Gazing Grain—
We passed the Setting Sun—   *12*

Or rather—He passed Us—
The Dews drew quivering and chill—
For only Gossamer, my Gown—
My Tippet°—only Tulle°—   *shawl; net of silk* *16*

We paused before a House that seemed
A Swelling of the Ground—
The Roof was scarcely visible—
The Cornice—in the Ground—   *20*

Since then—'tis Centuries—and yet
Feels shorter than the Day

---

[1]**Boanerges** a name said (in Mark 3.17) to mean "Sons of Thunder"

I first surmised the Horses' Heads
Were toward Eternity—   *24*

[c. 1863]

A narrow Fellow in the Grass

A narrow Fellow in the Grass
Occasionally rides—
You may have met Him—did you not
His notice sudden is—   *4*

The Grass divides as with a Comb—
A spotted shaft is seen—
And then it closes at your feet
And opens further on—   *8*

He likes a Boggy Acre
A Floor too cool for Corn—
Yet when a Boy, and Barefoot—
I more than once at Noon   *12*
Have passed, I thought, a Whip lash
Unbraiding in the Sun
When stopping to secure it
It wrinkled, and was gone—   *16*

Several of Nature's People
I know, and they know me—
I feel for them a transport
Of cordiality—   *20*

But never met this Fellow
Attended, or alone
Without a tighter breathing
And Zero at the Bone—   *24*

[c. 1865]

Further in Summer than the Birds

Further in Summer than the Birds
Pathetic from the Grass

A minor Nation celebrates
Its unobtrusive Mass.   *4*

No Ordinance° be seen   *religious rite of Holy Communion*
So gradual the Grace
A pensive Custom it becomes
Enlarging Loneliness.   *8*

Antiquest felt at Noon
When August burning low
Arise this spectral Canticle°   *hymn*
Repose to typify   *12*

Remit as yet no Grace
No Furrow on the Glow
Yet a Druidic° Difference   *pertaining to pre-Christian Celtic priests*
Enhances Nature now   *16*

[1866]

Tell all the Truth but tell it slant

Tell all the Truth but tell it slant—
Success in Circuit lies
Too bright for our infirm Delight
The Truth's superb surprise   *4*

As Lightning to the Children eased
With explanation kind
The Truth must dazzle gradually
Or every man be blind—   *8*

[c. 1868]

A Route of Evanescence

A Route of Evanescence
With a revolving Wheel—
A Resonance of Emerald—
A Rush of Cochineal¹—   *4*

¹**Cochineal**   bright red

And every Blossom on the Bush
Adjusts its tumbled Head—
The mail from Tunis,[2] probably,
An easy Morning's Ride—   *8*

[c. 1879]

Those—dying, then

Those—dying, then
Knew where they went
They went to God's Right Hand—
The Hand is amputated now   *4*
And God cannot be found—

The abdication of Belief
Makes the Behavior small—
Better an ignis fatuus[1]   *8*
Than no illume at all—

[1882]

Apparently with no surprise

Apparently with no surprise
To any happy Flower
The Frost beheads it at its play—
In accidental power—   *4*
The blonde Assassin passes on—
The Sun proceeds unmoved
To measure off another Day
For an Approving God.   *8*

[c. 1884]

We include three of Dickinson's letters, the first of which is addressed
to Susan Gilbert, probably her dearest friend and the wife of Dickinson's
brother, Austin. The two other letters are addressed to Thomas Wentworth
Higginson, a writer and leading abolitionist. After reading in *Atlantic*

---

[2]**Tunis**   city in North Africa, near the ancient site of Carthage
[1]**ignis fatuus**   a phosphorescent light that hovers over swampy ground, hence something
deceptive

Monthly (April 1862) Higginson's article offering advice to young authors, Dickinson (31 at the time) sent Higginson some of her poems along with a letter, and a correspondence ensued, lasting until Dickinson's death.

To Susan Gilbert (Dickinson)

late April 1852

So sweet and still, and Thee, Oh Susie, what need I more, to make my heaven whole?

Sweet Hour, blessed Hour, to carry me to you, and to bring you back to me, long enough to snatch one kiss, and whisper Good bye, again.

I have thought of it all day, Susie, and I fear of but little else, and when I was gone to meeting it filled my mind so full, I could not find a *chink* to put the worthy pastor; when he said "Our Heavenly Father," I said "Oh Darling Sue"; when he read the 100th Psalm, I kept saying your precious letter all over to myself, and Susie, when they sang — it would have made you laugh to hear one little voice, piping to the departed. I made up words and kept singing how I loved you, and you had gone, while all the rest of the choir were singing Hallelujahs. I presume nobody heard me, because I sang *so small,* but it was a kind of a comfort to think I might put them out, singing of you. I a'nt there this afternoon, tho', because I am here, writing a little letter to my dear Sue, and I am very happy. I think of ten weeks — Dear One, and I think of love, and you, and my heart grows full and warm, and my breath stands still. The sun does'nt shine at all, but I can feel a sunshine stealing into my soul and making it all summer, and every thorn, a *rose.* And I pray that such summer's sun shine on my Absent One, and cause her bird to sing!

You have been happy, Susie, and now are sad — and the whole world seems lone; but it wont be so always, "some days *must* be dark and dreary"! You wont cry any more, will you, Susie, for my father will be your father, and my home will be your home, and where you go, I will go, and we will lie side by side in the kirkyard.

I have parents on earth, dear Susie, but your's are in the skies, and I have an earthly fireside, but you have one above, and you have a "Father in Heaven," where I have *none* — and *sister* in heaven, and I know they love you dearly, and think of you every day.

Oh I wish I had half so many dear friends as you in heaven — I could'nt spare them now — but to know they had got there safely, and should suffer nevermore — Dear Susie! . . .

Emilie —

To T. W. Higginson

25 April 1862

Mr Higginson,

Your kindness claimed earlier gratitude—but I was ill—and write today, from my pillow.

Thank you for the surgery[1]—it was not so painful as a I supposed. I bring you others—as you ask—though they might not differ—

While my thought is undressed—I can make the distinction, but when I put them in the Gown—they look alike, and numb.

You asked how old I was? I made no verse—but one or two—until this winter—Sir—

I had a terror—since September—I could tell to none—and so I sing, as the Boy does by the Burying Ground—because I am afraid—You inquire my Books—For Poets—I have Keats—and Mr and Mrs Browning. For Prose—Mr Ruskin—Sir Thomas Browne—and the Revelations.[2] I went to school—but in your manner of the phrase—had no education. When a little Girl, I had a friend, who taught me Immortality—but venturing too near, himself—he never returned—Soon after, my Tutor, died—and for several years, my Lexicon—was my only companion—Then I found one more—but he was not contented I be his scholar—so he left the Land.

You ask of my Companions Hills—Sir—and the Sundown—and a Dog—large as myself, that my Father bought me—They are better than Beings—because they know—but do not tell—and the noise in the Pool, at Noon—excels my Piano. I have a Brother and Sister—My Mother does not care for thought—and Father, too busy with his Briefs[3]—to notice what we do—He buys me many Books—but begs me not to read them—because he fears they joggle the Mind. They are religious—except me—and address an Eclipse, every morning—whom they call their "Father." But I fear my story fatigues you—I would like to learn—Could you tell me how to grow—or is it unconveyed—like Melody—or Witchcraft?

You speak of Mr Whitman—I never read his Book[4]—but was told that he was disgraceful—

---

[1]**surgery**   probably cuts that Higginson suggested be made in her poems
[2]**Keats . . . Revelations**   John Keats, Robert Browning, and Elizabeth Barrett Browning were nineteenth-century English poets; Thomas Browne was a seventeenth-century English writer of prose; John Ruskin was a nineteenth-century English art critic and social critic; Revelations is the last book of the New Testament.
[3]**Briefs**   legal documents (Dickinson's father was a lawyer)
[4]**Mr Whitman . . . Book**   Walt Whitman's *Leaves of Grass* was first published in 1855. Its unconventional punctuation and its celebration of Whitman's passions shocked many readers.

I read Miss Prescott's "Circumstance,"[5] but it followed me, in the Dark—so I avoided her—

Two Editors of Journals came to my Father's House, this winter—and asked me for my Mind—and when I asked them "Why," they said I was penurious—and they, would use it for the World—

I could not weigh myself—Myself—

My size felt small—to me—I read your Chapters in the Atlantic—and experienced honor for you—I was sure you would not reject a confiding question—

Is this—Sir—what you asked me to tell you?

Your friend,
E—Dickinson.

To T. W. Higginson

1876

Nature is a Haunted House—but Art—a House that tries to be haunted.

Robert Frost

Robert Frost (1874–1963) was born in California. After his father's death in 1885 Frost's mother brought the family to New England, where she taught in high schools in Massachusetts and New Hampshire. Frost studied for part of one term at Dartmouth College in New Hampshire, then did odd jobs (including teaching), and from 1897 to 1899 was enrolled as a special student at Harvard. He then farmed in New Hampshire, published a few poems in local newspapers, left the farm and taught again, and in 1912 left for England, where he hoped to achieve more popular success as a writer. By 1915 he had won a considerable reputation, and he returned to the United States, settling on a farm in New Hampshire and cultivating the image of the country-wise farmer-poet. In fact he was well read in the classics, the Bible, and in English and American literature.

Among Frost's many comments about literature, here are three: "Writing is unboring to the extent that it is dramatic"; "Every poem is . . . a figure of the will braving alien entanglements"; and, finally, a poem "begins in delight and ends in wisdom . . . It runs a course of lucky events, and ends in a clarification of life—not necessarily a great clarification, such as sects and cults are founded on, but in a momentary stay against confusion."

---

[5] **Miss Prescott's "Circumstance"**   Harriet Prescott Spofford's story, published in *Atlantic Monthly* in May, 1860. It tells of a woman who, returning from a visit to a sick friend, is held hostage by a beast who is calmed only when she sings to him. Her husband eventually rescues her, but when they arrive home they find that their house has been burned down.

And for good measure, here is Frost, in a letter, writing about his own work. "You get more credit for thinking if you restate for-mulae or cite cases that fall in easily under formulae, but all the fun is outside[,] saying things that suggest formulae that won't formulate—that almost but don't quite formulate. I should like to be so subtle at this game as to seem to the casual person altogether obvious. The casual person would assume I meant nothing or else I came near enough meaning something he was familiar with to mean it for all practical purposes. Well, well, well."

The Pasture

I'm going out to clean the pasture spring;
I'll only stop to rake the leaves away
(And wait to watch the water clear, I may):
I sha'n't be gone long.—You come too.   *4*

I'm going out to fetch the little calf
That's standing by the mother. It's so young,
It totters when she licks it with her tongue.
I sha'n't be gone long.—You come too.   *8*

[1913]

Mending Wall

Something there is that doesn't love a wall,
That sends the frozen-ground-swell under it,
And spills the upper boulder in the sun;
And makes gaps even two can pass abreast.
The work of hunters is another thing: *5*
I have come after them and made repair
Where they have left not one stone on a stone,
But they would have the rabbit out of hiding,
To please the yelping dogs. The gaps I mean,
No one has seen them made or heard them made,   *10*
But at spring mending-time we find them there.
I let my neighbor know beyond the hill;
And on a day we meet to walk the line
And set the wall between us once again.
We keep the wall between us as we go.   *15*
To each the boulders that have fallen to each.
And some are loaves and some so nearly balls
We have to use a spell to make them balance:

'Stay where you are until our backs are turned!'
We wear our fingers rough with handling them.   20
Oh, just another kind of outdoor game,
One on a side. It comes to little more:
There where it is we do not need the wall:
He is all pine and I am apple orchard.
My apple trees will never get across   25
And eat the cones under his pines, I tell him.
He only says, 'Good fences make good neighbours.'
Spring is the mischief in me, and I wonder
If I could put a notion in his head:
'*Why* do they make good neighbours? Isn't it   30
Where there are cows? But here there are no cows.
Before I built a wall I'd ask to know
What I was walling in or walling out,
And to whom I was like to give offence.
Something there is that doesn't love a wall,   35
That wants it down.' I could say 'Elves' to him,
But it's not elves exactly, and I'd rather
He said it for himself. I see him there
Bringing a stone grasped firmly by the top
In each hand, like an old-stone savage armed.   40
He moves in darkness as it seems to me,
Not of woods only and the shade of trees.
He will not go behind his father's saying,
And he likes having thought of it so well
He says again, 'Good fences make good neighbours.'   45

[1914]

The Wood-Pile

Out walking in the frozen swamp one grey day,
I paused and said, 'I will turn back from here.
No, I will go on farther—and we shall see.'
The hard snow held me, save where now and then
One foot went through. The view was all in lines   5
Straight up and down of tall slim trees
Too much alike to mark or name a place by
So as to say for certain I was here
Or somewhere else: I was just far from home.
A small bird flew before me. He was careful   10
To put a tree between us when he lighted,
And say no word to tell me who he was

Who was so foolish as to think what *he* thought.
He thought that I was after him for a feather—
The white one in his tail; like one who takes   *15*
Everything said as personal to himself.
One flight out sideways would have undeceived him.
And then there was a pile of wood for which
I forgot him and let his little fear
Carry him off the way I might have gone,   *20*
Without so much as wishing him good-night.
He went behind it to make his last stand.
It was a cord of maple, cut and split
And piled—and measured, four by four by eight.
And not another like it could I see.   *25*
No runner tracks in this year's snow looped near it.
And it was older sure than this year's cutting,
Or even last year's or the year's before.
The wood was grey and the bark warping off it
And the pile somewhat sunken. Clematis   *30*
Has wound strings round and round it like a bundle.
What held it though on one side was a tree
Still growing, and on one a stake and prop,
These latter about to fall. I thought that only
Someone who lived in turning to fresh tasks   *35*
Could so forget his handiwork on which
He spent himself, the labour of his axe,
And leave it there far from a useful fireplace
To warm the frozen swamps as best it could
With the slow smokeless burning of decay.   *40*

[1914]

The Road Not Taken

Two roads diverged in a yellow wood,
And sorry I could not travel both
And be one traveler, long I stood
And looked down one as far as I could
To where it bent in the undergrowth;   *5*

Then took the other, as just as fair,
And having perhaps the better claim,
Because it was grassy and wanted wear;
Though as for that the passing there
Had worn them really about the same,   *10*

And both that morning equally lay
In leaves no step had trodden black.
Oh, I kept the first for another day!
Yet knowing how way leads on to way,
I doubted if I should ever come back.   15

I shall be telling this with a sigh
Somewhere ages and ages hence:
Two roads diverged in a wood, and I—
I took the one less traveled by,
And that has made all the difference.   20

[1916]

The Telephone

'When I was just as far as I could walk
From here to-day
There was an hour
All still
When leaning with my head against a flower   5
I heard you talk.
Don't say I didn't, for I heard you say—
You spoke from that flower on the window sill—
Do you remember what it was you said?'

'First tell me what it was you thought you heard.'   10

'Having found the flower and driven a bee away,
I leaned my head,
And holding by the stalk,
I listened and I thought I caught the word—
What was it? Did you call me by my name?   15
Or did you say—
Someone said "Come"—I heard it as I bowed.'

'I may have thought as much, but not aloud.'

'Well, so I came.'

[1916]

The Oven Bird

There is a singer everyone has heard,
Loud, a mid-summer and a mid-wood bird,
Who makes the solid tree trunks sound again.
He says that leaves are old and that for flowers
Mid-summer is to spring as one to ten.   *5*
He says the early petal-fall is past
When pear and cherry bloom went down in showers
On sunny days a moment overcast;
And comes that other fall we name the fall.
He says the highway dust is over all.   *10*
The bird would cease and be as other birds
But that he knows in singing not to sing.
The question that he frames in all but words
Is what to make of a diminished thing.

[1916]

Stopping by Woods on a Snowy Evening

Whose woods these are I think I know
His house is in the village though;
He will not see me stopping here
To watch his woods fill up with snow.   *4*

My little horse must think it queer
To stop without a farmhouse near
Between the woods and frozen lake
The darkest evening of the year.   *8*

He gives his harness bells a shake
To ask if there is some mistake.
The only other sound's the sweep
Of easy wind and downy flake.   *12*

The woods are lovely, dark and deep.
But I have promises to keep,
And miles to go before I sleep,
And miles to go before I sleep.   *16*

[1923]

The ~~steaming horses~~ think it queer

To ~~little~~ horse ~~~~ must
The ~~~~ ~~~~ to think it queer

To
We stop with not a farm house near

the woods   an a frozen
Between a ~~forest~~ ~~and a~~ lake

The darkest evening of the year

She   her
He gives harness bells a shake

To ask if there is some mistake

the
The only other sounds sweep

downy
Of easy wind and ~~falling~~ flake.

The woods are lovely dark and deep

But I have promises to keep

~~That bid me~~ ~~~~ ~~~~ ~~~~

And miles to go before I sleep

And miles to go before I sleep

Manuscript version of Frost's "Stopping by Woods on a Snowy Evening." The first part is lost.

The Need of Being Versed in Country Things

The house had gone to bring again
To the midnight sky a sunset glow.
Now the chimney was all of the house that stood,
Like a pistil after the petals go.   *4*

The barn opposed across the way,
That would have joined the house in flame
Had it been the will of the wind, was left
To bear forsaken the place's name.   *8*

No more it opened with all one end
For teams that came by the stony road
To drum on the floor with scurrying hoofs
And brush the mow with the summer load.   *12*

The birds that came to it through the air
At broken windows flew out and in,
Their murmur more like the sigh we sigh
From too much dwelling on what has been.   *16*

Yet for them the lilac renewed its leaf,
And the aged elm, though touched with fire;
And the dry pump flung up an awkward arm;
And the fence post carried a strand of wire.   *20*

For them there was really nothing sad.
But though they rejoiced in the nest they kept,
One had to be versed in country things
Not to believe the phoebes wept.   *24*

[1923]

Acquainted with the Night

I have been one acquainted with the night.
I have walked out in rain—and back in rain.
I have outwalked the furthest city light.
I have looked down the saddest city lane.   *4*
I have passed by the watchman on his beat
And dropped my eyes, unwilling to explain.

I have stood still and stopped the sound of feet
When far away an interrupted cry
Came over houses from another street,

But not to call me back or say good-bye;
And further still at an unearthly height,
One luminary clock against the sky

Proclaimed the time was neither wrong nor right
I have been one acquainted with the night.

[1928]

Desert Places

Snow falling and night falling fast oh fast
In a field I looked into going past,
And the ground almost covered smooth in snow,
But a few weeds and stubble showing last.

The woods around it have it—it is theirs.
All animals are smothered in their lairs.
I am too absent-spirited to count;
The loneliness includes me unawares.

And lonely as it is that loneliness
Will be more lonely ere it will be less—
A blanker whiteness of benighted snow
With no expression, nothing to express.

They cannot scare me with their empty spaces
Between stars—on stars where no human race is.
I have it in me so much nearer home
To scare myself with my own desert places.

[1936]

Design

I found a dimpled spider, fat and white,
On a white heal-all, holding up a moth
Like a white piece of rigid satin cloth—
Assorted characters of death and blight

Mixed ready to begin the morning right,
Like the ingredients of a witches' broth—
A snow-drop spider, a flower like froth,
And dead wings carried like a paper kite.   *8*

What had that flower to do with being white,
The wayside blue and innocent heal-all?
What brought the kindred spider to that height,
Then steered the white moth thither in the night?   *12*
What but design of darkness to appall?—
If design govern in a thing so small.

                                        [1936]

The Silken Tent

She is as in a field a silken tent
At midday when a sunny summer breeze
Has dried the dew and all its ropes relent,
So that in guys it gently sways at ease,   *4*
And its supporting central cedar pole,
That is its pinnacle to heavenward
And signifies the sureness of the soul,
Seems to owe naught to any single cord,   *8*
But strictly held by none, is loosely bound
By countless silken ties of love and thought
To everything on earth the compass round,
And only by one's going slightly taut   *12*
In the capriciousness of summer air
Is of the slightest bondage made aware.

                                        [1942]

Come In

As I came to the edge of the woods,
Thrush music—hark!
Now if it was dusk outside,
Inside it was dark.   *4*

Too dark in the woods for a bird
By sleight of wing

To better its perch for the night,
Though it still could sing.   *8*

The last of the light of the sun
That had died in the west
Still lived for one song more
In a thrush's breast.   *12*

Far in the pillared dark
Thrush music went—
Almost like a call to come in
To the dark and lament.   *16*

But no, I was out for stars:
I would not come in.
I meant not even if asked,
And I hadn't been.   *20*

[1942]

The Most of It

He thought he kept the universe alone;
For all the voice in answer he could wake
Was but the mocking echo of his own
From some tree-hidden cliff across the lake.
Some morning from the boulder-broken beach   *5*
He would cry out on life, that what it wants
Is not its own love back in copy speech,
But counter-love, original response.
And nothing ever came of what he cried
Unless it was the embodiment that crashed   *10*
In the cliff's talus on the other side,
And then in the far distant water splashed,
But after a time allowed for it to swim,
Instead of proving human when it neared
And someone else additional to him,   *15*
As a great buck it powerfully appeared,
Pushing the crumpled water up ahead,
And landed pouring like a waterfall,
And stumbled through the rocks with horny tread,
And forced the underbrush—and that was all.   *20*

[1942]

The Gift Outright

The land was ours before we were the land's.
She was our land more than a hundred years
Before we were her people. She was ours
In Massachusetts, in Virginia,
But we were England's, still colonials,   *5*
Possessing what we still were unpossessed by,
Possessed by what we now no more possessed.
Something we were withholding made us weak
Until we found it was ourselves
We were withholding from our land of living,   *10*
And forthwith found salvation in surrender.
Such as we were we gave ourselves outright
(The deed of gift was many deeds of war)
To the land vaguely realizing westward,
But still unstoried, artless, unenhanced,   *15*
Such as she was, such as she would become.

[1942]

Robert Frost on Poetry

We give four passages in which Frost talks about poetry. The first two
are letters addressed to John Bartlett, who had been a pupil when Frost
taught at Pinkerton Academy from 1907–09. Frost wrote these two letters during his stay in England, before he returned and established a career
in the United States.

In addition to the letters, an essay and a portion of another essay
are reprinted here. Frost wrote the first of these, "The Figure a Poem
Makes," for the 1939 edition of his *Collected Poems* (the 1930 edition did
not have the essay), and he reprinted it in later volumes. Our final selection is an extract—two paragraphs—from "The Constant Symbol," first
published in *The Atlantic Monthly* for October, 1946.

Dear John:—   Fourth of July [1913]   Beaconsfield
        Those initials you quote from T.P.'s belong to a fellow named Buckley
and the explanation of Buckley is this that he has recently issued a book
with David Nutt, but at his own expense, whereas in my case David Nutt
assumed the risks. *And* those other people Buckley reviewed are his personal friends or friends of his friends or if not that simply examples of
the kind of wrong horse most fools put their money on. You will be sorry
to hear me say so but they are not even craftsmen. Of course there are

two ways of using the word the good and the bad one. To be on the safe side it is best to call such dubs mechanics. To be perfectly frank with you I am one of the most notable craftsmen of my time. That will transpire presently. I am possibly the only person going who works on any but a worn out theory (principle I had better say) of versification. You see the great successes in recent poetry have been made on the assumption that the music of words was a matter of harmonised vowels and consonants. Both Swinburne and Tennyson arrived largely at effects in assonation. But they were on the wrong track or at any rate on a short track. They went the length of it. Any one else who goes that way must go after them. And that's where most are going. I alone of English writers have consciously set myself to make music out of what I may call the sound of sense. Now it is possible to have sense without the sound of sense (as in much prose that is supposed to pass muster but makes very dull reading) and the sound of sense without sense (as in Alice in Wonderland which makes anything but dull reading). The best place to get the abstract sound of sense is from voices behind a door that cuts off the words. Ask yourself how these sentences would sound without the words in which they are embodied:

> You mean to tell me you can't read?
> I said no such thing.
> Well read then.
> You're not my teacher.

———

> He says it's too late.
> Oh, say!
> Damn an Ingersoll watch anyway.

———

> One-two-three—go!
> No good! Come back—come back.
> Haslam go down there and make those kids get out of the track.

———

Those sounds are summoned by the audile [audial] imagination and they must be positive, strong, and definitely and unmistakeably indicated by the context. The reader must be at no loss to give his voice the posture proper to the sentence. The simple declarative sentence used in making a plain statement is one sound. But Lord love ye it mustn't be worked to death. It is against the law of nature that whole poems should be written in it. If they are written they won't be read. The sound of sense, then. You get that. It is the abstract vitality of our speech. It is pure sound— pure form. One who concerns himself with it more than the subject is an artist. But remember we are still talking merely of the raw material of poetry. An ear and an appetite for these sounds of sense is the first qualification of a writer, be it of prose or verse. But if one is to be a poet he must learn to get cadences by skillfully breaking the sounds of sense with all their irregularity of accent across the regular beat of the metre. Verse in which there is nothing but the beat of the metre furnished by the accents of the pollysyllabic words we call doggerel. Verse is not that. Neither is it the sound of sense alone. It is a resultant from those two. There are only two or three metres that are worth anything. We depend for variety on the infinite play of accents in the sound of sense. The high possibility of emotional expression all lets in this mingling of sense-sound and word-accent. A curious thing. And all this has its bearing on your prose me boy. Never if you can help it write down a sentence in which the voice will not know how to posture *specially.*

That letter head shows how far we have come since we left Pink. Editorial correspondent of the Montreal Star sounds to me. Gad, we get little mail from you.

Affectionately   R.F.

Maybe you'll keep this discourse on the sound of sense till I can say more on it.

Dear John: 22 February 1914   Beaconsfield

[. . .] I set a good deal of store by the magazine work you are doing or going to do. That is your way out of bondage. You can—must write better for a magazine than there is any inducement to do for a daily.

My notion is that your work is coming on. Your style tightens up. What you will have to guard against is the lingo of the newspaper, words that nobody but a journalist uses, and worse still, phrases. John Cournos who learned his trade on the Philadelphia Record, where he went by the nickname of Gorky, has come over here to write short stories. He is thirty. His worst enemy is going to be his habit of saying cuticle for skin.

I really liked what you wrote about me. Your sentences go their distance, straight and sure and they relay each other well. You always had ideas and apprehended ideas. You mustnt lose that merit. You must find some way to show people that you have initiative and judgement. You must "get up" new things as new even as a brand new department for some paper.

[. . .] I want to write down here two or three cardinal principles that I wish you would think over and turn over now and again till we *can* protract talk.

I give you a new definition of a sentence:

A sentence is a sound in itself on which other sounds called words may be strung.

You may string words together without a sentence-sound to string them on just as you may tie clothes together by the sleeves and stretch them without a clothes line between two trees, but—it is bad for the clothes.

The number of words you may string on one sentence-sound is not fixed but there is always danger of over loading.

The sentence-sounds are very definite entities. (This is no literary mysticism I am preaching.) They are as definite as words. It is not impossible that they could be collected in a book though I don't at present see on what system they would be catalogued.

They are apprehended by the ear. They are gathered by the ear from the vernacular and brought into books. Many of them are already familiar to us in books. I think no writer invents them. The most original writer only catches them fresh from talk, where they grow spontaneously.

A man is all a writer if *all* his words are strung on definite recognizable sentence sounds. The voice of the imagination, the speaking voice must know certainly how to behave how to posture in every sentence he offers.

A man is a marked writer if his words are largely strung on the more striking sentence sounds.

A word about recognition: In literature it is our business to give people the thing that will make them say, "Oh yes I know what you mean." It is never to tell them something they dont know, but something they know and hadnt thought of saying. It must be something they recognize.

A Patch of Old Snow

In the corner of the wall where the bushes haven't been trimmed, there is a patch of old snow like a blow-away newspaper that has come to rest there. And it is dirty as with the print and news of a day I have forgotten, if I ever read it.

Now that is no good except for what I may call certain points of recognition in it: patch of old snow in a corner of the wall,—you know what that is. You know what a blow-away newspaper is. You know the curious dirt on old snow and last of all you know how easily you forget what you read in papers.*

Now for the sentence sounds: We will look for the marked ones because they are easiest to discuss. The first sentence sound will do but

---

*Editors' note: Here is the final version of the poem, called "A Patch of Snow":

There's a patch of old snow in a corner,
    That I should have guessed
Was a blow-away paper the rain
    Had brought to rest.

It is speckled with grime as if
    Small print overspread it,
The news of a day I've forgotten—
    If I ever read it.

it is merely ordinary and bookish: it is entirely subordinate in interest to the meaning of the words strung on it. But half the effectiveness of the second sentence is in the very special tone with which you must say — news of a day I have forgotten — if I ever read it. You must be able to say Oh yes one knows how that goes. (There is some adjective to describe the intonation or cadence, but I won't hunt for it.)

One of the least successful of the poems in my book is almost saved by a final striking sentence-sound (Asking for Roses.)

Not caring so very much *what* she supposes.

Take My November Guest. Did you know at once how we say such sentences as these when we talk?

She thinks I have no eye for these.

———

Not yesterday I learned etc.

———

But it were vain to tell her so

———

Get away from the sing-song. You must hear and recognize in the last line the sentence sound that supports, No use in telling him so.

Let's have some examples pell-mell in prose and verse because I don't want you to think I am setting up as an authority on verse alone.

My father used to say —
You're a liar!
If a hen and a half lay an egg and a half etc.
A long long time ago —
Put it there, old man! (Offering your hand)
I aint a going [to] hurt you, so you needn't be scared.

Suppose Henry Horne says something offensive to a young lady named Rita when her brother Charles is by to protect her. Can you hear the two different tones in which she says their respective names. "Henry Horne! Charles!" I can hear it better than I can say it. And by oral practice I get further and further away from it.

Never you say a thing like that to a man!
And such they are and such they will be found.
Well I swan!
Unless I'm greatly mistaken —
Hence with denial vain and coy excuse
A soldier and afraid (afeared)
Come, child, come home.
The thing for me to do is to get right out of here while I am able.
No fool like an old fool.

It is so and not otherwise that we get the variety that makes it fun to write and read. *The ear does it.* The ear is the only true writer and the only true reader. I have known people who could read without hearing the sentence sounds and they were the fastest readers. Eye readers we call them. They can get the meaning by glances. But they are bad readers because they miss the best part of what a good writer puts into his work.

Remember that the sentence sound often says more than the words. It may even as in irony convey a meaning opposite to the words.

I wouldn't be writing all this if I didn't think it the most important thing I know. I write it partly for my own benefit, to clarify my ideas for an essay or two I am going to write some fine day (not far distant.)

To judge a poem or piece of prose you go the same way to work—apply the one test—greatest test. You listen for the sentence sounds. If you find some of those not bookish, caught fresh from the mouths of people, some of them striking, all of them definite and recognizable, so recognizable that with a little trouble you can place them and even name them, you know you have found a writer.[. . .]

The Figure a Poem Makes

Abstraction is an old story with the philosophers, but it has been like a new toy in the hands of the artists of our day. Why can't we have any one quality of poetry we choose by itself? We can have in thought. Then it will go hard if we can't in practice. Our lives for it.

Granted no one but a humanist much cares how sound a poem is if it is only *a* sound. The sound is the gold in the ore. Then we will have the sound out alone and dispense with the inessential. We do till we make the discovery that the object in writing poetry is to make all poems sound as different as possible from each other, and the resources for that of vowels, consonants, punctuation, syntax, words, sentences, meter are not enough. We need the help of context—meaning—subject matter. That is the greatest help towards variety. All that can be done with words is soon told. So also with meters—particularly in our language where there are virtually but two, strict iambic and loose iambic. The ancients with many were still poor if they depended on meters for all tune. It is painful to watch our sprung-rhythmists straining at the point of omitting one short from a foot for relief from monotony. The possibilities for tune from the dramatic tones of meaning struck across the rigidity of a limited meter are endless. And we are back in poetry as merely one more art of having something to say, sound or unsound. Probably better if sound, because deeper and from wider experience.

Then there is this wildness whereof it is spoken. Granted again that it has an equal claim with sound to being a poem's better half. If it is a wild tune, it is a poem. Our problem then is, as modern abstractionists, to have the wildness pure: to be wild with nothing to be wild about. We bring up as aberrationists, giving way to undirected associations and kicking ourselves from one chance suggestion to another in all directions as of a hot afternoon in the life of a grasshopper. Theme alone can steady us down. Just as the first mystery was how a poem could have a tune in such a straightness as meter, so the second mystery is how a poem can have wildness and at the same time a subject that shall be fulfilled.

It should be of the pleasure of a poem itself to tell how it can. The figure a poem makes. It begins in delight and ends in wisdom. The figure is the same as for love. No one can really hold that the ecstasy should be static and stand still in one place. It begins in delight, it inclines to the impulse, it assumes direction with the first line laid down, it runs a course of lucky events, and ends in a clarification of life—not necessarily a great clarification, such as sects and cults are founded on, but in a momentary stay against confusion. It has denouement. It has an outcome that though unforeseen was predestined from the first image of the original mood—and indeed from the very mood. It is but a trick poem and no poem at all if the best of it was thought of first and saved for the last. It finds its own name as it goes and discovers the best waiting for it in some final phrase at once wise and sad—the happy-sad blend of the drinking song.

No tears in the writer, no tears in the reader. No surprise for the writer, no surprise for the reader. For me the initial delight is in the surprise of remembering something I didn't know I knew. I am in a place, in a situation, as if I had materialized from cloud or risen out of the ground. There is a glad recognition of the long lost and the rest follows. Step by step the wonder of unexpected supply keeps growing. The impressions most useful to my purpose seem always those I was unaware of and so made no note of at the time when taken, and the conclusion is come to that like giants we are always hurling experience ahead of us to pave the future with against the day when we may want to strike a line of purpose across it for somewhere. The line will have the more charm for not being mechanically straight. We enjoy the straight crookedness of a good walking stick. Modern instruments of precision are being used to make things crooked as if by eye and hand in the old days.

I tell how there may be a better wildness of logic than of inconsequence. But the logic is backward, in retrospect, after the act. It must be more felt than seen ahead like prophecy. It must be a revelation, or a series of revelations, as much for the poet as for the reader. For it to be that there must have been the greatest freedom of the material to move about in it and to establish relations in it regardless of time and space, previous relation, and everything but affinity. We prate of freedom. We call our schools free because we are not free to stay away from them till we are sixteen years of age. I have given up my democratic prejudices and now willingly set the lower classes free to be completely taken care of by the upper classes. Political freedom is nothing to me. I bestow it right and left. All I would keep for myself is the freedom of my material—the condition of body and mind now and then to summons aptly from the vast chaos of all I have lived through.

Scholars and artists thrown together are often annoyed at the puzzle of where they differ. Both work from knowledge; but I suspect they differ most importantly in the way their knowledge is come by. Scholars get theirs with conscientious thoroughness along projected lines of logic; poets theirs cavalierly and as it happens in and out of books. They stick to nothing deliberately, but let what will stick to them like burrs where they walk in the fields. No acquirement is on assignment, or even self-assignment. Knowledge of the second kind is much more available in the wild free ways of wit and art. A school boy may be defined as one who can tell you what he knows in the order in which he learned it. The artist must value himself as he snatches a thing from some previous order in time and space into a new order with not so much as a ligature clinging to it of the old place where it was organic.

More than once I should have lost my soul to radicalism if it had been the originality it was mistaken for by young converts. Originality and initiative are what I ask for my country. For myself the originality need be no more than the freshness of a poem run in the way I have described: from delight to wisdom. The figure is the same as for love. Like a piece of ice on a hot stove the poem must ride on its own melting. A poem may be worked over once it is in being, but may not be worried into being. Its most precious quality will remain its having run itself and carried away the poet with it. Read it a hundred times: it will forever keep its freshness as a metal keeps its fragrance. It can never lose its sense of a meaning that once unfolded by suprise as it went.

from "The Constant Symbol"

There are many other things I have found myself saying about poetry, but the chiefest of these is that it is metaphor, saying one thing and meaning another, saying one thing in terms of another, the pleasure of ulteriority. Poetry is simply made of metaphor. So also is philosophy—and science, too, for that matter, if it will take the soft impeachment from a friend. Every poem is a new metaphor inside or it is nothing. And there is a sense in which all poems are the same old metaphor always.

Every single poem written regular is a symbol small or great of the way the will has to pitch into commitments deeper and deeper to a rounded conclusion and then be judged for whether any original intention it had has been strongly spent or weakly lost; be it in art, politics, school, church, business, love, or marriage—in a piece of work or in a career. Strongly spent is synonymous with kept.

19
A Collection of Poems

A NOTE ON FOLK BALLADS

Folk ballads, or **popular ballads,** are anonymous stories told in song. They acquired their distinctive flavor by being passed down orally from generation to generation, each singer consciously or unconsciously modifying his or her inheritance. Most ballad singers probably were composers only by accident; they intended to transmit what they had heard, but their memories were sometimes faulty and their imaginations active. The modifications effected by oral transmission generally give a ballad three noticeable qualities:

1. It is impersonal; even if there is an "I" who sings the tale, this "I" is usually characterless.
2. The ballad—like other oral literature such as the nursery rhyme or the counting-out rhyme ("one potato, two potato")—is filled with repetition, sometimes of lines, sometimes of words. Consider, for example, "Go saddle me the black, the black, / Go saddle me the brown," or "O wha is this has done this deid, / This ill deid don to me?" Sometimes, in fact, the story is told by repeating lines with only a few significant variations. This **incremental repetition** (repetition with slight variations advancing the narrative) is the heart of "Edward." Furthermore, **stock epithets** are repeated from ballad to ballad: "true love," "milk-white steed," "golden hair." Oddly, these clichés do not bore us, but by their impersonality often lend a simplicity that effectively contrasts with the violence of the tale.
3. Because the ballads are tranmitted orally, residing in the memory rather than on the printed page, weak stanzas have often been dropped, leaving a series of sharp scenes, frequently with dialogue:

> The king sits in Dumferling toune,
> Drinking the blude-reid wine:
> "O whar will I get guid sailor,
> To sail this schip of mine?"

Because ballads were sung rather than printed, and because singers made alterations, there is no one version of a ballad that is the "correct" one. The versions printed here have become such favorites that they are almost regarded as definitive, but the reader should cousult a collection of ballads to get some idea of the wide variety.

Popular ballads have been much imitated by professional poets, especially since the late eighteenth century. Two such **literary ballads** are Keats's "La Belle Dame sans Merci" (page 572), and Coleridge's "The Rime of the Ancient Mariner." In a literary ballad the story is often infused with multiple meanings, with insistent symbolic implications. Ambiguity is often found in the popular ballad also, but it is of a rather different sort. Whether it is due to the loss of stanzas or to the creator's unconcern with some elements of the narrative, the ambiguity of the popular ballad commonly lies in the narrative itself rather than in the significance of the narrative.

Here are five popular ballads:

Anonymous

Sir Patrick Spence

The king sits in Dumferling toune,
    Drinking the blude-reid wine:
"O whar will I get guid sailor,
    To sail this schip of mine?"

4

Up and spak an eldern knicht,
    Sat at the kings richt kne:
"Sir Patrick Spence is the best sailor,
    That sails upon the se."   *8*

The king has written a braid° letter,   *broad, open*
    And signed it wi' his hand,
And sent it to Sir Patrick Spence,
    Was walking on the sand.   *12*

The first line that Sir Patrick red,
    A loud lauch° lauched he;   *laugh*
The next line that Sir Patrick red,
    The teir blinded his ee.   *16*

"O wha is this has done this deid,
    This ill deid don to me,
To send me out this time o' the yeir,
    To sail upon the se?   *20*

"Mak hast, mak hast, my mirry men all,
    Our guid schip sails the morne":
"O say na sae, my master deir,
    For I feir a deadlie storme.   *24*

"Late late yestreen I saw the new moone,
    Wi' the auld moone in hir arme,
And I feir, I feir, my deir master,
    That we will cum to harme."   *28*

O our Scots nobles wer richt laith°   *loath*
    To weet their cork-heild schoone;°   *cork-heeled shoes*
Bot lang owre° a' the play wer playd,   *ere*
    Thair hats they swam aboone.°   *above* *32*

O lang, lang may their ladies sit,
    Wi' thair fans into their hand,
Or eir° they se Sir Patrick Spence   *ere*
    Cum sailing to the land.   *36*

O lang, lang may the ladies stand,
    Wi' thair gold kems in their hair,
Waiting for their ain deir lords,
    For they'll se thame na mair.   *40*

Have owre° have owre to Aberdour,   *half over*
    It's fiftie fadom deip,
And thair lies guid Sir Patrick Spence,
    Wi' the Scots lords at his feit.   **44**

Anonymous

The Three Ravens

*Alternate guitar chords transposing the tune into a key easier to play on a guitar are given in parentheses.

There were three ravens sat on a tree,
    Downe a downe, hay down, hay down
There were three ravens sat on a tree,
    With a downe
There were three ravens sat on a tree,   *5*
They were as blacke as they might be,
    With a downe derrie, derrie, derrie, downe, downe.

The one of them said to his mate,
"Where shall we our breakfast take?"

"Down in yonder greene field,   *10*
There lies a knight slain under his shield.

"His hounds they lie downe at his feete,
So well they can their master keepe.

"His haukes they flie so eagerly,
There's no fowle dare him come nie."   *15*

Downe there comes a fallow° doe,*   *brown*
As great with yong as she might goe.

She lift up his bloudy hed,
And kist his wounds that were so red.

She got him up upon her backe,   *20*
And carried him to earthen lake.°   *pit*

She buried him before the prime,°   *about nine* A.M.
She was dead herselfe ere even-song time.

God send every gentleman
Such haukes, such hounds, and such a leman.°   *sweetheart* *25*

---

*The "doe" (line 16), often taken as a suggestive description of the knight's beloved, is probably a vestige of the folk belief that an animal may be an enchanted human being.

Anonymous

The Twa Corbies

As I was walking all alane,
I heard twa corbies° making a mane;°   *two ravens; lament*
The tane° unto the t' other say,   *one*
"Where sall we gang° and dine to-day?"   *shall we go*   **4**

"In behint yon auld fail dyke,°   *old turf wall*
I wot° there lies a new-slain knight;   *know*
And naebody kens° that he lies there,   *knows*
But his hawk, his hound, and lady fair.   **8**

"His hound is to the hunting gane,
His hawk, to fetch the wild-fowl hame,
His lady's ta'en another mate,
So we may mak our dinner sweet.   **12**

"Ye'll sit on his white hause-bane,°   *neck bone*
And I'll pike out his bonny blue een.°   *eyes*
Wi' ae° lock o' his gowden° hair   *with one; golden*
We'll theek° our nest when it grows bare.   *thatch*   **16**

"Mony a one for him makes mane,
But nane sall ken whare he is gane;
O'er his white banes, when they are bare,
The wind sall blaw for evermair."   **20**

Anonymous

Edward

"Why dois you brand° sae° drap wi' bluid,   *sword; so*
    Edward, Edward?
Why dois your brand sae drap wi' bluid?
    And why sae sad gang° yee, O?"   *go*   **4**
"O, I hae killed my hauke sae guid,
    Mither, mither,
O, I hae killed my hauke sae guid,
    And I had nae mair bot hee, O."   **8**

"Your haukis bluid was nevir sae reid,
    Edward, Edward,
Your haukis bluid was nevir sae reid,
    My deir son I tell thee, O."   *12*
"O, I hae killed my reid-roan steid,
    Mither, mither,
O, I hae killed my reid-roan steid,
    That erst° was sae fair and frie,° O."   *once; spirited* *16*

"Your steid was auld, and ye hae gat mair,
    Edward, Edward,
Your steid was auld, and ye hae gat mair,
    Sum other dule° ye drie,° O."   *grief; suffer* *20*
"O, I hae killed my fadir deir,
    Mither, mither,
O, I hae killed my fadir deir,
    Alas, and wae is mee, O!"   *24*

"And whatten penance wul ye drie for that,
    Edward, Edward?
And whatten penance wul ye drie for that?
    My deir son, now tell me, O."   *28*
"Ile set my feit in yonder boat,
    Mither, mither,
Ile set my feit in yonder boat,
    And Ile fare ovir the sea, O."   *32*

"And what wul ye doe wi' your towirs and your ha',°   *hall*
    Edward, Edward,
And what wul ye doe wi' your towirs and your ha',
    That were sae fair to see, O?"   *36*
"Ile let thame stand tul they doun fa',°   *fall*
    Mither, mither,
Ile let thame stand tul they doun fa',
    For here nevir mair maun° I bee, O."   *must* *40*

"And what wul ye leive to your bairns° and your wife,   *children*
    Edward, Edward?
And what wul ye leive to your bairns and your wife,
    When ye gang ovir the sea, O?"   *44*
"The warldis° room, late° them beg thrae° life,   *world's; let; through*
    Mither, mither,
The warldis room, late them beg thrae life,
    For thame nevir mair wul I see, O."   *48*

"And what wul ye leive to your ain mither deir,
     Edward, Edward?
And what wul ye leive to your ain mither deir?
   My deir son, now tell me, O."   52
"The curse of hell frae me sall ye beir,
     Mither, mither,
The curse of hell frae me sall ye beir,
Sic° counseils ye gave to me, O."   such   56

Anonymous

John Henry*

John Henry was a very small boy,
Sitting on his mammy's knee;
He picked up a hammer and a little piece of steel,
Saying, "A hammer'll be the death of me, O Lord,
A hammer'll be the death of me."   5

John Henry went up on the mountain
And he came down on the side.
The mountain was so tall and John Henry was so small
That he laid down his hammer and he cried, "O Lord,"
He laid down his hammer and he cried.   10

John Henry was a man just six feet in height,
Nearly two feet and a half across the breast.
He'd take a nine-pound hammer and hammer all day long
And never get tired and want to rest, O Lord,
And never get tired and want to rest.   15

John Henry was a steel-driving man, O Lord,
He drove all over the world.
He come to Big Bend Tunnel on the C. & O. Road
Where he beat the steam drill down, O Lord,
Where he beat the steam drill down.   20

John Henry said to the captain,
"Captain, you go to town,

*John Henry, a black steel driver from West Virginia, worked on the Chesapeake and Ohio's
Big Bend Tunnel around 1870. The steel driver hammered a drill (held by his assistant, the
"shaker") into rocks so that explosives could then be poured in. In the 1870s, mechanical
steel drills were introduced, displacing the steel driver.

Bring me back a twelve-pound hammer
And I'll beat that steam drill down, O Lord,
And I'll beat that steam drill down." *25*

They place John Henry on the right-hand side,
The steam drill on the left;
He said, "Before I let that steam drill beat me down
I'll die with my hammer in my hand, O Lord,
And send my soul to rest." *30*

The white folks all got scared,
Thought Big Bend was a-fallin' in;
John Henry hollered out with a very loud shout,
"It's my hammer a-fallin' in the wind, O Lord,
It's my hammer a-fallin' in the wind." *35*

John Henry said to his shaker,
"Shaker, you better pray,
For if I miss that little piece of steel
Tomorrow'll be your buryin' day, O Lord,
Tomorrow'll be your buryin' day." *40*

The man that invented that steam drill
He thought he was mighty fine.
John Henry sunk the steel fourteen feet
While the steam drill only made nine, O Lord,
While the steam drill only made nine. *45*

John Henry said to his loving little wife,
"I'm sick and want to go to bed.
Fix me a place to lay down, Child;
There's a roarin' in my head, O Lord,
There's a roarin' in my head." *50*

Sir Thomas Wyatt (English; 1503–42)

They Flee from Me

They flee from me that sometime did me seek
With naked foot stalking in my chamber.
I have seen them gentle, tame, and meek
That now are wild and do not remember
That sometime they put themselves in danger *5*

To take bread at my hand; and now they range
Busily seeking with a continual change.

Thankèd be Fortune, it hath been otherwise
Twenty times better; but once in special,
In thin array after a pleasant guise,   10
When her loose gown from her shoulders did fall,
And she me caught in her arms long and small,°   *narrow*
And therewithall sweetly did me kiss,
And softly said, "Dear heart, how like you this?"

It was no dream; I lay broad waking.   15
But all is turned thorough my gentleness
Into a strange fashion of forsaking;
And I have leave to go of her goodness,
And she also to use newfangleness.
But since that I so kindely° am served,   *naturally, kindly (ironic)*   20
I fain would know what she hath deserved.

                              [1557]

William Shakespeare (English; 1564–1616)

Sonnet 29

When, in disgrace with Fortune and men's eyes,
I all alone beweep my outcast state,
And trouble deaf heaven with my bootless° cries,   *useless*
And look upon myself and curse my fate,   4
Wishing me like to one more rich in hope,
Featured like him, like him° with friends possessed,   *like a second man,*
Desiring this man's art and that man's scope,   *like a third man*
With what I most enjoy contented least;   8
Yet in these thoughts myself almost despising,
Haply° I think on thee, and then my state,   *perchance*
Like to the lark at break of day arising
From sullen earth, sings hymns at heaven's gate;   12
    For thy sweet love rememb'red such wealth brings,
    That then I scorn to change my state with kings.

Sonnet 73

That time of year thou mayst in me behold
When yellow leaves, or none, or few, do hang
Upon those boughs which shake against the cold,
Bare ruined choirs* where late the sweet birds sang. 4
In me thou see'st the twilight of such day
As after sunset fadeth in the west,
Which by-and-by black night doth take away,
Death's second self that seals up all in rest, 8
In me thou see'st the glowing of such fire
That on the ashes of his youth doth lie,
As the deathbed whereon it must expire,
Consumed with that which it was nourished by. 12
    This thou perceiv'st, which makes thy love more strong,
    To love that well which thou must leave ere long.

Sonnet 116

Let me not to the marriage of true minds
Admit impediments; love is not love
Which alters when it alteration finds,
Or bends with the remover to remove. 4
O, no, it is an ever-fixèd mark°   *guide to mariners*
That looks on tempests and is never shaken;
It is the star° to every wand'ring bark,   *the North Star*
Whose worth's unknown, although his height be taken. 8
Love's not Time's fool,° though rosy lips and cheeks   *plaything*
Within his bending sickle's compass° come;   *range*
Love alters not with his° brief hours and weeks   *Time's*
But bears° it out even to the edge of doom.° *endures; Judgment Day* 12
    If this be error and upon me proved,
    I never writ, nor no man ever loved.

*The part of the church where services were sung

Sonnet 146

Poor soul, the center of my sinful earth,
My sinful earth* these rebel pow'rs that thee array,
Why doest thou pine within and suffer dearth,
Painting thy outward walls so costly gay?   **4**
Why so large cost,° having so short a lease,   *expense*
Dost thou upon thy fading mansion spend?
Shall worms, inheritors of this excess,
Eat up thy charge? Is this thy body's end?   **8**
Then, soul, live thou upon thy servant's loss,
And let that pine to aggravate thy store;
Buy terms divine° in selling hours of dross;   *buy ages of immortality*
Within be fed, without be rich no more.   **12**
    So shalt thou feed on Death, that feeds on men,
    And death once dead, there's no more dying then.

John Donne (*English; 1572–1631*)

A Valediction: Forbidding Mourning

As virtuous men pass mildly away;
    And whisper to their souls, to go,
Whilst some of their sad friends do say,
    "The breath goes now," and some say, "No":   **4**

So let us melt, and make no noise.
    No tear-floods, nor sigh-tempests move.
'Twere profanation of our joys
    To tell the laity our love.   **8**

Moving of the earth° brings harms and fears,   *an earthquake*
    Men reckon what it did and meant;
But trepidation of the spheres,
    Though greater far, is innocent.†   **12**

---

*"My sinful earth," in line 2, is doubtless an error made by the printer of the first edition
(1609), who mistakenly repeated the end of the first line. Among suggested corrections
are "Thrall to," "Fooled by," "Rebuke these," "Leagued with," and "Feeding." Feel free to
offer your own conjectures.
† But the movement of the heavenly spheres (in Ptolemaic astronomy), though far greater,
is harmless.

Dull sublunary° lovers' love   *under the moon, i.e., earthly*
   (Whose soul is sense) cannot admit
Absence, because it doth remove
   Those things which elemented it.   **16**

But we, by a love so much refined
   That our selves know not what it is,
Inter-assurèd of the mind,
   Care less, eyes, lips, and hands to miss.   **20**

Our two souls therefore, which are one,
   Though I must go, endure not yet
A breach, but an expansion,
   Like gold to airy thinness beat.   **24**

If they be two, they are two so
   As stiff twin compasses° are two: *i.e., a carpenter's compass*
Thy soul, the fixed foot, makes no show
   To move, but doth, if the other do.   **28**

And though it in the center sit,
   Yet when the other far doth roam,
It leans, and hearkens after it,
   And grows erect, as that comes home.   **32**

Such wilt thou be to me, who must
   Like the other foot, obliquely run:
Thy firmness makes my circle just,
   And makes me end where I begun.   **36**

               [1633]

Robert Herrick (English; 1591–1674)

Upon Julia's Clothes

Whenas in silk my Julia goes,
Then, then, methinks, how sweetly flows
That liquefaction of her clothes.

Next, when I cast mine eyes, and see
That brave vibration, each way free
O, how that glittering taketh me!
            [1648]

Delight in Disorder

A sweet disorder in the dress	
Kindles in clothes a wantonness.	
A lawn° about the shoulders thrown	*a scarf*
Into a fine distraction;	4
An erring lace, which here and there	
Enthralls the crimson stomacher,°	*an ornamental cloth*
A cuff neglectful, and thereby	
Ribbons to flow confusedly;	8
A winning wave, deserving note,	
In the tempestuous petticoat;	
A careless shoestring, in whose tie	
I see a wild civility;	12
Do more bewitch me than when art	
Is too precise in every part.	

[1648]

John Milton (English; 1608–74)

When I consider how my light is spent

When I consider how my light is spent	
Ere half my days, in this dark world and wide,	
And that one talent which is death to hide*	
Lodged with me useless, though my soul more bent	4
To serve therewith my Maker, and present	
My true account, lest he returning chide;	
"Doth God exact day-labor, light denied?"	
I fondly° ask; but Patience to prevent°	*foolishly; forestall* 8
That murmur, soon replies, "God doth not need	
Either man's work or his own gifts; who best	
Bear his mild yoke, they serve him best. His state	

---

*There is a pun here, relating Milton's literary talent to Christ's "Parable of the Talents" (Matthew 25: 14 ff.), in which a servant is rebuked for not putting his talent (a unit of money) to use. Note also line 4, where "useless" includes a pun on "use," i.e., usury, interest.

Is kingly. Thousands at his bidding speed   *12*
    And post o'er land and ocean without rest:
    They also serve who only stand and wait."

                 [1673]

William Blake (English; 1757–1827)

The Lamb

    Little Lamb, who made thee?
    Dost thou know who made thee?
Gave thee life, and bid thee feed
By the stream and o'er the mead;   *4*
Gave thee clothing of delight,
Softest clothing, wooly, bright;
Gave thee such a tender voice,
Making all the vales rejoice?   *8*
    Little Lamb, who made thee?
    Dost thou know who made thee?

    Little Lamb, I'll tell thee,
    Little Lamb, I'll tell thee: *12*
He is callèd by thy name,
For he calls himself a Lamb.
He is meek, and he is mild;
He became a little child.   *16*
I a child, and thou a lamb,
We are callèd by his name.
    Little Lamb, God bless thee!
    Little Lamb, God bless thee!   *20*

                 [1789]

The Tyger

Tyger! Tyger! burning bright
In the forests of the night,
What immortal hand or eye
Could frame thy fearful symmetry?   *4*

In what distant deeps or skies
Burnt the fire of thine eyes?
On what wings dare he aspire?
What the hand dare seize the fire?   **8**

And what shoulder, and what art,
Could twist the sinews of thy heart?
And, when thy heart began to beat,
What dread hand? and what dread feet?   **12**

What the hammer? what the chain?
In what furnace was thy brain?
What the anvil? what dread grasp
Dare its deadly terrors clasp?   **16**

When the stars threw down their spears,
And watered heaven with their tears,
Did he smile his work to see?
Did he who made the lamb make thee?   **20**

Tyger! Tyger! burning bright
In the forests of the night,
What immortal hand or eye,
Dare frame thy fearful symmetry?   **24**

[1793]

London

I wander through each chartered street,
Near where the chartered Thames does flow,
And mark in every face I meet
Marks of weakness, marks of woe.   **4**

In every cry of every man,
In every Infant's cry of fear,
In every voice, in every ban,
The mind-forged manacles I hear.   **8**

How the Chimney-sweeper's cry
Every black'ning Church appalls;

And the hapless Soldier's sigh
Runs in blood down Palace walls.   *12*

But most through midnight streets I hear
How the youthful Harlot's curse
Blasts the new-born Infant's tear,
And blights with plagues the Marriage hearse.   *16*

[1794]

William Wordsworth *(English; 1770–1850)*

The World Is Too Much with Us

The world is too much with us; late and soon,
Getting and spending, we lay waste our powers;
Little we see in Nature that is ours;
We have given our hearts away, a sordid boon!°   *gift*   *4*
This Sea that bares her bosom to the moon,
The winds that will be howling at all hours,
And are up-gathered now like sleeping flowers,
For this, for everything, we are out of tune;   *8*
It moves us not.—Great God! I'd rather be
A Pagan suckled in a creed outworn;
So might I, standing on this pleasant lea,
Have glimpses that would make me less forlorn;   *12*
Have sight of Proteus* rising from the sea;
Or hear old Triton blow his wreathèd horn

[1807]

I Wandered Lonely as a Cloud

I wandered lonely as a cloud
That floats on high o'er vales and hills,
When all at once I saw a crowd,
A host, of golden daffodils,   *4*
Beside the lake, beneath the trees,
Fluttering and dancing in the breeze.

*Proteus** and **Triton** are sea gods.

Continuous as the stars that shine
And twinkle on the milky way,   *8*
They stretched in never-ending line
Along the margin of a bay;
Ten thousand saw I at a glance,
Tossing their heads in sprightly dance.   *12*

The waves beside them danced, but they
Outdid the sparkling waves in glee;
A poet could not but be gay,
In such a jocund company;   *16*
I gazed—and gazed—but little thought
What wealth the show to me had brought:

For oft, when on my couch I lie
In vacant or in pensive mood,   *20*
They flash upon that inward eye
Which is the bliss of solitude;
And then my heart with pleasure fills,
And dances with the daffodils.   *24*

[1807]

John Keats (Enlgish; 1795–1821)

La Belle Dame sans Merci

O what can ail thee, knight-at-arms,
    Alone and palely loitering?
The sedge has withered from the lake,
    And no birds sing.   *4*

O what can ail thee, knight-at-arms,
    So haggard and so woe-begone?
The squirrel's granary is full,
    And the harvest's done.   *8*

I see a lily on thy brow,
    With anguish moist and fever dew,
And on thy cheeks a fading rose
    Fast withereth too.   *12*

"I met a lady in the meads,
    Full beautiful—a faery's child,
Her hair was long, her foot was light,
    And her eyes were wild.   *16*

"I made a garland for her head,
    And bracelets too, and fragrant zone;°   *belt of flowers*
She looked at me as she did love,
    And made sweet moan.   *20*

"I set her on my pacing steed,
    And nothing else saw all day long,
For sidelong would she bend and sing
    A faery's song.   *24*

"She found me roots of relish sweet,
    And honey wild, and manna dew,
And sure in language strange she said
    'I love thee true.'   *28*

"She took me to her elfin grot,
    And there she wept and sighed full sore,
And there I shut her wild wild eyes
    With kisses four.   *32*

"And there she lullèd me asleep,
    And there I dreamed—Ah! woe betide!
The latest dream I ever dreamt
    On the cold hill side.   *36*

"I saw pale kings and princes too,
    Pale warriors, death-pale were they all;
They cried, 'La Belle Dame sans Merci°   *the beautiful pitiless lady*
    Hath thee in thrall!'   *40*

"I saw their starved lips in the gloam
    With horrid warning gapèd wide,
And I awoke, and found me here,
    On the cold hill's side.   *44*

"And this is why I sojourn here,
    Alone and palely loitering,
Though the sedge is withered from the lake,
    And no birds sing."   *48*

                         [1819]

To Autumn

I

Season of mists and mellow fruitfulness,
   Close bosom-friend of the maturing sun;
Conspiring with him how to load and bless
   With fruit the vines that round the thatch-eaves run;
To bend with apples the mossed cottage-trees,   5
   And fill all fruit with ripeness to the core;
      To swell the gourd, and plump the hazel shells
With a sweet kernel; to set budding more,
   And still more, later flowers for the bees,
   Until they think warm days will never cease,   10
      For summer has o'er-brimmed their clammy cells.

II

Who hath not seen thee oft amid thy store?
   Sometimes whoever seeks abroad may find
Thee sitting careless on a granary floor,
   Thy hair soft-lifted by the winnowing wind;   15
Or on a half-reaped furrow sound asleep,
   Drowsed with the fume of poppies, while thy hook
      Spares the next swath and all its twinèd flowers:
And sometime like a gleaner thou dost keep
   Steady thy laden head across a brook;   20
   Or by a cider-press, with patient look,
      Thou watchest the last oozings hours by hours.

III

Where are the songs of Spring? Ay, where are they?
   Think not of them, thou hast thy music too,—
While barred clouds bloom the soft-dying day,   25
   And touch the stubble-plains with rosy hue;
Then in a wailful choir the small gnats mourn
   Among the river sallows, borne aloft
      Or sinking as the light wind lives or dies;
And full-grown lambs loud bleat from hilly bourn;   30
   Hedge-crickets sing; and now with treble soft
   The red-breast whistles from a garden-croft;
      And gathering swallows twitter in the skies.

[1819]

Alfred, Lord Tennyson (English; 1809–92)

Ulysses

It little profits that an idle king,
By this still hearth, among these barren crags,
Matched with an aged wife, I mete and dole
Unequal laws unto a savage race,
That hoard, and sleep, and feed, and know not me.   *5*
I cannot rest from travel; I will drink
Life to the lees. All times I have enjoyed
Greatly, have suffered greatly, both with those
That loved me, and alone; on shore, and when
Thro' scudding drifts the rainy Hyades   *10*
Vext the dim sea. I am become a name;
For always roaming with a hungry heart
Much have I seen and known,—cities of men
And manners, climates, councils, governments,
Myself not least, but honored of them all,—   *15*
And drunk delight of battle with my peers,
Far on the ringing plains of windy Troy.
I am a part of all that I have met;
Yet all experience is an arch wherethro'
Gleams that untravelled world whose margin fades   *20*
For ever and for ever when I move.
How dull it is to pause, to make an end,
To rust unburnished, not to shine in use!
As tho' to breathe were life! Life piled on life
Were all too little, and of one to me   *25*
Little remains; but every hour is saved
From that eternal silence, something more,
A bringer of new things; and vile it were
For some three suns to store and hoard myself,
And this gray spirit yearning in desire   *30*
To follow knowledge like a sinking star,
Beyond the utmost bound of human thought.

    This is my son, mine own Telemachus,
To whom I leave the scepter and the isle,—
Well-loved of me, discerning to fulfill   *35*
This labor, by slow prudence to make mild
A rugged people, and thro' soft degrees
Subdue them to the useful and the good.

Most blameless is he, centered in the sphere
Of common duties, decent not to fail   *40*
In offices of tenderness, and pay
Meet adoration to my household gods,
When I am gone. He works his work, I mine.

    There lies the port; the vessel puffs her sail;
There gloom the dark, broad seas. My mariners,   *45*
Souls that have toiled, and wrought, and thought with me,—
That ever with a frolic welcome took
The thunder and the sunshine, and opposed
Free hearts, free foreheads,—you and I are old;
Old age hath yet his honor and his toil   *50*
Death closes all; but something ere the end,
Some work of noble note, may yet be done,
Not unbecoming men that strove with Gods.
The lights begin to twinkle from the rocks;
The long day wanes; the slow moon climbs; the deep   *55*
Moans round with many voices. Come, my friends.
'Tis not too late to seek a newer world.
Push off, and sitting well in order smite
The sounding furrows; for my purpose holds
To sail beyond the sunset, and the baths   *60*
Of all the western stars, until I die.
It may be that the gulfs will wash us down;
It may be we shall touch the Happy Isles,
And see the great Achilles, whom we knew.
Tho' much is taken, much abides; and tho'   *65*
We are not now that strength which in old days
Moved earth and heaven, that which we are, we are.
One equal temper of heroic hearts,
Made weak by time and fate, but strong in will
To strive, to seek, to find, and not to yield.   *70*

                                                    [1833]

Robert Browning (*English; 1812–89*)

Porphyria's Lover

The rain set early in tonight,
    The sullen wind was soon awake,

It tore the elm-tops down for spite,
　　And did its worst to vex the lake:
I listened with heart fit to break.　　　　　　　　　　　　5
When glided in Porphyria; straight
　　She shut the cold out and the storm,
And kneeled and made the cheerless grate
　　Blaze up, and all the cottage warm;
Which done, she rose, and from her form　　　　　　　10
Withdrew the dripping cloak and shawl,
　　And laid her soiled gloves by, untied
Her hat and let the damp hair fall,
　　And, last, she sat down by my side
And called me. When no voice replied,　　　　　　　　15
She put my arm about her waist,
　　And made her smooth white shoulder bare
And all her yellow hair displaced,
　　And stooping, made my cheek lie there,
And spread, o'er all, her yellow hair,　　　　　　　　　20
Murmuring how she loved me—she
　　Too weak, for all her heart's endeavor,
To set its struggling passion free
　　From pride, and vainer ties dissever,
And give herself to me forever.　　　　　　　　　　　　25
But passion sometimes would prevail,
　　Nor could tonight's gay feast restrain
A sudden thought of one so pale
　　For love of her, and all in vain:
So, she was come through wind and rain.　　　　　　30
Be sure I looked up at her eyes
　　Happy and proud; at last I knew
Porphyria worshipped me; surprise
　　Made my heart swell, and still it grew
While I debated what to do.　　　　　　　　　　　　35
That moment she was mine, mine, fair,
　　Perfectly pure and good: I found
A thing to do, and all her hair
　　In one long yellow string I wound
Three times her little throat around,　　　　　　　　40
And strangled her. No pain felt she;
　　I am quite sure she felt no pain.
As a shut bud that holds a bee,
　　I warily oped her lids: again
Laughed the blue eyes without a stain.　　　　　　　45
And I untightened next the tress
　　About her neck; her cheek once more

Blushed bright beneath my burning kiss:
    I propped her head up as before,
Only, this time my shoulder bore   *50*
Her head, which droops upon it still:
    The smiling rosy little head,
So glad it has its utmost will,
    That all it scorned at once is fled,
And I, its love, am gained instead!   *55*
Porphyria's love: she guessed not how
    Her darling one wish would be heard.
And thus we sit together now,
    And all night long we have not stirred,
And yet God has not said a word!   *60*

[1834]

Matthew Arnold (*English; 1822–88*)

Dover Beach

The sea is calm to-night.
The tide is full, the moon lies fair
Upon the straits;—on the French coast the light
Gleams and is gone; the cliffs of England stand,
Glimmering and vast, out in the tranquil bay.   *5*
Come to the window, sweet is the night-air!
Only, from the long line of spray
Where the sea meets the moon-blanch'd land,
Listen! you hear the grating roar
Of pebbles which the waves draw back, and fling, *10*
At their return, up the high strand,
Begin, and cease, and then again begin,
With tremulous cadence slow, and bring
The eternal note of sadness in.

Sophocles long ago   *15*
Heard it on the Ægean, and it brought
Into his mind the turbid ebb and flow
Of human misery; we
Find also in the sound a thought,
Hearing it by this distant northern sea.   *20*

The Sea of Faith
Was once, too, at the full, and round earth's shore
Lay like the folds of a bright girdle furl'd.
But now I only hear
Its melancholy, long, withdrawing roar,   *25*
Retreating, to the breath
Of the night-wind, down the vast edges drear
And naked shingles° of the world.   *pebbled beaches*

Ah, love, let us be true
To one another! for the world, which seems   *30*
To lie before us like a land of dreams,
So various, so beautiful, so new,
Hath really neither joy, nor love, nor light,
Nor certitude, nor peace, nor help for pain;
And we are here as on a darkling plain   *35*
Swept with confused alarms of struggle and flight,
Where ignorant armies clash by night.

[c. 1851]

Thomas Hardy *(English; 1840–1928)*

Ah, Are You Digging on My Grave?

"Ah, are you digging on my grave,
   My loved one?—planting rue?"
—"No: yesterday he went to wed
One of the brightest wealth has bred.   *4*
'It cannot hurt her now,' he said,
   'That I should not be true.'"

"Then who is digging on my grave?
   My nearest dearest kin?"   *8*
—"Ah, no: they sit and think, 'What use!
What good will planting flowers produce?
No tendance of her mound can loose
   Her spirit from Death's gin.'"   *12*

"But some one digs upon my grave?
   My enemy?—prodding sly?"

—"Nay: When she heard you had passed the Gate
That shuts on all flesh soon or late,   *16*
She thought you no more worth her hate,
    And cares not where you lie."

"Then, who is digging on my grave?
    Say—since I have not guessed!"   *20*
—"O it is I, my mistress dear,
Your little dog, who still lives near,
And much I hope my movements here
    Have not disturbed your rest?"   *24*

"Ah, yes! *You* dig upon my grave . . .
    Why flashed it not on me
That one true heart was left behind!
What feeling do we ever find   *28*
To equal among human kind
    A dog's fidelity!"

"Mistress, I dug upon your grave
    To bury a bone, in case   *32*
I should be hungry near this spot
When passing on my daily trot.
    I am sorry, but I quite forgot
It was your resting-place."   *36*

              [1914]

The Convergence of the Twain

Lines on the Loss of the Titanic

I

    In a solitude of the sea
    Deep from human vanity,
And the Pride of Life that planned her, stilly couches she.

II

    Steel chambers, late the pyres
    Of her salamandrine fires,   *5*
Cold currents thrid,° and turn to rhythmic tidal lyres.   *thread*

III

Over the mirrors meant
To glass the opulent
The sea-worm crawls—grotesque, slimed, dumb, indifferent.

IV

Jewels in joy designed   *10*
To ravish the sensuous mind
Lie lightless, all their sparkles bleared and black and blind.

V

Dim moon-eyed fishes near
Gaze at the gilded gear
And query: "What does this vaingloriousness down here?"   *15*

VI

Well: while was fashioning
This creature of cleaving wing,
The Immanent Will that stirs and urges everything

VII

Prepared a sinister mate
For her—so gaily great—   *20*
A Shape of Ice, for the time far and dissociate.

VIII

And as the smart ship grew
In stature, grace, and hue,
In shadowy silent distance grew the Iceberg too.

IX

Alien they seemed to be: *25*
No mortal eye could see
The intimate welding of their later history,

X

Or sign that they were bent
By paths coincident
On being anon twin halves of one august event,   *30*

XI

Till the Spinner of the Years
    Said "Now!" And each one hears,
And consummation comes, and jars two hemispheres.

[1912]

Gerard Manley Hopkins (*English; 1844–89*)

God's Grandeur

The world is charged with the grandeur of God.
    It will flame out, like shining from shook foil;
    It gathers to a greatness, like the ooze of oil
Crushed. Why do men then now not reck his rod?   *4*
Generations have trod, have trod, have trod;
    And all is seared with trade; bleared, smeared with toil;
    And wears man's smudge and shares man's smell: the soil
Is bare now, nor can foot feel, being shod.   *8*

And for all this, nature is never spent;
    There lives the dearest freshness deep down things;
And though the last lights off the black West went
    Oh, morning, at the brown brink eastward, springs—   *12*
Because the Holy Ghost over the bent
    World broods with warm breast and with ah! bright wings.

[1877]

Ezra Pound (*American; 1885–1972*)

In a Station of the Metro*

The apparition of these faces in the crowd;
Petals on a wet, black bough.

[1916]

*the Metro   the subway in Paris

A. E. Housman (*English; 1859–1936*)

Shropshire Lad #19
(To an Athlete Dying Young)

The time you won your town the race
We chaired you through the market-place;
Man and boy stood cheering by,
And home we brought you shoulder-high.   *4*

Today, the road all runners come,
Shoulder-high we bring you home,
And set you at your threshold down,
Townsman of a stiller town.   *8*

Smart lad, to slip betimes away
From fields where glory does not stay
And early though the laurel grows
It withers quicker than the rose.   *12*

Eyes the shady night has shut
Cannot see the record cut,
And silence sounds no worse than cheers
After earth has stopped the ears: *16*

Now you will not swell the rout
Of lads that wore their honors out,
Runners whom renown outran
And the name died before the man.   *20*

So set, before its echoes fade,
The fleet foot on the sill of shade,
And hold to the low lintel° up   *beam over a doorway*
The still-defended challenge-cup   *24*

And round that early-laureled head
Will flock to gaze the strengthless dead,
And find unwithered on its curls
The garland briefer than a girl's.   *28*

[1896]

William Butler Yeats *(Irish; 1865–1939)*

Leda and the Swan*

A sudden blow: the great wings beating still
Above the staggering girl, her thighs caressed
By the dark webs, her nape caught in his bill,
He holds her helpless breast upon his breast.   *4*

How can those terrified vague fingers push
The feathered glory from her loosening thighs?
And how can body, laid in that white rush,
But feel the strange heart beating where it lies?   *8*

A shudder in the loins engenders there
The broken wall, the burning roof and tower
And Agamemnon dead.
                          Being so caught up,
So mastered by the brute blood of the air,   *12*
Did she put on his knowledge with his power
Before the indifferent beak could let her drop?

                                        [1923]

The Second Coming

Turning and turning in the widening gyre°   *circular or spiral motion*
The falcon cannot hear the falconer;
Things fall apart; the center cannot hold;
Mere anarchy is loosed upon the world,
The blood-dimmed tide is loosed, and everywhere   *5*
The ceremony of innocence is drowned;
The best lack all conviction, while the worst
Are full of passionate intensity.

Surely some revelation is at hand;
Surely the Second Coming is at hand;   *10*
The Second Coming! Hardly are those words out
When a vast image out of *Spiritus Mundi*°   *Soul of the Universe*

---

*According to Greek mythology, Zeus fell in love with Leda, disguised himself as a swan, and raped her. Among the offspring of this union were Helen and Clytemnestra. Paris abducted Helen, causing the Greeks to raze Troy; Clytemnestra, wife of Agamemnon, murdered her husband on his triumphant return to Greece.

Troubles my sight: somewhere in the sands of the desert
A shape with lion body and the head of a man,
A gaze blank and pitiless as the sun,   *15*
Is moving its slow thighs, while all about it
Reel shadows of the indignant desert birds.
The darkness drops again; but now I know
That twenty centuries of stony sleep
Were vexed to nightmare by a rocking cradle,   *20*
And what rough beast, its hour come round at last,
Slouches towards Bethlehem to be born?

                                                    [1919]

Sailing to Byzantium*

I

That is no country for old men. The young
In one another's arms, birds in the trees
—Those dying generations—at their song,
The salmon-falls, the mackerel-crowded seas,   *4*
Fish, flesh, or fowl, commend all summer long
Whatever is begotten, born, and dies.
Caught in that sensual music all neglect
Monuments of unaging intellect.   *8*

II

An aged man is but a paltry thing,
A tattered coat upon a stick, unless
Soul clap its hands and sing, and louder sing
For every tatter in its mortal dress,   *12*
Nor is there singing school but studying
Monuments of its own magnificence;
And therefore I have sailed the seas and come
To the holy city of Bysantium.   *16*

III

O sages standing in God's holy fire
As in the gold mosaic of a wall,
Come from the holy fire, perne° in a gyre,   *whirl down*

*The modern Istanbul. Byzantium was the chief city of the Roman Empire in the east and
the capital of Eastern Christianity.

And be the singing-masters of my soul.   *20*
Consume my heart away; sick with desire
And fastened to a dying animal
It knows not what it is; and gather me
Into the artifice of eternity.   *24*

    IV

Once out of nature I shall never take
My bodily form from any natural thing,
But such a form as Grecian goldsmiths make
Of hammered gold and gold enameling   *28*
To keep a drowsy Emperor awake;
Or set upon a golden bough to sing
To lords and ladies of Byzantium
Of what is past, or passing, or to come.   *32*

                [1926]

For Anne Gregory*

"Never shall a young man,
Thrown into despair
By those great honey-coloured
Ramparts at your ear   *4*
Love you for yourself alone
And not your yellow hair."

"But I can get a hair-dye
And set such colour there,   *8*
Brown, or black, or carrot,
That young men in despair
May love me for myself alone
And not my yellow hair."   *12*

"I heard an old religious man
But yesternight declare
That he had found a text to prove
That only God, my dear,   *16*

---

*Yeats was 65 when he wrote this poem for Anne Gregory, the 19-year-old granddaughter of Lady Augusta Gregory, a woman whom Yeats had admired.

Could love you for yourself alone
And not your yellow hair."

[1930]

Edwin Arlington Robinson (American; 1869–1935)

Mr. Flood's Party

Old Eben Flood, climbing alone one night
Over the hill between the town below
And the forsaken upland hermitage
That held as much as he should ever know   *4*
On earth again of home, paused warily.
The road was his with not a native near;
And Eben, having leisure, said aloud;
For no man else in Tilbury Town to hear: *8*

"Well, Mr. Flood, we have the harvest moon
Again, and we may not have many more;
The bird is on the wing, the poet says,
And you and I have said it here before.   *12*
Drink to the bird." He raised up to the light
The jug that he had gone so far to fill,
And answered huskily: "Well, Mr. Flood,
Since you propose it, I believe I will."   *16*

Alone, as if enduring to the end
A valiant armor of scarred hopes outworn,
He stood there in the middle of the road
Like Roland's ghost winding a silent horn.*   *20*
Below him, in the town among the trees,
Where friends of other days had honored him,
A phantom salutation of the dead
Rang thinly till old Eben's eyes were dim.   *24*

Then, as a mother lays her sleeping child
Down tenderly, fearing it may awake,
He set the jug down slowly at his feet
With trembling care, knowing that most things break;   *28*

*__Roland's . . . horn__ in *The Song of Roland,* a medieval French poem, Roland dies after blow-
ing his horn to worn Charlemagne of the presence of enemy troops.

And only when assured that on firm earth
It stood, as the uncertain lives of men
Assuredly did not, he paced away,
And with his hand extended paused again: *32*

"Well, Mr. Flood, we have not met like this
In a long time; and many a change has come
To both of us, I fear, since last it was
We had a drop together. Welcome home!"   *36*
Convivially returning with himself.
Again he raised the jug up to the light;
And with an acquiescent quaver said:
"Well, Mr. Flood, if you insist, I might.   *40*

"Only a very little, Mr. Flood—
For auld lang syne. No more, sir; that will do."
So, for the time, apparently it did,
And Eben evidently thought so too;   *44*
For soon amid the silver loneliness
Of night he lifted up his voice and sang,
Secure, with only two moons listening,
Until the whole harmonious landscape rang—   *48*

"For auld lang syne." The weary throat gave out,
The last word wavered; and the song being done,
He raised again the jug regretfully
And shook his head, and was again alone.   *52*
There was not much that was ahead of him,
And there was nothing in the town below—
Where strangers would have shut the many doors
That many friends had opened long ago.   *56*

[1921]

William Carlos Williams (American; 1883–1963)

Spring and All

By the road to the contagious hospital
under the surge of the blue
mottled clouds driven from the
northeast—a cold wind. Beyond, the

waste of broad, muddy fields   5
brown with dried weeds, standing and fallen

patches of standing water
the scattering of tall trees

All along the road the reddish
purplish, forked, upstanding, twiggy   10
stuff of bushes and small trees
with dead, brown leaves under them
leafless vines—

Lifeless in appearance, sluggish
dazed spring approaches—   15

They enter the new world naked,
cold, uncertain of all
save that they enter. All about them
the cold, familiar wind—

Now the grass, tomorrow   20
the stiff curl of wildcarrot leaf
One by one objects are defined—
It quickens: clarity, outline of leaf

But now the stark dignity of
entrance—Still, the profound change   25
has come upon them: rooted, they
grip down and begin to awaken

[1923]

Marianne Moore (American; 1887–1972)

Poetry*

I, too, dislike it: there are things that are important beyond all
                                                        this fiddle.
        Reading it, however, with a perfect contempt for it, one
                                                        discovers in

---

*In a note to this poem, Moore says that the quotation in lines 17–18 is derived from *The Diaries of Leo Tolstoy;* the quotation in lines 21–22, from W. B. Yeats's *Ideas of Good and Evil.* A comment in *Predilections,* her volume of literary essays, affords some insights into

it after all, a place for the genuine.
         Hands that can grasp, eyes
           that can dilate, hair that can rise   5
           if it must, these things are important not because a
high sounding interpretation can be put upon them but because
                                they are
         useful. When they become so derivative as to become
                       unintelligible,
        the same thing may be said for all of us, that we
           do not admire what   10
           we cannot understand: the bat
           holding on upside down or in quest of something to
eat, elephants pushing, a wild horse taking a roll, a tireless
                        wolf under
      a tree, the immovable critic twitching his skin like a horse
                 that feels a flea, the base-
ball fan, the statistician—   15
         nor is it valid
             to discriminate against "business documents and
school-books"; all these phenomena are important. One must
                make a distinction
       however: when dragged into prominence by half poets, the
                 result is not poetry,
      nor till the poets among us can be   20
         "literalists of
          the imagination"—above
            insolence and triviality and can present

for inspection, "imaginary gardens with real toads in them"
                     shall we have
      it. In the meantime, if you demand on the one hand,   25
      the raw material of poetry in
         all its rawness and
         that which is on the other hand
            genuine, you are interested in poetry.

                            [1921]

---

her style: "My own fondness for the unaccepted rhyme derives, I think, from an instinctive effort to ensure naturalness. Even elate and fearsome rightness like Shakespeare's is only preserved from the offense of being 'poetic' by his well-nested effects of helpless naturalness."

T. S. Eliot (American; naturalized British citizen.
1888–1965)

The Love Song of J. Alfred Prufrock

S'io credesse che mia risposta fosse
A persona che mai tornasse al mondo,
Questa fiamma staria senza piu scosse.
Ma perciocchè giammai di questo fondo
Non torno vivo alcun, s' i' odo il vero,
Senza tema d'infama ti rispondo. *

Let us go then, you and I,
When the evening is spread out against the sky
Like a patient etherised upon a table;
Let us go, through certain half-deserted streets,
The muttering retreats   5
Of restless nights in one-night cheap hotels
And sawdust restaurants with oyster-shells:
Streets that follow like a tedious argument
Of insidious intent
To lead you to an overwhelming question . . .   10
Oh, do not ask, "What is it?"
Let us go and make our visit.

In the room the women come and go
Talking of Michelangelo.

The yellow fog that rubs its back upon the window-panes,   15
The yellow smoke that rubs its muzzle on the window-panes
Licked its tongue into the corners of the evening,
Lingered upon the pools that stand in drains,

*In Dante's *Inferno* XXVII:61–66, a damned soul who had sought absolution before committing a crime addresses Dante, thinking that his words will never reach the earth: "If I believed that my answer were to a person who could ever return to the world, this flame would no longer quiver. But because no one ever returned from this depth, if what I hear is true, without fear of infamy, I answer you."

  Explanations of allusions in the poem may be helpful. "Works and days" (line 29) is the title of a poem on farm life by Hesiod (eighth century B.C.); "dying fall" (line 52) echoes *Twelfth Night* I.i.4; lines 81–83 allude to John the Baptist (see Matthew 14:1–11); line 92 echoes lines 41–42 of Marvell's "To His Coy Mistress" (see page 540); for "Lazarus," (line 94) see Luke 16 and John 11; lines 112–17 allude to Polonius and perhaps to other figures in *Hamlet;* "full of high sentence" (line 117) comes from Chaucer's description of the Clerk of Oxford in the *Canterbury Tales.*

Let fall upon its back the soot that falls from chimneys,
Slipped by the terrace, made a sudden leap,   20
And seeing that it was a soft October night,
Curled once about the house, and fell asleep.

And indeed there will be time
For the yellow smoke that slides along the street,
Rubbing its back upon the window-panes;   25
There will be time, there will be time
To prepare a face to meet the faces that you meet;
There will be time to murder and create,
And time for all the works and days of hands
That lift and drop a question on your plate;   30
Time for you and time for me,
And time yet for a hundred indecisions,
And for a hundred visions and revisions,
Before the taking of a toast and tea.

In the room the women come and go   35
Talking of Michelangelo.
And indeed there will be time
To wonder, "Do I dare?" and, "Do I dare?"
Time to turn back and descend the stair,
With a bald spot in the middle of my hair—   40
[They will say: "How his hair is growing thin!"]
My morning coat, my collar mounting firmly to the chin,
My necktie rich and modest, but asserted by a simple pin—
[They will say: "But how his arms and legs are thin!"]
Do I dare   45
Disturb the universe?
In a minute there is time
For decisions and revisions which a minute will reverse.

For I have known them all already, known them all:—
Have known the evenings, mornings, afternoons,   50
I have measured out my life with coffee spoons;
I know the voices dying with a dying fall
Beneath the music from a farther room.
        So how should I presume?

And I have known the eyes already, known them all—   55
The eyes that fix you in a formulated phrase,
And when I am formulated, sprawling on a pin,
When I am pinned and wriggling on the wall,
Then how should I begin

To spit out all the butt-ends of my days and ways?   *60*
    And how should I presume?

And I have known the arms already, known them all—
Arms that are braceleted and white and bare
[But in the lamplight, downed with light brown hair!]
Is it perfume from a dress   *65*
That makes me so digress?
Arms that lie along a table, or wrap about a shawl.
    And should I then presume?
    And how should I begin?

    . . . . .

Shall I say, I have gone at dusk through narrow streets   *70*
And watched the smoke that rises from the pipes
Of lonely men in shirt-sleeves, leaning out of windows? . . .

I should have been a pair of ragged claws
Scuttling across the floors of silent seas.

    . . . . .

And the afternoon, the evening, sleeps so peacefully!   *75*
Smoothed by long fingers,
Asleep . . . tired . . . or it malingers,
Stretched on the floor, here beside you and me.
Should I, after tea and cakes and ices,
Have the strength to force the moment to its crisis?   *80*
But though I have wept and fasted, wept and prayed,
Though I have seen my head [grown slightly bald]
    brought in upon a platter,
I am no prophet—and here's no great matter;
I have seen the moment of my greatness flicker,
And I have seen the eternal Footman hold my coat, and
    snicker,   *85*
And in short, I was afraid.

And would it have been worth it, after all,
After the cups, the marmalade, the tea,
Among the porcelain, among some talk of you and me,
Would it have been worth while,   *90*
To have bitten off the matter with a smile,
To have squeezed the universe into a ball
To roll it toward some overwhelming question,
To say: "I am Lazarus, come from the dead,
Come back to tell you all, I shall tell you all"—   *95*
If one, settling a pillow by her head,

Should say: "That is not what I meant at all.
That is not it, at all."

And would it have been worth it, after all,
Would it have been worth while,   100
After the sunsets and the dooryards and the sprinkled streets,
After the novels, after the teacups, after the skirts
    that trail along the floor—
And this, and so much more?—
It is impossible to say just what I mean!
But as if a magic lantern threw the nerves in patterns
    on a screen: 105
Would it have been worth while
If one, settling a pillow or throwing off a shawl,
And turning toward the window, should say:
    "That is not it at all,
    That is not what I meant, at all."   110

                          . . . . .

No! I am not Prince Hamlet, nor was meant to be;
Am an attendant lord, one that will do
To swell a progress, start a scene or two,
Advise the prince; no doubt, an easy tool,
Deferential, glad to be of use,   115
Politic, cautious, and meticulous;
Full of high sentence, but a bit obtuse;
At times, indeed, almost ridiculous—
Almost, at times, the Fool.

I grow old . . . I grow old . . .   120
I shall wear the bottoms of my trousers rolled.

Shall I part my hair behind? Do I dare to eat a peach?
I shall wear white flannel trousers, and walk upon the beach.
I have heard the mermaids singing, each to each.

I do not think that they will sing to me.   125

I have seen them riding seaward on the waves
Combing the white hair of the waves blown back
When the wind blows the water white and black.

We have lingered in the chambers of the sea
By sea-girls wreathed with seaweed red and brown   130
Till human voices wake us, and we drown.
                                        [1917]

John Crowe Ransom *(American; 1888–1974)*

Piazza Piece

—I am a gentleman in a dustcoat trying
To make you hear. Your ears are soft and small
And listen to an old man not at all,
They want the young men's whispering and sighing.   *4*
But see the roses on your trellis dying
And hear the spectral singing of the moon;
For I must have my lovely lady soon,
I am a gentleman in a dustcoat trying.   *8*

—I am a lady young in beauty waiting
Until my truelove comes, and then we kiss.
But what gray man among the vines is this
Whose words are dry and faint as in a dream?   *12*
Back from my trellis, Sir, before I scream!
I am a lady young in beauty waiting.

[1925]

Archibald MacLeish *(American; 1892–1982)*

Ars Poetica

A poem should be palpable and mute
As a globed fruit,

Dumb
As old medallions to the thumb,   *4*

Silent as the sleeve-worn stone
Of casement ledges where the moss has grown—

A poem should be wordless
As the flight of birds.   *8*

A poem should be motionless in time
As the moon climbs,

Leaving, as the moon releases
Twig by twig the night-entangled trees,   *12*

Leaving, as the moon behind the winter leaves,
Memory by memory the mind —

A poem should be motionless in time
As the moon climbs.   *16*

A poem should be equal to:
Not true.

For all the history of grief
An empty doorway and a maple leaf.   *20*

For love
The leaning grasses and two lights above the sea —

A poem should not mean
But be.   *24*

                                   [1926]

Wilfred Owen *(English; 1893–1918)*

Dulce et Decorum Est[1]

Bent double, like old beggars under sacks,
Knock-kneed, coughing like hags, we cursed through sludge,
Till on the haunting flares we turned our backs
And towards our distant rest began to trudge.   *4*
Men marched asleep. Many had lost their boots
But limped on, blood-shod. All went lame; all blind;
Drunk with fatigue; deaf even to the hoots
Of tired, outstripped Five-Nines° that dropped behind.   *shells containing*   *8*
                                                         poison gas

Gas! Gas! Quick, boys! — An ecstasy of fumbling,
Fitting the clumsy helmets just in time;
But someone still was yelling out and stumbling
And flound'ring like a man in fire or lime . . .   *12*

Dim, through the misty panes and thick green light,
As under a green sea, I saw him drowning.

---

[1] From the Latin poet Horace's *Odes* (III:2.13): *Dulce et decorum est pro patria mori* — "It is sweet and honorable to die for your country."

In all my dreams, before my helpless sight,
He plunges at me, guttering, choking, drowning.   *16*

If in some smothering dreams you too could pace
Behind the wagon that we flung him in,
And watch the white eyes writhing in his face,
His hanging face, like a devil's sick of sin;   *20*
If you could hear, at every jolt, the blood
Come gargling from the forth-corrupted lungs,
Obscene as cancer, bitter as the cud
Of vile, incurable sores one innocent tongues,—   *24*
My friend,[2] you would not tell with such high zest
To children ardent for some desperate glory,
The old Lie: Dulce et decorum est
Pro patria mori.

                                        [1917]

E. E. Cummings (American; 1894–1962)

in Just-

in Just-
spring   when the world is mud-
luscious the little
lame balloonman   *4*

whistles   far   and wee

and eddieandbill come
running from marbles and
piracies and it's   *8*
spring

when the world is puddle-wonderful

the queer
old balloonman whistles   *12*
far   and   wee
and bettyandisbel come dancing

[2]Early drafts of the poem are dedicated to Jessie Pope, author of children's books and conventional patriotic verse.

from hop-scotch and jump-rope and

it's   *16*
spring
and
    the
          goat-footed   *20*
balloonMan   whistles
far
and
wee   *24*

[1920]

W. H. Auden (British; naturalized American citizen. 1907–73)

Musée des Beaux Arts

About suffering they were never wrong,
The Old Masters: how well they understood
Its human position; how it takes place
While someone else is eating or opening a window
   or just walking dully along;
How, when the aged are reverently, passionately waiting   *5*
For the miraculous birth, there always must be
Children who did not specially want it to happen, skating
On a pond at the edge of the wood:
They never forgot
That even the dreadful martyrdom must run its course   *10*
Anyhow in a corner, some untidy spot
Where the dogs go on with their doggy life and the torturer's
   horse
Scratches its innocent behind on a tree.

In Brueghel's *Icarus,* for instance: how everything turns away
Quite leisurely from the disaster; the plowman may   *15*
Have heard the splash, the forsaken cry,
But for him it was not an important failure; the sun shone
As it had to on the white legs disappearing into the green

The legs of the drowning Icarus are barely visible near the ship. Copyright ACL, Brussels.

Water; and the expensive delicate ship that must have seen
Something amazing, a boy falling out of the sky,   *20*
Had somewhere to get to and sailed calmly on.

[1940]

The Unknown Citizen

(To JS/07/M/378
This Marble Monument
Is Erected by the State)

He was found by the Bureau of Statistics to be
One against whom there was no official complaint,
And all the reports on his conduct agree
That, in the modern sense of an old-fashioned word, he was a
    saint,
For in everything he did he served the Greater Community.   *5*
Except for the War till the day he retired
He worked in a factory and never got fired,
But satisfied his employers, Fudge Motors Inc.
Yet he wasn't a scab or odd in his views,

For his Union reports that he paid his dues.   10
(Our report on his Union shows it was sound)
And our Social Psychology workers found
That he was popular with his mates and liked a drink.
The Press are convinced that he bought a paper every day
And that his reactions to advertisements were normal
   in every way.   15
Policies taken out in his name prove that he was fully insured,
And his Health-card shows he was once in hospital
   but left it cured.
Both Producers Research and High-Grade Living declare
He was fully sensible to the advantages of the Installment Plan
And had everything necessary to the Modern Man,   20
A phonograph, radio, a car and a frigidaire.
Our researchers into Public Opinion are content
That he held the proper opinions for the time of year;
When there was peace, he was for peace; when there
   was war, he went.
He was married and added five children
   to the population.   25
Which our Eugenist says was the right number
   for a parent of his generation,
And our teachers report that he never interfered
   with their education.
Was he free? Was he happy? The question is absurd:
Had anything been wrong, we should certainly have heard.

[1940]

Elizabeth Bishop (American; 1911–79)

The Fish

I caught a tremendous fish
and held him beside the boat
half out of water, with my hook
fast in a corner of his mouth.
He didn't fight.   5
He hadn't fought at all.
He hung a grunting weight,
battered and venerable
and homely. Here and there

his brown skin hung in strips   *10*
like ancient wall-paper,
and its pattern of darker brown
was like wall-paper:
shapes like full-blown roses
stained and lost through age.   *15*
He was speckled with barnacles,
fine rosettes of lime,
and infested
with tiny white sea-lice,
and underneath two or three   *20*
rags of green weed hung down.
While his gills were breathing in
the terrible oxygen
—the frightening gills,
fresh and crisp with blood,   *25*
that can cut so badly—
I thought of the coarse white flesh
packed in like feathers,
the big bones and the little bones,
the dramatic reds and blacks   *30*
of his shiny entrails,
and the pink swim-bladder
like a big peony.
I looked into his eyes
which were far larger than mine   *35*
but shallower, and yellowed,
the irises backed and packed
with tarnished tinfoil
seen through the lenses
of old scratched isinglass.   *40*
They shifted a little, but not
to return my stare.
—It was more like the tipping
of an object toward the light.
I admired his sullen face,   *45*
the mechanism of his jaw,
and then I saw
that from his lower lip
—if you could call it a lip—
grim, wet, and weapon-like,   *50*
hung five old pieces of fish-line,
or four and a wire leader
with the swivel still attached,
with all their five big hooks

grown firmly in his mouth.
A green line, frayed at the end   55
where he broke it, two heavier lines,
and a fine black thread
still crimped from the strain and snap
when it broke and he got away.   60
Like medals with their ribbons
frayed and wavering,
a five-haired beard of wisdom
trailing from his aching jaw.
I stared and stared   65
and victory filled up
the little rented boat,
from the pool of bilge
where oil had spread a rainbow
around the rusted engine   70
to the bailer rusted orange,
the sun-cracked thwarts,
the oarlocks on their strings,
the gunnels—until everything
was rainbow, rainbow, rainbow!   75
And I let the fish go.

[1946]

Poem

About the size of an old-style dollar bill,
American or Canadian,
mostly the same whites, gray greens, and steel grays
—this little painting (a sketch for a larger one?)
has never earned any money in its life.   5
Useless and free, it has spent seventy years
as a minor family relic
handed along collaterally to owners
who looked at it sometimes, or didn't bother to.

It must be Nova Scotia; only there   10
does one see gabled wooden houses
painted that awful shade of brown.
The other houses, the bits that show, are white.
Elm trees, low hills, a thin church steeple
—that gray-blue wisp—or is it? In the foreground   15
a water meadow with some tiny cows,

two brushstrokes each, but confidently cows;
two minuscule white geese in the blue water,
back-to-back, feeding, and a slanting stick.
Up closer, a wild iris, white and yellow,   20
fresh-squiggled from the tube.
The air is fresh and cold; cold early spring
clear as gray glass; a half inch of blue sky
below the steel-gray storm clouds.
(They were the artist's specialty.)   25
A specklike bird is flying to the left.
Or is it a flyspeck looking like a bird?

Heavens, I recognize the place, I know it!
It's behind—I can almost remember the farmer's name.
His barn backed on that meadow. There it is,   30
titanium white, one dab. The hint of steeple,
filaments of brush-hairs, barely there,
must be the Presbyterian church.
Would that be Miss Gillespie's house?
Those particular geese and cows   35
are naturally before my time.
A sketch done in an hour, "in one breath,"
once taken from a trunk and handed over.
Would you like this? I'll probably never
have room to hang these things again.   40
Your Uncle George, no, mine, my Uncle George,
he'd be your great-uncle, left them all with Mother
when he went back to England.
You know, he was quite famous, an R.A.° . . .   member of the Royal Academy

I never knew him. We both knew this place,   45
apparently, this literal small backwater,
looked at it long enough to memorize it,
our years apart. How strange. And it's still loved,
or its memory is (it must have changed a lot).
Our visions coincided—"visions" is   50
too serious a word—our looks, two looks:
art "copying from life" and life itself,
life and the memory of it so compressed
they've turned into each other. Which is which?
Life and the memory of it cramped,   55
dim, on a piece of Bristol board,
dim, but how live, how touching in detail
—the little that we get for free,
the little of our earthly trust. Not much.

About the size of our abidance   *60*
along with theirs: the munching cows,
the iris, crisp and shivering, the water
still standing from spring freshets,
the yet-to-be-dismantled elms, the geese.

[1976]

Robert Hayden (American; 1913–80)

Frederick Douglass*

When it is finally ours, this freedom, this liberty, this beautiful
and terrible thing, needful to man as air,
usable as earth; when it belongs at last to all,
when it is truly instinct, brain matter, diastole, systole,
reflex action; when it is finally won; when it is more   *5*
than the gaudy mumbo jumbo of politicians:
this man, this Douglass, this former slave, this Negro
beaten to his knees, exiled, visioning a world
where none is lonely, none hunted, alien,
this man, superb in love and logic, this man   *10*
shall be remembered. Oh, not with statues' rhetoric,
not with legends and poems and wreaths of bronze alone,
but with the lives grown out of his life, the lives
fleshing his dream of the beautiful, needful thing.

[1947]

Those Winter Sundays

Sundays too my father got up early
and put his clothes on in the blueblack cold,
then with cracked hands that ached
from labor in the weekday weather made
banked fires blaze. No one ever thanked him.   *5*

I'd wake and hear the cold splintering, breaking.
When the rooms were warm, he'd call,

*Frederick Douglass   Born a slave, Douglass (1817–95) escaped and became an impor-
tant spokesman for the abolitionist movement and later for civil rights for African-Americans.

and slowly I would rise and dress,
fearing the chronic angers of that house,

Speaking indifferently to him,   *10*
who had driven out the cold
and polished my good shoes as well.
What did I know, what did I know
of love's austere and lonely offices?

[1962]

Henry Reed *(English; b. 1914)*

Naming of Parts

To-day we have naming of parts. Yesterday,
We had daily cleaning. And to-morrow morning,
We shall have what to do after firing. But to-day,
To-day we have naming of parts. Japonica°   *Japanese quince*
Glistens like coral in all of the neighboring gardens,   *5*
    And to-day we have naming of parts.

This is the lower sling swivel. And this
Is the upper sling swivel, whose use you will see,
When you are given your slings. And this is the piling swivel,
Which in your case you have not got. The branches   *10*
Hold in the gardens their silent, eloquent gestures,
    Which in our case we have not got.

This is the safety-catch, which is always released
With an easy flick of the thumb. And please do not let me
See anyone using his finger. You can do it quite easy   *15*

If you have any strength in your thumb. The blossoms
Are fragile and motionless, never letting anyone see
    Any of them using their finger.

And this you can see is the bolt. The purpose of this
Is to open the breech, as you see. We can slide it   *20*
Rapidly backwards and forwards: we call this
Easing the spring. And rapidly backwards and forwards
The early bees are assaulting and fumbling the flowers:
    They call it easing the Spring.

They call it easing the Spring: it is perfectly easy   *25*
If you have any strength in your thumb: like the bolt,
And the breech, and the cocking-piece, and the point of balance,
Which in our case we have not got; and the almond-blossom
Silent in all of the gardens and the bees going backwards and
    forwards,
    For to-day we have naming of parts.   *30*

                                            [1946]

Dylan Thomas (Welsh; 1914–53)

Fern Hill

Now as I was young and easy under the apple boughs
About the lilting house and happy as the grass was green,
    The night above the dingle starry,
        Time let me hail and climb
      Golden in the heydays of his eyes,   *5*
And honored among wagons I was prince of the apple towns
And once below a time I lordly had the trees and leaves
        Trail with daisies and barley
      Down the rivers of the windfall light.

And as I was green and carefree, famous among the barns   *10*
About the happy yard and singing as the farm was home,
    In the sun that is young once only,
        Time let me play and be
      Golden in the mercy of his means,
And green and golden I was huntsman and herdsman,
        the calves   *15*
Sang to my horn, the foxes on the hills barked clear and cold,
        And the sabbath rang slowly
      In the pebbles of the holy streams.

All the sun long it was running, it was lovely, the hay
Fields high as the house, the tunes from the chimneys,
        it was air   *20*
    And playing, lovely and watery
        And fire green as grass.
      And nightly under the simple stars
As I rode to sleep the owls were bearing the farm away,

All the moon long I heard, blessed among stables, the night-
    jars   25
  Flying with the ricks, and the horses
    Flashing into the dark.

And then to awake, and the farm, like a wanderer white
With the dew, come back, the cock on his shoulder: it was all
  Shining, it was Adam and maiden,   30
    The sky gathered again
  And the sun grew round that very day.
So it must have been after the birth of the simple light
In the first, spinning place, the spellbound horses walking warm
  Out of the whinnying green stable   35
    On to the fields of praise.

And honored among foxes and pheasants by the gay house
Under the new made clouds and happy as the heart was long,
  In the sun born over and over,
    I ran my heedless ways,   40
  My wishes raced through the house high hay
And nothing I cared, at my sky blue trades, that time allows
In all his tuneful turning to few and such morning songs
  Before the children green and golden
    Follow him out of grace,   45

Nothing I cared, in the lamb white days, that time would take me
Up to the swallow thronged loft by the shadow of my hand,
  In the moon that is always rising,
    Nor that riding to sleep
  I should hear him fly with the high fields   50
And wake to the farm forever fled from the childless land.
Oh as I was young and easy in the mercy of his means,
    Time held me green and dying
  Though I sang in my chains like the sea.

                                               [1946]

Randall Jarrell (American; 1914–65)

The Woman at the Washington Zoo

The saris go by me from the embassies.

Cloth from the moon. Cloth from another planet.
They look back at the leopard like the leopard.

And I. . . .
          this print of mine, that has kept its color
Alive through so many cleanings; this dull null   5
Navy I wear to work, and wear from work, and so
To my bed, so to my grave, with no
Complaints, no comment: neither from my chief,
The Deputy Chief Assistant, nor his chief—
Only I complain. . . . this serviceable   10
Body that no sunlight dyes, no hand suffuses
But, dome-shadowed, withering among columns,
Wavy beneath fountains—small, far-off, shining
In the eyes of animals, these beings trapped
As I am trapped but no, themselves, the trap,   15
Aging, but without knowledge of their age,
Kept safe here, knowing not of death, for death—
Oh, bars of my own body, open, open!

The world goes by my cage and never sees me.
And there come not to me, as come to these,   20
The wild beasts, sparrows pecking the llamas' grain,
Pigeons settling on the bears' bread, buzzards
Tearing the meat the flies have clouded. . . .
                              Vulture,
When you come for the white rat that the foxes left,
Take off the red helmet of your head, the black   25
Wings that have shadowed me, and step to me as man:
The wild brother at whose feet the white wolves fawn,
To whose hand of power the great lioness
Stalks, purring. . . .
                  You know what I was,
You see what I am: change me, change me!   30

                         [1960]

William Stafford (American; b. 1914)

Traveling through the Dark

Traveling through the dark I found a deer
dead on the edge of the Wilson River road.

It is usually best to roll them into the canyon:
the road is narrow; to swerve might make more dead.   *4*

By glow of the tail-light I stumbled back of the car
and stood by the heap, a doe, a recent killing;
she had stiffened already, almost cold.
I dragged her off; she was large in the belly.   *8*

My fingers touching her side brought me the reason—
her side was warm; her fawn lay there waiting,
alive, still, never to be born.
Beside that mountain road I hesitated.   *12*

The car aimed ahead its lowered parking lights;
under the hood purred the steady engine.
I stood in the glare of the warm exhaust turning red;
around our group I could hear the wilderness listen.   *16*

I thought hard for us all—my only swerving—
then pushed her over the edge into the river.

[1960]

Lawrence Ferlinghetti *(American; b. 1919)*

Constantly risking absurdity

Constantly risking absurdity
                              and death
               whenever he performs
                         above the heads
                              of his audience   *5*
        the poet like an acrobat
                      climbs on rime
                           to a high wire of his own making
and balancing on eyebeams
                              above a sea of faces   *10*
               paces his way
                         to the other side of day
        performing *entrechats*°   *a leap in bal*
                         and sleight-of-foot tricks

and other high theatrics   15
                    and all without mistaking
          any thing
                    for what it may not be
       For he's the super realist
                              who must perforce perceive   20
                 taut truth
                              before the taking of each stance or step
     in his supposed advance
                              toward that still higher perch
where Beauty stands and waits   25
                         with gravity
                              to start her death-defying leap

       And he
           a little charleychaplin man
                              who may or may not catch   30
              her fair eternal form
                         spreadeagled in the empty air
              of existence

                                                             [1958]

Richard Wilbur *(American; b. 1921)*

Love Calls Us to the Things of This World

    The eyes open to a cry of pulleys,
And spirited from sleep, the astounded soul
Hangs for a moment bodiless and simple
As false dawn.
                    Outside the open window
The morning air is all awash with angels.   5

    Some are in bed-sheets, some are in blouses,
Some are in smocks: but truly there they are.
Now they are rising together in calm swells
Of halcyon feelings, filling whatever they wear
With the deep joy of their impersonal breathing;   10

    Now they are flying in place, conveying
The terrible speed of their omnipresence, moving

And staying like white water; and now of a sudden
They swoon down into so rapt a quiet
That nobody seems to be there.   15
                              The soul shrinks

    From all that it is about to remember,
From the punctual rape of every blessèd day,
And cries,
        "Oh, let there be nothing on earth but laundry,
Nothing but rosy hands in the rising steam
And clear dances done in the sight of heaven."   20

    Yet, as the sun acknowledges
With a warm look the world's hunks and colors,
The soul descends once more in bitter love
To accept the waking body, saying now
In a changed voice as the man yawns and rises,   25

"Bring them down from their ruddy gallows;
Let there be clean linen for the backs of thieves;
Let lovers go fresh and sweet to be undone,
And the heaviest nuns walk in a pure floating
Of dark habits,
              keeping their difficult balance."   30

                              [1956]

Anthony Hecht (American; b. 1923)

The Dover Bitch*

A Criticism of Life

For Andrews Wanning

So there stood Matthew Arnold and this girl
With the cliffs of England crumbling away behind them,
And he said to her, "Try to be true to me,
And I'll do the same for you, for things are bad
All over, etc., etc."   5

---

*Hecht's title alludes to Matthew Arnold's "Dover Beach" (p. 578).

Well now, I knew this girl. It's true she had read
Sophocles in a fairly good translation
And caught that bitter allusion to the sea,
But all the time he was talking she had in mind
The notion of what his whiskers would feel like   10
On the back of her neck. She told me later on
That after a while she got to looking out
At the lights across the channel, and really felt sad,
Thinking of all the wine and enormous beds
And blandishments in French and the perfumes.   15
And then she got really angry. To have been brought
All the way down from London, and then be addressed
As sort of a mournful cosmic last resort
Is really tough on a girl, and she was pretty.
Anyway, she watched him pace the room   20
And finger his watch-chain and seem to sweat a bit,
And then she said one or two unprintable things.
But you mustn't judge her by that. What I mean to say is,
She's really all right. I still see her once in a while
And she always treats me right.
We have a drink   25
And I give her a good time, and perhaps it's a year
Before I see her again, but there she is,
Running to fat, but dependable as they come,
And sometimes I bring her a bottle of *Nuit d'Amour.*

[1967]

Allen Ginsberg (American; b. 1926)

A Supermarket in California

What thoughts I have of you tonight, Walt Whitman, for I walked
down the sidestreets under the trees with a headache self-conscious looking
at the full moon.

In my hungry fatigue, and shopping for images, I went into
the neon fruit supermarket, dreaming of your enumerations!

What peaches and what penumbras! Whole families shopping
at night! Aisles full of husbands! Wives in the avocados, babies in
the tomatoes!—and you, Garcia Lorca,[1] what were you doing down by
the watermelons?

[1]Federico Garcia Lorca (1899–1936), Spanish poet

I saw you, Walt Whitman, childless, lonely old grubber, poking among the meats in the refrigerator and eyeing the grocery boys.

I heard you asking questions of each: Who killed the pork chops? What price bananas? Are you my Angel? 5

I wandered in and out of the brilliant stacks of cans following you, and followed in my imagination by the store detective.

We strode down the open corridors together in our solitary fancy tasting artichokes, possessing every frozen delicacy, and never passing the cashier.

Where are we going, Walt Whitman? The doors close in an hour. Which way does your beard point tonight?

(I touch your book and dream of our odyssey in the supermarket and feel absurd.)

Will we walk all night through solitary streets? The trees add shade to shade, lights out in the houses, we'll both be lonely. 10

Will we stroll dreaming of the lost America of love past blue automobiles in driveways, home to our silent cottage?

Ah, dear father, graybeard, lonely old courage-teacher, what America did you have when Charon[2] quit poling his ferry and you got out on a smoking bank and stood watching the boat disappear on the black water of Lethe?

[1956]

Adrienne Rich (American; b. 1929)

Living in Sin

She had thought the studio would keep itself,
not dust upon the furniture of love.
Half heresy, to wish the taps less vocal,
The panes relieved of grime. A plate of pears,
a piano with a Persian shawl, a cat   5
stalking the picturesque amusing mouse
had risen at his urging.
Not that at five each separate stair would writhe
under the milkman's tramp; that morning light
so coldly would delineate the scraps   10
of last night's cheese and three sepulchral bottles;

[2]In classical mythology, Charon ferried the souls of the dead across the river Styx, to Hades, where, after drinking from the river Lethe, they forget the life they had lived.

that on the kitchen shelf among the saucers
a pair of beetle-eyes would fix her own —
envoy from some black village in the mouldings . . .
Meanwhile, he, with a yawn,   15
sounded a dozen notes upon the keyboard,
declared it out of tune, shrugged at the mirror,
rubbed at his beard, went out for cigarettes;
while she, jeered by the minor demons,
pulled back the sheets and made the bed and found   20
a towel to dust the table-top,
and let the coffee-pot boil over on the stove.
By evening she was back in love again,
though not so wholly but throughout the night
she woke sometimes to feel the daylight coming   25
like a relentless milkman up the stairs.

                                            [1955]

Rape

There is a cop who is both prowler and father:
he comes from your block, grew up with your brothers,
had certain ideals.
You hardly know him in his boots and silver badge,
on horseback, one hand touching his gun.   5

You hardly know him but you have to get to know him:
he has access to machinery that could kill you.
He and his stallion clop like warlords among the trash,
his ideals stand in the air, a frozen cloud
from between his unsmiling lips.   10

And so, when the time comes, you have to turn to him,
the maniac's sperm still greasing your thighs,
your mind whirling like crazy. You have to confess
to him you are guilty of the crime
of having been forced.   15

And you see his blue eyes, the blue eyes of all the family
whom you used to know, grow narrow and glisten,
his hand types out the details
and he wants them all
but the hysteria in your voice pleases him best.   20

You hardly know him but now he thinks he knows you:
he has taken down your worst moment
on a machine and filed it in a file.
He knows, or thinks he knows, how much you imagined;
he knows, or thinks he knows, what you secretly wanted. *25*

He has access to machinery that could get you put away;
and if, in the sickening light of the precinct,
your details sound like a portrait of your confessor,
will you swallow, will you deny them, will you lie your way home? *30*

[1972]

Linda Pastan (American; b. 1932)

Marks

My husband gives me an A
for last night's supper,
an incomplete for my ironing,
a B plus in bed. *4*
My son says I am average,
an average mother, but if
I put my mind to it
I could improve. *8*
My daughter believes
in Pass/Fail and tells me
I pass. Wait 'til they learn
I'm dropping out. *12*

[1978]

Sylvia Plath (American; 1932–63)

Daddy

You do not do, you do not do
Any more, black shoe
In which I have lived like a foot
For thirty years, poor and white,
Barely daring to breathe or Achoo. *5*

Daddy, I have had to kill you.
You died before I had time—
Marble-heavy, a bag full of God,
Ghastly statue with one gray toe
Big as a Frisco seal   *10*

And a head in the freakish Atlantic
Where it pours bean green over blue
In the waters off beautiful Nauset.
I used to pray to recover you.
Ach, du.   *15*

In the German tongue, in the Polish town
Scraped flat by the roller
Of wars, wars, wars.
But the name of the town is common.
My Polack friend   *20*

Says there are a dozen or two.
So I never could tell where you
Put your foot, your root,
I never could talk to you.
The tongue stuck in my jaw.   *25*

It stuck in a barb wire snare.
Ich, ich, ich, ich,
I could hardly speak.
I thought every German was you.
And the language obscene   *30*

An engine, an engine
Chuffing me off like a Jew.
A Jew to Dachau, Auschwitz, Belsen.
I began to talk like a Jew.
I think I may well be a Jew.   *35*

The snows of the Tyrol, the clear beer of Vienna
Are not very pure or true.
With my gypsy ancestress and my weird luck
And my Taroc pack and my Taroc pack
I may be a bit of a Jew.   *40*

I have always been scared of *you*,
With your Luftwaffe, your gobbledygoo.
And your neat moustache

And your Aryan eye, bright blue,
Panzer-man, panzer-man, O You—   45

Not God but a swastika
So black no sky could squeak through.
Every woman adores a Fascist,
The boot in the face, the brute
Brute heart of a brute like you.   50

You stand at the blackboard, daddy,
In the picture I have of you,
A cleft in your chin instead of your foot
But no less a devil for that, no not
Any less the black man who   55

Bit my pretty red heart in two.
I was ten when they buried you.
At twenty I tried to die
And get back, back, back to you.
I thought even the bones would do.   60

But they pulled me out of the sack,
And they stuck me together with glue,
And then I knew what to do.
I made a model of you,
A man in black with a Meinkampf look   65

And a love of the rack and the screw.
And I said I do, I do.
So daddy, I'm finally through.
The black telephone's off at the root,
The voices just can't worm through.   70

If I've killed one man, I've killed two—
The vampire who said he was you
And drank my blood for a year,
Seven years, if you want to know.
Daddy, you can lie back now.   75

There's a stake in your fat black heart
And the villagers never liked you.
They are dancing and stamping on you.
They always *knew* it was you.
Daddy, daddy, you bastard, I'm through.   80

[1965]

N. Scott Momaday *(American; b. 1934)*

The Eagle-Feather Fan

The eagle is my power,
And my fan is an eagle.
It is strong and beautiful
In my hand. And it is real.
My fingers hold upon it   5
As if the beaded handle
Were the twist of bristlecone.
The bones of my hand are fine
And hollow; the fan bears them.
My hand veers in the thin air   10
Of the summits. All morning
It scuds on the cold currents;
All afternoon it circles
To the singing, to the drums.

[1976]

Lucille Clifton *(American; b. 1936)*

in the inner city

in the inner city
or
like we call it
home
we think a lot about uptown   5
and the silent nights
and the houses straight as
dead men
and the pastel lights
and we hang on to our no place   10
happy to be alive
and in the inner city
or
like we call it
home   15

[1969]

Pat Mora *(American; b. 1942)*

Sonrisas*

I live in a doorway
between two rooms. I hear
quiet clicks, cups of black
coffee, *click, click* like facts
    budgets, tenure, curriculum,   *5*
from careful women in crisp beige
suits, quick beige smiles
that seldom sneak into their eyes.

I peek
in the other room señoras   *10*
in faded dresses stir sweet
milk coffee, laughter whirls
with steam from fresh *tamales*
    sh, sh, mucho ruido,   *a lot of noise*
they scold one another   *15*
press their lips, trap smiles
in their dark, Mexican eyes.

          [1986]

Don L. Lee *(American; b. 1942)*

But He Was Cool
or: he even stopped for green lights

super–cool
ultrablack
a tan / purple
had a beautiful shade.
he had a double-natural   *5*
that wd put the sisters to shame.
his dashikis were tailor made
& his beads were imported sea shells
    (from some blk/country i never heard of)
he was triple-hip.   *10*

*smiles (Spanish)

his tikis were hand carved
out of ivory
& came express from the motherland.
he would greet u in swahili
& say good-bye in yoruba.   *15*

wooooooooooooo-jim he bes so cool & ill tel li gent
   cool-cool is so cool he was un-cooled by other niggers' cool
   cool-cool ultracool was bop-cool/ice box cool so cool cold
      cool
   his wine didn't have to be cooled, him was air conditioned
      cool
   cool-cool/real cool made me cool—now ain't that cool   *20*
   cool-cool so cool him nick-named refrigerator.

cool-cool so cool
he didn't know,
after detroit, newark, chicago &c.,
we had to hip   *25*
   cool-cool / super-cool / real cool
   that
to be black
is
to be   *30*
very-hot.

                       [1969]

Sharon Olds (American; b. 1942)

I Go Back to May 1937

I see them standing at the formal gates of their colleges,
I see my father strolling out
under the ochre sandstone arch, the
red tiles glinting like bent
plates of blood behind his head, I   *5*
see my mother with a few light books at her hip
standing at the pillar made of tiny bricks with the
wrought-iron gate still open behind her, its
sword-tips black in the May air,
they are about to graduate, they are about to get married,   *10*

they are kids, they are dumb, all they know is they are
innocent, they would never hurt anybody.
I want to go up to them and say Stop,
don't do it—she's the wrong woman,
he's the wrong man, you are going to do things   **15**
you cannot imagine you would ever do,
you are going to do bad things to children,
you are going to suffer in ways you never heard of,
you are going to want to die. I want to go
up to them there in the late May sunlight and say it,   **20**
her hungry pretty blank face turning to me,
her pitiful beautiful untouched body,
his arrogant handsome blind face turning to me,
his pitiful beautiful untouched body,
but I don't do it. I want to live. I   **25**
take them up like the male and female
paper dolls and bang them together
at the hips like chips of flint as if to
strike sparks from them, I say
Do what you are going to do, and I will tell about it.   **30**

[1987]

Nikki Giovanni (American; b. 1943)

Master Charge Blues

its wednesday night baby
and i'm all alone
wednesday night baby
and i'm all alone
sitting with myself   **5**
waiting for the telephone

wanted you baby
but you said you had to go
wanted you yeah
but you said you had to go   **10**
called your best friend
but he can't come 'cross no more

did you ever go to bed
at the end of a busy day

look over and see the smooth   *15*
where your hump usta lay
feminine odor and no reason why
i said feminine odor and no reason why
asked the lord to help me
he shook his head "not i"   *20*

but i'm a modern woman baby
ain't gonna let this get me down
i'm a modern woman
ain't gonna let this get me down
gonna take my master charge   *25*
and get everything in town

[1970]

Craig Raine (English; b. 1945)

A Martian Sends a Postcard Home

Caxtons[1] are mechanical birds with many wings
and some are treasured for their markings—

they cause the eyes to melt
or the body to shriek without pain.   *4*

I have never seen one fly, but
sometimes they perch on the hand.

Mist is when the sky is tired of flight
and rests its soft machine on ground: *8*

then the world is dim and bookish
like engravings under tissue paper.

Rain is when the earth is television.
It has the property of making colours darker.   *12*

Model T[2] is a room with the lock inside—
a key is turned to free the world

[1] William Caxton (c. 1422–91) was the first English printer of books.
[2] A Ford automobile made between 1908 and 1928

for movement, so quick there is a film
to watch for anything missed.   *16*

But time is tied to the wrist
or kept in a box, ticking with impatience.

In homes, a haunted apparatus sleeps,
that snores when you pick it up.   *20*

If the ghost cries, they carry it
to their lips and soothe it to sleep

with sounds. And yet, they wake it up
deliberately, by tickling with a finger.   *24*

Only the young are allowed to suffer
openly. Adults go to a punishment room

with water but nothing to eat.
They lock the door and suffer the noises   *28*

alone. No one is exempt
and everyone's pain has a different smell.

At night, when all the colours die,
they hide in pairs   *32*

and read about themselves—
in colour, with their eyelids shut.

[1979]

Joy Harjo (American; b. 1951)

Vision

The rainbow touched down
"somewhere in the Rio Grande,"
we said. And saw the light of it
from your mother's house in Isleta.*

****Isleta**   a pueblo in New Mexico

How it curved down between earth   5
and the deepest sky to give us horses
or color
          horses that were within us all of this time
but we didn't see them because
we wait for the easiest vision   10
                    to save us.

In Isleta the rainbow was a crack
In the universe. We saw the barest
of all life that is possible.
Bright horses rolled over   15
and over the dusking sky.
I heard the thunder of their beating
hearts. Their lungs hit air
and sang. All the colors of horses
formed the rainbow,   20
                    and formed us
watching them.

                                        [1983]

Rita Dove (American; b. 1952)

The Fish in the Stone

The fish in the stone
would like to fall
back into the sea.

He is weary   4
of analysis, the small
predictable truths.

He is weary of waiting
in the open,   8
his profile stamped
by a white light.

In the ocean the silence
moves and moves   12

and so much is unnecessary!
Patient, he drifts

until the moment comes
to cast his
skeletal blossom. 16

The fish in the stone
knows to fail is
to do the living 20
a favor.

He knows why the ant
engineers a gangster's
funeral, garish 24
and perfectly amber.
He knows why the scientist
in secret delight
strokes the fern's 28
voluptuous braille.

[1963]

Daystar

She wanted a little room for thinking:
but she saw diapers steaming on the line.
a doll slumped behind the door.
So she lugged a chair behind the garage
to sit out the children's naps. 5

Sometimes there were things to watch—
the pinched armor of a vanished cricket,
a floating maple leaf. Other days
she stared until she was assured
when she closed her eyes 10
she'd see only her own vivid blood.

She had an hour, at best, before Liza appeared
pouting from the top of the stairs.
And just *what* was mother doing
out back with the field mice? Why, 15

building a palace. Later
that night when Thomas rolled over and
lurched into her, she would open her eyes
and think of the place that was hers

for an hour—where   20
she was nothing,
pure nothing, in the middle of the day.

[1986]

Judith Ortiz Cofer (American; b. 1952)

My Father in the Navy:
A Childhood Memory

Stiff and immaculate
in the white cloth of his uniform
and a round cap on his head like a halo,
he was an apparition on leave from a shadow-world
and only flesh and blood when he rose from below   5
the waterline where he kept watch over the engines
and dials making sure the ship parted the waters
on a straight course.
Mother, brother and I kept vigil
on the nights and dawns of his arrivals,   10
watching the corner beyond the neon sign of a quasar
for the flash of white our father like an angel
heralding a new day.
His homecomings were the verses   15
we composed over the years making up
the siren's song that kept his coming back
from the bellies of iron whales
and into our nights
like the evening prayer.

[1987]

David Mura (American; b. 1952)

An Argument: On 1942

For my mother

Near Rose's Chop Suey and Jinosuke's grocery,
the temple where incense hovered and inspired

dense evening chants (prayers for Buddha's mercy,
colorless and deep), that day he was fired . . .   *4*

—No, no, no, she tells me. Why bring it back?
The camps are over. (Also overly dramatic.)
Forget *shoyu*[1]-stained *furoshiki,*[2] *mochi*[3] on a stick:
You're like a terrier, David, gnawing a bone, an old, old trick . . .   *8*

Mostly we were bored. Women cooked and sewed,
men played blackjack, dug gardens, a *benjo.*[4]
Who noticed barbed wire, guards in the towers?
We were children, hunting stones, birds, wild flowers.   *12*

Yes, Mother hid tins of *utskemono*[5] and eel
beneath the bed. And when the last was peeled,
clamped tight her lips, growing thinner and thinner.
But cancer not the camps made her throat blacker   *16*

. . . And she didn't die then . . . after the war, in St. Paul,
you weren't even born. Oh I know, I know, it's all
part of your job, your way, but why can't you glean
how far we've come, how much I can't recall—   *20*

David, it was so long ago—how useless it seems . . .

                                                                [1989]

[1] *shoyu* soy sauce;
[2] *furoshiki* a scarf that is used to carry things;
[3] *mochi* rice cakes
[4] *benjo* toilet
[5] *utskemono* Japanese pickles [Author's notes]

DRAMA

20
Some Elements of Drama

THINKING ABOUT THE LANGUAGE OF DRAMA

The earlier parts of this book have dealt with fiction and poetry. A third chief literary type is drama, texts written to be performed.

A play is written to be seen and to be heard. We go to *see* a play in a theater (*theater* is derived from a Greek word meaning "to watch"), but in the theater we *hear* it because we become an audience (*audience* is derived from a Latin word meaning "to hear.") Hamlet was speaking the ordinary language of his day when he said, "We'll hear a play tomorrow." When we read a play rather than see and hear it in a theater, we lose a good deal. We must try to see it in the mind's eye and hear it in the mind's ear.

In reading a play it's not enough mentally to hear the lines. We must try to see the characters, costumed and moving within a specified setting, and we must try to hear not only their words but their tone, their joy or hypocrisy or tentativeness or aggression, or whatever. Our job is much easier, of course, when we are in the theater and we have only to pay attention to the performers; as readers on our own, however, we must do what we can to perform the play in the theater under our hats.

If as a reader you develop the following principles into habits, you will get far more out of a play than if you read it as though it were a novel consisting only of dialogue.

1. *Pay attention to the* **list of characters** *and carefully read whatever* **descriptions** *the playwright has provided.* Early dramatists, such as Shakespeare, did not provide much in the way of description ("Othello, the Moor"

or "Iago, a villain" is about as much as we find in Elizabethan texts), but later playwrights often are very forthcoming. Here, for instance, is Tennessee Williams introducing us to Amanda Wingfield in *The Glass Menagerie.* (We give only the beginning of his longish description.)

> *Amanda Wingfield,* the mother. A little woman of great but confused vitality clinging frantically to another time and place.

And here is Susan Glaspell introducing us to all the characters in her one-act play, *Trifles:*

> . . . the Sheriff comes in followed by the County Attorney and Hale. The Sheriff and Hale are men in middle life, the County Attorney is a young man; all are much bundled up and go at once to the stove. They are followed by the two women—the Sheriff's wife, [Mrs. Peters] first; she is a slight wiry woman, a thin nervous face. Mrs. Hale is larger and would ordinarily be called more comfortable looking, but she is disturbed now and looks fearfully about as she enters. The women have come in slowly and stand close together near the door.

Glaspell's description of her characters is not nearly so explicit as Tennessee Williams's, but Glaspell does tell a reader a good deal. What do we know about the men? They differ in age, they are bundled up, and they "go at once to the stove." What do we know about the women? Mrs. Peters is slight, and she has a "nervous face"; Mrs. Hale is "larger" but she too is "disturbed." The women enter "slowly," and they "stand close together near the door." In short, the men, who take over the warmest part of the room, are more confident than the women, who nervously huddle together near the door. It's a man's world.

2. *Pay attention to* **gestures** *and* **costumes** *that are specified in stage directions or are implied by the dialogue.* We have just seen how Glaspell distinguishes between the men and the women by what they do—the men take over the warm part of the room, the women stand insecurely near the door. Most dramatists from the late nineteenth century to the present have been fairly generous with their stage directions, but when we read the works of earlier dramatists we often have to deduce the gestures from the speeches. For instance, although Shakespeare has an occasional direction such as "Othello kneels," he is very sparing. Consider this speech, spoken just before Othello solemnly vows to his companion, Iago, that he will be revenged on the man who (he mistakenly thinks) has slept with his wife:

> Look here, Iago,
> All my fond love thus do I blow to heaven.
> 'Tis gone.

We have no evidence of exactly what Othello does when he speaks these lines, but perhaps he touches his heart at "All my fond love," then extends his hand, palm upward, as though his "love" rested on the palm, then raises his hand toward his mouth and exhales upon the palm, seemingly blowing away whatever is on the palm. Probably he looks upward at "to heaven," and then perhaps at his still-extended palm when he says "'Tis gone."

In addition to thinking about gestures, don't forget the costumes that the characters wear. Costumes, of course, identify the characters as soldiers or farmers or whatever, and changes of costume can be especially symbolic. When we first meet Macbeth, for instance, he is dressed as a soldier. Later he wears the robes of a king, but at the end of the play, concluding a reign of terror, he appears again as a warrior. Presumably the sight of an armed Macbeth reminds the audience of the heroic soldier of the play's beginning.

3. *Keep in mind the **kind of theater** for which the play was written.* The plays in this book were written for various kinds of theaters. Sophocles, author of *Antigone* and *King Oedipus,* wrote for the ancient Greek theater, essentially a space where performers acted in front of an audience seated on a hillside. (See the illustration on page 777.) This theater was open to the heavens, with a structure representing a palace or temple behind the actors, in itself a kind of image of a society governed by the laws of the state and the laws of the gods. Moreover, the chorus enters the playing space by marching down the side aisles, close to the audience, thus helping to unite the world of the audience and of the players. On the other hand, the audience in most modern theaters sits in a darkened area and looks through a proscenium arch at performers who move in a boxlike setting. The box set of the late nineteenth century and the twentieth century is, it often seems, an appropriate image of the confined lives of the unheroic characters of the play.

4. *If the playwright describes a set, try to **envision the set** clearly.* Glaspell, for instance, tells us a good deal about the set. We quote only the first part.

> The kitchen in the now abandoned farmhouse of John Wright, a gloomy kitchen, and left without having been put in order. . . .

These details about a gloomy and disordered kitchen may seem to be mere realism—after all, the play has to take place *somewhere*—but it turns out that the disorder and, for that matter, the gloominess are extremely important. You'll have to read the play to find out why.

Another example of a setting that provides important information is Miller's in *Death of a Salesman.* Again we quote only the beginning of the description.

Before us is the Salesman's house. We are aware of towering, angular shapes behind it, surrounding it on all sides. Only the blue
light of the sky falls upon the house and forestage; the surrounding area shows an angry glow of orange.

If we read older drama, we find that playwrights do *not* give
us much help, but by paying attention to the words we can at least
to some degree visualize the locale. For instance, in the first scene
of *Othello* we learn from the dialogue that it is night and that two
people, raising a rumpus in the street, awaken someone who appears "above," i.e., at an upper-storey window. Or, to take another
example from the same play, when Othello finally learns of the
innocence of the wife whom a few minutes earlier he strangled in
their bed, he commits suicide by stabbing himself. As he dies he
says,

I kissed thee ere I killed thee. No way but this,
Killing myself, to die upon a kiss.

Surely we must see him kiss his wife, and die on the bed on which
she lies—the bed that he thought she had defiled.

5. *Pay attention to whatever* **sound effects** *are specified in the play.* The villain's lewd shouting in the first scene of *Othello* introduces a note
of chaos, and later he contrives a fight so that an alarm bell will be
sounded (when Othello arrives on the scene he gives an order: "Silence that dreadful bell"). These loud disturbances are appropriate,
even, we might say, symbolic, in a play in which the tragic hero says,
"And when I love thee not, / Chaos is come again."

In *Death of a Salesman,* before the curtain goes up, "A melody
is heard, played upon a flute. It is small and fine, telling of grass and
trees and the horizon." Then the curtain rises, revealing the Salesman's house, with "towering, angular shapes behind it, surrounding
it on all sides." Obviously the sound of the flute is meant to tell us
of the world that the Salesman is shut off from.

A sound effect, however, need not be so evidently symbolic
to be important in a play. In Glaspell's *Trifles,* for instance, almost
at the very end of the play we hear the "sound of a knob turning
in the other room." The sound has an electrifying effect on the audience, as it does on the two women on the stage, and it precedes
a decisive action.

6. *Pay attention, at least on second reading, to* **silences,** *including* **pauses within speeches** *or between speeches.* In *Othello,* for instance, old Brabantio, a senator in Venice, says to Iago, "Thou art a villian," and Iago
replies

You are—a senator.

Probably the dash indicates a significant pause, a change from something like "You are a fool," which is what Iago wants to say, to an acceptable polite response.

In *Trifles,* late in the play a stage direction tells us that "The women's eyes meet for an instant." We won't say what this exchange of looks indicates, but when you read the play you will see that the moment of silence is significant.

7. *Of course you will pay attention to what the characters say, and you will keep in mind that (like real people) dramatic characters are not always to be trusted.* An obvious case is Shakespeare's Iago, an utterly unscrupulous villain who knows that he is a liar, but a character may be self-deceived, or, to put it a bit differently, characters may say what they honestly thinks but may not know what they are talking about.

PLOT AND CHARACTER

Although **plot** is sometimes equated with the gist of the narrative—the story—it is sometimes reserved to denote the writer's *arrangement* of the happenings in the story. Thus, all plays about the assassination of Julius Caesar have pretty much the same story, but by beginning with a scene of workmen enjoying a holiday (and thereby introducing the motif of the fickleness of the mob), Shakespeare's play has a plot different from a play that omits such a scene.

Handbooks on the drama often suggest that a plot (arrangement of happenings) should have a **rising action,** a **climax,** and a **falling action.** This sort of plot can be diagrammed as a pyramid, the tension rising through complications, or **crises,** to a climax, at which point the fate of the **protagonist** (chief character) is firmly established; the climax is the apex, and the tension allegedly slackens as we witness the **dénouement** (unknotting). Shakespeare sometimes used a pyramidal structure, placing his climax neatly in the middle of what seems to us to be the third of five acts.*

---

*An **act** is a main division in a drama or opera. Act divisions probably stem from Roman theory and derive ultimately from the Greek practice of separating episodes in a play by choral interludes, but Greek (and probably Roman) plays were performed without interruption, for the choral interludes were part of the plays themselves. Elizabethan plays, too, may have been performed without breaks; the division of Elizabethan plays into five acts is usually the work of editors rather than of authors. Frequently an act division today (commonly indicated by lowering the curtain and turning up the houselights) denotes change in locale and lapse of time. A **scene** is a smaller unit, either (1) a division with no change of locale or abrupt shift of time, or (2) a division consisting of an actor or group of actors on the stage; according to the second definition, the departure or entrance of an actor changes the composition of the group and thus introduces a new scene. (In an entirely different sense, the scene is the locale where a work is set.)

Roughly the first half of *Julius Caesar* shows Brutus rising, reaching his height in 3.1 with the death of Caesar; but later in this scene he gives Marc Antony permission to speak at Caesar's funeral and thus he sets in motion his own fall, which occupies the second half of the play. In *Macbeth,* the protagonist attains his height in 3.1 ("Thou hast is now: King"), but he soon perceives that he is going downhill:

> I am in blood
> Stepped in so far, that, should I wade no more,
> Returning were as tedious as go o'er.

Of course, no law demands such a structure, and a hunt for the pyramid usually causes the hunter to overlook all the crises but the middle one. William Butler Yeats once suggestively diagramed a good plot not as a pyramid but as a line moving diagonally upward, punctuated by several crises. Perhaps it is sufficient to say that a good plot has its moments of tension, but the location of these will vary with the play. They are the product of **conflict,** but not all conflict produces tension; there is conflict but little tension in a ball game when the score is 10–0 in the ninth inning with two out and none on base.

Regardless of how a plot is diagramed, the **exposition** is that part that tells the audience what it has to know about the past, the **antecedent action.** When two gossiping servants tell each other that after a year away in Paris the young master is coming home tomorrow with a new wife, they are giving the audience the exposition by introducing characters and establishing relationships. The Elizabethans and the Greeks sometimes tossed out all pretense at dialogue and began with a **prologue,** like the one spoken by the Chorus at the outset of *Romeo and Juliet:*

> Two households, both alike in dignity
> In fair Verona, where we lay our scene,
> From ancient grudge break to new mutiny,
> Where civil blood makes civil hands unclean.
> From forth the fatal loins of these two foes
> A pair of star-crossed lovers take their life. . . .

And in Tennessee Williams's *The Glass Menagerie,* Tom's first speech is a sort of prologue. However, the exposition also may extend far into the play, so that the audience keeps getting bits of information that both clarify the present and build suspense about the future. Occasionally the **soliloquy** (speech of a character alone on the stage, revealing his thoughts) or the **aside** (speech in the presence of others but unheard by them) is used to do the job of putting the audience in possession of the essential facts. The soliloquy and the aside, of course, are not limited to esposition; they are used to reveal the private thoughts of characters who, like people in real life, do not always tell others what their inner thoughts are. The soliloquy is especially used for meditation, where we might say the character is interacting not with another character but with himself or herself.

Because a play is not simply words but words spoken with accompanying gestures by performers who are usually costumed and in a particular setting, it may be argued that to read a play (rather than to see and hear it) is to falsify it. Drama is not literature, some people hold, but theater. However, there are replies: a play can be literature as well as theater, and readers of a play can perhaps enact in the theater of their mind a more effective play than the one put on by imperfect actors. After all, as Shakespeare's Duke Theseus, in *A Midsummer Night's Dream,* says of actors, "The best in this kind are but shadows." In any case, we need not wait for actors to present a play; we can do a good deal on our own.

Susan Glaspell (American; 1882–1948)

Trifles

Scene: *The kitchen in the now abandoned farmhouse of John Wright, a gloomy kitchen, and left without having been put in order—unwashed pans under the sink, a loaf of bread outside the breadbox, a dish towel on the table—other signs of incompleted work. At the rear the outer door opens, and the Sheriff comes in, followed by the County Attorney and Hale. The Sheriff and Hale are men in middle life, the County Attorney is a young man; all are much bundled up and go at once to the stove. They are followed by the two women—the Sheriff's Wife first; she is a slight wiry woman, a thin nervous face. Mrs. Hale is larger and would ordinarily be called more comfortable looking, but she is disturbed now and looks fearfully about as she enters. The women have come in slowly and stand close together near the door.*

COUNTY ATTORNEY (*rubbing his hands*). This feels good. Come up to the fire, ladies.

MRS. PETERS (*after taking a step forward*). I'm not—cold.

SHERIFF (*unbuttoning his overcoat and stepping away from the stove as if to the beginning of official business*). Now, Mr. Hale, before we move things about, you explain to Mr. Henderson just what you saw when you came here yesterday morning.

COUNTY ATTORNEY. By the way, has anything been moved? Are things just as you left them yesterday?

SHERIFF (*looking about*). It's just the same. When it dropped below zero last night, I thought I'd better send Frank out this morning to make a fire for us—no use getting pneumonia with a big case on; but I told him not to touch anything except the stove—and you know Frank.

COUNTY ATTORNEY. Somebody should have been left here yesterday.

Marjorie Vonnegut, Elinor M. Cox, John King, Arthur F. Hole, and T. W. Gibson in a scene from Trifles, *as published in* Theatre Magazine, *January 1917. (Photograph courtesy of the New York Public Library Billy Rose Theatre Collection)*

SHERIFF. Oh—yesterday. When I had to send Frank to Morris Center for that man who went crazy—I want you to know I had my hands full yesterday. I knew you could get back from Omaha by today, and as long as I went over everything here myself—

COUNTY ATTORNEY. Well, Mr. Hale, tell just what happened when you came here yesterday morning.

HALE. Harry and I had started to town with a load of potatoes. We came along the road from my place; and as I got here, I said, "I'm going to see if I can't get John Wright to go in with me on a party telephone." I spoke to Wright about it once before, and he put me off, saying folks talked too much anyway, and all he asked was peace and quiet—I guess you know about how much he talked himself; but I thought maybe if I went to the house and talked about it before his wife, though I said to Harry that I didn't know as what his wife wanted made much difference to John—

COUNTY ATTORNEY. Let's talk about that later, Mr. Hale. I do want to talk about that, but tell now just what happened when you got to the house.

HALE. I didn't hear or see anything; I knocked at the door, and still it was all quiet inside. I knew they must be up, it was past eight o'clock. So I knocked again, and I thought I heard somebody say, "Come in." I wasn't sure, I'm not sure yet, but I opened the door—this door (*indicating the door by which the two women are still standing*), and there in that rocker—(*pointing to it*) sat Mrs. Wright. (*They all look at the rocker.*)

COUNTY ATTORNEY. What—was she doing?

HALE. She was rockin' back and forth. She had her apron in her hand and was kind of—pleating it.

COUNTY ATTORNEY. And how did she—look?

HALE. Well, she looked queer.

COUNTY ATTORNEY. How do you mean—queer?

HALE. Well, as if she didn't know what she was going to do next. And kind of done up.

COUNTY ATTORNEY. How did she seem to feel about your coming?

HALE. Why, I don't think she minded—one way or other. She didn't pay much attention. I said, "How do, Mrs. Wright, it's cold, ain't it?" And she said, "Is it?"—and went on kind of pleating at her apron. Well, I was surprised; she didn't ask me to come up to the stove, or to set down, but just sat there, not even looking at me, so I said, "I want to see John." And then she—laughed. I guess you would call it a laugh. I thought of Harry and the team outside, so I said a little sharp: "Can't I see John?" "No," she says, kind o' dull like. "Ain't he home?" says I. "Yes," says she, "he's home." "Then why can't I see him?" I asked her, out of patience. "'Cause he's dead," says she. "*Dead?*" says I. She just nodded her head, not getting a bit excited, but rockin' back and forth. "Why—where is he?" says I, not knowing what to say. She just pointed upstairs—like that (*himself pointing to the room above*). I got up, with the idea of going up there. I walked from there to here—then I says, "Why, what did he die of?" "He died of a rope around his neck," says she, and just went on pleatin' at her apron. Well, I went out and called Harry. I thought I might—need help. We went upstairs, and there he was lyin' —

COUNTY ATTORNEY. I think I'd rather have you go into that upstairs, where you can point it all out. Just go on now with the rest of the story.

HALE. Well, my first thought was to get that rope off. I looked . . . (*Stops, his face twitches.*) . . . but Harry, he went up to him, and he said, "No, he's dead all right, and we'd better not touch anything." So we went back downstairs. She was still sitting that same way. "Has anybody been notified?" I asked. "No," says she, unconcerned. "Who did this, Mrs. Wright?" said Harry. He said it businesslike—and she stopped pleatin' of her apron. "I don't know," she says. "You don't *know?*" says Harry. "No," says she, "Weren't you sleepin' in the bed with him?" says Harry. "Yes," says she, "but I was on the inside." "Somebody slipped a rope round his neck and strangled him, and you didn't wake up?" says Harry. "I didn't wake up," she said after him. We must 'a looked as if we didn't see how that could be, for after a minute she said, "I sleep sound." Harry was going to ask her more questions, but I said maybe we ought to let her tell her story first to the coroner, or the sheriff, so Harry went fast as he could to Rivers' place, where there's a telephone.

COUNTY ATTORNEY. And what did Mrs. Wright do when she knew that you had gone for the coroner?

HALE. She moved from that chair to this over here . . . (*Pointing to a small chair in the corner.*) . . . and just sat there with her hands held together and looking down. I got a feeling that I ought to make some conversation, so I said I had come in to see if John wanted to put in a telephone, and at that she started to laugh, and then she stopped and looked at me—scared. (*The County Attorney, who has had his notebook out, makes a note.*) I dunno, maybe it wasn't scared. I wouldn't like to say it was. Soon Harry got back, and then Dr. Lloyd came, and you, Mr. Peters, and so I guess that's all I know that you don't.

COUNTY ATTORNEY (*looking around*). I guess we'll go upstairs first—and then out to the barn and around there. (*To the Sheriff.*) You're convinced that there was nothing important here—nothing that would point to any motive?

SHERIFF. Nothing here but kitchen things.

(*The County Attorney, after again looking around the kitchen, opens the door of a cupboard closet. He gets up on a chair and looks on a shelf. Pulls his hand away, sticky.*)

COUNTY ATTORNEY. Here's a nice mess.

(*The women draw nearer.*)

MRS. PETERS (*to the other woman*). Oh, her fruit; it did freeze. (*To the Lawyer.*) She worried about that when it turned so cold. She said the fir'd go out and her jars would break.

SHERIFF. Well, can you beat the women! Held for murder and worryin' about her preserves.

COUNTY ATTORNEY. I guess before we're through she may have something more serious than preserves to worry about.

HALE. Well, women are used to worrying over trifles.

(*The two women move a little closer together.*)

COUNTY ATTORNEY (*with the gallantry of a young politician*). And yet, for all their worries, what would we do without the ladies? (*The women do not unbend. He goes to the sink, takes a dipperful of water from the pail and, pouring it into a basin, washes his hands. Starts to wipe them on the roller towel, turns it for a cleaner place.*) Dirty towels! (*Kicks his foot against the pans under the sink.*) Not much of a housekeeper, would you say, ladies?

MRS. HALE (*stiffly*). There's a great deal of work to be done on a farm.

COUNTY ATTORNEY. To be sure. And yet . . . (*With a little bow to her.*) . . . I know there are some Dickson county farmhouses which do not have such roller towels. (*He gives it a pull to expose its full length again.*)

MRS. HALE. Those towels get dirty awful quick. Men's hands aren't always as clean as they might be.

COUNTY ATTORNEY. Ah, loyal to your sex, I see. But you and Mrs. Wright were neighbors. I suppose you were friends, too.

MRS. HALE (*shaking her head*). I've not seen much of her of late years. I've not been in this house—it's more than a year.

COUNTY ATTORNEY. And why was that? You didn't like her?

MRS. HALE. I liked her all well enough. Farmers' wives have their hands full, Mr. Henderson. And then—

COUNTY ATTORNEY. Yes—?

MRS. HALE (*looking about*). It never seemed a very cheerful place.

COUNTY ATTORNEY. No—it's not cheerful. I shouldn't say she had the homemaking instinct.

MRS. HALE. Well, I don't know as Wright had, either.

COUNTY ATTORNEY. You mean that they didn't get on very well?

MRS. HALE. No, I don't mean anything. But I don't think a place'd be any cheerfuler for John Wright's being in it.

COUNTY ATTORNEY. I'd like to talk more of that a little later. I want to get the lay of things upstairs now. (*He goes to the left, where three steps lead to a stair door.*)

SHERIFF. I suppose anything Mrs. Peters does'll be all right. She was to take in some clothes for her, you know, and a few little things. We left in such a hurry yesterday.

COUNTY ATTORNEY. Yes, but I would like to see what you take, Mrs. Peters, and keep an eye out for anything that might be of use to us.

MRS. PETERS. Yes, Mr. Henderson.

(*The women listen to the men's steps on the stairs, then look about the kitchen.*)

MRS. HALE. I'd hate to have men coming into my kitchen, snooping around and criticizing. (*She arranges the pans under sink which the Lawyer had shoved out of place.*)

MRS. PETERS. Of course it's no more than their duty.

MRS. HALE. Duty's all right, but I guess that deputy sheriff that came out to make the fire might have got a little of this on. (*Gives the roller towel a pull.*) Wish I'd thought of that sooner. Seems mean to talk about her for not having things slicked up when she had to come away in such a hurry.

MRS. PETERS (*who has gone to a small table in the left rear corner of the room, and lifted one end of a towel that covers a pan*). She had bread set. (*Stands still.*)

MRS. HALE (*eyes fixed on a loaf of bread beside the breadbox, which is on a low shelf at the other side of the room. Moves slowly toward it*). She was going to put this in there. (*Picks up loaf, then abruptly drops it. In a manner of returning to familiar things.*) It's a shame about her fruit. I wonder if it's all gone. (*Gets up on the chair and looks.*) I think there's some here that's all right, Mrs. Peters. Yes—here; (*Holding it toward the window.*) this is cherries, too. (*Looking again.*) I declare I believe that's the only one. (*Gets down, bottle in her hand. Goes to the sink and wipes it off on the outside.*) She'll feel awful bad after all her hard work in the hot weather. I remember the afternoon I put up my cherries last summer. (*She puts the bottle on the big kitchen table, center of the room, front table. With a sigh, is about to sit down in the rocking chair. Before she is seated realizes what chair it is; with a slow look at it, steps back. The chair, which she has touched, rocks back and forth.*)

MRS. PETERS. Well, I must get those things from the front room closet. (*She goes to the door at the right, but after looking into the other room steps back.*) You coming with me, Mrs. Hale? You could help me carry them. (*They go into the other room; reappear, Mrs. Peters carrying a dress and skirt, Mrs. Hale following with a pair of shoes.*)

MRS. PETERS. My, it's cold in there. (*She puts the cloth on the big table, and hurries to the stove.*)

MRS. HALE (*examining the skirt*). Wright was close. I think maybe that's why she kept so much to herself. She didn't even belong to the Ladies' Aid. I suppose she felt she couldn't do her part, and then you don't enjoy things when you feel shabby. She used to wear pretty clothes and be lively, when she was Minnie Foster, one of the town girls singing in the choir. But that—oh, that was thirty years ago. This all you was to take in?

MRS. PETERS. She said she wanted an apron. Funny thing to want, for there isn't much to get you dirty in jail, goodness knows. But I suppose just to make her feel more natural. She said they was in the top drawer in this cupboard. Yes, here. And then her little shawl that always hung behind the door. (*Opens stair door and looks.*) Yes, here it is. (*Quickly shuts door leading upstairs.*)

MRS. HALE (*abruptly moving toward her*). Mrs. Peters?

MRS. PETERS. Yes, Mrs. Hale?

MRS. HALE. Do you think she did it?

MRS. PETERS (*in a frightened voice*). Oh, I don't know.

MRS. HALE. Well, I don't think she did. Asking for an apron and her little shawl. Worrying about her fruit.

MRS. PETERS (*starts to speak, glances up, where footsteps are heard in the room above. In a low voice*). Mr. Peters says it looks bad for her. Mr. Henderson is awful sarcastic in speech, and he'll make fun of her sayin' she didn't wake up.

MRS. HALE. Well, I guess John Wright didn't wake when they was slipping that rope under his neck.

MRS. PETERS. No, it's strange. It must have been done awful crafty and still. They say it was such a—funny way to kill a man, rigging it all up like that.

MRS. HALE. That's just what Mr. Hale said. There was a gun in the house. He says that's what he can't understand.

MRS. PETERS. Mr. Henderson said coming out that what was needed for the case was a motive; something to show anger, or—sudden feeling.

MRS. HALE (*who is standing by the table*). Well, I don't see any signs of anger around here. (*She puts her hand on the dish towel which lies on the table, stands looking down at the table, one half of which is clean, the other half messy.*) It's wiped here. (*Makes a move as if to finish work, then turns and looks at loaf of bread outside the breadbox. Drops towel. In that voice of coming back to familiar things.*) Wonder how they are finding things upstairs? I hope she had it a little more red-up there. You know, it seems kind of *sneaking*. Locking her up in town and then coming out here and trying to get her own house to turn against her!

MRS. PETERS. But, Mrs. Hale, the law is the law.

MRS. HALE. I s'pose 'tis. (*Unbuttoning her coat.*) Better loosen up your things, Mrs. Peters. You won't feel them when you go out.

(*Mrs. Peters takes off her fur tippet, goes to hang it on hook at the back of room, stands looking at the under part of the small corner table.*)

MRS. PETERS. She was piecing a quilt. (*She brings the large sewing basket, and they look at the bright pieces.*)

MRS. HALE. It's log cabin pattern. Pretty, isn't it? I wonder if she was goin' to quilt or just knot it?

(*Footsteps have been heard coming down the stairs. The Sheriff enters, followed by Hale and the County Attorney.*)

SHERIFF. They wonder if she was going to quilt it or just knot it. (*The men laugh, the women look abashed.*)

COUNTY ATTORNEY (*rubbing his hands over the stove*). Frank's fire didn't do much up there, did it? Well, let's go out to the barn and get that cleared up. (*The men go outside.*)

MRS. HALE (*resentfully*). I don't know as there's anything so strange, our takin' up our time with little things while we're waiting for them to get the evidence. (*She sits down at the big table, smoothing out a block with decision.*) I don't see as it's anything to laugh about.

MRS. PETERS (*apologetically*). Of course they've got awful important things on their minds. (*Pulls up a chair and joins Mrs. Hale at the table.*)

MRS. HALE (*examining another block*). Mrs. Peters, look at this one. Here, this is the one she was working on, and look at the sewing! All the rest of it has been so nice and even. And look at this! It's all over the place! Why, it looks as if she didn't know what she was about! (*After she has said this, they look at each other, then started to glance back at the door. After an instant Mrs. Hale has pulled at a knot and ripped the sewing.*)

MRS. PETERS. Oh, what are you doing, Mrs. Hale?

MRS. HALE (*mildly*). Just pulling out a stitch or two that's not sewed very good. (*Threading a needle.*) Bad sewing always made me fidgety.

MRS. PETERS (*nervously*). I don't think we ought to touch things.

MRS. HALE. I'll just finish up this end. (*Suddenly stopping and leaning forward.*) Mrs. Peters?

MRS. PETERS. Yes, Mrs. Hale?

MRS. HALE. What do you suppose she was so nervous about?

MRS. PETERS. Oh—I don't know. I don't know as she was nervous. I sometimes sew awful queer when I'm just tired. (*Mrs. Hale starts to say something, looks at Mrs. Peters, then goes on sewing.*) Well, I must get these things wrapped up. They may be through sooner than we think. (*Putting apron and other things together.*) I wonder where I can find a piece of paper, and string.

MRS. HALE. In that cupboard, maybe.

MRS. PETERS (*looking in cupboard*). Why, here's a birdcage. (*Holds it up.*) Did she have a bird, Mrs. Hale?

MRS. HALE. Why, I don't know whether she did or not—I've not been here for so long. There was a man around last year selling canaries cheap, but I don't know as she took one; maybe she did. She used to sing real pretty herself.

MRS. PETERS (*glancing around*). Seems funny to think of a bird here. But she must have had one, or why should she have a cage? I wonder what happened to it?

MRS. HALE. I s'pose maybe the cat got it.

MRS. PETERS. No, she didn't have a cat. She's got that feeling some people have about cats—being afraid of them. My cat got in her room, and she was real upset and asked me to take it out.

MRS. HALE. My sister Bessie was like that. Queer, ain't it?

MRS. PETERS (*examining the cage*). Why, look at this door. It's broke. One hinge is pulled apart.

MRS. HALE (*looking, too*). Looks as if someone must have been rough with it.

MRS. PETERS. Why, yes. (*She brings the cage forward and puts it on the table.*)

MRS. HALE. I wish if they're going to find any evidence they'd be about it. I don't like this place.

MRS. PETERS. But I'm awful glad you came with me, Mrs. Hale. It would be lonesome for me sitting here alone.

MRS. HALE. It would, wouldn't it? (*Dropping her sewing.*) But I tell you what I do wish, Mrs. Peters. I wish I had come over sometimes when *she* was here. I — (*Looking around the room.*) — wish I had.

MRS. PETERS. But of course you were awful busy, Mrs. Hale — your house and your children.

MRS. HALE. I could've come. I stayed away because it weren't cheerful — and that's why I ought to have come. I — I've never liked this place. Maybe because it's down in a hollow, and you don't see the road. I dunno what it is, but it's a lonesome place and always was. I wish I had come over to see Minnie Foster sometimes. I can see now — (*Shakes her head.*)

MRS. PETERS. Well, you mustn't reproach yourself, Mrs. Hale. Somehow we just don't see how it is with other folks until — something comes up.

MRS. HALE. Not having children makes less work — but it makes a quiet house, and Wright out to work all day, and no company when he did come in. Did you know John Wright, Mrs. Peters?

MRS. PETERS. Not to know him; I've seen him in town. They say he was a good man.

MRS. HALE. Yes — good; he didn't drink, and kept his word as well as most, I guess, and paid his debts. But he was a hard man, Mrs. Peters. Just to pass the time of day with him. (*Shivers.*) Like a raw wind that gets to the bone. (*Pauses, her eye falling on the cage.*) I should think she would 'a wanted a bird. But what do you suppose went with it?

MRS. PETERS. I don't know, unless it got sick and died. (*She reaches over and swings the broken door, swings it again; both women watch it.*)

MRS. HALE. You weren't raised round here, were you? (*Mrs. Peters shakes her head.*) You didn't know — her?

MRS. PETERS. Not till they brought her yesterday.

MRS. HALE. She — come to think of it, she was kind of like a bird herself — real sweet and pretty, but kind of timid and — fluttery. How — she — did — change. (*Silence; then as if struck by a happy thought and relieved to get back to everyday things.*) Tell you what, Mrs. Peters, why don't you take the quilt in with you? It might take up her mind.

MRS. PETERS. Why, I think that's a real nice idea, Mrs. Hale. There couldn't possible be any objection to it, could there? Now, just what would I take? I wonder if her patches are in here — and her things. (*They look in the sewing basket.*)

MRS. HALE. Here's some red. I expect this has got sewing things in it (*Brings out a fancy box.*) What a pretty box. Looks like something somebody would give you. Maybe her scissors are in here. (*Opens box. Suddenly puts her hand to her nose.*) Why — (*Mrs. Peters bends nearer, then turns her face away.*) There's something wrapped up in this piece of silk.

MRS. PETERS. Why, this isn't her scissors.

MRS. HALE (*lifting the silk*). Oh, Mrs. Peters—it's—(*Mrs. Peters bends closer.*)

MRS. PETERS. It's the bird.

MRS. HALE (*jumping up.*) But, Mrs. Peters—look at it. Its neck! Look at its neck! It's all—other side *to*.

MRS. PETERS. Somebody—wrung—its neck.

(*Their eyes meet. A look of growing comprehension of horror. Steps are heard outside. Mrs. Hale slips box under quilt pieces, and sinks into her chair. Enter Sheriff and County Attorney. Mrs. Peters rises.*)

COUNTY ATTORNEY (*as one turning from serious things to little pleasantries*). Well, ladies, have you decided whether she was going to quilt it or knot it?

MRS. PETERS. We think she was going to—knot it.

COUNTY ATTORNEY. Well, that's interesting, I'm sure. (*Seeing the birdcage.*) Has the bird flown?

MRS. HALE (*putting more quilt pieces over the box*). We think the—cat got it.

COUNTY ATTORNEY (*preoccupied*). Is there a cat?

(*Mrs. Hale glances in a quick covert way at Mrs. Peters.*)

MRS. PETERS. Well, not now. They're superstitious, you know. They leave.

COUNTY ATTORNEY (*to Sheriff Peters, continuing an interrupted conversation*). No sign at all of anyone having come from the outside. Their own rope. Now let's go up again and go over it piece by piece. (*They start upstairs.*) It would have to have been someone who knew just the—

(*Mrs. Peters sits down. The two women sit there not looking at one another, but as if peering into something and at the same time holding back. When they talk now, it is the manner of feeling their way over strange ground, as if afraid of what they are saying, but as if they cannot help saying it.*)

MRS. HALE. She liked the bird. She was going to bury it in that pretty box.

MRS. PETERS (*in a whisper*). When I was a girl—my kitten—there was a boy took a hatchet, and before my eyes—and before I could get there— (*Covers her face an instant.*) If they hadn't held me back, I would have— (*Catches herself, looks upstairs where steps are heard, falters weakly.*)—hurt him.

MRS. HALE (*with a slow look around her*). I wonder how it would seem never to have had any children around. (*Pause.*) No, Wright wouldn't like the bird—a thing that sang. She used to sing. He killed that, too.

MRS. PETERS (*moving uneasily*). We don't know who killed the bird.

MRS. HALE. I knew John Wright.

MRS. PETERS. It was an awful thing was done in this house that night, Mrs. Hale. Killing a man while he slept, slipping a rope around his neck that choked the life out of him.

MRS. HALE. His neck. Choked the life out of him.

(*Her hand goes out and rests on the birdcage.*)

MRS. PETERS (*with a rising voice*). We don't know who killed him. We don't *know*.

MRS. HALE (*her own feeling not interrupted*). If there'd been years and years of nothing, then a bird to sing to you, it would be awful—still, after the bird was still.

MRS. PETERS (*something within her speaking*). I know what stillness is. When we homesteaded in Dakota, and my first baby died—after he was two years old, and me with no other then—

MRS. HALE (*moving*). How soon do you suppose they'll be through, looking for evidence?

MRS. PETERS. I know what stillness is. (*Pulling herself back.*) The law has got to punish crime, Mrs. Hale.

MRS. HALE (*not as if answering that*). I wish you'd seen Minnie Foster when she wore a white dress with blue ribbons and stood up there in the choir and sang. (*A look around the room.*) Oh, I *wish* I'd come over here once in a while! That was a crime! That was a crime! Who's going to punish that?

MRS. PETERS (*looking upstairs*). We mustn't—take on.

MRS. HALE. I might have known she needed help! I know how things can be—for women. I tell you, it's queer, Mrs. Peters. We live close together and we live far apart. We all go through the same things—it's all just a different kind of the same thing. (*Brushes her eyes, noticing the bottle of fruit, reaches out for it.*) If I was you, I wouldn't tell her her fruit was gone. Tell her it *ain't*. Tell her it's all right. Take this in to prove it to her. She—she may never know whether it was broke or not.

MRS. PETERS (*takes the bottle, looks about for something to wrap it in; takes petticoat from the clothes brought from the other room, very nervously begins winding this around the bottle. In a false voice*). My, it's a good thing the men couldn't hear us. Wouldn't they just laugh! Getting all stirred up over a little thing like a—dead canary. As if that could have anything to do with—with—wouldn't they *laugh!*

(*The men are heard coming downstairs.*)

MRS. HALE (*under her breath*). Maybe they would—maybe they wouldn't.

COUNTY ATTORNEY. No, Peters, it's all perfectly clear except a reason for doing it. But you know juries when it comes to women. If there was some definite thing. Something to show—something to make a story about—a thing that would connect up with this strange way of doing it. (*The women's eyes meet for an instant. Enter Hale from outer door.*)

HALE. Well, I've got the team around. Pretty cold out there.

COUNTY ATTORNEY. I'm going to stay here awhile by myself. (*To the Sheriff.*) You can send Frank out for me, can't you? I want to go over everything. I'm not satisfied that we can't do better.

SHERIFF. Do you want to see what Mrs. Peters is going to take in?

(*The Lawyer goes to the table, picks up the apron, laughs.*)

COUNTY ATTORNEY. Oh I guess they're not very dangerous things the ladies have picked up. (*Moves a few things about, disturbing the quilt pieces which cover the box. Steps back.*) No, Mrs. Peters doesn't need supervising. For that matter, a sheriff's wife is married to the law. Ever think of it that way, Mrs. Peters?

MRS. PETERS. Not—just that way.

SHERIFF (*chuckling*). Married to the law. (*Moves toward the other room.*) I just
want you to come in here a minute, George. We ought to take a look
at these windows.

COUNTY ATTORNEY (*scoffingly*). Oh, windows!

SHERIFF. We'll be right out, Mr. Hale.

> (*Hale goes outside. The Sheriff follows the County Attorney into the other room.
> Then Mrs. Hale rises, hands tight together, looking intensely at Mrs. Peters, whose
> eyes take a slow turn, finally meeting Mrs. Hale's. A moment Mrs. Hale holds
> her, then her own eyes point the way to where the box is concealed. Suddenly
> Mrs. Peters throws back quilt pieces and tries to put the box in the bag she is
> wearing. It is too big. She opens box, starts to take the bird out, cannot touch
> it, goes to pieces, stands there helpless. Sound of a knob turning in the other room.
> Mrs. Hale snatches the box and puts it in the pocket of her big coat. Enter County
> Attorney and Sheriff.*)

COUNTY ATTORNEY (*facetiously*). Well, Henry, at least we found out that
she was not going to quilt it. She was going to—what is it you call
it, ladies?

MRS. HALE (*her hand against her pocket*). We call it—knot it, Mr. Henderson.

CURTAIN

[1916]

TOPICS FOR DISCUSSION AND WRITING

1. Briefly describe the setting, indicating what it "says" and what atmosphere it evokes.
2. How would you characterize Mr. Henderson, the county attorney?
3. In what way or ways are Mrs. Peters and Mrs. Hale different from
   each other?
4. Several times the men "laugh" or "chuckle." In their contexts, what
   do these expressions of amusement convey?
5. On page 647, "*the women's eyes meet for an instant.*" What do you think
   this bit of action "says"? What do you understand by the exchange
   of glances?
6. On page 646, when Mrs. Peters tells of the boy who killed her cat,
   she says, "If they hadn't held me back, I would have—(*catches herself,
   looks upstairs where steps are heard, falters weakly*)—hurt him." What
   do you think she was about to say before she faltered? Why do
   you suppose Glaspell included this speech about Mrs. Peters's
   girlhood?
7. On page 643, Mrs. Hale, looking at a quilt, wonders whether Mrs.
   Wright "was going to quilt it or just knot it." The men are amused

by the women's concern with this topic, and the last line of the play returns to the issue. What do you make of this emphasis on the matter?

8. We never see Mrs. Wright on stage. Nevertheless, by the end of *Trifles* we know a great deal about her. In an essay of 500–750 words explain both what we know about her—physical characteristics, habits, interests, personality, life before her marriage and after—and *how* we know these things.

9. The title of the play is ironic—the "trifles" are important. What other ironies do you find in the play? (On irony, see pages 652–53.)

10. Do you think the play is immoral? Explain.

11. Assume that the canary has been found, thereby revealing a possible motive, and that Minnie is indicted for murder. You are the defense attorney. In 500 words set forth your defense. (Take any position you wish. For instance, you may want to argue that she committed justifiable homicide or that—on the basis of her behavior as reported by Mr. Hale—she is innocent by reason of insanity.)

12. Assume that the canary had been found and Minnie Wright convicted. Compose the speech you think she might have delivered before the sentence was given.

21
Tragedy

Aristotle defined "tragedy" as a dramatization of a serious happening—not necessarily one ending with the death of the protagonist—and his definition remains among the best. But many plays have been written since Aristotle defined tragedy. When we think of Shakespeare's tragedies, we cannot resist narrowing Aristotle's definition by adding something like "showing a struggle that rends the protagonist's whole being"; and when we think of the "problem plays" of the last hundred years—the serious treatments of such sociological problems as alcoholism and race prejudice—we cannot resist excluding some of them by adding to the definition something about the need for universal appeal.

The question remains: Is there a single quality present in all works that we call tragedy and absent from works not called tragedy? If there is, no one has yet pointed it out to general satisfaction. But this failure does not mean that there is no such classification as "tragedy." We sense that tragedies resemble each other as members of the same family resemble each other: two children have the mother's coloring and eyes, a third child has the mother's coloring but the father's eyes, a fourth child has the mother's eyes but the father's coloring.

The next few pages will examine three comments on tragedy, none of which is entirely acceptable, but each of which seems to have some degree of truth, and each of which can help us detect resemblances and differences among tragedies. The first comment is by Cyril Tourneur, a tragic dramatist of the early seventeenth century:

> When the bad bleed, then is the tragedy good.

We think of Macbeth ("usurper," "butcher"). Macbeth, of course, is much more than a usurper and butcher, but it is undeniable that he is an offender against the moral order. Whatever the merits of Tourneur's statement, however, if we think of *Romeo and Juliet* (to consider only one play), we realize its inadequacy. Tourneur so stresses the guilt of the protagonist that his or her suffering becomes mere retributive justice. But we cannot plausibly say, for example, that Romeo and Juliet deserved to die because they married without their parents' consent; it is much too simple to call them "bad." Romeo and Juliet are young, in love, nobler in spirit than their parents.

Tourneur's view is probably derived ultimately from an influential passage in Aristotle's *Poetics* in which Aristotle speaks of **hamartia,** sometimes literally translated as "missing the target," sometimes as "vice" or "flaw" or "weakness," but perhaps best translated as "mistake." Aristotle seems to imply that the hero is undone because of some mistake he or she commits, but this mistake need not be the result of a moral fault; it may be simply a miscalculation—for example, failure to foresee the consequences of a deed. Brutus makes a strategic mistake when he lets Marc Antony speak at Caesar's funeral, but we can hardly call it a vice.

Because Aristotle's *hamartia* includes mistakes of this sort, the common translation "tragic flaw" is erroneous. In many Greek tragedies the hero's *hamartia* is **hybris** (or **hubris**), usually translated as "overweening pride." The hero forgets that he or she is fallible, acts as though he or she has the power and wisdom of the gods, and is later humbled for this arrogance. But one can argue that this self-assertiveness is not a vice but a virtue, not a weakness but a strength; if the hero is destroyed for self-assertion, he or she is nevertheless greater than the surrounding people, just as the person who tries to stem a lynch mob is greater than the mob, although that person also may be lynched for his or her virtue. Or a hero may be undone by a high-mindedness that makes him or her vulnerable. Hamlet is vulnerable because he is, as his enemy says, "most generous and free from all contriving"; because Hamlet is high-minded, he will not suspect that the proposed fencing match in a murderous plot. Othello can be tricked into murdering Desdemona not simply because he is jealous but because he is (in the words of the villainous Iago) "of a free and open nature / That thinks men honest that but seem so." Iago knows, too, that out of Desdemona's "goodness" he can "make the net / That shall enmesh them all."

Next, here is a statement more or less the reverse of Tourneur's, by a Soviet critic, L. I. Timofeev:

> Tragedy in Soviet literature arouses a feeling of pride for the man
> who has accomplished a great deed for the people's happiness;
> it calls for continued struggle against the things which brought
> about the hero's death.

The distortions in Soviet criticism are often amusing: Hamlet is sometimes seen as an incipient Communist, undone by the decadent aristocracy; or Romeo and Juliet as young people of the future, undone by bourgeois parents. Recent Soviet drama so consistently shows the triumph of the worker that Western visitors to Russia have commented on the absence of contemporary tragic plays. Still, there is much in the idea that the tragic hero accomplishes "a great deed" and perhaps we do resent "the things which brought about the hero's death." The stubbornness of the Montagues and Capulets, the fury of the mob that turns against Brutus, the crimes of Claudius in *Hamlet*—all these would seem in some measure to call for our indignation.

The third comment is by Arthur Miller:

> If it is true to say that in essence the tragic hero is intent upon claiming his whole due as a personality, and if this struggle must be total and without reservation, then it automatically demonstrates the indestructible will of man to achieve his humanity. . . . It is curious, although edifying, that the plays we revere, century after century, are the tragedies. In them, and in them alone, lies the belief—optimistic, if you will—in the perfectibility of man.

There is much in Miller's suggestions that the tragic hero makes a large and total claim and that the audience often senses triumph rather than despair in tragedies. We often feel that we have witnessed human greatness—that the hero, despite profound suffering, has lived according to his or her ideals. We may feel that we have achieved new insight into human greatness. But the perfectibility of man? Do we feel that *Julius Caesar* or *Macbeth* or *Hamlet* have to do with human perfectibility? Don't these plays suggest rather that people, whatever their nobility, have within them the seeds of their own destruction? Without overstressing the guilt of the protagonists, don't we feel that in part the plays dramatize the *im*perfectibility of human beings? In much tragedy, after all, the destruction comes from within, not from without:

> In tragic life, God wot,
> No villain need be! Passions spin the plot:
> We are betrayed by what is false within.
>
> —George Meredith

What we are talking about is **tragic irony,** the contrast between what is believed to be so and what is so, or between expectations and accomplishments.* Several examples from *Macbeth* illustrate something of the range of tragic irony within a single play. In the first act, King Duncan bestows on Macbeth the title of Thane of Cawdor. By his kindness Duncan seals his own doom, for Macbeth having achieved this rank, will next want to achieve a higher one. In the third act, Macbeth, knowing that Banquo will soon be murdered, hypocritically urges Banquo to "fail not our feast." But Macbeth's hollow request is ironically fulfilled: the ghost of Banquo

---

*Tragic irony is sometimes called **dramatic irony** or **Sophoclean irony.** The terms are often applied to speeches or actions that the audience understands in a sense fuller than or different from the sense in which the dramatic characters understand them.

terrorizes Macbeth during the feast. The most pervasive irony of all, of course, is that Macbeth aims at happiness when he kills Duncan and takes the throne, but he wins only sorrow.

Aristotle's discussion of **peripeteia (reversal)** and **anagnorisis (recognition)** may be a way of getting at this sort of irony. He may simply have meant a reversal of fortune (for example, good luck ceases) and a recognition of who is who (for example, the pauper is really the prince), but more likely he meant profounder things. One can say that the reversal in *Macbeth* lies in the sorrow that Macbeth's increased power brings; the recognition comes when he realizes the consequences of his deeds:

> I have lived long enough: my way of life
> Is fall'n into the sere, the yellow leaf;
> And that which should accompany old age,
> As honor, love, obedience, troops of friends,
> I must not look to have; but, in their stead,
> Curses, not loud but deep, mouth-honor, breath
> Which the poor heart would fain deny, and dare not.

That our deeds often undo us, that we can aim at our good and produce our ruin, was not, of course, a discovery of the tragic dramatists. The archetype is the story of Adam and Eve: these two aimed at becoming like God, and as a consequence, they brought upon themselves corruption, death, the loss of their earthly paradise. The Bible is filled with stories of tragic irony. A brief quotation from Ecclesiastes (10:8–9) can stand as an epitome of these stories:

> He that diggeth a pit shall fall into it; and whoso breaketh
> an hedge, a serpent shall bite him.
> Whoso removeth stones shall be hurt therewith; and he that
> cleaveth wood shall be endangered thereby.

"He that cleaveth wood shall be endangered thereby." Activity involves danger. To be inactive is, often, to be ignoble, but to be active is necessarily to imperil oneself. Perhaps we can attempt a summary of tragic figures: they act, and they suffer, usually as a consequence of their action. The question is not of the action's being particularly bad (Tourneur's view) or particularly good (Timofeev's view); the action is often both good and bad, a sign of courage and also of arrogance, a sign of greatness and also of limitations.

Finally, a brief consideration of the pleasure of tragedy: Why do we enjoy plays about suffering? Aristotle has some obscure comments on **catharsis (purgation)** that are often interpreted as saying that tragedy arouses in us both pity and fear and then purges us of these emotions. The idea, perhaps, is that just as we can harmlessly discharge our aggressive impulses by witnessing a prize fight or by shouting at an umpire, so we can harmlessly discharge our impulses to pity and to fear by witnessing the dramatization of a person's destruction. The theater in this view is an outlet for emotions that elsewhere would be harmful. But, it must be repeated, Aristotle's comments on catharsis are obscure; perhaps, too, they are wrong.

Most later theories on the pleasure of tragedy are footnotes to Aristotle's words on catharsis. Some say that our pleasure is sadistic (we enjoy the sight of suffering); some, that our pleasure is masochistic (we enjoy lacerating ourselves); some, that it lies in sympathy (we enjoy extending pity and benevolence to the wretched); some, that it lies in self-congratulation (we are reminded, when we see suffering, of our own good fortune); some, that we take pleasure in tragedy because the tragic hero acts out our secret desires, and we rejoice in his or her aggression, expiating our guilt in his or her suffering; and so on.

But this is all rather uncertain psychology, and it mostly neglects the distinction between real suffering and dramatized suffering. In the latter, surely, part of the pleasure is in the contemplation of an aesthetic object, an object that is unified and complete. The chaos of real life seems, for a few moments in drama, to be ordered: the protagonist's action, his or her subsequent suffering, and the total cosmos seem somehow related. Tragedy has no use for the passerby who is killed by a falling brick. The events (the person's walk, the brick's fall) have no meaningful relation. But suppose a person chooses to climb a mountain, and in making the ascent sets in motion an avalanche that destroys that person. Here we find (however simple the illustration) something closer to tragedy. We do not say that people should avoid mountains, or that mountain climbers deserve to die by avalanches. But we feel that the event is unified, as the accidental conjunction of brick and passerby is not.

Tragedy thus presents some sort of ordered action; tragic drama itself is orderly. As we see or read it, we feel it cannot be otherwise; word begets word, deed begets deed, and every moment is exquisitely appropriate. Whatever the relevance of sadism, masochism, sympathy, and the rest, the pleasure of tragedy surely comes in part from the artistic shaping of the material.

A NOTE ON THE ELIZABETHAN THEATER

Shakespeare's theater was wooden, round or polygonal (the Chorus in *Henry V* calls it a "wooden O"). About eight hundred spectators could stand in the yard in front of—and perhaps along the two sides of—the stage that jutted from the rear wall, and another fifteen hundred or so spectators could sit in the three roofed galleries that ringed the stage.

That portion of the galleries that was above the rear of the stage was sometimes used by actors. For instance, in the first scene of *Othello* Iago and Brabantio make a rumpus on the stage, awakening Brabantio,

Johannes de Witt, a Continental visitor to London, made a drawing of the Swan Theater in about the year 1596. The original drawing is lost; this is Arend van Buchel's copy of it.

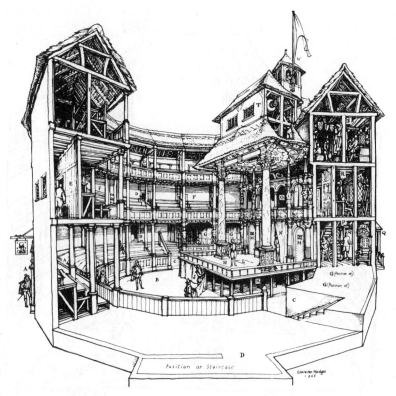

C. Walter Hodges's drawing (1965) of an Elizabethan playhouse.

who, the stage directions tell us, appears "above" or, in the words of another stage direction, "at a window."

Entry to the stage was normally gained by doors at the rear, but apparently on rare occasions use was made of a curtained alcove—or perhaps a booth—between the doors, which allowed characters to be "discovered" (revealed) as in the modern proscenium theater, which normally employs a curtain. But such "discovery" scenes are rare. In all probability, in *Othello* 1.3 the table was carried on stage, and so too in 5.2 was the bed: "Enter Othello and Desdemona in her bed."

Although the theater as a whole was unroofed, the stage was protected by a roof, supported by two pillars. These could serve (by an act of imagination) as trees behind which actors might pretend to conceal themselves. In *Othello* 5.1 Iago says to Roderigo, "Here stand behind this bulk" (i.e., behind this wooden stall projecting from a shop), presumably referring to one of the stage pillars.

A performance was probably uninterrupted by intermissions or by long pauses for the changing of scenery; a group of characters leaves the stage, another enters, and if the locale has changed the new characters somehow tell us. (Modern editors customarily add indications of locales to help a reader, but it should be remembered that the action on the Elizabethan stage was continuous.)

William Shakespeare (*English; 1564–1616*)

Othello*

List of Characters

OTHELLO, *the Moor*
BRABANTIO, [*a senator,*] *father to Desdemona*
CASSIO, *an honorable lieutenant* [*to Othello*]
IAGO, [*Othello's ancient,*] *a villain*
RODERIGO, *a gulled gentleman*
DUKE OF VENICE

---

*Edited by David Bevington. *Othello* was first published in 1622, in a small book of a type called a *quarto.* In 1623 it was published again, this time in the first collection of Shakespeare's plays, a large volume called the *First Folio.* Because the Folio text contains about 160 lines not found in the quarto, and also contains a number of small changes that seem to be Shakespeare's, it provides the basis for this edition. But the Folio also contains some errors, and in accordance with a law, it removes profanity. Bevington's text, therefore, though based on the Folio, occasionally adopts a reading from the quarto or a later emendation, and it modifies the punctuation in accordance with modern usage. Material added by the editor, such as in the list of *dramatis personae,* is indicated by square brackets [ ].

A degree sign (°) after a word means that the word is glossed in the footnotes.

Moses Gunn and Roberta Maxwell in Othello *at the American Shakespeare Festival Theatre in Stratford, Connecticut, 1970. (Photograph by Martha Swope.)*

SENATORS [*of Venice*]
MONTANO, *Governor of Cyprus*
GENTLEMEN *of Cyprus*
LODOVICO *and* GRATIANO, [*kinsmen to Brabantio,*] *two noble Venetians*
SAILORS
CLOWN

DESDEMONA, [*daughter to Brabantio and*] *wife to Othello*
EMILIA, *wife to Iago*
BIANCA, *a courtesan* [*and mistress to Cassio*]

[A MESSENGER
A HERALD
A MUSICIAN

Servants, Attendants, Officers, Senators, Musicians, Gentlemen

SCENE: *Venice; a seaport in Cyprus*]

[**1.1**] *Enter Roderigo and Iago.*

RODERIGO. Tush, never tell me!° I take it much unkindly   *1*
    That thou, Iago, who hast had my purse
    As if the strings were thine, shouldst know of this.°
IAGO. 'Sblood,° but you'll not hear me.
    If ever I did dream of such a matter,   *5*
    Abhor me.
RODERIGO. Thou toldst me thou didst hold him in thy hate.
IAGO. Despise me
    If I do not. Three great ones of the city,
    In personal suit to make me his lieutenant,   *10*
    Off-capped to him°; and by the faith of man,
    I know my price, I am worth no worse a place.
    But he, as loving his own pride and purposes,
    Evades them with a bombast° circumstance
    Horribly stuffed with epithets of war°,   *15*
    And, in conclusion,
    Nonsuits° my mediators. For, "Certes,"° says he,
    "I have already chose my officer."
    And what was he?
    Forsooth, a great arithmetician,°   *20*

1.1 Location: Venice. A street.
1 never tell me don't talk to me   **3 this** i.e., Desdemona's elopement   **4 'Sblood** by His
(Christ's) blood   **11 him** i.e., Othello   **14 bombast circumstance** wordy evasion. (*Bombast* is cotton padding.)   **15 epithets of war** military expressions   **17 Nonsuits** rejects the
petition of.   **Certes** certainly   **20 arithmetician** i.e., a man whose military knowledge
is merely theoretical, based on books of tactics

One Michael Cassio, a Florentine,
A fellow almost damned in a fair wife,°
That never set a squadron in the field
Nor the division° of a battle knows
More than a spinster°—unless the bookish theoric,°   *25*
Wherein the togaed° consuls° can propose°
As masterly as he. Mere prattle without practice
Is all his soldiership. But he, sir, had th' election;
And I, of whom his° eyes had seen the proof
At Rhodes, at Cyprus, and on other grounds   *30*
Christened° and heathen, must be beleed and calmed°
By debitor and creditor.° This countercaster,°
He, in good time,° must his lieutenant be,
And I—God bless the mark!°—his Moorship's ancient.°
RODERIGO. By heaven, I rather would have been his hangman.°   *35*
IAGO. Why, there's no remedy. 'Tis the curse of service;
Preferment° goes by letter and affection,°
And not by old gradation,° where each second
Stood heir to the first. Now, sir, be judge yourself
Whether I in any just term° am affined°   *40*
To love the Moor.
RODERIGO. I would not follow him, then.
IAGO. O sir, content you.°
I follow him to serve my turn upon him.
We cannot all be masters, nor all masters   *45*
Cannot be truly° followed. You shall mark
Many a duteous and knee-crooking knave
That, doting on his own obsequious bondage,
Wears out his time, much like his master's ass,
For naught but provender, and when he's old, cashiered°   *50*

---

22 A . . . wife (Cassio does not seem to be married, but his counterpart in Shakespeare's source does have a woman in his house. See also 4.1.131.)   **24 division of a battle** disposition of a military unit   **25 a spinster** i.e., a housewife, one whose regular occupation is spinning.   **theoric** theory   **26 togaed** wearing the toga.   **consuls** counselors, senators. **propose** discuss   **29 his** i.e., Othello's   **31 Christened** i.e., Christian. **beleed and calmed** left to leeward without wind, becalmed. (A sailing metaphor.)   **32 debitor and creditor** (A name for a system of bookkeeping, here used as a contemptuous nickname for Cassio.)   **countercaster** i.e., bookkeeper, one who tallies with *counters* or metal disks. (Said contemptuously.)   **33 in good time** i.e., forsooth   **34 God bless the mark** (Perhaps originally a formula to ward off evil; here an expression of impatience.)   **ancient** standard-bearer, ensign   **35 his hangman** the executioner of him   **37 Preferment** promotin **letter and affection** personal influence and favoritism   **38 old gradation** step-by-step seniority, the traditional way   **40 term** respect. **affined** bound   **43 content you** don't you worry about that   **46 truly** faithfully   **50 cashiered** dismissed from service

Whip me° such honest knaves. Others there are
Who, trimmed in forms and visages of duty,°
Keep yet their hearts attending on themselves,
And, throwing but shows of service on their lords,
Do well thrive by them, and when they have lined their coats,°   *55*
Do themselves homage.° These fellows have some soul,
And such a one do I profess myself. For, sir,
It is as sure as you are Roderigo,
Were I the Moor I would not be Iago.°
In following him, I follow but myself—   *60*
Heaven is my judge, not I for love and duty,
But seeming so for my peculiar° end.
For when my outward action doth demonstrate
The native° act and figure° of my heart
In compliment extern,° 'tis not long after   *65*
But I will wear my heart upon my sleeve
For daws to peck at. I am not what I am.°
RODERIGO. What a full° fortune does the thick-lips° owe°
     If he can carry 't thus!°
IAGO.   Call up her father.
     Rouse him, make after him, poison his delight,   *70*
     Proclaim him in the streets; incense her kinsmen,
     And, though he in a fertile climate dwell,
     Plague him with flies.° Though that his joy be joy,°
     Yet throw such changes of vexation° on 't
     As it may° lose some color.°   *75*
RODERIGO. Here is her father's house. I'll call aloud.
IAGO. Do, with like timorous° accent and dire yell
     As when, by night and negligence,° the fire
     Is spied in populous cities.
RODERIGO. What ho, Brabantio! Signor Brabantio, ho!   *80*

---

51 Whip me whip, as far as I'm concerned   **52 trimmed . . . duty** dressed up in the mere form and show of dutifulness   **55 lined their coats** i.e., stuffed their purses   **56 Do themselves homage** i.e., attend to self-interest solely   **59 Were . . . Iago** i.e., if I were able to assume command I certainly would not choose to remain a subordinate   **62 peculiar** particular, personal   **64 native** innate.   **figure** shape, intent   **65 compliment extern** outward show (conforming in this case to the inner workings and intention of the heart)   **67 I am not what I am** i.e., I am not one who wears his heart on his sleeve   **68 full** swelling.   **thick-lips** (Elizabethans often applied the term "Moor" to Negroes.)   **owe** own   **69 carry 't thus** carry this off   **72–73 though . . . flies** i.e., though he seems prosperous and happy now, vex him with misery   **73 Though . . . be joy** i.e., although he seems fortunate and happy. (Repeats the idea of 1.72.)   **74 changes of vexation** vexing changes   **75 As it may** that may cause it to.   **some color** i.e., some of its fresh gloss   **77 timorous** frightening   **78 and negligence** i.e., caused by negligence

IAGO. Awake! What ho, Brabantio! Thieves, thieves, thieves!
　　Look to your house, your daughter, and your bags!
　　Thieves, thieves!

Brabantio [enters] above [at a window].°

BRABANTIO. What is the reason of this terrible summons?
　　What is the matter° there?   *85*
RODERIGO. Signor, is all your family within?
IAGO. Are your doors locked?
BRABANTIO.　　　　　　　　　Why, wherefore ask you this?
IAGO. Zounds,° sir, you're robbed. For shame, put on your gown!
　　Your heart is burst; you have lost half your soul.
　　Even now, now, very now, an old black ram   *90*
　　Is tupping° your white ewe. Arise, arise!
　　Awake the snorting° citizens with the bell,
　　Or else the devil° will make a grandsire of you.
　　Arise, I say!
BRABANTIO.　　　What, have you lost your wits?
RODERIGO. Most reverend signor, do you know my voice?   *95*
BRABANTIO. Not I. What are you?
RODERIGO. My name is Roderigo.
BRABANTIO. The worser welcome.
　　I have charged thee not to haunt about my doors.
　　In honest plainness thou hast heard me say   *100*
　　My daughter is not for thee; and now, in madness,
　　Being full of supper and distempering° drafts,
　　Upon malicious bravery° dost thou come
　　To start° my quiet.
RODERIGO. Sir, sir, sir—
BRABANTIO.　　　　　　　But thou must needs be sure   *105*
　　My spirits and my place° have in° their power
　　To make this bitter to thee.
RODERIGO.　　　　　　　　　Patience, good sir.
BRABANTIO. What tell'st thou me of robbing? This is Venice;
　　My house is not a grange.°
RODERIGO.　　　　　　　　　Most grave Brabantio,
　　In simple° and pure soul I come to you.   *110*

---

83 **s.d. at a window** (This stage direction, from the quarto, probably calls for an appearance on the gallery above and rearstage.) 85 **the matter** your business 88 **Zounds** by His (Christ's) wounds 91 **tupping** covering, copulating with. (Said of sheep.) 92 **snorting** snoring 93 **the devil** (The devil was conventionally pictured as black.) 102 **distempering** intoxicating 103 **Upon malicious bravery** with hostile intent to defy me 104 **start** startle, disrupt 106 **My spirits and my place** my temperament and my authority of office. **have in** have it in 109 **grange** isolated farmhouse 110 **simple** sincere

IAGO. Zounds, sir, you are one of those that will not serve God if the devil
bid you. Because we come to do you service and you think we are
ruffians, you'll have your daughter covered with a Barbary horse;
you'll have your nephews° neigh to you; you'll have coursers° for
cousins° and jennets° for germans.° 115
BRABANTIO. What profane wretch art thou?
IAGO. I am one, sir, that comes to tell you your daughter and the
Moor are now making the beast with two backs.
BRABANTIO. Thou art a villain.
IAGO. You are—a senator.
BRABANTIO. This thou shalt answer.° I know thee, Roderigo. 120
RODERIGO. Sir, I will answer anything. But, I beseech you,
If 't be your pleasure and most wise consent—
As partly I find it is—that your fair daughter,
At this odd-even° and dull watch o' the night,
Transported with° no worse nor better guard 125
But with a knave° of common hire, a gondolier,
To the gross clasps of a lascivious Moor—
If this be known to you and your allowance°
We then have done you bold and saucy° wrongs.
But if you know not this, my manners tell me 130
We have your wrong rebuke. Do not believe
That, from° the sense of all civility,°
I thus would play and trifle with your reverence.°
Your daughter, if you have not given her leave,
I say again, hath made a gross revolt, 135
Tying her duty, beauty, wit,° and fortunes
In an extravagant° and wheeling° stranger°
Of here and everywhere. Straight° satisfy yourself.
If she be in her chamber or your house,
Let loose on me the justice of the state 140
For thus deluding you.
BRABANTIO. Strike on the tinder,° ho!
Give me a taper! Call up all my people!
This accident° is not unlike my dream.

---

114 nephews i.e., grandsons. **coursers** powerful horses **115 cousins** kinsmen.
jennets small Spanish horses. **germans** near relatives **120 answer** be held accountable for **124 odd-even** between one day and the next, i.e., about midnight **125 with** by
126 But with a knave than by a low fellow, a servant **128 allowance** permission
129 saucy insolent **131 from** contrary to. **civility** good manners, decency **133 your
reverence** the respect due to you **136 wit** intelligence **137 extravagant** expatriate,
wandering far from home. **wheeling** roving about, vagabond. **stranger** foreigner
138 Straight straightway **142 tinder** charred linen ignited by a spark from flint and steel,
used to light torches of *tapers* (143) **144 accident** occurrence, event

Belief of it oppresses me already.   145
Light, I say, light!   *Exit [above].*
IAGO.   Farewell, for I must leave you.
   It seems not meet nor wholesome to my place
   To be producted°—as, if I stay, I shall—
   Against the Moor. For I do know the state,   150
   However this may gall° him with some check,°
   Cannot with safety cast° him, for he's embarked°
   With such loud° reason to the Cyprus wars,
   Which even now stands in act,° that, for their souls,
   Another of his fathom° they have none   155
   To lead their business; in which regard,°
   Though I do hate him as I do hell pains,
   Yet for necessity of present life°
   I must show out a flag and sign of love,
   Which is indeed but sign. That you shall surely find him,   160
   Lead to the Sagittary° the raisèd search,°
   And there will I be with him. So farewell.   *Exit.*

Enter [below] Brabantio [in his nightgown°] with servants and torches.

BRABANTIO. It is too true an evil. Gone she is;
   And what's to come of my despisèd time°
   Is naught but bitterness. Now, Roderigo,   165
   Where didst thou see her?—O unhappy girl!—
   With the Moor, sayst thou?—Who would be a father!—
   How didst thou know 'twas she?—O, she deceives me
   Past thought!—What said she to you?—Get more tapers.
   Raise all my kindred.—Are they married, think you?   170
RODERIGO. Truly, I think they are.
BRABANTIO. O heaven! How got she out? O treason of the blood!
   Fathers, from hence trust not your daughters' minds
   By what you see them act. Is there not charms°
   By which the property° of youth and maidhood   175
   May be abused?° Have you not read, Roderigo,
   Of some such thing?
RODERIGO.   Yes, sir, I have indeed.

---

149 producted produced (as a witness) **151 gall** rub; oppress. **check** rebuke
152 cast dismiss. **embarked** engaged **153 loud** i.e., self-evident, boldly proclaimed
154 stands in act are going on **155 fathom** i.e., ability, depth of experience
156 in which regard out of regard for which **158 life** livelihood **161 Sagittary** (An
inn where Othello and Desdemona are staying.) **raisèd search** search party roused out
of sleep **162 s.d. nightgown** dressing gown. (This costuming is specified in the quarto
text.) **164 time** i.e., remainder of life **174 charms** spells **175 property** special quality, nature **176 abused** deceived

BRABANTIO. Call up my brother.—O, would you had had her!—
　　Some one way, some another.—Do you know
　　Where we may apprehend her and the Moor?   *180*
RODERIGO. I think I can discover° him, if you please
　　To get good guard and go along with me.
BRABANTIO. Pray you, lead on. At every house I'll call;
　　I may command° at most.—Get weapons, ho!
　　And raise some special officers of night.—   *185*
　　On, good Roderigo. I will deserve° your pains.   *Exeunt.*

　　　[1.2]　*Enter Othello, Iago, attendants with torches.*

IAGO. Though in the trade of war I have slain men,   *1*
　　Yet do I hold it very stuff° o' the conscience
　　To do no contrived° murder. I lack iniquity
　　Sometimes to do me service. Nine or ten times
　　I had thought t' have yerked° him° here under the ribs.   *5*
OTHELLO. 'Tis better as it is.
IAGO.　　　　　　　　　　Nay, but he prated,
　　And spoke such scurvy and provoking terms
　　Against your honor
　　That, with the little godliness I have,
　　I did full hard forbear him.° But, I pray you, sir,   *10*
　　Are you fast married? Be assured of this,
　　That the magnifico° is much beloved,
　　And hath in his effect° a voice potential°
　　As double° as the Duke's. He will divorce you,
　　Or put upon you what restraint and grievance   *15*
　　The law, with all his might to enforce it on,
　　Will give him cable.°
OTHELLO.　　　　　　Let him do his spite.
　　My services which I have done the seigniory°
　　Shall out-tongue his complaints. 'Tis yet to know°—

---

181 discover reveal, uncover　**184 command** demand assistance　**186 deserve** show
gratitude for

1.2 Location Venice. Another street, before Othello's lodgings.
2 very stuff essence, basic material (continuing the metaphor of *trade* from 1.1)
3 contrived premeditated　**5 yerked** stabbed.　**him** i.e., Roderigo　**10 I . . . him**I restrained myself with great difficulty from assaulting him　**12 magnifico** Venetian gran-
dee, i.e., Brabantio　**13 in his effect** at his command.　**potential** powerful　**14 double**
doubly powerful (in comparison with other senators)　**17 cable** i.e., scope　**18 seigniory**
Venetian government　**19 yet to know** not yet widely known

Which, when I know that boasting is an honor, 20
I shall promulgate—I fetch my life and being
From men of royal siege,° and my demerits°
May speak unbonneted° to as proud a fortune
As this that I have reached. For know, Iago,
But that I love the gentle Desdemona,
I would not my unhousèd free condition 25
Put into circumscription and confine°
For the sea's worth.° But look, what lights come yond?

Enter Cassio [and certain Officers] with torches.

IAGO. Those are the raisèd father and his friends.
You were best go in.

OTHELLO.   Not I. I must be found. 30
My parts, my title, and my perfect soul°
Shall manifest me rightly. Is it they?

IAGO. By Janus,° I think no.

OTHELLO. The servants of the Duke? And my lieutenant?
The goodness of the night upon you, friends! 35
What is the news?

CASSIO.   The Duke does greet you, General,
And he requires your haste-post-haste appearance
Even on the instant.

OTHELLO.   What is the matter,° think you?

CASSIO. Something from Cyprus, as I may divine.°
It is a business of some heat.° The galleys 40
Have sent a dozen sequent° messengers
This very night at one another's heels,
And many of the consuls,° raised and met,
Are at the Duke's already. You have been hotly called for;
When, being not at your lodging to be found, 45
The Senate hath sent about three several° quests
To search you out.

OTHELLO.   Tis well I am found by you.
I will but spend a word here in the house
And go with you.   [*Exit.*]

---

22 siege i.e., rank. (Literally, a *seat* used by a person of distinction.) **demerits** deserts **23 unbonneted** without removing the hat, i.e., on equal terms (? Or "with hat off," "in all due modesty.") **26 unhousèd** unconfined, undomesticated **27 circumscription and confine** restriction and confinement **28 the sea's worth** all the riches at the bottom of the sea **s.d. Officers** (The quarto text calls for "Cassio with lights, officers with torches.") **31 My . . . soul** my natural gifts, my position or reputation, and my un-flawed conscience **33 Janus** Roman two-faced god of beginnings **38 matter** business **39 divine** guess **40 heat** urgency **41 sequent** successive **43 consuls** senators **46 several** separate

CASSIO.   Ancient, what makes° he here?
IAGO. Faith, he tonight hath boarded° a land carrack.°   *50*
    If it prove lawful prize,° he's made forever.
CASSIO. I do not understand.
IAGO.   He's married.
CASSIO.   To who?

    [*Enter Othello.*]

IAGO. Marry,° to — Come, Captain, will you go?
OTHELLO. Have with you.°
CASSIO. Here comes another troop to seek for you.   *55*

    Enter Brabantio, Roderigo, with officers and torches.

IAGO. It is Brabantio. General, be advised.°
    He comes to bad intent.
OTHELLO.   Holla! Stand there!
RODERIGO. Signor, it is the Moor.
BRABANTIO.   Down with him, thief!

    [*They draw on both sides.*]

IAGO. You, Roderigo! Come, sir, I am for you.
OTHELLO. Keep up° your bright swords, for the dew will rust them.   *60*
    Good signor, you shall more command with years
    Than with your weapons.
BRABANTIO. O thou foul thief, where hast thou stowed my daughter?
    Damned as thou art, thou hast enchanted her!
    For I'll refer me° to all things of sense,°   *65*
    If she in chains of magic were not bound
    Whether a maid so tender, fair, and happy,
    So opposite to marriage that she shunned
    The wealthy curlèd darlings of our nation,
    Would ever have, t' incur a general mock,   *70*
    Run from her guardage° to the sooty bosom
    Of such a thing as thou — to fear, not to delight.
    Judge me the world if 'tis not gross in sense°
    That thou hast practiced on her with foul charms,
    Abused her delicate youth with drugs or minerals°   *75*

---

49 makes does   **50 boarded** gone aboard and seized as an act of piracy (with sexual suggestion).   **carrack** large merchant ship   **51 prize** booty   **53 Marry** (An oath, originally "by the Virgin Mary.")   **54 Have with you** i.e., let's go   **55 s.d officers and torches** (The quarto text calls for "others with lights and weapons.")   **56 be advised** be on your guard   **60 Keep up** i.e., sheathe   **65 refer me** submit my case. **things of sense** commonsense understandings, or, creatures possessing common sense   **71 guardage** guardianship   **73 gross in sense** obvious   **75 minerals** i.e., poisons

That weakens motion.° I'll have 't disputed on;°
'Tis probable, and palpable to thinking.
I therefore apprehend and do attach° thee
For an abuser of the world, a practicer
Of arts inhibited° and out of warrant°.—   80
Lay hold upon him! If he do resist,
Subdue him at his peril.

OTHELLO.   Hold your hands,
Both you of my inclining° and the rest.
Were it my cue to fight, I should have known it
Without a prompter.—Whither will you that I go   85
To answer this your charge?

BRABANTIO. To prison, till fit time
Of law and course of direct session°
Call thee to answer.

OTHELLO.   What if I do obey?
How may the Duke be therewith satisfied,   90
Whose messengers are here about my side
Upon some present business of the state
To bring me to him?

OFFICER.   —Tis true, most worthy signor.
The Duke's in council, and your noble self,
I am sure, is sent for.

BRABANTIO.   How? The Duke in council?   95
In this time of the night? Bring him away.°
Mine's not an idle° cause. The Duke himself,
Or any of my brothers of the state,
Cannot but feel this wrong as 'twere their own;
For if such actions may have passage free,   100
Bondslaves and pagans shall our statesmen be.   *Exeunt.*

[1.3] *Enter Duke [and] Senators [and sit at a table, with lights], and
Officers°. [The Duke and Senators are reading dispatches.]*

DUKE. There is no composition° in these news   1
That gives them credit.

---

76 weakens motion impair the vital faculties.   **disputed on** argued in court by professional counsel, discussed by experts   **78 attach** arrest   **80 inhibited** prohibited.   **out of
warrant** illegal   **83 inclining** following, party   **88 course of direct session** regular or
specially convened legal proceedings   **96 away** right along   **97 idle** trifling

1.3 Location: Venice. A council chamber.
s.d. Enter . . . Officers (The quarto text calls for the Duke and Senators to "sit at a table
with lights and attendants.")   **1 composition** consistency

FIRST SENATOR. Indeed, they are disproportioned.°
My letters say a hundred and seven galleys.
DUKE. And mine, a hundred forty.
SECOND SENATOR.   And mine, two hundred.   *5*
But though they jump° not on a just° account—
As in these cases, where the aim° reports
'Tis oft with difference—yet do they all confirm
A Turkish fleet, and bearing up to Cyprus.
DUKE. Nay, it is possible enough to judgment.   *10*
I do not so secure me in the error
But the main article I do approve°
In fearful sense.
SAILOR. (*Within*)   What ho, what ho, what ho!

Enter Sailor.

OFFICER. A messenger from the galleys.
DUKE. Now, what's the business?   *15*
SAILOR. The Turkish preparation° makes for Rhodes.
So was I bid report here to the state
By Signor Angelo.
DUKE. How say you by° this change?
FIRST SENATOR.   This cannot be
By no assay° of reason. 'Tis a pageant°   *20*
To keep us in false gaze.° When we consider
Th' importancy of Cyprus to the Turk,
And let ourselves again but understand
That, as it more concerns the Turk than Rhodes,
So may he with more facile question bear it,°   *25*
For that° it stands not in such warlike brace,°
But altogether lacks th' abilities°
That Rhodes is dressed in°—if we make thought of this,
We must not think the Turk is so unskillful°
To leave that latest° which concerns him first,   *30*
Neglecting an attempt of ease and gain
To wake° and wage° a danger profitless.
DUKE. Nay, in all confidence, he's not for Rhodes.
OFFICER. Here is more news.

---

3 disproportioned inconsistent   **6 jump** agree.   **just** exact   **7 the   aim** conjecture
11–12 I do not . . . approve I do not take such (false) comfort in the discrepancies that
I fail to perceive the main point, i.e., that the Turkish fleet is threatening   **16 preparation** fleet
prepared for battle   **19 by** about   **20 assay** test.   **pageant** mere show   **21 in false gaze**
looking the wrong way   **25 may . . . it** he (the Turk) can more easily capture it (Cyprus)
26 For that since.   **brace** state of defense   **27 abilities** means of self-defense   **28 dressed
in** equipped with   **29 unskillful** deficient in judgment   **30 latest** last   **32 wake** stir
up.   **wage** risk

Enter a Messenger.

MESSENGER. The Ottomites, reverend and gracious,   35
    Steering with due course toward the Isle of Rhodes,
    Have there injointed them° with an after° fleet.
FIRST SENATOR. Ay, so I thought. How many, as you guess?
MESSENGER. Of thirty sail; and now they do restem
    Their backward course,° bearing with frank appearance°   40
    Their purposes toward Cyprus. Signor Montano,
    Your trusty and most valiant servitor,°
    With his free duty° recommends° you thus,
    And prays you to believe him.
DUKE. 'Tis certain then for Cyprus.   45
    Marcus Luccicos, is not he in town?
FIRST SENATOR. He's now in Florence.
DUKE. Write from us to him, post-post-haste. Dispatch.
FIRST SENATOR. Here comes Brabantio and the valiant Moor.

Enter Brabantio, Othello, Cassio, Iago, Roderigo, and officers.

DUKE. Valiant Othello, we must straight° employ you   50
    Against the general° enemy Ottoman.
    [*To Brabantio.*]I did not see you; welcome, gentle° signor.
    We lacked your counsel and your help tonight.
BRABANTIO. So did I yours. Good Your Grace, pardon me;
    Neither my place° nor aught I heard of business   55
    Hath raised me from my bed, nor doth the general care
    Take hold on me, for my particular° grief
    Is of so floodgate° and overbearing nature
    That it engluts° and swallows other sorrows
    And it is still itself.°
DUKE.   Why, what's the matter?   60
BRABANTIO. My daughter! O, my daughter!
DUKE AND SENATORS.   Dead?
BRABANTIO.   Ay, to me.
    She is abused,° stol'n from me, and corrupted
    By spells and medicines bought of mountebanks;
    For nature so preposterously to err,

---

37 **injointed them** joined themselves. **after** second   **39–40 restem . . . course** retrace their original course   **40 frank appearance** i.e., undisguised intent   **42 servitor** officer under your command   **43 free duty** freely given and loyal service. **recommends** commends himself and reports to   **50 straight** straightway   **51 general** universal, i.e., against all Christendom   **52 gentle** noble   **55 place** official position   **57 particular** personal   **58 floodgate** i.e., overwhelming (as when floodgates are opened)   **59 engluts** engulfs   **60 is still itself** remains undiminished   **62 abused** deceived

Being not deficient,° blind, or lame of sense,   *65*
Sans° witchcraft could not.
DUKE. Whoe'er he be that in this foul proceeding
    Hath thus beguiled your daughter of herself,
    And you of her, the bloody book of law
    You shall yourself read in the bitter letter   *70*
    After your own sense°—yea, though our proper° son
    Stood in your action.°
BRABANTIO.   Humbly I thank Your Grace.
    Here is the man, this Moor, whom now it seems
    Your special mandate for the state affairs
    Hath hither brought.
ALL.   We are very sorry for 't.   *75*
DUKE [*To Othello*]. What, in your own part, can you say to this?
BRABANTIO. Nothing, but this is so.
OTHELLO. Most potent, grave, and reverend signors,
    My very noble and approved° good masters:
    That I have ta'en away this old man's daughter,   *80*
    It is most true; true, I have married her.
    The very head and front° of my offending
    Hath this extent, no more. Rude° am I in my speech,
    And little blessed with the soft phrase of peace;
    For since these arms of mine had seven years' pith,°   *85*
    Till now some nine moons wasted,° they have used
    Their dearest° action in the tented field;
    And little of this great world can I speak
    More than pertains to feats of broils and battle,
    And therefore little shall I grace my cause   *90*
    In speaking for myself. Yet, by your gracious patience,
    I will a round° unvarnished tale deliver
    Of my whole course of love—what drugs, what charms,
    What conjuration, and what mighty magic,
    For such proceeding I am charged withal,°   *95*
    I won his daughter.
BRABANTIO.   A maiden never bold;
    Of spirit so still and quiet that her motion
    Blushed at herself;° and she, in spite of nature,

---

65 deficient defective   **66 Sans** without   **71 After . . . sense** according to your own interpretation.   **our proper** my own   **72 Stood . . . action** were under your accusation **79 approved** proved, esteemed   **82 head and front** height and breadth, entire extent   **83 Rude** unpolished   **85 pith** strength, vigor (i.e., since I was seven)   **86 Till . . . wasted** until some nine months ago (since when Othello has evidently not been on active duty, but in Venice)   **87 dearest** most valuable   **92 round** plain   **95 withal** with **97–98 her . . . herself** her very emotions prompted her to blush at discovering such feelings in herself

Of years,° of country, credit,° everything,
To fall in love with what she feared to look on!   *100*
It is a judgment maimed and most imperfect
That will confess° perfection so could err
Against all rules of nature, and must be driven
To find out practices° of cunning hell
Why this should be. I therefore vouch° again   *105*
That with some mixtures powerful o'er the blood,°
Or with some dram conjured to this effect,°
He wrought upon her.

DUKE.   To vouch this is no proof,
Without more wider° and more overt test
Than these thin habits° and poor likelihoods   *110*
Of modern seeming° do prefer° against him.

FIRST SENATOR. But, Othello, speak.
Did you by indirect and forced courses
Subdue and poison this young maid's affections?
Or came it by request and such fair question°   *115*
As soul to soul affordeth?

OTHELLO.   I do beseech you,
Send for the lady to the Sagittary
And let her speak of me before her father.
If you do find me foul in her report,
The trust, the office I do hold of you   *120*
Not only take away, but let your sentence
Even fall upon my life.

DUKE.   Fetch Desdemona hither.

OTHELLO. Ancient, conduct them. You best know the place.
                    [*Exeunt Iago and attendants.*]
And, till she come, as truly as to heaven
I do confess the vices of my blood,°   *125*
So justly° to your grave ears I'll present
How I did thrive in this fair lady's love,
And she in mine.

DUKE. Say it, Othello.

OTHELLO. Her father loved me, oft invited me,   *130*
Still° questioned me the story of my life
From year to year—the battles, sieges, fortunes,

---

99 years i.e., difference in age. **credit** virtuous reputation **102 confess** concede (that)
104 practices plots **105 vouch** assert **106 blood** passions **107 conjured to this effect** made by magical spells to have this effect **109 more wider** fuller **110 habits** garments, i.e., appearances **111 modern seeming** commonplace assumption. **prefer** bring
forth **115 question** conversation **125 blood** passions, human nature **126 justly** truth-
fully, accurately **131 Still** continually

That I have passed.
I ran it through, even from my boyish days
To th' very moment that he bade me tell it,   *135*
Wherein I spoke of most disastrous chances,
Of moving accidents° by flood and field,
Of hairbreadth scapes i' th' imminent deadly breach,°
Of being taken by the insolent foe
And sold to slavery, of my redemption thence,   *140*
And portance° in my travels' history,
Wherein of antres° vast and deserts idle,°
Rough quarries,° rocks, and hills whose heads touch heaven,
It was my hint° to speak—such was my process—
And of the Cannibals that each other eat,   *145*
The Anthropophagi,° and men whose heads
Do grow beneath their shoulders. These things to hear
Would Desdemona seriously incline;
But still the house affairs would draw her thence,
Which ever as she could with haste dispatch   *150*
She'd come again, and with a greedy ear
Devour up my discourse. Which I, observing,
Took once a pliant° hour, and found good means
To draw from her a prayer of earnest heart
That I would all my pilgrimage dilate,°   *155*
Whereof by parcels° she had something heard,
But not intentively.° I did consent,
And often did beguile her of her tears,
When I did speak of some distressful stroke
That my youth suffered. My story being done,   *160*
She gave me for my pains a world of sighs.
She swore, in faith, 'twas strange, 'twas passing° strange,
'Twas pitiful, 'twas wondrous pitiful.
She wished she had not heard it, yet she wished
That heaven had made her such a man. She thanked me,   *165*
And bade me, if I had a friend that loved her,
I should but teach him how to tell my story,
And that would woo her. Upon this hint° I spake.
She loved me for the dangers I had passed,

---

137 accidents happenings **138 imminent . . . breach** death-threatening gaps made in a fortification **141 portance** conduct **142 antres** caverns. **idle** barren, desolate **143 Rough quarries** rugged rock formations **144 hint** occasion, opportunity **146 Anthropophagi** man-eaters. (A term from Pliny's *Natural History.*) **153 pliant** well-suiting **155 dilate** relate in detail **156 by parcels** piecemeal **157 intentively** with full attention **162 passing** exceedingly **168 hint** opportunity

And I loved her that she did pity them. 170
This only is the witchcraft I have used.
Here comes the lady. Let her witness it.

Enter Desdemona, Iago, [and] attendants.

DUKE. I think this tale would win my daughter too.
Good Brabantio,
Take up this mangled matter at the best.° 175
Men do their broken weapons rather use
Than their bare hands.

BRABANTIO.   I pray you, hear her speak.
If she confess that she was half the wooer,
Destruction on my head if my bad blame
Light on the man! Come hither, gentle mistress. 180
Do you perceive in all this noble company
Where most you owe obedience?

DESDEMONA.   My noble Father,
I do perceive here a divided duty.
To you I am bound for life and education;°
My life and education both do learn° me 185
How to respect you. You are the lord of duty;
I am hitherto your daughter. But here's my husband,
And so much duty as my mother showed
To you, preferring you before her father,
So much I challenge° that I may profess 190
Due to the Moor my lord.

BRABANTIO. God be with you! I have done.
Please it Your Grace, on to the state affairs.
I had rather to adopt a child than get° it.
Come hither, Moor. [*He joins the hands of Othello and Desdemona.*] 195
I here do give thee that with all my heart°
Which, but thou hast already, with all my heart°
I would keep from thee.—For your sake,° jewel,
I am glad at soul I have no other child,
For thy escape° would teach me tyranny, 200
To hang clogs° on them.—I have done, my lord.

DUKE. Let me speak like yourself,° and lay a sentence
Which, as a grece° or step, may help these lovers
Into your favor.

---

175 Take . . . best make the best of a bad bargain   **184 education** upbringing   **185 learn** teach   **190 challenge** claim   **194 get** beget   **196 with all my heart** wherein my whole affection has been engaged   **197 with all my heart** willingly, gladly   **198 For your sake** on your account   **200 escape** elopement   **201 clogs** (Literally, blocks of wood fastened to the legs of criminals or convicts to inhibit escape.)   **202 like yourself** i.e., as you would, in your proper temper.   **sentence maxim** (Also at l. 219)   **203 grece** step

When remedies° are past, the griefs are ended   *205*
By seeing the worst, which° late on hopes depended.°
To mourn a mischief° that is past and gone
Is the next° way to draw new mischief on.
What° cannot be preserved when fortune takes,
Patience her injury a mockery makes.°   *210*
The robbed that smiles steals something from the thief;
He robs himself that spends a bootless grief.°
BRABANTIO. So let the Turk of Cyprus us beguile,
We lose it not, so long as we can smile.
He bears the sentence well that nothing bears   *215*
But the free comfort which from thence he hears,
But he bears both the sentence and the sorrow
That, to pay grief, must of poor patience borrow.°
These sentences, to sugar or to gall,
Being strong on both sides, are equivocal.°   *220*
But words are words. I never yet did hear
That the bruised heart was piercèd through the ear.°
I humbly beseech you, proceed to th' affairs of state.
DUKE. The Turk with a most mighty preparation makes for Cyprus.
Othello, the fortitude° of the place is best known to you; and   *225*
though we have there a substitute° of most allowed° sufficiency, yet
opinion, a sovereign mistress of effects, throws a more safer voice
on you.° You must therefore be content to slubber° the gloss of
your new fortunes with this more stubborn° and boisterous expe-
dition.   *230*
OTHELLO. The tyrant custom, most grave senators,
Hath made the flinty and steel couch of war
My thrice-driven° bed of down. I do agnize°
A natural and prompt alacrity
I find in hardness,° and do undertake   *235*
These present wars against the Ottomites.

---

205 remedies hopes of remedy **206 which** i.e., the griefs. **late . . . depended** were sustained until recently by hopeful anticipation **207 mischief** misfortune, injury **208 next**
nearest **209 What** whatever **210 Patience . . . makes** patience laughs at the injury in-
flicted by fortune (and thus eases the pain) **212 spends a bootless grief** indulges in un-
availing grief **215–218 He bears . . . borrow** i.e., a person well bears out your maxim
who takes with him only the philosophic consolation it teaches him, a comfort free from
sorrow; but anyone whose grief bankrupts his poor patience is left with your saying and
his sorrow too. (*Bear the sentence* also plays on the meaning, "receives judicial sentence.")
219–220 These . . . equivocal i.e., these fine maxims are equivocal, either sweet or bitter
in their application **222 piercèd . . . ear** i.e., surgically lanced and cured by mere words
of advice **225 fortitude** strength **226 substitute** deputy. **allowed** acknowledged
227–28 opinion . . . on you general opinion, an important determiner of affairs, chooses
you as the best man **228 slubber** soil, sully **229 stubborn** harsh, rough **233 thrice-
driven** thrice sifted, winnowed. **agnize** know in myself, acknowledge **235 hardness**
hardship

Most humbly therefore bending to your state,°
I crave fit disposition for my wife,
Due reference of place and exhibition,°
With such accommodation° and besort°
As levels° with her breeding.

DUKE. Why, at her father's.

BRABANTIO.   I will not have it so.

OTHELLO. Nor I.

DESDEMONA.   Nor I. I would not there reside,
To put my father in impatient thoughts
By being in his eye. Most gracious Duke,
To my unfolding° lend your prosperous° ear,
And let me find a charter° in your voice
T' assist my simpleness.

DUKE. What would you, Desdemona?

DESDEMONA. That I did love the Moor to live with him,
My downright violence and storm of fortunes°
May trumpet to the world. My heart's subdued
Even to the very quality of my lord.°
I saw Othello's visage in his mind,
And to his honors and his valiant parts°
Did I my soul and fortunes consecrate.
So that, dear lords, if I be left behind
A moth° of peace, and he go to the war,
The rites° for why I love him are bereft me,
And I a heavy interim shall support
By his dear° absence. Let me go with him.

OTHELLO. Let her have your voice.°
Vouch with me, heaven, I therefor beg it not
To please the palate of my appetite,
Nor to comply with heat°—the young affects°
In me defunct—and proper° satisfaction,
But to be free° and bounteous to her mind.
And heaven defend° your good souls that you think°

240

245

250

255

260

265

---

237 bending . . . state bowing or kneeling to your authority   **239 reference . . . exhibition** provision of place to live and allowance of money   **240 accommodation** suitable provision.   **besort** attendance   **241 levels** equals, suits   **246 unfolding** explanation, proposal.   **prosperous** propitious   **247 charter** privilege, authorization   **251 My . . . fortunes** my plain and total breach of social custom, taking my future by storm and disrupting my whole life   **253 My heart's . . . lord** my heart is brought wholly into accord with Othello's virtues; I love him for his virtues   **255 parts** qualities   **258 moth** i.e., one who consumes merely   **259 rites** rites of love (with a suggestion too of *rights,* sharing)   **261 dear** (1) heartfelt (2) costly   **262 voice** consent   **265 heat** sexual passion. **young affects** passions of youth, desires   **266 proper** personal   **267 free** generous **268 defend** forbid.   **think** should think

I will your serious and great business scant
When she is with me. No, when light-winged toys   *270*
Of feathered Cupid seel° with wanton dullness
My speculative and officed instruments,°
That° my disports° corrupt and taint° my business,
Let huswives make a skillet of my helm,
And all indign° and base adversities   *275*
Make head° against my estimation!°

DUKE. Be it as you shall privately determine,
     Either for her stay or going. Th' affair cries haste,
     And speed must answer it.

A SENATOR.   You must away tonight.

DESDEMONA. Tonight, my lord?

DUKE.   This night.

OTHELLO.   With all my heart.   *280*

DUKE. At nine i' the morning here we'll meet again.
     Othello, leave some officer behind,
     And he shall our commission bring to you,
     With such things else of quality and respect°
     As doth import° you.

OTHELLO.   So please Your Grace, my ancient;   *285*
     A man he is of honesty and trust.
     To his conveyance I assign my wife,
     With what else needful Your Good Grace shall think
     To be sent after me.

DUKE.   Let it be so.
     Good night to everyone. [*To Brabantio.*] And, noble signor,   *290*
     If virtue no delighted° beauty lack,
     Your son-in-law is far more fair than black.

FIRST SENATOR. Adieu, brave Moor. Use Desdemona well.

BRABANTIO. Look to her, Moor, if thou hast eyes to see.
     She has deceived her father, and may thee.   *295*

               Exeunt [Duke, Brabantio, Cassio, Senators, and Officers].

OTHELLO. My life upon her faith! Honest Iago,
     My Desdemona must I leave to thee.
     I prithee, let thy wife attend on her,
     And bring them after in the best advantage.°
     Come, Desdemona. I have but an hour   *300*

---

271 seel i.e., make blind (as in falconry, by sewing up the eyes of the hawk during training) **272 speculative . . . instruments** i.e., perceptive faculties used in the performance of duty   **273 That** so that. **disports** sexual pastimes. **taint** impair   **275 indign** unworthy, shameful   **276 Make head** raise an army. **estimation** reputation   **284 of quality and respect** of importance and relevance   **285 import** concern   **291 delighted** capable of delighting   **299 in . . . advantage** at the most favorable opportunity

Of love, of worldly matters and direction,°
To spend with thee. We must obey the time.

Exit [with Desdemona].

RODERIGO. Iago—

IAGO. What sayst thou, noble heart?

RODERIGO. What will I do, think'st thou? 305

IAGO. Why, go to bed and sleep.

RODERIGO. I will incontinently° drown myself.

IAGO. If thou dost, I shall never love thee after. Why, thou silly gentleman?

RODERIGO. It is silliness to live when to live is torment and then have we
a prescription° to die when death is our physician. 310

IAGO. O villainous!° I have looked upon the world for four times seven
years, and, since I could distinguish betwixt a benefit and an injury,
I never found man that knew how to love himself. Ere I would say
I would drown myself for the love of a guinea hen,° I would change
my humanity with a baboon. 315

RODERIGO. What should I do? I confess it is my shame to be so fond°, but
it is not in my virtue° to amend it.

IAGO. Virtue? A fig!° 'Tis in ourselves that we are thus or thus. Our
bodies are our gardens, to the which our wills are gardeners; so that
if we will plant nettles or sow lettuce, set hyssop° and weed up 320
thyme, supply it with one gender° of herbs or distract it with°
many, either to have it sterile with idleness° or manured with
industry—why, the power and corrigible authority° of this lies in
our wills. If the beam° of our lives had not one scale of reason to
poise° another of sensuality, the blood° and baseness of our natures 325
would conduct us to most preposterous conclusions. But we have
reason to cool our raging motions,° our carnal stings, our unbitted°
lusts, whereof I take this that you call love to be a sect or scion.°

RODERIGO. It cannot be.

IAGO. It is merely a lust of the blood and a permission of the will. Come, 330
be a man. Drown thyself? Drown cats and blind puppies. I have
professed me thy friend, and I confess me knit to thy deserving with
cables of perdurable° toughness. I could never better stead° thee than
now. Put money in thy purse. Follow thou the wars; defeat thy

---

301 direction instructions **307 incontinently** immediately **310 prescription** (1) right
based on long-established custom (2) doctor's prescription **311 villainous** i.e., what perfect nonsense **314 guinea hen** (A slang term for a prostitute.) **316 fond** infatu-
ated **317 virtue** strength, nature **318 fig** (To give a fig is to thrust the thumb between
the first and second fingers in a vulgar and insulting gesture.) **320 hyssop** a herb of the
mint family **321 gender** kind. **distract it with** divide it among **322 idleness** want
of cultivation **323 corrigible authority** power to correct **324 beam** balance **325 poise**
counterbalance. **blood** natural passions **327 motions** appetites. **unbitted** unbridled,
uncontrolled **328 sect or scion** cutting or offshoot **333 perdurable** very durable.
stead assist

favor° with an usurped° beard. I say, put money in thy purse. It can- 335
not be long that Desdemona should continue her love to the
Moor—put money in thy purse—nor he his to her. It was a violent
commencement in her, and thou shalt see an answerable seques-
tration°—put but money in thy purse. These Moors are changea-
ble in their wills°—fill thy purse with money. The food that 340
to him now is as luscious as locusts° shall be to him shortly as bitter as coloquintida.° She must change for youth; when she is sated
with his body, she will find the error of her choice. She must have
change, she must. Therefore put money in thy purse. If thou wilt
needs damn thyself, do it a more delicate way than drowning. 345
Make° all the money thou canst. If sanctimony° and a frail vow betwixt an erring° barbarian and a supersubtle Venetian be not too
hard for my wits and all the tribe of hell, thou shalt enjoy her. Therefore make money. A pox of drowning thyself! It is clean out of the
way. Seek thou rather to be hanged in compassing° thy joy than to 350
be drowned and go without her.

RODERIGO. Wilt thou be fast° to my hopes if I depend on the issue?

IAGO. Thou art sure of me. Go, make money. I have told thee often, and
I retell thee again and again, I hate the Moor. My cause is hearted;°
thine hath no less reason. Let us be conjunctive° in our revenge 355
against him. If thou canst cuckold him, thou dost thyself a pleasure
me a sport. There are many events in the womb of time which will
be delivered. Traverse,° go, provide thy money. We will have more
of this tomorrow. Adieu.

RODERIGO. Where shall we meet i' the morning? 360

IAGO. At my lodging.

RODERIGO. I'll be with thee betimes.°   [*He starts to leave.*]

IAGO. Go to, farewell.—Do you hear, Roderigo?

RODERIGO. What say you?

IAGO. No more of drowning, do you hear? 365

RODERIGO. I am changed.

IAGO. Go to, farewell. Put money enough in your purse.

RODERIGO. I'll sell all my land.   *Exit.*

IAGO. Thus do I ever make my fool my purse;
    For I mine own gained knowledge should profane 370
    If I would time expend with such a snipe°

---

335 defeat thy favor disguise your face. **usurped** (The suggestion is that Roderigo is not
man enough to have a beard of his own.) **338–39 an answerable sequestration** a corresponding separation or estrangement **340 wills** carnal appetites **341 locusts** fruit of the
carob tree (see Matthew 3:4), or perhaps honeysuckle **342 coloquintida** colocynth or bitter
apple, a purgative **345 Make** raise, collect **346 sanctimony** sacred ceremony
347 erring wandering, vagabond, unsteady **350 compassing** encompassing, embracing
352 fast true **354 hearted** fixed in the heart, heartfelt **355 conjunctive** united
357 Traverse (A military marching term.) **362 betimes** early **371 snipe** woodcock, i.e.,
fool

But for my sport and profit. I hate the Moor;
And it is thought abroad° that twixt my sheets
He's done my office.° I know not if 't be true;
But I, for mere suspicion in that kind,   375
Will do as if for surety.° He holds me well;°
The better shall my purpose work on him.
Cassio's a proper° man. Let me see now:
To get his place and to plume up° my will
In double knavery—How, how?—Let's see: 380
After some time, to abuse° Othello's ear
That he° is too familiar with his wife.
He hath a person and a smooth dispose°
To be suspected, framed to make women false.
The Moor is of a free° and open° nature,   385
That thinks men honest that but seem to be so,
And will as tenderly° be led by the nose
As asses are.
I have 't. It is engendered. Hell and night
Must bring this monstrous birth to the world's light.   [*Exit.*]   390

[2.1]   *Enter Montano and two Gentlemen.*

MONTANO. What from the cape can you discern at sea?
FIRST GENTLEMAN. Nothing at all. It is a high-wrought flood.°
   I cannot, twixt the heaven and the main,°
   Descry a sail.
MONTANO. Methinks the wind hath spoke aloud at land;   5
   A fuller blast ne'er shook our battlements.
   If it hath ruffianed° so upon the sea,
   What ribs of oak, when mountains° melt on them,
   Can hold the mortise?° What shall we hear of this?
SECOND GENTLEMAN. A segregation° of the Turkish fleet.   10
   For do but stand upon the foaming shore,
   The chidden° billow seems to pelt the clouds;

---

373 **it is thought abroad** i.e., it is rumored   374 **my office** i.e., my sexual function as husband   376 **do . . . surety** act as if on certain knowledge.   **holds me well** regards me favorably   378 **proper** handsome   379 **plume up** glorify, gratify   381 **abuse** deceive 382 **he** i.e., Cassio   383 **dispose** manner, bearing   385 **free** frank, generous.   **open**. unsuspicious   387 **tenderly** readily

2.1. Location: A seaport in Cyprus. An open place near the quay.
2 **high-wrought flood** very agitated sea   3 **main** ocean (also at 1.41)   7 **ruffianed** raged 8 **mountains** i.e., of water   9 **hold the mortise** hold their joints together. (A *mortise* is the socket hollowed out in fitting timbers.)   10 **segregation** dispersion   12 **chidden** i.e., rebuked, repelled (by the shore), and thus shot into the air

The wind-shaked surge, with high and monstrous mane,°
Seems to cast water on the burning Bear°
And quench the guards of th' ever-fixèd pole.   *15*
I never did like molestation° view
On the enchafèd° flood.

MONTANO.   If that° the Turkish fleet
Be not ensheltered and embayed°, they are drowned;
It is impossible to bear it out.°   *20*

Enter a [Third] Gentleman.

THIRD GENTLEMAN. News, lads! Our wars are done.
The desperate tempest hath so banged the Turks
That their designment° halts.° A noble ship of Venice
Hath seen a grievous wreck° and sufferance°
On most part of their fleet.   *25*

MONTANO. How? Is this true?

THIRD GENTLEMAN. The ship is here put in,
A Veronesa;° Michael Cassio,
Lieutenant to the warlike Moor Othello,
Is come on shore; the Moor himself at sea,   *30*
And is in full commission here for Cyprus.

MONTANO. I am glad on 't. 'Tis a worthy governor.

THIRD GENTLEMAN. But this same Cassio, though he speak of comfort
Touching the Turkish loss, yet he looks sadly°
And prays the Moor be safe, for they were parted   *35*
With foul and violent tempest.

MONTANO.   Pray heaven he be,
For I have served him, and the man commands
Like a full° soldier. Let's to the seaside, ho!
As well to see the vessel that's come in
As to throw out our eyes for brave Othello,   *40*
Even till we make the main and th' aerial blue°
An indistinct regard.°

THIRD GENTLEMAN.   Come, let's do so,
For every minute is expectancy°
Of more arrivance.°

---

13 monstrous mane (The surf is like the mane of a wild beast.) **14 the burning Bear** i.e.,
the constellation Ursa Minor or the Little Bear, which includes the polestar (and hence
regarded as the *guards of th' ever-fixèd pole* in the next line; sometimes the term *guards* is applied to the two "pointers" of the Big Bear or Dipper, which may be intended here.) **16 like
molestation** comparable uproar **17 enchafèd** angry **18 If that** if **19 embayed** sheltered by a bay **20 bear it out** survive, weather the storm **23 designment** enterprise.
halts is lame **24 wreck** shipwreck. **sufferance** disaster **28 Veronesa** i.e., fitted out
in Verona for Venetian service, or possibly *Verennessa* (the Folio spelling), a cutter (from
verrinare, to cut through) **34 sadly** gravely **38 full** perfect **41 the main . . . blue** the
sea and the sky **42 An indistinct regard** indistinguishable in our view **43 is expectancy**
gives expectation **44 arrivance** arrival

Enter Cassio.

CASSIO. Thanks, you the valiant of this warlike isle,   45
That so approve° the Moor! O, let the heavens
Give him defense against the elements,
For I have lost him on a dangerous sea.
MONTANO. Is he well shipped?
CASSIO. His bark is stoutly timbered, and his pilot   50
Of very expert and approved allowance;°
Therefore my hopes, not surfeited to death,°
Stand in bold cure.°   [*A cry*] *within:* "A sail, a sail, a sail!"
CASSIO. What noise?
A GENTLEMAN. The town is empty. On the brow o' the sea   55
Stand ranks of people, and they cry "A sail!"
CASSIO. My hopes do shape him for the governor. [*A shot within.*]
SECOND GENTLEMAN. They do discharge their shot of courtesy;°
Our friends at least.
CASSIO.   I pray you, sir, go forth,
And give us truth who 'tis that is arrived.   60
SECOND GENTLEMAN. I shall.   *Exit.*
MONTANO. But, good Lieutenant, is your general wived?
CASSIO. Most fortunately. He hath achieved a maid
That paragons° description and wild fame,°
One that excels the quirks° of blazoning° pens,   65
And in th' essential vesture of creation
Does tire the enginer.°

Enter [Second] Gentleman.°
                    How now? Who has put in?°

SECOND GENTLEMAN. 'Tis one Iago, ancient to the General.
CASSIO. He's had most favorable and happy speed.
Tempests themselves, high seas, and howling winds,   70
The guttered° rocks and congregated sands—
Traitors ensteeped° to clog the guiltless keel—
As° having sense of beauty, do omit°

---

46 approve admire, honor   **51 approved allowance** tested reputation   **52 surfeited
to death** i.e., overextended, worn thin through repeated application or delayed fulfillment   **53 in bold cure** in strong hopes of fulfillment   **58 discharge . . . courtesy** fire
a salute in token of respect and courtesy   **64 paragons** surpasses.   **wild fame** extravagant
report   **65 quirks** witty conceits.   **blazoning** setting forth as though in heraldic language   **66–67 in . . . enginer** in her real beauty (she) defeats any attempt to praise her.
enginer engineer, i.e., poet, one who devises   **s.d. Second Gentleman** (So identified in
the quarto text here and in II. 58, 61, and 96; the Folio calls him a gentleman.)   **put in** i.e.,
to harbor   **71 guttered** jagged, trenched   **72 ensteeped** lying under water   **73 As** as
if.   **omit** forbear to exercise

Their mortal° natures, letting go safely by
The divine Desdemona.
MONTANO.   What is she?   75
CASSIO. She that I spake of, our great captain's captain,
    Left in the conduct of the bold Iago,
    Whose footing° here anticipates our thoughts
    A sennight's° speed. Great Jove, Othello guard,
    And swell his sail with thine own powerful breath,   80
    That he may bless this bay with his tall° ship,
    Make love's quick pants in Desdemona's arms,
    Give renewed fire to our extincted spirits,
    And bring all Cyprus comfort!

Enter Desdemona, Iago, Roderigo, and Emilia.

                            O, behold,
    The riches of the ship is come on shore!   [*He kneels.*] 85
    You men of Cyprus, let her have your knees.
    Hail to thee, lady! And the grace of heaven
    Before, behind thee, and on every hand
    Enwheel thee round!   [*He rises.*]
DESDEMONA.   I thank you, valiant Cassio.
    What tidings can you tell me of my lord?   90
CASSIO. He is not yet arrived, nor know I aught
    But that he's well and will be shortly here.
DESDEMONA. O, but I fear—How lost you company?
CASSIO. The great contention of the sea and skies
    Parted our fellowship.
                    (*Within*) "A sail, a sail!"   [*A shot.*]
                    But hark. A sail!   95
SECOND GENTLEMAN. They give their greeting to the citadel.
    This likewise is a friend.
CASSIO.   See for the news.
                                [*Exit Second Gentleman.*]
    Good Ancient, you are welcome. [*Kissing Emilia.*] Welcome, mistress.
    Let it not gall your patience, good Iago,
    That I extend° my manners. 'Tis my breeding   100
    That gives me this bold show of courtesy.
IAGO. Sir, would she give you so much of her lips
    As of her tongue she oft bestows on me,
    You would have enough.
DESDEMONA. Alas, she has no speech!   105

---

74 mortal deadly   **78 footing** landing   **79 sennight's** week's   **81 tall** splendid, gallant
100 extend show

IAGO. In faith, too much.
　　I find it still,° when I have list° to sleep.
　　Marry, before your ladyship, I grant,
　　She puts her tongue a little in her heart
　　And chides with thinking.°
EMILIA.　　　　　　　　　You have little cause to say so.　　　*110*
IAGO. Come on, come on. You are pictures out of doors,°
　　Bells° in your parlors, wildcats in your kitchens,°
　　Saints° in your injuries, devils being offended,
　　Players° in your huswifery,° and huswives° in your beds.
DESDEMONA. O, fie upon thee, slanderer!　　　　　　　　*115*
IAGO. Nay, it is true, or else I am a Turk.
　　You rise to play, and go to bed to work.
EMILIA. You shall not write my praise.
IAGO.　　　　　　　　　　No, let me not.
DESDEMONA. What wouldst write of me, if thou shouldst praise me?
IAGO. O gentle lady, do not put me to 't,　　　　　　　　*120*
　　For I am nothing if not critical.°
DESDEMONA. Come on, assay.°—There's one gone to the harbor?
IAGO. Ay, madam.
DESDEMONA. I am not merry, but I do beguile
　　The thing I am° by seeming otherwise.　　　　　　　　*125*
　　Come, how wouldst thou praise me?
IAGO. I am about it, but indeed my invention
　　Comes from my pate as birdlime° does from frieze°—
　　It plucks out brains and all. But my Muse labors,°
　　And thus she is delivered:　　　　　　　　　　　　　*130*
　　If she be fair and wise, fairness and wit,
　　The one's for use, the other useth it.°
DESDEMONA. Well praised! How if she be black° and witty?
IAGO. If she be black, and thereto have a wit,
　　She'll find a white° that shall her blackness fit.°　　　*135*
DESDEMONA. Worse and worse.
EMILIA.　　　　　　　　　How if fair and foolish?

107 still always. **list** desire　**110 with thinking** i.e., in her thoughts only　**111 pictures
out of doors** i.e., silent and well-behaved in public　**112 Bells** i.e., jangling, noisy, and
brazen.　**in your kitchens** i.e., in domestic affairs. (Ladies would not do the cooking.)
113 Saints martyrs　**114 Players** idlers, triflers, or deceivers.　**huswifery** housekeeping.　**huswives** hussies (i.e., woman are "busy" in bed, or thrifty in dispensing sexual
favors)　**121 critical** censorious　**122 assay** try　**125 The thing I am** i.e., my anxious
self　**128 birdlime** sticky substance used to catch small birds.　**frieze** coarse woolen
cloth　**129 labors** (1) exerts herself (2) prepares to deliver a child (with a following pun
on *delivered* in l. 130)　**132 The one's . . . it** i.e., her cleverness will make use of her
beauty　**133 black** dark complexioned, brunette　**135 white** a fair person (with word-
play on *wight,* a person).　**fit** (with sexual suggestion of mating)

IAGO. She never yet was foolish that was fair,
    For even her folly° helped her to an heir.°
DESDEMONA. These are old fond° paradoxes to make fools laugh i' th'
    alehouse. What miserable praise hast thou for her that's foul° and   *140*
    foolish?
IAGO. There's none so foul and foolish thereunto,
    But does foul° pranks which fair and wise ones do.
DESDEMONA. O heavy ignorance! Thou praisest the worst best. But what
    praise couldst thou bestow on a deserving woman indeed, one that,   *145*
    in the authority of her merit, did justly put on the vouch° of very
    malice itself?
IAGO. She that was ever fair, and never proud,
    Had tongue at will, and yet was never loud,
    Never lacked gold and yet went never gay,°   *150*
    Fled from her wish, and yet said, "Now I may,"°
    She that being angered, her revenge being nigh,
    Bade her wrong stay° and her displeasure fly,
    She that in wisdom never was so frail
    To change the cod's head for the salmon's tail,°   *155*
    She that could think and ne'er disclose her mind,
    See suitors following and not look behind,
    She was a wight, if ever such wight were—
DESDEMONA. To do what?
IAGO. To suckle fools° and chronicle small beer.°   *160*
DESDEMONA. O most lame and impotent conclusion! Do not learn of him,
    Emilia, though he be thy husband. How say you, Cassio? Is he
    not a most profane° and liberal° counselor?
CASSIO. He speaks home,° madam. You may relish° him more in° the
    soldier than in the scholar.   *165*

        [*Cassio and Desdemona stand together, conversing intimately.*]

IAGO. [*Aside*] He takes her by the palm. Ay, well said,° whisper. With as
    little a web as this will I ensnare as great a fly as Cassio. Ay, smile
    upon her, do; I will gyve° thee in thine own courtship.° You say

---

138 folly with added meaning of "lechery, wantonness"). **to an heir** i.e., to bear a
child **139 fond** foolish **140 foul** ugly **143 foul** sluttish **146 put . . . vouch**
compel the approval **150 gay** extravagantly clothed **151 Fled . . . may** avoided temptation where the choice was hers **153 Bade . . . stay** i.e., resolved to put up with her injury patiently **155 To . . . tail** i.e., to exchange a lackluster husband for a sexy lover (?)
(*Cod's head* is slang for penis, and *tail* for pudendum.) **160 suckle fools** breastfeed babies. **chronicle small beer** i.e., keep petty household accounts, keep track of trivial matters
163 profane irreverent, ribald. **liberal** licentious, free-spoken **164 home** i.e., without
reserve. **relish** appreciate. **in** in the character of **166 well said** well done **168 gyve**
fetter, shackle. **courtship** courtesy, show of courtly manners

true; 'tis so, indeed. If such tricks as these strip you out of your lieu-
tenantry, it had been better you had not kissed your three fingers   *170*
so oft, which now again you are most apt to play the sir° in. Very
good; well kissed! An excellent courtesy! 'Tis so, indeed. Yet again
your fingers to your lips? Would they were clyster pipes° for your
sake! [*Trumpet within.*] The Moor! I know his trumpet.
CASSIO. 'Tis truly so.   *175*
DESDEMONA. Let's meet him and receive him.
CASSIO. Lo, where he comes!

    Enter Othello and attendants.

OTHELLO. O my fair warrior!
DESDEMONA.   My dear Othello!
OTHELLO. It gives me wonder great as my content
    To see you here before me. O my soul's joy!   *180*
    If after every tempest come such calms,
    May the winds blow till they have wakened death!
    And let the laboring bark climb hills of seas
    Olympus-high, and duck again as low
    As hell's from heaven! If it were now to die,   *185*
    'Twere now to be most happy, for I fear
    My soul hath her content so absolute
    That not another comfort like to this
    Succeeds in unknown fate.°
DESDEMONA.   The heavens forbid
    But that our loves and comforts should increase   *190*
    Even as our days do grow!
OTHELLO. Amen to that, sweet powers!
    I cannot speak enough of this content.
    It stops me here; it is too much of joy.
    And this, and this, the greatest discords be   *195*
                                          [*They kiss°*]
    That e'er our hearts shall make!
IAGO. [*Aside*] O, you are well tuned now!
    But I'll set down° the pegs that make this music,
    As honest as I am.
OTHELLO. Come, let us to the castle.   *200*
    News, friends! Our wars are done, the Turks are drowned.
    How does my old acquaintance of this isle?—
    Honey, you shall be well desired° in Cyprus;

---

171 the sir i.e., the fine gentleman   **173 clyster pipes** tubes used for enemas and douches
189 Succeeds . . . fate i.e., can follow in the unknown future   **195 s.d. They kiss** (The
direction is from the quaro.)   **198 set down** loosen (and hence untune the instrument)
202 desired welcomed

I have found great love amongst them. O my sweet,
I prattle out of fashion,° and I dote   *205*
In mine own comforts.—I prithee, good Iago,
Go to the bay and disembark my coffers.°
Bring thou the master° to the citadel;
He is a good one, and his worthiness
Does challenge° much respect.—Come, Desdemona.—   *210*
Once more, well met at Cyprus!
            Exeunt Othello and Desdemona [and all but Iago and Roderigo].
IAGO. [*To an attendant*] Do thou meet me presently at the harbor. [*To
    Roderigo.*] Come hither. If thou be'st valiant—as, they say, base men°
    being in love have then a nobility in their natures more than is na-
    tive to them—list° me. The Lieutenant tonight watches on the court   *215*
    of guard.° First, I must tell thee this: Desdemona is directly in love
    with him.
RODERIGO. With him? Why, tis not possible.
IAGO. Lay thy finger thus,° and let thy soul be instructed. Mark me with
    what violence she first loved the Moor, but° for bragging and tell-   *220*
    ing her fantastical lies. To love him still for prating? Let not thy dis-
    creet heart think it. Her eye must be fed; and what delight shall she
    have to look on the devil? When the blood is made dull with the
    act of sport, there should be, again to inflame it and to give satiety
    a fresh appetite, loveliness in favor°, sympathy° in years, manners,   *225*
    and beauties—all which the Moor is defective in. Now, for want
    of these required conveniences,° her delicate tenderness will find it-
    self abused, begin to heave the gorge,° disrelish and abhor the Moor.
    Very nature will instruct her in it and compel her to some second
    choice. Now, sir, this granted—as it is a most pregnant° and un-   *230*
    forced position—who stands so eminent in the degree of this for-
    tune as Cassio does? A knave very voluble, no further conscionable°
    than in putting on the mere form of civil and humane° seeming for
    the better compassing of his salt° and most hidden loose affection.°
    Why, none, why, none. A slipper° and subtle knave, a finder out of   *235*
    occasions, that has an eye can stamp° and counterfeit advantages,°
    though true advantage never present itself; a devilish knave. Besides,
    the knave is handsome, young, and hath all those requisites in him

---

205 out of fashion irrelevantly (?) **207 coffers** chests, baggage **208 master** ship's
captain **210 challenge** lay claim to, deserve **213 base men** even lowly born men
215 list listen to **215–16 court of guard** guardhouse. (Cassio is in charge of the watch.)
219 thus i.e., on your lips **220 but** only **225 favor** appearance. **sympathy** correspondence, similarity **227 conveniences** compatibilities **228 heave the gorge** experience
nausea **230 pregnant** evident, cogent **232 conscionable** conscientious, concience-bound
233 humane polite,   courteous **234 salt** licentious. **affection** passion **235 slipper**
slippery **236 an eye can stamp** an eye that can coin, create. **advantages** favorable opportunities

that folly° and green° minds look after. A pestilent complete knave, and the woman hath found him° already. 240

RODERIGO. I cannot believe that in her. She's full of most blessed condition.°

IAGO. Blessed fig's end!° The wine she drinks is made of grapes. If she had been blessed, she would never have loved the Moor. Blessed pudding!° Didst thou not see her paddle with the palm of his hand? 245 Didst not mark that?

RODERIGO. Yes, that I did; but that was but courtesy.

IAGO. Lechery, by this hand. An index° and obscure° prologue to the history of lust and foul thoughts. They met so near with their lips that their breaths embraced together. Villainous thoughts, Roderigo! 250 When these mutualities° so marshal the way, hard at hand° comes the master and main exercise, th' incorporate° conclusion. Pish! But, sir, be you ruled by me. I have brought you from Venice. Watch you° tonight; for the command, I'll lay 't upon you.° Cassio knows you not. I'll not be far from you. Do you find some occasion to 255 anger Cassio, either by speaking too loud, or tainting° his discipline, or from what other course you please, which the time shall more favorably minister.°

RODERIGO. Well.

IAGO. Sir, he's rash and very sudden in choler,° and haply° may strike at 260 you. Provoke him that he may, for even out of that will I cause these of Cyprus to mutiny,° whose qualification° shall come into no true taste° again but by the displanting of Cassio. So shall you have a shorter journey to your desires by the means I shall then have to prefer° them, and the impediment most profitably removed, without 265 the which there were no expectation of our prosperity.

RODERIGO. I will do this, if you can bring it to any opportunity.

IAGO. I warrant° thee. Meet me by and by° at the citadel. I must fetch his necessaries ashore. Farewell.

RODERIGO. Adieu. *Exit.* 270

IAGO. That Cassio loves her, I do well believe 't;
    That she loves him, 'tis apt° and of great credit.°
    The Moor, howbeit that I endure him not,
    Is of a constant, loving, noble nature,

---

239 folly wantonness. **green** immature **240 found him** sized him up **242 condition** disposition **243 fig's end** (See 1.3.318 for the vulgar gesture of the fig.) **245 pudding** sausage **248 index** table of contents. **obscure** (i.e., the *lust and foul thoughts,* l. 249, are secret, hidden from view) **251 mutualities** exchanges, intimacies. **hard at hand** closely following **252 incorporate** carnal **253–54 Watch you** stand watch **255 for the command . . . you** I'll arrange for you to be appointed, given orders **256 tainting** disparaging **258 minister** provide **260 choler** wrath. **260 haply** perhaps **262 mutiny** riot. **qualification** appeasement **262–63 true taste** acceptable state **265 prefer** advance **267 warrant** assure. **by and by** immediately **272 apt** probable. **credit** credibility

And I dare think he'll prove to Desdemona   275
A most dear husband. Now, I do love her too,
Not out of absolute lust—though peradventure
I stand accountant° for as great a sin—
But partly led to diet° my revenge
For that I do suspect the lusty Moor   280
Hath leaped into my seat, the thought whereof
Doth, like a poisonous mineral, gnaw my innards;
And nothing can or shall content my soul
Till I am evened with him, wife for wife,
Or failing so, yet that I put the Moor   285
At least into a jealousy so strong
That judgment cannot cure. Which thing to do,
If this poor trash of Venice, whom I trace°
For° his quick hunting, stand the putting on,°
I'll have our Michael Cassio on the hip,°   290
Abuse° him to the Moor in the rank garb°—
For I fear Cassio with my nightcap° too—
Make the Moor thank me, love me, and reward me
For making him egregiously an ass
And practicing upon° his peace and quiet   295
Even to madness. 'Tis here, but yet confused.
Knavery's plain face is never seen till used.   *Exit.*

[2.2]   *Enter Othello's Herald with a proclamation.*

HERALD. It is Othello's pleasure, our noble and valiant general, that, upon
certain tidings now arrived, importing the mere perdition° of the
Turkish fleet, every man put himself into triumph: some to dance,
some to make bonfires, each man to what sport and revels his
addiction° leads him. For, besides these beneficial news, it is the   5
celebration of his nuptial. So much was his pleasure should be
proclaimed. All offices° are open, and there is full liberty of feast-
ing from this present hour of five till the bell have told eleven. Heaven
bless the isle of Cyprus and our noble general Othello!   *Exit.*

278 accountant accountable **279 diet** feed **288 trace** i.e., train, or follow (?), or perhaps
trash, a hunting term, meaning to put weights on a hunting dog in order to slow him
down **289 For** to make more eager. **stand . . . on** respond properly when I incite him
to quarrel **290 on the hip** at my mercy, where I can throw him. (A wrestling term.)
291 Abuse slander. **rank garb** coarse manner, gross fashion **292 with my nightcap** i.e.,
as a rival in my bed, as one who gives me cuckold's horns **295 practicing upon** plotting against

2.2 Location: Cyprus A street.
2 mere perdition complete destruction **5 addiction** inclination **7 offices** rooms where
food and drink are kept

[2.3] *Enter Othello, Desdemona, Cassio, and attendants.*

OTHELLO. Good Michael, look you to the guard tonight.   *1*
  Let's teach ourselves that honorable stop°
  Not to outsport° discretion.
CASSIO. Iago hath direction what to do,
  But notwithstanding, with my personal eye   *5*
  Will I look to 't.
OTHELLO.   Iago is most honest.
  Michael, good night. Tomorrow with your earliest°
  Let me have speech with you. [*To Desdemona.*] Come, my dear love,
  The purchase made, the fruits are to ensue;
  That profit's yet to come 'tween me and you.° —   *10*
  Good night.

  Exit [Othello, with Desdemona and attendants].

  Enter Iago.

CASSIO. Welcome, Iago. We must to the watch.
IAGO. Not this hour,° Lieutenant; 'tis not yet ten o' the clock. Our general
  cast° us thus early for the love of his Desdemona; who° let us not
  therefore blame. He hath not yet made wanton the night with her,   *15*
  and she is sport for Jove.
CASSIO. She's a most exquisite lady.
IAGO. And, I'll warrant her, full of game.
CASSIO. Indeed, she's a most fresh and delicate creature.
IAGO. What an eye she has! Methinks it sounds a parley° to provocation. *20*
CASSIO. An inviting eye, and yet methinks right modest.
IAGO. And when she speaks, is it not an alarum° to love?
CASSIO. She is indeed perfection.
IAGO. Well, happiness to their sheets! Come, Lieutenant, I have a stoup°
  of wine, and here without° are a brace° of Cyprus gallants that   *25*
  would fain have a measure° to the health of black Othello.
CASSIO. Not tonight, good Iago. I have very poor and unhappy brains for
  drinking. I could well wish courtesy would invent some other cus-
  tom of entertainment.
IAGO. O, they are our friends. But one cup! I'll drink for you.°   *30*

2.3 Location: Cyprus. The citadel.
2 stop restraint **3 outsport** celebrate beyond the bounds of **7 with your earliest** at
your earliest convenience **9–10 The purchase . . . you** i.e., though married, we haven't
yet consummated our love **13 Not this hour** not for an hour yet **14 cast** dismissed.
who i.e., Othello **20 sounds a parley** calls for a conference, issues an invitation
22 alarum signal calling men to arms (continuing the military metaphor of *parley,* l. 20)
24 stoup measure of liquor, two quarts **25 without** outside. **brace** pair **26 have a
measure** drink a toast **30 for you** in your place. (Iago will do the steady drinking to
keep the gallants company while Cassio has only one cup.)

CASSIO. I have drunk but one cup tonight, and that was craftily qualified°
    too, and behold what innovation° it makes here. I am unfortunate
    in the infirmity and dare not task my weakness with any more.
IAGO. What, man? 'Tis a night of revels. The gallants desire it.
CASSIO. Where are they?   35
IAGO. Here° at the door. I pray you, call them in.
CASSIO. I'll do 't, but it dislikes° me.   *Exit.*
IAGO. If I can fasten but one cup upon him,
    With that which he hath drunk tonight already,
    He'll be as full of quarrel and offense   40
    As my young mistress' dog. Now, my sick fool Roderigo,
    Whom love hath turned almost the wrong side out,
    To Desdemona hath tonight caroused°
    Potations pottle-deep°; and he's to watch.
    Three lads of Cyprus—noble swelling° spirits,   45
    That hold their honors in a wary distance,°
    The very elements° of this warlike isle—
    Have I tonight flustered with flowing cups,
    And they watch° too. Now, 'mongst this flock of drunkards
    Am I to put our Cassio in some action   50
    That may offend the isle.—But here they come.

Enter Cassio, Montano, and gentlemen; [servants following with wine].

    If consequence do but approve my dream,°
    My boat sails freely both with wind and stream.°
CASSIO. 'Fore God, they have given me a rouse° already.
MONTANO. Good faith, a little one; not past a pint, as I am a soldier.   55
IAGO. Some wine, ho!

    [*Sings.*] "And let me the cannikin° clink, clink,
            And let me the cannikin clink.
                A soldier's a man,
                O, man's life's but a span;°   60
            Why, then, let a soldier drink."

    Some wine, boys!
CASSIO. 'Fore God, an excellent song.

---

31 qualified diluted   **32 Innovation** disturbance, insurrection   **36 here** i.e., in my head
37 dislikes displeases   **43 caroused** drunk off   **44 pottle-deep** to the bottom of the
tankard   **45 swelling** proud   **46 hold . . . distance** i.e., are extremely sensitive of their
honor   **47 very elements** true representatives   **49 watch** are members of the guard
52 If . . . dream if subsequent events will only substantiate my scheme   **53 stream** current
54 rouse full draft of liquor   **57 cannikin** small drinking vessel   **60 span** i.e., brief span
of time. (Compare Psalm 39:5 as rendered in the Book of Common Prayer: "Thou hast
made my days as it were a span long.")

IAGO. I learned it in England, where indeed they are most potent in pot-
    ing.° Your Dane, your German, and your swag-bellied Hollander—   65
    drink, ho!—are nothing to your English.

CASSIO. Is your Englishman so exquisite in his drinking?

IAGO. Why, he drinks° you, with facility, your Dane° dead drunk; he
    sweats not to overthrow your Almain;° he gives your Hollander
    a vomit ere the next pottle can be filled.   70

CASSIO. To the health of our general!

MONTANO. I am for it, Lieutenant, and I'll do you justice.°

IAGO. O sweet England! [*Sings.*]

> "King Stephen was and-a worthy peer,
>   His breeches cost him but a crown;   75
> He held them sixpence all too dear;
>   With that he called the tailor lown.°
> He was a wight of high renown,
>   And thou art but of low degree.
> 'Tis pride° that pulls the country down;   80
>   Then take thy auld° cloak about thee."

Some wine, ho!

CASSIO. 'Fore God, this is a more exquisite song than the other.

IAGO. Will you hear 't again?

CASSIO. No, for I hold him to be unworthy of his place that does those   85
    things. Well, God's above all; and there be souls must be saved, and
    there be souls must not be saved.

IAGO. It's true, good Lieutenant.

CASSIO. For mine own part—no offense to the General, nor any man of
    quality°—I hope to be saved.   90

IAGO. And so do I too, Lieutenant.

CASSIO. Ay, but, by your leave, not before me. The lieutenant is to be
    saved before the ancient. Let's have no more of this. Let's to our af-
    fairs. God forgive us our sins! Gentlemen, let's look to our business.
    Do not think, gentlemen, I am drunk. This is my ancient; this is   95
    my right hand, and this is my left. I am not drunk now. I can stand
    well enough, and speak well enough.

GENTLEMEN. Excellent well.

CASSIO. Why, very well then. You must not think then that I am drunk.
                                                                Exit.

MONTANO. To th' platform, masters. Come, let's set the watch.°   100
                                             [*Exeunt Gentlemen.*]

64–65 potting drinking **68 drinks you** drinks. **your Dane** your typical Dane
69 Almain German **72 I'll . . . justice** i.e., I'll drink as much as you **77 lown** lout,
rascal **80 pride** i.e., extravagance in dress **81 auld** old **90 quality** rank **100 set the
watch** mount the guard

IAGO. You see this fellow that is gone before.
    He's a soldier fit to stand by Caesar
    And give direction; and do but see his vice.
    'Tis to his virtue a just equinox,°
    The one as long as th' other. 'Tis pity of him.   *105*
    I fear the trust Othello puts him in,
    On some odd time of his infirmity,
    Will shake this island.
MONTANO.   But is he often thus?
IAGO. 'Tis evermore the prologue to his sleep.
    He'll watch the horologe a double set,°   *110*
    If drink rock not his cradle.
MONTANO.   It were well
    The General were put in mind of it.
    Perhaps he sees it not, or his good nature
    Prizes the virtue that appears in Cassio
    And looks not on his evils. Is not this true?   *115*

Enter Roderigo.

IAGO. [*Aside to him*] How now, Roderigo?
    I pray you, after the Lieutenant; go.   [*Exit Roderigo.*]
MONTANO. And 'tis great pity that the noble Moor
    Should hazard such a place as his own second
    With° one of an engraffed° infirmity.   *120*
    It were an honest action to say so
    To the Moor.
IAGO.   Not I, for this fair island.
    I do love Cassio well and would do much
    To cure him of this evil.   [*Cry within:* "Help! Help!"]
                But hark! What noise?

Enter Cassio, pursuing° Roderigo.

CASSIO. Zounds, you rogue! You rascal!   *125*
MONTANO. What's the matter, Lieutenant?
CASSIO. A knave teach me my duty? I'll beat the knave into a twiggen°
    bottle.
RODERIGO. Beat me?
CASSIO. Dost thou prate, rogue?   [*He strikes Roderigo.*] *130*

---

104 just equinox exact counterpart. (*Equinox* is an equal length of days and nights.)
110 watch . . . set stay awake twice around the clock or *horologe* **119–20 hazard . . .
With** risk giving such an important position as his second in command to **120 en-
graffed** engrafted, inveterate **124 s.d. pursuing** (The quarto text reads, "driving in.")
127 twiggen wickercovered. (Cassio vows to assail Roderigo until his skin resembles wickerwork, or until he has driven Roderigo through the holes in a wickerwork.)

MONTANO. Nay, good Lieutenant. [*Staying him.*] I pray you, sir, hold your
    hand.

CASSIO. Let me go, sir, or I'll knock you o'er the mazard.°

MONTANO. Come, come, you're drunk.

CASSIO. Drunk?   [*They fight.*]   **135**

IAGO. [*Aside to Roderigo*]

    Away, I say. Go out and cry a mutiny.°   [*Exit Roderigo.*]

    Nay, good Lieutenant—God's will, gentlemen—

    Help, ho!—Lieutenant—sir—Montano—sir—

    Help, masters!°—Here's a goodly watch indeed!   [*A bell rings.*°]

    Who's that which rings the bell?—Diablo,° ho!   **140**

    The town will rise.° God's will, Lieutenant, hold!

    You'll be ashamed forever.

    Enter Othello and attendants [*with weapons*].

OTHELLO. What is the matter here?

MONTANO.   Zounds, I bleed still.

    I am hurt to th' death. He dies!   [*He thrusts at Cassio.*]

OTHELLO.   Hold, for your lives!

IAGO. Hold, ho! Lieutenant—sir—Montano—gentlemen—   **145**

    Have you forgot all sense of place and duty?

    Hold! The General speaks to you. Hold, for shame!

OTHELLO. Why, how now, ho! From whence ariseth this?

    Are we turned Turks, and to ourselves do that

    Which heaven hath forbid° the Ottomites?   **150**

    For Christian shame, put by this barbarous brawl!

    He that stirs next to carve for° his own rage

    Holds his soul light;° he dies upon his motion.°

    Silence that dreadful bell. It frights the isle

    From her propriety.° What is the matter, masters?   **155**

    Honest Iago, that looks dead with grieving,

    Speak. Who began this? On thy love, I charge thee.

IAGO. I do not know. Friends all but now, even now,

    In quarter° and in terms° like bride and groom

    Devesting them° for bed; and then, but now—   **160**

    As if some planet had unwitted men—

---

133 mazard i.e., head. (Literally, a drinking vessel.)   **136 mutiny** riot   **139 masters**
sirs   **s.d. A bell rings** (This direction is from the quarto, as are *They fight* at **135**, *Exit Roderigo*
at **136**, and *with weapons* at **142**.)   **140 Diablo** the devil   **141 rise** grow riotous   **150 forbid**
i.e., prevented, by destroying their fleet, so that the Venetians need not fight them   **152 carve**
for i.e., indulge, satisfy   **153 Holds . . . light** i.e., places little value on his life.   **upon**
his motion if he moves   **155 propriety** proper state or condition   **159 In quarter** in
friendly conduct, within bounds.   **in terms** on good terms   **160 Devesting them** un-
dressing themselves

Swords out, and tilting one at other's breast
In opposition bloody. I cannot speak°
Any beginning to this peevish odds;°
And would in action glorious I had lost   *165*
Those legs that brought me to a part of it!
OTHELLO. How comes it, Michael, you are thus forgot?°
CASSIO. I pray you, pardon me. I cannot speak.
OTHELLO. Worthy Montano, you were wont be° civil;
The gravity and stillness° of your youth   *170*
The world hath noted, and your name is great
In mouths of wisest censure.° What's the matter
That you unlace° your reputation thus
And spend your rich opinion° for the name
Of a night-brawler? Give me answer to it.   *175*
MONTANO. Worthy Othello, I am hurt to danger.
Your officer, Iago, can inform you—
While I spare speech, which something° now offends° me—
Of all that I do know; nor know I aught
By me that's said or done amiss this night,   *180*
Unless self-charity be sometimes a vice,
And to defend ourselves it be a sin
When violence assails us.
OTHELLO.   Now, by heaven,
My blood° begins my safer guides° to rule,
And passion, having my best judgment collied,°   *185*
Assays° to lead the way. Zounds, if I stir,
Or do but lift this arm, the best of you
Shall sink in my rebuke. Give me to know
How this foul rout° began, who set it on;
And he that is approved in° this offense,   *190*
Though he had twinned with me, both at a birth,
Shall lose me. What? In a town of war
Yet wild, the people's hearts brim full of fear,
To manage° private and domestic quarrel?
In night, and on the court and guard of safety?°   *195*
'Tis monstrous. Iago, who began 't?

---

163 speak explain   **164 peevish odds** childish quarrel   **167 are thus forgot** have forgotten yourself thus   **169 wont be** accustomed to be   **170 stillness** sobriety
172 censure judgment   **173 unlace** undo, lay open (as one might loose the strings of a
purse containing reputation)   **174 opinion** reputation   **178 something** somewhat.
offends pains   **184 blood** passion (of anger). **guides** i.e., reason   **185 collied** darkened
186 Assays undertakes   **189 rout** riot   **190 approved in** found guilty of   **194 manage**
undertake   **195 on . . . safety** the main guardhouse or headquarters and on watch

MONTANO. [*To Iago*] If partially affined,° or leagued in office,°
    Thou dost deliver more or less than truth,
    Thou art no soldier.
IAGO.   Touch me not so near.
    I had rather have this tongue cut from my mouth   *200*
    Than it should do offense to Michael Cassio;
    Yet, I persuade myself, to speak the truth
    Shall nothing wrong him. Thus it is, General.
    Montano and myself being in speech,
    There comes a fellow crying out for help,   *205*
    And Cassio following him with determined sword
    To execute° upon him. Sir, this gentleman   [*Indicating Montano*]
    Steps in to Cassio and entreats his pause.
    Myself the crying fellow did pursue,
    Lest by his clamor—as it so fell out—   *210*
    The town might fall in fright. He, swift of foot
    Outran my purpose, and I returned, the rather°
    For that I heard the clink and fall of swords
    And Cassio high in oath, which till tonight
    I ne'er might say before. When I came back—   *215*
    For this was brief—I found them close together
    At blow and thrust, even as again they were
    When you yourself did part them.
    More of this matter cannot I report.
    But men are men; the best sometimes forget.°   *220*
    Though Cassio did some little wrong to him,
    As men in rage strike those that wish them best,°
    Yet surely Cassio, I believe, received
    From him that fled some strange indignity,
    Which patience could not pass.°
OTHELLO.   I know, Iago,   *225*
    Thy honesty and love doth mince this matter,
    Making it light to Cassio. Cassio, I love thee,
    But nevermore be officer of mine.

    Enter Desdemona, attended.

    Look if my gentle love be not raised up.
    I'll make thee an example.   *230*
DESDEMONA. What is the matter, dear?

---

197 partially affined made partial by some personal relationship.   **leagued in office** in
league as fellow officers   **207 execute** give effect to (his anger)   **212 rather** sooner
220 forget forget themselves   **222 those . . . best** i.e., even those who are well disposed   **225 pass** pass over, overlook

OTHELLO.   All 's well now, sweeting;
    Come away to bed. [*To Montano.*] Sir, for your hurts,
    Myself will be your surgeon.° — Lead him off.

                                          [*Montano is led off.*]

    Iago, look with care about the town
    And silence those whom this vile brawl distracted.   235
    Come, Desdemona. 'Tis the soldiers' life
    To have their balmy slumbers waked with strife.

                              Exit [*with all but Iago and Cassio*].

IAGO. What, are you hurt, Lieutenant?

CASSIO. Ay, past all surgery.

IAGO. Marry, God forbid!   240

CASSIO. Reputation, reputation, reputation! O, I have lost my reputation!
    I have lost the immortal part of myself, and what remains is bestial.
    My reputation, Iago, my reputation!

IAGO. As I am an honest man, I thought you had received some bodily
    wound; there is more sense in that than in reputation. Reputation 245
    is an idle and most false imposition,° oft got without merit and lost
    without deserving. You have lost no reputation at all, unless you
    repute yourself such a loser. What, man, there are ways to recover°
    the General again. You are but now cast in his mood° — a punish-
    ment more in policy° than in malice, even so as one would beat his 250
    offenseless dog to affright an imperious lion.° Sue° to him again and
    he's yours.

CASSIO. I will rather sue to be despised than to deceive so good a com-
    mander with so slight,° so drunken, and so indiscreet an officer.
    Drunk? And speak parrot?° And squabble? Swagger? Swear? And 255
    discourse fustian with one's own shadow? O thou invisible spirit
    of wine, if thou hast no name to be known by, let us call thee devil!

IAGO. What was he that you followed with your sword? What had he done
    to you?

CASSIO. I know not.   260

IAGO. Is 't possible?

CASSIO. I remember a mass of things, but nothing distinctly; a quarrel,
    but nothing wherefore.° O God, that men should put an enemy in
    their mouths to steal away their brains! That we should, with joy,
    pleasance, revel, and applause transform ourselves into beasts!   265

---

233 be your surgeon i.e., make sure you receive medical attention **246 imposition**
thing artificially imposed and of no real value **248 recover** regain favor with **249 cast
in his mood** dismissed in a moment of anger **250 in policy** done for expediency's sake
and as a public gesture **250–51 would . . . lion** i.e., would make an example of a minor
offender in order to deter more important and dangerous offenders **251 Sue** petition
254 slight worthless **255 speak parrot** talk nonsense, rant. (*Discourse fustian,* **256,** has much
the same meaning.) **263 wherefore** why

IAGO. Why, but you are now well enough. How came you thus recovered?

CASSIO. It hath pleased the devil drunkenness to give place to the devil wrath. One unperfectness shows me another, to make me frankly despise myself.

IAGO. Come, you are too severe a moraler.° As the time, the place, and   270 the condition of this country stands, I could heartily wish this had not befallen; but since it is as it is, mend it for your own good.

CASSIO. I will ask him for my place again; he shall tell me I am a drunkard! Had I as many mouths as Hydra,° such an answer would stop them all. To be now a sensible man, by and by a fool, and presently a   275 beast! O, strange! Every inordinate cup is unblessed, and the ingredient is a devil.

IAGO. Come, come, good wine is a good familiar creature, if it be well used. Exclaim no more against it. And, good Lieutenant, I think you think I love you.   280

CASSIO. I have well approved° it, sir. I drunk!

IAGO. You or any man living may be drunk at a time,° man. I'll tell you what you shall do. Our general's wife is now the general—I may say so in this respect, for that° he hath devoted and given up himself to the contemplation, mark, and denotement° of her parts° and   285 graces. Confess yourself freely to her; importune her help to put you in your place again. She is of so free,° so kind, so apt, so blessed a disposition, she holds it a vice in her goodness not to do more than she is requested. This broken joint between you and her husband entreat her to splinter;° and, my fortunes against any lay°   290 worth naming, this crack of your love shall grow stronger than it was before.

CASSIO. You advise me well.

IAGO. I protest,° in the sincerity of love and honest kindness.

CASSIO. I think it freely;° and betimes in the morning I will beseech   295 the virtuous Desdemona to undertake for me. I am desperate of my fortunes if they check° me here.

IAGO. You are in the right. Good night, Lieutenant. I must to the watch.

CASSIO. Good night, honest Iago.   *Exit Cassio.*   300

IAGO. And what's he then that says I play the villain,
    When this advice is free° I give and honest,

---

270 **moraler** moralizer   274 **Hydra** the Lernaean Hydra, a monster with many heads and the ability to grow two heads when one was cut off; slain by Hercules as the second of his twelve labors   281 **approved** proved   282 **at a time** at one time or another   284 **in . . . that** in view of this fact, that   285 **mark, and denotement** (Both words mean "observation"). **parts** qualities   287 **free** generous   290 **splinter** bind with splints. **lay** stake, wager   294 **protest** insist, declare   295 **freely** unreservedly   297 **check** repulse   302 **free** (1) free from guile (2) freely given

Probal° to thinking, and indeed the course
To win the Moor again? For 'tis most easy
Th' inclining° Desdemona to subdue°   *305*
In any honest suit; she's framed as fruitful°
As the free elements.° And then for her
To win the Moor—were 't to renounce his baptism,
All seals and symbols of redeemèd sin—
His soul is so enfettered to her love   *310*
That she may make, unmake, do what she list,
Even as her appetite shall play the god
With his weak function.° How am I then a villain,
To counsel Cassio to this parallel° course
Directly to his good? Divinity of hell!°   *315*
When devils will the blackest sins put on,°
They do suggest° at first with heavenly shows,
As I do now. For whiles this honest fool
Plies Desdemona to repair his fortune,
And she for him pleads strongly to the Moor,   *320*
I'll pour this pestilence into his ear,
That she repeals him° for her body's lust;
And by how much she strives to do him good,
She shall undo her credit with the Moor.
So will I turn her virtue into pitch,   *325*
And out of her own goodness make the net
That shall enmesh them all.

Enter Roderigo.

                              How now, Roderigo?
RODERIGO. I do follow here in the chase, not like a hound that hunts, but
    one that fills up the cry.° My money is almost spent; I have been
    tonight exceedingly well cudgeled; and I think the issue will be I   *330*
    shall have so much° experience for my pains, and so, with no
    money at all and a little more wit, return again to Venice.
IAGO. How poor are they that have not patience!
    What wound did ever heal but by degrees?
    Thou know'st we work by wit, and not by witchcraft,   *335*
    And wit depends on dilatory time.

---

303 Probal probable, reasonable   **305 Inclining** favorably disposed. **subdue** persuade
306 fruitful generous   **307 free elements** i e., earth, air, fire, and water, which sustain
life (?)   **313 function** exercise of faculties (weakened by his fondness for her)   **314 parallel**
corresponding to these facts and to his best interests   **315 Divinity of hell** inverted the-
ology of hell (which seduces the soul to its damnation)   **316 put on** further, instigate
317 suggest tempt   **322 repeals him** i.e., attempts to get him restored   **329 fills up the
cry** merely takes part as one of the pack   **331 so much** just so much and no more

Does 't not go well? Cassio hath beaten thee,
And thou, by that small hurt, hast cashiered° Cassio.
Though other things grow fair against the sun,
Yet fruits that blossom first will first be ripe.°   340
Content thyself awhile. By the Mass, 'tis morning!
Pleasure and action make the hours seem short.
Retire thee; go where thou art billeted.
Away, I say! Thou shalt know more hereafter.
Nay, get thee gone.   *Exit Roderigo.*
                Two things are to be done.   345
My wife must move° for Cassio to her mistress;
I'll set her on;
Myself the while to draw the Moor apart
And bring him jump° when he may Cassio find
Soliciting his wife. Ay, that's the way.   350
Dull not device° by coldness° and delay.   *Exit.*

[3.1]   *Enter Cassio [and] Musicians.*

CASSIO. Masters, play here—I will content° your pains°—
     Something that's brief, and bid "Good morrow, General."
                                  [They play.]

[Enter] Clown.

CLOWN. Why, masters, have your instruments been in Naples, that they
     speak i' the nose° thus?
A MUSICIAN. How, sir, how?   5
CLOWN. Are these, I pray you, wind instruments?
A MUSICIAN. Ay, marry, are they, sir.
CLOWN. O, thereby hangs a tail.
A MUSICIAN. Whereby hangs a tale, sir?
CLOWN. Marry, sir, by many a wind instrument° that I know. But,   10
     masters, here's money for you. *[He gives money.]* And the General
     so likes your music that he desires you, for love's sake,° to make
     no more noise with it.

---

338 cashiered dismissed from service   **339–40 Though . . . ripe** i.e., the first part of our
plan has already ripened to fruition, and other parts are maturing in their own good
time   **346 move** plead   **349 jump** precisely   **351 device** plot. **coldness** lack of zeal

3.1. Location: Before the chamber of Othello and Desdemona.
1 content reward. **pains** efforts   **4 speak i' the nose** (1) sound nasal (2) sound like one
whose nose has been attacked by syphilis. (Naples was popularly supposed to have a high
incidence of venereal disease.)   **10 wind instrument** (With a joke on flatulence. The *tail,*
l. 8, that hangs nearby the *wind instrument* suggests the penis.)   **12 for love's sake** (1) out
of friendship and affection (2) for the sake of lovemaking in Othello's marriage

A MUSICIAN. Well, sir, we will not.

CLOWN. If you have any music that may not° be heard, to 't again; but,   15
as they say, to hear music the General does not greatly care.

A MUSICIAN. We have none such, sir.

CLOWN. Then put up your pipes in your bag, for I'll away.° Go, vanish
into air, away!   *Exeunt Musicians.*

CASSIO. Dost thou hear, mine honest friend?   20

CLOWN. No, I hear not your honest friend; I hear you.

CASSIO. Prithee, keep up° thy quillets.° There's a poor piece of gold for
thee. [*He gives money.*] If the gentlewoman that attends the General's
wife be stirring, tell her there's one Cassio entreats her a little favor
of speech.° Wilt thou do this?   25

CLOWN. She is stirring, sir. If she will stir hither, I shall seem° to notify
unto her.

CASSIO. Do, good my friend.   *Exit Clown.*

Enter Iago.

                    In happy time,° Iago.

IAGO. You have not been abed, then?

CASSIO. Why, no. The day had broke   30
Before we parted. I have made bold, Iago,
To send in to your wife. My suit to her
Is that she will to virtuous Desdemona
Procure me some access.

IAGO. I'll send her to you presently;   35
And I'll devise a means to draw the Moor
Out of the way, that your converse and business
May be more free.

CASSIO. I humbly thank you for 't.   *Exit [Iago].*
                    I never knew
A Florentine° more kind and honest.   40

Enter Emilia.

EMILIA. Good morrow, good Lieutenant. I am sorry
For your displeasure;° but all will sure be well.
The General and his wife are talking of it,
And she speaks for you stoutly. The Moor replies
That he you hurt is of great fame in Cyprus   45
And great affinity,° and that in wholesome wisdom

---

15 may not cannot **18 I'll away** (Possibly a misprint, or a snatch of song?) **22 keep
up** do not bring out, do not use. **quillets** quibbles, puns **24–25 a little . . . speech** the
favor of a brief talk **26 seem** deem it good, think fit **28 In happy time** i.e., well
met **40 Florentine** i.e., even a fellow Florentine. (Iago is a Venetian, Cassio a Florentine.) **42 displeasure** fall from favor **46 affinity** kindred, family connection

He might not but refuse you; but he protests he loves you
And needs no other suitor but his likings
To take the safest occasion by the front°
To bring you in again.
CASSIO.   Yet I beseech you,   50
If you think fit, or that it may be done,
Give me advantage of some brief discourse
With Desdemon alone.
EMILIA.   Pray you, come in.
I will bestow you where you shall have time
To speak your bosom° freely.   55
CASSIO. I am much bound to you.   [*Exeunt.*]

[3.2] *Enter Othello, Iago, and Gentlemen.*

OTHELLO. [*Giving letters*]
These letters give, Iago, to the pilot,
And by him do my duties° to the Senate.
That done, I will be walking on the works;°
Repair° there to me.
IAGO.   Well, my good lord, I'll do 't.
OTHELLO. This fortification, gentlemen, shall we see 't?   5
GENTLEMEN. We'll wait upon° your lordship.   *Exeunt.*

[3.3] *Enter Desdemona, Cassio, and Emilia.*

DESDEMONA. Be thou assured, good Cassio, I will do
All my abilities in thy behalf.
EMILIA. Good madam, do. I warrant it grieves my husband
As if the cause were his.
DESDEMONA. O, that's an honest fellow. Do not doubt, Cassio   5
But I will have my lord and you again
As friendly as you were.
CASSIO.   Bounteous madam,
Whatever shall become of Michael Cassio,
He's never anything but your true servant.
DESDEMONA. I know 't. I thank you. You do love my lord;   10
You have known him long, and be you well assured

---

49 occasion . . . front opportunity by the forelock   **55 bosom** inmost thoughts

3.2 Location: The citadel.
2 do my duties convey my respects   **3 works** breastworks, fortifications   **4 Repair**
return, come   **6 wait upon** attend

3.3 Location: The garden of the citadel.

He shall in strangeness° stand no farther off
Than in a politic° distance.
CASSIO.   Ay, but, lady,
    That policy may either last so long,
    Or feed upon such nice and waterish diet,°   *15*
    Or breed itself so out of circumstance,°
    That, I being absent and my place supplied,°
    My general will forget my love and service.
DESDEMONA. Do not doubt° that. Before Emilia here
    I give thee warrant of thy place. Assure thee,   *20*
    If I do vow a friendship I'll perform it
    To the last article. My lord shall never rest.
    I'll watch him tame° and talk him out of patience;°
    His bed shall seem a school, his board a shrift;°
    I'll intermingle everything he does   *25*
    With Cassio's suit. Therefore be merry, Cassio,
    For thy solicitor° shall rather die
    Than give thy cause away.°

    Enter Othello and Iago [at a distance].

EMILIA. Madam, here comes my lord.
CASSIO. Madam, I'll take my leave.   *30*
DESDEMONA. Why, stay, and hear me speak.
CASSIO. Madam, not now. I am very ill at ease,
    Unfit for mine own purposes.
DESDEMONA. Well, do your discretion.°   *Exit Cassio.*
IAGO. Ha? I like not that.   *35*
OTHELLO. What dost thou say?
IAGO. Nothing, my lord; or if—I know not what.
OTHELLO. Was not that Cassio parted from my wife?
IAGO. Cassio, my lord? No, sure, I cannot think it,
    That he would steal away so guiltylike,   *40*
    Seeing you coming.
OTHELLO. I do believe 'twas he.
DESDEMONA. How now, my lord?
    I have been talking with a suitor here,
    A man that languishes in your displeasure.   *45*

---

    12 strangeness aloofness   **13 politic** required by wise policy   **15 Or . . . diet** or sustain itself at length upon such a trivial and meager means of support   **16 breed . . . circumstance** continually renew itself so out of chance events, or yield so few chances for my being pardoned   **17 supplied** filled by another person   **19 doubt** fear   **23 watch him tame** tame him by keeping him from sleeping. (A term from falconry.)   **out of patience** past his endurance   **24 shrift** confessional   **27 solicitor** advocate   **28 away** up   **34 do your discretion** act according to your own discretion

OTHELLO. Who is 't you mean?

DESDEMONA. Why, your lieutenant, Cassio. Good my lord,
    If I have any grace or power to move you,
    His present° reconciliation take;
    For if he be not one that truly loves you,   *50*
    That errs in ignorance and not in cunning,°
    I have no judgment in an honest face.
    I prithee, call him back.

OTHELLO. Went he hence now?

DESDEMONA. Yes, faith, so humbled   *55*
    That he hath left part of his grief with me
    To suffer with him. Good love, call him back.

OTHELLO. Not now, sweet Desdemon. Some other time.

DESDEMONA. But shall 't be shortly?

OTHELLO. The sooner, sweet, for you.   *60*

DESDEMONA. Shall 't be tonight at supper?

OTHELLO. No, not tonight.

DESDEMONA. Tomorrow dinner,° then?

OTHELLO. I shall not dine at home.
    I meet the captains at the citadel.   *65*

DESDEMONA. Why, then, tomorrow night, or Tuesday morn,
    On Tuesday noon, or night, on Wednesday morn.
    I prithee, name the time, but let it not
    Exceed three days. In faith, he's penitent;
    And yet his trespass, in our common reason°—   *70*
    Save that, they say, the wars must make example
    Out of her best°—is not almost° a fault
    T' incur a private check.° When shall he come?
    Tell me, Othello. I wonder in my soul
    What you would ask me that I should deny,   *75*
    Or stand so mammering on.° What? Michael Cassio,
    That came a-wooing with you, and so many a time,
    When I have spoke of you dispraisingly,
    Hath ta'en your part—to have so much to do
    To bring him in!° By 'r Lady, I could do much—   *80*

OTHELLO. Prithee, no more. Let him come when he will;
    I will deny thee nothing.

---

49 present immediate   **51 in cunning** wittingly   **63 dinner** (The noon-time meal.)
70 common reason everyday judgments   **71–72 Save . . . best** were it not that, as the
saying goes, military discipline requires making an example of the very best men. (*Her* refers
to *wars* as a singular concept.)   **72 not almost** scarcely   **73 a private check** even a private reprimand   **76 mammering on** wavering about   **80 bring him in** restore him to
favor

DESDEMONA. Why, this is not a boon.
    'Tis as I should entreat you wear your gloves,
    Or feed on nourishing dishes, or keep you warm,   *85*
    Or sue to you to do a peculiar° profit
    To your own person. Nay, when I have a suit
    Wherein I mean to touch your love indeed,
    It shall be full of poise° and difficult weight,
    And fearful to be granted.   *90*
OTHELLO. I will deny thee nothing.
    Whereon,° I do beseech thee, grant me this,
    To leave me but a little to myself.
DESDEMONA. Shall I deny you? No. Farewell, my lord.
OTHELLO. Farewell, my Desdemona. I'll come to thee straight.°   *95*
DESDEMONA. Emilia, come.—Be as your fancies° teach you;
    Whate'er you be, I am obedient.   *Exit* [*with Emilia*].
OTHELLO. Excellent wretch!° Perdition catch my soul
    But I do° love thee! And when I love thee not,
    Chaos is come again.   *100*
IAGO. My noble lord—
OTHELLO. What dost thou say, Iago?
IAGO. Did Michael Cassio, when you wooed my lady,
    Know of your love?
OTHELLO. He did, from first to last. Why dost thou ask?   *105*
IAGO. But for a satisfaction of my thought;
    No further harm.
OTHELLO.   Why of thy thought, Iago?
IAGO. I did not think he had been acquainted with her.
OTHELLO. O, yes, and went between us very oft.
IAGO. Indeed?   *110*
OTHELLO. Indeed? Ay, indeed. Discern'st thou aught in that?
    Is he not honest?
IAGO. Honest, my lord?
OTHELLO. Honest. Ay, honest.
IAGO. My lord, for aught I know.   *115*
OTHELLO. What dost thou think?
IAGO. Think, my lord?
OTHELLO. "Think, my lord?" By heaven, thou echo'st me,
    As if there were some monster in thy thought
    Too hideous to be shown. Thou dost mean something.   *120*

---

86 peculiar particular, personal   **89 poise** weight, heaviness; or equipoise, delicate balance involving hard choice   **92 Whereon** in return for which   **95 straight** straightway   **96 fancies** inclinations   **98 wretch** (A term of affectionate endearment.)   **99 But I do** if I do not

I heard thee say even now, thou lik'st not that,
When Cassio left my wife. What didst not like?
And when I told thee he was of my counsel°
In my whole course of wooing, thou criedst "Indeed?"
And didst contract and purse° thy brow together   125
As if thou then hadst shut up in thy brain
Some horrible conceit.° If thou dost love me,
Show me thy thought.
IAGO. My lord, you know I love you.
OTHELLO. I think thou dost;   130
And, for I know thou'rt full of love and honesty,
And weigh'st thy words before thou giv'st them breath,
Therefore these stops° of thine fright me the more,
For such things in a false disloyal knave
Are tricks of custom,° but in a man that's just   135
They're close dilations,° working from the heart
That passion cannot rule.°
IAGO.   For Michael Cassio,
I dare be sworn I think that he is honest.
OTHELLO. I think so too.
IAGO.   Men should be what they seem;
Or those that be not, would they might seem none!°   140
OTHELLO. Certain, men should be what they seem.
IAGO. Why, then, I think Cassio's an honest man.
OTHELLO. Nay, yet there's more in this.
I prithee, speak to me as to thy thinkings,
As thou dost ruminate, and give thy worst of thoughts   145
The worst of words.
IAGO.   Good my lord, pardon me.
Though I am bound to every act of duty,
I am not bound to that° all slaves are free to.°
Utter my thoughts? Why, say they are vile and false,
As where's that palace whereinto foul things   150
Sometimes intrude not? Who has that breast so pure
But some uncleanly apprehensions
Keep leets and law days,° and in sessions sit
With° meditations lawful?°

---

123 of my counsel in my confidence   **125 purse** knit   **127 conceit** fancy   **133 stops**
pauses   **135 of custom** customary   **136 close dilations** secret or involuntary expressions
or delays   **137 That passion cannot rule** i.e., that are too passionately strong to be restrained (referring to the workings), or, that cannot rule its own passions (referring to the
heart)   **140 none** i.e., not to be men, or not seem to be honest   **148 that** that which.   **free
to** i.e. free with respect to   **153 Keep leets and law days** i.e., hold court, set up their
authority in one's heart. (*Leets* are a kind of manor court: *law days* are the days courts sit
in session, or those sessions.)   **154 With** along with.   **lawful** innocent

OTHELLO. Thou dost conspire against thy friend,° Iago,   *155*
      If thou but think'st him wronged and mak'st his ear
      A stranger to thy thoughts.
IAGO.   I do beseech you,
      Though I perchance am vicious° in my guess—
      As I confess it is my nature's plague
      To spy into abuses, and oft my jealousy°   *160*
      Shapes faults that are not—that your wisdom then,°
      From one° that so imperfectly conceits,°
      Would take no notice, nor build yourself a trouble
      Out of his scattering° and unsure observance.
      It were not for your quiet nor your good,   *165*
      Nor for my manhood, honesty, and wisdom,
      To let you know my thoughts.
OTHELLO.   What dost thou mean?
IAGO. Good name in man and woman, dear my lord,
      Is the immediate° jewel of their souls.
      Who steals my purse steals trash; 'tis something, nothing;   *170*
      'Twas mine, 'tis his, and has been slave to thousands;
      But he that filches from me my good name
      Robs me of that which not enriches him
      And makes me poor indeed.
OTHELLO. By heaven, I'll know thy thoughts.   *175*
IAGO. You cannot, if° my heart were in your hand,
      Nor shall not, whilst 'tis in my custody.
OTHELLO. Ha?
IAGO. O, beware, my lord, of jealousy!
      It is the green-eyed monster which doth mock
      The meat it feeds on.° That cuckold lives in bliss   *180*
      Who, certain of his fate, loves not his wronger;°
      But O, what damnèd minutes tells° he o'er
      Who dotes, yet doubts, suspects, yet fondly loves!
OTHELLO. O misery!
IAGO. Poor and content is rich, and rich enough,°   *185*
      But riches fineless° is as poor as winter
      To him that ever fears he shall be poor.

---

155 thy friend i.e., Othello   **158 vicious** wrong   **160 jealous** suspicion of evil   **161 then** on that account   **162 one** i.e., myself, Iago.   **conceits** judges, conjectures   **164 scattering** random   **169 immediate** essential, most precious   **176 if** even if   **179–180 doth mock . . . on** mocks and torments the heart of its victim the man who suffers jealousy   **181 his wronger** i.e. his faithless wife. (The unsuspecting cuckold is spared the misery of loving his wife only to discover she is cheating on him.)   **182 tells** counts   **185 Poor . . . enough** to be content with what little one has is the greatest wealth of all. (Proverbial.)   **186 fineless** boundless

Good God, the souls of all my tribe defend
From jealousy!
OTHELLO. Why, why is this?   *190*
  Think'st thou I'd make a life of jealousy,
  To follow still the changes of the moon
  With fresh suspicions?° No! To be once in doubt
  Is once° to be resolved.° Exchange me for a goat
  When I shall turn the business of my soul   *195*
  To such exsufflicate and blown° surmises
  Matching thy inference.° 'Tis not to make me jealous
  To say my wife is fair, feeds well, loves company,
  Is free of speech, sings, plays, and dances well;
  Where virtue is, these are more virtuous.   *200*
  Nor from mine own weak merits will I draw
  The smallest fear or doubt of her revolt,°
  For she had eyes, and chose me. No, Iago,
  I'll see before I doubt; when I doubt, prove;
  And on the proof, there is no more but this—   *205*
  Away at once with love or jealousy.
IAGO. I am glad of this, for now I shall have reason
  To show the love and duty that I bear you
  With franker spirit. Therefore, as I am bound,
  Receive it from me. I speak not yet of proof.   *210*
  Look to your wife; observe her well with Cassio.
  Wear your eyes thus, not° jealous nor secure.°
  I would not have your free and noble nature,
  Out of self-bounty,° be abused.° Look to 't.
  I know our country disposition well;   *215*
  In Venice they do let God see the pranks
  They dare not show their husbands; their best conscience
  Is not to leave 't undone, but keep 't unknown.
OTHELLO. Dost thou say so?
IAGO. She did deceive her father, marrying you;   *220*
  And when she seemed to shake and fear your looks,
  She loved them most.
OTHELLO.   And so she did.

192–193 To follow . . . suspicions to be constantly imagining new causes for suspicion, changing incessantly like the moon **194 once** once and for all. **resolved** free of doubt, having settled the matter **196 exsufflicate and blown** inflated and blown up, rumored about; or, spat out and flyblown, hence, loathsome, disgusting **197 inference** description or allegation **202 doubt . . . revolt** fear of her unfaithfulness **212 not** neither. **secure** free from uncertainty **214 self-bounty** inherent or natural goodness and generosity. **abused** deceived

IAGO.   Why, go to,° then!
    She that, so young, could give out such a seeming,°
    To seel° her father's eyes up close as oak,°
    He thought 'twas witchcraft! But I am much to blame.   225
    I humbly do beseech you of your pardon
    For too much loving you.
OTHELLO. I am bound° to thee forever.
IAGO. I see this hath a little dashed your spirits.
OTHELLO. Not a jot, not a jot.
IAGO.   I' faith, I fear it has.   230
    I hope you will consider what is spoke
    Comes from my love. But I do see you're moved.
    I am to pray you not to strain my speech
    To grosser issues° nor to larger reach°
    Than to suspicion.   235
OTHELLO. I will not.
IAGO. Should you do so, my lord,
    My speech should fall into such vile success°
    Which my thoughts aimed not. Cassio's my worthy friend.
    My lord, I see you're moved.
OTHELLO.   No, not much moved.   240
    I do not think but Desdemona's honest.°
IAGO. Long live she so! And long live you to think so!
OTHELLO. And yet, how nature erring from itself—
IAGO. Ay, there's the point! As—to be bold with you—
    Not to affect° many proposèd matches   245
    Of her own clime, complexion, and degree,
    Whereto we see in all things nature tends—
    Foh! One may smell in such a will° most rank,
    Foul disproportion,° thoughts unnatural.
    But pardon me. I do not in position°   250
    Distinctly speak of her, though I may fear
    Her will, recoiling° to her better° judgment,
    May fall to match you with her country forms°
    And happily repent.°

---

222 go to (An expression of impatience.) **223 seeming** false appearance **224 seel**
blind. (A term from falconry.) **oak** (A close-grained wood.) **228 bound** indebted (but
perhaps with ironic sense of "tied") **234 issues** significances. **reach** meaning,
scope **238 success** effect, result **241 honest** chaste **245 affect** prefer, desire **248 will**
sensuality, appetite **249 disproportion** abnormality **250 position** argument, proposition **252 recoiling** reverting. **better** i.e., more natural and reconsidered **253 fall . . .**
forms undertake to compare you with Venetian norms of handsomeness **254 happily**
repent haply repent her marriage

OTHELLO.   Farewell, farewell!
  If more thou dost perceive, let me know more.   *255*
  Set on thy wife to observe. Leave me, Iago.
IAGO. [*Going*] My lord, I take my leave.
OTHELLO. Why did I marry? This honest creature doubtless
  Sees and knows more, much more, than he unfolds.
IAGO. [*Returning*] My Lord, I would I might entreat your honor   *260*
  To scan this thing no farther. Leave it to time.
  Although 'tis fit that Cassio have his place—
  For, sure, he fills it up with great ability—
  Yet, if you please to hold him off awhile,
  You shall by that perceive him and his means.   *265*
  Note if your lady strain his entertainment°
  With any strong or vehement importunity;
  Much will be seen in that. In the meantime,
  Let me be thought too busy in my fears—
  As worthy cause I have to fear I am—   *270*
  And hold her free,° I do beseech your honor.
OTHELLO. Fear not my government.°
IAGO. I once more take my leave.   *Exit.*
OTHELLO. This fellow's of exceeding honesty,
  And knows all qualities,° with a learnèd spirit,   *275*
  Of human dealings. If I do prove her haggard,°
  Though that her jesses° were my dear heartstrings,
  I'd whistle her off and let her down the wind°
  To prey at fortune.° Haply, for° I am black
  And have not those soft parts of conversation°   *280*
  That chamberers° have, or for I am declined
  Into the vale of years—yet that's not much—
  She's gone. I am abused,° and my relief
  Must be to loathe her. O curse of marriage,   *285*
  That we can call these delicate creatures ours
  And not their appetites! I had rather be a toad
  And live upon the vapor of a dungeon
  Than keep a corner in the thing I love
  For others' uses. Yet, 'tis the plague of great ones;

---

266 strain his entertainment urge his reinstatement   **271 hold her free** regard her as innocent   **272 government** self-control, conduct   **275 qualities** natures, types   **276 haggard** wild (like a wild female hawk)   **277 jesses** straps fastened around the legs of a trained hawk   **278 I'd . . . wind** i.e., I'd let her go forever. (To release a hawk downwind was to invite it not to return.)   **279 prey at fortune** fend for herself in the wild.   **Haply, for** perhaps because   **280 soft . . . conversation** pleasing graces of social behavior   **281 chamberers** gallants   **283 abused** deceived

Prerogatived° are they less than the base.°   *290*
'Tis destiny unshunnable, like death.
Even then this forkèd° plague is fated to us
When we do quicken.° Look where she comes.

Enter Desdemona and Emilia.

If she be false, O, then heaven mocks itself!
I'll not believe 't.
DESDEMONA.   How now, my dear Othello?   *295*
Your dinner, and the generous° islanders
By you invited, do attend° your presence.
OTHELLO. I am to blame.
DESDEMONA.   Why do you speak so faintly?
Are you not well?
OTHELLO. I have a pain upon my forehead here.   *300*
DESDEMONA. Faith, that's with watching.° 'Twill away again.
                          [*She offers her handkerchief*]
Let me but bind it hard, within this hour
It will be well.
OTHELLO.   Your napkin° is too little.
Let it alone.° Come, I'll go in with you.
[*He puts the handkerchief from him, and it drops.*]
DESDEMONA. I am very sorry that you are not well.   *305*
                          Exit [*with Othello*].

EMILIA. [*Picking up the handkerchief*]
I am glad I have found this napkin.
This was her first remembrance from the Moor.
My wayward° husband hath a hundred times
Wooed me to steal it, but she so loves the token—
For he conjured her she should ever keep it—   *310*
That she reserves it evermore about her
To kiss and talk to. I'll have the work ta'en out,°
And give 't Iago. What he will do with it
Heaven knows, not I;
I nothing but to please his fantasy.°   *315*

---

290 Prerogatived privileged (to have honest wives). **the base** ordinary citizens
292 forkèd (An allusion to the horns of the cuckold.)   **293 quicken** receive life. (*Quicken*
may also mean to swarm with maggots as the body festers, as in 4.2.69, in which case ll.
292–293 suggest that *even then,* in death, we are cuckolded by *forkèd* worms.)   **296 gen-**
rous noble   **297 attend** await   **301 watching** too little sleep   **303 napkin** handkerchief   **304 Let it alone** i.e., never mind   **308 wayward** capricious   **312 work ta'en**
out design of the embroidery copied   **315 fantasy** whim

Enter Iago.

IAGO. How now? What do you here alone?

EMILIA. Do not you chide. I have a thing for you.

IAGO. You have a thing for me? It is a common thing°—

EMILIA. Ha?

IAGO. To have a foolish wife.   320

EMILIA. O, is that all? What will you give me now
    For that same handkerchief?

IAGO. What handkerchief?

EMILIA. What handkerchief?
    Why, that the Moor first gave to Desdemona;   325
    That which so often you did bid me steal.

IAGO. Hast stolen it from her?

EMILIA. No, faith. She let it drop by negligence,
    And to th' advantage° I, being here, took 't up.
    Look, here 'tis.

IAGO.   A good wench! Give it me.   330

EMILIA. What will you do with 't, that you have been so earnest
    To have me filch it?

IAGO. [*Snatching it*]   Why, what is that to you?

EMILIA. If it be not for some purpose of import,
    Give 't me again. Poor lady, she'll run mad
    When she shall lack it.

IAGO.   Be not acknown on 't.°   335
    I have use for it. Go, leave me.   *Exit Emilia.*
    I will in Cassio's lodging lose° this napkin
    And let him find it. Trifles light as air
    Are to the jealous confirmations strong
    As proofs of Holy Writ. This may do something.   340
    The Moor already changes with my poison.
    Dangerous conceits° are in their natures poisons,
    Which at the first are scarce found to distaste,°
    But with a little act° upon the blood
    Burn like the mines of sulfur.

Enter Othello.

                       I did say so.   345
Look where he comes! Not poppy nor mandragora°

---

318 common thing (with bawdy suggestion; *common* suggests coarseness and availability
to all comers, and *thing* is a slang term for the pudendum) **329 to th' advantage** taking
the opportunity **335 Be . . . on 't** do not confess knowledge of it **337 lose** (The Folio
spelling, *loose,* is a normal spelling for "lose," but it may also contain the idea of "let go,"
"release.") **342 conceits** fancies, ideas **343 distaste** be distasteful **344 act** action, working **346 mandragora** an opiate made of the mandrake root

Nor all the drowsy syrups of the world
Shall ever medicine thee to that sweet sleep
Which thou owedst° yesterday.
OTHELLO.   Ha, ha, false to me?
IAGO. Why, how now, General? No more of that.   *350*
OTHELLO. Avaunt! Begone! Thou hast set me on the rack.
   I swear tis better to be much abused
   Than but to know 't a little.
IAGO.   How now, my lord?
OTHELLO. What sense had I of her stolen hours of lust?
   I saw 't not, thought it not, it harmed not me.   *355*
   I slept the next night well, fed well, was free° and merry;
   I found not Cassio's kisses on her lips.
   He that is robbed, not wanting° what is stolen,
   Let him not know 't and he's not robbed at all.
IAGO. I am sorry to hear this.   *360*
OTHELLO. I had been happy if the general camp,
   Pioners° and all, had tasted her sweet body,
   So I had nothing known. O, now, forever
   Farewell the tranquil mind! Farewell content!
   Farewell the plumèd troops and the big° wars   *365*
   That makes ambition virtue! O, farewell!
   Farewell the neighing steed and the shrill trump,
   The spirit-stirring drum, th' ear-piercing fife,
   The royal banner, and all quality,°
   Pride,° pomp, and circumstance° of glorious war!   *370*
   And O, you mortal engines,° whose rude throats
   Th' immortal Jove's dread clamors° counterfeit,
   Farewell! Othello's occupation's gone.
IAGO. Is 't possible, my lord?
OTHELLO. Villain, be sure thou prove my love a whore!   *375*
   Be sure of it. Give me the ocular proof,
   Or, by the worth of mine eternal soul,
   Thou hadst been better have been born a dog
   Than answer my waked wrath!
IAGO.   Is 't come to this?
OTHELLO. Make me to see 't, or at the least so prove it   *380*
   That the probation° bear no hinge nor loop
   To hang a doubt on, or woe upon thy life!

---

349 thou owedst you did own **356 free** carefree **358 wanting** missing **362 Pioners**
diggers of mines, the lowest grade of soldiers **363 So** provided **365 big** stately
369 quality character, essential nature **370 Pride** rich display. **circumstance** pageantry
371 mortal engines i.e., cannon. (*Mortal* means "deadly.") **372 Jove's dread clamors** i.e.,
thunder **381 probation** proof

IAGO. My noble lord—

OTHELLO. If thou dost slander her and torture me,
        Never pray more; abandon all remorse;°   *385*
        On horror's head horrors accumulate;°
        Do deeds to make heaven weep, all earth amazed;°
        For nothing canst thou to damnation add
        Greater than that.

IAGO.   O grace! O heaven forgive me!
        Are you a man? Have you a soul or sense?   *390*
        God b' wi' you; take mine office. O wretched fool,°
        That lov'st to make thine honesty a vice!°
        O monstrous world! Take note, take note, O world,
        To be direct and honest is not safe.
        I thank you for this profit,° and from hence°   *395*
        I'll love no friend, sith° love breeds such offense.°

OTHELLO. Nay, stay. Thou shouldst be° honest.

IAGO. I should be wise, for honesty's a fool
        And loses that° it works for.

OTHELLO.   By the world,
        I think my wife be honest and think she is not;   *400*
        I think that thou art just and think thou art not.
        I'll have some proof. My name, that was as fresh
        As Dian's° visage, is now begrimed and black
        As mine own face. If there be cords, or knives,
        Poison, or fire, or suffocating streams,   *405*
        I'll not endure it. Would I were satisfied!

IAGO. I see, sir, you are eaten up with passion.
        I do repent me that I put it to you.
        You would be satisfied?

OTHELLO.   Would? Nay, and I will.

IAGO. And may; but how? How satisfied, my lord?   *410*
        Would you, the supervisor,° grossly gape on?
        Behold her topped?

OTHELLO.   Death and damnation! O!

IAGO. It were a tedious difficulty, I think,
        To bring them to that prospect. Damn them then,°

---

385 remorse pity **386 horrors accumulate** add still more horrors **387 amazed** confounded with horror **391 O wretched fool** (Iago addresses himself as a fool for having carried honesty too far.) **392 vice** failing, something overdone **395 profit** profitable instruction. **hence** henceforth **396 sith** since. **offense** i.e., harm to the one who offers help and friendship **397 Thou shouldst be** it appears that you are. (But Iago replies in the sense of "ought to be.") **399 that** what **403 Dian** Diana, goddess of the moon and of chastity **411 supervisor** onlooker **414 Damn them then** i.e., they would have to be really incorrigible

If ever mortal eyes do see them bolster°   *415*
More° than their own. What then? How then?
What shall I say? Where's satisfaction?
It is impossible you should see this,
Were they as prime° as goats, as hot as monkeys,
As salt° as wolves in pride,° and fools as gross   *420*
As ignorance made drunk. But yet, I say,
If imputation and strong circumstances
Which lead directly to the door of truth
Will give you satisfaction, you might have 't.
OTHELLO. Give me a living reason she's disloyal.   *425*
IAGO. I do not like the office.
But sith° I am entered in this cause so far,
Pricked° to 't by foolish honesty and love,
I will go on. I lay with Cassio lately,
And being troubled with a raging tooth   *430*
I could not sleep. There are a kind of men
So loose of soul that in their sleeps will mutter
Their affairs. One of this kind is Cassio.
In sleep I heard him say, "Sweet Desdemona,
Let us be wary, let us hide our loves!"   *435*
And then, sir, would he grip and wring my hand,
Cry "O sweet creature!" then kiss me hard,
As if he plucked up kisses by the roots
That grew upon my lips; then laid his leg
Over my thigh, and sighed, and kissed, and then   *440*
Cried, "Cursèd fate that gave thee to the Moor!"
OTHELLO. O monstrous! Monstrous!
IAGO.   Nay, this was but his dream.
OTHELLO. But this denoted a foregone conclusion.°
'Tis a shrewd doubt,° though it be but a dream.
IAGO. And this may help to thicken other proofs   *445*
That do demonstrate thinly.
OTHELLO.   I'll tear her all to pieces.
IAGO. Nay, yet be wise. Yet we see nothing done;
She may be honest yet. Tell me but this:
Have you not sometimes seen a handkerchief
Spotted with strawberries° in your wife's hand?   *450*
OTHELLO. I gave her such a one. 'Twas my first gift.

---

415 bolster go to bed together, share a bolster **416 More** other **419 prime** lustful
420 salt wanton, sensual. **pride** heat **427 sith** since **428 Pricked** spurred **443 foregone** conclusion concluded experience or action **444 shewd doubt** suspicious circumstance **450 Spotted wtth strawberries** embroidered with a strawberry pattern

IAGO. I know not that; but such a handkerchief—
　　I am sure it was your wife's—did I today
　　See Cassio wipe his beard with.
OTHELLO.　　　　　　　　　　　　　　If it be that—
IAGO. If it be that, or any that was hers,   455
　　It speaks against her with the other proofs.
OTHELLO. O, that the slave° had forty thousand lives!
　　One is too poor, too weak for my revenge.
　　Now do I see 'tis true. Look here, Iago,
　　All my fond° love thus do I blow to heaven.   460
　　'Tis gone.
　　Arise, black vengeance, from the hollow hell!
　　Yield up, O love, thy crown and hearted° throne
　　To tyrannous hate! Swell, bosom, with thy freight,°
　　For 'tis of aspics'° tongues!   465
IAGO. Yet be content.°
OTHELLO. O, blood, blood, blood!
IAGO. Patience, I say. Your mind perhaps may change.
OTHELLO. Never, Iago. Like to the Pontic Sea,°
　　Whose icy current and compulsive course   470
　　Ne'er feels retiring ebb, but keeps due on
　　To the Propontic° and the Hellespont,
　　Even so my bloody thoughts with violent pace
　　Shall ne'er look back, ne'er ebb to humble love,
　　Till that a capable° and wide revenge   475
　　Swallow them up. Now, by yond marble° heaven,
　　[*Kneeling*] In the due reverence of a sacred vow
　　I here engage my words.
IAGO.　　　　　　　　　　　Do not rise yet.
　　[*He kneels.*°] Witness, you ever-burning lights above,
　　You elements that clip° us round about,   480
　　Witness that here Iago doth give up
　　The execution° of his wit, hands, heart,
　　To wronged Othello's service! Let him command,
　　And to obey shall be in me remorse,°
　　What bloody business ever.°   [*They rise.*]

---

457 the slave i.e., Cassio　**460 fond** foolish　**463 hearted** fixed in the heart　**464 freight**
burden　**465 aspics'** venomous serpents'　**466 content** calm　**469 Pontic Sea** Black Sea
472 Propontic body of water between the Bosporus and Hellespont　**475 capable** comprehensive　**476 marble** i.e., gleaming like marble　**479 s.d. He kneels** (In the quarto
text. Iago kneels here after Othello has knelt at l. 477.)　**480 clip** encompass　**482 execution**
exercise, action.　**wit** mind　**484 remorse** pity (for Othello's wrongs)　**485 ever** soever

OTHELLO.   I greet thy love,   485
    Not with vain thanks, but with acceptance bounteous,
    And will upon the instant put thee to 't.
    Within these three days let me hear thee say
    That Cassio's not alive.
IAGO.   My friend is dead;
    'Tis done at your request. But let her live.   490
OTHELLO. Damn her, lewd minx!° O, damn her, damn her!
    Come, go with me apart. I will withdraw
    To furnish me with some swift means of death
    For the fair devil. Now art thou my lieutenant.
IAGO. I am your own forever.   *Exeunt.*   495

    [3.4]   *Enter Desdemona, Emilia, and Clown.*

DESDEMONA. Do you know, sirrah,° where Lieutenant Cassio lies?°
CLOWN. I dare not say he lies anywhere.
DESDEMONA. Why, man?
CLOWN. He's a soldier, and for me to say a soldier lies, 'tis stabbing.
DESDEMONA. Go to. Where lodges he?   5
CLOWN. To tell you where he lodges is to tell you where I lie.
DESDEMONA. Can anything be made of this?
CLOWN. I know not where he lodges, and for me to devise a lodging and
    say he lies here, or he lies there, were to lie in mine own throat.°
DESDEMONA. Can you inquire him out, and be edified by report?   10
CLOWN. I will catechize the world for him; that is, make questions, and
    by them answer.
DESDEMONA. Seek him, bid him come hither. Tell him I have moved° my
    lord on his behalf and hope all will be well.
CLOWN. To do this is within the compass of man's wit, and therefore I   15
    will attempt the doing it.   *Exit Clown.*
DESDEMONA. Where should I lose that handkerchief, Emilia?
EMILIA. I know not, madam.
DESDEMONA. Believe me, I had rather have lost my purse
    Full of crusadoes;° and but my noble Moor   20
    Is true of mind and made of no such baseness
    As jealous creatures are, it were enough
    To put him to ill thinking.

---

491 minx wanton

3.4 Location: Before the citadel.
1 sirrah (A form of address to an inferior.)   **1 lies** lodges. (But the Clown makes the obvious pun.)   **9 lie . . . throat** lie egregiously and deliberately   **13 moved** petitioned
20 crusadoes Portuguese gold coins

EMILIA.   Is he not jealous?
DESDEMONA. Who, he? I think the sun where he was born
    Drew all such humors° from him.
EMILIA.   Look where he comes.   *25*

    Enter Othello.

DESDEMONA. I will not leave him now till Cassio
    Be called to him.—How is 't with you, my lord?
OTHELLO. Well, my good lady. [*Aside.*] O, hardness to dissemble!—
    How do you, Desdemona?
DESDEMONA.   Well, my good lord.
OTHELLO. Give me your hand. [*She gives her hand.*] This hand is moist,
    my lady.   *30*
DESDEMONA. It yet hath felt no age nor known no sorrow.
OTHELLO. This argues° fruitfulness° and liberal° heart.
    Hot, hot, and moist. This hand of yours requires
    A sequester° from liberty, fasting and prayer,
    Much castigation,° exercise devout;   *35*
    For here's a young and sweating devil here
    That commonly rebels. 'Tis a good hand,
    A frank° one.
DESDEMONA.   You may indeed say so,
    For 'twas that hand that gave away my heart.
OTHELLO. A liberal hand! The hearts of old gave hands,°   *40*
    But our new heraldry is hands, not hearts.°
DESDEMONA. I cannot speak of this. Come now, your promise.
OTHELLO. What promise, chuck?°
DESDEMONA. I have sent to bid Cassio come speak with you.
OTHELLO. I have a salt and sorry rheum° offends me;   *45*
    Lend me thy handkerchief.
DESDEMONA. Here, my lord. [*She offers a handkerchief.*]
OTHELLO. That which I gave you.
DESDEMONA.   I have it not about me.
OTHELLO. Not?
DESDEMONA. No, faith, my lord.   *50*
OTHELLO. That's a fault. That handkerchief
    Did an Egyptian to my mother give.

---

25 humors (Refers to the four bodily fluids thought to determine temperament.)
32 argues gives evidence of.   **fruitfulness** generosity, amorousness, and fecundity.
liberal generous and sexually free   **34 sequester** separation, sequestration   **35 casti-
gation** corrective discipline   **38 frank** generous, open (with sexual suggestion)   **40 The
hearts . . . hands** i.e., in former times people would give their hearts when they gave their
hands to something   **41 But . . . hearts** i.e., in our decadent times the joining of hands
is no longer a badge to signify the giving of hearts   **43 chuck** (A term of endearment.)
45 salt . . . rheum distressful head cold or watering of the eyes

She was a charmer,° and could almost read
The thoughts of people. She told her, while she kept it,
'Twould make her amiable° and subdue my father   *55*
Entirely to her love, but if she lost it
Or made a gift of it, my father's eye
Should hold her loathèd and his spirits should hunt
After new fancies.° She, dying, gave it me,
And bid me, when my fate would have me wived,   *60*
To give it her.° I did so; and take heed on 't;
Make it a darling like your precious eye.
To lose 't or give 't away were such perdition°
As nothing else could match.
DESDEMONA.   Is 't possible?
OTHELLO. 'Tis true. There's magic in the web° of it.   *65*
A sibyl, that had numbered in the world
The sun to course two hundred compasses,°
In her prophetic fury° sewed the work;
The worms were hallowed that did breed the silk,
And it was dyed in mummy° which the skillful   *70*
Conserved of° maidens' hearts.
DESDEMONA.   I' faith! Is 't true?
OTHELLO. Most veritable. Therefore look to 't well.
DESDEMONA. Then would to God that I had never seen 't!
OTHELLO. Ha? Wherefore?
DESDEMONA. Why do you speak so startingly and rash?°   *75*
OTHELLO. Is 't lost? Is 't gone? Speak, is 't out o' the way?°
DESDEMONA. Heaven bless us!
OTHELLO. Say you?
DESDEMONA. It is not lost; but what an if° it were?
OTHELLO. How?   *80*
DESDEMONA. I say it is not lost.
OTHELLO.   Fetch 't. Let me see 't.
DESDEMONA. Why, so I can, sir, but I will not now.
This is a trick to put me from my suit.
Pray you, let Cassio be received again.
OTHELLO. Fetch me the handkerchief! My mind misgives.   *85*
DESDEMONA. Come, come,
You'll never meet a more sufficient° man.

---

53 charmer sorceress **55 amiable** desirable **59 fancies** loves **61 her** i.e., to my wife
63 perdition loss **65 web** fabric, weaving **67 compasses** annual circlings. (The *sibyl,*
or prophetess, was 200 years old.) **68 prophetic fury** frenzy of prophetic inspiration **70 mummy** medicinal or magical preparation drained from mummified bodies
71 Conserved of prepared or preserved out of **75 startingly and rash** disjointedly and
impetuously, excitedly **76 out o' the way** lost, misplaced **79 an if** if **87 sufficient** able,
complete

OTHELLO. The handkerchief!

DESDEMONA.   I pray, talk° me of Cassio.

OTHELLO. The handkerchief!

DESDEMONA.   A man that all his time°

    Hath founded his good fortunes on your love,   *90*

    Shared dangers with you—

OTHELLO. The handkerchief!

DESDEMONA. I' faith, you are to blame.

OTHELLO. Zounds!   *Exit Othello.*

EMILIA. Is not this man jealous?   *95*

DESDEMONA. I ne'er saw this before.

    Sure, there's some wonder in this handkerchief.

    I am most unhappy in the loss of it.

EMILIA. 'Tis not a year or two shows us a man.°

    They are all but° stomachs, and we all but food;   *100*

    They eat us hungerly,° and when they are full

    They belch us.

    Enter Iago and Cassio.

               Look you, Cassio and my husband.

IAGO. There is no other way; 'tis she must do 't.

    And, lo, the happiness!° Go and importune her.

DESDEMONA. How now, good Cassio? What's the news with you?   *105*

CASSIO. Madam, my former suit. I do beseech you

    That by your virtuous° means I may again

    Exist, and be a member of his love

    Whom I with all the office° of my heart

    Entirely honor. I would not be delayed.   *110*

    If my offense be of such mortal° kind

    That nor my service past nor° present sorrows,

    Nor purposed merit in futurity,

    Can ransom me into his love again,

    But to know so must be my benefit;°   *115*

    So shall I clothe me in a forced content,

    And shut myself up in some other course,

    To fortune's alms.°

DESDEMONA.   Alas, thrice-gentle Cassio,

    My advocation° is not now in tune.

---

88 talk talk to   **89 all his time** throughout his career   **99 'Tis . . . man**   i.e., you can't
really know a man even in a year or two of experience (?) or, real men come along seldom (?)
100 but nothing but   **101 hungerly** hungrily   **104 the happiness** in happy time, fortunately   met   **107 virtuous** efficacious   **109 office** loyal   service   **111 mortal** fatal
112 nor . . . nor neither . . . nor   **115 But . . . benefit** merely to know that my case is
hopeless must be all I can expect   **118 To fortune's alms** throwing myself on the mercy
of fortune   **119 advocation** advocacy

My lord is not my lord; nor should I know him,   120
Were he in favor° as in humor altered.
So help me every spirit sanctified
As I have spoken for you all my best
And stood within the blank° of his displeasure
For my free speech! You must awhile be patient.   125
What I can do I will, and more I will
Than for myself I dare. Let that suffice you.

IAGO. Is my lord angry?

EMILIA.   He went hence but now,
And certainly in strange unquietness.

IAGO. Can he be angry? I have seen the cannon   130
When it hath blown his ranks into the air,
And like the devil from his very arm
Puffed his own brother — and is he angry?
Something of moment° then. I will go meet him.
There's matter in 't indeed, if he be angry.   135

DESDEMONA. I prithee, do so.   *Exit [Iago].*
                           Something, sure, of state,°
Either from Venice, or some unhatched practice°
Made demonstrable here in Cyprus to him,
Hath puddled° his clear spirit; and in such cases
Men's natures wrangle with inferior things,   140
Though great ones are their object. 'Tis even so;
For let our finger ache, and it indues°
Our other healthful members even to a sense
Of pain. Nay, we must think men are not gods,
Nor of them look for such observancy°   145
As fits the bridal.° Beshrew me° much, Emilia,
I was, unhandsome° warrior as I am,
Arraigning his unkindness with° my soul;
But now I find I had suborned the witness,°
And he's indicted falsely.

EMILIA.   Pray heaven it be   150
State matters, as you think, and no conception
Nor no jealous toy° concerning you.

DESDEMONA. Alas the day! I never gave him cause.

---

121 favor appearance   **124 within the blank** within point-blank range. (The *blank* is the
center of the target.)   **134 of moment** of immediate importance, momentous   **136 of
state** concerning state affairs   **137 unhatched practice** as yet unexecuted or undiscovered
plot   **139 puddled** muddied   **142 indues** brings to the same condition   **145 obser-
vancy** attentiveness   **146 bridal** wedding (when a bridegroom is newly attentive to his
bride).   **Beshrew me** (A mild oath.)   **147 unhandsome** insufficient, unskillful
148 with before the bar of   **149 suborned the witness** induced the witness to give false
testimony   **152 toy** fancy

EMILIA. But jealous souls will not be answered so;
    They are not ever jealous for the cause,   155
    But jealous for° they're jealous. It is a monster
    Begot upon itself,° born on itself.
DESDEMONA. Heaven keep that monster from Othello's mind!
EMILIA. Lady, amen.
DESDEMONA. I will go seek him. Cassio, walk hereabout.   160
    If I do find him fit, I'll move your suit
    And seek to effect it to my uttermost.
CASSIO. I humbly thank your ladyship.   *Exit* [*Desdemona with Emilia*].

    Enter Bianca.

BIANCA. Save° you, friend Cassio!
CASSIO.   What make° you from home?
    How is 't with you, my most fair Bianca?   165
    I' faith, sweet love, I was coming to your house.
BIANCA. And I was going to your lodging, Cassio.
    What, keep a week away? Seven days and nights?
    Eightscore-eight hours? And lovers' absent hours
    More tedious than the dial° eightscore times?   170
    O weary reckoning!
CASSIO.   Pardon me, Bianca.
    I have this while with leaden thoughts been pressed;
    But I shall, in a more continuate° time,
    Strike off this score° of absence. Sweet Bianca,
                          [*Giving her Desdemona's handkerchief*]
    Take me this work out.°
BIANCA.   O Cassio, whence came this?   175
    This is some token from a newer friend.°
    To the felt absence now I feel a cause.
    Is 't come to this? Well, well.
CASSIO.   Go to, woman!
    Throw your vile guesses in the devil's teeth,
    From whence you have them. You are jealous now   180
    That this is from some mistress, some remembrance.
    No, by my faith, Bianca.
BIANCA.   Why, whose is it?
CASSIO. I know not, neither. I found it in my chamber.
    I like the work well. Ere it be demanded° —

---

156 for because   **157 Begot upon itself** generated solely from itself   **164 Save** God
save.   **make** do   **170 the dial** a complete revolution of the clock   **173 continuate** uninterrupted   **174 Strike . . . score** settle this account   **175 Take . . . out** copy this embroidery for me   **176 friend** mistress   **184 demanded** inquired for

As like° enough it will—I would have it copied.   *185*
Take it and do 't, and leave me for this time.
BIANCA. Leave you? Wherefore?
CASSIO. I do attend here on the General,
    And think it no addition,° nor my wish,
    To have him see me womaned.   *190*
BIANCA. Why, I pray you?
CASSIO. Not that I love you not.
BIANCA. But that you do not love me.
    I pray you, bring° me on the way a little,
    And say if I shall see you soon at night.   *195*
CASSIO. 'Tis but a little way that I can bring you,
    For I attend here; but I'll see you soon.
BIANCA. 'Tis very good. I must be circumstanced.°

                                              Exeunt omnes.

    [4.1]   *Enter Othello and Iago.*

IAGO. Will you think so?
OTHELLO.   Think so, Iago?
IAGO.   What,
IAGO. To kiss in private?
OTHELLO.   An unauthorized kiss!
IAGO. Or to be naked with her friend in bed
    An hour or more, not meaning any harm?
OTHELLO. Naked in bed, Iago, and not mean harm?   *5*
    It is hypocrisy against the devil.
    They that mean virtuously, and yet do so,
    The devil their virtue tempts, and they tempt heaven.
IAGO. If they do nothing, 'tis a venial° slip.
    But if I give my wife a handkerchief—   *10*
OTHELLO. What then?
IAGO. Why then, 'tis hers, my lord, and being hers,
    She may, I think, bestow 't on any man.
OTHELLO. She is protectress of her honor too.
    May she give that?   *15*
IAGO. Her honor is an essence that's not seen;
    They have it° very oft that have it not.
    But, for the handkerchief—

---

185 like likely   **189 addition** i.e., addition to my reputation   **194 bring** accompany
198 be circumstanced be governed by circumstance, yield to your conditions

4.1. Location: Before the citadel.
9 venial pardonable   **7 They have it** i.e., they enjoy a reputation for it

OTHELLO. By heaven, I would most gladly have forgot it.
    Thou saidst—O, it comes o'er my memory   20
    As doth the raven o'er the infectious house,°
    Boding to all—he had my handkerchief.
IAGO. Ay, what of that?
OTHELLO.   That's not so good now.
IAGO.   What
    If I had said I had seen him do you wrong?
    Or heard him say—as knaves be such abroad,°   25
    Who having, by their own importunate suit,
    Or voluntary dotage° of some mistress,
    Convincèd or supplied them, cannot choose
    But they must blab—
OTHELLO.   Hath he said anything?
IAGO. He hath, my lord; but, be you well assured,   30
    No more than he'll unswear.
OTHELLO.   What hath he said?
IAGO. Faith, that he did—I know not what he did.
OTHELLO. What? What?
IAGO. Lie—
OTHELLO. With her?
IAGO.   With her, on her; what you will.
OTHELLO. Lie with her? Lie on her? We say "lie on her" when they belie°   35
    her. Lie with her? Zounds, that's fulsome.°—Handkerchief—
    confessions—handkerchief!—To confess and be hanged for his
    labor—first to be hanged and then to confess.°—I tremble at it. Na-
    ture would not invest herself in such shadowing passion without
    some instruction.° It is not words° that shakes me thus. Pish! Noses,   40
    ears, and lips.—Is 't possible?—Confess—handkerchief!—O devil!
                                               Falls in a trance.

IAGO. Work on,
    My medicine, work! Thus credulous fools are caught,
    And many worthy and chaste dames even thus,
    All guiltless, meet reproach.—What ho! My lord!   45
    My lord, I say! Othello!

---

21 raven . . . house (Allusion to the belief that the raven hovered over a house of sickness or infection, such as one visited by the plague.)   **25 abroad** around about   **27 voluntary dotage** willing infatuation   **28 Convincèd or supplied** seduced or gratified   **36 belie** slander   **36–37 fulsome** foul   **38 first . . . to confess** (Othello reverses the proverbial *confess and be hanged;* Cassio is to be given no time to confess before he dies.)   **38–40 Nature . . . instruction** i.e., without some foundation in fact, nature would not have dressed herself in such an overwhelming passion that comes over me now and fills my mind with images, or in such a life-like fantasy as Cassio had in his dream of lying with Desdemona   **40 words** mere words

Enter Cassio.

How now, Cassio?

CASSIO. What's the matter?

IAGO. My lord is fall'n into an epilepsy.
This is his second fit. He had one yesterday.

CASSIO. Rub him about the temples.

IAGO.   No, forbear.   50
The lethargy° must have his° quiet course.
If not, he foams at mouth, and by and by
Breaks out to savage madness. Look, he stirs.
Do you withdraw yourself a little while.
He will recover straight. When he is gone,   55
I would on great occasion° speak with you.   [*Exit Cassio.*]
How is it, General? Have you not hurt your head?

OTHELLO. Dost thou mock me?

IAGO.   I mock° you not, by heaven.
Would you would bear your fortune like a man!

OTHELLO. A hornèd man's a monster and a beast.   60

IAGO. There's many a beast then in a populous city,
And many a civil° monster.

OTHELLO. Did he confess it?

IAGO. Good sir, be a man.
Think every bearded fellow that's but yoked°   65
May draw with you.° There's millions now alive
That nightly lie in those unproper° beds
Which they dare swear peculiar.° Your case is better.°
O, 'tis the spite of hell, the fiend's arch-mock,
To lip° a wanton in a secure° couch   70
And to suppose her chaste! No, let me know,
And knowing what I am,° I know what she shall be.°

OTHELLO. O, thou art wise. 'Tis certain.

IAGO. Stand you awhile apart;
Confine yourself but in a patient list.°   75
Whilst you were here o'erwhelmèd with your grief—
A passion most unsuiting such a man—
Cassio came hither. I shifted him away,°

---

51 lethargy coma. **his** its **56 on great occasion** on a matter of great importance **58 mock** (Othello takes Iago's question about hurting his head to be a mocking
reference to the cuckold's horns.) **62 civil** i.e. dwelling in a city **65 yoked** (1) married
(2) put into the yoke of infamy and cuckoldry **66 draw with you** pull as you do like
oxen who are yoked, i.e., share your fate as cuckold **67 unproper** not exclusively their
own **68 peculiar** private, their own. **better** i.e., because you know the truth **70 lip**
kiss. **secure** free from suspicion **72 what I am** i.e., a cuckold. **she shall be** i.e., an
adulteress who must die **75 in . . . list** within the bounds of patience **78 shifted him
away** used a dodge to get rid of him

And laid good 'scuses upon your ecstasy,°
Bade him anon return and here speak with me,   80
The which he promised. Do but encave° yourself
And mark the fleers,° the gibes, and notable° scorns
That dwell in every region of his face;
For I will make him tell the tale anew,
Where, how, how oft, how long ago, and when   85
He hath and is again to cope° your wife.
I say, but mark his gesture. Marry, patience!
Or I shall say you're all-in-all in spleen,°
And nothing of a man.
OTHELLO.   Dost thou hear, Iago?
I will be found most cunning in my patience;   90
But—dost thou hear?—most bloody.
IAGO.   That's not amiss;
But yet keep time° in all. Will you withdraw?

> [*Othello stands apart.*]

Now will I question Cassio of Bianca
A huswife° that by selling her desires
Buys herself bread and clothes. It is a creature   95
That dotes on Cassio—as 'tis the strumpet's plague
To beguile many and be beguiled by one.
He, when he hears of her, cannot restrain°
From the excess of laughter. Here he comes.

Enter Cassio.

As he shall smile, Othello shall go mad;   100
And his unbookish° jealousy must conster°
Poor Cassio's smiles, gestures, and light behaviors
Quite in the wrong.—How do you now, Lieutenant?
CASSIO. The worser that you give me the addition°
Whose want even kills me.   105
IAGO. Ply Desdemona well and you are sure on 't.
[*Speaking lower.*] Now, if this suit lay in Bianca's power,
How quickly should you speed!
CASSIO. [*Laughing*] Alas, poor caitiff!°
OTHELLO. Look how he laughs already!
IAGO. I never knew a woman love man so.   110
CASSIO. Alas, poor rogue! I think, i' faith, she loves me.

---

79 ecstasy trance   **81 encave** conceal   **82 fleers** sneers.   **notable** obvious   **86 cope**
encounter with, have sex with   **88 all-in-all in spleen** utterly governed by passionate impulses   **92 keep time** keep yourself steady (as in music)   **94 huswife** hussy   **98 restrain**
refrain   **101 unbookish** uninstructed.   **conster** construe   **104 addition** title   **108 caitiff**
wretch

OTHELLO. Now he denies it faintly, and laughs it out.

IAGO. Do you hear, Cassio?

OTHELLO.   Now he importunes him
    To tell it o'er. Go to! Well said,° well said.

IAGO. She gives it out that you shall marry her.   115
    Do you intend it?

CASSIO. Ha, ha, ha!

OTHELLO. Do you triumph, Roman?° Do you triumph?

CASSIO. I marry her? What? A customer?° Prithee, bear some charity to
    my wit;° do not think it so unwholesome. Ha, ha, ha!   120

OTHELLO. So, so, so, so! They laugh that win.°

IAGO. Faith, the cry° goes that you shall marry her.

CASSIO. Prithee, say true.

IAGO. I am a very villain else.

OTHELLO. Have you scored me?° Well.   125

CASSIO. This is the monkey's own giving out. She is persuaded I will
    marry her, out of her own love and flattery,° not out of my promise.

OTHELLO. Iago beckons° me. Now he begins the story.

CASSIO. She was here even now; she haunts me in every place. I was the
    other day talking on the seabank with certain Venetians, and thither   130
    comes the bauble,° and, by this hand, she falls me thus about my
    neck—   [*He embraces Iago.*]

OTHELLO. Crying, "O dear Cassio!" as it were; his gesture imports it.

CASSIO. So hangs and lolls and weeps upon me, so shakes and pulls me.
    Ha, ha, ha!   135

OTHELLO. Now he tells how she plucked him to my chamber. O, I see
    that nose of yours, but not that dog I shall throw it to.

CASSIO. Well, I must leave her company.

IAGO. Before me,° look where she comes.

    Enter Bianca [*with Othello's handkerchief*].

CASSIO. 'Tis such another fitchew!° Marry, a perfumed one.—What do   140
    you mean by this haunting of me?

BIANCA. Let the devil and his dam° haunt you! What did you mean by
    that same handkerchief you gave me even now? I was a fine fool
    to take it. I must take out the work? A likely piece of work,° that

---

114 Well said well done   **118 Roman** (The Romans were noted for their *triumphs* or triumphal processions.)   **119 customer** i.e., prostitute   **119–20 bear . . . wit** be more charitable to my judgment   **121 They . . . win** i.e., they that laugh last laugh best   **122 cry** rumor   **125 scored me** scored off me, beaten me, made up my reckoning, branded me   **127 flattery** self-flattery, self-deception   **128 beckons** signals   **131 bauble** plaything   **139 Before me** i.e., on my soul   **140 'Tis . . . fitchew** what a polecat she is! Just like all the others. (Polecats were often compared with prostitutes because of their rank smell and presumed lechery.)   **142 dam** mother   **144 A likely . . . work** a fine story

you should find it in your chamber and know not who left it there!   *145*
This is some minx's token, and I must take out the work? There;
give it your hobbyhorse.° [*She gives him the handkerchief.*] Where-
soever you had it, I'll take out no work on 't.

CASSIO. How now, my sweet Bianca? How now? How now?

OTHELLO. By heaven, that should be° my handkerchief!   *150*

BIANCA. If you'll come to supper tonight, you may; if you will not, come
when you are next prepared for.°   *Exit.*

IAGO. After her, after her.

CASSIO. Faith, I must. She'll rail in the streets else.

IAGO. Will you sup there?   *155*

CASSIO. Faith, I intend so.

IAGO. Well, I may chance to see you, for I would very fain speak with
you.

CASSIO. Prithee, come. Will you?

IAGO. Go to.° Say no more.   [*Exit Cassio.*]   *160*

OTHELLO. [*Advancing*] How shall I murder him, Iago?

IAGO. Did you perceive how he laughed at his vice?

OTHELLO. O, Iago!

IAGO. And did you see the handkerchief?

OTHELLO. Was that mine?   *165*

IAGO. Yours, by this hand. And to see how he prizes the foolish woman
your wife! She gave it him, and he hath given it his whore.

OTHELLO. I would have him nine years a-killing. A fine woman! A fair
woman! A sweet woman!

IAGO. Nay, you must forget that.   *170*

OTHELLO. Ay, let her rot, and perish, and be damned tonight, for she shall
not live. No, my heart is turned to stone; I strike it, and it hurts
my hand. O, the world hath not a sweeter creature! She might lie
by an emperor's side and command him tasks.

IAGO. Nay, that's not your way.°   *175*

OTHELLO. Hang her! I do but say what she is. So delicate with her
needle! An admirable musician! O, she will sing the savageness out
of a bear. Of so high and plenteous wit and invention!°

IAGO. She's the worse for all this.

OTHELLO. O, a thousand, a thousand times! And then, of so gentle a   *180*
condition!°

IAGO. Ay, too gentle.°

OTHELLO. Nay, that's certain. But yet the pity of it, Iago! O, Iago, the pity
of it, Iago!

---

147 hobbyhorse harlot **150 should be** must be **152 when . . . for** when I'm ready
for you (i.e., never) **160 Go to** (An expression of remonstrance.) **175 your way** i.e., the
way you should think of her **178 invention** imagination **180–81 gentle a condition**
wellborn and wellbred **182 gentle** generous, yielding (to other men)

IAGO. If you are so fond° over her iniquity, give her patent° to offend, for   *185*
    if it touch not you it comes near nobody.
OTHELLO. I will chop her into messes.° Cuckold me?
IAGO. O, 'tis foul in her.
OTHELLO. With mine officer?
IAGO. That's fouler.   *190*
OTHELLO. Get me some poison, Iago, this night. I'll not expostulate with
    her, lest her body and beauty unprovide° my mind again. This
    night, Iago.
IAGO. Do it not with poison. Strangle her in her bed, even the bed she
    hath contaminated.   *195*
OTHELLO. Good, good! The justice of it pleases. Very good.
IAGO. And for Cassio, let me be his undertaker.° You shall hear more by
    midnight.
OTHELLO. Excellent good. [*A trumpet within.*] What trumpet is that
    same?   *200*
IAGO. I warrant, something from Venice.

    Enter Lodovico, Desdemona, and attendants.

    'Tis Lodovico. This comes from the Duke.
    See, your wife's with him.
LODOVICO. God save you, worthy General!
OTHELLO.   With all my heart,° sir.
LODOVICO. [*Giving him a letter*]
    The Duke and the senators of Venice greet you.   *205*
OTHELLO. I kiss the instrument of their pleasures.
                            [*He opens the letter, and reads.*]
DESDEMONA. And what's the news, good cousin Lodovico?
IAGO. I am very glad to see you, signor.
    Welcome to Cyprus.
LODOVICO. I thank you. How does Lieutenant Cassio?   *210*
IAGO. Lives, sir.
DESDEMONA. Cousin, there's fall'n between him and my lord
    An unkind° breach; but you shall make all well.
OTHELLO. Are you sure of that?
DESDEMONA. My lord?   *215*
OTHELLO. [*Reads*] "This fail you not to do, as you will—"
LODOVICO. He did not call; he's busy in the paper.
    Is there division twixt my lord and Cassio?

---

185 fond foolish. **patent** license **187 messes** portions of meat, i.e., bits **192 unprovide**
weaken, render unfit **197 be his undertaker** undertake to dispatch him **204 With all
my heart** i.e., I thank you most heartily **213 unkind** unnatural, contrary to their
natures; hurtful

DESDEMONA. A most unhappy one. I would do much
    T' atone° them, for the love I bear to Cassio.   *220*
OTHELLO. Fire and brimstone!
DESDEMONA. My lord?
OTHELLO. Are you wise?
DESDEMONA. What, is he angry?
LODOVICO.   Maybe the letter moved him;
    For, as I think, they do command him home,   *225*
    Deputing Cassio in his government.°
DESDEMONA. By my troth, I am glad on 't.°
OTHELLO. Indeed?
DESDEMONA. My lord?
OTHELLO. I am glad to see you mad.   *230*
DESDEMONA. Why, sweet Othello—
OTHELLO. [*Striking her*] Devil!
DESDEMONA. I have not deserved this.
LODOVICO. My lord, this would not be believed in Venice,
    Though I should swear I saw 't. 'Tis very much.°   *235*
    Make her amends; she weeps.
OTHELLO.   O devil, devil!
    If that the earth could teem° with woman's tears,
    Each drop she falls° would prove a crocodile.°
    Out of my sight!
DESDEMONA.   I will not stay to offend you.   [*Going.*]
LODOVICO. Truly, an obedient lady.   *240*
    I do beseech your lordship, call her back.
OTHELLO. Mistress!
DESDEMONA. [*Returning*] My lord?
OTHELLO. What would you with her, sir?°
LODOVICO. Who, I, my lord?   *245*
OTHELLO. Ay, you did wish that I would make her turn.
    Sir, she can turn, and turn, and yet go on
    And turn again; and she can weep, sir, weep;
    And she's obedient,° as you say, obedient,
    Very obedient.—Proceed you in your tears.—   *250*
    Concerning this, sir—O well-painted passion!°—
    I am commanded home.—Get you away;
    I'll send for you anon.—Sir, I obey the mandate

---

220 **atone** reconcile   226 **government** office   227 **on 't** of it   230 **I am . . . mad** i.e.,
I am glad to see that you are insane enough to rejoice in Cassio's promotion (? Othello
bitterly plays on Desdemona's *I am glad.*)   235 **very much** too much, outrageous
237 **teem** breed, be impregnant   238 **falls** lets fall.   **crocodile** (Crocodiles were supposed to weep hypocritical tears for their victims.)   244 **What . . . sir** (Othello implies
that Desdemona is pliant and will do a *turn*, ll. 246–48, for any man.)   249 **obedient** (with
much the same sexual connotation as *turn* in ll. 246–48)   251 **passion** i.e., grief

And will return to Venice.—Hence, avaunt!   [*Exit Desdemona.*]
Cassio shall have my place. And, sir, tonight   255
I do entreat that we may sup together.
You are welcome, sir, to Cyprus.—Goats and monkeys!°   *Exit.*
LODOVICO. Is this the noble Moor whom our full Senate
Call all in all sufficient? Is this the nature
Whom passion could not shake? Whose solid virtue   260
The shot of accident nor dart of chance
Could neither graze nor pierce?
IAGO.   He is much changed.
LODOVICO. Are his wits safe? Is he not light of brain?
IAGO. He's that he is. I may not breathe my censure
What he might be. If what he might he is not,   265
I would to heaven he were!°
LODOVICO.   What, strike his wife?
IAGO. Faith, that was not so well; yet would I knew
That stroke would prove the worst!
LODOVICO.   Is it his use?°
Or did the letters work upon his blood°
And new-create his fault?
IAGO.   Alas, alas!   270
It is not honesty in me to speak
What I have seen and known. You shall observe him,
And his own courses will denote him so
That I may save my speech. Do but go after,
And mark how he continues.   275
LODOVICO. I am sorry that I am deceived in him.   *Exeunt.*

[**4.2**]   *Enter Othello and Emilia*

OTHELLO. You have seen nothing then?
EMILIA. Nor ever heard, nor ever did suspect.
OTHELLO. Yes, you have seen Cassio and she together.
EMILIA. But then I saw no harm, and then I heard
Each syllable that breath made up between them.   5
OTHELLO. What, did they never whisper?
EMILIA. Never, my lord.
OTHELLO. Nor send you out o' the way?
EMILIA. Never.

---

257 Goats and monkeys (See 3.3.194.)   **264–66 I may . . . were** i.e., I dare not venture
an opinion as to whether he's of unsound mind, as you suggest; but if he isn't, then it might
be better to wish he were in fact insane, since only that could excuse his wild
behavior   **268 use** custom   **269 blood** passions

4.2 Location: The citadel.

OTHELLO. To fetch her fan, her gloves, her mask, nor nothing? 10
EMILIA. Never, my lord.
OTHELLO. That's strange.
EMILIA. I durst, my lord, to wager she is honest
 Lay down my soul at stake.° If you think other,
 Remove your thought; it doth abuse your bosom. 15
 If any wretch have put this in your head,
 Let heaven requite it with the serpent's curse!°
 For if she be not honest, chaste, and true,
 There's no man happy; the purest of their wives
 Is foul as slander.
OTHELLO.   Bid her come hither. Go. *Exit Emilia.* 20
 She says enough; yet she's a simple bawd
 That cannot say as much.° This° is a subtle whore,
 A closet lock and key° of villainous secrets.
 And yet she'll kneel and pray; I have seen her do 't.

 Enter Desdemona and Emilia.

DESDEMONA. My lord, what is your will? 25
OTHELLO. Pray you, chuck, come hither.
DESDEMONA. What is your pleasure?
OTHELLO.   Let me see your eyes.
 Look in my face.
DESDEMONA.   What horrible fancy's this?
OTHELLO. [*To Emilia*] Some of your function,° mistress.
 Leave procreants° alone and shut the door; 30
 Cough or cry "hem" if anybody come.
 Your mystery,° your mystery! Nay, dispatch. *Exit Emilia.*
DESDEMONA. [*Kneeling*]
 Upon my knees, what doth your speech import?
 I understand a fury in your words,
 But not the words. 35
OTHELLO. Why, what art thou?
DESDEMONA.   Your wife, my lord, your true
 And loyal wife.
OTHELLO.   Come, swear it, damn thyself,
 Lest, being like one of heaven,° the devils themselves

---

14 **at stake** as the wager   17 **the serpent's curse** the curse pronounced by God on the serpent for deceiving Eve, just as some man has done to Othello and Desdemona. (See Genesis 3:14.)   21–22 **she's . . . much** i.e., any procuress or go-between who couldn't make up as convincing a story as Emilia's would have to be pretty stupid   22 **This** i.e., Desdemona   23 **closet lock and key** i.e., concealer   29 **Some . . . function** i.e., practice your chosen profession, that of bawd (by guarding the door)   30 **procreants** mating couples   32 **mystery** trade, occupation   38 **being . . . heaven** looking like an angel

    Should fear to seize thee. Therefore be double damned:
    Swear thou art honest.
DESDEMONA.   Heaven doth truly know it.   *40*
OTHELLO. Heaven truly knows that thou art false as hell.
DESDEMONA. To whom, my lord? With whom? How am I false?
OTHELLO. [*Weeping*] Ah, Desdemon! Away, away, away!
DESDEMONA. Alas the heavy day! Why do you weep?
    Am I the motive° of these tears, my lord?   *45*
    If haply you my father do suspect
    An instrument of this your calling back,
    Lay not your blame on me. If you have lost him,
    I have lost him too.
OTHELLO.   Had it pleased heaven
    To try me with affliction, had they° rained   *50*
    All kinds of sores and shames on my bare head,
    Steeped me in poverty to the very lips,
    Given to captivity me and my utmost hopes,
    I should have found in some place of my soul
    A drop of patience. But, alas, to make me   *55*
    A fixèd figure for the time of scorn°
    To point his° slow and moving finger at!
    Yet could I bear that too, well, very well.
    But there where I have garnered° up my heart,
    Where either I must live or bear no life,   *60*
    The fountain° from the which my current runs
    Or else dries up—to be discarded thence!
    Or keep it as a cistern° for foul toads
    To knot° and gender° in! Turn thy complexion there,°
    Patience, thou young and rose-lipped cherubin—   *65*
    Ay, there look grim as hell!°
DESDEMONA. I hope my noble lord esteems me honest.°
OTHELLO. O, ay, as summer flies are in the shambles,°
    That quicken° even with blowing.° O thou weed,
    Who art so lovely fair and smell'st so sweet   *70*
    That the sense aches at thee, would thou hadst ne'er been born!

---

45 motive cause   **50 they** i.e., heavenly powers   **56 time of scorn** i.e., scornful world
57 his its.   **slow and moving finger** i.e., hour hand of the clock, moving so slowly it
seems hardly to move at all. (Othello envisages himself as being eternally pointed at
by the scornful world as the numbers on a clock are pointed at by the hour hand.)
59 garnered stored   **61 fountain** spring   **63 cistern** cesspool   **64 knot** i.e., couple.
gender engender.   **Turn. . .there** change your color, grow pale, at such a sight
65–66 Patience . . . hell (Even Patience, that rose-lipped cherub, will look grim and pale
at this spectacle.)   **67 honest** chaste   **68 shambles** slaughterhouse   **69 quicken** come
to life.   **with blowing** i.e., with the puffing up of something rotten in which maggots
are breeding

DESDEMONA. Alas, what ignorant sin° have I committed?
OTHELLO. Was this fair paper, this most goodly book,
      Made to write "whore" upon? What committed?
      Committed? O thou public commoner!°   75
      I should make very forges of my cheeks,
      That would to cinders burn up modesty,
      Did I but speak thy deeds. What committed?
      Heaven stops the nose at it and the moon winks;°
      The bawdy wind, that kisses all it meets,   80
      Is hushed within the hollow mine° of earth
      And will not hear 't. What committed?
      Impudent strumpet!
DESDEMONA.   By heaven, you do me wrong.
OTHELLO. Are not you a strumpet?
DESDEMONA. No, as I am a Christian.   85
      If to preserve this vessel° for my lord
      From any other foul unlawful touch
      Be not to be a strumpet, I am none.
OTHELLO. What, not a whore?
DESDEMONA. No, as I shall be saved.   90
OTHELLO. Is 't possible?
DESDEMONA. O, heaven forgive us!
OTHELLO.   I cry you mercy,° then.
      I took you for that cunning whore of Venice
      That married with Othello. [*Calling out.*] You, mistress,
      That have the office opposite to Saint Peter   95
      And keep the gate of hell!

      Enter Emilia.

                        You, you, ay, you!
      We have done our course.° There's money for your pains.
                                        [*He gives money.*]
      I pray you, turn the key and keep our counsel.   *Exit.*
EMILIA. Alas, what does this gentleman conceive?°
      How do you, madam? How do you, my good lady?   100
DESDEMONA. Faith, half asleep.°
EMILIA. Good madam, what's the matter with my lord?
DESDEMONA. With who?
EMILIA. Why, with my lord, madam.
DESDEMONA. Who is thy lord?

---

72 ignorant sin sin in ignorance **75 commoner** prostitute **79 winks** closes her eyes.
(The moon symbolizes chastity.) **80 bawdy** kissing one and all **81 mine** cave (where
the winds were thought to dwell) **86 vessel** i.e., body **92 cry you mercy** beg your
pardon **97 course** business (with an indecent suggestion of "trick," turn at sex)
99 conceive suppose, think **101 half asleep** i.e., dazed

EMILIA.   He that is yours, sweet lady.   *105*
DESDEMONA. I have none. Do not talk to me, Emilia.
    I cannot weep, nor answers have I none
    But what should go by water.° Prithee, tonight
    Lay on my bed my wedding sheets, remember;
    And call thy husband hither.   *110*
EMILIA. Here's a change indeed!   *Exit.*
DESDEMONA. 'Tis meet° I should be used so, very meet.
    How have I been behaved, that he might stick°
    The small'st opinion° on my least misuse?°

    Enter Iago and Emilia.

IAGO. What is your pleasure, madam? How is 't with you?   *115*
DESDEMONA. I cannot tell. Those that do teach young babes
    Do it with gentle means and easy tasks.
    He might have chid me so, for, in good faith,
    I am a child to chiding.
IAGO. What is the matter, lady?   *120*
EMILIA. Alas, Iago, my lord hath so bewhored her,
    Thrown such despite and heavy terms upon her,
    That true hearts cannot bear it.
DESDEMONA. Am I that name, Iago?
IAGO. What name, fair lady?   *125*
DESDEMONA. Such as she said my lord did say I was.
EMILIA. He called her whore. A beggar in his drink
    Could not have laid such terms upon his callet.°
IAGO. Why did he so?
DESDEMONA. [*Weeping*] I do not know. I am sure I am none such.   *130*
IAGO. Do not weep, do not weep. Alas the day!
EMILIA. Hath she forsook so many noble matches,
    Her father and her country and her friends,
    To be called whore? Would it not make one weep?
DESDEMONA. It is my wretched fortune.
IAGO.   Beshrew° him for 't!   *135*
    How comes this trick° upon him?
DESDEMONA.   Nay, heaven doth know.
EMILIA. I will be hanged if some eternal° villain,
    Some busy and insinuating° rogue,
    Some cogging,° cozening° slave, to get some office,
    Have not devised this slander. I will be hanged else.   *140*

---

108 go by water be expressed by tears   **112 meet** fitting   **113 stick** attach   **114 opinion** censure. **least misuse** slightest misconduct   **128 callet** whore   **135 Beshrew** curse **136 trick** strange behavior, delusion   **137 eternal** inveterate   **138 insinuating** ingratiating, fawning, wheedling   **139 cogging** cheating. **cozening** defrauding

IAGO. Fie, there is no such man. It is impossible.

DESDEMONA. If any such there be, heaven pardon him!

EMILIA. A halter° pardon him! And hell gnaw his bones!
  Why should he call her whore? Who keeps her company?
  What place? What time? What form?° What likelihood?   *145*
  The Moor's abused by some most villainous knave,
  Some base notorious knave, some scurvy fellow.
  O heavens, that such companions° thou'dst unfold,°
  And put in every honest hand a whip
  To lash the rascals naked through the world   *150*
  Even from the east to th' west!

IAGO.   Speak within door.°

EMILIA. O, fie upon them! Some such squire° he was
  That turned your wit the seamy side° without
  And made you to suspect me with the Moor.

IAGO. You are a fool. Go to.°

DESDEMONA.   Alas, Iago,   *155*
  What shall I do to win my lord again?
  Good friend, go to him; for, by this light of heaven,
  I know not how I lost him. Here I kneel. [*She kneels.*]
  If e'er my will did trespass 'gainst his love,
  Either in discourse of thought° or actual deed,   *160*
  Or that° mine eyes, mine ears, or any sense
  Delighted them° in any other form;
  Or that I do not yet,° and ever did,
  And ever will—though he do shake me off
  To beggarly divorcement—love him dearly,   *165*
  Comfort forswear° me! Unkindness may do much,
  And his unkindness may defeat° my life,
  But never taint my love. I cannot say "whore."
  It does abhor° me now I speak the word;
  To do the act that might the addition° earn   *170*
  Not the world's mass of vanity° could make me.

IAGO. I pray you, be content. 'Tis but his humor.°
  The business of the state does him offense,
  And he does chide with you.

---

143 halter hangman's noose   **145 form** appearance, circumstance   **148 companions**
fellows.   **unfold** expose   **151 within door** i.e., not so loud   **152 squire** fellow
153 seamy side without wrong side out   **155 Go to** i.e., that's enough   **160 discourse
of thought** process of thinking   **161 that** if (also in l. 163)   **162 Delighted them** took
delight   **163 yet** still   **166 Comfort forswear** may heavenly comfort forsake   **167 defeat**
destroy   **169 abhor** (i) fill me with abhorrence (2) make me whorelike   **170 addition**
title   **171 vanity** showy splendor   **172 humor** mood

DESDEMONA. If 'twere no other—   *175*
IAGO. It is but so, I warrant.   [*Trumpets within.*]
      Hark, how these instruments summon you to supper!
      The messengers of Venice stays the meat.°
      Go in, and weep not. All things shall be well.
                                          Exeunt Desdemona and Emilia.

      Enter Roderigo.

      How now, Roderigo?   *180*
RODERIGO. I do not find that thou deal'st justly with me.
IAGO. What in the contrary?
RODERIGO. Every day thou daff'st me° with some device,° Iago, and
      rather, as it seems to me now, keep'st from me all conveniency° than
      suppliest me with the least advantage° of hope. I will indeed no   *185*
      longer endure it, nor am I yet persuaded to put up° in peace what
      already I have foolishly suffered.
IAGO. Will you hear me, Roderigo?
RODERIGO. Faith, I have heard too much, for your words and perfor-
      mances are no kin together.   *190*
IAGO. You charge me most unjustly.
RODERIGO. With naught but truth. I have wasted myself out of my means.
      The jewels you have had from me to deliver° Desdemona would
      half have corrupted a votarist.° You have told me she hath received
      them and returned me expectations and comforts of sudden respect°   *195*
      and acquaintance, but I find none.
IAGO. Well, go to, very well.
RODERIGO. "Very well"! "Go to"! I cannot go to,° man, nor 'tis not very
      well. By this hand, I think it is scurvy, and begin to find myself
      fopped° in it.   *200*
IAGO. Very well.
RODERIGO. I tell you 'tis not very well.° I will make myself known to
      Desdemona. If she will return me my jewels, I will give over my
      suit and repent my unlawful solicitation; if not, assure yourself I will
      seek satisfaction° of you.   *205*
IAGO. You have said now?°

---

178 stays the meat are waiting to dine   **183 thou daff'st me** you put me off.
device excuse, trick   **184 conveniency** advantage, opportunity   **185 advantage** increase
186 put up submit to, tolerate   **193 deliver** deliver to   **194 votarist** nun   **195 sudden
respect** immediate consideration   **198 I cannot go to** (Roderigo changes Iago's *go to,* an
expression urging patience, to *I cannot go to,* "I have no opportunity for sex.")
200 fopped fooled, duped   **202 not very well** (Roderigo changes Iago's *very well,* "all right,
then," to *not very well,* "not at all good.")   **205 satisfaction** repayment. (The term normally means the settling of accounts in a duel.)   **206 You . . . now** have you finished

RODERIGO. Ay, and said nothing but what I protest intendment° of doing.

IAGO. Why, now I see there's mettle in thee, and even from this instant do build on thee a better opinion than ever before. Give me thy hand, Roderigo. Thou hast taken against me a most just exception; but yet   *210* I protest I have dealt most directly in thy affair.

RODERIGO. It hath not appeared.

IAGO. I grant indeed it hath not appeared, and your suspicion is not without wit and judgment. But, Roderigo, if thou hast that in thee indeed which I have greater reason to believe now than ever—I mean   *215* purpose, courage, and valor—this night show it. If thou the next night following enjoy not Desdemona, take me from this world with treachery and devise engines for° my life.

RODERIGO. Well, what is it? Is it within reason and compass?

IAGO. Sir, there is especial commission come from Venice to depute Cassio   *220* in Othello's place.

RODERIGO. Is that true? Why, then Othello and Desdemona return again to Venice.

IAGO. O, no; he goes into Mauritania and takes away with him the fair Desdemona, unless his abode be lingered here by some accident;   *225* wherein none can be so determinate° as the removing of Cassio.

RODERIGO. How do you mean, removing of him?

IAGO. Why, by making him uncapable of Othello's place—knocking out his brains.

RODERIGO. And that you would have me to do?   *230*

IAGO. Ay, if you dare do yourself a profit and a right. He sups tonight with a harlotry,° and thither will I go to him. He knows not yet of his honorable fortune. If you will watch his going thence, which I will fashion to fall out° between twelve and one, you may take him at your pleasure. I will be near to second your attempt, and he   *235* shall fall between us. Come stand not amazed at it, but go along with me. I will show you such a necessity in his death that you shall think yourself bound to put it on him. It is now high° suppertime, and the night grows to waste.° About it.

RODERIGO. I will hear further reason for this.   *240*

IAGO. And you shall be satisfied.   *Exeunt.*

[4.3]   *Enter Othello, Lodovico, Desdemona, Emilia, and attendants.*

LODOVICO. I do beseech you, sir, trouble yourself no further.

OTHELLO. O, pardon me; 'twill do me good to walk.

---

207 intendment intention   **218 engines for** plots against   **226 determinate** effective
232 harlotry slut   **234 fall out** occur   **238 high** fully   **239 grows to waste** wastes away

4.3 Location: The citadel.

DESDEMONA. Your honor is most welcome.
OTHELLO.   Will you walk, sir?
    O, Desdemona!   5
DESDEMONA. My lord?
OTHELLO. Get you to bed on th' instant. I will be returned forthwith.
    Dismiss your attendant there. Look 't be done.
DESDEMONA. I will, my lord. *Exit* [*Othello, with Lodovico and attendants*].
EMILIA. How goes it now? He looks gentler than he did.   10
DESDEMONA. He says he will return incontinent,°
    And hath commanded me to go to bed,
    And bid me to dismiss you.
EMILIA. Dismiss me?
DESDEMONA. It was his bidding. Therefore, good Emilia,   15
    Give me my nightly wearing, and adieu.
    We must not now displease him.
EMILIA. I would you had never seen him!
DESDEMONA. So would not I. My love doth so approve him
    That even his stubbornness,° his checks,° his frowns—   20
    Prithee, unpin me—have grace and favor in them.
                              [*Emilia prepares Desdemona for bed.*]
EMILIA. I have laid those sheets you bade me on the bed.
DESDEMONA. All's one.° Good faith, how foolish are our minds!
    If I do die before thee, prithee shroud me   25
    In one of these same sheets.
EMILIA.   Come, come, you talk.°
DESDEMONA. My mother had a maid called Barbary.
    She was in love, and he she loved proved mad°
    And did forsake her. She had a song of "Willow."
    An old thing 'twas, but it expressed her fortune,   30
    And she died singing it. That song tonight
    Will not go from my mind; I have much to do
    But to go hang° my head all at one side
    And sing it like poor Barbary. Prithee, dispatch.
EMILIA. Shall I go fetch your nightgown?°   35
DESDEMONA. No, unpin me here.
    This Lodovico is a proper° man.
EMILIA. A very handsome man.
DESDEMONA. He speaks well.

---

11 incontinent immediately   **20 stubborness** roughness.   **checks** rebukes   **24 All's
one** all right. It doesn't really matter   **26 talk** i.e., prattle   **28 mad** wild, i.e., faithless
32–33 I . . . hang I can scarcely keep myself from hanging   **35 nightgown** dressing
gown   **37 proper** handsome

EMILIA. I know a lady in Venice would have walked barefoot to Palestine
    for a touch of his nether lip.
DESDEMONA. [*Singing*]
        "The poor soul sat sighing by a sycamore tree,
           Sing all a green willow;°
        Her hand on her bosom, her head on her knee,
           Sing willow, willow, willow.   *45*
        The fresh streams ran by her and murmured her moans;
           Sing willow, willow, willow;
        Her salt tears fell from her, and softened the stones—"
    Lay by these.
    [*Singing*.] "Sing willow, willow, willow—"   *50*
    Prithee, hie thee.° He'll come anon.
    [*Singing*.] "Sing all a green willow must be my garland.
        Let nobody blame him; his scorn I approve—"
    Nay, that's not next.—Hark! Who is 't that knocks?
EMILIA. It's the wind.   *55*
DESDEMONA. [*Singing*]
        "I called my love false love; but what said he then?
           Sing willow, willow, willow;
        If I court more women, you'll couch with more men."

    So, get thee gone. Good night. Mine eyes do itch;
    Doth that bode weeping?
EMILIA.   'Tis neither here nor there.   *60*
DESDEMONA. I have heard it said so. O, these men, these men!
    Dost thou in conscience think—tell me, Emilia—
    That there be women do abuse° their husbands
    In such gross kind?
EMILIA.   There be some such, no question.
DESDEMONA. Wouldst thou do such a deed for all the world?   *65*
EMILIA. Why, would not you?
DESDEMONA.   No, by this heavenly light!
EMILIA. Nor I neither by this heavenly light;
    I might do 't as well i' the dark.
DESDEMONA. Wouldst thou do such a deed for all the world?
EMILIA. The world's a huge thing. It is a great price   *70*
    For a small vice.
DESDEMONA. Good troth, I think thou wouldst not.
EMILIA. By my troth, I think I should, and undo 't when I had done.
    Marry, I would not do such a thing for a joint ring,° nor for

---

43 willow (A conventional emblem of disappointed love.)   **51 hie thee** hurry. **anon** right
away **63 abuse** deceive **75 joint ring** a ring made in separate halves.

measures of lawn,° nor for gowns, petticoats, nor caps, nor any 75
petty exhibition.° But for all the whole world! Uds° pity, who
would not make her husband a cuckold to make him a monarch?
I should venture purgatory for 't.
DESDEMONA. Beshrew me if I would do such a wrong
For the whole world.   80
EMILIA. Why, the wrong is but a wrong i' the world, and having the world
for your labor, 'tis a wrong in your own world, and you might
quickly make it right.
DESDEMONA. I do not think there is any such woman.
EMILIA. Yes, a dozen, and as many   85
To th' vantage° as would store° the world they played° for.
But I do think it is their husbands' faults
If wives do fall. Say that they slack their duties°
And pour our treasures into foreign laps,°
Or else break out in peevish jealousies,   90
Throwing restraint upon us?° Or say they strike us,
Or scant our former having in despite?°
Why, we have galls,° and though we have some grace,
Yet have we some revenge. Let husbands know
Their wives have sense° like them. They see, and smell,   95
And have their palates both for sweet and sour,
As husbands have. What is it that they do
When they change us for others? Is it sport?°
I think it is. And doth affection° breed it?
I think it doth. Is 't frailty that thus errs?   100
It is so too. And have not we affections,
Desires for sport, and frailty, as men have?
Then let them use us well, else let them know,
The ills we do, their ills instruct us so.
DESDEMONA. Good night, good night. God me such uses° send   105
Not to pick bad from bad, but by bad mend!°

                                                            Exeunt.

---

lawn fine linen **75–76 exhibition** gift **76 Uds** i.e., God's **86 To th' vantage** in addition, to boot. **store** populate. **played** (1) gambled (2) sported sexually **88 duties** marital duties **89 pour . . . laps** i.e., are unfaithful, give what is rightfully ours (semen) to other women **91 Throwing . . . us** i.e., jealously restricting our freedom to see other men **92 scant . . . despite** reduce our allowance to spite us **93 have galls** i.e., are capable of resenting injury and insult **95 sense** physical sense **98 sport** sexual pastime **99 affection** passion **105 uses** habit, practice **106 Not . . . mend** i.e., not to learn bad conduct from others' badness (as Emilia has suggested women learn from men), but to mend my ways by perceiving what badness is, making spiritual benefit out of evil and adversity

[5.1]   *Enter Iago and Roderigo.*

IAGO. Here stand behind this bulk.° Straight will he come.   1
    Wear thy good rapier bare,° and put it home.
    Quick, quick! Fear nothing. I'll be at thy elbow.
    It makes us or it mars us. Think on that,
    And fix most firm thy resolution.   5
RODERIGO. Be near at hand. I may miscarry in 't.
IAGO. Here, at thy hand. Be bold, and take thy stand.
                          [Iago stands aside. Roderigo conceals himself.]
RODERIGO. I have no great devotion to the deed;
    And yet he hath given me satisfying reasons.
    'Tis but a man gone. Forth, my sword! He dies.   10
                                            [He draws.]
IAGO. I have rubbed this young quat° almost to the sense,°
    And he grows angry. No, whether he kill Cassio
    Or Cassio him, or each do kill the other,
    Every way makes my gain. Live Roderigo,°
    He calls me to a restitution large   15
    Of gold and jewels that I bobbed° from him
    As gifts to Desdemona.
    It must not be. If Cassio do remain,
    He hath a daily beauty in life
    That makes me ugly; and besides, the Moor   20
    May unfold° me to him; there stand I in much peril.
    No, he must die. Be 't so. I hear him coming.

    Enter Cassio.

RODERIGO. *[Coming forth]*
    I know his gait, 'tis he.—Villain, thou diest!
                         [He makes a pass at Cassio.]
CASSIO. That thrust had been mine enemy indeed,
    But that my coat° is better than thou know'st.   25
    I will make proof° of thine.
                   [He draws, and wounds Roderigo.]
RODERIGO.   O, I am slain!   *[He falls.]*
       [Iago from behind wounds Cassio in the leg, and exit.]
CASSIO. I am maimed forever. Help, ho! Murder! Murder!

5.1 Location: A street in Cyprus.
1 bulk framework projecting from the front of a shop   **2 bare** unsheathed   **11 quat**
pimple, pustule.   **to the sense** to the quick   **14 Live Roderigo** if Roderigo live
16 bobbed swindled   **21 unfold** expose   **25 coat** (Possibly a garment of mail under the
outer clothing, or simply a tougher coat than Roderigo expected.)   **26 proof** a test

Enter Othello.

OTHELLO. The voice of Cassio! Iago keeps his word.
RODERIGO. O, villain that I am!
OTHELLO. It is even so.   30
CASSIO. O, help, ho! Light! A surgeon!
OTHELLO. 'Tis he. O brave Iago, honest and just
    That hast such noble sense of thy friend's wrong!
    Thou teachest me. Minion,° your dear lies dead,
    And your unblest fate hies.° Strumpet, I come.   35
    Forth of my heart those charms, thine eyes, are blotted;
    Thy bed, lust-stained, shall with lust's blood be spotted.
                             Exit Othello.

Enter Lodovico and Gratiano.

CASSIO. What ho! No watch? No passage?° Murder! Murder!
GRATIANO. 'Tis some mischance. The voice is very direful.
CASSIO. O, help!   40
LODOVICO. Hark!
RODERIGO. O wretched villain!
LODOVICO. Two or three groan. 'Tis heavy° night;
    These may be counterfeits. Let's think 't unsafe
    To come in to° the cry without more help.   45
               [They remain near the entrance.]
RODERIGO. Nobody come? Then shall I bleed to death.

Enter Iago [in his shirtsleeves, with a light].

LODOVICO. Hark!
GRATIANO. Here's one comes in his shirt, with light and weapons.
IAGO. Who's there? Whose noise is this that cries on° murder?
LODOVICO. We do not know.   50
IAGO.   Did not you hear a cry?
CASSIO. Here, here! For heaven's sake, help me!
IAGO.   What's the matter?
                        [He moves toward Cassio.]
GRATIANO. [*To Lodovico*] This is Othello's ancient, as I take it.
LODOVICO. [*To Gratiano*] The same indeed, a very valiant fellow.
IAGO. [*To Cassio*] What° are you here that cry so grievously?
CASSIO. Iago? O, I am spoiled,° undone by villains!   55
    Give me some help.
IAGO. O me, Lieutenant! What villains have done this?

---

34 Minion hussy (i.e., Desdemona) **35 hies** hastens on **36 Forth of** from out
38 passage people passing by **43 heavy** thick, dark **45 come in to** approach
49 cries on cries out **54 What** who (also at ll. 60 and 66) **55 spoiled** ruined, done for

CASSIO. I think that one of them is hereabout,
    And cannot make° away.
IAGO.   O treacherous villains!
    [*To Lodovico and Gratiano.*] What are you there? Come in, and
    give some help.   [*They advance.*]   60
RODERIGO. O, help me there!
CASSIO. That's one of them.
IAGO.   O murderous slave! O villain!
    [*He stabs Roderigo.*]
RODERIGO. O damned Iago! O inhuman dog!
IAGO. Kill men i' the dark?—Where be these bloody thieves?—
    How silent is this town!—Ho! Murder, murder!—   65
    [*To Lodovico and Gratiano.*] What may you be? Are you of good
    or evil?
LODOVICO. As you shall prove us, praise° us.
IAGO. Signor Lodovico?
LODOVICO. He, sir.
IAGO. I cry you mercy.° Here's Cassio hurt by villains.   70
GRATIANO. Cassio?
IAGO. How is 't, brother?
CASSIO. My leg is cut in two.
IAGO. Marry, heaven forbid!
    Light, gentlemen! I'll bind it with my shirt.   75
        [*He hands them the light, and tends to Cassio's wound.*]

    Enter Bianca.

BIANCA. What is the matter, ho? Who is 't that cried?
IAGO. Who is 't that cried?
BIANCA.   O my dear Cassio!
    My sweet Cassio! O Cassio, Cassio, Cassio!
IAGO. O notable strumpet! Cassio, may you suspect
    Who they should be that have thus mangled you?   80
CASSIO. No.
GRATIANO. I am sorry to find you thus. I have been to seek you.
IAGO. Lend me a garter. [*He applies a tourniquet.*] So.—O, for a chair,°
    To bear him easily hence!
BIANCA. Alas, he faints! O Cassio, Cassio, Cassio!   85
IAGO. Gentlemen all, I do suspect this trash
    To be a party in this injury.—
    Patience awhile, good Cassio.—Come, come;
    Lend me a light. [*He shines the light on Roderigo.*] Know we this
    face or no?

---

59 make get **67 praise** appraise **70 I cry you mercy** I beg your pardon **83 chair** litter

Alas, my friend and my dear countryman   90
Roderigo! No.—Yes, sure.—O heaven! Roderigo!
GRATIANO. What, of Venice?
IAGO. Even he, sir. Did you know him?
GRATIANO. Know him? Ay.
IAGO. Signor Gratiano? I cry your gentle pardon.   95
These bloody accidents must excuse my manners
That so neglected you.
GRATIANO.   I am glad to see you.
IAGO. How do you, Cassio? O, a chair, a chair!
GRATIANO. Roderigo!
IAGO. He, he, 'tis he. [*A litter is brought in.*] O, that's well said; the
chair.   100
Some good man bear him carefully from hence;
I'll fetch the General's surgeon. [*To Bianca.*] For you, mistress,
Save you your labor.—He that lies slain here, Cassio,
Was my dear friend. What malice was between you?
CASSIO.
None in the world, nor do I know the man.   105
IAGO. [*To Bianca*]
What, look you pale?—, bear him out o' th' air.
                [*Cassio and Roderigo are borne off.*]
Stay you, good gentlemen.—Look you pale, mistress?—
Do you perceive the gastness of her eye?—
Nay, if you stare, we shall hear more anon.—
Behold her well; I pray you, look upon her.   110
Do you see, gentlemen? Nay, guiltiness
Will speak, though tongues were out of use.

[*Enter Emilia.*]

EMILIA. 'Las, what's the matter? What's the matter, husband?
IAGO. Cassio hath here been set on in the dark
By Roderigo and fellows that are scaped.   115
He's almost slain, and Roderigo dead.
EMILIA. Alas, good gentleman! Alas, good Cassio!
IAGO. This is the fruits of whoring. Prithee, Emilia
Go know° of Cassio where he supped tonight.
[*To Bianca.*] What, do you shake at that?   120

---

95 gentle noble **96 accidents** sudden events **100 well said** well done **103 Save
. . . labor** i.e., never you mind tending Cassio **104 malice** enmity **106 bear . . . air**
(Fresh air was thought to be dangerous for a wound.) **107 Stay you** (Lodovico and
Gratiano are evidently about to leave.) **108 gastness** terror **109 stare** (Iago pretends to
interpret Bianca's wild looks as an involuntary confession of guilt.) **119 know** learn

BIANCA. He supped at my house, but I therefore shake not.
IAGO. O, did he so? I charge you go with me.
EMILIA. O, fie upon thee, strumpet!
BIANCA. I am no strumpet, but of life as honest°
    As you that thus abuse me.   125
EMILIA. As I? Faugh! Fie upon thee!
IAGO. Kind gentlemen, let's go see poor Cassio dressed.° —
    Come, mistress, you must tell 's another tale.
    Emilia, run you to the citadel
    And tell my lord and lady what hath happed. —   130
    Will you go on afore? [*Aside.*] This is the night
    That either makes me or fordoes° me quite.   *Exeunt.*

[**5.2**]   *Enter Othello [with a light], and Desdemona in her bed.°*

OTHELLO. It is the cause,° it is the cause, my soul.   1
    Let me not name it to you, you chaste stars!
    It is the cause. Yet I'll not shed her blood,
    Nor scar that whiter skin of hers than snow,
    And smooth as monumental° alabaster.   5
    Yet she must die, else she'll betray more men.
    Put out the light, and then put out the light.°
    If I quench thee, thou flaming minister,°
    I can again thy former light restore,
    Should I repent me;° but once put out thy light,   10
    Thou cunning'st pattern° of excelling nature,
    I know not where is that Promethean heat°
    That can thy light relume.° When I have plucked thy rose,
    I cannot give it vital growth again;
    It needs must wither. I'll smell thee on the tree   15
                         [*He kisses her.*]
    O balmy breath, that dost almost persuade
    Justice to break her sword! One more one more.

---

124 honest chaste   **127 Cassio dressed** Cassio's wounds dressed   **132 fordoes** undoes, ruins

5.2. Location: A bedchamber in the citadel.
s.d. in her bed (The bed is presumably "thrust out" onstage as the scene begins.)
1 cause i.e., cause of justice, the offense itself, which Othello must correct as an agent of justice **5 monumental** i.e., used in making tombs and funeral monuments **7 the light . . . light** the torch or lamp . . . Desdemona's life **8 flaming minister** torch or lamp that serves me **10 repent me** change my mind **11 Thou . . . pattern** you skillfully wrought perfect example **12 Promethean heat** divine fire. (Alluding to the theft of fire from heaven by Prometheus.) **13 relume** rekindle

Be thus when thou art dead, and I will kill thee,
And love thee after. One more, and that's the last.

[He kisses her.]

So sweet was ne'er so fatal. I must weep,   20
But they are cruel° tears. This sorrow's heavenly;
It strikes where it doth love.° She wakes.
DESDEMONA. Who's there? Othello?
OTHELLO. Ay, Desdemona.
DESDEMONA. Will you come to bed, my lord?   25
OTHELLO. Have you prayed tonight, Desdemon?
DESDEMONA. Ay, my lord.
OTHELLO. If you bethink yourself of any crime°
  Unreconciled as yet to heaven and grace,
  Solicit° for it straight.°   30
DESDEMONA. Alack, my lord, what may you mean by that?
OTHELLO. Well, do it, and be brief. I will walk by.
  I would not kill thy unpreparèd spirit.
  No, heaven forfend!° I would not kill thy soul.
DESDEMONA. Talk you of killing?
OTHELLO.   Ay, I do.
DESDEMONA.   Then heaven   35
  Have mercy on me!
OTHELLO.   Amen, with all my heart!
DESDEMONA. If you say so, I hope you will not kill me.
OTHELLO. Humh!
DESDEMONA. And yet I fear you; for you're fatal then
  When your eyes roll so. Why I should fear I know not   40
  Since guiltiness I know not; but yet I feel I fear.
OTHELLO. Think on thy sins.
DESDEMONA.   They are loves I bear to you.°
OTHELLO. Ay, and for that thou diest.
DESDEMONA. That death's unnatural that kills for loving.
  Alas, why gnaw you so your nether lip?   45
  Some bloody passion shakes your very frame.
  These are portents; but yet I hope, I hope,
  They do not point on° me.
OTHELLO. Peace, and be still!
DESDEMONA. I will so. What's the matter?   50

---

21 cruel unrelenting   **22 It . . . love** (Compare Hebrews 12:6: "For whom the Lord loveth
he chasteneth.")   **28 crime** sin   **30 Solicit** petition, pray.   **straight** immediately
34 forfend forbid   **42 They are . . . you** i.e., if I sinned, it was in loving you more than
my father, or more than God   **point on** point at, predict what is to happen to

OTHELLO. That handkerchief which I so loved and gave thee
    Thou gav'st to Cassio.
DESDEMONA.   No, by my life and soul!
    Send for the man and ask him.
OTHELLO. Sweet soul, take heed, take heed of perjury.
    Thou art on thy deathbed.   *55*
DESDEMONA. Ay, but not yet to die.
OTHELLO.   Yes, presently.°
    Therefore confess thee freely of thy sin;
    For to deny each article with oath
    Cannot remove nor choke the strong conception°
    That I do groan withal.° Thou art to die.   *60*
DESDEMONA. Then Lord have mercy on me!
OTHELLO.   I say, amen.
DESDEMONA. And have you mercy too! I never did
    Offend° you in my life; never loved Cassio
    But with such general warranty° of heaven
    As I might love. I never gave him token.   *65*
OTHELLO. By heaven, I saw my handkerchief in 's hand.
    O perjured woman! Thou dost stone° my heart,
    And makes me call what I intend to do
    A murder, which I thought a sacrifice.
    I saw the handkerchief.
DESDEMONA.   He found it, then.   *70*
    I never gave it him. Send for him hither;
    Let him confess a truth.
OTHELLO.   He hath confessed.
DESDEMONA. What, my lord?
OTHELLO. That he hath used thee.
DESDEMONA.   How? Unlawfully?
OTHELLO.   Ay.
DESDEMONA. He will not say so.
OTHELLO.   No, his mouth is stopped;   *75*
    Honest Iago hath ta'en order° for 't.
DESDEMONA. O, my fear interprets. What, is he dead?
OTHELLO. Had all his hairs been lives, my great revenge
    Had stomach for them all.
DESDEMONA. Alas, he is betrayed and I undone!   [*She weeps.*]   *80*
OTHELLO. Out, strumpet! Weep'st thou for him to my face?
DESDEMONA. O, banish me, my lord, but kill me not!

---

56 presently immediately   **59 conception** (1) belief in your guilt (2) plan in my mind
60 groan withal (1) groan at in sorrow (2) groan as in giving birth   **63 Offend** wrong
64 warranty sanction   **67 stone** turn to stone, harden   **76 ta'en order** taken measures

OTHELLO. Down, strumpet!

DESDEMONA. Kill me tomorrow; let me live tonight!

OTHELLO. Nay, if you strive— 85

DESDEMONA. But half an hour!

OTHELLO.   Being done,° there is no pause.

DESDEMONA. But while I say one prayer!

OTHELLO.   It is too late.

Smothers her.

EMILIA. [*At the door*] My lord, my lord! What ho! My lord, my lord!

OTHELLO. What noise is this? Not dead? Not yet quite dead?

I that am cruel am yet merciful; 90

I would not have thee linger in thy pain.   [*He dispatches her.*]

So, so.

EMILIA. [*Within*] What ho! My lord, my lord!

OTHELLO.   Who's there?

EMILIA. [*Within*] O, good my lord, I would speak a word with you!

OTHELLO. Yes, 'tis Emilia.—By and by.—She's dead.

'Tis like° she comes to speak of Cassio's death.— 95

The noise was here.° Ha! No more moving?

Still as the grave. Shall she come in? Were 't good?—

I think she stirs again. No. What's best to do?

If she come in, she'll sure speak to my wife.

My wife! My wife! What wife? I have no wife. 100

O, insupportable! O heavy hour!

Methinks it should be now a huge eclipse

Of sun and moon, and that th' affrighted globe

Should yawn° at alteration.°

EMILIA. [*Within*]   I do beseech you

That I may speak with you, O, good my lord! 105

OTHELLO. I had forgot thee. O, come in, Emilia.—

Soft,° by and by. Let me the curtains draw.—

[*He closes the bed-curtains and opens the door.*]

Where art thou?

Enter Emilia.

                What's the matter with thee now?

EMILIA. O, my good lord, yonder's foul murders done!

OTHELLO. What, now? 110

EMILIA. But now, my lord.

---

86 Being done i.e., since justice has begun its relentless course   **95 like** likely that
96 here (The Folio's *high* is possible, suggesting that the commotion of the attack on
Cassio was loud.)   **104 yawn** gape in amazement, i.e., move in an earthquake. (According
to Pliny, earthquakes often happen during eclipses.)   **at alteration** at these cataclysmic events
in nature, well suited to express the horror of Desdemona's death   **107 Soft** wait a minute

OTHELLO. It is the very error° of the moon;
    She comes more nearer earth than she was wont,
    And makes men mad.
EMILIA. Cassio, my lord, hath killed a young Venetian   *115*
    Called Roderigo.
OTHELLO.   Roderigo killed?
    And Cassio killed?
EMILIA.   No, Cassio is not killed.
OTHELLO. Not Cassio killed? Then murder's out of tune,
    And sweet revenge grows harsh.
DESDEMONA. O, falsely, falsely murdered!   *120*
EMILIA. O Lord, what cry is that?
OTHELLO. That? What?
EMILIA. Out° and alas, that was my lady's voice.
                           [She opens the bed-curtains.]
    Help, help, ho, help! O lady, speak again!
    Sweet Desdemona! O sweet mistress, speak!   *125*
DESDEMONA. A guiltless death I die.
EMILIA. O, who hath done this deed?
DESDEMONA. Nobody; I myself. Farewell.
    Commend me to my kind lord. O, farewell!   *[She dies.]*
OTHELLO. Why, how should she be murdered?
EMILIA.   Alas, who knows?   *130*
OTHELLO. You heard her say herself it was not I.
EMILIA. She said so. I must needs report the truth.
OTHELLO. She's like a liar gone to burning hell!
    'Twas I that killed her.
EMILIA.   O, the more angel she,
    And you the blacker devil!   *135*
OTHELLO. She turned to folly,° and she was a whore.
EMILIA. Thou dost belie° her, and thou art a devil.
OTHELLO. She was false as water.
EMILIA. Thou art rash as fire to say
    That she was false. O, she was heavenly true!   *140*
OTHELLO. Cassio did top her. Ask thy husband else.°
    O, I were damned beneath all depth in hell
    But that I did proceed upon just grounds
    To this extremity. Thy husband knew it all.
EMILIA. My husband?   *145*
OTHELLO. Thy husband.
EMILIA. That she was false to wedlock?

---

112 error aberration, irregularity   **123 Out** (A cry of dismay, intensifying *alas.*)   **136 folly**
i.e., wantonness, fleshly sin   **137 belie** slander   **141 else** i.e., if you don't believe me

OTHELLO. Ay, with Cassio. Nay, had she been true,
    If heaven would make me such another world
    Of one entire and perfect chrysolite,°   *150*
    I'd not have sold her for it.
EMILIA. My husband?
OTHELLO. Ay, 'twas he that told me on her first.
    An honest man he is, and hates the slime
    That sticks on filthy deeds.   *155*
EMILIA. My husband?
OTHELLO. What needs this iterance,° woman? I say thy husband.
EMILIA. O mistress, villainy hath made mocks° with love!
    My husband say she was false?
OTHELLO.   He, woman;
    I say thy husband. Dost understand the word?   *160*
    My friend, thy husband, honest, honest Iago.
EMILIA. If he say so, may his pernicious soul
    Rot half a grain a day! He lies to th' heart.
    She was too fond of her most filthy bargain.
OTHELLO. Ha?   [*He draws.*] *165*
EMILIA. Do thy worst!
    This deed of thine is no more worthy heaven
    Than thou wast worthy her.
OTHELLO.   Peace, you were best.°
EMILIA. Thou hast not half that power to do me harm
    As I have to be hurt.° O gull!° O dolt!   *170*
    As ignorant as dirt! Thou hast done a deed—
    I care not for thy sword; I'll make thee known
    Though I lost twenty lives.—Help! Help, ho, help!
    The Moor hath killed my mistress! Murder, murder!

    Enter Montano, Gratiano, and Iago.

MONTANO. What is the matter? How now, General?   *175*
EMILIA. O, are you come, Iago? You have done well,
    That men must lay their murders on your neck.
GRATIANO. What is the matter?
EMILIA. [*To Iago*] Disprove this villain, if thou be'st a man.
    He says thou toldst him that his wife was false.   *180*
    I know thou didst not; thou'rt not such a villain.
    Speak, for my heart is full.
IAGO. I told him what I thought, and told no more
    Than what he found himself was apt° and true.

---

150 chrysolite precious topaz   **157 iterance** iteration, repetition   **158 made mocks with** derided, made sport of   **168 you were best** it would be best for you   **170 to be hurt** i.e., to endure hunt. **gull** dupe   **184 apt** plausible

EMILIA. But did you ever tell him she was false?   *185*
IAGO. I did.
EMILIA. You told a lie, an odious, damnèd lie!
    Upon my soul, a lie, a wicked lie.
    She false with Cassio? Did you say with Cassio?
IAGO. With Cassio, mistress. Go to, charm° your tongue.   *190*
EMILIA. I will not charm my tongue; I am bound to speak.
    My mistress here lies murdered in her bed—
ALL. O heavens forfend!
EMILIA. And your reports have set the murder on.
OTHELLO. Nay, stare not, masters. It is true indeed.   *195*
GRATIANO. 'Tis a strange truth.
MONTANO. O monstrous act!
EMILIA.   Villainy, villainy, villainy!
    I think upon 't—I think I smell 't! O villainy!
    I thought so then°—I'll kill myself for grief—
    O villainy, villainy!   *200*
IAGO. What, are you mad? I charge you, get you home.
EMILIA. Good gentlemen, let me have leave to speak.
    'Tis proper I obey him, but not now.
    Perchance, Iago, I will ne'er go home.
OTHELLO. O! O! O!   [*Othello falls on the bed.*]
EMILIA.   Nay, lay thee down and roar,   *205*
    For thou hast killed the sweetest innocent
    That e'er did lift up eye.°
OTHELLO. [*Rising*]   O, she was foul!
    I scarce did know you, uncle. There lies your niece,
    Whose breath indeed these hands have newly stopped.
    I know this act shows° horrible and grim.   *210*
GRATIANO. Poor Desdemon! I am glad thy father's dead.
    Thy match was mortal to him, and pure grief
    Shore° his old thread in twain. Did he live now,
    This sight would make him do a desperate turn,°
    Yea, curse his better angel from his side,   *215*
    And fall to reprobance.°
OTHELLO. 'Tis pitiful. But yet Iago knows
    That she with Cassio hath the act of shame
    A thousand times committed. Cassio confessed it;
    And she did gratify° his amorous works   *220*

---

190 charm keep silent (as though by a magic spell)   **199 then** (Perhaps at 3.3.331–332
and 4.2.137–154.)   **205 s.d. Othello . . . bed** (This direction is from the quarto, as also
He kisses her at l. 19 and *She dies* at l. 129.)   **207 lift up eye** i.e., lift her eyes to heaven
210 shows looks   **213 Shore** sheared, cut   **214 turn** deed   **216 reprobance** damnation,
i.e., suicide   **220 gratify** reward

With that recognizance° and pledge of love
Which I first gave her. I saw it in his hand;
It was a handkerchief, an antique token
My father gave my mother.
EMILIA. O God! O heavenly God!   225
IAGO. Zounds, hold your peace.
EMILIA.   Twill out, twill out! I peace?
No, I will speak as liberal as the north.°
Let heaven and men and devils, let them all,
All, all, cry shame against me, yet I'll speak.
IAGO. Be wise, and get you home.   230
EMILIA.   I will not.   [*Iago threatens Emilia.*]
GRATIANO.   Fie,
Your sword upon a woman?
EMILIA. O thou dull Moor! That handkerchief thou speak'st of
I found by fortune and did give my husband;
For often, with a solemn earnestness,
More than indeed belonged° to such a trifle,   235
He begged of me to steal 't.
IAGO.   Villainous whore!
EMILIA. She give it Cassio? No, alas! I found it,
And I did give 't my husband.
IAGO.   Filth, thou liest!
EMILIA. By heaven, I do not, I do not, gentlemen.
O murderous coxcomb!° What should such a fool   240
Do with so good a wife?
OTHELLO. Are there no stones° in heaven
But what serves for the thunder?—Precious° villain!
[*He runs at Iago; Montano disarms Othello. Iago, from behind, stabs
Emilia.°*]
GRATIANO. The woman falls! Sure he hath killed his wife.
EMILIA. Ay, ay. O, lay me by my mistress' side.   [*Exit Iago.*]   245
GRATIANO. He's gone, but his wife's killed.
MONTANO. 'Tis a notorious villain. Take you this weapon
Which I have here recovered from the Moor.
Come, guard the door without. Let him not pass,
But kill him rather. I'll after that same villain,   250
For 'tis a damnèd slave.
                    Exit [*with all but Othello and Emilia,
                    who has been laid by Desdemona's side*].

221 **recognizance** token   227 **liberal as the north** freely as the north wind (blows)
235 **belonged** was appropriate   240 **coxcomb** fool. (Addressed to Othello.)   242 **stones**
bolts, such as those used for thunderbolts   243 **Precious** i.e., arrant, utter   **s.d. He . . .
Emilia** (The quarto text reads, "The Moor runs at Iago. Iago kills his wife." The quarto
also specifies the exit of Iago at l.245 and the death of Emilia at l.260.)

OTHELLO. I am not valiant neither,
But every puny whipster° gets my sword.
But why should honor° outlive honesty?°
Let it go all.
EMILIA.   What did thy song bode, lady?   *255*
Hark, canst thou hear me? I will play the swan,
And die in music. [*She sings.*] "Willow, willow, willow."
Moor, she was chaste. She loved thee, cruel Moor.
So come my soul to bliss as I speak true.
So speaking as I think, alas, I die.   [*She dies.*]   *260*
OTHELLO. I have another weapon in this chamber;
It was a sword of Spain, the ice-brook's temper°—
O, here it is. [*He finds a sword.*] Uncle, I must come forth.
GRATIANO. [*Within*] If thou attempt it, it will cost thee dear.
Thou hast no weapon, and perforce must suffer.   *265*
OTHELLO. Look in upon me then and speak with me,
Or, naked° as I am, I will assault thee.

[*Enter Gratiano.*]

GRATIANO. What is the matter?
OTHELLO.   Behold, I have a weapon;
A better never did itself sustain
Upon a soldier's thigh. I have seen the day   *270*
That, with this little arm and this good sword,
I have made my way through more impediments
Than twenty times your stop.° But O, vain boast!
Who can control his fate? 'Tis not so now.
Be not afraid, though you do see me weaponed;   *275*
Here is my journey's end, here is my butt°
And very seamark° of my utmost sail.   [*Gratiano steps back.*]
Do you go back dismayed? 'Tis a lost° fear;
Man but a rush° against Othello's breast
And he retires. Where should Othello go?   *280*
                    [*He turns to Desdemona.*]
Now, how dost thou look now? O ill-starred wench!
Pale as thy smock! When we shall meet at compt,°
This look of thine will hurl my soul from heaven,
And fiends will snatch at it. Cold, cold, my girl?
Even like thy chastity. O cursèd, cursèd slave!°   *285*

---

253 **whipster** contemptible fellow   254 **honor** i.e., the bravery for which one enjoys a soldier's reputation.   **honesty** true integrity   262 **the ice-brook's temper** tempered in ice-cold water   267 **naked** unarmed   273 **stop** power (to stop)   276 **butt** goal, limit. (An archery term.)   277 **seamark** beacon (marking his destination or limit)   278 **lost** wasted, unneeded   279 **Man . . . rush** wield no more than a reed   282 **compt** account, judgment day   285 **slave** i.e., Othello himself

Whip me, ye devils,
From the possession of this heavenly sight!
Blow me about in winds! Roast me in sulfur!
Wash me in steep-down gulfs of liquid fire!
O Desdemon! Dead, Desdemon! Dead! O! O!   *290*

Enter Lodovico, Cassio [carried in a litter°], Montano, and Iago
[prisoner], with officers.

LODOVICO. Where is this rash and most unfortunate man?
OTHELLO. That's he that was Othello. Here I am.
LODOVICO. Where is that viper? Bring the villain forth.
                                    [*Iago is led forward.*]
OTHELLO. I look down towards his feet;° but that's a fable.
    If that thou be'st a devil, I cannot kill thee.   *295*
                                    [*He wounds Iago.*]
LODOVICO. Wrench his sword from him.   [*Othello is disarmed.*]
IAGO.   I bleed, sir, but not killed.
OTHELLO. I am not sorry neither. I'd have thee live,
    For in my sense° 'tis happiness to die.
LODOVICO. O thou Othello, that was once so good,
    Fall'n in the practice° of a cursèd slave,°   *300*
    What shall be said to thee?
OTHELLO.   Why, anything.
    An honorable murderer, if you will,
    For naught I did in hate, but all in honor.
LODOVICO. This wretch hath part confessed his villainy.
    Did you and he consent° in Cassio's death?   *305*
OTHELLO. Ay.
CASSIO. Dear General, I never gave you cause.
OTHELLO. I do believe it, and I ask your pardon.
    Will you, I pray, demand that demi-devil
    Why he hath thus ensnared my soul and body?   *310*
IAGO. Demand me nothing. What you know, you know.
    From this time forth I never will speak word.
LODOVICO. What, not to pray?
GRATIANO. Torments° will ope your lips.
OTHELLO. Well, thou dost best.   *315*
LODOVICO. Sir, you shall understand what hath befall'n
    Which, as I think, you know not. Here is a letter
    Found in the pocket of the slain Roderigo;

---

290 s.d. in a litter (The quarto specifies that Cassio is "in a chair.") **294 towards his
feet** i.e., to see if they are cloven like the devil's **298 in my sense** to one who feel as
I do **300 in the practice** through the plotting. **slave** villain **305 consent** agree
314 Torments torture

And here another. [*He produces letters.*] The one of them imports
The death of Cassio, to be undertook   *320*
By Roderigo.
OTHELLO. O villain!
CASSIO.   Most heathenish and most gross!°
LODOVICO. [*Showing another paper*]
        Now here's another discontented° paper
        Found in his pocket too. And this, it seems,
        Roderigo meant t' have sent this damnèd villain;   *325*
        But that belike° Iago in the interim
        Came in° and satisfied him.
OTHELLO. O thou pernicious caitiff!—
        How came you, Cassio, by that handkerchief
        That was my wife's?
CASSIO.   I found it in my chamber;   *330*
        And he himself confessed it but even now
        That there he dropped it for a special purpose
        Which wrought to his desire.°
OTHELLO.   O fool, fool, fool!
CASSIO. There is besides in Roderigo's letter
        How he upbraids Iago, that he made him   *335*
        Brave° me upon the watch, whereon it came
        That I was cast;° and even but now he spake,
        After long seeming dead, Iago hurt him,
        Iago set him on.
LODOVICO. [*To Othello*] You must forsake this room and go with us.   *340*
        Your power and your command is taken off,°
        And Cassio rules in Cyprus. For this slave,
        If there be any cunning cruelty
        That can torment him much and hold him long,°
        It shall be his. You shall close prisoner rest°   *345*
        Till that the nature of your fault be known
        To the Venetian state.—Come, bring away.
OTHELLO. Soft you;° a word or two before you go.
        I have done the state some service, and they know 't.
        No more of that. I pray you, in your letters,   *350*
        When you shall these unlucky° deeds relate,
        Speak of me as I am; nothing extenuate,

---

322 gross monstrous   **323 discontented** full of discontent   **326 belike** most likely
327 Came in interposed   **333 wrought . . . desire** worked out as he wished, fitted in
with his plan   **336 Brave** defy   **337 cast** dismissed   **341 taken off** taken away
344 hold him long keep him alive a long time (during his torture)   **345 rest** remain
348 Soft you one moment   **351 unlucky** unfortunate

Nor set down aught in malice. Then must you speak
Of one that loved not wisely but too well;
Of one not easily jealous but, being wrought,° 355
Perplexed° in the extreme; of one whose hand,
Like the base Indian,° threw a pearl away
Richer than all his tribe; of one whose subdued° eyes,
Albeit unusèd to the melting mood,
Drops tears as fast as the Arabian trees 360
Their medicinable gum.° Set you down this;
And say besides that in Aleppo once,
Where a malignant and a turbaned Turk
Beat a Venetian and traduced the state
I took by th' throat the circumcisèd dog 365
And smote him, thus.   [*He stabs himself.*°]

LODOVICO. O bloody period!°

GRATIANO. All that is spoke is marred.

OTHELLO. I kissed thee ere I killed thee. No way but this,
Killing myself, to die upon a kiss. 370
            [*He kisses Desdemona and*]*dies.*

CASSIO. This did I fear, but thought he had no weapon;
For he was great of heart.

LODOVICO. [*To Iago*]   O Spartan dog,°
More fell° than anguish, hunger, or the sea!
Look on the tragic loading of this bed.
This is thy work. The object poisons sight; 375
Let it be hid.° Gratiano, keep° the house,
            [*The bed-curtains are drawn*]
And seize upon° the fortunes of the Moor,
For they succeed on° you. [*To Cassio.*] To you, Lord Governor,
Remains the censure° of this hellish villain,
The time, the place, the torture. O, enforce it! 380
Myself will straight aboard, and to the state
This heavy act with heavy heart relate.   *Exeunt.*

---

355 wrought worked upon   **356 Perplexed** distraught   **357 Indian** (This reading from the quarto pictures an ignorant savage who cannot recognize the value of a precious jewel. The Folio reading, *Iudean* or *Judean,* i.e., infidel or disbeliever, may refer to Herod, who slew Miriamne in a fit of jealousy, or to Judas Iscariot, the betrayer of Christ.) **358 subdued** i.e., overcome by grief   **361 gum** i.e., myrrh   **366 s.d. He stabs himself** (This direction is in the quarto text.)   **367 period** termination, conclusion   **372 Spartan dog** (Spartan dogs were noted for their savagery and silence.)   **373 fell** cruel   **376 Let it be hid** i.e., draw the bed-curtains. (No stage direction specifies that the dead are to be carried offstage at the end of the play.)   **keep** remain in   **377 seize upon** take legal possession of   **378 succeed on** pass as though by inheritance to   **379 censure** sentencing

TOPICS FOR DISCUSSION AND WRITING

Act 1

1. Iago, contemptuous of dutiful servants, compares them in 1.1.49 to asses. What other animal images does he use in the first scene? In your opinion, what does the use of such images suggest about Iago?
2. Is there any need to do more than knock loudly at Brabantio's door? What does 1.1.77–79 suggest about Iago?
3. In 1.1.111ff. and in his next speech, Iago uses prose instead of blank verse. What effect, in your opinion, is gained?
4. What do you think Iago is trying to do to Othello in the first speech of 1.2? In 1.2.29 why does Iago urge Othello to "go in"? When Othello first speaks (1.2.6) does he speak as you might have expected him to, given Iago's earlier comments about Othello? In Othello's second speech, is there anything that resembles Iago's earlier description of him?
5. Do you find it incredible that a girl who has rejected "the wealthy, curlèd darlings" (1.2.69) of Venice should choose Othello? Why, or why not?
6. Brabantio in 1.3.213–22 speaks in couplets (pairs of rhyming lines), as the Duke has just done. What is the effect of the verse? Does it suggest grief? Mockery?
7. Do you think that the love of Othello and Desdemona is impetuous and irrational? What do you think is its basis?
8. The last speech in 1.3. is in verse, though previous speeches are in prose. What is the effect of the change?
9. Do you think it is a fault that Othello "thinks men honest that but seem to be so" (1.3.386)? Explain.

Act 2

1. In 2.1.1–20 Shakespeare introduces a description of a storm? What symbolic overtones, if any, do you think it may have?
2. What does Iago's description (2.1.148–60) of a good woman suggest to you about his attitude toward goodness?
3. In Iago's last speech in this act, he gives several reasons why he hates Othello. List them, and add to the list any reasons he gave earlier. How convincing do you find them?
4. Again (2.1.272ff.), Shakespeare gives Iago verse when alone, after prose dialogue. Why?
5. In 2.3.13–24, what sort of thing do you suppose Iago is trying to get Cassio to say?

6. How does 2.3.183–196 prepare us for Othello's later tragic deed of killing Desdemona?

Act 3

1. What is the point of the repetition (3.3.106–42) of "thought," "think," "know," and "honest"?
2. Are you surprised that Othello speaks (3.3.194) of a goat? Explain your response. In later scenes keep an eye out for his use of animal imagery.
3. Do you smell "a will most rank" (3.3.248–54) in Desdemona's choice? Or do you think her choice was based on other qualities?
4. Emilia gets possession of the handkerchief by accident (3.3.304–06). Is it fair, then, to say that the tragic outcome is based on mere accident? Why, or why not?

Act 4

1. In 4.1.35ff. Othello uses prose. What do you think this shift suggests about Othello's state of mind?
2. Othello says (4.1.187) "I will chop her into messes! Cuckold me!" Do you feel that in this scene Othello's ferocity toward Desdemona is chiefly motivated by a sense of personal injury? What, if anything, does Shakespeare do here to prevent you from merely loathing Othello?
3. How would you characterize Othello's emotional state in the first 24 lines of 4.2?
4. In 4.2 Othello's baseness, very evident in the previous scene, continues here. But what lines—if any—in this scene tend to work against the view that he is merely base and instead give him the stature of a tragic hero?
5. In literary criticism a distinction is often made between the "tragic" and the "pathetic." A pathetic character—i.e., a character who evokes in the spectator feelings of pathos—is usually said to be pitifully weak, a mere victim. In 4.3 do you regard Desdemona as merely pathetic? Why, or why not?

Act 5

1. What do you 5.1.19–20 tell us about Iago? How much "daily beauty" have we seen in Cassio's life? Do we assume Iago judges him incorrectly?
2. What does 5.2.16–17 tell us about the spirit with which Othello is about to kill Desdemona? Is he acting from a sense of wounded pride?

3. In 5.2.128–29 Desdemona dies with a lie on her lips. Do we think the worse of her? Why?

4. Emilia calls Othello "gull," "dolt," "ignorant as dirt" (5.2.170–71). Has she a point? Do these words prevent Othello from being a tragic hero?

5. T. S. Eliot, in "Shakespeare and the Stoicism of Seneca," *Selected Essays,* says of 5.2.348–66: "Othello . . . is *cheering himself up.* He is endeavoring to escape reality, he has ceased to think about Desdemona and is thinking about himself." What do you think of this view?

6. Suicide is sometimes thought to be a sin, and it is sometimes said to be the "coward's way out." How do you judge it in this specific context?

GENERAL QUESTIONS

1. W. H. Auden, in *The Dyer's Hand,* says that "in most tragedies the fall of the hero from glory to misery and death is the work either of the gods, or of his own freely chosen acts, or, more commonly, a mixture of both. But the fall of Othello is the work of another human being; nothing he says or does originates with himself. In consequence we feel pity for him but no respect; our esthetic respect is reserved for Iago." Evaluate Auden's view.

2. Harley Granville-Barker, in *Prefaces to Shakespeare,* says: "The mere sight of such beauty and nobility and happiness, all wickedly destroyed, must be a harrowing one. Yet the pity and terror of it come short of serving for the purgation of our souls, since Othello's own soul stays unpurged. . . . It is a tragedy without meaning, and that is the ultimate horror of it." Evaluate this view.

3. How far are you willing to go with the idea that the play sets forth a contrast between a warm, intimate society of women (Desdemona and Emilia) and the cold, competitive, and hypocritical society of men?

4. Before the middle of the twentieth century it was most unusual for a black actor to play Othello, other than in all-black productions. A notable exception, however, was Ira Aldridge (c. 1805–67), a black American actor who, because his opportunities in the United States were severely limited, established a career as a Shakespearean actor in England and in Europe. He achieved fame for his performances of Othello and other tragic roles, but his Othello sometimes evoked an interesting objection. Some viewers thought that when a black performed the role, the play became too "real," too close to life, and thus the viewers could not enjoy it as a work of art. (If this objection seems odd, perhaps it will become more understandable if you

imagine seeing a play in which a blind and deaf person plays Helen Keller, or someone with polio plays Franklin Roosevelt, or a holocaust survivor plays Shylock.) In your opinion, does it matter whether the role of Othello is performed by a black or a white (or, for that matter, by an Asian or a Native American)?

5. H. Rap Brown says, in *Die Nigger Die,* "After I read *Othello,* it was obvious that Shakespeare was a racist." To what extent, if any, do you agree? Why?

22
Comedy

Though etymology is not always helpful (after all, is it really illuminating to say that "tragedy" may come from a Greek word meaning "goat song"?), the etymology of "comedy" helps to reveal comedy's fundamental nature. **Comedy** (Greek: *komoidia*) is a revel-song; ancient Greek comedies are descended from fertility rituals that dramatized the joy of renewal, the joy of triumphing over obstacles, the joy of being (in a sense) reborn. Whereas the movement of tragedy, speaking roughly, is from prosperity to disaster, the movement of comedy is from some sort of minor disaster to prosperity.

Consider *A Midsummer Night's Dream*. In the first act Egeus appears:

> Full of vexation come I, with complaint
> Against my child, my daughter Hermia.

Egeus wants Hermia to marry Demetrius, but she is in love with Lysander, and so Egeus threatens her with the law, which holds that she must obey her father's will or suffer either death or life in a cloister. We begin, then, in an oppressive patriarchal world. The play ends, of course, with Hermia marrying her beloved Lysander. In the words of Puck (who here summarizes the plots of most comedies),

> Jack shall have Jill,
> Nought shall go ill. . . .

To say, however, that comedy dramatizes the triumph over obstacles is to describe it as though it were melodrama, a play in which, after hairbreadth adventures, good prevails over evil, often in the form of the hero's unlikely last-minute rescue of the fair Belinda from the clutches of the villain. What distinguishes comedy from melodrama is the pervasive high spirits of comedy. The joyous ending in comedy—usually a marriage—is in the spirit of what has gone before; the entire play, not only the end, is a celebration of fecundity.

The threats in the world of comedy are not taken very seriously; the parental tyranny that helps make *Romeo and Juliet* and *Antigone* tragedies is, in comedy, laughable throughout. Parents may fret, fume, and lock doors, but in doing so they make themselves ridiculous, for love will find a way. Villains may threaten, but the audience never takes the threats seriously.

In the first act of Shakespeare's *As You Like It,* Rosalind, at the mercy of a cruel uncle who has driven her father from his own dukedom, says: "O, how full of briers is this working-day world." The immediate reply is, "They are but burrs, cousin, thrown upon thee in holiday foolery." And this spirit of holiday foolery dominates the whole play and culminates in marriage, the symbol of life renewing itself. In the last act of a comedy things work out—as from the start we knew they would; whereas *Antigone* concludes with Creon looking at the corpses of his wife, son, and intended daughter-in-law, a comedy usually concludes with preparation for a marriage, or even, as in *A Midsummer Night's Dream,* several marriages.

These marriages and renewals of society, so usual at the end of comedy, are most improbable, but they do not therefore weaken the comedy. The stuff of comedy is, in part, improbability. In *A Midsummer Night's Dream,* Puck speaks for the spectator when he says:

And those things do best please me
That befall preposterously.

In tragedy, probability is important; in comedy, the improbable is often desirable, for at least three reasons. First, comedy seeks to include as much as possible, to reveal the rich abundance of life. The motto of comedy (and the implication in the weddings with which it usually concludes) is the more the merrier. Second, the improbable is the surprising; surprise often evokes laughter, and laughter surely has a central place in comedy. Third, by getting his or her characters into improbable situations, the dramatist can show off the absurdity of their behavior. This point needs amplification.

Comedy often shows the absurdity of ideals. The miser, the puritan, the health-faddist, and so on, are people of ideals, but their ideals are suffocating. The miser, for example, treats everything in terms of money; the miser's ideal causes him or her to renounce much of the abundance and joy of life. He or she is in love, but is unwilling to support a spouse; or he or she has a headache, but will not be so extravagant as to take an aspirin tablet. If a thief accosts the miser with "Your money or your life," the miser will prefer to give up life—and that is what in fact he or she has been doing all the while. Now, by putting this miser in a series of improbable situations, the dramatist can continue to demonstrate entertainingly the miser's absurdity.*

*A character who is dominated by a single trait—avarice, jealousy, timidity, and so forth—is sometimes called a **humor character.** Medieval and Renaissance psychology held that an individual's personality depended on the mixture of four liquids (humors): blood (Latin:

The comic protagonist's tenacious hold on his or her ideals is not very far from that of the tragic protagonist. In general, however, tragedy suggests the nobility of ideals; the tragic hero's ideals undo him or her, and they may be ideals about which we have serious reservations, but still we admire the nobility of these ideals. Romeo and Juliet will not put off their love for each other; Antigone will not yield to Creon, and Creon holds almost impossibly long to his stern position. But the comic protagonist who is always trying to keep his or her hands clean is funny; we laugh at this refusal to touch dirt with the rest of us, this refusal to enjoy the abundance life has to offer. The comic protagonist who is always talking about his or her beloved is funny; we laugh at the failure to see that the world is filled with people more attractive than the one who obsesses him or her.

In short, the ideals for which the tragic protagonist loses the world seem important to us and gain, in large measure, our sympathy, but the ideals for which the comic protagonist loses the world seem trivial compared with the rich variety that life has to offer, and we laugh at their absurdity. The tragic figure makes a claim on our sympathy. The absurd comic figure continually sets up obstacles to our sympathetic interest; we feel detached from, superior to, and amused by him or her. Something along these lines is behind William Butler Yeats's insistence that character is always present in comedy but not in tragedy. Though Yeats is eccentric in his notion that individual character is obliterated in tragedy, he interestingly gets at one of the important elements in comedy:

> When the tragic reverie is at its height . . . [we do not say,] "How well that man is realized. I should know him were I to meet him in the street," for it is always ourselves that we see upon the [tragic] stage. . . . Tragedy must always be a drowning and breaking of the dikes that separate man from man, and . . . it is upon these dikes comedy keeps house.

Most comic plays can roughly be sorted into one of two types: romantic comedy and satiric comedy. **Romantic comedy** presents an ideal world, a golden world, a world more delightful than our own; if there are difficulties in it, they are not briers but "burrs . . . thrown . . . in holiday foolery." It is the world of most of Shakespeare's comedies, a world of Illyria, of the Forest of Arden, of Belmont of the moonlit Athens in *A Midsummer Night's Dream*. The chief figures are lovers; the course of their

---

sanguis), choler, phlegm, and bile. An overabundance of one fluid produced a dominant trait, and even today "sanguine," "choleric," "phlegmatic," and "bilious" describe personalities.

Not all comedy, of course, depends on humor characters placed in situations that exhibit their absurdity. **High comedy** is largely verbal, depending on witty language; **farce,** at the other extreme, is dependent on inherently ludicrous situations, for example, a hobo is mistaken for a millionaire. Situation comedy, then, may use humor characters, but it need not do so.

love is not smooth, but the outcome is never in doubt and the course is the more fun for being bumpy. Occasionally in this golden world there is a villain, but if so, the villain is a great bungler who never really does any harm; the world seems to be guided by a benevolent providence who prevents villains from seriously harming even themselves. In these plays, the world belongs to golden lads and lasses. When we laugh, we laugh not so much *at* them as *with* them.

If romantic comedy shows us a world with more attractive people than we find in our own, **satiric comedy** shows us a world with less attractive people. The satiric world seems dominated by morally inferior people—the decrepit wooer, the jealous spouse, the demanding parent. These unengaging figures go through their paces, revealing again and again their absurdity. The audience laughs *at* (rather than *with*) such figures, and writers justify this kind of comedy by claiming to reform society: antisocial members of the audience will see their grotesque images on the stage and will reform themselves when they leave the theater. But it is hard to believe that this theory is rooted in fact. Jonathan Swift (as we mentioned earlier) was probably right when he said, "Satire is a sort of glass wherein beholders do generally discover everybody's face but their own."

Near the conclusion of a satiric comedy, the obstructing characters are dismissed, often perfunctorily, allowing for a happy ending—commonly the marriage of figures less colorful than the obstructionist. And so all-encompassing are the festivities at the end that even obstructionists are invited to join in the wedding feast. If they refuse to join, we may find them—yet again—laughable rather than sympathetic, though admittedly one may also feel lingering regret that this somewhat shabby world of ours cannot live up to the exalted (even if rigid and rather crazy) standards of the outsider who refuses to go along with the way of the world.

Wendy Wasserstein (American; b. 1950)

The Man in a Case

List of Characters

BYELINKOV
VARINKA

Scene: A small garden in the village of Mironitski. 1898.

Byelinkov is pacing. Enter Varinka out of breath.

BYELINKOV. You are ten minutes late.
VARINKA. The most amazing thing happened on my way over here. You
    know the woman who runs the grocery store down the road. She wears

The Man in a Case. *The Acting Company, Champaign-Urbana, Illinois, 1985. Photo by Diane Gorodnitzki. All rights reserved.*

a black wig during the week, and a blond wig on Saturday nights. And she has the daughter who married an engineer in Moscow who is doing very well thank you and is living, God bless them, in a three-room apartment. But he really is the most boring man in the world. All he talks about is his future and his station in life. Well, she heard we were to be married and she gave me this basket of apricots to give to you.

BYELINKOV. That is a most amazing thing!

VARINKA. She said to me, Varinka, you are marrying the most honorable man in the entire village. In this village he is the only man fit to speak with my son-in-law.

BYELINKOV. I don't care for apricots. They give me hives.

VARINKA. I can return them. I'm sure if I told her they give you hives she would give me a basket of raisins or a cake.

BYELINKOV. I don't know this woman or her pompous son-in-law. Why would she give me her cakes?

VARINKA. She adores you!

BYELINKOV. She is emotionally loose.

VARINKA. She adores you by reputation. Everyone adores you by reputation. I tell everyone I am to marry Byelinkov, the finest teacher in the county.

BYELINKOV. You tell them this?

VARINKA. If they don't tell me first.

BYELINKOV. Pride can be an imperfect value.

VARINKA. It isn't pride. It is the truth. You are a great man!

BYELINKOV. I am the master of Greek and Latin at a local school at the end of the village of Mironitski.

(*Varinka kisses him*)

VARINKA. And I am to be the master of Greek and Latin's wife!

BYELINKOV. Being married requires a great deal of responsibility. I hope I am able to provide you with all that a married man must properly provide a wife.

VARINKA. We will be very happy.

BYELINKOV. Happiness is for children. We are entering into a social contract, an amicable agreement to provide us with a secure and satisfying future.

VARINKA. You are so sweet! You are the sweetest man in the world!

BYELINKOV. I'm a man set in his ways who saw a chance to provide himself with a small challenge.

VARINKA. Look at you! Look at you! Your sweet round spectacles, your dear collar always starched, always raised, your perfectly pressed pants always creasing at right angles perpendicular to the floor, and my most favorite part, the sweet little galoshes, rain or shine, just in case. My Byelinkov, never taken by surprise. Except by me.

BYELINKOV. You speak about me as if I were your pet.

VARINKA. You are my pet! My little school mouse.

BYELINKOV. A mouse?

VARINKA. My sweetest dancing bear with galoshes, my little stale babka.[1]

BYELINKOV. A stale babka?

VARINKA. I am not Pushkin.[2]

BYELINKOV (*Laughs*). That depends what you think of Pushkin.

VARINKA. You're smiling. I knew I could make you smile today.

BYELINKOV. I am a responsible man. Every day I have for breakfast black bread, fruit, hot tea, and every day I smile three times. I am halfway into my translation of the *Aeneid*[3] from classical Greek hexameter into Russian alexandrines. In twenty years I have never been late to school. I am a responsible man, but no dancing bear.

VARINKA. Dance with me.

BYELINKOV. Now? It is nearly four weeks before the wedding!

VARINKA. It's a beautiful afternoon. We are in your garden. The roses are in full bloom.

BYELINKOV. The roses have beetles.

VARINKA. Dance with me!

BYELINKOV. You are a demanding woman.

VARINKA. You chose me. And right. And left. And turn. And right. And left.

BYELINKOV. And turn. Give me your hand. You dance like a school mouse. It's a beautiful afternoon! We are in my garden. The roses are in full bloom! And turn. And turn. (*Twirls Varinka around*)

VARINKA. I am the luckiest woman!

(*Byelinkov stops dancing*)

Why are you stopping?

BYELINKOV. To place a lilac in your hair. Every year on this day I will place a lilac in your hair.

VARINKA. Will you remember?

BYELINKOV. I will write it down. (*Takes a notebook from his pocket*) Dear Byelinkov, don't forget the day a young lady, your bride, entered your garden, your peace, and danced on the roses. On that day every year you are to place a lilac in her hair.

VARINKA. I love you.

BYELINKOV. It is convenient we met.

VARINKA. I love you.

BYELINKOV. You are a girl.

VARINKA. I am thirty.

BYELINKOV. But you think like a girl. That is an attractive attribute.

---

[1] *babka* cake with almonds and raisins
[2] **Pushkin** Alexander Pushkin (1799–1837), Russian poet
[3] *Aeneid* Latin epic poem by the Roman poet Virgil (70–19 B.C.)

VARINKA. Do you love me?

BYELINKOV. We've never spoken about housekeeping.

VARINKA. I am an excellent housekeeper. I kept house for my family on the farm in Gadyatchsky. I can make a beetroot soup with tomatoes and aubergines which is so nice. Awfully awfully nice.

BYELINKOV. You are fond of expletives.

VARINKA. My beet soup, sir, is excellent!

BYELINKOV. Please don't be cross. I too am an excellent housekeeper. I have a place for everything in the house. A shelf for each pot, a cubby for every spoon, a folder for favorite recipes. I have cooked for myself for twenty years. Though my beet soup is not outstanding, it is sufficient.

VARINKA. I'm sure it's very good.

BYELINKOV. No. It is awfully, awfully not. What I am outstanding in, however, what gives me greatest pleasure, is preserving those things which are left over. I wrap each tomato slice I haven't used in a wet cloth and place it in the coolest corner of the house. I have had my shoes for seven years because I wrap them in the galoshes you are so fond of. And every night before I go to sleep I wrap my bed in quilts and curtains so I never catch a draft.

VARINKA. You sleep with curtains on your bed?

BYELINKOV. I like to keep warm.

VARINKA. I will make you a new quilt.

BYELINKOV. No. No new quilt. That would be hazardous.

VARINKA. It is hazardous to sleep under curtains.

BYELINKOV. Varinka, I don't like change very much. If one works out the arithmetic the final fraction of improvement is at best less than an eighth of value over the total damage caused by disruption. I never thought of marrying till I saw your eyes dancing among the familiar faces at the headmaster's tea. I assumed I would grow old preserved like those which are left over, wrapped suitably in my case of curtains and quilts.

VARINKA. Byelinkov, I want us to have dinners with friends and summer country visits. I want people to say, "Have you spent time with Varinka and Byelinkov? He is so happy now that they are married. She is just what he needed."

BYELINKOV. You have already brought me some happiness. But I never was a sad man. Don't ever think I thought I was a sad man.

VARINKA. My sweetest darling, you can be whatever you want! If you are sad, they'll say she talks all the time, and he is softspoken and kind.

BYELINKOV. And if I am difficult?

VARINKA. Oh, they'll say he is difficult because he is highly intelligent. All great men are difficult. Look at Lermontov, Tchaikovsky, Peter the Great.

BYELINKOV. Ivan the Terrible.[4]

VARINKA. Yes, him too.

BYELINKOV. Why are you marrying me? I am none of these things.

VARINKA. To me you are.

BYELINKOV. You have imagined this. You have constructed an elaborate romance for yourself. Perhaps you are the great one. You are the one with the great imagination.

VARINKA. Byelinkov, I am a pretty girl of thirty. You're right, I am not a woman. I have not made myself into a woman because I do not deserve that honor. Until I came to this town to visit my brother I lived on my family's farm. As the years passed I became younger and younger in fear that I would never marry. And it wasn't that I wasn't pretty enough or sweet enough, it was just that no man ever looked at me and saw a wife. I was not the woman who would be there when he came home. Until I met you I thought I would lie all my life and say I never married because I never met a man I loved. I will love you, Byelinkov. And I will help you to love me. We deserve the life everyone else has. We deserve not to be different.

BYELINKOV. Yes. We are the same as everyone else.

VARINKA. Tell me you love me.

BYELINKOV. I love you.

VARINKA (*Takes his hands*). We will be very happy. I am very strong. (*Pauses*) It is time for tea.

BYELINKOV. It is too early for tea. Tea is at half past the hour.

VARINKA. Do you have heavy cream? It will be awfully nice with apricots.

BYELINKOV. Heavy cream is too rich for teatime.

VARINKA. But today is special. Today you placed a lilac in my hair. Write in your note pad. Every year we will celebrate with apricots and heavy cream. I will go to my brother's house and get some.

BYELINKOV. But your brother's house is a mile from here.

VARINKA. Today it is much shorter. Today my brother gave me his bicycle to ride. I will be back very soon.

BYELINKOV. You rode to my house by bicycle! Did anyone see you!

VARINKA. Of course. I had such fun. I told you I saw the grocery store lady with the son-in-law who is doing very well thank you in Moscow, and the headmaster's wife.

BYELINKOV. You saw the headmaster's wife!

VARINKA. She smiled at me.

BYELINKOV. Did she laugh or smile?

---

[4]**Lermontov . . . Ivan the Terrible**   Mikhail Lermontov (1814–41), poet and novelist; Peter Ilich Tchaikovsky (1840–93), composer; Peter the Great (1672–1725) and Ivan the Terrible (1530–84), czars credited with making Russia a great European power.

VARINKA. She laughed a little. She said, "My dear, you are very progressive to ride a bicycle." She said you and your fiancé Byelinkov must ride together sometime. I wonder if he'll take off his galoshes when he rides a bicycle.

BYELINKOV. She said that?

VARINKA. She adores you. We had a good giggle.

BYELINKOV. A woman can be arrested for riding a bicycle. That is not progressive, it is a premeditated revolutionary act. Your brother must be awfully, awfully careful on behalf of your behavior. He has been careless — oh so careless — in giving you the bicycle.

VARINKA. Dearest Byelinkov, you are wrapping yourself under curtains and quilts! I made friends on the bicycle.

BYELINKOV. You saw more than the headmaster's wife and the idiot grocery woman.

VARINKA. She is not an idiot.

BYELINKOV. She is a potato-vending, sausage-armed fool!

VARINKA. Shhhh! My school mouse. Shhh!

BYELINKOV. What other friends did you make on this bicycle?

VARINKA. I saw students from my brother's classes. They waved and shouted, "Anthropos in love! Anthropos in love!!"

BYELINKOV. Where is that bicycle?

VARINKA. I left it outside the gate. Where are you going?

BYELINKOV (*Muttering as he exits*). Anthropos in love, anthropos in love.

VARINKA. They were cheering me on. Careful, you'll trample the roses.

BYELINKOV (*Returning with the bicycle*). Anthropos is the Greek singular for man. Anthropos in love translates as the Greek and Latin master in love. Of course they cheered you. Their instructor, who teaches them the discipline and contained beauty of the classics, is in love with a sprite on a bicycle. It is a good giggle, isn't it? A very good giggle! I am returning this bicycle to your brother.

VARINKA. But it is teatime.

BYELINKOV. Today we will not have tea.

VARINKA. But you will have to walk back a mile.

BYELINKOV. I have my galoshes on. (*Gets on the bicycle*) Varinka, we deserve not to be different. (*Begins to pedal. The bicycle doesn't move*)

VARINKA. Put the kickstand up.

BYELINKOV. I beg your pardon.

VARINKA (*Giggling*). Byelinkov, to make the bicycle move, you must put the kickstand up.

(*Byelinkov puts it up and awkwardly falls off the bicycle as it moves*)

(*Laughing*) Ha ha ha. My little school mouse. You look so funny! You are the sweetest dearest man in the world. Ha ha ha!

(*Pause*)

BYELINKOV. Please help me up. I'm afraid my galosh is caught.

VARINKA (*Trying not to laugh*). Your galosh is caught! (*Explodes in laughter again*) Oh, you are so funny! I do love you so. (*Helps Byelinkov up*) You were right, my pet, as always. We don't need heavy cream for tea. The fraction of improvement isn't worth the damage caused by the disruption.

BYELINKOV. Varinka, it is still too early for tea. I must complete two stanzas of my translation before late afternoon. That is my regular schedule.

VARINKA. Then I will watch while you work.

BYELINKOV. No. You had a good giggle. That is enough.

VARINKA. Then while you work I will work too. I will make lists of guests for our wedding.

BYELINKOV. I can concentrate only when I am alone in my house. Please take your bicycle home to your brother.

VARINKA. But I don't want to leave you. You look so sad.

BYELINKOV. I never was a sad man. Don't ever think I was a sad man.

VARINKA. Byelinkov, it's a beautiful day, we are in your garden. The roses are in bloom.

BYELINKOV. Allow me to help you on to your bicycle. (*Takes Varinka's hand as she gets on the bike*)

VARINKA. You are such a gentleman. We will be very happy.

BYELINKOV. You are very strong. Good day, Varinka.

(*Varinka pedals off. Byelinkov, alone in the garden, takes out his pad and rips up the note about the lilac, strews it over the garden, then carefully picks up each piece of paper and places them in all in a small envelope as lights fade to black*)

TOPICS FOR DISCUSSION AND WRITING

1. You will probably agree that the scene where Byelinkov gets on the bicycle and pedals but goes nowhere is funny. But *why* is it funny? Can you formulate some sort of theory of comedy based on this episode?

2. At the end of the play Byelinkov tears up the note but then collects the pieces. What do you interpret these actions to mean?

23

In Brief: Getting Ideas for Writing about Drama

The following questions may help you to formulate ideas for an essay on a play.

PLOT AND CONFLICT

1. Does the exposition introduce elements that will be ironically fulfilled? During the exposition do you perceive things differently from the way the characters perceive them?
2. Are certain happenings or situations recurrent? If so, what significance do you attach to them?
3. If there is more than one plot, do the plots seem to you to be related? Is one plot clearly the main plot and another plot a sort of subplot, a minor variation on the theme?
4. Do any scenes strike you as irrelevant?
5. Are certain scenes so strongly foreshadowed that you anticipated them? If so, did the happenings in these scenes merely fulfill your expectations, or did they also in some way surprise you?
6. What kinds of conflict are there? One character against another, one group against another, one part of a personality against another part in the same person?
7. How is the conflict resolved? By an unambiguous triumph of one side or by a triumph that is also in some degree a loss for the triumphant side? Do you find the resolution satisfying, or unsettling, or what? Why?

CHARACTER

1. A dramatic character is not likely to be thoroughly realistic, a copy of someone we might know. Still, we can ask if the character is consistent and coherent. We can also ask if the character is complex or is, on the other hand, a rather simple representative of some human type.
2. How is the character defined? Consider what the character says and does and what others say about him or her and do to him or her. Also consider other characters who more or less resemble the character in question, because the similarities — and the differences — may be significant.
3. How trustworthy are the characters when they characterize themselves? When they characterize others?
4. Do characters change as the play goes on, or do we simply know them better at the end?
5. What do you make of the minor characters? Are they merely necessary to the plot, or are they foils to other characters? Or do they serve some other functions?
6. If a character is tragic, does the tragedy seem to you to proceed from a moral flaw, from an intellectual error, from the malice of others, from sheer chance, or from some combination of these?
7. What are the character's goals? To what degree do you sympathize with them. If a character is comic, do you laugh *with* or *at* the character?
8. Do you think the characters are adequately motivated?
9. Is a given character so meditative that you feel he or she is engaged less in a dialogue with others than in a dialogue with the self? If so, do you feel that this character is in large degree a spokesperson for the author, commenting not only on the world of the play but also on the outside world?

NONVERBAL LANGUAGE

1. If the playwright does not provide full stage directions, try to imagine for at least one scene what gestures and tones might accompany each speech. (The first scene is usually a good one to try your hand at.)
2. What do you make of the setting? Does it help to reveal character? Do changes of scene strike you as symbolic? If so, symbolic of what?
3. Do certain costumes (dark suits, flowery shawls, stiff collars, etc.) or certain properties (books, pictures, toys, candlesticks, etc.) strike you as symbolic? If so, symbolic of what?

THE PLAY ON FILM

1. If the play has been turned into a film, what has been added? What has been omitted? Why?
2. Has the film medium been used to advantage—for example, in focusing attention through close-ups or reaction shots (shots showing not the speaker but a person reacting to the speaker). Or do some of the inventions, for example outdoor scenes that were not possible in the play, seem mere busywork, distracting from the urgency or the conflict or the unity of the play?

24
Plays for Further Study

A NOTE ON GREEK TRAGEDY

Little or nothing is known for certain of the origin of Greek tragedy. The most common hypothesis holds that it developed from improvised speeches during choral dances honoring Dionysus, a Greek nature god associated with spring, fertility, and wine. Thespis (who perhaps never existed) is said to have introduced an actor into these choral performances in the sixth century B.C. Aeschylus (525–456 B.C.), Greece's first great writer of tragedies, added the second actor, and Sophocles (496?–406 B.C.) added the third actor and fixed the size of the chorus at fifteen. (Because the chorus leader often functioned as an additional actor, and because the actors sometimes doubled in their parts, a Greek tragedy could have more characters than might at first be thought.)

All the extant great Greek tragedy is of the fifth century B.C. It was performed at religious festivals in the winter and early spring, in large outdoor amphitheaters built on hillsides. Some of these theaters were enormous; the one at Epidaurus held about fifteen thousand people. The audience sat in tiers, looking down on the **orchestra** (a dancing place), with the acting area behind it and the **skene** (the scene building) yet farther back. The scene building served as dressing room, background (suggesting a palace or temple), and place for occasional entrances and exits. Furthermore, this building helped to provide good acoustics, for speech travels well if there is a solid barrier behind the speakers and a hard, smooth surface in front of them, and if the audience sits in tiers. The wall of the scene building provided the barrier; the orchestra provided the surface in front of the actors; and the seats on the hillside fulfilled the third requirement. Moreover, the acoustics were somewhat improved by slightly elevating the actors above the orchestra, but it is not known exactly when this platform was first constructed in front of the scene building.

Greek Theatre of Epidaurus on the Peloponnesus east of Nauplia.
(Photograph: Frederick Ayer, Photo Researchers, Inc.)

A tragedy commonly begins with a **prologos** (prologue), during which the exposition is given. Next comes the **párodos,** the chorus's ode of entrance, sung while the chorus marches into the theater through the side aisles and onto the orchestra. The **epeisodion** (episode) is the ensuing scene; it is followed by a **stasimon** (choral song, ode). Usually there are four or five *epeisodia,* alternating with *stasima.* Each of these choral odes has a **strophe** (lines presumably sung while the chorus dances in one direction) and an **antistrophe** (lines presumably sung while the chorus retraces its steps). Sometimes a third part, an **epode,** concludes an ode. (In addition to odes that are *stasima,* there can be odes within episodes; the fourth episode of *Antigonê* contains an ode complete with *epode.*) After the last part of the last ode comes the **exodos,** the epilogue or final scene.

The actors (all male) wore masks, and they seem to have chanted much of the play. Perhaps the total result of combining speech with music and dancing was a sort of music–drama roughly akin to opera with some spoken dialogue, such as Mozart's *Magic Flute.*

Sophocles (Greek; 496? B.C–406 B.C.)

Oedipus Rex

An English Version by Dudley Fitts and Robert Fitzgerald

List of Characters
OEDIPUS
A PRIEST
CREON
TEIRESIAS
IOCASTÊ
MESSENGER
SHEPHERD OF LAÏOS
SECOND MESSENGER
CHORUS OF THEBAN ELDERS

Scene.   *Before the palace of Oedipus, King of Thebes. A central door and two lateral doors open onto a platform which runs the length of the façade. On the platform, right and left, are altars; and three steps lead down into the "orchestra," or chorus-ground. At the beginning of the action these steps are crowded by Suppliants who have brought branches and chaplets of olive leaves and who lie in various attitudes of despair. Oedipus enters.*

Laurence Olivier as Oedipus in the Old Vic production, 1945. (Photograph by John Vickers.)

Prologue

OEDIPUS. My children, generations of the living
    In the line of Kadmos,° nursed at his ancient hearth:
    Why have you strewn yourselves before these altars
    In supplication, with your boughs and garlands?
    The breath of incense rises from the city   *5*
    With a sound of prayer and lamentation.
                          Children,
    I would not have you speak through messengers,
    And therefore I have come myself to hear you—
    I, Oedipus, who bear the famous name.
    (*To a priest.*) You, there, since you are eldest in the company,   *10*
    Speak for them all, tell me what preys upon you,
    Whether you come in dread, or crave some blessing:
    Tell me, and never doubt that I will help you
    In every way I can; I should be heartless
    Were I not moved to find you suppliant here.   *15*
PRIEST. Great Oedipus, O powerful King of Thebes!
    You see how all the ages of our people
    Cling to your altar steps: here are boys
    Who can barely stand alone, and here are priests
    By weight of age, as I am a priest of God,   *20*
    And young men chosen from those yet unmarried;
    As for the others, all that multitude,
    They wait with olive chaplets in the squares,
    At the two shrines of Pallas,° and where Apollo°
    Speaks in the glowing embers.
                      Your own eyes   *25*
    Must tell you: Thebes is in her extremity
    And cannot lift her head from the surge of death.
    A rust consumes the buds and fruits of the earth;
    The herds are sick; children die unborn,
    And labor is vain. The god of plague and pyre   *30*
    Raids like detestable lightning through the city,
    And all the house of Kadmos is laid waste,
    All emptied, and all darkened: Death alone
    Battens upon the misery of Thebes.
    You are not one of the immortal gods, we know;   *35*
    Yet we have come to you to make our prayer
    As to the man of all men best in adversity

---

2 Kadmos mythical founder of Thebes
24 Pallas Athena, goddess of wisdom, protectress of Athens **24 Apollo** god of light and
healing

And wisest in the ways of God. You saved us
From the Sphinx,° that flinty singer, and the tribute
We paid to her so long; yet you were never   **40**
Better informed than we, nor could we teach you:
It was some god breathed in you to set us free.

Therefore, O mighty King, we turn to you:
Find us our safety, find us a remedy,
Whether by counsel of the gods or the men.   **45**
A king of wisdom tested in the past
Can act in a time of troubles, and act well.
Noblest of men, restore
Life to your city! Think how all men call you
Liberator for your triumph long ago;   **50**
Ah, when your years of kingship are remembered,
Let them not say *We rose, but later fell—*
Keep the State from going down in the storm!
Once, years ago, with happy augury,
You brought us fortune; be the same again!   **55**
No man questions your power to rule the land:
But rule over men, not over a dead city!
Ships are only hulls, citadels are nothing,
When no life moves in the empty passageways.

OEDIPUS. Poor children! You may be sure I know   **60**
All that you longed for in your coming here.
I know that you are deathly sick; and yet,
Sick as you are, not one is as sick as I.
Each of you suffers in himself alone
His anguish, not another's; but my spirit   **65**
Groans for the city, for myself, for you.

I was not sleeping, you are not waking me.
No, I have been in tears for a long while
And in my restless thought walked many ways.
In all my search, I found one helpful course,   **70**
And that I have taken: I have sent Creon,
Son of Menoikeus, brother of the Queen,
To Delphi, Apollo's place of revelation,

---

39 Sphinx a monster (body of a lion, wings of a bird, face of a woman) who asked the
riddle, "What goes on four legs in the morning, two at noon, and three in the evening?"
and who killed those who could not answer. When Oedipus responded correctly that man
crawls on all fours in infancy, walks upright in maturity, and uses a staff in old age, the
Sphinx destroyed herself.

To learn there, if he can,
What act or pledge of mine may save the city.   *75*
I have counted the days, and now, this very day,
I am troubled, for he has overstayed his time.
What is he doing? He has been gone too long.
Yet whenever he comes back, I should do ill
To scant whatever hint the god may give.   *80*

PRIEST. It is a timely promise. At this instant
They tell me Creon is here.

OEDIPUS.   O Lord Apollo!
May his news be fair as his face is radiant!

PRIEST. It could not be otherwise: he is crowned with bay,
The chaplet is thick with berries.

OEDIPUS.   We shall soon know;   *85*
He is near enough to hear us now.

Enter Creon.

                              O Prince:
Brother: son of Menoikeus:
What answer do you bring us from the god?

CREON. It is favorable. I can tell you, great afflictions
Will turn out well, if they are taken well.   *90*

OEDIPUS. What was the oracle? These vague words
Leave me still hanging between hope and fear.

CREON. Is it your pleasure to hear me with all these
Gathered around us? I am prepared to speak,
But should we not go in?

OEDIPUS.   Let them all hear it.   *95*
It is for them I suffer, more than myself.

CREON. Then I will tell you what I heard at Delphi.

In plain words
The god commands us to expel from the land of Thebes
An old defilement that it seems we shelter.   *100*
It is a deathly thing, beyond expiation.
We must not let it feed up on us longer.

OEDIPUS. What defilement? How shall we rid ourselves of it?

CREON. By exile or death, blood for blood. It was
Murder that brought the plague-wind on the city.   *105*

OEDIPUS. Murder of whom? Surely the god has named him?

CREON. My lord: long ago Laïos was our king,
Before you came to govern us.

OEDIPUS.   I know;
I learned of him from others; I never saw him.

CREON. He was murdered; and Apollo commands us now   *110*
    To take revenge upon whoever killed him.
OEDIPUS. Upon whom? Where are they? Where shall we find a clue
    To solve that crime, after so many years?
CREON. Here in this land, he said.
                      If we make enquiry,
    We may touch things that otherwise escape us.   *115*
OEDIPUS. Tell me: Was Laïos murdered in his house,
    Or in the fields, or in some foreign country?
CREON. He said he planned to make a pilgrimage.
    He did not come home again.
OEDIPUS.   And was there no one,
    No witness, no companion, to tell what happened?   *120*
CREON. They were all killed but one, and he got away
    So frightened that he could remember one thing only.
OEDIPUS. What was that one thing? One may be the key
    To everything, if we resolve to use it.
CREON. He said that a band of highwaymen attacked them,   *125*
    Outnumbered them, and overwhelmed the King.
OEDIPUS. Strange, that a highwayman should be so daring —
    Unless some faction here bribed him to do it.
CREON. We thought of that. But after Laïos' death
    New troubles arose and we had no avenger.   *130*
OEDIPUS. What troubles could prevent your hunting down the killers?
CREON. The riddling Sphinx's song
    Made us deaf to all mysteries but her own.
OEDIPUS. Then once more I must bring what is dark to light.
    It is most fitting that Apollo shows,   *135*
    As you do, this compunction for the dead.
    You shall see how I stand by you, as I should,
    To avenge the city and the city's god,
    And not as though it were for some distant friend,
    But for my own sake, to be rid of evil.   *140*
    Whoever killed King Laïos might — who knows? —
    Decide at any moment to kill me as well.
    By avenging the murdered king I protect myself.
    Come, then, my children: leave the altar steps,
    Lift up your olive boughs!
                      One of you go   *145*
    And summon the people of Kadmos to gather here.
    I will do all that I can; you may tell them that.   (*Exit a Page.*)
    So, with the help of God,
    We shall be saved — or else indeed we are lost.
PRIEST. Let us rise, children. It was for this we came,   *150*
    And now the King has promised it himself.

Phoibos° has sent us an oracle; may he descend
Himself to save us and drive out the plague.

*Exeunt Oedipus and Creon into the palace by the central door. The
Priest and the Suppliants disperse right and left. After a short pause the
Chorus enters the orchestra.*

Párodos

CHORUS. What is God singing in his profound   *Strophe 1*
    Delphi of gold and shadow?
What oracle for Thebes, the sunwhipped city?
Fear unjoints me, the roots of my heart tremble.
Now I remember, O Healer, your power, and wonder;   *5*
Will you send doom like a sudden cloud, or weave it
Like nightfall of the past?
Speak, speak to us, issue of holy sound:
Dearest to our expectancy: be tender!

Let me pray to Athenê, the immortal daughter   *Antistrophe 1*
    of Zeus,
And to Artemis her sister
Who keeps her famous throne in the market ring,
And to Apollo, bowman at the far butts of heaven—

O gods, descend! Like three streams leap against
The fires of our grief, the fires of darkness;   *15*
Be swift to bring us rest!

As in the old time from the brilliant house
Of air you stepped to save us, come again!

Now our afflictions have no end,   *Strophe 2*
Now all our stricken host lies down   *20*
And no man fights off death with his mind;

The noble plowland bears no grain,
And groaning mothers cannot bear—
See, how our lives like birds take wing,
Like sparks that fly when a fire soars,   *25*
To the shore of the god of evening.

152 Phoibos Phoebus Apollo, the sun god

The plague burns on, it is pitiless   *Antistrophe 2*
Though pallid children laden with death
Lie unwept in the stony ways,
And old gray women by every path   30
Flock to the strand about the altars

There to strike their breasts and cry
Worship of Phoibos in wailing prayers:
Be kind, God's golden child!

There are no swords in this attack by fire,   *Strophe 3* 35
No shields, but we are ringed with cries.
Send the besieger plunging from our homes
Into the vast sea-room of the Atlantic
Or into the waves that foam eastward of Thrace—
For the day ravages what the night spares—   40

Destroy our enemy, lord of the thunder!
Let him be riven by lightning from heaven!

Phoibos Apollo, stretch the sun's bowstring,   *Antistrophe 3*
That golden cord, until it sing for us,
Flashing arrows in heaven!
                  Artemis, Huntress,   45
Race with flaring lights upon our mountains!
O scarlet god, O golden-banded brow,
O Theban Bacchos° in a storm of Maenads,°

Enter Oedipus, center.

Whirl upon Death, that all the Undying hate!
Come with blinding cressets, come in joy!   50

Scene I

OEDIPUS. Is this your prayer? It may be answered. Come,
    Listen to me, act as the crisis demands,
    And you shall have relief from all these evils.

    Until now I was a stranger to this tale,
    As I had been a stranger to the crime.   5
    Could I track down the murderer without a clue?

---

48 Bacchos Dionysos, god of wine, thus scarlet-faced   **48 Maenads** Dionysos's female
attendants

But now, friends,
As one who became a citizen after the murder,
I make this proclamation to all Thebans:
If any man knows by whose hand Laïos, son of Labdakos,   *10*
Met his death, I direct that man to tell me everything,
No matter what he fears for having so long withheld it.
Let it stand as promised that no further trouble
Will come to him, but he may leave the land in safety.

Moreover: If anyone knows the murderer to be foreign,   *15*
Let him not keep silent: he shall have his reward from me.
However, if he does conceal it; if any man
Fearing for his friend or for himself disobeys this edict,
Hear what I propose to do:

I solemnly forbid the people of this country,   *20*
Where power and throne are mine, ever to receive that man
Or speak to him, no matter who he is, or let him
Join in sacrifice, lustration, or in prayer.
I decree that he be driven from every house,

Being, as he is, corruption itself to us: the Delphic   *25*
Voice of Zeus has pronounced this revelation.
Thus I associate myself with the oracle
And take the side of the murdered king.

As for the criminal, I pray to God—
Whether it be a lurking thief, or one of a number—   *30*
I pray that that man's life be consumed in evil and wretch-
edness.
And as for me, this curse applies no less
If it should turn out that the culprit is my guest here,
Sharing my hearth.
                    You have heard the penalty.
I lay it on you now to attend to this   *35*
For my sake, for Apollo's, for the sick
Sterile city that heaven has abandoned.
Suppose the oracle had given you no command:
Should this defilement go uncleansed for ever?
You should have found the murderer: your king,   *40*
A noble king, had been destroyed!
                    Now I,
Having the power that he held before me,
Having his bed, begetting children there

Upon his wife, as he would have, had he lived—
Their son would have been my children's brother,   45
If Laïos had had luck in fatherhood!
(But surely ill luck rushed upon his reign)—
I say I take the son's part, just as though
I were his son, to press the fight for him
And see it won! I'll find the hand that brought   50
Death to Labdakos' and Polydoros' child,
Heir of Kadmos' and Agenor's line.
And as for those who fail me,
May the gods deny them the fruit of the earth,
Fruit of the womb, and may they rot utterly!   55
Let them be wretched as we are wretched, and worse!

For you, for loyal Thebans, and for all
Who find my actions right, I pray the favor
Of justice, and of all the immortal gods.
CHORAGOS.° Since I am under oath, my lord, I swear   60
    I did not do the murder, I cannot name
    The murderer. Might not the oracle
    That has ordained the search tell where to find him?
OEDIPUS. An honest question. But no man in the world
    Can make the gods do more than the gods will.   65
CHORAGOS. There is one last expedient—
OEDIPUS.   Tell me what it is.
    Though it seem slight, you must not hold it back.
CHORAGOS. A lord clairvoyant to the lord Apollo,
    As we all know, is the skilled Teiresias.
    One might learn much about this from him, Oedipus.   70
OEDIPUS. I am not wasting time:
    Creon spoke of this, and I have sent for him—
    Twice, in fact; it is strange that he is not here.
CHORAGOS. The other matter—that old report—seems useless.
OEDIPUS. Tell me. I am interested in all reports.   75
CHORAGOS. The King was said to have been killed by highwaymen.
OEDIPUS. I know. But we have no witnesses to that.
CHORAGOS. If the killer can feel a particle of dread,
    Your curse will bring him out of hiding!
OEDIPUS.   No.
    The man who dared that act will fear no curse.   80

Enter the blind seer Teiresias, led by a Page.

60 Choragos leader of the Chorus

CHORAGOS. But there is one man who may detect the criminal.
    This is Teiresias, this is the holy prophet
    In whom, alone of all men, truth was born.
OEDIPUS. Teiresias: seer: student of mysteries,
    Of all that's taught and all that no man tells,   *85*
    Secrets of Heaven and secrets of the earth:
    Blind though you are, you know the city lies
    Sick with plague; and from this plague, my lord,
    We find that you alone can guard or save us.

    Possibly you did not hear the messengers?   *90*
    Apollo, when we sent to him,
    Sent us back word that this great pestilence
    Would lift, but only if we established clearly
    The identity of those who murdered Laïos.
    They must be killed or exiled.
                                Can you use   *95*
    Birdflight or any art of divination
    To purify yourself, and Thebes, and me
    From this contagion? We are in your hands.
    There is no fairer duty
    Than that of helping others in distress.   *100*
TEIRESIAS. How dreadful knowledge of the truth can be
    When there's no help in truth! I knew this well,
    But did not act on it: else I should not have come.
OEDIPUS. What is troubling you? Why are your eyes so cold?
TEIRESIAS. Let me go home. Bear your own fate, and I'll   *105*
    Bear mine. It is better so: trust what I say.
OEDIPUS. What you say is ungracious and unhelpful
    To your native country. Do not refuse to speak.
TEIRESIAS. When it comes to speech, your own is neither
        temperate
    Nor opportune. I wish to be more prudent.   *110*
OEDIPUS. In God's name, we all beg you—
TEIRESIAS.   You are all ignorant.
    No; I will never tell you what I know.
    Now it is my misery; then, it would be yours.
OEDIPUS. What! You do know something, and will not tell us?
    You would betray us all and wreck the State?   *115*
TEIRESIAS. I do not intend to torture myself, or you.
    Why persist in asking? You will not persuade me.
OEDIPUS. What a wicked man you are! You'd try a stone's
    Patience! Out with it! Have you no feeling at all?
TEIRESIAS. You call me unfeeling. If you could only see   *120*
    The nature of your feelings . . .

OEDIPUS.   Why,
  Who would not feel as I do? Who could endure
  Your arrogance toward the city?
TEIRESIAS.   What does it matter!
  Whether I speak or not, it is bound to come.
OEDIPUS. Then, if "it" is bound to come, you are bound to tell me.   *125*
TEIRESIAS. No, I will not go on. Rage as you please
OEDIPUS. Rage? Why not!
                              And I'll tell you what I think:
  You planned it, you had it done, you all but
  Killed him with your own hands: if you had eyes,
  I'd say the crime was yours, and yours alone.   *130*
TEIRESIAS. So? I charge you, then,
  Abide by the proclamation you have made.
  From this day forth
  Never speak again to these men or to me;
  You yourself are the pollution of this country.   *135*
OEDIPUS. You dare say that! Can you possibly think you have
  Some way of going free, after such insolence?
TEIRESIAS. I have gone free. It is the truth sustains me.
OEDIPUS. Who taught you shamelessness? It was not your craft.
TEIRESIAS. You did. You made me speak. I did not want to.   *140*
OEDIPUS. Speak what? Let me hear it again more clearly.
TEIRESIAS. Was it not clear before? Are you tempting me?
OEDIPUS. I did not understand it. Say it again.
TEIRESIAS. I say that you are the murderer whom you seek.
OEDIPUS. Now twice you have spat out infamy. You'll pay for it!   *145*
TEIRESIAS. Would you care for more? Do you wish to be really angry?
OEDIPUS. Say what you will. Whatever you say is worthless.
TEIRESIAS. I say you live in hideous shame with those
  Most dear to you. You cannot see the evil.
OEDIPUS. It seems you can go on mouthing like this for ever.   *150*
TEIRESIAS. I can, if there is power in truth.
OEDIPUS.   There is:
  But not for you, not for you,
  You sightless, witless, senseless, mad old man!
TEIRESIAS. You are the madman. There is no one here
  Who will not curse you soon, as you curse me.   *155*
OEDIPUS. You child of endless night! You cannot hurt me
  Or any other man who sees the sun.
TEIRESIAS. True: it is not from me your fate will come.
  That lies within Apollo's competence,
  As it is his concern.
OEDIPUS.   Tell me: *160*
  Are you speaking for Creon, or for yourself?

TEIRESIAS. Creon is no threat. You weave your own doom.
OEDIPUS. Wealth, power, craft of statesmanship!
    Kingly position, everywhere admired!
    What savage envy is stored up against these,   *165*
    If Creon, whom I trusted, Creon my friend,
    For this great office which the city once
    Put in my hands unsought—if for this power
    Creon desires in secret to destroy me!

    He has brought this decrepit fortune-teller, this   *170*
    Collector of dirty pennies, this prophet fraud—
    Why, he is no more clairvoyant than I am!
                                  Tell us:
    Has your mystic mummery ever approached the truth?
    When that hellcat the Sphinx was performing here,
    What help were you to these people?   *175*
    Her magic was not for the first man who came along:
    It demanded a real exorcist. Your birds—
    What good were they? or the gods, for the matter of that?
    But I came by,
    Oedipus, the simple man, who knows nothing—   *180*
    I thought it out for myself, no birds helped me!
    And this is the man you think you can destroy,
    That you may be close to Creon when he's king!
    Well, you and your friend Creon, it seems to me,
    Will suffer most. If you were not an old man,   *185*
    You would have paid already for your plot.
CHORAGOS. We cannot see that his words or yours
    Have spoken except in anger, Oedipus,
    And of anger we have no need. How can God's will
    Be accomplished best? That is what most concerns us.   *190*
TEIRESIAS. You are a king. But where argument's concerned
    I am your man, as much a king as you.
    I am not your servant, but Apollo's.
    I have no need of Creon to speak for me.

    Listen to me. You mock my blindness, do you?   *195*
    But I say that you, with both your eyes, are blind:
    You cannot see the wretchedness of your life,
    Not in whose house you live, no, nor with whom.
    Who are your father and mother? Can you tell me?
    You do not even know the blind wrongs   *200*
    That you have done them, on earth and in the world below.
    But the double lash of your parents' curse will whip you
    Out of this land some day, with only night

Upon your precious eyes.
Your cries then—where will they not be heard?   *205*
What fastness of Kithairon° will not echo them?
And that bridal-descant of yours—you'll know it then,
The song they sang when you came here to Thebes
And found your misguided berthing.
All this, and more, that you cannot guess at now,   *210*
Will bring you to yourself among your children.
Be angry, then. Curse Creon. Curse my words.
I tell you, no man that walks upon the earth
Shall be rooted out more horribly than you.
OEDIPUS. Am I to bear this from him?—Damnation   *215*
    Take you! Out of this place! Out of my sight!
TEIRESIAS. I would not have come at all if you had not asked me.
OEDIPUS. Could I have told that you'd talk nonsense, that
    You'd come here to make a fool of yourself, and of me?
TEIRESIAS. A fool? Your parents thought me sane enough.   *220*
OEDIPUS. My parents again!—Wait: who were my parents?
TEIRESIAS. This day will give you a father, and break your heart.
OEDIPUS. Your infantile riddles! Your damned abracadabra!
TEIRESIAS. You were a great man once at solving riddles.
OEDIPUS. Mock me with that if you like; you will find it true.   *225*
TEIRESIAS. It was true enough. It brought about your ruin.
OEDIPUS. But if it saved this town.
TEIRESIAS *(to the Page)*. Boy, give me your hand.
OEDIPUS. Yes, boy; lead him away.
                —While you are here
    We can do nothing. Go; leave us in peace.
TEIRESIAS. I will go when I have said what I have to say.   *230*
    How can you hurt me? And I tell you again:
    The man you have been looking for all this time,
    The damned man, the murderer of Laïos,
    That man is in Thebes. To your mind he is foreignborn,
    But it will soon be shown that he is a Theban,   *235*
    A revelation that will fail to please.
                  A blind man,
    Who has his eyes now; a penniless man, who is rich now;
    And he will go tapping the strange earth with his staff;
    To the children with whom he lives now he will be
    Brother and father—the very same; to her   *240*
    Who bore him, son and husband—the very same
    Who came to his father's bed, wet with his father's blood.

206 fastness of Kithairon stronghold in a mountain near Thebes

Enough. Go think that over.
If later you find error in what I have said,
You may say that I have no skill in prophecy.   *245*

Exit Teiresias, led by his Page. Oedipus goes into the palace.

Ode I

CHORUS. The Delphic stone of prophecies   *Strophe 1*
    Remembers ancient regicide
    And a still bloody hand.
    That killer's hour of flight has come.
    He must be stronger than riderless   *5*
    Coursers of untiring wind,
    For the son of Zeus° armed with his father's thunder
    Leaps in lightning after him;
    And the Furies° follow him, the sad Furies.

    Holy Parnossos' peak of snow   *Antistrophe 1*   *10*
    Flashes and blinds that secret man,
    That all shall hunt him down:
    Though he may roam the forest shade
    Like a bull gone wild from pasture
    To rage through glooms of stone.   *15*
    Doom comes down on him; flight will not avail him;
    For the world's heart calls him desolate,
    And the immortal Furies follow, for ever follow.

    But now a wilder thing is heard   *Strophe 2*
    From the old man skilled at hearing Fate in the wingbeat of a bird.   *20*
    Bewildered as a blown bird, my soul hovers and cannot find
    Foothold in this debate, or any reason or rest of mind.
    But no man ever brought—none can bring
    Proof of strife between Thebes' royal house,
    Labdakos' line,° and the son of Polybos;°   *25*
    And never until now has any man brought word
    Of Laïos' dark death staining Oedipus the King.

    Divine Zeus and Apollo hold   *Antistrophe 2*
    Perfect intelligence alone of all tales ever told;
    And well though this diviner works, he works in his own night;   *30*

---

7 son of Zeus Apollo   **9 Furies** avenging deities   **25 Labdakos' line** family of Laïos
25 son of Polybos Oedipus (so the Chorus believes)

No man can judge that rough unknown or trust in second sight,
For wisdom changes hands among the wise.
Shall I believe my great lord criminal.
At a raging word that a blind old man let fall?
I saw him, when the carrion woman faced him of old,   *35*
Prove his heroic mind! These evil words are lies.

Scene II

CREON. Men of Thebes:
      I am told that heavy accusations
      Have been brought against me by King Oedipus.
      I am not the kind of man to bear this tamely.

      If in these present difficulties   *5*
      He holds me accountable for any harm to him
      Through anything I have said or done—why, then,
      I do not value life in this dishonor.
      It is not as though this rumor touched upon
      Some private indiscretion. The matter is grave.   *10*
      The fact is that I am being called disloyal
      To the State, to my fellow citizens, to my friends.
CHORAGOS. He may have spoken in anger, not from his mind.
CREON. But did you hear him say I was the one
      Who seduced the old prophet into lying?   *15*
CHORAGOS. The thing was said; I do not know how seriously.
CREON. But you were watching him! Were his eyes steady?
      Did he look like a man in his right mind?
CHORAGOS.   I do not know.
      I cannot judge the behavior of great men.
      But here is the King himself.

      (*Enter Oedipus.*)

OEDIPUS.   So you dared come back.   *20*
      Why? How brazen of you to come to my house,
      You murderer!
                    Do you think I do not know
      That you plotted to kill me, plotted to steal my throne?
      Tell me, in God's name: am I coward, a fool,
      That you should dream you could accomplish this?   *25*
      A fool who could not see your slippery game?
      A coward, not to fight back when I saw it?
      You are the fool, Creon, are you not? hoping
      Without support or friends to get a throne?

Thrones may be won or bought: you could do neither.   *30*
CREON. Now listen to me. You have talked; let me talk, too.
    You cannot judge unless you know the facts.
OEDIPUS. You speak well: there is one fact; but I find it hard
    To learn from the deadliest enemy I have.
CREON. That above all I must dispute with you.   *35*
OEDIPUS. That above all I will not hear you deny.
CREON. If you think there is anything good in being stubborn
    Against all reason, then I say you are wrong.
OEDIPUS. If you think a man can sin against his own kind
    And not be punished for it, I say you are mad.   *40*
CREON. I agree. But tell me: what have I done to you?
OEDIPUS. You advised me to send for that wizard, did you not?
CREON. I did. I should do it again.
OEDIPUS.   Very well. Now tell me:
    How long has it been since Laïos—
CREON.   What of Laïos?
OEDIPUS. Since he vanished in that onset by the road?   *45*
CREON. It was long ago, a long time.
OEDIPUS.   And this prophet,
    Was he practicing here then?
CREON.   He was; and with honor, as now.
OEDIPUS. Did he speak of me at that time?
CREON.   He never did;
    At least, not when I was present.
OEDIPUS.   But . . . the enquiry?
    I suppose you held one?
CREON.   We did, but we learned nothing.   *50*
OEDIPUS. Why did the prophet not speak against me then?
CREON. I do not know; and I am the kind of man
    Who holds his tongue when he has no facts to go on.
OEDIPUS. There's one fact that you know, and you could tell it.
CREON. What fact is that? If I know it, you shall have it.   *55*
OEDIPUS. If he were not involved with you, he could not say
    That it was I who murdered Laïos.
CREON. If he says that, you are the one that knows it!—
    But now it is my turn to question you.
OEDIPUS. Put your questions. I am no murderer.   *60*
CREON. First, then: You married my sister?
OEDIPUS.   I married your sister.
CREON. And you rule the kingdom equally with her?
OEDIPUS. Everything that she wants she has from me.
CREON. And I am the third, equal to both of you?
OEDIPUS. That is why I call you a bad friend.   *65*
CREON. No. Reason it out, as I have done.

Think of this first. Would any sane man prefer
Power, with all a king's anxieties,
To that same power and the grace of sleep?
Certainly not I.   70
I have never longed for the king's power—only his rights.
Would any wise man differ from me in this?
As matters stand, I have my way in everything
With your consent, and no responsibilities.
If I were king, I should be a slave to policy.   75
How could I desire a scepter more
Than what is now mine—untroubled influence?
No, I have not gone mad; I need no honors,
Except those with the perquisites I have now.
I am welcome everywhere; every man salutes me,   80
And those who want your favor seek my ear,
Since I know how to manage what they ask.
Should I exchange this ease for that anxiety?
Besides, no sober mind is treasonable.
I hate anarchy   85
And never would deal with any man who likes it.

Test what I have said. Go to the priestess
At Delphi, ask if I quoted her correctly.
And as for this other thing: if I am found
Guilty of treason with Teiresias,   90
Then sentence me to death! You have my word
It is a sentence I should cast my vote for—
But not without evidence!
                              You do wrong
When you take good men for bad, bad men for good.
A true friend thrown aside—why, life itself   95
Is not more precious!
                              In time you will know this well:
For time, and time alone, will show the just man,
Though scoundrels are discovered in a day.
CHORAGOS. This is well said, and a prudent man would ponder it.
    Judgments too quickly formed are dangerous.   100
OEDIPUS. But is he not quick in his duplicity?
    And shall I not be quick to parry him?
    Would you have me stand still, hold my peace, and let
    This man win everything, through my inaction?
CREON. And you want—what is it, then? To banish me?   105
OEDIPUS. No, not exile. It is your death I want,
    So that all the world may see what treason means.

CREON. You will persist, then? You will not believe me?

OEDIPUS. How can I believe you?

CREON.   Then you are a fool.

OEDIPUS. To save myself?

CREON.   In justice, think of me.   *110*

OEDIPUS. You are evil incarnate.

CREON.   But suppose that you are wrong?

OEDIPUS. Still I must rule.

CREON.   But not if you rule badly.

OEDIPUS. O city, city!

CREON.   It is my city, too!

CHORAGOS. Now, my lords, be still. I see the Queen,
    Iocastê, coming from her palace chambers;   *115*
    And it is time she came, for the sake of you both.
    This dreadful quarrel can be resolved through her.

    Enter Iocastê.

IOCASTÊ. Poor foolish men, what wicked din is this?
    With Thebes sick to death, is it not shameful
    That you should rake some private quarrel up?   *120*
    (*To Oedipus.*) Come into the house.
                           —And you, Creon, go now:
    Let us have no more of this tumult over nothing.

CREON. Nothing? No, sister: what your husband plans for me
    Is one of two great evils: exile or death.

OEDIPUS. He is right.
                Why, woman, I have caught him squarely   *125*
    Plotting against my life.

CREON.   No! Let me die
    Accurst if ever I have wished you harm!

IOCASTÊ. Ah, believe it, Oedipus!
    In the name of the gods, respect this oath of his
    For my sake, for the sake of these people here!   *130*

CHORAGOS. Open your mind to her, my lord. Be ruled   *Strophe 1*
            by her, I beg you!

OEDIPUS. What would you have me do?

CHORAGOS. Respect Creon's word. He has never spoken like a fool,
    And now he has sworn an oath.

OEDIPUS. You know what you ask?

CHORAGOS.   I do.

OEDIPUS.   Speak on, then.

CHORAGOS. A friend so sworn should not be baited so,   *135*
    In blind malice, and without final proof.

OEDIPUS. You are aware, I hope, that what you say
    Means death for me, or exile at the least.

CHORAGOS. No, I swear by Helios,° first in Heaven!   *Strophe 2*
    May I die friendless and accurst,   *140*
    The worst of deaths, if ever I meant that!
        It is the withering fields
           That hurt my sick heart:
        Must we bear all these ills,
           And now your bad blood as well?   *145*
OEDIPUS. Then let him go. And let me die, if I must,
    Or be driven by him in shame from the land of Thebes.
    It is your unhappiness, and not his talk,
    That touches me.
           As for him—
    Wherever he is, I will hate him as long as I live.   *150*
CREON. Ugly in yielding, as you were ugly in rage!
    Natures like yours chiefly torment themelves.
OEDIPUS. Can you not go? Can you not leave me?
CREON.   I can.
    You do not know me; but the city knows me,
    And in its eyes I am just, if not in yours.   (*Exit Creon.*) *155*

CHORAGOS. Lady Iocastê, did you not ask the King   *Antistrophe 1*
        to go to his chambers?
IOCASTÊ. First tell me what has happened.
CHORAGOS. There was suspicion without evidence; yet it rankled
    As even false charges will.
IOCASTÊ. On both sides?
CHORAGOS.   On both.
IOCASTÊ.   But what was said?
CHORAGOS. Oh let it rest, let it be done with!   *160*
    Have we not suffered enough?
OEDIPUS. You see to what your decency has brought you:
    You have made difficulties where my heart saw none.

CHORAGOS. Oedipus, it is not once only I have told you—*Antistrophe 2*
    You must know I should count myself unwise   *165*
    To the point of madness, should I now forsake you—
        You, under whose hand,
           In the storm of another time,

139 Helios sun god

    Our dear land sailed out free,
      But now stand fast at the helm!   *170*
IOCASTÊ. In God's name, Oedipus, inform your wife as well:
  Why are you so set in this hard anger?
OEDIPUS. I will tell you, for none of these men deserves
  My confidence as you do. It is Creon's work,
  His treachery, his plotting against me.   *175*
IOCASTÊ. Go on, if you can make this clear to me.
OEDIPUS. He charges me with the murder of Laïos.
IOCASTÊ. Has he some knowledge? Or does he speak from hearsay?
OEDIPUS. He would not commit himself to such a charge,
  But he has brought in that damnable soothsayer   *180*
  To tell his story.
IOCASTÊ.   Set your mind at rest.
  If it is a question of soothsayers, I tell you
  That you will find no man whose craft gives knowledge
  Of the unknowable.
        Here is my proof.

  An oracle was reported to Laïos once   *185*
  (I will not say from Phoibos himself, but from
  His appointed ministers, at any rate)
  That his doom would be death at the hands of his own son—
  His son, born of his flesh and of mine!

  Now, you remember the story: Laïos was killed   *190*
  By marauding strangers where three highways meet;
  But his child had not been three days in this world
  Before the King had pierced the baby's ankles
  And left him to die on a lonely mountainside.

  Thus, Apollo never caused that child   *195*
  To kill his father, and it was not Laïos fate
  To die at the hands of his son, as he had feared.
  This is what prophets and prophecies are worth!
  Have no dread of them.
       It is God himself
  Who can show us what he wills, in his own way.   *200*
OEDIPUS. How strange a shadowy memory crossed my mind,
  Just now while you were speaking; it chilled my heart.
IOCASTÊ. What do you mean? What memory do you speak of?
OEDIPUS. If I understand you, Laïos was killed
  At a place where three roads meet.
IOCASTÊ.   So it was said;   *205*
  We have no later story.

OEDIPUS.　　　　　　　　Where did it happen?

IOCASTÊ. Phokis, it is called: at a place where the Theban Way
　　Divides into the roads towards Delphi and Daulia.

OEDIPUS. When?

IOCASTÊ.　　　　We had the news not long before you came
　　And proved the right to your succession here.　　　　　　210

OEDIPUS. Ah, what net has God been weaving for me?

IOCASTÊ. Oedipus! Why does this trouble you?

OEDIPUS.　　　　　　　　　　　　　Do not ask me yet.
　　First, tell me how Laïos looked, and tell me
　　How old he was.

IOCAST E.　　　　　　　He was tall, his hair just touched
　　With white; his form was not unlike your own.　　　　　215

OEDIPUS. I think that I myself may be accurst
　　By my own ignorant edict.

IOCASTÊ.　　　　　　　　　You speak strangely.
　　It makes me tremble to look at you, my King.

OEDIPUS. I am not sure that the blind man cannot see.
　　But I should know better if you were to tell me—　　　　220

IOCASTÊ. Anything—though I dread to hear you ask it.

OEDIPUS. Was the King lightly escorted, or did he ride
　　With a large company, as a ruler should?

IOCASTÊ. There were five men with him in all: one was
　　　　a herald;
　　And a single chariot, which he was driving.　　　　　　225

OEDIPUS. Alas, that makes it plain enough!
　　　　　　　　　　　　　　But who—
　　Who told you how it happened?

IOCASTÊ.　　　　　　　　　A household servant,
　　The only one to escape.

OEDIPUS.　　　　　　　And is he still
　　A servant of ours?

IOCASTÊ.　　　　　　No; for when he came back at last
　　And found you enthroned in the place of the dead king,　　230
　　He came to me, touched my hand with his, and begged
　　That I would send him away to the frontier district
　　Where only the shepherds go—
　　As far away from the city as I could send him.
　　I granted his prayer; for although the man was a slave,　　235
　　He had earned more than this favor at my hands.

OEDIPUS. Can he be called back quickly?

IOCASTÊ.　　　　　　　　　　Easily.
　　But why?

OEDIPUS.　　　I have taken too much upon myself
　　Without enquiry; therefore I wish to consult him.

IOCASTÊ. Then he shall come.
                                    But am I not one also   *240*
        To whom you might confide these fears of yours!
OEDIPUS. That is your right; it will not be denied you,
        Now least of all; for I have reached a pitch
        Of wild foreboding. Is there anyone
        To whom I should sooner speak?   *245*
        Polybos of Corinth is my father.
        My mother is a Dorian: Meropê.
        I grew up chief among the men of Corinth
        Until a strange thing happened—
        Not worth my passion, it may be, but strange.   *250*

        At a feast, a drunken man maundering in his cups
        Cries out that I am not my father's son!

        I contained myself that night, though I felt anger
        And a sinking heart. The next day I visited
        My father and mother, and questioned them. They stormed,   *255*
        Calling it all the slanderous rant of a fool;
        And this relieved me. Yet the suspicion
        Remained always aching in my mind;
        I knew there was talk; I could not rest;
        And finally, saying nothing to my parents,   *260*
        I went to the shrine at Delphi.
        The god dismissed my question without reply;
        He spoke of other things.
                                    Some were clear,
        Full of wretchedness, dreadful, unbearable:
        As, that I should lie with my own mother, breed   *265*
        Children from whom all men would turn their eyes;
        And that I should be my father's murderer.
        I heard all this, and fled. And from that day
        Corinth to me was only in the stars
        Descending in that quarter of the sky,   *270*
        As I wandered farther and farther on my way
        To a land where I should never see the evil
        Sung by the oracle. And I came to this country
        Where, so you say, King Laïos was killed.
        I will tell you all that happened there, my lady.   *275*

        There were three highways
        Coming together at a place I passed;
        And there a herald came towards me, and a chariot

Drawn by horses, with a man such as you describe
Seated in it. The groom leading the horses   *280*
Forced me off the road at his lord's command;
But as this charioteer lurched over toward me
I struck him in my rage. The old man saw me
And brought his double goad down upon my head
As I came abreast.
                He was paid back, and more!   *285*
Swinging my club in this right hand I knocked him
Out of his car, and he rolled on the ground.
                              I killed him.

I killed them all.
Now if that stranger and Laïos were—kin,
Where is a man more miserable than I?   *290*
More hated by the gods? Citizen and alien alike
Must never shelter me or speak to me—
I must be shunned by all.
                 And I myself
Pronounced this malediction upon myself!

Think of it: I have touched you with these hands,   *295*
These hands that killed your husband. What defilement!

Am I all evil, then? It must be so,
Since I must flee from Thebes, yet never again
See my own countrymen, my own country,
For fear of joining my mother in marriage   *300*
And killing Polybos, my father.
                Ah,
If I was created so, born to this fate,
Who could deny the savagery of God?

O holy majesty of heavenly powers!
May I never see that day! Never!   *305*
Rather let me vanish from the race of men
Than know the abomination destined me!
CHORAGOS. We too, my lord, have felt dismay at this.
    But there is hope: you have yet to hear the shepherd.
OEDIPUS. Indeed, I fear no other hope is left me.   *310*
IOCASTÊ . What do you hope from him when he comes?
OEDIPUS.   This much:
    If his account of the murder tallies with yours,
    Then I am cleared.
IOCASTÊ.   What was it that I said
    Of such importance?

OEDIPUS.   Why, "marauders," you said,
    Killed the King, according to this man's story.   315
    If he maintains that still, if there were several,
    Clearly the guilt is not mine: I was alone.
    But if he says one man, singlehanded, did it,
    Then the evidence all points to me.
IOCASTÊ. You may be sure that he said there were several;   320
    And can he call back that story now? He cannot.
    The whole city heard it as plainly as I.
    But suppose he alters some detail of it:
    He cannot ever show that Laïos' death
    Fulfilled the oracle: for Apollo said   325
    My child was doomed to kill him; and my child—
    Poor baby!—it was my child that died first.

    No. From now on, where oracles are concerned,
    I would not waste a second thought on any.
OEDIPUS. You may be right.
                     But come: let someone go   330
    For the shepherd at once. This matter must be settled.
IOCASTÊ. I will send for him.
    I would not wish to cross you in anything,
    And surely not in this.—Let us go in.   *Exeunt into the palace.*

Ode II

CHORUS. Let me be reverent in the ways of right,   *Strophe 1*
    Lowly the paths I journey on;
    Let all my words and actions keep
    The laws of the pure universe
    From highest Heaven handed down.   5
    For Heaven is their bright nurse,
    Those generations of the realms of light;
    Ah, never of mortal kind were they begot,
    Nor are they slaves of memory, lost in sleep:
    Their Father is greater than Time, and ages not.   10

    The tyrant is a child of Pride   *Antistrophe 1*
    Who drinks from his great sickening cup
    Recklessness and vanity,
    Until from his high crest headlong
    He plummets to the dust of hope.   15
    That strong man is not strong.
    But let no fair ambition be denied;

May God protect the wrestler for the State
In government, in comely policy,
Who will fear God, and on His ordinance wait.   *20*

Haughtiness and the high hand of disdain   *Strophe 2*
Tempt and outrage God's holy law;
And any mortal who dares hold
No immortal Power in awe
Will be caught up in a net of pain: *25*
The price for which his levity is sold.
Let each man take due earnings, then,
And keep his hands from holy things,
And from blasphemy stand apart—
Else the crackling blast of heaven   *30*
Blows on his head, and on his desperate heart;
Though fools will honor impious men,
In their cities no tragic poet sings.

Shall we lose faith in Delphi's obscurities,   *Antistrophe 2*
We who have heard the world's core   *35*
Discredited, and the sacred wood
Of Zeus at Elis praised no more?
The deeds and the strange prophecies
Must make a pattern yet to be understood.
Zeus, if indeed you are lord of all,   *40*
Throned in light over night and day,
Mirror this in your endless mind:
Our masters call the oracle
Words on the wind, and the Delphic vision blind!
Their hearts no longer know Apollo,   *45*
And reverence for the gods has died away.

Scene III

Enter Iocastê.

IOCASTÊ. Princes of Thebes, it has occurred to me
    To visit the altars of the gods, bearing
    These branches as a suppliant, and this incense.
    Our King is not himself: his noble soul
    Is overwrought with fantasies of dread,   *5*
    Else he would consider
    The new prophecies in the light of the old.

He will listen to any voice that speaks disaster,
And my advice goes for nothing.

She approaches the altar, right.

                                    To you, then, Apollo,
Lycean lord, since you are nearest, I turn in prayer.   *10*
Receive these offerings, and grant us deliverance
From defilement. Our hearts are heavy with fear
When we see our leader distracted, as helpless sailors
Are terrified by the confusion of their helmsman.

Enter Messenger.

MESSENGER. Friends, no doubt you can direct me: *15*
    Where shall I find the house of Oedipus,
    Or, better still, where is the King himself?
CHORAGOS. It is this very place, stranger; he is inside.
    This is his wife and mother of his children.
MESSENGER. I wish her happiness in a happy house,   *20*
    Blest in all the fulfillment of her marriage.
IOCASTÊ. I wish as much for you: your courtesy
    Deserves a like good fortune. But now, tell me:
    Why have you come? What have you to say to us?
MESSENGER. Good news, my lady, for your house and your husband.   *25*
IOCASTÊ. What news? Who sent you here?
MESSENGER.   I am from Corinth.
    The news I bring ought to mean joy for you,
    Though it may be you will find some grief in it.
IOCASTÊ. What is it? How can it touch us in both ways?
MESSENGER. The people of Corinth, they say,   *30*
    Intend to call Oedipus to be their king.
IOCASTÊ. But old Polybos—is he not reigning still?
MESSENGER. No. Death holds him in his sepulchre.
IOCASTÊ. What are you saying? Polybos is dead?
MESSENGER. If I am not tellling the truth, may I die myself.   *35*
IOCASTÊ (*To a Maidservant*). Go in, go quickly; tell this to your master.
    O riddlers of God's will, where are you now!
    This was the man whom Oedipus, long ago,
    Feared so, fled so, in dread of destroying him—
    But it was another fate by which he died.   *40*

Enter Oedipus, center.

OEDIPUS. Dearest Iocastê, why have you sent for me?
IOCASTÊ. Listen to what this man says, and then tell me
    What has become of the solemn prophecies.
OEDIPUS. Who is this man? What is his news for me?

IOCASTÊ. He has come from Corinth to announce your father's death! *45*
OEDIPUS. Is it true, stranger? Tell me in your own words.
MESSENGER. I cannot say it more clearly: the King is dead.
OEDIPUS. Was it by treason? Or by an attack of illness?
MESSENGER. A little thing brings old men to their rest.
OEDIPUS. It was sickness, then?
MESSENGER.   Yes, and his many years. *50*
OEDIPUS. Ah!
    Why should a man respect the Pythian hearth,° or
    Give heed to the birds that jangle above his head?
    They prophesied that I should kill Polybos,
    Kill my own father; but he is dead and buried, *55*
    And I am here—I never touched him, never,
    Unless he died in grief for my departure,
    And thus, in a sense, through me. No Polybos
    Has packed the oracles off with him underground.
    They are empty words.
IOCASTÊ.   Had I not told you so? *60*
OEDIPUS. You had; it was my faint heart that betrayed me.
IOCASTÊ. From now on never think of those things again.
OEDIPUS. And yet—must I not fear my mother's bed?
IOCASTÊ.Why should anyone in this world be afraid,
    Since Fate rules us and nothing can be foreseen? *65*
    A man should live only for the present day.
    Have no more fear of sleeping with your mother
    How many men, in dreams, have lain with their mothers!
    No reasonable man is troubled by such things.
OEDIPUS. That is true; only— *70*
    If only my mother were not still alive!
    But she is alive. I cannot help my dread.
IOCASTÊ. Yet this news of your father's death is wonderful.
OEDIPUS. Wonderful. But I fear the living woman.
MESSENGER. Tell me, who is this woman that you fear? *75*
OEDIPUS. It is Meropê, man; the wife of King Polybos.
MESSENGER. Meropê? Why should you be afraid of her?
OEDIPUS. An oracle of the gods, a dreadful saying.
MESSENGER. Can you tell me about it or are you sworn to silence?
OEDIPUS. I can tell you, and I will. *80*
    Apollo said through his prophet that I was the man
    Who should marry his own mother, shed his father's blood
    With his own hands. And so, for all these years

52 Pythian hearth Delphi (also called Pytho became a great snake had lived there), where
Apollo spoke through a priestess

I have kept clear of Corinth, and no harm has come—
Though it would have been sweet to see my parents again. 85
MESSENGER. And is this the fear that drove you out of Corinth?
OEDIPUS. Would you have me kill my father?
MESSENGER.   As for that
You must be reassured by the news I gave you.
OEDIPUS. If you could reassure me, I would reward you.
MESSENGER. I had that in mind, I will confess: I thought 90
I could count on you when you returned to Corinth.
OEDIPUS. No: I will never go near my parents again.
MESSENGER. Ah, son, you still do not know what you are doing—
OEDIPUS. What do you mean? In the name of God tell me!
MESSENGER. —If these are your reasons for not going home, 95
OEDIPUS. I tell you, I fear the oracle may come true.
MESSENGER. And guilt may come upon you through your parents?
OEDIPUS. That is the dread that is always in my heart.
MESSENGER. Can you not see that all your fears are groundless?
OEDIPUS. How can you say that? They are my parents, surely? 100
MESSENGER. Polybos was not your father.
OEDIPUS.   Not my father?
MESSENGER. No more your father than the man speaking to you.
OEDIPUS. But you are nothing to me!
MESSENGER.   Neither was he.
OEDIPUS. Then why did he call me son?
MESSENGER.   I will tell you:
Long ago he had you from my hands, as a gift. 105
OEDIPUS. Then how could he love me so, if I was not his?
MESSENGER. He had no children, and his heart turned to you.
OEDIPUS. What of you? Did you buy me?
Did you find me by chance?
MESSENGER. I came upon you in the crooked pass of Kithairon.
OEDIPUS. And what were you doing there?
MESSENGER.   Tending my flocks. 110
OEDIPUS. A wandering shepherd?
MESSENGER.   But your savior, son, that day.
OEDIPUS. From what did you save me?
MESSENGER.   Your ankles should tell you that.
OEDIPUS. Ah, stranger, why do you speak of that childhood pain?
MESSENGER. I cut the bonds that tied your ankles together.
OEDIPUS. I have had the mark as long as I can remember. 115
MESSENGER. That was why you were given the name you bear.°

---

116 name you bear "Oedipus" means "swollen-foot"

OEDIPUS. God! Was it my father or my mother who did it?
    Tell me!
MESSENGER. I do not know. The man who gave you to me
    Can tell you better than I.   120
OEDIPUS. It was not you that found me, but another?
MESSENGER. It was another shepherd gave you to me.
OEDIPUS. Who was he? Can you tell me who he was?
MESSENGER. I think he was said to be one of Laïos' people.
OEDIPUS. You mean the Laïos who was king here years ago?   125
MESSENGER. Yes; King Laïos; and the man was one of his herdsmen.
OEDIPUS. Is he still alive? Can I see him?
MESSENGER.   These men here
    Know best about such things.
OEDIPUS.   Does anyone here
    Know this shepherd that he is talking about?
    Have you seen him in the fields, or in the town?   130
    If you have, tell me. It is time things were made plain.
CHORAGOS. I think the man he means is that same shepherd
    You have already asked to see. Iocastê perhaps
    Could tell you something.
OEDIPUS.   Do you know anything
    About him, Lady? Is he the man we have summoned?   135
    Is that the man this shepherd means?
IOCASTÊ.   Why think of him?
    Forget this herdsman. Forget it all.
    This talk is a waste of time.
OEDIPUS.   How can you say that,
    When the clues to my true birth are in my hands?
IOCASTÊ. For God's love, let us have no more questioning!   140
    Is your life nothing to you?
    My own is pain enough for me to bear.
OEDIPUS. You need not worry. Suppose my mother a slave,
    And born of slaves: no baseness can touch you.
IOCASTÊ. Listen to me, I beg you: do not do this thing!   145
OEDIPUS. I will not listen; the truth must be made known.
IOCASTÊ. Everything that I say is for your own good!
OEDIPUS.   My own good
    Snaps my patience, then: I want none of it.
IOCASTÊ. You are fatally wrong! May you never learn who your are!
OEDIPUS. Go, one of you, and bring the shepherd here.   150
    Let us leave this woman to brag of her royal name.
IOCASTÊ. Ah, miserable!
    That is the only word I have for you now.
    That is the only word I can ever have.   *Exit into the palace.*

CHORAGOS. Why has she left us, Oedipus? Why has she gone   *155*
    In such a passion of sorrow? I fear this silence:
    Something dreadful may come of it.
OEDIPUS.   Let it come!
    However base my birth, I must know about it.
    The Queen, like a woman, is perhaps ashamed
    To think of my low origin. But I   *160*
    Am a child of luck; I cannot be dishonored.
    Luck is my mother; the passing months, my brothers,
    Have seen me rich and poor.
                  If this is so,
    How could I wish that I were someone else?
    How could I not be glad to know my birth?   *165*

Ode III

CHORUS. If ever the coming time were known   *Strophe*
    To my heart's pondering,
    Kithairon, now by Heaven I see the torches
    At the festival of the next full moon,
    And see the dance, and hear the choir sing   *5*
    A grace to your gentle shade:
    Mountain where Oedipus was found,
    O mountain guard of a noble race!
    May the god who heals us lend his aid,
    And let that glory come to pass   *10*
    For our king's cradling-ground.

    Of the nymphs that flower beyond the years.   *Antistrophe*
    Who bore you, royal child,
    To Pan of the hills or the timberline Apollo,
    Cold in delight where the upland clears.   *15*
    Or Hermês for whom Kyllenê's° heights are piled?
    Or flushed as evening cloud,
    Great Dionysos, roamer of mountains,
    He—was it he who found you there,
    And caught you up in his own proud   *20*
    Arms from the sweet god-ravisher
    Who laughed by the Muses' fountains?

---

16 Hermês . . . Kyllenê's Hermês messenger of the gods, was said to have been born on
Mt. Kyllenê.

Scene IV

OEDIPUS. Sirs: though I do not know the man,
    I think I see him coming, this shepherd we want:
    He is old, like our friend here, and the men
    Bringing him seem to be servants of my house.
    But you can tell, if you have ever seen him.   *5*

Enter Shepherd escorted by servants.

CHORAGOS. I know him, he was Laïos' man. You can trust him.
OEDIPUS. Tell me first, you from Corinth: is this the shepherd
    We were discussing?
MESSENGER.   This is the very man.
OEDIPUS *(To Shepherd).* Come here. No, look at me. You must answer
    Everything I ask.—You belonged to Laïos?   *10*
SHEPHERD. Yes: born his slave, brought up in his house.
OEDIPUS. Tell me: what kind of work did you do for him?
SHEPHERD. I was a shepherd of his, most of my life.
OEDIPUS. Where mainly did you go for pasturage?
SHEPHERD. Sometimes Kithairon, sometimes the hills near-by.   *15*
OEDIPUS. Do you remember ever seeing this man out there?
SHEPHERD. What would he be doing there? This man?
OEDIPUS. This man standing here. Have you ever seen him before?
SHEPHERD. No. At least, not to my recollection.
MESSENGER. And that is not strange, my lord. But I'll refresh   *20*
    His memory: he must remember when we two
    Spent three whole seasons together, March to September,
    On Kithairon or thereabouts. He had two flocks;
    I had one. Each autumn I'd drive mine home
    And he would go back with his to Laïos' sheepfold.—   *25*
    Is this not true, just as I have described it?
SHEPHERD. True, yes; but it was all so long ago.
MESSENGER. Well, then: do you remember, back in those days
    That you gave me a baby boy to bring up as my own?
SHEPHERD. What if I did? What are you trying to say?   *30*
MESSENGER. King Oedipus was once that little child.
SHEPHERD. Damn you, hold your tongue!
OEDIPUS.   No more of that!
    It is your tongue needs watching, not this man's.
SHEPHERD. My King, my Master, what is it I have done wrong?
OEDIPUS. You have not answered his question about the boy.   *35*
SHEPHERD. He does not know . . . He is only making trouble . . .
OEDIPUS. Come, speak plainly, or it will go hard with you.
SHEPHERD. In God's name, do not torture an old man!
OEDIPUS. Come here, one of you; bind his arms behind him.

SHEPHERD. Unhappy king! What more do you wish to learn?   40
OEDIPUS. Did you give this man the child he speaks of?
SHEPHERD.   I did.
    And I would to God I had died that very day.
OEDIPUS. You will die now unless you speak the truth.
SHEPHERD. Yet if I speak the truth, I am worse than dead.
OEDIPUS. Very well; since you insist upon delaying—   45
SHEPHERD. No! I have told you already that I gave him the boy.
OEDIPUS. Where did you get him? From your house? From somewhere else?
SHEPHERD. Not from mine, no. A man gave him to me.
OEDIPUS. Is that man here? Do you know whose slave he was?
SHEPHERD. For God's love, my King, do not ask me any more!   50
OEDIPUS. You are a dead man if I have to ask you again.
SHEPHERD. Then . . . Then the child was from the palace of Laïos.
OEDIPUS. A slave child? or a child of his own line?
SHEPHERD. Ah, I am on the brink of dreadful speech!
OEDIPUS. And I of dreadful hearing. Yet I must hear.   55
SHEPHERD. If you must be told, then . . .
                                    They said it was Laïos' child,
    But it is your wife who can tell you about that.
OEDIPUS. My wife!—Did she give it to you?
SHEPHERD.   My lord, she did.
OEDIPUS. Do you know why?
SHEPHERD.   I was told to get rid of it.
OEDIPUS. An unspeakable mother!
SHEPHERD.   There had been prophecies . . .   60
OEDIPUS. Tell me.
SHEPHERD.   It was said that the boy would kill his own father.
OEDIPUS. Then why did you give him over to this old man?
SHEPHERD. I pitied the baby, my King,
    And I thought that this man would take him far away
    To his own country.
                  He saved him—but for what a fate!   65
    For if you are what this man says you are,
    No man living is more wretched than Oedipus.
OEDIPUS. Ah God!
          It was true!
                  All the prophecies!
                          —Now,
    O Light, may I look on you for the last time!   70
    I, Oedipus,
    Oedipus, damned in his birth, in his marriage damned,
    Damned in the blood he shed with his own hand!
He rushes into the palace.

Ode IV

CHORUS. Alas for the seed of men.   *Strophe 1*

What measure shall I give these generations
That breathe on the void and are void
And exist and do not exist?

Who bears more weight of joy   *5*
Than mass of sunlight shifting in images,
Or who shall make his thought stay on
That down time drifts away?

Your splendor is all fallen.

O naked brow of wrath and tears,   *10*
O change of Oedipus!
I who saw your days call no man blest—
Your great days like ghósts góne.

That mind was a strong bow.   *Antistrophe 1*
Deep, how deep you drew it then, hard archer,   *15*
At a dim fearful range,
And brought dear glory down!

You overcame the stranger—
The virgin with her hooking lion claws—
And though death sang, stood like a tower   *20*
To make pale Thebes take heart.

Fortress against our sorrow!

Divine king, giver of laws,
Majestic Oedipus!
No prince in Thebes had ever such renown,   *25*
No prince won such grace of power.

And now of all men ever known   *Strophe 2*
Most pitiful is this man's story:
His fortunes are most changed, his state
Fallen to a low slave's   *30*
Ground under bitter fate.

O Oedipus, most royal one!
The great door that expelled you to the light

Gave it night—ah, gave night to your glory:
As to the father, to the fathering son.   *35*

All understood too late.

How could that queen whom Laïos won,
The garden that he harrowed at his height,
Be silent when that act was done?

But all eyes fail before time's eye,   *Antistrophe 2* *40*
All actions come to justice there.
Though never willed, though far down the deep past,
Your bed, your dread sirings,
Are brought to book at last.
Child by Laïos doomed to die,   *45*
Then doomed to lose that fortunate little death,
Would God you never took breath in this air
That with my wailing lips I take to cry:

For I weep the world's outcast.

I was blind, and now I can tell why: *50*
Asleep, for you had given ease of breath
To Thebes, while the false years went by.

Exodos

Enter, from the palace, Second Messenger.

SECOND MESSENGER. Elders of Thebes, most honored in this land,
What horrors are yours to see and hear, what weight
Of sorrow to be endured, if, true to your birth,
You venerate the line of Labdakos!
I think neither Istros nor Phasis, those great rivers,   *5*
Could purify this place of the corruption
It shelters now, or soon must bring to light—
Evil not done unconsciously, but willed.

The greatest griefs are those we cause ourselves.
CHORAGOS. Surely, friend, we have grief enough already;   *10*
What new sorrow do you mean?
SECOND MESSENGER.   The Queen is dead.
CHORAGOS. Iocastê? Dead? But at whose hand?
SECOND MESSENGER.   Her own.
The full horror of what happened you cannot know,

For you did not see it; but I, who did, will tell you
As clearly as I can how she met her death.   *15*

When she had left us,
In passionate silence, passing through the court,
She ran to her apartment in the house,
Her hair clutched by the fingers of both hands.
She closed the doors behind her; then, by that bed   *20*
Where long ago the fatal son was conceived—
That son who should bring about his father's death—
We heard her call upon Laïos, dead so many years,
And heard her wail for the double fruit of her marriage,
A husband by her husband, children by her child.   *25*

Exactly how she died I do not know:
For Oedipus burst in moaning and would not let us
Keep vigil to the end: it was by him
As he stormed about the room that our eyes were caught.
From one to another of us he went, begging a sword,   *30*
Cursing the wife who was not his wife, the mother
Whose womb had carried his own children and himself.
I do not know: it was none of us aided him,
But surely one of the gods was in control!
For with a dreadful cry   *35*
He hurled his weight, as though wrenched out of himself,
At the twin doors: the bolts gave, and he rushed in.
And there we saw her hanging, her body swaying
From the cruel cord she had noosed about her neck.
A great sob broke from him heartbreaking to hear,   *40*
As he loosed the rope and lowered her to the ground.

I would blot out from my mind what happened next!
For the King ripped from her gown the golden brooches
That were her ornament, and raised them, and plunged them down
Straight into his own eyeballs, crying, "No more,   *45*
No more shall you look on the misery about me,
The horrors of my own doing! Too long you have known
The faces of those whom I should never have seen,
Too long been blind to those for whom I was searching!
From this hour, go in darkness!" And as he spoke,   *50*
He struck at his eyes—not once, but many times;
And the blood spattered his beard,
Bursting from his ruined sockets like red hail.
So from the unhappiness of two this evil has sprung,
A curse on the man and woman alike. The old   *55*

Happiness of the house of Labdakos
Was happiness enough: where is it today?
It is all wailing and ruin, disgrace, death—all
The misery of mankind that has a name—
And it is wholly and for ever theirs.   *60*

CHORAGOS. Is he in agony still? Is there no rest for him?

SECOND MESSENGER. He is calling for someone to lead him to the gates
So that all the children of Kadmos may look upon
His father's murderer, his mother's—no,
I cannot say it!
             And then he will leave Thebes,   *65*
Self-exiled, in order that the curse
Which he himself pronounced may depart from the house.
He is weak, and there is none to lead him,
So terrible is his suffering.
             But you will see:
Look, the doors are opening; in a moment   *70*
You will see a thing that would crush a heart of stone.

The central door is opened; Oedipus, blinded, is led in.

CHORAGOS. Dreadful indeed for men to see.
Never have my own eyes
Looked on a sight so full of fear.

Oedipus!   *75*
What madness came upon you, what daemon°
Leaped on your life with heavier
Punishment than a mortal man can bear?
No: I cannot even
Look at you, poor ruined one.   *80*
And I would speak, question, ponder,
If I were able. No.
You make me shudder.

OEDIPUS. God. God.
Is there a sorrow greater?   *85*
Where shall I find harbor in this world?
My voice is hurled far on a dark wind.
What has God done to me?

CHORAGOS. Too terrible to think of, or to see.

OEDIPUS. O cloud of night,   *Strophe 1*   *90*
Never to be turned away: night coming on,
I cannot tell how: night like a shroud!

---

76 daemon a spirit, not necessarily evil

My fair winds brought me here.
                                        Oh God. Again
The pain of the spikes where I had sight,
The flooding pain   *95*
Of memory, never to be gouged out.
CHORAGOS. This is not strange.
        You suffer it all twice over, remorse in pain,
        Pain in remorse.

OEDIPUS. Ah dear friend   *Antistrophe 1* *100*
        Are you faithful even yet, you alone?
        Are you still standing near me, will you stay here,
        Patient, to care for the blind?
                                        The blind man!
        Yet even blind I know who it is attends me,
        By the voice's tone—   *105*
        Though my new darkness hide the comforter.
CHORAGOS. Oh fearful act!
        What god was it drove you to rake black
        Night across your eyes?
OEDIPUS. Apollo. Apollo. Dear   *Strophe 2* *110*
        Children, the god was Apollo.
        He brought my sick, sick fate upon me.
        But the blinding hand was my own!
        How could I bear to see
        When all my sight was horror everywhere?   *115*
CHORAGOS. Everywhere; that is true.
OEDIPUS. And now what is left?
        Images? Love? A greeting even,
        Sweet to the senses? Is there anything?
        Ah, no, friends: lead me away.   *120*
        Lead me away from Thebes.
                                        Lead the great wreck
        And hell of Oedipus, whom the gods hate.
CHORAGOS. Your fate is clear, you are not blind to that.
        Would God you had never found it out!

OEDIPUS. Death take the man who unbound   *Antistrophe 2* *125*
        My feet on that hillside
        And delivered me from death to life! What life?
        If only I had died,
        This weight of monstrous doom
        Could not have dragged me and my darlings down.   *130*
CHORAGOS. I would have wished the same.

OEDIPUS. Oh never to have come here
    With my father's blood upon me! Never
    To have been the man they call his mother's husband!
    Oh accurst! O child of evil,   135
    To have entered that wretched bed—
                         the selfsame one!
    More primal than sin itself, this fell to me.
CHORAGOS. I do not know how I can answer you.
    You were better dead than alive and blind.
OEDIPUS. Do not counsel me any more. This punishment   140
    That I have laid upon myself is just.
    If I had eyes,
    I do not know how I could bear the sight
    Of my father, when I came to the house of Death,
    Or my mother: for I have sinned against them both   145
    So vilely that I could not make my peace
    By strangling my own life.
                  Or do you think my children,
    Born as they were born, would be sweet to my eyes?
    Ah never, never! Nor this town with its high walls,
    Nor the holy images of the gods.
                 For I,   150
    Thrice miserable—Oedipus, noblest of all the line
    Of Kadmos, have condemned myself to enjoy
    These things no more, by my own malediction
    Expelling that man whom the gods declared
    To be a defilement in the house of Laïos.   155
    After exposing the rankness of my own guilt,
    How could I look men frankly in the eyes?
    No, I swear it,
    If I could have stifled my hearing at its source,
    I would have done it and made all this body   160
    A tight cell of misery, blank to light and sound:
    So I should have been safe in a dark agony
    Beyond all recollection.
               Ah Kithairon!
    Why did you shelter me? When I was cast upon you,
    Why did I not die? Then I should never   165
    Have shown the world my execrable birth.

    Ah Polybos! Corinth, city that I believed
    The ancient seat of my ancestors: how fair
    I seemed, your child! And all the while this evil
    Was cancerous within me!

For I am sick   *170*
In my daily life, sick in my origin.

O three roads, dark ravine, woodland and way
Where three roads met: you, drinking my father's blood,
My own blood, spilled by my own hand: can you remember
The unspeakable things I did there, and the things   *175*
I went on from there to do?
                          O marriage, marriage!
The act that engendered me, and again the act
Performed by the son in the same bed—
                                    Ah, the net
Of incest, mingling fathers, brothers, sons,
With brides, wives, mothers: the last evil   *180*
That can be known by men: no tongue can say
How evil!
         No. For the love of God, conceal me
Somewhere far from Thebes; or kill me; or hurl me
Into the sea, away from men's eyes for ever.
Come, lead me. You need not fear to touch me.   *185*
Of all men, I alone can bear this guilt.

Enter Creon.

CHORAGOS. We are not the ones to decide; but Creon here
     May fitly judge of what you ask. He only
     Is left to protect the city in your place.
OEDIPUS. Alas, how can I speak to him? What right have I   *190*
     To beg his courtesy whom I have deeply wronged?
CREON. I have not come to mock you, Oedipus,
     Or to reproach you, either.
     (*To Attendants.*)   —You, standing there:
     If you have lost all respect for man's dignity,
     At least respect the flame of Lord Helios: *195*
     Do not allow this pollution to show itself
     Openly here, an affront to the earth
     And Heaven's rain and the light of day. No, take him
     Into the house as quickly as you can.
     For it is proper   *200*
     That only the close kindred see his grief.
OEDIPUS. I pray you in God's name, since your courtesy
     Ignores my dark expectation, visiting
     With mercy this man of all men most execrable:
     Give me what I ask—for your good, not for mine.   *205*
CREON. And what is it that you would have me do?

OEDIPUS. Drive me out of this country as quickly as may be
　　To a place where no human voice can ever greet me.
CREON. I should have done that before now—only,
　　God's will had not been wholly revealed to me.　　　　　　　210
OEDIPUS. But his command is plain: the parricide
　　Must be destroyed. I am that evil man.
CREON. That is the sense of it, yes; but as things are,
　　We had best discover clearly what is to be done.
OEDIPUS. You would learn more about a man like me?　　　　215
CREON. You are ready now to listen to the god.
OEDIPUS. I will listen. But it is to you.
　　That I must turn for help. I beg you, hear me.

　　The woman in there—
　　Give her whatever funeral you think proper:　　　　　　　220
　　She is your sister.
　　　　　　　　　—But let me go, Creon!
　　Let me purge my father's Thebes of the pollution
　　Of my living here, and go out to the wild hills,
　　To Kithairon, that has won such fame with me,
　　The tomb my mother and father appointed for me,　　　　225
　　And let me die there, as they willed I should.
　　And yet I know
　　Death will not ever come to me through sickness
　　Or in any natural way: I have been preserved
　　For some unthinkable fate. But let that be.　　　　　　　230
　　As for my sons, you need not care for them.
　　They are men, they will find some way to live.
　　But my poor daughters, who have shared my table,
　　Who never before have been parted from their father—
　　Take care of them, Creon; do this for me.　　　　　　　235
　　And will you let me touch them with my hands
　　A last time, and let us weep together?
　　Be kind, my lord,
　　Great prince, be kind!
　　　　　　　　Could I but touch them,
　　They would be mine again, as when I had my eyes.　　　　240

Enter Antigonê and Ismenê, attended.

　　Ah, God!
　　Is it my dearest children I hear weeping?
　　Has Creon pitied me and sent my daughters?
CREON. Yes, Oedipus: I knew that they were dear to you
　　In the old days, and know you must love them still.　　　245

OEDIPUS. May God bless you for this—and be a friendlier
    Guardian to you than he has been to me!

    Children, where are you?
    Come quickly to my hands: they are your brother's—
    Hands that have brought your father's once clear eyes   *250*
    To this way of seeing—
                         Ah dearest ones,
    I had neither sight nor knowledge then, your father
    By the woman who was the source of his life!
    And I weep for you—having no strength to see you—
    I weep for you when I think of the bitterness   *255*
    That men will visit upon you all your lives.
    What homes, what festivals can you attend
    Without being forced to depart again in tears?
    And when you come to marriageable age,
    Where is the man, my daughters, who would dare   *260*
    Risk the bane that lies on all my children?
    Is there any evil wanting? Your father killed
    His father; sowed the womb of her who bore him;
    Engendered you at the fount of his own existence!
    That is what they will say of you.
                                   Then, whom   *265*
    Can you ever marry? There are no bridegrooms for you,
    And your lives must wither away in sterile dreaming.
    O Creon, son of Menoikeus!
    You are the only father my daughters have,
    Since we, their parents, are both of us gone for ever.   *270*
    They are your own blood: you will not let them
    Fall into beggary and loneliness;
    You will keep them from the miseries that are mine!
    Take pity on them; see, they are only children,
    Friendless except for you. Promise me this,   *275*
    Great Prince, and give me your hand in token of it.

    Creon clasps his right hand.

    Children:
    I could say much, if you could understand me,
    But as it is, I have only this prayer for you:
    Live where you can, be as happy as you can—   *280*
    Happier, please God, than God has made your father!
CREON. Enough. You have wept enough. Now go within.
OEDIPUS. I must; but it is hard.
CREON.   Time eases all things.
OEDIPUS. But you must promise—

CREON.   Say what you desire.
OEDIPUS. Send me from Thebes!
CREON.   God grant that I may!   *285*
OEDIPUS. But since God hates me . . .
CREON.   No, he will grant your wish.
OEDIPUS. You promise?
CREON.   I cannot speak beyond my knowledge.
OEDIPUS. Then lead me in.
CREON.   Come now, and leave your children.
OEDIPUS. No! Do not take them from me!
CREON.   Think no longer
     That you are in command here, but rather think   *290*
     How, when you were, you served your own destruction.

*Exeunt into the house all but the Chorus; the Choragos chants directly
to the audience.*

CHORAGOS. Men of Thebes: look upon Oedipus.
     This is the king who solved the famous riddle
     And towered up, most powerful of men.
     No mortal eyes but looked on him with envy,   *295*
     Yet in the end ruin swept over him.
     Let every man in mankind's frailty
     Consider his last day; and let none
     Presume on his good fortune until he find
     Life, at his death, a memory without pain.   *300*

TOPICS FOR DISCUSSION AND WRITING

1. On the basis of the Prologue, characterize Oedipus. What additional
   traits are revealed in Scene I and Ode I?
2. How fair is it to say that Oedipus is morally guilty? Does he argue
   that he is morally innocent because he did not intend to do immoral
   deeds? Can it be said that he is guilty of *hubris* but that *hubris* has
   nothing to do with his fall?
3. Oedipus says that he blinds himself in order not to look upon people he should not. What further reasons can be given? Why does
   he not (like his mother) commit suicide?
4. How fair is it to say that the play shows the contemptibleness of
   man's efforts to act intelligently?
5. How fair is it to say that in *Oedipus* the gods are evil?
6. Are the choral odes lyrical interludes that serve to separate the scenes,
   or do they advance the dramatic action?
7. Matthew Arnold said that Sophocles saw life steadily and saw it
   whole. But in this play is Sophocles facing the facts of life, or, on

the contrary, is he avoiding life as it usually is and presenting a series of unnatural and outrageous coincidences?
8. Can you describe your emotions at the end of the play? Do they
   include pity for Oedipus? Pity for all human beings, including yourself? Fear that you might be punished for some unintended trans-
   gression? Awe, engendered by a perception of the interrelatedness
   of things? Relief that the story is only a story? Exhilaration?

Sophocles *(496?–406 B.C.)*

ANTIGONÊ

An English Version by Dudley Fitts and Robert Fitzgerald

List of Characters

ANTIGONÊ
ISMENÊ
EURYDICÊ
CREON
HAIMON
TEIRESIAS
A SENTRY
A MESSENGER
CHORUS

Scene.   *Before the palace of Creon, king of Thebes. A central double door, and
two lateral doors A platform extends the length of the facade, and from this platform
three steps lead down into the "orchestra," or chorus-ground.*

Time.   *Dawn of the day after the repulse of the Argive army from the assault
on Thebes.*

Prologue

Antigonê and Ismenê enter from the central door of the palace.

ANTIGONÊ. Ismenê, dear sister,
You would think that we had already suffered enough
For the curse on Oedipus.°

3 Oedipus, once King of Thebes, was the father of Antigonê and Ismenê, and of their
brothers Polyneicês and Eteoclês. Oedipus unwittingly killed his father, Laïos, and married
his own mother, Iocastê. When he learned what he had done, he blinded himself and left
Thebes. Eteoclês and Polyneicês quarreled. Polyneicês was driven out but returned to assault Thebes. In the battle each brother killed the other; Creon became king and ordered
that Polyneicês be left to rot unburied on the battlefield as a traitor.

The 1984 production of Antigonê at Cottesloe with Jane Lapotaire as Antigonê. Directed by John Burgess and Peter Gill. (Photo by Donald Cooper © PHOTOSTAGE.)

I cannot imagine any grief
That you and I have not gone through. And now—   5
Have they told you of the new decree of our King Creon?
ISMENÊ. I have heard nothing: I know
     That two sisters lost two brothers, a double death
     In a single hour; and I know that the Argive army
     Fled in the night; but beyond this, nothing.   10
ANTIGONÊ. I thought so. And that is why I wanted you
     To come out here with me. There is something we must do.
ISMENÊ. Why do you speak so strangely?
ANTIGONÊ. Listen, Ismenê:
     Creon buried our brother Eteoclês   15
     With military honors, gave him a soldier's funeral,
     And it was right that he should; but Polyneicês,
     Who fought as bravely and died as miserably,—
     They say that Creon has sworn
     No one shall bury him, no one mourn for him,   20
     But his body must lie in the fields, a sweet treasure
     For carrion birds to find as they search for food.
     That is what they say, and our good Creon is coming here
     To announce it publicly; and the penalty—
     Stoning to death in the public square!
                          There it is,   25
     And now you can prove what you are:
     A true sister, or a traitor to your family.
ISMENÊ. Antigonê, you are mad! What could I possibly do?
ANTIGONÊ. You must decide whether you will help me or not.
ISMENÊ. I do not understand you. Help you in what?   30
ANTIGONÊ. Ismenê, I am going to bury him. Will you come?
ISMENÊ. Bury him! You have just said the new law forbids it.
ANTIGONÊ. He is my brother. And he is your brother, too.
ISMENÊ. But think of the danger! Think what Creon will do!
ANTIGONÊ. Creon is not strong enough to stand in my way.   35
ISMENÊ. Ah sister!
     Oedipus died, everyone hating him
     For what his own search brought to light, his eyes
     Ripped out by his own hand; and Iocastê died,
     His mother and wife at once: she twisted the cords   40
     That strangled her life; and our two brothers died,
     Each killed by the other's sword. And we are left:
     But oh, Antigonê,
     Think how much more terrible than these
     Our own death would be if we should go against Creon   45
     And do what he has forbidden! We are only women,
     We cannot fight with men, Antigonê!

The law is strong, we must give in to the law
In this thing, and in worse. I beg the Dead
To forgive me, but I am helpless: I must yield   50
To those in authority. And I think it is dangerous business
To be always meddling.
ANTIGONÊ.   If that is what you think,
I should not want you, even if you asked to come.
You have made your choice, you can be what you want to be.
But I will bury him; and if I must die,   55
I say that this crime is holy: I shall lie down
With him in death, and I shall be as dear
To him as he to me.
                    It is the dead,
Not the living, who make the longest demands:
We die for ever . . .
                    You may do as you like,   60
Since apparently the laws of the gods mean nothing to you.
ISMENÊ. They mean a great deal to me; but I have no strength
To break laws that were made for the public good.
ANTIGONÊ. That must be your excuse, I suppose. But as for me,
I will bury the brother I love.
ISMENÊ.   Antigonê,   65
I am so afraid for you!
ANTIGONÊ.   You need not be:
You have yourself to consider, after all.
ISMENÊ. But no one must hear of this, you must tell no one!
I will keep it a secret, I promise!
ANTIGONÊ.   O tell it! Tell everyone!
Think how they'll hate you when it all comes out   70
If they learn that you knew about it all the time!
ISMENÊ. So fiery! You should be cold with fear.
ANTIGONÊ. Perhaps. But I am doing only what I must.
ISMENÊ. But can you do it? I say that you cannot.
ANTIGONÊ. Very well: when my strength gives out,
I shall do no more.   75
ISMENÊ. Impossible things should not be tried at all.
ANTIGONÊ. Go away, Ismenê:
I shall be hating you soon, and the dead will too,
For your words are hateful. Leave me my foolish plan:
I am not afraid of the danger; if it means death,   80
It will not be the worst of deaths—death without honor.
ISMENÊ. Go then, if you feel that you must.
You are unwise,
But a loyal friend indeed to those who love you.
Exit into the palace. Antigonê goes off, left. Enter the Chorus.

Párodos

CHORUS. Now the long blade of the sun, lying   *Strophe 1*
     Level east to west, touches with glory
     Thebes of the Seven Gates. Open, unlidded
     Eye of golden day! O marching light
     Across the eddy and rush of Dirce's stream,°   5
     Striking the white shields of the enemy
     Thrown headlong backward from the blaze of morning!
CHORAGOS.° Polyneicês their commander
     Roused them with windy phrases,
     He the wild eagle screaming   10
     Insults above our land,
     His wings their shields of snow,
     His crest their marshalled helms.

CHORUS. Against our seven gates in a yawning ring   *Antistrophe 1*
     The famished spears came onward in the night;   15
     But before his jaws were sated with our blood,
     Or pine fire took the garland of our towers,
     He was thrown back; and as he turned, great Thebes—
     No tender victim for his noisy power—
     Rose like a dragon behind him, shouting war.   20
CHORAGOS. For God hates utterly
     The bray of bragging tongues;
     And when he beheld their smiling,
     Their swagger of golden helms,
     The frown of his thunder blasted   25
     Their first man from our walls.

CHORUS. We heard his shout of triumph high in the air   *Strophe 2*
     Turn to a scream; far out in a flaming arc
     He fell with his windy torch, and the earth struck him.
     And others storming in fury no less than his   30
     Found shock of death in the dusty joy of battle.
CHORAGOS. Seven captains at seven gates
     Yielded their clanging arms to the god
     That bends the battle-line and breaks it.
     These two only, brothers in blood,   35
     Face to face in matchless rage,
     Mirroring each the other's death,
     Clashed in long combat.

5 Dircê's stream a stream west of Thebes   **8 Choragos** leader of the Chorus

CHORUS. But now in the beautiful morning of victory   *Antistrophe 2*
    Let Thebes of the many chariots sing for joy!   *40*
    With hearts for dancing we'll take leave of war:
    Our temples shall be sweet with hymns of praise,
    And the long nights shall echo with our chorus.

Scene I

CHORAGOS. But now at last our new King is coming:
    Creon of Thebes, Menoikeus' son.
    In this auspicious dawn of his rein
    What are the new complexities
    That shifting Fate has woven for him?   *5*
    What is his counsel? Why has he summoned
    The old men to hear him?

*Enter Creon from the palace, center. He addresses the Chorus from the
top step.*

CREON. Gentlemen: I have the honor to inform you that our Ship of State,
which recent storms have threatened to destroy, has come safely to
harbor at last, guided by the merciful wisdom of Heaven. I have   *10*
summoned you here this morning because I know that I can depend upon you: your devotion to King Lalos was absolute; you never
hesitated in your duty to our late ruler Oedipus; and when Oedipus
died, your loyalty was transferred to his children. Unfortunately, as
you know, his two sons, the princes Eteoclês and Polyneicês, have   *15*
killed each other in battle; and I, as the next in blood, have succeeded
to the full power of the throne.

    I am aware, of course, that no Ruler can expect complete loyalty
from his subjects until he has been tested in office. Nevertheless, I
say to you at the very outset that I have nothing but contempt for   *20*
the kind of Governor who is afraid, for whatever reason, to follow
the course that he knows is best for the State; and as for the man
who sets private friendship above the public welfare,—I have no use
for him, either. I call God to witness that if I saw my country headed
for ruin, I should not be afraid to speak out plainly; and I need hardly *25*
remind you that I would never have any dealings with an enemy
of the people. No one values friendship more highly than I; but we
must remember that friends made at the risk of wrecking our Ship
are not real friends at all.

    These are my principles, at any rate, and that is why I have   *30*
made the following decision concerning the sons of Oedipus: Eteoclês, who died as a man should die, fighting for his country, is to

be buried with full military honors, with all the ceremony that is usual when the greatest heroes die; but his brother Polyneicês, who broke his exile to come back with fire and sword against his native 35 city and the shrines of his fathers' gods, whose one idea was to spill the blood of his blood and sell his own people into slavery— Polyneicês, I say, is to have no burial: no man is to touch him or say the least prayer for him; he shall lie on the plain, unburied; and the birds and the scavenging dogs can do with him whatever they like. 40

> This is my command, and you can see the wisdom behind it. As long as I am King, no traitor is going to be honored with the loyal man. But whoever shows by word and deed that he is on the side of the State,—he shall have my respect while he is living and my reverence when he is dead. 45

CHORAGOS. If that is your will, Creon son of Menoikeus,
> You have the right to enforce it: we are yours.

CREON. That is my will. Take care that you do your part.

CHORAGOS. We are old men: let the younger ones carry it out.

CREON. I do not mean that: the sentries have been appointed. 50

CHORAGOS. Then what is it that you would have us do?

CREON. You will give no support to whoever breaks this law.

CHORAGOS. Only a crazy man is in love with death!

CREON. And death it is; yet money talks, and the wisest
> Have sometimes been known to count a few coins too many. 55

Enter Sentry from left.

SENTRY. I'll not say that I'm out of breath from running, King, because every time I stopped to think about what I have to tell you, I felt like going back. And all the time a voice kept saying, "You fool, don't you know you're walking straight into trouble?"; and then another voice: "Yes, but if you let somebody else get the news to 60 Creon first, it will be even worse than that for you!" But good sense won out, at least I hope it was good sense, and here I am with a story that makes no sense at all; but I'll tell it anyhow, because, as they say, what's going to happen's going to happen and—

CREON. Come to the point. What have you to say? 65

SENTRY. I did not do it. I did not see who did it. You must not punish me for what someone else has done.

CREON. A comprehensive defense! More effective, perhaps.
> If I knew its purpose. Come: what is it?

SENTRY. A dreadful thing . . . I don't know how to put it— 70

CREON. Out with it!

SENTRY.   Well, then;
> The dead man—
>   Polyneicês—

Pause. The Sentry is overcome, fumbles for words. Creon waits impassively.

                                                      out there —
                                                                      someone, —
New dust on the slimy flesh!

Pause. No sign from Creon.

Someone has given it burial that way, and
Gone . . .   75

Long pause. Creon finally speaks with deadly control.

CREON. And the man who dared do this?
SENTRY.   I swear I
Do not know! You must believe me!
                                                      Listen:
The ground was dry, not a sign of digging, no,
Not a wheeltrack in the dust, no trace of anyone.
It was when they relieved us this morning: and one of them,   80
The corporal, pointed to it.
                                            There it was,
The strangest —
                              Look:
The body, just mounded over with light dust: you see?
Not buried really, but as if they'd covered it
Just enough for the ghost's peace. And no sign   85
Of dogs or any wild animal that had been there.

And then what a scene there was! Every man of us
Accusing the other: we all proved the other man did it,
We all had proof that we could not have done it.
We were ready to take hot iron in our hands,   90
Walk through fire, swear by all the gods,
It was not I!
I do not know who it was, but it was not I!

*Creon's rage has been mounting steadily, but the Sentry is too intent
upon his story to notice it.*

And then, when this came to nothing, someone said
A thing that silenced us and made us stare   95
Down at the ground: you had to be told the news,
And one of us had to do it! We threw the dice,
And the bad luck fell to me. So here I am,
No happier to be here than you are to have me:
Nobody likes the man who brings bad news.   100

CHORAGOS. I have been wondering, King: can it be that the gods
    have done this?
CREON (*furiously*). Stop!
    Must you doddering wrecks
    Go out of your heads entirely? "The gods"!   *105*
    Intolerable!
    The gods favor this corpse? Why? How had he served them?
    Tried to loot their temples, burn their images,
    Yes, and the whole State, and its laws with it!
    Is it your senile opinion that the gods love to honor bad men?   *110*
    A pious thought!—
              No, from the very beginning
    There have been those who have whispered together,
    Stiff-necked anarchists, putting their heads together,
    Scheming against me in alleys. These are the men,
    And they have bribed my own guard to do this thing.   *115*
    (*Sententiously.*) Money!
    There's nothing in the world so demoralizing as money.
    Down go your cities,
    Homes gone, men gone, honest hearts corrupted,
    Crookedness of all kinds, and all for money!
    (*To Sentry.*)   But you—!   *120*
    I swear by God and by the throne of God,
    The man who has done this thing shall pay for it!
    Find that man, bring him here to me, or your death
    Will be the least of your problems: I'll string you up
    Alive, and there will be certain ways to make you   *125*
    Discover your employer before you die;
    And the process may teach you a lesson you seem to have
        missed:
    The dearest profit is sometimes all too dear:
    That depends on the source. Do you understand me?
    A fortune won is often misfortune.   *130*
SENTRY. King, may I speak?
CREON.   Your very voice distresses me.
SENTRY. Are you sure that it is my voice, and not your conscience?
CREON. By God, he wants to analyze me now!
SENTRY. It is not what I say, but what has been done, that hurts you.
CREON. You talk too much.
SENTRY.   Maybe; but I've done nothing.   *135*
CREON. Sold your soul for some silver: that's all you've done.
SENTRY. How dreadful it is when the right judge judges wrong!
CREON. Your figures of speech
    May entertain you now; but unless you bring me the man,
    You will get little profit from them in the end.   *140*

Exit Creon into the palace.

SENTRY. "Bring me the man"—!
    I'd like nothing better than bringing him the man!
    But bring him or not, you have seen the last of me here.
    At any rate, I am safe!   (*Exit Sentry.*)

Ode I

CHORUS. Numberless are the world's wonders, but none   *Strophe 1*
    More wonderful than man; the stormgray sea
    Yields to his prows, the huge crests bear him high;
    Earth, holy and inexhaustible, is graven
    With shining furrows where his plows have gone   5
    Year after year, the timeless labor of stallions.

    The lightboned birds and beasts that cling to cover,   *Antistrophe 1*
    The lithe fish lighting their reaches of dim water,
    All are taken, tamed in the net of his mind;
    The lion on the hill, the wild horse windy-maned,   10
    Resign to him; and his blunt yoke has broken
    The sultry shoulders of the mountain bull.

    Words also, and thought as rapid as air,!   *Strophe 2*
    He fashions to his good use; statecraft is his,
    And his the skill that deflects the arrows of snow,   15
    The spears of winter rain: from every wind
    He has made himself secure—from all but one:
    In the late wind of death he cannot stand.

    O clear intelligence, force beyond all measure!   *Antistrophe 2*
    O fate of man, working both good and evil!   20
    When the laws are kept, how proudly his city stands!
    When the laws are broken, what of his city then?
    Never may the anárchic man find rest at my hearth,
    Never be it said that my thoughts are his thoughts.

Scene II

Reenter Sentry leading Antigonê.

CHORAGOS. What does this mean? Surely this captive woman
    Is the Princess, Antigonê. Why should she be taken?
SENTRY. Here is the one who did it! We caught her
    In the very act of burying him.—Where is Creon?

CHORAGOS. Just coming from the house.

Enter Creon, center.

CREON.   What has happened?   5
    Why have you come back so soon?
SENTRY (*expansively*).   O King,
    A man should never be too sure of anything:
    I would have sworn
    That you'd not see me here again: your anger
    Frightened me so, and the things you threatened me with;   10
    But how could I tell then
    That I'd be able to solve the case so soon?
    No dice-throwing this time: I was only too glad to come!
    Here is this woman. She is the guilty one:
    We found her trying to bury him.   15
    Take her, then; question her; judge her as you will.
    I am through with the whole thing now, and glad of it.
CREON. But this is Antigonê! Why have you brought her here?
SENTRY. She was burying him, I tell you!
CREON (*severely*).   Is this the truth?
SENTRY. I saw her with my own eyes. Can I say more?   20
CREON. The details: come, tell me quickly!
SENTRY.   It was like this:
    After those terrible threats of yours, King,
    We went back and brushed the dust away from the body.
    The flesh was soft by now, and stinking,
    So we sat on a hill to windward and kept guard.   25
    No napping this time! We kept each other awake.
    But nothing happened until the white round sun
    Whirled in the center of the round sky over us:
    Then, suddenly,
    A storm of dust roared up from the earth, and the sky   30
    Went out, the plain vanished with all its trees
    In the stinging dark. We closed our eyes and endured it.
    The whirlwind lasted a long time, but it passed;
    And then we looked, and there was Antigonê!
    I have seen   35
    A mother bird come back to a stripped nest, heard
    Her crying bitterly a broken note or two
    For the young ones stolen. Just so, when this girl
    Found the bare corpse, and all her love's work wasted,
    She wept, and cried on heaven to damn the hands   40
    That had done this thing.
                     And then she brought more dust
    And sprinkled wine three times for her brother's ghost.

We ran and took her at once. She was not afraid,
Not even when we charged her with what she had done.
She denied nothing.
                              And this was a comfort to me,   *45*
And some uneasiness: for it is a good thing
To escape from death, but it is no great pleasure
To bring death to a friend.
                              Yet I always say
There is nothing so comfortable as your own safe skin!
CREON (*slowly, dangerously*). And you, Antigonê,   *50*
    You with your head hanging,—do you confess this thing?
ANTIGONÊ. I do. I deny nothing.
CREON (*to Sentry*).   You may go.   (*Exit Sentry.*)
    (*To Antigonê.*) Tell me, tell me briefly:
    Had you heard my proclamation touching this matter?
ANTIGONÊ. It was public. Could I help hearing it?   *55*
CREON. And yet you dared defy the law.
ANTIGONÊ. I dared.
    It was not God's proclamation. That final Justice
    That rules the world below makes no such laws.

    Your edict, King, was strong,
    But all your strength is weakness itself against   *60*
    The immortal unrecorded laws of God.
    They are not merely now: they were, and shall be,
    Operative for ever, beyond man utterly.

    I knew I must die, even without your decree:
    I am only mortal. And if I must die   *65*
    Now, before it is my time to die,
    Surely this is no hardship: can anyone
    Living, as I live, with evil all about me,
    Think Death less than a friend? This death of mine
    Is of no importance; but if I had left my brother   *70*
    Lying in death unburied, I should have suffered.
    Now I do not.
                    You smile at me. Ah Creon,
    Think me a fool, if you like; but it may well be
    That a fool convicts me of folly.
CHORAGOS. Like father, like daughter: both headstrong, deaf to reason!   *75*
    She has never learned to yield:
CREON.   She has much to learn.
    The inflexible heart breaks first, the toughest iron
    Cracks first, and the wildest horses bend their necks
    At the pull of the smallest curb.

Pride? In a slave?
This girl is guilty of a double insolence,   *80*
Breaking the given laws and boasting of it.
Who is the man here,
She or I, if this crime goes unpunished?
Sister's child, or more than sister's child,
Or closer yet in blood—she and her sister   *85*
Win bitter death for this!
(*To Servants.*)   Go, some of you,
Arrest Ismenê. I accuse her equally.
Bring her: you will find her sniffling in the house there.

Her mind's a traitor: crimes kept in the dark
Cry for light, and the guardian brain shudders;   *90*
But how much worse than this
Is brazen boasting of barefaced anarchy!
ANTIGONÊ. Creon, what more do you want than my death?
CREON.   Nothing.
That gives me everything.
ANTIGONÊ.   Then I beg you: kill me.
This talking is a great weariness: your words   *95*
Are distasteful to me, and I am sure that mine
Seem so to you. And yet they should not seem so:
I should have praise and honor for what I have done.
All these men here would praise me
Were their lips not frozen shut with fear of you.   *100*
(*Bitterly.*) Ah the good fortune of kings,
Licensed to say and do whatever they please!
CREON. You are alone here in that opinion.
ANTIGONÊ. No, they are with me. But they keep their tongues in
          leash.
CREON. Maybe. But you are guilty, and they are not.   *105*
ANTIGONÊ. There is no guilt in reverence for the dead.
CREON. But Eteoclês—was he not your brother too?
ANTIGONÊ. My brother too.
CREON.   And you insult his memory?
ANTIGONÊ (*softly*). The dead man would not say that I insult it.
CREON. He would: for you honor a traitor as much as him.   *110*
ANTIGONÊ. His own brother, traitor or not, and equal in blood.
CREON. He made war on his country. Eteoclês defended it.
ANTIGONÊ. Nevertheless, there are honors due all the dead.
CREON. But not the same for the wicked as for the just.
ANTIGONÊ. Ah Creon, Creon,   *115*
     Which of us can say what the gods hold wicked?
CREON. An enemy is an enemy, even dead.

ANTIGONÊ. It is my nature to join in love, not hate.

CREON (_finally losing patience_). Go join them then; if you must have
   your love,
   Find it in hell!   120

CHORAGOS. But see, Ismenê comes:

   Enter Ismenê, guarded.

   Those tears are sisterly, the cloud
   That shadows her eyes rains down gentle sorrow.

CREON. You too, Ismenê,
   Snake in my ordered house, sucking my blood   125
   Stealthily—and all the time I never knew
   That these two sisters were aiming at my throne!

                                                             Ismenê,
   Do you confess your share in this crime, or deny it?
   Answer me.

ISMENÊ. Yes, if she will let me say so. I am guilty.   130

ANTIGONÊ (_coldly_). No, Ismenê. You have no right to say so.
   You would not help me, and I will not have you help me.

ISMENÊ. But now I know what you meant; and I am here
   To join you, to take my share of punishment.

ANTIGONÊ. The dead man and the gods who rule the dead   135
   Know whose act this was. Words are not friends.

ISMENÊ. Do you refuse me, Antigonê? I want to die with you:
   I too have a duty that I must discharge to the dead.

ANTIGONÊ. You shall not lessen my death by sharing it.

ISMENÊ. What do I care for life when you are dead?   140

ANTIGONÊ. Ask Creon. You're always hanging on his opinions.

ISMENÊ. You are laughing at me. Why, Antigonê?

ANTIGONÊ. It's a joyless laughter, Ismenê.

ISMENÊ.   But can I do nothing?

ANTIGONÊ. Yes. Save yourself. I shall not envy you.
   There are those who will praise you; I shall have honor, too.   145

ISMENÊ. But we are equally guilty!

ANTIGONÊ.   No more, Ismenê.
   You are alive, but I belong to Death.

CREON (_to the Chorus_). Gentlemen, I beg you to observe these girls:
   One has just now lost her mind; the other,
   It seems, has never had a mind at all.   150

ISMENÊ. Grief teaches the steadiest minds to waver, King.

CREON. Yours certainly did, when you assumed guilt with the guilty!

ISMENÊ. But how could I go on living without her?

CREON.   You are.
   She is already dead.

ISMENÊ.   But your own son's bride!

CREON. There are places enough for him to push his plow.   *155*
    I want no wicked women for my sons!
ISMENÊ. O dearest Haimon, how your father wrongs you!
CREON. I've had enough of your childish talk of marriage!
CHORAGOS. Do you really intend to steal this girl from your son?
CREON. No; Death will do that for me.
CHORAGOS.   Then she must die?   *160*
CREON (*ironically.*) You dazzle me.
                    —But enough of this talk!
    (*To Guards.*) You, there, take them away and guard them well:
For they are but women, and even brave men run
When they see Death coming.
                 Exeunt Ismenê, Antigonê, and Guards.

Ode II

CHORUS. Fortunate is the man who has never tasted God's
       vengeance!   *Strophe 1*
    Where once the anger of heaven has struck, that house is
       shaken
    For ever: damnation rises behind each child
    Like a wave cresting out of the black northeast,
    When the long darkness under sea roars up   *5*
    And bursts drumming death upon the windwhipped sand.

    I have seen this gathering sorrow from time   *Antistrophe 1*
       long past
    Loom upon Oedipus' children: generation from generation
    Takes the compulsive rage of the enemy god.
    So lately this last flower of Oedipus' line   *10*
    Drank the sunlight! but now a passionate word
    And a handful of dust have closed up all its beauty.

        What mortal arrogance   *Strophe 2*
        Transcends the wrath of Zeus?
    Sleep cannot lull him nor the effortless long months   *15*
    Of the timeless gods: but he is young for ever,
    And his house is the shining day of high Olympos.
        All that is and shall be,
        And all the past, is his.
    No pride on earth is free of the curse of heaven.   *20*

    The straying dreams of men   *Antistrophe 2*
       May bring them ghosts of joy:

But as they drowse, the waking embers burn them;
Or they walk with fixed eyes, as blind men walk.
But the ancient wisdom speaks for our own time: 25
    Fate works most for woe
    With Folly's fairest show.
Man's little pleasure is the spring of sorrow.

Scene III

CHORAGOS. But here is Haimon, King, the last of all your sons.
    Is it grief for Antigonê that brings him here,
    And bitterness at being robbed of his bride?

    Enter Haimon.

CREON. We shall soon see, and no need of diviners.
                              —Son,
    You have heard my final judgment on that girl: 5
    Have you come here hating me, or have you come
    With deference and with love, whatever I do?
HAIMON. I am your son, father. You are my guide.
    You make things clear for me, and I obey you.
    No marriage means more to me than your continuing wisdom.   10
CREON. Good. That is the way to behave: subordinate
    Everything else, my son, to your father's will.
    This is what a man prays for, that he may get
    Sons attentive and dutiful in his house,
    Each one hating his father's enemies,   15
    Honoring his father's friends. But if his sons
    Fail him, if they turn out unprofitably,
    What has he fathered but trouble for himself
    And amusement for the malicious?

                           So you are right
    Not to lose your head over this woman.
    Your pleasure with her would soon grow cold, Haimon,   20
    And then you'd have a hellcat in bed and elsewhere.
    Let her find her husband in Hell!
    Of all the people in this city, only she
    Has had contempt for my law and broken it.   25

    Do you want me to show myself weak before the people?
    Or to break my sworn word? No, and I will not.
    The woman dies.
    I suppose she'll plead "family ties." Well, let her.
    If I permit my own family to rebel,   30
    How shall I earn the world's obedience?

Show me the man who keeps his house in hand,
He's fit for public authority.
                I'll have no dealings
With lawbreakers, critics of the government:
Whoever is chosen to govern should be obeyed—   *35*
Must be obeyed, in all things, great and small,
Just and unjust! O Haimon,
The man who knows how to obey, and that man only,
Knows how to give commands when the time comes.
You can depend on him, no matter how fast   *40*
The spears come: he's a good soldier, he'll stick it out.

Anarchy, anarchy! Show me a greater evil!
This is why cities tumble and the great houses rain down,
This is what scatters armies!
No, no: good lives are made so by discipline.   *45*
We keep the laws then, and the lawmakers,
And no woman shall seduce us. If we must lose,
Let's lose to a man, at least! Is a woman stronger than we?
CHORAGOS. Unless time has rusted my wits,
     What you say, King, is said with point and dignity.   *50*
HAIMON (*boyishly earnest*). Father:
Reason is God's crowning gift to man, and you are right
To warn me against losing mine. I cannot say—
I hope that I shall never want to say!—that you
Have reasoned badly. Yet there are other men   *55*
Who can reason, too; and their opinions might be helpful.
You are not in a position to know everything
That people say or do, or what they feel:
Your temper terrifies—everyone
Will tell you only what you like to hear.   *60*
But I, at any rate, can listen; and I have heard them
Muttering and whispering in the dark about this girl.
They say no woman has ever, so unreasonably,
Died so shameful a death for a generous act:
"She covered her brother's body. Is this indecent?   *65*
She kept him from dogs and vultures. Is this a crime?
Death?—She should have all the honor that we can give her!"

This is the way they talk out there in the city.

You must believe me:
Nothing is closer to me than your happiness.   *70*
What could be closer? Must not any son
Value his father's fortune as his father does his?

I beg you, do not be unchangeable:
Do not believe that you alone can be right.
The man who thinks that,   *75*
The man who maintains that only he has the power
To reason correctly, the gift to speak, the soul—
A man like that, when you know him, turns out empty.

It is not reason never to yield to reason!

In flood time you can see how some trees bend,   *80*
And because they bend, even their twigs are safe,
While stubborn trees are torn up, roots and all.
And the same thing happens in sailing:
Make your sheet fast, never slacken,—and over you go,
Head over heels and under: and there's your voyage.   *85*
Forget you are angry! Let yourself be moved!
I know I am young; but please let me say this:
The ideal condition
Would be, I admit, that men should be right by instinct;
But since we are all too likely to go astray,   *90*
The reasonable thing is to learn from those who can teach.
CHORAGOS. You will do well to listen to him, King,
    If what he says is sensible. And you, Haimon,
    Must listen to your father.—Both speak well.
CREON. You consider it right for a man of my years and experience   *95*
    To go to school to a boy?
HAIMON.   It is not right
    If I am wrong. But if I am young, and right,
    What does my age matter?
CREON. You think it right to stand up for an anarchist?
HAIMON. Not at all. I pay no respect to criminals.   *100*
CREON. Then she is not a criminal?
HAIMON. The City would deny it, to a man.
CREON. And the City proposes to teach me how to rule?
HAIMON. Ah. Who is it that's talking like a boy now?
CREON. My voice is the one voice giving orders in this City!   *105*
HAIMON. It is no City if it takes orders from one voice.
CREON. The State is the King!
HAIMON.   Yes, if the State is a desert.

    Pause.

CREON. This boy, it seems, has sold out to a woman.
HAIMON. If you are a woman: my concern is only for you.
CREON. So? Your "concern"! In a public brawl with your father!   *110*
HAIMON. How about you, in a public brawl with justice?

CREON. With justice, when all that I do is within my rights?
HAIMON. You have no right to trample on God's right.
CREON (*completely out of control*). Fool, adolescent fool! Taken in by a
      woman!
HAIMON. You'll never see me taken in by anything vile.   115
CREON. Every word you say is for her!
HAIMON (*quietly, darkly*).   And for you.
    And for me. And for the gods under the earth.
CREON. You'll never marry her while she lives.
HAIMON. Then she must die.—But her death will cause another.
CREON. Another?   120
    Have you lost your senses? Is this an open threat?
HAIMON. There is no threat in speaking to emptiness.
CREON. I swear you'll regret this superior tone of yours!
    You are the empty one!
HAIMON.   If you were not my father,
    I'd say you were perverse.   125
CREON. You girlstruck fool, don't play at words with me!
HAIMON. I am sorry. You prefer silence.
CREON.   Now, by God—!
    I swear, by all the gods in heaven above us,
    You'll watch it, I swear you shall!
    (*To the Servants*)   Bring her out!
    Bring the woman out! Let her die before his eyes!   130
    Here, this instant, with her bridegroom beside her!
HAIMON. Not here, no; she will not die here, King.
    And you will never see my face again.
    Go on raving as long as you've a friend to endure you.

                            (*Exit Haimon.*)

CHORAGOS. Gone, gone.   135
    Creon, a young man in a rage is dangerous!
CREON. Let him do, or dream to do, more than a man can.
    He shall not save these girls from death.
CHORAGOS.   These girls?
    You have sentenced them both?
CREON.   No, you are right.
    I will not kill the one whose hands are clean.   140
CHORAGOS. But Antigonê?
CREON (*somberly*).   I will carry her far away
    Out there in the wilderness, and lock her
    Living in a vault of stone. She shall have food,
    As the custom is, to absolve the State of her death.
    And there let her pray to the gods of hell: 145
    They are her only gods:

Perhaps they will show her an escape from death,
Or she may learn,
                        though late,
That piety shown the dead is pity in vain.   (*Exit Creon.*)

Ode III

CHORUS. Love, unconquerable   *Strophe*
    Waster of rich men, keeper
    Of warm lights and all-night vigil
    In the soft face of a girl:
    Sea-wanderer, forest-visitor!   *5*
    Even the pure Immortals cannot escape you,
    And mortal man, in his one day's dusk,
    Trembles before your glory.

    Surely you swerve upon ruin   *Antistrophe*
    The just man's consenting heart,   *10*
    As here you have made bright anger
    Strike between father and son—
    And none has conquered but Love!
    A girl's glánce wórking the will of heaven:
    Pleasure to her alone who mocks us,   *15*
    Merciless Aphrodite.°

Scene IV

CHORAGOS (*as Antigonê enters guarded*). But I can no longer stand in
        awe of this,
    Nor, seeing what I see, keep back my tears.
    Here is Antigonê, passing to that chamber
    Where all find sleep at last.

ANTIGONÊ. Look upon me, friends, and pity me   *Strophe 1* *5*
    Turning back at the night's edge to say
    Good-by to the sun that shines for me no longer;
    Now sleepy Death
    Summons me down to Acheron,° that cold shore:
    There is no bridesong there, nor any music.   *10*

Ode III. **16 Aphroditê** goddess of love
Scene IV. **9 Acheron** a river of the underworld, which was ruled by Hades

CHORUS. Yet not unpraised, not without a kind of honor,
    You walk at last into the underworld;
    Untouched by sickness, broken by no sword.
    What woman has ever found your way to death?

ANTIGONÊ. How often I have heard the story of Niobê,°   *Antistrophe 1* **15**
    Tantalos' wretched daughter, how the stone
    Clung fast about her, ivy-close: and they say
    The rain falls endlessly
    And sifting soft snow; her tears are never done.
    I feel the loneliness of her death in mine.   **20**
CHORUS. But she was born of heaven, and you
    Are woman, woman-born. If her death is yours,
    A mortal woman's, is this not for you
    Glory in our world and in the world beyond?

ANTIGONÊ. You laugh at me. Ah, friends, friends,   *Strophe 2* **25**
    Can you not wait until I am dead? O Thebes,
    O men many-charioted, in love with Fortune,
    Dear springs of Dircê, sacred Theban grove,
    Be witnesses for me, denied all pity,
    Unjustly judged! and think a word of love   **30**
    For her whose path turns
    Under dark earth, where there are no more tears.
CHORUS. You have passed beyond human daring and come at last
    Into a place of stone where Justice sits.
    I cannot tell   **35**
    What shape of your father's guilt appears in this.

ANTIGONÊ. You have touched it at last: that bridal bed   *Antistrophe 2*
    Unspeakable, horror of son and mother mingling:
    Their crime, infection of all our family!
    O Oedipus, father and brother!   **40**
    Your marriage strikes from the grave to murder mine.
    I have been a stranger here in my own land:
    All my life
    The blasphemy of my birth has followed me.
CHORUS. Reverence is a virtue, but strength   **45**
    Lives in established law: that must prevail.
    You have made your choice,
    Your death is the doing of your conscious hand.

---

15 Niobê Niobê boasted of her numerous children, provoking Leto, the mother of Apollo, to destroy them. Niobê wept profusely, and finally was turned into a stone on Mount Sipylus, whose streams are her tears.

ANTIGONÊ. Then let me go, since all your words are bitter,   *Epode*
    And the very light of the sun is cold to me.   50
    Lead me to my vigil, where I must have
    Neither love nor lamentation; no song, but silence.

    Creon interrupts impatiently.

CREON. If dirges and planned lamentations could put off death,
    Men would be singing for ever.
    (*To the Servants.*)   Take her, go!
    You know your orders: take her to the vault   55
    And leave her alone there. And if she lives or dies,
    That's her affair, not ours: our hands are clean.

ANTIGONÊ. O tomb, vaulted bride-bed in eternal rock,
    Soon I shall be with my own again
    Where Persephonê° welcomes the thin ghosts underground: 60
    And I shall see my father again, and you, mother,
    And dearest Polyneicês—
                    dearest indeed
    To me, since it was my hand
    That washed him clean and poured the ritual wine:
    And my reward is death before my time!   65

    And yet, as men's hearts know, I have done no wrong,
    I have not sinned before God. Or if I have,
    I shall know the truth in death. But if the guilt
    Lies upon Creon who judged me, then, I pray,
    May his punishment equal my own.
CHORAGOS. O passionate heart,   70
    Unyielding, tormented still by the same winds!
CREON. Her guards shall have good cause to regret their delaying.
ANTIGONÊ. Ah! That voice is like the voice of death!
CREON. I can give you no reason to think you are mistaken.
ANTIGONÊ. Thebes, and you my fathers' gods,   75
    And rulers of Thebes, you see me now, the last
    Unhappy daughter of a line of kings,
    Your kings, led away to death. You will remember
    What things I suffer, and at what men's hands,
    Because I would not transgress the laws of heaven.   80
    (*To the Guards, simply.*) Come: let us wait no longer.

                    (*Exit Antigonê, left, guarded.*)

60 Persephonê queen of the underworld

Ode IV

CHORUS. All Danaê's beauty was locked away   *Strophe 1*
    In a brazen cell where the sunlight could not come:
    A small room still as any grave, enclosed her.
    Yet she was a princess too,
    And Zeus in a rain of gold poured love upon her.   *5*
    O child, child,
    No power in wealth or war
    Or tough sea-blackened ships
    Can prevail against untiring Destiny!

    And Dryas' son° also, that furious king,   *Antistrophe 1* *10*
    Bore the god's prisoning anger for his pride:
    Sealed up by Dionysos in deaf stone,
    His madness died among echoes.
    So at the last he learned what dreadful power
    His tongue had mocked: *15*
    For he had profaned the revels,
    And fired the wrath of the nine
    Implacable Sisters° that love the sound of the flute.

    And old men tell a half-remembered tale   *Strophe 2*
    Of horror where a dark ledge splits the sea   *20*
    And a double surf beats on the gráy shóres:
    How a king's new woman,° sick
    With hatred for the queen he had imprisoned,
    Ripped out his two sons' eyes with her bloody hands
    While grinning Arês° watched the shuttle plunge   *25*
    Four times: four blind wounds crying for revenge,

    Crying, tears and blood mingled.— Piteously born,   *Antistrophe 2*
    Those sons whose mother was of heavenly birth!
    Her father was the god of the North Wind
    And she was cradled by gales,   *30*
    She raced with young colts on the glittering hills
    And walked untrammeled in the open light:
    But in her marriage deathless Fate found means
    To build a tomb like yours for all her joy.

---

10 Dyras' son Lycurgus, King of Thrace   **18 Sisters** the Muses   **22 king's new woman**
Eidothea, second wife of King Phineus, blinded her stepsons. Their mother, Cleopatra. had
beenimprisoned in a cave. Phineus was the son of a king, and Cleopatra, his first wife, was
the daughter of Boreas, the North wind, but this illustrious ancestry could not protect his
sons from violence and darkness.   **25 Arês** god of war

Scene V

Enter blind Teiresias, led by a boy. The opening speeches of Teiresias should be in singsong contrast to the realistic lines of Creon.

TEIRESIAS. This is the way the blind man comes, Princes,
       Princes,
Lock-step, two heads lit by the eyes of one.
CREON. What new thing have you to tell us, old Teiresias?
TEIRESIAS. I have much to tell you: listen to the prophet, Creon.
CREON. I am not aware that I have ever failed to listen.   *5*
TEIRESIAS. Then you have done wisely, King, and ruled well.
CREON. I admit my debt to you. But what have you to say?
TEIRESIAS. This, Creon: you stand once more on the edge of fate.
CREON. What do you mean? Your words are a kind of dread.
TEIRESIAS. Listen, Creon: *10*
    I was sitting in my chair of augury, at the place
    Where the birds gather about me. They were all a-chatter,
    As is their habit, when suddenly I heard
    A strange note in their jangling, a scream, a
    Whirring fury; I knew that they were fighting,   *15*
    Tearing each other, dying
    In a whirlwind of wings clashing. And I was afraid.
    I began the rites of burnt-offering at the altar,
    But Hephaistos° failed me: instead of bright flame,
    There was only the sputtering slime of the fat thigh-flesh   *20*
    Melting: the entrails dissolved in gray smoke,
    The bare bone burst from the welter. And no blaze!

    This was a sign from heaven. My boy described it,
    Seeing for me as I see for others.

    I tell you, Creon, you yourself have brought   *25*
    This new calamity upon us. Our hearths and altars
    Are stained with the corruption of dogs and carrion birds
    That glut themselves on the corpse of Oedipus' son.
    The gods are deaf when we pray to them, their fire
    Recoils from our offering, their birds of omen   *30*
    Have no cry of comfort, for they are gorged
    With the thick blood of the dead.
                         O my son,
    These are no trifles! Think: all men make mistakes,

19 Hephaistos god of fire

But a good man yields when he knows his course is wrong,
And repairs the evil. The only crime is pride.   *35*
Give in to the dead man, then: do not fight with a corpse—
What glory is it to kill a man who is dead?
Think, I beg you:
It is for your own good that I speak as I do.
You should be able to yield for your own good.   *40*

CREON. It seems that prophets have made me their especial province.
      All my life long
      I have been a kind of butt for the dull arrows
      Of doddering fortune-tellers!
                              No, Teiresias:
      If your birds—if the great eagles of God himself   *45*
      Should carry him stinking bit by bit to heaven,
      I would not yield. I am not afraid of pollution:
      No man can defile the gods.
                              Do what you will,
      Go into business, make money, speculate
      In India gold or that synthetic gold from Sardis,   *50*
      Get rich otherwise than by my consent to bury him.
      Teiresias, it is a sorry thing when a wise man
      Sells his wisdom, lets out his words for hire!

TEIRESIAS. Ah Creon! Is there no man left in the world—
CREON. To do what?—Come, let's have the aphorism!   *55*
TEIRESIAS. No man who knows that wisdom outweighs any wealth?
CREON. As surely as bribes are baser than any baseness.
TEIRESIAS. You are sick, Creon! You are deathly sick!
CREON. As you say: it is not my place to challenge a prophet.
TEIRESIAS. Yet you have said my prophecy is for sale.   *60*
CREON. The generation of prophets has always loved gold.
TEIRESIAS. The generation of kings has always loved brass.
CREON. You forget yourself! You are speaking to your King.
TEIRESIAS. I know it. You are a king because of me.
CREON. You have a certain skill; but you have sold out.   *65*
TEIRESIAS. King, you will drive me to words that—
CREON.   Say them, say them!
      Only remember: I will not pay you for them.
TEIRESIAS. No, you will find them too costly.
CREON.   No doubt. Speak:
      Whatever you say, you will not change my will.
TEIRESIAS. Then take this, and take it to heart!   *70*
      The time is not far off when you shall pay back
      Corpse for corpse, flesh of your own flesh.
      You have thrust the child of this world into living night,

You have kept from the gods below the child that is theirs:
The one in a grave before her death, the other,   75
Dead, denied the grave. This is your crime:
And the Furies and the dark gods of Hell
Are swift with terrible punishment for you.

Do you want to buy me now, Creon?

                            Not many days,
And your house will be full of men and women weeping,   80
And curses will be hurled at you from far
Cities grieving for sons unburied, left to rot
Before the walls of Thebes.

These are my arrows, Creon: they are all for you.

(*To Boy*) But come, child: lead me home.   85
Let him waste his fine anger upon younger men.
Maybe he will learn at last
To control a wiser tongue in a better head.   (*Exit Teiresias.*)
CHORAGOS. The old man has gone, King, but his words
    Remain to plague us. I am old, too,   90
    But I cannot remember that he was ever false.
CREON. That is true. . . . It troubles me.
    Oh it is hard to give in! but it is worse
    To risk everything for stubborn pride.
CHORAGOS. Creon: take my advice.
CREON.   What shall I do?   95
CHORAGOS. Go quickly: free Antigonê from her vault
    And build a tomb for the body of Polyneicês.
CREON. You would have me do this!
CHORAGOS.   Creon, yes!
    And it must be done at once: God moves
    Swiftly to cancel the folly of stubborn men.   100
CREON. It is hard to deny the heart! But I
    Will do it: I will not fight with destiny.
CHORAGOS. You must go yourself, you cannot leave it to others.
CREON. I will go.
           —Bring axes, servants: Come with me to the tomb.
       I buried her, I   105
Will set her free.
           Oh quickly! My mind misgives—
The laws of the gods are mighty, and a man must serve them
To the last day of his life!   (*Exit Creon.*)

Paean°

CHORAGOS. God of many names   *Strophe 1*
CHORUS.   O Iacchos
                     son
    of Kadmeian Sémelê
           O born of the Thunder!
    Guardian of the West
           Regent
    of Eleusis' plain
           O Prince of maenad Thebes
    and the Dragon Field by rippling Ismenós:°   5

CHORAGOS. God of many names   *Antistrophe 1*
CHORUS.   the flame of torches
    flares on our hills
           the nymphs of Iacchos
    dance at the spring of Castalia:°
    from the vine-close mountain
           come ah come in ivy:
    Evohé evohé! sings through the streets of Thebes   10

CHORAGOS. God of many names   *Strophe 2*
CHORUS.   Iacchos of Thebes
    heavenly Child
           of Sémelê bride of the Thunderer!
    The shadow of plague is upon us:
               come
    with clement feet
           oh come from Parnasos
    down the long slopes
           across the lamenting water   15

CHORAGOS. Iô Fire! Chorister of the throbbing stars!   *Antistrophe 2*
    O purest among the voices of the night!
    Thou son of God, blaze for us!
CHORUS. Come with choric rapture of circling Maenads
    Who cry *Iô Iacche!*
           God of many names!   20

Paean a hymn (here dedicated to Iacchos, also called Dionysos. His father was Zeus, his mother was Sémelê, daughter of Kadmos. Iacchos's worshipers were the Maenads, whose cry was "*Evohé evohé.*"   **5 Ismenós** a river east of Thebes. From a dragon's teeth, sown near the river, there sprang men who became the ancestors of the Theban nobility.   **8 Castalia** a spring on Mount Parnasos

Exodos

Enter Messenger from left.

MESSENGER. Men of the line of Kadmos,° you who live
    Near Amphion's citadel,°
               I cannot say
    Of any condition of human life "This is fixed,
    This is clearly good, or bad." Fate raises up,
    And Fate casts down the happy and unhappy alike: 5
    No man can foretell his Fate.
                    Take the case of Creon:
    Creon was happy once, as I count happiness:
    Victorious in battle, sole governor of the land,
    Fortunate father of children nobly born.
    And now it has all gone from him! Who can say   10
    That a man is still alive when his life's joy fails?
    He is a walking dead man. Grant him rich,
    Let him live like a king in his great house:
    If his pleasure is gone, I would not give
    So much as the shadow of smoke for all he owns.   15
CORAGOS. Your words hint at sorrow: what is your news for us?
MESSENGER. They are dead. The living are guilty of their death.
CHORAGOS. Who is guilty? Who is dead? Speak!
MESSENGER.   Haimon.
    Haimon is dead; and the hand that killed him
    Is his own hand.
CHORAGOS. His father's? or his own?   20
MESSENGER. His own, driven mad by the murder his father had
    done.
CHORAGOS. Teiresias, Teiresias, how clearly you saw it all!
MESSENGER. This is my news: you must draw what conclusions
    you can from it.
CHORAGOS. But look: Eurydicê, our Queen:
    Has she overheard us?   25

Enter Eurydicê from the palace, center.

EURYDICÊ. I have heard something, friends:
    As I was unlocking the gate of Pallas'° shrine,
    For I needed her help today, I heard a voice

---

1 Kadmos, who sowed the dragon's teeth, was founder of Thebes. **2 Amphion's
citadel** Amphion played so sweetly on his lyre that he charmed stones to form a wall around
Thebes. **27 Pallas** Pallas Athene, goddess of wisdom

Telling of some new sorrow. And I fainted
There at the temple with all my maidens about me.   *30*
But speak again: whatever it is, I can bear it:
Grief and I are no strangers.
MESSENGER.   Dearest Lady,
I will tell you plainly all that I have seen.
I shall not try to comfort you: what is the use,
Since comfort could lie only in what is not true?   *35*
The truth is always best.
                        I went with Creon
To the outer plain where Polyneicês was lying,
No friend to pity him, his body shredded by dogs.
We made our prayers in that place to Hecatê
And Pluto,° that they would be merciful. And we bathed   *40*
The corpse with holy water, and we brought
Fresh-broken branches to burn what was left of it,
And upon the urn we heaped up a towering barrow
Of the earth of his own land.
                        When we were done, we ran
To the vault where Antigonê lay on her couch of stone.   *45*
One of the servants had gone ahead,
And while he was yet far off he heard a voice
Grieving within the chamber, and he came back
And told Creon. And as the King went closer,
The air was full of wailing, the words lost,   *50*
And he begged us to make all haste. "Am I a prophet?"
He said, weeping, "And must I walk this road,
The saddest of all that I have gone before?
My son's voice calls me on. Oh quickly, quickly!
Look through the crevice there, and tell me   *55*
If it is Haimon, or some deception of the gods!"

We obeyed; and in the cavern's farthest corner
We saw her lying:
She had made a noose of her fine linen veil
And hanged herself. Haimon lay beside her,   *60*
His arms about her waist, lamenting her,
His love lost under ground, crying out
That his father had stolen her away from him.

---

40 Hecatê / And Pluto Hecatê and Pluto (also known as Hades) were deities of the underworld.

When Creon saw him the tears rushed to his eyes
And he called to him: "What have you done, child? Speak to me.   *65*
What are you thinking that makes your eyes so strange?
O my son, my son, I come to you on my knees!"
But Haimon spat in his face. He said not a word,
Staring—
             And suddenly drew his sword
And lunged. Creon shrank back, the blade missed; and the boy,   *70*
Desperate against himself, drove it half its length
Into his own side, and fell. And as he died
He gathered Antigonê close in his arms again,
Choking, his blood bright red on her white cheek.
And now he lies dead with the dead, and she is his   *75*
At last, his bride in the house of the dead.

                       Exit Eurydicê into the palace.

CHORAGOS. She has left us without a word. What can this mean?
MESSENGER. It troubles me, too; yet she knows what is best,
    Her grief is too great for public lamentation,
    And doubtless she has gone to her chamber to weep   *80*
    For her dead son, leading her maidens in his dirge.

    Pause.

CHORAGOS. It may be so: but I fear this deep silence.
MESSENGER. I will see what she is doing. I will go in.

                       Exit Messenger into the palace.

    Enter Creon with attendants, bearing Haimon's body.

CHORAGOS. But here is the king himself: oh look at him,
    Bearing his own damnation in his arms.   *85*
CREON. Nothing you say can touch me any more.
    My own blind heart has brought me
    From darkness to final darkness. Here you see
    The father murdering, the murdered son—
    And all my civic wisdom!   *90*

    Haimon my son, so young, so young to die,
    I was the fool, not you; and you died for me.
CHORAGOS. That is the truth; but you were late in learning it.
CREON. This truth is hard to bear. Surely a god
    Has crushed me beneath the hugest weight of heaven,   *95*
    And driven me headlong a barbaric way
    To trample out the thing I held most dear.

    The pains that men will take to come to pain!

Enter Messenger from the palace.

MESSENGER. The burden you carry in your hands is heavy,
    But it is not all: you will find more in your house.   100
CREON. What burden worse than this shall I find there?
MESSENGER. The Queen is dead.
CREON. O port of death, deaf world,
    Is there no pity for me? And you, Angel of evil,
    I was dead, and your words are death again.   105
    Is it true, boy? Can it be true?
    Is my wife dead? Has death bred death?
MESSENGER. You can see for yourself.

The doors are opened and the body of Eurydicê is disclosed within.

CREON. Oh pity!
    All true, all true, and more than I can bear!   110
    O my wife, my son!
MESSENGER. She stood before the altar, and her heart
    Welcomed the knife her own hand guided,
    And a great cry burst from her lips for Megareus° dead,
    And for Haimon dead, her sons; and her last breath   115
    Was a curse for their father, the murderer of her sons.
    And she fell, and the dark flowed in through her closing eyes.
CREON. O God, I am sick with fear.
    Are there no swords here? Has no one a blow for me?
MESSENGER. Her curse is upon you for the deaths of both.   120
CREON. It is right that it should be. I alone am guilty.
    I know it, and I say it. Lead me in,
      Quickly, friends.
    I have neither life nor substance. Lead me in.
CHORAGOS. You are right, if there can be right in so much wrong.   125
    The briefest way is best in a world of sorrow.
CREON. Let it come,
    Let death come quickly, and be kind to me.
    I would not ever see the sun again.
CHORAGOS. All that will come when it will; but we, meanwhile,   130
    Have much to do. Leave the future to itself.
CREON. All my heart was in that prayer!
CHORAGOS. Then do not pray any more: the sky is deaf.
CREON. Lead me away. I have been rash and foolish.
    I have killed my son and my wife.   135
    I look for comfort; my comfort lies here dead.
    Whatever my hands have touched has come to nothing.
    Fate has brought all my pride to a thought of dust.

114 Megareus Megareus, brother of Haimon, had died in the assault on Thebes.

As Creon is being led into the house, the Choragos advances and speaks directly to the audience.

CHORAGOS. There is no happiness where there is no wisdom;
No wisdom but in submission to the gods.   *140*
Big words are always punished,
And proud men in old age learn to be wise.

TOPICS FOR DISCUSSION AND WRITING

1. Although Sophocles called his play Antigonê, many critics say that Creon is the real tragic hero, pointing out that Antigonê is absent from the last third of the play. Evaluate this view.

2. In some Greek tragedies, fate plays a great role in bringing about the downfall of the tragic hero. Though there are references to the curse on the House of Oedipus in *Antigonê*, do we feel that Antigonê goes to her death as a result of the workings of fate? Do we feel that fate is responsible for Creon's fall? Is the Messenger right to introduce the notion of "fate" (*Exodos,* line 4)? Or are both Antigonê and Creon the creators of their own tragedy?

3. Are the words *hamartia* and *hubris* (page 651) relevant to Antigonê? To Creon?

4. Why does Creon, contrary to the Chorus's advice (Scene V, lines 96–97), bury the body of Polyneicês before he releases Antigonê? Does his action show a zeal for piety as shortsighted as his earlier zeal for law? Is his action plausible , in view of the facts that Teiresias has dwelt on the wrong done to Polyneicês, and that Antigonê has ritual food to sustain her? Or are we not to worry about Creon's motive?

5. A *foil* is a character who, by contrast, sets off or helps to define another character. To what extent is Ismenê a foil to Antigonê? Is she entirely without courage?

6. What function does Eurydicê serve? How deeply do we feel about her fate?

William Shakespeare (English; 1564–1616)

A Midsummer Night's Dream

[*Dramatis Personae*

THESEUS, *Duke of Athens*
HIPPOLYTA, *Queen of the Amazons, betrothed to Theseus*
PHILOSTRATE, *Master of the Revels*
EGEUS, *father of Hermia*

HERMIA, *daughter of Egeus, in love with Lysander*
LYSANDER, *in love with Hermia*
DEMETRIUS, *in love with Hermia and favored by Egeus*
HELENA, *in love with Demetrius*

OBERON, *King of the Fairies*
TITANIA, *Queen of the Fairies*
PUCK, *or* ROBIN GOODFELLOW
PEASEBLOSSOM,
COBWEB,   *fairies attending*
MOTE,   *Titania*
MUSTARDSEED,
Other FAIRIES *attending*

PETER QUINCE, *a carpenter,*   PROLOGUE
NICK BOTTOM, *a weaver,*   PYRAMUS
FRANCIS FLUTE, *a bellows mender,* *representing* THISBE
TOM SNOUT, *a tinker,*   WALL
SNUG, *a joiner,*   LION
ROBIN STARVELING, *a tailor,*   MOONSHINE

Lords and Attendants on Theseus and Hippolyta

Scene: *Athens, and a wood near it*]

[**1.1**]   *Enter Theseus, Hippolyta,* [*and Philostrate,*] *with others.*

THESEUS. Now, fair Hippolyta, our nuptial hour
    Draws on apace. Four happy days bring in
    Another moon; but, O, methinks, how slow

Edited by David Bevington. *A Midsummer Night's Dream* was first published in 1600 in a small book of a type called a quarto. A second quarto edition, printed in 1616 but based on the 1600 text, introduces a few corrections, but it also introduces many errors. The 1619 text in turn was the basis for the text in the first collected edition of Shakespeare's plays, the First Folio (1623). Bevington's edition is of course based on the text of 1600, but it includes a few corrections, and it modifies the punctuation in accordance with modern usage. Material added by the editor, such as amplifications in the *dramatis personae,* is enclosed within square brackets [ ].
1.1 Location: Athens, Theseus' court

Above: Oberon (Alan Howard), Puck (John Kane); below: Titania (Sara Kestelman), and Nick Bottom (David Waller) in a 1970 Stratford-upon-Avon production of A Midsummer Night's Dream *directed by Peter Brook. (Photo by David Farrell, Shakespeare Centre Library, Stratford-upon-Avon.)*

This old moon wanes! She lingers° my desires,
Like to a stepdame° or a dowager°   5
Long withering out° a young man's revenue.
HIPPOLYTA. Four days will quickly steep themselves in night,
Four nights will quickly dream away the time;
And then the moon, like to a silver bow
New bent in heaven, shall behold the night   10
Of our solemnities.
THESEUS.   Go, Philostrate,
Stir up the Athenian youth to merriments,
Awake the pert and nimble spirit of mirth,
Turn melancholy forth to funerals;
The pale companion° is not for our pomp.°   *[Exit Philostrate.]* 15
Hippolyta, I wooed thee with my sword°
And won thy love doing thee injuries;
But I will wed thee in another key,
With pomp, with triumph,° and with reveling.

Enter Egeus and his daughter Hermia, and Lysander, and Demetrius.

EGEUS. Happy be Theseus, our renowned duke!   20
THESEUS. Thanks, good Egeus. What's the news with thee?
EGEUS. Full of vexation come I, with complaint
Against my child, my daughter Hermia.
Stand forth, Demetrius. My noble lord,
This man hath my consent to marry her.   25
Stand forth, Lysander. And, my gracious Duke,
This man hath bewitched the bosom of my child.
Thou, thou, Lysander, thou hast given her rhymes
And interchanged love tokens with my child.
Thou hast by moonlight at her window sung   30
With feigning voice verses of feigning° love,
And stol'n the impression of her fantasy°
With bracelets of thy hair, rings, gauds,° conceits,°
Knacks,° trifles, nosegays, sweetmeats — messengers
Of strong prevailment in° unhardened youth.   35
With cunning hast thou filched my daughter's heart,

---

4 lingers postpones, delays the fulfillment of **5 stepdame** stepmother. **dowager** i.e., a
widow (whose right of inheritance from her dead husband is eating into her son's estate)
6 withering out causing to dwindle **15 companion** fellow. **pomp** ceremonial magnificence **16 with my sword** i e., in a military engagement against the Amazons, when Hippolyta was taken captive **19 triumph** public festivity **31 feigning** (1) counterfeiting
(2) faining, desirous **32 And . . . fantasy** and made her fall in love with you (imprinting
your image on her imagination) by stealthy and dishonest means **33 gauds** playthings.
conceits fanciful trifles **34 Knacks** knickknacks **35 prevailment in** influence on

Turned her obedience, which is due to me,
To stubborn harshness. And, my gracious Duke,
Be it so° she will not here before Your Grace
Consent to marry with Demetrius,　　　　　　　　　　　40
I beg the ancient privilege of Athens:
As she is mine, I may dispose of her,
Which shall be either to this gentleman
Or to her death, according to our law
Immediately° provided in that case.　　　　　　　　　　45

THESEUS. What say you, Hermia? Be advised, fair maid.
To you your father should be as a god—
One that composed your beauties, yea, and one
To whom you are but as a form in wax
By him imprinted, and within his power　　　　　　　　50
To leave° the figure or disfigure° it.
Demetrius is a worthy gentleman.

HERMIA. So is Lysander.

THESEUS.　　　　　　　　In himself he is;
But in this kind,° wanting° your father's voice,°
The other must be held the worthier.　　　　　　　　　55

HERMIA. I would my father looked but with my eyes.

THESEUS. Rather your eyes must with his judgment look.

HERMIA. I do entreat Your Grace to pardon me.
I know not by what power I am made bold,
Nor how it may concern° my modesty　　　　　　　　60
In such a presence here to plead my thoughts;
But I beseech Your Grace that I may know
The worst that may befall me in this case
If I refuse to wed Demetrius.

THESEUS. Either to die the death or to abjure　　　　　65
Forever the society of men.
Therefore, fair Hermia, question your desires,
Know of your youth, examine well your blood,°
Whether, if you yield not to your father's choice,
You can endure the livery° of a nun,　　　　　　　　70
For aye° to be in shady cloister mewed,°
To live a barren sister all your life,
Chanting faint hymns to the cold fruitless moon.
Thrice blessèd they that master so their blood
To undergo such maiden pilgrimage;　　　　　　　　75
But earthlier happy° is the rose distilled

---

39 Be it so if　**45 Immediately** directly, with nothing intervening　**51 leave** i.e., leave
unaltered.　**disfigure** obliterate　**54 kind** respect.　**wanting** lacking.　**voice** approval
60 concern befit　**68 blood** passions　**70 livery** habit　**71 aye** ever.　**mewed** shut in.
(Said of a hawk, poultry, etc.)　**76 earthlier happy** happier as respects this world

Than that which, withering on the virgin thorn,
Grows, lives, and dies in single blessedness.
HERMIA. So will I grow, so live, so die, my lord,
    Ere I will yield my virgin patent° up   *80*
    Unto his lordship, whose unwishèd yoke
    My soul consents not to give sovereignty.
THESEUS. Take time to pause, and by the next new moon—
    The sealing day betwixt my love and me
    For everlasting bond of fellowship—   *85*
    Upon that day either prepare to die
    For disobedience to your father's will,
    Or° else to wed Demetrius, as he would,
    Or on Diana's altar to protest°
    For aye austerity and single life.   *90*
DEMETRIUS. Relent, sweet Hermia, and, Lysander, yield
    Thy crazèd° title to my certain right.
LYSANDER. You have her father's love, Demetrius;
    Let me have Hermia's. Do you marry him.
EGEUS. Scornful Lysander! True, he hath my love,   *95*
    And what is mine my love shall render him.
    And she is mine, and all my right of her
    I do estate unto° Demetrius.
LYSANDER. I am, my lord, as well derived° as he,
    As well possessed;° my love is more than his;   *100*
    My fortunes every way as fairly° ranked,
    If not with vantage,° as Demetrius';
    And, which is more than all these boasts can be,
    I am beloved of beauteous Hermia.
    Why should not I then prosecute my right?   *105*
    Demetrius, I'll avouch it to his head,°
    Made love to Nedar's daughter, Helena
    And won her soul; and she, sweet lady, dotes,
    Devoutly dotes, dotes in idolatry,
    Upon this spotted° and inconstant man.   *110*
THESEUS. I must confess that I have heard so much,
    And with Demetrius thought to have spoke thereof;
    But, being overfull of self-affairs,°
    My mind did lose it. But, Demetrius, come,
    And come, Egeus, you shall go with me;   *115*
    I have some private schooling° for you both.

---

80 patent privilege   **88 Or** either   **89 protest** vow   **92 crazèd** cracked, unsound
98 estate unto settle or bestow upon   **99 derived** descended, i.e., as well born
100 possessed endowed with wealth   **101 fairly** handsomely   **102 vantage** superiority
106 head i.e., face   **110 spotted** i.e., morally stained   **113 self-affairs** my own concerns
116 schooling admonition

For you, fair Hermia, look you arm° yourself
To fit your fancies° to your father's will;
Or else the law of Athens yields you up—
Which by no means we may extenuate°—   *120*
To death or to a vow of single life.
Come, my Hippolyta. What cheer, my love?
Demetrius and Egeus, go° along.
I must employ you in some business
Against° our nuptial and confer with you   *125*
Of something nearly that° concerns yourselves.

EGEUS. With duty and desire we follow you.

> *Exeunt [all but Lysander and Hermia].*

LYSANDER. How now, my love, why is your cheek so pale?
How chance the roses there do fade so fast?

HERMIA. Belike for want of rain, which I could well   *135*
Beteem° them from the tempest of my eyes.

LYSANDER. Ay me! For aught that I could ever read,
Could ever hear by tale or history,
The course of true love never did run smooth
But either it was different in blood°—   *135*

HERMIA. O cross!° Too high to be enthralled to low.

LYSANDER. Or else misgrafted in respect of years—

HERMIA. O spite! Too old to be engaged to young.

LYSANDER. Or else it stood upon the choice of friends°—

HERMIA. O hell, to choose love by another's eyes!   *140*

LYSANDER. Or if there were a sympathy° in choice,
War, death, or sickness did lay siege to it,
Making it momentary° as a sound,
Swift as a shadow, short as any dream,
Brief as the lightning in the collied° night,   *145*
That in a spleen° unfolds° both heaven and earth,
And ere a man hath power to say "Behold!"
The jaws of darkness do devour it up.
So quick° bright things come to confusion.°

HERMIA. If then true lovers have been ever crossed,°   *150*
It stands as an edict in destiny.
Then let us teach our trial patience,°

117 look you arm take care you prepare **118 fancies** likings, thoughts of love **120 extenuate** mitigate **123 go** i.e., come **125 Against** in preparation for **126 nearly that** that closely **130 Belike** very likely **131 Beteem** grant, afford **135 blood** hereditary station **136 cross** vexation **137 misgrafted** ill grafted, badly matched **139 friends** relatives **141 sympathy** agreement **143 momentany** lasting but a moment **145 collied** blackened (as with coal dust), darkened **146 in a spleen** in a swift impulse, in a violent flash. **unfolds** discloses **149 quick** quickly; or, perhaps, living, alive. **confusion** ruin **150 ever crossed** always thwarted **152 teach . . . patience** i.e., teach ourselves patience in this trial

Because it is a customary cross,
As due to love as thoughts and dreams and sighs,
Wishes and tears, poor fancy's° followers.   155
LYSANDER. A good persuasion.° Therefore, hear me, Hermia:
I have a widow aunt, a dowager
Of great revenue, and she hath no child.
From Athens is her house remote seven leagues;
And she respects° me as her only son.   160
There, gentle Hermia, may I marry thee,
And to that place the sharp Athenian law
Cannot pursue us. If thou lovest me, then,
Steal forth thy father's house tomorrow night;
And in the wood, a league without the town,   165
Where I did meet thee once with Helena
To do observance to a morn of May,°
There will I stay for thee.
HERMIA.   My good Lysander!
I swear to thee by Cupid's strongest bow,
By his best arrow° with the golden head,   170
By the simplicity° of Venus' doves,°
By that which knitteth souls and prospers loves,
And by that fire which burned the Carthage queen°
When the false Trojan° under sail was seen,
By all the vows that ever men have broke,   175
In number more than ever women spoke,
In that same place thou hast appointed me
Tomorrow truly will I meet with thee.
LYSANDER. Keep promise, love. Look, here comes Helena.

Enter Helena.

HERMIA. God speed, fair° Helena! Whither away?   180
HELENA. Call you me fair? That "fair" again unsay.
Demetrius loves your fair.° O happy fair!°
Your eyes are lodestars,° and your tongue's sweet air°
More tunable° than lark to shepherd's ear
When wheat is green, when hawthorn buds appear.   185

---

155 fancy's amorous passion's **156 persuasion** conviction **160 respects** regards
167 do . . . May perform the ceremonies of May Day **170 best arrow** (Cupid's best gold-pointed arrows were supposed to induce love, his blunt leaden arrows, aversion.)
171 simplicity innocence. **doves** i.e., those that drew Venus' chariot **173, 174 Carthage queen, false Trojan** (Dido, Queen of Carthage, immolated herself on a funeral pyre after having been deserted by the Trojan hero Aeneas.) **180 fair** fair-complexioned (generally regarded by the Elizabethans as more beautiful than dark complexioned) **182 your fair** your beauty (even though Hermia is dark-complexioned). **happy fair** lucky fair one **183 lodestars** guiding stars. **air** music **184 tunable** tuneful, melodious

Sickness is catching. O, were favor° so!
Yours would I catch, fair Hermia, ere I go;
My ear should catch your voice, my eye your eye,
My tongue should catch your tongue's sweet melody.
Were the world mine, Demetrius being bated,° 190
The rest I'd give to be to you translated.°
O, teach me how you look and with what art
You sway the motion° of Demetrius' heart.

HERMIA. I frown upon him, yet he loves me still.

HELENA. O, that your frowns would teach my smiles such skill! 195

HERMIA. I give him curses, yet he gives me love.

HELENA. O, that my prayers could such affection° move!°

HERMIA. The more I hate, the more he follows me.

HELENA. The more I love, the more he hateth me.

HERMIA. His folly, Helena, is no fault of mine. 200

HELENA. None but your beauty. Would that fault were mine!

HERMIA. Take comfort. He no more shall see my face.
Lysander and myself will fly this place.
Before the time I did Lysander see
Seemed Athens as a paradise to me. 205
O, then, what graces in my love do dwell
That he hath turned a heaven unto a hell!

LYSANDER. Helen, to you our minds we will unfold.
Tomorrow night, when Phoebe° doth behold
Her silver visage in the watery glass,° 210
Decking with liquid pearl the bladed grass,
A time that lovers' flights doth still° conceal,
Through Athens' gates have we devised to steal.

HERMIA. And in the wood, where often you and I
Upon faint° primrose beds were wont to lie, 215
Emptying our bosoms of their counsel° sweet,
There my Lysander and myself shall meet;
And thence from Athens turn away our eyes,
To seek new friends and stranger companies.
Farewell, sweet playfellow. Pray thou for us, 220
And good luck grant thee thy Demetrius!
Keep word, Lysander. We must starve our sight
From lovers' food till morrow deep midnight.

LYSANDER. I will, my Hermia.   *Exit Hermia.*
                    Helena, adieu.
As you on him, Demetrius dote on you! 225
                    Exit Lysander.

---

186 favor appearance, looks   **190 bated** excepted   **191 translated** transformed   **193 motion** impulse   **197 affection** passion.   **move** arouse   **209 Phoebe** Diana, the moon   **210 glass** mirror   **212 still** always   **215 faint** pale   **216 counsel** secret thought

HELENA. How happy some o'er other some can be!°
    Through Athens I am thought as fair as she.
    But what of that? Demetrius thinks not so;
    He will not know what all but he do know.
    And as he errs, doting on Hermia's eyes,   230
    So I, admiring° of his qualities.
    Things base and vile, holding no quantity,°
    Love can transpose to form and dignity.
    Love looks not with the eyes, but with the mind,
    And therefore is winged Cupid painted blind.   235
    Nor hath Love's mind of any judgment taste;°
    Wings, and no eyes, figure° unheedy haste.
    And therefore is Love said to be a child,
    Because in choice he is so oft beguiled.
    As waggish° boys in game° themselves forswear,   240
    So the boy Love is perjured everywhere.
    For ere Demetrius looked on Hermia's eyne,°
    He hailed down oaths that he was only mine;
    And when this hail some heat from Hermia felt,
    So he dissolved, and showers of oaths did melt.   245
    I will go tell him of fair Hermia's flight.
    Then to the wood will he tomorrow night
    Pursue her; and for this intelligence°
    If I have thanks, it is a dear expense.°
    But herein mean I to enrich my pain,   250
    To have his sight thither and back again.   *Exit.*

[**1.2**]   *Enter Quince the carpenter, and Snug the joiner, and Bottom*
    the weaver, and Flute the bellows mender, and Snout the
    tinker, and Starveling the tailor.

QUINCE. Is all our company here?
BOTTOM. You were best to call them generally,° man by man, accord-
    ing to the scrip.°
QUINCE. Here is the scroll of every man's name which is thought fit,
    through all Athens, to play in our interlude before the Duke and   5
    the Duchess on his wedding day at night.

---

226 o'er . . . can be can be in comparison to some others   **231 admiring of** wondering at   **232 holding no quantity** i.e., unsubstantial, unshapely   **236 Nor . . .**
taste i.e., nor has Love, which dwells in the fancy or imagination, any *taste* or least bit of
judgment or reason   **237 figure** are a symbol of   **240 waggish** playful, mischievous.
game sport, jest   **242 eyne** eyes. (Old form of plural.)   **248 intelligence** information
249 a dear expense i.e., a trouble worth taking.   **dear** costly

1.2 Location: Athens
2 generally (Bottom's blunder for *individually*.)   **3 scrip** scrap. (Bottom's error for *script*.)

BOTTOM. First, good Peter Quince, say what the play treats on, then read the names of the actors, and so grow to° a point.

QUINCE. Marry,° our play is "The most lamentable comedy and most cruel death of Pyramus and Thisbe." 10

BOTTOM. A very good piece of work, I assure you, and a merry. Now, good Peter Quince, call forth your actors by the scroll. Masters, spread yourselves.

QUINCE. Answer as I call you. Nick Bottom,° the weaver.

BOTTOM. Ready. Name what part I am for, and proceed. 15

QUINCE. You, Nick Bottom, are set down for Pyramus.

BOTTOM. What is Pyramus? A lover or a tyrant?

QUINCE. A lover, that kills himself most gallant for love.

BOTTOM. That will ask some tears in the true performing of it. If I do it, let the audience look to their eyes. I will move storms; I will 20 condole° in some measure. To the rest—yet my chief humor° is for a tyrant. I could play Ercles° rarely, or a part to tear a cat° in, to make all split.°

> "The raging rocks
> And shivering shocks 25
> Shall break the locks
> Of prison gates:
> And Phibbus' car°
> Shall shine from far
> And make and mar 30
> The foolish Fates."

This was lofty! Now name the rest of the players. This is Ercles' vein, a tyrants vein. A lover is more condoling.

QUINCE. Francis Flute, the bellows mender.

FLUTE. Here, Peter Quince. 35

QUINCE. Flute, you must take Thisbe on you.

FLUTE. What is Thisbe? A wandering knight?

QUINCE. It is the lady that Pyramus must love.

FLUTE. Nay, faith, let not me play a woman. I have a beard coming.

QUINCE. That's all one.° You shall play it in a mask, and you may speak 40 as small° as you will.

BOTTOM. An° I may hide my face, let me play Thisbe too. I'll speak in a monstrous little voice, "Thisne, Thisne!" "Ah Pyramus, my lover dear! Thy Thisbe dear, and lady dear!"

---

8 grow to come to   **9 Marry** (A mild oath originally the name of the Virgin Mary.)
14 Bottom (As a weaver's term, a *bottom* was an object around which thread was wound.)   **21 condole** lament, arouse pity   **humor** inclination, whim   **22 Ercles** Hercules. (The tradition of ranting came from Seneca's *Hercules Furens*.)   **tear a cat** i.e., rant   **23 make all split** i.e., cause a stir, bring the house down   **28 Phibbus' car** Phoebus', the sun-god's, chariot   **40 That's all one** it makes no difference   **41 small** high-pitched   **42 An** if (also at l.67)

QUINCE. No, no, you must play Pyramus, and, Flute, you Thisbe. 45
BOTTOM. Well, proceed.
QUINCE. Robin Starveling, the tailor.
STARVELING. Here, Peter Quince.
QUINCE. Robin Starveling, you must play Thisbe's mother. Tom Snout, the tinker. 50
SNOUT. Here, Peter Quince.
QUINCE. You, Pyramus' father; myself, Thisbe's father; Snug, the joiner, you, the lion's part, and I hope here is a play fitted.
SNUG. Have you the lion's part written? Pray you, if it be, give it me, for I am slow of study. 55
QUINCE. You may do it extempore, for it is nothing but roaring.
BOTTOM. Let me play the lion too. I will roar that I will do any man's heart good to hear me. I will roar that I will make the Duke say, "Let him roar again, let him roar again."
QUINCE. An you should do it too terribly, you would fright the Duchess 60
and the ladies, that they would shriek; and that were enough to hang us all.
ALL. That would hang us, every mother's son.
BOTTOM. I grant you, friends, if you should fright the ladies out of their wits, they would have no more discretion but to hang us; but I will 65
aggravate° my voice so that I will roar you° as gently as any suck-ing dove;° I will roar you an 'twere any nightingale.
QUINCE. You can play no part but Pyramus; for Pyramus is a sweet-faced man, a proper° man as one shall see in a summer's day, a most lovely gentlemanlike man. Therefore you must needs play Pyramus. 70
BOTTOM. Well, I will undertake it. What beard were I best to play it in?
QUINCE. Why, what you will.
BOTTOM. I will discharge° it in either your° straw-color beard, your orange-tawny beard, your purple-in-grain° beard, or your French-crown color° beard, your perfect yellow. 75
QUINCE. Some of your French crowns° have no hair at all, and then you will play barefaced. But, masters, here are your parts. [*He distributes parts.*] And I am to entreat you, request you, and desire you to con° them by tomorrow night; and meet me in the palace wood, a mile without the town, by moonlight. There will we rehearse; for if we 80
meet in the city, we shall be dogged with company, and our

___

66 aggravate (Bottom's blunder for *moderate.*) **roar you** i.e., roar for you. **66–67 sucking dove** (Bottom conflates *sitting dove* and *sucking lamb,* two proverbial images of inno-cence.) **69 proper** handsome **73 discharge** perform. **your** i.e., you know the kind I mean **74 purple-in-grain** dyed a very deep red. (From *grain,* the name applied to the dried insect used to make the dye.) **74–75 French-crown-color** i.e., color of a French crown, a gold coin **76 crowns** heads bald from syphilis, the "French disease" **78 con** learn by heart

devices° known. In the meantime I will draw a bill° of properties, such as our play wants. I pray you, fail me not.

BOTTOM. We will meet, and there we may rehearse most obscenely° and
courageously. Take pains, be perfect;° adieu.   *85*

QUINCE. At the Duke's oak we meet.

BOTTOM. Enough. Hold, or cut bowstrings.°   *Exeunt.*

     [2.1]   *Enter a Fairy at one door, and Robin Goodfellow [Puck] at
another.*

PUCK. How now, spirit, whither wander you?

FAIRY.
         Over hill, over dale,
           Thorough° bush, thorough brier,
         Over park, over pale,°
           Thorough flood, thorough fire,   *5*
         I do wander everywhere,
         Swifter than the moon's sphere;°
         And I serve the Fairy Queen,
         To dew her orbs° upon the green.
         The cowslips tall her pensioners° be.   *10*
         In their gold coats spots you see:
         Those be rubies, fairy favors;°
         In those freckles live their savors.°
         I must go seek some dewdrops here
         And hang a pearl in every cowslip's ear.   *15*
         Farewell, thou lob° of spirits; I'll be gone.
         Our Queen and all her elves come here anon.°

PUCK. The King doth keep his revels here tonight.
         Take heed the Queen come not within his sight.
         For Oberon is passing fell° and wrath,°   *20*
         Because that she as her attendant hath
         A lovely boy, stolen from an Indian king;

---

82 devices plans   **bill** list   **84 obscenely** (An unintentionally funny blunder, whatever
Bottom meant to say.)   **85 perfect** i.e., letter-perfect in memorizing your parts
87 Hold . . . bowstrings (An archers' expression not definitely explained, but probably
meaning here "keep your promises, or give up the play.")

2.1. Location: A wood near Athens.
3 Thorough through   **4 pale** enclosure   **7 sphere** orbit   **9 orbs** circles, i.e., fairy rings
(circular bands of grass, darker than the surrounding area, caused by fungi enriching the
soil)   **10 pensioners** retainers, members of the royal bodyguard   **12 favors** love tokens
13 savors sweet smells   **16 lob** country bumpkin   **17 anon** at once   **20 passing fell** exceedingly angry.   **wrath** wrathful

She never had so sweet a changeling.°
And jealous Oberon would have the child
Knight of his train, to trace° the forests wild.   25
But she perforce° withholds the lovèd boy,
Crowns him with flowers, and makes him all her joy.
And now they never meet in grove or green,
By fountain° clear, or spangled starlight sheen,°
But they do square,° that all their elves for fear   30
Creep into acorn cups and hide them there.

FAIRY. Either I mistake your shape and making quite,
Or else you are that shrewd° and knavish sprite°
Called Robin Goodfellow. Are not you he
That frights the maidens of the villagery,°   35
Skim milk, and sometimes labor in the quern,°
And bootless° make the breathless huswife° churn,
And sometimes make the drink to bear no barm,°
Mislead night wanderers, laughing at their harm?
Those that "Hobgoblin" call you, and "Sweet Puck,"   40
You do their work, and they shall have good luck.
Are you not he?

PUCK.   Thou speakest aright;
I am that merry wanderer of the night.
I jest to Oberon and make him smile
When I a fat and bean-fed horse beguile,   45
Neighing in likeness of a filly foal;
And sometimes lurk I in a gossip's° bowl,
In very likeness of a roasted crab,
And when she drinks, against her lips I bob
And on her withered dewlap° pour the ale.   50
The wisest aunt,° telling the saddest° tale,
Sometimes for three-foot stool mistaketh me;
Then slip I from her bum, down topples she,
And "Tailor"° cries, and falls into a cough;
And then the whole choir° hold their hips and laugh,   55
And waxen° in their mirth, and neeze,° and swear
A merrier hour was never wasted there.
But, room,° fairy! Here comes Oberon.

---

23 changeling child exchanged for another by the fairies **25 trace** range through
26 perforce forcibly **29 fountain** spring. **starlight sheen** shining starlight **30 square**
quarrel **33 shrewd** mischievous. **sprite** spirit **35 villagery** village population
36 quern handmill **37 bootless** in vain. **huswife** housewife **38 barm** yeast, head on
the ale **47 gossip's** old woman's **48 crab** crab apple **50 dewlap** loose skin on neck
51 aunt old woman. **saddest** most serious **54 Tailor** (Possibly because she ends up sitting cross-legged on the floor, looking like a tailor.) **55 choir** company **56 waxen**
increase. **neeze** sneeze **58 room** stand aside, make room

FAIRY. And here my mistress. Would that he were gone!

Enter [Oberon] the King of Fairies at one door, with his train; and
[Titania] the Queen at another, with hers.

OBERON. Ill met by moonlight, proud Titania. 60

TITANIA. What, jealous Oberon? Fairies, skip hence.
I have forsworn his bed and company.

OBERON. Tarry, rash wanton.° Am not I thy lord?

TITANIA. Then I must be thy lady; but I know
When thou hast stolen away from Fairyland 65
And in the shape of Corin° sat all day,
Playing on pipes of corn° and versing love
To amorous Phillida.° Why art thou here
Come from the farthest step° of India
But that, forsooth, the bouncing Amazon, 70
Your buskined° mistress and your warrior love,
To Theseus must be wedded, and you come
To give their bed joy and prosperity.

OBERON. How canst thou thus for shame, Titania,
Glance at my credit with Hippolyta,° 75
Knowing I know thy love to Theseus?
Didst not thou lead him through the glimmering night
From Perigenia,° whom he ravishèd?
And make him with fair Aegles° break his faith,
With Ariadne° and Antiopa?°

TITANIA. These are the forgeries of jealousy;
And never, since the middle summer's spring,°
Met we on hill, in dale, forest, or mead,
By pavèd° fountain or by rushy° brook,
Or in the beachèd margent° of the sea, 85
To dance our ringlets° to the whistling wind,
But with thy brawls thou hast disturbed our sport.
Therefore the winds, piping to us in vain,

---

63 wanton headstrong creature   **66, 68 Corin, Phillida** (Conventional names of pastoral lovers.)   **67 corn** (Here, oat stalks.)   **69 step** farthest limit of travel, or, perhaps, *steep,* mountain range   **71 buskined** wearing half-boots called buskins   **75 Glance . . . Hippolyta** make insinuations about my favored relationship with Hippolyta   **78 Perigenia** i.e., Perigouna, one of Theseus' conquests. (This and the following women are named in Thomas North's translation of Plutarch's "Life of Theseus.")   **79 Aegles** i.e., Aegle, for whom Theseus deserted Ariadne according to some accounts   **80 Ariadne** the daughter of Minos, King of Crete, who helped Theseus to escape the labyrinth after killing the Minotaur; later she was abandoned by Theseus.   **Antiopa** Queen of the Amazons and wife of Theseus; elsewhere identified with Hippolyta, but here thought of as a separate woman   **82 middle summer's spring** beginning of midsummer   **84 pavèd** with pebbled bottom.   **rushy** bordered with rushes   **85 in** on.   **margent** edge, border   **86 ringlets** dances in a ring. (See *orbs* in l.9.)

As in revenge, have sucked up from the sea
Contagious° fogs; which, falling in the land,   *90*
Hath every pelting° river made so proud
That they have overborne their continents.°
The ox hath therefore stretched his yoke in vain,
The plowman lost his sweat, and the green corn°
Hath rotted ere his youth attained a beard;   *95*
The fold° stands empty in the drownèd field,
And crows are fatted with the murrain° flock;
The nine-men's-morris° is filled up with mud,
And the quaint mazes° in the wanton° green
For lack of tread are undistinguishable.   *100*
The human mortals want° their winter° here;
No night is now with hymn or carol blessed.
Therefore° the moon, the governess of floods,
Pale in her anger, washes all the air,
That rheumatic diseases° do abound.   *105*
And thorough this distemperature° we see
The seasons alter: hoary-headed frosts
Fall in the fresh lap of the crimson rose,
And on old Hiems'° thin and icy crown
An odorous chaplet of sweet summer buds   *110*
Is, as in mockery, set. The spring, the summer,
The childing° autumn, angry winter, change
Their wonted liveries,° and the mazèd° world
By their increase° now knows not which is which.
And this same progeny of evils comes   *115*
From our debate,° from our dissension;
We are their parents and original.°
OBERON. Do you amend it, then; it lies in you.
Why should Titania cross her Oberon?
I do but beg a little changeling boy   *120*
To be my henchman.°

---

90 Contagious noxious **91 pelting** paltry **92 continents** banks that contain them
94 corn grain of any kind **96 fold** pen for sheep or cattle **97 murrain** having died of
the plague **98 nine-men's-morris** i.e., portion of the village green marked out in a square
for a game played with nine pebbles or pegs **99 quaint mazes** i.e., intricate paths marked
out on the village green to be followed rapidly on foot as a kind of contest. **wanton**
luxuriant **101 want** lack. **winter** i.e., regular winter season; or, proper observances of
winter, such as the *hymn or carol* in the next line (?) **103 Therefore** i.e., as a result of our
quarrel **105 rheumatic diseases** colds, flu, and other respiratory infections **106 distem-
perature** disturbance in nature **109 Hiems'** the winter god's **112 childing** fruitful,
pregnant **113 wonted liveries** usual apparel. **mazèd** bewildered **114 their increase**
their yield, what they produce **116 debate** quarrel **117 original** origin **121 henchman**
attendant, page

TITANIA.   Set your heart at rest.
    The fairy land buys not the child of me.
    His mother was a vot'ress of my order,
    And in the spicèd Indian air by night
    Full often hath she gossiped by my side   125
    And sat with me on Neptune's yellow sands,
    Marking th' embarkèd traders° on the flood,°
    When we have laughed to see the sails conceive
    And grow big-bellied with the wanton° wind;
    Which she, with pretty and with swimming° gait,   130
    Following—her womb then rich with my young squire—
    Would imitate, and sail upon the land
    To fetch me trifles, and return again
    As from a voyage, rich with merchandise.
    But she, being mortal, of that boy did die;   135
    And for her sake do I rear up her boy,
    And for her sake I will not part with him.
OBERON. How long within this wood intend you stay?
TITANIA. Perchance till after Theseus' wedding day.
    If you will patiently dance in our round°   140
    And see our moonlight revels, go with us;
    If not, shun me, and I will spare° your haunts.
OBERON. Give me that boy and I will go with thee.
TITANIA. Not for thy fairy kingdom. Fairies, away!
    We shall chide downright if I longer stay.   145
                      Exeunt [*Titania with her train*].

OBERON. Well, go thy way. Thou shalt not from° this grove
    Till I torment thee for this injury.
    My gentle Puck, come hither. Thou rememb'rest
    Since° once I sat upon a promontory,
    And heard a mermaid on a dolphin's back   150
    Uttering such dulcet and harmonious breath°
    That the rude° sea grew civil at her song,
    And certain stars shot madly from their spheres
    To hear the sea-maid's music.
PUCK.   I remember.
OBERON. That very time I saw, but thou couldst not,   155
    Flying between the cold moon and the earth,
    Cupid all° armed. A certain aim he took

---

127 traders trading vessels. **flood** flood tide **129 wanton** sportive **130 swimming**
smooth, gliding **140 round** circular dance **142 spare** shun **146 from** go from
149 Since when **151 breath** voice, song **152 rude** rough **157 all** fully

At a fair vestal° thronèd by the west,
And loosed° his love shaft smartly from his bow
As° it should pierce a hundred thousand hearts;   160
But I might° see young Cupid's fiery shaft
Quenched in the chaste beams of the watery moon,
And the imperial vot'ress passèd on
In maiden meditation, fancy-free.°
Yet marked I where the bolt° of Cupid fell: 165
It fell upon a little western flower,
Before milk-white, now purple with love's wound,
And maidens call it "love-in-idleness."°
Fetch me that flower; the herb I showed thee once.
The juice of it on sleeping eyelids laid   170
Will make or man or° woman madly dote
Upon the next live creature that it sees.
Fetch me this herb, and be thou here again
Ere the leviathan° can swim a league.

PUCK. I'll put a girdle round about the earth   175
In forty° minutes.   [*Exit.*]

OBERON.   Having once this juice,
I'll watch Titania when she is asleep
And drop the liquor of it in her eyes.
The next thing then she waking looks upon,
Be it on lion, bear, or wolf, or bull,   180
On meddling monkey, or on busy ape,
She shall pursue it with the soul of love.
And ere I take this charm from off her sight,
As I can take it with another herb,
I'll make her render up her page to me.   185
But who comes here? I am invisible,
And I will overhear their conference.

Enter Demetrius, Helena following him.

DEMETRIUS. I love thee not; therefore pursue me not.
Where is Lysander and fair Hermia?
The one I'll slay; the other slayeth me.   190
Thou toldst me they were stol'n unto this wood;
And here am I, and wode° within this wood,

---

158 vestal vestal virgin. (Contains a complimentary allusion to Queen Elizabeth as a votaress of Diana and probably refers to an actual entertainment in her honor at Elvetham in 1591.)   **159 loosed** released   **160 As** as if   **161 might** could   **164 fancy-free** free of love's spell   **165 bolt** arrow   **168 love-in-idleness** pansy, heartsease   **171 or . . . or** either . . . or   **174 leviathan** sea monster, whale   **176 forty** (Used indefinitely.)   **192 wode** mad. (Pronounced "wood" and often spelled so.)

Because I cannot meet my Hermia.
Hence, get thee gone, and follow me no more.
HELENA. You draw me, you hardhearted adamant!° 195
But yet you draw not iron, for my heart
Is true as steel. Leave° you your power to draw,
And I shall have no power to follow you.
DEMETRIUS. Do I entice you? Do I speak you fair?° 200
Or rather do I not in plainest truth
Tell you I do not nor I cannot love you?
HELENA. And even for that do I love you the more.
I am your spaniel; and, Demetrius,
The more you beat me, I will fawn on you.
Use me but as your spaniel, spurn me, strike me, 205
Neglect me, lose me; only give me leave,
Unworthy as I am, to follow you.
What worser place can I beg in your love—
And yet a place of high respect with me—
Than to be usèd as you use your dog? 210
DEMETRIUS. Tempt not too much the hatred of my spirit,
For I am sick when I do look on thee.
HELENA. And I am sick when I look not on you.
DEMETRIUS. You do impeach° your modesty too much
To leave the city and commit yourself 215
Into the hands of one that loves you not,
To trust the opportunity of night
And the ill counsel of a desert° place
With the rich worth of your virginity.
HELENA. Your virtue° is my privilege. For that° 220
It is not night when I do see your face,
Therefore I think I am not in the night;
Nor doth this wood lack worlds of company,
For you, in my respect,° are all the world.
Then how can it be said I am alone 225
When all the world is here to look on me?
DEMETRIUS. I'll run from thee and hide me in the brakes,°
And leave thee to the mercy of wild beasts.
HELENA. The wildest hath not such a heart as you.
Run when you will, the story shall be changed: 230

---

195 adamant lodestone, magnet (with pun on *hardhearted,* since adamant was also thought to be the hardest of all stones and was confused with the diamond) **197 Leave** give up **199 fair** courteously **214 impeach** call into question **218 desert** deserted **220 virtue** goodness or power to attract. **privilege** safeguard, warrant. **For that** because **224 in my respect** as far as I am concerned **227 brakes** thickets

Apollo flies and Daphne holds the chase,°
The dove pursues the griffin,° the mild hind°
Makes speed to catch the tiger—bootless° speed,
When cowardice pursues and valor flies!

DEMETRIUS. I will not stay° thy questions.° Let me go!   235
Or if thou follow me, do not believe
But I shall do thee mischief in the wood.

HELENA. Ay, in the temple, in the town, the field,
You do me mischief. Fie, Demetrius!
Your wrongs do set a scandal on my sex.°   240
We cannot fight for love, as men may do;
We should be wooed and were not made to woo.

                                        [*Exit Demetrius.*]

I'll follow thee and make a heaven of hell,
To die upon° the hand I love so well.   [*Exit.*]

OBERON. Fare thee well, nymph. Ere he do leave this grove,   245
Thou shalt fly him and he shall seek thy love.

Enter Puck.

Hast thou the flower there? Welcome, wanderer.

PUCK. Ay, there it is.   [*He offers the flower.*]

OBERON.   I pray thee, give it me.
I know a bank where the wild thyme blows,°
Where oxlips° and the nodding violet grows,   250
Quite overcanopied with luscious woodbine,°
With sweet muskroses° and with eglantine.°
There sleeps Titania sometimes of the night,
Lulled in these flowers with dances and delight;
And there the snake throws° her enameled skin,   255
Weed° wide enough to wrap a fairy in.
And with the juice of this I'll streak° her eyes
And make her full of hateful fantasies.
Take thou some of it, and seek through this grove.

                                        [*He gives some love juice.*]

---

231 Apollo . . . chase (In the ancient myth, Daphne fled from Apollo and was saved from rape by being transformed into a laurel tree, here it is the female *who holds the chase,* or pursues, instead of the male.) **232 griffin** a fabulous monster with the head of an eagle and the body of a lion. **hind** female deer **233 bootless** fruitless **235 stay** wait for. **questions** talk or argument **240 Your . . . sex** i.e., the wrongs that you do me cause me to act in a manner that disgraces my sex **244 upon** by **249 blows** blooms **250 oxlips** flowers resembling cowslip and primrose **251 woodbine** honeysuckle **252 muskroses** a kind of large, sweet-scented rose. **eglantine** sweetbrier, another kind of rose **255 throws** sloughs off, sheds **256 Weed** garment **257 streak** anoint, touch gently

A sweet Athenian lady is in love   260
With a disdainful youth. Anoint his eyes,
But do it when the next thing he espies
May be the lady. Thou shalt know the man
By the Athenian garments he hath on.
Effect it with some care, that he may prove   265
More fond on° her than she upon her love;
And look thou meet me ere the first cock crow.
PUCK. Fear not, my lord, your servant shall do so.

                                                   Exeunt.

[2.2] *Enter Titania, Queen of Fairies, with her train.*

TITANIA. Come, now a roundel° and a fairy song;
Then, for the third part of a minute, hence—
Some to kill cankers° in the muskrose buds,
Some war with reremice° for their leathern wings
To make my small elves coats, and some keep back   5
The clamorous owl, that nightly hoots and wonders
At our quaint° spirits. Sing me now asleep.
Then to your offices, and let me rest.

Fairies sing.

FIRST FAIRY.
                You spotted snakes with double° tongue,
                    Thorny hedgehogs, be not seen;   10
                Newts° and blindworms, do no wrong,
                    Come not near our Fairy Queen.
CHORUS.
                    Philomel,° with melody
                    Sing in our sweet lullaby;
                Lulla, lulla, lullaby, lulla, lulla, lullaby.   15
                    Never harm
                    Nor spell nor charm
                    Come our lovely lady nigh.
                    So good night, with lullaby.

266 fond on doting on

2.2 Location: The wood.
1 roundel dance in a ring   **3 cankers** cankerworms (i.e., caterpillars or grubs)   **4 reremice**
bats   **7 quaint** dainty   **9 double** forked   **11 Newts** water lizards (considered poisonous,
as were *blindworms*— small snakes with tiny eyes—and spiders)   **13 Philomel** the nightingale. (Philomela, daughter of King Pandion, was transformed into a nightingale, according to Ovid's *Metamorphoses* 6, after she had been raped by her sister Procne's husband, Tereus.)

FIRST FAIRY.
> Weaving spiders, come not here;   20
>> Hence, you long-legged spinners, hence!
> Beetles black, approach not near;
>> Worm nor snail, do no offense.

CHORUS.
>> Philomel, with melody
>>> Sing in our sweet lullaby;   25
> Lulla, lulla, lullaby, lulla, lulla, lullaby.
>>> Never harm
>>> Nor spell nor charm
>> Come our lovely lady nigh.
>> So good night, with lullaby.   30

             [*Titania sleeps.*]

SECOND FAIRY.
> Hence, away! Now all is well.
> One aloof stand sentinel.

             [*Exeunt Fairies.*]

Enter Oberon [and squeezes the flower on Titania's eyelids].
OBERON.
> What thou seest when thou dost wake,
> Do it for thy true love take;
> Love and languish for his sake.   35
> Be it ounce,° or cat, or bear,
> Pard,° or boar with bristled hair,
> In thy eye that shall appear
> When thou wak'st, it is thy dear.
> Wake when some vile thing is near.   [*Exit.*] 40

Enter Lysander and Hermia.

LYSANDER. Fair love, you faint with wandering in the wood;
> And to speak truth, I have forgot our way.
> We'll rest us, Hermia, if you think it good,
> And tarry for the comfort of the day.
HERMIA. Be it so, Lysander. Find you out a bed,   45
> For I upon this bank will rest my head.
LYSANDER. One turf shall serve as pillow for us both;
> One heart, one bed, two bosoms, and one troth.°
HERMIA. Nay, good Lysander, for my sake, my dear,
> Lie further off yet; do not lie so near.   50
LYSANDER. O, take the sense, sweet, of my innocence!°

---

36 ounce lynx   **37 Pard** leopard   **48 troth** faith, trothplight   **51 take . . . innocence**
i.e., interpret my intention as innocent

Love takes the meaning in love's conference.°
I mean that my heart unto yours is knit
So that but one heart we can make of it;
Two bosoms interchainèd with an oath—   55
So then two bosoms and a single troth.
Then by your side no bed-room me deny,
For lying so, Hermia, I do not lie.°
HERMIA. Lysander riddles very prettily.
     Now much beshrew° my manners and my pride   60
If Hermia meant to say Lysander lied.
But, gentle friend, for love and courtesy
Lie further off, in human° modesty;
Such separation as may well be said
Becomes a virtuous bachelor and a maid,   65
So far be distant; and good night, sweet friend.
Thy love ne'er alter till thy sweet life end!
LYSANDER. Amen, amen, to that fair prayer, say I,
     And then end life when I end loyalty!
Here is my bed. Sleep give thee all his rest!   70
HERMIA. With half that wish the wisher's eyes be pressed!°
                [*They sleep, separated by a short distance.*]

     Enter Puck.

PUCK.
       Through the forest have I gone,
       But Athenian found I none
       On whose eyes I might approve°
       This flower's force in stirring love.   75
       Night and silence.—Who is here?
       Weeds of Athens he doth wear.
       This is he, my master said,
       Despisèd the Athenian maid;
       And here the maiden, sleeping sound,   80
       On the dank and dirty ground.
       Pretty soul, she durst not lie
       Near this lack-love, this kill-courtesy.
       Churl, upon thy eyes I throw
       All the power this charm doth owe.°   85
                   [*He applies the love juice.*]

---

52 Love . . . conference i.e., when lovers confer, love teaches each lover to interpret the other's meaning lovingly   **58 lie** tell a falsehood (with a riddling pun on *lie,* recline)   **60 beshrew** curse. (But mildly meant.)   **63 human** courteous   **71 With . . . pressed** i.e., may we share your wish, so that your eyes too are *pressed,* closed, in sleep   **74 approve** test   **85 owe** own

When thou wak'st, let love forbid
Sleep his seat on thy eyelid.
So awake when I am gone,
For I must now to Oberon.   *Exit.*

Enter Demetrius and Helena, running.

HELENA. Stay, though thou kill me, sweet Demetrius!   *90*
DEMETRIUS. I charge thee, hence, and do not haunt me thus.
HELENA. O, wilt thou darkling° leave me? Do not so.
DEMETRIUS. Stay, on thy peril!° I alone will go.   [*Exit.*]
HELENA. O, I am out of breath in this fond° chase!
    The more my prayer, the lesser is my grace.°   *95*
    Happy is Hermia, wheresoe'er she lies,
    For she hath blessèd and attractive eyes.
    How came her eyes so bright? Not with salt tears;
    If so, my eyes are oftener washed than hers.
    No, no, I am as ugly as a bear;   *100*
    For beasts that meet me run away for fear.
    Therefore no marvel though Demetrius
    Do, as a monster, fly my presence thus.°
    What wicked and dissembling glass of mine
    Made me compare° with Hermia's sphery eyne?°   *105*
    But who is here? Lysander, on the ground?
    Dead, or asleep? I see no blood, no wound.
    Lysander, if you live, good sir, awake.
LYSANDER. [*Awaking*] And run through fire I will for thy
    sweet sake.
    Transparent° Helena! Nature shows art,   *110*
    That through thy bosom makes me see thy heart.
    Where is Demetrius? O, how fit a word
    Is that vile name to perish on my sword!
HELENA. Do not say so, Lysander, say not so.
    What though he love your Hermia? Lord, what though?   *115*
    Yet Hermia still loves you. Then be content.
LYSANDER. Content with Hermia? No! I do repent
    The tedious minutes I with her have spent.
    Not Hermia but Helena I love.
    Who will not change a raven for a dove?   *120*

---

92 darkling in the dark   **93 on thy peril** i.e., on pain of danger to you if you don't obey
me and stay   **94 fond** doting   **95 my grace** the favor I obtain   **96 lies** dwells
102–103 no marvel . . . thus i.e., no wonder that Demetrius flies from me as from a monster
105 compare vie.   **sphery eyne** eyes as bright as stars in their spheres   **110 Transparent** (1) radiant (2) able to be seen through

The will of man is by his reason swayed,
And reason says you are the worthier maid.
Things growing are not ripe until their season;
So I, being young, till now ripe not° to reason.
And touching° now the point° of human skill,°   *125*
Reason becomes the marshal to my will
And leads me to your eyes, where I o'erlook°
Love's stories written in love's richest book.

HELENA. Wherefore° was I to this keen mockery born?
   When at your hands did I deserve this scorn?   *130*
   Is 't not enough, is 't not enough, young man,
   That I did never, no, nor never can,
   Deserve a sweet look from Demetrius' eye,
   But you must flout my insufficiency?
   Good troth,° you do me wrong, good sooth,° you do,   *135*
   In such disdainful manner me to woo.
   But fare you well. Perforce I must confess
   I thought you lord of° more true gentleness.°
   O, that a lady, of° one man refused,
   Should of another therefore be abused!°   *Exit.*   *140*

LYSANDER. She sees not Hermia. Hermia, sleep thou there,
   And never mayst thou come Lysander near!
   For as a surfeit of the sweetest things
   The deepest loathing to the stomach brings,
   Or as the heresies that men do leave   *145*
   Are hated most of those they did deceive,°
   So thou, my surfeit and my heresy,
   Of all be hated, but the most of me!
   And, all my powers, address° your love and might
   To honor Helen and to be her knight!   *Exit.*   *150*

HERMIA. [*Awaking*] Help me, Lysander, help me! Do thy best
   To pluck this crawling serpent from my breast!
   Ay me, for pity! What a dream was here!
   Lysander, look how I do quake with fear.
   Methought a serpent ate my heart away,   *155*
   And you sat smiling at his cruel prey.°
   Lysander! What, removed? Lysander! Lord!
   What, out of hearing? Gone? No sound, no word?

---

124 ripe not (am) not ripened   **125 touching** reaching. **point** summit. **skill** judgment   **127 o'erlook** read   **129 Wherefore** why   **135 Good troth, good sooth** i.e., indeed, truly   **138 lord of** i.e., possessor of. **gentleness** courtesy   **139 of** by   **140 abused** ill treated   **145–146 as . . . deceive** as renounced heresies are hated most by those persons who formerly were deceived by them   **149 address** direct, apply   **156 prey** act of preying

Alack, where are you? Speak, an if° you hear;
Speak, of all loves!° I swoon almost with fear.   160
No? Then I well perceive you are not nigh.
Either death, or you, I'll find immediately.

                                        Exit. [The sleeping Titania remains.]

[3.1]   *Enter the clowns [Quince, Snug, Bottom, Flute, Snout, and
          Starveling].*

BOTTOM. Are we all met?

QUINCE. Pat, pat;° and here's a marvelous convenient place for our
     rehearsal. This green plot shall be our stage, this hawthorn brake°
     our tiring-house,° and we will do it in action as we will do it be-
     fore the Duke.   5

BOTTOM. Peter Quince?

QUINCE. What sayest thou, bully° Bottom?

BOTTOM. There are things in this comedy of Pyramus and Thisbe that will
     never please. First, Pyramus must draw a sword to kill himself, which
     the ladies cannot abide. How answer you that?   10

SNOUT. By 'r lakin,° a parlous° fear.

STARVELING. I believe we must leave the killing out, when all is done.°

BOTTOM. Not a whit. I have a device to make all well. Write me° a pro-
     logue, and let the prologue seem to say we will do no harm with
     our swords, and that Pyramus is not killed indeed; and for the more   15
     better assurance, tell them that I, Pyramus, am not Pyramus but Bot-
     tom the weaver. This will put them out of fear.

QUINCE. Well, we will have such a prologue, and it shall be written in
     eight and six.°

BOTTOM. No, make it two more; let it be written in eight and eight.   20

SNOUT. Will not the ladies be afeard of the lion?

STARVELING. I fear it, I promise you.

BOTTOM. Masters, you ought to consider with yourselves, to bring in—
     God shield us!—a lion among ladies° is a most dreadful thing. For

---

159 an if if   **160 of loves** for all love's sake

3.1. Location: The action is continuous.
2 Pat on the dot, punctually   **3 brake** thicket   **4 tiring-house** attiring area, hence backstage   **8 bully** i.e., worthy, jolly, fine fellow   **11 By 'r lakin** by our ladykin, i.e., the Virgin
Mary.   **parlous** alarming   **12 when all is done** i.e., when all is said and done   **13 Write
me** i.e., write at my suggestion. (*Me* is used colloquially.)   **19 eight and six** alternate lines
of eight and six syllables, a common ballad measure   **24 lion among ladies** (A contemporary pamphlet tells how at the christening in 1594 of Prince Henry, eldest son of King
James VI of Scotland, later James I of England, a "blackamoor" instead of a lion drew the
triumphal chariot, since the lion's presence might have "brought some fear to the nearest.")

there is not a more fearful° wildfowl than your lion living; and we   25
ought to look to 't.

SNOUT. Therefore another prologue must tell he is not a lion.

BOTTOM. Nay, you must name his name, and half his face must be seen
through the lion's neck, and he himself must speak through, saying
thus, or to the same defect:° "Ladies"—or "Fair ladies—I would   30
wish you"—or "I would request you"—or "I would entreat you—
not to fear, not to tremble; my life for yours.° If you think I come
hither as a lion, it were pity of my life.° No, I am no such thing;
I am a man as other men are." And there indeed let him name his
name and tell them plainly he is Snug the joiner.   35

QUINCE. Well, it shall be so. But there is two hard things: that is, to bring
the moonlight into a chamber; for, you know, Pyramus and Thisbe
meet by moonlight.

SNOUT. Doth the moon shine that night we play our play?

BOTTOM. A calendar, a calendar! Look in the almanac. Find out moon-   40
shine, find out moonshine.   [*They consult an almanac.*]

QUINCE. Yes, it doth shine that night.

BOTTOM. Why, then, may you leave a casement of the great chamber window, where we play, open, and the moon may shine in at the
casement.   45

QUINCE. Ay; or else one must come in with a bush of thorns° and a lantern and say he comes to disfigure,° or to present,° the person of
Moonshine. Then there is another thing: we must have a wall in the
great chamber; for Pyramus and Thisbe, says the story, did talk
through the chink of a wall.   50

SNOUT. You can never bring in a wall. What say you, Bottom?

BOTTOM. Some man or other must present Wall. And let him have some
plaster, or some loam, or some roughcast° about him, to signify
wall; or let him hold his fingers thus, and through that cranny shall
Pyramus and Thisbe whisper.   55

QUINCE. If that may be, then all is well. Come, sit down, every mother's
son, and rehearse your parts. Pyramus, you begin. When you have
spoken your speech, enter into that brake, and so everyone according to his cue.

Enter Robin [*Puck*].

---

25 fearful fear inspiring   **30 defect** (Bottom's blunder for *effect.*)   **32 my life for yours**
i.e., I pledge my life to make your lives safe   **33 it were . . . life** my life would be endangered   **46 bush of thorns** bundle of thornbush faggots (part of the accoutrements of the
man in the moon, according to the popular notions of the time, along with his lantern and
his dog)   **47 disfigure** (Quince's blunder for *figure.*)   **present** represent   **53 roughcast** a
mixture of lime and gravel used to plaster the outside of buildings

PUCK. What hempen homespuns° have we swaggering here   60
    So near the cradle° of the Fairy Queen?
    What, a play toward?° I'll be an auditor;
    An actor too perhaps, if I see cause.
QUINCE. Speak, Pyramus. Thisbe, stand forth.
BOTTOM. [*As Pyramus*]
    "Thisbe, the flowers of odious savors sweet—"   65
QUINCE. Odors, odors.
BOTTOM. "—Odors savors sweet;
    So hath thy breath, my dearest Thisbe dear.
    But hark, a voice! Stay thou but here awhile,   70
    And by and by I will to thee appear."   *Exit.*
PUCK. A stranger Pyramus than e'er played here.°   [*Exit.*]
FLUTE. Must I speak now?
QUINCE. Ay, marry, must you; for you must understand he goes but
    to see a noise that he heard, and is to come again.
FLUTE. [*As Thisbe*]
    "Most radiant Pyramus, most lily-white of hue,   75
    Of color like the red rose on triumphant° brier,
    Most brisky juvenal° and eke° most lovely Jew,°
    As true as truest horse, that yet would never tire.
    I'll meet thee, Pyramus, at Ninny's tomb."
QUINCE. "Ninus'° tomb," man. Why, you must not speak that yet.   80
    That you answer to Pyramus. You speak all your part° at once, cues
    and all. Pyramus, enter. Your cue is past; it is "never tire."
PLUTE. O—"As true as truest horse, that yet would never tire."

[*Enter Puck, and Bottom as Pyramus with the ass head.°*]

BOTTOM.
    "If I were fair,° Thisbe, I were° only thine."
QUINCE. O, monstrous! O, strange! We are haunted.   85
    Pray, masters! Fly, masters! Help!
        [*Exeunt Quince, Snug, Flute, Snout, and Starveling.*]

---

60 hempen homespuns i.e., rustics dressed in clothes woven of coarse, homespun fabric
made from hemp **61 cradle** i.e. Titania's bower **62 toward** about to take place
71 A stranger . . . here (Puck indicates that he has conceived of his plan to present a
"stranger" Pyramus than ever seen before, and so Puck exits to put his plan into effect.)
76 triumphant magnificent **77 brisky juvenal** lively youth. **eke** also. **Jew** (Probably
an absurd repetition of the first syllable of *juvenal*, or Flute's error for *jewel*.) **80 Ninus**
mythical founder of Nineveh (whose wife, Semiramis, was supposed to have built the walls
of Babylon where the story of Pyramus and Thisbe takes place) **81 part** (An actor's *part*
was a script consisting only of his speeches and their cues.) **83 s.d. with the ass head** (This
stage direction, taken from the Folio, presumably refers to a standard stage property.)
84 fair handsome. **were** would be

PUCK. I'll follow you, I'll lead you about a round,°
  Through bog, through bush, through brake, through brier.
 Sometimes a horse I'll be, sometimes a hound,
  A hog, a headless bear, sometimes a fire;°   *90*
 And neigh, and bark, and grunt, and roar, and burn,
 Like horse, hound, hog, bear, fire, at every turn. *Exit.*
BOTTOM. Why do they run away? This is a knavery of them to make me
 afeard.

 Enter Snout.

SNOUT. O Bottom, thou art changed! What do I see on thee?   *95*

BOTTOM. What do you see? You see an ass head of your own, do
 you?   [*Exit Snout.*]

 Enter Quince.

QUINCE. Bless thee, Bottom, bless thee! Thou art translated.°
                     Exit.
BOTTOM. I see their knavery. This is to make an ass of me, to fright me,
 if they could. But I will not stir from this place, do what they can. *100*
 I will walk up and down here, and will sing, that they shall hear
 I am not afraid.   [*Sings.*]
   The ouzel cock° so black of hue,
    With orange-tawny bill,
   The throstle° with his note so true,   *105*
    The wren with little quill°—
TITANIA. [*Awaking*] What angel wakes me from my flowery bed?
BOTTOM. [*Sings*]
   The finch, the sparrow, and the lark,
    The plainsong° cuckoo gray,
   Whose note full many a man doth mark,   *110*
    And dares not answer nay°—
 For, indeed, who would set his wit to so foolish a bird? Who would
 give a bird the lie,° though he cry "cuckoo" never so?°
TITANIA. I pray thee, gentle mortal, sing again.
 Mine ear is much enamored of thy note;   *115*
 So is mine eye enthrallèd to thy shape;
 And thy fair virtue's force° perforce doth move me
 On the first view to say, to swear, I love thee.

---

87 about a round roundabout **90 fire** will-o'-the wisp **98 translated** transformed
103 ouzel cock male blackbird **105 throstle** song thrush **106 quill** (Literally, a reed
pipe; hence, the bird's piping song.) **109 plainsong** singing a melody without variations
111 dares . . . nay i.e., cannot deny that he is a cuckold **113 give . . . lie** call the bird
a liar. **never so** ever so much **117 thy . . . force** the power of your beauty

BOTTOM. Methinks, mistress, you should have little reason for that. And
    yet, to say the truth, reason and love keep little company together *120*
    nowadays. The more the pity that some honest neighbors will not
    make them friends. Nay, I can gleek° upon occasion.
TITANIA. Thou art as wise as thou art beautiful.
BOTTOM. Not so, neither. But if I had wit enough to get out of this wood,
    I have enough to serve mine own turn.° *125*
TITANIA. Out of this wood do not desire to go.
    Thou shalt remain here, whether thou wilt or no.
    I am a spirit of no common rate.°
    The summer still° doth tend upon my state,°
    And I do love thee. Therefore go with me. *130*
    I'll give thee fairies to attend on thee
    And they shall fetch thee jewels from the deep,
    And sing while thou on pressèd flowers dost sleep.
    And I will purge thy mortal grossness° so
    That thou shalt like an airy spirit go. *135*
    Peaseblossom, Cobweb, Mote,° and Mustardseed!

Enter four Fairies [Peaseblossom, Cobweb, Mote, and Mustardseed].

PEASEBLOSSOM. Ready.
COBWEB. And I.
MOTE.   And I.
MUSTARDSEED.   And I.
ALL.   Where shall we go?
TITANIA. Be kind and courteous to this gentleman.
    Hop in his walks and gambol in his eyes;° *140*
    Feed him with apricots and dewberries,°
    With purple grapes, green figs, and mulberries;
    The honey bags steal from the humble-bees,
    And for night tapers crop their waxen thighs
    And light them at the fiery glowworms' eyes, *145*
    To have my love to bed and to arise;
    And pluck the wings from painted butterflies
    To fan the moonbeams from his sleeping eyes.
    Nod to him, elves, and do him courtesies.
PEASEBLOSSOM. Hail, mortal! *150*
COBWEB. Hail!
MOTE. Hail!
MUSTARDSEED. Hail!

---

122 gleek scoff, jest **125 serve . . .turn** answer my purpose **128 rate** rank, value
129 still ever, always. **doth . . . state** waits upon me as a part of my royal retinue
134 mortal grossness materiality (i.e., the corporal nature of a mortal being) **136 Mote** i.e.,
speck. (The two words *moth* and *mote* were pronounced alike, and both meanings may be
present.) **140 in his eyes** in his sight (i.e., before him) **141 dewberries** blackberries

BOTTOM. I cry your worships mercy, heartily. I beseech your worship's
    name.   155
COBWEB. Cobweb.
BOTTOM. I shall desire you of more acquaintance, good Master Cobweb.
    If I cut my finger, I shall make bold with you.°—Your name, honest
    gentleman?
PEASEBLOSSOM. Peaseblossom.   160
BOTTOM. I pray you, commend me to Mistress Squash,° your mother,
    and to Master Peascod,° your father. Good Master Peaseblossom,
    I shall desire you of more acquaintance too.—Your name, I beseech
    you, sir?
MUSTARDSEED. Mustardseed.   165
BOTTOM. Good Master Mustardseed I know your patience° well. That
    same cowardly giantlike ox-beef hath devoured many a gentleman
    of your house. I promise you, your kindred hath made my eyes
    water° ere now. I desire you of more acquaintance, good Master
    Mustardseed.   170
TITANIA. Come, wait upon him; lead him to my bower.
      The moon methinks looks with a watery eye;
  And when she weeps,° weeps every little flower,
      Lamenting some enforcèd° chastity.
      Tie up my lover's tongue,° bring him silently.   175

                                       [Exeunt.]

    [3.2]   *Enter [Oberon,] King of Fairies.*

OBERON. I wonder if Titania be awaked;
      Then what it was that next came in her eye,
      Which she must dote on in extremity.

    [Enter] Robin Goodfellow [Puck].

      Here comes my messenger. How now, mad spirit?
      What night-rule° now about this haunted° grove?   5
PUCK. My mistress with a monster is in love.
      Near to her close° and consecrated bower,
      While she was in her dull° and sleeping hour,

---

158 If . . . you (Cobwebs were used to stanch bleeding.)   **161 Squash** unripe pea
pod   **162 Peascod** ripe pea pod   **166 your patience** what you have endured   **169 water**
(1) weep for sympathy (2) smart, sting   **173 she weeps** i.e., she causes dew   **174 enforcèd**
forced, violated; or, possibly, constrained (since Titania at this moment is hardly concerned
about chastity)   **175 The . . . tongue** (Presumably Bottom is braying like an ass.)

3.2. Location: The wood.
5 night-rule diversion for the night.   **haunted** much frequented   **7 close** secret, private
8 dull drowsy

A crew of patches,° rude mechanicals,°
That work for bread upon Athenian stalls,°   *10*
Were met together to rehearse a play
Intended for great Theseus' nuptial day.
The shallowest thick-skin of that barren sort,°
Who Pyramus presented° in their sport,
Forsook his scene° and entered in a brake.   *15*
When I did him at this advantage take,
An ass's noll° I fixèd on his head.
Anon his Thisbe must be answered,
And forth my mimic° comes. When they him spy,
As wild geese that the creeping fowler° eye,   *20*
Or russet-pated choughs,° many in sort,°
Rising and cawing at the gun's report,
Sever° themselves and madly sweep the sky,
So, at his sight, away his fellows fly;
And, at our stamp, here o'er and o'er one falls;   *25*
He "Murder!" cries and help from Athens calls.
Their sense thus weak, lost with their fears thus strong,
Made senseless things begin to do them wrong,
For briers and thorns at their apparel snatch;
Some, sleeves—some, hats; from yielders all things catch.°   *30*
I led them on in this distracted fear
And left sweet Pyramus translated there,
When in that moment, so it came to pass,
Titania waked and straightway loved an ass.
OBERON. This falls out better than I could devise.   *35*
    But hast thou yet latched° the Athenian's eyes
    With the love juice, as I did bid thee do?
PUCK. I took him sleeping—that is finished too—
    And the Athenian woman by his side,
    That, when he waked, of force° she must be eyed.   *40*

Enter Demetrius and Hermia.

OBERON. Stand close. This is the same Athenian.
PUCK. This is the woman, but not this the man.
                                  [They stand aside.]

---

9 patches clowns, fools. **rude mechanicals** ignorant artisans **10 stalls** market booths
13 barren sort stupid company or crew **14 presented** acted **15 scene** playing area
17 noll noddle, head **19 mimic** burlesque actor **20 fowler** hunter of game birds
21 russet-pated choughs reddish brown or gray-headed jackdaws. **in sort** in a flock
23 Sever i.e., scatter **30 from . . . catch** i.e. everything preys on those who yield to fear
36 latched fastened, snared **40 of force** perforce

DEMETRIUS. O, why rebuke you him that loves you so?
　　Lay breath so bitter on your bitter foe.
HERMIA. Now I but chide; but I should use thee worse,　　45
　　For thou, I fear, hast given me cause to curse.
　　If thou hast slain Lysander in his sleep,
　　Being o'er shoes° in blood, plunge in the deep,
　　And kill me too.
　　The sun was not so true unto the day　　　　　　50
　　As he to me. Would he have stolen away
　　From sleeping Hermia? I'll believe as soon
　　This whole° earth may be bored, and that the moon
　　May through the center creep, and so displease
　　Her brother's° noontide with th' Antipodes.°　　55
　　It cannot be but thou hast murdered him;
　　So should a murderer look, so dead,° so grim.
DEMETRIUS. So should the murdered look, and so should I
　　Pierced through the heart with your stern cruelty.
　　Yet you, the murderer, look as bright, as clear,　　60
　　As yonder Venus in her glimmering sphere.
HERMIA. What's this to° my Lysander? Where is he?
　　Ah, good Demetrius, wilt thou give him me?
DEMETRIUS. I had rather give his carcass to my hounds.
HERMIA. Out, dog! Out, cur! Thou driv'st me past the bounds　　65
　　Of maiden's patience. Hast thou slain him, then?
　　Henceforth be never numbered among men.
　　O, once tell true, tell true, even for my sake:
　　Durst thou have looked upon him being awake?
　　And hast thou killed him sleeping? O brave touch!°　　70
　　Could not a worm,° an adder, do so much?
　　An adder did it; for with doubler tongue
　　Than thine, thou serpent, never adder stung.
DEMETRIUS. You spend your passion° on a misprised mood.°
　　I am not guilty of Lysander's blood,　　　　　　75
　　Nor is he dead, for aught that I can tell.
HERMIA. I pray thee, tell me then that he is well.
DEMETRIUS. An if I could, what should I get therefor?
HERMIA. A privilege never to see me more.
　　And from thy hated presence part I so.　　　　　80
　　See me no more, whether he be dead or no.　　　　*Exit.*

---

48 o'er shoes i.e., so far gone　**53 whole** solid　**55 Her brother's** i.e., the sun's.　**th'
Antipodes** the people on the opposite side of the earth (where the moon is imagined bringing
night to noontime)　**57 dead** deadly, or deathly pale　**62 to** to do with　**70 brave touch**
noble exploit. (Said ironically.)　**71 worm** serpent　**74 passion** violent feelings.　**misprised mood** anger based on misconception

DEMETRIUS. There is no following her in this fierce vein.
    Here therefore for a while I will remain.
    So sorrow's heaviness doth heavier° grow
    For debt that bankrupt° sleep doth sorrow owe;   *85*
    Which now in some slight measure it will pay,
    If for his tender here I make some stay.°

                       Lie[s] down [and sleeps].

OBERON. What hast thou done? Thou hast mistaken quite
    And laid the love juice on some true love's sight.
    Of thy misprision° must perforce ensue   *90*
    Some true love turned, and not a false turned true.
PUCK. Then fate o'errules, that, one man holding troth,°
    A million fail, confounding oath on oath.°
OBERON. About the wood go swifter than the wind,
    And Helena of Athens look° thou find.   *95*
    All fancy-sick° she is and pale of cheer°
    With sighs of love, that cost the fresh blood° dear.
    By some illusion see thou bring her here.
    I'll charm his eyes against she do appear.°
PUCK. I go, I go, look how I go,   *100*
    Swifter than arrow from the Tartar's bow.°

                        [Exit].

OBERON. *[Applying love juice to Demetrius' eyes]*
        Flower of this purple dye,
        Hit with Cupid's archery,
        Sink in apple of his eye.
        When his love he doth espy,   *105*
    Let her shine as gloriously
    As the Venus of the sky.
    When thou wak'st, if she be by,
    Beg of her for remedy.

    Enter Puck.

PUCK.
        Captain of our fairy band,   *110*
        Helena is here at hand,
        And the youth, mistook by me,

---

84 heavier (1) harder to bear (2) more drowsy **85 bankrupt** (Demetrius is saying that his sleepiness adds to the weariness caused by sorrow.) **86–87 Which . . . stay** i.e., to a small extent I will be able to "pay back" and hence find some relief from sorrow, if I pause here awhile (*make some stay*) while sleep "tenders" or offers itself by way of paying the debt owed to sorrow **90 misprision** mistake **92 troth** faith **93 confounding . . . oath** i.e., invalidating one oath with another **95 look** i.e., be sure **96 fancy-sick** lovesick. **cheer** face **97 sighs . . . blood** (An allusion to the physiological theory that each sigh costs the heart a drop of blood.) **99 against . . . appear** in anticipation of her coming **101 Tartars bow** (Tartars were famed for their skill with the bow.)

Pleading for a lover's fee.°
Shall we their fond pageant° see?
Lord, what fools these mortals be!   *115*

OBERON.

Stand aside. The noise they make
Will cause Demetrius to awake.

PUCK.

Then will two at once woo one;
That must needs be sport alone.°
And those things do best please me   *120*
That befall preposterously.°

                                          [*They stand aside.*]

Enter Lysander and Helena.

LYSANDER. Why should you think that I should woo in scorn?
    Scorn and derision never come in tears.
    Look when° I vow, I weep; and vows so born,
        In their nativity all truth appears.°   *125*
    How can these things in me seem scorn to you,
    Bearing the badge° of faith to prove them true?

HELENA. You do advance° your cunning more and more.
    When truth kills truth,° O, devilish-holy fray!
    These vows are Hermia's. Will you give her o'er?   *130*
        Weigh oath with oath, and you will nothing weigh.
    Your vows to her and me, put in two scales,
        Will even weigh, and both as light as tales.°

LYSANDER. I had no judgment when to her I swore.

HELENA. Nor none, in my mind, now you give her o'er.   *135*

LYSANDER. Demetrius loves her, and he loves not you.

DEMETRIUS. [*Awaking*] O Helen, goddess, nymph, perfect, divine!
    To what, my love, shall I compare thine eyne?
    Crystal is muddy. O, how ripe in show°
    Thy lips, those kissing cherries, tempting grow!   *140*
    That pure congealèd white, high Taurus'° snow,
    Fanned with the eastern wind, turns to a crow°
    When thou hold'st up thy hand. O, let me kiss
    This princess of pure white, this seal° of bliss!

---

113 fee privilege, reward   **114 fond pageant** foolish exhibition   **119 alone** unequaled
121 preposterously out of the natural order   **124 Look when** whenever   **124–125 vows
. . . appears** i.e., vows made by one who is weeping give evidence thereby of their sincerity   **127 badge** identifying device such as that worn on servants' livery (here, his tears)
128 advance carry forward display   **129 truth kills truth** i.e., one of Lysander's vows
must invalidate the other   **133 tales** lies   **139 show** appearance   **141 Taurus** a lofty
mountain range in Asia Minor   **142 turns to a crow** i.e., seems black by contrast
144 seal pledge

HELENA. O spite! O hell! I see you all are bent   *145*
  To set against° me for your merriment.
  If you were civil and knew courtesy,
  You would not do me thus much injury.
  Can you not hate me, as I know you do,
  But you must join in souls to mock me too?   *150*
  If you were men, as men you are in show,
  You would not use a gentle lady so—
  To vow, and swear, and superpraise° my parts,°
  When I am sure you hate me with your hearts.
  You both are rivals, and love Hermia;   *155*
  And now both rivals, to mock Helena.
  A trim° exploit, a manly enterprise,
  To conjure tears up in a poor maid's eyes
  With your derision! None of noble sort°
  Would so offend a virgin and extort°   *160*
  A poor soul's patience, all to make you sport.
LYSANDER. You are unkind, Demetrius. Be not so;
  For you love Hermia; this you know I know.
  And here, with all good will, with all my heart,
  In Hermia's love I yield you up my part;   *165*
  And yours of Helena to me bequeath,
  Whom I do love and will do till my death.
HELENA. Never did mockers waste more idle breath.
DEMETRIUS. Lysander, keep thy Hermia; I will none.°
  If e'er I loved her, all that love is gone.   *170*
  My heart to her but as guest-wise sojourned,°
  And now to Helen is it home returned,
  There to remain.
LYSANDER.   Helen, it is not so.
DEMETRIUS. Disparage not the faith thou dost not know,
  Lest, to thy peril, thou aby° it dear.   *175*
  Look where thy love comes; yonder is thy dear.

  Enter Hermia.

HERMIA. Dark night, that from the eye his° function takes,
  The ear more quick of apprehension makes;
  Wherein it doth impair the seeing sense
  It pays the hearing double recompense.   *180*
  Thou art not by mine eye, Lysander, found;

---

146 set against attack **153 superpraise** overpraise. **parts** qualities **157 trim** pretty,
fine. (Said ironically.) **159 sort** character, quality **160 extort** twist, torture **169 will
none** i.e., want no part of her **171 to . . . sojourned** only visited with her **175 aby** pay
for **177 his** its

Mine ear, I thank it, brought me to thy sound.
But why unkindly didst thou leave me so?
LYSANDER. Why should he stay whom love doth press to go?
HERMIA. What love could press Lysander from my side? 185
LYSANDER. Lysander's love, that would not let him bide —
    Fair Helena, who more engilds° the night
    Than all yon fiery oes° and eyes of light.
    Why seek'st thou me? Could not this make thee know,
    The hate I bear thee made me leave thee so? 190
HERMIA. You speak not as you think. It cannot be.
HELENA. Lo, she is one of this confederacy!
    Now I perceive they have conjoined all three
    To fashion this false sport in spite of me.°
    Injurious Hermia, most ungrateful maid! 195
    Have you conspired, have you with these contrived°
    To bait° me with this foul derision?
    Is all the counsel° that we two have shared,
    The sisters' vows, the hours that we have spent,
    When we have chid the hasty-footed time 200
    For parting us — O, is all forgot?
    All schooldays' friendship, childhood innocence?
    We, Hermia, like two artificial° gods,
    Have with our needles created both one flower,
    Both on one sampler, sitting on one cushion, 205
    Both warbling of one song, both in one key,
    As if our hands, our sides, voices, and minds
    Had been incorporate.° So we grew together
    Like to a double cherry, seeming parted
    But yet an union in partition, 210
    Two lovely° berries molded on one stem;
    So with two seeming bodies but one heart,
    Two of the first, like coats in heraldry,
    Due but to one and crownèd with one crest.°
    And will you rend our ancient love asunder 215
    To join with men in scorning your poor friend?
    It is not friendly, 'tis not maidenly.
    Our sex, as well as I, may chide you for it,
    Though I alone do feel the injury.

---

187 **engilds** brightens with a golden light   188 **oes** spangles (here, stars)   194 **in spite of me** to vex me   196 **contrived** plotted   197 **bait** torment, as one sets on dogs to bait a bear   198 **counsel** confidential talk   203 **artificial** skilled in art or creation   208 **incorporate** of one body   211 **lovely** loving   213–214 **Two . . . crest** i.e., we have two separate bodies, just as a coat of arms in heraldry can be represented twice on a shield but surmounted by a single crest

HERMIA. I am amazèd at your passionate words. 220
    I scorn you not. It seems that you scorn me.
HELENA. Have you not set Lysander, as in scorn,
    To follow me and praise my eyes and face?
    And made your other love, Demetrius,
    Who even but now did spurn me with his foot, 225
    To call me goddess, nymph, divine and rare,
    Precious, celestial? Wherefore speaks he this
    To her he hates? And wherefore doth Lysander
    Deny your love, so rich within his soul,
    And tender° me, forsooth, affection, 230
    But by your setting on, by your consent?
    What though I be not so in grace° as you,
    So hung upon with love, so fortunate,
    But miserable most, to love unloved?
    This you should pity rather than despise. 235
HERMIA. I understand not what you mean by this.
HELENA. Ay, do! Persever, counterfeit sad° looks,
    Make mouths° upon° me when I turn my back,
    Wink each at other, hold the sweet jest up.°
    This sport, well carried,° shall be chronicled. 240
    If you have any pity, grace, or manners,
    You would not make me such an argument.°
    But fare ye well. 'Tis partly my own fault,
    Which death, or absence, soon shall remedy.
LYSANDER. Stay, gentle Helena; hear my excuse, 245
    My love, my life, my soul, fair Helena!
HELENA. O excellent!
HERMIA. [*To Lysander*] Sweet, do not scorn her so.
DEMETRIUS. If she cannot entreat,° I can compel.
LYSANDER. Thou canst compel no more than she entreat.
    Thy threats have no more strength than her weak prayers. 250
    Helen, I love thee, by my life I do!
    I swear by that which I will lose for thee,
    To prove him false that says I love thee not.
DEMETRIUS. I say I love thee more than he can do.
LYSANDER. If thou say so, withdraw, and prove it too. 255
DEMETRIUS. Quick, come!
HERMIA.   Lysander, whereto tends all this?

---

230 tender offer **232 grace** favor **237 sad** grave, serious **238 mouths** i.e., mows, faces, grimaces. **upon** at **239 hold . . . up** keep up the joke **240 carried** managed **242 argument** subject for a jest **248 entreat** i.e., succeed by entreaty

LYSANDER. Away, you Ethiop!°

                  [*He tries to break away from Hermia.*]

DEMETRIUS.   No, no; he'll

    Seem to break loose; take on as° you would follow,

    But yet come not. You are a tame man, go!

LYSANDER. Hang off,° thou cat, thou burr! Vile thing, let

    loose,   260

    Or I will shake thee from me like a serpent!

HERMIA. Why are you grown so rude? What change is this,

    Sweet love?

LYSANDER.   Thy love? Out, tawny Tartar, out!

    Out, loathèd med'cine!° O hated potion, hence!

HERMIA. Do you not jest?

HELENA.   Yes, sooth,° and so do you.   265

LYSANDER. Demetrius, I will keep my word with thee.

DEMETRIUS. I would I had your bond, for I perceive

    A weak bond° holds you. I'll not trust your word.

LYSANDER. What, should I hurt her, strike her, kill her dead?

    Although I hate her, I'll not harm her so.   270

HERMIA. What, can you do me greater harrm than hate?

    Hate me? Wherefore? O me, what news,° my love?

    Am not I Hermia? Are not you Lysander?

    I am as fair now as I was erewhile.°

    Since night you loved me; yet since night you left me.   275

    Why, then you left me—O, the gods forbid!—

    In earnest, shall I say?

LYSANDER.   Ay, by my life!

    And never did desire to see thee more.

    Therefore be out of hope, of question, of doubt;

    Be certain, nothing truer. 'Tis no jest   280

    That I do hate thee and love Helena.

HERMIA. [*To Helena*] O me! You juggler! You cankerblossom!°

    You thief of love! What, have you come by night

    And stol'n my love's heart from him?

HELENA.   Fine, i faith!

    Have you no modesty, no maiden shame,   285

    No touch of bashfulness? What, will you tear

---

257 **Ethiop** (Referring to Hermia's relatively dark hair and complexion; see also *tawny Tartar* six lines later.) 258 **take on as** act as if 260 **Hang off** let go 264 **med'cine** i.e., poison 265 **sooth** truly 268 **weak bond** i.e., Hermia's arm (with a pun on *bond,* oath, in the previous line) 272 **what news** what is the matter 274 **erewhile** just 282 **cankerblossom** worm that destroys the flower bud (?)

Impatient answers from my gentle tongue?
Fie, fie! You counterfeit, you puppet,° you!
HERMIA. "Puppet"? Why, so!° Ay, that way goes the game.
    Now I perceive that she hath made compare   *290*
    Between our statures: she hath urged her height,
    And with her personage, her tall personage,
    Her height, forsooth, she hath prevailed with him.
    And are you grown so high in his esteem
    Because I am so dwarfish and so low?   *295*
    How low am I, thou painted maypole? Speak!
    How low am I? I am not yet so low
    But that my nails can reach unto thine eyes.
                [*She flails at Helena but is restrained.*]
HELENA. I pray you, though you mock me, gentlemen,
    Let her not hurt me. I was never curst;°   *300*
    I have no gift at all in shrewishness;
    I am a right° maid for my cowardice.
    Let her not strike me. You perhaps may think,
    Because she is something° lower than myself,
    That I can match her.
HERMIA.   Lower? Hark, again!   *305*
HELENA. Good Hermia, do not be so bitter with me.
    I evermore did love you, Hermia,
    Did ever keep your counsels, never wronged you;
    Save that, in love unto Demetrius,
    I told him of your stealth° unto this wood.   *310*
    He followed you; for love I followed him.
    But he hath chid me hence° and threatened me
    To strike me, spurn me, nay, to kill me too.
    And now, so° you will let me quiet go,
    To Athens will I bear my folly back   *315*
    And follow you no further. Let me go.
    You see how simple and how fond° I am.
HERMIA. Why, get you gone. Who is 't that hinders you?
HELENA. A foolish heart, that I leave here behind.
HERMIA. What, with Lysander?
HELENA.   With Demetrius.   *320*
LYSANDER. Be not afraid; she shall not harm thee, Helena.
DEMETRIUS. No, sir, she shall not, though you take her part.

---

288 puppet (1) counterfeit (2) dwarfish woman (in reference to Hermia's smaller stature)
289 Why, so i.e., Oh, so that's how it is **300 curst** shrewish **302 right** true
304 something somewhat **310 stealth** stealing away **312 chid me hence** driven me
away with his scolding **314 so** if only **317 fond** foolish

HELENA. O, when she is angry, she is keen° and shrewd.°
　　　She was a vixen when she went to school,
　　　And though she be but little, she is fierce.　　　　　　325
HERMIA. "Little" again? Nothing but "low" and "little"?
　　　Why will you suffer her to flout me thus?
　　　Let me come to her.
LYSANDER.　　　　　　　　Get you gone, you dwarf!
　　　You minimus,° of hindering knotgrass° made!
　　　You bead, you acorn!
DEMETRIUS.　　　　　　　You are too officious　　　　　　330
　　　In her behalf that scorns your services.
　　　Let her alone. Speak not of Helena;
　　　Take not her part. For, if thou dost intend°
　　　Never so little show of love to her,
　　　Thou shalt aby° it.
LYSANDER.　　　　　　　Now she holds me not;　　　　　335
　　　Now follow, if thou dar'st, to try whose right,
　　　Of thine or mine, is most in Helena.　　　　　[*Exit.*]
DEMETRIUS. Follow? Nay, I'll go with thee, cheek by jowl.°
　　　　　　　　　　　　　　[*Exit, following Lysander.*]
HERMIA. You, mistress, all this coil° is 'long of° you.
　　　Nay, go not back.°
HELENA.　　　　　　　I will not trust you, I　　　　　340
　　　Nor longer stay in your curst company.
　　　Your hands than mine are quicker for a fray;
　　　My legs are longer, though, to run away.　　　[*Exit.*]
HERMIA. I am amazed and know not what to say.　　　*Exit.*

　　　[*Oberon and Puck come forward.*]

OBERON. This is thy negligence. Still thou mistak'st,　　　345
　　　Or else committ'st thy knaveries willfully.
PUCK. Believe me, king of shadows, I mistook.
　　　Did not you tell me I should know the man
　　　By the Athenian garments he had on?
　　　And so far blameless proves my enterprise　　　350
　　　That I have 'nointed an Athenian's eyes;
　　　And so far am I glad it so did sort,°
　　　As° this their jangling I esteem a sport.

---

323 **keen** fierce, cruel.　**shrewd** shrewish　329 **minimus** diminutive creature.　**knotgrass** a weed, an infusion of which was thought to stunt the growth　333 **intend** give sign of　335 **aby** pay for　338 **cheek by jowl** i.e., side by side　339 **coil** turmoil, dissension.　**'long of** on account of　340 **go not back** i.e., don't retreat. (Hermia is again proposing a fight.)　352 **sort** turn out　353 **As** that (also at l. 359)

OBERON. Thou seest these lovers seek a place to fight.
Hie° therefore, Robin, overcast the night;   355
The starry welkin° cover thou anon
With drooping fog as black as Acheron,°
And lead these testy rivals so astray
As one come not within another's way.
Like to Lysander sometimes frame thy tongue,   360
Then stir Demetrius up with bitter wrong;°
And sometimes rail thou like Demetrius.
And from each other look thou lead them thus,
Till o'er their brows death-counterfeiting sleep
With leaden legs and batty° wings doth creep.   365
Then crush this herb° into Lysander's eye,   [*Giving herb*]
Whose liquor hath this virtuous° property,
To take from thence all error with his° might
And make his eyeballs roll with wonted° sight.
When they next wake, all this derision°   370
Shall seem a dream and fruitless vision,
And back to Athens shall the lovers wend
With league whose date° till death shall never end.
Whiles I in this affair do thee employ,
I'll to my queen and beg her Indian boy;   375
And then I will her charmèd eye release
From monster's view, and all things shall be peace.
PUCK. My fairy lord, this must be done with haste,
For night's swift dragons° cut the clouds full fast,
And yonder shines Aurora's harbinger,°   380
At whose approach, ghosts, wand'ring here and there,
Troop home to churchyards. Damnèd spirits all,
That in crossways and floods have burial,°
Already to their wormy beds are gone.
For fear lest day should look their shames upon,   385
They willfully themselves exile from light
And must for aye° consort with black-browed night.

---

355 Hie hasten **356 welkin** sky **357 Acheron** river of Hades (here representing Hades
itself) **361 wrong** insults **365 batty** batlike **366 this herb** i.e., the antidote (mentioned
in 2.1.184) to love-in-idleness **367 virtuous** efficacious **368 his** its **369 wonted**
accustomed **370 derision** laughable business **373 date** term of existence **379 dragons**
(Supposed by Shakespeare to be yoked to the car of the goddess of night.) **380 Aurora's
harbinger** the morning star, precursor of dawn **383 crossways . . . burial** (Those who
had committed suicide were buried at crossways, with a stake driven through them; those
drowned, i e., buried in floods or great waters, would be condemned to wander disconsolate for want of burial rites.) **387 for aye** forever

OBERON. But we are spirits of another sort.
    I with the Morning's love° have oft made sport,
    And, like a forester,° the groves may tread   *390*
    Even till the eastern gate, all fiery red,
    Opening on Neptune with fair blessèd beams,
    Turns into yellow gold his salt green streams.
    But notwithstanding, haste, make no delay.
    We may effect this business yet ere day.   [*Exit.*] *395*
PUCK.
        Up and down, up and down,
        I will lead them up and down.
        I am feared in field and town.
        Goblin, lead them up and down.
        Here comes one.   *400*

    Enter Lysander.

LYSANDER. Where art thou, proud Demetrius? Speak thou now.
PUCK. [*Mimicking Demetrius*]
    Here, villain, drawn° and ready. Where art thou?
LYSANDER. I will be with thee straight.°
PUCK.   Follow me, then,
    To plainer° ground.

               [*Lysander wanders about, following the voice.*]

    Enter Demetrius.

DEMETRIUS.   Lysander! Speak again!
    Thou runaway, thou coward, art thou fled?   *405*
    Speak! In some bush? Where dost thou hide thy head?
PUCK. [*Mimicking Lysander*]
    Thou coward, art thou bragging to the stars,
    Telling the bushes that thou look'st for wars,
    And wilt not come? Come, recreant;° come, thou child,
    I'll whip thee with a rod. He is defiled   *410*
    That draws a sword on thee.
DEMETRIUS.   Yea, art thou there?
PUCK. Follow my voice. We'll try° no manhood here.

                          Exeunt.

    [*Lysander returns.*]

---

389 Morning's love Cephalus, a beautiful youth beloved by Aurora; or perhaps the goddess of the dawn herself   **390 forester** keeper of a royal forest   **402 drawn** with drawn sword   **403 straight** immediately   **404 plainer** more open   **s.d. Lysander wanders about** (It is not clearly necessary that Lysander exit at this point; neither exit nor re-entrance is indicated in the early texts.)   **409 recreant** cowardly wretch   **412 try** test

LYSANDER. He goes before me and still dares me on.
    When I come where he calls, then he is gone.
    The villain is much lighter-heeled than I.   *415*
    I followed fast, but faster he did fly,
    That fallen am I in dark uneven way,
    And here will rest me. [*He lies down.*] Come, thou gentle day!
    For if but once thou show me thy gray light,
    I'll find Demetrius and revenge this spite. [*He sleeps.*]   *420*

    [*Enter*] *Robin* [*Puck*] *and Demetrius.*

PUCK. Ho, ho, ho! Coward, why com'st thou not?
DEMETRIUS. Abide° me, if thou dar'st; for well I wot°
    Thou runn'st before me, shifting every place,
    And dar'st not stand nor look me in the face.
    Where art thou now?
PUCK.   Come hither. I am here.   *425*
DEMETRIUS. Nay, then, thou mock'st me. Thou shalt buy°
       this dear,°
    If ever I thy face by daylight see.
    Now, go thy way. Faintness constraineth me
    To measure out my length on this cold bed.
    By day's approach look to be visited.   *430*
                          [*He lies down and sleeps.*]

    Enter Helena.

HELENA.
    O weary night, O long and tedious night,
        Abate° thy hours! Shine comforts from the east,
    That I may back to Athens by daylight,
        From these that my poor company detest;
    And sleep, that sometimes shuts up sorrow's eye,   *435*
    Steal me awhile from mine own company.
                     [*She lies down and*] *sleep*[*s*].

PUCK.
        Yet but three? Come one more;
        Two of both kinds makes up four.
        Here she comes, curst° and sad.
        Cupid is a knavish lad,   *440*
        Thus to make poor females mad.

    [*Enter Hermia.*]

---

422 Abide confront, face. **wot** know   **426 buy** aby, pay for.   **dear** dearly   **432 Abate**
lessen, shorten   **439 curst** ill-tempered

HERMIA.
> Never so weary, never so in woe,
>> Bedabbled with the dew and torn with briers
> I can no further crawl, no further go;
>> My legs can keep no pace with my desires.   *445*
> Here will I rest me till the break of day.
> Heavens shield Lysander, if they mean a fray!

PUCK.   [*She lies down and sleeps.*]
>> On the ground
>> Sleep sound.
>> I'll apply   *450*
>> To your eye,
> Gentle lover, remedy.

                              [*Squeezing the juice on Lysander's eyes.*]
>> When thou wak'st,
>> Thou tak'st
>> True delight   *455*
>> In the sight
> Of thy former lady's eye;
> And the country proverb known,
> That every man should take his own,
> In your waking shall be shown: *460*
>> Jack shall have Jill;°
>> Naught shall go ill;
> The man shall have his mare again, and all shall be well.

                          [*Exit. The four sleeping lovers remain.*]

[4.1] *Enter [Titania] Queen of Fairies, and [Bottom the] clown, and
Fairies; and [Oberon,] the King, behind them.*

TITANIA.
> Come, sit thee down upon this flowery bed,
>> While I thy amiable° cheeks do coy,°
> And stick muskroses in thy sleek smooth head,
>> And kiss thy fair large ears, my gentle joy.

                                              [*They recline.*]

BOTTOM. Where's Peaseblossom?   *5*
PEASEBLOSSOM. Ready.

---

461 Jack shall have Jill (Proverbial for "boy gets girl.")

**4.1 Location: The action is continuous. The four lovers are still asleep onstage.
2 amiable** lovely. **coy** caress

BOTTOM. Scratch my head, Peaseblossom. Where's Monsieur Cobweb?

COBWEB. Ready.

BOTTOM. Monsieur Cobweb, good monsieur, get you your weapons in
　　　your hand, and kill me a red-hipped humble-bee on the top of a　10
　　　thistle; and, good monsieur, bring me the honey bag. Do not fret
　　　yourself too much in the action, monsieur, and, good monsieur, have
　　　a care the honey bag break not; I would be loath to have you over-
　　　flown with a honey bag, signor. [*Exit Cobweb.*] Where's Monsieur
　　　Mustardseed?　15

MUSTARDSEED. Ready.

BOTTOM. Give me your neaf,° Monsieur Mustardseed. Pray you, leave
　　　your courtesy,° good monsieur.

MUSTARDSEED. What's your will?

BOTTOM. Nothing, good monsieur, but to help Cavalery°Cobweb° to　20
　　　scratch. I must to the barber's, monsieur, for methinks I am mar-
　　　velous hairy about the face; and I am such a tender ass, if my hair
　　　do but tickle me, I must scratch.

TITANIA. What, wilt thou hear some music, my sweet love?

BOTTOM. I have a reasonable good ear in music. Let's have the tongs and　25
　　　the bones.°

　　　　　　　　　　　　　　　　　[*Music: tongs, rural music.*°]

TITANIA. Or say, sweet love, what thou desirest to eat.

BOTTOM. Truly, a peck of provender.° I could munch your good dry oats.
　　　Methinks I have a great desire to a bottle° of hay. Good hay, sweet
　　　hay, hath no fellow.°　30

TITANIA. I have a venturous fairy that shall seek
　　　The squirrel's hoard, and fetch thee new nuts.

BOTTOM. I had rather have a handful or two of dried peas. But, I pray you,
　　　let none of your people stir° me. I have an exposition° of sleep come
　　　upon me.　35

TITANIA. Sleep thou, and I will wind thee in my arms.
　　　Fairies, begone, and be all ways° away.

　　　　　　　　　　　　　　　　　　[*Exeunt Fairies.*]

　　　So doth the woodbine the sweet honeysuckle
　　　Gently entwist; the female ivy so

---

17 neaf fist   **17–18 leave your courtesy** i.e., stop bowing, or put on your hat   **20 Caval-
ery** cavalier. (Form of address for a gentleman.)   **Cobweb** (Seemingly an error, since Cobweb has been sent to bring honey while Peaseblossom has been asked to scratch.)
25–26 tongs . . . bones instruments for rustic music. (The tongs were played like a tri-
angle, whereas the bones were held between the fingers and used as clappers.)   **s.d.
Music . . . music** (This stage direction is added from the Folio.)   **28 peck of
provender** one-quarter bushel of grain   **29 bottle** bundle   **30 fellow** equal   **34 stir**
disturb.   **exposition** (Bottom's word for *disposition*.)   **37 all ways** in all directions

Enrings the barky fingers of the elm.   40
O, how I love thee! How I dote on thee!

                                               [*They sleep.*]

Enter Robin Goodfellow [Puck].

OBERON. [*Coming forward*]
   Welcome, good Robin. Seest thou this sweet sight?
   Her dotage now I do begin to pity.
   For, meeting her of late behind the wood,
   Seeking sweet favors° for this hateful fool,   45
   I did upbraid her and fall out with her.
   For she his hairy temples then had rounded
   With coronet of fresh and fragrant flowers;
   And that same dew, which sometime° on the buds
   Was wont to swell like round and orient pearls,°   50
   Stood now within the pretty flowerets' eyes
   Like tears that did their own disgrace bewail.
   When I had at my pleasure taunted her,
   And she in mild terms begged my patience,
   I then did ask of her her changeling child,   55
   Which straight she gave me, and her fairy sent
   To bear him to my bower in Fairyland.
   And, now I have the boy, I will undo
   This hateful imperfection of her eyes.
   And, gentle Puck, take this transformèd scalp   60
   From off the head of this Athenian swain,
   That he, awaking when the other° do,
   May all to Athens back again repair,°
   And think no more of this night's accidents
   But as the fierce vexation of a dream.   65
   But first I will release the Fairy Queen.
                          [*He squeezes a herb on her eyes.*]
      Be as thou wast wont to be;
      See as thou wast wont to see.
      Dian's bud° o'er Cupid's flower
      Hath such force and blessèd power.   70
   Now, my Titania, wake you, my sweet queen.
TITANIA. [*Waking*] My Oberon! What visions have I seen!
   Methought I was enamored of an ass.

---

45 favors i.e., gifts of flowers   **49 sometime** formerly   **50 orient pearls** i.e., the most
beautiful of all pearls, those coming from the Orient   **62 other** others   **63 repair** return
69 Dian's bud (Perhaps the flower of the *agnus castus* or chaste-tree, supposed to preserve
chastity; or perhaps referring simply to Oberon's herb by which he can undo the effects
of "Cupid's flower," the love-in-idleness of 2.1.166–168.)

OBERON. There lies your love.
TITANIA.   How came these things to pass?
   O, how mine eyes do loathe his visage now!   75
OBERON. Silence awhile. Robin, take off this head.
   Titania, music call, and strike more dead
   Than common sleep of all these five° the sense.
TITANIA. Music, ho! Music, such as charmeth° sleep!

                                                    [*Music.*]

PUCK. [*Removing the ass head*]
   Now, when thou wak'st, with thine own fool's eyes peep.   80
OBERON. Sound, music! Come, my queen, take hands with me,
   And rock the ground whereon these sleepers be.   [*They dance.*]
   Now thou and I are new in amity,
   And will tomorrow midnight solemnly°
   Dance in Duke Theseus' house triumphantly,   85
   And bless it to all fair prosperity.
   There shall the pairs of faithful lovers be
   Wedded, with Theseus, all in jollity.
PUCK.
         Fairy King, attend, and mark:
         I do hear the morning lark.   90
OBERON.
         Then, my queen, in silence sad,°
         Trip we after night's shade.
         We the globe can compass soon,
         Swifter than the wandering moon.
TITANIA.
         Come, my lord, and in our flight   95
         Tell me how it came this night
         That I sleeping here was found
         With these mortals on the ground.
                                                    Exeunt.
                                        Wind horn [*within*].

   Enter Theseus and all his train; [*Hippolyta, Egeus*].

THESEUS. Go, one of you, find out the forester,
   For now our observation° is performed;   100
   And since we have the vaward° of the day,
   My love shall hear the music of my hounds.
   Uncouple° in the western valley, let them go.
   Dispatch, I say, and find the forester.   [*Exit an Attendant.*]
   We will, fair queen, up to the mountain's top   105

78 these five i.e., the four lovers and Bottom   **79 charmeth** brings about, as though by
a charm   **84 solemnly** ceremoniously   **91 sad** sober   **100 observation** i.e., observance
to a morn of May (1.1.167)   **101 vaward** vanguard, i.e, earliest part   **103 Uncouple** set
free for the hunt

And mark the musical confusion
Of hounds and echo in conjunction.

HIPPOLTYA. I was with Hercules and Cadmus° once,
When in a wood of Crete they bayed° the bear
With hounds of Sparta.° Never did I hear   110
Such gallant chiding;° for, besides the groves,
The skies, the fountains, every region near
Seemed all one mutual cry. I never heard
So musical a discord, such sweet thunder.

THESEUS. My hounds are bred out of the Spartan kind,°   115
So flewed,° so sanded;° and their heads are hung
With ears that sweep away the morning dew;
Crook-kneed, and dewlapped° like Thessalian bulls;
Slow in pursuit, but matched in mouth like bells,
Each under each.° A cry° more tunable°   120
Was never holloed to, nor cheered° with horn,
In Crete, in Sparta, nor in Thessaly.
Judge when you hear. [*He sees the sleepers.*] But, soft!
What nymphs are these?

EGEUS. My lord, this is my daughter here asleep,   125
And this Lysander; this Demetrius is,
This Helena, old Nedar's Helena.
I wonder of° their being here together.

THESEUS. No doubt they rose up early to observe
The rite of May, and hearing our intent,   130
Came here in grace of our solemnity.°
But speak, Egeus. Is not this the day
That Hermia should give answer of her choice?

EGEUS. It is, my lord.

THESEUS. Go, bid the huntsmen wake them with their horns.   135

[*Exit an Attendant.*]

Shout within. Wind horns. They all start up.

Good morrow, friends. Saint Valentine° is past.
Begin these woodbirds but to couple now?

---

108 Cadmus mythical founder of Thebes. (This story about him is unknown.)   **109 bayed**
brought to bay   **110 hounds of Sparta** (A breed famous in antiquity for their hunting skill.)
111 chiding i.e., yelping   **115 kind** strain, breed   **116 So flewed** similarly having large
hanging chaps or fleshy covering of the jaw.   **sanded** of sandy color   **118 dewlapped**
having pendulous folds of skin under the neck   **119–20 matched . . . each** i.e., harmoni-
ously matched in their various cries like a set of bells, from treble down to bass   **120 cry** pack
of hounds.   **tunable** well tuned, melodious   **121 cheered** encouraged   **128 wonder of**
wonder at   **131 in . . . solemnity** in honor of our wedding   **136 Saint Valentine** (Birds
were supposed to choose their mates on Saint Valentine's Day.)

LYSANDER. Pardon, my lord.   [*They kneel.*]
THESEUS.   I pray you all, stand up.
    I know you two are rival enemies;
    How comes this gentle concord in the world,   140
    That hatred is so far from jealousy°
    To sleep by hate and fear no enmity?
LYSANDER. My lord, I shall reply amazedly,
    Half sleep, half waking; but as yet, I swear,
    I cannot truly say how I came here.   145
    But, as I think—for truly would I speak,
    And now I do bethink me, so it is—
    I came with Hermia hither. Our intent
    Was to be gone from Athens, where° we might,
    Without° the peril of the Athenian law—   150
EGEUS. Enough, enough, my lord; you have enough.
    I beg the law, the law, upon his head.
    They would have stol'n away; they would, Demetrius,
    Thereby to have defeated° you and me,
    You of your wife and me of my consent,   155
    Of my consent that she should be your wife.
DEMETRIUS. My lord, fair Helen told me of their stealth,
    Of this their purpose hither° to this wood,
    And I in fury hither followed them,
    Fair Helena in fancy following me.   160
    But, my good lord, I wot not by what power—
    But by some power it is—my love to Hermia,
    Melted as the snow, seems to me now
    As the remembrance of an idle gaud°
    Which in my childhood I did dote upon;   165
    And all the faith, the virtue of my heart,
    The object and the pleasure of mine eye,
    Is only Helena. To her, my lord,
    Was I betrothed ere I saw Hermia,
    But like a sickness did I loathe this food;   170
    But, as in health, come to my natural taste,
    Now I do wish it, love it, long for it,
    And will for evermore be true to it.
THESEUS. Fair lovers, you are fortunately met.
    Of this discourse we more will hear anon.   175
    Egeus, I will overbear your will;
    For in the temple, by and by, with us

---

141 jealousy suspicion   **149 where** wherever; or, to where   **150 Without** outside of,
beyond   **154 defeated** defrauded   **158 hither** in coming hither   **164 idle gaud** worthless
trinket

These couples shall eternally be knit.
And, for° the morning now is something° worn,
Our purposed hunting shall be set aside.   180
Away with us to Athens. Three and three,
We'll hold a feast in great solemnity.
Come, Hippolyta.

> [*Exeunt Theseus, Hippolyta, Egeus, and train.*]

DEMETRIUS. These things seem small and undistinguishable,
Like far-off mountains turnèd into clouds.   185
HERMIA. Methinks I see these things with parted° eye,
When everything seems double.
HELENA.   So methinks;
And I have found Demetrius like a jewel,
Mine own, and not mine own.°
DEMETRIUS.   Are you sure
That we are awake? It seems to me   190
That yet we sleep, we dream. Do not you think
The Duke was here, and bid us follow him?
HERMIA. Yea, and my father.
HELENA.   And Hippolyta.
LYSANDER. And he did bid us follow to the temple.
DEMETRIUS. Why, then, we are awake. Let's follow him,   195
And by the way let us recount our dreams.   [*Exeunt.*]
BOTTOM. [*Awaking*] When my cue comes, call me, and I will answer. My
next is, "Most fair Pyramus." Heigh — ho! Peter Quince! Flute, the
bellows mender! Snout, the tinker! Starveling! God's° my life, stolen hence and left me asleep! I have had a most rare vision. I have   200
had a dream, past the wit of man to say what dream it was. Man
is but an ass if he go about° to expound this dream. Methought I
was—there is no man can tell what. Methought I was—and
methought I had—but man is but a patched° fool if he will offer°
to say what methought I had. The eye of man hath not heard, the   205
ear of man hath not seen, man's hand is not able to taste, his tongue
to conceive, nor his heart to report,° what my dream was. I will get
Peter Quince to write a ballad of this dream. It shall be called "Bottom's Dream," because it hath no bottom; and I will sing it in the
latter end of a play, before the Duke. Peradventure, to make it the   210
more gracious, I shall sing it at her° death.   [*Exit.*]

---

179 for since. **something** somewhat   **186 parted** improperly focused   **188–89 like . . .
mine own** i.e., like a jewel that one finds by chance and therefore possesses but cannot
certainly consider one's own property   **199 God's** may God save   **202 go about** attempt
204 patched wearing motley, i.e., a dress of various colors.   **offer** venture
205–207 The eye . . . report (Bottom garbles the terms of 1 Corinthians 2:9)
211 her Thisbe's (?)

[**4.2**]   *Enter Quince, Flute, [Snout, and Starveling].*

QUINCE. Have you sent to Bottom's house? Is he come home yet?

STARVELING. He cannot be heard of. Out of doubt he is transported.°

FLUTE. If he come not, then the play is marred. It goes not forward, doth
    it?

QUINCE. It is not possible. You have not a man in all Athens able to   *5*
    discharge° Pyramus but he.

FLUTE. No, he hath simply the best wit° of any handicraft man in Athens.

QUINCE. Yea, and the best person° too, and he is a very paramour for a
    sweet voice.

FLUTE. You must say "paragon." A paramour is, God bless us, a thing of   *10*
    naught.°

    Enter Snug the joiner.

SNUG. Masters, the Duke is coming from the temple and there is two
    or three lords and ladies more married. If our sport had gone for-
    ward, we had all been made men.°

FLUTE. O sweet bully Bottom! Thus hath he lost sixpence a day during   *15*
    his life; he could not have scaped sixpence a day. An the Duke had
    not given him sixpence a day° for playing Pyramus, I'll be hanged.
    He would have deserved it. Sixpence a day in Pyramus, or nothing.

    Enter Bottom.

BOTTOM. Where are these lads? Where are these hearts?°

QUINCE. Bottom! O most courageous day! O most happy hour!   *20*

BOTTOM. Masters, I am to discourse wonders.° But ask me not what; for
    if I tell you, I am no true Athenian. I will tell you everything, right
    as it fell out.

QUINCE. Let us hear, sweet Bottom.

BOTTOM. Not a word of° me. All that I will tell you is—that the Duke   *25*
    hath dined. Get your apparel together, good strings° to your beards,
    new ribbons to your pumps;° meet presently° at the palace; every
    man look o'er his part; for the short and the long is, our play is
    preferred.° In any case, let Thisbe have clean linen; and let not him
    that plays the lion pare his nails, for they shall hang out for the lion's   *30*

4.2 Location: Athens

2 transported carried off by fairies; or, possibly, transformed **6 discharge** perform **7 wit**
intellect **8 person** appearance **10–11 a . . . naught** a shameful thing **14 we . . .
men** i.e., we would have had our fortunes made **17 sixpence a day** i.e., as a royal pension **19 hearts** good fellows **21 am . . . wonders** have wonders to relate **25 of**
out of **26 strings** (to attach the beards) **27 pumps** light shoes or slippers. **presently**
immediately **29 preferred** selected for consideration

claws. And, most dear actors, eat no onions nor garlic, for we are
to utter sweet breath; and I do not doubt but to hear them say it
is a sweet comedy. No more words. Away! Go, away!

            [*Exeunt.*]

   [5.1]   *Enter Theseus, Hippolyta, and Philostrate, [lords, and attendants].*

HIPPOLTYA. 'Tis strange, my Theseus, that° these lovers speak of.
THESEUS. More strange than true. I never may° believe
     These antique° fables nor these fairy toys.°
     Lovers and madmen have such seething brains,
     Such shaping fantasies,° that apprehend°   5
     More than cool reason ever comprehends.°
     The lunatic, the lover, and the poet
     Are of imagination all compact.°
     One sees more devils than vast hell can hold;
     That is the madman. The lover, all as frantic,   10
     Sees Helen's° beauty in a brow of Egypt.°
     The poet's eye, in a fine frenzy rolling,
     Doth glance from heaven to earth, from earth to heaven;
     And as imagination bodies forth
     The forms of things unknown, the poet's pen   15
     Turns them to shapes and gives to airy nothing
     A local habitation and a name.
     Such tricks hath strong imagination
     That, if it would but apprehend some joy,
     It comprehends some bringer° of that joy;   20
     Or in the night, imagining some fear,°
     How easy is a bush supposed a bear!
HIPPOLYTA. But all the story of the night told over,
     And all their minds transfigured so together,
     More witnesseth than fancy's images°   25
     And grows to something of great constancy;°
     But, howsoever,° strange and admirable.°

5.1. Location: Athens. The palace of Theseus.
1 that that which   **2 may** can   **3 antique** old-fashioned (punning too on *antic,* strange,
grotesque).   **fairy toys** trifling stories about fairies   **5 fantasies** imaginations.   **apprehend**
conceive, imagine   **6 comprehends** understands   **8 compact** formed, composed
11 Helen's i.e., of Helen of Troy, pattern of beauty.   **brow of Egypt** i.e., face of a gypsy
20 bringer i.e., source   **21 fear** object of fear   **25 More . . . images** testifies to something more substantial than mere imaginings   **26 constancy** certainty   **27 howsoever** in any case   **admirable** a source of wonder

Enter lovers: Lysander, Demetrius, Hermia, and Helena.

THESEUS. Here come the lovers, full of joy and mirth.
　　Joy, gentle friends! Joy and fresh days of love
　　Accompany your hearts!
LYSANDER. 　　　　　　More than to us   *30*
　　Wait in your royal walks, your board, your bed!
THESEUS. Come now, what masques,° what dances shall we have
　　To wear away this long age of three hours
　　Between our after-supper and bedtime?
　　Where is our usual manager of mirth?   *35*
　　What revels are in hand? Is there no play
　　To ease the anguish of a torturing hour?
　　Call Philostrate.
PHILOSTRATE. 　　　　Here, mighty Theseus.
THESEUS. Say what abridgment° have you for this evening?
　　What masque? What music? How shall we beguile   *40*
　　The lazy time, if not with some delight?
PHILOSTRATE. [*Giving him a paper*]
　　There is a brief° how many sports are ripe.
　　Make choice of which Your Highness will see first.
THESEUS. [*Reads*] "The battle with the Centaurs,° to be sung
　　By an Athenian eunuch to the harp"?   *45*
　　We'll none of that. That have I told my love,
　　In glory of my kinsman° Hercules.
　　[*Reads*] "The riot of the tipsy Bacchanals,
　　Tearing the Thracian singer in their rage"?°
　　That is an old device;° and it was played   *50*
　　When I from Thebes came last a conqueror.
　　[*Reads.*] "The thrice three Muses mourning for the death
　　Of Learning, late deceased in beggary"?°
　　That is some satire, keen and critical,
　　Not sorting with° a nuptial ceremony.   *55*
　　[*Reads.*] "A tedious brief scene of young Pyramus
　　And his love Thisbe; very tragical mirth"?
　　Merry and tragical? Tedious and brief?

32 masques courtly entertainments　**39 abridgment** pastime (to abridge or shorten the evening)　**42 brief** short written statement, summary　**44 battle . . . Centaurs** (Probably refers to the battle of the Centaurs and the Lapithae, when the Centaurs attempted to carry off Hippodamia, bride of Theseus' friend Pirothous.)　**47 kinsman** (Plutarch's "Life of Theseus" states that Hercules and Theseus were near kinsmen. Theseus is referring to a version of the battle of the Centaurs in which Hercules was said to be present.)　**48–49 The riot . . . rage** (This was the story of the death of Orpheus, as told in *Metamorphoses* 9.)　**50 device** show, performance　**52–53 The thrice . . . beggary** (Possibly an allusion to Spenser's *Teares of the Muses,* 1591, though "satires" deploring the neglect of learning and the creative arts were commonplace.)　**55 sorting with** befitting

That is hot ice and wondrous strange° snow.
How shall we find the concord of this discord?   *60*
PHILOSTRATE. A play there is, my lord, some ten words long,
      Which is as brief as I have known a play;
      But by ten words, my lord, it is too long,
      Which makes it tedious. For in all the play
      There is not one word apt, one player fitted.   *65*
      And tragical, my noble lord, it is,
      For Pyramus therein doth kill himself.
      Which, when I saw rehearsed, I must confess,
      Made mine eyes water; but more merry tears
      The passion of loud laughter never shed.   *70*
THESEUS. What are they that do play it?
PHILOSTRATE. Hard-handed men that work in Athens here,
      Which never labored in their minds till now,
      And now have toiled° their unbreathed° memories
      With this same play, against° your nuptial.   *75*
THESEUS. And we will hear it.
PHILOSTRATE.   No, my noble lord,
      It is not for you. I have heard it over,
      And it is nothing, nothing in the world;
      Unless you can find sport in their intents,
      Extremely stretched° and conned° with cruel pain   *80*
      To do you service.
THESEUS.   I will hear that play;
      For never anything can be amiss
      When simpleness° and duty tender it.
      Go bring them in; and take your places, ladies.
            [*Philostrate goes to summon the players.*]
HIPPOLYTA. I love not to see wretchedness o'ercharged,°   *85*
      And duty in his service° perishing.
THESEUS. Why, gentle sweet, you shall see no such thing.
HIPPOLTYA. He says they can do nothing in this kind.°
THESEUS. The kinder we, to give them thanks for nothing.
      Our sport shall be to take what they mistake;   *90*
      And what poor duty cannot do, noble respect°
      Takes it in might, not merit.°
      Where I have come, great clerks° have purposèd

---

59 strange (Sometimes emended to an adjective that would contrast with *snow,* just as *hot*
contrasts with *ice.*) **74 toiled** taxed. **unbreathed** unexercised **75 against** in preparation for **80 stretched** strained. **conned** memorized **83 simpleness** simplicity
85 wretchedness o'ercharged incompetence overburdened **86 his service** its attempt
to serve **88 kind** kind of thing **91 respect** evaluation, consideration **92 Takes . . .
merit** values it for the effort made rather than for the excellence achieved **93 clerks** learned
men

To greet me with premeditated welcomes;
Where I have seen them shiver and look pale,   *95*
Make periods in the midst of sentences,
Throttle their practiced accent° in their fears,
And in conclusion dumbly have broke off,
Not paying me a welcome. Trust me, sweet,
Out of this silence° yet I picked a welcome;   *100*
And in the modesty of fearful duty
I read as much as from the rattling tongue
Of saucy and audacious eloquence.
Love, therefore, and tongue-tied simplicity
In least° speak most, to my capacity.°   *105*

[*Philostrate returns.*]

PHILOSTRATE. So please Your Grace, the Prologue° is addressed.°
THESEUS. Let him approach.   [*A flourish of trumpets.*]

Enter the Prologue [Quince].

PROLOGUE.
    If we offend, it is with our good will.
        That you should think, we come not to offend,
    But with good will. To show our simple skill,   *110*
        That is the true beginning of our end.
    Consider then, we come but in despite.
        We do not come, as minding° to content you,
    Our true intent is. All for your delight.
        We are not here. That you should here repent you,   *115*
    The actors are at hand, and, by their show,
    You shall know all that you are like to know.
THESEUS. This fellow doth not stand upon points.°
LYSANDER. He hath rid° his prologue like a rough° colt; he knows not
    the stop.° A good moral, my lord: it is not enough to speak, but   *120*
    to speak true.
HIPPOLYTA. Indeed he hath played on his prologue like a child on a re-
    corder;° a sound, but not in government.°
THESEUS. His speech was like a tangled chain: nothing° impaired, but all
    disordered. Who is next?   *125*

---

97 practiced accent i.e., rehearsed speech or, usual way of speaking   **105 least** i.e., saying least.   **to my capacity** in my judgment and understanding   **106 Prologue** speaker of the prologue.   **addressed** ready   **113 minding** intending   **118 stand upon points** (1) heed niceties or small points (2) pay attention to punctuation in his reading. (The humor of Quince's speech is in the blunders of its punctuation.)   **119 rid** ridden.   **rough** unbroken   **120 stop** (1) the stopping of a colt by reining it in (2) punctuation mark   **122–23 recorder** a wind instrument like a flute or flageolet   **123 government** control   **124 nothing** not at all

Enter Pyramus [Bottom] and Thisbe [Flute], and Wall [Snout], and Moon-shine [Starveling], and Lion [Snug].

PROLOGUE.
    Gentles, perchance you wonder at this show,
        But wonder on, till truth make all things plain.
    This man is Pyramus, if you would know;
        This beauteous lady Thisbe is certain.
    This man with lime and roughcast doth present   *130*
        Wall, that vile Wall which did these lovers sunder;
    And through Wall's chink, poor souls, they are content
        To whisper. At the which let no man wonder.
    This man, with lantern, dog, and bush of thorn,
        Presenteth Moonshine; for, if you will know,   *135*
    By moonshine did these lovers think no scorn°
        To meet at Ninus' tomb, there, there to woo.
    This grisly beast, which Lion hight° by name,
        The trusty Thisbe coming first by night
    Did scare away, or rather did affright;   *140*
    And as she fled, her mantle she did fall,°
        Which Lion vile with bloody mouth did stain.
    Anon comes Pyramus, sweet youth and tall,°
        And finds his trusty Thisbe's mantle slain;
    Whereat, with blade, with bloody blameful blade,   *145*
        He bravely broached° his boiling bloody breast.
    And Thisbe, tarrying in mulberry shade,
        His dagger drew, and died. For all the rest,
    Let Lion, Moonshine, Wall, and lovers twain
    At large° discourse while here they do remain.   *150*
                Exeunt Lion, Thisbe, and Moonshine.
THESEUS. I wonder if the lion be to speak.
DEMETRIUS. No wonder. my lord. One lion may, when many asses do.
WALL. In this same interlude° it doth befall
    That I, one Snout by name, present a wall;
    And such a wall as I would have you think   *155*
    That had in it a crannied hole or chink,
    Through which the lovers, Pyramus and Thisbe,
    Did whisper often, very secretly.
    This loam, this roughcast, and this stone doth show
    That I am that same wall; the truth is so.   *160*

---

136 think no scorn think it no disgraceful matter   **138 hight** is called   **141 fall** let fall
143 tall courageous   **146 broached** stabbed   **150 At large** in full, at length   **153 inter-lude** play

And this the cranny is, right and sinister,°
Through which the fearful lovers are to whisper.
THESEUS. Would you desire lime and hair to speak better?
DEMETRIUS. It is the wittiest partition° that ever I heard discourse, my lord.

[*Pyramus comes forward.*]

THESEUS. Pyramus draws near the wall. Silence!   165
PYRAMUS.
    O grim-looked° night! O night with hue so black!
      O night, which ever art when day is not!
    O night, O night! Alack, alack, alack,
      I fear my Thisbe's promise is forgot.
    And thou, O wall, O sweet, O lovely wall,   170
      That stand'st between her father's ground and mine,
    Thou wall, O wall, O sweet and lovely wall,
      Show me thy chink to blink through with mine eyne!
                  [*Wall makes a chink with his fingers.*]
    Thanks, courteous wall. Jove shield thee well for this.
      But what see l? No Thisbe do I see.   175
    O wicked wall, through whom I see no bliss!
      Cursed be thy stones for thus deceiving me!
THESEUS. The wall, methinks, being sensible,° should curse again.
PYRAMUS. No, in truth, sir he should not. "Deceiving me" is Thisbe's
    cue: she is to enter now, and I am to spy her through the wall.   180
    You shall see, it will fall pat° as I told you. Yonder she comes.

Enter Thisbe.

THISBE.
    O wall, full often hast thou heard my moans,
      For parting my fair Pyramus and me.
    My cherry lips have often kissed thy stones,
      Thy stones with lime and hair knit up in thee.   185
PYRAMUS.
    I see a voice. Now will I to the chink,
      To spy an° I can hear my Thisbe's face.
    Thisbe!
THISBE. My love! Thou art my love, I think.
PYRAMUS.
    Think what thou wilt, I am thy lover's grace,°   190
    And like Limander° am I trusty still.

---

161 right and sinister i.e., the right side of it and the left; or, running from right to
left, horizontally **163 partition** (1) wall (2) section of a learned treatise or oration
166 grim-looked grim-looking **178 sensible** capable of feeling **181 pat** exactly
187 an if **190 lover's grace** i.e. gracious lover **191, 192 Limander, Helen** (Blunders

THISBE.

    And I like Helen,° till the Fates me kill.

PYRAMUS.

    Not Shafalus to Procrus° was so true.

THISBE.

    As Shafalus to Procrus, I to you.

PYRAMUS.

    O, kiss me through the hole of this vile wall!   195

THISBE.

    I kiss the wall's hole, not your lips at all.

PYRAMUS.

    Wilt thou at Ninny's tomb meet me straightway?

THISBE.

    'Tide° life, 'tide death, I come without delay.

                          [Exeunt Pyramus and Thisbe.]

WALL.

    Thus have I, Wall, my part dischargèd so;

    And, being done, thus Wall away doth go.   *[Exit.]* 200

THESEUS. Now is the mural down between the two neighbors.

DEMETRIUS. No remedy, my lord, when walls are so willful° to hear
    without warning.°

HIPPOLTYA. This is the silliest stuff that ever I heard.

THESEUS. The best in this kind° are but shadows;° and the worst are 205
    no worse, if imagination amend them.

HIPPOLTYA. It must be your imagination then, and not theirs.

THESEUS. If we imagine no worse of them than they of themselves, they
    may pass for excellent men. Here come two noble beasts in, a man
    and a lion.   210

    Enter Lion and Moonshine.

LION.

    You, ladies, you whose gentle hearts do fear

        The smallest monstrous mouse that creeps on floor,

    May now perchance both quake and tremble here,

        When lion rough in wildest rage doth roar.

    Then know that I, as Snug the joiner, am   215

    A lion fell,° nor else no lion's dam;

    For, if I should as lion come in strife

    Into this place, 'twere pity on my life.

---

for *Leander* and *Hero*.) **193 Shafalus, Procrus** (Blunders for *Cephalus* and *Procris*, also famous
lovers.) **198 'Tide** betide, come **202 willful** willing **203 without warning** ie., without
warning the parents. (Demetrius makes a joke on the proverb "Walls have ears.") **205 in
this kind** of this sort. **shadows** likenesses, representations **216 lion fell** fierce lion (with
a play on the idea of "lion skin")

THESEUS. A very gentle beast, and of a good conscience.
DEMETRIUS. The very best at a beast, my lord, that e'er I saw.   *220*
LYSANDER. This lion is a very fox for his valor.°
THESEUS. True; and a goose for his discretion.°
DEMETRIUS. Not so, my lord; for his valor cannot carry his discretion; and the fox carries the goose.
THESEUS. His discretion, I am sure, cannot carry his valor; for the goose   *225*
carries not the fox. It is well. Leave it to his discretion, and let us listen to the moon.
MOON. This lanthorn° doth the hornèd moon present—
DEMETRIUS. He should have worn the horns on his head.°
THESEUS. He is no crescent, and his horns are invisible within the   *230*
circumference.
MOON. This lanthorn doth the hornèd moon present;
   Myself the man i' the moon do seem to be.
THESEUS. This is the greatest error of all the rest. The man should be put into the lanthorn. How is it else the man i' the moon?   *235*
DEMETRIUS. He dares not come there for the° candle, for you see, it is already in snuff.°
HIPPOLTYA. I am aweary of this moon. Would he would change!
THESEUS. It appears, by his small light of discretion, that he is in the wane; but yet, in courtesy, in all reason, we must stay the time.   *240*
LYSANDER. Proceed, Moon.
MOON. All that I have to say is to tell you that the lanthorn is the moon, the man i' the moon, this thornbush my thornbush, and this dog my dog.
DEMETRIUS. Why, all these should be in the lanthorn, for all these are in   *245*
the moon. But silence! Here comes Thisbe.

   Enter Thisbe.

THISE. This is old Ninny's tomb. Where is my love?
LION. [*Roaring*] O!
DEMETRIUS. Well roared, Lion.
          [*Thisbe runs off, dropping her mantle.*]
THESEUS. Well run, Thisbe.   *250*
HIPPOLTYA. Well shone, Moon. Truly, the moon shines with a good grace.
          [*The Lion worries Thisbe's mantle.*]

---

221 is . . . valor i.e., his valor consists of craftiness and discretion   **222 goose . . . dis-cretion** i.e., as discreet as a goose, that is, more foolish than discreet   **228 lanthorn** (This original spelling, *lanthorn,* may suggest a play on the *horn* of which lanterns were made, and also on a cuckold's horns; but the spelling *lanthorn* is not used consistently for comic effect in this play or elsewhere. At 5.1.134, for example, the word is *lantern* in the original.)   **229 on his head** (as a sign of cuckoldry)   **236 for the** because of the   **237 in snuff** (1) offended (2) in need of snuffing or trimming

THESEUS. Well moused,° Lion.

   Enter Pyramus.   *[Exit Lion.]*

DEMETRIUS. And then came Pyramus.

LYSANDER. And so the lion vanished.

PYRAMUS.

    Sweet Moon, I thank thee for thy sunny beams;   *255*

       I thank thee, Moon, for shining now so bright;

    For, by thy gracious, golden, glittering gleams,

       I trust to take of truest Thisbe sight.

            But stay, O spite!

            But mark, poor knight,   *260*

       What dreadful dole° is here?

            Eyes, do you see?

            How can it be?

       O dainty duck! O dear!

            Thy mantle good,   *265*

         What, stained with blood!

       Approach, ye Furies° fell!°

          O Fates,° come, come,

          Cut thread and thrum;°

       Quail,° crush, conclude, and quell!°   *270*

THESEUS. This passion, and the death of a dear friend, would go near to

   make a man look sad.°

HIPPOLTYA. Beshrew my heart, but I pity the man.

PYRAMUS.

    O, wherefore, Nature, didst thou lions frame?

    Since lion vile hath here deflowered my dear,   *275*

    Which is—no, no, which was—the fairest dame

    That lived, that loved, that liked, that looked with cheer.°

          Come, tears, confound,

          Out, sword, and wound

       The pap° of Pyramus;   *280*

          Ay, that left pap,

          Where heart doth hop.   *[He stabs himself.]*

       Thus die I, thus, thus, thus.

          Now am I dead,

          Now am I fled;   *285*

---

252 moused shaken, torn, bitten   **261 dole** grievous event   **267 Furies** avenging goddesses of Greek myth. **fell** fierce   **268 Fates** the three goddesses (Clotho, Lachesis, Atropos) of Greek myth who drew and cut the thread of human life   **269 thread and thrum** the warp in weaving and the loose end of the warp   **270 Quail** overpower. **quell** kill, destroy   **271–72 This . . . sad** i.e., if one had other reason to grieve, one might be sad, but not from this absurd portrayal of passion   **277 cheer** countenance   **280 pap** breast

My soul is in the sky.
　　Tongue, lose thy light;
　　Moon, take thy flight.　　　　　[*Exit Moonshine.*]
　Now die, die, die, die, die.　　　[*Pyramus dies.*]
DEMETRIUS. No die, but an ace,° for him; for he is but one.°　　　*290*
LYSANDER. Less than an ace, man; for he is dead, he is nothing.
THESEUS. With the help of a surgeon he might yet recover, and yet prove
　　an ass.°
HIPPOLTYA. How chance Moonshine is gone before Thisbe comes back
　　and finds her lover?　　　　　*295*
THESEUS. She will find him by starlight.

　[*Enter Thisbe.*]

　Here she comes, and her passion ends the play.
HIPPOLTYA. Methinks she should not use a long one for such a Pyramus.
　　I hope she will be brief.
DEMETRIUS. A mote° will turn the balance, which Pyramus, which°　*300*
　　Thisbe, is the better: he for a man, God warrant us; she for a
　　woman, God bless us.
LYSANDER. She hath spied him already with those sweet eyes.
DEMETRIUS. And thus she means,° videlicet:°
THISBE.

　　Asleep, my love?　　　　　*305*
　　What, dead, my dove?
　O Pyramus, arise!
　　Speak, speak. Quite dumb?
　　Dead, dead? A tomb
　Must cover thy sweet eyes.　　　*310*
　　These lily lips,
　　This cherry nose,
　These yellow cowslip cheeks,
　　Are gone, are gone!
　　Lovers, make moan.　　　　　*315*
　His eyes were green as leeks.
　　O Sisters Three,°
　　Come, come to me,
　With hands as pale as milk;
　　Lay them in gore,　　　　　*320*
　　Since you have shore°

---

290 ace the side of the die featuring the single pip, or spot. (The pun is on *die* as a singular
of *dice;* Bottom's performance is not worth a whole *die* but rather one single face of it, one
small portion.) **one** (1) an individual person (2) unique　**293 ass** (with a pun on *ace*)
300 mote small particle. **which . . . which** whether . . . or　**304 means** moans, laments.
videlicet to wit　**317 Sisters Three** the Fates　**321 shore** shorn

With shears his thread of silk.
    Tongue, not a word.
    Come, trusty sword,
  Come, blade, my breast imbrue!° [*Stabs herself.*]   325
    And farewell, friends.
    Thus Thisbe ends.
    Adieu, adieu, adieu.   [*She dies.*]

THESEUS. Moonshine and Lion are left to bury the dead.

DEMETRIUS. Ay, and Wall too.   330

BOTTOM. [*Starting up, as Flute does also*] No, I assure you, the wall is down
    that parted their fathers. Will it please you to see the epilogue,
    or to hear a Bergomask dance° between two of our company?
                          [*The other players enter.*]

THESEUS. No epilogue, I pray you; for your play needs no excuse. Never
    excuse; for when the players are all dead, there need none to be   335
    blamed. Marry, if he that writ it had played Pyramus and
    hanged himself in Thisbe's garter, it would have been a fine
    tragedy; and so it is, truly, and very notably discharged. But,
    come, your Bergomask. Let your epilogue alone.   [*A dance.*]
    The iron tongue° of midnight hath told° twelve.   340
    Lovers, to bed, 'tis almost fairy time.
    I fear we shall outsleep the coming morn
    As much as we this night have overwatched.°
    This palpable-gross° play hath well beguiled
    The heavy° gait of night. Sweet friends, to bed.   345
    A fortnight hold we this solemnity.
    In nightly revels and new jollity.   *Exeunt.*

Enter Puck [*carrying a broom*].

PUCK.
    Now the hungry lion roars,
      And the wolf behowls the moon;
    Whilst the heavy° plowman snores,   350
      All with weary task fordone.°
    Now the wasted brands° do glow,
      Whilst the screech owl, screeching loud
    Puts the wretch that lies in woe
      In remembrance of a shroud.   355

---

325 imbrue stain with blood   **333 Bergomask dance** a rustic dance named from Ber-
gamo, a province in the state of Venice   **340 iron tongue** i.e., of a bell.   **told** counted,
struck ("tolled")   **343 over-watched** stayed up too late   **344 palpable-gross** gross,
obviously crude   **345 heavy** drowsy, dull   **350 heavy** tired   **351 fordone** exhausted
352 wasted brands burned-out logs

Now it is the time of night
    That the graves, all gaping wide,
Every one lets forth his sprite,°
    In the church-way paths to glide.
And we fairies, that do run   *360*
    By the triple Hecate's° team
From the presence of the sun,
    Following darkness like a dream,
Now are frolic.° Not a mouse
    Shall disturb this hallowed house.   *365*
I am sent with broom before,
To sweep the dust behind° the door.

Enter [Oberon and Titania,] King and Queen of Fairies, with all their
train.

OBERON.

Through the house give glimmering light,
    By the dead and drowsy fire;
Every elf and fairy sprite   *370*
    Hop as light as bird from brier;
And this ditty, after me,
Sing, and dance it trippingly.

TITANIA.

First, rehearse your song by rote,
To each word a warbling note.   *375*
Hand in hand, with fairy grace,
Will we sing, and bless this place.

                                        [*Song and dance.*]

OBERON.

Now, until the break of day,
Through this house each fairy stray.
To the best bride-bed will we,   *380*
Which by us shall blessèd be;
And the issue there create°
Ever shall be fortunate.
So shall all the couples three
Ever true in loving be;   *385*
And the blots of Nature's hand
Shall not in their issue stand;
Never mole, harelip, nor scar,

---

358 Every . . . sprite every grave lets forth its ghost **361 triple Hecate's** (Hecate
ruled in three capacities: as Luna or Cynthia in heaven, as Diana on earth, and as Proserpina
in hell.) **364 frolic** merry **367 behind** from behind. (Robin Goodfellow was a household spirit who helped good housemaids and punished lazy ones.) **382 create** created

Nor mark prodigious,° such as are
Despisèd in nativity,   *390*
Shall upon their children be.
With this field dew consecrate°
Every fairy take his gait,°
And each several° chamber bless,
Through this palace, with sweet peace;   *395*
And the owner of it blest
Ever shall in safety rest.
Trip away; make no stay;
Meet me all by break of day.
                Exeunt [*Oberon, Titania, and train*].
PUCK. [*To the audience*]
If we shadows have offended,   *400*
Think but this, and all is mended,
That you have but slumbered here°
While these visions did appear.
And this weak and idle theme,
No more yielding but° a dream,   *405*
Gentles, do not reprehend.
If you pardon, we will mend.°
And, as I am an honest Puck,
If we have unearnèd luck
Now to scape the serpent's tongue,°   *410*
We will make amends ere long;
Else the Puck a liar call.
So, good night unto you all.
Give me your hands,° if we be friends,
And Robin shall restore amends.°   [*Exit.*] *415*

TOPICS FOR DISCUSSION AND WRITING

Act 1

1. On the basis of the first scene, how would you characterize Theseus? Egeus? Hermia? Do you agree with some critics that Egeus is presented comically? (Support your view.)
2. What connections can you make between 1.2 and the first scene?

389 prodigious monstrous, unnatural   **392 consecrate** consecrated   **393 take his gait** go his way   **394 several** separate   **402 That . . . here** i.e., that it is a "midsummer night's dream"   **405 No . . . but** yielding no more than   **407 mend** improve   **410 serpent's tongue** i.e., hissing   **414 Give . . . hands** applaud   **415 restore amends** give satisfaction in return

Act 2

1. Why do you suppose that in 2.1 Shakespeare included material about Theseus's past (lines 76–80)?
2. When the play is staged, audiences invariably laugh loudly at 2.2.109, when Lysander awakens and sees Helena. What's so funny about this?

Act 3

1. What assumptions does Bottom seem to make about the nature of drama? How do they compare with your own?
2. Puck himself has said that he is mischievous, but how mischievous is he? Why did he anoint the eyes of the wrong lover?

Act 4

1. Bottom is the only mortal who sees the fairies. What can we make of this? Or should we not try to make anything of it?

Act 5

1. What do you make of the debate between Theseus and Hippolyta (lines 1–27)? Which of the two seems to you to come closer to the truth? Explain.
2. Do you think it is cruel to laugh at the unintentional antics of the rustic performers? Why, or why not?
3. Puck is sometimes played by a female. What advantages or disadvantages do you see to giving the part to a woman?

General Questions

1. Some critics speak of the play as a delightful fantasy that is engaging because it has so little connection with real life, but others find in it intimations of dark and dangerous elements in human beings. Where do you stand, and why?
2. Today Shakespeare's plays are sometimes done in modern dress or in costumes that reflect a particular time and place, such as the Wild West of the mid-nineteenth century or the South before the Civil War. How would you costume the play? What advantages might there be in your choice?

Henrik Ibsen *(Norwegian; 1828–1906)*

A Doll's House

Translated by Michael Meyer

List of Characters

TORVALD HELMER, *a lawyer*
NORA, his wife
DR. RANK
MRS. LINDE
NILS KROGSTAD, *also a lawyer*
The Helmers' three small children
ANNE-MARIE, *their nurse*
HELEN, *the maid*
A Porter

Scene: *The action takes place in the Helmers' apartment.*

ACT 1

A comfortably and tastefully, but not expensively furnished room. Backstage right a door leads out to the hall; backstage left, another door to Helmer's study. Between these two doors stands a piano. In the middle of the left-hand wall is a door, with a window downstage of it. Near the window, a round table with armchairs and a small sofa. In the right-hand wall, slightly upstage, is a door; downstage of this, against the same wall, a stove lined with porcelain tiles, with a couple of armchairs and a rocking-chair in front of it. Between the stove and the side door is a small table. Engravings on the wall. A what-not with china and other bric-a-brac; a small bookcase with leather-bound books. A carpet on the floor; a fire in the stove. A winter day.

A bell rings in the hall outside. After a moment, we hear the front door being opened. Nora enters the room, humming contentedly to herself. She is wearing outdoor clothes and carrying a lot of parcels, which she puts down on the table right. She leaves the door to the hall open; through it, we can see a Porter carrying a Christmas tree and a basket. He gives these to the Maid, who has opened the door for them.

NORA. Hide that Christmas tree away, Helen. The children mustn't see it before I've decorated it this evening. (*To the Porter, taking out her purse.*) How much—?
PORTER. A shilling.
NORA. Here's half a crown. No, keep it.

The Porter touches his cap and goes. Nora closes the door. She continues to laugh happily to herself she removes her coat, etc. She takes from her pocket

A Doll's House: *a symbolic gesture. (Photograph: Harvard Theatre Collection.)*

a bag containing macaroons and eats a couple. Then, she tiptoes across and listens at her husband's door.

NORA. Yes, he's here. (*Starts humming again as she goes over to the table, right.*)

HELMER (*from his room*). Is that my skylark twittering out there?

NORA (*opening some of the parcels*). It is!

HELMER. Is that my squirrel rustling?

NORA. Yes!

HELMER. When did my squirrel come home?

NORA. Just now. (*Pops the bag of macaroons in her pocket and wipes her mouth.*) Come out here, Torvald, and see what I've bought.

HELMER. You mustn't disturb me! (*Short pause; then he opens the door and looks in, his pen in his hand.*) Bought, did you say? All that? Has my little squanderbird been overspending again?

NORA. Oh, Torvald, surely we can let ourselves go a little this year! It's the first Christmas we don't have to scrape.

HELMER. Well, you know, we can't afford to be extravagant.

NORA. Oh yes, Torvald, we can be a little extravagant now. Can't we? Just a tiny bit? You've got a big salary now, and you're going to make lots and lots of money.

HELMER. Next year, yes. But my new salary doesn't start till April.

NORA. Pooh; we can borrow till then.

HELMER. Nora! (*Goes over to her and takes her playfully by the ear.*) What a little spendthrift you are! Suppose I were to borrow fifty pounds today, and you spent it all over Christmas, and then on New Year's Eve a tile fell off a roof onto my head—

NORA (*puts her hand over his mouth*). Oh, Torvald! Don't say such dreadful things!

HELMER. Yes, but suppose something like that did happen? What then?

NORA. If any thing as frightful as that happened, it wouldn't make much difference whether I was in debt or not.

HELMER. But what about the people I'd borrowed from?

NORA. Them? Who cares about them? They're strangers.

HELMER. Oh, Nora, Nora, how like a woman! No, but seriously, Nora, you know how I feel about this. No debts! Never borrow! A home that is founded on debts can never be a place of freedom and beauty. We two have stuck it out bravely up to now; and we shall continue to do so for the short time we still have to.

NORA (*goes over towards the stove*). Very well, Torvald. As you say.

HELMER (*follows her*). Now, now! My little song bird mustn't droop her wings. What's this? Is little squirrel sulking? (*Takes out his purse.*) Nora; guess what I've got here!

NORA (*turns quickly*). Money!

HELMER. Look. (*Hands her some banknotes.*) I know how these small expenses crop up at Christmas.

HELMER. Look. (*Hands her some banknotes.*) I know how these small expenses crop up at Christmas.

NORA (*counts them*). One—two—three—four. Oh, thank you, Torvald, thank you! I should be able to manage with this.

HELMER. You'll have to.

NORA. Yes, yes, of course I will. But come over here, I want to show you everything I've bought. And so cheaply! Look, here are new clothes for Ivar—and a sword. And a horse and a trumpet for Bob. And a doll and a cradle for Emmy—they're nothing much, but she'll pull them apart in a few days. And some bits of material and handkerchiefs for the maids. Old Anne-Marie ought to have had something better, really.

HELMER. And what's in that parcel?

NORA (*cries*). No, Torvald, you mustn't see that before this evening!

HELMER. Very well. But now, tell me, you little spendthrift, what do you want for Christmas?

NORA. Me? Oh, pooh, I don't want anything.

HELMER. Oh, yes, you do. Now tell me, what, within reason, would you most like?

NORA. No, I really don't know. Oh, yes—Torvald—!

HELMER. Well?

NORA (*plays with his coat-buttons; not looking at him*). If you really want to give me something, you could—you could—

HELMER. Come on, out with it.

NORA (*quickly*). You could give me money, Torvald. Only as much as you feel you can afford; then later I'll buy something with it.

HELMER. But, Nora—

NORA. Oh yes, Torvald dear, please! Please! Then I'll wrap up the notes in pretty gold paper and hang them on the Christmas tree. Wouldn't that be fun?

HELMER. What's the name of that little bird that can never keep any money?

NORA. Yes, yes, squanderbird; I know. But let's do as I say, Torvald; then I'll have time to think about what I need most. Isn't that the best way? Mm?

HELMER (*smiles*). To be sure it would be, if you could keep what I give you and really buy yourself something with it. But you'll spend it on all sorts of useless things for the house, and then I'll have to put my hand in my pocket again.

NORA. Oh, but Torvald—

HELMER. You can't deny it, Nora dear. (*Puts his arm round her waist.*) The squanderbird's a pretty little creature, but she gets through an awful lot of money. It's incredible what an expensive pet she is for a man to keep.

NORA. For shame! How can you say such a thing? I save every penny I can.

HELMER *(laughs)*. That's quite true. Every penny you can. But you can't.

NORA *(hums and smiles, quietly gleeful)*. Hm. If you only knew how many expenses we larks and squirrels have, Torvald.

HELMER. You're a funny little creature. Just like your father used to be. Always on the look-out for some way to get money, but as soon as you have any it just runs through your fingers, and you never know where it's gone. Well, I suppose I must take you as you are. It's in your blood. Yes, yes, yes, these things are hereditary, Nora.

NORA. Oh, I wish I'd inherited more of Papa's qualities.

HELMER. And I wouldn't wish my darling little songbird to be any different from what she is. By the way, that reminds me. You look awfully—how shall I put it?—awfully guilty today.

NORA. Do I?

HELMER. Yes, you do. Look me in the eyes.

NORA *(looks at him)*. Well?

HELMER *(wags his finger)*. Has my little sweet-tooth been indulging herself in town today, by any chance?

NORA. No, how can you think such a thing?

HELMER. Not a tiny little digression into a pastry shop?

NORA. No, Torvald, I promise—

HELMER. Not just a wee jam tart?

NORA. Certainly not.

HELMER. Not a little nibble at a macaroon?

NORA. No, Torvald—I promise you, honestly—

HELMER. There, there. I was only joking.

NORA *(goes over to the table, right)*. You know I could never act against your wishes.

HELMER. Of course not. And you've given me your word—*(Goes over to her.)* Well, my beloved Nora, you keep your little Christmas secrets to yourself. They'll be revealed this evening, I've no doubt, once the Christmas tree has been lit.

NORA. Have you remembered to invite Dr. Rank?

HELMER. No. But there's no need; he knows he'll be dining with us. Anyway, I'll ask him when he comes this morning. I've ordered some good wine. Oh Nora, you can't imagine how I'm looking forward to this evening.

NORA. So am I. And, Torvald, how the children will love it!

HELMER. Yes, it's a wonderful thing to know that one's position is assured and that one has an ample income. Don't you agree? It's good to know that, isn't it?

NORA. Yes, it's almost like a miracle.

HELMER. Do you remember last Christmas? For three whole weeks you shut yourself away every evening to make flowers for the Christmas tree, and all those other things you were going to surprise us with. Ugh, it was the most boring time I've ever had in my life.

NORA. I didn't find it boring.

HELMER (*smiles*). But it all came to nothing in the end, didn't it?

NORA. Oh, are you going to bring that up again? How could I help the cat getting in and tearing everything to bits?

HELMER. No, my poor little Nora, of course you couldn't. You simply wanted to make us happy, and that's all that matters. But it's good that those hard times are past.

NORA. Yes, it's wonderful.

HELMER. I don't have to sit by myself and be bored. And you don't have to tire your pretty eyes and your delicate little hands—

NORA (*claps her hands*). No, Torvald, that's true, isn't it—I don't have to any longer? Oh, it's really all just like a miracle. (*Takes his arm.*) Now, I'm going to tell you what I thought we might do, Torvald. As soon as Christmas is over—(*A bell rings in the hall.*) Oh, there's the doorbell. (*Tidies up one or two things in the room.*) Someone's coming. What a bore.

HELMER. I'm not at home to any visitors. Remember!

MAID (*in the doorway*). A lady's called, madam. A stranger.

NORA. Well, ask her to come in.

MAID. And the doctor's here too, sir.

HELMER. Has he gone to my room?

MAID. Yes, sir.

Helmer goes into his room. The Maid shows in Mrs. Linde, who is dressed in traveling clothes, and closes the door.

MRS. LINDE (*shyly and a little hesitantly*). Good evening, Nora.

NORA (*uncertainly*). Good evening—

MRS. LINDE. I don't suppose you recognize me.

NORA. No, I'm afraid I—Yes, wait a minute—surely—(*Exclaims.*) Why, Christine! Is it really you?

MRS. LINDE. Yes, it's me.

NORA. Christine! And I didn't recognize you! But how could I—? (*More quietly.*) How you've changed, Christine!

MRS. LINDE. Yes, I know. It's been nine years—nearly ten—

NORA. Is it so long? Yes, it must be. Oh, these last eight years have been such a happy time for me! So you've come to town? All that way in winter! How brave of you!

MRS. LINDE. I arrived by the steamer this morning.

NORA. Yes, of course—to enjoy yourself over Christmas. Oh, how splendid! We'll have to celebrate! But take off your coat. You're not cold, are you? (*Helps her off with it.*) There! Now let's sit down here by the stove and be comfortable. No, you take the armchair. I'll sit here in the rocking-chair. (*Clasps Mrs. Linde's hands.*) Yes, now you look like your old self. It was just at first that—you've got a little paler, though, Christine. And perhaps a bit thinner.

MRS. LINDE. And older, Nora. Much, much older.

NORA. Yes, perhaps a little older. Just a tiny bit. Not much. (*Checks herself suddenly and says earnestly.*) Oh, but how thoughtless of me to sit here and chatter away like this! Dear, sweet Christine, can you forgive me?

MRS. LINDE. What do you mean, Nora?

NORA (*quietly*). Poor Christine, you've become a widow.

MRS. LINDE. Yes. Three years ago.

NORA. I know, I know—I read it in the papers. Oh, Christine, I meant to write to you so often, honestly. But I always put it off, and something else always cropped up.

MRS. LINDE. I understand, Nora dear.

NORA. No, Christine, it was beastly of me. Oh, my poor darling, what you've gone through! And he didn't leave you anything?

MRS. LINDE. No.

NORA. No children, either?

MRS. LINDE. No.

NORA. Nothing at all, then?

MRS. LINDE. Not even a feeling of loss or sorrow.

NORA (*looks incredulously at her*). But, Christine, how is that possible?

MRS. LINDE (*smiles sadly and strokes Nora's hair*). Oh, these things happen, Nora.

NORA. All alone. How dreadful that must be for you. I've three lovely children. I'm afraid you can't see them now, because they're out with nanny. But you must tell me everything—

MRS. LINDE. No, no, no. I want to hear about you.

NORA. No, you start. I'm not going to be selfish today, I'm just going to think about you. Oh, but there's one thing I *must* tell you. Have you heard of the wonderful luck we've just had?

MRS. LINDE. No. What?

NORA. Would you believe it—my husband's just been made manager of the bank!

MRS. LINDE. Your husband? Oh, how lucky—!

NORA. Yes, isn't it? Being a lawyer is so uncertain, you know, especially if one isn't prepared to touch any case that isn't—well—quite nice. And of course Torvald's been very firm about that—and I'm absolutely with him. Oh, you can imagine how happy we are! He's joining the bank in the New Year, and he'll be getting a big salary, and lots of percentages too. From now on we'll be able to live quite differently—we'll be able to do whatever we want. Oh, Christine, it's such a relief! I feel so happy! Well, I mean, it's lovely to have heaps of money and not to have to worry about anything. Don't you think?

MRS. LINDE. It must be lovely to have enough to cover one's needs, anyway.

NORA. Not just our needs! We're going to have heaps and heaps of money!

MRS. LINDE (*smiles*). Nora, Nora, haven't you grown up yet? When we were at school you were a terrible little spendthrift.

NORA (*laughs quietly*). Yes, Torvald still says that. (*Wags her finger.*) But "Nora, Nora" isn't as silly as you think. Oh, we've been in no position for me to waste money. We've both had to work.

MRS. LINDE. You too?

NORA. Yes, little things—fancy work, crocheting, embroidery and so forth. (*Casually.*) And other things too. I suppose you know Torvald left the Ministry when we got married? There were no prospects of promotion in his department, and of course he needed more money. But the first year he overworked himself quite dreadfully. He had to take on all sorts of extra jobs, and worked day and night. But it was too much for him, and he became frightfully ill. The doctors said he'd have to go to a warmer climate.

MRS. LINDE. Yes, you spent a whole year in Italy, didn't you?

NORA. Yes. It wasn't easy for me to get away, you know. I'd just had Ivar. But of course we had to do it. Oh, it was a marvelous trip! And it saved Torvald's life. But it cost an awful lot of money, Christine.

MRS. LINDE. I can imagine.

NORA. Two hundred and fifty pounds. That's a lot of money, you know.

MRS. LINDE. How lucky you had it.

NORA. Well, actually, we got it from my father.

MRS. LINDE. Oh, I see. Didn't he die just about that time?

NORA. Yes, Christine, just about then. Wasn't it dreadful, I couldn't go and look after him. I was expecting little Ivar any day. And then I had my poor Torvald to care for—we really didn't think he'd live. Dear, kind Papa! I never saw him again, Christine. Oh, it's the saddest thing that's happened to me since I got married.

MRS. LINDE. I know you were very fond of him. But you went to Italy—?

NORA. Yes. Well, we had the money, you see, and the doctors said we mustn't delay. So we went the month after Papa died.

MRS. LINDE. And your husband came back completely cured?

NORA. Fit as a fiddle!

MRS. LINDE. But—the doctor?

NORA. How do you mean?

MRS. LINDE. I thought the maid said that the gentleman who arrived with me was the doctor.

NORA. Oh yes, that's Doctor Rank, but he doesn't come because anyone's ill. He's our best friend, and he looks us up at least once every day. No, Torvald hasn't had a moment's illness since we went away. And the children are fit and healthy and so am I. (*Jumps up and claps her hands.*) Oh God, oh God, Christine, isn't it a wonderful thing to be alive and happy! Oh, but how beastly of me! I'm only talking about myself. (*Sits on a footstool and rests her arms on Mrs. Linde's knee.*) Oh, please don't be angry with me! Tell me, is it really true you didn't love your husband? Why did you marry him, then?

MRS. LINDE. Well, my mother was still alive; and she was helpless and bedridden. And I had my two little brothers to take care of. I didn't feel I could say no.

NORA. Yes, well, perhaps you're right. He was rich then, was he?

MRS. LINDE. Quite comfortably off, I believe. But his business was unsound, you see, Nora. When he died it went bankrupt, and there was nothing left.

NORA. What did you do?

MRS. LINDE. Well, I had to try to make ends meet somehow, so I started a little shop, and a little school, and anything else I could turn my hand to. These last three years have been just one endless slog for me, without a moment's rest. But now it's over, Nora. My poor dear mother doesn't need me any more; she's passed away. And the boys don't need me either; they've got jobs now and can look after themselves.

NORA. How relieved you must feel—

MRS. LINDE. No, Nora. Just unspeakably empty. No one to live for any more. (*Gets up restlessly.*) That's why I couldn't bear to stay out there any longer, cut off from the world. I thought it'd be easier to find some work here that will exercise and occupy my mind. If only I could get a regular job—office work of some kind—

NORA. Oh but, Christine, that's dreadfully exhausting; and you look practically finished already. It'd be much better for you if you could go away somewhere.

MRS. LINDE (*goes over to the window*). I have no Papa to pay for my holidays, Nora.

NORA (*gets up*). Oh, please don't be angry with me.

MRS. LINDE. My dear Nora, it's I who should ask you not to be angry. That's the worst thing about this kind of situation—it makes one so bitter. One has no one to work for; and yet one has to be continually sponging for jobs. One has to live; and so one becomes completely egocentric. When you told me about this luck you've just had with Torvald's new job—can you imagine?—I was happy not so much on your account, as on my own.

NORA. How do you mean? Oh, I understand. You mean Torvald might be able to do something for you?

MRS. LINDE. Yes, I was thinking that.

NORA. He will too, Christine. Just you leave it to me. I'll lead up to it so delicately, so delicately; I'll get him in the right mood. Oh, Christine, I do so want to help you.

MRS. LINDE. It's sweet of you to bother so much about me, Nora. Especially since you know so little of the worries and hardships of life.

NORA. I? You say *I* know little of—?

MRS. LINDE (*smiles*). Well, good heavens—those bits of fancy work of yours—well, really—! You're a child, Nora.

NORA (*tosses her head and walks across the room*). You shouldn't say that so patronizingly.

MRS. LINDE. Oh?

NORA. You're like the rest. You all think I'm incapable of getting down to anything serious—

MRS. LINDE. My dear—

NORA. You think I've never had any worries like the rest of you

MRS. LINDE. Nora dear, you've just told me about all your difficulties—

NORA. Pooh—that! (*Quietly.*) I haven't told you about the big thing.

MRS. LINDE. What big thing? What do you mean?

NORA. You patronize me, Christine; but you shouldn't. You're proud that you've worked so long and so hard for your mother.

MRS. LINDE. I don't patronize anyone, Nora. But you're right—I am both proud and happy that I was able to make my mother's last months on earth comparatively easy.

NORA. And you're also proud of what you've done for your brothers.

MRS. LINDE. I think I have a right to be.

NORA. I think so too. But let me tell you something, Christine. I too have done something to be proud and happy about.

MRS. LINDE. I don't doubt it. But—how do you mean?

NORA. Speak quietly! Suppose Torvald should hear! He mustn't, at any price—no one must know, Christine—no one but you.

MRS. LINDE. But what is this?

NORA. Come over here. (*Pulls her down on to the sofa beside her.*) Yes, Christine—I too have done something to be happy and proud about. It was I who saved Torvald's life.

MRS. LINDE. Saved his—? How did you save it?

NORA. I told you about our trip to Italy. Torvald couldn't have lived if he hadn't managed to get down there—

MRS. LINDE. Yes, well—your father provided the money—

NORA (*smiles*). So Torvald and everyone else thinks. But—

MRS. LINDE. Yes?

NORA. Papa didn't give us a penny. It was I who found the money.

MRS. LINDE. You? All of it?

NORA. Two hundred and fifty pounds. What do you say to that?

MRS. LINDE. But Nora, how could you? Did you win a lottery or something?

NORA (*scornfully*). Lottery? (*Sniffs*) What would there be to be proud of in that?

MRS. LINDE. But where did you get it from, then?

NORA (*hums and smiles secretively*). Hm; tra-la-la-la

MRS. LINDE. You couldn't have borrowed it.

NORA. Oh? Why not?

MRS. LINDE. Well, a wife can't borrow money without her husband's consent.

NORA (*tosses her head*). Ah, but when a wife has a little business sense, and knows how to be clever—

MRS. LINDE. But Nora, I simply don't understand—

NORA. You don't have to. No one has said I borrowed the money. I could have got it in some other way. (*Throws herself back on the sofa.*) I could have got it from an admirer. When a girl's as pretty as I am—

MRS. LINDE. Nora, you're crazy!

NORA. You're dying of curiosity now, aren't you, Christine?

MRS. LINDE. Nora dear, you haven't done anything foolish?

NORA (*sits up again*). Is it foolish to save one's husband's life?

MRS. LINDE. I think it's foolish if without his knowledge, you—

NORA. But the whole point was that he mustn't know! Great heavens, don't you see? He hadn't to know how dangerously ill he was. I was the one they told that his life was in danger and that only going to a warm climate could save him. Do you suppose I didn't try to think of other ways of getting him down there? I told him how wonderful it would be for me to go abroad like other young wives; I cried and prayed; I asked him to remember my condition, and said he ought to be nice and tender to me; and then I suggested he might quite easily borrow the money. But then he got almost angry with me, Christine. He said I was frivolous, and that it was his duty as a husband not to pander to my moods and caprices—I think that's what he called them. Well, well, I thought, you've got to be saved somehow. And then I thought of a way—

MRS. LINDE. But didn't your husband find out from your father that the money hadn't come from him?

NORA. No, never. Papa died just then. I'd thought of letting him into the plot and asking him not to tell. But since he was so ill—! And as things turned out, it didn't become necessary.

MRS. LINDE. And you've never told your husband about this?

NORA. For heaven's sake, no! What an idea! He's frightfully strict about such matters. And besides—he's so proud of being a *man*—it'd be so painful and humiliating for him to know that he owed anything to me. It'd completely wreck our relationship. This life we have built together would no longer exist.

MRS. LINDE. Will you never tell him?

NORA (*thoughtfully, half-smiling*). Yes—some time, perhaps. Years from now, when I'm no longer pretty. You mustn't laugh! I mean of course, when Torvald no longer loves me as he does now; when it no longer amuses him to see me dance and dress up and play the fool for him. Then it might be useful to have something up my sleeve. (*Breaks off.*) Stupid, stupid, stupid! That time will never come. Well, what do you think of my big secret, Christine? I'm not completely useless, am I? Mind you, all this has caused me a frightful lot of worry. It hasn't been easy for me to meet my obligations punctually. In case you don't know, in the world of business there are things called quarterly installments and interest, and they're a terrible problem to cope with. So I've had to scrape a little here and save a little there as best I can. I haven't been able to save much on the housekeeping money, because Torvald likes to live well; and I couldn't let the children go short of clothes—I couldn't take anything out of what he gives me for them. The poor little angels!

MRS. LINDE. So you've had to stint yourself, my poor Nora?

NORA. Of course. Well, after all, it was my problem. Whenever Torvald gave me money to buy myself new clothes, I never used more than half of it; and I always bought what was cheapest and plainest. Thank heaven anything suits me, so that Torvald's never noticed. But it made me a bit sad sometimes, because it's lovely to wear pretty clothes. Don't you think?

MRS. LINDE. Indeed it is.

NORA. And then I've found one or two other sources of income. Last winter I managed to get a lot of copying to do. So I shut myself away and wrote every evening, late into the night. Oh, I often got so tired, so tired. But it was great fun, though, sitting there working and earning money. It was almost like being a man.

MRS. LINDE. But how much have you managed to pay off like this?

NORA. Well, I can't say exactly. It's awfully difficult to keep an exact check on these kind of transactions. I only know I've paid everything I've managed to scrape together. Sometimes I really didn't know where to turn. (*Smiles.*) Then I'd sit here and imagine some rich old gentleman had fallen in love with me—

MRS. LINDE. What! What gentleman?

NORA. Silly! And that now he'd died and when they opened his will it said in big letters: "Everything I possess is to be paid forthwith to my beloved Mrs. Nora Helmer in cash."

MRS. LINDE. But, Nora dear, who was this gentleman?

NORA. Great heavens, don't you understand? There wasn't any old gentleman, he was just something I used to dream up as I sat here evening after evening wondering how on earth I could raise some money. But what does it matter? The old bore can stay imaginary as far as I'm concerned, because now I don't have to worry any longer! (*Jumps up.*) Oh, Christine, isn't it wonderful? I don't have to worry any more! No more troubles! I can play all day with the children, I can fill the house with pretty things, just the way Torvald likes. And, Christine, it will soon be spring, and the air will be fresh and the skies blue—and then perhaps we'll be able to take a little trip somewhere. I shall be able to see the sea again. Oh, yes, yes, it's a wonderful thing to be alive and happy!

The bell rings in the hall.

MRS. LINDE (*gets up*). You've a visitor. Perhaps I'd better go.

NORA. No stay. It won't be for me. It's someone for Torvald—

MAID (*in the doorway*). Excuse me, madam, a gentleman's called who says he wants to speak to the master. But I didn't know—seeing as the doctor's with him—

NORA. Who is this gentleman?

KROGSTAD (*in the doorway*). It's me, Mrs. Helmer.

Mrs. Linde starts, composes herself; and turns away to the window.

NORA (*takes a step toward him and whispers tensely*). You? What is it? What do you want to talk to my husband about?

KROGSTAD. Business—you might call it. I hold a minor post in the bank, and I hear your husband is to become our new chief—

NORA. Oh—then it isn't—?

KROGSTAD. Pure business, Mrs. Helmer. Nothing more.

NORA. Well, you'll find him in his study.

Nods indifferently as she closes the hall door behind him. Then she walks across the room and sees to the stove.

MRS. LINDE. Nora, who was that man?

NORA. A lawyer called Krogstad.

MRS. LINDE. It was him, then.

NORA. Do you know that man?

MRS. LINDE. I used to know him—some years ago. He was a solicitor's clerk in our town, for a while.

NORA. Yes, of course, so he was.

MRS. LINDE. How he's changed!

NORA. He was very unhappily married, I believe.

MRS. LINDE. Is he a widower now?

NORA. Yes, with a lot of children. Ah, now it's alight.

She closes the door of the stove and moves the rocking-chair a little to one side.

MRS. LINDE. He does—various things now, I hear?

NORA. Does he? It's quite possible—I really don't know. But don't let's talk about business. It's so boring.

Dr. Rank enters from Helmer's study.

RANK (*still in the doorway*). No, no, my dear chap, don't see me out. I'll go and have a word with your wife. (*Closes the door and notices Mrs. Linde.*) Oh, I beg your pardon. I seem to be *de trop* here too.

NORA. Not in the least. (*Introduces them.*) Dr. Rank. Mrs. Linde.

RANK. Ah! A name I have often heard in this house. I believe I passed you on the stairs as I came up.

MRS. LINDE. Yes. Stairs tire me; I have to take them slowly.

RANK. Oh, have you hurt yourself?

MRS. LINDE. No, I'm just a little run down.

RANK. Ah, is that all? Then I take it you've come to town to cure yourself by a round of parties?

MRS. LINDE. I have come here to find work.

RANK. Is that an approved remedy for being run down?

MRS. LINDE. One has to live, Doctor.

RANK. Yes, people do seem to regard it as a necessity.

NORA. Oh, really, Dr. Rank. I bet you want to stay alive.

RANK. You bet I do. However miserable I sometimes feel, I still want to go on being tortured for as long as possible. It's the same with all my patients; and with people who are morally sick, too. There's a moral cripple in with Helmer at this very moment—

MRS. LINDE (*softly*). Oh!

NORA. Whom do you mean?

RANK. Oh, a lawyer fellow called Krogstad—you wouldn't know him. He's crippled all right; morally twisted. But even he started off by announcing, as though it were a matter of enormous importance, that he had to live.

NORA. Oh? What did he want to talk to Torvald about?

RANK. I haven't the faintest idea. All I heard was something about the bank.

NORA. I didn't know that Krog—that this man Krogstad had any connection with the bank.

RANK. Yes, he's got some kind of job down there. (*To Mrs. Linde.*) I wonder if in your part of the world you too have a species of human being that spends its time fussing around trying to smell out moral corruption? And when they find a case they give him some nice, comfortable position so that they can keep a good watch on him. The healthy ones just have to lump it.

MRS. LINDE. But surely it's the sick who need care most?

RANK (*shrugs his shoulders*). Well, there we have it. It's that attitude that's turning human society into a hospital.

Nora, lost in her own thoughts, laughs half to herself and claps her hands.

RANK. Why are you laughing? Do you really know what society is?

NORA. What do I care about society? I think it's a bore. I was laughing at something else—something frightfully funny. Tell me, Dr. Rank—will everyone who works at the bank come under Torvald now?

RANK. Do you find that particularly funny?

NORA (*smiles and hums*). Never you mind! Never you mind! (*Walks around the room.*) Yes, I find it very amusing to think that we—I mean, Torvald—has obtained so much influence over so many people. (*Takes the paper bag from her pocket.*) Dr. Rank, would you like a small macaroon?

RANK. Macaroons! I say! I thought they were forbidden here.

NORA. Yes, well, these are some Christine gave me.

MRS. LINDE. What? I—?

NORA. All right, all right, don't get frightened. You weren't to know Torvald had forbidden them. He's afraid they'll ruin my teeth. But, dash it — for once —! Don't you agree, Dr. Rank? Here! (*Pops a macaroon into his mouth.*) You too, Christine. And I'll have one too. Just a little one. Two at the most. (*Begins to walk round again.*) Yes, now I feel really, really happy. Now there's just one thing in the world I'd really love to do.

RANK. Oh? And what is that?

NORA. Just something I'd love to say to Torvald.

RANK. Well, why don't you say it?

NORA. No, I daren't. It's too dreadful.

MRS. LINDE. Dreadful?

RANK. Well, then, you'd better not. But you can say it to us. What is it you'd so love to say to Torvald?

NORA. I've the most extraordinary longing to say: "Bloody hell!"

RANK. Are you mad?

MRS. LINDE. My dear Nora —!

RANK. Say it. Here he is.

NORA (*hiding the bag of macaroons*). Ssh! Ssh!

Helmer, with his overcoat on his arm and his hat in his hand, enters from his study.

NORA (*goes to meet him*). Well, Torvald dear, did you get rid of him?

HELMER. Yes, he's just gone.

NORA. May I introduce you —? This is Christine. She's just arrived in town.

HELMER. Christine —? Forgive me, but I don't think —

NORA. Mrs. Linde, Torvald dear. Christine Linde.

HELMER. Ah. A childhood friend of my wife's, I presume?

MRS. LINDE. Yes, we knew each other in earlier days.

NORA. And imagine, now she's traveled all this way to talk to you.

HELMER. Oh?

MRS. LINDE. Well, I didn't really —

NORA. You see, Christine's frightfully good at office work, and she's mad to come under some really clever man who can teach her even more than she knows already —

HELMER. Very sensible, madam.

NORA. So when she heard you'd become head of the bank — it was in her local paper — she came here as quickly as she could and — Torvald, you will, won't you? Do a little something to help Christine? For my sake?

HELMER. Well, that shouldn't be impossible. You are a widow, I take it, Mrs. Linde?

MRS. LINDE. Yes.

HELMER. And you have experience of office work?

MRS. LINDE. Yes, quite a bit.

HELMER. Well then, it's quite likely I may be able to find some job for you —

NORA (*claps her hands*). You see, you see!

HELMER. You've come at a lucky moment, Mrs. Linde.

MRS. LINDE. Oh, how can I ever thank you—?

HELMER. There's absolutely no need. (*Puts on his overcoat.*) But now I'm afraid I must ask you to excuse me—

RANK. Wait. I'll come with you.

He gets his fur coat from the hall and warms it at the stove.

NORA. Don't be long, Torvald dear.

HELMER. I'll only be an hour.

NORA. Are you going too, Christine?

MRS. LINDE (*puts on her outdoor clothes*). Yes, I must start to look round for a room.

HELMER. Then perhaps we can walk part of the way together.

NORA (*helps her*). It's such a nuisance we're so cramped here—I'm afraid we can't offer to—

MRS. LINDE. Oh, I wouldn't dream of it. Goodbye, Nora dear, and thanks for everything.

NORA. *Au revoir.* You'll be coming back this evening, of course. And ,you too, Dr. Rank. What? If you're well enough? Of course you'll be well enough. Wrap up warmly, though.

They go out, talking, into the hall. Children's voices are heard from the stairs.

NORA. Here they are! Here they are!

She runs out and opens the door. Anne-Marie, the nurse, enters with the children.

NORA. Come in, come in! (*Stoops down and kisses them.*) Oh, my sweet darlings—! Look at them, Christine! Aren't they beautiful?

RANK. Don't stand here chattering in this draught!

HELMER. Come, Mrs. Linde. This is for mothers only.

Dr. Rank, Helmer, and Mrs. Linde go down the stairs. The nurse brings the children into the room. Nora follows, and closes the door to the hall.

NORA. How well you look! What red cheeks you've got! Like apples and roses! (*The children answer her inaudibly as she talks to them.*) Have you had fun? That's splendid. You gave Emmy and Bob a ride on the sledge? What, both together? I say! What a clever boy you are, Ivar! Oh, let me hold her for a moment, Anne-Marie! My sweet little baby doll! (*Takes the smallest child from the nurse and dances with her.*) Yes, yes, Mummy will dance with Bob too. What? Have you been throwing snowballs? Oh, I wish I'd been there! No, don't—I'll undress them myself, Anne-Marie. No, please let me; it's such fun. Go inside and warm yourself; you look frozen. There's some hot coffee on the stove. (*The nurse goes into the room on the left. Nora takes off the children's outdoor clothes and throws them anywhere while they all chatter simultaneously.*) What? A big dog ran after you? But he didn't bite you? No, dogs don't bite lovely little baby dolls. Leave those parcels alone, Ivar. What's in them? Ah, wouldn't you like to know! No, no; it's nothing nice. Come on, let's play a game. What shall we play? Hide and seek. Yes, let's play hide and seek. Bob shall hide first. You want me to? All right, let, me hide first.

Nora and the children play around the room, and in the adjacent room to the left, laughing and shouting. At length Nora hides under the table. The children rush in, look, but cannot find her. Then they hear her half-stifled laughter, run to the table, lift up the cloth, and see her. Great excitement. She crawls out as though to frighten them. Further excitement. Meanwhile, there has been a knock on the door leading from the hall, but no one has noticed it. Now the door is half-opened and Krogstad enters. He waits for a moment; the game continues.

KROGSTAD. Excuse me, Mrs. Helmer—

NORA (*turns with a stifled cry and half jumps up*). Oh! What do you want?

KROGSTAD. I beg your pardon; the front door was ajar. Someone must have forgotten to close it.

NORA (*gets up*). My husband is not at home, Mr. Krogstad.

KROGSTAD. I know.

NORA. Well, what do want here, then?

KROGSTAD. A word with you.

NORA. With—? (*To the children, quietly.*) Go inside to Anne-Marie. What? No, the strange gentleman won't do anything to hurt Mummy. When he's gone we'll start playing again.

She takes the children into the room on the left and closes the door behind them.

NORA (*uneasy, tense*). You want to speak to me?

KROGSTAD. Yes.

NORA. Today? But it's not the first of the month yet.

KROGSTAD. No, it is Christmas Eve. Whether or not you have a merry Christmas depends on you.

NORA. What do you want? I can't give you anything today—

KROGSTAD. We won't talk about that for the present. There's something else. You have a moment to spare?

NORA. Oh, yes. Yes, I suppose so; though—

KROGSTAD. Good. I was sitting in the café down below and I saw your husband cross the street—

NORA. Yes.

KROGSTAD. With a lady.

NORA. Well?

KROGSTAD. Might I be so bold as to ask: was not that lady a Mrs. Linde?

NORA. Yes.

KROGSTAD. Recently arrived in town?

NORA. Yes, today.

KROGSTAD. She is a good friend of yours, is she not?

NORA. Yes, she is. But I don't see—

KROGSTAD. I used to know her too once.

NORA. I know.

KROGSTAD. Oh? You've discovered that. Yes, I thought you would. Well then, may I ask you a straight question: is Mrs. Linde to be employed at the bank?

NORA. How dare you presume to cross-examine me, Mr. Krogstad? You, one of my husband's employees? But since you ask, you shall have an answer. Yes, Mrs. Linde is to be employed by the bank. And I arranged it, Mr. Krogstad. Now you know.

KROGSTAD. I guessed right, then.

NORA (*walks up and down the room*). Oh, one has a little influence, you know. Just because one's a woman it doesn't necessarily mean that— When one is in a humble position, Mr. Krogstad, one should think twice before offending someone who—hm—

KROGSTAD. —who has influence?

NORA. Precisely.

KROGSTAD (*changes his tone*). Mrs. Helmer, will you have the kindness to use your influence on my behalf?

NORA. What? What do you mean?

KROGSTAD. Will you be so good as to see that I keep my humble position at the bank?

NORA. What do you mean? Who is thinking of removing you from your position?

KROGSTAD. Oh, you don't need to play innocent with me. I realize it can't be very pleasant for your friend to risk bumping into me; and now I also realize whom I have to thank for being hounded out like this.

NORA. But I assure you—

KROGSTAD. Look, let's not beat about the bush. There's still time, and I'd advise you to use your influence to stop it.

NORA. But, Mr. Krogstad, I have no influence

KROGSTAD. Oh? I thought you just said—

NORA. But I didn't mean it like that! I? How on earth could you imagine that I would have any influence over my husband?

KROGSTAD. Oh, I've known your husband since we were students together. I imagine he has his weaknesses like other married men.

NORA. If you speak impertinently of my husband, I shall show you the door.

KROGSTAD. You're a bold woman, Mrs. Helmer.

NORA. I'm not afraid of you any longer. Once the New Year is in, I'll soon be rid of you.

KROGSTAD (*more controlled*). Now listen to me, Mrs. Helmer. If I'm forced to, I shall fight for my little job at the bank as I would fight for my life.

NORA. So it sounds.

KROGSTAD. It isn't just the money; that's the last thing I care about. There's something else — well, you might as well know. It's like this, you see. You know of course, as every one else does, that some years ago I committed an indiscretion.

NORA. I think I did hear something —

KROGSTAD. It never came into court; but from that day, every opening was barred to me. So I turned my hand to the kind of business you know about. I had to do something; and I don't think I was one of the worst. But now I want to give up all that. My sons are growing up; for their sake, I must try to regain what respectability I can. This job in the bank was the first step on the ladder. And now your husband wants to kick me off that ladder back into the dirt.

NORA. But my dear Mr. Krogstad, it simply isn't in my power to help you.

KROGSTAD. You say that because you don't want to help me. But I have the means to make you.

NORA. You don't mean you'd tell my husband that I owe you money?

KROGSTAD. And if I did?

NORA. That'd be a filthy trick! (*Almost in tears.*) This secret that is my pride and my joy — that he should hear about it in such a filthy, beastly way — hear about it from you! It'd involve me in the most dreadful unpleasantness —

KROGSTAD. Only — unpleasantness?

NORA (*vehemently*). All right, do it! You'll be the one who'll suffer. It'll show my husband the kind of man you are, and then you'll never keep your job.

KROGSTAD. I asked you whether it was merely domestic unpleasantness you were afraid of.

NORA. If my husband hears about it, he will of course immediately pay you whatever is owing. And then we shall have nothing more to do with you.

KROGSTAD (*takes a step closer*). Listen, Mrs. Helmer. Either you've a bad memory or else you know very little about financial transactions. I had better enlighten you.

NORA. What do you mean?

KROGSTAD. When your husband was ill, you came to me to borrow two hundred and fifty pounds.

NORA. I didn't know anyone else.

KROGSTAD. I promised to find that sum for you —

NORA. And you did find it.

KROGSTAD. I promised to find that sum for you on certain conditions. You were so worried about your husband's illness and so keen to get the money to take him abroad that I don't think you bothered much about the details. So it won't be out of place if I refresh your memory. Well — I promised to get you the money in exchange for an I.O.U., which I drew up.

NORA. Yes, and which I signed.

KROGSTAD. Exactly. But then I added a few lines naming your father as security for the debt. This paragraph was to be signed by your father.

NORA. Was to be? He did sign it.

KROGSTAD. I left the date blank for your father to fill in when he signed this paper. You remember, Mrs. Helmer?

NORA. Yes, I think so—

KROGSTAD. Then I gave you back this I.O.U. for you to post to your father. Is that not correct?

NORA. Yes.

KROGSTAD. And of course you posted it at once; for within five or six days you brought it along to me with your father's signature on it. Whereupon I handed you the money.

NORA. Yes, well. Haven't I repaid the installments as agreed?

KROGSTAD. Mm—yes, more or less. But to return to what we were speaking about—that was a difficult time for you just then, wasn't it, Mrs. Helmer?

NORA. Yes, it was.

KROGSTAD. And your father was very ill, if I am not mistaken.

NORA. He was dying.

KROGSTAD. He did in fact die shortly afterwards?

NORA. Yes.

KROGSTAD. Tell me, Mrs. Helmer, do you by any chance remember the date of your father's death? The day of the month, I mean.

NORA. Papa died on the twenty-ninth of September.

KROGSTAD. Quite correct; I took the trouble to confirm it. And that leaves me with a curious little problem—(*Takes out a paper.*)—which I simply cannot solve.

NORA. Problem? I don't see—

KROGSTAD. The problem, Mrs. Helmer, is that your father signed this paper three days after his death.

NORA. What? I don't understand—

KROGSTAD. Your father died on the twenty-ninth of September. But look at this. Here your father has dated his signature the second of October. Isn't that a curious little problem, Mrs. Helmer? (*Nora is silent.*) Can you suggest any explanation? (*She remains silent.*) And there's another curious thing. The words "second of October" and the year are written in a hand which is not your father's, but which I seem to know. Well, there's a simple explanation to that. Your father could have forgotten to write in the date when he signed, and someone else could have added it before the news came of his death. There's nothing criminal about that. It's the signature itself I'm wondering about. It is genuine, I suppose, Mrs. Helmer? It was your father who wrote his name here?

NORA (*after a short silence, throws back her head and looks defiantly at him*). No, it was not. It was I who wrote Papa's name there.

KROGSTAD. Look, Mrs. Helmer, do you realize this is a dangerous admission?

NORA. Why? You'll get your money.

KROGSTAD. May I ask you a question? Why didn't you send this paper to your father?

NORA. I couldn't. Papa was very ill. If I'd asked him to sign this, I'd have had to tell him what the money was for. But I couldn't have told him in his condition that my husband's life was in danger. I couldn't have done that!

KROGSTAD. Then you would have been wiser to have given up your idea of a holiday.

NORA. But I couldn't! It was to save my husband's life. I couldn't put it off.

KROGSTAD. But didn't it occur to you that you were being dishonest towards me?

NORA. I couldn't bother about that. I didn't care about you. I hated you because of all the beastly difficulties you'd put in my way when you knew how dangerously ill my husband was.

KROGSTAD. Mrs. Helmer, you evidently don't appreciate exactly what you have done. But I can assure you that it is no bigger nor worse a crime than the one I once committed, and thereby ruined my whole social position.

NORA. You? Do you expect me to believe that you would have taken a risk like that to save your wife's life?

KROGSTAD. The law does not concern itself with motives.

NORA. Then the law must be very stupid.

KROGSTAD. Stupid or not, if I show this paper to the police, you will be judged according to it.

NORA. I don't believe that. Hasn't a daughter the right to shield her father from worry and anxiety when he's old and dying? Hasn't a wife the right to save her husband's life? I don't know much about the law but there must be something somewhere that says that such things are allowed. You ought to know about that, you're meant to be a lawyer, aren't you? You can't be a very good lawyer, Mr. Krogstad.

KROGSTAD. Possibly not. But business, the kind of business we two have been transacting—I think you'll admit I understand something about that? Good. Do as you please. But I tell you this. If I get thrown into the gutter for a second time, I shall take you with me.

He bows and goes out through the hall.

NORA (*stands for a moment in thought, then tosses her head*). What nonsense! He's trying to frighten me! I'm not that stupid. (*Busies herself gathering together the children's clothes; then she suddenly stops.*) But—? No, it's impossible. I did it for love, didn't I?

CHILDREN (*in the doorway, left*). Mummy, the strange gentleman's gone out into the street.

NORA. Yes, yes, I know. But don't talk to anyone about the strange gentleman. You hear? Not even to Daddy.

CHILDREN. No, Mummy. Will you play with us again now?

NORA. No, no. Not now.

CHILDREN. Oh but, Mummy, you promised!

NORA. I know, but I can't just now. Go back to the nursery. I've a lot to do. Go away, my darlings, go away. (*She pushes them gently into the other room and closes the door behind them. She sits on the sofa, takes up her embroidery, stitches for a few moments, but soon stops.*) No! (*Throws the embroidery aside, gets up, goes to the door leading to the hall, and calls.*) Helen! Bring in the Christmas tree! (*She goes to the table on the left and opens the drawer in it; then pauses again.*) No, but it's utterly impossible!

MAID (*enters with the tree*). Where shall I put it, madam?

NORA. There, in the middle of the room.

MAID. Will you be wanting anything else?

NORA. No, thank you, I have everything I need.

The maid puts down the tree and goes out.

NORA (*busy decorating the tree*). Now—candles here—and flowers here. That loathsome man! Nonsense, nonsense, there's nothing to be frightened about. The Christmas tree must be beautiful. I'll do everything that you like, Torvald. I'll sing for you, dance for you—

Helmer, with a bundle of papers under his arm, enters.

NORA. Oh—are you back already?

HELMER. Yes. Has anyone been here?

NORA. Here? No.

HELMER. That's strange. I saw Krogstad come out of the front door.

NORA. Did you? Oh yes, that's quite right—Krogstad was here for a few minutes.

HELMER. Nora, I can tell from your face, he's been here and asked you to put in a good word for him.

NORA. Yes.

HELMER. And you were to pretend you were doing it of your own accord? You weren't going to tell me he'd been here? He asked you to do that too, didn't he?

NORA. Yes, Torvald. But—

HELMER. Nora, Nora! And you were ready to enter into such a conspiracy? Talking to a man like that, and making him promises—and then, on top of it all, to tell me an untruth!

NORA. An untruth?

HELMER. Didn't you say no one had been here? (*Wags his finger.*) My little songbird must never do that again. A songbird must have a clean beak to sing with; otherwise she'll start twittering out of tune. (*Puts his arm round her waist.*) Isn't that the way we want things? Yes, of course it is.

(*Lets go of her.*) So let's hear no more about that. (*Sits down in front of the stove.*) Ah, how cozy and peaceful it is here. (*Glances for a few moments at his papers.*)

NORA (*busy with the tree; after a short silence*). Torvald.

HELMER. Yes.

NORA. I'm terribly looking forward to that fancy dress ball at the Stenborgs on Boxing Day.

HELMER. And I'm terribly curious to see what you're going to surprise me with.

NORA. Oh, it's so maddening.

HELMER. What is?

NORA. I can't think of anything to wear. It all seems so stupid and meaningless.

HELMER. So my little Nora's come to that conclusion, has she?

NORA (*behind his chair, resting her arms on its back*). Are you very busy, Torvald?

HELMER. Oh—

NORA. What are those papers?

HELMER. Just something to do with the bank.

NORA. Already?

HELMER. I persuaded the trustees to give me authority to make certain immediate changes in the staff and organization. I want to have everything straight by the New Year.

NORA. Then that's why this poor man Krogstad—

HELMER. Hm.

NORA (*still leaning over his chair, slowly strokes the back of his head*). If you hadn't been so busy, I was going to ask you an enormous favor, Torvald.

HELMER. Well, tell me. What was it to be?

NORA. You know I trust your taste more than anyone's. I'm so anxious to look really beautiful at the fancy dress ball. Torvald, couldn't you help me to decide what I shall go as, and what kind of costume I ought to wear?

HELMER. Aha! So little Miss Independent's in trouble and needs a man to rescue her, does she?

NORA. Yes, Torvald. I can't get anywhere without your help.

HELMER. Well, well, I'll give the matter thought. We'll find something.

NORA. Oh, how kind of you! (*Goes back to the tree. Pause.*) How pretty these red flowers look! But, tell me, is it so dreadful, this thing that Krogstad's done?

HELMER. He forged someone else's name. Have you any idea what that means?

NORA. Mightn't he have been forced to do it by some emergency?

HELMER. He probably just didn't think—that's what usually happens. I'm not so heartless as to condemn a man for an isolated action.

NORA. No, Torvald, of course not!

HELMER. Men often succeed in re-establishing themselves if they admit their crime and take their punishment.

NORA. Punishment?

HELMER. But Krogstad didn't do that. He chose to try and trick his way out of it; and that's what has morally destroyed him.

NORA. You think that would—?

HELMER. Just think how a man with that load on his conscience must always be lying and cheating and dissembling; how he must wear a mask even in the presence of those who are dearest to him, even his own wife and children! Yes, the children. That's the worst danger, Nora.

NORA. Why?

HELMER. Because an atmosphere of lies contaminates and poisons every corner of the home. Every breath that the children draw in such a house contains the germs of evil.

NORA (*comes closer behind him*). Do you really believe that?

HELMER. Oh, my dear, I've come across it so often in my work at the bar. Nearly all young criminals are the children of mothers who are constitutional liars.

NORA. Why do you say mothers?

HELMER. It's usually the mother; though of course the father can have the same influence. Every lawyer knows that only too well. And yet this fellow Krogstad has been sitting at home all these years poisoning his children with his lies and pretenses. That's why I say that, morally speaking, he is dead. (*Stretches out his hands towards her.*) So my pretty little Nora must promise me not to plead his case. Your hand on it. Come, come, what's this? Give me your hand. There. That's settled, now. I assure you it'd be quite impossible for me to work in the same building as him. I literally feel physically ill in the presence of a man like that.

NORA (*draws her hand from his and goes over to the other side of the Christmas tree*). How hot it is in here! And I've so much to do.

HELMER (*gets up and gathers his papers*). Yes, and I must try to get some of this read before dinner. I'll think about your costume too. And I may even have something up my sleeve to hang in gold paper on the Christmas tree. (*Lays his hand on her head.*) My precious little songbird!

He goes into his study and closes the door.

NORA (*softly, after a pause*). It's nonsense. It must be. It's impossible. It *must* be impossible!

NURSE (*in the doorway, left*). The children are asking if they can come in to Mummy.

NORA. No, no, no; don't let them in! You stay with them, Anne-Marie.

NURSE. Very good, madam. (*Closes the door.*)

NORA (*pale with fear*). Corrupt my little children—! Poison my home! (*Short pause. She throws back her head.*) It isn't true! It *couldn't* be true!

ACT 2

The same room. In the corner by the piano the Christmas tree stands, stripped and disheveled, its candles burned to their sockets. Nora's outdoor clothes lie on the sofa. She is alone in the room, walking restlessly to and fro. At length she stops by the sofa and picks up her coat.

NORA (*drops the coat again*). There's someone coming! (*Goes to the door and listens.*) No, it's no one. Of course—no one'll come today, it's Christmas Day. Nor tomorrow. But perhaps—! (*Opens the door and looks out.*) No. Nothing in the letter-box. Quite empty. (*Walks across the room.*) Silly, silly. Of course he won't do anything. It couldn't happen. It isn't possible. Why, I've three small children.

The Nurse, carrying a large cardboard box, enters from the room on the left.

NURSE. I found those fancy dress clothes at last, madam.

NORA. Thank you. Put them on the table.

NURSE (*does so*). They're all rumpled up.

NORA. Oh, I wish I could tear them into a million pieces!

NURSE. Why, madam! They'll be all right. Just a little patience.

NORA. Yes, of course. I'll go and get Mrs. Linde to help me.

NURSE. What, out again? In this dreadful weather? You'll catch a chill, madam.

NORA. Well, that wouldn't be the worst. How are the children?

NURSE. Playing with their Christmas presents, poor little dears. But—

NORA. Are they still asking to see me?

NURSE. They're so used to having their Mummy with them.

NORA. Yes, but, Anne-Marie, from now on I shan't be able to spend so much time with them.

NURSE. Well, children get used to anything in time.

NORA. Do you think so? Do you think they'd forget their mother if she went away from them—for ever?

NURSE. Mercy's sake, madam! For ever!

NORA. Tell me, Anne-Marie—I've so often wondered. How could you bear to give your child away—to strangers?

NURSE. But I had to when I came to nurse my little Miss Nora.

NORA. Do you mean you wanted to?

NURSE. When I had the chance of such a good job? A poor girl what's got into trouble can't afford to pick and choose. That good-for-nothing didn't lift a finger.

NORA. But your daughter must have completely forgotten you.

NURSE. Oh no, indeed she hasn't. She's written to me twice, once when she got confirmed and then again when she got married.

NORA (*hugs her*). Dear old Anne-Marie, you were a good mother to me.

NURSE. Poor little Miss Nora, you never had any mother but me.

NORA. And if my little ones had no one else, I know you would—no, silly, silly, silly! (*Opens the cardboard box.*) Go back to them, Anne-Marie.

Now I must—Tomorrow you'll see how pretty I shall look.

NURSE. Why, there'll be no one at the ball as beautiful as my Miss Nora.

She goes into the room, left.

NORA (*begins to unpack the clothes from the box, but soon throws them down again*). Oh, if only I dared to go out! If I could be sure no one would come, and nothing would happen while I was away! Stupid, stupid! No one will come. I just mustn't think about it. Brush this muff. Pretty gloves, pretty gloves! Don't think about it, don't think about it! One, two, three, four, five, six—(*Cries.*) Ah—they're coming—!

She begins to run toward the door, but stops uncertainly. Mrs. Linde enters from the hall, where she has been taking off her outdoor clothes.

NORA. Oh, it's you, Christine. There's no one else out there, is there? Oh, I'm so glad you've come.

MRS. LINDE. I hear you were at my room asking for me.

NORA. Yes, I just happened to be passing. I want to ask you to help me with something. Let's sit down here on the sofa. look at this. There's going to be a fancy dress ball tomorrow night upstairs at Consul Stenborg's, and Torvald wants me to go as a Neapolitan fisher-girl and dance the tarantella. I learned it on Capri.

MRS. LINDE. I say, are you going to give a performance?

NORA. Yes, Torvald says I should. Look, here's the dress. Torvald had it made for me in Italy; but now it's all so torn, I don't know—

MRS. LINDE. Oh, we'll soon put that right; the stitching's just come away. Needle and thread? Ah, here we are.

NORA. You're being awfully sweet.

MRS. LINDE (*sews*). So you're going to dress up tomorrow, Nora? I must pop over for a moment to see how you look. Oh, but I've completely forgotten to thank you for that nice evening yesterday.

NORA (*gets up and walks across the room*). Oh, I didn't think it was as nice as usual. You ought to have come to town a little earlier, Christine. . . . Yes, Torvald understands how to make a home look attractive.

MRS. LINDE. I'm sure you do, too. You're not your father's daughter for nothing. But, tell me. Is Dr. Rank always in such low spirits as he was yesterday?

NORA. No, last night it was very noticeable. But he's got a terrible disease; he's got spinal tuberculosis, poor man. His father was a frightful creature who kept mistresses and so on. As a result Dr. Rank has been sickly ever since he was a child—you understand—

MRS. LINDE (*puts down her sewing*). But, my dear Nora, how on earth did you get to know about such things?

NORA (*walks about the room*). Oh, don't be silly, Christine—when one has three children, one comes into contact with women who—well, who know about medical matters, and they tell one a thing or two.

MRS. LINDE *(sews again; a short silence)*. Does Dr. Rank visit you every day?

NORA. Yes, every day. He's Torvald's oldest friend, and a good friend to me too. Dr. Rank's almost one of the family.

MRS. LINDE. But, tell me—is he quite sincere? I mean, doesn't he rather say the sort of thing he thinks people want to hear?

NORA. No, quite the contrary. What gave you that idea?

MRS. LINDE. When you introduced me to him yesterday, he said he'd often heard my name mentioned here. But later I noticed your husband had no idea who I was. So how could Dr. Rank—?

NORA. Yes, that's quite right, Christine. You see, Torvald's so hopelessly in love with me that he wants to have me all to himself—those were his very words. When we were first married, he got quite jealous if I as much as mentioned any of my old friends back home. So naturally, I stopped talking about them. But I often chat with Dr. Rank about that kind of thing. He enjoys it, you see.

MRS. LINDE. Now listen, Nora. In many ways you're still a child; I'm a bit older than you and have a little more experience of the world. There's something I want to say to you. You ought to give up this business with Dr. Rank.

NORA. What business?

MRS. LINDE. Well, everything. Last night you were speaking about this rich admirer of yours who was going to give you money—

NORA. Yes, and who doesn't exist—unfortunately. But what's that got to do with—?

MRS. LINDE. Is Dr. Rank rich?

NORA. Yes.

MRS. LINDE. And he has no dependents?

NORA. No, no one. But—

MRS. LINDE. And he comes here to see you every day?

NORA. Yes, I've told you.

MRS. LINDE. But how dare a man of his education be so forward?

NORA. What on earth are you talking about?

MRS. LINDE. Oh, stop pretending, Nora. Do you think I haven't guessed who it was who lent you that two hundred pounds?

NORA. Are you out of your mind? How could you imagine such a thing? A friend someone who comes here every day! Why, that'd be an impossible situation!

MRS. LINDE. Then it really wasn't him?

NORA. No, of course not. I've never for a moment dreamed of—anyway, he hadn't any money to lend then. He didn't come into that till later.

MRS. LINDE. Well, I think that was a lucky thing for you, Nora dear.

NORA. No, I could never have dreamed of asking Dr. Rank—Though I'm sure that if I ever did ask him—

MRS. LINDE. But of course you won't.

NORA. Of course not. I can't imagine that it should ever become necessary. But I'm perfectly sure that if I did speak to Dr. Rank—

MRS. LINDE. Behind your husband's back?

NORA. I've got to get out of this other business; and *that's* been going
on behind his back. I've *got* to get out of it.

MRS. LINDE. Yes, well, that's what I told you yesterday. But—

NORA (*walking up and down*). It's much easier for a man to arrange these
things than a woman—

MRS. LINDE. One's own husband, yes.

NORA. Oh, bosh. (*Stops walking.*) When you've completely repaid a debt,
you get your I.O.U. back, don't you?

MRS. LINDE. Yes, of course.

NORA. And you can tear it into a thousand pieces and burn the filthy,
beastly thing!

MRS. LINDE (*looks hard at her, puts down her sewing, and gets up slowly*). Nora,
you're hiding something from me.

NORA. Can you see that?

MRS. LINDE. Something has happened since yesterday morning. Nora,
what is it?

NORA (*goes toward her*). Christine! (*Listens.*) Ssh! There's Torvald. Would
you mind going into the nursery for a few minutes? Torvald can't bear
to see sewing around. Anne-Marie'll help you.

MRS. LINDE (*gathers some of her things together*). Very well. But I shan't leave
this house until we've talked this matter out.

She goes into the nursery, left. As she does so, Helmer enters from the hall.

NORA (*runs to meet him*). Oh, Torvald dear, I've been so longing for you
to come back!

HELMER. Was that the dressmaker?

NORA. No, it was Christine. She's helping me mend my costume. I'm
going to look rather splendid in that.

HELMER. Yes, that was quite a bright idea of mine, wasn't it?

NORA. Wonderful! But wasn't it nice of me to give in to you?

HELMER (*takes her chin in his hand*). Nice—to give in to your husband? All
right, little silly, I know you didn't mean it like that. But I won't disturb you. I expect you'll be wanting to try it on.

NORA. Are you going to work now?

HELMER. Yes. (*Shows her a bundle of papers.*) Look at these. I've been down
to the bank—(*Turns to go into his study.*)

NORA. Torvald.

HELMER (*stops*). Yes.

NORA. If little squirrel asked you really prettily to grant her a wish—

HELMER. Well?

NORA. Would you grant it to her?

HELMER. First I should naturally have to know what it was.

NORA. Squirrel would do lots of pretty tricks for you if you granted her wish.

HELMER. Out with it, then.

NORA. Your little skylark would sing in every room—

HELMER. My little skylark does that already.

NORA. I'd turn myself into a little fairy and dance for you in the moonlight, Torvald.

HELMER. Nora, it isn't that business you were talking about this morning?

NORA (*comes closer*). Yes, Torvald—oh, please! I beg of you!

HELMER. Have you really the nerve to bring that up again?

NORA. Yes, Torvald, yes, you must do as I ask ! You must let Krogstad keep his place at the bank!

HELMER. My dear Nora, his is the job I'm giving to Mrs. Linde.

NORA. Yes, that's terribly sweet of you. But you can get rid of one of the other clerks instead of Krogstad.

HELMER. Really, you're being incredibly obstinate. Just because you thoughtlessly promised to put in a word for him, you expect me to—

NORA. No, it isn't that, Helmer. It's for your own sake. That man writes for the most beastly newspapers—you said so yourself. He could do you tremendous harm. I'm so dreadfully frightened of him—

HELMER. Oh, I understand. Memories of the past. That's what's frightening you.

NORA. What do you mean?

HELMER. You're thinking of your father, aren't you?

NORA. Yes, yes. Of course. Just think what those dreadful men wrote in the papers about Papa! The most frightful slanders. I really believe it would have lost him his job if the Ministry hadn't sent you down to investigate, and you hadn't been so kind and helpful to him.

HELMER. But my dear little Nora, there's a considerable difference between your father and me. Your father was not a man of unassailable reputation. But I am; and I hope to remain so all my life.

NORA. But no one knows what spiteful people may not dig up. We could be so peaceful and happy now, Torvald—we could be free from every worry—you and I and the children. Oh, please, Torvald, please—!

HELMER. The very fact of your pleading his cause makes it impossible for me to keep him. Everyone at the bank already knows that I intend to dismiss Krogstad. If the rumor got about that the new manager had allowed his wife to persuade him to change his mind—

NORA. Well, what then?

HELMER. Oh, nothing, nothing. As long as my little Miss Obstinate gets her way—Do you expect me to make a laughing-stock of myself before my entire staff—give people the idea that I am open to outside influence? Believe me, I'd soon feel the consequences! Besides—there's something else that makes it impossible for Krogstad to remain in the bank while I am its manager.

NORA. What is that?

HELMER. I might conceivably have allowed myself to ignore his moral obloquies—

NORA. Yes, Torvald, surely?

HELMER. And I hear he's quite efficient at his job. But we—well, we were school friends. It was one of those friendships that one enters into over hastily and so often comes to regret later in life. I might as well confess the truth. We—well, we're on Christian name terms. And the tactless idiot makes no attempt to conceal it when other people are present. On the contrary, he thinks it gives him the right to be familiar with me. He shows off the whole time, with "Torvald this," and "Torvald that." I can tell you, I find it damned annoying. If he stayed, he'd make my position intolerable.

NORA. Torvald, you can't mean this seriously.

HELMER. Oh? And why not?

NORA. But it's so petty.

HELMER. What did you say? Petty? You think *I* am petty?

NORA. No, Torvald dear, of course you're not. That's just why—

HELMER. Don't quibble! You call my motives petty. Then I must be petty too. Petty! I see. Well, I've had enough of this. (*Goes to the door and calls into the hall.*) Helen!

NORA. What are you going to do?

HELMER (*searching among his papers*). I'm going to settle this matter once and for all. (*The Maid enters*) Take this letter downstairs at once. Find a messenger and see that he delivers it. Immediately! The address is on the envelope. Here's the money.

MAID. Very good, sir. (*Goes out with the letter.*)

HELMER (*putting his papers in order*). There now, little Miss Obstinate.

NORA (*tensely*). Torvald—what was in that letter?

HELMER. Krogstad's dismissal.

NORA. Call her back, Torvald! There's still time. Oh, Torvald, call her back! Do it for my sake—for your own sake—for the children! Do you hear me, Torvald? Please do it! You don't realize what this may do to us all!

HELMER. Too late.

NORA. Yes. Too late.

HELMER. My dear Nora, I forgive you this anxiety. Though it is a bit of an insult to me. Oh, but it is! Isn't it an insult to imply that I should be frightened by the vindictiveness of a depraved hack journalist? But I forgive you, because it so charmingly testifies to the love you bear me. (*Takes her in his arms.*) Which is as it should be, my own dearest Nora. Let what will happen, happen. When the real crisis comes, you will not find me lacking in strength or courage. I am man enough to bear the burden for us both.

NORA. (*fearfully*) What do you mean?

HELMER. The whole burden, I say—

NORA (*calmly*). I shall never let you do that.

HELMER. Very well. We shall share it, Nora—as man and wife. And that is as it should be. (*Caresses her.*) Are you happy now? There, there, there; don't look at me with those frightened little eyes. You're simply imagining things. You go ahead now and do your tarantella, and get some practice on that tambourine. I'll sit in my study and close the door. Then I won't hear anything, and you can make all the noise you want. (*Turns in the doorway.*) When Dr. Rank comes, tell him where to find me. (*He nods to her, goes into his room with his papers, and closes the door.*)

NORA (*desperate with anxiety, stands as though transfixed, and whispers*). He said he'd do it. He will do it. He will do it, and nothing'll stop him. No, never that. I'd rather anything. There must be some escape—Some way out—! (*The bell rings in the hall.*) Dr. Rank—! Anything but that! Anything, I don't care—!

She passes her hand across her face, composes herself, walks across, and opens the door to the hall. Dr. Rank is standing there, hanging up his fur coat. During the following scene, it begins to grow dark.

NORA. Good evening, Dr. Rank. I recognized your ring. But you mustn't go to Torvald yet. I think he's busy.

RANK. And—you?

NORA (*as he enters the room and she closes the door behind him*). Oh, you know very well I've always time to talk to you.

RANK. Thank you. I shall avail myself of that privilege as long as I can.

NORA. What do you mean by that? As long as you *can?*

RANK. Yes. Does that frighten you?

NORA. Well, it's rather a curious expression. Is something going to happen?

RANK. Something I've been expecting to happen for a long time. But I didn't think it would happen quite so soon.

NORA (*seizes his arm*). What is it? Dr. Rank, you must tell me!

RANK (*sits down by the stove*). I'm on the way out. And there's nothing to be done about it.

NORA (*sighs with relief*). Oh, it's you—?

RANK. Who else? No, it's no good lying to oneself. I am the most wretched of all my patients, Mrs. Helmer. These last few days I've been going through the books of this poor body of mine, and I find I am bankrupt. Within a month I may be rotting up there in the churchyard.

NORA. Ugh, what a nasty way to talk!

RANK. The facts aren't exactly nice. But the worst is that there's so much else that's nasty to come first. I've only one more test to make. When that's done I'll have a pretty accurate idea of when the final disintegration is likely to begin. I want to ask you a favour. Helmer's a sensitive chap, and I know how he hates anything ugly. I don't want him to visit me when I'm in hospital—

NORA. Oh but, Dr. Rank—

RANK. I don't want him there. On any pretext. I shan't have him allowed
  in. As soon as I know the worst, I'll send you my visiting card with
  a black cross on it, and then you'll know that the final filthy process
  has begun.

NORA. Really, you're being quite impossible this evening. And I did hope
  you'd be in a good mood.

RANK. With death on my hands? And all this to atone for someone else's
  sin? Is there justice in that? And in every single family, in one way or
  another, the same merciless law of retribution is at work—

NORA (*holds her hands to her ears*). Nonsense! Cheer up! Laugh!

RANK. Yes, you're right. Laughter's all the damned thing's fit for. My poor
  innocent spine must pay for the fun my father had as a gay young lieutenant.

NORA (*at the table, left*). You mean he was too fond of asparagus and *foie gras?*

RANK. Yes, and truffles too.

NORA. Yes, of course, truffles, yes. And oysters too, I suppose?

RANK. Yes, oysters, oysters. Of course.

NORA. And all that port and champagne to wash them down. It's too sad
  that all those lovely things should affect one's spine.

RANK. Especially a poor spine that never got any pleasure out of them.

NORA. Oh yes, that's the saddest thing of all.

RANK (*looks searchingly at her*). Hm—

NORA (*after a moment*). Why did you smile?

RANK. No, it was you who laughed.

NORA. No, it was you who smiled, Dr. Rank!

RANK (*gets up*). You're a worse little rogue than I thought.

NORA. Oh, I'm full of stupid tricks today.

RANK. So it seems.

NORA (*puts both her hands on his shoulders*). Dear, dear Dr. Rank, you mustn't
  die and leave Torvald and me.

RANK. Oh, you'll soon get over it. Once one is gone, one is soon forgotten.

NORA (*looks at him anxiously*). Do you believe that?

RANK. One finds replacements, and then—

NORA. Who will find a replacement?

RANK. You and Helmer both will, when I am gone. You seem to have
  made a start already, haven't you? What was this Mrs. Linde doing here
  yesterday evening?

NORA. Aha! But surely you can't be jealous of poor Christine?

RANK. Indeed I am. She will be my successor in this house. When I have
  moved on, this lady will—

NORA. Ssh—don't speak so loud! She's in there!

RANK. Today again? You see!

NORA. She's only come to mend my dress. Good heavens, how unreasonable you are! (*Sits on the sofa.*) Be nice now, Dr. Rank. Tomorrow

you'll see how beautifully I shall dance; and you must imagine that I'm
doing it just for you. And for Torvald of course; obviously. (*Takes some
things out of the box.*) Dr. Rank, sit down here and I'll show you something.

RANK (*sits*). What's this?

NORA. Look here! Look!

RANK. Silk stockings!

NORA. Flesh-colored. Aren't they beautiful? It's very dark in here now,
of course, but tomorrow—No, no, no; only the soles. Oh well, I suppose you can look a bit higher if you want to.

RANK. Hm—

NORA. Why are you looking so critical? Don't you think they'll fit me?

RANK. I can't really give you a qualified opinion on that.

NORA (*looks at him for a moment*). Shame on you! (*Flicks him on the ear with
the stockings.*) Take that. (*Puts them back in the box.*)

RANK. What other wonders are to be revealed to me?

NORA. I shan't show you anything else. You're being naughty.

She hums a little and looks among the things in the box.

RANK (*after a short silence*). When I sit here like this being so intimate with
you, I can't think—I cannot imagine what would have become of me
if I had never entered this house.

NORA (*smiles*). Yes, I think you enjoy being with us, don't you?

RANK (*more quietly, looking into the middle distance*). And now to have to leave
it all—

NORA. Nonsense. You're not leaving us.

RANK (*as before*). And not to be able to leave even the most wretched token
of gratitude behind; hardly even a passing sense of loss; only an empty
place, to be filled by the next comer.

NORA. Suppose I were to ask you to—? No—

RANK. To do what?

NORA. To give me proof of your friendship—

RANK. Yes, yes?

NORA. No, I mean—to do me a very great service—

RANK. Would you really for once grant me that happiness?

NORA. But you've no idea what it is.

RANK. Very well, tell me, then.

NORA. No, but, Dr. Rank, I can't. It's far too much—I want your help
and advice, and I want you to do something for me.

RANK. The more the better. I've no idea what it can be. But tell me. You
do trust me, don't you?

NORA. Oh, yes, more than anyone. You're my best and truest friend.
Otherwise I couldn't tell you. Well then, Dr. Rank—there's something
you must help me to prevent. You know how much Torvald loves me—
he'd never hesitate for an instant to lay down his life for me—

RANK (*leans over towards her*). Nora—do you think he is the only one—?

NORA (*with a slight start*). What do you mean?

RANK. Who would gladly lay down his life for you?

NORA (*sadly*). Oh, I see.

RANK. I swore to myself I would let you know that before I go. I shall never have a better opportunity. . . . Well, Nora, now you know that. And now you also know that you can trust me as you can trust nobody else.

NORA (*rises; calmly and quietly*). Let me pass, please.

RANK (*makes room for her but remains seated*). Nora—

NORA (*in the doorway to the hall*). Helen, bring the lamp. (*Goes over to the stove.*) Oh, dear Dr. Rank, this was really horrid of you.

RANK (*gets up*). That I have loved you as deeply as anyone else has? Was that horrid of me?

NORA. No—but that you should go and tell me. That was quite unnecessary—

RANK. What do you mean? Did you know, then—?

The Maid enters with the lamp, puts it on the table, and goes out.

RANK. Nora—Mrs. Helmer—I am asking you, did you know this?

NORA. Oh, what do I know, what did I know, what didn't I know—I really can't say. How could you be so stupid, Dr. Rank? Everything was so nice.

RANK. Well, at any rate now you know that I am ready to serve you, body and soul. So—please continue.

NORA (*looks at him*). After this?

RANK. Please tell me what it is.

NORA. I can't possibly tell you now.

RANK. Yes, yes! You mustn't punish me like this. Let me be allowed to do what I can for you.

NORA. You can't do anything for me now. Anyway; I don't need any help. It was only my imagination—you'll see. Yes, really. Honestly. (*Sits in the rocking chair, looks at him, and smiles.*)Well, upon my word you *are* a fine gentleman, Dr. Rank. Aren't you ashamed of yourself, now that the lamp's been lit?

RANK. Frankly, no. But perhaps I ought to say—*adieu?*

NORA. Of course not. You will naturally continue to visit us as before. You know quite well how Torvald depends on your company.

RANK. Yes, but you?

NORA. Oh, I always think it's enormous fun having you here.

RANK. That was what misled me. You're a riddle to me, you know. I'd often felt you'd just as soon be with me as with Helmer.

NORA. Well, you see, there are some people whom one loves, and others whom it's almost more fun to be with.

RANK. Oh yes, there's some truth in that.

NORA. When I was at home, of course I loved Papa best. But I always used to think it was terribly amusing to go down and talk to the servants; because they never told me what I ought to do; and they were such fun to listen to.

RANK. I see. So I've taken their place?

NORA (*jumps up and runs over to him*). Oh, dear, sweet Dr. Rank, I didn't mean that at all. But I'm sure you understand — I feel the same about Torvald as I did about Papa.

MAID (*enters from the hall*). Excuse me, madam. (*Whispers to her and hands her a visiting card.*)

NORA (*glances at the card*). Oh! (*Puts it quickly in her pocket.*)

RANK. Anything wrong?

NORA. No, no, nothing at all. It's just something that — it's my new dress.

RANK. What? But your costume is lying over there.

NORA. Oh — that, yes — but there's another — I ordered it specially — Torvald mustn't know —

RANK. Ah, so that's your big secret?

NORA. Yes, yes. Go in and talk to him — he's in his study — keep him talking for a bit —

RANK. Don't worry. He won't get away from me. (*Goes into Helmer's study.*)

NORA (*to the Maid*). Is he waiting in the kitchen?

MAID. Yes, madam, he came up the back way —

NORA. But didn't you tell him I had a visitor?

MAID. Yes, but he wouldn't go.

NORA. Wouldn't go?

MAID. No, madam, not until he'd spoken with you.

NORA. Very well, show him in; but quietly. Helen, you mustn't tell anyone about this. It's a surprise for my husband.

NORA. Very good, madam. I understand. (*Goes.*)

NORA It's happening. It's happening after all. No, no, no, it can't happen, it mustn't happen.

She walks across and bolts the door of Helmer's study. The Maid opens the door from the hall to admit Krogstad, and closes it behind him. He is wearing an overcoat, heavy boots, and a fur cap.

NORA (*goes towards him*). Speak quietly. My husband's at home.

KROGSTAD. Let him hear.

NORA. What do you want from me?

KROGSTAD. Information.

NORA. Hurry up, then. What is it?

KROGSTAD. I suppose you know I've been given the sack.

NORA. I couldn't stop it, Mr. Krogstad. I did my best for you, but it didn't help.

KROGSTAD. Does your husband love you so little? He knows what I can do to you, and yet he dares to —

NORA. Surely you don't imagine I told him?

KROGSTAD. No. I didn't really think you had. It wouldn't have been like my old friend Torvald Helmer to show that much courage—

NORA. Mr. Krogstad, I'll trouble you to speak respectfully of my husband.

KROGSTAD. Don't worry, I'll show him all the respect he deserves. But since you're so anxious to keep this matter hushed up, I presume you're better informed than you were yesterday of the gravity of what you've done?

NORA. I've learned more than you could ever teach me.

KROGSTAD. Yes, a bad lawyer like me—

NORA. What do you want from me?

KROGSTAD. I just wanted to see how things were with you, Mrs. Helmer. I've been thinking about you all day. Even duns and hack journalists have hearts, you know.

NORA. Show some heart, then. Think of my little children.

KROGSTAD. Have you and your husband thought of mine? Well, let's forget that. I just wanted to tell you, you don't need to take this business too seriously. I'm not going to take any action, for the present.

NORA. Oh, no—you won't, will you? I knew it.

KROGSTAD. It can all be settled quite amicably. There's no need for it to become public. We'll keep it among the three of us.

NORA. My husband must never know about this.

KROGSTAD. How can you stop him? Can you pay the balance of what you owe me?

NORA. Not immediately.

KROGSTAD. Have you any means of raising the money during the next few days?

NORA. None that I would care to use.

KROGSTAD. Well, it wouldn't have helped anyway. However much money you offered me now I wouldn't give you back that paper.

NORA. What are you going to do with it?

KROGSTAD. Just keep it. No one else need ever hear about it. So in case you were thinking of doing anything desperate—

NORA. I am.

KROGSTAD. Such as running away—

NORA. I am.

KROGSTAD. Or anything more desperate—

NORA. How did you know?

KROGSTAD. —just give up the idea.

NORA. How did you know?

KROGSTAD. Most of us think of that at first. I did. But I hadn't the courage—

NORA (*dully*). Neither have I.

KROGSTAD (*relieved*). It's true, isn't it? You haven't the courage either?

NORA. No. I haven't. I haven't.

KROGSTAD. It'd be a stupid thing to do anyway. Once the first little domestic explosion is over. . . . I've got a letter in my pocket here addressed to your husband—

NORA. Telling him everything?

KROGSTAD. As delicately as possible.

NORA (*quickly*). He must never see that letter. Tear it up. I'll find the money somehow—

KROGSTAD. I'm sorry, Mrs. Helmer, I thought I'd explained—

NORA. Oh, I don't mean the money I owe you. Let me know how much you want from my husband, and I'll find it for you.

KROGSTAD. I'm not asking your husband for money.

NORA. What do you want, then?

KROGSTAD. I'll tell you. I want to get on my feet again, Mrs. Helmer. I want to get to the top. And your husband's going to help me. For eighteen months now my record's been clean. I've been in hard straits all that time; I was content to fight my way back inch by inch. Now I've been chucked back into the mud, and I'm not going to be satisfied with just getting back my job. I'm going to get to the top, I tell you. I'm going to get back into the bank, and it's going to be higher up. Your husband's going to create a new job for me—

NORA. He'll never do that!

KROGSTAD. Oh, yes he will. I know him. He won't dare to risk a scandal. And once I'm in there with him, you'll see! Within a year I'll be his right-hand man. It'll be Nils Krogstad who'll be running that bank, not Torvald Helmer!

NORA. That will never happen.

KROGSTAD. Are you thinking of—?

NORA. Now I *have* the courage.

KROGSTAD. Oh, you can't frighten me. A pampered little pretty like you—

NORA. You'll see! You'll see!

KROGSTAD. Under the ice? Down in the cold, black water? And then, in the spring, to float up again, ugly, unrecognizable, hairless—?

NORA. You can't frighten me.

KROGSTAD. And you can't frighten me. People don't do such things, Mrs. Helmer. And anyway, what'd be the use? I've got him in my pocket.

NORA. But afterwards? When I'm no longer—?

KROGSTAD. Have you forgotten that then your reputation will be in my hands? (*She looks at him speechlessly.*) Well, I've warned you. Don't do anything silly. When Helmer's read my letter, he'll get in touch with me. And remember, it's your husband who's forced me to act like this. And for that I'll never forgive him. Goodbye, Mrs. Helmer. (*He goes out through the hall.*)

NORA (*runs to the hall door, opens it a few inches, and listens*). He's going. He's not going to give him the letter. Oh, no, no, it couldn't possibly happen. (*Opens the door a little wider.*) What's he doing? Standing outside the front door. He's not going downstairs. Is he changing his mind? Yes, he—!

A letter falls into the letter-box. Krogstad's footsteps die away down the stairs.

NORA (*with a stifled cry runs across the room towards the table by the sofa. A pause*). In the letter-box. (*Steals timidly over towards the hall door.*) There it is! Oh, Torvald, Torvald! Now we're lost!

MRS. LINDE (*enters from the nursery with Nora's costume*). Well, I've done the best I can. Shall we see how it looks—?

NORA (*whispers hoarsely*). Christine, come here.

MRS. LINDE (*throws the dress on the sofa*). What's wrong with you? You look as though you'd seen a ghost!

NORA. Come here. Do you see that letter? There—look—through the glass of the letter-box.

MRS. LINDE. Yes, yes, I see it.

NORA. That letter's from Krogstad—

MRS. LINDE. Nora! It was Krogstad who lent you the money!

NORA. Yes. And now Torvald's going to discover everything.

MRS. LINDE. Oh, believe me, Nora, it'll be best for you both.

NORA. You don't know what's happened. I've committed a forgery—

MRS. LINDE. But, for heaven's sake—!

NORA. Christine, all I want is for you to be my witness.

MRS. LINDE. What do you mean? Witness what?

NORA. If I should go out of my mind—and it might easily happen—

MRS. LINDE. Nora!

NORA. Or if anything else should happen to me—so that I wasn't here any longer—

MRS. LINDE. Nora, Nora, you don't know what you're saying!

NORA. If anyone should try to take the blame, and say it was all his fault—you understand—?

MRS. LINDE. Yes, yes—but how can you think?

NORA. Then you must testify that it isn't true, Christine. I'm not mad—I know exactly what I'm saying—and I'm telling you, no one else knows anything about this. I did it entirely on my own. Remember that.

MRS. LINDE. All right. But I simply don't understand—

NORA. Oh, how could you understand? A—miracle—is about to happen.

MRS. LINDE. Miracle?

NORA. Yes. A miracle. But it's so frightening, Christine. It *musn't* happen, not for anything in the world.

MRS. LINDE. I'll go over and talk to Krogstad.

NORA. Don't go near him. He'll only do something to hurt you.

MRS. LINDE. Once upon a time he'd have done anything for my sake.

NORA. He?

MRS. LINDE. Where does he live?

NORA. Oh, how should I know—? Oh, yes, wait a moment—! (*Feels in her pocket.*) Here's his card. But the letter, the letter—!

HELMER (*from his study, knocks on the door*). Nora!

NORA (*cries in alarm*). What is it?

HELMER. Now, now, don't get alarmed. We're not coming in; you've closed the door. Are you trying on your costume?

NORA. Yes, yes—I'm trying on my costume. I'm going to look so pretty for you, Torvald.

MRS. LINDE (*who has been reading the card*). Why, he lives just around the corner.

NORA. Yes; but it's no use. There's nothing to be done now. The letter's lying there in the box.

MRS. LINDE. And your husband has the key?

NORA. Yes, he always keeps it.

MRS. LINDE. Krogstad must ask him to send the letter back unread. He must find some excuse—

NORA. But Torvald always opens the box at just about this time—

MRS. LINDE. You must stop him. Go in and keep him talking. I'll be back as quickly as I can.

She hurries out through the hall.

NORA (*goes over to Helmer's door, opens it and peeps in*). Torvald!

HELMER (*offstage*). Well, may a man enter his own drawing-room again? Come on, Rank, now we'll see what—(*In the doorway.*) But what's this?

NORA. What, Torvald dear?

HELMER. Rank's been preparing me for some great transformation scene.

RANK (*in the doorway*). So I understood. But I seem to have been mistaken.

NORA. Yes, no one's to be allowed to see me before tomorrow night.

HELMER. But, my dear Nora, you look quite worn out. Have you been practicing too hard?

NORA. No, I haven't practiced at all yet.

HELMER. Well, you must.

NORA. Yes, Torvald, I must, I know. But I can't get anywhere without your help. I've completely forgotten everything.

HELMER. Oh, we'll soon put that to rights.

NORA. Yes, help me, Torvald. Promise me you will? Oh, I'm so nervous. All those people—! You must forget everything except me this evening. You mustn't think of business—I won't even let you touch a pen. Promise me, Torvald?

HELMER. I promise. This evening I shall think of nothing but you—my poor, helpless little darling. Oh, there's just one thing I must see to—(*Goes towards the hall door.*)

NORA. What do you want out there?

HELMER. I'm only going to see if any letters have come.

NORA. No, Torvald, no!

HELMER. Why, what's the matter?

NORA. Torvald, I beg you. There's nothing there.

HELMER. Well, I'll just make sure.

He moves towards the door. Nora runs to the piano and plays the first bars of the tarantella.

HELMER (*at the door, turns*). Aha!

NORA. I can't dance tomorrow if I don't practice with you now.

HELMER (*goes over to her*). Are you really so frightened, Nora dear?

NORA. Yes, terribly frightened. Let me start practicing now, at once— we've still time before dinner. Oh, do sit down and play for me, Torvald dear. Correct me, lead me, the way you always do.

HELMER. Very well, my dear, if you wish it.

He sits down at the piano. Nora seizes the tambourine and a long multi-colored shawl from the cardboard box, wraps the latter hastily around her, then takes a quick leap into the center of the room.

NORA. Play for me! I want to dance!

Helmer plays and Nora dances. Dr. Rank stands behind Helmer at the piano and watches her.

HELMER (*as he plays*). Slower, slower!

NORA. I can't!

HELMER. Not so violently, Nora.

NORA. I must!

HELMER (*stops playing*). No, no, this won't do at all.

NORA (*laughs and swings her tambourine*). Isn't that what I told you?

RANK. Let me play for her.

HELMER (*gets up*). Yes, would you? Then it'll be easier for me to show her.

Rank sits down at the piano and plays. Nora dances more and more wildly. Helmer has stationed himself by the stove and tries repeatedly to correct her, but she seems not to hear him. Her hair works loose and falls over her shoulders; she ignores it and continues to dance. Mrs. Linde enters.

MRS. LINDE (*stands in the doorway as though tongue-tied*). Ah—!

NORA (*as she dances*). Oh, Christine, we're having such fun!

HELMER. But, Nora darling, you're dancing as if your life depended on it.

NORA. It does.

HELMER. Rank, stop it! This is sheer lunacy. Stop it, I say!

Rank ceases playing. Nora suddenly stops dancing.

HELMER (*goes over to her*). I'd never have believed it. You've forgotten everything I taught you.

NORA (*throws away the tambourine*). You see!

HELMER. I'll have to show you every step.

NORA. You see how much I need you! You must show me every step of the way. Right to the end of the dance. Promise me you will, Torvald?

HELMER. Never fear. I will.

NORA. You mustn't think about anything but me—today or tomorrow. Don't open any letters—don't even open the letter-box—

HELMER. Aha, you're still worried about that fellow—

NORA. Oh, yes, yes, him too.

HELMER. Nora, I can tell from the way you're behaving, there's a letter from him already lying there.

NORA. I don't know. I think so. But you mustn't read it now. I don't want anything ugly to come between us till it's all over.

RANK (*quietly, to Helmer*). Better give her her way.

HELMER (*puts his arm round her*). My child shall have her way. But tomorrow night, when your dance is over—

NORA. Then you will be free.

MAID (*appears in the doorway, right*). Dinner is served, madam.

NORA. Put out some champagne, Helen.

MAID. Very good, madam. (*Goes.*)

HELMER. I say! What's this, a banquet?

NORA. We'll drink champagne until dawn! (*Calls.*) And, Helen! Put out some macaroons! Lots of macaroons—for once!

HELMER (*takes her hands in his*). Now, now, now. Don't get so excited. Where's my little songbird, the one I know?

NORA. All right. Go and sit down—and you too, Dr. Rank. I'll be with you in a minute. Christine, you must help me put my hair up.

RANK (*quietly, as they go*). There's nothing wrong, is there? I mean, she isn't—er—expecting—?

HELMER. Good heavens no, my dear chap. She just gets scared like a child sometimes—I told you before—

They go out right.

NORA. Well?

MRS. LINDE. He's left town.

NORA. I saw it from your face.

MRS. LINDE. He'll be back tomorrow evening. I left a note for him.

NORA. You needn't have bothered. You can't stop anything now. Anyway, it's wonderful really, in a way—sitting here and waiting for the miracle to happen.

MRS. LINDE. Waiting for what?

NORA. Oh, you wouldn't understand. Go in and join them. I'll be with you in a moment.

Mrs. Linde goes into the dining-room.

NORA (*stands for a moment as though collecting herself. Then she looks at her watch*). Five o'clock. Seven hours till midnight. Then another twenty-four hours till midnight tomorrow. And then the tarantella will be finished. Twenty-four and seven? Thirty-one hours to live.

HELMER *(appears in the doorway, right)*. What's happened to my little songbird?
NORA *(runs to him with her arms wide)*. Your songbird is here!

ACT 3

The same room. The table which was formerly by the sofa has been moved into the center of the room; the chairs surround it as before. The door to the hall stands open. Dance music can be heard from the floor above. Mrs. Linde is seated at the table, absent-mindedly glancing through a book. She is trying to read, but seems unable to keep her mind on it. More than once she turns and listens anxiously towards the front door.

MRS. LINDE *(looks at her watch)*. Not here yet. There's not much time left. Please God he hasn't—! *(Listens again.)* Ah, here he is. *(Goes out into the hall and cautiously opens the front door. Footsteps can be heard softly ascending the stairs. She whispers.)* Come in. There's no one here.
KROGSTAD *(in the doorway)*. I found a note from you at my lodgings. What does this mean?
MRS. LINDE. I must speak with you.
KROGSTAD. Oh? And must our conversation take place in this house?
MRS. LINDE. We couldn't meet at my place; my room has no separate entrance. Come in. We're quite alone. The maid's asleep, and the Helmers are at the dance upstairs.
KROGSTAD *(comes into the room)*. Well, well! So the Helmers are dancing this evening? Are they indeed?
MRS. LINDE. Yes. why not?
KROGSTAD. True enough. Why not?
MRS. LINDE. Well, Krogstad. You and I must have a talk together.
KROGSTAD. Have we two anything further to discuss?
MRS. LINDE. We have a great deal to discuss.
KROGSTAD. I wasn't aware of it.
MRS. LINDE. That's because you've never really understood me.
KROGSTAD. Was there anything to understand? It's the old story, isn't it—a woman chucking a man because something better turns up?
MRS. LINDE. Do you really think I'm so utterly heartless? You think it was easy for me to give you up?
KROGSTAD. Wasn't it?
MRS. LINDE. Oh, Nils, did you really believe that?
KROGSTAD. Then why did you write to me the way you did?
MRS. LINDE. I had to. Since I had to break with you, I thought it my duty to destroy all the feelings you had for me.
KROGSTAD *(clenches his fists)*. So that was it. And you did this for money!
MRS. LINDE. You mustn't forget I had a helpless mother to take care of, and two little brothers. We couldn't wait for you, Nils. It would have been so long before you'd had enough to support us.

KROGSTAD. Maybe. But you had no right to cast me off for someone else.

MRS. LINDE. Perhaps not. I've often asked myself that.

KROGSTAD (*more quietly*). When I lost you, it was just as though all solid ground had been swept from under my feet. Look at me. Now I am a shipwrecked man, clinging to a spar.

MRS. LINDE. Help may be near at hand.

KROGSTAD. It was near. But then you came, and stood between it and me.

MRS. LINDE. I didn't know, Nils. No one told me till today that this job I'd found was yours.

KROGSTAD. I believe you, since you say so. But now you know, won't you give it up?

MRS. LINDE. No—because it wouldn't help you even if I did.

KROGSTAD. Wouldn't it? I'd do it all the same.

MRS. LINDE. I've learned to look at things practically. Life and poverty have taught me that.

KROGSTAD. And life has taught me to distrust fine words.

MRS. LINDE. Then it's taught you a useful lesson. But surely you still believe in actions?

KROGSTAD. What do you mean?

MRS. LINDE. You said you were like a shipwrecked man clinging to a spar.

KROGSTAD. I have good reason to say it.

MRS. LINDE. I'm in the same position as you. No one to care about, no one to care for.

KROGSTAD. You made your own choice.

MRS. LINDE. I had no choice—then.

KROGSTAD. Well?

MRS. LINDE. Nils, suppose we two shipwrecked souls could join hands?

KROGSTAD. What are you saying?

MRS. LINDE. Castaways have a better chance of survival together than on their own.

KROGSTAD. Christine!

MRS. LINDE. Why do you suppose I came to this town?

KROGSTAD. You mean—you came because of me?

MRS. LINDE. I must work if I'm to find life worth living. I've always worked, for as long as I can remember; it's been the greatest joy of my life—my only joy. But now I'm alone in the world, and I feel so dreadfully lost and empty. There's no joy in working just for oneself Oh, Nils, give me something— someone—to work for.

KROGSTAD. I don't believe all that. You're just being hysterical and romantic. You want to find an excuse for self-sacrifice.

MRS. LINDE. Have you ever known me to be hysterical?

KROGSTAD. You mean you really—? Is it possible? Tell me—you know all about my past?

MRS. LINDE. Yes.

KROGSTAD. And you know what people think of me here?

MRS. LINDE. You said just now that with me you might have become a different person.

KROGSTAD. I know I could have.

MRS. LINDE. Couldn't it still happen?

KROGSTAD. Christine—do you really mean this? Yes—you do—I see it in your face. Have you really the courage—?

MRS. LINDE. I need someone to be a mother to; and your children need a mother. And you and I need each other. I believe in you, Nils. I am afraid of nothing—with you.

KROGSTAD (*clasps her hands*). Thank you, Christine—thank you! Now I shall make the world believe in me as you do! Oh—but I'd forgotten—

MRS. LINDE (*listens*). Ssh! The tarantella! Go quickly, go!

KROGSTAD. Why? What is it?

MRS. LINDE. You hear that dance? As soon as it's finished, they'll be coming down.

KROGSTAD. All right, I'll go. It's no good, Christine. I'd forgotten—you don't know what I've just done to the Helmers.

MRS. LINDE. Yes, Nils. I know.

KROGSTAD. And yet you'd still have the courage to—?

MRS. LINDE. I know what despair can drive a man like you to.

KROGSTAD. Oh, if only I could undo this!

MRS. LINDE. You can. Your letter is still lying in the box.

KROGSTAD. Are you sure?

MRS. LINDE. Quite sure. But—

KROGSTAD (*looks searchingly at her*). Is that why you're doing this? You want to save your friend at any price? Tell me the truth. Is that the reason?

MRS. LINDE. Nils, a woman who has sold herself once for the sake of others doesn't make the same mistake again.

KROGSTAD. I shall demand my letter back.

MRS. LINDE. No, no.

KROGSTAD. Of course I shall. I shall stay here till Helmer comes down. I'll tell him he must give me back my letter—I'll say it was only to do with my dismissal, and that I don't want him to read it—

MRS. LINDE. No, Nils, you mustn't ask for that letter back.

KROGSTAD. But—tell me—wasn't that the real reason you asked me to come here?

MRS. LINDE. Yes—at first, when I was frightened. But a day has passed since then, and in that time I've seen incredible things happen in this house. Helmer must know the truth. This unhappy secret of Nora's must be revealed. They must come to a full understanding; there must be an end of all these shiftings and evasions.

KROGSTAD. Very well. If you're prepared to risk it. But one thing I can do—and at once—

MRS. LINDE (*listens*). Hurry! Go, go! The dance is over. We aren't safe here another moment.

KROGSTAD. I'll wait for you downstairs.

MRS. LINDE. Yes, do. You can see me home.

KROGSTAD. I've never been so happy in my life before!

He goes out through the front door. The door leading from the room into the hall remains open.

MRS. LINDE (*tidies the room a little and gets her hat and coat*). What a change! Oh, what a change! Someone to work for—to live for! A home to bring joy into! I won't let this chance of happiness slip through my fingers. Oh, why don't they come? (*Listens.*) Ah, here they are. I must get my coat on.

She takes her hat and coat. Helmer's and Nora's voices become audible outside. A key is turned in the lock and Helmer leads Nora almost forcibly into the hall. She is dressed in an Italian costume with a large black shawl. He is in evening dress, with a black cloak.

NORA (*still in the doorway, resisting him*). No, no, no—not in here! I want to go back upstairs. I don't want to leave so early.

HELMER. But my dearest Nora—

NORA. Oh, please, Torvald, please! Just another hour!

HELMER. Not another minute, Nora, my sweet. You know what we agreed. Come along, now. Into the drawing-room. You'll catch cold if you stay out here.

He leads her, despite her efforts to resist him, gently into the room.

MRS. LINDE. Good evening.

NORA Christine!

HELMER. Oh, hullo, Mrs. Linde. You still here?

MRS. LINDE. Please forgive me. I did so want to see Nora in her costume.

NORA. Have you been sitting here waiting for me?

MRS. LINDE. Yes. I got here too late, I'm afraid. You'd already gone up. And I felt I really couldn't go back home without seeing you.

HELMER (*takes off Nora's shawl*). Well, take a good look at her. She's worth looking at, don't you think? Isn't she beautiful, Mrs. Linde?

MRS. LINDE. Oh, yes, indeed—

HELMER. Isn't she unbelievably beautiful? Everyone at the party said so. But dreadfully stubborn she is, bless her pretty little heart. What's to be done about that? Would you believe it, I practically had to use force to get her away!

NORA. Oh, Torvald, you're going to regret not letting me stay—just half an hour longer.

HELMER. Hear that, Mrs. Linde? She dances her tarantella—makes a roaring success—and very well deserved—though possibly a trifle too realistic—more so than was aesthetically necessary, strictly speaking. But never mind that. Main thing is—she had a success—roaring success. Was I going to let her stay on after that and spoil the impression? No, thank you. I took my beautiful little Capri signorina—my capricious little Capricienne, what?—under my arm—a swift round of the ballroom, a curtsey to the company, and, as they say in novels, the beautiful apparition disappeared! An exit should always be dramatic, Mrs. Linde. But unfortunately that's just what I can't get Nora to realize. I say, it's hot in here. (*Throws his cloak on a chair and opens the door to his study.*) What's this? It's dark in here. Ah, yes, of course— excuse me. (*Goes in and lights a couple of candles.*)

NORA (*whispers swiftly, breathlessly*). Well?

MRS. LINDE (*quietly*). I've spoken to him.

NORA. Yes?

MRS. LINDE. Nora—you must tell your husband everthing.

NORA (*dully*). I knew it.

MRS. LINDE. You've nothing to fear from Krogstad. But you must tell him.

NORA. I shan't tell him anything.

MRS. LINDE. Then the letter will.

NORA. Thank you, Christine. Now I know what I must do. Ssh!

HELMER (*returns*). Well, Mrs. Linde, finished admiring her?

MRS. LINDE. Yes. Now I must say good night.

HELMER. Oh, already? Does this knitting belong to you?

MRS. LINDE (*takes it*). Thank you, yes. I nearly forgot it.

HELMER. You knit, then?

MRS. LINDE. Why, yes.

HELMER. Know what? You ought to take up embroidery.

MRS. LINDE. Oh? Why?

HELMER. It's much prettier. Watch me, now. You hold the embroidery in your left hand, like this, and then you take the needle in your right hand and go in and out in a slow, easy movement—like this. I am right, aren't I?

MRS. LINDE. Yes, I'm sure—

HELMER. But knitting, now—that's an ugly business—can't help it. Look—arms all huddled up—great clumsy needles going up and down—makes you look like a damned Chinaman. I say, that really was a magnificent champagne they served us.

MRS. LINDE. Well, good night, Nora. And stop being stubborn. Remember!

HELMER. Quite right, Mrs. Linde!

MRS. LINDE. Good night, Mr. Helmer.

HELMER (*accompanies her to the door*). Good night, good night! I hope you'll manage to get home all right? I'd gladly—but you haven't far to go, have you? Good night, good night. (*She goes. He closes the door behind her and returns.*) Well, we've got rid of her at last. Dreadful bore that woman is!

NORA. Aren't you very tired, Torvald?

HELMER. No, not in the least.

NORA. Aren't you sleepy?

HELMER. Not a bit. On the contrary, I feel extraordinarily exhilarated. But what about you? Yes, you look very sleepy and tired.

NORA. Yes, I am very tired. Soon I shall sleep.

HELMER. You see, you see! How right I was not to let you stay longer!

NORA. Oh, you're always right, whatever you do.

HELMER (*kisses her on the forehead*). Now my little songbird's talking just like a real big human being. I say, did you notice how cheerful Rank was this evening?

NORA. Oh? Was he? I didn't have a chance to speak with him.

HELMER. I hardly did. But I haven't seen him in such a jolly mood for ages. (*Looks at her for a moment, then comes closer.*) I say, it's nice to get back to one's home again, and be all alone with you. Upon my word, you're a distractingly beautiful young woman.

NORA. Don't look at me like that, Torvald!

HELMER. What, not look at my most treasured possession? At all this wonderful beauty that's mine, mine alone, all mine.

NORA (*goes round to the other side of the table*). You mustn't talk to me like that tonight.

HELMER (*follows her*). You've still the tarantella in your blood, I see. And that makes you even more desirable. Listen! Now the other guests are beginning to go. (*More quietly.*) Nora—soon the whole house will be absolutely quiet.

NORA. Yes, I hope so.

HELMER. Yes, my beloved Nora, of course you do! Do you know—when I'm out with you among other people like we were tonight, do you know why I say so little to you, why I keep so aloof from you, and just throw you an occasional glance? Do you know why I do that? It's because I pretend to myself that you're my secret mistress, my clandestine little sweetheart, and that nobody knows there's anything at all between us.

NORA. Oh, yes, yes, yes—I know you never think of anything but me.

HELMER. And then when we're about to go, and I wrap the shawl round your lovely young shoulders, over this wonderful curve of your neck—then I pretend to myself that you are my young bride, that we've just come from the wedding, that I'm taking you to my house for the first time—that, for the first time, I am alone with you—quite alone with you, as you stand there young and trembling and beautiful. All evening I've had no eyes for anyone but you. When I saw you dance the tarantella, like a huntress, a temptress, my blood grew hot, I couldn't stand it any longer! That was why I seized you and dragged you down here with me—

NORA. Leave me, Torvald! Get away from me! I don't want all this.

HELMER. What? Now, Nora, you're joking with me. Don't want, don't want—? Aren't I your husband—?

There is a knock on the front door.

NORA (*starts*). What was that?

HELMER (*goes towards the hall*). Who is it?

RANK (*outside*). It's me. May I come in for a moment?

HELMER (*quietly, annoyed*). Oh, what does he want now? (*Calls.*) Wait a moment. (*Walks over and opens the door.*) Well! Nice of you not to go by without looking in.

RANK. I thought I heard your voice, so l felt I had to say goodbye. (*His eyes travel swiftly around the room.*) Ah, yes—these dear rooms, how well I know them. What a happy, peaceful home you two have.

HELMER. You seemed to be having a pretty happy time yourself upstairs.

RANK. Indeed I did. Why not? Why shouldn't one make the most of this world? As much as one can, and for as long as one can. The wine was excellent—

HELMER. Especially the champagne.

RANK. You noticed that too? It's almost incredible how much I managed to get down.

NORA. Torvald drank a lot of champagne too, this evening.

RANK. Oh?

NORA. Yes. It always makes him merry afterwards.

RANK. Well, why shouldn't a man have a merry evening after a well-spent day?

HELMER. Well-spent? Oh, I don't know that I can claim that.

RANK (*slaps him across the back*). I can though, my dear fellow!

NORA. Yes, of course, Dr. Rank—you've been carrying out a scientific experiment today, haven't you?

RANK. Exactly.

HELMER. Scientific experiment! Those are big words for my little Nora to use!

NORA. And may I congratulate you on the finding?

RANK. You may indeed.

NORA. It was good, then?

RANK. The best possible finding—both for the doctor and the patient. Certainty.

NORA (*quickly*). Certainty?

RANK. Absolute certainty. So aren't I entitled to have a merry evening after that?

NORA. Yes, Dr. Rank. You were quite right to.

HELMER. I agree. Provided you don't have to regret it tomorrow.

RANK. Well, you never get anything in this life without paying for it.

NORA. Dr. Rank—you like masquerades, don't you?

RANK. Yes, if the disguises are sufficiently amusing.

NORA. Tell me. What shall we two wear at the next masquerade?

HELMER. You little gadabout! Are you thinking about the next one already?

RANK. We two? Yes, I'll tell you. You must go as the Spirit of Happiness —

HELMER. You try to think of a costume that'll convey that.

RANK. Your wife need only appear as her normal, everyday self —

HELMER. Quite right! Well said! But what are you going to be? Have you decided that?

RANK. Yes, my dear friend. I have decided that.

HELMER. Well?

RANK. At the next masquerade, I shall be invisible.

HELMER. Well, that's a funny idea.

RANK. There's a big, black hat — haven't you heard of the invisible hat? Once it's over your head, no one can see you any more.

HELMER (*represses a smile*). Ah yes, of course.

RANK. But I'm forgetting what I came for. Helmer, give me a cigar. One of your black Havanas.

HELMER. With the greatest pleasure. (*Offers him the box.*)

RANK (*takes one and cuts off the tip*). Thank you.

NORA (*strikes a match*). Let me give you a light.

RANK. Thank you. (*She holds out the match for him. He lights his cigar.*) And now — goodbye.

HELMER. Goodbye, my dear chap, goodbye.

NORA. Sleep well, Dr. Rank.

RANK. Thank you for that kind wish.

NORA. Wish me the same.

RANK. You? Very well — since you ask. Sleep well. And thank you for the light. (*He nods to them both and goes.*)

HELMER (*quietly*). He's been drinking too much.

NORA (*abstractedly*). Perhaps.

Helmer takes his bunch of keys from his pocket and goes out into the hall.

NORA. Torvald, what do you want out there?

HELMER. I must empty the letter-box. It's absolutely full. There'll be no room for the newspapers in the morning.

NORA. Are you going to work tonight?

HELMER. You know very well I'm not. Hullo, what's this? Someone's been at the lock.

NORA. At the lock —?

HELMER. Yes, I'm sure of it. Who on earth —? Surely not one of the maids? Here's a broken hairpin. Nora, it's yours —

NORA (*quickly*). Then it must have been the children.

HELMER. Well, you'll have to break them of that habit. Hm, hm. Ah, that's done it. (*Takes out the contents of the box and calls into the kitchen.*) Helen! Put out the light on the staircase. (*Comes back into the drawing-room with the letters in his hand and closes the door to the hall.*) Look at this! You see how they've piled up? (*Glances through them.*) What on earth's this?

NORA (*at the window*). The letter! Oh, no, Torvald, no!

HELMER. Two visiting cards—from Rank.

NORA. From Dr. Rank?

HELMER (*looks at them*). Peter Rank, M.D. They were on top. He must have dropped them in as he left.

NORA. Has he written anything on them?

HELMER. There's a black cross above his name. Look. Rather gruesome, isn't it? It looks just as though he was announcing his death.

NORA. He is.

HELMER. What? Do you know something? Has he told you anything?

NORA. Yes. When these cards come, it means he's said goodbye to us. He wants to shut himself up in his house and die.

HELMER. Ah, poor fellow. I knew I wouldn't be seeing him for much longer. But so soon—! And now he's going to slink away and hide like a wounded beast.

NORA. When the time comes, it's best to go silently. Don't you think so, Torvald?

HELMER (*walks up and down*). He was so much a part of our life. I can't realize that he's gone. His suffering and loneliness seemed to provide a kind of dark background to the happy sunlight of our marriage. Well, perhaps it's best this way. For him, anyway. (*Stops walking.*) And perhaps for us too, Nora. Now we have only each other. (*Embraces her.*) Oh, my beloved wife—I feel as though I could never hold you close enough. Do you know, Nora, often I wish some terrible danger might threaten you, so that I could offer my life and my blood, everything, for your sake.

NORA (*tears herself loose and says in a clear, firm voice*). Read your letters now, Torvald.

HELMER. No, no. Not tonight. Tonight I want to be with you, my darling wife—

NORA. When your friend is about to die—?

HELMER. You're right. This news has upset us both. An ugliness has come between us; thoughts of death and dissolution. We must try to forget them. Until then—you go to your room; I shall go to mine.

NORA (*throws her arms round his neck*). Good night, Torvald! Good night!

HELMER (*kisses her on the forehead*). Good night, my darling little songbird. Sleep well, Nora. I'll go and read my letters.

He goes into the study with the letters in his hand, and closes the door.

NORA (*wild-eyed, fumbles around, seizes Helmer's cloak, throws it round herself and whispers quickly, hoarsely*). Never see him again. Never. Never. Never. (*Throws the shawl over her head.*) Never see the children again. Them too. Never. Never. Oh—the icy black water! Oh—that bottomless—that—!

Oh, if only it were all over! Now he's got it—he's reading it. Oh, no, no! Not yet! Goodbye, Torvald! Goodbye, my darlings!

She turns to run into the hall. As she does so, Helmer throws open his door and stands there with an open letter in his hand.

HELMER. Nora!

NORA (*shrieks*). Ah—!

HELMER. What is this? Do you know what is in this letter?

NORA. Yes, I know. Let me go! Let me go!

HELMER (*holds her back*). Go? Where?

NORA. (*tries to tear herself loose*) You mustn't try to save me, Torvald!

HELMER (*staggers back*). Is it true? Is it true, what he writes? Oh, my God! No, no—it's impossible, it can't be true!

NORA. It *is* true. I've loved you more than anything else in the world.

HELMER. Oh, don't try to make silly excuses.

NORA (*takes a step towards him*). Torvald—

HELMER. Wretched woman! What have you done?

NORA. Let me go! You're not going to suffer for my sake. I won't let you!

HELMER. Stop being theatrical. (*Locks the front door.*) You're going to stay here and explain yourself. Do you understand what you've done? Answer me! Do you understand?

NORA (*looks unflinchingly at him and, her expression growing colder, says*). Yes. Now I am beginning to understand.

HELMER (*walking around the room*). Oh, what a dreadful awakening! For eight whole years—she who was my joy and my pride—a hypocrite, a liar—worse, worse—a criminal! Oh, the hideousness of it! Shame on you, shame!

Nora is silent and stares unblinkingly at him.

HELMER (*stops in front of her*). I ought to have guessed that something of this sort would happen. I should have foreseen it. All your father's recklessness and instability—be quiet!—I repeat, all your father's recklessness and instability he has handed on to you. No religion, no morals, no sense of duty! Oh, how I have been punished for closing my eyes to his faults! I did it for your sake. And now you reward me like this.

NORA. Yes. Like this.

HELMER. Now you have destroyed all my happiness. You have ruined my whole future. Oh, it's too dreadful to contemplate! I am in the power of a man who is completely without scruples. He can do what he likes with me, demand what he pleases, order me to do anything—I dare not disobey him. I am condemned to humiliation and ruin simply for the weakness of a woman.

NORA. When I am gone from this world, you will be free.

HELMER. Oh, don't be melodramatic. Your father was always ready with that kind of remark. How would it help me if you were "gone from this world," as you put it? It wouldn't assist me in the slightest. He can still make all the facts public; and if he does, I may quite easily be suspected of having been an accomplice in your crime. People may think that I was behind it—that it was I who encouraged you! And for all this I have to thank you, you whom I have carried on my hands through all the years of our marriage! Now do you realize what you've done to me?

NORA (*coldly calm*). Yes.

HELMER. It's so unbelievable I can hardly credit it. But we must try to find some way out. Take off that shawl. Take it off, I say! I must try to buy him off somehow. This thing must be hushed up at any price. As regards our relationship—we must appear to be living together just as before. Only *appear*, of course. You will therefore continue to reside here. That is understood. But the children shall be taken out of your hands. I dare no longer entrust them to you. Oh, to have to say this to the woman I once loved so dearly— and whom I still—! Well, all that must be finished. Henceforth there can be no question of happiness; we must merely strive to save what shreds and tatters—(*The front door bell rings. Helmer starts.*) What can that be? At this hour? Surely not—? He wouldn't—? Hide yourself, Nora. Say you're ill.

Nora does not move. Helmer goes to the door of the room and opens it. The maid is standing half-dressed in the hall.

MAID. A letter for madam.

HELMER. Give it to me. (*Seizes the letter and shuts the door.*) Yes, it's from him. You're not having it. I'll read this myself.

NORA. Read it.

HELMER (*by the lamp*). I hardly dare to. This may mean the end for us both. No, I must know. (*Tears open the letter hastily; reads a few lines; looks at a piece of paper which is enclosed with it; utters a cry of joy.*) Nora! (*She looks at him questioningly.*) Nora! No—I must read it once more. Yes, yes, it's true! I am saved! Nora, I am saved!

NORA. What about me?

HELMER. You too, of course. We're both saved, you and I. Look! He's returning your I.O.U. He writes that he is sorry for what has happened—a happy accident has changed his life—oh, what does it matter what he writes? We are saved, Nora! No one can harm you now. Oh, Nora, Nora—no, first let me destroy this filthy thing. Let me see—! (*Glances at the I.O.U.*) No, I don't want to look at it. I shall merely regard the whole business as a dream. (*He tears the I.O.U. and both letters into pieces, throws them into the stove, and watches them burn.*) There. Now they're destroyed. He wrote that ever since Christmas Eve you've been—oh, these must have been three dreadful days for you, Nora.

NORA. Yes. It's been a hard fight.

HELMER. It must have been terrible—seeing no way out except—no, we'll forget the whole sordid business. We'll just be happy and go on telling ourselves over and over again: "It's over! It's over!" Listen to me, Nora. You don't seem to realize. It's over! Why are you looking so pale? Ah, my poor little Nora, I understand. You can't believe that I have forgiven you. But I have, Nora. I swear it to you. I have forgiven you everything. I know that what you did you did for your love of me.

NORA. That is true.

HELMER. You have loved me as a wife should love her husband. It was simply that in your inexperience you chose the wrong means. But do you think I love you any the less because you don't know how to act on your own initiative? No, no. Just lean on me. I shall counsel you. I shall guide you. I would not be a true man if your feminine helplessness did not make you doubly attractive in my eyes. You mustn't mind the hard words I said to you in those first dreadful moments when my whole world seemed to be tumbling about my ears. I have forgiven you, Nora. I swear it to you; I have forgiven you.

NORA. Thank you for your forgiveness.

She goes out through the door, right.

HELMER. No, don't go—(*Looks in.*) What are you doing there?

NORA (*offstage*). Taking off my fancy dress.

HELMER (*by the open door*). Yes, do that. Try to calm yourself and get your balance again, my frightened little songbird. Don't be afraid. I have broad wings to shield you. (*Begins to walk around near the door.*) How lovely and peaceful this little home of ours is, Nora. You are safe here; I shall watch over you like a hunted dove which I have snatched unharmed from the claws of the falcon. Your wildly beating little heart shall find peace with me. It will happen, Nora; it will take time, but it will happen, believe me. Tomorrow all this will seem quite different. Soon everything will be as it was before. I shall no longer need to remind you that I have forgiven you; your own heart will tell you that it is true. Do you really think I could ever bring myself to disown you, or even to reproach you? Ah, Nora, you don't understand what goes on in a husband's heart. There is something indescribably wonderful and satisfying for a husband in knowing that he has forgiven his wife—forgiven her unreservedly, from the bottom of his heart. It means that she has become his property in a double sense; he has, as it were, brought her into the world anew; she is now not only his wife but also his child. From now on that is what you shall be to me, my poor, helpless, bewildered little creature. Never be frightened of anything again, Nora. Just open your heart to me. I shall be both your will and your conscience. What's this? Not in bed? Have you changed?

NORA. (*in her everyday dress*). Yes, Torvald. I've changed.

HELMER. But why now—so late—?

NORA. I shall not sleep tonight.

HELMER. But, my dear Nora—

NORA (*looks at her watch*). It isn't that late. Sit down here, Torvald. You and I have a lot to talk about.

She sits down on one side of the table.

HELMER. Nora, what does this mean? You look quite drawn—

NORA. Sit down. It's going to take a long time. I've a lot to say to you.

HELMER (*sits down on the other side of the table*). You alarm me, Nora. I don't understand you.

NORA. No, that's just it. You don't understand me. And I've never understood you—until this evening. No, don't interrupt me. Just listen to what I have to say. You and I have got to face facts, Torvald.

HELMER. What do you mean by that?

NORA (*after a short silence*). Doesn't anything strike you about the way we're sitting here?

HELMER. What?

NORA. We've been married for eight years. Does it occur to you that this is the first time that we two, you and I, man and wife, have ever had a serious talk together?

HELMER. Serious? What do you mean, serious?

NORA. In eight whole years—no, longer—ever since we first met—we have never exchanged a serious word on a serious subject.

HELMER. Did you expect me to drag you into all my worries—worries you couldn't possibly have helped me with?

NORA. I'm not talking about worries. I'm simply saying that we have never sat down seriously to try to get to the bottom of anything.

HELMER. But, my dear Nora, what on earth has that got to do with you?

NORA. That's just the point. You have never understood me. A great wrong has been done to me, Torvald. First by Papa, and then by you.

HELMER. What? But we two have loved you more than anyone in the world!

NORA (*shakes her head*). You have never loved me. You just thought it was fun to be in love with me.

HELMER. Nora, what kind of a way is this to talk?

NORA. It's the truth, Torvald. When I lived with Papa, he used to tell me what he thought about everything, so that I never had any opinions but his. And if I did have any of my own, I kept them quiet, because he wouldn't have liked them. He called me his little doll, and he played with me just the way I played with my dolls. Then I came here to live in your house—

HELMER. What kind of a way is that to describe our marriage?

NORA (*undisturbed*). I mean, then I passed from Papa's hands into yours. You arranged everything the way you wanted it, so that I simply took over your taste in everything—or pretended I did—I don't really know—I think it was a little of both—first one and then the other. Now I look back on it, it's as if I've been living here like a pauper, from hand to mouth. I performed tricks for you, and you gave me food and drink. But that was how you wanted it. You and Papa have done me a great wrong. It's your fault that I have done nothing with my life.

HELMER. Nora, how can you be so unreasonable and ungrateful? Haven't you been happy here?

NORA. No; never. I used to think I was; but I haven't ever been happy.

HELMER. Not—not happy?

NORA. No. I've just had fun. You've always been very kind to me. But our home has never been anything but a playroom. I've been your doll-wife, just as I used to be Papa's doll-child. And the children have been my dolls. I used to think it was fun when you came in and played with me, just as they think it's fun when I go in and play games with them. That's all our marriage has been, Torvald.

HELMER. There may be a little truth in what you say, though you exaggerate and romanticize. But from now on it'll be different. Playtime is over. Now the time has come for education.

NORA. Whose education? Mine or the children's?

HELMER. Both yours and the children's, my dearest Nora.

NORA. Oh, Torvald, you're not the man to educate me into being the right wife for you.

HELMER. How can you say that?

NORA. And what about me? Am I fit to educate the children?

HELMER. Nora!

NORA. Didn't you say yourself a few minutes ago that you dare not leave them in my charge?

HELMER. In a moment of excitement. Surely you don't think I meant it seriously?

NORA. Yes. You were perfectly right. I'm not fitted to educate them. There's something else I must do first. I must educate myself. And you can't help me with that. It's something I must do by myself. That's why I'm leaving you.

HELMER (*jumps up*). What did you say?

NORA. I must stand on my own feet if I am to find out the truth about myself and about life. So I can't go on living here with you any longer.

HELMER. Nora, Nora!

NORA. I'm leaving you now, at once. Christine will put me up for tonight—

HELMER. You're out of your mind! You can't do this! I forbid you!

NORA. It's no use your trying to forbid me any more. I shall take with me nothing but what is mine. I don't want anything from you, now or ever.

HELMER. What kind of madness is this?

NORA. Tomorrow I shall go home—I mean, to where I was born. It'll be easiest for me to find some kind of a job there.

HELMER. But you're blind! You've no experience of the world—

NORA. I must try to get some, Torvald.

HELMER. But to leave your home, your husband, your children! Have you thought what people will say?

NORA. I can't help that. I only know that I must do this.

HELMER. But this is monstrous! Can you neglect your most sacred duties?

NORA. What do you call my most sacred duties?

HELMER. Do I have to tell you? Your duties towards your husband, and your children.

NORA. I have another duty which is equally sacred.

HELMER. You have not. What on earth could that be?

NORA. My duty towards myself.

HELMER. First and foremost you are a wife and a mother.

NORA. I don't believe that any longer. I believe that I am first and foremost a human being, like you—or anyway, that I must try to become one. I know most people think as you do, Torvald, and I know there's something of the sort to be found in books. But I'm no longer prepared to accept what people say and what's written in books. I must think things out for myself, and try to find my own answer.

HELMER. Do you need to ask where your duty lies in your own home? Haven't you an infallible guide in such matters—your religion?

NORA. Oh, Torvald, I don't really know what religion means.

HELMER. What are you saying?

NORA. I only know what Pastor Hansen told me when I went to confirmation. He explained that religion meant this and that. When I get away from all this and can think things out on my own, that's one of the questions I want to look into. I want to find out whether what Pastor Hansen said was right—or anyway, whether it is right for me.

HELMER. But it's unheard of for so young a woman to behave like this! If religion cannot guide you, let me at least appeal to your conscience. I presume you have some moral feelings left? Or—perhaps you haven't? Well, answer me.

NORA. Oh, Torvald, that isn't an easy question to answer. I simply don't know. I don't know where I am in these matters. I only know that these things mean something quite different to me from what they do to you. I've learned now that certain laws are different from what I'd imagined them to be; but I can't accept that such laws can be right. Has a woman really not the right to spare her dying father pain, or save her husband's life? I can't believe that.

HELMER. You're talking like a child. You don't understand how society works.

NORA. No, I don't. But now I intend to learn. I must try to satisfy myself which is right, society or I.

HELMER. Nora, you're ill; you're feverish. I almost believe you're out of your mind.

NORA. I've never felt so sane and sure in my life.

HELMER. You feel sure that it is right to leave your husband and your children?

NORA. Yes. I do.

HELMER. Then there is only one possible explanation.

NORA. What?

HELMER. That you don't love me any longer.

NORA. No, that's exactly it.

HELMER. Nora! How can you say this to me?

NORA. Oh, Torvald, it hurts me terribly to have to say it, because you've always been so kind to me. But I can't help it. I don't love you any longer.

HELMER (*controlling his emotions with difficulty.*) And you feel quite sure about this too?

NORA. Yes, absolutely sure. That's why I can't go on living here any longer.

HELMER. Can you also explain why I have lost your love?

NORA. Yes, I can. It happened this evening, when the miracle failed to happen. It was then that I realized you weren't the man I'd thought you to be.

HELMER. Explain more clearly. I don't understand you.

NORA. I've waited so patiently, for eight whole years—well, good heavens, I'm not such a fool as to suppose that miracles occur every day. Then this dreadful thing happened to me, and then I *knew:* "Now the miracle will take place!" When Krogstad's letter was lying out there, it never occurred to me for a moment that you would let that man trample over you. I *knew* that you would say to him: "Publish the facts to the world." And when he had done this—

HELMER. Yes, what then? When I'd exposed my wife's name to shame and scandal—

NORA. Then I was certain that you would step forward and take all the blame on yourself, and say: "I am the one who is guilty!"

HELMER. Nora!

NORA. You're thinking I wouldn't have accepted such a sacrifice from you? No, of course I wouldn't! But what would my word have counted for against yours? That.was the miracle I was hoping for, and dreading. And it was to prevent it happening that I wanted to end my life.

HELMER. Nora, I would gladly work for you night and day, and endure sorrow and hardship for your sake. But no man can be expected to sacrifice his honor, even for the person he loves.

NORA. Millions of women have done it.

HELMER. Oh, you think and talk like a stupid child.

NORA. That may be. But you neither think nor talk like the man I could share my life with. Once you'd got over your fright—and you weren't frightened of what might threaten me, but only of what threatened you—once the danger was past, then as far as you were concerned it was exactly as though nothing had happened. I was your little song-bird just as before—your doll whom henceforth you would take particular care to protect from the world because she was so weak and fragile. (*Gets up.*) Torvald, in that moment I realized that for eight years I had been living here with a complete stranger, and had borne him three children—! Oh, I can't bear to think of it! I could tear myself to pieces!

HELMER (*sadly*). I see it, I see it. A gulf has indeed opened between us. Oh, but Nora—couldn't it be bridged?

NORA. As I am now, I am no wife for you.

HELMER. I have the strength to change.

NORA. Perhaps—if your doll is taken from you.

HELMER. But to be parted—to be parted from you! No, no, Nora, I can't conceive of it happening!

NORA (*goes into the room, right*). All the more necessary that it should happen.

She comes back with her outdoor things and a small traveling-bag, which she puts down on a chair by the table.

HELMER. Nora, Nora, not now! Wait till tomorrow!

NORA (*puts on her coat*). I can't spend the night in a strange man's house.

HELMER. But can't we live here as brother and sister, then—?

NORA (*fastens her hat*). You know quite well it wouldn't last. (*Puts on her shawl.*) Goodbye, Torvald. I don't want to see the children. I know they're in better hands than mine. As I am now, I can be nothing to them.

HELMER. But some time, Nora—some time—?

NORA. How can I tell? I've no idea what will happen to me.

HELMER. But you are my wife, both as you are and as you will be.

NORA. Listen, Torvald. When a wife leaves her husband's house, as I'm doing now, I'm told that according to the law he is freed of any obligations towards her. In any case, I release you from any such obligations. You mustn't feel bound to me in any way, however small, just as I shall not feel bound to you. We must both be quite free. Here is your ring back. Give me mine.

HELMER. That too?

NORA. That too.

HELMER. Here it is.

NORA. Good. Well, now it's over. I'll leave the keys here. The servants know about everything to do with the house—much better than I do. Tomorrow, when I have left town, Christine will come to pack the things I brought here from home. I'll have them sent on after me.

HELMER. This is the end then! Nora, will you never think of me any more?

NORA. Yes, of course. I shall often think of you and the children and this house.

HELMER. May I write to you, Nora?

NORA. No. never. You mustn't do that.

HELMER. But at least you must let me send you—

NORA. Nothing. Nothing.

HELMER. But if you should need help?—

NORA. I tell you, no. I don't accept things from strangers.

HELMER. Nora—can I never be anything but a stranger to you?

NORA (*picks up her bag*). Oh, Torvald! Then the miracle of miracles would have to happen.

HELMER. The miracle of miracles?

NORA. You and I would both have to change so much that—oh, Torvald, I don't believe in miracles any longer.

HELMER. But I want to believe in them. Tell me. We should have to change so much that—?

NORA. That life together between us two could become a marriage. Goodbye.

She goes out through the hall.

HELMER (*sinks down on a chair by the door and buries his face in his hands*). Nora! Nora! (*Looks round and gets up.*) Empty! She's gone! (*A hope strikes him.*) The miracle of miracles—?

The street door is slammed shut downstairs.

[1879]

TOPICS FOR DISCUSSION AND WRITING

1. Near the beginning of the play, how does Mrs. Linde's presence help to define Nora's character? How does Nora's response to Krogstad's entrance tell us something about Nora?

2. What does Dr. Rank contribute to the play? If he were eliminated, what would be lost?

3. In view of the fact that the last act several times seems to be moving toward a "happy ending" (e.g., Krogstad promises to recall his letter), what is wrong with the alternate ending (see page 978) that Ibsen reluctantly provided for a German production?

4. Can it be argued that although at the end Nora goes out to achieve self-realization, her abandonment of her children— especially to Torvald's loathsome conventional morality—is a crime? (By the way, exactly why does Nora leave the children? She seems to imply, in some passages, that because she forged a signature she is unfit to bring them up. But do you agree with her?)

5. Michael Meyer, in his splendid biography *Henrik Ibsen,* says that the play is not so much about women's rights as about "the need of every individual to find out the kind of person he or she really is, and to strive to become that person." What evidence can you offer to support or refute this interpretation?

6. In *The Quintessence of Ibsenism* Bernard Shaw says that Ibsen, reacting against a common theatrical preference for strange situations, "saw that . . . the more familiar the situation, the more interesting the play. Shakespear had put ourselves on the stage but not our situations. Our uncles seldom murder our fathers and . . . marry our mothers. . . . Ibsen . . . gives us not only ourselves, but ourselves in our own situations. The things that happen to his stage figures are things that happen to us. One consequence is that his plays are much more important to us than Shakespear's. Another is that they are capable both of hurting us cruelly and of filling us with excited hopes of escape from idealistic tyrannies, and with visions of intenser life in the future." How much of this do you believe?

Contexts for *A Doll's House:* Remarks by Ibsen

The University Library, Oslo, has the following preliminary notes for a *A Doll's House:*

Notes for the tragedy of modern times

Rome 19.10.78

There are two kinds of moral law, two kinds of conscience, one in man and a completely different one in woman. They do not understand each other; but in matters of practical living the woman is judged by man's law, as if she were not a woman but a man.

The wife in the play ends up quite bewildered and not knowing right from wrong; her natural instincts on the one side and her faith in authority on the other leave her completely confused.

A woman cannot be herself in contemporary society, it is an exclusively male society with laws drafted by men, and with counsel and judges who judge feminine conduct from the male point of view.

She has committed a crime, and she is proud of it; because she did it for love of her husband and to save his life. But the husband, with his conventional views of honour, stands on the side of the law and looks at the affair with male eyes.

Mental conflict. Depressed and confused by her faith in authority, she loses faith in her moral right and ability to bring up her children.

Bitterness. A mother in contemporary society, just as certain insects go away and die when she has done her duty in the propagation of the race [*sic*]. Love of life, of home and husband and children and family. Now and then, woman-like, she shrugs off her thoughts. Sudden return of dread and terror. Everything must be borne alone. The catastrophe approaches, ineluctably, inevitably. Despair, resistance, defeat.

[*The following note was later added in the margin:*]

Krogstad has done some dishonest business, and thus made a bit of money; but his prosperity does not help him, he cannot recover his honour.

Because Norwegian works were not copyrighted in Germany, German theaters could stage and freely adapt Ibsen's works without his consent. When he heard that a German director was going to change the ending to a happy one, Ibsen decided that he had better do the adaptation himself, though he characterized it as a "a barbaric outrage" against the play.

NORA. . . . Where we could make a real marriage out of our lives together. Goodbye. (*Begins to go.*)

HELMER. Go then! (*Seizes her arm.*) But first you shall see your children for the last time!

NORA. Let me go! I will not see them! I cannot!

HELMER (*draws her over to the door, left*). You shall see them. (*Opens the door and says softly.*) Look, there they are asleep, peaceful and carefree. Tomorrow, when they wake up and call for their mother, they will be— motherless.

NORA (*trembling*). Motherless . . . !

HELMER. As you once were.

NORA. Motherless! (*Struggles with herself, lets her travelling bag fall, and says*) Oh, this is a sin against myself, but I cannot leave them. (*Half sinks down by the door.*)

HELMER (*joyfully, but softly*). Nora!

(*The curtain falls.*)

Speech at the Banquet of the Norwegian League for Women's Rights

Christiania, May 26, 1898

[A month after the official birthday celebrations were over, Ibsen and his wife were invited to a banquet in his honor given by the leading Norwegian feminist society.]

I am not a member of the Women's Rights League. Whatever I have written has been without any conscious thought of making propaganda. I have been more the poet and less the social philosopher than people generally seem inclined to believe. I thank you for the toast, but must disclaim the honor of having consciously worked for the women's rights movement. I am not even quite clear as to just what this women's rights movement really is. To me it has seemed a problem of mankind in general. And if you read my books carefully you will understand this. True enough, it is desirable to solve the woman problem, along with all the others; but that has not been the whole purpose. My task has been the *description of humanity*. To be sure, whenever such a description is felt to be reasonably true, the reader will read his own feelings and sentiments into the work of the poet. These are then attributed to the poet; but incorrectly so. Every reader remolds the work beautifully and neatly, each according to his own personality. Not only those who write but also those who read are poets. They are collaborators. They are often more poetical than the poet himself.

Tennessee Williams (American; 1914–83)

The Glass Menagerie

Nobody, not even the rain, has such small hands.
—*E. E. Cummings*

List of Characters

AMANDA WINGFIELD, the mother. A little woman of great but confused vitality clinging frantically to another time and place. Her characterization must be carefully created, not copied from type. She is not paranoiac, but her life is paranoia. There is much to admire in Amanda, and as much to love and pity as there is to laugh at. Certainly she has endurance and a kind of heroism, and though her foolishness makes her unwittingly cruel at times, there is tenderness in her slight person.

LAURA WINGFIELD, her daughter. Amanda, having failed to establish contact with reality, continues to live vitally in her illusions, but Laura's situation is even graver. A childhood illness has left her crippled, one leg slightly shorter than the other, and held in a brace. This defect need not be more than suggested on the stage. Stemming from this, Laura's separation increases till she is like a piece of her own glass collection, too exquisitely fragile to move from the shelf.

TOM WINGFIELD, her son. And the narrator of the play. A poet with a job in a warehouse. His nature is not remorseless, but to escape from a trap he has to act without pity.

This is a scene from the opening production of The Glass Menagerie at The Playhouse
in New York on March 31, 1945, starring Lorette Taylor, Julie Hayden, Eddie Dowling,
and Anthony Ross. Reproduced by courtesy of the New York Public Library, The Billy Rose
Theater Collection.

JIM O'CONNOR, the gentleman caller. A nice, ordinary, young man.

Scene. An alley in St. Louis.

Part I. Preparation for a Gentleman Caller.
Part II. The Gentleman Calls.

Time. Now and the Past.

SCENE 1

The Wingfield apartment is in the rear of the building, one of those vast hive-like conglomerations of cellular living-units that flower as warty growths in overcrowded urban centers of lower middle-class population and are symptomatic of the impulse of this largest and fundamentally enslaved section of American society to avoid fluidity and differentiation and to exist and function as one interfused mass of automatism.

The apartment faces an alley and is entered by a fire-escape, a structure whose name is a touch of accidental poetic truth, for all of these huge buildings are always burning with the slow and implacable fires of human desperation. The fire-escape is included in the set—that is, the landing of it and steps descending from it.

The scene is memory and is therefore nonrealistic. Memory takes a lot of poetic license. It omits some details; others are exaggerated, according to the emotional value of the articles it touches, for memory is seated predominantly in the heart. The interior is therefore rather dim and poetic.

At the rise of the curtain, the audience is faced with the dark, grim rear wall of the Wingfield tenement. This building, which runs parallel to the footlights, is flanked on both sides by dark, narrow alleys which run into murky canyons of tangled clotheslines, garbage cans and the sinister latticework of neighboring fire-escapes. It is up and down these side alleys that exterior entrances and exits are made, during the play. At the end of Tom's opening commentary, the dark tenement wall slowly reveals (by means of a transparency) the interior of the ground floor Wingfield apartment.

Downstage is the living room, which also serves as a sleeping room for Laura, the sofa unfolding to make her bed. Upstage, center, and divided by a wide arch or second proscenium with transparent faded portieres (or second curtain), is the dining room. In an old-fashioned what-not in the living room are seen scores of transparent glass animals. A blown-up photograph of the father hangs on the wall of the living room, facing the audience, to the left of the archway. It is the face of a very handsome young man in a doughboy's First World War cap. He is gallantly smiling, ineluctably smiling, as if to say, "I will be smiling forever."

The audience hears and sees the opening scene in the dining room through both the transparent fourth wall of the building and the transparent gauze portieres of the dining-room arch. It is during this revealing scene that the fourth wall slowly ascends, out of sight.

This transparent exterior wall is not brought down again until the very end of the play, during Tom's final speech.

The narrator is an undisguised convention of the play. He takes whatever license with dramatic convention as is convenient to his purposes.

Tom enters dressed as a merchant sailor from alley, stage left, and strolls across the front of the stage to the fire-escape. There he stops and lights a cigarette. He addresses the audience.

TOM. Yes, I have tricks in my pocket, I have things up my sleeve. But I am the opposite of a stage magician. He gives you illusion that has the appearance of truth. I give you truth in the pleasant disguise of illusion. To begin with, I turn back time. I reverse it to that quaint period, the thirties, when the huge middle class of America was matriculating in a school for the blind. Their eyes had failed them, or they had failed their eyes, and so they were having their fingers pressed forcibly down on the fiery Braille alphabet of a dissolving economy. In Spain there was revolution. Here there was only shouting and confusion. In Spain there was Guernica. Here there were disturbances of labor, sometimes pretty violent, in otherwise peaceful cities such as Chicago, Cleveland, Saint Louis. . . . This is the social background of the play.

(Music.)

The play is memory. Being a memory play, it is dimly lighted, it is sentimental, it is not realistic. In memory everything seems to happen to music. That explains the fiddle in the wings. I am the narrator of the play, and also a character in it. The other characters are my mother, Amanda, my sister, Laura, and a gentleman caller who appears in the final scenes. He is the most realistic character in the play, being an emissary from a world of reality that we were somehow set apart from. But since I have a poet's weakness for symbols, I am using this character also as a symbol; he is the long delayed but always expected something that we live for. There is a fifth character in the play who doesn't appear except in this larger-than-life photograph over the mantel. This is our father who left us a long time ago. He was a telephone man who fell in love with long distances; he gave up his job with the telephone company and skipped the light fantastic out of town. . . . The last we heard of him was a picture post-card from Mazatlan, on the Pacific coast of Mexico, containing a message of two words—"Hello—Goodbye!" and no address. I think the rest of the play will explain itself. . . .

Amanda's voice becomes audible through the portieres.

(Legend on Screen: "Où Sont les Neiges?")

He divides the portieres and enters the upstage area.

Amanda and Laura are seated at a drop-leaf table. Eating is indicated by gestures without food or utensils. Amanda faces the audience. Tom and Laura are seated in profile.

The interior has lit up softly and through the scrim we see Amanda and Laura seated at the table in the upstage area.

AMANDA (*calling*). Tom?

TOM. Yes, Mother.

AMANDA. We can't say grace until you come to the table!

TOM. Coming, Mother. (*He bows slightly and withdraws, reappearing a few moments later in his place at the table.*)

AMANDA (*to her son*). Honey, don't *push* with your *fingers.* If you have to push with something, the thing to push with is a crust of bread. And chew—chew! Animals have sections in their stomachs which enable them to digest food without mastication, but human beings are supposed to chew their food before they swallow it down. Eat food leisurely, son, and really enjoy it. A well-cooked meal has lots of delicate flavors that have to be held in the mouth for appreciation. So chew your food and give your salivary glands a chance to function!

Tom deliberately lays his imaginary fork down and pushes his chair back from the table.

TOM. I haven't enjoyed one bite of this dinner because of your constant directions on how to eat it. It's you that makes me rush through meals with your hawk-like attention to every bite I take. Sickening—spoils my appetite—all this discussion of animals' secretion—salivary glands— mastication!

AMANDA (*lightly*). Temperament like a Metropolitan star! (*He rises and crosses downstage.*) You're not excused from the table.

TOM. I am getting a cigarette.

AMANDA. You smoke too much.

Laura rises.

LAURA. I'll bring in the blanc mange.

He remains standing with his cigarette by the portieres during the following.

AMANDA (*rising*). No, sister, no, sister—you be the lady this time and I'll be the darky.

LAURA. I'm already up.

AMANDA. Resume your seat, little sister—I want you to stay fresh and pretty—for gentlemen callers!

LAURA. I'm not expecting any gentlemen callers.

AMANDA (*crossing out to kitchenette. Airily*). Sometimes they come when they are least expected! Why, I remember one Sunday afternoon in Blue Mountain—(*Enters kitchenette.*)

TOM. I know what's coming!

LAURA. Yes. But let her tell it.

TOM. Again?

LAURA. She loves to tell it.

Amanda returns with bowl of dessert.

AMANDA. One Sunday afternoon in Blue Mountain — your mother received — *seventeen!* — gentlemen callers! Why, sometimes there weren't chairs enough to accommodate them all. We had to send the nigger over to bring in folding chairs from the parish house.

TOM (*remaining at portieres*). How did you entertain those gentlemen callers?

AMANDA. I understood the art of conversation!

TOM. I bet you could talk.

AMANDA. Girls in those days *knew* how to talk, I can tell you.

TOM. Yes?

(*Image: Amanda as a Girl on a Porch Greeting Callers.*)

AMANDA. They knew how to entertain their gentlemen callers. It wasn't enough for a girl to be possessed of a pretty face and a graceful figure — although I wasn't slighted in either respect. She also needed to have a nimble wit and a tongue to meet all occasions.

TOM. What did you talk about?

AMANDA. Things of importance going on in the world! Never anything coarse or common or vulgar. (*She addresses Tom as though he were seated in the vacant chair at the table though he remains by portieres. He plays this scene as though he held the book.*) My callers were gentlemen — all! Among my callers were some of the most prominent young planters of the Mississippi Delta — planters and sons of planters!

Tom motions for music and a spot of light on Amanda.

Her eyes lift, her face glows, her voice becomes rich and elegiac.

(*Screen Legend: "Où Sont les Neiges?"*)

There was young Champ Laughlin who later became vice-president of the Delta Planters Bank. Hadley Stevenson who was drowned in Moon Lake and left his widow one hundred and fifty thousand in Government bonds. There were the Cutrere brothers, Wesley and Bates. Bates was one of my bright particular beaux! He got in a quarrel with that wild Wainright boy. They shot it out on the floor of Moon Lake Casino. Bates was shot through the stomach. Died in the ambulance on his way to Memphis. His widow was also well-provided for, came into eight or ten thousand acres, that's all. She married him on the rebound — never loved her — carried my picture on him the night he died! And there was that boy that every girl in Delta had set her cap for! That beautiful, brilliant young Fitzhugh boy from Green County!

TOM. What did he leave his widow?

AMANDA. He never married! Gracious, you talk as though all of my old admirers had turned up their toes to the daisies!

TOM. Isn't this the first you mentioned that still survives?

AMANDA. That Fitzhugh boy went North and made a fortune—came to be known as the Wolf of Wall Street! He had the Midas touch, whatever he touched turned to gold! And I could have been Mrs. Duncan J. Fitzhugh, mind you! But—I picked your *father!*

LAURA (*rising*). Mother, let me clear the table.

AMANDA. No dear, you go in front and study your typewriter chart. Or practice your shorthand a little. Stay fresh and pretty!—It's almost time for our gentlemen callers to start arriving. (*She flounces girlishly toward the kitchenette.*) How many do you suppose we're going to entertain this afternoon?

Tom throws down the paper and jumps up with a groan.

LAURA (*alone in the dining room*). I don't believe we're going to receive any, Mother.

AMANDA (*reappearing, airily*). What? No one—not one? You must be joking! (*Laura nervously echoes her laugh. She slips in a fugitive manner through the half-open portieres and draws them gently behind her. A shaft of very clear light is thrown on her face against the faded tapestry of the curtains.*) (*Music: "The Glass Menagerie" Under Faintly.*) (*Lightly.*) Not one gentleman caller? It can't be true! There must be a flood, there must have been a tornado!

LAURA. It isn't a flood, it's not a tornado, Mother. I'm just not popular like you were in Blue Mountain. . . . (*Tom utters another groan. Laura glances at him with a faint, apologetic smile. Her voice catching a little.*) Mother's afraid I'm going to be an old maid.

(*The Scene Dims Out with "Glass Menagerie" Music.*)

SCENE 2

"Laura, Haven't You Ever Liked Some Boy?"

On the dark stage the screen is lighted with the image of blue roses.

Gradually Laura's figure becomes apparent and the screen goes out. The music subsides.

Laura is seated in the delicate ivory chair at the small clawfoot table.

She wears a dress of soft violet material for a kimono—her hair tied back from her forehead with a ribbon.

She is washing and polishing her collection of glass.

Amanda appears on the fire-escape steps. At the sound of her ascent, Laura catches her breath, thrusts the bowl of ornaments away and seats herself stiffly before the diagram of the typewriter keyboard as though it held her spellbound. Something has happened to Amanda. It is written in her face as she climbs to the landing: a look that is grim and hopeless and a little absurd.

She has on one of those cheap or imitation velvety-looking cloth coats with imitation fur collar. Her hat is five or six years old, one of those dreadful cloche hats that were worn in the late twenties, and she is clasping an enormous black patent-leather pocketbook with nickel clasp and initials. This is her full-dress outfit, the one she usually wears to the D.A.R.

Before entering she looks through the door.

She purses her lips, opens her eyes wide, rolls them upward and shakes her head.

Then she slowly lets herself in the door. Seeing her mother's expression Laura touches her lips with a nervous gesture.

LAURA. Hello, Mother, I was—(*She makes a nervous gesture toward the chart on the wall. Amanda leans against the shut door and stares at Laura with a martyred look.*)

AMANDA. Deception? Deception? (*She slowly removes her hat and gloves, continuing the swift suffering stare. She lets the hat and gloves fall on the floor—a bit of acting.*)

LAURA (*shakily*). How was the D.A.R. meeting? (*Amanda slowly opens her purse and removes a dainty white handkerchief which she shakes out delicately and delicately touches to her lips and nostrils.*) Didn't you go to the D.A.R. meeting, Mother?

AMANDA (*faintly, almost inaudibly*).—No.—No. (*Then more forcibly.*) I did not have the strength—to go to the D.A.R. In fact, I did not have the courage! I wanted to find a hole in the ground and hide myself in it forever! (*She crosses slowly to the wall and removes the diagram of the typewriter keyboard. She holds it in front of her for a second, staring at it sweetly and sorrowfully—then bites her lips and tears it in two pieces.*)

LAURA (*faintly*). Why did you do that, Mother? (*Amanda repeats the same procedure with the chart of the Gregg Alphabet.*) Why are you—

AMANDA. Why? Why? How old are you, Laura?

LAURA. Mother, you know my age.

AMANDA. I thought that you were an adult; it seems that I was mistaken. (*She crosses slowly to the sofa and sinks down and stares at Laura.*)

LAURA. Please don't stare at me, Mother.

Amanda closes her eyes and lowers her head. Count ten.

AMANDA. What are we going to do, what is going to become of us, what is the future?

Count ten.

LAURA. Has something happened, Mother? (*Amanda draws a long breath and takes out the handkerchief again. Dabbing process.*) Mother, has — something happened?

AMANDA. I'll be all right in a minute. I'm just bewildered — (*count five*) — by life. . . .

LAURA. Mother, I wish that you would tell me what's happened.

AMANDA. As you know, I was supposed to be inducted into my office at the D.A.R. this afternoon. (*Image: A Swarm of Typewriters.*) But I stopped off at Rubicam's Business College to speak to your teachers about your having a cold and ask them what progress they thought you were making down there.

LAURA. Oh. . . .

AMANDA. I went to the typing instructor and introduced myself as your mother. She didn't know who you were. Wingfield, she said. We don't have any such student enrolled at the school! I assured her she did, that you had been going to classes since early in January. "I wonder," she said, "if you could be talking about that terribly shy little girl who dropped out of school after only a few days' attendance?" "No," I said, "Laura, my daughter, has been going to school every day for the past six weeks!" "Excuse me," she said. She took the attendance book out and there was your name, unmistakably printed, and all the dates you were absent until they decided that you had dropped out of school. I still said, "No, there must have been some mistake! There must have been some mix-up in the records!" And she said, "No — I remember her perfectly now. Her hand shook so that she couldn't hit the right keys! The first time we gave a speed-test, she broke down completely — was sick at the stomach and almost had to be carried into the washroom! After that morning she never showed up any more. We phoned the house but never got any answer" — while I was working at Famous and Barr, I suppose, demonstrating those — Oh! I felt so weak I could barely keep on my feet. I had to sit down while they got me a glass of water! Fifty dollars' tuition, all of our plans — my hopes and ambitions for you — just gone up the spout, just gone up the spout like that. (*Laura draws a long breath and gets awkwardly to her feet. She crosses to the victrola and winds it up.*) What are you doing?

LAURA. Oh! (*She releases the handle and returns to her seat.*)

AMANDA. Laura, where have you been going when you've gone out pretending that you were going to business college?

LAURA. I've just been going out walking.

AMANDA. That's not true.

LAURA. It is. I just went walking.

AMANDA. Walking? Walking? In winter? Deliberately courting pneumonia in that light coat? Where did you walk to, Laura?

LAURA. It was the lesser of two evils, Mother. (*Image: Winter Scene in Park.*) I couldn't go back up. I — threw up — on the floor!

AMANDA. From half past seven till after five every day you mean to tell me you walked around in the park, because you wanted to make me think that you were still going to Rubicam's Business College?

LAURA. It wasn't as bad as it sounds. I went inside places to get warmed up.

AMANDA. Inside where?

LAURA. I went in the art museum and the bird-houses at the Zoo. I visited the penguins every day! Sometimes I did without lunch and went to the movies. Lately I've been spending most of my afternoons in the Jewel-box, that big glass house where they raise the tropical flowers.

AMANDA. You did all this to deceive me, just for the deception? (*Laura looks down.*) Why?

LAURA. Mother, when you're disappointed, you get that awful suffering look on your face, like the picture of Jesus' mother in the museum!

AMANDA. Hush!

LAURA. I couldn't face it.

Pause. A whisper of strings.

(*Legend: "The Crust of Humility."*)

AMANDA (*hopelessly fingering the huge pocketbook*). So what are we going to do the rest of our lives? Stay home and watch the parades go by? Amuse ourselves with the glass menagerie, darling? Eternally play those worn-out phonograph records your father left as a painful reminder of him? We won't have a business career—we've given that up because it gave us nervous indigestion! (*Laughs wearily.*) What is there left but dependency all our lives? I know so well what becomes of unmarried women who aren't prepared to occupy a position. I've seen such pitiful cases in the South—barely tolerated spinsters living upon the grudging patronage of sister's husband or brother's wife!—stuck away in some little mousetrap of a room—encouraged by one in-law to visit another—little birdlike women without any nest—eating the crust of humility all their life! Is that the future that we've mapped out for ourselves? I swear it's the only alternative I can think of! It isn't a very pleasant alternative, is it? Of course—some girls *do* marry. (*Laura twists her hands nervously.*) Haven't you ever liked some boy?

LAURA. Yes. I liked one once. (*Rises.*) I came across his picture a while ago.

AMANDA (*with some interest*). He gave you his picture?

LAURA. No, it's in the year-book.

AMANDA. (*disappointed*). Oh—a high-school boy.

(*Screen Image: Jim as a High-School Hero Bearing a Silver Cup.*)

LAURA. Yes. His name was Jim. (*Laura lifts the heavy annual from the claw-foot table.*) Here he is in *The Pirates of Penzance.*

AMANDA (*absently*). The what?

LAURA. The operetta the senior class put on. He had a wonderful voice and we sat across the aisle from each other Mondays, Wednesdays and Fridays in the Aud. Here he is with the silver cup for debating! See his grin?

AMANDA (*absently*). He must have had a jolly disposition.

LAURA. He used to call me—Blue Roses.

(*Image: Blue Roses.*)

AMANDA. Why did he call you such a name as that?

LAURA. When I had that attack of pleurosis—he asked me what was the matter when I came back. I said pleurosis—he thought that I said Blue Roses! So that's what he always called me after that. Whenever he saw me, he'd holler, "Hello, Blue Roses!" I didn't care for the girl that he went out with. Emily Meisenbach. Emily was the best-dressed girl at Soldan. She never struck me, though, as being sincere. . . . It says in the Personal Section—they're engaged. That's—six years ago! They must be married by now.

AMANDA. Girls that aren't cut out for business careers usually wind up married to some nice man. (*Gets up with a spark of revival.*) Sister, that's what you'll do!

Laura utters a startled, doubtful laugh. She reaches quickly for a piece of glass.

LAURA. But, Mother—

AMANDA. Yes? (*Crossing to photograph.*)

LAURA (*in a tone of frightened apology*). I'm—crippled!

(*Image: Screen.*)

AMANDA. Nonsense! Laura, I've told you never, never to use that word. Why, you're not crippled, you just have a little defect—hardly noticeable, even! When people have some slight disadvantage like that, they cultivate other things to make up for it—develop charm—and vivacity—and—*charm!* That's all you have to do! (*She turns again to the photograph.*) One thing your father had *plenty of*—was *charm!*

Tom motions to the fiddle in the wings.

(*The Scene Fades out with Music.*)

SCENE 3

(*Legend on the Screen: "After the Fiasco—"*)

Tom speaks from the fire-escape landing.

TOM. After the fiasco at Rubicam's Business College, the idea of getting a gentleman caller for Laura began to play a more important part in Mother's calculations. It became an obsession. Like some archetype of the universal unconscious, the image of the gentleman caller haunted our small apartment. . . . (*Image: Young Man at Door with Flowers.*) An evening at home rarely passed without some allusion to this image, this specter, this hope. . . . Even when he wasn't mentioned, his presence hung in Mother's preoccupied look and in my sister's frightened, apologetic manner—hung like a sentence passed upon the Wingfields! Mother was a woman of action as well as words. She began to take logical steps in the planned direction. Late that winter and in the early spring—realizing that extra money would be needed to properly feather the nest and plume the bird—she conducted a vigorous campaign on the telephone, roping in subscribers to one of those magazines for matrons called *The Home-maker's Companion,* the type of journal features the serialized sublimations of ladies of letters who think in terms of delicate cuplike breasts, slim, tapering waists, rich, creamy thighs, eyes like woodsmoke in autumn, fingers that soothe and caress like strains of music, bodies as powerful as Etruscan sculpture.

(*Screen Image: Glamor Magazine Cover.*)

Amanda enters with phone on long extension cord. She is spotted in the dim stage.

AMANDA. Ida Scott? This is Amanda Wingfield! We *missed* you at the D.A.R. last Monday! I said to myself: She's probably suffering with that sinus condition! How is that sinus condition? Horrors! Heaven have mercy!—You're a Christian martyr, yes, that's what you are, a Christian martyr! Well, I just now happened to notice that your subscription to the *Companion's* about to expire! Yes, it expires with the next issue, honey!—just when that wonderful new serial by Bessie Mae Hopper is getting off to such an exciting start. Oh, honey, it's something that you can't miss! You remember how *Gone With the Wind* took everybody by storm? You simply couldn't go out if you hadn't read it. All everybody *talked* was Scarlett O'Hara. Well, this is a book that critics already compare to *Gone With the Wind.* It's the *Gone With the Wind* of the post-World War generation!—What?—Burning?—Oh, honey, don't let them burn, go take a look in the oven and I'll hold the wire! Heavens—I think she's hung up!

(*Dim Out.*)

(*Legend on Screen: "You Think I'm in Love with Continental Shoemakers?"*)

Before the stage is lighted, the violent voices of Tom and Amanda are heard. They are quarreling behind the portieres. In front of them stands Laura with clenched hands and panicky expression.

A clear pool of light on her figure throughout this scene.

TOM. What in Christ's name am I—
AMANDA (*shrilly*). Don't you use that—

TOM. Supposed to do!

AMANDA. Expression! Not in my—

TOM. Ohhh!

AMANDA. Presence! Have you gone out of your senses?

TOM. I have, that's true, *driven* out!

AMANDA. What is the matter with you, you—big—big—IDIOT!

TOM. Look—I've got *no thing,* no single thing—

AMANDA. Lower your voice!

TOM. In my life here that I can call my OWN! Everything is—

AMANDA. Stop that shouting!

TOM. Yesterday you confiscated my books! You had the nerve to—

AMANDA. I took that horrible novel back to the library—yes! That hideous book by that insane Mr. Lawrence. (*Tom laughs wildly.*) I cannot control the output of diseased minds or people who cater to them— (*Tom laughs still more wildly.*) BUT I WON'T ALLOW SUCH FILTH BROUGHT INTO MY HOUSE! No, no, no, no, no!

TOM. House, house! Who pays rent on it, who makes a slave of himself to—

AMANDA (*fairly screeching*). Don't you DARE to—

TOM. No, no, *I* musn't say things! *I've* got to just—

AMANDA. Let me tell you—

TOM. I don't want to hear any more! (*He tears the portieres open. The upstage area is lit with a turgid smoky red glow.*)

Amanda's hair is in metal curlers and she wears a very old bathrobe, much too large for her slight figure, a relic of the faithless Mr. Wingfield.

An upright typewriter and a wild disarray of manuscripts are on the drop-leaf table. The quarrel was probably precipitated by Amanda's interruption of his creative labor. A chair lying overthrown on the floor.

Their gesticulating shadows are cast on the ceiling by the fiery glow.

AMANDA. You *will* hear more, you—

TOM. No, I won't hear more, I'm going out!

AMANDA. You come right back in—

TOM. Out, out, out! Because I'm—

AMANDA. Come back here, Tom Wingfield! I'm not through talking to you!

TOM. Oh, go—

LAURA (*desperately*). Tom!

AMANDA. You're going to listen, and no more insolence from you! I'm at the end of my patience! (*He comes back toward her.*)

TOM. What do you think I'm at? Aren't I supposed to have any patience to reach the end of, Mother? I know, I know. It seems unimportant to you, what I'm *doing*—what I *want* to do—having a little *difference* between them! You don't think that—

AMANDA. I think you've been doing things that you're ashamed of. That's why you act like this. I don't believe that you go every night to the movies. Nobody goes to the movies night after night. Nobody in their right minds goes to the movies as often as you pretend to. People don't go to the movies at nearly midnight, and movies don't let out at two A.M. Come in stumbling. Muttering to yourself like a maniac! You get three hours' sleep and then go to work. Oh, I can picture the way you're doing down there. Moping, doping, because you're in no condition.

TOM (*wildly*). No, I'm in no condition!

AMANDA. What right have you got to jeopardize your job? Jeopardize the security of us all? How do you think we'd manage if you were—

TOM. Listen! You think I'm crazy *about* the *warehouse*? (*He bends fiercely toward her slight figure.*) You think I'm in love with the Continental Shoe-makers? You think I want to spend fifty-five *years* down there in that— *celotex interior!* with—*fluorescent—tubes!* Look! I'd rather somebody picked up a crowbar and battered out my brains—than go back mornings! I go! Every time you come in yelling that God damn "*Rise and Shine!*" "*Rise and Shine!*" I say to myself "How *lucky dead* people are!" But I get up. I *go!* For sixty-five dollars a month I give up all that I dream of doing and being *ever!* And you say self—*self's* all I ever think of. Why, listen, if self is what I thought of, Mother, I'd be where he is— GONE! (*Pointing to father's picture.*) As far as the system of transportation reaches! (*He starts past her. She grabs his arm.*) Don't grab at me, Mother!

AMANDA. Where are you going?

TOM. I'm going to the *movies!*

AMANDA. I don't believe that lie!

TOM (*crouching toward her, overtowering her tiny figure. She backs away, gasping*). I'm going to opium dens! Yes, opium dens, dens of vice and criminals' hang-outs, Mother. I've joined the Hogan gang, I'm a hired assassin, I carry a tommy-gun in a violin case! I run a string of cat-houses in the Valley! They call me Killer, Killer Wingfield, I'm leading a double life, a simple, honest warehouse worker by day, by night a dynamic *czar* of the *underworld, Mother.* I go to gambling casinos, I spin away fortunes on the roulette table! I wear a patch over one eye and a false mustache, sometimes I put on green whiskers. On those occasions they call me—*El Diablo!* Oh, I could tell you things to make you sleepless! My enemies plan to dynamite this place. They're going to blow us all sky-high some night! I'll be glad, very happy, and so will you! You'll go up, up on a broomstick, over Blue Mountain with seventeen gentlemen callers! You ugly—babbling old—*witch....* (*He goes through a series of violent, clumsy movements, seizing his overcoat, lunging to the door, pulling it fiercely open. The women watch him, aghast. His arm catches in the sleeve of the coat as he struggles to pull it on. For a moment he is pinioned by the bulky garment. With an outraged groan he tears the coat off again, splitting the shoulders of it, and hurls it across the room. It strikes against the shelf of Laura's glass collection, there is a tinkle of shattering glass. Laura cries out as if wounded.)*

(Music Legend: "The Glass Menagerie.")

LAURA *(shrilly)*. My glass!—menagerie. . . . *(She covers her face and turns away.)*

But Amanda is still stunned and stupefied by the "ugly witch" so that she barely notices this occurrence. Now she recovers her speech.

AMANDA *(in an awful voice)*. I won't speak to you—until you apologize! *(She crosses through portieres and draws them together behind her. Tom is left with Laura. Laura clings weakly to the mantel with her face averted. Tom stares at her stupidly for a moment. Then he crosses to shelf. Drops awkwardly to his knees to collect the fallen glass, glancing at Laura as if he would speak but couldn't.)*

"The Glass Menagerie" steals in as

(The Scene Dims Out.)

SCENE 4

The interior is dark. Faint light in the alley.

A deep-voiced bell in a church is tolling the hour of five as the scene commences.

Tom appears at the top of the alley. After each solemn boom of the bell in the tower, he shakes a little noise-maker or rattle as if to express the tiny spasm of man in contrast to the sustained power and dignity of the Almighty. This and the unsteadiness of his advance make it evident that he has been drinking.

As he climbs the few steps to the fire-escape landing light steals up inside. Laura appears in night-dress, observing Tom's empty bed in the front room.

Tom fishes in his pockets for the door-key, removing a motley assortment of articles in the search, including a perfect shower of movie-ticket stubs and an empty bottle. At last he finds the key, but just as he is about to insert it, it slips from his fingers. He strikes a match and crouches below the door.

TOM *(bitterly)*. One crack—and it falls through!

Laura opens the door.

LAURA. Tom! Tom, what are you doing?
TOM. Looking for a door-key.
LAURA. Where have you been all this time?
TOM. I have been to the movies.
LAURA. All this time at the movies?
TOM. There was a very long program. There was a Garbo picture and a Mickey Mouse and a travelogue and a newsreel and a preview of coming attractions. And there was an organ solo and a collection for the milk-fund—simultaneously—which ended up in a terrible fight between a fat lady and an usher!

LAURA (*innocently*). Did you have to stay through everything?

TOM. Of course! And, oh, I forgot! There was a big stage show! The headliner on this stage show was Malvolio the Magician. He performed wonderful tricks, many of them, such as pouring water back and forth between pitchers. First it turned to wine and then it turned to beer and then it turned to whiskey. I know it was whiskey it finally turned into because he needed somebody to come up out of the audience to help him, and I came up—both shows! It was Kentucky Straight Bourbon. A very generous fellow, he gave souvenirs. (*He pulls from his back pocket a shimmering rainbow-colored scarf.*) He gave me this. This is his magic scarf. You can have it, Laura. You wave it over a canary cage and you get a bowl of gold-fish. You wave it over the gold-fish bowl and they fly away canaries. . . . But the wonderfullest trick of all was the coffin trick. We nailed him into a coffin and he got out of the coffin without removing one nail. (*He has come inside.*) There is a trick that would come in handy for me—get me out of this 2 by 4 situation! (*Flops onto bed and starts removing shoes.*)

LAURA. Tom—Shhh!

TOM. What you shushing me for?

LAURA. You'll wake up Mother.

TOM. Goody, goody! Pay 'er back for all those "Rise an' Shines." (*Lies down, groaning.*) You know it don't take much intelligence to get yourself into a nailed-up coffin, Laura. But who in hell ever got himself out of one without removing one nail?

As if in answer, the father's grinning photograph lights up.

(*Scene Dims Out.*)

Immediately following: The church bell is heard striking six. At the sixth stroke the alarm clock goes off in Amanda's room, and after a few moments we hear her calling: "Rise and Shine! Rise and Shine! Laura, go tell your brother to rise and shine!"

TOM (*sitting up slowly*). I'll rise—but I won't shine.

The light increases.

AMANDA. Laura, tell your brother his coffee is ready.

Laura slips into front room.

LAURA. Tom! it's nearly seven. Don't make Mother nervous. (*He stares at her stupidly. Beseechingly.*) Tom, speak to Mother this morning. Make up with her, apologize, speak to her!

TOM. She won't to me. It's her that started not speaking.

LAURA. If you just say you're sorry she'll start speaking.

TOM. Her not speaking—is that such a tragedy?

LAURA. Please—please!

AMANDA (*calling from kitchenette*). Laura, are you going to do what I asked you to do, or do I have to get dressed and go out myself?

LAURA. Going, going—soon as I get on my coat! (*She pulls on a shapeless felt hat with nervous, jerky movement, pleadingly glancing at Tom. Rushes awkwardly for coat. The coat is one of Amanda's, inaccurately made-over, the sleeves too short for Laura.*) Butter and what else?

AMANDA (*entering upstage*). Just butter. Tell them to charge it.

LAURA. Mother, they make such faces when I do that.

AMANDA. Sticks and stones may break my bones, but the expression on Mr. Garfinkel's face won't harm us! Tell your brother his coffee is getting cold.

LAURA (*at door*). Do what I asked you, will you, will you, Tom?

He looks sullenly away.

AMANDA. Laura, go now or just don't go at all!

LAURA (*rushing out*). Going—going! (*A second later she cries out. Tom springs up and crosses to the door. Amanda rushes anxiously in. Tom opens the door.*)

TOM. Laura?

LAURA. I'm all right. I slipped, but I'm all right.

AMANDA (*peering anxiously after her*). If anyone breaks a leg on those fire-escape steps, the landlord ought to be sued for every cent he possesses! (*She shuts door. Remembers she isn't speaking and returns to other room.*)

As Tom enters listlessly for his coffee, she turns her back to him and stands rigidly facing the window on the gloomy gray vault of the areaway. Its light on her face with its aged but childish features is cruelly sharp, satirical as a Daumier print.

(*Music Under: "Ave Maria."*)

Tom glances sheepishly but sullenly at her averted figure and slumps at the table. The coffee is scalding hot; he sips it and gasps and spits it back in the cup. At his gasp, Amanda catches her breath and half turns. Then catches herself and turns back to window.

Tom blows on his coffee, glancing sidewise at his mother. She clears her throat. Tom clears his. He starts to rise. Sinks back down again, scratches his head, clears his throat again. Amanda coughs. Tom raises his cup in both hands to blow on it, his eyes staring over the rim of it at his mother for several moments. Then he slowly sets the cup down and awkwardly and hesitantly rises from the chair.

TOM (*hoarsely*). Mother. I—I apologize. Mother. (*Amanda draws a quick, shuddering breath. Her face works grotesquely. She breaks into childlike tears.*) I'm sorry for what I said, for everything that I said, I didn't mean it.

AMANDA (*sobbingly*). My devotion has made me a witch and so I make myself hateful to my children!

TOM. No, you *don't*.

AMANDA. I worry so much, don't sleep, it makes me nervous!

TOM (*gently*). I understand that.

AMANDA. I've had to put up a solitary battle all these years. But you're my right-hand bower! Don't fall down, don't fail!

TOM (*gently*). I try Mother.

AMANDA (*with great enthusiasm*). Try and you will SUCCEED! (*The notion makes her breathless.*) Why, you—you're just *full* of natural endowments! Both of my children—they're *unusual* children! Don't you think I know it? I'm so—*proud!* Happy and—feel I've—so much to be thankful for but—Promise me one thing, son!

TOM. What, Mother?

AMANDA. Promise, son, you'll—never be a drunkard!

TOM (*turns to her grinning*). I will never be a drunkard, Mother.

AMANDA. That's what frightened me so, that you'd be drinking! Eat a bowl of Purina!

TOM. Just coffee, Mother.

AMANDA. Shredded wheat biscuit?

TOM. No. No, Mother, just coffee.

AMANDA. You can't put in a day's work on an empty stomach. You've got ten minutes—don't gulp! Drinking too-hot liquids makes cancer of the stomach. . . . Put cream in.

TOM. No, thank you.

AMANDA. To cool it.

TOM. No! No, thank you, I want it black.

AMANDA. I know, but it's not good for you. We have to do all that we can to build ourselves up. In these trying times we live in, all that we have to cling to is—each other. . . . That's why it's so important to—Tom, I—I sent out your sister so I could discuss something with you. If you hadn't spoken I would have spoken to you. (*Sits down.*)

TOM (*gently*). What is it, Mother, that you want to discuss?

AMANDA. Laura!

Tom puts his cup down slowly.

(*Legend on Screen: "Laura."*)

(*Music: "The Glass Menagerie."*)

TOM. —Oh.—Laura . . .

AMANDA (*touching his sleeve*). You know how Laura is. So quiet but—still water runs deep! She notices things and I think she—broods about them. (*Tom looks up.*) A few days ago I came in and she was crying.

TOM. What about?

AMANDA. You.

TOM. Me?

AMANDA. She has an idea that you're not happy here.

TOM. What gave her that idea?

AMANDA. What gives her any idea? However, you do act strangely. I—
I'm not criticizing, understand *that!* I know your ambitions do not lie
in the warehouse, that like everybody in the whole wide world—you've
had to—make sacrifices, but—Tom—Tom—life's not easy, it calls for—
Spartan endurance! There's so many things in my heart that I cannot
describe to you! I've never told you but I—*loved* your father. . . .

TOM (*gently*). I know that, Mother.

AMANDA. And you—when I see you taking after his ways! Staying out
late—and—well, you *had* been drinking the night you were in that—
terrifying condition! Laura says that you hate the apartment and that
you go out nights to get away from it! Is that true, Tom?

TOM. No. You say there's so much in your heart that you can't describe
to me. That's true of me, too. There's so much in my heart that I can't
describe to *you!* So let's respect each other's—

AMANDA. But, why—*why*, Tom—are you always so *restless?* Where do you
go to, nights?

TOM. I—go to the movies.

AMANDA. Why do you go to the movies so much, Tom?

TOM. I go to the movies because—I like adventure. Adventure is something I don't have much of at work, so I go to the movies.

AMANDA. But, Tom, you go to the movies *entirely too much!*

TOM. I like a lot of adventure

*Amanda looks baffled, then hurt. As the familiar inquisition resumes he becomes
hard and impatient again. Amanda slips back into her querulous attitude toward
him.*

(Image on Screen: Sailing Vessel with Jolly Roger.)

AMANDA. Most young men find adventure in their careers.

TOM. Then most young men are not employed in a warehouse.

AMANDA. The world is full of young men employed in warehouses and
offices and factories.

TOM. Do all of them find adventure in their careers?

AMANDA. They do or they do without it! Not everybody has a craze for
adventure.

TOM. Man is by instinct a lover, a hunter, a fighter, and none of those
instincts are given much play at the warehouse!

AMANDA. Man is by instinct! Don't quote instinct to me! Instinct is something that people have got away from! It belongs to animals! Christian
adults don't want it!

TOM. What do Christian adults want, then, Mother?

AMANDA. Superior things! Things of the mind and the spirit! Only
animals have to satisfy instincts! Surely your aims are somewhat higher
than theirs! Than monkeys—pigs—

TOM. I reckon they're not.

AMANDA. You're joking. However, that isn't what I wanted to discuss.

TOM (*rising*). I haven't much time.

AMANDA (*pushing his shoulders*). Sit down.

TOM. You want me to punch in red at the warehouse, Mother?

AMANDA. You have five minutes. I want to talk about Laura.

(*Legend: "Plans and Provisions."*)

TOM. All right! What about Laura?

AMANDA. We have to be making plans and provisions for her. She's older than you, two years, and nothing has happened. She just drifts along doing nothing. It frightens me terribly how she just drifts along.

TOM. I guess she's the type that people call home girls.

AMANDA. There's no such type, and if there is, it's a pity! That is unless the home is hers, with a husband!

TOM. What?

AMANDA. Oh, I can see the handwriting on the wall as plain as I see the nose in the front of my face! It's terrifying! More and more you remind me of your father! He was out all hours without explanation— Then *left!* Goodbye! And me with the bag to hold. I saw that letter you got from the Merchant Marine. I know what you're dreaming of. I'm not standing here blindfolded. Very well, then. Then *do* it! But not till there's somebody to take your place.

TOM. What do you mean?

AMANDA. I mean that as soon as Laura has got somebody to take care of her, married, a home of her own, independent—why, then you'll be free to go wherever you please, on land, on sea, whichever way the wind blows! But until that time you've got to look out for your sister. I don't say me because I'm old and don't matter! I say for your sister because she's young and dependent. I put her in business college—a dismal failure! Frightened her so it made her sick to her stomach. I took her over to the Young People's League at the church. Another fiasco. She spoke to nobody, nobody spoke to her. Now all she does is fool with those pieces of glass and play those worn-out records. What kind of a life is that for a girl to lead!

TOM. What can I do about it?

AMANDA. Overcome selfishness! Self, self, self is all that you ever think of! (*Tom springs up and crosses to get his coat. It is ugly and bulky. He pulls on a cap with earmuffs.*) Where is your muffler? Put your wool muffler on! (*He snatches it angrily from the closet and tosses it around his neck and pulls both ends tight.*) Tom! I haven't said what I had in mind to ask you.

TOM. I'm too late to—

AMANDA (*catching his arms—very importunately. Then shyly*). Down at the warehouse, aren't there some—nice young men?

TOM. No!

AMANDA. There *must* be—*some*.

TOM. Mother—

Gesture.

AMANDA. Find out one that's clean-living—doesn't drink and—ask him out for sister!

TOM. What?

AMANDA. For *sister!* To *meet!* Get *acquainted!*

TOM (*stamping to door*). Oh, my *go-osh!*

AMANDA. Will you? (*He opens door. Imploringly.*) Will you? (*He starts down.*) Will you? *Will* you dear?

TOM (*calling back*). YES!

Amanda closes the door hesitantly and with a troubled but faintly hopeful expression.

(*Screen Image: Glamor Magazine Cover.*)

Spot Amanda at phone.

AMANDA. Ella Cartwright? This is Amanda Wingfield! How are you honey? How is that kidney condition? (*Count five.*) Horrors! (*Count five.*) You're a Christian martyr, yes, honey, that's what you are, a Christian martyr! Well, I just happened to notice in my little red book that your subscription to the *Companion* has just run out! I knew that you wouldn't want to miss out on the wonderful serial starting in this new issue. It's by Bessie Mae Hopper, the first thing she's written since *Honeymoon for Three.* Wasn't that a strange and interesting story? Well, this one is even lovelier, I believe. It has a sophisticated society background. It's all about the horsey set on Long Island!

(*Fade Out.*)

SCENE 5

(*Legend on Screen: "Annunciation."*) *Fade with music.*

It is early dusk of a spring evening. Supper has just been finished at the Wingfield apartment. Amanda and Laura in light colored dresses are removing dishes from the table, in the upstage area, which is shadowy, their movements formalized almost as a dance or ritual, their moving forms as pale and silent as moths.

Tom, in white shirt and trousers, rises from the table and crosses toward the fire-escape.

AMANDA (*as he passes her*). Son, will you do me a favor?

TOM. What?

AMANDA. Comb your hair! You look so pretty when your hair is combed! (*Tom slouches on sofa with evening paper. Enormous caption "Franco Triumphs."*) There is only one respect in which I would like you to emulate your father.

TOM. What respect is that?

AMANDA. The care he always took of his appearance. He never allowed himself to look untidy. (*He throws down the paper and crosses to fire-escape.*) Where are you going?

TOM. I'm going out to smoke.

AMANDA. You smoke too much. A pack a day at fifteen cents a pack. How much would that amount to in a month? Thirty times fifteen is how much, Tom? Figure it out and you will be astounded at what you could save. Enough to give you a night-school course in accounting at Washington U! Just think what a wonderful thing that would be for you, son!

Tom is unmoved by the thought.

TOM. I'd rather smoke. (*He steps out on landing, letting the screen door slam.*)

AMANDA (*sharply*). I know! That's the tragedy of it. . . . (*Alone, she turns to look at her husband's picture.*)

(*Dance Music: "All the World Is Waiting for the Sunrise!"*)

TOM (*to the audience*). Across the alley from us was the Paradise Dance Hall. On evenings in spring the windows and doors were open and the music came outdoors. Sometimes the lights were turned out except for a large glass sphere that hung from the ceiling. It would turn slowly about and filter the dusk with delicate rainbow colors. Then the orchestra played a waltz or a tango, something that had a slow and sensuous rhythm. Couples would come outside, to the relative privacy of the alley. You could see them kissing behind ashpits and telephone poles. This was the compensation for lives that passed like mine, without any change or adventure. Adventure and change were imminent in this year. They were waiting around the corner for all these kids. Suspended in the mist over Berchtesgaden, caught in the folds of Chamberlain's umbrella — In Spain there was Guernica! But here there was only hot swing music and liquor, dance halls, bars, and movies, and sex that hung in the gloom like a chandelier and flooded the world with brief, deceptive rainbows. . . . All the world was waiting for bombardments!

Amanda turns from the picture and comes outside.

AMANDA (*sighing*). A fire-escape landing's a poor excuse for a porch. (*She spreads a newspaper on a step and sits down, gracefully and demurely as if she were settling into a swing on a Mississippi veranda.*) What are you looking at?

TOM. The moon.

AMANDA. Is there a moon this evening?

TOM. It's rising over Garfinkel's Delicatessen.

AMANDA. So it is! A little silver slipper of a moon. Have you made a wish on it yet?

TOM. Um-hum.

AMANDA. What did you wish for?

TOM. That's a secret.

AMANDA. A secret, huh? Well, I won't tell mine either. I will be just as mysterious as you.

TOM. I bet I can guess what yours is.

AMANDA. Is my head so transparent?

TOM. You're not a sphinx.

AMANDA. No, I don't have secrets. I'll tell you what I wished for on the moon. Success and happiness for my precious children! I wish for that whenever there's a moon, and when there isn't a moon, I wish for it, too.

TOM. I thought perhaps you wished for a gentleman caller.

AMANDA. Why do you say that?

TOM. Don't you remember asking me to fetch one?

AMANDA. I remember suggesting that it would be nice for your sister if you brought some nice young man from the warehouse. I think I've made that suggestion more than once.

TOM. Yes, you have made it repeatedly.

AMANDA. Well?

TOM. We are going to have one.

AMANDA. *What?*

TOM. A gentleman caller!

(*The Annunciation Is Celebrated with Music.*)

Amanda rises.

(*Image on Screen: Caller with Bouquet.*)

AMANDA. You mean you have asked some nice young man to come over?

TOM. Yep. I've asked him to dinner.

AMANDA. You really did?

TOM. I did!

AMANDA. You did, and did he—*accept?*

TOM. He did!

AMANDA. Well, well—well, well! That's—lovely!

TOM. I thought that you would be pleased.

AMANDA. It's definite, then?

TOM. Very definite.

AMANDA. Soon?

TOM. Very soon.

AMANDA. For heaven's sake, stop putting on and tell me some things, will you?

TOM. What things do you want me to tell you?

AMANDA. Naturally I would like to know when he's *coming!*

TOM. He's coming tomorrow.

AMANDA. *Tomorrow?*

TOM. Yep. Tomorrow.

AMANDA. But, Tom!

TOM. Yes, Mother?

AMANDA. Tomorrow gives me no time!

TOM. Time for what?

AMANDA. Preparations! Why didn't you phone me at once, as soon as you asked him, the minute that he accepted? Then, don't you see, I could have been getting ready!

TOM. You don't have to make any fuss.

AMANDA. Oh, Tom, Tom, Tom, of course I have to make a fuss! I want things nice, not sloppy! Not thrown together. I'll certainly have to do some fast thinking, won't I?

TOM. I don't see why you have to think at all.

AMANDA. You just don't know. We can't have a gentleman caller in a pig-sty! All my wedding silver has to be polished, the monogrammed table linen ought to be laundered! The windows have to be washed and fresh curtains put up. And how about clothes? We have to *wear* something, don't we?

TOM. Mother, this boy is no one to make a fuss over!

AMANDA. Do you realize he's the first young man we've introduced to your sister? It's terrible, dreadful, disgraceful that poor little sister has never received a single gentleman caller! Tom, come inside! (*She opens the screen door.*)

TOM. What for?

AMANDA. I want to ask you some things.

TOM. If you're going to make such a fuss, I'll call it off, I'll tell him not to come.

AMANDA. You certainly won't do anything of the kind. Nothing offends people worse than broken engagements. It simply means I'll have to work like a Turk! We won't be brilliant, but we'll pass inspection. Come on inside. (*Tom follows, groaning.*) Sit down.

TOM. Any particular place you would like me to sit?

AMANDA. Thank heavens I've got that new sofa! I'm also making payments on a floor lamp I'll have sent out! And put the chintz covers on, they'll brighten things up! Of course I'd hoped to have these walls re-papered. . . . What is the young man's name?

TOM. His name is O'Connor.

AMANDA. That, of course, means fish—tomorrow is Friday! I'll have that salmon loaf—with Durkee's dressing! What does he do? He works at the warehouse?

TOM. Of course! How else would I—

AMANDA. Tom, he—doesn't drink?

TOM. Why do you ask me that?

AMANDA. Your father *did!*

TOM. Don't get started on that!

AMANDA. He *does* drink, then?

TOM. Not that I know of!

AMANDA. Make sure, be certain! The last thing I want for my daughter's a boy who drinks!

TOM. Aren't you being a little premature? Mr. O'Connor has not yet appeared on the scene!

AMANDA. But will tomorrow. To meet your sister, and what do I know about his character? Nothing! Old maids are better off than wives of drunkards!

TOM. Oh, my God!

AMANDA. Be still!

TOM (*leaning forward to whisper*). Lots of fellows meet girls whom they don't marry!

AMANDA. Oh, talk sensibly, Tom—and don't be sarcastic! (*She has gotten a hairbrush.*)

TOM. What are you doing?

AMANDA. I'm brushing that cow-lick down! What is this young man's position at the warehouse?

TOM (*submitting grimly to the brush and the interrogation*). This young man's position is that of a shipping clerk, Mother.

AMANDA. Sounds to me like a fairly responsible job, the sort of a job *you* would be in if you just had more *get-up*. What is his salary? Have you got any idea?

TOM. I would judge it to be approximately eighty-five dollars a month.

AMANDA. Well—not princely, but—

TOM. Twenty more than I make.

AMANDA. Yes, how well I know! But for a family man, eighty-five dollars a month is not much more than you can just get by on. . . .

TOM. Yes, but Mr. O'Connor is not a family man.

AMANDA. He might be, mightn't he? Some time in the future?

TOM. I see. Plans and provisions.

AMANDA. You are the only man that I know of who ignores the fact that the future becomes the present, the present the past, and the past turns into everlasting regret if you don't plan for it!

TOM. I will think that over and see what I can make of it.

AMANDA. Don't be supercilious with your mother! Tell me some more about this—what do you call him?

TOM. James D. O'Connor. The D. is for Delaney.

AMANDA. Irish on *both* sides! *Gracious!* And doesn't drink?

TOM. Shall I call him up and ask him right this minute?

AMANDA. The only way to find out about those things is to make discreet inquiries at the proper moment. When I was a girl in Blue Mountain and it was suspected that a young man drank, the girl whose attentions he had been receiving, if any girl *was*, would sometimes speak to the minister of his church, or rather her father would if her father was living, and sort of feel him out on the young man's character. That is the way such things are discreetly handled to keep a young woman from making a tragic mistake!

TOM. Then how did you happen to make a tragic mistake?

AMANDA. That innocent look of your father's had everyone fooled! He *smiled*—the world was *enchanted!* No girl can do worse than put herself at the mercy of a handsome appearance! I hope that Mr. O'Connor is not too good-looking.

TOM. No, he's not too good-looking. He's covered with freckles and hasn't too much of a nose.

AMANDA. He's not right-down homely, though?

TOM. Not right-down homely. Just medium homely, I'd say.

AMANDA. Character's what to look for in a man.

TOM. That's what I've always said, Mother.

AMANDA. You've never said anything of the kind and I suspect you would never give it a thought.

TOM. Don't be suspicious of me.

AMANDA. At least I hope he's the type that's up and coming.

TOM. I think he really goes in for self-improvement.

AMANDA. What reason have you to think so?

TOM. He goes to night school.

AMANDA (*beaming*). Splendid! What does he do, I mean study?

TOM. Radio engineering and public speaking!

AMANDA. Then he has visions of being advanced in the world! Any young man who studies public speaking is aiming to have an executive job some day! And radio engineering? A thing for the future! Both of these facts are very illuminating. Those are the sort of things that a mother should know concerning any young man who comes to call on her daughter. Seriously or—not.

TOM. One little warning. He doesn't know about Laura. I didn't let on that we had dark ulterior motives. I just said, why don't you come have dinner with us? He said okay and that was the whole conversation.

AMANDA. I bet it was! You're eloquent as an oyster. However, he'll know about Laura when he gets here. When he sees how lovely and sweet and pretty she is, he'll thank his lucky stars he was asked to dinner.

TOM. Mother, you mustn't expect too much of Laura.

AMANDA. What do you mean?

TOM. Laura seems all those things to you and me because she's ours and we love her. We don't even notice she's crippled any more.

AMANDA. Don't say crippled! You know that I never allow that word to be used!

TOM. But face facts, Mother. She is and—that's not all—

AMANDA. What do you mean "not all"?

TOM. Laura is very different from other girls.

AMANDA. I think the difference is all to her advantage.

TOM. Not quite all—in the eyes of others—strangers—she's terribly shy and lives in a world of her own and those things make her seem a little peculiar to people outside the house.

AMANDA. Don't say peculiar.

TOM. Face the facts. She is.

(*The Dance-Hall Music Changes to a Tango that Has a Minor and Somewhat Ominous Tone.*)

AMANDA. In what way is she peculiar—may I ask?

TOM (*gently*). She lives in a world of her own—a world of—little glass ornaments, Mother. . . . (*Gets up. Amanda remains holding brush, looking at him, troubled.*) She plays old phonograph records and—that's about all—(*He glances at himself in the mirror and crosses to door.*)

AMANDA (*sharply*). Where are you going?

TOM. I'm going to the movies. (*Out screen door.*)

AMANDA. Not to the movies, every night to the movies! (*Follows quickly to screen door.*) I don't believe you always go to the movies! (*He is gone. Amanda looks worriedly after him for a moment. Then vitality and optimism return and she turns from the door. Crossing to portieres.*) Laura! Laura! (*Laura answers from kitchenette.*)

LAURA. Yes, Mother.

AMANDA. Let those dishes go and come in front! (*Laura appears with dish towel. Gaily.*) Laura, come here and make a wish on the moon!

LAURA (*entering*). Moon—moon?

AMANDA. A little silver slipper of a moon. Look over your left shoulder, Laura, and make a wish! (*Laura looks faintly puzzled as if called out of sleep. Amanda seizes her shoulders and turns her at angle by the door.*) Now! Now, darling, *wish!*

LAURA. What shall I wish for, Mother?

AMANDA (*her voice trembling and her eyes suddenly filling with tears*). Happiness! Good Fortune!

The violin rises and the stage dims out.

SCENE 6

(*Image: High School Hero.*)

TOM. And so the following evening I brought Jim home to dinner. I had known Jim slightly in high school. In high school Jim was a hero. He had tremendous Irish good nature and vitality with the scrubbed and polished look of white chinaware. He seemed to move in a continual spotlight. He was a star in basketball, captain of the debating club, president of the senior class and the glee club and he sang the male lead in the annual light operas. He was always running or bounding, never just walking. He seemed always at the point of defeating the law of gravity. He was shooting with such velocity through his adolescence that you would logically expect him to arrive at nothing short of the White House by the time he was thirty. But Jim apparently ran into more interference after his graduation from Soldan. His speed had definitely slowed. Six years after he left high school he was holding a job that wasn't much better than mine.

(Image: Clerk.)

He was the only one at the warehouse with whom I was on friendly terms. I was valuable to him as someone who could remember his former glory, who had seen him win basketball games and the silver cup in debating. He knew of my secret practice of retiring to a cabinet of the washroom to work on poems when business was slack in the warehouse. He called me Shakespeare. And while the other boys in the warehouse regarded me with suspicious hostility, Jim took a humorous attitude toward me. Gradually his attitude affected the others, their hostility wore off and they also began to smile at me as people smile at an oddly fashioned dog who trots across their path at some distance.

I knew that Jim and Laura had known each other at Soldan, and I had heard Laura speak admiringly of his voice. I didn't know if Jim remembered her or not. In high school Laura had been as unobtrusive as Jim had been astonishing. If he did remember Laura, it was not as my sister, for when I asked him to dinner, he grinned and said, "You know, Shakespeare, I never thought of you as having folks!"

He was about to discover that I did. . . .

(Light up Stage.)

(Legend on Screen: "The Accent of a Coming Foot.")

Friday evening. It is about five o'clock of a late spring evening which comes "scattering poems in the sky."

A delicate lemony light is in the Wingfield apartment.

Amanda has worked like a Turk in preparation for the gentleman caller. The results are astonishing. The new floor lamp with its rose-silk shade is in place, a colored paper lantern conceals the broken light fixture in the ceiling, new billowing white curtains are at the windows, chintz covers are on chairs and sofa, a pair of new sofa pillows make their initial appearance.

Open boxes and tissue paper are scattered on the floor.

Laura stands in the middle with lifted arms while Amanda crouches before her, adjusting the hem of the new dress, devout and ritualistic. The dress is colored and designed by memory. The arrangement of Laura's hair is changed; it is softer and more becoming. A fragile, unearthly prettiness has come out in Laura: she is like a piece of translucent glass touched by light, given a momentary radiance, not actual, not lasting.

AMANDA (*impatiently*). Why are you trembling?

LAURA. Mother, you've made me so nervous!

AMANDA. How have I made you nervous?

LAURA. By all this fuss! You make it seem so important!

AMANDA. I don't understand you, Laura. You couldn't be satisfied with just sitting home, and yet whenever I try to arrange something for you, you seem to resist it. (*She gets up.*) Now take a look at yourself. No, wait! Wait just a moment—I have an idea!

LAURA. What is it now?

Amanda produces two powder puffs which she wraps in handkerchiefs and stuffs in Laura's bosom.

LAURA. Mother, what are you doing?

AMANDA. They call them "Gay Deceivers"!

LAURA. I won't wear them!

AMANDA. You will!

LAURA. Why should I?

AMANDA. Because, to be painfully honest, your chest is flat.

LAURA. You make it seem like we were setting a trap.

AMANDA. All pretty girls are a trap, a pretty trap, and men expect them to be. (*Legend: "A Pretty Trap."*) Now look at yourself, young lady. This is the prettiest you will ever be! I've got to fix myself now! You're going to be surprised by your mother's appearance! (*She crosses through portieres, humming gaily.*)

Laura moves slowly to the long mirror and stares solemnly at herself.

A wind blows the white curtains inward in a slow, graceful motion and with a faint, sorrowful sighing.

AMANDA (*off stage*). It isn't dark enough yet. (*She turns slowly before the mirror with a troubled look.*)

(*Legend on Screen: "This Is My Sister: Celebrate Her with Strings!" Music.*)

AMANDA (*laughing, off*). I'm going to show you something. I'm going to make a spectacular appearance!

LAURA. What is it, Mother?

AMANDA. Possess your soul in patience—you will see! Something I've resurrected from that old trunk! Styles haven't changed so terribly much after all. . . . (*She parts the portieres.*) Now just look at your mother! (*She wears a girlish frock of yellowed voile with a blue silk sash. She carries a bunch of jonquils—the legend of her youth is nearly revived. Feverishly.*) This is the dress in which I led the cotillion. Won the cakewalk twice at Sunset

Hill, wore one spring to the Governor's ball in Jackson! See how I sashayed around the ballroom, Laura? (*She raises her skirt and does a mincing step around the room.*) I wore it on Sundays for my gentlemen callers! I had it on the day I met your father—I had malaria fever all that spring. The change of climate from East Tennessee to the Delta—weakened resistance—I had a little temperature all the time—not enough to be serious—just enough to make me restless and giddy! Invitations poured in—parties all over the Delta!—"Stay in bed," said Mother, "you have fever!"—but I just wouldn't.—I took quinine but kept on going, going!—Evenings, dances!—Afternoons, long, long rides! Picnics—lovely!—So lovely, that country in May.—All lacy with dogwood, literally flooded with jonquils!—That was the spring I had the craze for jonquils. Jonquils became an absolute obsession. Mother said, "Honey, there's no more room for jonquils." And still I kept bringing in more jonquils. Whenever, wherever I saw them, I'd say, "Stop! Stop! I see jonquils!" I made the young men help me gather the jonquils! It was a joke, Amanda and her jonquils! Finally there were no more vases to hold them, every available space was filled with jonquils. No vases to hold them? All right, I'll hold them myself! And then I—(*She stops in front of the picture.*) (*Music.*) met your father! Malaria fever and jonquils and then—this—boy. . . . (*She switches on the rose-colored lamp.*) I hope they get here before it starts to rain. (*She crosses upstage and places the jonquils in bowl on table.*) I gave your brother a little extra change so he and Mr. O'Connor could take the service car home.

LAURA (*with altered look*). What did you say his name was?
AMANDA. O'Connor.
LAURA. What is his first name?
AMANDA. I don't remember. Oh, yes, I do. It was—Jim!

Laura sways slightly and catches hold of a chair.

(*Legend on Screen: "Not Jim!"*)

LAURA (*faintly*). Not—Jim!
AMANDA. Yes, that was it, it was Jim! I've never known a Jim that wasn't nice!

(*Music: Ominous.*)

LAURA. Are you sure his name is Jim O'Connor?
AMANDA. Yes. Why?
LAURA. Is he the one that Tom used to know in high school?
AMANDA. He didn't say so. I think he just got to know him at the warehouse.
LAURA. There was a Jim O'Connor we both knew in high school—(*Then, with effort.*) If that is the one that Tom is bringing to dinner—you'll have to excuse me, I won't come to the table.

AMANDA. What sort of nonsense is this?

LAURA. You asked me once if I'd ever liked a boy. Don't you remember I showed you this boy's picture?

AMANDA. You mean the boy you showed me in the year book?

LAURA. Yes, that boy.

AMANDA. Laura, Laura, were you in love with that boy?

LAURA. I don't know, Mother. All I know is I couldn't sit at the table if it was him!

AMANDA. It won't be him! It isn't the least bit likely. But whether it is or not, you will come to the table. You will not be excused.

LAURA. I'll have to be, Mother.

AMANDA. I don't intend to humor your silliness, Laura. I've had too much from you and your brother, both! So just sit down and compose yourself till they come. Tom has forgotten his key so you'll have to let them in, when they arrive

LAURA (*panicky*). Oh, Mother—*you* answer the door!

AMANDA (*lightly*). I'll be in the kitchen—busy!

LAURA. Oh, Mother, please answer the door, don't make me do it!

AMANDA (*crossing into kitchenette*). I've got to fix the dressing for the salmon. Fuss, fuss—silliness!—over a gentleman caller!

Door swings shut. Laura is left alone.

(Legend: "Terror!")

She utters a low moan and turns off the lamp—sits stiffly on the edge of the sofa, knotting her fingers together.

(Legend on Screen: "The Opening of a Door!")

Tom and Jim appear on the fire-escape steps and climb to landing. Hearing their approach, Laura rises with a panicky gesture. She retreats to the portieres.

The doorbell. Laura catches her breath and touches her throat. Low drums.

AMANDA (*calling*). Laura, sweetheart! The door!

Laura stares at it without moving.

JIM. I think we just beat the rain.

TOM. Uh-huh. (*He rings again, nervously. Jim whistles and fishes for a cigarette.*)

AMANDA (*very, very gaily*). Laura, that is your brother and Mr. O'Connor! Will you let them in, darling?

Laura crosses toward kitchenette door.

LAURA (*breathlessly*). Mother—you go to the door!

Amanda steps out of kitchenette and stares furiously at Laura. She points imperiously at the door.

LAURA. Please, please!

AMANDA (*in a fierce whisper*). What is the matter with you, you silly thing?

LAURA (*desperately*). Please, you answer it, *please!*

AMANDA. I told you I wasn't going to humor you, Laura. Why have you chosen this moment to lose your mind?

LAURA. Please, please, please, you go!

AMANDA. You'll have to go to the door because I can't!

LAURA (*despairingly*). I can't either!

AMANDA. Why?

LAURA. I'm *sick!*

AMANDA. I'm sick, too—of your nonsense! Why can't you and your brother be normal people? Fantastic whims and behavior! (*Tom gives a long ring.*) Preposterous goings on! Can you give me one reason—(*Calls out lyrically.*) COMING! JUST ONE SECOND!—why should you be afraid to open a door? Now you answer it, Laura!

LAURA. Oh, oh, oh . . . (*She returns through the portieres. Darts to the victrola and winds it frantically and turns it on.*)

AMANDA. Laura Wingfield, you march right to that door!

LAURA. Yes—yes, Mother!

A faraway, scratchy rendition of "Dardanella" softens the air and gives her strength to move through it. She slips to the door and draws it cautiously open.

Tom enters with caller, Jim O'Connor.

TOM. Laura, this is Jim. Jim, this is my sister, Laura.

JIM (*stepping inside*). I didn't know that Shakespeare had a sister!

LAURA (*retreating stiff and trembling from the door*). How—how do you do?

JIM (*heartily extending his hand*). Okay!

Laura touches it hesitantly with hers.

JIM. Your hand's *cold*, Laura!

LAURA. Yes, well—I've been playing the victrola. . . .

JIM. Must have been playing classical music on it! You ought to play a little hot swing music to warm you up!

LAURA. Excuse me—I haven't finished playing the victrola. . . .

She turns awkwardly and hurries into the front room. She pauses a second by the victrola. Then catches her breath and darts through the portieres like a frightened deer.

JIM (*grinning*). What was the matter?

TOM. Oh—with Laura? Laura is—terribly shy.

JIM. Shy, huh? It's unusual to meet a shy girl nowadays. I don't believe you ever mentioned you had a sister.

TOM. Well, now you know. I have one. Here is the *Post Dispatch*. You want a piece of it?

JIM. Uh-huh.

TOM. What piece? The comics?

JIM. Sports! (*Glances at it.*) Ole Dizzy Dean is on his bad behavior.

TOM (*disinterest*). Yeah? (*Lights cigarette and crosses back to fire-escape door.*)

JIM. Where are *you* going?

TOM. I'm going out on the terrace.

JIM (*goes after him*). You know, Shakespeare—I'm going to sell you a bill of goods!

TOM. What goods?

JIM. A course I'm taking.

TOM. Huh?

JIM. In public speaking! You and me, we're not the warehouse type.

TOM. Thanks—that's good news. But what has public speaking got to do with it?

JIM. It fits you for—executive positions!

TOM. Awww.

JIM. I tell you it's done a helluva lot for me.

(*Image: Executive at Desk.*)

TOM. In what respect?

JIM. In every! Ask yourself what is the difference between you an' me and men in the office down front? Brains?—No!—Ability?—No! Then what? Just one little thing—

TOM. What is that one little thing?

JIM. Primarily it amounts to—social poise! Being able to square up to people and hold your own on any social level!

AMANDA (*off stage*). Tom?

TOM. Yes, Mother?

AMANDA. Is that you and Mr. O'Connor?

TOM. Yes, Mother.

AMANDA. Well, you just make yourselves comfortable in there.

TOM. Yes, Mother.

AMANDA. Ask Mr. O'Connor if he would like to wash his hands.

JIM. Aw—no—no—thank you—I took care of that at the warehouse. Tom—

TOM. Yes?

JIM. Mr. Mendoza was speaking to me about you.

TOM. Favorably?

JIM. What do you think?

TOM. Well—

JIM. You're going to be out of a job if you don't wake up.

TOM. I am waking up—

JIM. You show no signs.

TOM. The signs are interior.

(*Image on Screen: The Sailing Vessel with Jolly Roger Again.*)

TOM. I'm planning to change. (*He leans over the rail speaking with quiet exhilaration. The incandescent marquees and signs of the first-run movie houses light his face from across the alley. He looks like a voyager.*) I'm right at the point of committing myself to a future that doesn't include the warehouse and Mr. Mendoza or even a night-school course in public speaking.

JIM. What are you gassing about?

TOM. I'm tired of the movies.

JIM. Movies!

TOM. Yes, movies! Look at them—(*a wave toward the marvels of Grand Avenue.*) All of those glamorous people—having adventures—hogging it all, gobbling the whole thing up! You know what happens? People go to the *movies* instead of *moving!* Hollywood characters are supposed to have all the adventures for everybody in America, while everybody in America sits in a dark room and watches them have them! Yes, until there's a war. That's when adventure becomes available to the masses! *Everyone's* dish, not only Gable's! Then the people in the dark room come out of the dark room to have some adventures themselves—Goody, goody—It's our turn now, to go to the South Sea Island—to make a safari—to be exotic, far-off—But I'm not patient. I don't want to wait till then. I'm tired of the *movies* and I am *about* to *move!*

JIM (*incredulously*). Move?

TOM. Yes.

JIM. When?

TOM. Soon!

JIM. Where? Where?

(*Theme Three: Music Seems to Answer the Question, while Tom Thinks it Over. He Searches among his Pockets.*)

TOM. I'm starting to boil inside. I know I seem dreamy, but inside—well, I'm boiling! Whenever I pick up a shoe, I shudder a little thinking how short life is and what I am doing!—Whatever that means. I know it doesn't mean shoes—except as something to wear on a traveler's feet (*Finds paper.*) Look—

JIM. What?

TOM. I'm a member.

JIM (*reading*). The Union of Merchant Seamen.

TOM. I paid my dues this month, instead of the light bill.

JIM. You will regret it when they turn the lights off.

TOM. I won't be here.

JIM. How about your mother?

TOM. I'm like my father. The bastard son of a bastard! See how he grins? And he's been absent going on sixteen years!

JIM. You're just talking, you drip. How does your mother feel about it?

TOM. Shhh—Here comes Mother! Mother is not acquainted with my plans!

AMANDA (*enters portieres*). Where are you all?
TOM. On the terrace, Mother.

They start inside. She advances to them. Tom is distinctly shocked at her appearance. Even Jim blinks a little. He is making his first contact with girlish Southern vivacity and in spite of the night-school course in public speaking is somewhat thrown off the beam by the unexpected outlay of social charm.

Certain responses are attempted by Jim but are swept aside by Amanda's gay laughter and chatter. Tom is embarrassed but after the first shock Jim reacts very warmly. Grins and chuckles, is altogether won over.

(*Image: Amanda as a Girl.*)

AMANDA (*coyly smiling, shaking her girlish ringlets*). Well, well, well, so this is Mr. O'Connor. Introductions entirely unnecessary. I've heard so much about you from my boy. I finally said to him, Tom — good gracious! — why don't you bring this paragon to supper? I'd like to meet this nice young man at the warehouse! — Instead of just hearing him sing your praises so much! I don't know why my son is so standoffish — that's not Southern behavior! Let's sit down and — I think we could stand a little more air in here! Tom, leave the door open. I felt a nice fresh breeze a moment ago. Where has it gone? Mmm, so warm already! And not quite summer, even. We're going to burn up when summer really gets started. However, we're having — we're having a very light supper. I think light things are better fo' this time of year. The same as light clothes are. Light clothes an' light food are what warm weather calls fo'. You know our blood gets so thick during th' winter — it takes a while fo' us to *adjust* ou'selves! — when the season changes . . . It's come so quick this year. I wasn't prepared. All of a sudden — heavens! Already summer! — I ran to the trunk an' pulled out this light dress — Terribly old! Historical almost! But feels so good — so good an' co-ol, y'know. . . .
TOM. Mother —
AMANDA. Yes, honey?
TOM. How about — supper?
AMANDA. Honey, you go ask Sister if supper is ready! You know that Sister is in full charge of supper! Tell her you hungry boys are waiting for it. (*To Jim.*) Have you met Laura?
JIM. She —
AMANDA. Let you in? Oh, good, you've met already! It's rare for a girl as sweet an' pretty as Laura to be domestic! But Laura is, thank heavens, not only pretty but also very domestic. I'm not at all. I never was a bit. I never could make a thing but angel-food cake. Well, in the South we had so many servants. Gone, gone, gone. All vestiges of gracious living! Gone completely! I wasn't prepared for what the future brought me. All of my gentlemen callers were sons of planters and so of course I assumed that I would be married to one and raise my family on a

large piece of land with plenty of servants. But man proposes—and woman accepts the proposal!—To vary that old, old saying a little bit—I married no planter! I married a man who worked for the telephone company!—that gallantly smiling gentleman over there! (*Points to the picture.*) A telephone man who—fell in love with long distance!—Now he travels and I don't even know where!—But what am I going on for about my—tribulations! Tell me yours—I hope you don't have any! Tom?

TOM (*returning*). Yes, Mother?

AMANDA. Is supper nearly ready?

TOM. It looks to me like supper is on the table.

AMANDA. Let me look—(*She rises prettily and looks through portieres.*) Oh, lovely—But where is Sister?

TOM. Laura is not feeling well and she says that she thinks she'd better not come to the table.

AMANDA. What?—Nonsense!—Laura? Oh, Laura!

LAURA (*off stage, faintly*). Yes, Mother.

AMANDA. You really must come to the table. We won't be seated until you come to the table! Come in, Mr. O'Connor. You sit over there and I'll—Laura? Laura Wingfield! You're keeping us waiting, honey! We can't say grace until you come to the table!

The back door is pushed weakly open and Laura comes in. She is obviously quite faint, her lips trembling, her eyes wide and staring. She moves unsteadily toward the table.

(*Legend: "Terror!"*)

Outside a summer storm is coming abruptly. The white curtains billow inward at the windows and there is a sorowful murmur and deep blue dusk.

Laura suddenly stumbles—She catches a chair with a faint moan.

TOM. Laura!

AMANDA. Laura! (*There is a clap of thunder.*) (*Legend: "Ah!"*) (*Despairingly.*) Why, Laura, you *are* sick, darling! Tom, help your sister into the living room, dear! Sit in the living room, Laura—rest on the sofa. Well! (*To the gentleman caller.*) Standing over the hot stove made her ill!—I told her that it was just too warm this evening, but—(*Tom comes back in. Laura is on the sofa.*) Is Laura all right now?

TOM. Yes.

AMANDA. What *is* that? Rain? A nice cool rain has come up! (*She gives the gentleman caller a frightened look.*) I think we may—have grace—now . . . (*Tom looks at her stupidly.*) Tom, honey—you say grace!

TOM. Oh . . . "For these and all thy mercies—" (*They bow their heads, Amanda stealing a nervous glance at Jim. In the living room Laura, stretched on the sofa, clenches her hand to her lips, to hold back a shuddering sob.*) God's Holy Name be praised—

(*The Scene Dims Out.*)

SCENE 7

A Souvenir

Half an hour later. Dinner is just being finished in the upstage area which is concealed by the drawn portieres.

As the curtain rises Laura is still huddled upon the sofa, her feet drawn under her, her head resting on a pale blue pillow, her eyes wide and mysteriously watchful. The new floor lamp with its shade of rose-colored silk gives a soft, becoming light to her face, bringing out the fragile, unearthly prettiness which usually escapes attention. There is a steady murmur of rain, but it is slackening and stops soon after the scene begins; the air outside becomes pale and luminous as the moon breaks out.

A moment after the curtain rises, the lights in both rooms flicker and go out.

JIM. Hey, there, Mr. Light Bulb!

Amanda laughs nervously.

(*Legend: "Suspension of a Public Service."*)

AMANDA. Where was Moses when the lights went out? Ha-ha. Do you know the answer to that one, Mr. O'Connor?

JIM. No, Ma'am, what's the answer?

AMANDA. In the dark! (*Jim laughs appreciatively.*) Everybody sit still. I'll light the candles. Isn't it lucky we have them on the table? Where's a match? Which of you gentlemen can provide a match?

JIM. Here.

AMANDA. Thank you, sir.

JIM. Not at all, Ma'am!

AMANDA. I guess the fuse has burnt out. Mr. O'Connor, can you tell a burnt-out fuse? I know I can't and Tom is a total loss when it comes to mechanics. (*Sound: Getting Up: Voices Recede a Little to Kitchenette.*) Oh, be careful you don't bump into something. We don't want our gentleman caller to break his neck. Now wouldn't that be a fine howdy-do?

JIM. Ha-ha! Where is the fuse-box?

AMANDA. Right here next to the stove. Can you see anything?

JIM. Just a minute.

AMANDA. Isn't electricity a mysterious thing? Wasn't it Benjamin Franklin who tied a key to a kite? We live in such a mysterious universe, don't we? Some people say that science clears up all the mysteries for us. In my opinion it only creates more! Have you found it yet?

JIM. No, Ma'am. All these fuses look okay to me.

AMANDA. Tom!

TOM. Yes, Mother?

AMANDA. That light bill I gave you several days ago. The one I told you we got the notices about?

TOM. Oh.—Yeah.

(*Legend: "Ha!"*)

AMANDA. You didn't neglect to pay it by any chance?

TOM. Why, I—

AMANDA. Didn't! I might have known it!

JIM. Shakespeare probably wrote a poem on that light bill, Mrs. Wingfield.

AMANDA. I might have known better than to trust him with it! There's such a high price for negligence in this world!

JIM. Maybe the poem will win a ten-dollar prize.

AMANDA. We'll just have to spend the remainder of the evening in the nineteenth century, before Mr. Edison made the Mazda lamp!

JIM. Candlelight is my favorite kind of light.

AMANDA. That shows you're romantic! But that's no excuse for Tom. Well, we got through dinner. Very considerate of them to let us get through dinner before they plunged us into everlasting darkness, wasn't it, Mr. O'Connor?

JIM. Ha-ha!

AMANDA. Tom, as a penalty for your carelessness you can help me with the dishes.

JIM. Let me give you a hand.

AMANDA. Indeed you will not!

JIM. I ought to be good for something.

AMANDA. Good for something? (*Her tone is rhapsodic.*) You? Why, Mr. O'Connor, nobody, *nobody's* given me this much entertainment in years—as you have!

JIM. Aw, now, Mrs. Wingfield!

AMANDA. I'm not exaggerating, not one bit! But Sister is all by her lonesome. You go keep her company in the parlor! I'll give you this lovely old candelabrum that used to be on the altar at the church of the Heavenly Rest. It was melted a little out of shape when the church burnt down. Lightning struck it one spring. Gypsy Jones was holding a revival at the time and he intimated that the church was destroyed because the Episcopalians gave card parties.

JIM. Ha-ha.

AMANDA. And how about coaxing Sister to drink a little wine? I think it would be good for her! Can you carry both at once?

JIM. Sure. I'm Superman!

AMANDA. Now, Thomas, get into this apron!

The door of kitchenette swings closed on Amanda's gay laughter; the flickering light approaches the portieres.

Laura sits up nervously as he enters. Her speech at first is low and breathless from the almost intolerable strain of being alone with a stranger.

(Legend: "I Don't Suppose You Remember Me at All!")

In her first speeches in this scene, before Jim's warmth overcomes her paralyzing shyness, Laura's voice is thin and breathless as though she has run up a steep flight of stairs.

Jim's attitude is gently humorous. In playing this scene it should be stressed that while the incident is apparently unimportant, it is to Laura the climax of her secret life.

JIM. Hello, there, Laura.

LAURA (*faintly*). Hello. (*She clears her throat.*)

JIM. How are you feeling now? Better?

LAURA. Yes. Yes, thank you.

JIM. This is for you. A little dandelion wine. (*He extends it toward her with extravagant gallantry.*)

LAURA. Thank you.

JIM. Drink it—but don't get drunk! (*He laughs heartily. Laura takes the glass uncertainly; laughs shyly.*) Where shall I set the candles?

LAURA. Oh—oh, anywhere . . .

JIM. How about here on the floor? Any objections?

LAURA. No.

JIM. I'll spread a newspaper under to catch the drippings. I like to sit on the floor. Mind if I do?

LAURA. Oh, no.

JIM. Give me a pillow?

LAURA. What?

JIM. A pillow!

LAURA. Oh . . . (*Hands him one quickly.*)

JIM. How about you? Don't you like to sit on the floor?

LAURA. Oh—yes.

JIM. Why don't you, then?

LAURA. I—will.

JIM. Take a pillow! (*Laura does. Sits on the other side of the candelabrum. Jim crosses his legs and smiles engagingly at her.*) I can't hardly see you sitting way over there.

LAURA. I can—see you.

JIM. I know, but that's not fair, I'm in the limelight. (*Laura moves her pillow closer.*) Good! Now I can see you! Comfortable?

LAURA. Yes.

JIM. So am I. Comfortable as a cow. Will you have some gum?

LAURA. No, thank you.

JIM. I think that I will indulge, with your permission. (*Musingly unwraps it and holds it up.*) Think of the fortune made by the guy that invented the first piece of chewing gum. Amazing, huh? The Wrigley Building is one of the sights of Chicago.—I saw it summer before last when I went up to the Century of Progress. Did you take in the Century of Progress?

LAURA. No, I didn't.

JIM. Well, it was quite a wonderful exposition. What impressed me most was the Hall of Science. Gives you an idea of what the future will be in America, even more wonderful than the present time is! (*Pause. Smiling at her.*) Your brother tells me you're shy. Is that right, Laura?

LAURA. I—don't know.

JIM. I judge you to be an old-fashioned type of girl. Well, I think that's a pretty good type to be. Hope you don't think I'm being too personal—do you?

LAURA (*hastily, out of embarrassment*). I believe I *will* take a piece of gum, if you—don't mind. (*Clearing her throat.*) Mr. O'Connor, have you—kept up with your singing?

JIM. Singing? Me?

LAURA. Yes. I remember what a beautiful voice you had.

JIM. When did you hear me sing?

(*Voice Offstage in the Pause*)

VOICE (*offstage*).
    O blow, ye winds, heigh-ho.
    A-roving I will go!
    I'm off to my love
    With a boxing glove—
    Ten thousand miles away!

JIM. You say you've heard me sing?

LAURA. Oh, yes! Yes, very often . . . I—don't suppose you remember me—at all?

JIM (*smiling doubtfully*). You know I have an idea I've seen you before. I had that idea soon as you opened the door. It seemed almost like I was about to remember your name. But the name that I started to call you—wasn't a name! And so I stopped myself before I said it.

LAURA. Wasn't it—Blue Roses?

JIM (*springs up, grinning*). Blue Roses! My gosh, yes—Blue Roses! That's what I had on my tongue when you opened the door! Isn't it funny what tricks your memory plays? I didn't connect you with the high school somehow or other. But that's where it was; it was high school. I didn't even know you were Shakespeare's sister! Gosh, I'm sorry.

LAURA. I didn't expect you to. You—barely knew me!

JIM. But we did have a speaking acquaintance, huh?

LAURA. Yes, we—spoke to each other.

JIM. When did you recognize me?

LAURA. Oh, right away!

JIM. Soon as I came in the door?

LAURA. When I heard your name I thought it was probably you. I knew that Tom used to know you a little in high school. So when you came in the door—Well, then I was—sure.

JIM. Why didn't you *say* something, then?

LAURA (*breathlessly*). I didn't know what to say, I was—too surprised!

JIM. For goodness' sakes! You know, this sure is funny!

LAURA. Yes! Yes, isn't it, though. . . .

JIM. Didn't we have a class in something together?

LAURA. Yes, we did.

JIM. What class was that?

JIM. It was—singing—Chorus!

JIM. Aw!

LAURA. I sat across the aisle from you in the Aud.

JIM. Aw.

LAURA. Mondays, Wednesdays and Fridays.

JIM. Now I remember—you always came in late.

LAURA. Yes, it was so hard for me, getting upstairs. I had a brace on my leg—it clumped so loud!

JIM. I never heard any clumping

LAURA (*wincing at the recollection*). To me it sounded like—thunder!

JIM. Well, well, well. I never even noticed.

LAURA. And everybody was seated before I came in. I had to walk in front of all those people. My seat was in the back row. I had to go clumping all the way up the aisle with everyone watching!

JIM. You shouldn't have been self-conscious.

LAURA. I know, but I was. It was always such a relief when the singing started.

JIM. Aw, yes, I've placed you now! I used to call you Blue Roses. How was it that I got started calling you that?

LAURA. I was out of school a little while with pleurosis. When I came back you asked me what was the matter. I said I had pleurosis—you thought I said Blue Roses. That's what you always called me after that!

JIM. I hope you didn't mind.

LAURA. Oh, no—I liked it. You see, I wasn't acquainted with many—people. . . .

JIM. As I remember you sort of stuck by yourself.

LAURA. I—I—never had much luck at—making friends.

JIM. I don't see why you wouldn't.

LAURA. Well, I—started out badly.

JIM. You mean being—

LAURA. Yes, it sort of—stood between me—

JIM. You shouldn't have let it!

LAURA. I know, but it did, and—

JIM. You were shy with people!

LAURA. I tried not to be but never could—

JIM. Overcome it?

LAURA. No, I—I never could!

JIM. I guess being shy is something you have to work out of kind of gradually.

LAURA (*sorrowfully*). Yes—I guess it—

JIM. Takes time!

LAURA. Yes—

JIM. People are not so dreadful when you know them. That's what you have to remember! And everybody has problems, not just you, but practically everybody has got some problems. You think of yourself as having the only problems, as being the only one who is disappointed. But just look around you and you will see lots of people as disappointed as you are. For instance, I hoped when I was going to high school that I would be further along at this time, six years after, than I am now— You remember that wonderful write-up I had in *The Torch?*

LAURA. Yes! (*She rises and crosses to table.*)

JIM. It said I was bound to succeed in anything I went into! (*Laura returns with the annual.*) Holy Jeez! *The Torch!* (*He accepts it reverently. They smile across it with mutual wonder. Laura crouches beside him and they begin to turn through it. Laura's shyness is dissolving in his warmth.*)

LAURA. Here you are in *Pirates of Penzance!*

JIM (*wistfully*). I sang the baritone lead in that operetta.

LAURA (*rapidly*). So—*beautifully!*

JIM (*protesting*). Aw—

LAURA. Yes, yes—beautifully—beautifully!

JIM. You heard me?

LAURA. All three times!

JIM. No!

LAURA. Yes!

JIM. All three performances?

LAURA (*looking down*). Yes.

JIM. Why?

LAURA. I—wanted to ask you to—autograph my program.

JIM. Why didn't you ask me to?

LAURA. You were always surrounded by your own friends so much that I never had a chance to.

JIM. You should have just—

LAURA. Well, I—thought you might think I was—

JIM. Thought I might think you was—what?

LAURA. Oh—

JIM (*with reflective relish*). I was beleaguered by females in those days.

LAURA. You were terribly popular!

JIM. Yeah—

LAURA. You had such a—friendly way—

JIM. I was spoiled in high school.

LAURA. Everybody—liked you!

JIM. Including you?

LAURA. I—yes, I—I did, too—(*She gently closes the book in her lap.*)

JIM. Well, well, well!—Give me that program, Laura. (*She hands it to him. He signs it with a flourish.*) There you are—better late than never!

LAURA. Oh, I—what a—surprise!

JIM. My signature isn't worth very much right now. But some day—maybe—it will increase in value! Being disappointed is one thing and being discouraged is something else. I am disappointed but I'm not discouraged. I'm twenty-three years old. How old are you?

LAURA. I'll be twenty-four in June.

JIM. That's not old age!

LAURA. No, but—

JIM. You finished high school?

LAURA (*with difficulty*). I didn't go back.

JIM. You mean you dropped out?

LAURA. I made bad grades in my final examinations. (*She rises and replaces the book and the program. Her voice strained.*) How is—Emily Meisenbach getting along?

JIM. Oh, that kraut-head!

LAURA. Why do you call her that?

JIM. That's what she was.

LAURA. You're not still—going with her?

JIM. I never see her.

LAURA. It said in the Personal Section that you were—engaged!

JIM. I know, but I wasn't impressed by that—propaganda!

LAURA. It wasn't—the truth?

JIM. Only in Emily's optimistic opinion!

LAURA. Oh—

(*Legend: "What Have You Done since High School?"*)

Jim lights a cigarette and leans indolently back on his elbows smiling at Laura with a warmth and charm which light her inwardly with altar candles. She remains by the table and turns in her hands a piece of glass to cover her tumult.

JIM (*after several reflective puffs on a cigarette*). What have you done since high school? (*She seems not to hear him.*) Huh? (*Laura looks up.*) I said what have you done since high school, Laura?

LAURA. Nothing much.

JIM. You must have been doing something these six long years.

LAURA. Yes.

JIM. Well, then, such as what?

LAURA. I took a business course at business college—

JIM. How did that work out?

LAURA. Well, not very—well—I had to drop out, it gave me—indigestion—

Jim laughs gently.

JIM. What are you doing now?

LAURA. I don't do anything—much. Oh, please don't think I sit around doing nothing! My glass collection takes up a good deal of my time. Glass is something you have to take good care of.

JIM. What did you say—about glass?

LAURA. Collection I said—I have one—(*She clears her throat and turns away again, acutely shy.*)

JIM (*abruptly*). You know what I judge to be the trouble with you? Inferiority complex! Know what that is? That's what they call it when someone low-rates himself! I understand it because I had it, too. Although my case was not so aggravated as yours seems to be. I had it until I took up public speaking, developed my voice, and learned that I had an aptitude for science. Before that time I never thought of myself as being outstanding in any way whatsoever! Now I've never made a regular study of it, but I have a friend who says I can analyze people better than doctors that make a profession of it. I don't claim that to be necessarily true, but I can sure guess a person's psychology, Laura! (*Takes out his gum.*) Excuse me, Laura. I always take it out when the flavor is gone. I'll use this scrap of paper to wrap it in. I know how it is to get it stuck on a shoe. Yep—that's what I judge to be your principal trouble. A lack of confidence in yourself as a person. You don't have the proper amount of faith in yourself. I'm basing that fact on a number of your remarks and also on certain observations I've made. For instance that clumping you thought was so awful in high school. You say that you even dreaded to walk into class. You see what you did? You dropped out of school, you gave up an education because of a clump, which as far as I know was practically nonexistent! A little physical defect is what you have. Hardly noticeable even! Magnified thousands of times by imagination! You know what my strong advice to you is? Think of yourself as *superior* in some way!

LAURA. In what way would I think?

JIM. Why, man alive, Laura! Just look about you a little. What do you see? A world full of common people! All of 'em born and all of 'em going to die! Which of them has one-tenth of your good points! Or mine! Or anyone else's, as far as that goes—Gosh! Everybody excels in some one thing. Some in many! (*Unconsciously glances at himself in the mirror.*) All you've got to do is discover in *what*! Take me, for instance. (*He adjusts his tie at the mirror.*) My interest happens to lie in electrodynamics. I'm taking a course in radio engineering at night school, Laura, on top of a fairly responsible job at the warehouse. I'm taking that course and studying public speaking.

LAURA. Ohhhh.

JIM. Because I believe in the future of television! (*Turning back to her.*) I wish to be ready to go up right along with it. Therefore I'm planning to get in on the ground floor. In fact, I've already made the right connections and all that remains is for the industry itself to get under way! Full steam—(*His eyes are starry.*) *Knowledge*—Zzzzzp! *Money*—Zzzzzzp!— *Power!* That's the cycle democracy is built on! (*His attitude is convincingly dynamic. Laura stares at him, even her shyness eclipsed in her absolute wonder. He suddenly grins.*) I guess you think I think a lot of myself!

LAURA. No—o-o-o, I—

JIM. Now how about you? Isn't there something you take more interest in than anything else?

LAURA. Well, I do—as I said—have my—glass collection—

A peal of girlish laughter from the kitchen.

JIM. I'm not right sure I know what you're talking about. What kind of glass is it?

LAURA. Little articles of it, they're ornaments mostly! Most of them are little animals made out of glass, the tiniest little animals in the world. Mother calls them a glass menagerie! Here's an example of one, if you'd like to see it! This one is one of the oldest. It's nearly thirteen. (*He stretches out his hand.*) (*Music: "The Glass Menagerie."*) Oh, be careful—if you breathe, it breaks!

JIM. I'd better not take it. I'm pretty clumsy with things.

LAURA. Go on, I trust you with him! (*Places it in his palm.*) There now— you're holding him gently! Hold him over the light, he loves the light! You see how the light shines through him?

JIM. It sure does shine!

LAURA. I shouldn't be partial, but he is my favorite one.

JIM. What kind of a thing is this one supposed to be?

LAURA. Haven't you noticed the single horn on his forehead?

JIM. A unicorn, huh?

LAURA. Mmm-hmmm!

JIM. Unicorns, aren't they extinct in the modern world?

LAURA. I know!

JIM. Poor little fellow, he must feel sort of lonesome.

LAURA (*smiling*). Well, if he does he doesn't complain about it. He stays on a shelf with some horses that don't have horns and all of them seem to get along nicely together.

JIM. How do you know?

LAURA (*lightly*). I haven't heard any arguments among them!

JIM (*grinning*). No arguments, huh? Well, that's a pretty good sign! Where shall I set him?

LAURA. Put him on the table. They all like a change of scenery once in a while!

JIM (*stretching*). Well, well, well, well—Look how big my shadow is when I stretch!

LAURA. Oh, oh, yes—it stretches across the ceiling!

JIM (*crossing to door*). I think it's stopped raining. (*Opens fire-escape door.*) Where does the music come from?

LAURA. From the Paradise Dance Hall across the alley.

JIM. How about cutting the rug a little, Miss Wingfield?

LAURA. Oh, I—

JIM. Or is your program filled up? Let me have a look at it. (*Grasps imaginary card.*) Why, every dance is taken! I'll just have to scratch some out. (*Waltz Music: "La Golondrina."*) Ahhh, a waltz! (*He executes some sweeping turns by himself then holds his arms toward Laura.*)

LAURA (*breathlessly*). I—can't dance!

JIM. There you go, that inferiority stuff!

LAURA. I've never danced in my life!

JIM. Come on, try!

LAURA. Oh, but I'd step on you!

JIM. I'm not made out of glass.

LAURA. How—how—how do we start?

JIM. Just leave it to me. You hold your arms out a little.

LAURA. Like this?

JIM. A little bit higher. Right. Now don't tighten up, that's the main thing about it—relax.

LAURA (*laughing breathlessly*). It's hard not to.

JIM. Okay.

LAURA. I'm afraid you can't budge me.

JIM. What do you bet I can't? (*He swings her into motion.*)

LAURA. Goodness, yes, you can!

JIM. Let yourself go, now, Laura, just let yourself go.

LAURA. I'm—

JIM. Come on!

LAURA. Trying!

JIM. Not so stiff—Easy does it!

LAURA. I know but I'm—

JIM. Loosen th' backbone! There now, that's a lot better.

LAURA. Am I?

JIM. Lots, lots better! (*He moves her about the room in a clumsy waltz.*)

LAURA. Oh, my!

JIM. Ha-ha!

LAURA. Goodness, yes you can!

JIM. Ha-ha-ha! (*They suddenly bump into the table. Jim stops.*) What did we hit on?

LAURA. Table.

JIM. Did something fall off it? I think—

LAURA. Yes.

JIM. I hope that it wasn't the little glass horse with the horn!

LAURA. Yes.

JIM. Aw, aw, aw. Is it broken?

LAURA. Now it is just like all the other horses.

JIM. It's lost its—

LAURA. Horn! It doesn't matter. Maybe it's a blessing in disguise.

JIM. You'll never forgive me. I bet that that was your favorite piece of glass.

LAURA. I don't have favorites much. It's no tragedy, Freckles. Glass breaks so easily. No matter how careful you are. The traffic jars the shelves and things fall off them.

JIM. Still I'm awfully sorry that I was the cause.

LAURA (*smiling*). I'll just imagine he had an operation. The horn was removed to make him feel less—freakish! (*They both laugh.*) Now he will feel more at home with the other horses, the ones that don't have horns . . .

JIM. Ha-ha, that's very funny! (*Suddenly serious.*) I'm glad to see that you have a sense of humor. You know—you're—well—very different! Surprisingly different from anyone else I know! (*His voice becomes soft and hesitant with a genuine feeling.*) Do you mind me telling you that? (*Laura is abashed beyond speech.*) You make me feel sort of—I don't know how to put it! I'm usually pretty good at expressing things, but—This is something that I don't know how to say! (*Laura touches her throat and clears it—turns the broken unicorn in her hands.*) (*Even softer.*) Has anyone ever told you that you were pretty? (*Pause: Music.*) (*Laura looks up slowly, with wonder, and shakes her head.*) Well, you are! In a very different way from anyone else. And all the nicer because of the difference, too. (*His voice becomes low and husky. Laura turns away, nearly faint with the novelty of her emotions.*) I wish that you were my sister. I'd teach you to have some confidence in yourself. The different people are not like other people, but being different is nothing to be ashamed of. Because other people are not such wonderful people. They're one hundred times one thousand. You're one times one! They walk all over the earth. You just stay here. They're common as—weeds, but—you—well, you're *Blue Roses!*

(*Image on Screen: Blue Roses.*)

(*Music Changes.*)

LAURA. But blue is wrong for—roses . . .

JIM. It's right for you—You're—pretty!

LAURA. In what respect am I pretty?

JIM. In all respects—believe me! Your eyes—your hair—are pretty! Your hands are pretty! (*He catches hold of her hand.*) You think I'm making this up because I'm invited to dinner and have to be nice. Oh, I could do that! I could put on an act for you, Laura, and say lots of things without being very sincere. But this time I am. I'm talking to you sincerely. I happened to notice you had this inferiority complex that keeps you from feeling comfortable with people. Somebody needs to build your confidence up and make you proud instead of shy and turning away and—blushing—Somebody ought to—ought to—*kiss* you. Laura! (*His hand slips slowly up her arm to her shoulder.*) (*Music Swells Tumultuously.*) (*He suddenly turns her about and kisses her on the lips. When he releases her Laura sinks on the sofa with a bright, dazed look. Jim backs away and fishes in his pocket for a cigarette.*) (*Legend on Screen: "Souvenir."*) Stumble-john! (*He lights the cigarette, avoiding her look. There is a peal of girlish laughter from Amanda in the kitchen. Laura slowly raises and opens her hand. It still contains the little broken glass animal. She looks at it with a tender, bewildered expression.*) Stumble-john! I shouldn't have done that—That was way off the beam. You don't smoke, do you? (*She looks up, smiling, not hearing the question. He sits beside her a little gingerly. She looks at him speechlessly—waiting. He coughs decorously and moves a little farther aside as he considers the situation and senses her feelings, dimly, with perturbation. Gently.*) Would you—care for a—mint? (*She doesn't seem to hear him but her look grows brighter even.*) Peppermint—Life Saver? My pocket's a regular drug store—wherever I go . . . (*He pops a mint in his mouth. Then gulps and decides to make a clean breast of it. He speaks slowly and gingerly.*) Laura, you know, if I had a sister like you, I'd do the same thing as Tom. I'd bring out fellows—introduce her to them. The right type of boys of a type to—appreciate her. Only—well—he made a mistake about me. Maybe I've got no call to be saying this. That may not have been the idea in having me over. But what if it was? There's nothing wrong about that. The only trouble is that in my case—I'm not in a situation to—do the right thing. I can't take down your number and say I'll phone. I can't call up next week and—ask for a date. I thought I had better explain the situation in case you misunderstood it and—hurt your feelings. . . . (*Pause. Slowly, very slowly, Laura's look changes, her eyes returning slowly from his to the ornament in her palm.*)

Amanda utters another gay laugh in the kitchen.

LAURA (*faintly*). You—won't—call again?
JIM. No, Laura, I can't. (*He rises from the sofa.*) As I was just explaining, I've—got strings on me, Laura, I've—been going steady! I go out all the time with a girl named Betty. She's a home-girl like you, and Catholic, and Irish, and in a great many ways we—get along fine. I met her last summer on a moonlight boat trip up the river to Alton, on the *Majestic.* Well—right away from the start it was—love! (*Legend: Love!*) (*Laura sways slightly forward and grips the arm of the sofa. He fails to notice, now enrapt in his own comfortable being.*) Being in love has made a new man of me! (*Leaning stiffly forward, clutching the arm of the sofa, Laura struggles visibly with her storm. But Jim is oblivious, she is a long way off.*) The power of love is really pretty tremendous! Love is something that—

changes the whole world, Laura! (*The storm abates a little and Laura leans back. He notices her again.*) It happened that Betty's aunt took sick, she got a wire and had to go to Centralia. So Tom—when he asked me to dinner—I naturally just accepted the invitation, not knowing that you—that he—that I—(*He stops awkwardly.*) Huh—I'm a stumble-john! (*He flops back on the sofa. The holy candles in the altar of Laura's face have been snuffed out! There is a look of almost infinite desolation. Jim glances at her uneasily.*) I wish that you would—say something. (*She bites her lip which was trembling and then bravely smiles. She opens her hand again on the broken glass ornament. Then she gently takes his hand and raises it level with her own. She carefully places the unicorn in the palm of his hand, then pushes his fingers closed upon it.*) What are you—doing that for? You want me to have him?—Laura? (*She nods.*) What for?

LAURA. A—souvenir . . .

She rises unsteadily and crouches beside the victrola to wind it up.

(*Legend on Screen: "Things Have a Way of Turning Out So Badly."*)

(*Or Image: "Gentleman Caller Waving Good-Bye!—Gaily."*)

At this moment Amanda rushes brightly back in the front room. She bears a pitcher of fruit punch in an old-fashioned cut-glass pitcher and a plate of macaroons. The plate has a gold border and poppies painted on it.

AMANDA. Well, well, well! Isn't the air delightful after the shower? I've made you children a little liquid refreshment. (*Turns gaily to the gentleman caller.*) Jim, do you know that song about lemonade?

"Lemonade, lemonade
Made in the shade and stirred with a spade—
Good enough for any old maid!"

JIM (*uneasily*). Ha-ha! No—I never heard it.

AMANDA. Why, Laura! You look so serious!

JIM. We were having a serious conversation.

AMANDA. Good! Now you're better acquainted!

JIM (*uncertainly*). Ha-ha! Yes.

AMANDA. You modern young people are much more serious-minded than my generation. I was so gay as a girl!

JIM. You haven't changed, Mrs. Wingfield.

AMANDA. Tonight I'm rejuvenated! The gaiety of the occasion, Mr. O'Connor! (*She tosses her head with a peal of laughter. Spills lemonade.*) Oooo! I'm baptizing myself!

JIM. Here—let me—

AMANDA (*setting the pitcher down*). There now. I discovered we had some maraschino cherries. I dumped them in, juice and all!

JIM. You shouldn't have gone to that trouble, Mrs. Wingfield.

AMANDA. Trouble, trouble? Why it was loads of fun! Didn't you hear me cutting up in the kitchen? I bet your ears were burning! I told Tom how outdone with him I was for keeping you to himself so long a time! He should have brought you over much, much sooner! Well, now that you've found your way, I want you to be a very frequent caller! Not just occasional but all the time. Oh, we're going to have a lot of gay times together! I see them coming! Mmm, just breathe that air! So fresh, and the moon's so pretty! I'll skip back out—I know where my place is when young folks are having a—serious conversation!

JIM. Oh, don't go out, Mrs. Wingfield. The fact of the matter is I've got to be going.

AMANDA. Going, now? You're joking! Why, it's only the shank of the evening, Mr. O'Connor!

JIM. Well, you know how it is.

AMANDA. You mean you're a young workingman and have to keep workingmen's hours. We'll let you off early tonight. But only on the condition that next time you stay later. What's the best night for you? Isn't Saturday night the best night for you workingmen?

JIM. I have a couple of time-clocks to punch, Mrs. Wingfield. One at morning, another one at night!

AMANDA. My, but you *are* ambitious! You work at night, too?

JIM. No, Ma'am, not work but—Betty! (*He crosses deliberately to pick up his hat. The band at the Paradise Dance Hall goes into a tender waltz.*)

AMANDA. Betty? Betty? Who's—Betty! (*There is an ominous cracking sound in the sky.*)

JIM. Oh, just a girl. The girl I go steady with! (*He smiles charmingly. The sky falls.*)

(*Legend: "The Sky Falls."*)

AMANDA (*a long-drawn exhalation*). Ohhhh . . . Is it a serious romance, Mr. O'Connor?

JIM. We're going to be married the second Sunday in June.

AMANDA. Ohhhh—how nice! Tom didn't mention that you were engaged to be married.

JIM. The cat's not out of the bag at the warehouse yet. You know how they are. They call you Romeo and stuff like that. (*He stops at the oval mirror to put on his hat. He carefully shapes the brim and the crown to give a discreetly dashing effect.*) It's been a wonderful evening, Mrs. Wingfield. I guess this is what they mean by Southern hospitality.

AMANDA. It really wasn't anything at all.

JIM. I hope it don't seem like I'm rushing off. But I promised Betty I'd pick her up at the Wabash depot, an' by the time I get my jalopy down there her train'll be in. Some women are pretty upset if you keep 'em waiting.

AMANDA. Yes, I know—The tyranny of women! (*Extends her hand.*) Good-
bye, Mr. O'Connor. I wish you luck—and happiness—and success! All
three of them, and so does Laura!—Don't you, Laura?

LAURA. Yes!

JIM (*taking her hand*). Goodbye, Laura. I'm certainly going to treasure that
souvenir. And don't you forget the good advice I gave you. (*Raises his
voice to a cheery shout.*) So long, Shakespeare! Thanks again, ladies—good
night!

He grins and ducks jauntily out.

*Still bravely grimacing, Amanda closes the door on the gentleman caller. Then
she turns back to the room with a puzzled expression. She and Laura don't dare
to face each other. Laura crouches beside the victrola to wind it.*

AMANDA (*faintly*). Things have a way of turning out so badly. I don't believe that I would play the victrola. Well, well—well—Our gentleman
caller was engaged to be married! Tom!

TOM (*from back*). Yes, Mother?

AMANDA. Come in here a minute. I want to tell you something awfully
funny.

TOM (*enters with macaroon and a glass of the lemonade*). Has the gentleman
caller gotten away already?

AMANDA. The gentleman caller has made an early departure. What a wonderful joke you played on us!

TOM. How do you mean?

AMANDA. You didn't mention that he was engaged to be married.

TOM. Jim? Engaged?

AMANDA. That's what he just informed us.

TOM. I'll be jiggered! I didn't know about that.

AMANDA. That seems very peculiar.

TOM. What's peculiar about it?

AMANDA. Didn't you call him your best friend down at the warehouse?

TOM. He is, but how did I know?

AMANDA. It seems extremely peculiar that you wouldn't know your best
friend was going to be married!

TOM. The warehouse is where I work, not where I know things about
people!

AMANDA. You don't know things anywhere! You live in a dream; you
manufacture illusions! (*He crosses to door.*) Where are you going?

TOM. I'm going to the movies.

AMANDA. That's right, now that you've had us make such fools of ourselves. The effort, the preparations, all the expense! The new floor lamp,
the rug, the clothes for Laura! All for what? To entertain some other
girl's fiancé! Go to the movies, go! Don't think about us, a mother

deserted, an unmarried sister who's crippled and has no job! Don't let anything interfere with your selfish pleasure! Just go, go, go—to the movies!

TOM. All right, I will! The more you shout about my selfishness to me the quicker I'll go, and I won't go to the movies!

AMANDA. Go, then! Then go to the moon—you selfish dreamer!

Tom smashes his glass on the floor. He plunges out on the fire-escape, slamming the door. Laura screams—cut by door.

Dance-hall music up. Tom goes to the rail and grips it desperately, lifting his face in the chill white moonlight penetrating the narrow abyss of the alley.

(Legend on Screen: "And So Good-Bye . . .")

Tom's closing speech is timed with the interior pantomime. The interior scene is played as though viewed through sound-proof glass. Amanda appears to be making a comforting speech to Laura who is huddled upon the sofa. Now that we cannot hear the mother's speech, her silliness is gone and she has dignity and tragic beauty. Laura's dark hair hides her face until at the end of the speech she lifts it to smile at her mother. Amanda's gestures are slow and graceful, almost dancelike, as she comforts the daughter. At the end of her speech she glances a moment at the father's picture—then withdraws through the portieres. At close of Tom's speech, Laura blows out the candles, ending the play.

TOM. I didn't go to the moon, I went much further—for time is the longest distance between two places—Not long after that I was fired for writing a poem on the lid of a shoe-box. I left Saint Louis. I descended the steps of this fire-escape for a last time and followed, from then on, in my father's footsteps, attempting to find in motion what was lost in space—I traveled around a great deal. The cities swept about me like dead leaves, leaves that were brightly colored but torn away from the branches. I would have stopped, but I was pursued by something. It always came upon me unawares, taking me altogether by surprise. Perhaps it was a familiar bit of music. Perhaps it was only a piece of transparent glass—Perhaps I am walking along a street at night, in some strange city, before I have found companions. I pass the lighted window of a shop where perfume is sold. The window is filled with pieces of colored glass, tiny transparent bottles in delicate colors, like bits of a shattered rainbow. Then all at once my sister touches my shoulder. I turn around and look into her eyes . . . Oh, Laura, Laura, I tried to leave you behind me, but I am more faithful than I intended to be! I reach for a cigarette, I cross the street, I run into the movies or a bar, I buy a drink, I speak to the nearest stranger—anything that can blow your candles out! *(Laura bends over the candles.)*—for nowadays the world is lit by lightning! Blow out your candles, Laura—and so goodbye . . .

She blows the candles out.

(*The Scene Dissolves.*)

[1944]

TOPICS FOR DISCUSSION AND WRITING

1. When produced in New York, the magic-lantern slides were omitted. Is the device an extraneous gimmick? Might it even interfere with the play, by oversimplifying and thus in a way belittling the actions?

2. What does the victrola offer to Laura? Why is the typewriter a better symbol (for the purposes of the play) than, say, a piano? After all, Laura could have been taking piano lessons. Explain the symbolism of the unicorn, and the loss of its horn. What is Laura saying to Jim in the gesture of giving him the unicorn?

3. Laura escapes to her glass menagerie. To what do Amanda and Tom escape? How complete is Tom's escape at the end of the play?

4. What is meant at the end when Laura blows out the candles? Is she blowing out illusions? Or life? Or both?

5. Did Williams make a slip in having Amanda say Laura is "crippled" on page 1030?

6. There is an implication that had Jim not been going steady he might have rescued Laura, but Jim also seems to represent (for example, in his lines about money and power) the corrupt outside world that no longer values humanity. Is this a slip on Williams's part, or is it an interesting complexity?

7. On page 1030 Williams says, in a stage direction, "Now that we cannot hear the mother's speech, her silliness is gone and she has dignity and tragic beauty." Is Williams simply dragging in the word "tragic" because of its prestige, or is it legitimate? "Tragedy" is often distinguished from "pathos": in the tragic, the suffering is experienced by persons who act and are in some measure responsible for their suffering; in the pathetic, the suffering is experienced by the passive and the innocent. For example, in discussing Aeschylus's *The Suppliants* (in *Greek Tragedy*), H. D. F. Kitto says: "The Suppliants are not only pathetic, as the victims of outrage, but also tragic, as the victims of their own misconceptions." Given this distinction, to what extent are Amanda and Laura tragic? Pathetic?

CONTEXTS FOR *THE GLASS MENAGERIE*

Production Notes [by Tennessee Williams]

Being a "memory play," *The Glass Menagerie* can be presented with unusual freedom of convention. Because of its considerably delicate or tenuous material, atmospheric touches and subtleties of direction play a particularly important part. Expressionism and all other unconventional techniques in drama have only one valid aim, and that is a closer approach to truth. When a play employs unconventional techniques, it is not, or certainly shouldn't be, trying to escape its responsibility of dealing with reality, or interpreting experience, but is actually or should be attempting to find a closer approach, a more penetrating and vivid expression of things as they are. The straight realistic play with its genuine frigidaire and authentic ice cubes, its characters that speak exactly as its audience speaks, corresponds to the academic landscape and has the same virtue of a photographic likeness. Everyone should know nowadays the unimportance of the photographic in art: that truth, life, or reality is an organic thing which the poetic imagination can represent or suggest, in essence, only through transformation, through changing into other forms than those which were merely present in appearance.

These remarks are not meant as comments only on this particular play. They have to do with a conception of a new, plastic theater which must take the place of the exhausted theater of realistic conventions if the theater is to resume vitality as a part of our culture.

The Screen Device

There is *only one important difference between the original and acting version of the play* and that is the *omission* in the latter of the device which I tentatively included in my *original* script. This device was the use of a screen on which were projected magic-lantern slides bearing images or titles. I do not regret the omission of this device from the . . . Broadway production. The extraordinary power of Miss Taylor's performance made it suitable to have the utmost simplicity in the physical production. But I think it may be interesting to some readers to see how this device was conceived. So I am putting it into the published manuscript. These images and legends, projected from behind, were cast on a section of wall between the front-room and dining-room areas, which should be indistinguishable from the rest when not in use.

The purpose of this will probably be apparent. It is to give accent to certain values in each scene. Each scene contains a particular point (or several) which is structurally the most important. In an episodic play, such as this, the basic structure or narrative line may be obscured from the audience; the effect may seem fragmentary rather than architectural. This may not be the fault of the play so much as a lack of attention in the audience.

The legend or image upon the screen will strengthen the effect of what is merely allusion in the writing and allow the primary point to be made more simply and lightly than if the entire responsibility were on the spoken lines. Aside from this structural value, I think the screen will have a definite emotional appeal, less definable but just as important. An imaginative producer or director may invent many other uses for this device than those indicated in the present script. In fact the possibilities of the device seem much larger to me than the instance of this play can possibly utilize.

The Music

Another extra-literary accent in this play is provided by the use of music. A single recurring tune, "The Glass Menagerie," is used to give emotional emphasis to suitable passages. This tune is like circus music, not when you are on the grounds or in the immediate vicinity of the parade, but when you are at some distance and very likely thinking of something else. It seems under those circumstances to continue almost interminably and it weaves in and out of your preoccupied consciousness; then it is the lightest, most delicate music in the world and perhaps the saddest. It expresses the surface vivacity of life with the underlying strain of immutable and inexpressible sorrow. When you look at a piece of delicately spun glass you think of two things: how beautiful it is and how easily it can be broken. Both of those ideas should be woven into the recurring tune, which dips in and out of the play as if it were carried on a wind that changes. It serves as a thread of connection and allusion between the narrator with his separate point in time and space and the subject of his story. Between each episode it returns as reference to the emotion, nostalgia, which is the first condition of the play. It is primarily Laura's music and therefore comes out most clearly when the play focuses upon her and the lovely fragility of glass which is her image.

The Lighting

The lighting in the play is not realistic. In keeping with the atmosphere of memory, the stage is dim. Shafts of light are focused on selected areas or actors, sometimes in contradistinction to what is the apparent center. For instance, in the quarrel scene between Tom and Amanda, in which Laura has no active part, the clearest pool of light is on her figure. This is also true of the supper scene. The light upon Laura should be distinct from the others, having a peculiar pristine clarity such as light used in early religious portraits of female saints or madonnas. A certain correspondence to light in religious paintings, such as El Greco's, where the figures are radiant in atmosphere that is relatively dusky, could be effectively used throughout the play. (It will also permit a more effective use of the screen.) A free, imaginative use of light can be of enormous value in giving a mobile, plastic quality to plays of a more or less static nature.

Tennessee Williams, on The Timeless World of a Play

Carson McCullers concludes one of her lyric poems with the line: "Time, the endless idiot, runs screaming 'round the world." It is this continual rush of time, so violent that it appears to be screaming, that deprives our actual lives of so much dignity and meaning, and it is, perhaps more than anything else, the *arrest of time* which has taken place in a completed work of art that gives to certain plays their feeling of depth and significance. In the London notices of *Death of a Salesman* a certain notoriously skeptical critic made the remark that Willy Loman was the sort of man that almost any member of the audience would have kicked out of an office had he applied for a job or detained one for conversation about his troubles. The remark itself possibly holds some truth. But the implication that Willy Loman is consequently a character with whom we have no reason to concern ourselves in drama, reveals a strikingly false conception of what plays are. Contemplation is something that exists outside of time, and so is the tragic sense. Even in the actual world of commerce, there exists in some persons a sensibility to the unfortunate situations of others, a capacity for concern and compassion, surviving from a more tender period of life outside the present whirling wire-cage of business activity. Facing Willy Loman across an office desk, meeting his nervous glance and hearing his querulous voice, we would be very likely to glance at our wrist watch and our schedule of other appointments. We would not kick him out of the office, no, but we would certainly *ease* him out with more expedition than Willy had feebly hoped for. But suppose there had been no wrist watch or office clock and suppose there had *not* been the schedule of pressing appointments, and suppose that we were not actually facing Willy across a desk — and facing a person is *not* the best way to *see* him! — suppose, in other words, that the meeting with Willy Loman had somehow occurred in a world *outside* of time. Then I think we would receive him with concern and kindness and even with respect. If the world of a play did not offer us this occasion to view its characters under that special condition of a *world without time*, then, indeed, the characters and occurrences of drama would become equally pointless, equally trivial, as corresponding meetings and happenings in life.

The classic tragedies of Greece had tremendous nobility. The actors wore great masks, movements were formal, dancelike, and the speeches had an epic quality which doubtless was as removed from the normal conversation of their contemporary society as they seem today. Yet they did not seem false to the Greek audiences: the magnitude of the events and the passions aroused by them did not seem ridiculously out of proportion to common experience. And I wonder if this was not because the Greek audiences knew, instinctively or by training, that the created world of a play is removed from that element which makes people *little* and their emotions fairly inconsequential.

Great sculpture often follows the lines of the human body: yet the repose of great sculpture suddenly transmutes those human lines to something that has an absoluteness, a purity, a beauty, which would not be possible in a living mobile form.

A play may be violent, full of motion: yet it has that special kind of repose which allows contemplation and produces the climate in which tragic importance is a possible thing, provided that certain modern conditions are met.

In actual existence the moments of love are succeeded by the moments of satiety and sleep. The sincere remark is followed by a cynical distrust. Truth is fragmentary, at best: we love and betray each other in not quite the same breath but in two breaths that occur in fairly close sequence. But the fact that passion occurred in *passing,* that it then declined into a more familiar sense of indifference, should not be regarded as proof of its inconsequence. And this is the very truth that drama wished to bring us. . . .

Whether or not we admit it to ourselves, we are all haunted by a truly awful sense of impermanence. I have always had a particularly keen sense of this at New York cocktail parties, and perhaps that is why I drink the martinis almost as fast as I can snatch them from the tray. This sense is the febrile thing that hangs in the air. Horror of insincerity, of *not meaning,* overhangs these affairs like the cloud of cigarette smoke and the hectic chatter. This horror is the only thing, almost, that is left unsaid at such functions. All social functions involving a group of people not intimately known to each other are always under this shadow. They are almost always (in an unconscious way) like that last dinner of the condemned: where steak or turkey, whatever the doomed man wants, is served in his cell as a mockingly cruel reminder of what the great-big-little-transitory world had to offer.

In a play, time is arrested in the sense of being confined. By a sort of legerdemain, events are made to remain *events,* rather than being reduced so quickly to mere *occurrences.* The audience can sit back in a comforting dusk to watch a world which is flooded with light and in which emotion and action have a dimension and dignity that they would likewise have in real existence, if only the shattering intrusion of time could be locked out.

About their lives, people ought to remember that when they are finished, everything in them will be contained in a marvelous state of repose which is the same as that which they unconsciously admired in drama. The rush is temporary. The great and only possible dignity of man lies in his power deliberately to choose certain moral values by which to live as steadfastly as if he, too, like a character in a play, were immured against the corrupting rush of time. Snatching the eternal out of the desperately fleeting is the great magic trick of human existence. As far as we know, as far as there exists any kind of empiric evidence, there is no way to beat the game of *being* against *non-being,* in which non-being is the predestined victor on realistic levels.

Yet plays in the tragic tradition offer us a view of certain moral values in violent juxtaposition. Because we do not participate, except as spectators, we can view them clearly, within the limits of our emotional equipment. These people on the stage do not return our looks. We do not have to answer their questions nor make any sign of being in company with them, nor do we have to compete with their virtues nor resist their offenses. All at once, for this reason, we are able to *see* them! Our hearts are wrung by recognition and pity, so that the dusky shell of the auditorium where we are gathered anonymously together is flooded with an almost liquid warmth of unchecked human sympathies, relieved of selfconsciousness, allowed to function. . . .

Men pity and love each other more deeply than they permit themselves to know. The moment after the phone has been hung up, the hand reaches for a scratch pad and scrawls a notation: "Funeral Tuesday at five, Church of the Holy Redeemer, don't forget flowers." And the same hand is only a little shakier than usual as it reaches, some minutes later, for a highball glass that will pour a stupefaction over the kindled nerves. Fear and evasion are the two little beasts that chase each other's tails in the revolving wire-cage of our nervous world. They distract us from feeling too much about things. Time rushes toward us with its hospital tray of infinitely varied narcotics, even while it is preparing us for its inevitably fatal operation. . . .

So successfully have we disguised from ourselves the intensity of our own feelings, the sensibility of our own hearts, that plays in the tragic tradition have begun to seem untrue. For a couple of hours we may surrender ourselves to a world of fiercely illuminated values in conflict, but when the stage is covered and the auditorium lighted, almost immediately there is a recoil of disbelief. "Well, well!" we say as we shuffle back up the aisle, while the play dwindles behind us with the sudden perspective of an early Chirico painting. By the time we have arrived at Sardi's, if not as soon as we pass beneath the marquee, we have convinced ourselves once more that life has as little resemblance to the curiously stirring and meaningful occurrences on the stage as a jingle has to an elegy of Rilke.

This modern condition of his theater audience is something that an author must know in advance. The diminishing influence of life's destroyer, time, must be somehow worked into the context of his play. Perhaps it is a certain foolery, a certain distortion toward the grotesque, which will solve the problem for him. Perhaps it is only restraint, putting a mute on the strings that would like to break all bounds. But almost surely, unless he contrives in some way to relate the dimensions of his tragedy to the dimensions of a world in which time is *included*—he will be left among his magnificent debris on a dark stage, muttering to himself: "Those fools . . ."

And if they could hear him above the clatter of tongues, glasses, chinaware and silver, they would give him this answer: "But you have shown us a world not ravaged by time. We admire your innocence. But we have seen our photographs, past and present. Yesterday evening we passed our first wife on the street. We smiled as we spoke but we didn't really see her! It's too bad, but we know what is true and not true, and at 3 A.M. your disgrace will be in print!"

[1951]

Arthur Miller *(American; b. 1915)*

Death of a Salesman

Certain Private Conversations in Two Acts and a Requiem

List of Characters

WILLY LOMAN
LINDA
BIFF
HAPPY
BERNARD
THE WOMAN
CHARLEY
UNCLE BEN
HOWARD WAGNER
JENNY
STANLEY
MISS FORSYTHE
LETTA

Scene. *The action takes place in Willy Loman's house and yard and in various places he visits in the New York and Boston of today.*

ACT 1

Scene: *A melody is heard played upon a flute. It is small and fine telling of grass and trees and the horizon. The curtain rises.*

Before us is the Salesman's house. We are aware of towering, angular shapes behind it, surrounding it on all sides. Only the blue light of the sky falls upon the house and forestage; the surrounding area shows an angry glow of orange. As more light appears, we see a solid vault of apartment houses around the small,

Top: *Lee J. Cobb starred as Willy Loman in the 1949 original Broadway production of* Death of a Salesman. *Photograph reproduced courtesy of the Theatre Arts Library, Harry Ransom Humanities Research Center, The University of Texas at Austin.* Bottom: *Dustin Hoffman, as Willy Loman, and John Malkovich, as Biff, face each other in this scene from the 1984 production. Photograph by Inge Morath; reproduced by permission of Magnum Photos, Inc.*

fragile-seeming home. An air of the dream clings to the place, a dream rising out of reality. The kitchen at center seems actual enough, for there is a kitchen table with three chairs, and a refrigerator. But no other fixtures are seen. At the back of the kitchen there is a draped entrance, which leads to the living room. To the right of the kitchen, on a level raised two feet, is a bedroom furnished only with a brass bedstead and a straight chair. On a shelf over the bed a silver athletic trophy stands. A window opens onto the apartment house at the side.

Behind the kitchen, on a level raised six and a half feet, is the boys' bedroom, at present barely visible. Two beds are dimly seen, and at the back of the room a dormer window. (This bedroom is above the unseen living room.) At the left a stairway curves up to it from the kitchen.

The entire setting is wholly or, in some places, partially transparent. The roof-line of the house is one-dimensional; under and over it we see the apartment build-ings. Before the house lies an apron, curving beyond the forestage into the orches-tra. This forward area serves as the back yard as well as the locale of all Willy's imaginings and of his city scenes. Whenever the action is in the present the actors observe the imaginary wall-lines, entering the house only through its door at the left. But in the scenes of the past these boundaries are broken, and characters enter or leave a room by stepping "through" a wall onto the forestage.

From the right, Willy Loman, the Salesman, enters, carrying two large sample cases. The flute plays on. He hears but is not aware of it. He is past sixty years of age, dressed quietly. Even as he crosses the stage to the doorway of the house, his exhaustion is apparent. He unlocks the door, comes into the kitchen, and thank-fully lets his burden down, feeling the soreness of his palms. A word-sigh escapes his lips — it might be "Oh, boy, oh, boy." He closes the door, then carries his cases out into the living room, through the draped kitchen doorway.

Linda, his wife, has stirred in her bed at the right. She gets out and puts on a robe, listening. Most often jovial, she has developed an iron repression of her exceptions to Willy's behavior — she more than loves him, she admires him, as though his mercurial nature, his temper, his massive dreams and little cruelties, served her only as sharp reminders of the turbulent longings within him, longings which she shares but lacks the temperament to utter and follow to their end.

LINDA (*hearing Willy outside the bedroom, calls with some trepidation*). Willy!
WILLY. It's all right. I came back.
LINDA. Why? What happened? (*Slight pause.*) Did something happen, Willy?
WILLY. No, nothing happened.
LINDA. You didn't smash the car, did you?
WILLY (*with casual irritation*). I said nothing happened. Didn't you hear me?
LINDA. Don't you feel well?
WILLY. I'm tired to the death. (*The flute has faded away. He sits on the bed beside her, a little numb.*) I couldn't make it. I just couldn't make it, Linda.
LINDA (*very carefully, delicately*). Where were you all day? You look terrible.

WILLY. I got as far as a little above Yonkers. I stopped for a cup of coffee. Maybe it was the coffee.

LINDA. What?

WILLY (*after a pause*). I suddenly couldn't drive any more. The car kept going off onto the shoulder, y'know?

LINDA (*helpfully*). Oh. Maybe it was the steering again. I don't think Angelo knows the Studebaker.

WILLY. No, it's me, it's me. Suddenly I realize I'm goin' sixty miles an hour and I don't remember the last five minutes. I'm—I can't seem to—keep my mind to it.

LINDA. Maybe it's your glasses. You never went for your new glasses.

WILLY. No, I see everything. I came back ten miles an hour. It took me nearly four hours from Yonkers.

LINDA (*resigned*). Well, you'll just have to take a rest, Willy, you can't continue this way.

WILLY. I just got back from Florida.

LINDA. But you didn't rest your mind. Your mind is overactive, and the mind is what counts, dear.

WILLY. I'll start out in the morning. Maybe I'll feel better in the morning. (*She is taking off his shoes.*) These goddam arch supports are killing me.

LINDA. Take an aspirin. Should I get you an aspirin? It'll soothe you.

WILLY (*with wonder*). I was driving along, you understand? And I was fine. I was even observing the scenery. You can imagine, me looking at scenery, on the road every week of my life. But it's so beautiful up there, Linda, the trees are so thick, and the sun is warm. I opened the windshield and just let the warm air bathe over me. And then all of a sudden I'm goin' off the road! I'm tellin' ya, I absolutely forgot I was driving. If I'd've gone the other way over the white line I might've killed somebody. So I went on again—and five minutes later I'm dreamin' again, and I nearly . . . (*He presses two fingers against his eyes.*) I have such thoughts, I have such strange thoughts.

LINDA. Willy, dear. Talk to them again. There's no reason why you can't work in New York.

WILLY. They don't need me in New York. I'm the New England man. I'm vital in New England.

LINDA. But you're sixty years old. They can't expect you to keep traveling every week.

WILLY. I'll have to send a wire to Portland. I'm supposed to see Brown and Morrison tomorrow morning at ten o'clock to show the line. Goddammit, I could sell them! (*He starts putting on his jacket.*)

LINDA (*taking the jacket from him*). Why don't you go down to the place tomorrow and tell Howard you've simply got to work in New York? You're too accommodating, dear.

WILLY. If old man Wagner was alive I'd a been in charge of New York now! That man was a prince, he was a masterful man. But that boy of his, that Howard, he don't appreciate. When I went north the first time, the Wagner Company didn't know where New England was!

LINDA. Why don't you tell those things to Howard, dear?

WILLY (*encouraged*). I will, I definitely will. Is there any cheese?

LINDA. I'll make you a sandwich.

WILLY. No, go to sleep. I'll take some milk. I'll be up right away. The boys in?

LINDA. They're sleeping. Happy took Biff on a date tonight.

WILLY (*interested*). That so?

LINDA. It was so nice to see them shaving together, one behind the other, in the bathroom. And going out together. You notice? The whole house smells of shaving lotion.

WILLY. Figure it out. Work a lifetime to pay off a house. You finally own it, and there's nobody to live in it.

LINDA. Well, dear, life is a casting off. It's always that way.

WILLY. No, no, some people—some people accomplish something. Did Biff say anything after I went this morning?

LINDA. You shouldn't have criticized him, Willy, especially after he just got off the train. You mustn't lose your temper with him.

WILLY. When the hell did I lose my temper? I simply asked him if he was making any money. Is that a criticism?

LINDA. But, dear, how could he make any money?

WILLY (*worried and angered*). There's such an undercurrent in him. He became a moody man. Did he apologize when I left this morning?

LINDA. He was crestfallen, Willy. You know how he admires you. I think if he finds himself, then you'll both be happier and not fight any more.

WILLY. How can he find himself on a farm? Is that a life? A farm hand? In the beginning, when he was young, I thought, well, a young man, it's good for him to tramp around, take a lot of different jobs. But it's more than ten years now and he has yet to make thirty-five dollars a week!

LINDA. He's finding himself, Willy.

WILLY. Not finding yourself at the age of thirty-four is a disgrace!

LINDA. Shh!

WILLY. The trouble is he's lazy, goddammit!

LINDA. Willy, please!

WILLY. Biff is a lazy bum!

LINDA. They're sleeping. Get something to eat. Go on down.

WILLY. Why did he come home? I would like to know what brought him home.

LINDA. I don't know. I think he's still lost, Willy. I think he's very lost.

WILLY. Biff Loman is lost. In the greatest country in the world a young man with such—personal attractiveness, gets lost. And such a hard worker. There's one thing about Biff—he's not lazy.

LINDA. Never.

WILLY (*with pity and resolve*). I'll see him in the morning; I'll have a nice talk with him. I'll get him a job selling. He could be big in no time. My God! Remember how they used to follow him around in high school? When he smiled at one of them their faces lit up. When he walked down the street . . . (*He loses himself in reminiscences.*)

LINDA (*trying to bring him out of it*). Willy, dear, I got a new kind of American-type cheese today. It's whipped.

WILLY. Why do you get American when I like Swiss?

LINDA. I just thought you'd like a change . . .

WILLY. I don't want a change! I want Swiss cheese. Why am I always being contradicted?

LINDA (*with a covering laugh*). I thought it would be a surprise.

WILLY. Why don't you open a window in here, for God's sake?

LINDA (*with infinite patience*). They're all open, dear.

WILLY. The way they boxed us in here. Bricks and windows, windows and bricks.

LINDA. We should've bought the land next door.

WILLY. The street is lined with cars. There's not a breath of fresh air in the neighborhood. The grass don't grow any more, you can't raise a carrot in the back yard. They should've had a law against apartment houses. Remember those two beautiful elm trees out there? When I and Biff hung the swing between them?

LINDA. Yeah, like being a million miles from the city.

WILLY. They should've arrested the builder for cutting those down. They massacred the neighborhood. (*Lost.*) More and more I think of those days, Linda. This time of year it was lilac and wisteria. And then the peonies would come out, and the daffodils. What fragrance in this room!

LINDA. Well, after all, people had to move somewhere.

WILLY. No, there's more people now.

LINDA. I don't think there's more people. I think . . .

WILLY. There's more people! That's what's ruining this country! Population is getting out of control. The competition is maddening! Smell the stink from that apartment house! And another one on the other side . . . How can they whip cheese?

On Willy's last line, Biff and Happy raise themselves up in their beds, listening.

LINDA. Go down, try it. And be quiet.

WILLY (*turning to Linda, guiltily*). You're not worried about me, are you, sweetheart?

BIFF. What's the matter?

HAPPY. Listen!

LINDA. You've got too much on the ball to worry about.

WILLY. You're my foundation and my support, Linda.

LINDA. Just try to relax, dear. You make mountains out of molehills.

WILLY. I won't fight with him any more. If he wants to go back to Texas, let him go.

LINDA. He'll find his way.

WILLY. Sure. Certain men just don't get started till later in life. Like Thomas Edison, I think. Or B. F. Goodrich. One of them was deaf. (*He starts for the bedroom doorway.*) I'll put my money on Biff.

LINDA. And Willy—if it's warm Sunday we'll drive in the country. And we'll open the windshield, and take lunch.

WILLY. No, the windshields don't open on the new cars.

LINDA. But you opened it today.

WILLY. Me? I didn't. (*He stops.*) Now isn't that peculiar! Isn't that a remarkable . . . (*He breaks off in amazement and fright as the flute is heard distantly.*)

LINDA. What, darling?

WILLY. That is the most remarkable thing.

LINDA. What, dear?

WILLY. I was thinking of the Chevvy. (*Slight pause.*) Nineteen twenty-eight . . . when I had that red Chevvy . . . (*Breaks off.*) That funny? I coulda sworn I was driving that Chevvy today.

LINDA. Well, that's nothing. Something must've reminded you.

WILLY. Remarkable. Ts. Remember those days? The way Biff used to simonize that car? The dealer refused to believe there was eighty thousand miles on it. (*He shakes his head.*) Heh! (*To Linda.*) Close your eyes, I'll be right up. (*He walks out of the bedroom.*)

HAPPY (*to Biff*). Jesus, maybe he smashed up the car again!

LINDA (*calling after Willy*). Be careful on the stairs, dear! The cheese is on the middle shelf. (*She turns, goes over to the bed, takes his jacket, and goes out of the bedroom.*)

Light has risen on the boys' room. Unseen, Willy is heard talking to himself, "Eighty thousand miles," and a little laugh. Biff gets out of bed, comes downstage a bit, and stands attentively. Biff is two years older than his brother Happy, well built, but in these days bears a worn air and seems less self-assured. He has succeeded less, and his dreams are stronger and less acceptable than Happy's. Happy is tall, powerfully made. Sexuality is like a visible color on him, or a scent that many women have discovered. He, like his brother, is lost, but in a different way, for he has never allowed himself to turn his face toward defeat and is thus more confused and hard-skinned, although seemingly more content.

HAPPY (*getting out of bed*). He's going to get his license taken away if he keeps that up. I'm getting nervous about him, y'know, Biff?

BIFF. His eyes are going.

HAPPY. No, I've driven with him. He sees all right. He just doesn't keep his mind on it. I drove into the city with him last week. He stops at a green light and then it turns red and he goes. (*He laughs.*)

BIFF. Maybe he's color-blind.

HAPPY. Pop? Why he's got the finest eye for color in the business. You know that.

BIFF (*sitting down on his bed*). I'm going to sleep.

HAPPY. You're not still sour on Dad, are you, Biff?

BIFF. He's all right, I guess.

WILLY (*underneath them, in the living room*). Yes, sir, eighty thousand miles—eighty-two thousand!

BIFF. You smoking?

HAPPY (*holding out a pack of cigarettes*). Want one?

BIFF (*taking a cigarette*). I can never sleep when I smell it.

WILLY. What a simonizing job, heh!

HAPPY (*with deep sentiment*). Funny, Biff, y'know? Us sleeping in here again? The old beds. (*He pats his bed affectionately.*) All the talk that went across those two beds, huh? Our whole lives.

BIFF. Yeah. Lotta dreams and plans.

HAPPY (*with a deep and masculine laugh*). About five hundred women would like to know what was said in this room. (*They share a soft laugh.*)

BIFF. Remember that big Betsy something—what the hell was her name—over on Bushwick Avenue?

HAPPY (*combing his hair*). With the collie dog!

BIFF. That's the one. I got you in there, remember?

HAPPY. Yeah, that was my first time—I think. Boy, there was a pig. (*They laugh, almost crudely.*) You taught me everything I know about women. Don't forget that.

BIFF. I bet you forgot how bashful you used to be. Especially with girls.

HAPPY. Oh, I still am, Biff.

BIFF. Oh, go on.

HAPPY. I just control it, that's all. I think I got less bashful and you got more so. What happened, Biff? Where's the old humor, the old confidence? (*He shakes Biff's knee. Biff gets up and moves restlessly about the room.*) What's the matter?

BIFF. Why does Dad mock me all the time?

HAPPY. He's not mocking you, he . . .

BIFF. Everything I say there's a twist of mockery on his face. I can't get near him.

HAPPY. He just wants you to make good, that's all. I wanted to talk to you about Dad for a long time, Biff. Something's—happening to him. He—talks to himself.

BIFF. I noticed that this morning. But he always mumbled.

HAPPY. But not so noticeable. It got so embarrassing I sent him to Florida. And you know something? Most of the time he's talking to you.

BIFF. What's he say about me?

HAPPY. I can't make it out.

BIFF. What's he say about me?

HAPPY. I think the fact that you're not settled, that you're still kind of up in the air . . .

BIFF. There's one or two other things depressing him, Happy.

HAPPY. What do you mean?

BIFF. Never mind. Just don't lay it all to me.

HAPPY. But I think if you just got started—I mean—is there any future for you out there?

BIFF. I tell ya, Hap, I don't know what the future is. I don't know—what I'm supposed to want.

HAPPY. What do you mean?

BIFF. Well, I spent six or seven years after high school trying to work myself up. Shipping clerk, salesman, business of one kind or another. And it's a measly manner of existence. To get on that subway on the hot mornings in summer. To devote your whole life to keeping stock, or making phone calls, or selling or buying. To suffer fifty weeks of the year for the sake of a two-week vacation, when all you really desire is to be outdoors, with your shirt off. And always to have to get ahead of the next fella. And still—that's how you build a future.

HAPPY. Well, you really enjoy it on a farm? Are you content out there?

BIFF (*with rising agitation*). Hap, I've had twenty or thirty different kinds of jobs since I left home before the war, and it always turns out the same. I just realized it lately. In Nebraska when I herded cattle, and the Dakotas, and Arizona, and now in Texas. It's why I came home now, I guess, because I realized it. This farm I work on, it's spring there now, see? And they've got about fifteen new colts. There's nothing more inspiring or—beautiful than the sight of a mare and a new colt. And it's cool there now, see? Texas is cool now, and it's spring. And whenever spring comes to where I am, I suddenly get the feeling, my God, I'm not gettin' anywhere! What the hell am I doing, playing around with horses, twenty-eight dollars a week! I'm thirty-four years old, I oughta be makin' my future. That's when I come running home. And now, I get here, and I don't know what to do with myself. (*After a pause.*) I've always made a point of not wasting my life, and everytime I come back here I know that all I've done is to waste my life.

HAPPY. You're a poet, you know that, Biff? You're a—you're an idealist!

BIFF. No, I'm mixed up very bad. Maybe I oughta get married. Maybe I oughta get stuck into something. Maybe that's my trouble. I'm like a boy. I'm not married, I'm not in business, I just—I'm like a boy. Are you content, Hap? You're a success, aren't you? Are you content?

HAPPY. Hell, no!

BIFF. Why? You're making money, aren't you?

HAPPY (*moving about with energy, expressiveness*). All I can do now is wait for the merchandise manager to die. And suppose I get to be merchandise manager? He's a good friend of mine, and he just built a terrific estate on Long Island. And he lived there about two months and sold it, and now he's building another one. He can't enjoy it once it's finished. And I know that's just what I would do. I don't know what the hell I'm workin' for. Sometimes I sit in my apartment—all alone. And I think of the rent I'm paying. And it's crazy. But then, it's what I always wanted. My own apartment, a car, and plenty of women. And still, goddammit, I'm lonely.

BIFF (*with enthusiasm*). Listen, why don't you come out West with me?

HAPPY. You and I, heh?

BIFF. Sure, maybe we could buy a ranch. Raise cattle, use our muscles. Men built like we are should be working out in the open.

HAPPY (*avidly*). The Loman Brothers, heh?

BIFF (*with vast affection*). Sure, we'd be known all over the counties!

HAPPY (*enthralled*). That's what I dream about, Biff. Sometimes I want to just rip my clothes off in the middle of the store and outbox that goddam merchandise manager. I mean I can outbox, outrun, and outlift anybody in that store, and I have to take orders from those common, petty sons-of-bitches till I can't stand it any more.

BIFF. I'm tellin' you, kid, if you were with me I'd be happy out there.

HAPPY (*enthused*). See, Biff, everybody around me is so false that I'm constantly lowering my ideals . . .

BIFF. Baby, together we'd stand up for one another, we'd have someone to trust.

HAPPY. If I were around you . . .

BIFF. Hap, the trouble is we weren't brought up to grub for money. I don't know how to do it.

HAPPY. Neither can I!

BIFF. Then let's go!

HAPPY. The only thing is—what can you make out there?

BIFF. But look at your friend. Builds an estate and then hasn't the peace of mind to live in it.

HAPPY. Yeah, but when he walks into the store the waves part in front of him. That's fifty-two thousand dollars a year coming through the revolving door, and I got more in my pinky finger than he's got in his head.

BIFF. Yeah, but you just said . . .

HAPPY. I gotta show some of those pompous, self-important executives over there that Hap Loman can make the grade. I want to walk into the store the way he walks in. Then I'll go with you, Biff. We'll be together yet, I swear. But take those two we had tonight. Now weren't they gorgeous creatures?

BIFF. Yeah, yeah, most gorgeous I've had in years.

HAPPY. I get that any time I want, Biff. Whenever I feel disgusted. The only trouble is, it gets like bowling or something. I just keep knockin' them over and it doesn't mean anything. You still run around a lot?

BIFF. Naa. I'd like to find a girl—steady, somebody with substance.

HAPPY. That's what I long for.

BIFF. Go on! You'd never come home.

HAPPY. I would! Somebody with character, with resistance! Like Mom, y'know? You're gonna call me a bastard when I tell you this. That girl Charlotte I was with tonight is engaged to be married in five weeks. (*He tries on his new hat.*)

BIFF. No kiddin'!

HAPPY. Sure, the guy's in line for the vice-presidency of the store. I don't know what gets into me, maybe I just have an over-developed sense of competition or something, but I went and ruined her, and furthermore I can't get rid of her. And he's the third executive I've done that to. Isn't that a crummy characteristic? And to top it all, I go to their weddings! (*Indignantly, but laughing.*) Like I'm not supposed to take bribes. Manufacturers offer me a hundred-dollar bill now and then to throw an order their way. You know how honest I am, but it's like this girl, see. I hate myself for it. Because I don't want the girl, and, still, I take it and—I love it!

BIFF. Let's go to sleep.

HAPPY. I guess we didn't settle anything, heh?

BIFF. I just got one idea that I think I'm going to try.

HAPPY. What's that?

BIFF. Remember Bill Oliver?

HAPPY. Sure, Oliver is very big now. You want to work for him again?

BIFF. No, but when I quit he said something to me. He put his arm on my shoulder, and he said, "Biff, if you ever need anyting, come to me."

HAPPY. I remember that. That sounds good.

BIFF. I think I'll go to see him. If I could get ten thousand or even seven or eight thousand dollars I could buy a beautiful ranch.

HAPPY. I bet he'd back you, 'Cause he thought highly of you, Biff. I mean, they all do. You're well liked, Biff. That's why I say to come back here, and we both have the apartment. And I'm tellin' you, Biff, any babe you want . . .

BIFF. No, with a ranch I could do the work I like and still be something. I just wonder though. I wonder if Oliver still thinks I stole that carton of basketballs.

HAPPY. Oh, he probably forgot that long ago. It's almost ten years. You're too sensitive. Anyway, he didn't really fire you.

BIFF. Well, I think he was going to. I think that's why I quit. I was never sure whether he knew or not. I know he thought the world of me, though. I was the only one he'd let lock up the place.

WILLY (*below*). You gonna wash the engine, Biff?

HAPPY. Shh!

Biff looks at Happy, who is gazing down, listening. Willy is mumbling in the parlor.

HAPPY. You hear that?

They listen. Willy laughs warmly.

BIFF (*growing angry*). Doesn't he know Mom can hear that?

WILLY. Don't get your sweater dirty, Biff!

A look of pain crosses Biff's face.

HAPPY. Isn't that terrible? Don't leave again, will you? You'll find a job here. You gotta stick around. I don't know what to do about him, it's getting embarrassing.

WILLY. What a simonizing job!

BIFF. Mom's hearing that!

WILLY. No kiddin', Biff, you got a date? Wonderful!

HAPPY. Go on to sleep. But talk to him in the morning, will you?

BIFF (*reluctantly getting into bed*). With her in the house. Brother!

HAPPY (*getting into bed*). I wish you'd have a good talk with him.

The light on their room begins to fade.

BIFF (*to himself in bed*). That selfish, stupid . . .

HAPPY. Sh . . . Sleep, Biff.

Their light is out. Well before they have finished speaking, Willy's form is dimly seen below in the darkened kitchen. He opens the refrigerator, searches in there, and takes out a bottle of milk. The apartment houses are fading out, and the entire house and surroundings become covered with leaves. Music insinuates itself as the leaves appear.

WILLY. Just wanna be careful with those girls, Biff, that's all. Don't make any promises. No promises of any kind. Because a girl, y'know, they always believe what you tell 'em, and you're very young, Biff, you're too young to be talking seriously to girls.

Light rises on the kitchen. Willy, talking, shuts the refrigerator door and comes downstage to the kitchen table. He pours milk into a glass. He is totally immersed in himself, smiling faintly.

WILLY. Too young entirely, Biff. You want to watch your schooling first. Then when you're all set, there'll be plenty of girls for a boy like you. (*He smiles broadly at a kitchen chair.*) That so? The girls pay for you? (*He laughs.*) Boy, you must really be makin' a hit.

Willy is gradually addressing—physically—a point offstage, speaking through the wall of the kitchen, and his voice has been rising in volume to that of a normal conversation.

WILLY. I been wondering why you polish the care so careful. Ha! Don't leave the hubcaps, boys. Get the chamois to the hubcaps. Happy, use newspaper on the windows, it's the easiest thing. Show him how to do it, Biff! You see, Happy? Pad it up, use it like a pad. That's it, that's it, good work. You're doin' all right, Hap. (*He pauses, then nods in approbation for a few seconds, then looks upward.*) Biff, first thing we gotta do when we get time is clip that big branch over the house. Afraid it's gonna fall in a storm and hit the roof. Tell you what. We get a rope and sling her around, and then we climb up there with a couple of saws and take her down. Soon as you finish the car, boys, I wanna see ya. I got a surprise for you, boys.

BIFF (*offstage*). Whatta ya got, Dad?

WILLY. No, you finish first. Never leave a job till you're finished — remember that. (*Looking toward the "big trees."*) Biff, up in Albany I saw a beautiful hammock. I think I'll buy it next trip, and we'll hang it right between those two elms. Wouldn't that be something? Just swinging' there under those branches. Boy, that would be . . .

Young Biff and Young Happy appear from the direction Willy was addressing. Happy carries rags and a pail of water. Biff, wearing a sweater with a block "S," carries a football.

BIFF (*pointing in the direction of the car offstage*). How's that, Pop, professional?

WILLY. Terrific. Terrific job, boys. Good work, Biff.

HAPPY. Where's the surprise, Pop?

WILLY. In the back seat of the car.

HAPPY. Boy! (*He runs off.*)

BIFF. What is it, Dad? Tell me, what'd you buy?

WILLY (*laughing, cuffs him*). Never mind, something I want you to have.

BIFF (*turns and starts off*). What is it, Hap?

HAPPY (*offstage*). It's a punching bag!

BIFF. Oh, Pop!

WILLY. It's got Gene Tunney's signature on it!

Happy runs onstage with a punching bag.

BIFF. Gee, how'd you know we wanted a punching bag?

WILLY. Well, it's the finest thing for the timing.

HAPPY (*lies down on his back and pedals with his feet*). I'm losing weight, you notice, Pop?

WILLY (*to Happy*). Jumping rope is good too.

BIFF. Did you see the new football I got?

WILLY (*examining the ball*). Where'd you get a new ball?

BIFF. The coach told me to practice my passing.

WILLY. That so? And he gave you the ball, heh?

BIFF. Well, I borrowed it from the locker room. (*He laughs confidentially.*)

WILLY (*laughing with him at the theft*). I want you to return that.

HAPPY. I told you he wouldn' like it!

BIFF (*angrily*). Well, I'm bringing it back!

WILLY (*stopping the incipient argument, to Happy*). Sure, he's gotta practice with a regulation ball, doesn't he? (*To Biff.*) Coach'll probably congratulate you on your initiative!

BIFF. Oh, he keeps congratulating my initiative all the time, Pop.

WILLY. That's because he likes you. If somebody else took that ball there'd be an uproar. So what's the report, boys, what's the report?

BIFF. Where'd you go this time, Dad? Gee we were lonesome for you.

WILLY (*pleased, puts an arm around each boy and they come down to the apron*). Lonesome, heh?

BIFF. Missed you every minute.

WILLY. Don't say? Tell you a secret, boys. Don't breathe it to a soul. Someday I'll have my own business, and I'll never have to leave home any more.

HAPPY. Like Uncle Charley, heh?

WILLY. Bigger than Uncle Charley! Because Charley is not—liked. He's liked, but he's not—well liked.

BIFF. Where'd you go this time, Dad?

WILLY. Well, I got on the road, and I went north to Providence. Met the Mayor.

BIFF. The Mayor of Providence!

WILLY. He was sitting in the hotel lobby.

BIFF. What'd he say?

WILLY. He said, "Morning!" And I said, "You got a fine city here, Mayor." And then he had coffee with me. And then I went to Waterbury. Waterbury is a fine city. Big clock city, the famous Waterbury clock. Sold a nice bill there. And then Boston—Boston is the cradle of the Revolution. A fine city. And a couple of other towns in Mass., and on to Portland and Bangor and straight home!

BIFF. Gee, I'd love to go with you sometime, Dad.

WILLY. Soon as summer comes.

HAPPY. Promise?

WILLY. You and Hap and I, and I'll show you all the towns. America is full of beautiful towns and fine, upstanding people. And they know me, boys, they know me up and down New England. The finest people. And when I bring you fellas up, there'll be open sesame for all of us, 'cause one thing, boys: I have friends. I can park my car in any street in New England, and the cops protect it like their own. This summer, heh?

BIFF AND HAPPY (*together*). Yeah! You bet!

WILLY. We'll take our bathing suits.

HAPPY. We'll carry your bags, Pop!

WILLY. Oh, won't that be something! Me comin' into the Boston stores with you boys carryin' my bags. What a sensation!

Biff is prancing around, practicing passing the ball.

WILLY. You nervous, Biff, about the game?

BIFF. Not if you're gonna be there.

WILLY. What do they say about you in school, now that they made you captain?

HAPPY. There's a crowd of girls behind him everytime the classes change.

BIFF (*taking Willy's hand*). This Saturday, Pop, this Saturday—just for you, I'm going to break through for a touchdown.

HAPPY. You're supposed to pass.

BIFF. I'm takin' one play for Pop. You watch me, Pop, and when I take off my helmet, that means I'm breakin' out. Then you watch me crash through that line!

WILLY (*kisses Biff*). Oh, wait'll I tell this in Boston!

Bernard enters in knickers. He is younger than Biff, earnest and loyal, a worried boy.

BERNARD. Biff, where are you? You're supposed to study with me today.

WILLY. Hey, looka Bernard. What're you lookin' so anemic about, Bernard?

BERNARD. He's gotta study. Uncle Willy. He's got Regents next week.

HAPPY (*tauntingly, spinning Bernard around*). Let's box, Bernard!

BERNARD. Biff! (*He gets away from Happy.*) Listen, Biff, I heard Mr. Birnbaum say that if you don't start studyin' math he's gonna flunk you, and you won't graduate. I heard him!

WILLY. You better study with him, Biff. Go ahead now.

BERNARD. I heard him!

BIFF. Oh, Pop, you didn't see my sneakers! (*He holds up a foot for Willy to look at.*)

WILLY. Hey, that's a beautiful job of printing!

BERNARD (*wiping his glasses*). Just because he printed University of Virginia on his sneakers doesn't mean they've got to graduate him, Uncle Willy!

WILLY (*angrily*). What're you talking about? With scholarships to three universities they're gonna flunk him?

BERNARD. But I heard Mr. Birnbaum say . . .

WILLY. Don't be a pest, Bernard! (*To his boys.*) What an anemic!

BERNARD. Okay, I'm waiting for you in my house, Biff.

Bernard goes off. The Lomans laugh.

WILLY. Bernard is not well liked, is he?

BIFF. He's liked, but he's not well liked.

HAPPY. That's right, Pop.

WILLY. That's just what I mean. Bernard can get the best marks in school, y'understand, but when he gets out in the business would y'understand, you are going to be five times ahead of him. That's why I thank Almighty God you're both built like Adonises. Because the man who makes an appearance in the business world, the man who creates personal interest, is the man who gets ahead. Be liked and you will never want. You take me, for instance. I never have to wait in line to see a buyer. "Willy Loman is here!" That's all they have to know, and I go right through.

BIFF. Did you knock them dead, Pop?

WILLY. Knocked 'em cold in Providence, slaughtered 'em in Boston.

HAPPY (*on his back, pedaling again*). I'm losing weight, you notice, Pop?

Linda enters as of old, a ribbon in her hair, carrying a basket of washing.

LINDA (*with youthful energy*). Hello, dear!

WILLY. Sweetheart!

LINDA. How'd the Chevvy run?

WILLY. Chevrolet, Linda, is the greatest car ever built. (*To the boys.*) Since when do you let your mother carry wash up the stairs?

BIFF. Grab hold there, boy!

HAPPY. Where to, Mom?

LINDA. Hang them up on the line. And you better go down to your friends, Biff. The cellar is full of boys. They don't know what to do with themselves.

BIFF. Ah, when Pop comes home they can wait!

WILLY (*laughs appreciatively*). You better go down and tell them what to do, Biff.

BIFF. I think I'll have them sweep out the furnace room.

WILLY. Good work, Biff.

BIFF (*goes through wall-line of kitchen to doorway at back and calls down*). Fellas! Everybody sweep out the furnace room! I'll be right down!

VOICES. All right! Okay, Biff.

BIFF. George and Sam and Frank, come out back! We're hangin' up the wash! Come on, Hap, on the double! (*He and Happy carry out the basket.*)

LINDA. The way they obey him!

WILLY. Well, that's training, the training. I'm tellin' you, I was sellin' thousands and thousands, but I had to come home.

LINDA. Oh, the whole block'll be at that game. Did you sell anything?

WILLY. I did five hundred gross in Providence and seven hundred gross in Boston.

LINDA. No! Wait a minute. I've got a pencil. (*She pulls pencil and paper out of her apron pocket.*) That makes your commission . . . Two hundred— my God! Two hundred and twelve dollars!

WILLY. Well, I didn't figure it yet, but . . .

LINDA. How much did you do?

WILLY. Well, I—I did—about a hundred and eighty gross in Providence. Well, no—it came to—roughly two hundred gross on the whole trip.

LINDA (*without hesitation*). Two hundred gross. That's . . . (*She figures.*)

WILLY. The trouble was that three of the stores were half-closed for inventory in Boston. Otherwise I woulda broke records.

LINDA. Well, it makes seventy dollars and some pennies. That's very good.

WILLY. What do we owe?

LINDA. Well, on the first there's sixteen dollars on the refrigerator . . .

WILLY. Why sixteen?

LINDA. Well, the fan belt broke, so it was a dollar eighty.

WILLY. But it's brand new.

LINDA. Well, the man said that's the way it is. Till they work themselves in, y'know.

They move through the wall-line into the kitchen.

WILLY. I hope we didn't get stuck on that machine.

LINDA. They got the biggest ads of any of them!

WILLY. I know, it's a fine machine. What else?

LINDA. Well, there's nine-sixty for the washing machine. And for the vacuum cleaner there's three and a half due on the fifteenth. Then the roof, you got twenty-one dollars remaining.

WILLY. It don't leak, does it?

LINDA. No, they did a wonderful job. Then you owe Frank for the carburetor.

WILLY. I'm not going to pay that man! That goddam Chevrolet, they ought to prohibit the manufacture of that car!

LINDA. Well, you owe him three and a half. And odds and ends, comes to around a hundred and twenty dollars by the fifteenth.

WILLY. A hundred and twenty dollars! My God, if business don't pick up I don't know what I'm gonna do!

LINDA. Well, next week you'll do better.

WILLY. Oh, I'll knock 'em dead next week. I'll go to Hartford. I'm very well liked in Hartford. You know, the trouble is, Linda, people don't seem to take to me.

They move onto the forestage.

LINDA. Oh, don't be foolish.

WILLY. I know it when I walk in. They seem to laugh at me.

LINDA. Why? Why would they laugh at you? Don't talk that way, Willy.

Willy moves to the edge of the stage. Linda goes into the kitchen and starts to darn stockings.

WILLY. I don't know the reason for it, but they just pass me by. I'm not noticed.

LINDA. But you're doing wonderful, dear. You're making seventy to a hundred dollars a week.

WILLY. But I gotta be at it ten, twelve hours a day. Other men—I don't know—they do it easier. I don't know why—I can't stop myself—I talk too much. A man oughta come in with a few words. One thing about Charley. He's a man of few words, and they respect him.

LINDA. You don't talk too much, you're just lively.

WILLY (*smiling*). Well, I figure, what the hell, life is short, a couple of jokes. (*To himself:*) I joke too much! (*The smile goes.*)

LINDA. Why? You're . . .

WILLY. I'm fat. I'm very—foolish to look at, Linda. I didn't tell you, but Christmas time I happened to be calling on F. H. Stewarts, and a salesman I know, as I was going in to see the buyer I heard him say something about—walrus. And I—I cracked him right across the face. I won't take that. I simply will not take that. But they do laugh at me. I know that.

LINDA. Darling . . .

WILLY. I gotta overcome it. I know I gotta overcome it. I'm not dressing to advantage, maybe.

LINDA. Willy, darling, you're the handsomest man in the world . . .

WILLY. Oh, no, Linda.

LINDA. To me you are. (*Slight pause.*) The handsomest.

From the darkness is heard the laughter of a woman. Willy doesn't turn to it, but it continues through Linda's lines.

LINDA. And the boys, Willy. Few men are idolized by their children the way you are.

Music is heard as behind a scrim, to the left of the house; The Woman, dimly seen, is dressing.

WILLY (*with great feeling*). You're the best there is, Linda, you're a pal, you know that? On the road—on the road I want to grab you sometimes and just kiss the life outa you.

The laughter is loud now, and he moves into a brightening area at the left, where The Woman has come from behind the scrim and is standing, putting on her hat, looking into a "mirror" and laughing.

WILLY. 'Cause I get so lonely—especially when business is bad and there's nobody to talk to. I get the feeling that I'll never sell anything again, that I won't make a living for you, or a business, a business for the boys. (*He talks through The Woman's subsiding laughter; The Woman primps at the "mirror."*) There's so much I want to make for . . .

THE WOMAN. Me? You didn't make me, Willy. I picked you.

WILLY (*pleased*). You picked me?

THE WOMAN (*who is quite proper-looking, Willy's age*). I did. I've been sitting at that desk watching all the salesmen go by, day in, day out. But you've got such a sense of humor, and we do have such a good time together, don't we?

WILLY. Sure, sure. (*He takes her in his arms.*) Why do you have to go now?

THE WOMAN. It's two o'clock . . .

WILLY. No, come on in! (*He pulls her.*)

THE WOMAN . . . . my sisters'll be scandalized. When'll you be back?

WILLY. Oh, two weeks about. Will you come up again?

THE WOMAN. Sure thing. You do make me laugh. It's good for me. (*She squeezes his arm, kisses him.*) And I think you're a wonderful man.

WILLY. You picked me, heh?

THE WOMAN. Sure. Because you're so sweet. And such a kidder.

WILLY. Well, I'll see you next time I'm in Boston.

THE WOMAN. I'll put you right through to the buyers.

WILLY (*slapping her bottom*). Right. Well, bottoms up!

THE WOMAN (*slaps him gently and laughs*). You just kill me, Willy. (*He suddenly grabs her and kisses her roughly.*) You kill me. And thanks for the stockings. I love a lot of stockings. Well, good night.

WILLY. Good night. And keep your pores open!

THE WOMAN. Oh, Willy!

The Woman bursts out laughing, and Linda's laughter blends in. The Woman disappears into the dark. Now the area at the kitchen table brightens. Linda is sitting where she was at the kitchen table, but now is mending a pair of her silk stockings.

LINDA. You are, Willy. The handsomest man. You've got no reason to feel that . . .

WILLY (*coming out of The Woman's dimming area and going over to Linda*). I'll make it all up to you, Linda, I'll . . .

LINDA. There's nothing to make up, dear. You're doing fine, better than . . .

WILLY (*noticing her mending*). What's that?

LINDA. Just mending my stockings. They're so expensive . . .

WILLY (*angrily, taking them from her*). I won't have you mending stockings in this house! Now throw them out!

Linda puts the stockings in her pocket.

BERNARD (*entering on the run*). Where is he? If he doesn't study!

WILLY (*moving to the forestage, with great agitation*). You'll give him the answers!

BERNARD. I do, but I can't on a Regents! That's a state exam! They're liable to arrest me!

WILLY. Where is he? I'll whip him, I'll whip him!

LINDA. And he'd better give back that football, Willy, it's not nice.

WILLY. Biff! Where is he? Why is he taking everything?

LINDA. He's too rough with the girls, Willy. All the mothers are afraid of him!

WILLY. I'll whip him!

BERNARD. He's driving the car without a license!

The Woman's laugh is heard.

WILLY. Shut up!

LINDA. All the mothers . . .

WILLY. Shut up!

BERNARD (*backing quietly away and out*). Mr. Birnbaum says he's stuck up.

WILLY. Get outa here!

BERNARD. If he doesn't buckle down he'll flunk math! (*He goes off.*)

LINDA. He's right, Willy, you've gotta . . .

WILLY (*exploding at her*). There's nothing the matter with him! You want him to be a worm like Bernard? He's got spirit, personality . . .

As he speaks, Linda, almost in tears, exits into the living room. Willy is alone in the kitchen, wilting and staring. The leaves are gone. It is night again, and the apartment houses look down from behind.

WILLY. Loaded with it. Loaded! What is he stealing? He's giving it back, isn't he? Why is he stealing? What did I tell him? I never in my life told him anything but decent things.

Happy in pajamas has come down the stairs; Willy suddenly becomes aware of Happy's presence.

HAPPY. Let's go now, come on.

WILLY (*sitting down at the kitchen table*). Huh! Why did she have to wax the floors herself? Everytime she waxes the floors she keels over. She knows that!

HAPPY. Shh! Take it easy. What brought you back tonight?

WILLY. I got an awful scare. Nearly hit a kid in Yonkers. God! Why didn't I go to Alaska with my brother Ben that time! Ben! That man was a genius, that man was success incarnate! What a mistake! He begged me to go.

HAPPY. Well, there's no use in . . .

WILLY. You guys! There was a man started with the clothes on his back and ended up with diamond mines!

HAPPY. Boy, someday I'd like to know how he did it.

WILLY. What's the mystery? The man knew what he wanted and went out and got it! Walked into a jungle, and comes out, the age of twenty-one, and he's rich! The world is an oyster, but you don't crack it open on a mattress!

HAPPY. Pop, I told you I'm gonna retire you for life.

WILLY. You'll retire me for life on seventy goddam dollars a week? And your women and your car and your apartment, and you'll retire me for life! Christ's sake, I couldn't get past Yonkers today! Where are you guys, where are you? The woods are burning! I can't drive a car!

Charley has appeared in the doorway. He is a large man, slow of speech, laconic, immovable. In all he says, despite what he says, there is pity, and, now, trepidation. He has a robe over pajamas, slippers on his feet. He enters the kitchen.

CHARLEY. Everything all right?

HAPPY. Yeah, Charley, everything's . . .

WILLY. What's the matter?

CHARLEY. I heard some noise. I thought something happened. Can't we do something about the walls? You sneeze in here, and in my house hats blow off.

HAPPY. Let's go to bed, Dad. Come on.

Charley signals to Happy to go.

WILLY. You go ahead, I'm not tired at the moment.

HAPPY (*to Willy*). Take it easy, huh? (*He exits.*)

WILLY. What're you doin' up?

CHARLEY (*sitting down at the kitchen table opposite Willy*). Couldn't sleep good. I had a heartburn.

WILLY. Well, you don't know how to eat.

CHARLEY. I eat with my mouth.

WILLY. No, you're ignorant. You gotta know about vitamins and things like that.

CHARLEY. Come on, let's shoot. Tire you out a little.

WILLY (*hesitantly*). All right. You got cards?

CHARLEY (*taking a deck from his pocket*). Yeah, I got them. Someplace. What is it with those vitamins?

WILLY (*dealing*). They build up your bones. Chemistry.

CHARLEY. Yeah, but there's no bones in a heartburn.

WILLY. What are you talkin' about? Do you know the first thing about it?

CHARLEY. Don't get insulted.

WILLY. Don't talk about something you don't know anything about.

They are playing. Pause.

CHARLEY. What're you doin' home?

WILLY. A little trouble with the car.

CHARLEY. Oh. (*Pause.*) I'd like to take a trip to California.

WILLY. Don't say.

CHARLEY. You want a job?

WILLY. I got a job, I told you that. (*After a slight pause.*) What the hell are you offering me a job for?

CHARLEY. Don't get insulted.

WILLY. Don't insult me.

CHARLEY. I don't see no sense in it. You don't have to go on this way.

WILLY. I got a good job. (*Slight pause.*) What do you keep comin' in here for?

CHARLEY. You want me to go?

WILLY (*after a pause, withering*). I can't understand it. He's going back to
  Texas again. What the hell is that?

CHARLEY. Let him go.

WILLY. I got nothin' to give him, Charley, I'm clean, I'm clean.

CHARLEY. He won't starve. None a them starve. Forget about him.

WILLY. Then what have I got to remember?

CHARLEY. You take it too hard. To hell with it. When a deposit bottle
  is broken you don't get your nickel back.

WILLY. That's easy enough for you to say.

CHARLEY. That ain't easy for me to say.

WILLY. Did you see the ceiling I put up in the living room?

CHARLEY. Yeah, that's a piece of work. To put up a ceiling is a mystery
  to me. How do you do it?

WILLY. What's the difference?

CHARLEY. Well, talk about it.

WILLY. You gonna put up a ceiling?

CHARLEY. How could I put up a ceiling?

WILLY. Then what the hell are you bothering me for?

CHARLEY. You're insulted again.

WILLY. A man who can't handle tools is not a man. You're disgusting.

CHARLEY. Don't call me disgusting, Willy.

*Uncle Ben, carrying a valise and an umbrella, enters the forestage from around
the right corner of the house. He is a stolid man, in his sixties, with a mustache
and an authoritative air. He is utterly certain of his destiny, and there is an aura
of far places about him. He enters exactly as Willy speaks.*

WILLY. I'm getting awfully tired, Ben.

Ben's music is heard. Ben looks around at everything.

CHARLEY. Good, keep playing; you'll sleep better. Did you call me Ben?

Ben looks at his watch.

WILLY. That's funny. For a second there you reminded me of my brother Ben.

BEN. I only have a few minutes. (*He strolls, inspecting the place. Willy and
  Charley continue playing.*)

CHARLEY. You never heard from him again, heh? Since that time?

WILLY. Didn't Linda tell you? Couple of weeks ago we got a letter from
  his wife in Africa. He died.

CHARLEY. That so.

BEN (*chuckling*). So this is Brooklyn, eh?

CHARLEY. Maybe you're in for some of his money.

WILLY. Naa, he had seven sons. There's just one opportunity I had with
  that man . . .

BEN. I must make a train, William. There are several properties I'm looking
  at in Alaska.

WILLY. Sure, sure! If I'd gone with him to Alaska that time, everything would've been totally different.

CHARLEY. Go on, you'd froze to death up there.

WILLY. What're you talking about?

BEN. Opportunity is tremendous in Alaska, William. Surprised you're not up there.

WILLY. Sure, tremendous.

CHARLEY. Heh?

WILLY. There was the only man I ever met who knew the answers.

CHARLEY. Who?

BEN. How are you all?

WILLY (*taking a pot, smiling*). Fine, fine.

CHARLEY. Pretty sharp tonight.

BEN. Is Mother living with you?

WILLY. No, she died a long time ago.

CHARLEY. Who?

BEN. That's too bad. Fine specimen of a lady, Mother.

WILLY (*to Charley*). Heh?

BEN. I'd hoped to see the old girl.

CHARLEY. Who died?

BEN. Heard anything from Father, have you?

WILLY (*unnerved*). What do you mean, who died?

CHARLEY (*taking a pot*). What're you talkin' about?

BEN (*looking at his watch*). William, it's half-past eight!

WILLY (*as though to dispel his confusion he angrily stops Charley's hand*). That's my build!

CHARLEY. I put the ace . . .

WILLY. If you don't know how to play the game I'm not gonna throw my money away on you!

CHARLEY (*rising*). It was my ace, for God's sake!

WILLY. I'm through, I'm through!

BEN. When did Mother die?

WILLY. Long ago. Since the beginning you never knew how to play cards.

CHARLEY (*picks up the cards and goes to the door*). All right! Next time I'll bring a deck with five aces.

WILLY. I don't play that kind of game!

CHARLEY (*turning to him*). You ought to be ashamed of yourself!

WILLY. Yeah?

CHARLEY. Yeah! (*He goes out.*)

WILLY (*slamming the door after him*). Ignoramus!

BEN (*as Willy comes toward him through the wall-line of the kitchen*). So you're William.

WILLY (*shaking Ben's hand*). Ben! I've been waiting for you so long! What's the answer? How did you do it?

BEN. Oh, there's a story in that.

Linda enters the forestage, as of old, carrying the wash basket.

LINDA. Is this Ben?

BEN (*gallantly*). How do you do, my dear.

LINDA. Where've you been all these years? Willy's always wondered why you . . .

WILLY (*pulling Ben away from her impatiently*). Where is Dad? Didn't you follow him? How did you get started?

BEN. Well, I don't know how much you remember.

WILLY. Well, I was just a baby, of course, only three or four years old . . .

BEN. Three years and eleven months.

WILLY. What a memory, Ben!

BEN. I have many enterprises, William, and I have never kept books.

WILLY. I remember I was sitting under the wagon in—was it Nebraska?

BEN. It was South Dakota, and I gave you a bunch of wild flowers.

WILLY. I remember you walking away down some open road.

BEN (*laughing*). I was going to find Father in Alaska.

WILLY. Where is he?

BEN. At that age I had a very faulty view of geography, William. I discovered after a few days that I was heading due south, so instead of Alaska, I ended up in Africa.

LINDA. Africa!

WILLY. The Gold Coast!

BEN. Principally diamond mines.

LINDA. Diamond mines!

BEN. Yes, my dear. But I've only a few minutes . . .

WILLY. No! Boys! Boys! (*Young Biff and Happy appear.*) Listen to this. This is your Uncle Ben, a great man! Tell my boys, Ben!

BEN. Why, boys, when I was seventeen I walked into the jungle, and when I was twenty-one I walked out. (*He laughs.*) And by God I was rich.

WILLY (*to the boys*). You see what I been talking about? The greatest things can happen!

BEN (*glancing at his watch*). I have an appointment in Ketchikan Tuesday week.

WILLY. No, Ben! Please tell about Dad. I want my boys to hear. I want them to know the kind of stock they spring from. All I remember is a man with a big beard, and I was in Mamma's lap, sitting around a fire, and some kind of high music.

BEN. His flute. He played the flute.

WILLY. Sure, the flute, that's right!

New music is heard, a high, rollicking tune.

BEN. Father was a very great and a very wild-hearted man. We would start in Boston, and he'd toss the whole family into the wagon, and then he'd drive the team right across the country; through Ohio, and

Indiana, Michigan, Illinois, and all the Western states. And we'd stop in the towns and sell the flutes that he'd made on the way. Great inventor, Father. With one gadget he made more in a week than a man like you could make in a lifetime.

WILLY. That's just the way I'm bringing them up, Ben—rugged, well liked, all-around.

BEN. Yeah? (*To Biff.*) Hit that, boy—hard as you can. (*He pounds his stomach.*)

BIFF. Oh, no, sir!

BEN (*taking boxing stance*). Come on, get to me! (*He laughs.*)

WILLY. Go to it. Biff! Go ahead, show him!

BIFF. Okay! (*He cocks his fists and starts in.*)

LINDA (*to Willy*). Why must he fight, dear?

BEN (*sparring with Biff*). Good boy! Good boy!

WILLY. How's that, Ben, heh?

HAPPY. Give him the left, Biff!

LINDA. Why are you fighting?

BEN. Good boy! (*Suddenly comes in, trips Biff, and stands over him, the point of his umbrella poised over Biff's eye.*)

LINDA. Look out, Biff!

BIFF. Gee!

BEN (*patting Biff's knee*). Never fight fair with a stranger, boy. You'll never get out of the jungle that way. (*Taking Linda's hand and bowing.*) It was an honor and a pleasure to meet you, Linda.

LINDA (*withdrawing her hand coldly, frightened*). Have a nice—trip.

BEN (*to Willy*). And good luck with your—what do you do?

WILLY. Selling.

BEN. Yes. Well . . . (*He raises his hand in farewell to all.*)

WILLY. No, Ben, I don't want you to think . . . (*He takes Ben's arm to show him.*) It's Brooklyn, I know, but we hunt too.

BEN. Really, now.

WILLY. Oh, sure, there's snakes and rabbits and—that's why I moved out here. Why, Biff can fell any one of these trees in no time! Boys! Go right over to where they're building the apartment house and get some sand. We're gonna rebuild the entire front stoop right now! Watch this, Ben!

BIFF. Yes, sir! On the double, Hap!

HAPPY (*as he and Biff run off*). I lost weight, Pop, you notice?

Charley enters in knickers, even before the boys are gone.

CHARLEY. Listen, if they steal any more from that building the watchman'll put the cops on them!

LINDA (*to Willy*). Don't let Biff . . .

Ben laughs lustily.

WILLY. You shoulda seen the lumber they brought home last week. At least a dozen six-by-tens worth all kinds a money.

CHARLEY. Listen, if that watchman . . .

WILLY. I gave them hell, understand. But I got a couple of fearless characters there.

CHARLEY. Willy, the jails are full of fearless characters.

BEN (*clapping Willy on the back, with a laugh at Charley*). And the stock exchange, friend!

WILLY (*joining in Ben's laughter*). Where are the rest of your pants?

CHARLEY. My wife bought them.

WILLY. Now all you need is a golf club and you can go upstairs and go to sleep. (*To Ben.*) Great athlete! Between him and his son Bernard they can't hammer a nail!

BERNARD (*rushing in*). The watchman's chasing Biff!

WILLY (*angrily*). Shut up! He's not stealing anything!

LINDA (*alarmed, hurrying off left*). Where is he? Biff, dear! (*She exits.*)

WILLY (*moving toward the left, away from Ben*). There's nothing wrong. What's the matter with you?

BEN. Nervy boy. Good!

WILLY (*laughing*). Oh, nerves of iron, that Biff!

CHARLEY. Don't know what it is. My New England man comes back and he's bleedin', they murdered him up there.

WILLY. It's contacts, Charley, I got important contacts!

CHARLEY (*sarcastically*). Glad to hear it, Willy. Come in later, we'll shoot a little casino. I'll take some of your Portland money. (*He laughs at Willy and exits.*)

WILLY (*turning to Ben*). Business is bad, it's murderous. But not for me, of course.

BEN. I'll stop by on my way back to Africa.

WILLY (*longingly*). Can't you stay a few days? You're just what I need, Ben, because I—I have a fine position here, but I—well, Dad left when I was such a baby and I never had a chance to talk to him and I still feel—kind of temporary about myself.

BEN. I'll be late for my train.

They are at opposite ends of the stage.

WILLY. Ben, my boys—can't we talk? They'd go into the jaws of hell for me, see, but I . . .

BEN. William, you're being first-rate with your boys. Outstanding, manly chaps!

WILLY (*hanging on to his words*). Oh, Ben, that's good to hear! Because sometimes I'm afraid that I'm not teaching them the right kind of— Ben, how should I teach them?

BEN (*giving great weight to each word, and with a certain vicious audacity*). William, when I walked into the jungle, I was seventeen. When I walked out I was twenty-one. And, by God, I was rich! (*He goes off into darkness around the right corner of the house.*)

WILLY. . . . was rich! That's just the spirit I want to imbue them with! To walk into a jungle! I was right! I was right! I was right!

Ben is gone, but Willy is still speaking to him as Linda, in nightgown and robe, enters the kitchen, glances around for Willy, then goes to the door of the house, looks out and sees him. Comes down to his left. He looks at her.

LINDA. Willy, dear? Willy?

WILLY I was right!

LINDA. Did you have some cheese? (*He can't answer.*) It's very late, darling. Come to bed, heh?

WILLY (*looking straight up*). Gotta break your neck to see a star in this yard.

LINDA. You coming in?

WILLY Whatever happened to that diamond watch fob? Remember? When Ben came from Africa that time? Didn't he give me a watch fob with a diamond in it?

LINDA. You pawned it, dear. Twelve, thirteen years ago. For Biff's radio correspondence course.

WILLY. Gee, that was a beautiful thing. I'll take a walk.

LINDA. But you're in your slippers.

WILLY (*starting to go around the house at the left*). I was right! I was! (*Half to Linda, as he goes, shaking his head.*) What a man! There was a man worth talking to. I was right!

LINDA (*calling after Willy*). But in your slippers, Willy!

Willy is almost gone when Biff, in his pajamas, comes down the stairs and enters the kitchen.

BIFF. What is he doing out there?

LINDA. Sh!

BIFF. God Almighty, Mom, how long has he been doing this?

LINDA. Don't, he'll hear you.

BIFF. What the hell is the matter with him?

LINDA. It'll pass by morning.

BIFF. Shouldn't we do anything?

LINDA. Oh, my dear, you should do a lot of things, but there's nothing to do, so go to sleep.

Happy comes down the stair and sits on the steps.

HAPPY. I never heard him so loud, Mom.

LINDA. Well, come around more often; you'll hear him. (*She sits down at the table and mends the lining of Willy's jacket.*)

BIFF. Why didn't you ever write me about this, Mom?

LINDA. How would I write to you? For over three months you had no address.

BIFF. I was on the move. But you know I thought of you all the time. You know that, don't you, pal?

LINDA. I know, dear, I know. But he likes to have a letter. Just to know that there's still a possibility for better things.

BIFF. He's not like this all the time, is he?

LINDA. It's when you come home he's always the worst.

BIFF. When I come home?

LINDA. When you write you're coming, he's all smiles, and talks about the future, and—he's just wonderful. And then the closer you seem to come, the more shaky he gets, and then, by the time you get here, he's arguing, and he seems angry at you. I think it's just that maybe he can't bring himself to—to open up to you. Why are you so hateful to each other? Why is that?

BIFF (*evasively*). I'm not hateful, Mom.

LINDA. But you no sooner come in the door than you're fighting!

BIFF. I don't know why. I mean to change. I'm tryin', Mom, you understand?

LINDA. Are you home to stay now?

BIFF. I don't know. I want to look around, see what's doin'.

LINDA. Biff, you can't look around all your life, can you?

BIFF. I just can't take hold, Mom. I can't take hold of some kind of a life.

LINDA. Biff, a man is not a bird, to come and go with the spring time.

BIFF. Your hair . . . (*He touches her hair.*) Your hair got so gray.

LINDA. Oh, it's been gray since you were in high school. I just stopped dyeing it, that's all.

BIFF. Dye it again, will ya? I don't want my pal looking old. (*He smiles.*)

LINDA. You're such a boy! You think you can go away for a year and . . . You've got to get it into your head now that one day you'll knock on this door and there'll be strange people here . . .

BIFF. What are you talking about? You're not even sixty, Mom.

LINDA. But what about your father?

BIFF (*lamely*). Well, I meant him too.

HAPPY. He admires Pop.

LINDA. Biff, dear, if you don't have any feeling for him, then you can't have any feeling for me.

BIFF. Sure I can, Mom.

LINDA. No. You can't just come to see me, because I love him. (*With a threat, but only a threat, of tears.*) He's the dearest man in the world to me, and I won't have anyone making him feel unwanted and low and blue. You've got to make up your mind now, darling, there's no leeway any more. Either he's your father and you pay him that respect, or else you're not to come here. I know he's not easy to get along with— nobody knows that better than me—but . . .

WILLY (*from the left, with a laugh*). Hey, hey, Biffo!

BIFF (*starting to go out after Willy*). What the hell is the matter with him? (*Happy stops him.*)

LINDA. Don't — don't go near him!

BIFF. Stop making excuses for him! He always, always wiped the floor with you. Never had an ounce of respect for you.

HAPPY. He's always had respect for . . .

BIFF. What the hell do you know about it?

HAPPY (*surlily*). Just don't call him crazy!

BIFF. He's got no character — Charley wouldn't do this. Not in his own house — spewing out that vomit from his mind.

HAPPY. Charley never had to cope with what he's got to.

BIFF. People are worse off than Willy Loman. Believe me, I've seen them!

LINDA. Then make Charley your father, Biff. You can't do that, can you? I don't say he's a great man. Willy Loman never made a lot of money. His name was never in the paper. He's not the finest character that ever lived. But he's a human being, and a terrible thing is happening to him. So attention must be paid. He's not to be allowed to fall into his grave like an old dog. Attention, attention must be finally paid to such a person. You called him crazy . . .

BIFF. I didn't mean . . .

LINDA. No, a lot of people think he's lost his — balance. But you don't have to be very smart to know what his trouble is. The man is exhausted.

HAPPY. Sure!

LINDA. A small man can be just as exhausted as a great man. He works for a company thirty-six years this March, opens up unheard-of territories to their trademark, and now in his old age they take his salary away.

HAPPY (*indignantly*). I didn't know that, Mom.

LINDA. You never asked, my dear! Now that you get your spending money someplace else you don't trouble your mind with him.

HAPPY. But I gave you money last . . .

LINDA. Christmas time, fifty dollars! To fix the hot water it cost ninety-seven fifty! For five weeks he's been on straight commission, like a beginner, an unknown!

BIFF. Those ungrateful bastards!

LINDA. Are they any worse than his sons? When he brought them business, when he was young, they were glad to see him. But now his old friends, the old buyers that loved him so and always found some order to hand him in a pinch — they're all dead, retired. He used to be able to make six, seven calls a day in Boston. Now he takes his valises out of the car and puts them back and takes them out again and he's exhausted. Instead of walking he talks now. He drives seven hundred miles, and when he gets there no one knows him any more, no one welcomes him. And what goes through a man's mind, driving seven hundred miles home without having earned a cent? Why shouldn't he talk to himself? Why? When he has to go to Charley and borrow fifty dollars a week and pretend to me that it's his pay? How long can that go on? How long? You see what I'm sitting here and waiting for? And you tell me he has no character? The man who never worked a day but for your benefit? When does he get the medal for that? Is this his reward—to turn around at the age of sixty-three and find his sons, who he loved better than his life, one a philandering bum . . .

HAPPY. Mom!

LINDA. That's all you are, my baby! (*To Biff.*) And you! What happened to the love you had for him? You were such pals! How you used to talk to him on the phone every night! How lonely he was till he could come home to you!

BIFF. All right, Mom. I'll live here in my room, and I'll get a job. I'll keep away from him, that's all.

LINDA. No, Biff. You can't stay here and fight all the time.

BIFF. He threw me out of this house, remember that.

LINDA. Why did he do that? I never knew why.

BIFF. Because I know he's a fake and he doesn't like anybody around who knows!

LINDA. Why a fake? In what way? What do you mean?

BIFF. Just don't lay it all at my feet. It's between me and him—that's all I have to say. I'll chip in from now on. He'll settle for half my paycheck. He'll be all right. I'm going to bed. (*He starts for the stairs.*)

LINDA. He won't be all right.

BIFF (*turning on the stairs, furiously*). I hate this city and I'll stay here. Now what do you want?

LINDA. He's dying, Biff.

Happy turns quickly to her, shocked.

BIFF (*after a pause*). Why is he dying?

LINDA. He's been trying to kill himself.

BIFF (*with great horror*). How?

LINDA. I live from day to day.

BIFF. What're you talking about?

LINDA. Remember I wrote you that he smashed up the car again? In February?

BIFF. Well?

LINDA. The insurance inspector came. He said that they have evidence. That all these accidents in the last year—weren't—weren't—accidents.

HAPPY. How can they tell that? That's a lie.

LINDA. It seems there's a woman . . . (*She takes a breath as:*)

BIFF (*sharply but contained*). What woman?

LINDA (*simultaneously*). . . . and this woman . . .

LINDA. What?

BIFF. Nothing. Go ahead.

LINDA. What did you say?

BIFF. Nothing. I just said what woman?

HAPPY. What about her?

LINDA. Well, it seems she was walking down the road and saw his car. She says that he wasn't driving fast at all, and that he didn't skid. She says he came to that little bridge, and then deliberately smashed into the railing, and it was only the shallowness of the water that saved him.

BIFF. Oh, no, he probably just fell asleep again.

LINDA. I don't think he fell asleep.

BIFF. Why not?

LINDA. Last month . . . (*With great difficulty.*) Oh, boys, it's so hard to say a thing like this! He's just a big stupid man to you, but I tell you there's more good in him than in many other people. (*She chokes, wipes her eyes.*) I was looking for a fuse. The lights blew out, and I went down the cellar. And behind the fuse box—it happened to fall out—was a length of rubber pipe—just short.

HAPPY. No kidding!

LINDA. There's a little attachment on the end of it. I knew right away. And sure enough, on the bottom of the water heater there's a new little nipple on the gas pipe.

HAPPY (*angrily*). That—jerk.

BIFF. Did you have it taken off?

LINDA. I'm—I'm ashamed to. How can I mention it to him? Every day I go down and take away that little rubber pipe. But, when he comes home, I put it back where it was. How can I insult him that way? I don't know what to do. I live from day to day, boys. I tell you, I know every thought in his mind. It sounds so old-fashioned and silly, but I tell you he put his whole life into you and you've turned your backs on him. (*She is bent over in the chair, weeping, her face in her hands.*) Biff, I swear to God! Biff, his life is in your hands!

HAPPY (*to Biff*). How do you like that damned fool!

BIFF (*kissing her*). All right, pal, all right. It's all settled now. I've been remiss. I know that, Mom. But now I'll stay, and I swear to you, I'll apply myself. (*Kneeling in front of her, in a fever of self-reproach.*) It's just— you see, Mom, I don't fit in business. Not that I won't try. I'll try, and I'll make good.

HAPPY. Sure you will. The trouble with you in business was you never tried to please people.

BIFF. I know, I . . .

HAPPY. Like when you worked for Harrison's. Bob Harrison said you were tops, and then you go and do some damn fool thing like whistling whole songs in the elevator like a comedian.

BIFF (*against Happy*). So what? I like to whistle sometimes.

HAPPY. You don't raise a guy to a responsible job who whistles in the elevator!

LINDA. Well, don't argue about it now.

HAPPY. Like when you'd go off and swim in the middle of the day instead of taking the line around.

BIFF (*his resentment rising*). Well, don't you run off? You take off sometimes, don't you? On a nice summer day?

HAPPY. Yeah, but I cover myself!

LINDA. Boys!

HAPPY. If I'm going to take a fade the boss can call any number where I'm supposed to be and they'll swear to him that I just left. I'll tell you something that I hate to say, Biff, but in the business world some of them think you're crazy.

BIFF (*angered*). Screw the business world!

HAPPY. All right, screw it! Great, but cover yourself!

LINDA. Hap, Hap!

BIFF. I don't care what they think! They've laughed at Dad for years, and you know why? Because we don't belong in this nuthouse of a city! We should be mixing cement on some open plain or—or carpenters. A carpenter is allowed to whistle!

Willy walks in from the entrance of the house, at left.

WILLY. Even your grandfather was better than a carpenter. (*Pause. They watch him.*) You never grew up. Bernard does not whistle in the elevator, I assure you.

BIFF (*as though to laugh Willy out of it*). Yeah, but you do, Pop.

WILLY. I never in my life whistled an elevator! And who in the business world thinks I'm crazy?

BIFF. I didn't mean it like that, Pop. Now don't make a whole thing out of it, will ya?

WILLY. Go back to the West! Be a carpenter, a cowboy, enjoy yourself!

LINDA. Willy, he was just saying . . .

WILLY. I heard what he said!

HAPPY (*trying to quiet Willy*). Hey, Pop, come on now . . .

WILLY (*continuing over Happy's line*). They laugh at me, heh? Go to Filene's, go to the Hub, go to Slattery's, Boston. Call out the name Willy Loman and see what happens! Big shot!

BIFF. All right, Pop.

WILLY. Big!

BIFF. All right!

WILLY. Why do you always insult me?

BIFF. I didn't say a word. (*To Linda.*) Did I say a word?

LINDA. He didn't say anything, Willy.

WILLY (*going to the doorway of the living room*). All right, good night, good
  night.
LINDA. Willy, dear, he just decided . . .
WILLY (*to Biff*). If you get tired hanging around tomorrow, paint the ceil-
  ing I put up in the living room.
BIFF. I'm leaving early tomorrow.
HAPPY. He's going to see Bill Oliver, Pop.
WILLY (*interestedly*). Oliver? For what?
BIFF (*with reserve, but trying, trying*). He always said he'd stake me. I'd like
  to go into business, so maybe I can take him up on it.
LINDA. Isn't that wonderful?
WILLY. Don't interrupt. What's wonderful about it? There's fifty men in
  the City of New York who'd stake him. (*To Biff.*) Sporting goods?
BIFF. I guess so. I know something about it and . . .
WILLY. He knows something about it! You know sporting goods better
  than Spalding, for God's sake! How much is he giving you?
BIFF. I don't know, I didn't even see him yet, but . . .
WILLY. Then what're you talkin' about?
BIFF (*getting angry*). Well, all I said was I'm gonna see him, that's all!
WILLY (*turning away*). Ah, you're counting your chickens again.
BIFF (*starting left for the stairs*). Oh, Jesus, I'm going to sleep!
WILLY (*calling after him*). Don't curse in this house!
BIFF (*turning*). Since when did you get so clean?
HAPPY (*trying to stop them*). Wait a . . .
WILLY. Don't use that language to me! I won't have it!
HAPPY (*grabbing Biff, shouts*). Wait a minute! I got an idea. I got a feasible
  idea. Come here, Biff, let's talk this over now, let's talk some sense here.
  When I was down in Florida last time, I thought of a great idea to sell
  sporting goods. It just came back to me. You and I, Biff—we have a
  line, the Loman Line. We train a couple of weeks, and put on a couple
  of exhibitions, see?
WILLY. That's an idea!
HAPPY. Wait! We form two basketball teams, see? Two waterpolo teams.
  We play each other. It's a million dollars' worth of publicity. Two
  brothers, see? The Loman Brothers. Displays in the Royal Palms—all
  the hotels. And banners over the ring and the basketball court: "Loman
  Brothers." Baby, we could sell sporting goods!
WILLY. That is a one-million-dollar idea!
LINDA. Marvelous!
BIFF. I'm in great shape as far as that's concerned.
HAPPY. And the beauty of it is, Biff, it wouldn't be like a business. We'd
  be out playin' ball again.
BIFF (*enthused*). Yeah, that's . . .
WILLY. Million-dollar . . .

HAPPY. And you wouldn't get fed up with it, Biff. It'd be the family again. There'd be the old honor, and comradeship, and if you wanted to go off for a swim or somethin'—well, you'd do it! Without some smart cooky gettin' up ahead of you!

WILLY. Lick the world! You guys together could absolutely lick the civilized world.

BIFF. I'll see Oliver tomorrow. Hap, if we could work that out . . .

LINDA. Maybe things are beginning to . . .

WILLY (*wildly enthused, to Linda*). Stop interrupting! (*To Biff.*) But don't wear sport jacket and slacks when you see Oliver.

BIFF. No, I'll . . .

WILLY. A business suit, and talk as little as possible, and don't crack any jokes.

BIFF. He did like me. Always liked me.

LINDA. He loved you!

WILLY (*to Linda*). Will you stop! (*To Biff.*) Walk in very serious. You are not applying for a boy's job. Money is to pass. Be quiet, fine, and serious. Everybody likes a kidder, but nobody lends him money.

HAPPY. I'll try to get some myself, Biff. I'm sure I can.

WILLY. I see great things for you kids, I think your troubles are over. But remember, start big and you'll end big. Ask for fifteen. How much you gonna ask for?

BIFF. Gee, I don't know . . .

WILLY. And don't say "Gee." "Gee" is a boy's word. A man walking in for fifteen thousand dollars does not say "Gee!"

BIFF. Ten, I think, would be top though.

WILLY. Don't be so modest. You always started too low. Walk in with a big laugh. Don't look worried. Start off with a couple of your good stories to lighten things up. It's not what you say, it's how you say it— because personality always wins the day.

LINDA. Oliver always thought the highest of him . . .

WILLY. Will you let me talk?

BIFF. Don't yell at her, Pop, will ya?

WILLY (*angrily*). I was talking, wasn't I?

BIFF. I don't like you yelling at her all the time, and I'm tellin' you, that's all.

WILLY. What're you, takin' over this house?

LINDA. Willy . . .

WILLY (*turning to her*). Don't take his side all the time, goddammit!

BIFF (*furiously*). Stop yelling at her!

WILLY (*suddenly pulling on his cheek, beaten down, guilt ridden*). Give my best to Bill Oliver—he may remember me. (*He exits through the living room doorway.*)

LINDA (*her voice subdued*). What'd you have to start that for? (*Biff turns away.*) You see how sweet he was as soon as you talked hopefully? (*She goes over to Biff.*) Come up and say good night to him. Don't let him go to bed that way.

HAPPY. Come on, Biff, let's buck him up.

LINDA. Please, dear. Just say good night. It takes so little to make him happy. Come. (*She goes through the living room doorway, calling upstairs from within the living room.*) Your pajamas are hanging in the bathroom, Willy!

HAPPY (*looking toward where Linda went out*). What a woman! They broke the mold when they made her. You know that, Biff.

BIFF. He's off salary. My God, working on commission!

HAPPY. Well, let's face it: he's no hot-shot selling man. Except that sometimes, you have to admit, he's a sweet personality.

BIFF (*deciding*). Lend me ten bucks, will ya? I want to buy some new ties.

HAPPY. I'll take you to a place I know. Beautiful stuff. Wear one of my striped shirts tomorrow.

BIFF. She got gray. Mom got awful old. Gee, I'm gonna go in to Oliver tomorrow and knock him for a . . .

HAPPY. Come on up. Tell that to Dad. Let's give him a whirl. Come on.

BIFF (*steamed up*). You know, with ten thousand bucks, boy!

HAPPY (*as they go into the living room*). That's the talk, Biff, that's the first time I've heard the old confidence out of you! (*From within the living room, fading off*) You're gonna live with me, kid, and any babe you want just say the word . . . (*The last lines are hardly heard. They are mounting the stairs to their parents' bedroom.*)

LINDA (*entering her bedroom and addressing Willy, who is in the bathroom. She is straightening the bed for him*). Can you do anything about the shower? It drips.

WILLY (*from the bathroom*). All of a sudden everything falls to pieces. Goddam plumbing, oughta be sued, those people. I hardly finished putting it in and the thing . . . (*His words rumble off.*)

LINDA. I'm just wondering if Oliver will remember him. You think he might?

WILLY (*coming out of the bathroom in his pajamas*). Remember him? What's the matter with you, you crazy? If he'd've stayed with Oliver he'd be on top by now! Wait'll Oliver gets a look at him. You don't know the average caliber any more. The average young man today — (*he is getting into bed*) — is got a caliber of zero. Greatest thing in the world for him was to bum around.

Biff and Happy enter the bedroom. Slight pause.

WILLY (*stops short, looking at Biff*). Glad to hear it, boy.

HAPPY. He wanted to say good night to you, sport.

WILLY (*to Biff*). Yeah. Knock him dead, boy. What'd you want to tell me?

BIFF. Just take it easy, Pop. Good night. (*He turns to go.*)

WILLY (*unable to resist*). And if anything falls off the desk while you're talking to him — like a package or something — don't you pick it up. They have office boys for that.

LINDA. I'll make a big breakfast . . .

WILLY. Will you let me finish? (*To Biff.*) Tell him you were in the business in the West. Not farm work.

BIFF. All right, Dad.

LINDA. I think everything . . .

WILLY (*going right through her speech*). And don't undersell yourself. No less than fifteen thousand dollars.

BIFF (*unable to bear him*). Okay. Good night, Mom. (*He starts moving.*)

WILLY. Because you got a greatness in you, Biff, remember that. You got all kinds of greatness . . . (*He lies back, exhausted. Biff walks out.*)

LINDA (*calling after Biff*). Sleep well, darling!

HAPPY. I'm gonna get married, Mom. I wanted to tell you.

LINDA. Go to sleep, dear.

HAPPY (*going*). I just wanted to tell you.

WILLY. Keep up the good work. (*Happy exits.*) God . . . remember that Ebbets Field game? The championship of the city?

LINDA. Just rest. Should I sing to you?

WILLY. Yeah. Sing to me. (*Linda hums a soft lullaby.*) When that team came out—he was the tallest, remember?

LINDA. Oh, yes. And in gold.

Biff enters the darkened kitchen, takes a cigarette, and leaves the house. He comes downstage into a golden pool of light. He smokes, staring at the night.

WILLY. Like a young god. Hercules—something like that. And the sun, the sun all around him. Remember how he waved to me? Right up from the field, with the representatives of three colleges standing by? And the buyers I brought, and the cheers when he came out—Loman, Loman, Loman! God Almighty, he'll be great yet. A star like that, magnificent, can never really fade away!

The light on Willy is fading. The gas heater begins to glow through the kitchen wall, near the stairs, a blue flame beneath red coils.

LINDA (*timidly*). Willy dear, what has he got against you?

WILLY. I'm so tired. Don't talk any more.

Biff slowly returns to the kitchen. He stops, stares toward the heater.

LINDA. Will you ask Howard to let you work in New York?

WILLY. First thing in the morning. Everything'll be all right.

Biff reaches behind the heater and draws out a length of rubber tubing. He is horrified and turns his head toward Willy's room, still dimly lit, from which the strains of Linda's desperate but monotonous humming rise.

WILLY (*staring through the window into the moonlight*). Gee, look at the moon moving between the buildings!

Biff wraps the tubing around his hand and quickly goes up the stairs.

ACT 2

Scene: *Music is heard, gay and bright. The curtain rises as the music fades away. Willy, in shirt sleeves, is sitting at the kitchen table, sipping coffee, his hat in his lap. Linda is filling his cup when she can.*

WILLY. Wonderful coffee. Meal in itself.

LINDA. Can I make you some eggs?

WILLY. No. Take a breath.

LINDA. You look so rested, dear.

WILLY. I slept like a dead one. First time in months. Imagine, sleeping till ten on a Tuesday morning. Boys left nice and early, heh?

LINDA. They were out of here by eight o'clock.

WILLY. Good work!

LINDA. It was so thrilling to see them leaving together. I can't get over the shaving lotion in this house!

WILLY (*smiling*). Mmm . . .

LINDA. Biff was very changed this morning. His whole attitude seemed to be hopeful. He couldn't wait to get downtown to see Oliver.

WILLY. He's heading for a change. There's no question, there simply are certain men that take longer to get—solidified. How did he dress?

LINDA. His blue suit. He's so handsome in that suit. He could be a— anything in that suit!

Willy gets up from the table. Linda holds his jacket for him.

WILLY. There's no question, no question at all. Gee, on the way home tonight I'd like to buy some seeds.

LINDA (*laughing*). That'd be wonderful. But not enough sun gets back there. Nothing'll grow any more.

WILLY. You wait, kid, before it's all over we're gonna get a little place out in the country, and I'll raise some vegetables, a couple of chickens . . .

LINDA. You'll do it yet, dear.

Willy walks out of his jacket. Linda follows him.

WILLY. And they'll get married, and come for a weekend. I'd build a little guest house. 'Cause I got so many fine tools, all I'd need would be a little lumber and some peace of mind.

LINDA (*joyfully*). I sewed the lining . . .

WILLY. I could build two guest houses, so they'd both come. Did he decide how much he's going to ask Oliver for?

LINDA (*getting him into the jacket*). He didn't mention it, but I imagine ten or fifteen thousand. You going to talk to Howard today?

WILLY. Yeah. I'll put it to him straight and simple. He'll just have to take me off the road.

LINDA. And Willy, don't forget to ask for a little advance, because we've got the insurance premium. It's the grace period now.

WILLY. That's a hundred . . . ?

LINDA. A hundred and eight, sixty-eight. Because we're a little short again.

WILLY. Why are we short?

LINDA. Well, you had the motor job on the car . . .

WILLY. That goddam Studebaker!

LINDA. And you got one more payment on the refrigerator . . .

WILLY. But it just broke again!

LINDA. Well, it's old, dear.

WILLY. I told you we should've bought a well-advertised machine. Charley bought a General Electric and it's twenty years old and it's still good, that son-of-a-bitch.

LINDA. But, Willy . . .

WILLY. Whoever heard of a Hastings refrigerator? Once in my life I would like to own something outright before it's broken! I'm always in a race with the junkyard! I just finished paying for the car and it's on its last legs. The refrigerator consumes belts like a goddamn maniac. They time those things. They time them so when you finally paid for them, they're used up.

LINDA (*buttoning up his jacket as he unbuttons it*). All told, about two hundred dollars would carry us, dear. But that includes the last payment on the mortgage. After this payment, Willy, the house belongs to us.

WILLY. It's twenty-five years!

LINDA. Biff was nine years old when we bought it.

WILLY. Well, that's a great thing. To weather a twenty-five year mortgage is . . .

LINDA. It's an accomplishment.

WILLY. All the cement, the lumber, the reconstruction I put in this house! There ain't a crack to be found in it any more.

LINDA. Well, it served its purpose.

WILLY. What purpose? Some stranger'll come along, move in, and that's that. If only Biff would take this house, and raise a family . . . (*He starts to go.*) Good-by, I'm late.

LINDA (*suddenly remembering*). Oh, I forgot! You're supposed to meet them for dinner.

WILLY. Me?

LINDA. At Frank's Chop House on Forty-eighth near Sixth Avenue.

WILLY. Is that so! How about you?

LINDA. No, just the three of you. They're gonna blow you to a big meal!

WILLY. Don't say! Who thought of that?

LINDA. Biff came to me this morning, Willy, and he said, "Tell Dad, we want to blow him to a big meal." Be there six o'clock. You and your two boys are going to have dinner.

WILLY. Gee whiz! That's really somethin'. I'm gonna knock Howard for a loop, kid. I'll get an advance, and I'll come home with a New York job. Goddammit, now I'm gonna do it!

LINDA. Oh, that's the spirit, Willy!

WILLY. I will never get behind a wheel the rest of my life!

LINDA. It's changing, Willy, I can feel it changing!

WILLY. Beyond a question. G'by, I'm late. (*He starts to go again.*)

LINDA (*calling after him as she runs to the kitchen table for a handkerchief*). You got your glasses?

WILLY (*feels for them, then comes back in*). Yeah, yeah, got my glasses.

LINDA (*giving him the handkerchief*). And a handkerchief.

WILLY. Yeah, handkerchief.

LINDA. And your saccharine?

WILLY. Yeah, my saccharine.

LINDA. Be careful on the subway stairs.

She kisses him, and a silk stocking is seen hanging from her hand. Willy notices it.

WILLY. Will you stop mending stockings? At least while I'm in the house. It gets me nervous. I can't tell you. Please.

Linda hides the stocking in her hand as she follows Willy across the forestage in front of the house.

LINDA. Remember, Frank's Chop House.

WILLY (*passing the apron*). Maybe beets would grow out there.

LINDA (*laughing*). But you tried so many times.

WILLY. Yeah. Well, don't work hard today. (*He disappears around the right corner of the house.*)

LINDA. Be careful!

As Willy vanishes, Linda waves to him. Suddenly the phone rings. She runs across the stage and into the kitchen and lifts it.

LINDA. Hello? Oh, Biff! I'm so glad you called, I just . . . Yes, sure, I just told him. Yes, he'll be there for dinner at six o'clock, I didn't forget. Listen, I was just dying to tell you. You know that little rubber pipe I told you about? That he connected to the gas heater? I finally decided to go down the cellar this morning and take it away and destroy it. But it's gone! Imagine? He took it away himself, it isn't there! (*She listens.*) When? Oh, then you took it. Oh—nothing, it's just that I'd hoped he'd taken it away himself. Oh, I'm not worried, darling, because this morning he left in such high spirits, it was like the old days! I'm not afraid any more. Did Mr. Oliver see you? . . . Well, you wait there then. And make a nice impression on him, darling. Just don't perspire too much before you see him. And have a nice time with Dad. He may have big news too! . . . That's right, a New York job. And be sweet to him tonight, dear. Be loving to him. Because he's only a little boat looking for a harbor. (*She is trembling with sorrow and joy.*) Oh, that's wonderful, Biff, you'll save his life. Thanks, darling. Just put your arm around him when he comes into the restaurant. Give him a smile. That's the boy . . . Good-by, dear. . . . You got your comb? . . . That's fine. Good-by, Biff dear.

In the middle of her speech, Howard Wagner, thirty-six, wheels in a small type-writer table on which is a wire-recording machine and proceeds to plug it in. This is on the left forestage. Light slowly fades on Linda as it rises on Howard. Howard is intent on threading the machine and only glances over his shoulder as Willy appears.

WILLY. Pst! Pst!

HOWARD. Hello, Willy, come in.

WILLY. Like to have a little talk with you, Howard.

HOWARD. Sorry to keep you waiting. I'll be with you in a minute.

WILLY. What's that, Howard?

HOWARD. Didn't you ever see one of these? Wire recorder.

WILLY. Oh. Can we talk a minute?

HOWARD. Records things. Just got delivery yesterday. Been driving me crazy, the most terrific machine I ever saw in my life. I was up all night with it.

WILLY. What do you do with it?

HOWARD. I bought it for dictation, but you can do anything with it. Listen to this. I had it home last night. Listen to what I picked up. The first one is my daughter. Get this. (*He flicks the switch and "Roll out the Barrel" is heard being whistled.*) Listen to that kid whistle.

WILLY. That is lifelike, isn't it?

HOWARD. Seven years old. Get that tone.

WILLY. Ts, ts. Like to ask a little favor if you . . .

The whistling breaks off, and the voice of Howard's daughter is heard.

HIS DAUGHTER. "Now you, Daddy."

HOWARD. She's crazy for me! (*Again the same song is whistled.*) That's me! Ha! (*He winks.*)

WILLY. You're very good!

The whistling breaks off again. The machine runs silent for a moment.

HOWARD. Sh! Get this now, this is my son.

HIS SON. "The capital of Alabama is Montgomery; the capital of Arizona is Phoenix; the capital of Arkansas is Little Rock; the capital of California is Sacramento . . ." (*and on, and on.*)

HOWARD (*holding up five fingers*). Five years old, Willy!

WILLY. He'll make an announcer some day!

HIS SON (*continuing*). "The capital . . ."

HOWARD. Get that—alphabetical order! (*The machine breaks off suddenly.*) Wait a minute. The maid kicked the plug out.

WILLY. It certainly is a . . .

HOWARD. Sh, for God's sake!

HIS SON. "It's nine o'clock, Bulova watch time. So I have to go to sleep."

WILLY. That really is . . .

HOWARD. Wait a minute! The next is my wife.

They wait.

HOWARD'S VOICE. "Go on, say something." (*pause.*) "Well, you gonna talk?"

HIS WIFE. "I can't think of anything."

HOWARD'S VOICE. "Well, talk—it's turning."

HIS WIFE (*shyly, beaten*). "Hello." (*Silence.*) "Oh, Howard, I can't talk into this . . ."

HOWARD (*snapping the machine off*). That was my wife.

WILLY. That is a wonderful machine. Can we . . .

HOWARD. I tell you, Willy, I'm gonna take my camera, and my bandsaw, and all my hobbies, and out they go. This is the most fascinating relaxation I ever found.

WILLY. I think I'll get one myself.

HOWARD. Sure, they're only a hundred and a half. You can't do without it. Supposing you wanna hear Jack Benny, see? But you can't be at home at that hour. So you tell the maid to turn the radio on when Jack Benny comes on, and this automatically goes on with the radio . . .

WILLY. And when you come home you . . .

HOWARD. You can come home twelve o'clock, one o'clock, any time you like, and you get yourself a Coke and sit yourself down, throw the switch, and there's Jack Benny's program in the middle of the night!

WILLY. I'm definitely going to get one. Because lots of times I'm on the road, and I think to myself, what I must be missing on the radio!

HOWARD. Don't you have a radio in the car?

WILLY. Well, yeah, but who ever thinks of turning it on?

HOWARD. Say, aren't you supposed to be in Boston?

WILLY. That's what I want to talk to you about, Howard. You got a minute? (*He draws a chair in from the wing.*)

HOWARD. What happened? What're you doing here?

WILLY. Well . . .

HOWARD. You didn't crack up again, did you?

WILLY. Oh, no. No . . .

HOWARD. Geez, you had me worried there for a minute. What's the trouble?

WILLY. Well, tell you the truth, Howard. I've come to the decision that I'd rather not travel any more.

HOWARD. Not travel! Well, what'll you do?

WILLY. Remember, Christmas time, when you had the party here? You said you'd try to think of some spot for me here in town.

HOWARD. With us?

WILLY. Well, sure.

HOWARD. Oh, yeah, yeah. I remember. Well, I couldn't think of anything for you, Willy.

WILLY. I tell ya, Howard. The kids are all grown up, y'know. I don't need much any more. If I could take home—well, sixty-five dollars a week, I could swing it.

HOWARD. Yeah, but Willy, see I . . .

WILLY. I tell ya why, Howard. Speaking frankly and between the two of us, y'know—I'm just a little tired.

HOWARD. Oh, I could understand that, Willy. But you're a road man, Willy, and we do a road business. We've only got a half-dozen salesmen on the floor here.

WILLY. God knows, Howard. I never asked a favor of any man. But I was with the firm when your father used to carry you in here in his arms.

HOWARD. I know that, Willy, but . . .

WILLY. Your father came to me the day you were born and asked me what I thought of the name Howard, may he rest in peace.

HOWARD. I appreciate that, Willy, but there just is no spot here for you. If I had a spot I'd slam you right in, but I just don't have a single solitary spot.

He looks for his lighter. Willy has picked it up and gives it to him. Pause.

WILLY (*with increasing anger*). Howard, all I need to set my table is fifty dollars a week.

HOWARD. But where am I going to put you, kid?

WILLY. Look, it isn't a question of whether I can sell merchandise, is it?

HOWARD. No, but it's business, kid, and everybody's gotta pull his own weight.

WILLY (*desperately*). Just let me tell you a story, Howard . . .

HOWARD. 'Cause you gotta admit, business is business.

WILLY (*angrily*). Business is definitely business, but just listen for a minute. You don't understand this. When I was a boy—eighteen, nineteen—I was already on the road. And there was a question in my mind as to whether selling had a future for me. Because in those days I had a yearning to go to Alaska. See, there were three gold strikes in one month in Alaska, and I felt like going out. Just for the ride, you might say.

HOWARD (*barely interested*). Don't say.

WILLY. Oh, yeah, my father lived many years in Alaska. He was an adventurous man. We've got quite a little streak of self-reliance in our family. I thought I'd go out with my older brother and try to locate him, and maybe settle in the North with the old man. And I was almost decided to go, when I met a salesman in the Parker House. His name was Dave Singleman. And he was eighty-four years old, and he'd drummed merchandise in thirty-one states. And old Dave, he'd go up to his room, y'understand, put on his green velvet slippers—I'll never forget—and pick up his phone and call the buyers, and without ever leaving his room, at the age of eighty-four, he made his living. And when I saw that, I realized that selling was the greatest career a man could want. 'Cause what could be more satisfying than to be able to go, at the age of eighty-four, into twenty or thirty different cities, and pick up a phone, and be remembered and loved and helped by so many different people? Do you know? when he died—and by the way he died the death of a salesman, in his green velvet slippers in the smoker of the New York, New Haven and Hartford, going into Boston —when he died, hundreds of salesmen and buyers were at his funeral. Things were sad on a lotta trains for months after that. (*He stands up. Howard has not looked at him.*) In those days there was personality in it, Howard. There was respect, and comradeship, and gratitude in it. Today, it's all cut and dried, and there's no chance for bringing friendship to bear— or personality. You see what I mean? They don't know me any more.

HOWARD (*moving away, to the right*). That's just the thing, Willy.

WILLY. If I had forty dollars a week—that's all I'd need. Forty dollars, Howard.

HOWARD. Kid, I can't take blood from a stone, I . . .

WILLY (*desperation is on him now*). Howard, the year Al Smith was nominated, your father came to me and . . .

HOWARD (*starting to go off*). I've got to see some people, kid.

WILLY (*stopping him*). I'm talking about your father! There were promises made across this desk! You mustn't tell me you've got people to see—I put thirty-four years into this firm, Howard, and now I can't pay my insurance! You can't eat the orange and throw the peel away—a man is not a piece of fruit! (*After a pause.*) Now pay attention. Your father—in 1928 I had a big year. I averaged a hundred and seventy dollars a week in commissions.

HOWARD (*impatiently*). Now, Willy, you never averaged . . .

WILLY (*banging his hand on the desk*). I averaged a hundred and seventy dollars a week in the year of 1928! And your father came to me—or rather, I was in the office here—it was right over this desk—and he put his hand on my shoulder . . .

HOWARD (*getting up*). You'll have to excuse me, Willy, I gotta see some people. Pull yourself together. (*Going out.*) I'll be back in a little while.

On Howard's exit, the light on his chair grows very bright and strange.

WILLY. Pull myself together! What the hell did I say to him? My God, I was yelling at him! How could I? (*Willy breaks off, staring at the light, which occupies the chair, animating it. He approaches this chair, standing across the desk from it.*) Frank, Frank, don't you remember what you told me that time? How you put your hand on my shoulder, and Frank . . . (*He leans on the desk and as he speaks the dead man's name he accidentally switches on the recorder, and instantly*)

HOWARD'S SON. "... of New York is Albany. The capital of Ohio is Cincinnati, the capital of Rhode Island is ..." (*The recitation continues.*)

WILLY (*leaping away with fright, shouting*). Ha! Howard! Howard! Howard!

HOWARD (*rushing in*). What happened?

WILLY (*pointing at the machine, which continues nasally, childishly, with the capital cities*). Shut it off! Shut it off!

HOWARD (*pulling the plug out*). Look, Willy ...

WILLY (*pressing his hands to his eyes*). I gotta get myself some coffee. I'll get some coffee ...

Willy starts to walk out. Howard stops him.

HOWARD (*rolling up the cord*). Willy, look ...

WILLY. I'll go to Boston.

HOWARD. Willy, you can't go to Boston for us.

WILLY. Why can't I go?

HOWARD. I don't want you to represent us. I've been meaning to tell you for a long time now.

WILLY. Howard, are you firing me?

HOWARD. I think you need a good long rest, Willy.

WILLY. Howard ...

HOWARD. And when you feel better, come back, and we'll see if we can work something out.

WILLY. But I gotta earn money, Howard. I'm in no position to ...

HOWARD. Where are your sons? Why don't your sons give you a hand?

WILLY. They're working on a very big deal.

HOWARD. This is no time for false pride, Willy. You go to your sons and you tell them that you're tired. You've got two great boys, haven't you?

WILLY. Oh, no question, no question, but in the meantime ...

HOWARD. Then that's that, heh?

WILLY. All right, I'll go to Boston tomorrow.

HOWARD. No, no.

WILLY. I can't throw myself on my sons. I'm not a cripple!

HOWARD. Look, kid, I'm busy this morning.

WILLY (*grasping Howard's arm*). Howard, you've got to let me go to Boston!

HOWARD (*hard, keeping himself under control*). I've got a line of people to see this morning. Sit down, take five minutes, and pull yourself together, and then go home, will ya? I need the office, Willy. (*He starts to go, turns, remembering the recorder, starts to push off the table holding the recorder.*) Oh, yeah. Whenever you can this week, stop by and drop off the samples. You'll feel better, Willy, and then come back and we'll talk. Pull yourself together, kid, there's people outside.

Howard exits, pushing the table off left. Willy stares into space, exhausted. Now the music is heard—Ben's music—first distantly, then closer, closer. As Willy speaks, Ben enters from the right. He carries valise and umbrella.

WILLY. Oh, Ben, how did you do it? What is the answer? Did you wind
up the Alaska deal already?

BEN. Doesn't take much time if you know what you're doing. Just a short
business trip. Boarding ship in an hour. Wanted to say good-by.

WILLY. Ben, I've got to talk to you.

BEN (*glancing at his watch*). Haven't the time, William.

WILLY (*crossing the apron to Ben*). Ben, nothing's working out. I don't know
what to do.

BEN. Now, look here, William. I've bought timberland in Alaska and I
need a man to look after things for me.

WILLY. God, timberland! Me and my boys in those grand outdoors!

BEN. You've a new continent at your doorstep, William. Get out of these
cities, they're full of talk and time payments and courts of law. Screw
on your fists and you can fight for a fortune up there.

WILLY. Yes, yes! Linda, Linda!

Linda enters as of old, with the wash.

LINDA. Oh, you're back?

BEN. I haven't much time.

WILLY. No, wait! Linda, he's got a proposition for me in Alaska.

LINDA. But you've got . . . (*To Ben.*) He's got a beautiful job here.

WILLY. But in Alaska, kid, I could . . .

LINDA. You're doing well enough, Willy!

BEN (*to Linda*). Enough for what, my dear?

LINDA (*frightened of Ben and angry at him*). Don't say those things to him!
Enough to be happy right here, right now. (*To Willy, while Ben laughs.*)
Why must everybody conquer the world? You're well liked, and the
boys love you, and someday—(*To Ben*)—why, old man Wagner told him
just the other day that if he keeps it up he'll be a member of the firm,
didn't he, Willy?

WILLY. Sure, sure. I am building something with this firm, Ben, and if
a man is building something he must be on the right track, mustn't he?

BEN. What are you building? Lay your hand on it. Where is it?

WILLY (*hesitantly*). That's true, Linda, there's nothing.

LINDA. Why? (*To Ben.*) There's a man eighty-four years old . . .

WILLY. That's right, Ben, that's right. When I look at that man I say, what
is there to worry about?

BEN. Bah!

WILLY. It's true, Ben. All he has to do is go into any city, pick up the
phone, and he's making his living and you know why?

BEN (*picking up his valise*). I've got to go.

WILLY (*holding Ben back*). Look at this boy!

*Biff, in his high school sweater, enters carrying suitcase. Happy carries Biff's shoul-
der guards, gold helmet, and football pants.*

WILLY. Without a penny to his name, three great universities are begging for him, and from there the sky's the limit, because it's not what you do, Ben. It's who you know and the smile on your face! It's contacts, Ben, contacts! The whole wealth of Alaska passes over the lunch table at the Commodore Hotel, and that's the wonder, the wonder of this country, that a man can end with diamonds here on the basis of being liked! (*He turns to Biff.*) And that's why when you get out on that field today it's important. Because thousands of people will be rooting for you and loving you. (*To Ben, who has again begun to leave.*) And Ben! when he walks into a business office his name will sound out like a bell and all the doors will open to him! I've seen it, Ben, I've seen it a thousand times! You can't feel it with your hand like timber, but it's there!

BEN. Good-by, William.

WILLY. Ben, am I right? Don't you think I'm right? I value your advice.

BEN. There's a new continent at your doorstep, William. You could walk out rich. Rich! (*He is gone.*)

WILLY. We'll do it here, Ben! You hear me? We're gonna do it here!

Young Bernard rushes in. The gay music of the Boys is heard.

BERNARD. Oh, gee, I was afraid you left already!

WILLY. Why? What time is it?

BERNARD. It's half-past one!

WILLY. Well, come on, everybody! Ebbets Field next stop! Where's the pennants? (*He rushes through the wall-line of the kitchen and out into the living room.*)

LINDA (*to Biff*). Did you pack fresh underwear?

BIFF (*who has been limbering up*). I want to go!

BERNARD. Biff, I'm carrying your helmet, ain't I?

HAPPY. No, I'm carrying the helmet.

BERNARD. Oh, Biff, you promised me.

HAPPY. I'm carrying the helmet.

BERNARD. How am I going to get in the locker room?

LINDA. Let him carry the shoulder guards. (*She puts her coat and hat on in the kitchen.*)

BERNARD. Can I, Biff? 'Cause I told everybody I'm going to be in the locker room.

HAPPY. In Ebbets Field it's the clubhouse.

BERNARD. I meant the clubhouse. Biff!

HAPPY. Biff!

BIFF (*grandly, after a slight pause*). Let him carry the shoulder guards.

HAPPY (*as he gives Bernard the shoulder guards*). Stay close to us now.

Willy rushes in with the pennants.

WILLY (*handing them out*). Everybody wave when Biff comes out on the field. (*Happy and Bernard run off.*) You set now, boy?

The music has died away.

BIFF. Ready to go, Pop. Every muscle is ready.

WILLY (*at the edge of the apron*). You realize what this means?

BIFF. That's right, Pop.

WILLY (*feeling Biff's muscles*). You're comin' home this afternoon captain of the All-Scholastic Championship Team of the City of New York.

BIFF. I got it, Pop. And remember, pal, when I take off my helmet, that touchdown is for you.

WILLY. Let's go! (*He is starting out, with his arm around Biff, when Charley enters, as of old, in knickers.*) I got no room for you, Charley.

CHARLEY. Room? For what?

WILLY. In the car.

CHARLEY. You goin' for a ride? I wanted to shoot some casino.

WILLY (*furiously*). Casino! (*Incredulously.*) Don't you realize what today is?

LINDA. Oh, he knows, Willy. He's just kidding you.

WILLY. That's nothing to kid about!

CHARLEY. No, Linda, what's goin' on?

LINDA. He's playing in Ebbets Field.

CHARLEY. Baseball in this weather?

WILLY. Don't talk to him. Come on, come on! (*He is pushing them out.*)

CHARLEY. Wait a minute, didn't you hear the news?

WILLY. What?

CHARLEY. Don't you listen to the radio? Ebbets Field just blew up.

WILLY. You go to hell! (*Charley laughs. Pushing them out.*) Come on, come on! We're late.

CHARLEY (*as they go*). Knock a homer, Biff, knock a homer!

WILLY (*the last to leave, turning to Charley*). I don't think that was funny, Charley. This is the greatest day of his life.

CHARLEY. Willy, when are you going to grow up?

WILLY. Yeah, heh? When this game is over, Charley, you'll be laughing out of the other side of your face. They'll be calling him another Red Grange. Twenty-five thousand a year.

CHARLEY (*kidding*). Is that so?

WILLY. Yeah, that's so.

CHARLEY. Well, then, I'm sorry, Willy. But tell me something.

WILLY. What?

CHARLEY. Who is Red Grange?

WILLY. Put up your hands. Goddam you, put up your hands!

Charley, chuckling, shakes his head and walks away, around the left corner of the stage. Willy follows him. The music rises to a mocking frenzy.

WILLY. Who the hell do you think you are, better than everybody else? You don't know everything, you big, ignorant, stupid . . . Put up your hands!

Light rises, on the right side of the forestage, on a small table in the reception room of Charley's office. Traffic sounds are heard. Bernard, now mature, sits whistling to himself. A pair of tennis rackets and an old overnight bag are on the door beside him.

WILLY (*offstage*). What are you walking away for? Don't walk away! If you're going to say something say it to my face! I know you laugh at me behind my back. You'll laugh out of the other side of your god-dam face after this game. Touchdown! Touchdown! Eighty thousand people! Touchdown! Right between the goal posts.

Bernard is a quiet, earnest, but self-assured young man. Willy's voice is coming from right upstage now. Bernard lowers his feet off the table and listens. Jenny, his father's secretary, enters.

JENNY (*distressed*). Say, Bernard, will you go out in the hall?

BERNARD. What is that noise? Who is it?

JENNY. Mr. Loman. He just got off the elevator.

BERNARD (*getting up*). Who's he arguing with?

JENNY. Nobody. There's nobody with him. I can't deal with him any more, and your father gets all upset every time he comes. I've got a lot of typing to do, and your father's waiting to sign it. Will you see him?

WILLY (*entering*). Touchdown! Touch—(*He sees Jenny.*) Jenny, Jenny, good to see you. How're ya? Workin'? Or still honest?

JENNY. Fine. How've you been feeling?

WILLY. Not much any more, Jenny. Ha, ha! (*He is surprised to see the rackets.*)

BERNARD. Hello, Uncle Willy.

WILLY (*almost shocked*). Bernard! Well, look who's here! (*He comes quickly, guiltily, to Bernard and warmly shakes his hand.*)

BERNARD. How are you? Good to see you.

WILLY. What are you doing here?

BERNARD. Oh, just stopped by to see Pop. Get off my feet till my train leaves. I'm going to Washington in a few minutes.

WILLY. Is he in?

BERNARD. Yes, he's in his office with the accountant. Sit down.

WILLY (*sitting down*). What're you going to do in Washington?

BERNARD. Oh, just a case I've got there, Willy.

WILLY. That so? (*Indicating the rackets.*) You going to play tennis there?

BERNARD. I'm staying with a friend who's got a court.

WILLY. Don't say. His own tennis court. Must be fine people, I bet.

BERNARD. They are, very nice. Dad tells me Biff's in town.

WILLY (*with a big smile*). Yeah, Biff's in. Working on a very big deal, Bernard.

BERNARD. What's Biff doing?

WILLY. Well, he's been doing very big things in the West. But he decided to establish himself here. Very big. We're having dinner. Did I hear your wife had a boy?

BERNARD. That's right. Our second.

WILLY. Two boys! What do you know!

BERNARD. What kind of a deal has Biff got?

WILLY. Well, Bill Oliver—very big sporting-goods man—he wants Biff very badly. Called him in from the West. Long distance, carte blanche, special deliveries. Your friends have their own private tennis court?

BERNARD. You still with the old firm, Willy?

WILLY (*after a pause*). I'm—I'm overjoyed to see how you made the grade, Bernard, overjoyed. It's an encouraging thing to see a young man really—really . . . Looks very good for Biff—very . . . (*He breaks off, then.*) Bernard . . . (*He is so full of emotion, he breaks off again.*)

BERNARD. What is it, Willy?

WILLY (*small and alone*). What—what's the secret?

BERNARD. What secret?

WILLY. How—how did you? Why didn't he ever catch on?

BERNARD. I wouldn't know that, Willy.

WILLY (*confidentially, desperately*). You were his friend, his boyhood friend. There's something I don't understand about it. His life ended after that Ebbets Field game. From the age of seventeen nothing good ever happened to him.

BERNARD. He never trained himself for anything.

WILLY. But he did, he did. After high school he took so many correspondence courses. Radio mechanics; television; God knows what, and never made the slightest mark.

BERNARD (*taking off his glasses*). Willy, do you want to talk candidly?

WILLY (*rising, faces Bernard*). I regard you as a very brilliant man, Bernard. I value your advice.

BERNARD. Oh, the hell with the advice, Willy. I couldn't advise you. There's just one thing I've always wanted to ask you. When he was supposed to graduate, and the math teacher flunked him . . .

WILLY. Oh, that son-of-a-bitch ruined his life.

BERNARD. Yeah, but, Willy, all he had to do was go to summer school and make up that subject.

WILLY. That's right, that's right.

BERNARD. Did you tell him not to go to summer school?

WILLY. Me? I begged him to go. I ordered him to go!

BERNARD. Then why wouldn't he go?

WILLY. Why? Why! Bernard, that question has been trailing me like a ghost for the last fifteen years. He flunked the subject, and laid down and died like a hammer hit him!

BERNARD. Take it easy, kid.

WILLY. Let me talk to you—I got nobody to talk to. Bernard, Bernard, was it my fault? Y'see? It keeps going around in my mind, maybe I did something to him. I got nothing to give him.

BERNARD. Don't take it so hard.

WILLY. Why did he lay down? What is the story there? You were his friend!

BERNARD. Willy, I remember, it was June, and our grades came out. And he'd flunked math.

WILLY. That son-of-a-bitch!

BERNARD. No, it wasn't right then. Biff just got very angry, I remember, and he was ready to enroll in summer school.

WILLY (*surprised*). He was?

BERNARD. He wasn't beaten by it at all. But then, Willy, he disappeared from the block for almost a month. And I got the idea that he'd gone up to New England to see you. Did he have a talk with you then?

Willy stares in silence.

BERNARD. Willy?

WILLY (*with a strong edge of resentment in his voice*). Yeah, he came to Boston. What about it?

BERNARD. Well, just that when he came back — I'll never forget this, it always mystifies me. Because I'd thought so well of Biff, even though he'd always taken advantage of me. I loved him, Willy, y'know? And he came back after that month and took his sneakers — remember those sneakers with "University of Virginia" printed on them? He was so proud of those, wore them every day. And he took them down in the cellar, and burned them up in the furnace. We had a fist fight. It lasted at least half an hour. Just the two of us, punching each other down the cellar, and crying right through it. I've often thought of how strange it was that I knew he'd given up his life. What happened in Boston, Willy?

Willy looks at him as at an intruder.

BERNARD. I just bring it up because you asked me.

WILLY (*angrily*). Nothing. What do you mean, "What happened?" What's that got to do with anything?

BERNARD. Well, don't get sore.

WILLY. What are you trying to do, blame it on me? If a boy lays down is that my fault?

BERNARD. Now, Willy, don't get . . .

WILLY. Well, don't — don't talk to me that way! What does that mean, "What happened?"

Charley enters. He is in his vest, and he carries a bottle of bourbon.

CHARLEY. Hey, you're going to miss that train. (*He waves the bottle.*)

BERNARD. Yeah, I'm going. (*He takes the bottle.*) Thanks, Pop. (*He picks up his rackets and bag.*) Good-by, Willy, and don't worry about it. You know, "If at first you don't succeed . . ."

WILLY. Yes, I believe in that.

BERNARD. But sometimes, Willy, it's better for a man just to walk away.

WILLY. Walk away?

BERNARD. That's right.

WILLY. But if you can't walk away?

BERNARD (*after a slight pause*). I guess that's when it's tough. (*Extending his hand.*) Good-by, Willy.

WILLY (*shaking Bernard's hand*). Good-by, boy.

CHARLEY (*an arm on Bernard's shoulder*). How do you like this kid? Gonna argue a case in front of the Supreme Court.

BERNARD (*protesting*). Pop!

WILLY (*genuinely shocked, pained, and happy*). No! The Supreme Court!

BERNARD. I gotta run. 'By, Dad!

CHARLEY. Knock 'em dead, Bernard!

Bernard goes off.

WILLY (*as Charley takes out his wallet*). The Supreme Court! And he didn't even mention it!

CHARLEY (*counting out money on the desk*). He don't have to—he's gonna do it.

WILLY. And you never told him what to do, did you? You never took any interest in him.

CHARLEY. My salvation is that I never took any interest in anything. There's some money—fifty dollars. I got an accountant inside.

WILLY. Charley, look . . . (*With difficulty.*) I got my insurance to pay. If you can manage it—I need a hundred and ten dollars.

Charley doesn't reply for a moment; merely stops moving.

WILLY. I'd draw it from my bank but Linda would know, and I . . .

CHARLEY. Sit down, Willy.

WILLY (*moving toward the chair*). I'm keeping an account of everything, remember. I'll pay every penny back. (*He sits.*)

CHARLEY. Now listen to me, Willy.

WILLY. I want you to know I appreciate . . .

CHARLEY (*sitting down on the table*). Willy, what're you doin'? What the hell is going on in your head?

WILLY. Why? I'm simply . . .

CHARLEY. I offered you a job. You make fifty dollars a week. And I won't send you on the road.

WILLY. I've got a job.

CHARLEY. Without pay? What kind of a job is a job without pay? (*He rises.*) Now, look, kid, enough is enough. I'm no genius but I know when I'm being insulted.

WILLY. Insulted!

CHARLEY. Why don't you want to work for me?

WILLY. What's the matter with you? I've got a job.

CHARLEY. Then what're you walkin' in here every week for?

WILLY (*getting up*). Well, if you don't want me to walk in here . . .

CHARLEY. I'm offering you a job.

WILLY. I don't want your goddam job!

CHARLEY. When the hell are you going to grow up?

WILLY (*furiously*). You big ignoramus, if you say that to me again I'll rap you one! I don't care how big you are! (*He's ready to fight.*)

Pause.

CHARLEY (*kindly, going to him*). How much do you need, Willy?

WILLY. Charley, I'm strapped. I'm strapped. I don't know what to do. I was just fired.

CHARLEY. Howard fired you?

WILLY. That snotnose. Imagine that? I named him. I named him Howard.

CHARLEY. Willy, when're you gonna realize that them things don't mean anything? You named him Howard, but you can't sell that. The only thing you got in this world is what you can sell. And the funny thing is that you're a salesman, and you don't know that.

WILLY. I've always tried to think otherwise, I guess. I always felt that if a man was impressive, and well liked, that nothing . . .

CHARLEY. Why must everybody like you? Who liked J.P. Morgan? Was he impressive? In a Turkish bath he'd look like a butcher. But with his pockets on he was very well liked. Now listen, Willy, I know you don't like me, and nobody can say I'm in love with you, but I'll give you a job because—just for the hell of it, put it that way. Now what do you say?

WILLY. I—I just can't work for you, Charley.

CHARLEY. What're you, jealous of me?

WILLY. I can't work for you, that's all, don't ask me why.

CHARLEY (*angered, takes out more bills*). You been jealous of me all your life, you dammed fool! Here, pay your insurance. (*He puts the money in Willy's hand.*)

WILLY. I'm keeping strict accounts.

CHARLEY. I've got some work to do. Take care of yourself. And pay your insurance.

WILLY (*moving to the right*). Funny, y'know? After all the highways, and the trains, and the appointments, and the years, you end up worth more dead than alive.

CHARLEY. Willy, nobody's worth nothin' dead. (*After a slight pause.*) Did you hear what I said?

Willy stands still, dreaming.

CHARLEY. Willy!

WILLY. Apologize to Bernard for me when you see him. I didn't mean to argue with him. He's a fine boy. They're all fine boys, and they'll end up big—all of them. Someday they'll all play tennis together. Wish me luck, Charley. He saw Bill Oliver today.

CHARLEY. Good luck.

WILLY (*on the verge of tears*). Charley, you're the only friend I got. Isn't that a remarkable thing? (*He goes out.*)

CHARLEY. Jesus!

Charley stares after him a moment and follows. All light blacks out. Suddenly raucous music is heard, and a red glow rises behind the screen at right. Stanley, a young waiter, appears, carrying a table, followed by Happy, who is carrying two chairs.

STANLEY (*putting the table down*). That's all right, Mr. Loman, I can handle it myself. (*He turns and takes the chairs from Happy and places them at the table.*)

HAPPY (*glancing around*). Oh, this is better.

STANLEY. Sure, in the front there you're in the middle of all kinds of noise. Whenever you got a party, Mr. Loman, you just tell me and I'll put you back here. Y'know, there's a lotta people they don't like it private, because when they go out they like to see a lotta action around them because they're sick and tired to stay in the house by theirself. But I know you, you ain't from Hackensack. You know what I mean?

HAPPY (*sitting down*). So how's it coming, Stanley?

STANLEY. Ah, it's a dog life. I only wish during the war they'd a took me in the Army. I coulda been dead by now.

HAPPY. My brother's back, Stanley.

STANLEY. Oh, he come back, heh? From the Far West.

HAPPY. Yeah, big cattle man, my brother, so treat him right. And my father's coming too.

STANLEY. Oh, your father too!

HAPPY. You got a couple of nice lobsters?

STANLEY. Hundred per cent, big.

HAPPY. I want them with the claws.

STANLEY. Don't worry, I don't give you no mice. (*Happy laughs.*) How about some wine? It'll put a head on the meal.

HAPPY. No. You remember, Stanley, that recipe I brought you from overseas? With the champagne in it?

STANLEY. Oh, yeah, sure. I still got it tacked up yet in the kitchen. But that'll have to cost a buck apiece anyways.

HAPPY. That's all right.

STANLEY. What'd you, hit a number or somethin'?

HAPPY. No, it's a little celebration. My brother is—I think he pulled off a big deal today. I think we're going into business together.

STANLEY. Great! That's the best for you. Because a family business, you know what I mean?—that's the best.

HAPPY. That's what I think.

STANLEY. 'Cause what's the difference? Somebody steals? It's in the family. Know what I mean? (*Sotto voce.*) Like this bartender here. The boss is goin' crazy what kinda leak he's got in the cash register. You put it in but it don't come out.

HAPPY (*raising his head*). Sh!

STANLEY. What?

HAPPY. You notice I wasn't lookin' right or left, was I?

STANLEY. No.

HAPPY. And my eyes are closed.

STANLEY. So what's the . . . ?

HAPPY. Strudel's comin'.

STANLEY (*catching on, looks around*). Ah, no, there's no . . .

He breaks off as a furred, lavishly dressed Girl enters and sits at the next table. Both follow her with their eyes.

STANLEY. Geez, how'd ya know?

HAPPY. I got radar or something. (*Staring directly at her profile.*) Oooooooo . . . Stanley.

STANLEY. I think that's for you, Mr. Loman.

HAPPY. Look at that mouth. Oh, God. And the binoculars.

STANLEY. Geez, you got a life, Mr. Loman.

HAPPY. Wait on her.

STANLEY (*going to the Girl's table*). Would you like a menu, ma'am?

GIRL. I'm expecting someone, but I'd like a . . .

HAPPY. Why don't you bring her—excuse me, miss, do you mind? I sell champagne, and I'd like you to try my brand. Bring her a champagne, Stanley.

GIRL. That's awfully nice of you.

HAPPY. Don't mention it. It's all company money. (*He laughs.*)

GIRL. That's a charming product to be selling, isn't it?

HAPPY. Oh, gets to be like everything else. Selling is selling, y'know.

GIRL. I suppose.

HAPPY. You don't happen to sell, do you?

GIRL. No, I don't sell.

HAPPY. Would you object to a compliment from a stranger? You ought to be on a magazine cover.

GIRL (*looking at him a little archly*). I have been.

Stanley comes in with a glass of champagne.

HAPPY. What'd I say before, Stanley? You see? She's a cover girl.

STANLEY. Oh, I could see, I could see.

HAPPY (*to the Girl*). What magazine?

GIRL. Oh, a lot of them. (*She takes the drink.*) Thank you.

HAPPY. You know what they say in France, don't you? "Champagne is the drink of the complexion"—Hya, Biff!

Biff has entered and sits with Happy.

BIFF. Hello, kid. Sorry I'm late.

HAPPY. I just got here. Uh, Miss . . . ?

GIRL. Forsythe.

HAPPY. Miss Forsythe, this is my brother.

BIFF. Is Dad here?

HAPPY. His name is Biff. You might've heard of him. Great football player.

GIRL. Really? What team?

HAPPY. Are you familiar with football?

GIRL. No, I'm afraid I'm not.

HAPPY. Biff is quarterback with the New York Giants.

GIRL. Well, that is nice, isn't it? (*She drinks.*)

HAPPY. Good health.

GIRL. I'm happy to meet you.

HAPPY. That's my name. Hap. It's really Harold, but at West Point they called me Happy.

GIRL (*now really impressed*). Oh, I see. How do you do? (*She turns her profile.*)

BIFF. Isn't Dad coming?

HAPPY. You want her?

BIFF. Oh, I could never make that.

HAPPY. I remember the time that idea would never come into your head. Where's the old confidence, Biff?

BIFF. I just saw Oliver . . .

HAPPY. Wait a minute. I've got to see that old confidence again. Do you want her? She's on call.

BIFF. Oh, no. (*He turns to look at the Girl.*)

HAPPY. I'm telling you. Watch this. (*Turning to the Girl.*) Honey? (*She turns to him.*) Are you busy?

GIRL. Well, I am . . . but I could make a phone call.

HAPPY. Do that, will you, honey? And see if you can get a friend. We'll be here for a while. Biff is one of the greatest football players in the country.

GIRL (*standing up*). Well, I'm certainly happy to meet you.

HAPPY. Come back soon.

GIRL. I'll try.

HAPPY. Don't try, honey, try hard.

The Girl exits. Stanley follows, shaking his head in bewildered admiration.

HAPPY. Isn't that a shame now? A beautiful girl like that? That's why I can't get married. There's not a good woman in a thousand. New York is loaded with them, kid!

BIFF. Hap, look . . .

HAPPY. I told you she was on call!

BIFF (*strangely unnerved*). Cut it out, will ya? I want to say something to you.

HAPPY. Did you see Oliver?

BIFF. I saw him all right. Now look, I want to tell Dad a couple of things and I want you to help me.

HAPPY. What? Is he going to back you?

BIFF. Are you crazy? You're out of your goddam head, you know that?

HAPPY. Why? What happened?

BIFF (*breathlessly*). I did a terrible thing today, Hap. It's been the strangest day I ever went through. I'm all numb, I swear.

HAPPY. You mean he wouldn't see you?

BIFF. Well, I waited six hours for him, see? All day. Kept sending my name in. Even tried to date his secretary so she'd get me to him, but no soap.

HAPPY. Because you're not showin' the old confidence, Biff. He remembered you, didn't he?

BIFF (*stopping Happy with a gesture*). Finally, about five o'clock, he comes out. Didn't remember who I was or anything. I felt like such an idiot, Hap.

HAPPY. Did you tell him my Florida idea?

BIFF. He walked away. I saw him for one minute. I got so mad I could've torn the walls down! How the hell did I ever get the idea I was a salesman there? I even believed myself that I'd been a salesman for him! And then he gave me one look and—I realized what a ridiculous lie my whole life has been! We've been talking in a dream for fifteen years. I was a shipping clerk.

HAPPY. What'd you do?

BIFF (*with great tension and wonder*). Well, he left, see. And the secretary went out. I was all alone in the waiting room. I don't know what came over me, Hap. The next thing I know I'm in his office—paneled walls, everything. I can't explain it. I—Hap, I took his fountain pen.

HAPPY. Geez, did he catch you?

BIFF. I ran out. I ran down all eleven flights. I ran and ran and ran.

HAPPY. That was an awful dumb—what'd you do that for?

BIFF (*agonized*). I don't know, I just—wanted to take something, I don't know. You gotta help me, Hap. I'm gonna tell Pop.

HAPPY. You crazy? What for?

BIFF. Hap, he's got to understand that I'm not the man somebody lends that kind of money to. He thinks I've been spiting him all these years and its' eating him up.

HAPPY. That's just it. You tell him something nice.

BIFF. I can't.

HAPPY. Say you got a lunch date with Oliver tomorrow.

BIFF. So what do I do tomorrow?

HAPPY. You leave the house tomorrow and come back at night and say Oliver is thinking it over. And he thinks it over for a couple of weeks, and gradually it fades away and nobody's the worse.

BIFF. But it'll go on forever!

HAPPY. Dad is never so happy as when he's looking forward to something!

Willy enters.

HAPPY. Hello, scout!

WILLY. Gee, I haven't been here in years!

Stanley has followed Willy in and sets a chair for him. Stanley starts off but Happy stops him.

HAPPY. Stanley!

Stanley stands by, waiting for an order.

BIFF (*going to Willy with guilt, as to an invalid*). Sit down, Pop. You want a drink?

WILLY. Sure, I don't mind.

BIFF. Let's get a load on.

WILLY. You look worried.

BIFF. N-no. (*To Stanley.*) Scotch all around. Make it doubles.

STANLEY. Doubles, right. (*He goes.*)

WILLY. You had a couple already, didn't you?

BIFF. Just a couple, yeah.

WILLY. Well, what happened, boy? (*Nodding affirmatively, with a smile.*) Everything go all right?

BIFF (*takes a breath, then reaches out and grasps Willy's hand*). Pal . . . (*He is smiling bravely, and Willy is smiling too.*) I had an experience today.

HAPPY. Terrific, Pop.

WILLY. That so? What happened?

BIFF (*high, slightly alcoholic, above the earth*). I'm going to tell you everything from first to last. It's been a strange day. (*Silence. He looks around, composes himself as best he can, but his breath keeps breaking the rhythm of his voice.*) I had to wait quite a while for him, and . . .

WILLY. Oliver?

BIFF. Yeah, Oliver. All day, as a matter of cold fact. And a lot of—instances—facts, Pop, facts about my life came back to me. Who was it, Pop? Who ever said I was a salesman with Oliver?

WILLY. Well, you were.

BIFF. No, Dad, I was a shipping clerk.

WILLY. But you were practically . . .

BIFF (*with determination*). Dad, I don't know who said it first, but I was never a salesman for Bill Oliver.

WILLY. What're you talking about?

BIFF. Let's hold on to the facts tonight, Pop. We're not going to get anywhere bullin' around. I was a shipping clerk.

WILLY (*angrily*). All right, now listen to me . . .

BIFF. Why don't you let me finish?

WILLY. I'm not interested in stories about the past or any crap of that kind because the woods are burning, boys, you understand? There's a big blaze going on all around. I was fired today.

BIFF (*shocked*). How could you be?

WILLY. I was fired, and I'm looking for a little good news to tell your mother, because the woman has waited and the woman has suffered. The gist of it is that I haven't got a story left in my head, Biff. So don't give me a lecture about facts and aspects. I am not interested. Now what've you got to say to me?

Stanley enters with three drinks. They wait until he leaves.

WILLY. Did you see Oliver?

BIFF. Jesus, Dad!

WILLY. You mean you didn't go up there?

HAPPY. Sure he went up there.

BIFF. I did. I—saw him. How could they fire you?

WILLY (*on the edge of his chair*). What kind of a welcome did he give you?

BIFF. He won't even let you work on commission?

WILLY. I'm out! (*Driving.*) So tell me, he gave you a warm welcome?

HAPPY. Sure, Pop, sure!

BIFF (*driven*). Well, it was kind of . . .

WILLY. I was wondering if he'd remember you. (*To Happy.*) Imagine, man doesn't see him for ten, twelve years and gives him that kind of a welcome!

HAPPY. Damn right!

BIFF (*trying to return to the offensive*). Pop, look . . .

WILLY. You know why he remembered you, don't you? Because you impressed him in those days.

BIFF. Let's talk quietly and get this down to the facts, huh?

WILLY (*as though Biff had been interrupting*). Well, what happened? It's great news, Biff. Did he take you into his office or'd you talk in the waiting room?

BIFF. Well, he came in, see, and . . .

WILLY (*with a big smile*). What'd he say? Betcha he threw his arm around you.

BIFF. Well, he kinda . . .

WILLY. He's a fine man. (*To Happy.*) Very hard man to see, y'know.

HAPPY (*agreeing*). Oh, I know.

WILLY (*to Biff*). Is that where you had the drinks?

BIFF. Yeah, he gave me a couple of—no, no!

HAPPY (*cutting in*). He told him my Florida idea.

WILLY. Don't interrupt. (*To Biff.*) How'd he react to the Florida idea?

BIFF. Dad, will you give me a minute to explain?

WILLY. I've been waiting for you to explain since I sat down here! What happened? He took you into his office and what?

BIFF. Well—I talked. And—and he listened, see.

WILLY. Famous for the way he listens, y'know. What was his answer?

BIFF. His answer was—(*He breaks off, suddenly angry.*) Dad, you're not letting me tell you what I want to tell you!

WILLY (*accusing, angered*). You didn't see him, did you?

BIFF. I did see him!

WILLY. What'd you insult him or something? You insulted him, didn't you?

BIFF. Listen, will you let me out of it, will you just let me out of it!

HAPPY. What the hell!

WILLY. Tell me what happened!

BIFF (*to Happy*). I can't talk to him!

A single trumpet note jars the ear. The light of green leaves stains the house, which holds the air of night and a dream. Young Bernard enters and knocks on the door of the house.

YOUNG BERNARD (*frantically*). Mrs. Loman, Mrs. Loman!

HAPPY. Tell him what happened!

BIFF (*to Happy*). Shut up and leave me alone!

WILLY. No, no! You had to go and flunk math!

BIFF. What math? What're you talking about?

YOUNG BERNARD. Mrs. Loman, Mrs. Loman!

Linda appears in the house, as of old.

WILLY (*wildly*). Math, math, math!

BIFF. Take it easy, Pop!

YOUNG BERNARD. Mrs. Loman!

WILLY (*furiously*). If you hadn't flunked you'd've been set by now!

BIFF. Now, look, I'm gonna tell you what happened, and you're going to listen to me.

YOUNG BERNARD. Mrs. Loman!

BIFF. I waited six hours . . .

HAPPY. What the hell are you saying?

BIFF. I kept sending in my name but he wouldn't see me. So finally he . . .(*He continues unheard as light fades low on the restaurant.*)

YOUNG BERNARD. Biff flunked math!

LINDA. No!

YOUNG BERNARD. Birnbaum flunked him! They won't graduate him!

LINDA. But they have to. He's gotta go to the university. Where is he? Biff! Biff!

YOUNG BERNARD. No, he left. He went to Grand Central.

LINDA. Grand—You mean he went to Boston!

YOUNG BERNARD. Is Uncle Willy in Boston?

LINDA. Oh, maybe Willy can talk to the teacher. Oh, the poor, poor boy!

Light on house area snaps out.

BIFF (*at the table, now audible, holding up a gold fountain pen*) . . . so I'm washed up with Oliver, you understand? Are you listening to me?

WILLY (*at a loss*). Yeah, sure. If you hadn't flunked . . .

BIFF. Flunked what? What're you talking about?

WILLY. Don't blame everything on me! I didn't flunk math—you did! What pen?

HAPPY. That was awful dumb, Biff, a pen like that is worth—

WILLY (*seeing the pen for the first time*). You took Oliver's pen?

BIFF (*weakening*). Dad, I just explained it to you.

WILLY. You stole Bill Oliver's fountain pen!

BIFF. I didn't exactly steal it! That's just what I've been explaining to you!

HAPPY. He had it in his hand and just then Oliver walked in, so he got nervous and stuck it in his pocket!

WILLY. My God, Biff!

BIFF. I never intended to do it, Dad!

OPERATOR'S VOICE. Standish Arms, good evening!

WILLY (*shouting*). I'm not in my room!

BIFF (*frightened*). Dad, what's the matter? (*He and Happy stand up.*)

OPERATOR. Ringing Mr. Loman for you!

WILLY. I'm not there, stop it!

BIFF (*horrified, gets down on one knee before Willy*). Dad, I'll make good, I'll make good. (*Willy tries to get to his feet. Biff holds him down.*) Sit down now.

WILLY. No, you're no good, you're no good for anything.

BIFF. I am, Dad, I'll find something else, you understand? Now don't worry about anything. (*He holds up Willy's face.*) Talk to me, Dad.

OPERATOR. Mr. Loman does not answer. Shall I page him?

WILLY (*attempting to stand, as though to rush and silence the Operator*). No, no, no!

HAPPY. He'll strike something, Pop.

WILLY. No, no . . .

BIFF (*desperately, standing over Willy*). Pop, listen! Listen to me! I'm telling you something good. Oliver talked to his partner about the Florida idea. You listening? He—he talked to his partner, and he came to me . . . I'm going to be all right, you hear? Dad, listen to me, he said it was just a question of the amount!

WILLY. Then you . . . got it?

HAPPY. He's gonna be terrific, Pop!

WILLY (*trying to stand*). Then you got it, haven't you? You got it! You got it!

BIFF (*agonized, holds Willy down*). No, no. Look, Pop. I'm supposed to have lunch with them tomorrow. I'm just telling you this so you'll know that I can still make an impression, Pop. And I'll make good somewhere, but I can't go tomorrow, see.

WILLY. Why not? You simply . . .

BIFF. But the pen, Pop!

WILLY. You give it to him and tell him it was an oversight!

HAPPY. Sure, have lunch tomorrow!

BIFF. I can't say that . . .

WILLY. You were doing a crossword puzzle and accidentally used his pen!

BIFF. Listen, kid, I took those balls years ago, now I walk in with his fountain pen? That clinches it, don't you see? I can't face him like that! I'll try elsewhere.

PAGE'S VOICE. Paging Mr. Loman!

WILLY. Don't you want to be anything?

BIFF. Pop, how can I go back?

WILLY. You don't want to be anything, is that what's behind it?

BIFF (*now angry at Willy for not crediting his sympathy*). Don't take it that way! You think it was easy walking into that office after what I'd done to him? A team of horses couldn't have dragged me back to Bill Oliver!

WILLY. Then why'd you go?

BIFF. Why did I go? Why did I go! Look at you! Look at what's become of you!

Off left, The Woman laughs.

WILLY. Biff, you're going to go to that lunch tomorrow, or . . .

BIFF. I can't go. I've got no appointment!

HAPPY. Biff, for . . . !

WILLY. Are you spiting me?

BIFF. Don't take it that way! Goddammit!

WILLY (*strikes Biff and falters away from the table*). You rotten little louse! Are you spiting me?

THE WOMAN. Someone's at the door, Willy!

BIFF. I'm no good, can't you see what I am?

HAPPY (*separating them*). Hey, you're in a restaurant! Now cut it out, both of you! (*The girls enter.*) Hello, girls, sit down.

The Woman laughs, off left.

MISS FORSYTHE. I guess we might as well. This is Letta.

THE WOMAN. Willy, are you going to wake up?

BIFF (*ignoring Willy*). How're ya, miss, sit down. What do you drink?

MISS FORSYTHE. Letta might not be able to stay long.

LETTA. I gotta get up very early tomorrow. I got jury duty. I'm so excited! Were you fellows ever on a jury?

BIFF. No, but I been in front of them! (*The girls laugh.*) This is my father.

LETTA. Isn't he cute? Sit down with us, Pop.

HAPPY. Sit him down, Biff!

BIFF (*going to him*). Come on, slugger, drink us under the table. To hell with it! Come on, sit down, pal.

On Biff's last insistence, Willy is about to sit.

THE WOMAN (*now urgently*). Willy, are you going to answer the door!

The Woman's call pulls Willy back. He starts right, befuddled.

BIFF. Hey, where are you going?
WILLY. Open the door.
BIFF. The door?
WILLY. The washroom . . . the door . . . where's the door?
BIFF (*leading Willy to the left*). Just go straight down.

Willy moves left.

THE WOMAN. Willy, Willy, are you going to get up, get up, get up, get up?

Willy exits left.

LETTA. I think it's sweet you bring your daddy along.
MISS FORSYTHE. Oh, he isn't really your father!
BIFF (*at left, turning to her resentfully*). Miss Forsythe, you've just seen a prince walk by. A fine, troubled prince. A hardworking, unappreciated prince. A pal, you understand? A good companion. Always for his boys.
LETTA. That's so sweet.
HAPPY. Well, girls, what's the program? We're wasting time. Come on, Biff. Gather round. Where would you like to go?
BIFF. Why don't you do something for him?
HAPPY. Me!
BIFF. Don't you give a damn for him, Hap?
HAPPY. What're you talking about? I'm the one who . . .
BIFF. I sense it, you don't give a good goddam about him. (*He takes the rolled-up hose from his pocket and puts it on the table in front of Happy.*) Look what I found in the cellar, for Christ's sake. How can you bear to let it go on?
HAPPY. Me? Who goes away? Who runs off and . . .
BIFF. Yeah, but he doesn't mean anything to you. You could help him—I can't! Don't you understand what I'm talking about? He's going to kill himself, don't you know that?
HAPPY. Don't I know it! Me!
BIFF. Hap, help him! Jesus . . . help him . . . Help me, help me, I can't bear to look at his face! (*Ready to weep, he hurries out, up right.*)
HAPPY (*starting after him*). Where are you going?
MISS FORSYTHE. What's he so mad about?
HAPPY. Come on, girls, we'll catch up with him.
MISS FORSYTHE (*as Happy pushes her out*). Say, I don't like that temper of his!
HAPPY. He's just a little overstrung, he'll be all right!
WILLY (*off left, as The Woman laughs*). Don't answer! Don't answer!

LETTA. Don't you want to tell your father . . .

HAPPY. No, that's not my father. He's just a guy. Come on, we'll catch
Biff, and, honey, we're going to paint this town! Stanley, where's the
check! Hey, Stanley!

They exit. Stanley looks toward left.

STANLEY (*calling to Happy indignantly*). Mr. Loman! Mr. Loman!

*Stanley picks up a chair and follows them off. Knocking is heard off left. The
Woman enters, laughing. Willy follows her. She is in a black slip; he is buttoning
his shirt. Raw, sensuous music accompanies their speech:*

WILLY. Will you stop laughing? Will you stop?

THE WOMAN. Aren't you going to answer the door? He'll wake the whole
hotel.

WILLY. I'm not expecting anybody.

THE WOMAN. Whyn't you have another drink, honey, and stop being so
damn self-centered?

WILLY. I'm so lonely.

THE WOMAN. You know you ruined me, Willy? From now on, whenever
you come to the office, I'll see that you go right through to the buyers.
No waiting at my desk anymore, Willy. You ruined me.

WILLY. That's nice of you to say that.

THE WOMAN. Gee, you are self-centered! Why so sad? You are the saddest, self-centeredest soul I ever did see-saw. (*She laughs. He kisses
her.*) Come on inside, drummer boy. It's silly to be dressing in the middle of the night. (*As knocking is heard.*) Aren't you going to answer the
door?

WILLY. They're knocking on the wrong door.

THE WOMAN. But I felt the knocking. And he heard us talking in here.
Maybe the hotel's on fire!

WILLY (*his terror rising*). It's a mistake.

THE WOMAN. Then tell him to go away!

WILLY. There's nobody there.

THE WOMAN. It's getting on my nerves, Willy. There's somebody standing out there and it's getting on my nerves!

WILLY (*pushing her away from him*). All right, stay in the bathroom here,
and don't come out. I think there's a law in Massachusetts about it,
so don't come out. It may be that new room clerk. He looked very
mean. So don't come out. It's a mistake, there's no fire.

*The knocking is heard again. He takes a few steps away from her, and she van-
ishes into the wing. The light follows him, and now he is facing Young Biff,
who carries a suitcase. Biff steps toward him. The music is gone.*

BIFF. Why didn't you answer?

WILLY. Biff! What are you doing in Boston?

BIFF. Why didn't you answer? I've been knocking for five minutes, I called you on the phone . . .

WILLY. I just heard you. I was in the bathroom and had the door shut. Did anything happen home?

BIFF. Dad — I let you down.

WILLY. What do you mean?

BIFF. Dad . . .

WILLY. Biffo, what's this about? (*putting his arm around Biff.*) Come on, let's go downstairs and get you a malted.

BIFF. Dad, I flunked math.

WILLY. Not for the term?

BIFF. The term. I haven't got enough credits to graduate.

WILLY. You mean to say Bernard wouldn't give you the answers?

BIFF. He did, he tried, but I only got a sixty-one.

WILLY. And they wouldn't give you four points?

BIFF. Birnbaum refused absolutely. I begged him, Pop, but he won't give me those points. You gotta talk to him before they close the school. Because if he saw the kind of man you are, and you just talked to him in your way, I'm sure he'd come through for me. The class came right before practice, see, and I didn't go enough. Would you talk to him? He'd like you, Pop. You know the way you could talk.

WILLY. You're on. We'll drive right back.

BIFF. Oh, Dad, good work! I'm sure he'll change it for you!

WILLY. Go downstairs and tell the clerk I'm checkin' out. Go right down.

BIFF. Yes, sir! See, the reason he hates me, Pop — one day he was late for class so I got up at the blackboard and imitated him. I crossed my eyes and talked with a lithp.

WILLY (*laughing*). You did? The kids like it?

BIFF. They nearly died laughing!

WILLY. Yeah? What'd you do?

BIFF. The thquare root of thixthy twee is . . . (*Willy bursts out laughing; Biff joins.*) And in the middle of it he walked in!

Willy laughs and The Woman joins in offstage.

WILLY (*without hesitation*). Hurry downstairs and . . .

BIFF. Somebody in there?

WILLY. No, that was next door.

The Woman laughs offstage.

BIFF. Somebody got in your bathroom!

WILLY. No, it's the next room, there's a party . . .

THE WOMAN (*enters, laughing; she lisps this*). Can I come in? There's something in the bathtub, Willy, and it's moving!

Willy looks at Biff; who is staring open-mouthed and horrified at The Woman.

WILLY. Ah—you better go back to your room. They must be finished painting by now. They're painting her room so I let her take a shower here. Go back, go back . . . (*He pushes her.*)

THE WOMAN (*resisting*). But I've got to get dressed, Willy, I can't . . .

WILLY. Get out of here! Go back, go back . . . (*Suddenly striving for the ordinary.*) This is Miss Francis, Biff, she's a buyer. They're painting her room. Go back, Miss Francis, go back . . .

THE WOMAN. But my clothes, I can't go out naked in the hall!

WILLY (*pushing her offstage*). Get outa here! Go back, go back!

Biff slowly sits down on his suitcase as the argument continues offstage.

THE WOMAN. Where's my stockings? You promised me stockings, Willy!

WILLY. I have no stockings here!

THE WOMAN. You had two boxes of size nine sheers for me, and I want them!

WILLY. Here, for God's sake, will you get outa here!

THE WOMAN (*enters holding a box of stockings*). I just hope there's nobody in the hall. That's all I hope. (*To Biff.*) Are you football or baseball?

BIFF. Football.

THE WOMAN (*angry, humiliated*). That's me too. G'night. (*She snatches her clothes from Willy, and walks out.*)

WILLY (*after a pause*). Well, better get going. I want to get to the school first thing in the morning. Get my suits out of the closet. I'll get my valise. (*Biff doesn't move.*) What's the matter! (*Biff remains motionless, tears falling.*) She's a buyer. Buys for J. H. Simmons. She lives down the hall— they're painting. You don't imagine—(*He breaks off. After a pause.*) Now listen, pal, she's just a buyer. She sees merchandise in her room and they have to keep it looking just so . . .(*Pause. Assuming command.*) All right, get my suits. (*Biff doesn't move.*) Now stop crying and do as I say. I gave you an order. Biff, I gave you an order! Is that what you do when I give you an order? How dare you cry! (*putting his arm around Biff.*) Now look, Biff, when you grow up you'll understand about these things. You mustn't—you mustn't overemphasize a thing like this. I'll see Birnbaum first thing in the morning.

BIFF. Never mind.

WILLY (*getting down beside Biff.*) Never mind! He's going to give you those points. I'll see to it.

BIFF. He wouldn't listen to you.

WILLY. He certainly will listen to me. You need those points for the U. of Virginia.

BIFF. I'm not going there.

WILLY. Heh? If I can't get him to change that mark you'll make it up in summer school. You've got all summer to . . .

BIFF (*his weeping breaking from him*). Dad . . .

WILLY (*infected by it*). Oh, my boy . . .

BIFF. Dad . . .

WILLY. She's nothing to me, Biff. I was lonely, I was terribly lonely.

BIFF. You—you gave her Mama's stockings! (*His tears break through and he rises to go.*)

WILLY (*grabbing for Biff*). I gave you an order!

BIFF. Don't touch me, you—liar!

WILLY. Apologize for that!

BIFF. You fake! You phony little fake! You fake! (*Overcome, he turns quickly and weeping fully goes out with his suitcase. Willy is left on the floor on his knees.*)

WILLY. I gave you an order! Biff, come back here or I'll beat you! Come back here! I'll whip you!

Stanley comes quickly in from the right and stands in front of Willy.

WILLY (*shouts at Stanley*). I gave you an order . . .

STANLEY. Hey, let's pick it up, pick it up, Mr. Loman. (*He helps Willy to his feet.*) Your boys left with the chippies. They said they'll see you home.

A second waiter watches some distance away.

WILLY. But we were supposed to have dinner together.

Music is heard, Willy's theme.

STANLEY. Can you make it?

WILLY. I'll—sure, I can make it. (*Suddenly concerned about his clothes.*) Do I—I look all right?

STANLEY. Sure, you look all right. (*He flicks a speck off Willy's lapel.*)

WILLY. Here—here's a dollar.

STANLEY. Oh, your son paid me. It's all right.

WILLY (*putting it in Stanley's hand*). No, take it. You're a good boy.

STANLEY. Oh, no, you don't have to . . .

WILLY. Here—here's some more, I don't need it any more. (*After a slight pause.*) Tell me—is there a seed store in the neighborhood?

STANLEY. Seeds? You mean like to plant?

As Willy turns, Stanley slips the money back into his jacket pocket.

WILLY. Yes. Carrots, peas . . .

STANLEY. Well, there's hardware stores on Sixth Avenue, but it may be too late now.

WILLY (*anxiously*). Oh, I'd better hurry. I've got to get some seeds. (*He starts off to the right.*) I've got to get some seeds, right away. Nothing's planted. I don't have a thing in the ground.

Willy hurries out as the light goes down. Stanley moves over to the right after him, watches him off. The other waiter has been staring at Willy.

STANLEY (*to the waiter*). Well, whatta you looking at?

The waiter picks up the chairs and moves off right. Stanley takes the table and follows him. The light fades on this area. There is a long pause, the sound of the flute coming over. The light gradually rises on the kitchen, which is empty. Happy appears at the door of the house, followed by Biff. Happy is carrying a large bunch of long-stemmed roses. He enters the kitchen, looks around for Linda. Not seeing her, he turns to Biff, who is just outside the house door, and makes a gesture with his hands, indicating "Not here, I guess." He looks into the living room and freezes. Inside, Linda, unseen, is seated, Willy's coat on her lap. She rises ominously and quietly and moves toward Happy, who backs up into the kitchen, afraid.

HAPPY. Hey, what're you doing up? (*Linda says nothing but moves toward him implacably.*) Where's Pop? (*He keeps backing to the right, and now Linda is in full view in the doorway to the living room.*) Is he sleeping?

LINDA. Where were you?

HAPPY (*trying to laugh it off*). We met two girls, Mom, very fine types. Here, we brought you some flowers. (*Offering them to her.*) Put them in your room, Ma.

She knocks them to the floor at Biff's feet. He has now come inside and closed the door behind him. She stares at Biff, silent.

HAPPY. Now what'd you do that for? Mom, I want you to have some flowers . . .

LINDA (*cutting Happy off, violently to Biff*). Don't you care whether he lives or dies?

HAPPY (*going to the stairs*). Come upstairs, Biff.

BIFF (*with a flare of disgust, to Happy*). Go away from me! (*To Linda.*) What do you mean, lives or dies? Nobody's dying around here, pal.

LINDA. Get out of my sight! Get out of here!

BIFF. I wanna see the boss.

LINDA. You're not going near him!

BIFF. Where is he? (*He moves into the living room and Linda follows.*)

LINDA (*shouting after Biff*). You invite him for dinner. He looks forward to it all day—(*Biff appears in his parents' bedroom, looks around, and exits*)—and then you desert him there. There's no stranger you'd do that to!

HAPPY. Why? He had a swell time with us. Listen, when I— (*Linda comes back into the kitchen*)—desert him I hope I don't outlive the day!

LINDA. Get out of here!

HAPPY. Now look, Mom . . .

LINDA. Did you have to go to women tonight? You and your lousy rotten whores!

Biff re-enters the kitchen.

HAPPY. Mom, all we did was follow Biff around trying to cheer him up! (*To Biff.*) Boy, what a night you gave me!

LINDA. Get out of here, both of you, and don't come back! I don't want you tormenting him any more. Go on now, get your things together! (*To Biff.*) You can sleep in his apartment. (*She starts to pick up the flowers and stops herself*) Pick up this stuff, I'm not your maid any more. Pick it up, you bum, you!

Happy turns his back to her in refusal. Biff slowly moves over and gets down on his knees, picking up the flowers.

LINDA. You're a pair of animals! Not one, not another living soul would have had the cruelty to walk out on that man in a restaurant!

BIFF (*not looking at her*). Is that what he said?

LINDA. He didn't have to say anything. He was so humiliated he nearly limped when he came in.

HAPPY. But, Mom, he had a great time with us . . .

BIFF (*cutting him off violently*). Shut up!

Without another word, Happy goes upstairs.

LINDA. You! You didn't even go in to see if he was all right!

BIFF (*still on the floor in front of Linda, the flowers in his hand; with self-loathing*). No. Didn't. Didn't do a damned thing. How do you like that, heh? Left him babbling in a toilet.

LINDA. You louse. You . . .

BIFF. Now you hit it on the nose! (*He gets up, throws the flowers in the waste-basket.*) The scum of the earth, and you're looking at him!

LINDA. Get out of here!

BIFF. I gotta talk to the boss, Mom. Where is he?

LINDA. You're not going near him. Get out of this house!

BIFF (*with absolute assurance, determination*). No. We're gonna have an abrupt conversation, him and me.

LINDA. You're not talking to him.

Hammering is heard from outside the house, off right. Biff turns toward the noise.

LINDA (*suddenly pleading*). Will you please leave him alone?

BIFF. What's he doing out there?

LINDA. He's planting the garden!

BIFF (*quietly*). Now? Oh, my God!

Biff moves outside, Linda following. The light dies down on them and comes up on the center of the apron as Willy walks into it. He is carrying a flashlight, a hoe, and a handful of seed packets. He raps the top of the hoe sharply to fix it firmly, and then moves to the left, measuring off the distance with his foot. He holds the flashlight to look at the seed packets, reading off the instructions. He is in the blue of night.

WILLY. Carrots . . . quarter-inch apart. Rows . . . one-foot rows. (*He measures it off.*) One foot. (*He puts down a package and measures off.*) Beets.

(*He puts down another package and measures again.*) Lettuce. (*He reads the package, puts it down.*) One foot — (*He breaks off as Ben appears at the right and moves slowly down to him.*) What a proposition, ts, ts. Terrific, terrific. 'Cause she's suffered, Ben, the woman has suffered. You understand me? A man can't go out the way he came in, Ben, a man has got to add up to something. You can't, you can't — (*Ben moves toward him as though to interrupt.*) You gotta consider now. Don't answer so quick. Remember, it's a guaranteed twenty-thousand-dollar proposition. Now look, Ben, I want you to go through the ins and outs of this thing with me. I've got nobody to talk to, Ben, and the woman has suffered, you hear me?

BEN (*standing still, considering*). What's the proposition?

WILLY. It's twenty thousand dollars on the barrelhead. Guaranteed, gilt-edged, you understand?

BEN. You don't want to make a fool of yourself. They might not honor the policy.

WILLY. How can they dare refuse? Didn't I work like a coolie to meet every premium on the nose? And now they don't pay off? Impossible!

BEN. It's called a cowardly thing, William.

WILLY. Why? Does it take more guts to stand here the rest of my life ringing up a zero?

BEN (*yielding*). That's a point, William. (*He moves, thinking, turns.*) And twenty thousand — that is something one can feel with the hand, it is there.

WILLY (*now assured, with rising power*). Oh, Ben, that's the whole beauty of it! I see it like a diamond, shining in the dark, hard and rough, that I can pick up and touch in my hand. Not like — like an appointment! This would not be another damned-fool appointment, Ben, and it changes all the aspects. Because he thinks I'm nothing, see, and so he spites me. But the funeral . . . (*Straightening up.*) Ben, that funeral will be massive! They'll come from Maine, Massachusetts, Vermont, New Hampshire! All the old-timers with the strange license plates — that boy will be thunderstruck, Ben, because he never realized — I am known! Rhode Island, New York, New Jersey — I am known, Ben, and he'll see it with his eyes once and for all. He'll see what I am, Ben! He's in for a shock, that boy!

BEN (*coming down to the edge of the garden*). He'll call you a coward.

WILLY (*suddenly fearful*). No, that would be terrible.

BEN. Yes. And a damned fool.

WILLY. No, no, he mustn't, I won't have that! (*He is broken and desperate.*)

BEN. He'll hate you, William.

The gay music of the Boys is heard.

WILLY. Oh, Ben, how do we get back to all the great times? Used to be so full of light, and comradeship, the sleigh-riding in winter, and the ruddiness on his cheeks. And always some kind of good news coming up, always something nice coming up ahead. And never even let me carry the valises in the house, and simonizing, simonizing that little red car! Why, why can't I give him something and not have him hate me?

BEN. Let me think about it. (*He glances at his watch.*) I still have a little time. Remarkable proposition, but you've got to be sure you're not making a fool of yourself.

Ben drifts off upstage and goes out of sight. Biff comes down from the left.

WILLY (*suddenly conscious of Biff, turns and looks up at him, then begins picking up the packages of seeds in confusion.*) Where the hell is that seed? (*Indignantly.*) You can't see nothing out here! They boxed in the whole goddam neighborhood!

BIFF. There are people all around here. Don't you realize that?

WILLY. I'm busy. Don't bother me.

BIFF (*taking the hoe from Willy*). I'm saying good-by to you, Pop. (*Willy looks at him, silent, unable to move.*) I'm not coming back any more.

WILLY. You're not going to see Oliver tomorrow?

BIFF. I've got no appointment, Dad.

WILLY. He put his arm around you, and you've got no appointment?

BIFF. Pop, get this now, will you? Everytime I've left it's been a—fight that sent me out of here. Today I realized something about myself and I tried to explain it to you and I—I think I'm just not smart enough to make any sense out of it for you. To hell with whose fault it is or anything like that. (*He takes Willy's arm.*) Let's just wrap it up, heh? Come on in, we'll tell Mom. (*He gently tries to pull Willy to left.*)

WILLY (*frozen, immobile, with guilt in his voice*). No, I don't want to see her.

BIFF. Come on! (*He pulls again, and Willy tries to pull away.*)

WILLY (*highly nervous*). No, no, I don't want to see her.

BIFF (*tries to look into Willy's face, as if to find the answer there*). Why don't you want to see her?

WILLY (*more harshly now*). Don't bother me, will you?

BIFF. What do you mean, you don't want to see her? You don't want them calling you yellow, do you? This isn't your fault; it's me, I'm a bum. Now come inside! (*Willy strains to get away.*) Did you hear what I said to you?

Willy pulls away and quickly goes by himself into the house. Biff follows.

LINDA (*to Willy*). Did you plant, dear?

BIFF (*at the door, to Linda*). All right, we had it out. I'm going and I'm not writing any more.

LINDA (*going to Willy in the kitchen*). I think that's the best way, dear. 'Cause there's no use drawing it out, you'll just never get along.

Willy doesn't respond.

BIFF. People ask where I am and what I'm doing, you don't know, and you don't care. That way it'll be off your mind and you can start brightening up again. All right? That clears it, doesn't it? (*Willy is silent, and Biff goes to him.*) You gonna wish me luck, scout? (*He extends his hand.*) What do you say?

LINDA. Shake his hand, Willy.

WILLY (*turning to her, seething with hurt*). There's no necessity—to mention the pen at all, y'know.

BIFF (*gently*). I've got no appointment, Dad.

WILLY (*erupting fiercely*). He put his arm around . . . ?

BIFF. Dad, you're never going to see what I am, so what's the use of arguing? If I strike oil I'll send you a check. Meantime forget I'm alive.

WILLY (*to Linda*). Spite, see?

BIFF. Shake hands, Dad.

WILLY. Not my hand.

BIFF. I was hoping not to go this way.

WILLY. Well, this is the way you're going. Good-by.

Biff looks at him a moment, then turns sharply and goes to the stairs.

WILLY (*stops him with*). May you rot in hell if you leave this house!

BIFF (*turning*). Exactly what is it that you want from me?

WILLY. I want you to know, on the train, in the mountains, in the valleys, wherever you go, that you cut down your life for spite!

BIFF. No, no.

WILLY. Spite, spite, is the word of your undoing! And when you're down and out, remember what did it. When you're rotting somewhere beside the railroad tracks, remember, and don't you dare blame it on me!

BIFF. I'm not blaming it on you!

WILLY. I won't take the rap for this, you hear?

Happy comes down the stairs and stands on the bottom step, watching.

BIFF. That's just what I'm telling you!

WILLY (*sinking into a chair at a table, with full accusation*). You're trying to put a knife in me—don't think I don't know what you're doing!

BIFF. All right, phony! Then let's lay it on the line. (*He whips the rubber tube out of his pocket and puts it on the table.*)

HAPPY. You crazy . . .

LINDA. Biff! (*She moves to grab the hose, but Biff holds it down with his hand.*)

BIFF. Leave it there! Don't move it!

WILLY. (*not looking at it*). What is that?

BIFF. You know goddam well what that is.

WILLY. (*caged, wanting to escape*). I never saw that.

BIFF. You saw it. The mice didn't bring it into the cellar! What is this supposed to do, make a hero out of you? This supposed to make me sorry for you?

WILLY. Never heard of it.

BIFF. There'll be no pity for you, you hear it? No pity!

WILLY (*to Linda*). You hear the spite!

BIFF. No, you're going to hear the truth—what you are and what I am!

LINDA. Stop it!

WILLY. Spite!

HAPPY (*coming down toward Biff*). You cut it now!

BIFF (*to Happy*). The man don't know who we are! The man is gonna know! (*To Willy.*) We never told the truth for ten minutes in this house!

HAPPY. We always told the truth!

BIFF (*turning on him*). You big blow, are you the assistant buyer? You're one of the two assistants to the assistant, aren't you?

HAPPY. Well, I'm practically . . .

BIFF. You're practically full of it! We all are! and I'm through with it. (*To Willy.*) Now hear this, Willy, this is me.

WILLY. I know you!

BIFF. You know why I had no address for three months? I stole a suit in Kansas City and I was in jail. (*To Linda, who is sobbing.*) Stop crying. I'm through with it.

Linda turns away from them, her hands covering her face.

WILLY. I suppose that's my fault!

BIFF. I stole myself out of every good job since high school!

WILLY. And whose fault is that?

BIFF. And I never got anywhere because you blew me so full of hot air I could never stand taking orders from anybody! That's whose fault it is!

WILLY. I hear that!

LINDA. Don't, Biff!

BIFF. It's goddam time you heard that! I had to be boss big shot in two weeks, and I'm through with it!

WILLY. Then hang yourself! For spite, hang yourself!

BIFF. No! Nobody's hanging himself, Willy! I ran down eleven flights with a pen in my hand today. And suddenly I stopped, you hear me? And in the middle of that office building, do you hear this? I stopped in the middle of that building and I saw—the sky. I saw the things that I love in this world. The work and the food and time to sit and smoke. And I looked at the pen and said to myself, what the hell am I grabbing this for? Why am I trying to become what I don't want to be? What am I doing in an office, making a contemptuous, begging fool of myself, when all I want is out there, waiting for me the minute I say I know who I am! Why can't I say that, Willy? (*He tries to make Willy face him, but Willy pulls away and moves to the left.*)

WILLY (*with hatred, threateningly*). The door of your life is wide open!

BIFF. Pop! I'm a dime a dozen, and so are you!

WILLY (*turning on him now in an uncontrolled outburst*). I am not a dime a dozen! I am Willy Loman, and you are Biff Loman!

Biff starts for Willy, but is blocked by Happy. In his fury, Biff seems on the verge of attacking his father.

BIFF. I am not a leader of men, Willy, and neither are you. You were never anything but a hard-working drummer who landed in the ash can like all the rest of them! I'm one dollar an hour, Willy! I tried seven states and couldn't raise it. A buck an hour! Do you gather my meaning? I'm not bringing home any prizes any more, and you're going to stop waiting for me to bring them home!

WILLY (*directly to Biff*). You vengeful, spiteful mutt!

Biff breaks from Happy. Willy, in fright, starts up the stairs. Biff grabs him.

BIFF (*at the peak of his fury*). Pop! I'm nothing! I'm nothing, Pop. Can't you understand that? There's no spite in it any more. I'm just what I am, that's all.

Biff's fury has spent itself and he breaks down, sobbing, holding on to Willy, who dumbly fumbles for Biff's face.

WILLY (*astonished*). What're you doing? What're you doing? (*To Linda.*) Why is he crying?

BIFF (*crying, broken*). Will you let me go, for Christ's sake? Will you take that phony dream and burn it before something happens? (*Struggling to contain himself he pulls away and moves to the stairs.*) I'll go in the morning. Put him—put him to bed. (*Exhausted, Biff moves up the stairs to his room.*)

WILLY (*after a long pause, astonished, elevated*). Isn't that—isn't that remarkable? Biff—he likes me!

LINDA. He loves you, Willy!

HAPPY (*deeply moved*). Always did, Pop.

WILLY. Oh, Biff! (*Staring wildly.*) He cried! Cried to me. (*He is choking with his love, and now cries out his promise.*) That boy—that boy is going to be magnificent!

Ben appears in the light just outside the kitchen.

BEN. Yes, outstanding, with twenty thousand behind him.

LINDA (*sensing the racing of his mind, fearfully, carefully*). Now come to bed, Willy. It's all settled now.

WILLY (*finding it difficult not to rush out of the house*). Yes, we'll sleep. Come on. Go to sleep, Hap.

BEN. And it does take a great kind of a man to crack the jungle.

In accents of dread, Ben's idyllic music starts up.

HAPPY (*his arm around Linda*). I'm getting married, Pop, don't forget it. I'm changing everything. I'm gonna run that department before the year is up. You'll see, Mom. (*He kisses her.*)

BEN. The jungle is dark but full of diamonds, Willy.

Willy turns, moves, listening to Ben.

LINDA. Be good. You're both good boys, just act that way, that's all.

HAPPY. 'Night, Pop. (*He goes upstairs.*)

LINDA (*to Willy*). Come, dear.

BEN (*with greater force*). One must go in to fetch a diamond out.

WILLY (*to Linda, as he moves slowly along the edge of kitchen, toward the door*). I just want to get settled down, Linda. Let me sit alone for a little.

LINDA (*almost uttering her fear*). I want you upstairs.

WILLY (*taking her in his arms*). In a few minutes, Linda. I couldn't sleep right now. Go on, you look awful tired. (*He kisses her.*)

BEN. Not like an appointment at all. A diamond is rough and hard to the touch.

WILLY. Go on now. I'll be right up.

LINDA. I think this is the only way, Willy.

WILLY. Sure, it's the best thing.

BEN. Best thing!

WILLY. The only way. Everything is gonna be—go on, kid, get to bed. You look so tired.

LINDA. Come right up.

WILLY. Two minutes.

Linda goes into the living room, then reappears in her bedroom. Willy moves just outside the kitchen door.

WILLY. Loves me. (*Wonderingly.*) Always loved me. Isn't that a remarkable thing? Ben, he'll worship me for it!

BEN (*with promise*). It's dark there, but full of diamonds.

WILLY. Can you imagine that magnificence with twenty thousand dollars in his pocket?

LINDA (*calling from her room*). Willy! Come up!

WILLY (*calling into the kitchen*). Yes! yes. Coming! It's very smart, you realize that, don't you, sweetheart? Even Ben sees it. I gotta go, baby. 'By! 'By! (*going over to Ben, almost dancing.*) Imagine? When the mail comes he'll be ahead of Bernard again!

BEN. A perfect proposition all around.

WILLY. Did you see how he cried to me? Oh, if I could kiss him, Ben!

BEN. Time, William, time!

WILLY. Oh, Ben, I always knew one way or another we were gonna make it, Biff and I.

BEN (*looking at his watch*). The boat. We'll be late. (*He moves slowly off into the darkness.*)

WILLY (*elegiacally, turning to the house*). Now when you kick off, boy, I want a seventy-yard boot, and get right down the field under the ball, and when you hit, hit low and hit hard, because it's important, boy. (*He swings around and faces the audience.*) There's all kinds of important people in the stands, and the first thing you know . . . (*Suddenly realizing he is alone.*) Ben! Ben, where do I . . . ? (*He makes a sudden movement of search.*) Ben, how do I . . . ?

LINDA (*calling*). Willy, you coming up?

WILLY (*uttering a gasp of fear, whirling about as if to quiet her*). Sh! (*He turns around as if to find his way; sounds, faces, voices, seem to be swarming in upon him and he flicks at them, crying.*) Sh! Sh! (*Suddenly music, faint and high, stops him. It rises in intensity, almost to an unbearable scream. He goes up and down on his toes, and rushes off around the house.*) Shhh!

LINDA. Willy?

There is no answer. Linda waits. Biff gets up off his bed. He is still in his clothes. Happy sits up. Biff stands listening.

LINDA (*with real fear*). Willy, answer me! Willy!

There is the sound of a car starting and moving away at full speed.

LINDA. No!

BIFF (*rushing down the stairs*). Pop!

As the car speeds off the music crashes down in a frenzy of sound, which becomes the soft pulsation of a single cello string. Biff slowly returns to his bedroom. He and Happy gravely don their jackets. Linda slowly walks out of her room. The music has developed into a dead march. The leaves of day are appearing over everything. Charley and Bernard, somberly dressed, appear and knock on the kitchen door. Biff and Happy slowly descend the stairs to the kitchen as Charley and Bernard enter. All stop a moment when Linda, in clothes of mourning, bearing a little bunch of roses, comes through the draped doorway into the kitchen. She goes to Charley and takes his arm. Now all move toward the audience, through the wall-line of the kitchen. At the limit of the apron, Linda lays down the flowers, kneels, and sits back on her heels. All stare down at the grave.

REQUIEM

CHARLEY. It's getting dark, Linda.

Linda doesn't react. She stares at the grave.

BIFF. How about it, Mom? Better get some rest, heh? They'll be closing the gate soon.

Linda makes no move. Pause.

HAPPY (*deeply angered*). He had no right to do that. There was no necessity for it. We would've helped him.

CHARLEY (*grunting*). Hmmm.

BIFF. Come along, Mom.

LINDA. Why didn't anybody come?

CHARLEY. It was a very nice funeral.

LINDA. But where are all the people he knew? Maybe they blame him.

CHARLEY. Naa. It's a rough world, Linda. They wouldn't blame him.

LINDA. I can't understand it. At this time especially. First time in thirty-five years we were just about free and clear. He only needed a little salary. He was even finished with the dentist.

CHARLEY. No man only needs a little salary.

LINDA. I can't understand it.

BIFF. There were a lot of nice days. When he'd come home from a trip; or on Sundays, making the stoop; finishing the cellar; putting on the new porch; when he built the extra bathroom; and put up the garage. You know something, Charley, there's more of him in that front stoop than in all the sales he ever made.

CHARLEY. Yeah. He was a happy man with a batch of cement.

LINDA. He was so wonderful with his hands.

BIFF. He had the wrong dreams. All, all, wrong.

HAPPY (*almost ready to fight Biff*). Don't say that!

BIFF. He never knew who he was.

CHARLEY (*stopping Happy's movement and reply; to Biff*). Nobody dast blame this man. You don't understand: Willy was a salesman. And for a salesman, there is no rock bottom to the life. He don't put a bolt to a nut, he don't tell you the law or give you medicine. He's a man way out there in the blue, riding on a smile and a shoeshine. And when they start not smiling back—that's an earthquake. And then you get yourself a couple of spots on your hat, and you're finished. Nobody dast blame this man. A salesman is got to dream, boy. It comes with the territory.

BIFF. Charley, the man didn't know who he was.

HAPPY (*infuriated*). Don't say that!

BIFF. Why don't you come with me, Happy?

HAPPY. I'm not licked that easily. I'm staying right in this city, and I'm gonna beat this racket! (*He looks at Biff, his chin set.*) The Loman Brothers!

BIFF. I know who I am, kid.

HAPPY. All right, boy. I'm gonna show you and everybody else that Willy Loman did not die in vain. He had a good dream. It's the only dream you can have—to come out number-one man. He fought it out here, and this is where I'm gonna win it for him.

BIFF (*with a hopeless glance at Happy, bends toward his mother*). Let's go, Mom.

LINDA. I'll be with you in a minute. Go on, Charley. (*He hesitates.*) I want to, just for a minute. I never had a chance to say good-by.

Charley moves away, followed by Happy. Biff remains a slight distance up and left of Linda. She sits there, summoning herself. The flute begins, not far away, playing behind her speech.

LINDA. Forgive me, dear. I can't cry. I don't know what it is, but I can't cry. I don't understand it. Why did you ever do that? Help me, Willy, I can't cry. It seems to me that you're just on another trip. I keep expecting you. Willy, dear, I can't cry. Why did you do it? I search and search and I search, and I can't understand it, Willy. I made the last payment on the house today. Today, dear. And there'll be nobody home. (*A sob rises in her throat.*) We're free and clear. (*Sobbing mournfully, released.*) We're free. (*Biff comes slowly toward her.*) We're free . . . We're free . . .

Biff lifts her to her feet and moves out up right with her in his arms. Linda sobs quietly. Bernard and Charley come together and follow them, followed by Happy. Only the music of the flute is left on the darkening stage as over the house the hard towers of the apartment buildings rise into sharp focus and the curtain falls.

[1949]

TOPICS FOR DISCUSSION AND WRITING

1. Miller said in the *New York Times* (February 27, 1949, Sec. II, p. 1) that tragedy shows man's struggle to secure "his sense of personal dignity," and that "his destruction in the attempt posits a wrong or an evil in his environment." Does this make sense when applied to some earlier tragedy (for example, *Oedipus Rex* or *Hamlet*), and does it apply convincingly to *Death of a Salesman?* Is this the tragedy of an individual's own making? Or is society at fault for corrupting and exploiting Willy? Or both?
2. Do you find Willy pathetic rather than tragic? If pathetic, does this imply that the play is less worthy than if he is tragic?
3. Do you feel that Miller is straining too hard to turn a play about a little man into a big, impressive play? For example, do the musical themes, the unrealistic setting, the appearances of Ben, and the speech at the grave seem out of keeping in a play about the death of a salesman?
4. We don't know what Willy sells, and we don't know whether or not the insurance will be paid after his death. Do you consider these uncertainties to be faults in the play?
5. Is Howard a villain?
6. Characterize Linda.
7. The critic Kenneth Tynan has written, in *Tynan Right and Left:* "*Death of a Salesman* . . . is not a tragedy. Its catastrophe depends entirely on the fact that the company Willy Loman works for has no pension

scheme for its employees. What ultimately destroys Willy is economic injustice, which is curable, as the ills that plague Oedipus are not." What do you think of Tynan's view?

CONTEXTS FOR *DEATH OF A SALESMAN*

Arthur Miller, on Tragedy and the Common Man

In this age few tragedies are written. It has often been held that the lack is due to a paucity of heroes among us, or else that modern man has had the blood drawn out of his organs of belief by the skepticism of science, and the heroic attack on life cannot feed on an attitude of reserve and circumspection. For one reason or another, we are often held to be below tragedy—or tragedy above us. The inevitable conclusion is, of course, that the tragic mode is archaic, fit only for the very highly placed, the kings or the kingly, and where this admission is not made in so many words it is most often implied.

I believe that the common man is as apt a subject for tragedy in its highest sense as kings were. On the face of it this ought to be obvious in the light of modern psychiatry, which bases its analysis upon classic formulations, such as the Oedipus and Orestes complexes, for instances, which were enacted by royal beings, but which apply to everyone in similar emotional situations.

More simply, when the question of tragedy in art is not at issue, we never hesitate to attribute to the well-placed and the exalted the very same mental processes as the lowly. And finally, if the exaltation of tragic action were truly a property of the high-bred character alone, it is inconceivable that the mass of mankind should cherish tragedy above all other forms, let alone be capable of understanding it.

As a general rule, to which there may be exceptions unknown to me, I think the tragic feeling is evoked in us when we are in the presence of a character who is ready to lay down his life, if need be, to secure one thing—his sense of personal dignity. From Orestes to Hamlet, Medea to Macbeth, the underlying struggle is that of the individual attempting to gain his "rightful" position in his society.

Sometimes he is one who has been displaced from it, sometimes one who seeks to attain it for the first time, but the fateful wound from which the inevitable events spiral is the wound of indignity, and its dominant force is indignation. Tragedy, then, is the consequence of a man's total compulsion to evaluate himself justly.

In the sense of having been initiated by the hero himself, the tale always reveals what has been called his "tragic flaw," a failing that is not peculiar to grand or elevated characters. Nor is it necessarily a weakness. The flaw, or crack in the character, is really nothing — and need be nothing, but his inherent unwillingness to remain passive in the face of what he conceives to be a challenge to his dignity, his image of his rightful status. Only the passive, only those who accept their lot without active retaliation, are "flawless." Most of us are in that category.

But there are among us today, as there always have been, those who act against the scheme of things that degrades them, and in the process of action everything we have accepted out of fear or insensitivity or ignorance is shaken before us and examined, and from this total onslaught by an individual against the seemingly stable cosmos surrounding us — from this total examination of the "unchangeable" environment — comes the terror and the fear that is classically associated with tragedy.

More important, from this total questioning of what has previously been unquestioned, we learn. And such a process is not beyond the common man. In revolutions around the world, these past thirty years, he has demonstrated again and again this inner dynamic of all tragedy.

Insistence upon the rank of the tragic hero, or the so-called nobility of his character, is really but a clinging to the outward forms of tragedy. If rank or nobility of character was indispensable, then it would follow that the problems of those with rank were the particular problems of tragedy. But surely the right of one monarch to capture the domain from another no longer raises our passions, nor are our concepts of justice what they were to the mind of an Elizabethan king.

The quality in such plays that does shake us, however, derives from the underlying fear of being displaced, the disaster inherent in being torn away from our chosen image of what and who we are in this world. Among us today this fear is as strong, and perhaps stronger, than it ever was. In fact, it is the common man who knows this fear best.

Now, if it is true that tragedy is the consequence of a man's total compulsion to evaluate himself justly, his destruction in the attempts posits a wrong or an evil in his environment. And this is precisely the morality of tragedy and its lesson. The discovery of the moral law, which is what the enlightenment of tragedy consists of, is not the discovery of some abstract or metaphysical quantity.

The tragic right is a condition of life, a condition in which the human personality is able to flower and realize itself. The wrong is the condition which suppresses man, perverts the flowing out of his love and creative instinct. Tragedy enlightens — and it must, in that it points the heroic finger at the enemy of man's freedom. The thrust for freedom is the quality in tragedy which exalts. The revolutionary questioning of the stable environment is what terrifies. In no way is the common man debarred from such thoughts or such actions.

Seen in this light, our lack of tragedy may be partially accounted for by the turn which modern literature has taken toward the purely psychiatric view of life, or the purely sociological. If all our miseries, our indignities, are born and bred within our minds, then all action, let alone the heroic action, is obviously impossible.

And if society alone is responsible for the cramping of our lives, then the protagonist must needs be so pure and faultless as to force us to deny his validity as a character. From neither of these views can tragedy derive, simply because neither represents a balanced concept of life. Above all else, tragedy requires the finest appreciation by the writer of cause and effect.

No tragedy can therefore come about when its author fears to question absolutely everything, when he regards any institution, habit or custom as being either everlasting, immutable or inevitable. In the tragic view the need of man to wholly realize himself is the only fixed star, and whatever it is that hedges his nature and lowers it is ripe for attack and examination. Which is not to say that tragedy must preach revolution.

The Greeks could probe the very heavenly origin of their ways and return to confirm the rightness of laws. And Job could face God in anger, demanding his right and end in submission. But for a moment everything is in suspension, nothing is accepted, and in this stretching and tearing apart of the cosmos, in the very action of so doing, the character gains "size," the tragic stature which is spuriously attached to the royal or the highborn in our minds. The commonest of men may take on that stature to the extent of his willingness to throw all he has into the contest, the battle to secure his rightful place in his world.

There is a misconception of tragedy with which I have been struck in review after review, and in many conversations with writers and readers alike. It is the idea that tragedy is of necessity allied to pessimism. Even the dictionary says nothing more about the word than that it means a story with a sad or unhappy ending. This impression is so firmly fixed that I almost hesitate to claim that in truth tragedy implies more optimism in its author than does comedy, and that its final result ought to be the reinforcement of the onlooker's brightest opinions of the human animal.

For, if it is true to say that in essence the tragic hero is intent upon claiming his whole due as a personality, and if this struggle must be total and without reservation, then it automatically demonstrates the indestructible will of man to achieve his humanity.

The possibility of victory must be there in tragedy. Where pathos rules, where pathos is finally derived, a character has fought a battle he could not possibly have won. The pathetic is achieved when the protagonist is, by virtue of his witlessness, his insensitivity or the very air he gives off, incapable of grappling with a much superior force.

Pathos truly is the mode for the pessimist. But tragedy requires a nicer balance between what is possible and what is impossible. And it is curious, although edifying, that the plays we revere, century after century, are the tragedies. In them, and in them alone, lies the belief—optimistic, if you will, in the perfectibility of man.

It is time, I think, that we who are without kings, took up this bright thread of our history and followed it to the only place it can possibly lead in our time—the heart and spirit of the average man.

[1949]

Arthur Miller on Willy Loman's Ideals

[In 1958 Arthur Miller made these comments during the course of a symposium on *Death of a Salesman*. The title is the editors'.]

Miller: The trouble with Willy Loman is that he has tremendously powerful ideals. We're not accustomed to speaking of ideals in his terms; but, if Willy Loman, for instance, had not had a very profound sense that his life as lived had left him hollow, he would have died contentedly polishing his car on some Sunday afternoon at a ripe old age. The fact is he has values. The fact that they cannot be realized is what is driving him mad—just as, unfortunately, it's driving a lot of other people mad. The truly valueless man, a man without ideals, is always perfectly at home anywhere . . . because there cannot be a conflict between nothing and something. Whatever negative qualities there are in the society or in the environment don't bother him, because they are not in conflict with what positive sense one may have. I think Willy Loman, on the other hand, is seeking for a kind of ecstasy in life, which the machine-civilization deprives people of. He's looking for his selfhood, for his immortal soul, so to speak. People who don't know the intensity of that quest, possibly, think he's odd. Now an extraordinarily large number of salesmen particularly, who are in a line of work where a large measure of ingenuity and individualism are required, have a very intimate understanding of this problem. More so, I think, than literary critics who probably need strive less after a certain point. A salesman is a kind of creative person (*it's possibly idiotic to say so on a literary program, but they are*), they have to get up in the morning and conceive a plan of attack and use all kinds of ingenuity all day long, just the way a writer does.

Joyce Carol Oates *(American; b. 1938)*

Tone Clusters

A Play in Nine Scenes

List of Characters

FRANK GULICK, *fifty-three years old*
EMILY GULICK, *fifty-one years old*
VOICE, *male, indeterminate age*

> These are white Americans of no unusual distinction, nor are they
> in any self-evident way "representative."

Tone Clusters is not intended to be a realistic work, thus any inclination
toward the establishment of character should be resisted. Its primary effect should be visual (the dominance of the screen at center stage, the
play of lights of sharply contrasting degrees of intensity) and audio (the
Voice, the employment of music — "tone clusters" of Henry Cowell and/or
Charles Ives, and electronic music, etc.) The mood is one of fragmentation, confusion, yet, at times, strong emotion. A fractured narrative emerges
which the audience will have no difficulty piecing together even as — and
this is the tragicomedy of the piece — the characters Mr. and Mrs. Gulick
deny it.

In structure, *Tone Clusters* suggests an interview; but a stylized interview in which questions and answers are frequently askew. Voices trail
off into silence or may be mocked or extended by strands of music. The
Voice is sometimes overamplified and booming; sometimes marred by
static; sometimes clear, in an ebullient tone, like that of a talk-show host.
The Voice has no identity but must be male. It should not be represented
by any actual presence on the stage or within view of the audience. At
all times, the Voice is in control: the principals on the stage are dominated
by their interrogator and by the screen, which is seemingly floating in
the air above them, at center stage. Indeed the screen emerges as a character.

The piece is divided into nine uneven segments. When one ends,
the lights dim, then come up again immediately. (After the ninth segment
the lights go out completely and darkness is extended for some seconds
to indicate that the piece is ended: it ends on an abrupt cutoff of lights
and images on the screen and the monitors.)

By degree the Gulicks become somewhat accustomed to the experience of being interviewed and filmed, but never wholly accustomed: they
are always slightly disoriented, awkward, confused, inclined to speak slowly
and methodically or too quickly, "unprofessionally," often with inappropri-
ate emotion (fervor, enthusiasm, hope, sudden rage) or no emotion at all
(like "computer voices"). The Gulicks may at times speak in unison (as if

In Darkest America (Tone Clusters) *by Joyce Carol Oates (1990 Humana Festival of New American Plays). Photo: Richard Trigg/Actors Theatre of Louisville.*

one were an echo of the other); they may mimic the qualities of tone-cluster music or electronic music (I conceive of their voices, and that of the Voice, as music of a kind); should the director wish, there may be some clear–cut relationship between subject and emotion or emphasis—but the piece should do no more than approach "realism," and then withdraw. The actors must conceive of themselves as elements in a dramatic structure, not as "human characters" wishing to establish rapport with an audience.

Tone Clusters is about the absolute mystery—the *not knowing*—at the core of our human experience. That the mystery is being exploited by a television documentary underscores its tragicomic nature.

SCENE 1

Lights up. Initially very strong, near-blinding. On a bare stage, middle-aged Frank and Emily Gulick sit ill-at-ease in "comfortable" modish cushioned swivel chairs, trying not to squint or grimace in the lights (which may be represented as the lights of a camera crew provided the human figures involved can be kept shadowy, even indistinct.) They wear clip-on microphones, to which they are unaccustomed. They are "dressed up" for the occasion, and clearly nervous: they continually touch their faces, or clasp their hands firmly in their laps, or fuss with fingernails, buttons, the microphone cords, their hair. The nervous mannerisms continue throughout the piece but should never be too distracting and never comic.

Surrounding the Gulicks, dominating their human presence, are the central screen and the TV monitors and/or slide screens upon which, during the course of the play, disparate images, words, formless flashes of light are projected. Even when the Gulicks' own images appear on the screens they are upstaged by it: they glance at it furtively, with a kind of awe.

The rest of the time, the monitors always show the stage as we see it: the Gulicks seated, glancing uneasily up at the large screen. Thus there is a "screen within a screen."

The employment of music is entirely at the director's discretion. The opening might be accompanied by classical tone cluster piano pieces—Henry Cowell's "Advertisement," for instance. The music should never be intrusive. The ninth scene might well be completely empty of music. There should certainly be no "film-music" effect. (The Gulicks do not hear the music.)

The Voice too in its modulations is at the discretion of the director. Certainly at the start the Voice is booming and commanding. There should be intermittent audio trouble (whistling, static, etc.); the Voice, wholly in control, can exude any number of effects throughout the play—pomposity, charity, condescension, bemusement, false chattiness, false pedantry, false sympathy, mild incredulity (like that of a television emcee), affectless "computer talk." The Gulicks are entirely intimidated by the Voice and try very hard to answer its questions.

Screen shifts from its initial image to words: IN A CASE OF MUR-DER—*large black letters on white.*

VOICE

In a case of murder   (taking murder as an abstraction)   there is
always a sense of the Inevitable   once the identity of the murderer
    is   established. Beforehand there   is   a sense   of
disharmony.
And humankind fears and loathes disharmony,
Mr. and Mrs. Gulick of Lakepointe, New Jersey, would you comment?

FRANK

. . . Yes I would say.   I think that

EMILY

What is that again, exactly?   I . . .

FRANK

My wife and I, we . . .

EMILY

Disharmony . . . ?

FRANK

I don't like disharmony.   I mean, all the family,
we are a law-abiding family.

VOICE

A religious family   I believe?

FRANK

Oh yes.   Yes,
We go to church every

EMILY

We almost never miss a,   a Sunday
For a while,   I helped with Sunday School classes
The children,   the children don't always go but they believe,
our daughter Judith for instance she   and Carl

FRANK

oh yes   yessir

EMILY

and Dennis.   they do believe they were raised to
believe in God and, and Jesus Christ

FRANK

We raised them that way because   we were raised that way,

EMILY

there *is* a God whether you agree with Him   or not.

VOICE

"Religion" may be defined as   a sort of adhesive matter invisibly
holding together   nation-states, nationalities, tribes, families
        for   the   good   of   those   so
                                        held together,
                            would you comment?

FRANK

Oh,   oh yes.

EMILY

For the good of . . .

FRANK

Yes I would say so,   I think so.

EMILY

My husband and I, we were married in church, in

FRANK

In the Lutheran Church.

EMILY

In Penns Neck.

FRANK

In New Jersey.

EMILY

All our children,

BOTH

they believe.

EMILY

God sees into the human heart.

VOICE

Mr. and Mrs. Gulick   from your experience would you   theorize for
our audience: is the Universe "predestined"   in every particular
        or   is   man   capable   of   acts   of   "freedom"?

BOTH

. . .

EMILY

. . . I would say,   that is hard to say.

FRANK

Yes. I believe that man is free.

EMILY

If you mean like, I guess   choosing good and evil?   Yes

FRANK

I would have to say   yes.   You would have to say
mankind is free.

FRANK

Like moving my hand. (*moves hand*)

EMILY

If nobody is free   it wouldn't be right would it
to punish anybody?

FRANK

There is always   Hell.
I believe in Hell.

EMILY

Anybody at all

FRANK

Though I am not free to, to   fly up in the air am I? (*laughs*)
because   Well I'm not built right for that am I? (*laughs*)

VOICE

Man is free.   Thus man is   responsible for his acts.

EMILY

Except, oh   sometime if,   maybe for instance if
A baby born without

FRANK

Oh one of those "AIDS" babies

EMILY

poor thing

FRANK

"crack" babies
Or if you were captured   by some enemy, y'know   and tortured
Some people never have a chance.

EMILY

But God sees into the human heart,
God knows who to forgive   and who not.

   Lights down.

SCENE 2

Lights up. Screen shows a suburban street of lower-income homes; the Gulicks stare at the screen and their answers are initially distracted.

VOICE

Here we have Cedar Street   in Lakepointe, New Jersey   neatly kept homes (as you can see)   American suburb   low crime rate, single-family homes   suburb of Newark, New Jersey   population twelve thousand   the neighborhood of Mr. and Mrs. Frank Gulick the parents of   Carl Gulick Will you introduce yourselves to our audience please?

(*House lights come up.*)

FRANK

. . . Go on, you first

EMILY

I, I don't know what to say

FRANK

My name is   Frank Gulick, I   I am fifty-three years old that's our house there   2368 Cedar Street

EMILY

My name is Emily Gulick, fifty-one years old,

VOICE

How employed,   would you care to say?   Mr. Gulick?

FRANK

I work for the post office,   I'm a supervisor for

EMILY

He has worked for the post office for twenty-five years

FRANK

. . . The Terhune Avenue branch.

VOICE

And how long have you resided   in your attractive home   on Cedar Street?

(*House lights begin to fade down.*)

FRANK

. . . Oh I guess, how long   if this is this is 1990?

EMILY

(oh just think: 1990!)

FRANK

we moved there in, uh   Judith wasn't born yet so

EMILY

Oh there was our thirtieth anniversary a year ago,

FRANK

wedding
no that was two years ago

EMILY

was it?

FRANK

or three, I   twenty-seven years, this is 1990

EMILY

Yes: Judith is twenty-six,   now I'm a grandmother

FRANK

Carl is twenty-two

EMILY

Denny is seventeen, he's a senior in high school
No none of them are living at home now

FRANK

not now

EMILY

Right now poor Denny is staying with my sister in

VOICE

Frank and Emily Gulick you have been happy here   in Lakepointe
raising your family like any   American couple   with your
hopes and aspirations
until recently?

FRANK

. . . Yes, oh yes.

EMILY

Oh for a long time we *were*

FRANK

oh yes.

EMILY

It's so strange to,   to think of
The years go by so

VOICE

You have led a   happy family life   like so many millions
of Americans

EMILY

Until this,   this terrible thing

FRANK

Innocent until proven guilty—that's a laugh!

EMILY

Oh it's a, a terrible thing

FRANK

Never any hint beforehand of   the meanness of people's hearts.
I mean the neighbors.

EMILY

Oh now don't start that,   this isn't the

FRANK

Oh God you just try to   comprehend

EMILY

this isn't the place, I

FRANK

Like last night: this carload of kids
drunk, beer-drinking   foul language in the night

EMILY

oh don't, my hands are

FRANK

Yes but you know it's the parents   set them going
And telephone calls   our number is changed now, but

EMILY

my hands are shaking so
we are both on medication   the doctor says,

FRANK

oh you would not believe, you would not   believe   the hatred
like Nazi Germany

EMILY

Denny had to drop out of school,   he loved school he is
an honor student

FRANK

everybody turned against us

EMILY

My sister in Yonkers, he's staying with

FRANK

Oh he'll never be the same   boy again.
none of us will.

VOICE

In the development of   human identity   there's the element
of chance,   and there is genetic determinism.
    Would you comment please?

FRANK

The thing is,   you try your best.

EMILY

oh dear God yes.

FRANK

Your best.

EMILY

You give all that's in your heart

FRANK

you
can't do more than that can you?

EMILY

Yes but there is certain to be   justice.
There *is* a, a sense of things.

FRANK

Sometimes there is a chance, the way they   turn out
but also   what they *are.*

EMILY

Your own babies

VOICE

Frank Gulick   and Mary   what is your assessment of
    American civilization   today?

EMILY

. . . it's Emily.

FRANK

My wife's name is,

EMILY

it's
Emily.

VOICE

Frank and EMILY   Gulick.

FRANK

. . . The state of the   civilization?

EMILY

It's so big,

FRANK

We are here to   tell our side of,

EMILY

. . . I don't know: it's a,   a Democracy

FRANK

the truth is,   do you want the truth?
the truth is where we live
Lakepointe
it's changing too

EMILY

it has changed

FRANK

Yes but it's all over, it's
terrible, just terrible

EMILY

Now we are grandparents we fear for

FRANK

Yes what you read and see on TV

EMILY

You don't know what to think,

FRANK

Look: in this country   half the crimes
are committed by the,   by half the population against

the other half.   (*laughs*)
You have your law-abiding citizens,

                          EMILY

taxpayers

                          FRANK
and you have the   rest of them
Say you went downtown into a city like   Newark, some night

                          EMILY
you'd be crazy if you got out of your car

                          FRANK
you'd be dead.   That's what.

                          VOICE
Is it possible,   probable   or in your assessment *im*probable
that the slaying of   fourteen-year-old   Edith Kaminsky
        on February 12, 1990   is related to
                              the social malaise
                          of which you speak?

                          FRANK
. . . "ma-lezz"?

                          EMILY
. . . oh it's hard to,   I would say yes

                          FRANK
. . . whoever did it, he

                          EMILY
Oh it's terrible the things that
keep happening

                          FRANK
If only the police would arrest the right person,

                          VOICE
Frank and Emily Gulick   you remain adamant in your belief
in your faith in your twenty-two-year-old son   Carl
        that he is innocent   in the death of
              fourteen-year-old Edith Kaminsky
                  on February 12, 1990?

                          EMILY
Oh yes,

FRANK

oh yes that is
the single thing we are convinced of

EMILY

On this earth.

BOTH

With God as our witness,

FRANK

yes

EMILY

Yes.

FRANK

The single thing.

Lights down.

SCENE 3

Lights up. Screen shows violent movement: urban scenes, police patrol cars, a fire burning out of control, men being arrested and herded into vans; a body lying in the street. The Gulicks stare at the screen.

VOICE

Of today's pressing political issues   the rise in violent crime
most concerns American citizens   Number-one political issue of
        Mr. and Mrs. Gulick   tell our viewers your opinion?

FRANK

In this state,
the state of New Jersey

EMILY

Oh it's everywhere

FRANK

there's capital punishment supposedly

EMILY

But the lawyers   the lawyers get them off.

FRANK

you bet
There's public defenders the taxpayer pays

EMILY

Oh, it's   it's out of control
(like that, what is it   "acid rain"

FRANK

it can fall on you anywhere,

EMILY

the sun is too hot too:

BOTH

the "greenhouse effect")

FRANK

It's a welfare state by any other name

EMILY

Y'know who pays:

BOTH

the taxpayer

FRANK

The same God damn criminal, you pay for him   then he
That's the joke of it (*laughs*)
the same criminal who slits your throat (*laughs*)
He's the one you pay bail for, to get out.
But it sure isn't funny.   (*laughs*)

EMILY

Oh God.

FRANK

It sure isn't funny.

VOICE

Many Americans have come to believe   this past decade   that
capital punishment is one of the   answers: would you
comment please?

FRANK

Oh in cases of actual, proven   murder

EMILY

Those drug dealers

FRANK

Yes *I* would have to say, definitely   yes

                              EMILY

I would say so yes

                              FRANK

You always hear them say   opponents of the death penalty
"The death penalty doesn't stop crime"

                              EMILY

Oh that's what they say!

                              FRANK

Yes but *I* say, once a man is dead   he sure ain't gonna commit
any more crimes, is he.   *(laughs)*

                              VOICE

The death penalty *is* a deterrent to crime   in those cases
when the criminal has been   executed

                              FRANK

But you have to find the right,
the actual murderer.

                              EMILY

Not some poor innocent*   some poor innocent*

   Lights down.

SCENE 4

   *Lights up. Screen shows a grainy magnified snapshot of a boy about ten. Quick
   jump to a snapshot of the same boy a few years older. Throughout this scene
   images of "Carl Gulick" appear and disappear on the screen though not in strict
   relationship to what is being said, nor in chronological order. "Carl Gulick" in
   his late teens and early twenties is muscular but need not have any other outstanding characteristics: he may look like any American boy at all.*

                              VOICE

Carl Gulick, twenty-two years old   the second-born child of Frank
and Emily Gulick   of Lakespointe, New Jersey   How would you
describe your son, Frank and Emily

                              FRANK

D'you mean how he looks or . . . ?

                              EMILY

He's a shy boy, he's   shy   Not backward just

---

*"innocent" is an adjective here, not a noun.

FRANK

He's about my height I guess   brown hair, eyes

EMILY

Oh! no I think   no he's much taller Frank
he's been taller than you   for years

FRANK

Well that depends on how we're both standing.
How we're both   standing
Well in one newspaper it said six feet one inch, in the other
six feet three inches, that's the kind of

EMILY

accuracy

FRANK

reliability of the news media
you can expect!

EMILY

And oh that terrible picture of,
in the paper
that face he was making   the police carrying him
against his will   laying their hands on him

FRANK

handcuffs

EMILY

Oh that isn't *him*

BOTH

that isn't our son

   (*Gulicks respond dazedly to snapshots flashed on screen.*)

EMILY

Oh! that's Carl   age I guess about

FRANK

four?

EMILY

that's at the beach one summer

FRANK

only nine or ten, he was big for

FRANK

that's my brother George

EMILY

That's

EMILY

With his sister Judith

FRANK

He loved Boy Scouts,

EMILY

but
Oh when you are the actual parents it's
a different

FRANK

Oh it is so different!
from something just on TV.

VOICE

In times of disruption   of fracture   it is believed that
human behavior moves   in unchartable leaps   History is a formal
record of such   leaps   but in large-scale demographical   terms
      in which the   individual   is   lost
            Frank and Emily Gulick it's said your son   Carl   charged
in the savage slaying of   fourteen-year-old   shows no sign of
      remorse   that is to say, *awareness* of the act:
thus the question we pose to you   Can guilt reside in those
      without conscience,
or is memory   conscience, and conscience memory?
      can "the human" reside in those
            devoid of "memory"

EMILY

. . . Oh the main thing is,
he is innocent.

FRANK

. . . Stake my life on it.

EMILY

He has always been   cheerful, optimistic

FRANK

a good boy, of course he has not
forgotten

BOTH

He is innocent.

EMILY

How could our son "forget" when he has nothing to

BOTH

"forget"

FRANK

He took that lie detector test voluntarily didn't he

EMILY

Oh there he is   weight-lifting, I don't remember
who took that picture?

FRANK

When you are the actual parents you see them every day,
you don't form judgments.

VOICE

And how is your son employed, Mr. and Mrs. Kaminsky?
Excuse me: GULICK.

FRANK

Up until Christmas he was working in
This butcher shop in East Orange

EMILY

... it isn't easy, at that age

FRANK

Before that, loading and unloading

EMILY

at Sear's at the mall

FRANK

No: that was before, that was before the other

EMILY

No: the job at Sear's was

FRANK

... Carl was working for that Italian, y'know that

EMILY

the lawn service

FRANK

Was that before?   or after
Oh in this butcher shop   his employer

EMILY

yes there were hard feelings, on both sides

FRANK

Look: you can't believe a single thing   in the newspaper or TV

EMILY

it's not that they lie

FRANK

Oh yes they lie

EMILY

not that they lie, they just   get everything wrong

FRANK

Oh they do lie!   and it's printed and you can't stop them.

EMILY

In this meat shop, I never wanted him to work there

FRANK

In this shop there was pressure on him
to join the union.

EMILY

Then the other side, his employer
did not want him to join.
He's a sensitive boy,   his stomach and nerves
He lost his appetite for weeks, he'd say "oh if you could see
some of the things I see"   "the insides of things"
and so much blood

VOICE

There was always a loving   relationship   in the household?

EMILY

. . . When they took him away he said,   he was so brave
he said Momma I'll be back soon
I'll be right back,   I am innocent he said
I don't know how she came to be in   our house
I don't know,   I don't know he said
I looked into my son's eyes and saw   truth shining
His eyes have always been   dark green,
like mine.

VOICE

On the afternoon of   February 12 you have told police that
no one was home   in your house?

EMILY

I, I was . . . I had a doctor's appointment,
My husband was working, he doesn't get home until

FRANK

Whoever did it,   and brought her body in

EMILY

No: they say she was   they say it,   it happened there

FRANK

No I don't buy that,   He brought her in   carried her
whoever that was,
I believe he tried   other houses
seeing who was home and who   wasn't
and then he

EMILY

Oh it was like lightning striking

VOICE

Your son Dennis   was at Lakepointe High School attending a meeting
of the yearbook staff,   your son Carl has told police he
     was   riding   his   motor scooter
          in the park,

FRANK

They dragged him like   an animal
put their hands on him like
Like Nazi Germany,

EMILY

it couldn't be any worse

FRANK

And that judge
it's a misuse of power, it's

EMILY

I just don't understand

VOICE

Your son Carl on and after   February 12   did not exhibit
(in your presence) any unusual sign of   emotion?
     agitation? guilt?

EMILY

Every day in a house,   a household
is like the other days.   Oh you never step back,   never *see.*
Like I told them, the   police,   everybody. *He did not.*

Lights down.

SCENE 5

Lights up. Screen shows snapshots, photographs, of the murdered girl Kaminsky. Like Carl Gulick, she is anyone at all of that age: white, neither strikingly beautiful nor unattractive.

VOICE

Sometime in the evening of February 12 of this year forensic reports
say   fourteen-year-old Edith Kaminsky daughter of   neighbors
2361 Cedar Street, Lakepointe, New Jersey   multiple stab wounds,
sexual assault   strangulation
An arrest has been made but   legally or otherwise,   the absolute
identity of the murderer has yet to be

EMILY

Oh it's so unjust,

FRANK

the power of a single man
That judge

EMILY

Carl's birthday is   next week
Oh God he'll be in that terrible   cold place

FRANK

"segregated" they call it
How can a judge refuse to set bail

EMILY

oh I would borrow a million dollars
if I could

FRANK

Is this America or   Russia?

EMILY

I can't stop crying

FRANK

. . . we are both under medication you see but

EMILY

Oh it's true he wasn't himself   sometimes.

FRANK

But that day when it happened, that wasn't one of the times.

VOICE

You hold out for the possibility that   the true murderer
     carried Edith Kaminsky into your house,   into your basement
thus meaning to throw suspicion on your son?

FRANK

Our boy is guiltless that's the main thing, I will never doubt that.

EMILY

Our body is innocent . . .   What did I say?

FRANK

Why the hell do they make so much of
Carl lifting weights, his   muscles
He is not a freak.

EMILY

There's lots of them   and women too, today   like that,

FRANK

He has other interests he used to collect stamps   play baseball

EMILY

Oh there's so much misunderstanding

FRANK

actual lies
Because the police do not know who the murderer *is*
of course they will blame   anyone they can.

Lights down.

SCENE 6

*Lights up. Screen shows the exterior of the Gulick house seen from various an-
gles; then the interior (the basement, evidently, and the "storage area" where the
young girl's body was found).*

VOICE

If, as is believed, "premeditated" acts arise   out of a
mysterious sequence of neuron discharges   (in the brain)
out of what source   do
     "unpremeditated"   acts   arise?

EMILY

Nobody was down in,   in the basement
until the police came.   The storage space is behind the
water heater,   but

FRANK

My God if my son is   so shiftless   like people are saying
just look: he helped me paint the house last summer

EMILY

Yes Carl and Denny both,

FRANK

Why are they telling such   lies, our neighbors?   We have never
wished them harm,

EMILY

I believed a certain neighbor was my friend,   her and I, we
we'd go shopping together   took my car
Oh my heart is broken

FRANK

It's robin's-egg blue,   the paint turned out brighter than
when it dried, a little brighter than we'd   expected

EMILY

I think it's pretty

FRANK

Well.   We'll have to sell the house,   there's no choice
the legal costs   Mr. Filco our attorney has said

EMILY

He told us

FRANK

he's going to fight all the way, he believes Carl is   innocent

EMILY

My heart is broken.

FRANK

My heart isn't,
I'm going to fight this all the way

EMILY

A tragedy like this,   you learn fast who is your friend and who
is your enemy

FRANK

Nobody's your friend.

VOICE

The Gulicks and Kaminskys were   well acquainted?

EMILY

We lived on Cedar first,   when they moved in I don't remember:
my mind isn't right these days

FRANK

Oh yes   we knew them

EMILY

I'd have said Mrs. Kaminsky   was my friend, but
that's how people are

FRANK

Yes

EMILY

Carl knew her,   Edith
I mean, we all did

FRANK

but not well.

EMILY

just neighbors
Now they're our declared enemies, the Kaminskys

FRANK

well,   so be it.

EMILY

Oh! that poor girl   if only she hadn't,
I mean, there's no telling who   she was with,   walking home
walking home from school I guess

FRANK

Well she'd been missing overnight,

EMILY

yes overnight

FRANK

of course we were aware

FRANK

The Kaminskys came around ringing doorbells,

EMILY

then the police,

FRANK

then
they got a search party going,   Carl helped them out

EMILY

Everybody said how much he helped

FRANK

he kept at it for hours
They walked miles and miles,
he's been out of work for a while,

EMILY

he'd been looking
in the *help wanted* ads but

FRANK

. . . He doesn't like to use the telephone.

EMILY

People laugh at him he says,

FRANK

I told him no he was imagining it.

EMILY

This neighborhood:

FRANK

you would not believe it.

EMILY

Call themselves Christians

FRANK

Well   some are Jews.

EMILY

Well it's still white isn't it   a white neighborhood,   you expect
better.

VOICE

The murder weapon   has yet to be found?

FRANK

One of the neighbors had to offer an opinion,   something sarcastic
I guess

EMILY

Oh don't go into *that*

FRANK

the color of the paint   on our house
So Carl said, You don't like it, wear sunglasses.

EMILY

But,
he was smiling.

VOICE

A young man with a sense of   humor.

FRANK

Whoever hid that poor girl's
body
in the storage space of our
basement well clearly it
obviously it was   to deceive
to cast blame on our son.

EMILY

Yes   if there were fingerprints down there,

BOTH

that handprint they found on the wall

FRANK

well for God's sake it was from when Carl
was down there

BOTH

helping them

FRANK

He cooperated with them,

EMILY

Frank wasn't home,

FRANK

Carl led them downstairs

EMILY

Why they came to our house, I don't know.
Who was saying things   I don't know,
it was like everybody had gone   crazy
casting blame on all sides.

VOICE

Mr. and Mrs. Gulick   it's said that from your son's room
Lakepointe police officers confiscated   comic books, military
magazines, pornographic magazines   a cache of more than one dozen
       knives including   switchblades   plus
a U.S. Army bayonet (World War II)   Nazi memorabilia
     including a "souvenir" SS helmet   (manufactured in Taiwan)
a pink plastic skull   with lightbulbs in eyes
      a naked Barbie doll, badly scratched   bitten
        numerous pictures of naked women
      and women in fashion magazines,   their eyes
breasts   crotches   cut out with a scissors
     (*pause*)
Do you have any comment   Mr. and Mrs. Gulick?

FRANK

. . . .
Mainly they were hobbies,

EMILY

I guess I don't,

FRANK

we didn't know about

EMILY

Well   he wouldn't allow me in his room,   to vacuum, or

FRANK

You know how boys are

EMILY

Didn't want his mother

FRANK

poking her nose in

EMILY

So . . .

    (*Emily upsets a glass of water on the floor.*)

VOICE

Police forensic findings   bloodstains, hairs, semen
     and DNA 'fingerprinting'   constitute a tissue of
      circumstance   linking your son to

EMILY (*interrupting*)
Mr. Filco says   it's all pieced together
'Circumstantial evidence,' he says   not proof

FRANK

I call it bullshit   (*laughs*)

EMILY

Oh Frank

FRANK

I call it bullshit (*laughs*)

VOICE

Eyewitness accounts disagree,   two parties report
having seen Carl Gulick and Edith Kaminsky   walking together
in the afternoon, in the alley   behind Cedar Street
      a third party   a neighbor   claims to have seen
the girl   in the company of a   stranger   at approximately
      4:15 PM   And Carl Gulick insists
he was 'riding his motor scooter'   all afternoon

FRANK

He is a boy

EMILY

not capable of lying

FRANK

Look: I would have to discipline him sometimes,

EMILY

You have to, with boys

FRANK

Oh yes you have to, otherwise

EMILY

He was always a good eater   didn't fuss

FRANK

He's a quiet boy

EMILY

You can't guess his thoughts

FRANK

But he loved his mother and father   respected

EMILY

Always well behaved at home
That ugly picture in the paper, oh

FRANK

THAT WASN'T HIM

EMILY

You can't believe   the cruelty in the human heart

FRANK

Giving interviews! his own teachers from the school

EMILY

Telling lies   cruel   nasty

FRANK

His own teachers from the   school

VOICE

Mr. and Mrs. Gulick   you had no suspicion
             no   awareness
   you had no sense   of   the   fact
      that the battered   raped   mutilated body of
             fourteen-year-old Edith Kaminsky
         was hidden in your basement   in a storage space
             wrapped in plastic garbage bags
for approximately   forty   hours

GULICKS

. . . .

VOICE

No consciousness of   disharmony
   in your household?

FRANK

It was a day like

EMILY

   It *was,*   I mean, it wasn't

FRANK

I keep the cellar clean, I   There's leakage

EMILY

Oh
Last week at my sister's   where we were staying,
we had to leave   this terrible place

in Yonkers I was crying,   I could not stop   crying
downstairs in the kitchen   three in the morning
I was standing by a window and there was suddenly   it looked
like snow!
it was moonlight moving in the window and there came a   shadow I
guess
like an eclipse?   was there an eclipse?
Oh I felt so, I felt   my heart stopped Oh but I, I wasn't scared
I was thinking   I was seeing how the world is
how the universe *is*
it's so hard to say, I feel like a   a fool
I was gifted by this, by   seeing   how the world *is* not
how you see it   with your eyes, or talk   talk about it
I mean names you give to,   parts of it   No I mean how it *is*
when there is nobody there.

VOICE

A subliminal conviction of disharmony   may be nullified by   a
     transcendental leap of   consciousness: to a "higher plane"
          of celestial harmony,
          would you comment   Mr. and Mrs. Gulick?

EMILY

Then Sunday night it was,

FRANK

this last week

EMILY

they came again

FRANK

threw trash on our lawn

EMILY

screamed
Murderers! they were drunk, yelling   in the night *Murderers!*

FRANK

There was the false report that Carl was released on   bail
that he was home with us

EMILY

Oh dear God if only that was true

FRANK

I've lost fifteen pounds since February

EMILY

Oh Frank has worked so hard   on that lawn,
it's his pride and joy and in the neighborhood   everybody knows,
they compliment him,   and now
Yes he squats right out there, he pulls out crabgrass   by hand
Dumping such such ugly nasty disgusting things
Then in the A&P a woman followed me   up and down the aisles
I could hear people   *That's her, that's the mother of*
the murderer   I could hear them   everywhere in the store
Is that her,   is that the mother of the murderer? they were saying
Lived in this neighborhood, in this town   for so many years
we thought we were welcome here and now
Aren't you ashamed to show your face!   a voice screamed
What can I do with my face,   can I hide it forever?

FRANK

And all this when our boy is   innocent.

VOICE

Perceiving the inviolate nature of   the Universe   apart from human
suffering   rendered you happy, Mrs. Gulick   is this so?
                    for some precious moments?

EMILY

Oh yes, I was crying but
not because of
no   I was crying because
I was happy I think.

   Lights down.

SCENE 7

   *Lights up. Screen shows neurological X-rays, medical diagrams, charts as of EEG
   and CAT-scan tests.*

VOICE

Is it possible that in times of   fracture, of evolutionary
unease   or, perhaps, at any time   human behavior mimics that
of minute   particles   of light?   The atom is primarily emptiness
          the neutron dense-packed
The circuitry of the human brain   circadian rhythms   can be tracked
but never,   it's said comprehended.   And then   in descent
from "identity"—(memory?)   to tissue to cells to cell-particles
     electrical impulses   axon-synapse-dendrite
               and beyond, be-
                    neath

to subatomic bits
Where is "Carl Gulick"?

(Gulicks turn to each other in bewilderment. Screen flashes images: kitchen interior; weight-lifting paraphernalia; a shelf of trophies; photographs; domestic scenes, etc.)

VOICE

Mr. and Mrs. Gulick you did not notice anything   unusual   in your son's behavior on the night of February 12   or the following day,   to the best   of your recollection?

EMILY

... Oh we've told the police this so many   many times

FRANK

Oh you forget what you remember,

EMILY

That night, before we knew there was anyone missing   I mean, in the neighborhood   anyone we knew

FRANK

I can't remember.

EMILY

Yes but Carl had supper with us like always

FRANK

No I think,   he was napping up in his room

EMILY

he was at the table with us:

FRANK

I remember   he came down around nine o'clock,   but he did eat.

EMILY

Him and Denny, they were at the table with us

FRANK

We've told the police this so many times, it's
I don't know any longer

EMILY

I'm sure it was Denny too.   Both our sons.
We had meatloaf   ketchup baked on top, it's the boys'
favorite dish just about   isn't it?

FRANK

Oh anything with hamburger and ketchup!

EMILY

Of course he was at the table with us,   he had his usual appetite.

FRANK

... he was upstairs, said he had a touch of   flu

EMILY

Oh no he was there.

FRANK

It's hard to speak of your own flesh and blood,   as if
they are other people
it's hard   without giving false testimony against your will.

VOICE

Is the intrusion of the "extra-ordinary"   into the dimension of the
"ordinary"   an indication that such Aristotelian categories are
invalid?   If one day fails to resemble the preceding
          what does it resemble?

FRANK

... He has sworn to us, we are his parents
He did not touch a hair of that poor child's head   let alone the rest.
Anybody who knew him, they'd know

EMILY

Oh those trophies!   he was so proud
one of them is from the, I guess the Lakepointe YMCA
there's some from the New Jersey competition   at Atlantic City
two years ago?

FRANK

no, he was in high school
the first was, Carl was only fifteen years old

EMILY

Our little muscleman!

VOICE

Considering the evidence of thousands of years   of human culture
of language   art   religion   the judicial system   "The family
unit"   athletics   hobbies   fraternal organizations
charitable impulses   gods of all species
is   it   possible   that   humankind   desires
          not   to   know
               its   place   in
                    the
                         food cycle?

EMILY

One day he said
He wasn't going back to school,
my heart was broken.

FRANK

Only half his senior year ahead
but you can't argue,   not with

EMILY

oh his temper!   he takes after,
oh I don't know who

FRANK

we always have gotten along together
in this household   haven't we

EMILY

yes but the teachers would laugh at him he said
girls laughed at him he said   stared and pointed at him he said
and there was this pack of   oh we're not prejudiced
against Negroes,   it's just that
the edge of the Lakepointe school district
well

FRANK

Carl got in fights sometimes
in the school cafeteria and   I guess the park?

EMILY

the park isn't safe for law-abiding people these days
they see the color of your skin,   they'll attack
some of them are just like animals   yes they *are*

FRANK

Actually our son was attacked first   it isn't like he got
into fights by himself

EMILY

Who his friends are now, I don't   remember

FRANK

He is a quiet boy, keeps to himself

EMILY

he wanted to work
he was looking for work

FRANK

Well: our daughter Judith was misquoted about that

EMILY

also about Carl having a bad temper   she never said that
the reporter for the paper twisted her words
Mr. Filco says   we might sue

FRANK

Look: our son never raised a hand against anybody let alone against

EMILY

He loves his mother and father,   he respects us

FRANK

He is a religious boy at heart

EMILY

He looked me in the eyes he said   Momma you believe me don't
you?   and I said Oh yes   Oh yes   he's just my baby

FRANK

nobody knows him

EMILY

nobody knows him the way we do

FRANK

who would it be, if they did?
I ask you.

SCENE 8

House lights come up, TV screen shows video rewind. Sounds of audio rewind.
Screen shows Gulicks on stage.

VOICE

Frank and Mary Gulick we're very sorry   something happened to
the tape we're going to have to re-shoot   Let's go back just to,
we're showing an interior   Carl's room   the trophies
     I will say,   I'll be repeating
          Are you ready?

(House lights out, all tech returns to normal.)
          Well Mr. and Mrs. Gulick your son has
               quite a collection of trophies!

FRANK

. . . I,   I don't remember what I

EMILY

. . . yes he,

FRANK

Carl was proud of   he had other hobbies though

EMILY

Oh he was so funny, didn't want his mother   poking in his room
he said

FRANK

Yes but that's   how boys are

EMILY

That judge refuses to set bail, which I don't   understand

FRANK

Is this the United States or   is this the Soviet Union?

EMILY

we are willing to sell our house to stand up for what is

VOICE

You were speaking of your son Carl   having quit school,
     his senior year?   and then?

EMILY

. . . He had a hard time, the teachers   were down on him.

FRANK

I don't know why,

EMILY

we were never told
And now in the newspapers

FRANK

the kinds of lies they are saying

EMILY

that he got into fights, that he was

EMILY

that kind of thing is all a distortion

EMILY

He was always a quiet boy

FRANK

but he had his own friends

EMILY

they came over to the house sometime, I don't remember   who

FRANK

there was that one boy what was his name

EMILY

Oh Frank   Carl hasn't seen him in years
he had friends in grade school

FRANK

Look: in the newspaper there were false statements

EMILY

Mr. Filco says   we might sue

FRANK

Oh no: he says we can't,   we have to prove "malice"

EMILY

Newspapers and TV are filled with lies

FRANK

Look: our son Carl never raised a hand against anybody let alone against

EMILY

He loves his mother and father,

FRANK

he respects us

VOICE

Frank and,   it's Emily isn't it   Frank and Emily Gulick
that is very moving.

Lights down.

SCENE 9

Lights up. Screen shows Gulicks in theater.

VOICE

The discovery of radioactive elements   in the late nineteenth
century enabled scientists to set back the estimated age of the Earth
to several billion years,   and the discovery in more
recent decades   that the Universe is expanding,   thus that .
there is a point in Time when the Universe   was tightly
compressed   smaller than your tiniest fingernail!
thus that the age of the Universe is many billions

    of   years
    uncountable.
Yet   humankind resides in Time,   God bless us.
    Frank and Emily Gulick as we wind down *our* time together
        What are your plans for the future?

FRANK

. . . Oh that is, that's hard to   that's hard to answer.

EMILY

It depends I guess on

FRANK

Mr. Filco has advised

EMILY

I guess it's,
next is the grand jury

FRANK

Yes: the grand jury.
Mr. Filco cannot be present for the session   to protect our boy
I don't understand the law, just the prosecutor is there
swaying the jurors' minds
Oh I try to understand but I can't,

EMILY

he says we should be prepared
we should be prepared for a trial

VOICE

You are ready for the trial   to clear your son's name?

FRANK

Oh yes . . .

EMILY

yes that is a way of,   of putting it
Yes.   To clear Carl's name.

FRANK

. . . Oh yes you have to be realistic.

EMILY

Yes but before that   the true murderer of Edith Kaminsky
might come forward.
If the true murderer is watching this   *Please come forward.*

FRANK

... Well we both believe Carl is protecting someone, some
friend   another boy

EMILY

the one who really   committed the terrible crime

FRANK

So all we can do is pray.   Pray Carl will come
to his senses   give police the other boy's name, or
I believe this: if it's a friend of Carl's
he must have some decency   in his heart

VOICE

Your faith   in your son remains unshaken?

EMILY

You would have had to see his   toes,
his tiny baby toes in his bath.
His curly hair,   splashing in the bath.
His yellow rompers or no: I guess that was Denny

FRANK

If your own flesh and blood looks you in the eye,
you believe

EMILY

Oh yes.

VOICE

Human personality, it might be theorized, is a phenomenon of memory
yet memory   built up from cells, and   atoms does not "exist":
     thus memory   like mind   like personality
          is but a fiction?

EMILY

Oh   remembering backward is so hard!
oh it's,

FRANK

it pulls your brain in two.

EMILY

This medication the doctor gave me, my mouth   my mouth is so
dry
In the middle of the night I wake up drenched in

FRANK

You don't know who you are   until a thing like this happens,
then you don't know.

EMILY

It tears your brain in two, trying to   remember,
like even looking at the pictures
Oh you are lost

FRANK

in Time you are lost

EMILY

You fall and fall,
. . . ever since the,   the butcher shop
he wasn't always himself   but
who he was then, I don't know.   But
it's so hard, remembering why.

FRANK

Yes my wife means thinking backward the way   the way the police
make you, so many questions   you start forgetting right away
it comes out crazy.
Like now,   right here   I don't remember anything up to now
I mean, I can't swear to it: the first time, you see, we just
lived. We lived in our house. I am a, I am a post office employee
I guess I said that?   well, we live in our,   our house.
I mean, it was the first time through.   Just living
Like the TV, the picture's always on if nobody's watching it
you know?   So,   the people we were then,
I guess I'm trying to say
those actual people, me and her   the ones you see *here*
aren't them. (*laughs*)
I guess that sounds crazy,

VOICE

We have here the heartbeat   of parental love and faith, it's
a beautiful thing   Frank and Molly Gullick, please comment?

FRANK

We are that boy's father and mother.
We know that our son is not a murderer and a,   a rapist

EMILY

We know, if that girl came to harm,   there is some reason
for it to be revealed, but
they never found the knife, for one thing

FRANK

or whatever it was

EMILY

They never found the knife, the murderer could tell them where
it's buried, or   whatever it was.
Oh he could help us so   if he just would.

VOICE

And your plans for the future,   Mr. and Mrs. Gulick of Lakepointe,
New Jersey?

FRANK

. . . Well.
I guess,   I guess we don't have any.

   (*Long silence, to the point of awkwardness.*)

VOICE

. . . Plans for the future, Mr. and Mr. Gulick of Lakepointe, New Jersey?

FRANK

The thing is, you discover   you need to be protected
from your own thoughts sometimes,   but
who is there to do it?

EMILY

God didn't make any of us strong enough I guess.

FRANK

Look: one day in a family like this, it's   like the next day
and the day before.

EMILY

You could say it *is* the next day, I mean the same   the same day.

FRANK

Until one day it isn't

   Lights slowly down, then out.

(THE END)

[1991]

TOPICS FOR DISCUSSION AND WRITING

1. In her introductory note Oates says that in *Tone Clusters* "A fractured narrative emerges which the audience will have no difficulty piecing together even as — and this is the tragi-comedy of the piece — the characters Mr. and Mrs. Gulick deny it." In a few sentences set forth the narrative, and then evaluate Oates's view that the piece is a "tragi-comedy."

2. The first stage direction begins, "Lights up. Initially very strong, near blinding." Why do you suppose Oates begins this way? Later in the first stage direction we are told that the Gulicks "are 'dressed up' for the occasion." If you were the director, exactly how might you dress them?

3. On the basis of the Voice's first speech (two sentences), how would you characterize the Voice? (Incidentally, Oates in her initial stage direction says that the Voice "has no identity but must be male." Do you think that if the Voice were female the play would be substantially changed? Why?)

4. In "On Writing Drama" Oates says (page 1161): ". . . *Tone Clusters,* which exists in my imagination as a purely experimental work about the fracturing of reality in an electronic era, is always, for others, 'about' a crime." What do you take Oates to mean when she speaks of "the fracturing of reality in an electronic era"?

A CONTEXT FOR *TONE CLUSTERS*

Joyce Carol Oates, *On Writing Drama*

Writing for the stage when one has written primarily for publication, to be read, is an extremely challenging task, though it's difficult to say why. The written word and the spoken word are both *words* — aren't they?

Yet, as the fiction writer begins the task of writing drama, he or she discovers that the techniques of prose fiction simply do not apply to the stage. Still more, the task of "adapting" fiction for the stage is problematic, for one quickly discovers that it is not "adapting" so much as "transposing" that must be done. How much easier, how much more expedient, simply to set aside the fiction and begin anew, from a new angle of vision!

The essential difference between prose fiction and drama is that in prose fiction, it is the narrative voice, the writerly voice, that tells the story; in drama, of course, characters' voices are usually unmediated, direct. In a memory play, the central character may speak to the audience as a narrator, but only to introduce the action in which, then, he or she will participate. The prose writer's sheltering cocoon of language dissolves in the theater, and what is exposed is the bare skeleton of dialogue—action—subterranean/subtextual movement. Suddenly, everything must be dramatized for the eye and the ear; nothing can be summarized. Description simply *is*. Does that sound easy?

Many a gifted prose writer has failed at writing plays for lack of, not talent exactly, but an elusive quality that might just be humility. In itself, humility won't make a fiction writer or a poet into a playwright, but it is a helpful starting place.

Drama, unlike prose fiction, is not an interior esthetic phenomenon. It is communal; its meeting ground is the juncture at which the sheerly imaginary (the playwright's creation) is brought into being by the incontestably real (the living stage). Unlike prose fiction, with its many strategies of advance and retreat, flashbacks, flashforwards, digressions, analyses, interruptions, drama depends upon immediately establishing and sustaining visceral tension; in powerful plays, force fields of emotion are virtually visible on stage. When tension is resolved, it must be in purely emotional terms.

Drama remains our highest communal celebration of the mystery of being, and of our being together, in relationships we struggle to define, and which define us. It makes the point, ceaselessly, that our lives are *now;* there is no history that is not *now.*

When I write poetry and prose fiction, every punctuation mark is debated over in my head; my poetry is a formalist's obsession, in which even margins and blank spaces function as part of the poem. (Not that anyone else would notice, or that I would expect anyone else to notice. Poets quickly learn, and come to be content in, the loneliness of their obsessions.) When I write for the stage, however, I write for others; especially in the hope of striking an imaginative chord in a director whose sensibility is as quirky as my own. Which is not to imply that I am without a deep, abiding, and frequently stubborn sense of what a play of mine is, or an interior vision with which it is inextricably bound. It's simply that, to me, a text is a text—inviolable, yet without life. A play is something else entirely, and so is a film. It is this mysterious "something else"—the something that is others' imaginations in collaboration with my own—that arouses my interest.

Well-intentioned, print-oriented people are forever asking, "Doesn't it upset you to see your characters taken over by other people, out of your control?" My reply is generally a mild one: "But isn't that the point of writing for the theater?"

As soon ask of a novelist, "Doesn't it upset you if strangers read your books, and impose their own interpretations on them?"

In 1985 I attended the West Coast premiere of my play *The Triumph of the Spider Monkey* at the Los Angeles Theatre Center. As directed by

Al Rossi and featuring the popular young actor Shaun Cassidy, my grimly satirical posthumous-confessional play about a youthful mass murderer who becomes a fleeting media celebrity in Southern California had been transformed into a fluid succession of brief scenes, with a rock music score and arresting stage devices—a sort of showcase for Cassidy, whose energetic presence in this unknown work by a little-known playwright assured sellout performances for the play's limited run, and some enthusiastic reviews by critics who might otherwise have been skeptical about the credentials of a prose writer turned playwright. My collaboration with Mr. Rossi had been by way of telephone and through the mail, and my pleasure in the production was enormous, both because it was very well done and because it was in the nature of a surprise. *The Triumph of the Spider Monkey,* reimagined by another, was no longer my play; "my" play, published in book form (in *Three Plays,* Ontario Review Press, 1980), consists of words, a text. This was something else. And it may have been that my fascination with it was in direct proportion to the degree to which I was surprised by it.

Of course, over the years, since I first began writing plays (in 1967, at the invitation of Frank Corsaro, who directed my first play, *The Sweet Enemy,* for the Actors Studio), I have had a few stunning surprises too. Yet, in fact, very few—and even these have been instructive.

In the spring of 1990 I learned with much gratitude what can work—and what can't—on the stage. At the invitation of Jon Jory and Michael Dixon, I accepted a commission to write two linked one-act plays for the Humana Festival of New Plays at the Actors' Theatre of Louisville, *Tone Clusters* and *The Eclipse.* The first began as a purely conceptual piece, devoid of story: an idea, a mood, a sequence of jarring and discordant sounds. "Tone clusters" refers to the eerie, haunting, dissonant music, primarily for piano, composed by Charles Ives and Henry Cowell in the early twentieth century. The music is unsettling and abrades the nerves, suggesting as it does a radical disjuncture of perception; a sense that the universe is not after all harmonious or logical. In conjunction with these tone clusters of sound I envisioned philosophical inquiries of the kind humankind has posed since the pre-Socratic philosophers, but rarely answered—"Is the universe predetermined in every particular, or is mankind 'free'?"; "Where does identity reside?"—being put to an ordinary American couple of middle age, as in a hallucinatory television interview. The horror of the piece arises from its revelation that we reside in ignorance, not only of most of the information available to us, but of our own lives, our own motives: *Death wrapped in plastic garbage bags! in the basement! and we never knew, never had a premonition!* Only later, by degrees, in the writing of the play, did the nightmare interview become linked with a crime, thus with the specific, the time-bound and finite. It is subsequently ironic to me that *Tone Clusters,* which exists in my imagination as a purely experimental work about the fracturing of reality in an electronic era, is always, for others, "about" a crime.

When rehearsals were begun in Louisville, however, under the direction of Steve Albreezi, and I saw actors inhabiting the roles (Adale O'Brien and Peter Michael Goetz), I soon realized the impracticability of my original vision. Why, I thought, there the Gulicks are, and they're *real.*

In my original idealism, or naiveté, I had even wanted the play's dialogue to be random, with no lines assigned to either speaker; a kind of aleatory music. What madness!

Equally impractical was my notion, for the second play, *The Eclipse,* that an actual eclipse—a "blade of darkness"—move from left to light across the stage, in mimicry of an older woman's relentless gravitation toward death. As soon as the gifted actresses Beth Dixon and Madeleine Sherwood inhabited their roles, this purely symbolic device became unnecessary. (I have left the direction in the play, however. My impractical idealism remains—maybe, somehow, it might be made to work?)

In my writing for the theater I always have in mind, as an undercurrent shaping and guiding the surface action, the ancient structure of drama as sacrificial rite. Stories are being told not by us but by way of us—"drama" is our formal acknowledgment of this paradox, which underscores our common humanity. Obviously, this phenomenon involves not only performers on a stage but an audience as well, for there is no ritual without community, and, perhaps, no community without ritual. To experience the play, the playwright must become a part of the audience, and this can occur only when there is an actual stage, living actors, voices other than one's own.

The question of how a writer knows when a work is fully realized is rather more of a riddle than a question. In terms of prose fiction and poetry, one writes, and rewrites, until there seems quite literally nothing more to say, or to feel; the mysterious inner integrity of the work has been expressed, and that phase of the writer's life is over. (Which is why writers so frequently occupy melancholy zones—always, we are being expelled from phases of our lives that, for sheer intensity and drama, can rarely be replicated in the real world.) Theater is the same, yet different: for the living work is communal, and there can be no final, fully realized performance.

I sense that my work is done when I feel, as I sit in the audience, that I am, not the playwright, nor even a quivering network of nerves invisibly linked to what is happening on the stage, but a member of the audience. In the theater, such distance, and such expulsion, is the point.

February 1991

Scene from the TV adaptation, "El Teatro Campesino Special: Los Vendidos." KNBC, Los Angeles, 1972.

Luis Valdez *(American; b. 1940)*

In 1965, after some experience with the San Francisco Mime Troupe, a left-wing group that performed in parks and streets, Valdez returned to his birthplace, Delano, California, where Cesar Chavez had organized a strike of farm workers and a boycott against grape growers. In Delano, under the wing of the United Farm Workers, Valdez established El Teatro Campesino (the Farm Workers' Theater), which at first specialized in doing short, improvised, satirical skits called *actos.* The actors included striking farm workers, and the plays were performed on college campuses and on flatbed trucks at the edges of vineyards rather than in theaters.

Los Vendidos*

List of Characters

HONEST SANCHO
SECRETARY
FARM WORKER
JOHNNY
REVOLUCIONARIO
MEXICAN-AMERICAN

Scene: *Honest Sancho's Used Mexican Lot and Mexican Curio Shop. Three models are on display in Honest Sancho's shop: to the right, there is a Revolucionario, complete with sombrero, carrilleras[1] and carabina 30–30. At center, on the floor, there is the Farm Worker, under a broad straw sombrero. At stage left is the Pachuco,[2] filero[3] in hand.*

(Honest Sancho is moving among his models, dusting them off and preparing for another day of business.)

SANCHO. Bueno, bueno, mis monos, vamos a ver a quien vendemos ahora, ¿no?[4] *(To audience.)* ¡Quihubo! I'm Honest Sancho and this is my shop. Antes fui contratista pero ahora logré tener mi negocito[5] All I need now is a customer. *(A bell rings offstage.)* Ay, a customer!
SECRETARY *(Entering).* Good morning, I'm Miss Jiménez from—
SANCHO. ¡Ah, una chicana! Welcome, welcome Señorita Jiménez.

---

*Los Vendidos   the sellouts
[1] carrilleras   cartridge belts
[2] Pachuco   an urban tough guy
[3] filero   blade
[4] Bueno . . . no?   Well, well, darlings, let's see who we can sell now, O.K.?
[5] Antes . . . negocito   I used to be a contractor, but now I've succeeded in having my little business.

SECRETARY (*Anglo pronunciation*). JIM-enez.

SANCHO. ¿Qué?

SECRETARY. My name is Miss JIM-enez. Don't you speak English? What's wrong with you?

SANCHO. Oh, nothing, Señorita JIM-enez. I'm here to help you.

SECRETARY. That's better. As I was starting to say, I'm a secretary from Governor Reagan's office, and we're looking for a Mexican type for the administration.

SANCHO. Well, you come to the right place, lady. This is Honest Sancho's Used Mexican lot, and we got all types here. Any particular type you want?

SECRETARY. Yes, we were looking for somebody suave—

SANCHO. Suave.

SECRETARY. Debonair.

SANCHO. De buen aire.

SECRETARY. Dark.

SANCHO. Prieto.

SECRETARY. But of course not too dark.

SANCHO. No muy prieto.

SECRETARY. Perhaps, beige.

SANCHO. Beige, just the tone. Así como cafecito con leche,[6] ¿no?

SECRETARY. One more thing. He must be hard-working.

SANCHO. That could only be one model. Step right over here to the center of the shop, lady. (*They cross to the Farm Worker.*) This is our standard farm worker model. As you can see, in the words of our beloved Senator George Murphy, he is "built close to the ground." Also take special notice of his four-ply Goodyear huaraches, made from the rain tire. This wide-brimmed sombrero is an extra added feature—keeps off the sun, rain, and dust.

SECRETARY. Yes, it does look durable.

SANCHO. And our farmworker model is friendly. Muy amable.[7] Watch. (*Snaps his fingers.*)

FARM WORKER (*Lifts up head*). Buenos días, señorita. (*His head drops.*)

SECRETARY. My, he's friendly.

SANCHO. Didn't I tell you? Loves his patrones! But his most attractive feature is that he's hard working. Let me show you. (*Snaps fingers. Farm Worker stands.*)

FARM WORKER. ¡El jale![8] (*He begins to work.*)

SANCHO. As you can see, he is cutting grapes.

SECRETARY. Oh, I wouldn't know.

SANCHO. He also picks cotton. (*Snap. Farm Worker begins to pick cotton.*)

---

[6]**Así . . . leche**   like coffee with milk
[7]**Muy amable**   very friendly
[8]**El jale**   The job

SECRETARY. Versatile isn't he?

SANCHO. He also picks melons. (*Snap. Farm Worker picks melons.*) That's his slow speed for late in the season. Here's his fast speed. (*Snap. Farm Worker picks faster.*)

SECRETARY. ¡Chihuahua! . . . I mean, goodness, he sure is a hard worker.

SANCHO (*Pulls the Farm Worker to his feet*). And that isn't the half of it. Do you see these little holes on his arms that appear to be pores? During those hot sluggish days in the field, when the vines or the branches get so entangled, it's almost impossible to move; these holes emit a certain grease that allow our model to slip and slide right through the crop with no trouble at all.

SECRETARY. Wonderful. But is he economical?

SANCHO. Economical? Señorita, you are looking at the Volkswagen of Mexicans. Pennies a day is all it takes. One plate of beans and tortillas will keep him going all day. That, and chile. Plenty of chile. Chile jalapenos, chile verde, chile colorado. But, of course, if you do give him chile (*Snap. Farm Worker turns left face. Snap. Farm Worker bends over.*) then you have to change his oil filter once a week.

SECRETARY. What about storage?

SANCHO. No problem. You know these new farm labor camps our Honorable Governor Reagan has built out by Parlier or Raisin City? They were designed with our model in mind. Five, six, seven, even ten in one of those shacks will give you no trouble at all. You can also put him in old barns, old cars, river banks. You can even leave him out in the field overnight with no worry!

SECRETARY. Remarkable.

SANCHO. And here's an added feature: Every year at the end of the season, this model goes back to Mexico and doesn't return, automatically, until next Spring.

SECRETARY. How about that. But tell me: does he speak English?

SANCHO. Another outstanding feature is that last year this model was programmed to go out on STRIKE! (*Snap.*)

FARM WORKER. ¡HUELGA! ¡HUELGA! Hermanos, sálganse de esos files.[9] (*Snap. He stops.*)

SECRETARY. No! Oh no, we can't strike in the State Capitol.

SANCHO. Well, he also scabs. (*Snap.*)

FARM WORKER. Me vendo barato, ¿y qué?[10] (*Snap.*)

SECRETARY. That's much better, but you didn't answer my question. Does he speak English?

SANCHO. Bueno . . . no, pero[11] he has other—

SECRETARY. No.

---

[9]**Huelga . . . files.**   Strike! Strike! Brothers, leave those rows.
[10]**Me . . . qué**   I come cheap. So what?
[11]**Bueno . . . no, pero**   Well, no, but

SANCHO. Other features.

SECRETARY. NO! He just won't do!

SANCHO. Okay, okay pues. We have other models.

SECRETARY. I hope so. What we need is something a little more sophisticated.

SANCHO. Sophisti — ¿qué?

SECRETARY. An urban model.

SANCHO. Ah, from the city! Step right back. Over here in this corner of the shop is exactly what you're looking for. Introducing our new 1969 JOHNNY PACHUCO model! This is our fast-back model. Streamlined. Built for speed, low-riding, city life. Take a look at some of these features. Mag shoes, dual exhausts, green chartreuse paint-job, dark-tint windshield, a little poof on top. Let me just turn him on. (*Snap. Johnny walks to stage center with a pachuco bounce.*)

SECRETARY. What was that?

SANCHO. That, señorita, was the Chicano shuffle.

SECRETARY. Okay, what does he do?

SANCHO. Anything and everything necessary for city life. For instance, survival: He knife fights. (*Snap. Johnny pulls out switch blade and swings at Secretary.*)

(*Secretary screams.*)

SANCHO. He dances. (*Snap.*)

JOHNNY (*Singing*). "Angel Baby, my Angel Baby . . ." (*Snap.*)

SANCHO. And here's a feature no city model can be without. He gets arrested, but not without resisting, of course. (*Snap.*)

JOHNNY. ¡En la madre, la placa![12] I didn't do it! I didn't do it! (*Johnny turns and stands up against an imaginary wall, legs spread out, arms behind his back.*)

SECRETARY. Oh no, we can't have arrests! We must maintain law and order.

SANCHO. But he's bilingual!

SECRETARY. Bilingual?

SANCHO. Simón que yes.[13] He speaks English! Johnny, give us some English. (*Snap.*)

JOHNNY (*Comes downstage*). Fuck-you!

SECRETARY (*Gasps*). Oh! I've never been so insulted in my whole life!

SANCHO. Well, he learned it in your school.

SECRETARY. I don't care where he learned it.

SANCHO. But he's economical!

SECRETARY. Economical?

SANCHO. Nickels and dimes. You can keep Johnny running on hamburgers, Taco Bell tacos, Lucky Lager beer, Thunderbird wine, yesca —

---

[12]**¡En . . . la placa!** Wow, the cops!

[13]**Simón que yes.** Yea, sure.

SECRETARY. Yesca?

SANCHO. Mota.

SECRETARY. Mota?

SANCHO. Leños[14] . . . Marijuana. (*Snap; Johnny inhales on an imaginary joint.*)

SECRETARY. That's against the law!

JOHNNY (*Big smile, holding his breath*). Yeah.

SANCHO. He also sniffs glue. (*Snap. Johnny inhales glue, big smile.*)

JOHNNY. Tha's too much man, ése.[15]

SECRETARY. No, Mr. Sancho, I don't think this—

SANCHO. Wait a minute, he has other qualities I know you'll love. For example, an inferiority complex. (*Snap.*)

JOHNNY (*To Sancho*). You think you're better than me, huh ése? (*Swings switch blade.*)

SANCHO. He can also be beaten and he bruises, cut him and he bleeds; kick him and he—(*He beats, bruises and kicks Pachuco.*) would you like to try it?

SECRETARY. Oh, I couldn't.

SANCHO. Be my guest. He's a great scapegoat.

SECRETARY. No, really.

SANCHO. Please.

SECRETARY. Well, all right. Just once. (*She kicks Pachuco.*) Oh, he's so soft.

SANCHO. Wasn't that good? Try again.

SECRETARY (*Kicks Pachuco*). Oh, he's so wonderful! (*She kicks him again.*)

SANCHO. Okay, that's enough, lady. You ruin the merchandise. Yes, our Johnny Pachuco model can give you many hours of pleasure. Why, the L.A.P.D. just bought twenty of these to train their rookie cops on. And talk about maintenance. Señorita, you are looking at an entirely self-supporting machine. You're never going to find our Johnny Pachuco model on the relief rolls. No, sir, this model knows how to liberate.

SECRETARY. Liberate?

SANCHO. He steals. (*Snap. Johnny rushes the Secretary and steals her purse.*)

JOHNNY. ¡Dame esa bolsa, vieja![16] (*He grabs the purse and runs. Snap by Sancho. He stops.*)

(*Secretary runs after Johnny and grabs purse away from him, kicking him as she goes.*)

SECRETARY. No, no, no! We can't have any *more* thieves in the State Administration. Put him back.

SANCHO. Okay, we still got other models. Come on, Johnny, we'll sell you to some old lady. (*Sancho takes Johnny back to his place.*)

---

[14]**Leños** joints (marijuana)

[15]**ése** fellow

[16]**Dame . . . vieja** Give me that bag, old lady!

SECRETARY. Mr. Sancho, I don't think you quite understand what we need. What we need is something that will attract the women voters. Something more traditional, more romantic.

SANCHO. Ah, a lover. (*He smiles meaningfully.*) Step right over here, señorita. Introducing our standard Revolucionario and/or Early California Bandit type. As you can see he is well-built, sturdy, durable. This is the International Harvester of Mexicans.

SECRETARY. What does he do?

SANCHO. You name it, he does it. He rides horses, stays in the mountains, crosses deserts, plains, rivers, leads revolutions, follows revolutions, kills, can be killed, serves as a martyr, hero, movie star—did I say movie star? Did you ever see *Viva Zapata? Viva Villa? Villa Rides? Pancho Villa Returns? Pancho Villa Goes Back? Pancho Villa Meets Abbott and Costello*—

SECRETARY. I've never seen any of those.

SANCHO. Well, he was in all of them. Listen to this. (*Snap.*)

REVOLUCIONARIO (Scream). ¡VIVA VILLAAAAA!

SECRETARY. That's awfully loud.

SANCHO. He has a volume control. (*He adjusts volume. Snap.*)

REVOLUCIONARIO (Mousey voice). ¡Viva Villa!

SECRETARY. That's better.

SANCHO. And even if you didn't see him in the movies, perhaps you saw him on TV. He makes commercials. (*Snap.*)

REVOLUCIONARIO. Is there a Frito Bandito in your house?

SECRETARY. Oh yes, I've seen that one!

SANCHO. Another feature about this one is that he is economical. He runs on raw horsemeat and tequila!

SECRETARY. Isn't that rather savage?

SANCHO. Al contrario,[17] it makes him a lover. (*Snap.*)

REVOLUCIONARIO (*To Secretary*). ¡Ay, mamasota, cochota, ven pa'ca![18] (*He grabs Secretary and folds her back—Latin-Lover style.*)

SANCHO (*Snap. Revolucionario goes back upright.*). Now wasn't that nice?

SECRETARY. Well, it was rather nice.

SANCHO. And finally, there is one outstanding feature about this model I KNOW the ladies are going to love: He's a GENUINE antique! He was made in Mexico in 1910!

SECRETARY. Made in Mexico?

SANCHO. That's right. Once in Tijuana, twice in Guadalajara, three times in Cuernavaca.

SECRETARY. Mr. Sancho, I thought he was an American product.

SANCHO. No, but—

---

[17]**Al contrario** On the contrary
[18]**Ay . . . pa'ca!** ----, get over here!

SECRETARY. No, I'm sorry. We can't buy anything but American-made products. He just won't do.

SANCHO. But he's an antique!

SECRETARY. I don't care. You still don't understand what we need. It's true we need Mexican models such as these, but it's more important that he be *American.*

SANCHO. American?

SECRETARY. That's right, and judging from what you've shown me, I don't think you have what we want. Well, my lunch hour's almost over; I better—

SANCHO. Wait a minute! Mexican but American?

SECRETARY. That's correct.

SANCHO. Mexican but . . . (*A sudden flash.*) AMERICAN! Yeah, I think we've got exactly what you want. He just came in today! Give me a minute. (*He exits. Talks from backstage.*) Here he is in the shop. Let me just get some papers off. There. Introducing our new 1970 Mexican-American! Ta-ra-ra-ra-ra-ra-RA-RAAA!

(*Sancho brings out the Mexican-American model, a clean-shaven middle-class type in a business suit, with glasses.*)

SECRETARY (*Impressed*). Where have you been hiding this one?

SANCHO. He just came in this morning. Ain't he a beauty? Feast your eyes on him! Sturdy US STEEL frame, streamlined, modern. As a matter of fact, he is built exactly like our Anglo models except that he comes in a variety of darker shades: naugahyde, leather, or leatherette.

SECRETARY. Naugahyde.

SANCHO. Well, we'll just write that down. Yes, señorita, this model represents the apex of American engineering! He is bilingual, college educated, ambitious! Say the word "acculturate" and he accelerates. He is intelligent, well-mannered, clean—did I say clean? (*Snap. Mexican-American raises his arm.*) Smell.

SECRETARY (*Smells*). Old Sobaco, my favorite.

SANCHO (*Snap. Mexican-American turns toward Sancho.*). Eric! (*To Secretary.*) We call him Eric García. (*To Eric.*) I want you to meet Miss JIM-enez, Eric.

MEXICAN-AMERICAN. Miss JIM-enez, I am delighted to make your acquaintance. (*He kisses her hand.*)

SECRETARY. Oh, my, how charming!

SANCHO. Did you feel the suction? He has seven especially engineered suction cups right behind his lips. He's a charmer all right!

SECRETARY. How about boards? Does he function on boards?

SANCHO. You name them, he is on them. Parole boards, draft boards, school boards, taco quality control boards, surf boards, two-by-fours.

SECRETARY. Does he function in politics?

SANCHO. Señorita, you are looking at a political MACHINE. Have you ever heard of the OEO, EOC, COD, WAR ON POVERTY? That's our model! Not only that, he makes political speeches.

SECRETARY. May I hear one?

SANCHO. With pleasure. (*Snap.*) Eric, give us a speech.

MEXICAN-AMERICAN. Mr. Congressman, Mr. Chairman, members of the board, honored guests, ladies and gentlemen. (*Sancho and Secretary applaud.*) Please, please. I come before you as a Mexican-American to tell you about the problems of the Mexican. The problems of the Mexican stem from one thing and one thing alone: He's stupid. He's uneducated. He needs to stay in school. He needs to be ambitious, forward-looking, harder-working. He needs to think American, American, American, AMERICAN, AMERICAN, AMERICAN. GOD BLESS AMERICA! GOD BLESS AMERICA! GOD BLESS AMERICA!! (*He goes out of control.*)

(*Sancho snaps frantically and the Mexican-American finally slumps forward, bending at the waist.*)

SECRETARY. Oh my, he's patriotic too!

SANCHO. Sí, señorita, he loves his country. Let me just make a little adjustment here. (*Stands Mexican-American up.*)

SECRETARY. What about upkeep? Is he economical?

SANCHO. Well, no, I won't lie to you. The Mexican-American costs a little bit more, but you get what you pay for. He's worth every extra cent. You can keep him running on dry Martinis, Langendorf bread.

SECRETARY. Apple pie?

SANCHO. Only Mom's. Of course, he's also programmed to eat Mexican food on ceremonial functions, but I must warn you: an overdose of beans will plug up his exhaust.

SECRETARY. Fine! There's just one more question: HOW MUCH DO YOU WANT FOR HIM?

SANCHO. Well, I tell you what I'm gonna do. Today and today only, because you've been so sweet, I'm gonna let you steal this model from me! I'm gonna let you drive him off the lot for the simple price of— let's see taxes and license included—$15,000.

SECRETARY. Fifteen thousand DOLLARS? For a MEXICAN!

SANCHO. Mexican? What are you talking, lady? This is a Mexican-AMERICAN! We had to melt down two pachucos, a farm worker and three gabachos[19] to make this model! You want quality, but you gotta pay for it! This is no cheap run-about. He's got class!

SECRETARY. Okay, I'll take him.

SANCHO. You will?

SECRETARY. Here's your money.

---

[19]**gabachos** whites

SANCHO. You mind if I count it?

SECRETARY. Go right ahead.

SANCHO. Well, you'll get your pink slip in the mail. Oh, do you want me to wrap him up for you? We have a box in the back.

SECRETARY. No, thank you. The Governor is having a luncheon this afternoon, and we need a brown face in the crowd. How do I drive him?

SANCHO. Just snap your fingers. He'll do anything you want.

(Secretary snaps. Mexican-American steps forward.)

MEXICAN-AMERICAN. RAZA QUERIDA, ¡VAMOS LEVANTANDO ARMAS PARA LIBERARNOS DE ESTOS DESGRACIADOS GABACHOS QUE NOS EXPLOTAN! VAMOS.[20]

SECRETARY. What did he say?

SANCHO. Something about lifting arms, killing white people, etc.

SECRETARY. But he's not supposed to say that!

SANCHO. Look, lady, don't blame me for bugs from the factory. He's your Mexican-American; you bought him, now drive him off the lot!

SECRETARY. But he's broken!

SANCHO. Try snapping another finger.

(Secretary snaps. Mexican-American comes to life again.)

MEXICAN-AMERICAN. ¡ESTA GRAN HUMANIDAD HA DICHO BASTA! Y SE HA PUESTO EN MARCHA! ¡BASTA! ¡BASTA! ¡VIVA LA RAZA! ¡VIVA LA CAUSA! ¡VIVA LA HUELGA! ¡VIVAN LOS BROWN BERETS! ¡VIVAN LOS ESTUDIANTES![21] ¡CHICANO POWER!

(The Mexican-American turns toward the Secretary, who gasps and backs up. He keeps turning toward the Pachuco, Farm Worker, and Revolucionario, snapping his fingers and turning each of them on, one by one.)

PACHUCO *(Snap. To Secretary).* I'm going to get you, baby! ¡Viva La Raza!

FARM WORKER *(Snap. To Secretary).* ¡Viva la huelga! ¡Viva la Huelga! ¡VIVA LA HUELGA!

REVOLUCIONARIO *(Snap. To Secretary).* ¡Viva la revolución! ¡VIVA LA REVOLUCIÓN!

(The three models join together and advance toward the Secretary who backs up and runs out of the shop screaming. Sancho is at the other end of the shop holding his money in his hand. All freeze. After a few seconds of silence, the Pachuco moves and stretches, shaking his arms and loosening up. The Farm Worker and Revolucionario do the same. Sancho stays where he is, frozen to his spot.)

[20]**Raza . . . Vamos.** Beloved Raza [persons of Mexican descent], let's take up arms to liberate ourselves from those damned whites who exploit us. Let's get going.

[21]**¡Esta . . . Estudiantes!** This great mass of humanity has said enough! And it has begun to march. Enough! Enough! Long live La Raza! Long live the Cause! Long live the strike! Long live the Brown Berets! Long live the students!

JOHNNY. Man, that was a long one, ése.[22] (*Others agree with him.*)

FARM WORKER. How did we do?

JOHNNY. Perty good, look at all that lana,[23] man! (*He goes over to Sancho and removes the money from his hand. Sancho stays where he is.*)

REVOLUCIONARIO. En la madre, look at all the money.

JOHNNY. We keep this up, we're going to be rich.

FARM WORKER. They think we're machines.

REVOLUCIONARIO. Burros.

JOHNNY. Puppets.

MEXICAN-AMERICAN. The only thing I don't like is—how come I always got to play the godamn Mexican-American?

JOHNNY. That's what you get for finishing high school.

FARM WORKER. How about our wages, ése?

JOHNNY. Here it comes right now. $3,000 for you, $3,000 for you, $3,000 for you, and $3,000 for me. The rest we put back into the business.

MEXICAN-AMERICAN. Too much, man. Heh, where you vatos[24] going tonight?

FARM WORKER. I'm going over to Concha's. There's a party.

JOHNNY. Wait a minute, vatos. What about our salesman? I think he needs an oil job.

REVOLUCIONARIO. Leave him to me.

(*The Pachuco, Farm Worker, and Mexican-American exit, talking loudly about their plans for the night. The Revolucionario goes over to Sancho, removes his derby hat and cigar, lifts him up and throws him over his shoulder. Sancho hangs loose, lifeless.*)

REVOLUCIONARIO (*To audience*). He's the best model we got! ¡Ajua![25] (*Exit.*)

(*End.*)

TOPICS FOR DISCUSSION AND WRITING

1. If you are an Anglo (shorthand for a Caucasian with traditional Northern European values), do you find the play deeply offensive? Why, or why not? If you are a Mexican-American, do you find the play entertaining—or do you find parts of it offensive? What might Anglos enjoy in the play, and what might Mexican-Americans find offensive?

---

[22]**ése**   man
[23]**lana**   money
[24]**vatos**   guys
[25]**Ajua!**   Wow!

2. What stereotypes of Mexican-Americans are presented here? At the end of the play what image of the Mexican-American is presented? How does it compare with the stereotypes?

3. If you are a member of some other minority group, in a few sentences indicate how *Los Vendidos* might be adapted into a play about that group.

4. Putting aside the politics of the play (and your own politics), what do you think are the strengths of *Los Vendidos?* What do you think are the weaknesses?

5. The play was written in 1967. Putting aside a few specific references, for instance to Governor Reagan, do you find it dated? If not, why not?

6. In 1971 when *Los Vendidos* was produced by El Teatro de la Esperanza, the group altered the ending by having the men decide to use the money to build a community center. Evaluate this ending.

7. When the play was videotaped by KNBC in Los Angeles for broadcast in 1973, Valdez changed the ending. In the revised version we discover that a scientist (played by Valdez) masterminds the operation, placing Mexican-American models wherever there are persons of Mexican descent. These models soon will become Chicanos (as opposed to persons with Anglo values) and will aid rather than work against their fellows. Evaluate this ending.

8. In his short essay, "The Actos," Valdez says that "Actos: Inspire the audience to social action. Illuminate specific points about social problems. Satirize the opposition. Show or hint at a solution. Express what people are feeling." How many of these do you think *Los Vendidos* does?

9. Many people assume that politics get in the way of serious art. That is, they assume that artists ought to be concerned with issues that transcend politics. Does this point make any sense to you? Why or why not?

A CONTEXT FOR *LOS VENDIDOS*

Luis Valdez, The *Actos*

Nothing represents the work of El Teatro Campesino (and other teatros Chicanos) better than the acto. In a sense, the acto is Chicano theatre, though we are now moving into a new, more mystical dramatic form we have begun to call the mito. The two forms are, in fact, cuates[1] that complement and balance each other as day goes into night, el sol la sombra,

[1]**cuates** twins

la vida la muerte, el pájaro la serpiente.[2] Our rejection of white western European (gabacho) proscenium theatre makes the birth of new Chicano forms necessary, thus, los actos y los mitos; one through the eyes of man, the other through the eyes of God.

The actos were born quite matter of factly in Delano. Nacieron hambrientos de la realidad. Anything and everything that pertained to the daily life, la vida cotidiana, of the huelguistas[3] became food for thought, material for actos. The reality of campesinos on strike had become dramatic, (and theatrical as reflected by newspapers, TV newscasts, films, etc.) and so the actos merely reflected the reality. Huelguistas portrayed huelguistas, drawing their improvised dialogue from real words they exchanged with the esquiroles (scabs) in the fields everyday.[4]

"Hermanos, compañeros, sálganse de esos files."
"Tenemos comida y trabajo para ustedes afuera de la huelga."
"Esquirol, ten verguenza."
"Unidos venceremos."
"¡Sal de ahi barrigón!"

The first huelguista to portray an esquirol in the teatro did it to settle a score with a particularly stubborn scab he had talked with in the fields that day. Satire became a weapon that was soon aimed at known and despised contractors, growers and mayordomos. The effect of those early actos on the huelguistas de Delano packed into Filipino Hall was immediate, intense and cathartic. The actos rang true to the reality of the huelga.

Looking back at those early, crude, vital, beautiful, powerful actos of 1965, certain things have now become clear about the dramatic form we were just beginning to develop. There was, of course, no conscious deliberate plan to develop the acto as such. Even the name we gave our small presentations reflects the hard pressing expediency under which we worked from day to day. We could have called them "skits," but we lived and talked in San Joaquin Valley Spanish (with a strong Tejano influence), so we needed a name that made sense to the raza. Cuadros, pasquines, autos, entremeses[5] all seemed too highly intellectualized. We began to call them actos for lack of a better word, lack of time and lack of interest in trying to sound like classical Spanish scholars. De todos modos éramos raza, ¿quién se iba a fijar?[6]

---

[2]**el sol . . . serpiente**   sun and shade, life and death, the bird and the serpent
[3]**huelguistas**   strikers
[4]The following five lines of dialogue can be translated thus: Brothers, friends, leave those rows. / We have food and work for you outside of the strike. / Scab, you ought to be ashamed. / United we will conquer. / Get out of here, fatso!
[5]**Cuadros . . . entremeses**   various Spanish words for short plays
[6]**De todos . . . fijar**   In all ways we are the Race (i.e., indigenous Americans mixed with European and African blood); who was going to pay attention?

The acto, however, developed its own structure through five years of experimentation. It evolved into a short dramatic form now used primarily by los teatros de Aztlán, but utilized to some extent by other non Chicano guerrilla theatre companies throughout the U.S., including the San Francisco Mime Troupe and the Bread and Puppet Theatre. (Considerable creative crossfeeding has occurred on other levels, I might add, between the Mime Troupe, the Bread and Puppet, and the Campesino.) Each of these groups may have their own definition of the acto, but the following are some of the guidelines we have established for ourselves over the years:

> Actos: Inspire the audience to social action. Illuminate specific
> points about social problems. Satirize the opposition.
> Show or hint at a solution. Express what people are
> feeling.

So what's new, right? Plays have been doing that for thousands of years. True, except that the major emphasis in the acto is the social vision, as opposed to the individual artist or playwright's vision. Actos are not written; they are created collectively, through improvisation by a group. The reality reflected in an acto is thus a social reality, whether it pertains to campesinos or to batos locos, not psychologically deranged self-projections, but rather, group archetypes. Don Sotaco, Don Coyote, Johnny Pachuco, Juan Raza, Jorge el Chingón, la Chicana, are all group archtypes that have appeared in actos.

The usefulness of the acto extended well beyond the huelga into the Chicano movement, because Chicanos in general want to identify themselves as a group. The teatro archtypes symbolize the desire for unity and group identity through Chicano heroes and heroines. One character can thus represent the entire Raza, and the Chicano audience will gladly respond to his triumphs or defeats. What to a non-Chicano audience may seem like oversimplification in an acto, is to the Chicano a true expression of his social state and therefore reality.

[1970]

August Wilson *(American; b. 1945)*

Fences

for Lloyd Richards,
who adds to whatever he touches

> *When the sins of our fathers visit us*
> *We do not have to play host.*
> *We can banish them with forgiveness*
> *As God, in His Largeness and Laws.*
>
> *—August Wilson*

List of Characters

TROY MAXSON
JIM BONO, *Troy's friend*
ROSE, *Troy's wife*
LYONS, *Troy's oldest son by previous marriage*
GABRIEL, *Troy's brother*
CORY, *Troy and Rose's son*
RAYNELL, *Troy's daughter*

Setting: *The setting is the yard which fronts the only entrance to the Maxson household, an ancient two-story brick house set back off a small alley in a big-city neighborhood. The entrance to the house is gained by two or three steps leading to a wooden porch badly in need of paint.*

   A relatively recent addition to the house and running its full width, the porch lacks congruence. It is a sturdy porch with a flat roof. One or two chairs of dubious value sit at one end where the kitchen window opens onto the porch. An old-fashioned icebox stands silent guard at the opposite end.

   The yard is a small dirt yard, partially fenced, except for the last scene, with a wooden saw horse, a pile of lumber, and other fence-building equipment set off to the side. Opposite is a tree from which hangs a ball made of rags. A baseball bat leans against the tree. Two oil drums serve as garbage receptacles and sit near the house at right to complete the setting.

The Play: *Near the turn of the century, the destitute of Europe sprang on the city with tenacious claws and an honest and solid dream. The city devoured them. They swelled its belly until it burst into a thousand furnaces and sewing machines, a thousand butcher shops and bakers' ovens, a thousand churches and hospitals and funeral parlors and money-lenders. The city grew. It nourished itself and offered each man a partnership limited only by his talent, his guile, and his willingness and capacity for hardwork. For the immigrants of Europe, a dream dared and won true.*

Seattle Repertory Theatre production with (left to right) Francis Foster as Rose Maxon, Keith Amos as Cory Maxon, William Jay as Gabriel, and Gilbert Lewis as Troy Maxon. (Photo © Chris Bennion.)

The descendants of African slaves were offered no such welcome or participation. They came from places called the Carolinas and the Virginias, Georgia, Alabama, Mississippi, and Tennessee. They came strong, eager, searching. The city rejected them and they fled and settled along the riverbanks and under bridges in shallow, ramshackle houses made of sticks and tarpaper. They collected rags and wood. They sold the use of their muscles and their bodies. They cleaned houses and washed clothes, they shined shoes, and in quiet desperation and vengeful pride, they stole, and lived in pursuit of their own dream. That they could breathe free, finally, and stand to meet life with the force of dignity and whatever eloquence the heart could call upon.

By 1957, the hard-won victories of the European immigrants had solidified the industrial might of America. War had been confronted and won with new energies that used loyalty and patriotism as its fuel. Life was rich, full, and flourishing. The Milwaukee Braves won the World Series, and the hot winds of change that would make the sixties a turbulent, racing, dangerous, and provocative decade had not yet begun to blow full.

ACT 1

SCENE 1

It is 1957. Troy and Bono enter the yard, engaged in conversation. Troy is fifty-three years old, a large man with thick, heavy hands; it is this largeness that he strives to fill out and make an accommodation with. Together with his blackness, his largeness informs his sensibilities and the choices he has made in his life.

Of the two men, Bono is obviously the follower. His commitment to their friendship of thirty-odd years is rooted in his admiration of Troy's honesty, capacity for hard work, and his strength, which Bono seeks to emulate.

It is Friday night, payday, and the one night of the week the two men engage in a ritual of talk and drink. Troy is usually the most talkative and at times he can be crude and almost vulgar, though he is capable of rising to profound heights of expression. The men carry lunch buckets and wear or carry burlap aprons and are dressed in clothes suitable to their jobs as garbage collectors.

BONO. Troy, you ought to stop that lying!

TROY. I ain't lying! The nigger had a watermelon this big. (*He indicates with his hands.*) Talking about . . . "What watermelon, Mr. Rand?" I liked to fell out! "What watermelon, Mr. Rand?" . . . And it sitting there big as life.

BONO. What did Mr. Rand say?

TROY. Ain't said nothing. Figure if the nigger too dumb to know he carrying a watermelon, he wasn't gonna get much sense out of him. Trying to hide that great big old watermelon under his coat. Afraid to let the white man see him carry it home.

BONO. I'm like you . . . I ain't got no time for them kind of people.

TROY. Now what he look like getting mad cause he see the man from the union talking to Mr. Rand?

BONO. He come to me talking about . . . "Maxson gonna get us fired." I told him to get away from me with that. He walked away from me calling you a troublemaker. What Mr. Rand say?

TROY. Ain't said nothing. He told me to go down the Commissioner's office next Friday. They called me down there to see them.

BONO. Well, as long as you got your complaint filed, they can't fire you. That's what one of them white fellows tell me.

TROY. I ain't worried about them firing me. They gonna fire me cause I asked a question? That's all I did. I went to Mr. Rand and asked him, "Why? Why you got the white mens driving and the colored lifting?" Told him, "what's the matter, don't I count? You think only white fellows got sense enough to drive a truck. That ain't no paper job! Hell, anybody can drive a truck. How come you got all whites driving and the colored lifting?" He told me "take it to the union." Well, hell, that's what I done! Now they wanna come up with this pack of lies.

BONO. I told Brownie if the man come and ask him any questions . . . just tell the truth! It ain't nothing but something they done trumped up on you cause you filed a complaint on them.

TROY. Brownie don't understand nothing. All I want them to do is change the job description. Give everybody a chance to drive the truck. Brownie can't see that. He ain't got that much sense.

BONO. How you figure he be making out with that gal be up at Taylors' all the time . . . that Alberta gal?

TROY. Same as you and me. Getting just as much as we is. Which is to say nothing.

BONO. It is, huh? I figure you doing a little better than me . . . and I ain't saying what I'm doing.

TROY. Aw, nigger, look here . . . I know you. If you had got anywhere near that gal, twenty minutes later you be looking to tell somebody. And the first one you gonna tell . . . that you gonna want to brag to . . . is me.

BONO. I ain't saying that. I see where you be eyeing her.

TROY. I eye all the women. I don't miss nothing. Don't never let nobody tell you Troy Maxson don't eye the women.

BONO. You been doing more than eyeing her. You done bought her a drink or two.

TROY. Hell yeah, I bought her a drink! What that mean? I bought you one, too. What that mean cause I buy her a drink? I'm just being polite.

BONO. It's all right to buy her one drink. That's what you call being polite. But when you wanna be buying two or three . . . that's what you call eyeing her.

TROY. Look here, as long as you known me . . . you ever known me to chase after women?

BONO. Hell yeah! Long as I done known you. You forgetting I knew you when.

TROY. Naw, I'm talking about since I been married to Rose?

BONO. Oh, not since you been married to Rose. Now, that's the truth, there. I can say that.

TROY. All right then! Case closed.

BONO. I see you be walking up around Alberta's house. You supposed to be at Taylors' and you be walking up around there.

TROY. What you watching where I'm walking for? I ain't watching after you.

BONO. I seen you walking around there more than once.

TROY. Hell, you liable to see me walking anywhere! That don't mean nothing cause you see me walking around there.

BONO. Where she come from anyway? She just kinda showed up one day.

TROY. Tallahassee. You can look at her and tell she one of them Florida gals. They got some big healthy women down there. Grow them right up out the ground. Got a little bit of Indian in her. Most of them niggers down in Florida got some Indian in them.

BONO. I don't know about that Indian part. But she damn sure big and healthy. Woman wear some big stockings. Got them great big old legs and hips as wide as the Mississippi River.

TROY. Legs don't mean nothing. You don't do nothing but push them out of the way. But them hips cushion the ride!

BONO. Troy, you ain't got no sense.

TROY. It's the truth! Like you riding on Goodyears!

Rose enters from the house. She is ten years younger than Troy, her devotion to him stems from her recognition of the possibilities of her life without him: a succession of abusive men and their babies, a life of partying and running the streets, the Church, or aloneness with its attendant pain and frustration. She recognizes Troy's spirit as a fine and illuminating one and she either ignores or forgives his faults, only some of which she recognizes. Though she doesn't drink, her presence is an integral part of the Friday night rituals. She alternates between the porch and the kitchen, where supper preparations are under way.

ROSE. What you all out here getting into?

TROY. What you worried about what we getting into for? This is men talk, woman.

ROSE. What I care what you all talking about? Bono, you gonna stay for supper?

BONO. No, I thank you, Rose. But Lucille say she cooking up a pot of pigfeet.

TROY. Pigfeet! Hell, I'm going home with you! Might even stay the night if you got some pigfeet. You got something in there to top them pigfeet, Rose?

ROSE. I'm cooking up some chicken. I got some chicken and collard greens.

TROY. Well, go on back in the house and let me and Bono finish what we was talking about. This is men talk. I got some talk for you later. You know what kind of talk I mean. You go on and powder it up.

ROSE. Troy Maxson, don't you start that now!

TROY (*puts his arm around her*). Aw, woman . . . come here. Look here, Bono . . . when I met this woman . . . I got out that place, say, "Hitch up my pony, saddle up my mare . . . there's a woman out there for me somewhere. I looked here. Looked there. Saw Rose and latched on to her." I latched on to her and told her—I'm gonna tell you the truth—I told her, "Baby, I don't wanna marry, I just wanna be your man." Rose told me . . . tell him what you told me, Rose.

ROSE. I told him if he wasn't the marrying kind, then move out the way so the marrying kind could find me.

TROY. That's what she told me. "Nigger, you in my way. You blocking the view! Move out the way so I can find me a husband." I thought it over two or three days. Come back—

ROSE. Ain't no two or three days nothing. You was back the same night.

TROY. Come back, told her . . . "Okay, baby . . . but I'm gonna buy me a banty rooster and put him out there in the backyard . . . and when he see a stranger come, he'll flap his wings and crow . . ." Look here, Bono, I could watch the front door by myself . . . it was that back door I was worried about.

ROSE. Troy, you ought not talk like that. Troy ain't doing nothing but telling a lie.

TROY. Only thing is . . . when we first got married . . . forget the rooster . . . we ain't had no yard!

BONO. I hear you tell it. Me and Lucille was staying down there on Logan Street. Had two rooms with the outhouse in the back. I ain't mind the outhouse none. But when that goddamn wind blow through there in the winter . . . that's what I'm talking about! To this day I wonder why in the hell I ever stayed down there for six long years. But see, I didn't know I could do no better. I thought only white folks had inside toilets and things.

ROSE. There's a lot of people don't know they can do no better than they doing now. That's just something you got to learn. A lot of folks still shop at Bella's.

TROY. Ain't nothing wrong with shopping at Bella's. She got fresh food.

ROSE. I ain't said nothing about if she got fresh food. I'm talking about what she charge. She charge ten cents more than the A&P.

TROY. The A&P ain't never done nothing for me. I spends my money where I'm treated right. I go down to Bella, say, "I need a loaf of bread, I'll pay you Friday." She give it to me. What sense that make when I got money to go and spend it somewhere else and ignore the person who done right by me? That ain't in the Bible.

ROSE. We ain't talking about what's in the Bible. What sense it make to shop there when she overcharge?

TROY. You shop where you want to. I'll do my shopping where the people been good to me.

ROSE. Well, I don't think it's right for her to overcharge. That's all I was saying.

BONO. Look here . . . I got to get on. Lucille going be raising all kind of hell.

TROY. Where you going, nigger? We ain't finished this pint. Come here, finish this pint.

BONO. Well, hell, I am . . . if you ever turn the bottle loose.

TROY (*hands him the bottle*). The only thing I say about the A&P is I'm glad Cory got that job down there. Help him take care of his school clothes and things. Gabe done moved out and things getting tight around here. He got that job . . . He can start to look out for himself.

ROSE. Cory done went and got recruited by a college football team.

TROY. I told that boy about that football stuff. The white man ain't gonna let him get nowhere with that football. I told him when he first come to me with it. Now you come telling me he done went and got more tied up in it. He ought to go and get recruited in how to fix cars or something where he can make a living.

ROSE. He ain't talking about making no living playing football. It's just something the boys in school do. They gonna send a recruiter by to talk to you. He'll tell you he ain't talking about making no living playing football. It's a honor to be recruited.

TROY. It ain't gonna get him nowhere. Bono'll tell you that.

BONO. If he be like you in the sports . . . he's gonna be all right. Ain't but two men ever played baseball as good as you. That's Babe Ruth and Josh Gibson.[1] Them's the only two men ever hit more home runs than you.

TROY. What it ever get me? Ain't got a pot to piss in or a window to throw it out of.

ROSE. Times have changed since you was playing baseball, Troy. That was before the war. Times have changed a lot since then.

TROY. How in hell they done changed?

ROSE. They got lots of colored boys playing ball now. Baseball and football.

BONO. You right about that, Rose. Times have changed, Troy. You just come along too early.

TROY. There ought not never have been no time called too early! Now you take that fellow . . . what's that fellow they had playing right field for the Yankees back then? You know who I'm talking about, Bono. Used to play right field for the Yankees.

ROSE. Selkirk?

TROY. Selkirk! That's it! Man batting .269, understand? .269. What kind of sense that make? I was hitting .432 with thirty-seven home runs!

---

[1]**Josh Gibson** African-American ballplayer (1911–47), known as the Babe Ruth of the Negro leagues

Man batting .269 and playing right field for the Yankees! I saw Josh Gibson's daughter yesterday. She walking around with raggedy shoes on her feet. Now I bet you Selkirk's daughter ain't walking around with raggedy shoes on her feet! I bet you that!

ROSE. They got a lot of colored baseball players now. Jackie Robinson[2] was the first. Folks had to wait for Jackie Robinson.

TROY. I done seen a hundred niggers play baseball better than Jackie Robinson. Hell, I know some teams Jackie Robinson couldn't even make! What you talking about Jackie Robinson. Jackie Robinson wasn't nobody. I'm talking about if you could play ball then they ought to have let you play. Don't care what color you were. Come telling me I come along too early. If you could play . . . then they ought to have let you play.

Troy takes a long drink from the bottle.

ROSE. You gonna drink yourself to death. You don't need to be drinking like that.

TROY. Death ain't nothing. I done seen him. Done wrassled with him. You can't tell me nothing about death. Death ain't nothing but a fastball on the outside corner. And you know what I'll do to that! Lookee here, Bono . . . am I lying? You get one of them fastballs, about waist high, over the outside corner of the plate where you can get the meat of the bat on it . . . and good god! You can kiss it goodbye. Now, am I lying?

BONO. Naw, you telling the truth there. I seen you do it.

TROY. If I'm lying . . . that 450 feet worth of lying! (*Pause.*) That's all death is to me. A fastball on the outside corner.

ROSE. I don't know why you want to get on talking about death.

TROY. Ain't nothing wrong with talking about death. That's part of life. Everybody gonna die. You gonna die, I'm gonna die. Bono's gonna die. Hell, we all gonna die.

ROSE. But you ain't got to talk about it. I don't like to talk about it.

TROY. You the one brought it up. Me and Bono was talking about baseball . . . you tell me I'm gonna drink myself to death. Ain't that right, Bono? You know I don't drink this but one night out of the week. That's Friday night. I'm gonna drink just enough to where I can handle it. Then I cuts it loose. I leave it alone. So don't you worry about me drinking myself to death. 'Cause I ain't worried about Death. I done seen him. I done wrestled with him.

Look here, Bono . . . I looked up one day and Death was marching straight at me. Like Soldiers on Parade! The Army of Death was marching straight at me. The middle of July, 1941. It got real cold just

---

[2]**Jackie Robinson** In 1947 Robinson (1919–72) became the first African-American to play baseball in the major leagues.

like it be winter. It seem like Death himself reached out and touched me on the shoulder. He touch me just like I touch you. I got cold as ice and Death standing there grinning at me.

ROSE. Troy, why don't you hush that talk.

TROY. I say . . . what you want, Mr. Death? You be wanting me? You done brought your army to be getting me? I looked him dead in the eye. I wasn't fearing nothing. I was ready to tangle. Just like I'm ready to tangle now. The Bible say be ever vigilant. That's why I don't get but so drunk. I got to keep watch.

ROSE. Troy was right down there in Mercy Hospital. You remember he had pneumonia? Laying there with a fever talking plumb out of his head.

TROY. Death standing there staring at me . . . carrying that sickle in his hand. Finally he say, "You want bound over for another year?" See, just like that . . . "You want bound over for another year?" I told him, "Bound over hell! Let's settle this now!"

It seem like he kinda fell back when I said that, and all the cold went out of me. I reached down and grabbed that sickle and threw it just as far as I could throw it . . . and me and him commenced to wrestling.

We wrestled for three days and three nights. I can't say where I found the strength from. Everytime it seemed like he was gonna get the best of me, I'd reach way down deep inside myself and find the strength to do him one better.

ROSE. Everytime Troy tell that story he find different ways to tell it. Different things to make up about it.

TROY. I ain't making up nothing. I'm telling you the facts of what happened. I wrestled with Death for three days and three nights and I'm standing here to tell you about it. (*Pause.*) All right. At the end of the third night we done weakened each other to where we can't hardly move. Death stood up, throwed on his robe . . . had him a white robe with a hood on it. He throwed on that robe and went off to look for his sickle. Say, "I'll be back." Just like that. "I'll be back." I told him, say, "Yeah, but . . . you gonna have to find me!" I wasn't no fool. I wan't going looking for him. Death ain't nothing to play with. And I know he's gonna get me. I know I got to join his army . . . his camp followers. But as long as I keep my strength and see him coming . . . as long as I keep up my vigilance . . . he's gonna have to fight to get me. I ain't going easy.

BONO. Well, look here, since you got to keep up your vigilance . . . let me have the bottle.

TROY. Aw hell, I shouldn't have told you that part. I should have left out that part.

ROSE. Troy be talking that stuff and half the time don't even know what he be talking about.

TROY. Bono know me better than that.

BONO. That's right. I know you. I know you got some Uncle Remus[3] in your blood. You got more stories than the devil got sinners.

TROY. Aw hell, I done seen him too! Done talked with the devil.

ROSE. Troy, don't nobody wanna be hearing all that stuff.

Lyons enters the yard from the street. Thirty-four years old, Troy's son by a previous marriage, he sports a neatly trimmed goatee, sport coat, white shirt, tieless and buttoned at the collar. Though he fancies himself a musician, he is more caught up in the rituals and "idea" of being a musician than in the actual practice of the music. He has come to borrow money from Troy, and while he knows he will be successful, he is uncertain as to what extent his lifestyle will be held up to scrutiny and ridicule.

LYONS. Hey, Pop.

TROY. What you come "Hey, Popping" me for?

LYONS. How you doing, Rose? (*He kisses her.*) Mr. Bono. How you doing?

BONO. Hey, Lyons . . . how you been?

TROY. He must have been doing all right. I ain't seen him around here last week.

ROSE. Troy, leave your boy alone. He come by to see you and you wanna start all that nonsense.

TROY. I ain't bothering Lyons. (*Offers him the bottle.*) Here . . . get you a drink. We got an understanding. I know why he come by to see me and he know I know.

LYONS. Come on, Pop . . . I just stopped by to say hi . . . see how you was doing.

TROY. You ain't stopped by yesterday.

ROSE. You gonna stay for supper, Lyons? I got some chicken cooking in the oven.

LYONS. No, Rose . . . thanks. I was just in the neighborhood and thought I'd stop by for a minute.

TROY. You was in the neighborhood all right, nigger. You telling the truth there. You was in the neighborhood cause it's my payday.

LYONS. Well, hell, since you mentioned it . . . let me have ten dollars.

TROY. I'll be damned! I'll die and go to hell and play blackjack with the devil before I give you ten dollars.

BONO. That's what I wanna know about . . . that devil you done seen.

LYONS. What . . . Pop done seen the devil? You too much, Pops.

TROY. Yeah, I done seen him. Talked to him too!

ROSE. You ain't seen no devil. I done told you that man ain't had nothing to do with the devil. Anything you can't understand, you want to call it the devil.

TROY. Look here, Bono . . . I went down to see Hertzberger about some furniture. Got three rooms for two-ninety-eight. That what it say on

---

[3]**Uncle Remus** Narrator of traditional black tales in a book by Joel Chandler Harris

the radio. "Three rooms . . . two-ninety-eight." Even made up a little song about it. Go down there . . . man tell me I can't get no credit. I'm working every day and can't get no credit. What to do? I got an empty house with some raggedy furniture in it. Cory ain't got no bed. He's sleeping on a pile of rags on the floor. Working every day and can't get no credit. Come back here — Rose'll tell you — madder than hell. Sit down . . . try to figure what I'm gonna do. Come a knock on the door. Ain't been living here but three days. Who know I'm here? Open the door . . . devil standing there bigger than life. White fellow . . . white fellow . . . got on good clothes and everything. Standing there with a clipboard in his hand. I ain't had to say nothing. First words come out of his mouth was . . . "I understand you need some furniture and can't get no credit." I liked to fell over. He say, "I'll give you all the credit you want, but you got to pay the interest on it." I told him, "Give me three rooms worth and charge whatever you want." Next day a truck pulled up here and two men unloaded them three rooms. Man what drove the truck give me a book. Say send ten dollars, first of every month to the address in the book and every thing will be all right. Say if I miss a payment the devil was coming back and it'll be hell to pay. That was fifteen years ago. To this day . . . the first of the month I send my ten dollars, Rose'll tell you.

ROSE. Troy lying.

TROY. I ain't never seen that man since. Now you tell me who else that could have been but the devil? I ain't sold my soul or nothing like that, you understand. Naw, I wouldn't have truck with the devil about nothing like that. I got my furniture and pays my ten dollars the first of the month just like clockwork.

BONO. How long you say you been paying this ten dollars a month?

TROY. Fifteen years!

BONO. Hell, ain't you finished paying for it yet? How much the man done charged you?

TROY. Ah hell, I done paid for it. I done paid for it ten times over! The fact is f I'm scared to stop paying it.

ROSE. Troy lying. We got that furniture from Mr. Glickman. He ain't paying no ten dollars a month to nobody.

TROY. Aw hell, woman. Bono know I ain't that big a fool.

LYONS. I was just getting ready to say . . . I know where there's a bridge for sale.

TROY. Look here, I'll tell you this . . . it don't matter to me if he was the devil. It don't matter if the devil give credit. Somebody has got to give it.

ROSE. It ought to matter. You going around talking about having truck with the devil . . . God's the one you gonna have to answer to. He's the one gonna be at the Judgment.

LYONS. Yeah, well, look here, Pop . . . let me have that ten dollars. I'll give it back to you. Bonnie got a job working at the hospital.

TROY. What I tell you, Bono? The only time I see this nigger is when he wants something. That's the only time I see him.

LYONS. Come on, Pop, Mr. Bono don't want to hear all that. Let me have the ten dollars. I told you Bonnie working.

TROY. What that mean to me? "Bonnie working." I don't care if she working. Go ask her for the ten dollars if she working. Talking about "Bonnie working." Why ain't you working?

LYONS. Aw, Pop, you know I can't find no decent job. Where am I gonna get a job at? You know I can't get no job.

TROY. I told you I know some people down there. I can get you on the rubbish if you want to work. I told you that the last time you came by here asking me for something.

LYONS. Naw, Pop . . . thanks. That ain't for me. I don't wanna be carrying nobody's rubbish. I don't wanna be punching nobody's time clock.

TROY. What's the matter, you too good to carry people's rubbish? Where you think that ten dollars you talking about come from? I'm just supposed to haul people's rubbish and give my money to you cause you too lazy to work. You too lazy to work and wanna know why you ain't got what I got.

ROSE. What hospital Bonnie working at? Mercy?

LYONS. She's down at Passavant working in the laundry.

TROY. I ain't got nothing as it is. I give you that ten dollars and I got to eat beans the rest of the week. Naw . . . you ain't getting no ten dollars here.

LYONS. You ain't got to be eating no beans. I don't know why you wanna say that.

TROY. I ain't got no extra money. Gabe done moved over to Miss Pearl's paying her the rent and things done got tight around here. I can't afford to be giving you every payday.

LYONS. I ain't asked you to give me nothing. I asked you to loan me ten dollars. I know you got ten dollars.

TROY. Yeah, I got it. You know why I got it? Cause I don't throw my money away out there in the streets. You living the fast life . . . wanna be a musician . . . running around in them clubs and things . . . then, you learn to take care of yourself. You ain't gonna find me going and asking nobody for nothing. I done spent too many years without.

LYONS. You and me is two different people, Pop.

TROY. I done learned my mistake and learned to do what's right by it. You still trying to get something for nothing. Life don't owe you nothing. You owe it to yourself. Ask Bono. He'll tell you I'm right.

LYONS. You got your way of dealing with the world . . . I got mine. The only thing that matters to me is the music.

TROY. Yeah, I can see that! It don't matter how you gonna eat . . . where your next dollar is coming from. You telling the truth there.

LYONS. I know I got to eat. But I got to live too. I need something that gonna help me to get out of the bed in the morning. Make me feel like I belong in the world. I don't bother nobody. I just stay with the music cause that's the only way I can find to live in the world. Otherwise there ain't no telling what I might do. Now I don't come criticizing you and how you live. I just come by to ask you for ten dollars. I don't wanna hear all that about how I live.

TROY. Boy, your mamma did a hell of a job raising you.

LYONS. You can't change me, Pop. I'm thirty-four years old. If you wanted to change me, you should have been there when I was growing up. I come by to see you . . . ask for ten dollars and you want to talk about how I was raised. You don't know nothing about how I was raised.

ROSE. Let the boy have ten dollars, Troy.

TROY (*to Lyons*). What the hell you looking at me for? I ain't got no ten dollars. You know what I do with my money. (*To Rose.*) Give him ten dollars if you want him to have it.

ROSE. I will. Just as soon as you turn it loose.

TROY (*handing Rose the money*). There it is. Seventy-six dollars and forty-two cents. You see this, Bono? Now, I ain't gonna get but six of that back.

ROSE. You ought to stop telling that lie. Here, Lyons. (*She hands him the money.*)

LYONS. Thanks, Rose. Look . . . I got to run . . . I'll see you later.

TROY. Wait a minute. You gonna say, "thanks, Rose" and ain't gonna look to see where she got that ten dollars from? See how they do me, Bono?

LYONS. I know she got it from you, Pop. Thanks. I'll give it back to you.

TROY. There he go telling another lie. Time I see that ten dollars . . . he'll be owing me thirty more.

LYONS. See you, Mr. Bono.

BONO. Take care, Lyons!

LYONS. Thanks, Pop. I'll see you again.

Lyons exits the yard.

TROY. I don't know why he don't go and get him a decent job and take care of that woman he got.

BONO. He'll be all right, Troy. The boy is still young.

TROY. The *boy* is thirty-four years old.

ROSE. Let's not get off into all that.

BONO. Look here . . . I got to be going. I got to be getting on. Lucille gonna be waiting.

TROY (*puts his arm around Rose*). See this woman, Bono? I love this woman. I love this woman so much it hurts. I love her so much . . . I done run out of ways of loving her. So I got to go back to basics. Don't you come by my house Monday morning talking about time to go to work . . . 'cause I'm still gonna be stroking!

ROSE. Troy! Stop it now!

BONO. I ain't paying him no mind, Rose. That ain't nothing but gin-talk. Go on, Troy. I'll see you Monday.

TROY. Don't you come by my house, nigger! I done told you what I'm gonna be doing.

The lights go down to black.

SCENE 2

The lights come up on Rose hanging up clothes. She hums and sings softly to herself. It is the following morning.

ROSE (*sings*). Jesus, be a fence all around me every day
Jesus, I want you to protect me as I travel on my way.
Jesus, be a fence all around me every day.

Troy enters from the house.

Jesus, I want you to protect me
As I travel on my way.
(*To Troy.*) 'Morning, You ready for breakfast? I can fix it soon as I finish hanging up these clothes?

TROY. I got the coffee on. That'll be all right. I'll just drink some of that this morning.

ROSE. That 651 hit yesterday. That's the second time this month. Miss Pearl hit for a dollar . . . seem like those that need the least always get lucky. Poor folks can't get nothing.

TROY. Them numbers don't know nobody. I don't know why you fool with them. You and Lyons both.

ROSE. It's something to do.

TROY. You ain't doing nothing but throwing your money away.

ROSE. Troy, you know I don't play foolishly. I just play a nickel here and a nickel there.

TROY. That's two nickels you done thrown away.

ROSE. Now I hit sometimes . . . that makes up for it. It always comes in handy when I do hit. I don't hear you complaining then.

TROY. I ain't complaining now. I just say it's foolish. Trying to guess out of six hundred ways which way the number gonna come. If I had all the money niggers, these Negroes, throw away on numbers for one week—just one week—I'd be a rich man.

ROSE. Well, you wishing and calling it foolish ain't gonna stop folks from playing numbers. That's one thing for sure. Besides . . . some good things come from playing numbers. Look where Pope done bought him that restaurant off of numbers.

TROY. I can't stand niggers like that. Man ain't had two dimes to rub together. He walking around with his shoes all run over bumming money for cigarettes. All right. Got lucky there and hit the numbers . . .

ROSE. Troy, I know all about it.

TROY. Had good sense, I'll say that for him. He ain't throwed his money away. I seen niggers hit the numbers and go through two thousand dollars in four days. Man bought him that restaurant down there . . . fixed it up real nice . . . and then didn't want nobody to come in it! A Negro go in there and can't get no kind of service. I seen a white fellow come in there and order a bowl of stew. Pope picked all the meat out the pot for him. Man ain't had nothing but a bowl of meat! Negro come behind him and ain't got nothing but the potatoes and carrots. Talking about what numbers do for people, you picked a wrong example. Ain't done nothing but make a worser fool out of him than he was before.

ROSE. Troy, you ought to stop worrying about what happened at work yesterday.

TROY. I ain't worried. Just told me to be down there at the Commissioner's office on Friday. Everybody think they gonna fire me. I ain't worried about them firing me. You ain't got to worry about that. (*Pause.*) Where's Cory? Cory in the house? (*Calls.*) Cory?

ROSE. He gone out.

TROY. Out, huh? He gone out 'cause he know I want him to help me with this fence. I know how he is. That boy scared of work.

Gabriel enters. He comes halfway down the alley and, hearing Troy's voice, stops.

TROY (*continues*). He ain't done a lick of work in his life.

ROSE. He had to go to football practice. Coach wanted them to get in a little extra practice before the season start.

TROY. I got his practice . . . running out of here before he get his chores done.

ROSE. Troy, what is wrong with you this morning? Don't nothing set right with you. Go on back in there and go to bed . . . get up on the other side.

TROY. Why something got to be wrong with me? I ain't said nothing wrong with me.

ROSE. You got something to say about everything. First it's the numbers . . . then it's the way the man runs his restaurant . . . then you done got on Cory. What's it gonna be next? Take a look up there and see if the weather suits you . . . or is it gonna be how you gonna put up the fence with the clothes hanging in the yard.

TROY. You hit the nail on the head then.

ROSE. I know you like I know the back of my hand. Go on in there and get you some coffee . . . see if that straighten you up. 'Cause you ain't right this morning.

Troy starts into the house and sees Gabriel. Gabriel starts singing. Troy's brother, he is seven years younger than Troy. Injured in World War II, he has a metal-plate in his head. He carries an old trumpet tied around his waist and believes with every fiber of his being that he is the Archangel Gabriel. He carries a chipped basket with an assortment of discarded fruits and vegetables he has picked up in the strip district and which he attempts to sell.

GABRIEL. (*Singing*). Yes, ma'am I got plums
    You ask me how I sell them
    Oh ten cents apiece
    Three for a quarter
    Come and buy now
    'Cause I'm here today
    And tomorrow I'll be gone

Gabriel enters.

    Hey, Rose!
ROSE. How you doing Gabe?
GABRIEL. There's Troy . . . Hey, Troy!
TROY. Hey, Gabe.

Exit into kitchen.

ROSE (*to Gabriel*). What you got there?
GABRIEL. You know what I got, Rose. I got fruits and vegetables.
ROSE (*looking in basket*). Where's all these plums you talking about?
GABRIEL. I ain't got no plums today, Rose. I was just singing that. Have
    some tomorrow. Put me in a big order for plums. Have enough plums
    tomorrow for St. Peter and everybody.

Troy reenters from kitchen, crosses to steps.

(*To Rose.*) Troy's mad at me.
TROY. I ain't mad at you. What I got to be mad at you about? You ain't
    done nothing to me.
GABRIEL. I just moved over to Miss Pearl's to keep out from in you way.
    I ain't mean no harm by it.
TROY. Who said anything about that? I ain't said anything about that.
GABRIEL. You ain't mad at me, is you?
TROY. Naw . . . I ain't mad at you, Gabe. If I was mad at you I'd tell you
    about it.
GABRIEL. Got me two rooms. In the basement. Got my own door too.
    Wanna see my key? (*He holds up a key.*) That's my own key! My two
    rooms!
TROY. Well, that's good, Gabe. You got you own key . . . that's good.
ROSE. You hungry, Gabe? I was just fixing to cook Troy his breakfast.
GABRIEL. I'll take some biscuits. You got some biscuits? Did you know
    when I was in heaven . . . every morning me and St. Peter would sit
    down by the gate and eat some big fat biscuits? Oh, yeah! We had us
    a good time. We'd sit there and eat us them biscuits and then St. Peter
    would go off to sleep and tell me to wake him up when it's time to
    open the gates for the judgment.
ROSE. Well, come on . . . I'll make up a batch of biscuits.

Rose exits into the house.

GABRIEL. Troy . . . St. Peter got your name in the book. I seen it. It say . . . Troy Maxson. I say . . . I know him! He got the same name like what I got. That's my brother!

TROY. How many times you gonna tell me that, Gabe?

GABRIEL. Ain't got my name in the book. Don't have to have my name. I done died and went to heaven. He got your name though. One morning St. Peter was looking at his book . . . marking it up for the judgment . . . and he let me see your name. Got it in there under M. Got Rose's name . . . I ain't seen it like I seen yours . . . but I know it's in there. He got a great big book. Got everybody's name what was ever been born. That's what he told me. But I seen your name. Seen it with my own eyes.

TROY. Go on in the house there. Rose going to fix you something to eat.

GABRIEL. Oh, I ain't hungry. I done had breakfast with Aunt Jemimah. She come by and cooked me up a whole mess of flapjacks. Remember how we used to eat them flapjacks?

TROY. Go on in the house and get you something to eat now.

GABRIEL. I got to sell my plums. I done sold some tomatoes. Got me two quarters. Wanna see? (*He shows Troy his quarters.*) I'm gonna save them and buy me a new horn so St. Peter can hear me when it's time to open the gates. (*Gabriel stops suddenly. Listens.*) Hear that? That's the hellhounds. I got to chase them out of here. Go on get out of here! Get out!

Gabriel exits singing.

Better get ready for the judgment
Better get ready for the judgment
My Lord is coming down

Rose enters from the house.

TROY. He's gone off somewhere.

GABRIEL (*offstage*). Better get ready for the judgment
Better get ready for the judgment morning
Better get ready for the judgment
My God is coming down

ROSE. He ain't eating right. Miss Pearl say she can't get him to eat nothing.

TROY. What you want me to do about it, Rose? I done did everything I can for the man. I can't make him get well. Man got half his head blown away . . . what you expect?

ROSE. Seem like something ought to be done to help him.

TROY. Man don't bother nobody. He just mixed up from that metal plate he got in his head. Ain't no sense for him to go back into the hospital.

ROSE. Least he be eating right. They can help him take care of himself.

TROY. Don't nobody wanna be locked up, Rose. What you wanna lock him up for? Man go over there and fight the war . . . messin' around with them Japs, get half his head blown off . . . and they give him a lousy three thousand dollars. And I had to swoop down on that.

ROSE. Is you fixing to go into that again?

TROY. That's the only way I got a roof over my head . . . cause of that metal plate.

ROSE. Ain't no sense you blaming yourself for nothing. Gabe wasn't in no condition to manage that money. You done what was right by him. Can't nobody say you ain't done what was right by him. Look how long you took care of him . . . till he wanted to have his own place and moved over there with Miss Pearl.

TROY. That ain't what I'm saying, woman! I'm just stating the facts. If my brother didn't have that metal plate in his head . . . I wouldn't have a pot to piss in or a window to throw it out of. And I'm fifty-three years old. Now see if you can understand that!

Troy gets up from the porch and starts to exit the yard.

ROSE. Where you going off to? You been running out of here every Saturday for weeks. I thought you was gonna work on this fence?

TROY. I'm gonna walk down to Taylors'. Listen to the ball game. I'll be back in a bit. I'll work on it when I get back.

He exits the yard. The lights go to black.

SCENE 3

The lights come up on the yard. It is four hours later. Rose is taking down the clothes from the line. Cory enters carrying his football equipment.

ROSE. Your daddy like to had a fit with you running out of here this morning without doing your chores.

CORY. I told you I had to go to practice.

ROSE. He say you were supposed to help him with this fence.

CORY. He been saying that the last four or five Saturdays, and then he don't never do nothing, but go down to Taylors. Did you tell him about the recruiter?

ROSE. Yeah, I told him.

CORY. What he say?

ROSE. He ain't said nothing too much. You get in there and get started on your chores before he gets back. Go on and scrub down them steps before he gets back here hollering and carrying on.

CORY. I'm hungry. What you got to eat, Mama?

ROSE. Go on and get started on your chores. I got some meat loaf in there. Go on and make you a sandwich . . . and don't leave no mess in there.

Cory exits into the house. Rose continues to take down the clothes. Troy enters the yard and sneaks up and grabs her from behind.

Troy! Go on, now. You liked to scared me to death. What was the score of the game? Lucille had me on the phone and I couldn't keep up with it.

TROY. What I care about the game? Come here, woman. (*He tries to kiss her.*)

ROSE. I thought you went down Taylors' to listen to the game. Go on, Troy! You supposed to be putting up this fence.

TROY (*attempting to kiss her again*). I'll put it up when I finish with what is at hand.

ROSE. Go on, Troy. I ain't studying you.

TROY (*chasing after her*). I'm studying you . . . fixing to do my homework!

ROSE. Troy, you better leave me alone.

TROY. Where's Cory? That boy brought his butt home yet?

ROSE. He's in the house doing his chores.

TROY (*calling*). Cory! Get your butt out here, boy!

> *Rose exits into the house with the laundry. Troy goes over to the pile of wood, picks up a board, and starts sawing. Cory enters from the house.*

TROY. You just now coming in here from leaving this morning?

CORY. Yeah, I had to go to football practice.

TROY. Yeah, what?

CORY. Yessir.

TROY. I ain't but two seconds off you noway. The garbage sitting in there overflowing . . . you ain't done none of your chores . . . and you come in here talking about "Yeah."

CORY. I was just getting ready to do my chores now, Pop . . .

TROY. Your first chore is to help me with this fence on Saturday. Everything else come after that. Now get that saw and cut them boards.

> *Cory takes the saw and begins cutting the boards. Troy continues working. There is a long pause.*

CORY. Hey, Pop . . . why don't you buy a TV?

TROY. What I want with a TV? What I want one of them for?

CORY. Everybody got one. Earl, Ba Bra . . . Jesse!

TROY. I ain't asked you who had one. I say what I want with one?

CORY. So you can watch it. They got lots of things on TV. Baseball games and everything. We could watch the World Series.

TROY. Yeah . . . and how much this TV cost?

CORY. I don't know. They got them on sale for around two hundred dollars.

TROY. Two hundred dollars, huh?

CORY. That ain't that much, Pop.

TROY. Naw, it's just two hundred dollars. See that roof you got over your head at night? Let me tell you something about that roof. It's been over ten years since that roof was last tarred. See now . . . the snow come this winter and sit up there on that roof like it is . . . and it's gonna seep inside. It's just gonna be a little bit . . . ain't gonna hardly notice it. Then the next thing you know, it's gonna be leaking all over the house. Then the wood rot from all that water and you gonna need a whole new roof. Now, how much you think it cost to get that roof tarred?

CORY. I don't know.

TROY. Two hundred and sixty-four dollars . . . cash money. While you thinking about a TV, I got to be thinking about the roof . . . and whatever else go wrong here. Now if you had two hundred dollars, what would you do . . . fix the roof or buy a TV?

CORY. I'd buy a TV. Then when the roof started to leak . . . when it needed fixing . . . I'd fix it.

TROY. Where you gonna get the money from? You done spent it for a TV. You gonna sit up and watch the water run all over your brand new TV.

CORY. Aw, Pop. You got money. I know you do.

TROY. Where I got it at, huh?

CORY. You got it in the bank.

TROY. You wanna see my bankbook? You wanna see that seventy-three dollars and twenty-two cents I got sitting up in there.

CORY. You ain't got to pay for it all at one time. You can put a down payment on it and carry it on home with you.

TROY. Not me. I ain't gonna owe nobody nothing if I can help it. Miss a payment and they come and snatch it right out your house. Then what you got? Now, soon as I get two hundred dollars clear, then I'll buy a TV. Right now, as soon as I get two hundred and sixty-four dollars, I'm gonna have this roof tarred.

CORY. Aw . . . Pop!

TROY. You go on and get you two hundred dollars and buy one if ya want it. I got better things to do with my money.

CORY. I can't get no two hundred dollars. I ain't never seen two hundred dollars.

TROY. I'll tell you what . . . you get you a hundred dollars and I'll put the other hundred with it.

CORY. All right, I'm gonna show you.

TROY. You gonna show me how you can cut them boards right now.

Cory begins to cut the boards. There is a long pause.

CORY. The Pirates won today. That makes five in a row.

TROY. I ain't thinking about the Pirates. Got an all-white team. Got that boy . . . that Puerto Rican boy . . . Clemente. Don't even half-play him. That boy could be something if they give him a chance. Play him one day and sit him on the bench the next.

CORY. He gets a lot of chances to play.

TROY. I'm talking about playing regular. Playing every day so you can get your timing. That's what I'm talking about.

CORY. They got some white guys on the team that don't play every day. You can't play everybody at the same time.

TROY. If they got a white fellow sitting on the bench . . . you can bet your last dollar he can't play! The colored guy got to be twice as good before he get on the team. That's why I don't want you to get all tied up in them sports. Man on the team and what it get him? They got colored on the team and don't use them. Same as not having them. All them teams the same.

CORY. The Braves got Hank Aaron and Wes Covington. Hank Aaron hit two home runs today. That makes forty-three.

TROY. Hank Aaron ain't nobody. That what you supposed to do. That's how you supposed to play the game. Ain't nothing to it. It's just a matter of timing . . . getting the right follow-through. Hell, I can hit forty-three home runs right now!

CORY. Not off no major-league pitching, you couldn't.

TROY. We had better pitching in the Negro leagues. I hit seven home runs off of Satchel Paige.[4] You can't get no better than that!

CORY. Sandy Koufax. He's leading the league in strikeouts.

TROY. I ain't thinking of no Sandy Koufax.

CORY. You got Warren Spahn and kew Burdette. I bet you couldn't hit no home runs off of Warren Spahn.

TROY. I'm through with it now. You go on and cut them boards. (*Pause.*) Your mama tell me you done got recruited by a college football team? Is that right?

CORY. Yeah. Coach Zellman say the recruiter gonna be coming by to talk to you. Get you to sign the permission papers.

TROY. I thought you supposed to be working down there at the A&P. Ain't you suppose to be working down there after school?

CORY. Mr. Stawicki say he gonna hold my job for me until after the football season. Say starting next week I can work weekends.

TROY. I thought we had an understanding about this football stuff? You suppose to keep up with your chores and hold that job down at the A&P. Ain't been around here all day on a Saturday. Ain't none of your chores done . . . and now you telling me you done quit your job.

CORY. I'm going to be working weekends.

TROY. You damn right you are! And ain't no need for nobody coming around here to talk to me about signing nothing.

CORY. Hey, Pop . . . you can't do that. He's coming all the way from North Carolina.

TROY. I don't care where he coming from. The white man ain't gonna let you get nowhere with that football noway. You go on and get your book-learning so you can work yourself up in that A&P or learn how to fix cars or build houses or something, get you a trade. That way

---

[4] **Satchel Paige** (1906–82) pitcher in the Negro leagues

you have something can't nobody take away from you. You go on and learn how to put your hands to some good use. Besides hauling people's garbage.

CORY. I get good grades, Pop. That's why the recruiter wants to talk with you. You got to keep up your grades to get recruited. This way I'll be going to college. I'll get a chance . . .

TROY. First you gonna get your butt down there to the A&P and get your job back.

CORY. Mr. Stawicki done already hired somebody else 'cause I told him I was playing football.

TROY. You a bigger fool than I thought . . . to let somebody take away your job so you can play some football. Where you gonna get your money to take out your girlfriend and whatnot? What kind of foolishness is that to let somebody take away your job?

CORY. I'm still gonna be working weekends.

TROY. Naw . . . naw. You getting your butt out of here and finding you another job.

CORY. Come on, Pop! I got to practice. I can't work after school and play football too. The team needs me. That's what Coach Zellman say . . .

TROY. I don't care what nobody else say. I'm the boss . . . you understand? I'm the boss around here. I do the only saying what counts.

CORY. Come on, Pop!

TROY. I asked you . . . did you understand?

CORY. Yeah . . .

TROY. What?!

CORY. Yessir.

TROY. You go on down there to that A&P and see if you can get your job back. If you can't do both . . . then you quit the football team. You've got to take the crookeds with the straights.

CORY. Yessir. *(Pause.)* Can I ask you a question?

TROY. What the hell you wanna ask me? Mr. Stawicki the one you got the questions for.

CORY. How come you ain't never liked me?

TROY. Liked you? Who the hell say I got to like you? What law is there say I got to like you? Wanna stand up in my face and ask a damn fool-ass question like that. Talking about liking somebody. Come here, boy, when I talk to you.

Cory comes over to where Troy is working. He stands slouched over and Troy shoves him on his shoulder.

Straighten up, goddammit! I asked you a question . . . what law is there say I got to like you?

CORY. None.

TROY. Well, all right then! Don't you eat every day? *(Pause.)* Answer me when I talk to you! Don't you eat every day?

CORY. Yeah.

TROY. Nigger, as long as you in my house, you put that sir on the end of it when you talk to me

CORY. Yes . . . sir.

TROY. You eat every day.

CORY. Yessir!

TROY. Got a roof over your head.

CORY. Yessir!

TROY. Got clothes on your back.

CORY. Yessir.

TROY. Why you think that is?

CORY. Cause of you.

TROY. Ah, hell I know it's cause of me . . . but why do you think that is?

CORY (*hesitant*). Cause you like me.

TROY. Like you? I go out of here every morning . . . bust my butt . . . putting up with them crackers every day . . . cause I like you? You are the biggest fool I ever saw. (*Pause.*) It's my job. It's my responsibility! You understand that? A man got to take care of his family. You live in my house . . . sleep you behind on my bedclothes . . . fill you belly up with my food . . . cause you my son. You my flesh and blood. Not cause I like you! Cause it's my duty to take care of you. I owe a responsibility to you! Let's get this straight right here . . . before it go along any further . . . I ain't got to like you. Mr. Rand don't give me my money come payday cause he likes me. He give me cause he owe me. I done give you everything I had to give you. I gave you your life! Me and your mama worked that out between us. And liking your black ass wasn't part of the bargain. Don't you try and go through life worrying about if somebody like you or not. You best be making sure they doing right by you. You understand what I'm saying boy?

CORY. Yessir.

TROY. Then get the hell out of my face, and get on down to that A&P.

Rose has been standing behind the screen door for much of the scene. She enters as Cory exits.

ROSE. Why don't you let the boy go ahead and play football, Troy? Ain't no harm in that. He's just trying to be like you with the sports.

TROY. I don't want him to be like me! I want him to move as far away from my life as he can get. You the only decent thing that ever happened to me. I wish him that. But I don't wish him a thing else from my life. I decided seventeen years ago that boy wasn't getting involved in no sports. Not after what they did to me in the sports.

ROSE. Troy, why don't you admit you was too old to play in the major leagues? For once . . . why don't you admit that?

TROY. What do you mean too old? Don't come telling me I was too old. I just wasn't the right color. Hell, I'm fifty-three years old and can do better than Selkirk's .269 right now!

ROSE. How's was you gonna play ball when you were over forty? Sometimes I can't get no sense out of you.

TROY. I got good sense, woman. I got sense enough not to let my boy get hurt over playing no sports. You been mothering that boy too much. Worried about if people like him.

ROSE. Everything that boy do . . . he do for you. He wants you to say "Good job, son." That's all.

TROY. Rose, I ain't got time for that. He's alive. He's healthy. He's got to make his own way. I made mine. Ain't nobody gonna hold his hand when he get out there in that world.

ROSE. Times have changed from when you was young, Troy. People change. The world's changing around you and you can't even see it.

TROY (*slow, methodical*). Woman . . . I do the best I can do. I come in here every Friday. I carry a sack of potatoes and a bucket of lard. You all line up at the door with your hands out. I give you the lint from my pockets. I give you my sweat and my blood. I ain't got no tears. I done spent them. We go upstairs in that room at night . . . and I fall down on you and try to blast a hole into forever. I get up Monday morning . . . find my lunch on the table. I go out. Make my way. Find my strength to carry me through to the next Friday. (*Pause.*) That's all I got, Rose. That's all I got to give. I can't give nothing else.

Troy exits into the house. The lights go down to black.

SCENE 4

It is Friday. Two weeks later. Cory starts out of the house with his football equipment. The phone rings.

CORY (*calling*). I got it! (*He answers the phone and stands in the screen door talking.*) Hello? Hey, Jesse. Naw . . . I was just getting ready to leave now.

ROSE (*calling*). Cory!

CORY. I told you, man, them spikes is all tore up. You can use them if you want, but they ain't no good. Earl got some spikes.

ROSE (*calling*). Cory!

CORY (*calling to Rose*). Mam? I'm talking to Jesse. (*Into phone.*) When she say that? (*Pause.*) Aw, you lying, man. I'm gonna tell her you said that.

ROSE (*calling*). Cory, don't you go nowhere!

CORY. I got to go to the game, Ma! (*Into the phone.*) Yeah, hey, look, I'll talk to you later. Yeah, I'll meet you over Earl's house. Later. Bye, Ma.

Cory exits the house and starts out the yard.

ROSE. Cory, where you going off to? You got that stuff all pulled out and thrown all over your room.

CORY (*in the yard*). I was looking for my spikes. Jesse wanted to borrow my spikes.

ROSE. Get up there and get that cleaned up before your daddy get back in here.

CORY. I got to go to the game! I'll clean it up *when I get back.*

Cory exits.

ROSE. That's all he need to do is see that room all messed up.

Rose exits into the house. Troy and Bono enter the yard. Troy is dressed in clothes other than his work clothes.

BONO. He told him the same thing he told you. Take it to the union.

TROY. Brownie ain't got that much sense. Man wasn't thinking about nothing. He wait until I confront them on it . . . then he wanna come crying seniority. (*Calls.*) Hey, Rose!

BONO. I wish I could have seen Mr. Rand's face when he told you.

TROY. He couldn't get it out of his mouth! Liked to bit his tongue! When they called me down there to the Commissioner's office . . . he thought they was gonna fire me. Like everybody else.

BONO. I didn't think they was gonna fire you. I thought they was gonna put you on the warning paper.

TROY. Hey, Rose! (*To Bono.*) Yeah, Mr. Rand like to bit his tongue.

Troy breaks the seal on the bottle, takes a drink, and hands it to Bono.

BONO. I see you run right down to Taylors' and told that Alberta gal.

TROY (*calling*). Hey Rose! (*To Bono.*) I told everybody. Hey, Rose! I went down there to cash my check.

ROSE (*entering from the house*). Hush all that hollering, man! I know you out here. What they say down there at the Commissioner's office?

TROY. You supposed to come when I call you, woman. Bono'll tell you that. (*To Bono.*) Don't Lucille come when you call her?

ROSE. Man, hush your mouth. I ain't no dog . . . talk about "come when you call me."

TROY (*puts his arm around Rose*). You hear this, Bono? I had me an old dog used to get uppity like that. You say, "C'mere, Blue!" . . . and he just lay there and look at you. End up getting a stick and chasing him away trying to make him come.

ROSE. I ain't studying you and your dog. I remember you used to sing that old song.

TROY (*he sings*). Hear it ring! Hear it ring! I had a dog his name was Blue.

ROSE. Don't nobody wanna hear you sing that old song.

TROY (*sings*). You know Blue was mighty true.

ROSE. Used to have Cory running around here singing that song.

BONO. Hell, I remember that song myself.

TROY (*sings*). You know Blue was a good old dog.

   Blue treed a possum in a hollow log.

   That was my daddy's song. My daddy made up that song.

ROSE. I don't care who made it up. Don't nobody wanna hear you sing it.

TROY (*makes a song like calling a dog*). Come here, woman.

ROSE. You come in here carrying on, I reckon they ain't fired you. What they say down there at the Commissioner's office?

TROY. Look here, Rose . . . Mr. Rand called me into his office today when I got back from talking to them people down there . . . it come from up top . . . he called me in and told me they was making me a driver.

ROSE. Troy, you kidding!

TROY. No I ain't. Ask Bono.

ROSE. Well, that's great, Troy. Now you don't have to hassle them people no more.

   Lyons enters from the street.

TROY. Aw hell, I wasn't looking to see you today. I thought you was in jail. Got it all over the front page of the *Courier* about them raiding Sefus's place . . . where you be hanging out with all them thugs.

LYONS. Hey, Pop . . . that ain't got nothing to do with me. I don't go down there gambling. I go down there to sit in with the band. I ain't got nothing to do with the gambling part. They got some good music down there.

TROY. They got some rogues . . . is what they got.

LYONS. How you been, Mr. Bono? Hi, Rose.

BONO. I see where you playing down at the Crawford Grill tonight.

ROSE. How come you ain't brought Bonnie like I told you? You should have brought Bonnie with you, she ain't been over in a month of Sundays.

LYONS. I was just in the neighborhood . . . thought I'd stop by.

TROY. Here he come . . .

BONO. Your daddy got a promotion on the rubbish. He's gonna be the first colored driver. Ain't got to do nothing but sit up there and read the paper like them white fellows.

LYONS. Hey, Pop . . . if you knew how to read you'd be all right.

BONO. Naw . . . naw . . . you mean if the nigger knew how to drive he'd be all right. Been fighting with them people about driving and ain't even got a license. Mr. Rand know you ain't got no driver's license?

TROY. Driving ain't nothing. All you do is point the truck where you want it to go. Driving ain't nothing.

BONO. Do Mr. Rand know you ain't got no driver's license? That's what I'm talking about. I ain't asked if driving was easy. I asked if Mr. Rand know you ain't got no driver's license.

TROY. He ain't got to know. The man ain't got to know my business. Time he find out, I have two or three driver's licenses.

LYONS (*going into his pocket*). Say, look here, Pop . . .

TROY. I knew it was coming. Didn't I tell you, Bono? I know what kind of "Look here, Pop" that was. The nigger fixing to ask me for some money. It's Friday night. It's my payday. All them rogues down there on the avenue . . . the ones that ain't in jail . . . and Lyons is hopping in his shoes to get down there with them.

LYONS. See, Pop . . . if you give somebody else a chance to talk sometimes, you'd see that I was fixing to pay you back your ten dollars like I told you. Here . . . I told you I'd pay you when Bonnie got paid.

TROY. Naw . . . you go ahead and keep that ten dollars. Put it in the bank. The next time you feel like you wanna come by here and ask me for something . . . you go on down there and get that.

LYONS. Here's your ten dollars, Pop. I told you I don't want you to give me nothing. I just wanted to borrow ten dollars.

TROY. Naw . . . you go on and keep that for the next time you want to ask me.

LYONS. Come on, Pop . . . here go your ten dollars.

ROSE. Why don't you go on and ler the boy pay you back, Troy?

LYONS. Here you go, Rose. If you don't take it I'm gonna have to hear about it for the next six months. (*He hands her the money.*)

ROSE. You can hand yours over here too, Troy.

TROY. You see this, Bono. You see how they do me.

BONO. Yeah, Lucille do me the same way.

Gabriel is heard singing off stage. He enters.

GABRIEL. Better get ready for the Judgment! Better get ready for . . . Hey! . . . Hey! . . . There's Troy's boy!

LYONS. How are you doing, Uncle Gabe?

GABRIEL. Lyons . . . The King of the Jungle! Rose . . . hey, Rose. Got a flower for you. (*He takes a rose from his pocket.*) Picked it myself. That's the same rose like you is!

ROSE. That's right nice of you, Gabe.

LYONS. What you been doing, Uncle Gabe?

GABRIEL. Oh, I been chasing hellhounds and waiting on the time to tell St. Peter to open the gates.

LYONS. You been chasing hellhounds, huh? Well . . . you doing the right thing, Uncle Gabe. Somebody got to chase them.

GABRIEL. Oh, yeah . . . I know it. The devil's strong. The devil ain't no pushover. Hellhounds snipping at everybody's heels. But I got my trumpet waiting on the judgment time.

LYONS. Waiting on the Battle of Armageddon, huh?

GABRIEL. Ain't gonna be too much of a battle when God get to waving

that Judgment sword. But the people's gonna have a hell of a time trying to get into heaven if them gates ain't open.

LYONS (*putting his arm around Gabriel*). You hear this, Pop. Uncle Gabe,
you all right!

GABRIEL (*laughing with Lyons*). Lyons! King of the Jungle.

ROSE. You gonna stay for supper, Gabe? Want me to fix you a plate?

GABRIEL. I'll take a sandwich, Rose. Don't want no plate. Just wanna eat
with my hands. I'll take a sandwich.

ROSE. How about you, Lyons? You staying? Got some short ribs cooking.

LYONS. Naw, I won't eat nothing till after we finished playing. (*Pause.*) You
ought to come down and listen to me play, Pop.

TROY. I don't like that Chinese music. All that noise.

ROSE. Go on in the house and wash up, Gabe . . . I'll fix you a sandwich.

GABRIEL (*to Lyons, as he exits*). Troy's mad at me.

LYONS. What you mad at Uncle Gabe for, Pop?

ROSE. He thinks Troy's mad at him cause he moved over to Miss Pearl's.

TROY. I ain't mad at the man. He can live where he want to live at.

LYONS. What he move over there for? Miss Pearl don't like nobody.

ROSE. She don't mind him none. She treats him real nice. She just don't
allow all that singing.

TROY. She don't mind that rent he be paying . . . that's what she don't
mind.

ROSE. Troy, I ain't going through that with you no more. He's over there
cause he want to have his own place. He can come and go as he
please.

TROY. Hell, he could come and go as he please here. I wasn't stopping
him. I ain't put no rules on him.

ROSE. It ain't the same thing, Troy. And you know it.

Gabriel comes to the door.

Now, that's the last I wanna hear about that. I don't wanna hear nothing else about Gabe and Miss Pearl. And next week . . .

GABRIEL. I'm ready for my sandwich, Rose.

ROSE. And next week . . . when that recruiter come from that school . . . I
want you to sign that paper and go on and let Cory play football. Then
that'll be the last I have to hear about that.

TROY (*to Rose as she exits into the house*). I ain't thinking about Cory nothing.

LYONS. What . . . Cory got recruited? What school he going to?

TROY. That boy walking around here smelling his piss . . . thinking he's
grown. Thinking he's gonna do what he want, irrespective of what I
say. Look here, Bono . . . I left the Commissioner's office and went
down to the A&P . . . that boy ain't working down there. He lying to
me. Telling me he got his job back . . . telling me he working weekends . . . telling me he working after school . . . Mr. Stawicki tell me
he ain't working down there at all!

LYONS. Cory just growing up. He's just busting at the seams trying to fill out your shoes.

TROY. I don't care what he's doing. When he get to the point where he wanna disobey me . . . then it's time for him to move on. Bono'll tell you that. I bet he ain't never disobeyed his daddy without paying the consequences.

BONO. I ain't never had a chance. My daddy came on through . . . but I ain't never knew him to see him . . . or what he had on his mind or where he went. Just moving on through. Searching out the New Land. That's what the old folks used to call it. See a fellow moving around from place to place . . . woman to woman . . . called it searching out the New Land. I can't say if he ever found it. I come along, didn't want no kids. Didn't know if I was gonna be in one place long enough to fix on them right as their daddy. I figured I was going searching too. As it turned out I been hooked up with Lucille near about as long as your daddy been with Rose. Going on sixteen years.

TROY. Sometimes I wish I hadn't known my daddy. He ain't cared nothing about no kids. A kid to him wasn't nothing. All he wanted was for you to learn how to walk so he could start you to working. When it come time for eating . . . he ate first. If there was anything left over, that's what you got. Man would sit down and eat two chickens and give you the wing.

LYONS. You ought to stop that, Pop. Everybody feed their kids. No matter how hard times is . . . everybody care about their kids. Make sure they have something to eat.

TROY. The only thing my daddy cared about was getting them bales of cotton in to Mr. Lubin. That's the only thing that mattered to him. Sometimes I used to wonder why he was living. Wonder why the devil hadn't come and got him. "Get them bales of cotton in to Mr. Lubin" and find out he owe him money . . .

LYONS. He should have just went on and left when he saw he couldn't get nowhere. That's what I would have done.

TROY. How he gonna leave with eleven kids? And where he gonna go? He ain't knew how to do nothing but farm. No, he was trapped and I think he knew it. But I'll say this for him . . . he felt a responsibility toward us. Maybe he ain't treated us the way I felt he should have . . . but without that responsibility he could have walked off and left us . . . made his own way.

BONO. A lot of them did. Back in those days what you talking about . . . they walk out their front door and just take on down one road or another and keep on walking.

LYONS. There you go! That's what I'm talking about.

BONO. Just keep on walking till you come to something else. Ain't you never heard of nobody having the walking blues? Well, that's what you call it when you just take off like that.

TROY. My daddy ain't had them walking blues! What you talking about? He stayed right there with his family. But he was just as evil as he could be. My mama couldn't stand him. Couldn't stand that evilness. She run off when I was about eight. She sneaked off one night after he had gone to sleep. Told me she was coming back for me. I ain't never seen her no more. All his women run off and left him. He wasn't good for nobody.

When my turn come to head out, I was fourteen and got to sniffing around Joe Canewell's daughter. Had us an old mule we called Greyboy. My daddy sent me out to do some plowing and I tied up Greyboy and went to fooling around with Joe Canewell's daughter. We done found us a nice little spot, got real cozy with each other. She about thirteen and we done figured we was grown anyway . . . so we down there enjoying ourselves . . . ain't thinking about nothing. We didn't know Greyboy had got loose and wandered back to the house and my daddy was looking for me. We down there by the creek enjoying ourselves when my daddy come up on us. Surprised us. He had them leather straps off the mule and commenced to whupping me like there was no tomorrow. I jumped up, mad and embarrassed. I was scared of my daddy. When he commenced to whupping on me . . . quite naturally I run to get out of the way. (*Pause.*) Now I thought he was mad cause I ain't done my work. But I see where he was chasing me off so he could have the gal for himself. When I see what the matter of it was, I lost all fear of my daddy. Right there is where I become a man . . . at fourteen years of age. (*Pause.*) Now it was my turn to run him off. I picked up them same reins that he had used on me. I picked up them reins and commenced to whupping on him. The gal jumped up and run off . . . and when my daddy turned to face me, I could see why the devil had never come to get him . . . cause he was the devil himself. I don't know what happened. When I woke up, I was laying right there by the creek, and Blue . . . this old dog we had . . . was licking my face. I thought I was blind. I couldn't see nothing. Both my eyes were swollen shut. I laid there and cried. I didn't know what I was gonna do. The only thing I knew was the time had come for me to leave my daddy's house. And right there the world suddenly got big. And it was a long time before I could cut it down to where I could handle it.

Part of that cutting down was when I got to the place where I could feel him kicking in my blood and knew that the only thing that separated us was the matter of a few years.

Gabriel enters from the house with a sandwich.

LYONS. What you got there, Uncle Gabe?
GABRIEL. Got me a ham sandwich. Rose gave me a ham sandwich.
TROY. I don't know what happened to him. I done lost touch with everybody except Gabriel. But I hope he's dead. I hope he found some peace.

LYONS. That's a heavy story, Pop. I didn't know you left home when you was fourteen.

TROY. And didn't know nothing. The only part of the world I knew was the forty-two acres of Mr. Lubin's land. That's all I knew about life.

LYONS. Fourteen's kinda young to be out on your own. (*Phone rings.*) I don't even think I was ready to be out on my own at fourteen. I don't know what I would have done.

TROY. I got up from the creek and walked on down to Mobile. I was through with farming. Figured I could do better in the city. So I walked the two hundred miles to Mobile.

LYONS. Wait a minute . . . you ain't walked no two hundred miles, Pop. Ain't nobody gonna walk no two hundred miles. You talking about some walking there.

BONO. That's the only way you got anywhere back in them days.

LYONS. Shhh. Damn if I wouldn't have hitched a ride with somebody!

TROY. Who you gonna hitch it with? They ain't had no cars and things like they got now. We talking about 1918.

ROSE (*entering*). What you all out here getting into?

TROY (*to Rose*). I'm telling Lyons how good he got it. He don't know nothing about this I'm talking.

ROSE. Lyons, that was Bonnie on the phone. She say you supposed to pick her up.

LYONS. Yeah, okay, Rose.

TROY. I walked on down to Mobile and hitched up with some of them fellows that was heading this way. Got up here and found out . . . not only couldn't you get a job . . . you couldn't find no place to live. I thought I was in freedom. Shhh. Colored folks living down there on the riverbanks in whatever kind of shelter they could find for themselves. Right down there under the Brady Street Bridge. Living in shacks made of sticks and tarpaper. Messed around there and went from bad to worse. Started stealing. First it was food. Then I figured, hell, if I steal money I can buy me some food. Buy me some shoes too! One thing led to another. Met your mama. I was young and anxious to be a man. Met your mama and had you. What I do that for? Now I got to worry about feeding you and her. Got to steal three times as much. Went out one day looking for somebody to rob . . . that's what I was, a robber. I'll tell you the truth. I'm ashamed of it today. But it's the truth. Went to rob this fellow . . . pulled out my knife . . . and he pulled out a gun. Shot me in the chest. I felt just like somebody had taken a hot branding iron and laid it on me. When he shot me I jumped at him with my knife. They told me I killed him and they put me in the penitentiary and locked me up for fifteen years. That's where I met Bono. That's where I learned how to play baseball. Got out that place and your mama had taken you and went on to make life without me. Fifteen years was a long time for her to wait. But that fifteen years cured me of that robbing stuff. Rose'll tell you. She asked me when I met her if I had gotten all that foolishness out of my system. And I told her, "Baby, it's you and baseball all what count with me." You hear me, Bono? I meant it too. She say, "Which one comes first?" I told her, "Baby, ain't no doubt it's baseball . . . but you stick and get old with me and we'll both outlive this baseball." Am I right, Rose? And it's true.

ROSE. Man, hush your mouth. You ain't said no such thing. Talking about, "Baby you know you'll always be number one with me." That's what you was talking.

TROY. You hear that, Bono. That's why I love her.

BONO. Rose'll keep you straight. You get off the track, she'll straighten you up.

ROSE. Lyons, you better get on up and get Bonnie. She waiting on you.

LYONS (*gets up to go*). Hey, Pop, why don't you come on down to the Grill and hear me play?

TROY. I ain't going down there. I'm too old to be sitting around in them clubs.

BONO. You got to be good to play down at the Grill.

LYONS. Come on, Pop . . .

TROY. I got to get up in the morning.

LYONS. You ain't got to stay long.

TROY. Naw, I'm gonna get my supper and go on to bed.

LYONS. Well, I got to go. I'll see you again.

TROY. Don't you come around my house on my payday.

ROSE. Pick up the phone and let somebody know you coming. And bring Bonnie with you. You know I'm always glad to see her.

LYONS. Yeah, I'll do that, Rose. You take care now. See you, Pop. See you, Mr. Bono. See you, Uncle Gabe.

GABRIEL. Lyons! King of the Jungle!

Lyons exits.

TROY. Is supper ready, woman? Me and you got some business to take care of. I'm gonna tear it up too.

ROSE. Troy, I done told you now!

TROY (*puts his arm around Bono*). Aw hell, woman . . . this is Bono. Bono like family. I done known this nigger since . . . how long I done know you?

BONO. It's been a long time.

TROY. I done know this nigger since Skippy was a pup. Me and him done been through some times.

BONO. You sure right about that.

TROY. Hell, I done know him longer than I known you. And we still standing shoulder to shoulder. Hey, look here, Bono . . . a man can't ask for no more than that. (*Drinks to him.*) I love you, nigger.

BONO. Hell, I love you too . . . I got to get home see my woman. You got yours in hand. I got to go get mine.

Bono starts to exit as Cory enters the yard, dressed in his football uniform. He gives Troy a hard, uncompromising look.

CORY. What you do that for, Pop?

He throws his helmet down in the direction of Troy.

ROSE. What's the matter? Cory . . . what's the matter?

CORY. Papa done went up to the school and told Coach Zellman I can't play football no more. Wouldn't even let me play the game. Told him to tell the recruiter not to come.

ROSE. Troy . . .

TROY. What you Troying me for. Yeah, I did it. And the boy know why I did it.

CORY. Why you wanna do that to me? That was the one chance I had.

ROSE. Ain't nothing wrong with Cory playing football, Troy.

TROY. The boy lied to me. I told the nigger if he wanna play football . . . to keep up his chores and hold down that job at the A&P. That was the conditions. Stopped down there to see Mr. Stawicki . . .

CORY. I can't work after school during the football season, Pop! I tried to tell you that Mr. Stawicki's holding my job for me. You don't never want to listen to nobody. And then you wanna go and do this to me!

TROY. I ain't done nothing to you. You done it to yourself.

CORY. Just cause you didn't have a chance! You just scared I'm gonna be better than you, that's all.

TROY. Come here.

ROSE. Troy . . .

Cory reluctantly crosses over to Troy.

TROY. All right! See. You done made a mistake.

CORY. I didn't even do nothing!

TROY. I'm gonna tell you what your mistake was. See . . . you swung at the ball and didn't hit it. That's strike one. See, you in the batter's box now. You swung and you missed. That's strike one. Don't you strike out!

Lights fade to black.

ACT 2

SCENE 1

The following morning. Cory is at the tree hitting the ball with the bat. He tries to mimic Troy, but his swing is awkward, less sure. Rose enters from the house.

ROSE. Cory, I want you to help me with this cupboard.

CORY. I ain't quitting the team. I don't care what Poppa say.

ROSE. I'll talk to him when he gets back. He had to go see about your Uncle Gabe. The police done arrested him. Say he was disturbing the peace. He'll be back directly. Come on in here and help me clean out the top of this cupboard.

Cory exits into the house. Rose sees Troy and Bono coming down the alley.

Troy . . . what they say down there?

TROY. Ain't said nothing. I give them fifty dollars and they let him go. I'll talk to you about it. Where's Cory?

ROSE. He's in there helping me clean out these cupboards.

TROY. Tell him to get his butt out here.

Troy and Bono go over to the pile of wood. Bono picks up the saw and begins sawing.

TROY (*to Bono*). All they want is the money. That makes six or seven times I' done went down there and got him. See me coming they stick out their hands.

BONO. Yeah. I know what you mean. That's all they care about . . . that money. They don't care about what's right. (*Pause.*) Nigger, why you got to go and get some hard wood? You ain't doing nothing but building a little old fence. Get you some soft pine wood. That's all you need.

TROY. I know what I'm doing. This is outside wood. You put pine wood inside the house. Pine wood is inside wood. This here is outside wood. Now you tell me where the fence is gonna be?

BONO. You don't need this wood. You can put it up with pine wood and it'll stand as long as you gonna be here looking at it.

TROY. How you know how long I'm gonna be here, nigger? Hell, I might just live forever. Live longer than old man Horsely.

BONO. That's what Magee used to say.

TROY. Magee's a damn fool. Now you tell me who you ever heard of gonna pull their own teeth with a pair of rusty pliers.

BONO. The old folks . . . my granddaddy used to pull his teeth with pliers. They ain't had no dentists for the colored folks back then.

TROY. Get clean pliers! You understand? Clean pliers! Sterilize them! Besides we ain't living back then. All Magee had to do was walk over to Doc Goldblum's.

BONO. I see where you and that Tallahassee gal . . . that Alberta . . . I see where you all done got tight.

TROY. What you mean "got tight"?

BONO. I see where you be laughing and joking with her all the time.

TROY. I laughs and jokes with all of them, Bono. You know me.

BONO. That ain't the kind of laughing and joking I'm talking about.

Cory enters from the house.

CORY. How you doing, Mr. Bono?

TROY. Cory? Get that saw from Bono and cut some wood. He talking about the wood's too hard to cut. Stand back there, Jim, and let that young boy show you how it's done.

BONO. He's sure welcome to it.

Cory takes the saw and begins to cut the wood.

Whew-e-e! Look at that. Big old strong boy. Look like Joe Louis. Hell, must be getting old the way I'm watching that boy whip through that wood.

CORY. I don't see why Mama want a fence around the yard noways.

TROY. Damn if I know either. What the hell she keeping out with it? She ain't got nothing nobody want.

BONO. Some people build fences to keep people out . . . and other people build fences to keep people in. Rose wants to hold on to you all. She loves you.

TROY. Hell, nigger, I don't need nobody to tell me my wife loves me. Cory . . . go on in the house and see if you can find that other saw.

CORY. Where's it at?

TROY. I said find it! Look for it till you find it!

Cory exits into the house.

What's that supposed to mean? Wanna keep us in?

BONO. Troy . . . I done known you seem like damn near my whole life. You and Rose both. I done know both of you all for a long time. I remember when you met Rose. When you was hitting them baseball out the park. A lot of them old gals was after you then. You had the pick of the litter. When you picked Rose, I was happy for you. That was the first time I knew you had any sense. I said . . . My man Troy knows what he's doing . . . I'm gonna follow this nigger . . . he might take me somewhere. I been following you too. I done learned a whole heap of things about life watching you. I done learned how to tell where the shit lies. How to tell it from the alfalfa. You done learned me a lot of things. You showed me how to not make the same mistakes . . . to take life as it comes along and keep putting one foot in front of the other. (*Pause.*) Rose a good woman, Troy.

TROY. Hell, nigger, I know she a good woman. I been married to her for eighteen years. What you got on your mind, Bono?

BONO. I just say she a good woman. Just like I say anything. I ain't got to have nothing on my mind.

TROY. You just gonna say she a good woman and leave it hanging out there like that? Why you telling me she a good woman?

BONO. She loves you, Troy. Rose loves you.

TROY. You saying I don't measure up. That's what you trying to say. I don't measure up cause I'm seeing this other gal. I know what you trying to say.

BONO. I know what Rose means to you, Troy. I'm just trying to say I don't want to see you mess up.

TROY. Yeah, I appreciate that, Bono. If you was messing around on Lucille I'd be telling you the same thing.

BONO. Well, that's all I got to say. I just say that because I love you both.

TROY. Hell, you know me . . . I wasn't out there looking for nothing. You can't find a better woman than Rose. I know that. But seems like this woman just stuck onto me where I can't shake her loose. I done wrestled with it, tried to throw her off me . . . but she just stuck on tighter. Now she's stuck on for good.

BONO. You's in control . . . that's what you tell me all the time. You responsible for what you do.

TROY. I ain't ducking the responsibility of it. As long as it sets right in my heart . . . then I'm okay. Cause that's all I listen to. It'll tell me right from wrong every time. And I ain't talking about doing Rose no bad turn. I love Rose. She done carried me along ways and I love and respect her for that.

BONO. I know you do. That's why I don't want to see you hurt her. But what you gonna do when she find out? What you got then? If you try and juggle both of them . . . sooner or later you gonna drop one of them. That's common sense.

TROY. Yeah, I hear what you saying, Bono. I been trying to figure away to work it out.

BONO. Work it out right, Troy. I don't want to be getting all up between you and Rose's business . . . but work it so it come out right.

TROY. Ah hell, I get all up between you and Lucille's business. When you gonna get that woman that refrigerator she been wanting? Don't tell me you ain't got no money now. I know who your banker is. Mellon don't need that money bad as Lucille want that refrigerator. I'll tell you that.

BONO. Tell you what I'll do . . . when you finish building this fence for Rose . . . I'll buy Lucille that refrigerator.

TROY. You done stuck your foot in your mouth now!

Troy grabs up a board and begins to saw. Bono starts to walk out the yard.

Hey, nigger . . . where you going?

BONO. I'm going home. I know you don't expect me to help you now. I'm protecting my money. I wanna see you put that fence up by yourself. That's what I want to see. You'll be here another six months without me.

TROY. Nigger, you ain't right.

BONO. When it comes to my money . . . I'm right as fireworks on the Fourth of July.

TROY. All right, we gonna see now. You better get out your bankbook.

Bono exits, and Troy continues to work. Rose enters from the house.

ROSE. What they say down there? What's happening with Gabe?

TROY. I went down there and got him out. Cost me fifty dollars. Say he was disturbing the peace. Judge set up a hearing for him in three weeks. Say to show cause why he shouldn't be recommitted.

ROSE. What was he doing that cause them to arrest him?

TROY. Some kids was teasing him and he run them off home. Say he was howling and carrying on. Some folks seen him and called the police. That's all it was.

ROSE. Well, what's you say? What'd you tell the judge?

TROY. Told him I'd look after him. It didn't make no sense to recommit the man. He stuck out his big greasy palm and told me to give him fifty dollars and take him on home.

ROSE. Where's he at now? Where'd he go off to?

TROY. He's gone about his business. He don't need nobody to hold his hand.

ROSE. Well, I don't know. Seem like that would be the best place for him if they did put him into the hospital. I know what you're gonna say. But that's what I think would be best.

TROY. The man done had his life ruined fighting for what? And they wanna take and lock him up. Let him be free. He don't bother nobody.

ROSE. Well, everybody got their own way of looking at it I guess. Come on and get your lunch. I got a bowl of lima beans and some cornbread in the oven. Come and get something to eat. Ain't no sense you fretting over Gabe.

Rose turns to go into the house.

TROY. Rose . . . got something to tell you.

ROSE. Well, come on . . . wait till I get this food on the table.

TROY. Rose!

She stops and turns around.

I don't know how to say this. (*Pause.*) I can't explain it none. It just sort of grows on you till it gets out of hand. It starts out like a little bush . . . and the next thing you know it's a whole forest.

ROSE. Troy . . . what is you talking about?

TROY. I'm talking, woman, let me talk. I'm trying to find a way to tell you . . . I'm gonna be a daddy. I'm gonna be somebody's daddy.

ROSE. Troy . . . you're not telling me this? You're gonna be . . . what?

TROY. Rose . . . now . . . see . . .

ROSE. You telling me you gonna be somebody's daddy? You telling your *wife* this?

Gabriel enters from the street. He carries a rose in his hand.

GABRIEL. Hey, Troy! Hey, Rose!

ROSE. I have to wait eighteen years to hear something like this.

GABRIEL. Hey, Rose . . . I got a flower for you. (*He hands it to her.*) That's a rose. Same rose like you is.

ROSE. Thanks, Gabe.

GABRIEL. Troy, you ain't mad at me is you? Them bad mens come and put me away. You ain't mad at me is you?

TROY. Naw, Gabe, I ain't mad at you.

ROSE. Eighteen years and you wanna come with this.

GABRIEL (*takes a quarter out of his pocket*). See what I got? Got a brand new quarter.

TROY. Rose . . . it's just . . .

ROSE. Ain't nothing you can say, Troy. Ain't no way of explaining that.

GABRIEL. Fellow that give me this quarter had a whole mess of them. I'm gonna keep this quarter till it stop shining.

ROSE. Gabe, go on in the house there. I got some watermelon in the Frigidaire. Go on and get you a piece.

GABRIEL. Say, Rose . . . you know I was chasing hellhounds and them bad mens come and get me and take me away. Troy helped me. He come down there and told them they better let me go before he beat them up. Yeah, he did!

ROSE. You go on and get you a piece of watermelon, Gabe. Them bad mens is gone now.

GABRIEL. Okay, Rose . . . gonna get me some watermelon. The kind with the stripes on it.

Gabriel exits into the house.

ROSE. Why, Troy? Why? After all these years to come dragging this in to me now. It don't make no sense at your age. I could have expected this ten or fifteen years ago, but not now.

TROY. Age ain't got nothing to do with it, Rose.

ROSE. I done tried to be everything a wife should be. Everything a wife could be. Been married eighteen years and I got to live to see the day you tell me you been seeing another woman and done fathered a child by her. And you know I ain't never wanted no half nothing in my family. My whole family is half. Everybody got different fathers and mothers . . . my two sisters and my brother. Can't hardly tell who's who. Can't never sit down and talk about Papa and Mama. It's your papa and your mama and my papa and my mama . . .

TROY. Rose . . . stop it now.

ROSE. I ain't never wanted that for none of my children. And now you wanna drag your behind in here and tell me something like this.

TROY. You ought to know. It's time for you to know.

ROSE. Well, I don't want to know, goddamn it!

TROY. I can't just make it go away. It's done now. I can't wish the circumstance of the thing away.

ROSE. And you don't want to either. Maybe you want to wish me and my boy away. Maybe that's what you want? Well, you can't wish us away. I've got eighteen years of my life invested in you. You ought to have stayed upstairs in my bed where you belong.

TROY. Rose . . . now listen to me . . . we can get a handle on this thing. We can talk this out . . . come to an understanding.

ROSE. All of a sudden it's "we." Where was "we" at when you was down there rolling around with some godforsaken woman? "We" should have come to an understanding before you started making a damn fool of yourself. You're a day late and a dollar short when it comes to an understanding with me.

TROY. It's just . . . She gives me a different idea . . . a different understanding about myself. I can step out of this house and get away from the pressures and problems . . . be a different man. I ain't got to wonder how I'm gonna pay the bills or get the roof fixed. I can just be a part of myself that I ain't never been.

ROSE. What I want to know . . . is do you plan to continue seeing her. That's all you can say to me.

TROY. I can sit up in her house and laugh. Do you understand what I'm saying. I can laugh out loud . . . and it feels good. It reaches all the way down to the bottom of my shoes. (*Pause.*) Rose, I can't give that up.

ROSE. Maybe you ought to go on and stay down there with her . . . if she's a better woman than me.

TROY. It ain't about nobody being a better woman or nothing. Rose, you ain't the blame. A man couldn't ask for no woman to be a better wife than you've been. I'm responsible for it. I done locked myself into a pattern trying to take care of you all that I forgot about myself.

ROSE. What the hell was I there for? That was my job, not somebody else's.

TROY. Rose, I done tried all my life to live decent . . . to live a clean . . . hard . . . useful life. I tried to be a good husband to you. In every way I knew how. Maybe I come into the world backwards, I don't know. But . . . you born with two strikes on you before you come to the plate. You got to guard it closely . . . always looking for the curve ball on the inside corner. You can't afford to let none get past you. You can't afford a call strike. If you going down . . . you going down swinging. Everything lined up against you. What you gonna do. I fooled them, Rose. I bunted. When I found you and Cory and a halfway decent job . . . I was safe. Couldn't nothing touch me. I wasn't gonna strike out no more. I wasn't going back to the penitentiary. I wasn't gonna lay in the streets with a bottle of wine. I was safe. I had me a family. A job. I wasn't gonna get that last strike. I was on first looking for one of them boys to knock me in. To get me home.

ROSE. You should have stayed in my bed, Troy.

TROY. Then when I saw that gal . . . she firmed up my backbone. And I got to thinking that if I tried . . . I just might be able to steal second. Do you understand after eighteen years I wanted to steal second.

ROSE. You should have held me tight. You should have grabbed me and held on.

TROY. I stood on first base for eighteen years and I thought . . . well, goddamn it . . . go on for it!

ROSE. We're not talking about baseball! We're talking about you going off to lay in bed with another woman . . . and then bring it home to me. That's what we're talking about. We ain't talking about no baseball.

TROY. Rose, you're not listening to me. I'm trying the best I can to explain it to you. It's not easy for me to admit that I been standing in the same place for eighteen years.

ROSE. I been standing with you! I been right here with you, Troy. I got a life too. I gave eighteen years of my life to stand in the same spot with you. Don't you think I ever wanted other things? Don't you think I had dreams and hopes? What about my life? What about me. Don't you think it ever crossed my mind to want to know other men? That I wanted to lay up somewhere and forget about my responsibilities? That I wanted someone to make me laugh so I could feel good? You not the only one who's got wants and needs. But I held on to you, Troy. I took all my feelings, my wants and needs, my dreams . . . and I buried them inside you. I planted a seed and watched and prayed over it. I planted myself inside you and waited to bloom. And it didn't take me no eighteen years to find out the soil was hard and rocky and it wasn't never gonna bloom.

But I held on to you, Troy. I held you tighter. You was my husband. I owed you everything I had. Every part of me I could find to give you. And upstairs in that room . . . with the darkness falling in on me . . . I gave everything I had to try and erase the doubt that you wasn't the finest man in the world. And wherever you was going . . . I wanted to be there with you. Cause you was my husband. Cause that's the only way I was gonna survive as your wife. You always talking about what you give . . . and what you don't have to give. But you take too. You take . . . and don't even know nobody's giving!

Rose turns to exit into the house; Troy grabs her arm.

TROY. You say I take and don't give!

ROSE. Troy! You're hurting me!

TROY. You say I take and don't give!

ROSE. Troy . . . you're hurting my arm! Let go!

TROY. I done give you everything I got. Don't you tell that lie on me.

ROSE. Troy!

TROY. Don't you tell that lie on me!

Cory enters from the house.

CORY. Mama!

ROSE. Troy. You're hurting me.

TROY. Don't you tell me about no taking and giving.

Cory comes up behind Troy and grabs him. Troy, surprised, is thrown off balance just as Cory throws a glancing blow that catches him on the chest and knocks him down. Troy is stunned, as is Cory.

ROSE. Troy. Troy. No!

Troy gets to his feet and starts at Cory.

Troy . . . no. Please! Troy!

Rose pulls on Troy to hold him back. Troy stops himself.

TROY (*to Cory*). All right. That's strike two. You stay away from around me, boy. Don't you strike out. You living with a full count. Don't you strike out.

Troy exits out the yard as the lights go down.

SCENE 2

It is six months later, early afternoon. Troy enters from the house and starts to exit the yard. Rose enters from the house.

ROSE. Troy, I want to talk to you.

TROY. All of a sudden, after all this time, you want to talk to me, huh? You ain't wanted to talk to me for months. You ain't wanted to talk to me last night. You ain't wanted no part of me then. What you wanna talk to me about now?

ROSE. Tomorrow's Friday.

TROY. I know what day tomorrow is. You think I don't know tomorrow's Friday? My whole life I ain't done nothing but look to see Friday coming and you got to tell me it's Friday.

ROSE. I want to know if you're coming home.

TROY. I always come home, Rose. You know that. There ain't never been a night I ain't come home.

ROSE. That ain't what I mean . . . and you know it. I want to know if you're coming straight home after work.

TROY. I figure I'd cash my check . . . hang out at Taylors' with the boys . . . maybe play a game of checkers . . .

ROSE. Troy, I can't live like this. I won't live like this. You livin' on borrowed time with me. It's been going on six months now you ain't been coming home.

TROY. I be here every night. Every night of the year. That's 365 days.

ROSE. I want you to come home tomorrow after work.

TROY. Rose . . . I don't mess up my pay. You know that now. I take my pay and I give it to you. I don't have no money but what you give me back. I just want to have a little time to myself . . . a little time to enjoy life.

ROSE. What about me? When's my time to enjoy life?

TROY. I don't know what to tell you, Rose. I'm doing the best I can.

ROSE. You ain't been home from work but time enough to change your clothes and run out . . . and you wanna call that the best you can do?

TROY. I'm going over to the hospital to see Alberta. She went into the hospital this afternoon. Look like she might have the baby early. I won't be gone long.

ROSE. Well, you ought to know. They went over to Miss Pearl's and got Gabe today. She said you told them to go ahead and lock him up.

TROY. I ain't said no such thing. Whoever told you that is telling a lie. Pearl ain't doing nothing but telling a big fat lie.

ROSE. She ain't had to tell me. I read it on the papers.

TROY. I ain't told them nothing of the kind.

ROSE. I saw it right there on the papers.

TROY. What it say, huh?

ROSE. It said you told them to take him.

TROY. Then they screwed that up, just the way they screw up everything. I ain't worried about what they got on the paper.

ROSE. Say the government send part of his check to the hospital and the other part to you.

TROY. I ain't got nothing to do with that if that's the way it works. I ain't made up the rules about how it work.

ROSE. You did Gabe just like you did Cory. You wouldn't sign the paper for Cory . . . but you signed for Gabe. You signed that paper.

The telephone is heard ringing inside the house.

TROY. I told you I ain't signed nothing, woman! The only thing I signed was the release form. Hell, I can't read, I don't know what they had on that paper! I ain't signed nothing about sending Gabe away.

ROSE. I said send him to the hospital . . . you said let him be free . . . now you done went down there and signed him to the hospital for half his money. You went back on yourself, Troy. You gonna have to answer for that.

TROY. See now . . . you been over there talking to Miss Pearl. She done got mad cause she ain't getting Gabe's rent money. That's all it is. She's liable to say anything.

ROSE. Troy, I seen where you signed the paper.

TROY. You ain't seen nothing I signed. What she doing got papers on my brother anyway? Miss Pearl telling a big fat lie. And I'm gonna tell her about it too! You ain't seen nothing I signed. Say . . . you ain't seen nothing I signed.

Rose exits into the house to answer the telephone. Presently she returns.

ROSE. Troy . . . that was the hospital. Alberta had the baby.

TROY. What she have? What is it?

ROSE. It's a girl.

TROY. I better get on down to the hospital to see her.

ROSE. Troy . . .

TROY. Rose . . . I got to go see her now. That's only right . . . what's the matter . . . the baby's all right, ain't it?

ROSE. Alberta died having the baby.

TROY. Died . . . you say she's dead? Alberta's dead?

ROSE. They said they done all they could. They couldn't do nothing for her.

TROY. The baby? How's the baby?

ROSE. They say it's healthy. I wonder who's gonna bury her.

TROY. She had family, Rose. She wasn't living in the world by herself.

ROSE. I know she wasn't living in the world by herself.

TROY. Next thing you gonna want to know if she had any insurance.

ROSE. Troy, you ain't got to talk like that.

TROY. That's the first thing that jumped out your mouth. "Who's gonna bury her?" Like I'm fixing to take on that task for myself.

ROSE. I am your wife. Don't push me away.

TROY. I ain't pushing nobody away. Just give me some space. That's all. Just give me some room to breathe.

Rose exits into the house. Troy walks about the yard.

TROY (*with a quiet rage that threatens to consume him*). All right . . . Mr. Death. See now . . . I'm gonna tell you what I'm gonna do. I'm gonna take and build me a fence around this yard. See? I'm gonna build me a fence around what belongs to me. And then I want you to stay on the other side. See? You stay over there until you're ready for me. Then you come on. Bring your army. Bring your sickle. Bring your wrestling clothes. I ain't gonna fall down on my vigilance this time. You ain't gonna sneak up on me no more. When you ready for me . . . when the top of your list say Troy Maxson . . . that's when you come around here. You come up and knock on the front door. Ain't nobody else got nothing to do with this. This is between you and me. Man to man. You stay on the other side of that fence until you ready for me. Then you come up and knock on the front door. Anytime you want. I'll be ready for you.

The lights go down to black.

SCENE 3

The lights come up on the porch. It is late evening three days later. Rose sits listening to the ball game waiting for Troy. The final out of the game is made and Rose switches off the radio. Troy enters the yard carrying an infant wrapped in blankets. He stands back from the house and calls.

Rose enters and stands on the porch. There is a long, awkward silence, the weight of which grows heavier with each passing second.

TROY. Rose . . . I'm standing here with my daughter in my arms. She ain't but a wee bittie little old thing. She don't know nothing about grown-ups' business. She innocent . . . and she ain't got no mama.

ROSE. What you telling me for, Troy?

She turns and exits into the house.

TROY. Well . . . I guess we'll just sit out here on the porch.

He sits down on the porch. There is an awkward indelicateness about the way he handles the baby. His largeness engulfs and seems to swallow it. He speaks loud enough for Rose to hear.

A man's got to do what's right for him. I ain't sorry for nothing I done. It felt right in my heart. (*To the baby.*) What you smiling at? Your daddy's a big man. Got these great big old hands. But sometimes he's scared. And right now your daddy's scared cause we sitting out here and ain't got no home. Oh, I been homeless before. I ain't had no little baby with me. But I been homeless. You just be out on the road by your lonesome and you see one of them trains coming and you just kinda go like this . . .

He sings as a lullaby.

Please, Mr. Engineer let a man ride the line
Please, Mr. Engineer let a man ride the line
I ain't got no ticket please let me ride the blinds

Rose enters from the house. Troy, hearing her steps behind him, stands and faces her.

She's my daughter, Rose. My own flesh and blood. I can't deny her no more than I can deny them boys. (*Pause.*) You and them boys is my family. You and them and this child is all I got in the world. So I guess what I'm saying is . . . I'd appreciate it if you'd help me take care of her.

ROSE. Okay, Troy . . . you're right. I'll take care of your baby for you . . . cause . . . like you say . . . she's innocent . . . and you can't visit the sins of the father upon the child. A motherless child has got a hard time. (*She takes the baby from him.*) From right now . . . this child got a mother. But you a womanless man.

Rose turns and exits into the house with the baby. Lights go down to black.

SCENE 4

It is two months later. Lyons enters the street. He knocks on the door and calls.

LYONS. Hey, Rose! (*Pause.*) Rose!

ROSE (*from inside the house*). Stop that yelling. You gonna wake up Raynell. I just got her to sleep.

LYONS. I just stopped by to pay Papa this twenty dollars I owe him. Where's Papa at?

ROSE. He should be here in a minute. I'm getting ready to go down to the church. Sit down and wait on him.

LYONS. I got to go pick up Bonnie over her mother's house.

ROSE. Well, sit it down there on the table. He'll get it.

LYONS (*enters the house and sets the money on the table*). Tell Papa I said thanks. I'll see you again.

ROSE. All right, Lyons. We'll see you.

Lyons starts to exit as Cory enters.

CORY. Hey, Lyons.

LYONS. What's happening, Cory? Say man, I'm sorry I missed your graduation. You know I had a gig and couldn't get away. Otherwise, I would have been there, man. So what you doing?

CORY. I'm trying to find a job.

LYONS. Yeah I know how that go, man. It's rough out here. Jobs are scarce.

CORY. Yeah, I know.

LYONS. Look here, I got to run. Talk to Papa . . . he know some people. He'll be able to help get you a job. Talk to him . . . see what he say.

CORY. Yeah . . . all right, Lyons.

LYONS. You take care. I'll talk to you soon. We'll find some time to talk.

Lyons exits the yard. Cory wanders over to the tree, picks up the bat, and assumes a batting stance. He studies an imaginary pitcher and swings. Dissatisfied with the result, he tries again. Troy enters. They eye each other for a beat. Cory puts the bat down and exits the yard. Troy starts into the house as Rose exits with Raynell. She is carrying a cake.

TROY. I'm coming in and everybody's going out.

ROSE. I'm taking this cake down to the church for the bake sale. Lyons was by to see you. He stopped by to pay you your twenty dollars. It's laying in there on the table.

TROY (*going into his pocket*). Well . . . here go this money.

ROSE. Put it in there on the table, Troy. I'll get it.

TROY. What time you coming back?

ROSE. Ain't no use in you studying me. It don't matter what time I come back.

TROY. I just asked you a question, woman. What's the matter . . . can't I ask you a question?

ROSE. Troy, I don't want to go into it. Your dinner's in there on the stove. All you got to do is heat it up. And don't you be eating the rest of them cakes in there. I'm coming back for them. We having a bake sale at the church tomorrow.

Rose exits the yard. Troy sits down on the steps, takes a pint bottle from his pocket, opens it, and drinks. He begins to sing.

TROY. Hear it ring! Hear it ring!
  Had an old dog his name was Blue
  You know Blue was mighty true
  You know Blue as a good old dog
  Blue trees a possum in a hollow log
  You know from that he was a good old dog

Bono enters the yard.

BONO. Hey, Troy.
TROY. Hey, what's happening, Bono?
BONO. I just thought I'd stop by to see you.
TROY. What you stop by and see me for? You ain't stopped by in a month of Sundays. Hell, I must owe you money or something.
BONO. Since you got your promotion I can't keep up with you. Used to see you every day. Now I don't even know what route you working.
TROY. They keep switching me around. Got me out in Greentree now . . . hauling white folks' garbage.
BONO. Greentree, huh? You lucky, at least you ain't got to be lifting them barrels. Damn if they ain't getting heavier. I'm gonna put in my two years and call it quits.
TROY. I'm thinking about retiring myself.
BONO. You got it easy. You can drive for another five years.
TROY. It ain't the same, Bono. It ain't like working the back of the truck. Ain't got nobody to talk to . . . feel like you working by yourself. Naw, I'm thinking about retiring. How's Lucille?
BONO. She all right. Her arthritis get to acting up on her sometime. Saw Rose on my way in. She going down to the church, huh?
TROY. Yeah, she took up going down there. All them preachers looking for somebody to fatten their pockets. (*Pause.*) Got some gin here.
BONO. Naw, thanks. I just stopped by to say hello.
TROY. Hell, nigger . . . you can take a drink. I ain't never known you to say no to a drink. You ain't got to work tomorrow.
BONO. I just stopped by. I'm fixing to go over to Skinner's. We got us a domino game going over his house every Friday.
TROY. Nigger, you can't play no dominoes. I used to whup you four games out of five.
BONO. Well, that learned me. I'm getting better.
TROY. Yeah? Well, that's all right.
BONO. Look here . . . I got to be getting on. Stop by sometime, huh?

TROY. Yeah, I'll do that, Bono. Lucille told Rose you bought her a new refrigerator.

BONO. Yeah, Rose told Lucille you had finally built your fence . . . so I figured we'd call it even.

TROY. I knew you would.

BONO. Yeah . . . okay. I'll be talking to you.

TROY. Yeah, take care, Bono. Good to see you. I'm gonna stop over.

BONO. Yeah. Okay, Troy.

Bono exits. Troy drinks from the bottle.

TROY. Old Blue died and I dig his grave
Let him down with a golden chain
Every night when I hear old Blue bark
I know Blue treed a possum in Noah's Ark.
Hear it ring! Hear it ring!

Cory enters the yard. They eye each other for a beat. Troy is sitting in the middle of the steps. Cory walks over.

CORY. I got to get by.

TROY. Say what? What's you say?

CORY. You in my way. I got to get by.

TROY. You got to get by where? This is my house. Bought and paid for. In full. Took me fifteen years. And if you wanna go in my house and I'm sitting on the steps . . . you say excuse me. Like your mama taught you.

CORY. Come on, Pop . . . I got to get by.

Cory starts to maneuver his way past Troy. Troy grabs his leg and shoves him back.

TROY. You just gonna walk over top of me?

CORY. I live here too!

TROY (*advancing toward him*). You just gonna walk over top of me in my own house?

CORY. I ain't scared of you.

TROY. I ain't asked if you was sacred of me. I asked you if you was fixing to walk over top of me in my own house? That's the question. You ain't gonna say excuse me? You just gonna walk over top of me?

CORY. If you wanna put it like that.

TROY. How else am I gonna put it?

CORY. I was walking by you to go into the house cause you sitting on the steps drunk, singing to yourself. You can put it like that.

TROY. Without saying excuse me???

Cory doesn't respond.

I asked you a question. Without saying excuse me???

CORY. I ain't got to say excuse me to you. You don't count around here no more.

TROY. Oh, I see . . . I don't count around here no more. You ain't got to say excuse me to your daddy. All of a sudden you done got so grown that your daddy don't count around here no more . . . Around here in his own house and yard that he done paid for with the sweat of his brow. You done got so grown to where you gonna take over. You gonna take over my house. Is that right? You gonna wear my pants. You gonna go in there and stretch out on my bed. You ain't got to say excuse me cause I don't count around here no more. Is that right?

CORY. That's right. You always talking this dumb stuff. Now, why don't you just get out my way?

TROY. I guess you got someplace to sleep and something to put in your belly. You got that, huh? You got that? That's what you need. You got that, huh?

CORY. You don't know what I got. You ain't got to worry about what I got.

TROY. You right! You one hundred percent right! I done spent the last seventeen years worrying about what you got. Now it's your turn, see? I'll tell you what to do. You grown . . . we done established that. You a man. Now, let's see you act like one. Turn your behind around and walk out this yard. And when you get out there in the alley . . . you can forget about this house. See? Cause this is my house. You go on and be a man and get your own house. You can forget about this. Cause this is mine. You go on and get yours cause I'm through with doing for you.

CORY. You talking about what you did for me . . . what'd you ever give me?

TROY. Them feet and bones! That pumping heart, nigger! I give you more than anybody else is ever gonna give you.

CORY. You ain't never gave me nothing! You ain't never done nothing but hold me back. Afraid I was gonna be better than you. All you ever did was try and make me scared of you. I used to tremble every time you called my name. Every time I heard your footsteps in the house. Wondering all the time . . . what's Papa gonna say if I do this? . . . What's he gonna say if I do that? . . . What's Papa gonna say if I turn on the radio? And Mama, too . . . she tries . . . but she's scared of you.

TROY. You leave your mama out of this. She ain't got nothing to do with this.

CORY. I don't know how she stand you . . . after what you did to her.

TROY. I told you to leave your mama out of this!

He advances toward Cory.

CORY. What you gonna do . . . give me a whupping? You can't whup me no more. You're too old. You just an old man.

TROY (*shoves him on his shoulder*). Nigger! That's what you are. You just another nigger on the street to me!

CORY. You crazy! You know that?

TROY. Go on now! You got the devil in you. Get on away from me!

CORY. You just a crazy old man . . . talking about I got the devil in me.

TROY. Yeah, I'm crazy! If you don't get on the other side of that yard . . . I'm gonna show you how crazy I am! Go on . . . get the hell out of my yard.

CORY. It ain't your yard. You took Uncle Gabe's money he got from the army to buy this house and then you put him out.

TROY (*advances on Cory*). Get your black ass out of my yard!

Troy's advance backs Cory up against the tree. Cory grabs up the bat.

CORY. I ain't going nowhere! Come on . . . put me out! I ain't scared of you.

TROY. That's my bat!

CORY. Come on!

TROY. Put my bat down!

CORY. Come on, put me out.

Cory swings at Troy, who backs across the yard.

What's the matter? You so bad . . . put me out!

Troy advances toward Cory.

CORY (*backing up*). Come on! Come on!

TROY. You're gonna have to use it! You wanna draw that bat back on me . . . you're gonna have to use it.

CORY. Come on! . . . Come on!

Cory swings the bat at Troy a second time. He misses. Troy continues to advance toward him.

TROY. You're gonna have to kill me! You wanna draw that bat back on me. You're gonna have to kill me.

Cory, backed up against the tree, can go no farther. Troy taunts him. He sticks out his head and offers him a target.

Come on! Come on!

Cory is unable to swing the bat. Troy grabs it.

TROY. Then I'll show you.

Cory and Troy struggle over the bat. The struggle is fierce and fully engaged. Troy ultimately is the stronger and takes the bat from Cory and stands over him ready to swing. He stops himself.

Go on and get away from around my house.

Cory, stung by his defeat, picks himself up, walks slowly out of the yard and up the alley.

CORY. Tell Mama I'll be back for my things.
TROY. They'll be on the other side of that fence.

Cory exits.

TROY. I can't taste nothing. Helluljah! I can't taste nothing no more. (*Troy assumes a batting posture and begins to taunt Death, the fastball on the outside corner.*) Come on! It's between you and me now! Come on! Anytime you want! Come on! I be ready for you . . . but I ain't gonna be easy.

The lights go down on the scene.

SCENE 5

The time is 1965. The lights come up in the yard. It is the morning of Troy's funeral. A funeral plaque with a light hangs beside the door. There is a small garden plot off to the side. There is noise and activity in the house as Rose, Gabriel, and Bono have gathered. The door opens and Raynell, seven years old enters dressed in a flannel nightgown. She crosses to the garden and pokes around with a stick. Rose calls from the house.

ROSE. Raynell!
RAYNELL. Mam?
ROSE. What you doing out there?
RAYNELL. Nothing.

Rose comes to the door.

ROSE. Girl, get in here and get dressed. What you doing?
RAYNELL. Seeing if my garden growed.
ROSE. I told you it ain't gonna grow overnight. You got to wait.
RAYNELL. It don't look like it never gonna grow. Dag!
ROSE. I told you a watched pot never boils. Get in here and get dressed.
RAYNELL. This ain't even no pot, Mama.
ROSE. You just have to give it a chance. It'll grow. Now you come on and do what I told you. We got to be getting ready. This ain't no morning to be playing around. You hear me?
RAYNELL. Yes, mam.

Rose exits into the house. Raynell continues to poke at her garden with a stick. Cory enters. He is dressed in a Marine corporal's uniform, and carries a duffel-bag. His posture is that of a military man, and his speech has a clipped sternness.

CORY (*to Raynell*). Hi. (*Pause.*) I bet your name is Raynell.
RAYNELL. Uh huh.
CORY. Is your mama home?

Raynell runs up on the porch and calls through the screen door.

RAYNELL. Mama . . . there's some man out here. Mama?

Rose comes to the door.

ROSE. Cory? Lord have mercy! Look here, you all!

Rose and Cory embrace in a tearful reunion as Bono and Lyons enter from the house dressed in funeral clothes.

BONO. Aw, looka here . . .

ROSE. Done got all grown up!

CORY. Don't cry, Mama. What you crying about?

ROSE. I'm just so glad you made it.

CORY. Hey Lyons. How you doing, Mr. Bono.

Lyons goes to embrace Cory.

LYONS. Look at you, man. Look at you. Don't he look good, Rose. Got them Corporal stripes.

ROSE. What took you so long?

CORY. You know how the Marines are, Mama. They got to get all their paperwork straight before they let you do anything.

ROSE. Well, I'm sure glad you made it. They let Lyons come. Your Uncle Gabe's still in the hospital. They don't know if they gonna let him out or not. I just talked to them a little while ago.

LYONS. A Corporal in the United States Marines.

BONO. Your daddy knew you had it in you. He used to tell me all the time.

LYONS. Don't he look good, Mr. Bono?

BONO. Yeah, he remind me of Troy when I first met him. (*Pause.*) Say, Rose, Lucille's down at the church with the choir. I'm gonna go down and get the pallbearers lined up. I'll be back to get you all.

ROSE. Thanks, Jim.

CORY. See you, Mr. Bono.

LYONS (*with his arm around Raynell*). Cory . . . look at Raynell. Ain't she precious? She gonna break a whole lot of hearts.

ROSE. Raynell, come and say hello to your brother. This is your brother, Cory. You remember Cory.

RAYNELL. No, Mam.

CORY. She don't remember me, Mama.

ROSE. Well, we talk about you. She heard us talk about you. (*To Raynell.*) This is your brother, Cory. Come on and say hello.

RAYNELL. Hi.

CORY. Hi. So you're Raynell. Mama told me a lot about you.

ROSE. You all come on into the house and let me fix you some breakfast. Keep up your strength.

CORY. I ain't hungry, Mama.

LYONS. You can fix me something, Rose. I'll be in there in a minute.

ROSE. Cory, you sure you don't want nothing? I know they ain't feeding you right.

CORY. No, Mama . . . thanks. I don't feel like eating. I'll get something later.

ROSE. Raynell . . . get on upstairs and get that dress on like I told you.

Rose and Raynell exit into the house.

LYONS. So . . . I hear you thinking about getting married.

CORY. Yeah, I done found the right one, Lyons. It's about time.

LYONS. Me and Bonnie been split up about four years now. About the time Papa retired. I guess she just got tired of all them changes I was putting her through. (*Pause.*) I always knew you was gonna make something out yourself. Your head was always in the right direction. So . . . you gonna stay in . . . make it a career . . . put in your twenty years?

CORY. I don't know. I got six already, I think that's enough.

LYONS. Stick with Uncle Sam and retire early. Ain't nothing out here. I guess Rose told you what happened with me. They got me down the workhouse. I thought I was being slick cashing other people's checks.

CORY. How much time you doing?

LYONS. They give me three years. I got that beat now. I ain't got but nine more months. It ain't so bad. You learn to deal with it like anything else. You got to take the crookeds with the straights. That's what Papa used to say. He used to say that when he struck out. I seen him strike out three times in a row . . . and the next time up he hit the ball over the grandstand. Right out there in Homestead Field. He wasn't satisfied hitting in the seats . . . he want to hit it over everything! After the game he had two hundred people standing around waiting to shake his hand. You got to take the crookeds with the straights. Yeah, Papa was something else.

CORY. You still playing?

LYONS. Cory . . . you know I'm gonna do that. There's some fellows down there we got us a band . . . we gonna try and stay together when we get out . . . but yeah, I'm still playing. It still helps me to get out of bed in the morning. As long as it do that I'm gonna be right there playing and trying to make some sense out of it.

ROSE (*Rose calling*). Lyons, I got these eggs in the pan.

LYONS. Let me go on and get these eggs, man. Get ready to go bury Papa. (*Pause.*) How you doing? You doing all right?

Cory nods. Lyons touches him on the shoulder and they share a moment of silent grief. Lyons exits into the house. Cory wanders about the yard. Raynell enters.

RAYNELL. Hi.

CORY. Hi.

RAYNELL. Did you used to sleep in my room?

CORY. Yeah . . . that used to be my room.

RAYNELL. That's what Papa call it. "Cory's room." It got your football in the closet.

Rose comes to the door.

ROSE. Raynell, get in there and get them good shoes on.

RAYNELL. Mama, can't I wear these? Them other one hurt my feet.

ROSE. Well, they just gonna have to hurt your feet for a while. You ain't said they hurt your feet when you went down to the store and got them.

RAYNELL. They didn't hurt then. My feet done got bigger.

ROSE. Don't you give me no backtalk now. You get in there and get them shoes on.

Raynell exits into the house.

Ain't too much changed. He still got that piece of rag tied to that tree. He was out here swinging that bat. I was just ready to go back in the house. He swung that bat and then he just fell over. Seem like he swung it and stood there with this grin on his face . . . and then he just fell over. They carried him on down to the hospital, but I knew there wasn't no need . . . why don't you come on in the house?

CORY. Mama . . . I got something to tell you. I don't know how to tell you this . . . but I've got to tell you . . . I'm not going to Papa's funeral.

ROSE. Boy, hush your mouth. That's your daddy you talking about. I don't want hear that kind of talk this morning. I done raised you to come to this? You standing there all healthy and grown talking about you ain't going to your daddy's funeral?

CORY. Mama . . . listen . . .

ROSE. I don't want to hear it, Cory. You just get that thought out of your head.

CORY. I can't drag Papa with me everywhere I go. I've got to say no to him. One time in my life I've got to say no.

ROSE. Don't nobody have to listen to nothing like that. I know you and your daddy ain't seen eye to eye, but I ain't got to listen to that kind of talk this morning. Whatever was between you and your daddy . . . the time has come to put it aside. Just take it and set it over there on the shelf and forget about it. Disrespecting your daddy ain't gonna make you a man, Cory. You got to find a way to come to that on your own. Not going to your daddy's funeral ain't gonna make you a man.

CORY. The whole time I was growing up . . . living in his house . . . Papa was like a shadow that followed you everywhere. It weighed on you and sunk into your flesh. It would wrap around you and lay there until you couldn't tell which one was you anymore. That shadow digging in your flesh. Trying to crawl in. Trying to live through you. Everywhere I looked, Troy Maxson was staring back at me . . . hiding under the bed . . . in the closet. I'm just saying I've got to find a way to get rid of that shadow, Mama.

ROSE. You just like him. You got him in you good.

CORY. Don't tell me that, Mama.

ROSE. You Troy Maxson all over again.

CORY. I don't want to be Troy Maxson. I want to be me.

ROSE. You can't be nobody but who you are, Cory. That shadow wasn't nothing but you growing into yourself. You either got to grow into it or cut it down to fit you. But that's all you got to make life with. That's all you got to measure yourself against that world out there. Your daddy wanted you to be everything he wasn't . . . and at the same time he tried to make you into everything he was. I don't know if he was right or wrong . . . but I do know he meant to do more good than he meant to do harm. He wasn't always right. Sometimes when he touched he bruised. And sometimes when he took me in his arms he cut.

When I first met your daddy I thought . . . Here is a man I can lay down with and make a baby. That's the first thing I thought when I seen him. I was thirty years old and had done seen my share of men. But when he walked up to me and said, "I can dance a waltz that'll make you dizzy," I thought, Rose Lee, here is a man that you can open yourself up to and be filled to bursting. Here is a man that can fill all them empty spaces you been tipping around the edges of. One of them empty spaces was being somebody's mother.

I married your daddy and settled down to cooking his supper and keeping clean sheets on the bed. When your daddy walked through the house he was so big he filled it up. That was my first mistake. Not to make him leave some room for me. For my part in the matter. But at that time I wanted that. I wanted a house that I could sing in. And that's what your daddy gave me. I didn't know to keep up his strength I had to give up little pieces of mine. I did that. I took on his life as mine and mixed up the pieces so that you couldn't hardly tell which was which anymore. It was my choice. It was my life and I didn't have to live it like that. But that's what life offered me in the way of being a woman and I took it. I grabbed hold of it with both hands.

By the time Raynell came into the house, me and your daddy had done lost touch with one another. I didn't want to make my blessing off of nobody's misfortune . . . but I took on to Raynell like she was all them babies I had wanted and never had.

The phone rings.

Like I'd been blessed to relive a part of my life. And if the Lord see fit to keep up my strength . . . I'm gonna do her just like your daddy did you . . . I'm gonna give her the best of what's in me.

RAYNELL (*entering, still with her old shoes*). Mama . . . Reverend Tollivier on the phone.

Rose exits into the house.

RAYNELL. Hi.

CORY. Hi.

RAYNELL. You in the Army or the Marines?
CORY. Marines.
RAYNELL. Papa said it was the Army. Did you know Blue?
CORY. Blue? Who's Blue?
RAYNELL. Papa's dog what he sing about all the time.
CORY (*singing*). Hear it ring! Hear it ring!
    I had a dog his name was Blue
    You know Blue was mighty true
    You know Blue was a good old dog
    Blue treed a possum in a hollow log
    You know from that he was a good old dog.
    Hear it ring! Hear it ring!

Raynell joins in singing.

CORY AND RAYNELL. Blue treed a possum out on a limb
    Blue looked at me and I looked at him
    Grabbed that possum and put him in a sack
    Blue stayed there till I came back
    Old Blue's feets was big and round
    Never allowed a possum to touch the ground.

    Old Blue died and I dug his grave
    I dug his grave with a silver spade
    Let him down with a golden chain
    And every night I call his name
    Go on Blue, you good dog you
    Go on Blue, you good dog you
RAYNELL. Blue laid down and died like a man
    Blue laid down and died . . .
BOTH. Blue laid down and died like a man
    Now he's treeing possums in the Promised Land
    I'm gonna tell you this to let you know
    Blue's gone where the good dogs go
    When I hear old Blue bark
    When I hear old Blue bark
    Blue treed a possum in Noah's Ark
    Blue treed a possum in Noah's Ark.

Rose comes to the screen door.

ROSE. Cory, we gonna be ready to go in a minute.
CORY (*to Raynell*). You go on in the house and change them shoes like
    Mama told you so we can go to Papa's funeral.
RAYNELL. Okay, I'll be back.

*Raynell exits into the house. Cory gets up and crosses over to the tree. Rose stands
in the screen door watching him. Gabriel enters from the alley.*

GABRIEL (*calling*). Hey, Rose!

ROSE. Gabe?

GABRIEL. I'm here, Rose. Hey Rose, I'm here!

Rose enters from the house.

ROSE. Lord . . . Look here, Lyons!

LYONS. See, I told you, Rose . . . I told you they'd let him come.

CORY. How you doing, Uncle Gabe?

LYONS. How you doing, Uncle Gabe?

GABRIEL. Hey, Rose. It's time. It's time to tell St. Peter to open the gates. Troy, you ready? You ready, Troy. I'm gonna tell St. Peter to open the gates. You get ready now.

Gabriel, with great fanfare, braces himself to blow. The trumpet is without a mouthpiece. He puts the end of it into his mouth and blows with great force, like a man who has been waiting some twenty-odd years for this single moment. No sound comes out of the trumpet. He braces himself and blows again with the same result. A third time he blows. There is a weight of impossible description that falls away and leaves him bare and exposed to a frightful realization. It is a trauma that a sane and normal mind would be unable to withstand. He begins to dance. A slow, strange dance, eerie and life-giving. A dance of atavistic signature and ritual. Lyons attempts to embrace him. Gabriel pushes Lyons away. He begins to howl in what is an attempt at song, or perhaps a song turning back into itself in an attempt at speech. He finishes his dance and the gates of heaven stand open as wide as God's closet.

That's the way that go!

(*Blackout*)

[1987]

TOPICS FOR DISCUSSION AND WRITING

1. What do you think Bono means when he says, early in Act II (page 1211), "Some people build fences to keep people out . . . and some people build fences to keep people in"? Why is the play called *Fences*? What is Troy fencing in? (You'll want to take account of Troy's last speech in 2.2, but don't limit your response to this speech.)

2. Would you agree that Troy's refusal to encourage his son's aspirations is one of the "fences" of the play? What do you think Troy's reasons are — conscious and unconscious — for not wanting Cory to play football at college?

3. Compare and contrast Cory and Lyons. Consider, too, in what ways they resemble Troy, and in what ways they differ from him.

4. In what ways is Troy like his father, and in what ways unlike?

5. What do you make of the prominence given to the song about Blue?

6. There is a good deal of anger in the play, but there is also humor. Which passages do you find humorous, and why?
7. Characterize Rose Maxson.
8. Some scenes begin by specifying that "the lights come up." Others do not, presumably beginning with an illuminated stage. All scenes except the last one—which ends with a sudden blackout—end with the lights slowly going down to blackness. How would you explain Wilson's use of lighting?

A CONTEXT FOR *FENCES*

August Wilson, Talking about *Fences*

[Part of an interview conducted with David Savran, on March 13, 1987]

In reading **Fences,** *I came to view Troy more and more critically as the play progressed, sharing Rose's point of view. We see that Troy has been crippled by his father. That's being replayed in Troy's relationship with Cory. Do you think there's a way out of that cycle?*

Surely. First of all, we're all like our parents. The things we are taught early in life, how to respond to the world, our sense of morality—everything, we get from them. Now you can take that legacy and do with it anything you want to do. It's in your hands. Cory is Troy's son. How can he be Troy's son without sharing Troy's values? I was trying to get at why Troy made the choices he made, how they have influenced his values and how he attempts to pass those along to his son. Each generation gives the succeeding generation what they think they need. One question in the play is, "Are the tools we are given sufficient to compete in a world that is different from the one our parents knew?" I think they are—it's just that we have to do different things with the tools. That's all Troy has to give. Troy's flaw is that he does not recognize that the world was changing. That's because he spent fifteen years in a penitentiary.

As African-Americans, we should demand to participate in society as Africans. That's the way out of the vicious cycle of poverty and neglect that exists in 1987 in America, where you have a huge percentage of blacks living in the equivalent of South African townships, in housing projects. No one is inviting these people to participate in society. Look at the poverty levels—$8,500 for a family of four, if you have $8,501 you're not counted. Those statistics would go up enormously if we had an honest assessment of the cost of living in America. I don't know how anybody can support a family of four on $8,500. What I'm saying is that 85 or 90 percent of blacks in America are living in abject poverty and, for the most part, are crowded into what amount to concentration camps. The situation for blacks in America is worse than it was forty years ago. Some sociologists will tell you about the tremendous progress we've made. They didn't put me out when I walked in the door. And you can always point to someone who works on Wall Street, or is a doctor. But they don't count in the larger scheme of things.

Do you have any idea how these political changes could take place?

I'm not sure. I know that blacks must be allowed their cultural differences. I think the process of assimilation to white American society was a big mistake. We don't want to be like you. Blacks living in housing projects are isolated from the society, for the most part — living as they choose, as Africans. Only they don't realize the value in what they're doing because they have accepted their victimization. They've marked themselves as victims. Once they recognize that, they can begin to move through society in a different manner, from a stronger position, and claim what is theirs.

A project of yours is to point up what happens when oppression is internalized.

Yes, transfer of aggression to the wrong target. I think it's interesting that the two roads open to blacks for "full participation" are entertainment and sports. *Ma Rainey* and *Fences,* and I didn't plan it that way. I don't think that they're the correct roads. I think Troy's right. Now with the benefit of historical perspective, I can say that the athletic scholarship was actually a way of exploiting. Now you've got two million kids who think they're going to play in the NBA. In the sixties the universities made a lot of money off of athletics. You had kids playing for free who, by and large, were not getting educated, were taking courses in basketweaving. Some of them could barely read.

Troy may be right about that issue, but it seems that he has passed on certain destructive traits in spite of himself. Take the hostility between father and son.

I think every generation says to the previous generation: you're in my way, I've got to get by. The father–son conflict is actually a normal generational conflict that happens all the time.

So it's a healthy and a good thing?

Oh, sure. Troy is seeing this boy walk around, smelling his piss. Two men cannot live in the same household. Troy would have been tremendously disappointed if Cory had not challenged him. Troy knows that this boy has to go out and do battle with that world: "So I had best prepare him because I know that's a harsh, cruel place out there. But that's going to be easy compared to what he's getting here. Ain't nobody gonna whip your ass like I'm gonna whip it." He has a tremendous love for the kid. But he's not going to say, "I love you," he's going to demonstrate it. He's carrying garbage for seventeen years just for the kid. The only world Troy knows is the one that he made. Cory's going to go on to find another one, he's going to arrive at the same place as Troy. I think one of the most important lines in the play is when Troy is talking about his father: "I got to the place where I could feel him kicking in my blood and knew that the only thing that separated us was the matter of a few years."

Hopefully, Cory will do things a bit differently with his son. For Troy, sports was not the way to go, the white man wouldn't let him get away with that. "Get you a job, with your hands, something that nobody can take away from you." The idea of school—he doesn't know what that is. That's for white folks. Very few blacks had paperwork jobs. But if you knew how to fix cars, you could always make some money. That's what Troy wants for Cory. There aren't many people who ever jumped up in Troy's face. So he's proud of the kid at the same time that he expresses a hurt that all men feel. You got to cut your kid loose at some point. There's that sense of loss and separation. You find out how Troy left his father's house and you see how Cory leaves his house. I suspect with Cory it will repeat with some differences and maybe, after five or six generations, they'll find a different way to do it.

Where Cory ends up is very ambiguous, as a marine in 1965.

Yes. For the average black kid on the street, that was an alternative. You went into the army because you could learn how to do something. I can remember my parents talking about the son of some friends: "He's in the navy. He *did* something"—as opposed to standing on the street corner, shooting drugs, drinking wine, and robbing stores. Lyons says to Cory, "I always knew you were going to make something out of yourself." It really wounds me. He's a corporal in the marines. For blacks, that is a sense of accomplishment. Therein lies one of the tragedies of blacks in America. Cory says, "I don't know. I put in six years. That's enough." Anyone who goes into the army and makes a career out of it is a loser. They sit there and are nurtured by the army and they don't have to confront life. Then they get out of the army and find there's nothing to do. They didn't learn any skills. And if they did, they can't find a job. Four months later, they're shooting dope. In the sixties a whole bunch of blacks went over, fought and died in the Vietnam War. The survivors came back to the same street corners and found out nothing had changed. They still couldn't get a job.

At the end of *Fences* every person, with the exception of Raynell, is institutionalized. Rose is in a church. Lyons is in a penitentiary. Gabriel's in a mental hospital and Cory's in the marines. The only free person is the girl, Troy's daughter, the hope for the future. That was conscious on my part because in '57 that's what I saw. Blacks have relied on institutions which are really foreign—except for the black church, which has been our saving grace. I have some problems with it but I recognize it as a central social organization and sometimes an economic organization for the black community. I would like to see blacks develop their own institutions that respond to their needs.

APPENDIX A
Writing Essays about Literature

WHY WRITE?

People write about literature to clarify and account for their responses to works that interest or excite or frustrate them. In putting words on paper you will have to take a second and third look at what is in front of you and what is within you. And so writing is a way of learning. The last word about complex thoughts and feelings is never said, but when we write we hope to make at least a little progress in the difficult but rewarding job of talking about our responses. We learn, and then we hope to interest our readers because we are communicating to them our responses to something that for one reason or another is worth talking about.

This communication is, in effect, teaching. You may think that you are writing for the teacher, but that is a misconception; when you write, *you* are the teacher. An essay on literature is an attempt to help someone see the work as you see it. If this chapter had to be boiled down to a single sentence, that sentence would be: Because you are teaching, your essay should embody those qualities that you value in teachers—probably intelligence, openmindedness, and effort; and certainly a desire to offer what help one can.

PRE-WRITING: GETTING IDEAS

"All there is to writing," Robert Frost said, "is having ideas. To learn to write is to learn to have ideas." But how does one "learn to have ideas"? Among the methods are these: reading with a pen or pencil in hand, so that you can annotate the text; keeping a journal, in which you jot down reflections about your reading; talking with others (including your instructor) about the reading. Let's look at the first of these, annotating.

Annotating a Text

In reading, if you own the book don't hesitate to mark it up, indicating (by highlighting or underlining or by making marginal notes) what puzzles you, what pleases or interests you, and what displeases or bores you. Later, of course, you'll want to think further about these responses, asking yourself, on rereading, if you still feel that way, and if not, why not, but these first responses will get you started.

For an example of a student's annotations of Langston Hughes's "Harlem," see page 413.

Brainstorming for Ideas for Writing

Unlike annotating, which consists of making brief notes and small marks on the printed page, "brainstorming"—the free jotting down of ideas—asks that you jot down whatever comes to mind, without inhibition. Don't worry about spelling, about writing complete sentences, or about unifying your thoughts; just let one thought lead to another. Later you can review your jottings, deleting some, connecting with arrows others that are related, expanding still others, but for now you want to get going, and so there is no reason to look back. Thus you might jot down something about the title. Let's assume that you have read Kate Chopin's "The Story of an Hour" (page 40):

```
Title speaks of an hour, and story covers an hour,
but maybe takes five minutes to read
```

And then, perhaps prompted by "an hour," you might happen to add something to this effect:

```
Doubt that a woman who got news of the death of her
husband could move from grief to joy within an hour
```

Your next jotting might have little or nothing to do with this issue; it might simply say

```
Enjoyed "Hour" more than "Ripe Figs" partly because
"Hour" is so shocking
```

And then you might ask yourself

```
By shocking, do I mean "improbable," or what? Come
to think of it, maybe it's not so improbable. A lot
depends on what the marriage was like.
```

Focused Free Writing

Focused, or directed, free writing is a method related to brainstorming that some writers use to uncover ideas they may want to write about. Concentrating on one issue—for instance, a question that strikes them as worth puzzling over (What kind of person is Mrs. Mallard?)—they write at length, nonstop, for perhaps five or ten minutes.

Writers who find free writing helpful put down everything they can think of that has bearing on the one issue or question they are examining. They do not stop at this stage to evaluate the results, and they do not worry about niceties of sentence structure or of spelling. They just pour out their ideas in a steady stream of writing, drawing on whatever associations come to mind. If they pause in their writing, it is only to refer to the text, to search for more detail—perhaps a quotation—that will help them answer their question.

After the free-writing session, these writers usually go back and reread what they have written, highlighting or underlining what seems to be of value. Of course they find much that is of little or no use, but they also usually find that some strong ideas have surfaced and have received some development. At this point the writers are often able to make a scratch outline and then begin a draft.

Here is an example of one student's focused free writing, again on Chopin's "The Story of an Hour."

What do I know about Mrs. Mallard? Let me put everything down here I know about her or can figure out
from what Kate Chopin tells me. When she finds herself alone after the death of her husband, she
says,"Free. Body and soul free" and before that she
said, "Free, free, free." Three times. So she has
suddenly perceived that she has not been free; she
has been under the influence of a "powerful will."
In this case it has been her husband, but she says
no one, man nor woman, should impose their will on
anyone else. So it's not a feminist issue--it's a
power issue. No one should push anyone else around
is what I guess Chopin means, force someone to do
what the other person wants. I used to have a friend
that did that to me all the time; he had to run
everything. They say that fathers--before the women's movement--used to run things, with the father
in charge of all the decisions, so maybe this is an
honest reaction to having been pushed around by a
husband. I think Mrs. Mallard is a believable

character, even if the plot is not all that believ-
able--all those things happening in such quick succession.

Listing

In your preliminary thinking you may find it useful to make lists. For "The
Story of an Hour" you might list Mrs. Mallard's traits; or you might list the
stages in her development. (Such a list is not the same as a summary of a
plot. The list helps the writer to see the sequence of psychological changes.)

```
weeps (when she gets the news)
goes to room, alone
"pressed down by a physical exhaustion"
"dull stare"
"something coming to her"
strives to beat back "this thing"
"Free, free, free!" The "vacant stare went from her
eyes"
"A clear and exalted perception"
rejects Josephine
"she was drinking in the very elixir of life"
gets up, opens door, "a feverish triumph in her eyes"
sees B, and dies
```

Of course, unlike brainstorming and annotating, which let you go in all directions, listing requires that you first make a decision about what you will
be listing—traits of character, images, puns, or whatever. Once you make
the decision, you can then construct the list, and, with a list in front of you,
you will probably see patterns that you were not earlier fully conscious of.

Asking Questions

If you feel stuck, ask yourself questions. We suggest questions for fiction
on page 97, for poetry on page 521, and for drama on page 631. If, for
instance, you are thinking about a work of fiction, you might ask yourself
questions about the plot and the characters—are they believable, are they
interesting, and what does it all add up to? What does the story mean *to
you?* One student found it helpful to jot down the following questions:

```
Plot
    Ending false? unconvincing? or prepared for?
Character?
    Mrs. M. unfeeling? Immoral?
    Mrs. M. unbelievable character?
```

```
What might her marriage have been like? Many
    gaps. (Can we tell what her husband was like?)
    "And yet she loved him--sometimes." Fickle?
    Realistic?
What is "this thing that was approaching to
    possess her"?
Symbolism
    Set on spring day = symbolic of new life?
```

But, again, you don't have to be as tidy as this student was. You can begin by jotting down notes and queries about what you like or dislike and about what puzzles or amuses you. Here are the jottings of another student. They are, obviously, in no particular order—the student is "brainstorming," putting down whatever occurs to her—though it is equally obvious that one note sometimes led to the next:

```
Title nothing special. What might be better title?
Could a woman who loved her husband be so heartless?
Is she heartless? Did she love him?
What are (were) Louise's feelings about her husband?
Did she want too much? What did she want?
Could this story happen today? Feminist interpreta-
    tion?
Sister (Josephine)--a busybody?
Tricky ending--but maybe it could be true
"And yet she loved him--sometimes. Often she had
    not."
Why does one love someone "sometimes"?
Irony: plot has reversal. Are characters ironic too?
```

These jottings will help the reader-writer to think about the story, to find a special point of interest and to develop a thoughtful argument about it.

Keeping a Journal

A journal is not a diary, a record of what the writer did each day ("today I read Chopin's 'Hour'"); rather, a journal is a place to store some of the thoughts that you may have inscribed on a scrap of paper or in the margin of the text—for instance, your initial response to the title of a work or to the ending. It's also a place to jot down some further reflections. These reflections may include thoughts about what the work means to you or what was said in the classroom about writing in general or about specific works. You, may for instance, want to reflect on why your opinion is so different from that of another student, or you may want to apply a concept such as "character" or "irony" or "plausibility" to a story that later you may write an essay about.

You might even make an entry in the form of a letter to the author or in the form of a letter from one character to another. Similarly, you might write a dialogue between characters in two works or between two authors, or you might record an experience of your own that is comparable to something in the work.

A student who wrote about "The Story of an Hour" began with the following entry in his journal. In reading this entry, notice that one idea stimulates another. The student was, quite rightly, concerned with getting and exploring ideas, not with writing a unified paragraph.

> Apparently a "well-made" story, but seems
> clever rather than moving or real. Doesn't seem
> plausible. Mrs. M's change comes out of the blue--
> maybe some women might respond like this, but
> probably not most.
>
> Does literature deal with unusual people, or
> with usual (typical?) people? Shouldn't it deal with
> typical? Maybe not. (Anyway, how can I know?) Is
> "typical" same as "plausible"? Come to think of it,
> prob. not.
>
> Anyway, whether Mrs. M. is typical or not, is
> her change plausible, believable?
>
> Why did she change? Her husband dominated her
> life and controlled her action; he did "impose a
> private will upon a fellow creature." She calls this
> a crime? Why? Why not?

Arriving at a Thesis

Having raised some questions, a reader goes back to the story, hoping to read it now with increased awareness. Some of the jottings will be dead ends, but some will lead to further ideas that can be arranged in lists. What the **thesis** of the essay will be—the idea that will be asserted and supported—is still in doubt, but there is no doubt about one thing: A good essay will have a thesis, a point, an argument. You ought to be able to state your point in a **thesis sentence.**

Consider these candidates as possible thesis sentences:

1. Mrs. Mallard dies soon after hearing that her husband has died.

     True, but scarcely a point that can be argued, or even developed. About the most the essayist can do with this sentence is to amplify it by summarizing the plot of the story, a task not worth doing. An analysis may include a sentence or two of summary, to give readers their bearings, but a summary is not an essay.

2. The story is a libel on women.

In contrast to the first statement, this one can be developed into an argument. Probably the writer will try to demonstrate that Mrs. Mallard's behavior is despicable. Whether this point can be convincingly argued is another matter; the thesis may be untenable, but it is a thesis. A second problem, however, is this: Even if the writer demonstrates that Mrs. Mallard's behavior is despicable, he or she will have to go on to demonstrate that the presentation of one despicable woman constitutes a libel on women in general. That's a pretty big order.

3. The story is clever but superficial because it is based on an unreal character.

Here, too, is a thesis, a point of view that can be argued. Whether or not this thesis is true is another matter. The writer's job will be to support it by presenting evidence. Probably the writer will have no difficulty in finding evidence that the story is "clever"; the difficulty probably will be in establishing a case that the characterization of Mrs. Mallard is "unreal." The writer will have to set forth some ideas about what makes a character real and then will have to show that Mrs. Mallard is an "unreal" (unbelievable) figure.

4. The irony of the ending is believable partly because it is consistent with earlier ironies in the story.

It happens that the student who wrote the essay printed on page 1247 began by drafting an essay based on the third of these thesis topics, but as she worked on a draft she found that she couldn't support her assertion that the character was unconvincing. In fact, she came to believe that although Mrs. Mallard's joy was the reverse of what a reader might expect, several early reversals in the story helped to make Mrs. Mallard's shift from grief to joy acceptable.

WRITING A DRAFT

After jotting down notes and then adding more notes stimulated by rereading and further thinking, you'll probably be able to formulate a tentative thesis. At this point most writers find it useful to clear the air by glancing over their preliminary notes and by jotting down the thesis and a few especially promising notes—brief statements of what they think their key points may be. These notes may include some brief key quotations that the writer thinks will help to support the thesis.

Here are the notes (not the original brainstorming notes, but a later selection from them, with additions) and a draft (below) that makes use of them. The final version of the essay—the product produced by the process—is given on page 1247.

```
title? Ironies in an Hour (?) An Hour of Irony (?)
Kate Chopin's Irony (?)

thesis: irony at the end is prepared for by earlier
ironies

chief irony: Mrs. M. dies just as she is beginning
to enjoy life

smaller ironies: 1. "sad message" brings her joy
                 2. Richards is "too late" at end;
                 3. Richards is too early at start
```

Sample Draft of an Essay on Kate Chopin's "The Story of an Hour"

Now for the student's draft—not the first version, but a revised draft with some of the irrelevancies of the first draft omitted and some evidence added.

The digits within the parentheses refer to the page numbers from which the quotations are drawn, through with so short a work as "The Story of an Hour," page references are hardly necessary. Check with your instructor to find out if you must always give citations. (Detailed information about how to document a paper is given on pages 1266–76.)

```
                   Ironies in an Hour

     After we know how the story turns out, if we
reread it we find irony at the very start, as is
true of many other stories. Mrs. Mallard's friends
assume, mistakenly, that Mrs. Mallard was deeply in
love with her husband, Brently Mallard. They take
great care to tell her gently of his death. The
friends mean well, and in fact they do well. They
bring her an hour of life, an hour of freedom. They
think their news is sad. Mrs. Mallard at first ex-
presses grief when she hears the news, but soon she
finds joy in it. So Richard's "sad message" (40),
though sad in Richard's eyes, is in fact a happy
message.
     Among the ironic details is the statement that
when Mallard entered the house, Richards tried to
```

conceal him from Mrs. Mallard, but "Richards was too late" (42). This is ironic because earlier Richards "hastened" (40) to bring his sad message; if he had at the start been "too late" (42), Brently Mallard would have arrived at home first, and Mrs. Mallard's life would not have ended an hour later but would simply have gone on as it had before. Yet another irony at the end of the story is the diagnosis of the doctors. The doctors say she died of "heart disease--of joy that kills" (42). In one sense the doctors are right: Mrs. Mallard has experienced a great joy. But of course the doctors totally misunderstood the joy that kills her.

The central irony resides not in the well-intentioned but ironic actions of Richards, or in the unconsciously ironic words of the doctors, but in her own life. In a way she has been dead. She "sometimes" (41) loved her husband, but in a way she has been dead. Now, his apparent death brings her new life. This new life comes to her at the season of the year when "the tops of trees . . . were all aquiver with the new spring life" (40). But, ironically, her new life will last only an hour. She looks forward to "summer days" (42) but she will not see even the end of this spring day. Her years of marriage were ironic. They brought her a sort of living death instead of joy. Her new life is ironic too. It grows out of her moment of grief for her supposedly dead husband, and her vision of a new life is cut short.

Work Cited

Chopin, Kate. "The Story of an Hour." Introduction to Literature. 10th ed. Ed. Sylvan Barnet, Morton Berman, and William Burto. New York: HarperCollins, 1993, 40-42.

Revising a Draft

The draft, although thoughtful and clear, is not yet a finished essay. The student went on to improve it in many small but important ways.

First, the draft needs a good introductory paragraph, a paragraph that will let readers know where the writer will be taking them. Doubtless you know from your own experience as a reader that readers can follow an argument more easily—and with more pleasure—if early in the discussion the writer alerts them to the gist of the argument. (The title, too, can strongly suggest the thesis.) Second, some of the paragraphs could be clearer.

In revising paragraphs—or, or that matter, in revising an entire draft—writers unify, organize, clarify, and polish.

1. **Unity** is achieved partly by eliminating irrelevances. Notice that in the final version, printed on page 1247, the writer has deleted "as is true of many other stories."
2. **Organization** is largely a matter of arranging material into a sequence that will assist the reader to grasp the point.
3. **Clarity** is achieved largely by providing concrete details and quotations to support generalizations and by providing helpful transitions ("for instance," "furthermore," "on the other hand," "however").
4. **Polish** is small-scale revision. For instance, one deletes unnecessary repetitions. In the second paragraph of the draft, the phrase "the doctors" appears three times, but it appears only once in the final version of the paragraph. Similarly, in polishing, a writer combines choppy sentences into longer sentences and breaks overly long sentences into shorter sentences.

Later, after producing a draft that seems close to a finished essay, writers engage in yet another activity.

5. They **edit,** checking the accuracy of quotations by comparing them with the original, checking a dictionary for the spelling of doubtful words, checking a handbook for doubtful punctuation—for instance, whether a comma or a semicolon is needed in a particular sentence.

Peer Review

Your instructor may encourage (or even require) you to discuss your draft with another student or with a small group of students. That is, you may be asked to get a review from your peers. Such a procedure is helpful in several ways. First, it gives the writer a real audience, readers who can point to what pleases or puzzles them, who make suggestions, who may often disagree (with the writer or with each other), and who frequently, though not intentionally, *misread.* Though writers don't necessarily like everything they hear (they seldom hear "This is perfect. Don't change a word!"), reading and discussing their work with others almost always gives them a fresh perspective on their work, and a fresh perspective may stimulate thoughtful revision. (Having your intentions *misread* because your writing isn't clear enough can be particularly stimulating.)

The writer whose work is being reviewed is not the sole beneficiary. When students regularly serve as readers for each other, they become better readers of their own work and consequently better revisers.

If peer review is a part of the writing process in your course, the instructor may distribute a sheet with some suggestions and questions. Here is an example of such a sheet.

QUESTIONS FOR PEER REVIEW   ENGLISH 125a

Read each draft once, quickly. Then read it again, with the following questions in mind.

1. What is the essay's topic? Is it one of the assigned topics, or a variation from it? Does the draft show promise of fulfilling the assignment?
2. Looking at the essay as a whole, what thesis (main idea) is stated or implied? If implied, try to state it in your own words.
3. Is the thesis plausible? How might it be strengthened?
4. Looking at each paragraph separately:
   a. What is the basic point? (If it isn't clear to you, ask for clarification.)
   b. How does the paragraph relate to the essay's main idea or to the previous paragraph?
   c. Should some paragraphs be deleted? Be divided into two or more paragraphs? Be combined? Be put elsewhere? (If you outline the essay by jotting down the gist of each paragraph, you will get help in answering these questions.)
   d. Is each sentence clearly related to the sentence that precedes and to the sentence that follows?
   e. Is each paragraph adequately developed?
   f. Are there sufficient details, perhaps brief supporting quotations from the text?
5. What are the paper's chief strengths?
6. Make at least two specific suggestions that you think will assist the author to improve the paper.

THE FINAL VERSION

Here is the final version of the student's essay. The essay that was submitted to the instructor had been retyped, but here, so that you can easily see how the draft has been revised, we print the draft with the final changes written in by hand.

Ironies of Life in Kate Chopin's "The Story of an Hour"
~~Ironies in an Hour~~

Despite its title, Kate Chopin's "The Story of an Hour" ironically takes only a few minutes to read. In addition the story turns out to have an ironic ending, but on rereading it one sees that the irony is not concentrated only in the outcome of the plot — Mrs. Mallard dies just when she is beginning to live — but is also present in many details.

After we know how the story turns out, if we reread it we find irony at the very start/ ~~as is~~ ~~true of many other stories~~. *Because* Mrs. Mallard's friends *and her sister* assume, mistakenly, that ~~Mrs. Mallard~~ *she* was deeply in love with her husband, Brently Mallard, *;* ~~T~~They take great care to tell her gently of his death. ~~The friends~~ *They* mean well, and in fact they do well, ~~They~~ *but it is ironic* bring*ing* her an hour of life, an hour of *joyous* freedom *;* *that* They think their news is sad. *True,* Mrs. Mallard at first ex- *(unknown to her friends)* presses grief when she hears the news, but soon* she finds joy in it. So Richard's "sad message" (40), though sad in Richard's eyes, is in fact a happy message. *small but significant* *near the end of the story* Among the ironic details is the statement that when Mallard entered the house, Richards tried to conceal him from Mrs. Mallard, but "Richards was too late" (42). This is ironic because ~~earlier~~ *almost at the start of the story, in the second paragraph* Richards "hastened" (40) to bring his sad message; if he had at the start been "too late" (42), Brently Mallard would have arrived at home first, and Mrs. Mallard's life would not have ended an hour later but would simply have gone on as it had before. Yet another irony at the end of the story is the diagnosis of the doctors. ~~The doctors~~ *They* say she died of "heart disease--of joy that kills" (42). In one sense ~~the doctors~~ *they* are right: Mrs. Mallard has *for the last hour* experienced a great joy. But of course the doctors totally misunderstand the joy that kills her. *It is not joy at seeing her husband alive, but her realization that the great joy she experienced during the last hour is over.*

All of these ironic details add richness to the story, but ^The central irony resides not in the well-intentioned but ironic actions of Richards, or in the unconsciously ironic words of the doctors, but in ~~her~~ *Mrs. Mallard's* own life. ~~In a way she has been dead.~~ She "sometimes" (41) loved her husband, but in a way she has been dead, ^*a body subjected to her husband's will* Now, his apparent death brings her new life. ^*Appropriately* This new life comes to her at the season of the year when "the tops of trees . . . were all aquiver with the new spring life" (40). But, ironically, her new life will last only an hour. ^*She is "Free, free, free"—but only until her husband walks through the doorway.* She looks forward to "summer days" (41) but she will not see even the end of this spring day. ^*If* Her years of marriage were ironic/, ~~They brought~~ *bringing* her a sort of

living death instead of joy~~,~~ ~~H~~er new life is ironic
not only because
too~~,~~ ~~I~~t grows out of her moment of grief for her
but also because her vision of "a long progression of years"
supposedly dead husband,~~ and her vision of a new~~

~~life~~ is cut short~~,~~ *within an hour on a spring day.*

Work Cited
Chopin, Kate. "The Story of an Hour." <u>Introduction</u>
    <u>to Literature</u>. 10th ed. Ed. Sylvan Barnet,
    Morton Berman, and William Burto. New York:
    HarperCollins, 1993. 40-42.

A Brief Overview of the Final Version

Finally, as a quick review, let's look at several principles illustrated by this essay.

1. The **title of the essay** is not merely the title of the work discussed; rather, it gives the reader a clue, a small idea of the essayist's topic.
2. The **opening** or **introductory paragraph** does not begin by saying "In this story . . ." Rather, by naming the author and the title, it lets the reader know exactly what story is being discussed. It also develops the writer's thesis so readers know where they will be going.
3. The **organization** is effective. The smaller ironies are discussed in the second and third paragraphs, the central (chief) irony in the last paragraph. That is, the essay does not dwindle or become anticlimatic; rather, it builds up from the least important to the most important point.
4. Some **brief quotations** are used, both to provide evidence and to let the reader hear—even if only fleetingly—Kate Chopin's writing.
5. The essay is chiefly devoted to **analysis** (how the parts relate to each other), not to summary (a brief restatement of the happenings). The writer, properly assuming that the reader has read the work, does not tell the plot in great detail. But, aware that the reader has not memorized the story, the writer gives helpful reminders.
6. The **present tense** is used in narrating the action: "Mrs. Mallard dies"; "Mrs. Mallard's friends and relatives all assume."
7. Although a **concluding paragraph** is often useful—if it does more than merely summarize what has already been clearly said—it is not essential in a short analysis. In this essay, the last sentence explains the chief irony and therefore makes an acceptable ending.

A SECOND EXAMPLE: AN ESSAY ON THE STRUCTURE OF *THE GLASS MENAGERIE*

The following essay discusses the structure of *The Glass Menagerie*. It mentions various characters, but, since its concern is with the arrangement of scenes, it does not (for instance) examine any of the characters in detail. An essay might well be devoted to examining (for example) Williams's assertion that "There is much to admire in Amanda, and as much to love and pity as there is to laugh at," but an essay on the structure of the play is probably not the place to talk about Williams's characterization of Amanda.

Preliminary Notes

After deciding to write on the structure of the play, with an eye toward seeing the overall pattern, the student reread *The Glass Menagerie,* jotted down some notes briefly summarizing each of the seven scenes, with an occasional comment, and then typed them. On rereading the typed notes, he added a few observations in handwriting.

nagging

1. begins with Tom talking to audience;
~~says he is a magician~~
American, in 1930s
        "shouting and confusion"
Father deserted
Amanda nagging; ~~is she a bit cracked?~~
Tom: bored, angry
Laura: embarrassed, depressed

2. Laura: quit business school; sad, but Jim's name is mentioned, so, lighter tone introduced

out-and-out battle

3. Tom and Amanda argue
Tom almost destroys glass menagerie
Rage: Can things get any worse?

4. T and A reconciled

5. T tells A that Jim will visit things are looking up

reconciliation, and false hopes— then final collapse

6. Jim arrives; L terrified still, Amanda thinks things can work out

7. Lights go out (foreshadowing dark ending?) Jim a jerk, clumsy; breaks unicorn, but L doesn't seem to mind. Maybe he _is_ the right guy to draw her into normal world. Jim reveals

```
he is engaged:
    "Desolation."
Tom escapes into merchant marine,
but can't escape memories. Speaks to
audience. L. blows out candles (does
this mean he forgets her? No, be-
cause he is remembering her right
now. I don't get it, if the candles
are supposed to be symbolic.)
```

These notes enabled the student to prepare a rough draft, which he then submitted to some classmates for peer review. (On peer review, see page 1245.)

THE FINAL VERSION

Notice that the final version of the essay, printed below, is *not* merely a summary (a brief retelling of the plot). Although it does indeed include summary, it chiefly is devoted to showing *how* the scenes are related.

Title is focused; it announces topic and thesis.

The Solid Structure of

The Glass Menagerie

Opening paragraph closes in on thesis.

In the "Production Notes" Tennessee Williams calls The Glass Menagerie a "memory play," a term that the narrator in the play also uses. Memories often consist of fragments of episodes which are so loosely connected that they seem chaotic, and therefore we might think that The Glass Menagerie will consist of very loosely related episodes. However, the play covers only one episode and though it gives the illusion of random talk, it really has a firm structure and moves steadily toward a foregone conclusion.

Tennessee Williams divides the play into seven scenes. The first scene begins with a sort of prologue and the last scene concludes with a sort of epilogue that is related to the prologue. In the prologue Tom addresses the audience and comments on the 1930s as a time when America was

"blind" and was a place of "shouting and confusion." Tom also mentions that our lives consist of expectations, and though he does not say that our expectations are unfulfilled, near the end of the prologue he quotes a postcard that his father wrote to the family he deserted: "Hello--Goodbye," In the epilogue Tom tells us that he followed his "father's footsteps," deserting the family. And just before the epilogue, near the end of Scene 7, we see what can be considered another desertion: Jim explains to Tom's sister Laura that he is engaged and therefore can-

not visit Laura again. Thus the end is closely related to the beginning, and the play is the steady development of the initial implications.

Chronological organiza-
tion is reasonable.
Opening topic sentence
lets readers know where
they are going.

The first three scenes show things going from bad to worse. Amanda is a nagging mother who finds her only relief in talking about the past to her crippled daughter Laura and her frustrated son Tom. When she was young she was beautiful and was eagerly courted by rich young men, but now the family is poor and this harping on the past can only bore or infuriate Tom and embarrass or depress Laura, who have no happy past to look back to, who see no happy future, and who can only be upset by Amanda's insistence that they should behave as she behaved long ago. The

Brief plot summary
supports thesis.

second scene deepens the despair: Amanda learns that the timorous Laura has not been attending a business school but has retreated in terror from this confrontation with the contemporary world. Laura's helplessness is made clear to the audience, and so is Amanda's lack of understanding. Near the end of the second scene, however, Jim's name is introduced; he is a boy Laura had a crush on in high school, and so the audience gets a glimpse of a happier Laura and a sense that possibly Laura's world is wider than the stifling tenement in

which she and her mother and brother
live. But in the third scene things
get worse, when Tom and Amanda have
so violent an argument that they are
no longer on speaking terms. Tom is
so angry with his mother that he
almost by accident destroys his
sister's treasured collection of
glass animals, the fragile lifeless
world which is her refuge. The apartment is literally full of the
"shouting and confusion" that Tom
spoke of in his prologue.

*Useful summary and
transition.*

The first three scenes have revealed a progressive worsening of relations; the next three scenes reveal
a progressive improvement in relations. In Scene 4 Tom and his mother
are reconciled, and Tom reluctantly--
apparently in an effort to make up
with his mother--agrees to try to get
a friend to come to dinner so that
Laura will have "a gentleman caller."
In Scene 5 Tom tells his mother that
Jim will come to dinner on the next
night, and Amanda brightens, because
she sees a possibility of security
for Laura at last. In Scene 6 Jim
arrives, and despite Laura's initial
terror, there seems, at least in
Amanda's mind, to be the possibility

that things will go well.

The seventh scene, by far the longest, at first seems to be fulfilling Amanda's hopes. Despite the ominous fact that the lights go out because Tom has not paid the electric bill, Jim is at ease. He is an insensitive oaf, but that doesn't seem to bother Amanda, and almost miraculously he manages to draw Laura somewhat out of her sheltered world. Even when Jim in his clumsiness breaks the horn of Laura's treasured glass unicorn, she is not upset. In fact, she is almost relieved because the loss of the horn makes the animal less "freakish" and he "will feel more at home with the other horses." In a way, of course, the unicorn symbolizes the crippled Laura, who at least for the moment feels freakish and isolated now that she is somewhat reunited with society through Jim. But this is a play about life in a blind and confused world, and though in a previous age the father escaped, there can be no escape now. Jim reveals that he is engaged, Laura relapses into "desolation," Amanda relapses into rage and bitterness, and Tom relapses into dreams of escape. In a limited

sense Tom does escape. He leaves the
family and joins the merchant marine,
but his last speech or epilogue tells
us that he cannot escape the memory
of his sister: "Oh, Laura, Laura, I
tried to leave you behind me, but I

The essayist is thinking and commenting, not merely summarizing the plot.

am more faithful than I intended to
be!" And so the end of the last scene
brings us back again to the beginning
of the first scene: we are still in a
world of "the blind" and of
"confusion." But now at the end of
the play the darkness is deeper, the
characters are lost forever in their
unhappiness as Laura "blows the candles out," the darkness being literal
but also symbolic of their extin-
guished hopes.

    Numerous devices, such as
repeated references to the absent
father, to Amanda's youth, to Laura's
Victrola and of course to Laura's
glass menagerie help to tie the

Useful, thoughtful sum-mary of thesis.

scenes together into a unified play.
But beneath these threads of imagery,
and recurring motifs, is a fundamental pattern that involves the
movement from nagging (Scenes 1 and
2) to open hostilities (Scene 3) to
temporary reconciliation (Scene 4) to
false hopes (Scenes 5 and 6) to an

impossible heightening of false hopes
and then, in a swift descent, to an
inevitable collapse (Scene 7). Tennessee Williams has constructed his
play carefully. G. B. Tennyson says
that a "playwright must 'build' his
speeches, as the theatrical expression has it" (13). But a playwright
must do more, he must also build his
play out of scenes. Like Ibsen, if
Williams had been introduced to an
architect he might have said,
"Architecture is my business too."

Works Cited

Documentation

Tennyson, G. B. An Introduction to
        Drama, New York: Holt, 1967.
Williams, Tennessee. The Glass
        Menagerie. Introduction to
        Literature. 10th ed. Ed. Sylvan
        Barnet, Morton Berman, and
        William Burto. New York: Harper-
        Collins, 1993. 979-1031.

The danger in writing about structure, especially if one proceeds by
beginning at the beginning and moving steadily to the end, is that one
will simply tell the plot. This essay on *The Glass Menagerie* manages to
say things about the organization of the plot even as it tells the plot. It
has a point, hinted at in the pleasantly paradoxical title, developed in the
body of the essay, and wrapped up in the last line.

EXPLICATION

A line-by-line commentary on what is going on in a text is an explication (literally, unfolding, or spreading out). Although your explication will for the most part move steadily from the beginning to the end of the selection, try to avoid writing along these lines (or, one might say, along this one line): "In line one . . . In the second line . . . In the third line . . ." That is, don't hesitate to write such things as

```
The poem begins . . . In the next line . . . The
speaker immediately adds . . . He then intro-
duces . . . The next stanza begins by saying . . .
```

And of course you can discuss the second line before the first if that seems the best way of handling the passage.

An explication is not concerned with the writer's life or times, and it is not a paraphrase (a rewording)—though it may include paraphrase if a passage in the original seems unclear perhaps because of an unusual word or an unfamiliar expression. On the whole, however, an explication goes beyond paraphrase, seeking to make explicit what the reader perceives as implicit in the work. To this end it calls attention, as it proceeds, to the implications of words (for instance, to their tone), the function of rhymes (for instance, how they may connect ideas, as in *throne* and *alone*), the development of contrasts, and any other contributions to the meaning.

A good way to stimulate responses to the poem is to ask some of the questions given on pages 521–23.

A Sample Explication

Take this short poem (published in 1917) by the Irish poet William Butler Yeats (1865–1939). The "balloon" in the poem is a dirigible, a blimp.

William Butler Yeats

The Balloon of the Mind

Hands, do what you're bid:
Bring the balloon of the mind
That bellies and drags in the wind
Into its narrow shed.

[1917]

A student began thinking about the poem by copying it, double-spaced. Then she jotted down her first thoughts.

sounds abrupt
/
Hands, do what you're bid: — *balloon imagined by the mind? Or a mind*

Bring the balloon of the mind   *like a balloon?*

no real rhymes?

That bellies and drags in the wind

Into its narrow shed.   *line seems to drag — it's so long!*

Later she wrote some notes in a journal.

> I'm still puzzled about the meaning of the words, "The balloon of the mind." Does "balloon of the mind" mean a balloon that belongs to the mind, sort of like "a disease of the heart"? If so, it means a balloon that the mind has, a balloon that the mind possesses, I guess by imagining it. Or does it mean that the mind is like a balloon, as when you say "he's a pig of a man," meaning he is like a pig, he is a pig? Can it mean both? What's a balloon that the mind imagines? Something like dreams of fame, wealth? Castles in Spain.
>
> Is Yeats saying that the "hands" have to work hard to make dreams a reality? Maybe. But maybe the idea really is that the mind is like a balloon--hard to keep under control, floating around. Very hard to keep the mind on the job. If the mind is like a bal-loon, it's hard to get it into the hangar (shed).
>
> "Bellies." Is there such a verb? In this poem it seems to mean something like "puffs out" or "flops around in the wind." Just checked The Ameri-can Heritage Dictionary, and it says "belly" can be a verb, "to swell out," "to bulge." Well, you learn something every day.

A later entry:

> OK; I think the poem is about a writer trying to keep his balloon-like mind from floating around, trying to keep the mind under control, trying to keep it working at the job of writing something, maybe writing something with the "clarity, unity, and coherence" I keep hearing about in this course.

Here is the student's final version of the explication.

Yeat's "Balloon of the Mind" is about writing
poetry, specifically about the difficulty of getting
one's floating thoughts down in lines on the page.
The first line, a short, stern, heavily stressed
command to the speaker's hands, perhaps implies by
its severe or impatient tone that these hands will
be disobedient or inept or careless if not watched
closely: the poor bumbling body so often fails to
achieve the goals of the mind. The bluntness of the
command in the first line is emphasized by the fact
that all the subsequent lines have more syllables.
Furthermore, the first line is a grammatically complete sentence, whereas the thought of line 2 spills
over into the next lines, implying the difficulty of
fitting ideas into confining spaces, that is, of
getting one's thoughts into order, especially into a
coherent poem.

Lines 2 and 3 amplify the metaphor already
stated in the title (the product of the mind is an
airy but unwieldy balloon), and they also contain a
second command, "Bring." Alliteration ties this command, "Bring," to the earlier "bid"; it also ties
both of these verbs to their object, "balloon," and
to the verb that most effectively describes the balloon, "bellies." In comparison with the abrupt first
line of the poem, lines 2 and 3 themselves seem
almost swollen, bellying and dragging, an effect
aided by using adjacent unstressed syllables ("of
the," "[bell]ies and," "in the") and by using an eye
rhyme ("mind" and "wind") rather than an exact
rhyme. And then comes the short last line: almost

before we could expect it, the cumbersome balloon--
here, the idea that is to be packed into the
stanza--is successfully lodged in its "narrow shed."
Aside from the relatively colorless "into," the only
words of more than one syllable in the poem are
"balloon," "bellies," and "narrow," and all three
emphasize the difficulty of the task. But after
"narrow"--the word itself almost looks long and narrow, in this context like a hanger--we get the simplicity of the monosyllable "shed." The difficult
job is done, the thought is safely packed away, the
poem is completed--but again with an off rhyme
("bid" and "shed"), for neatness can go only so far
when hands and mind and a balloon are involved.

Note: The reader of an explication needs to see the text, and because the explicated text is usually short, it is advisable to quote it all. (Remember, your imagined audience probably consists of your classmates; even if they have already read the work you are explicating, they have not memorized it, and so you helpfully remind them of the work by quoting it.) You can quote the entire text at the outset, or you can quote the first unit (for example, a stanza), then explicate that unit, and then quote the next unit, and so on. And if the poem or passage of prose is longer than, say, six lines, it it advisable to number each line at the right for easy reference.

COMPARISON AND CONTRAST

Something should be said about an essay organized around a **compari-son** or a **contrast,** say, of the settings in two short stories, of two charac-ters in a novel, or of the symbolism in two poems. (A comparison em-phasizes resemblances and a contrast emphasizes differences, but we can use the word "comparison" to cover both kinds of writing.) Probably the student's first thought, after making some jottings, is to discuss one-half of the comparison and then go on to the second half. Instructors and text-books (though not this one) usually condemn such an organization, argu-ing that the essay breaks into two parts and that the second part involves a good deal of repetition of categories set up in the first part. Usually they recommend that the student organize his thoughts differently, somewhat along these lines:

1. First similarity
    a. first work (or character, or characteristic)
    b. second work
2. Second similarity
    a. first work
    b. second work
3. First difference
    a. first work
    b. second work
4. Second difference
    a. first work
    b. second work

and so on, for as many additional differences as seem relevant. For example, if one wishes to compare *Huckleberry Finn* with *The Catcher in the Rye*, one may organize the material thus:

1. First similarity: the narrator and his quest
    a. Huck
    b. Holden
2. Second similarity: the corrupt world surrounding the narrator
    a. society in *Huckleberry Finn*
    b. society in *Catcher*
3. First difference: degree to which the narrator fulfills his quest and escapes from society
    a. Huck's plan to "light out" to the frontier
    b. Holden's breakdown

Here is another way of organizing a comparison and contrast:

1. First point: the narrator and his quest
    a. similarities between Huck and Holden
    b. differences between Huck and Holden
2. Second point: the corrupt world
    a. similarities between the worlds in *Huck* and *Catcher*
    b. differences between the worlds in *Huck* and *Catcher*
3. Third point: degree of success
    a. similarities between Huck and Holden
    b. differences between Huck and Holden

But a comparison need not employ either of these structures. There is even the danger that an essay employing either of them may not come into focus until the essayist stands back from the seven-layer cake and announces, in the concluding paragraph, that the odd layers taste better. In one's preparatory thinking, one may want to make comparisons in pairs (good-natured humor: the clown in *Othello,* the clownish gravedigger in *Hamlet;* social satire: the clown in *Othello,* the gravedigger in *Hamlet;* relevance to main theme: . . . ; length of role: . . . ; comments by other characters: . . .), but one must come to some conclusions about what these add up to before writing the final version. This final version should not duplicate the thought processes; rather, it should be organized to make the point clearly and effectively. After reflection, one may believe that although there are superficial similarities between the clown in *Othello* and the clownish gravedigger in *Hamlet,* there are essential differences; then in the finished essay one probably will not wish to obscure the main point by jumping back and forth from play to play, working through a series of similarities and differences. It may be better to discuss the clown in *Othello* and then to point out that, although the gravedigger in *Hamlet* resembles him in A, B, and C, the gravedigger also has other functions (D, E, and F) and is of greater consequence to *Hamlet* than the clown is to *Othello.* Some repetition in the second half of the essay (for example, "The gravedigger's puns come even faster than the clown's. . . .") will serve to bind the two halves into a meaningful whole, making clear the degree of similarity or difference.

The point of the essay presumably is not to list pairs of similarities of differences, but to illuminate a work or works by making thoughtful comparisons. Although in a long essay one cannot postpone until page 30 a discussion of the second half of the comparison, in an essay of, say, fewer than ten pages nothing is wrong with setting forth one-half of the comparison and then, in light of it, the second half. The essay will break into two unrelated parts if the second half makes no use of the first or if it fails to modify the first half, but not if the second half looks back to the first half and calls attention to differences that the new material reveals. One ought to learn how to write an essay with interwoven comparisons, but one ought also to know that there is another, simpler and clearer way to write a comparison.

REVIEW: HOW TO WRITE AN EFFECTIVE ESSAY

Everyone must work out his or her own procedures and rituals (John C. Calhoun liked to plough his farm before writing), but the following suggestions may provide some help.

1. **Read the work carefully.**
2. **Choose a worthwhile and compassable subject,** something that interests you and is not so big that your handling of it must be

superficial. As you work, shape and narrow your topic—for example, from "The Character of Hester Prynne" to "The Effects of Alienation on Hester Prynne."

3. **Reread the work, jotting down notes** of all relevant matters. As you read, reflect on your reading and record your reflections. If you have a feeling or an idea, jot it down; don't assume that you will remember it when you get around to writing your essay. The margins of the book are a good place for initial jottings, but many people find that in the long run it is easiest to transfer these notes to 3 x 5 cards, writing on one side only.

4. **Sort out your cards into some kind of reasonable divisions,** and reject cards irrelevant to your topic. As you work you may discover a better way to group your notes. If so, start reorganizing. If you are writing an explication, the order probably is essentially the order of the lines or of the episodes, but if you are writing an analysis you may wish to organize your essay from the lesser material to the greater (to avoid anticlimax) or from the simple to the complex (to ensure intelligibility). If, for example, you are discussing the roles of three characters in a story, it may be best to build up to the one of the three that you think the most important. If you are comparing two characters it may be best to move from the most obvious contrasts to the least obvious. When you have arranged your notes into a meaningful sequence of packets, you have approximately divided your material into paragraphs.

5. **Get it down on paper.** Most essayists find it useful to jot down some sort of outline, indicating the main idea of each paragraph and, under each main idea, supporting details that give it substance. An outline—not necessarily anything highly formal with capital and lowercase letters and roman and arabic numerals but merely key phrases in some sort of order—will help you to overcome the paralysis called "writer's block" that commonly afflicts professionals as well as students. A page of paper with ideas in some sort of sequence, however rough, ought to encourage you to realize that you do have something to say. And so, despite the temptation to sharpen another pencil or put a new ribbon into the typewriter, the best thing to do at this point is to sit down and start writing.

If you don't feel that you can work from note cards and a rough outline, try another method: get something down on paper, writing freely, sloppily, automatically, or whatever, but allowing your ideas about what the work means to you and how it conveys its meaning—rough as your ideas may be—to begin to take visible form. If you are like most people, you can't do much precise thinking until you have committed to paper at least a rough sketch of your initial ideas. Later you can push and polish your ideas into shape, perhaps even deleting all of them and starting over, but it's a lot easier to improve your ideas once you see them in front of you than it is to do the job in your head. On paper one word leads to another; in your head one word often blocks another.

Just keep going; you may realize, as you near the end of a sentence, that you no longer believe it. O.K., be glad that your first idea led you to a better one, and pick up your better one and keep going with it. What you are doing is, in a sense, by trial and error pushing your way not only toward clear expression but also toward sharper ideas and richer responses.

6. If there is time, **reread the work,** looking for additional material that strengthens or weakens your main point; take account of it in your outline or draft.

7. **By now your thesis should be clear to you,** and you ought to be able to give your essay an informative title—*not* simply the title of the story, poem, or play, but something that lets your reader know where you will be going.

   With a thesis and title clearly in mind, improve your draft, checking your notes for fuller details, such as supporting quotations. If, as you work, you find that some of the points in your earlier jottings are no longer relevant, eliminate them, but make sure that the argument flows from one point to the next. As you write, your ideas will doubtless become clearer; some may prove to be poor ideas. (We rarely know exactly what our ideas are until we have them set down on paper. As the little girl said, replying to the suggestion that she should think before she spoke, "How do I know what I think until I say it?") Not until you have written a draft do you really have strong sense of how good your essay may be.

8. After a suitable interval, preferably a few days, **read the draft with a view toward revising it,** not with a view toward congratulating yourself. A revision, after all, is a re-vision, a second (and presumably sharper) view. When you revise, you will be in the company of Picasso, who said that in painting he advanced by a series of destructions. A revision—say, the substitution of a precise word for an imprecise one—is not a matter of prettifying but of thinking. As you read, correct things that disturb you (for example, awkward repetitions that bore, inflated utterances that grate), add supporting detail where the argument is undeveloped (a paragraph of only one or two sentences is usually an undeveloped paragraph), and ruthlessly delete irrelevancies however well written they may be. But remember that a deletion probably requires some adjustment in the preceding and subsequent material.

   Make sure that the argument, aided by **transitions,** runs smoothly. The **details** should be relevant, the organization reasonable, the argument clear. **Check all quotations** for accuracy. Quotations are evidence, usually intended to support your assertions, and it is not nice to alter the evidence, even unintentionally. If there is time (there almost never is), put the revision aside, reread it in a day or two, and revise it again, especially with a view toward deleting wordiness and, on the other hand, supporting generalizations with evidence.

9. **Type or write a clean copy,** following the principles concerning margins, pagination, footnotes, and so on set forth on pages 1277–78. If you have borrowed any ideas, be sure to give credit, usually in footnotes, to your sources. Remember that plagiarism is not limited to the unacknowledged borrowing or words; a borrowed idea, even when put into your own words, requires acknowledgment.

10. **Proofread and make corrections** as explained on pages 1278–79.

DOCUMENTATION: FOOTNOTES AND INTERNAL PARENTHETICAL CITATIONS

Documentation tells your reader exactly what your sources are. Until recently, the standard form was the footnote, which, for example, told the reader that the source of such-and-such a quotation was a book by So-and-so. But in 1984 the Modern Language Association, which had established the footnote form used in hundreds of journals, university presses, and classrooms, substituted a new form. It is this new form — parenthetical citation *within* the text (rather than at the foot of the page or the end of the essay) — that we will discuss at length. Keep in mind, though, that footnotes still have their uses.

Footnotes

If you are using only one source your instructor may advise you to give the source in a footnote. (Check with your instructors to find out their preferred forms of documentation.)

Let's say that your only source is this textbook. Let's say, too, that all of your quotations will be from a single story — Kate Chopin's "The Story of an Hour" — printed in this book on pages 40–42. The simplest way to cite your source is to type the digit 1 (elevated, and *without* a period after it) after your first reference to (or quotation from) the story, and then to put a footnote at the bottom of the page, explaining where the story can be found. After the last line of type on the page, triple-space, indent five spaces from the left-hand margin, raise the typewriter carriage half a line, and type the arabic number 1. Do *not* put a period after it. Then lower the carriage half a line and type a statement (double-spaced) to the effect that all references are to this book. Notice that although the footnote begins by being indented five spaces, if the note runs to more than one line the subsequent lines are given flush left.

    [1]Chopin's story appears in Sylvan Barnet, Morton Berman, and William Burto, <u>An Introduction to Literature</u>, 10th ed. (New York: HarperCollins, 1993), 40-42.

(If a book has more than three authors or editors, give the name of only the first author or editor, and follow it with a comma and et al., the Latin abbreviation for "and others.")

Even if you are writing a comparison of, say, two stories in this book, you can use a note of this sort. It might run thus:

    [1]All page references given parenthetically within the essay refer to stories in Sylvan Barnet, Morton Berman, and William Burto, eds., <u>An Introduction to Literature</u>, 10th ed. (New York: HarperCollins, 1993).

If you use such a note, you do not need to use a footnote after each quotation that follows. You can give the citations right in the body of the paper, by putting the page references in parentheses after the quotations.

Internal Parenthetical Citations

On pages 1280–81 we distinguish between embedded quotations (which are short, are run right into your own sentence, and are enclosed within quotation marks) and quotations that are set off on the page (for example, three or more lines of poetry, five or more lines of typed prose that are not enclosed within quotation marks).

For an embedded quotation, put the page reference in parentheses immediately after the closing quotation mark, *without* any intervening punctuation. Then, after the parenthesis that follows the number, put the necessary punctuation (for instance, a comma or a period).

    Woolf says that there was "something marvelous as well as pathetic" about the struggling moth (93). She goes on to explain . . .

Notice that the period comes *after* the parenthetical citation. Notice, similarly, that in the next example *no* punctuation comes after the first citation — because none is needed — and a comma comes *after* (not before or within) the second citation, because a comma is needed in the sentence.

```
This is ironic because almost at the start of the
story, in the second paragraph, Richards with the
best of motives "hastened" (40) to bring his sad
message; if he had at the start been "too late"
(42), Mallard would have arrived at home first.
```

For a quotation that is not embedded within the text but is set off (by being indented ten spaces), put the parenthetical citation on the last line of the quotation, two spaces *after* the period that ends the quoted sentence.

Four additional points:

1. "p.," "pg.," and "pp." are *not* used in citing pages.
2. If a story is very short—perhaps running for only a page or two—your instructor may tell you there is no need to keep citing the page reference for each quotation. Simply mention in the footnote that the story appears on, say, pages 200–02.
3. If you are referring to a poem, your instructor may tell you to use parenthetical citations of line numbers rather than of page numbers. But, again, your footnote will tell the reader that the poem can be found in this book, and on what page.
4. If you are referring to a play with numbered lines, your instructor may prefer that in your parenthetical citations you give act, scene, and line, rather than page numbers. Use arabic (not roman) numerals, separating the act from the scene, and the scene from the line, by periods. Here, then, is how a reference to act three, scene two, line 118 would be given:

$$(3.2.118)$$

Parenthetical Citations and List of Works Cited

Footnotes have fallen into disfavor. Parenthetical citations are now usually clarified not by means of a footnote but by means of a list, headed Works Cited, given at the end of the essay. In this list you give, alphabetically (last name first), the authors and titles that you have quoted or referred to in the essay.

Briefly, the idea is that the reader of your paper encounters an author's name and a parenthetical citation of pages. By checking the author's name in Works Cited, the reader can find the passage in the book. Suppose the writer is writing about Kate Chopin's "The Story of an Hour." Let's assume that the writer has already mentioned the author and title of the story—that is, has let the reader know what the subject of the essay is—and now uses a quotation from the story, in a sentence such as this. (Notice the parenthetical citation of page numbers immediately after the quotation.)

```
True, Mrs. Mallard at first expresses grief when she
hears the news, but soon (unknown to her friends)
she finds joy in it. So, Richard's "sad message"
(40), though sad in Richard's eyes, is in fact a
happy message.
```

Turning to Works Cited, the reader, knowing the quoted words are by Chopin, looks for Chopin and finds the following:

```
Chopin, Kate. "The Story of an Hour." An Introduction
    to Literature, 10th ed. Eds. Sylvan Barnet,
    Morton Berman, and William Burto. New York:
    HarperCollins, 1993. 40-42.
```

Thus the essayist is informing the reader that the quoted words ("sad message") are to be found on page 40 of this anthology.

If the writer had not mentioned Chopin's name in some sort of lead-in, the name would have to be given within the parentheses so that the reader would know the author of the quoted words:

```
What are we to make out of a story that ends by
telling us that the leading character has died "of
joy that kills" (Chopin 42)?
```

(Notice, by the way, that the closing quotation marks come immediately after the last word of the quotation; the citation and the final punctuation — in this case, the essayist's question mark — come *after* the closing quotation marks.)

If you are comparing Chopin's story with Gilman's "The Yellow Wallpaper," in Works Cited you will give a similar entry for Gilman — her name, the title of the story, the book in which it is reprinted, and the page numbers that the story occupies.

If you are referring to several works reprinted within one volume, instead of listing each item fully, it is acceptable in Works Cited to list each item simply by giving the author's name, the title of the work, then a period, two spaces, and the name of the anthologist followed by the page numbers that the selection spans. Thus a reference to Chopin's "The Story of an Hour" would be followed only by: Barnet, 40–42. This form, of course, requires that the anthology itself be cited under the name of the first-listed editor, thus:

```
Barnet, Sylvan, Morton Berman, and William Burto,
    eds. An Introduction to Literature. 10th ed.
    New York: HarperCollins, 1993.
```

If you are writing a research paper, you will of course use many sources. Within the essay itself you will mention an author's name, and then will quote or summarize from this author, and follow the quotation or summary with a parenthetical citation of the pages. In Works Cited, you will give the full title, place of publication, and other bibliographic material.

Forms of Citation in Works Cited

In looking over the following samples of entries in Works Cited, remember:

1. The list of Works Cited is arranged alphabetically by author (last name first).
2. If a work is anonymous, list it under the first word of the title unless the first word is *A, An,* or *The,* in which case list it under the second word.
3. If a work is by two authors, although the book is listed alphabetically under the first author's last name, the second author's name is given in the normal order, first name first.
4. If you list two or more works by the same author, the author's name is not repeated but is represented by three hyphens followed by a period and two spaces.
5. Each item begins flush left, but if an entry is longer than one line, subsequent lines in the entry are indented five spaces.

For details about almost every imaginable kind of citation, consult Joseph Gibaldi and Walter S. Achtert, *MLA Handbook for Writers of Research Papers,* 3rd ed. (New York: Modern Language Association, 1988).

Here are samples of the citations of the kinds of publications you are most likely to include in your list of Works Cited.

Entries (arranged alphabetically) begin flush with the left margin. If an entry runs more than one line, indent the subsequent lines or lines five spaces from the left margin.

A book by one author

```
Douglas, Ann. The Feminization of American Culture.
    New York: Knopf, 1977.
```

Notice that the author's last name is given first, but otherwise the name is given as on the title page. Do not substitute initials for names written out on the title page. But you may shorten the publisher's name—for example, from Little, Brown and Company to Little.

Take the title from the title page, not from the cover or the spine. But disregard unusual typography—for instance, the use of only capital letters, or the use of & for *and*. Underline the title and subtitle with one continuous underline, but do not underline the period. The place of publication is indicated by the name of the city. But if the city is not well known, or if several cities have the same name (for instance Cambridge, Massachusetts, and Cambridge, England) the name of the state is added. If the title page lists several cities, give only the first.

A book by more than one author

Gilbert, Sandra, and Susan Gubar, <u>The Madwoman in</u>

 <u>the Attic: The Woman Writer and the Nineteenth-</u>

 <u>Century Literary Imagination</u>. New Haven: Yale

 UP, 1979.

Notice that the book is listed under the last name of the first author (Gilbert) and the second author's name is then given with first name (Susan) first. *If the book has more than three authors,* give the name of the first author only (last name first) and follow it with et al. (Latin for "and others.")

A book in several volumes

McQuade, Donald, et al., eds. <u>The Harper American</u>

 <u>Literature</u>. 2 vols. New York: HarperCollins,

 1987.

Pope, Alexander. <u>The Correspondence of Alexander</u>

 <u>Pope</u>. 5 vols. Ed. George Sherburn. Oxford:

 Clarendon, 1956.

Notice that the total number of volumes is given after the title, regardless of the number that you have used.

If you have used more than one volume, within your essay you will parenthetically indicate a reference to, for instance, page 30 of volume 3 thus: (3: 30). But if you have used only one volume of a multivolume work—let's say you used only volume 2 of McQuade's anthology—in your entry in Works Cited write, after the period following the date, Vol. 2. In your parenthetical citation within the essay you will therefore cite only the page reference (without the volume number), since the reader will (on consulting Works Cited) understand that in this example the reference is in volume 2.

If, instead of using the volumes as whole, you used only an independent work within one volume—say a poem in volume 2—in Works Cited omit the abbreviation "Vol." Instead give an arabic 2 (indicating volume 2) followed by a colon, a space, and the page numbers that encompass the selection you used.

```
Didion, Joan. "Some Dreamers of the Golden Dream."

    The Harper American Literature. Ed. Donald

    McQuade et al. 2 vols. New York: HarperCollins,

    1987. 2: 2198-2210.
```

Notice that this entry for Didion specifies not only that the book consists of two volumes, but also that only one selection ("Some Dreamers," occupying pages 2198–2210 in volume 2) was used. If you use this sort of citation in Works Cited, in the body of your essay a documentary reference to this work will be only to the page; the volume number will *not* be added.

A revised edition of a book

```
Ellmann, Richard. James Joyce. Rev. ed. New York:

    Oxford UP, 1982.
```

A reprint, for instance, a paperback version of an older clothbound book

```
Rourke, Constance, American Humor. 1931. Garden

    City, New York: Doubleday, 1953.
```

Notice that the entry cites the original date (1931) but indicates that the writer is using the Doubleday reprint of 1953.

An edited book other than an anthology

```
Keats, John. The Letters of John Keats. Ed. Hyder

    Edward Rollins. 2 vols. Cambridge, Mass.:

    Harvard UP, 1958.
```

An anthology. You can list an anthology either under the editor's name or under the title.

A work in a volume of works by one author

```
Sontag, Susan, "The Aesthetics of Silence." In

    Styles of Radical Will. New York: Farrar,

    1969. 3-34.
```

This entry indicates that Sontag's essay, called "The Aesthetics of Silence," appears in a book of hers entitled *Styles of Radical Will.* Notice that the page numbers of the short work are cited (not page numbers that you may happen to refer to, but the page numbers of the entire piece).

A work in an anthology, that is, in a collection of works by several authors. Begin with the author and the title of the work you are citing, not with the name of the anthologist or the title of the anthology. The entry ends with the pages occupied by the selection you are citing.

Bowen, Elizabeth. "Hand in Glove." The Oxford Book

of English Ghost Stories. Ed. Michael Cox and

R. A. Gilbert. Oxford: Oxford UP, 1986. 444-52.

Porter, Katherine Anne. "The Jilting of Granny

Weatherall." An Introduction to Literature.

Eds. Sylvan Barnet, Morton Berman, and William

Burto. 10th ed. New York: HarperCollins. 1993.

233-40.

Normally you will give the title of the work you are citing (probably an essay, short story or poem) in quotation marks. But if you are referring to a book-length work (for instance, a novel of a full-length play), underline it to indicate italics. If the work is translated, after the period that follows the title, write "Trans." and give the name of the translator, followed by a period and the name of the anthology.

If the collection is a multivolume work, and you are using only one volume, in Works Cited you will specify the volume, as in the example (page 1272) of Didion's essay. Because the list of Works Cited specifies the volume, your parenthetical documentay reference within your essay will specify (as mentioned earlier) only the page numbers, not the volume. Thus, although Didion's essay appears on pages 2198–2210 in the second volume of a two-volume work, a parenthetical citation will refer only to the page numbers because the citation in Works Cited specifies the volume.

Remember that the pages specified in the entry in your list of Works Cited are to the *entire selection,* not simply to pages you may happen to refer to within your paper.

Two or more works in an anthology. If you are referring to more than one work in an anthology (for example, in this book), in order to avoid repeating all the information about the anthology in each entry in Works Cited, under each author's name (in the appropriate alphabetical place) you can give the author and title of the work, then a period, two spaces, and the name of the anthologist followed by the page numbers that the selection spans. Thus, a reference to Shakespeare's *Othello* would be followed only by

Barnet 657-757

rather than by a full citation of this book. But this form of course requires that the anthology itself also be listed, under Barnet.

Two or more works by the same author. Notice that the works are given in alphabetical order (*Fables* precedes *Fools*) and that the author's name is not repeated but is represented by three hyphens followed by a period and two spaces. If the author is the translator or editor of a volume, the three hyphens are followed not by a period but by a comma, then a space, then the appropriate abbreviation (trans. or ed.), then (two spaces after the period) the title.

Frye, Northrop. <u>Fables of Identity Studies in Poetic</u>

<u>Mythology</u>. New York: Harcourt, 1963.

---. <u>Fools of Time: Studies in Shakespearian Trag-</u>

<u>edy</u>. Toronto: U of Toronto P, 1967.

A translated book

Gogol, Nikolai, <u>Dead Souls</u>. Trans. Andrew McAndrew.

New York: New American Library. 1961.

If, however, you are discussing the translation itself, as opposed to the book, list the work under the translator's name. Then put a comma, a space, and "trans." After the period following "trans." skip two spaces, then give the title of the book, a period, two spaces, and then "by" and the author's name, first name first. Continue with information about the place of publication, publisher, and date, as in any entry to a book.

An introduction, foreword, or afterword, or other editorial apparatus

Fromm, Erich. Afterword. <u>1984</u>. By George Orwell. New

American Library, 1961.

Usually a book with an introduction or some such comparable material is listed under the name of the author of the book rather than the name of the author of the editorial material (see the citation to Pope on page 1271). But if you are referring to the editor's apparatus rather than to the work itself, use the form just given.

Words such as preface, introduction, afterword, and conclusion are capitalized in the entry but are neither enclosed within quotation marks nor underlined.

A book review. First, an example of a review that does not have a title.

Vendler, Helen. Rev. of <u>Essays on Style</u>. Ed. Roger

    Fowler. <u>Essays in Criticism</u> 16 (1966): 457-63.

If the review has a title, give the title after the period following the reviewer's name, before the word "Rev." If the review is unsigned, list it under the first word of the title, or the second word if the first word is *A, An,* or *The.* If an unsigned review has no title, begin the entry with "Rev. of" and alphabetize it under the title of the work being reviewed.

An encyclopedia. The first example is for a signed article, the second for an unsigned article:

Lang, Andrew. "Ballads." <u>Encyclopaedia Britannica</u>.

    1910 ed.

"Metaphor." <u>The New Encyclopaedia Britannica</u>:

    <u>Micropaedia</u>. 1974 ed.

An article in a scholarly journal. Some journals are paginated consecutively—that is, the pagination of the second issue picks up where the first issue left off. Other journals begin each issue with a new page one. The forms of the citations in Works Cited differ slightly.

    First, the citation of *a journal that uses continuous pagination:*

Burbick, Joan. "Emily Dickinson and the Economics of

    Desire." <u>American Literature</u> 58 (1986): 361-78.

This article appeared in volume 58, which was published in 1986. (Notice that the volume number is followed by a space, then by the year, in parentheses, then by a colon, a space, and the page numbers of the entire article.) Although each volume consists of four issues, you do *not* specify the issue number when the journal is paginated continuously.

    For *a journal that paginates each issue separately* (if the journal is a quarterly, there will be four page 1's each year), give the issue number directly after the volume number and a period, with no spaces before or after the period.

Spillers, Hortense J. "Martin Luther King and the

    Style of the Black Sermon." <u>The Black Scholar</u> 3.1

    (1971), 14-27.

An article in a weekly, biweekly, or monthly publication

```
McCabe, Bernard. "Taking Dickens Seriously."
     Commonweal 14 May 1965.
```

Notice that the volume number and the issue number are omitted for popular weeklies or monthlies such as *Time* and *Atlantic*.

An article in a newspaper. Because newspapers usually consist of several sections, a section number may precede the page number. The example indicates that an article begins on page 1 of section 2 and is continued on a later page.

```
Wu, Jim. "Authors Praise New Forms." New York Times
     8 March 1987, Sec. 2:1+.
```

APPENDIX B

Remarks about Manuscript Form

BASIC MANUSCRIPT FORM

Much of what follows is nothing more than common sense.

1. Use 8½ ″ x 11 ″ paper of good weight. Do *not* use pages torn out of a spiral notebook.
2. If you typewrite, use a reasonably fresh ribbon, double-space, and type on one side of the page only. If you submit a handwritten copy, use lined paper and write on one side of the page only, in black or dark blue ink, on every other line. Most instructors do *not* want papers to be enclosed in any sort of binder. And most instructors want papers to be clipped together in the upper left corner; do not crimp or crease corners and expect them to hold together.
3. Leave an adequate margin — an inch or an inch and a half — at top, bottom, and sides.
4. Number the pages consecutively, using arabic numerals in the upper right-hand corner.
5. Put your name and class or course number in the upper right-hand corner of the first page. It is a good idea to put your name in the upper corner of each page so that if a page gets separated it can easily be restored to the proper essay.
6. Create your own title — one that reflects your topic or thesis. For example, a paper on Shirley Jackson's "The Lottery" should *not* be called "The Lottery" but might be called

>   Suspense in Shirley Jackson's "The Lottery"

or

>   Is "The Lottery" Rigged?

or

```
    Jackson's "The Lottery" and Scapegoat Rituals
```

These titles do at least a little in the way of rousing a reader's interest.
7. Center the title of your essay below the top margin of the first page.
Begin the first word of the title with a capital letter, and capitalize
each subsequent word except articles (*a, an, the*) conjunctions (*and,
but, if, when,* etc.), and prepositions (*in, on, with,* etc.), thus:

```
        A Word on Behalf of Iago
```

Notice that you do *not* enclose you title within quotation marks, nor
do you underline it—though if it includes the title of a story, *that*
is enclosed within quotation marks, as in the following example:

```
        Illusion and Reality in
      Hawthorne's "Young Goodman Brown"
```

8. Begin the essay an inch or two below the title.
9. Your extensive revisions should have been made in your drafts, but
minor last-minute revisions may be made—neatly—on the finished
copy. Proofreading may catch some typographical errors, and you
may notice some small weaknesses. You can make corrections with
the following proofreader's symbols.

CORRECTIONS IN THE MANUSCRIPT

1. *Changes* in wording may be made by crossing through words and
rewriting them:

```
                              has
   The influence of Poe and Hawthorne have greatly
   diminished.
                                     ^
```

2. *Additions* should be made above the line, with a caret below the line
at the appropriate place:

```
                                      greatly
   The influence of Poe and Hawthorne has dimin-
   ished.                                 ^
```

3. *Transpositions* of letters may be made thus:

```
   The inlfluence of Poe and Hawthorne has greatly
   diminished.
```

4. *Deletions* are indicated by a horizontal line through the word or words
to be deleted. Delete a single letter by drawing a vertical or diagonal
line through it, and indicate whether the letters on either side are
to be closed up by drawing a connecting arc:

```
The influence of Poe and Hawthorne has
greatlɪy, diminished.
```

5. *Separation* of words accidentally run together is indicated by a vertical line, *closure* by a curved line connecting the letters to be closed up:

```
The influenceof Poe and Hawthorne has g reatly
diminished.
```

6. *Paragraphing* may be indicated by the symbol ¶ before the word
   that is to begin the new paragraph:

```
The influence of Poe and Hawthorne has greatly
diminished.¶The influence of Borges has very
largely replaced that of earlier writers of
fantasy.
```

QUOTATIONS AND QUOTATION MARKS

First, a word about the *point* of using quotations. Don't use quotations
to pad the length of a paper. Rather, give quotations from the work you
are discussing so that your readers will see the material you are discussing
and (especially in a research paper) so that your readers will know what
some of the chief interpretations are and what your responses to them are.

Note: The next few paragraphs do *not* discuss how to include citations of pages, a topic discussed in the preceding appendix under the heading "How to Document."

The Golden Rule: If you quote, *comment on* the quotation. Let the
reader know what you make of it and why you quote it.

Additional principles:

1. **Identify the speaker or writer or the quotation** so that the reader
   is not left with a sense of uncertainty. Usually, in accordance with
   the principle of letting readers know where they are going, this identification precedes the quoted material, but occasionally it may follow the quotation, expecially if it will provide something of a pleasant
   surprise. For instance, in a discussion of Flannery O'Connor's stories, you might quote a disparaging comment on one of the stories
   and then reveal that O'Connor herself was the speaker.

2. **If the quotation is part of your own sentence, be sure to fit the
   quotation grammatically and logically into your sentence.**

   Incorrect: Holden Caulfield tells us very little about "what
   my lousy childhood was like."

> *Correct:* Holden Caulfield tells us very little about what his "lousy childhood" was like.

3. **Indicate any omissions or additions.** The quotation must be exact. Any material that you add—even one or two words—must be enclosed within square bracket, thus:

```
Hawthorne tells us that "owing doubtless to the
depth of the gloom at that particular spot [in
the forest], neither the travellers nor their
steeds were visible."
```

If you wish to omit material from within a quotation, indicate the ellipsis by three spaced periods. If your sentence ends in an omission, add a closed-up period and then three spaced periods to indicate the omission. The following example is based on a quotation from the sentences immediately above this one:

```
The instructions say that "if you...omit
materials from within a quotation, [you must]
indicate the ellipsis.... If your sentence ends
in an omission, add a closed-up period and then
three spaced periods...."
```

Notice that although material preceded "If you," periods are not needed to indicate the ommission because "If you" began a sentence in the original. Customarily, initial and terminal omissions are indicated only when they are part of the sentence you are quoting. Even such omissions need not be indicated when the quoted material is obviously incomplete—when, for instance, it is a word or phrase.

4. **Distinguish between short and long quotations,** and treat each appropriately. *Short quotations* (usually defined as fewer than five lines of typed prose) are enclosed within quotation marks and are embedded, that is they are run into the text (rather than being set off, without quotation marks), as in the following example:

```
Hawthorne begins the story by telling us that
"Young Goodman Brown came forth at sunset into
the street at Salem village," thus at the outset
connecting the village with daylight. A few
paragraphs later, when Hawthorne tells us that
the road Brown takes was "darkened by all of the
gloomiest trees of the forest," he begins to as-
sociate the forest with darkness--and a very
little later with evil.
```

To set off a *long quotation* (more than four typed lines of prose), indent the entire quotation ten spaces from the left margin. Usually a long quotation is introduced by a clause ending with a colon; for instance, "The following passage will make this point clear:" or "The closest we come to hearing an editorial voice is a long passage in the middle of the story:" or some lead-in. After typing your lead-in, double-space, then type the quotation, indented and double-spaced.

5. **Commas and periods** go inside the quotation marks.

```
Chopin tells us in the first sentence that "Mrs.
Mallard was afflicted with heart trouble," and
in the last sentence the doctors say that Mrs.
Mallard "died of heart disease."
```

Exception: if the quotation is immediately followed by material in parentheses or in square brackets, close the quotation, then give the parenthetic or bracketed material, and then—after closing the parenthesis or bracket—put the comma or period.

```
Chopin tells us in the first sentence that "Mrs.
Mallard was afflicted with heart trouble" (17),
and in the last sentence the doctors say that
Mrs. Mallard "died of heart disease" (18).
```

6. **Semicolons, colons, and dashes** go outside the closing quotation marks.

7. **Question marks and exclamation points** go inside if they are part of the quotation, outside if they are your own.

   In the following passage from a student's essay, notice that because the second question mark is the student's, it comes after the closing quotation marks.

```
The older man says to Goodman Brown, "Sayest
thou so?" Doesn't a reader become uneasy when
the man immediately adds, "We are but a little
way in the forest yet"?
```

8. **Quotation marks versus underlining.** Use quotation marks around titles of short stories and other short works—that is, titles of chapters in books, essays, and poems that might not be published by themselves. Underline (to indicate italics) titles of books, periodicals, collections of essays, plays, and long poems such as *The Rime of the Ancient Mariner.*

(Continued from p. iv)

José Armas. "El Tonto del Barrio." First published in *DeColores.* Reprinted by permission of the author.

W. H. Auden. "The Unknown Citizen," "Musée des Beaux Arts." Copyright © 1940 and renewed 1968 by W. H. Auden. Reprinted from *W. H. Auden: Collected Poems,* edited by Edward Mendelson, by permission of Random House, Inc. and Faber and Faber Ltd.

Toni Cade Bambara. "The Lesson" from *Gorilla, My Love* by Toni Cade Bambara. Copyright © 1972 by Toni Cade Bambara. Reprinted by permission of Random House, Inc.

Elizabeth Bishop. "Filling Station," "The Fish," and "Poem" from *The Complete Poems 1927–1979* by Elizabeth Bishop. Copyright © 1979, 1983 by Alice Helen Methfessel. Reprinted by permission of Farrar, Straus & Giroux, Inc.

Gwendolyn Brooks. "We Real Cool" from *Blacks,* published by The David Company, Chicago. Copyright © 1987. Reprinted by permission of the author.

Raymond Carver. "Cathedral" from *Cathedral* by Raymond Carver. Copyright © 1981 by Raymond Carver. Reprinted by permission of Alfred A. Knopf, Inc.

Anton Chekhov. "Enemies" reprinted with the permission of Macmillan Publishing Company from *The Schoolmaster and Other Stories* by Anton Chekhov, translated from the Russian by Constance Garnett. Copyright 1921 The Macmillan Company, renewed 1949 by David Garnett. "Misery" reprinted with the permission of Macmillan Publishing Company from The Schoolmistress and Other Stories by Anton Chekhov, translated from the Russian by Constance Garnett. Copyright 1921 The Macmillan Company, renewed 1949 by David Garnett.

Kate Chopin. "The Storm" reprinted by permission of Louisiana State University Press from *The Complete Works of Kate Chopin,* edited by Per Seyersted. Copyright © 1969 by Louisiana State University Press.

Sandra Cisneros. "One Holy Night." Copyright © 1991 by Sandra Cisneros. Published in the United States in *Woman Hollering Creek,* Random House, Inc., New York, and simultaneously in Canada by Random House of Canada Limited, Toronto. First published in *The Village Voice Literary Supplement.* Reprinted by permission of Susan Bergholz Literary Services.

Lucille Clifton. "In the Inner City" from *Good Times* by Lucille Clifton. Copyright © 1969 by Lucille Clifton. Reprinted by permission of Random House, Inc.

Judith Ortiz Cofer. "My Father in the Navy" from *Triple Crown* by Judith Ortiz Cofer (1987). Reprinted by permission of Bilingual Press, Arizona State University, Tempe, AZ.

Countee Cullen: "For a Lady I Know" reprinted by permission of GRM Associates, Inc., Agents for the Estate of Ida M. Cullen. From the book *On These I Stand* by Countee Cullen. Copyright © 1925 by Harper & Brothers; copyright renewed 1953 by Ida M. Cullen.

E. E. Cummings. "anyone lived in a pretty how town," "next to of course god america i," and "in Just-" are reprinted from *Complete Poems, 1913–1962* by E. E. Cummings, by permission of Liveright Publishing Corporation. Copyright © 1923, 1925, 1931, 1935, 1938, 1939, 1940, 1944, 1945, 1946, 1947, 1948, 1949, 1950, 1951, 1952, 1953, 1954, 1955, 1956, 1957, 1958, 1959, 1960, 1961, 1962 by the Trustees for the E. E. Cummings Trust. Copyright © 1961, 1963, 1968 by Marion Morehouse Cummings.

Trifles is the sole property of the author and is fully protected under the copyright laws of the Unites States, the British Empire including the Dominion of Canada, and all other countries of the Copyright Union, and are subject to royalty. The play may not be acted by professionals or amateurs without formal permission in writing and the payment of royalty. All rights including professional, amateur, stock, radio and television broadcasting, motion picture, recitation, lecturing, public reading and the rights of translation in foreign languages are reserved. All inquiries should be directed to Baker's Plays, 100 Chauncy Street, Boston, Massachusetts 02111.

Joy Harjo. "Anchorage" from the book *She Had Some Horses* by Joy Harjo. Copyright © 1983 by Thunder's Mouth Press. Used by permission of the publisher, Thunder's Mouth Press.

Robert Hayden. "Frederick Douglass" and "Those Winter Sundays" are reprinted from *Angle of Ascent: New and Selected Poems,* by Robert Hayden, by permission of Liveright Publishing Corporation. Copyright © 1975, 1972, 1970, 1966 by Robert Hayden.

Seamus Heaney. "Digging" from *Selected Poems 1966–1987* by Seamus Heaney. Copyright © 1990 by Seamus Heaney. Reprinted by permission of Farrar, Straus & Giroux, Inc. and Faber and Faber Ltd.

Anthony Hecht. "The Dover Bitch" from *Collected Earlier Poems* by Anthony Hecht. Copyright © 1990 by Anthony E. Hecht. Reprinted by permission of Alfred A. Knopf, Inc.

Ernest Hemingway. "Cat in the Rain" reprinted with permission of Charles Scribner's Sons, an imprint of Macmillan Publishing Company, from *In Our Time* by Ernest Hemingway. Copyright 1925 by Charles Scribner's Sons; renewal copyright 1953 by Ernest Hemingway.

A. E. Housman. "To an Athlete Dying Young" and "Eight O'Clock" from *The Collected Poems* of A. E. Housman by A. E. Houseman. Copyright © 1922, 1939, 1940, 1965 by Holt, Rinehart and Winston, Inc. Copyright © 1950 by Barclays Bank Ltd. Copyright © 1967, 1968 by Robert E. Symons. Reprinted by permission of Henry Holt and Company, Inc.

Langston Hughes. "Evenin' Air Blues" from *Shakespeare in Harlem.* Copyright 1942 by Alfred A. Knopf Inc. Copyright renewed. "Dream Boogie" "Passing" and "Theme for English B" from *Montage of a Dream Deferred.* Copyright 1951 by Langston Hughes. Copyright renewed 1979 by George Houston Bass. Reprinted by permission of Harold Ober Associates. "Harlem (Dream Deferred)" from *The Panther and the Lash* by Langston Hughes. Copyright 1951 by Langston Hughes. Reprinted by permission of Alfred A. Knopf, Inc. "Negro" from *Selected Poems of Langston Hughes* by Langston Hughes. Copyright 1926 by Alfred A. Knopf, Inc. Copyright renewed 1954 by Langston Hughes. Reprinted by permission of Alfred A. Knopf, Inc.

Ted Hughes. "Hawk Roosting" from *New Selected Poems* by Ted Hughes. Copyright © 1959 by Ted Hughes. Reprinted by permission of HarperCollins Publishers and Faber and Faber Ltd.

Zora Neale Hurston. "Sweat" from *The Selected Stories of Zora Neale Hurston.* Reprinted by permission of Lucy Hurston.

Henrik Ibsen. Excerpt from "Speech at the Banquet of the Norwegian League for Women's Rights" from *Ibsen: Letters and Speeches* edited by Evert Sprinchorn. Copyright © 1964 by Evert Sprinchorn. "A Doll's House" from *Ghosts* *and Other Plays* by Henrik Ibsen, translated by Michael Meyer. Copyright © 1966 by Michael Meyer. Reprinted by permission of Harold Ober Associates Incorporated. Excerpts reprinted from *The Oxford Ibsen,* volume 5, translated and edited by J. W. McFarlane (1961) by permission of Oxford University Press.

Shirley Jackson. "The Lottery" from *The Lottery* by Shirley Jackson. Copyright © 1948, 1949 by Shirley Jackson. Renewal copyright © 1976, 1977 by Laurence Hyman, Barry Hyman, Mrs. Sarah Webster and Mrs. Joanne Schnurer. Reprinted by permission of Farrar, Straus & Giroux, Inc.

Randall Jarrell. "The Death of the Ball Turret Gunner" from *The Complete Poems* by Randall Jarrell. Copyright © 1945 and renewal copyright © 1972 by Mrs. Randall Jarrell. Reprinted by permission of Farrar, Straus & Giroux, Inc. "The Woman At the Washington Zoo" © 1960 by Randall Jarrell from *The Woman at the Washington Zoo,* reprinted in *The Complete Poems of Randall Jarrell,* Farrar, Straus & Giroux, 1989. Permission granted by Rhoda Weyr Agency, New York.

James Joyce. "Araby" from *Dubliners* by James Joyce. Copyright 1916 by B. W. Heubsch. Definitive text copyright © 1967 by the Estate of James Joyce. Used by permission of Viking Penguin, a division of Penguin Books USA, Inc.

Franz Kafka. "The Metamorphosis" from *The Metamorphosis, The Penal Colony and Other Stories* by Franz Kafka, translated by Willa and Edwin Muir. Copyright 1948 by Schocken Books, Inc. Copyright renewed 1975 by Schocken Books, Inc. Reprinted by permission of Schocken Books, published by Pantheon Books, a division of Random House.

X. J. Kennedy. "Nothing in Heaven Functions as it Ought" from *Cross Ties: Selected Poems* by X. J. Kennedy. Copyright © 1985 by X. J. Kennedy. Reprinted by permission of the University of Georgia Press.

Jamaica Kincaid. "Girl" from *At the Bottom of the River* by Jamaica Kincaid. Copyright © 1978, 1983 by Jamaica Kincaid. Reprinted by permission of Farrar, Straus & Giroux, Inc.

D. H. Lawrence. "Snake" from *The Complete Poems of D. H. Lawrence,* by D. H. Lawrence. Copyright © 1964, 1971 by Angelo Ravagli and C. M. Weekley, Executors of the Estate of Frieda Lawrence Ravagli. Used by permission of Viking Penguin, a division of Penguin Books USA, Inc.

Don L. Lee. "But He Was Cool" from *Don't Cry Scream.* Reprinted by permission of the author and Third World Press.

Li-Young Lee. "I Ask My Mother to Sing" from *Rose: Poems by Li-Young Lee* copyright © 1986 by Li-Young Lee. Reprinted with permission of BOA Editions, Ltd.

John Lennon and Paul McCartney. "Eleanor Rigby" words and music by John Lennon and Paul McCartney. © Copyright 1966 by *Northern Songs.* All Rights Controlled and Administered by MCA Music Publishing, A Division of MCA, Inc., New York, NY 10019 under license from *Northern Songs.* USED BY PERMISSION. INTERNATIONAL COPYRIGHT SECURED. ALL RIGHTS RESERVED.

Archibald MacLeish. "Ars Poetica" from *New and Collected Poems 1917–1982* by Archibald MacLeish. Copyright © 1985 by the Estate of Archibald MacLeish. Reprinted by permission of Houghton Mifflin Company. All rights reserved.

Edna St. Vincent Millay. Sonnet XXX of *Fatal Interview* ("Love is Not All") and "The Spring and the Fall" by Edna St. Vincent Millay. From *Collected Poems,* Harper & Row. Copyright © 1923, 1931, 1951, 1958 by Edna St. Vincent Millay and Norma Millay Ellis. Reprinted by permission of Elizabeth Barnett, literary executor.

Pastan, by permission of W. W. Norton & Company, Inc. Copyright © 1978 by Linda Pastan.

Marge Piercy. "Barbie Doll," "What's That Smell in the Kitchen," and "A Work of Artifice" from *Circles on the Water* by Marge Piercy. Copyright 1969, 1971, 1973, 1982 by Marge Piercy. Reprinted by permission of Alfred A. Knopf, Inc.

Sylvia Plath. "Metaphors" copyright © 1960 by Ted Hughes. "Daddy" copyright © 1963 by Ted Hughes. From *The Collected Poems of Sylvia Plath,* edited by Ted Hughes. Reprinted by permission of HarperCollins Publishers and Faber and Faber Ltd.

Katherine Anne Porter. "The Jilting of Granny Weatherall" from *The Flowering Judas and Other Stories,* copyright 1930 and renewed 1958 by Katherine Anne Porter, reprinted by permission of Harcourt Brace Jovanovich, Inc.

Ezra Pound. "An Immortality" from *Collected Early Poems of Ezra Pound.* Copyright © 1976 by the Trustees of The Ezra Pound Literary Property Trust. In a Station of the Metro" from *Personae* by Ezra Pound. Copyright 1926 by Ezra Pound. Reprinted by permission of New Directions Publishing Corporation.

Craig Raine. "A Martian Sends a Postcard Home" © Craig Raine 1979. Reprinted from *A Martian Sends a Postcard Home* by Craig Raine (1979) by permission of Oxford University Press.

John Crowe Ransom. "Piazza Piece" and "Bells for John Whiteside's Daughter" from *Selected Poems,* Third Edition, Revised and Enlarged by John Crowe Ransom. Copyright 1924, 1927 by Alfred A. Knopf, Inc. Copyright renewed 1952, 1955 by John Crowe Ransom. Reprinted by permission of Alfred A. Knopf, Inc.

Henry Reed. "Naming of Parts" from *A Map of Verona* by Henry Reed. Copyright Henry Reed, reproduced by permission of Curtis Brown Ltd, London.

Adrienne Rich. "Living in Sin," "Diving into the Wreck," "Rape" reprinted from *The Fact of a Doorframe, Poems Selected and New, 1950–1984* by Adrienne Rich, by permission of W. W. Norton & Company, Inc. Copyright © 1984 by Adrienne Rich. Copyright © 1975, 1978 by W. W. Norton & Company, Inc. Copyright © 1981 by Adrienne Rich.

Edwin Arlington Robinson. "Mr. Flood's Party" reprinted with permission of Macmillan Publishing Company from *Collected Poems of Edwin Arlington Robinson.* Copyright 1921 by Edwin Arlington Robinson, renewed 1949 by Ruth Nivison. "Richard Cory" from *The Children of the Night* by Edwin Arlington Robinson (New York: Charles Scribner's Sons, 1897).

Theodore Roethke. "My Papa's Waltz" copyright 1942 by Hearst Magazines, Inc., from *The Collected Poems of Theodore Roethke* by Theodore Roethke. Used by permission of Doubleday, a division of Bantam Doubleday Dell Publishing Group, Inc.

David Savran. "Talking About Fences" (editor's title) from *In Their Own Words* by David Savran. Reprinted by permission of Theatre Communications Group.

William Shakespeare. *A Midsummer Night's Dream* and *Othello* from *The Complete Works of Shakespeare,* edited by David Bevington. Reprinted by permission of HarperCollins Publishers, Inc.

Leslie Marmon Silko. "The Man to Send Rain Clouds" from *The Man to Send Rain Clouds* by Leslie Marmon Silko. Reprinted with the permission of Wylie, Aitken & Stone, Inc.

Stevie Smith. "Not Waving but Drowning" from *The Collected Poems of Stevie Smith* by Stevie Smith. Copyright © 1972 by Stevie Smith. Reprinted by permission of New Directions Publishing Corporation.

Sophocles. *The Antigone of Sophocles: An English Version* by Dudley Fitts and Robert Fitzgerald, copyright 1939 by Harcourt Brace Jovanovich, Inc. and renewed 1967 by Dudley Fitts and Robert Fitzgerald, reprinted by permission of the author. *The Oedipus Rex of Sophocles: An English Version* by Dudley Fitts and Robert Fitzgerald, copyright 1949 by Harcourt Brace Jovanovich, Inc. and renewed 1977 by Cornelia Fitts and Robert Fitzgerald, reprinted by permission of the publisher. CAUTION: For both plays, all rights, including professional, amateur, motion picture, recitation, lecturing, performance, public reading, radio broadcasting, and television are strictly reserved. Inquiries on all rights should be addressed to Harcourt Brace Jovanovich, Inc., Permissions Department, Orlando, Florida 32887.

William Stafford. "Traveling Through the Dark" from *Stories That Could Be True* by William Stafford (Harper & Row, 1977). Reprinted by permission of the author.

George Starbuck. "Fable for Blackboard" from *Bone Thoughts.* Copyright © 1960 by George Starbuck. Reprinted by permission of Yale University.

Wallace Stevens. "Anecdote of the Jar" and "Emperor of Ice Cream" from *The Collected Poems of Wallace Stevens* by Wallace Stevens. Copyright 1923 and renewed 1951 by Wallace Stevens. Reprinted by permission of Alfred A. Knopf, Inc.

Amy Tan. "Two Kinds" reprinted by permission of The Putnam Publishing Group from *The Joy Luck Club* by Amy Tan. Copyright © 1989 by Amy Tan.

Dylan Thomas. "Fern Hill" and "Do not go gentle into that good night" from Dylan Thomas, *The Poems of Dylan Thomas.* Copyright 1945 by the Trustees for the Copyrights of Dylan Thomas; 1952 by Dylan Thomas. Reprinted by permission of New Directions Publishing Corporation and David Higham Associates Ltd.

John Updike. "The Rumor." First appeared in *Esquire.* Reprinted by permission of the author.

Luis Valdez. "Los Vendidos" and "The Actos" from *Actos* by Luis Valdez. Reprinted by permission of Arte Publico Press.

Helena Maria Viramontes. "The Moth" from *The Moths and Other Stories* by Helena Maria Viramontes. Reprinted by permission of Arte Publico Press.

Alice Walker. "Everyday Use" from *In Love and Trouble,* copyright © 1973 by Alice Walker, reprinted by permission of Harcourt Brace Jovanovich, Inc.

Wendy Wasserstein. "The Man in a Case" from *Orchards: Seven Stories by Anton Chekhov and Seven Plays They Have Inspired* by Anton Chekhov et al. Copyright © 1986 by Wendy Wasserstein. Reprinted by permission of Alfred A. Knopf.

Eudora Welty. "Livvie" from *A Wide Net and Other Stories,* copyright 1942 and renewed 1970 by Eudora Welty, reprinted by permission of Harcourt Brace Jovanovich, Inc.

John Hall Wheelock. "Earth" reprinted with permission of Charles Scribner's Sons, an imprint of Macmillan Publishing Company, from *The Gardener and Other Poems* by John Hall Wheelock. Copyright © 1961 by John Hall Wheelock. Copyright renewed 1989.

Richard Wilbur. "A Simile for Her Smile" from *Ceremony and Other Poems,* copyright 1950 and renewed 1978 by Richard Wilbur, reprinted by permission of Harcourt Brace Jovanovich, Inc. "Love Calls Us to the Things of This World" from *Things of This World,* copyright © 1956 and renewed 1984 by Richard Wilbur, reprinted by permission of Harcourt Brace Jovanovich, Inc.

Index of Critical Terms

Index of Authors, Titles, and First Lines of Poems

Quotation marks indicate the first line of a poem.